W9-BJC-571

MANUAL OF CREDIT AND COMMERCIAL LAWS
97th Edition

NATIONAL ASSOCIATION OF CREDIT MANAGEMENT
COLUMBIA, MARYLAND

Contributors

Paige E. Barr
Jaffe Raitt Heuer & Weiss
Detroit, MI

Scott R. Blakeley, Esq.
Blakeley & Blakeley, LLP
Irvine, CA

Wanda Borges, Esq.
Borges & Associates, LLC
Syosset, NY

James Fullerton, Esq.
Fullerton & Associates
Clifton, VA

David Goch
Webster, Chamberlain & Bean
Washington, DC

James W. Hays, Esq.
Hays & Potter
Atlanta, GA

Tara Leberman, CPA
BDO Seidman, LLP
Denver, CO

Joseph A. Marino, Esq.
Marino & Mayers, LLC
Clifton, NJ

Max G. Moses
(Managing Editor)
Member Media
Chicago, IL

Jerry T. Myers
Smith Debnam Narron Wyche Story
& Myers, LLP
Raleigh, NC

Bruce S. Nathan, Esq.
Lowenstein Sandler, PC
New York, NY

Manual H. Newburger, Esq.
Barron & Newburger, PC
Austin, TX

Maria A. Rowan
Weltman, Weinberg & Reis, Co. LPA
Cleveland, OH

Richard J. Ruszat II
SulmeyerKupetz
Los Angeles, CA

Jonathan P. Sauer, Esq.
Sauer & Associates
Norwood, MA

Deborah Thorne
Barnes & Thornburg LLP
Chicago, IL

Caroline Zimmerman
NACM-National
Columbia, MD

ISBN 1-888505-22-2

Printed in the United States of America

10 9 8 7 6 5 4 3 2 1

Table of Contents

Chapter 2
PARTNERSHIPS AND JOINT VENTURES—THEIR LEGAL
OBLIGATIONS AND HOW TO DEAL WITH THEM

Chapter 3
CREATION OF AGREEMENTS WITH AGENTS AND PRINCIPALS

Chapter 4
DEALING WITH THE PARTY USING AN
ASSUMED OR FICTITIOUS NAME

Chapter 5
TRANSACTIONAL GUIDE TO THE FORMATION,
PERFORMANCE AND ENFORCEMENT OF CONTRACTS

Chapter 6
AN OVERVIEW OF THE UNIFORM COMPUTER INFORMATION TRANSACTIONS ACT

Chapter 7
UNIFORM COMMERCIAL CODE: AN OVERVIEW

Chapter 8
EQUIPMENT LEASING

Chapter 9
NEGOTIABLE INSTRUMENTS: NOTES, CHECKS, DRAFTS—
HOW THEY WORK—AND INTEREST RATES

Chapter 10
SECURED TRANSACTIONS: A STEP-BY-STEP EXPLANATION

Chapter 11
LIENS AFFECTING PERSONAL PROPERTY

Chapter 12
MECHANICS' LIENS

Chapter 13
CONSTRUCTION BONDS ON PUBLIC PROJECTS

Chapter 14
TRUST FUND AGREEMENTS

Chapter 15
RECLAMATION, STOPPAGE IN TRANSIT,
NEW ADMINISTRATIVE CLAIM IN FAVOR OF GOODS SUPPLIERS,
AND OTHER RETURN OF GOODS REMEDIES

Chapter 16
STEPS IN THE COLLECTION PROCESS

Chapter 17
BAD CHECK LAWS

Chapter 18
CLAIMS AGAINST DECEDENTS' ESTATES

Chapter 19
A CREDITOR'S GUIDE TO THE BANKRUPTCY PROCESS

Chapter 20
ALTERNATIVES TO FORCING A FINANCIALLY DISTRESSED DEBTOR INTO BANKRUPTCY

Chapter 21
RETAIL INSTALLMENT SALES LAWS

Chapter 22
CONSUMER PROTECTION LEGISLATION—AN OVERVIEW

Chapter 23
ANTITRUST AND TRADE REGULATION FOR CREDIT GROUPS
AND CREDIT GRANTORS

Chapter 24
ESCHEATMENT LAWS AND UNCLAIMED PROPERTY
REPORTING REQUIREMENTS

Chapter 25
COMPLIANCE ISSUES AND REGULATIONS

Chapter 26
U.S. DISTRICT COURT SYSTEM LOCATOR

Chapter 27
FORMS FOR REFERENCE AND USE

Appendix A
SECRETARIES OF STATE

Appendix B
MORE STATUTORY SUMMARIES

Appendix C
SELECTED TEXT OF THE UNIFORM COMMERCIAL CODE

Tables and Statutory Summaries

About the Editors and Contributors

Paige E. Barr is an Associate in the Insolvency and Reorganization practice of the Michigan law firm of Jaffe Raitt Heuer & Weiss. She earned her J.D. from DePaul University College of Law (2004) and her B.A. from the University of Pittsburgh (2001). A prolific writer, she prepared the 2004 update for Chapter 34: Inventory & Accounts Financing in *Commercial Law and Practice Guide* (Matthew Bender Publications). Her articles have been published in a number of law reviews and other legal publications including: "A Double Edged Sword: FCC v. NextWave," 2 *DePaul Bus. & Com L. J.* (2004); "The Facts & Fictions of Bankruptcy Reform," 1 *DePaul Bus. & Com. L. J. 361* (2003) (coauthor Catherine Vance); "Non-Dischargeability for an Intentional Tort Requires the Actor Intend the Consequences of the Act, Not Simply the Act Itself," Commercial Law League of America Bankruptcy Sec. Newsletter, Feb. 2004; "Ordinary Contract Damages vs. Non-Dischargeable Debts," Commercial Law League of America Bankruptcy Sec. Newsletter, Aug. 2003. She was awarded the American College of Bankruptcy's 2004 Seventh Circuit Distinguished Law Student.

Scott Blakeley is a partner in the law firm of Blakeley & Blakeley LLP, where he advises companies around the country regarding creditors' rights, commercial law, e-commerce and bankruptcy law. He was selected as one of the 50 most influential people in commercial credit by *Credit Today*. He is contributing editor for American Bankruptcy Institute's *Manual of Reclamation Laws*, and author of *A History of Bankruptcy Preference Law*, published by ABI. The Credit Research Foundation has published his manuals entitled *The Credit Professional's Guide to Bankruptcy, Serving on a Creditors' Committee* and *Commencing an Involuntary Bankruptcy Petition*. Scott has published dozens of articles and manuals in the area of creditors' rights, commercial law, e-commerce and bankruptcy in such publications as *Business Credit, Managing Credit, Receivables & Collections, Norton's Bankruptcy Review* and the *Practicing Law Institute*, and speaks frequently to credit industry groups regarding these topics throughout the country. Scott holds a B.S. from Pepperdine University, an M.B.A. from Loyola University and a law degree from Southwestern University.

Wanda Borges is a member of the Borges & Associates, LLC law firm. Ms. Borges has concentrated her practice on commercial litigation and creditors' rights in commercial insolvency matters representing corporate clients and creditors' committees throughout the United States in Chapter 11 proceedings, out of court settlements, commercial transactions and preference defenses, for an excess of 25 years. She serves the Commercial Law League of America as an Attorney Member of its National Board of Governors, a Past Chair of the Bankruptcy Section and a past member of the executive council of its Eastern Region. She is a member of INSOL, the American Bar Association, the American Bankruptcy Institute, the Turnaround Management Association and the Hispanic National Bar Association. She has become a regular lecturer for NACM-National and its affiliated associations on commercial and corporate law (including ECOA, the Uniform Commercial Code and FCRA), insolvency matters, creditors' rights issues, antitrust law, and the Sarbanes-

Oxley Act of 2002. She is one of the authors of the Comments of the Commercial Law League of America and its Bankruptcy Section to the Preliminary Draft of Proposed Amendments to the Federal Rules of Bankruptcy Procedure. Ms. Borges has authored, edited and contributed to numerous publications including Thomson West's *Enforcing Judgments and Collecting Debts in New York*, NACM's *Antitrust, Restraint of Trade and Unfair Competition: Myth Versus Reality*, NAB's *Out of the Red and Into the Black*, BCCA's *Credit & Collection Handbook*, the CLLA Bulletin, and Bankruptcy Section newsletters, including her treatise "Hidden Liens, Who Is Entitled to What?," NACM's *Principles of Business Credit* and NACM's *Manual of Credit and Commercial Laws.*

James D. Fullerton is an attorney licensed in Virginia, Maryland, and the District of Columbia and is the President of the law firm of Fullerton & Knowles, PC. The firm represents owners, design professionals, suppliers, subcontractors, general contractors and other members of the real estate and construction industries, filing mechanic's liens, surety bond and other construction claims across all of the states in the Mid Atlantic region. He also represents creditors in bankruptcy issues nationwide, particularly defense of bankruptcy preference claims; advises on all real estate and construction law issues; contract formation and disputes; defects in labor and materials; design defects in plans and specifications; inefficiency, impact and delay claims; litigation, arbitration and mediation in public and private projects. Mr. Fullerton is also a master brick mason, a licensed real estate broker and the President of Summit Real Estate, Inc. He is on Board of Directors of Northern Virginia Conservation Trust; is Counsel to Board of Directors, National Association of Credit Management, East Coast Corporation; and Counsel to Board of Directors, Virginia Precast Concrete Association. He graduated from the University of Colorado and the University of Virginia School of Law. The firm's *Construction Law Survival Manual* is well known and widely used by participants in the construction process. The 400-page manual provides valuable information about construction contract litigation, mechanic's liens, payment bond claims, bankruptcy and credit management and contains over 30 commonly used contract forms. All of this information and recent construction law issues are constantly updated on the website www.FullertonLaw.com.

David Goch is a Partner in the Washington, D.C. law firm of Webster, Chamberlain & Bean. His practice includes all aspects of nonprofit law including: corporate, tax, antitrust, intellectual property, standards and certification, employment matters, and government relations, for which the firm has established a national reputation as being the leader in the field. He has over 13 years' experience working with nonprofit organizations of all sizes. David has a bachelor's degree from the University of Michigan and a J.D., with honors, from the University of Maryland School of Law.

James W. "Beau" Hays is a partner in the firm of Hays & Potter, P.C. in Atlanta, Georgia, where he concentrates his practice in the areas of creditor representation in construction and bankruptcy cases. Beau was graduated from the University of North Carolina with a B.A. in Political Science and History and a J.D. from UNC's School of Law. He is a member of the Commercial Law League of America. He is a founding member of the State Bar of Georgia's Creditors' Rights Section and serves as legislative liaison for that Section to the Georgia Legislature. He has been a lecturer for National Association of Credit Management programs in Georgia on a variety of credit topics.

Tara Leberman, CPA, Engagement Senior Manager, has over 12 years of total experience, six years of which has been with BDO working exclusively on SAS 70 reviews. She is an alumnus of a Big 4 firm. She is responsible for managing and performing SAS 70 reviews for organizations throughout the United States and internationally. She has worked with diverse engagement involving such processes as payment processing, accounts receivable management, credit card issuing and merchant acquiring, administration of defined contributions plans, defined benefit plans, Section 125 flexible spending plans, pharmaceutical claims processing, health and welfare plans, COBRA, trustee/custodial services, non-qualified employee benefit plans, payroll processing, bill processing, web-based advertising, asset management and equity and loan servicing and broker/dealer services. She is a member of the AICPA and the Information Systems Audit and Control Association (ISACA).

Joseph A. Marino is the senior partner in the firm of Marino & Mayers, LLC, in Clifton, New Jersey. Mr. Marino received his J.D. from the New England School of Law, in 1976 and has been admitted to practice law in New Jersey, Florida and the District of Columbia. Mr. Marino has been an active member of the Commercial Law League of America (CLLA) since 1978, and has served on its Board of Governors as the Recording Secretary, the Creditor's Rights Section Board Representative, Chair of the Creditor Rights Section and Chair of the Eastern Region. He has contributed to numerous legal articles, was the Editor and contributing author of the CLLA *Creditors' Rights Collections Handbook*, has been a contributing author to the NACM *Manual of Credit and Commercial Laws* for several years, and has served educational programs and served on numerous educational panels over the past 20 years. In July 1994, Mr. Marino became a Board Certified Creditors Rights Specialist by the CLLA Academy of Commercial & Bankruptcy Law Specialists, which subsequently merged into the American Board of Certification. He currently serves on its Board of Governors. He is also currently serving as an Attorney Member to the Board of Governors of the Commercial Law League of America. Mr. Marino is also a Member of the Association of Certified Fraud Examiners and maintains a commercial and retail litigation and anti-fraud practice. Professionally, Mr. Marino has also been an active member of American Bar Association; New Jersey State Bar Association; and the Essex County Bar Association. Mr. Marino has served as an Arbitrator and Mediator for the Superior Court of New Jersey for over 13 years. Mr. Marino has been admitted as Special Counsel in numerous Bankruptcy Courts to handle the liquidations of receivables and portfolios.

Max G. Moses served the Commercial Law League of America, a national specialty bar association for business bankruptcy and creditors' rights professionals, for over 20 years, the last 15 as its Executive Vice President. *Credit Today* named him one of the 50 most influential people in credit. He is a Certified Public Accountant, licensed in Illinois. He is also an attorney admitted to practice law in Kansas. He earned his M.B.A. (with distinction) from the Keller Graduate School of Management. Currently, he is president of Max G. Moses & Associates, an organization that works with small businesses and not-for-profit organizations. Max G. Moses & Associates provides managing editor services on an outsource basis to periodicals and other publications. In addition, Max G. Moses & Associates work with professional service firms to help them present their expertise to target markets through trade and professional publications.

Jerry T. Myers is a partner with the law firm of Smith Debnam Narron Wyche Saintsing & Myers, LLP in Raleigh, North Carolina. His practice is concentrated primarily in the areas of commercial litigation and debt collection. Mr. Myers is certified as a Specialist in the field of Creditors Rights Law by the American Board of Specialization. Mr. Myers' book, *Collections and Enforcement of Judgments in North Carolina* was published by Lawyers Cooperative Publishing in 1997. Mr. Myers is also a contributing author to Judgment Enforcement, an authoritative treatise on enforcing judgments in the federal court system. Mr. Myers is an active member of Commercial Law League of America (CLLA), serving as its President in 2005-2006. For four years Mr. Myers served as the CLLA's Observer to the national legislative drafting committee that prepared the Uniform Computer Information Transactions Act (UCITA). Mr. Myers received an A.A. degree, summa cum laude, from Wingate University in 1978, a B.S. degree from Wake Forest University in 1980, and a J.D. degree from Wake Forest University School of Law in 1984.

Bruce S. Nathan is currently a member of the law firm of Lowenstein Sandler PC and is an active member of NACM. Mr. Nathan concentrates on all aspects of creditors' rights and workouts in bankruptcy, out of court matters, and other types of insolvency cases for secured creditors, creditors' committees, trustees and trade creditors, and in negotiating and preparing letters of credit, guaranties, security, consignment and other agreements. Mr. Nathan holds combined J.D./M.B.A. degrees from the University of Pennsylvania Law School and the Wharton School of Management. He is also an active member of the American Bankruptcy Institute ("ABI"), is a co-chair of ABI's Unsecured Trade Creditor Committee, is a contributing editor for the "Last In Line" column published in the *American Bankruptcy Institute Journal* and is the editor of ABI's *Second Circuit Update*. Mr. Nathan also is the author of *Manual on Trade Creditors' Rights of Reclamation and Stoppage of Delivery of Goods* published by ABI and is also the author of a monograph entitled *Protecting Corporate Creditors under the Bankruptcy Code* published by Matthew Bender. Mr. Nathan also frequently writes for NACM's *Business Credit* magazine and other credit-oriented periodicals. Mr. Nathan is a member of NACM's Editorial Advisory Board and is a yearly contributing editor of the *Manual of Credit and Commercial Laws*. Mr. Nathan also lectures at NACM Credit Congresses and Legislative Conferences, and at various credit groups affiliated with NACM on bankruptcy, UCC Article 9, letter of credit law, and other credit-related issues.

Manuel H. Newburger is the Vice-President of Barron & Newburger, P.C., the President of Fair Debt Consultants, LLC, and an adjunct professor at the University of Texas School of Law. A graduate of Trinity University and the University of Texas School of Law, Mr. Newburger is admitted to practice law before the Texas Supreme Court, the United States Supreme Court, the United States Court of Appeals for the Second, Fifth, Seventh and Ninth Circuits, all four United States District Courts for the State of Texas, and the United States District Courts for the Eastern District of Wisconsin and the Central District of California. He is board certified as a specialist in consumer and commercial law by the Texas Board of Legal Specialization. Mr. Newburger consults nationally and internationally on fair debt compliance, consumer litigation issues, and collection agency licensing. He defends and serves as an expert witness in FDCPA cases across the United States, and he provides FDCPA compliance training and reviews to collection industry members. He represented the Commercial Law League of America as an amicus curiae in *Heintz v. Jenkins*, 514 U.S. 291, 115 S.Ct. 1489 (1995), *White v. Goodman*, 200 F.3d 1016 (7th Cir. 2000), and *Riviere v. Banner Chevrolet, Inc.*, 184 F.3d 457 (5th Cir. 1999). Mr. Newburger is the co-author of M. Newburger and B. Barron, *Fair Debt Collection Practices: Federal and State Law and Regulation* (Sheshunoff & Pratt 2002).

Maria A. Rowan, associate of the Cleveland Office of Weltman, Weinberg & Reis, Co. LPA, concentrates her practice in the area of Probate (Deceased Collections). She is licensed in the state of Ohio and is a member of the American and Ohio Bar Associations. She earned a B.A. in History/Pre-law and a Minor in English from Ohio University in 1999 and received her J.D. from Case Western Reserve University School of Law in 2002.

Richard J. Ruszat II is an associate at the Los Angeles, California law firm of SulmeyerKupetz. Mr. Ruszat's practice areas concentrate on bankruptcy, business and commercial litigation including an insolvency practice through his representation of debtors and creditors' committees in Chapter 11 proceedings. Mr. Ruszat received his undergraduate degree *Summa Cum Laude* from the University of California, Irvine (1996) where he also received *Phi Beta Kappa* honors. He earned his law degree *Cum Laude* from the University of Minnesota Law School (2000) where he was recognized as Maynard Pirsig Moot Court Champion and participated on the Law School's elite American Bar Association Moot Court Competition Team. Mr. Ruszat is a contributing author to the *Manual of Credit and Commercial Laws*, 93rd through 97th Editions. Mr. Ruszat has also published numerous articles and manuals with trade publications involving the credit industry. Mr. Ruszat has served as a director on the Board of Directors for the University of California Alumni Association and is a member of the American Bankruptcy Institute and Los Angeles County Bar Association.

Jonathan P. Sauer practices law as Sauer & Associates, a Boston, Massachusetts area law firm which concentrates in the practice in the representation of equipment rental companies, material suppliers, subcontractors, general contractors, owners and sureties. A frequent seminar presenter, he publishes his own newsmagazine, *Scribbles*, several times per year, which combines articles of interest involving construction law issues as well as humor and continuing fictional story lines. A current issue, along with numerous articles and forms, can be found on his website at www.sauerconstructionlaw.com. An honors graduate of Northeastern University and of Suffolk University Law School, he is in his thirtieth year of practice. An avid reader, he enjoys riding his six motorcycles and hopes one day to publish a novel.

Deborah Thorne is a partner in the Chicago office of Barnes & Thornburg LLP. She concentrates her practice in the areas of creditors' rights, bankruptcy, financial restructurings, secured lending, and commercial transactions encompassing all phases of commercial litigation and representation of creditors seeking recovery for breach of contract and other claims; negotiation of restructuring plans, financing and other disputes; representation of secured creditors in UCC foreclosures, replevins of personal property, workouts of non-performing loans, representation of trade vendors in preference defense and reclamation claims, and representation of various parties in assignments for the benefit of creditors. Ms. Thorne received her B.A. degree in history from Macalester College, her M.A.T. degree from Duke University, and her J.D. with honors from the Illinois Institute of Technology, Chicago Kent College of Law. She is a frequent lecturer and has authored numerous articles for legal and business publications, including NACM's *Business Credit* and the *ABI Journal*. She is co-chair of the Unsecured Trade Creditors Committee for the American Bankruptcy Institute and a contributing editor of the *ABI Journal*.

NACM-National would like to thank the following for reviewing and/or providing material for sections to specific chapters:

Kimberly Ashby
Akerman Senterfitt
Orlando, FL

Shaaron Bangs, Esq.
Crawford & Bangs
Covina, CA

H. Lee Cook
Stewart Sokol & Gray, LLC
Seattle, WA

Alan C. Dobson
Cross, Gunter, Witherspoon
& Galchus, P.C.
Little Rock, AR

John F. Fatino
Whitfield & Eddy, PLC
Des Moines, IA

Andrew B. Faulkner
Cross, Gunter, Witherspoon
& Galchus, P.C.
Little Rock, AR

Carolyn E. Hayashi, Esq.
Char Sokamoto Ishii Lum & Ching
Honolulu, HI

Rebecca A. Hicks, Esq.
Bell, Nunnally & Martin, LLP
Dallas, TX

Nicholas D. Krawec, Esq.
Bernstein Law Firm, P.C.
Pittsburgh, PA

Randall K. Lindley, Esq.
Bell, Nunnally & Martin, LLP
Dallas, TX

Sue Figert Meyer, Esq.
Rubin & Levin, PC
Indianapolis, IN

William L. Norton III
Boult Cummings Conners
& Berry, PLC
Nashville, TN

Danial D. Pharris, Esq.
Lasher Holzapfel, Sperry & Ebberson
Seattle, WA

Protiviti
www.Protiviti.com

David K. Taylor
Boult Cummings Conners
& Berry, PLC
Nashville, TN

Benjamin B. Ullem
Whitfield & Eddy, PLC
Des Moines, IA

Diane L. Yetter
Yetter Consulting Services, Inc.
Chicago, IL

1 Understanding Corporations and How to Deal with Them

Corporations are artificial entities that are formed and maintained in accordance with state statutes. The officers, directors and shareholders are protected from personal liability if corporate formalities are met. Most business entities are corporations. All corporations must have shareholders, officers and directors, although the specific requirements as to the number of officers and directors vary from state to state.

Most business on a worldwide basis is transacted by and between corporate entities. The nature and structure of these entities is critical in determining the legal obligations and responsibilities of the parties to any agreement. Before being able to study in detail the nature of agreements and their enforceability, one must understand the structure of the entity with which one is doing business. A corporations is immortal so long as registration with the appropriate state authorities are current and taxes are paid.

In addition to having perpetual life, a corporation is a legal entity or artificial person, entirely separate and apart from the persons who comprise its members. A corporation has the power to receive, hold and convey property, enter into contracts, sue and be sued and otherwise exercise those rights and privileges which may be accorded by the laws under which it was created, in the same manner as a natural person.

A corporation, created pursuant to state statute, has no inherent rights or powers except within the framework of the law of its creation. Thus, the corporation must be organized in strict accordance with the legal requirements of the state of its domicile. While it is afforded protection as a "person" by our federal Constitution, including its right to engage in interstate commerce, it cannot step beyond the bounds of its domicile into another state without having that state confer upon it the authorization to do business within its borders. Its powers and purposes are fixed by charter or bylaws and cannot be changed at will as in the case of an individual or partnership. Such a change as entering into a new type of business or increasing its capitalization, in fact, any variation from the rights or powers conferred by its charter or bylaws, can be effected only by amending that charter or bylaws in accordance with the laws of the state that authorized the incorporation initially. Often, the bylaws themselves will state the methodology necessary to effectuate an amendment.

Since the corporation may only do that which it is legally authorized to do, when it does exceed its authority, the person or entity doing business with it may, in some instances, disregard the corporate authority and look to the individuals for liability. It is thus very important to examine in detail the structure and authority of the corporate entity with which one is doing business.

ADVANTAGES OF INCORPORATION

To the stockholders of a corporation this form of business organization affords two prime advantages which must be considered—protection from liability and potentially unlimited capital. The individual in business for himself—the sole proprietor—risks everything he owns in his venture, his capital being what he owns plus what he can borrow on his personal credit. A partnership does little more than increase the potential capital by the means of one or more additional individuals while at the same time it spreads the risk or liabilities among the several individuals (*see* Chapter 2). A stockholder of a corporation, however, who holds fully paid and nonassessable shares of stock, generally has no potential liability other than the loss of the money paid for the shares. An exception is the holder of banking corporation stock who in some states may be subject to a so-called "double liability" if the bank becomes insolvent. In general, a stockholder is not liable for the debts of the corporation in the absence of special circumstances. Liability may exist in the event of defective incorporation, irregularity in issuance of stock or under special statutory enactments such as those which in some states impose a liability on stockholders of an insolvent corporation unable to pay wage claims.

With the advantage of this limited liability, as well as the relative simplicity with which the shareholder can purchase or dispose of his interest in the corporation, this form of business organization has attracted investment of funds running into billions of dollars from millions of individuals.

Under the federal tax laws, however, a corporation may enjoy the tax advantages of a partnership if it meets special requirements of the Internal Revenue Code, 26 USC § 1371-1377. The entities enjoying this tax treatment are referred to as Subchapter S corporations. Limited Liability Companies are also entitled to special tax treatment under federal tax laws. If properly organized under state law, the LLC can file an election with the IRS to be classified for federal tax purposes as a sole proprietorship, or as a partnership.

DETERMINATION OF CORPORATE STATUS
AND ISSUES RELATING TO BUSINESS TRANSACTIONS

Credit grantors assume a business with a name carrying the suffix "Inc.," "Incorporated," "Co." and the like is a corporation. This is not always so. In particular, none of these suffixes are sufficient for a credit grantor to determine the exact status of the person or entity with whom the business transaction is being conducted. If a credit grantor does business with an entity and does not properly identify its corporate status or corporate name, enforcing the obligation may become impossible. It is critically important that care be taken to make sure of the correct business status of an entity where business is being transacted.

As noted elsewhere, corporations are created by an individual or individuals who seek to do business using the corporate structure. A corporation maintains its corporate status only by continuing to perform the acts necessary to keep its corporate status active on a yearly basis. The mere fact that a corporation filed initially with a particular state does not automatically mean that it continues in existence.

While most credit grantors do not need to examine corporate documents in order to extend credit, one must recognize that it is very much a "seller beware" situation when dealing with a corporation. A credit grantor should insist on receiving specific information to justify the existence of a corporation.

The office of the Secretary of State in each state is the facility whereby an interested party may retrieve copies of documents on file with respect to a corporation (see Appendix A for a state-by-state listing). These include articles of incorporation and filings which demonstrate that the corporation is then in good standing. Some states also keep these on record and will copy bylaws and other documents. Corporations that have met the legal requirements under state law and continue to do so are known as "de jure" corporations. That is, they have complied with the statutory requirements to maintain their status as a corporation.

However, it is important to note that a corporation may exist that has not complied with all the state's statutory requirements. Known as a "de facto" corporation, these entities gain their status as a corporation if the following three conditions exist:

1. There is a state statute under which the corporation can be validly incorporated
2. The parties must have made a good faith attempt to comply with that statute
3. The entity has undertaken to do business as a corporation

If the corporation is "de facto" only the state can successfully challenge the entity's existence as a corporation.

The use of commercial reports to verify corporate existence is one method, although extreme care should be taken to ensure that the credit reporting agency has specifically verified the current existence and good standing of the corporation, rather than simply relying on the representations of the principals of the corporation. There are serious implications when extending credit to a corporate entity which is not, in fact, in existence or in good standing.

The best method by which to verify corporate existence is the check of records with the respective Secretary of State. All incorporation information is now available electronically at no charge. Most states will also contain information as to whether or not the corporation is in "good standing," which refers to whether or not they have paid their required fees and franchise taxes.

Some confusion arises as to the importance of the place of incorporation for such an entity. In actuality, in dealing with the extension of credit, this is a relatively insignificant issue. For tax and other reasons, different states have different laws relating to corporations that are domiciled in that particular state. Irrespective of the state of incorporation, most corporations that do business throughout the country incorporate in one state and are qualified to do business as a "foreign" corporation in all of the other states. The fact that a corporation has not qualified to do business in a particular state has no major impact on the extension of credit or the corporation's ultimate liability for the debt. However, if it is learned that a corporation is not qualified to do business in a state where it does significant business, appropriate inquiry should be made as to the reason for this lack of registration. The credit grantor may find that corporate status has lapsed due to nonpayment of taxes. Clearly, if taxes are not paid, this bodes a warning to credit grantors whose debt holds a lesser level of priority than tax debt.

LIABILITY FOR CORPORATE DEBTS
BY OFFICERS, DIRECTORS OR STOCKHOLDERS

Officers and directors may be personally liable for the business obligations of the corporate entity if the formalities of corporate law have not been observed. In some instances, shareholders may also be involved. It is, therefore, very important that a determination be made that corporate formalities are being fully observed.

Generally, directors, officers and shareholders of a corporation are insulated from personal liability. Both statutory and common law exceptions exist, but proving the bases for these exceptions and enforcing them are often difficult.

Liability of Directors or Officers

Directors are in a position analogous to that of trustees; they have a fiduciary responsibility to stockholders and creditors. At common law, directors are liable to creditors and to the corporation for distribution of improper dividends provided such distribution resulted from willfulness, negligence, bad faith or fraud. If the directors act in good faith and with due care, no liability results unless imposed by statute. Some states hold a director liable for a portion of an unlawful distribution if that director fails to meet a certain standard of conduct.

Otherwise, directors and officers are not liable for corporate debts nor personally bound by corporate contracts unless the director or officer specifically agrees to become liable. It is not uncommon for a credit grantor to believe that a director or officer can be held liable for a check that does not clear. UCC 3-403(2)(a) contains an important provision that says: "An authorized representative who signs his own name to an instrument is personally obligated if the instrument neither names the person represented nor shows that the representative signed in a representative capacity." Case law has established, however, that while statute requires an individual to indicate he is signing a check in his corporate capacity in order to avoid personal liability, that capacity can otherwise be established between the parties; for example, the bank account upon which the check was drawn can be in the corporate name. Case law has established that an individual can become personally liable for corporate debts if he fails to make it clear that he is an agent of the corporation and is not acting in his personal capacity.

Since credit professionals today often wear many hats, one's responsibilities may include issuance and signing of corporate checks. The way to avoid the problems of potential personal liability is to follow three simple steps. First, the signer should have actual authority to sign. Second, the name of the corporation should be on the check. Third, the signer should always clearly indicate that he or she is signing in a representative capacity.

There are a number of state statutes that can subject a director or officer to personal liability. Many jurisdictions have a minimum capitalization requirement for incorporation. Often the threshold capitalization is very small compared with the potential liabilities. Therefore, it is important for a creditor to consider the integrity of management before extending credit. Failure to meet the minimum capitalization requirement can make the director, officer or shareholder personally liable for acts done prior to acquiring the minimum required capital.

Every jurisdiction imposes personal liability on directors who participate in the declaration and payment of illegal dividends or other distributions to shareholders. The liability may be enforced, depending on the state, by the corporation, or creditors or shareholders who did not benefit from the illegal dividends. A number of states have statutes that permit creditors to hold directors liable for the distribution of illegal dividends.

Shareholder Liability

In the absence of any specific statutory provisions, shareholders are generally not liable for the debts or obligations of a corporation. Persons dealing with the corporation must look to it and not to the individual stockholders for payment of claims. This is true despite the fact that an individual stockholder may own all or practically all of the shares of stock, except as noted below.

Many states provide for statutory liability of shareholders for the receipt of illegal dividends. Most of the statutes make the shareholder liable to the corporation. Louisiana explicitly allows creditors to enforce liability against shareholders; however, as a practical matter creditors are more likely to sue the directors or the corporation. A number of statutes condition shareholder liability upon the shareholder having knowledge that the dividend was illegal, or that the corporation had become insolvent.

Disregard of Corporate Entity

Although a corporation is a legal entity existing separate and apart from the persons comprising it, the courts will not permit this concept to be used for purposes of fraud and injustice. In appropriate cases the corporate entity will be disregarded (frequently referred to as "piercing the corporate veil") and the corporation and the individual or individuals owning all or substantially all of its stock and assets will be treated as one. In order to impose corporate liability on a shareholder, a strong showing of fraud, illegality, manipulation, injustice or wrongdoing by the shareholder must be clearly demonstrated.

Despite the fact that this matter is controlled by local law, which varies from state to state, the following are some common activities that could, taken in the aggregate, give rise to successfully "piercing the corporate veil":

1. Corporate debt is knowingly incurred when the company is already insolvent
2. Required annual shareholders or board of directors meetings are not held, or other corporate formalities are not observed
3. Corporate records, especially minutes of directors meetings, are not maintained correctly
4. Shareholders remove unreasonable amounts of money from the corporation impacting negatively the corporation's financial stability
5. There is a pattern of consistent nonpayment of dividends, or payment of excessive dividends
6. There is a general commingling of corporate activity and/or funds and those of the person or persons who control the corporation
7. There is a failure to maintain separate offices, the company has little or no other business and is only a facade for the activities of the dominant shareholder who is in fact, the corporate "alter ego"

DOMESTIC AND FOREIGN CORPORATIONS

A corporation is known as a domestic corporation within the state in which it is organized. As to all other states and countries, it is a foreign corporation. A foreign corporation may be broadly defined as one created by or organized and existing under the laws of another state or territory, or of a foreign government. Foreign corporations are subject to statutory regulation by every state in which they do business. Some states have provisions whereby a foreign corporation can become domesticated. For example, in Florida and Delaware, any non-United States corporation may become domesticated by filing with the Secretary of State: (a) a certificate of domestication; and (b) articles or certificate of incorporation, in compliance with the respective state's law. For the purposes of domestication of a non-United States corporation, the term "corporation" includes any incorporated organization, private law corporation, public law corporation, partnership, proprietorship, joint venture, foundation, trust, association or similar entity.

The 14th Amendment to the United States Constitution states "...No state shall make or enforce any law which shall abridge the privileges or immunities of citizens of the United States..." Immediately after the ratification of this Amendment in 1868, case law has dealt with the question of corporations as "citizens". It is well-settled law of this country that a corporation is not entitled to all the privileges and immunities of citizens in the several States, but that each state has the power and privilege of prescribing the terms upon which it will allow foreign corporations to transact business within its borders. Each state is entitled to determine its own conditions under which foreign companies or corporations may do business or maintain offices within its borders, provided always that such requisites do not interfere with any transactions by such corporations of interstate or foreign commerce.

This provision extends to the usage of the courts by a foreign business entity such as a corporation. Most states will require a corporation to be authorized to do business within a state and pay the requisite state taxes if it wishes to use the courts of that particular state. The alternative to being authorized to do business is generally to file a bond if a foreign corporation wishes to use a particular state's court system.

Constitutional Provision Regarding Interstate Commerce

Article I, section 8, of the Constitution of the United States, the power to regulate commerce with foreign nations and among the several states, is given exclusively to the federal government. This power has been reviewed frequently by the United States Supreme Court, and state statutes that have attempted to place burdens upon interstate commerce have been found to be unconstitutional and void.

The question that most frequently arises today under this section of the Constitution is whether or not a state may legally impose a tax upon foreign corporations, and whether or not the conditions it imposes, or attempts to impose, upon foreign corporations for the privilege of doing business interfere with the constitutional right of the corporation to transact interstate business free from local interference. When the state of South Dakota, in 1914, attempted by statute to restrict the use of the state courts by foreign corporations transacting strictly interstate business, the United States Supreme Court held the statute an unreasonable burden on interstate commerce. Additionally, when the state of Kansas, in 1910, attempted to levy a tax upon the entire authorized capital stock of the Western Union Telegraph Company, a foreign corporation, it was found that the tax was an attempt to place a burden upon interstate commerce and, therefore, was unconstitutional.

In later decisions of the United States Supreme Court, however, the restriction on the states' rights to tax interstate transactions has been relaxed. Since 1959, the imposition of a net income tax on income derived from interstate sales solicited by local salesmen has been upheld. In 1960 the United States Supreme Court upheld the state's right to collect use taxes from an out-of-state seller when it had agents in the taxing state soliciting orders for interstate shipment.

Discrimination against foreign corporations, however, is unlawful insofar as such discrimination violates constitutional provisions relating to interstate commerce and equal protection of the laws. This is contrasted, however, by a federal statute enacted in 1976 (15 USCA, §§ 381-384) which prohibits the imposition of such a tax where the seller is not engaged in business in the taxing state and his only activity there consists of soliciting orders that are accepted and filled outside the state. In that same year, a higher excise tax rate for foreign corporations than for domestic corporations was held to violate the state constitution's uniformity clause and was a denial of equal protection of laws under the United States Constitution. The court found that different tax rates may be acceptable but that arbitrary distinctions were discriminatory; therefore, it held that the Pennsylvania law was unconstitutional.

Restrictions Imposed on Foreign Corporations for the Transaction of Intrastate Business

The distinction between interstate business and intrastate business is not easily defined, and the decisions of the courts are conflicting in many instances as to whether a given course of procedure is properly defined as an interstate transaction, or amounts to intrastate business. It is of the highest importance that businesspeople be familiar with the restrictions imposed by the states upon the transaction of intrastate business by foreign corporations because the penalties imposed by the statutes are usually severe.

By the comity of nations, foreign corporations may make such contracts and transact business not contrary to the laws of the place where such contracts are made or such business is transacted, and there is a presumption of law in favor of the power of a foreign corporation to exercise all of the powers conferred by its charter; but the limitations contained in its charter follow it into every state in which it may do business.

Licensing of Foreign Corporations

The requirements with which a foreign corporation must comply to obtain a license or right to do business in any particular state, the fees incidental thereto, and the initial or annual franchise tax imposed upon such corporation by the state for a license or certificate of authority to do business within its borders vary greatly from state to state. Insurance and banking corporations are usually subject to special laws, and the limitations upon their powers are more severe than those which are placed upon ordinary business corporations. The Supreme Court determined in 1869 that insurance is not "commerce" which a foreign corporation has a right to engage in under federal laws.

The table at the end of this chapter indicates the penalties imposed by the various states for failure of a foreign corporation to qualify to do business in another state.

All states require a foreign corporation to qualify to do business in that state prior to transacting such business. Often, a foreign corporation can succeed in transacting business within the state without qualifying until it becomes necessary for the corporation to commence and maintain legal action within the courts of that state. Vermont's statute provides that any foreign entity can proceed with a legal action, if, prior to the commencement thereof, returns and appropriate registration fee have been filed and paid. Failure to do so can result in a fine. Alabama, on the other hand, requires registration prior to even conducting business within its state. In Alabama, the failure to file a certificate of authority prior to transacting business will result in having all contracts or agreements made or entered into deemed void. This will not impair, however, the foreign corporation seeking to enforce a contract or agreement involving a mortgage insured by the Federal Housing Administration or guaranteed by the Veteran's Administration.

In most other states, an unqualified foreign corporation is permitted to maintain its legal action by thereafter qualifying under the state law.

WHAT CONSTITUTES INTERSTATE BUSINESS?

Business transactions which traverse state lines are Interstate Business. Conducting interstate business triggers the applicability of a number of federal laws, federal requirements, some state requirements and additional reporting requirements. It also subjects entities to lawsuits in federal court and in the courts within any state where they do business.

It is impossible to formulate from the many decisions of the various states a comprehensive definition of the phrase "doing business" within the foreign state to such an extent, or in such a manner, that the business becomes intrastate as opposed to interstate, and renders the corporation liable to the taxes, restrictions and penalties imposed by state laws.

All states have attempted to define "doing business." Seven states—Alabama, Illinois, Iowa, Kansas, Louisiana, Oklahoma and Wyoming—define "doing business" through case law rather than statute. The majority of those states defining the term have done so negatively by enumerating activities which do not constitute the transaction of business, e.g., maintaining bank accounts or borrowing money, creating evidences of debts, transacting business in interstate commerce and conducting isolated transactions completed within 30 days.

Only three states, Kansas, Ohio and Vermont, have attempted affirmatively to define what constitutes doing business. These activities include owning property, committing a tort, maintaining a distribution point or performing a corporate function within the state.

Over 25 years ago, the United States Supreme Court considered this question in the case of *Allenberg Cotton Co., Inc. v. Pittman*, 419 U.S. 20 (1974). The issue in this case was whether or not the activities of Allenberg constituted intrastate business of sufficient magnitude to permit the state of Mississippi to apply its qualification statute without violating the commerce clause of the United States Constitution. The Allenberg Cotton Co. was a cotton merchant with its principal office in Memphis, Tennessee. It had arranged with a Mississippi resident to act for it to purchase cotton produced by cotton farmers in Mississippi. The agent would contact the farmers and relay the purchase terms to Allenberg's office in Tennessee, where, if acceptable, a contract would be prepared and signed by Allenberg. Thereafter, a copy would be sent to the agent in Mississippi to be executed by the farmer. The agent negotiated a contract with Pittman, who was to plant, cultivate and harvest a crop of cotton for Allenberg. Pittman, however, refused to deliver the cotton to Allenberg, who then commenced suit in Mississippi demanding injunctive relief and damages.

Pittman responded by claiming that Allenberg was a foreign corporation doing business in Mississippi and that it had not qualified to do so by securing a certificate of authority as required. Pittman alleged that Allenberg was not entitled to maintain its suit under the Mississippi statute, which provided that: "No foreign corporation transacting business in this state without a certificate of authority shall be permitted to maintain any action, suit or proceeding in any court of this state." Id. at 21 n.l.

The local court in Mississippi held that Allenberg was not doing business in that state within the meaning of the statute. The Supreme Court of Mississippi reversed that decision and held that Allenberg was doing business within the state. The United States Supreme Court in turn reversed. In an opinion by Mr. Justice Douglas, holding that Allenberg's local activities were inseparable from the overall interstate aspects of its transactions, the court stated that: "The cotton in this Mississippi sale...though temporarily in a warehouse [in Mississippi] was still in the stream of interstate commerce." Id. at 30.

The case is not a departure from prior law and remains good case law today for the premise that a foreign corporation engaged purely in interstate commerce cannot be prejudiced by a particular state's requirements. It rests on the factual determination that Allenberg did not have a sufficient corporate presence in Mississippi to require qualification. Generally, when a domestic corporation is being sued by an unqualified foreign corporation, the burden is on the domestic corporation to prove by competent evidence: (1) that the suer's activities are of a kind that constitute "doing business" in the state and require authorization; and (2) that the suer had not received authority to do business in the state.

Held to Be Interstate Business

The Supreme Court of Michigan has handed down several decisions which exemplify what is held to be Interstate Business. In a 1920 case a contract for certain ornamental plaster work in a building under construction in Michigan contained a stipulation that the material to be used was to be "furnished, delivered, and set in place by us." In a suit to recover the price of the material and work, the court held that the plaintiff could not collect because it was an unregistered foreign corporation engaged in interstate business. The court said in part:

> The record discloses that there are concerns in at least two or three cities of Michigan furnishing ornamental plaster work in competition with the plaintiff, and it is apparent that there are mechanics in the state entirely competent to erect such material. We think it is equally apparent that there is no such "intrinsic or peculiar quality or inherent complexity" in the article sold in the case at bar as would prevent its sale unless erected by the vendor. The test applied to contracts of this sort is whether or not the installation or construction of the article sold is such an essential requisite to the sale that it can be said that but for the installation by the seller, the sale could not take place.

Held Not to Be Interstate Business

It is difficult to find a case in which the sale of an article will necessarily fail unless the manufacturer agrees to install, erect or construct the material or apparatus within a foreign state. It is even more difficult to think of a case in which the plaintiff can offer proof that there are no mechanics within the state in question who are capable of erecting, installing or constructing material or apparatus. Yet in the absence of proof that such is the case, it would seem that the unregistered foreign corporation will be held to have entered into an interstate contract and will be denied the use of the courts of the foreign state to enforce payment.

A leading decision of the United States Supreme Court on the subject of the installation contract is the case of *York Mfg. Co. v. Colley*, 247 U.S. 21 (1910), which was an appeal from the Texas Court of Civil Appeals. The York Mfg. Co. was not qualified to do business in the state of Texas where it contracted to install certain ice machinery. The contract contained a stipulation to the effect that the York Mfg. Co. would send an engineer to supervise the installation of the machine, but his services were to be paid for by the purchaser, and all labor, material, etc., in connection therewith were to be performed and furnished by the purchaser. The Supreme Court, reversing the Texas court, held that the services of the engineer in assembling and erecting the machinery were relevant and appropriate to the interstate sale of the ice machinery and, because of its complexity, formed a part of the interstate transaction. Therefore, the interstate sale was entitled to the "protection" of the Constitution.

Sale of Goods Stored in State as Interstate Business

Where it appears that a foreign corporation is maintaining an agency for the sale of goods within another state, the authorities hold uniformly that the corporation is engaging in interstate commerce and is subject to taxation and regulation. But the mere storing of goods in a foreign state for some other purpose than that of sale does not amount to the transaction of interstate commerce and the goods do not lose their character as articles of intrastate commerce.

Free Port Laws

Numerous states and the District of Columbia have adopted "free port laws." These laws, intended to reduce the incidence of multiple taxation, exempt goods stored in the state while awaiting shipment to points outside the state from ad valorem property taxation. The specific rules vary from state to state; e.g., some states require that the goods remain in their original packages, whereas others do not. The reader is therefore advised to consult the statutes of those states with which he is concerned.

Consignment Sales

The question as to whether a foreign corporation is engaged in business within a given state is largely determined by whether it is in the actual ownership and possession of goods within the state for the purpose of barter and sale. A foreign corporation is doing business within the state when it consigns goods to a merchant to be sold *for the corporation* and not for himself, where the merchant does not purchase the goods, and the corporation does not actually part with the possession thereof. With respect to consignment sales, one should be very careful in determining the exact nature of the consignment agreement. Under the provisions of the Uniform Commercial Code, consignment sales may be deemed to be avoided and deemed a sale on credit if certain requirements are not met. Care must be taken to make the proper determination when dealing with a consignment sale.

The shipment of goods to a factor for sale by the factor on commission is ordinarily not doing business within the state. Nor is shipping goods in the state for sale in the name of the seller, although on commission, considered doing business within the states; nor is a foreign corporation doing business in the state by selling its products in the state by a factor in his own name, who is to make the sale, receive the consideration in his own name and guarantee the collection of any credit extended to purchasers.

Where a foreign corporation consigns goods to a factor for sale, but does maintain a warehouse, office or a place of business and does not pay any of the expense of receiving, handling, storing or selling its goods in a foreign state, and it is the factor who transacts local business and bears the expense of receiving, selling, handling and storing the goods, it is the factor who is doing business in the foreign state and *not the corporation.*

Office, Salesroom or Other Nexus in Foreign State

Corporations that maintain foreign offices or salesrooms must be careful to avoid adding other factors that may lead to the characterization of their business as interstate. These factors include the maintenance of a bank account, the carrying of a stock of goods for sale, the keeping of books of accounts, the hiring of employees, the making of collections by local agents within the state, the consummation of contracts in the foreign state or other acts that show an intention to carry on a local or interstate business. Isolated transactions are not interstate commerce within the meaning of the law, but even these should be guarded against for the reason that a suit on an isolated transaction, in a foreign state, of an unlicensed corporation is more than likely to be met with the defense that the corporation is engaged in interstate business and has no standing in the state courts. Even though the defense may be overruled, the corporation will be put to the expense of proving that it is not engaged in interstate business or that its transaction was an isolated one.

The U.S. Supreme Court dealt with this issue in 1987 in *Tyler Pipe Industries v. Washington State Department of Revenue* (483 U.S. 232, 107 S.Ct. 2810). Tyler Pipe Industries claimed that with no office, no ownership of property and no employees in a state, it should not be subjected to gross receipts tax in the state of Washington. The U.S. Supreme Court disagreed. Despite the apparent lack of nexus with the state, the court found that Tyler's in-state sales representative, which engaged in substantial activities that helped Tyler maintain its business in Washington, had a sufficient nexus to subject Tyler to tax.

Tyler argued that the representative was not an agent, but an independent contractor. Therefore, the representative's activities should not be considered in determining whether Tyler had sufficient nexus with the state. The court rejected this argument and determined that the crucial factor is "whether the activities performed in the state on behalf of the taxpayer are significantly associated with the taxpayer's ability to establish and maintain a market in this state for the sales." The court concluded that the representative's activities were significantly associated with Tyler's ability to maintain its business.

Principal Place of Business

The "principal place of business" of a corporation is of important significance. That phrase is one of the standards used in 28 USC § 1332 to determine if federal courts can acquire jurisdiction of a matter based on diversity of jurisdiction. The statute provides: "A corporation shall be deemed a citizen of any state by which it has been incorporated and of the state where it has its principal place of business." The courts are therefore frequently called upon to determine the location of a corporation's principal place of business in an effort to decide if the requirements of diversity jurisdiction have been fulfilled. The term "principal place of business" must be distinguished from the term "chief place of business" which is used for various other purposes in the Uniform Commercial Code, including, but not limited to, the requirements for the filing of UCC-1 financing statements.

Where a corporation has its principal place of business is a question of fact to be determined in each particular case by taking into consideration such factors as the character of the corporation, its purposes, the kind of business in which it is engaged and the situs of its operations. But the weight to apply to each of these particular facts is a question of law. The federal courts have not developed one test by which a place of business can be ascertained. Instead, three general theories have developed:

1. The "home office" or "nerve center" tests used for corporations engaged in far-flung and varied activities that are carried on in different states. The principal place of business is the location of the nerve center from which information and decisions radiate to constituent parts, and from which the nerve center office has direct control and coordinates all activities.
2. The "place of operations" test holds that a corporation's principal place of business for purposes of diversity jurisdiction is where the actual physical operations of the company are carried on and directed rather than where occasional high-level policy decisions are made. Under this test, the courts select the state in which the operations predominate in accordance with such factors as the location of real property, equipment, inventory and other tangible assets; and distribution of employees, payroll, production and other physical activities.
3. The "center of corporate activity" is the third test and it is similar to the place of operations test except that it stresses the site of the daily operational control of the corporation rather than the location of its actual physical operations. In that case, although the president and top executive officers had offices in New York where they spent substantial time; the board of directors met regularly in New York; the general counsel, secretary and treasurer had their offices in New York; and high-level decisions were made in that state, the operation policy committee of the corporation conducted its affairs in Pennsylvania and the day-to-day business of the corporation was conducted in that state. The court concluded that Pennsylvania was the corporation's principal place of business.

LIMITED LIABILITY COMPANIES

Limited liability companies are similar to corporations from a structural standpoint, but permit the owners or participants to have tax advantages as if they were partnerships. The symbols "LLC", "LLP", "PLLC" or "PLLP" signal that the credit grantor is dealing with an entity that may not be "traditional." Extending credit to these entities generally will be similar to extending credit to a corporation, but requires a comprehensive knowledge of how they are formed.

What Are They and How Are They Formed?

A limited liability company is a hybrid created by juxtaposing the basic concept of an unincorporated business association which desires to do business under a corporate structure with the benefits of a partnership. As in a traditional "C" corporation, the members (similar to stockholders) of LLCs enjoy liability protection from most liability. At the same time, a properly structured LLC avoids the double taxation of "C" corporations, thereby enjoying the pass-through tax advantages of a partnership. A single member LLC, permitted in many states, is treated as a sole proprietorship for tax purposes.

Among the other unique characteristics of LLCs are:

1. There is no limit to the number of members (although some states require there to be at least two members)
2. The LLC, itself, may be an owner, member or stockholder of shares in another legal entity or an entire legal entity
3. While the member enjoys limited liability, there is no limit to the ability of a member to participate in management of the LLC (contrast this to a limited partner)
4. Although variations will occur—state by state—generally, the formative document for an LLC (sometimes called Articles of Organization or a Certificate of Formation), must contain:
   a. The name of the LLC
   b. The name and address of the registered agent
   c. The county within the state in which the LLCs office is to be located, or if the business is to operate in more than one county, then the county in which the principal office is to be located
   d. Whether the LLC is to be managed by its members or by one or more managers
   e. The latest date on which the LLC is to be dissolved (in most states, if there is no date specified, the duration of an LLC is perpetual)
   f. If the LLC is to be a Professional Limited Liability Company, there must be provided, appropriate certificates of authority attached to the Articles of Organization (e.g., a Certificate of Good Standing is the appropriate certificate of authority for an attorney)

Similar to a Certificate of Incorporation, the Articles of Organization are filed with the Office of the Secretary of State. In addition, publication of notification of the formation of the LLC must be done within 120 days after the Articles of Incorporation are filed.

How Do They Operate?

The members of an LLC will adopt an Operating Agreement that complies with its particular state statutes. That Operating Agreement will specify how the business affairs will be conducted and will set forth the rights, powers, preferences, limitations or responsibilities of each of its members, managers, employees and agents.

While this would be an ideal document for a credit professional to view in order to understand exactly who at the LLC is performing what task and is responsible for what business decision, it is highly unlikely that this Operating Agreement will be released to the credit professional. The Operation Agreement does not have to be filed with the Secretary of State when the LLC is formed nor at any time thereafter.

It is more likely that the credit professional can obtain a letter from the LLC which informs the credit professional as to which member or manager of the LLC can be looked to for a specific function.

Throughout all of the discussion of LLCs, the credit professional should be constantly aware of the fact that LLCs are creatures created primarily for tax advantages and, by and large, do not differ in the overall corporate structure for those extending credit. The credit grantor does presumably receive a distinct advantage when dealing with an LLC in that revenues that may ordinarily be utilized for payment of corporate taxes could clearly be available in the form of cash flow to satisfy debts of creditors.

Considerations for Creditors

At first blush, an unsecured creditor would seem to think that dealing with an LLC would be no different than dealing with a corporation. In most instances this is true, as absent a personal guarantee from one of the principals, the creditor must look to the assets of the company in order to satisfy its obligations. In general, an LLC has the authority to conduct business, enter into contracts and transact any type of business in accordance with its articles of organization just as a corporation would act in accordance with its bylaws.

When the limited liability companies were first being utilized, and before each state had its own set of LLC statutes, credit professionals needed to be particularly wary of these entities that were generally "startup operations." Today, the LLC format is being utilized almost as often as a corporate format, and no particular concern should be attributed to the fact that the entity has chosen to be an LLC rather than a corporation.

There are, however, still some specific considerations which should be reviewed when dealing with an LLC:

1. While there are tax advantages for both profits and losses, the pass-through of losses to the members is a very distinct advantage. It is possible for an entity anticipating a break-even year to pre-pay expenses in order for the individual members to reap only minimal profits on which taxes must be paid. This can actually be advantageous to a creditor since the LLC may wish to pay its bills rather than have the members pay taxes. The credit professional might even encourage the LLC to pay its expenses prior to its year end to obtain this tax benefit for its members.

2. On the flip side of this advantage, a creditor will want to be aware of the cash flow habits of its LLC customer. While the LLC itself will escape tax liability as this will be "imposed" upon the members, a creditor must assume that provisions for these taxes will be somehow made by way of distributions to the members. Careful review of the annual financial statement of an LLC entity should be undertaken to make sure that cash is not removed at such a rate which, while satisfying the tax obligations of the members, depletes the entity of cash needed in order to carry out its functions and pay its creditors in the ordinary course of business.

3. If a credit grantor is hesitant to extend credit to an LLC after a careful review of the usual financial information, that credit grantor may seek a personal guarantee from the principal(s) of the LLC. If the principals of an LLC will not provide a credit grantor with personal guarantees, consideration should be given to securing a subordination agreement from the members that provides that the LLC may not distribute profit to them unless and until the debts due to the credit grantor are current. In many instances, this can have an even greater impact upon the individuals involved than would a personal guarantee, since the taking of the profit by the principals may be their means of paying personal income taxes. By selective monitoring of the financial statements of the entity, the credit grantor can "keep in touch" with the situation and make sure that the provisions are being honored.

4. If a substantial amount of credit is being extended, it may be wise to receive an opinion from the legal or accounting professional for the LLC that it has been properly structured in order to receive the tax advantages. Were the LLC to anticipate the tax benefits but not receive them because of improper struc-

turing, this could create a serious tax burden on the entity, which could interfere with the cash flow needed to pay debts in the ordinary course of business. There is no reason or prohibition why a creditor cannot seek such an opinion from the legal or tax professional of a substantial customer. Indeed, the reluctance to provide one could signal the possibility of a problem.

DEALING WITH AN S OR SUBCHAPTER S CORPORATION

Credit grantors often learn that the customer is an "S" corporation and wonder how this will affect the extension of credit.

The Internal Revenue Service defines an "S corporation" as a "small business corporation" which has "elected" to be an "S corporation." To be eligible, a "small business corporation" must have:

1. Less than 75 shareholders
2. Only one class of stock
3. Only individuals as shareholders (except for certain trusts and certain exempt organizations)

In addition, nonresident aliens may not be shareholders of this corporation.

The Internal Revenue Service regulations with respect to S corporations are extremely precise. The election to be an S corporation must be made by unanimous consent of all shareholders. The time period during which an election may be made is narrow. Further, the Internal Revenue Service has exact rules under which an S corporation election may be terminated.

The benefit of an S corporation election is that the corporate entity itself does not pay taxes on profits or gain the benefit of losses. Rather, the tax liability or benefits pass through to the stockholders. It is for this reason that the popularity of LLCs has developed, as most of the restrictions are not present with LLCs, yet all of the tax advantages are still present.

When creditors determine that a customer is an S corporation, the dealings with the corporation should not be directly impacted because of the tax structure of the corporation. Some considerations for dealing with an S corporation by credit grantors are the following:

1. A more careful viewing of distributions to principals (shareholders) of an S corporation should be made than in a situation with a C corporation. Especially if the entity is profitable, there is a tendency for the principals of an S corporation to try to have sufficient distributions flow through to the principals so that the taxes that are created as a result of the corporation's profits are paid for with corporate funds. This has the tendency to diminish cash, especially at year end, and interfere with the normal flow of the payment of debts to creditors in the ordinary course of business.
2. When dealing with an S corporation, there is even a greater impetus to try to secure personal guarantees from the principals. While there is always a reluctance of the corporate principals to give the guarantees, the rationale exists that such guarantees are appropriate, given the fact that the individuals will be directly benefiting from the profits and losses of the corporation, unlike a situation in a C corporation where dividends are the only method of a benefit, and these are subject to double taxation.

3. Consideration should be given to receiving a subordination agreement from the stockholders providing that distributions will not be made to the stockholders for any purpose other than normal salaries unless and until all debts to a particular trade creditor are current. Because of the direct taxation on the individual shareholders, there is a greater ability to pass through money to the individuals, thus draining the corporation of cash needed to operate. As noted above, this becomes most prevalent close to the end of the calendar year. Although a wonderful choice for credit grantors, obtaining this subordination agreement is highly unlikely.

EFFECTIVE USE OF GUARANTEES

Guarantees by individuals, partnerships or corporations provide a method to further help ensure collection of an indebtedness. Guarantees may be secured or unsecured. They may be joint or several, and they can be absolute or conditional. Since guarantees are contracts, in order to have them fully enforceable, the terms of the guarantee agreement must be clear and accurate. As structuring of credit becomes more and more complicated, the need for the effective use of guarantees becomes even more important. This, coupled with issues involving the Equal Credit Opportunity Act and the Fair Credit Reporting Act mandate that today's credit professional "be on top" of such issues. The old simple personal guarantee will no longer be effective. Specific provisions dealing with specific issues must be inserted in a document.

General Principles

Unfortunately, many credit professionals do not effectively use the benefits of guarantees to help ensure repayment of an obligation. Although there is little statutory law governing guarantees, and there are variations on a state-by-state basis as to particular provisions, they are, nevertheless, very effective tools which can be utilized by the prudent credit professional.

If one assumes that most business people are honest and intend to honor their corporate and personal obligations, the signing of a guarantee creates an additional moral or otherwise persuasive obligation on the part of the guarantors, in addition to the legal and moral obligation on the part of the customer or debtor. Many times, irrespective of the legal issues involved, a guarantor will do everything possible to first satisfy those obligations which are personally guaranteed, especially when there are a limited amount of funds available. By the creation of this additional "incentive," a credit grantor can effectively increase the opportunities to be paid.

A GUARANTEE IS NOT SECURITY

Many creditors who receive personal guarantees consider their account now to be "secured." Security exists only if the guarantor provides specific collateral by way of a mortgage on real property or security interest in personal property to back up the guarantee. Otherwise, the guarantee is nothing more than an unsecured promise to pay the obligation by the person, persons or entities,that sign the guarantee. Do not mistake the benefits of collateral with the benefits of a guarantee.

TYPES OF GUARANTEES

Guarantees may be in various forms and by individuals or entities. When dealing with a corporation which is a subsidiary of another or an affiliate of another, consideration should be given to securing the parent entity's or affiliate entity's guarantee. Oftentimes, a subsidiary is established for a particular purpose and is not fully funded with cash or assets. In such case, especially with a new venture or division, the creditor of the subsidiary may be left with less than adequate assets in which to effect repayment should difficulties arise. One may view not only the financial statements of the subsidiary where credit is to be extended, but also the financial statements of the parent or affiliate entities, to determine where appropriate financial strength may lie. When parent entities are properly approached for guarantees of the subsidiary entities, there is not necessarily a great hesitance in signing such a guarantee. Since there is no legal prohibition on a parent entity signing a guarantee for a subsidiary, if a credit professional encounters reluctance to signing a guarantee, this could indicate that further consideration should be given prior to the extension of any large amount of unsecured credit.

Conversely while there is nothing illegal or improper about a subsidiary guaranteeing the debt of a parent, should the subsidiary fall into financial difficulty, the signing of the guarantee can be subsequently treated as a fraudulent transfer. While there is certainly consideration for a parent guaranteeing the debt of a subsidiary, the courts have held that there may be an absence of consideration for the subsidiary's guarantee of the parent's debt. It may be beneficial to a creditor without a guarantee to seek to overturn a guarantee that has been previously executed by a subsidiary for a parent.

When taking a guarantee from a corporation, it is very important that there be an appropriate corporate resolution authorizing the execution of the guarantee, and a certified copy of the resolution should be obtained by the prudent credit professional.

The credit grantor will prefer receiving a guarantee which is unlimited as to the extent and duration. Guarantors will want to include language in a guarantee which limits the duration of the guarantee (it expires on a certain date) or provide that the guarantee is effective only up to a certain dollar limit. Furthermore, a provision should be inserted in the guarantee to make it clear that the creditor may pursue the guarantor without first being required to pursue the obligor or attempt recovery from the obligor as a precondition to pursuit of the guarantor. Too often, to the chagrin of a credit grantor, the guarantor will insert fine print in a guarantee that states, even in the event of a bankruptcy, nothing can be pursued on the guarantee until the expiration of a substantial period of time.

A Guarantee of Payment is one that requires nothing more than a debt remaining unpaid. A Guarantee of Collection requires the creditor to do whatever is necessary to attempt to collect the debt from the principal debtor before pursuing a guarantor. This could involve suing a debtor, obtaining a judgment and having an execution returned as uncollectible before any action can be taken against the guarantor. Creditors should always place language in the guarantee that assures it to be a Guarantee of Payment.

Section 362 of the Bankruptcy Code prohibits actions to collect a debt against the debtor. However, except in the limited situation of a co-debtor under Chapter 13, the filing of a bankruptcy proceeding by a principal obligor does not in and of itself, nor does the automatic stay preclude pursuit of the guarantors while the bankruptcy case is pending. Again, it is important to have clear language within the term of the guarantee to reinforce this provision, but, absent some limitation, the guarantors may be pursued during the pendency of the bankruptcy case.

Use of Personal Guarantees

Principals of a corporation are those who should be considered for a guarantee. Since those principals have a direct financial interest in the corporation's success, they should be willing to either fully or partially guarantee that success when seeking the extension of credit.

It is a prudent practice to secure a financial statement from a guarantor not only at the time of the signing of the guarantee, but also at subsequent annual intervals. At first, this will provide the credit grantor with the knowledge of the worth of the guarantor. Secondarily, this will assist the credit grantor in the event that assets are shifted or diverted, alerting the credit grantor to the fact that collection of the guarantee may be difficult if not impossible.

Personal guarantees should clearly state that they are unlimited, and shall continue in full force and effect until canceled. Of course, any debt that is incurred prior to the cancellation will continue to be the obligation of the guarantor. A personal guarantee should also provide that the creditor may modify, change, or extend credit terms or conditions without specific notification of the guarantor and without receiving the guarantor's consent. There have been a number of cases that have held that if a credit grantor modifies or extends credit terms (such as taking a promissory note on an open account), this change or modification will have the effect of totally eliminating the guarantor's obligation.

The California Supreme Court has held that a creditor must inform the guarantor if the risk level to the guarantor changes by virtue of a further extension of credit to the original debtor or by virtue of a change in the financial condition of the original debtor. A specific waiver of disclosure should be included in the personal guarantee which states: "Guarantor waives any right to receive disclosures of the debtor's financial condition and risk. Further, guarantor assumes all responsibility for staying advised as to the principal debtor's financial condition."

In many states because of various exemptions, the guarantee of one spouse does not provide access to marital assets in the event of an action on the guarantee. Thus, if at all possible, it is very important to consider securing the guarantee of both spouses. This, however, must be tempered with the fact that under Title 15 of the United States Code, the securing of a guarantee by a non-affiliated spouse may be an illegal credit discriminatory practice. All credit professionals should consult with knowledgeable and competent counsel as to what should be done in this situation, as it can become a "trap" for the unwary credit professional.

Secured Guarantees

An innovative technique is to have a guarantee secured by assets of the guarantor. For years, banks have taken a pledge of a savings account or other depository account or Certificate of Deposit of a guarantor to secure the guarantor's obligation. The creditor, in such a situation, may not proceed against the assets which are so pledged until a default and appropriate notice and time to cure, but it does give the creditor an opportunity to specifically look to other assets without resorting to lengthy litigation.

In a situation where the credit grantor desires to obtain collateral on the guarantee, normal security interest language should be inserted into the guarantee itself. It is a good idea to file a UCC financing statement to perfect the collateralization, although in many instances where assets are pledged, filing may not be necessary. Revised Article 9 of the Uniform Commercial Code sets forth the specific requirements for collateralization (*see* Chapter 10).

Waiver of Jury Trial

More and more credit professionals are using waivers of jury trial in various credit agreements, sales agreements and the like. This, too, can be a very effective tool in a guarantee, whether it is one from individuals or from other corporate entities.

Most states permit the waiver of jury trial in a non-consumer transaction. The language should be sufficiently clear and specific, and should unequivocally state that the jury trial is waived. It is suggested that the typeset for the waiver of jury trial be larger and be boldly printed. In that way, there can never be a question that the guarantor was well aware that the jury trial was being waived.

Appropriate Notice to Guarantors

Absent a specific provision in a guarantee which waives the right of notification (*see above* Use of Personal Guarantees), it is critical that the credit grantor keep all guarantors fully and completely advised as to all happenings with respect to the obligation which is guaranteed. Should a credit limit be initially or subsequently established, the guarantor must be made aware of it. If the amount of debt exceeds the credit limit at any point, it is critical that the guarantor be notified. Should the terms of credit be modified, extended or changed in any way, it is likewise imperative that the guarantors be notified.

In such instances, it is not necessary that the guarantors consent to any such changes or modifications, but it is necessary that notification be effected. Courts in many states have now provided that the modification or extension of credit terms or debt obligations without notification to the guarantor constitutes a basis for eliminating the guarantor's liability. This can be remedied by an appropriate provision in the guarantee, but absent reliance on such a provision, constant notification to the guarantor should be given. It should be remembered that there never can be too much notification to the guarantor.

Confession of Judgment

A number of states still permit confession of judgment in business transactions. Confession of judgment language in notes or other instruments permits the creditor, upon default, to proceed in an appropriate court and obtain a judgment almost immediately.

When drafting a guarantee agreement, one should investigate as to whether confession of judgment is permitted in the state of the guarantor's residence. If it is, such language should be inserted in the guarantee. If this is done properly, and if there is a default by the principal obligor, the creditor may proceed to obtain an almost immediate judgment against the guarantor on the guaranteed debt. This places the creditor in a unique position of being "first in line" and having a judgment which may effectively be a lien on the assets of the guarantor, thus helping to ensure that payment will be forthcoming or effected.

Form of Guarantee

Chapter 27 contains a form for a guarantee which may be used in an individual situation. Chapter 27 also contains a form for corporate guarantee.

There is no specific or "magic" form, and any appropriate language may be used in a guarantee. Caution should be used when attempting to include guarantee language in some other agreement. Some courts have held that the mere inclusion of guarantee language in some other form of agreement such as in a credit application is not sufficient to put the guarantor on notice of the signing of the guarantee, nor is there appropriate consideration for the execution of the guarantee. If a credit grantor believes that it is necessary to include guarantee provisions in some other agreement, the guarantee language should be separately set forth, be appropriately conspicuous, and have a signature separate from that of the agreement in which it is contained.

Guarantees by Corporations

Generally, a corporation has the power and authority to become a guarantor or surety or otherwise lend its credit to another person or corporation. Power to so act will be set forth in the statute of the incorporating state or in the certificate of incorporation of the entity. Some corporations may have a specific provision in its certificate of incorporation or its bylaws prohibiting it from proving a guarantee or surety. This power and authority to become a guarantor or surety has been denied to banking, loan and trust companies; to insurance companies; to railroad, plank road and other transportation companies; to land and irrigation companies. Some specific state statutes might likewise contain a specific prohibition for other types of corporate entities.

Appropriate documentation to determine that the guarantee has been properly authorized by the board of directors must be received by the credit grantor. If significant reliance is going to be made on the guarantee by a corporation, some investigation should be made as to the reason for the entity's providing such a guarantee. If the corporation will not directly benefit by the extension of credit to the customer, an argument could be made at a later time that the giving of the guarantee by the corporation was a fraudulent transfer. So-called "upstream guarantees" (when a subsidiary guarantees its parent's debt) has been held by some courts to be a fraudulent transfer since there is no consideration or basis for the guarantee since the subsidiary cannot receive a benefit from extension of credit to its parent. If the corporate guarantor is purported to be in shaky financial condition, information should be obtained which will support the consideration for the corporate guarantee.

The courts have held that a corporation cannot issue accommodation paper for the payment of, or as security for, an individual debt of another person in which it has no interest, and for which it is not responsible; that it cannot assume liability for the individual debt of a stockholder; that it cannot execute a guarantee for the purpose of promoting a sale by another corporation; and that it has no power to guarantee the payment of other persons' notes in which it has no interest.

Where a corporation is without power to become a surety on the note of another corporation, the fact that such contract of suretyship is based upon independent consideration does not render the corporation liable thereon. Nor does the fact that the corporation acting as surety has the same stockholders and officers as the corporation whose note it guarantees have any effect to validate the contract of suretyship.

The only safe way to assure the guarantee is authorized and valid is to receive a copy of a corporate resolution authorizing the guarantee. Absent the receipt of this corporate resolution or documentation to support the authority of the corporation to issue the guarantee, it may be null and void.

When Guarantee Is Authorized

Sometimes a corporation is expressly authorized by charter or statute to make contracts of guarantee or suretyship, and frequently corporations are created for that express purpose. Such a company cannot, however, escape the general rule of law that a corporation cannot guarantee the liability of others, except insofar as it becomes a guarantor in the ordinary course of its business, or unless it receives the proceeds of the paper which it guarantees. Nor has a corporation authorized by statute to guarantee contracts any authority thereunder to enter into contracts of indemnity, not even on the theory that the making of indemnity contracts falls within the implied powers of such a corporation.

A corporation has, however, implied power to enter into a contract of guarantee or suretyship whenever the transaction can reasonably be said to be incidental to the conduct of the business authorized by its charter. But it must appear that the giving of the guarantee or the making of the contract of suretyship is reasonably necessary to enable the corporation to accomplish the object for which it was created, or that the particular transaction is reasonably necessary or proper in the conduct of its business. The mere fact that a contract of suretyship or guarantee may or will result in gain or benefit to the corporation, by increasing its business or otherwise, is not alone sufficient to authorize the same.

Gathering Information on the Guarantors

In order to determine whether a potential individual guarantor has the financial wherewithal necessary to support the guarantee, a credit professional should purchase a consumer credit report. The Fair Credit Reporting Act ("FCRA") defines a "consumer report" as any written, oral or other communication of any information by a consumer reporting agency bearing on a consumer's creditworthiness, credit standing, credit capability, character, general reputation, personal characteristics or mode of living which is used or expected to be used or collected in whole or in part for the purpose of serving as a factor in establishing the consumer's eligibility for (a) credit or insurance to be used primarily for personal, family or household purposes; (b) employment purposes; or (c) any other purpose authorized under Section 604 of the statute. Since the law focuses on the use of the credit as opposed to the nature of the proposed or actual credit recipient, if one seeks to purchase or acquire a "consumer report" which deals with personal, family or household credit issues, the law requires that there be a written consent by the person whose credit is to be checked, as well as a statement to the consumer reporting agency as to the permissible purpose for which the report is being obtained. This presented a troublesome duality to trade credit grantors who dealt with sole proprietors, partnerships or personal guarantors. On the one hand, the FCRA defines each individual as a consumer. On the other hand, trade credit grantors are not extending credit for personal, family or household credit uses. It has now been determined that where the individual is one who is or will be personally liable on the extension of commercial trade credit, such as in the case of a sole proprietor, partner or guarantor, the obtaining and use of a consumer credit report is a permissible purpose under Section 604 of the FCRA.

Refer to Chapter 27 for the following forms:

- Application for Employer Identification Number
- Articles of Incorporation
- Articles of Organization for the Limited Liability Company
- Assignment by a Corporation
- Corporate Bylaws
- Corporate Guarantee
- Corporate Guarantee of Payment of Future Debts
- Employment Agreement
- Operating Agreement and Regulations
- Unconditional Personal Guarantee
- Written Action of Subscriber, First Board of Directors and Stockholders

PENALTIES FOR VIOLATIONS OF INTERSTATE BUSINESS STATUTES

Consequences which can be imposed on foreign corporations transacting interstate business in violation of applicable statutes

	Penalties Imposed on Corporation or its Agentsor Officers	Injunction to Enjoin Corporation from Transacting Business in State	Contracts Void, Voidable,[1] or Valid	Liability of Officers, Directors, Stockholders, or Agents for Debts or on Contracts
Alabama[7]	Yes	Yes	Void[4]	
Alaska	Yes	Yes	Valid	
Arizona	Yes	Yes	Valid	
Arkansas[7]	Yes		Valid[3]	Yes
California[8]	Yes	Yes	Valid[3a]	Yes
Colorado	Yes	Yes	Valid[3a]	Yes
Connecticut	Yes		Valid	
Delaware[2]	Yes		Valid	Yes
D.C.	Yes		Valid[3a]	
Florida	Yes		Valid	
Georgia	Yes		Voidable	
Hawaii	Yes		Valid[12]	Yes
Idaho[5,6]	Yes	Yes	Valid	
Illinois	Yes	Yes	Valid[3a]	
Indiana[8,13]	Yes	Yes	Valid[3]	
Iowa[7,8]	Yes		Valid	
Kansas	Yes	Yes	Valid[3a]	
Kentucky	Yes		Valid	No
Louisiana[8]	Yes		Valid[3a]	Yes
Maine	Yes	Repealed	Valid[3a]	Repealed
Maryland[8]	Yes		Valid[3a]	Yes
Massachusetts	Yes		Valid[3b]	
Michigan	Yes	Yes	Valid[3a]	
Minnesota[11]	Yes	Yes	Valid[3a]	
Mississippi	Yes		Valid[3a]	
Missouri	Yes		Valid[3b]	
Montana	Yes		Valid[3a]	
Nebraska	Yes		Valid[3a]	
Nevada	Yes		Valid[14]	Yes
New Hampshire	Yes		Valid	
New Jersey[11]	Yes	Yes	Valid[3a]	
New Mexico[7]	Yes		Valid[3a]	
New York	Yes	Yes	Valid[3a]	
North Carolina	Yes		Valid[3a]	
North Dakota	Yes		Valid[3a]	
Ohio[8]	Yes	Yes	Valid[3a]	Yes
Oklahoma[8]	Yes	Yes	Valid[3c]	Yes
Oregon	Yes		Valid[3a]	No
Pennsylvania[9]	No		Valid[3a]	
Puerto Rico	Yes		Valid	
Rhode Island	Yes		Valid[3a]	
South Carolina	Yes	Yes	Valid	
South Dakota	Yes		Valid[3a]	

PENALTIES FOR VIOLATIONS OF INTERSTATE BUSINESS STATUTES
(Continued)

	Penalties Imposed on Corporation or its Agents or Officers	Injunction to Enjoin Corporation from Transacting Business in State	Contracts Void, Voidable,[1] or Valid	Liability of Officers, Directors, Stockholders, or Agents for Debts or on Contracts
Tennessee	Yes		Valid[3a]	
Texas	Yes		Valid[3a]	
Utah	Yes	Repealed	Valid[3a]	
Vermont[3,7]	Yes	Yes	Valid[3b]	
Virginia[8,9]	No		Valid[3a]	Yes
Washington	Yes		Valid[3a]	
West Virginia	Yes		Valid[3a]	
Wisconsin[10]	Yes		Valid[3c]	
Wyoming	Yes		Valid[3a]	

[1] A contract otherwise void or voidable may frequently be cured by obtaining a certificate of qualification and the payment of any applicable fines.

[2] Delaware has a reciprocal penalties provision whereby penalties imposed upon Delaware corporations doing business in other states which are greater than those imposed by Delaware law under similar conditions are imposed on foreign corporations doing business in Delaware.

[3] If corporation is unqualified at time of making of contract, no suit may thereafter be maintained.

[3a] Unenforceable but defendable.

[3b] No action on contract.

[3c] Neither civil action nor defense is permitted.

[4] This does not include mortgages insured by the Federal Housing Administration or Veterans Administration.

[5] The Supreme Court of Idaho has held that a foreign corporation which is qualified at time of trial is able to maintain a suit. *Spokane Merchants' Association v. Olmstead,* 80 Idaho 166, 327 P.2d 385 (1958).

[6] In Idaho, real estate deeds of unlicensed foreign corporations are voidable.

[7] Statutes regulating contract enforcement by unlicensed foreign corporation are limited to contracts executed within the state.

[8] Violation is a misdemeanor.

[9] Corporation may not maintain action in any court until it obtains certificate.

[10] A foreign corporation which transacts business in Wisconsin without a certificate of authority may be required to forfeit not more than $5,000. This forfeiture is in addition to any other fees which may be collected.

[11] Non-resident corporations in Minnesota must file a one-page business activity report containing the extent of the company's local assets, sales, and other activities within three and a half months after calendar or fiscal year, or they will lose their right to sue. This requirement was modeled after a similar statute in New Jersey, which was recently challenged as being unconstitutional in *First Family Mortgage Corp. v. Durham,* 528 A.2d 1288 (1987). The sole question in this case was whether the Corporation Business Activities Reporting Act (the Reporting Act), N.J.S.A. 14:13-14 to 23, violates the commerce clause [U.S. Const. art.I par.8, cl.3], or the supremacy clause [U.S. Const. art.VI par.2]. A plurality of the N.J. Supreme Court decided that the statute was constitutional and that the state could withhold access to the courts, but only until the corporation complies. The court held that once a foreign corporation files an Activities Report, the commerce clause requires that the corporation be allowed access to the courts for any current cause of action regardless of when it arose. The U.S. Supreme Court granted a Writ of Certiorari and will be reviewing this case during the 1988-1989 term. If it reverses the N.J. court it is likely that other states will enact similar statutes.

[12] In Hawaii benefit of statute of limitations is denied; can't sue or appear in any court for any cause.

[13] In Indiana guilty of Class C violation.

[14] In Nevada benefit or statute of limitations is denied.

2 Partnerships and Joint Ventures—Their Legal Obligations and How to Deal with Them

PARTNERSHIPS

Partnerships and joint ventures are entities created under state law by which two or more individuals may do business without forming a corporation. Partnerships and Joint Ventures are generally established by written agreements. These agreements, which are in the nature of a contract are governed by state law, and the rights and responsibilities concerning these agreements vary from state to state.

Partnerships are not the same as corporations, and the issues involving the extension of credit to them create many difficulties. It is important to understand the nature of the partnership with whom one is doing business, as well as the separate intricacies involved with partnership law. Fortunately, the Uniform Partnership Act has been adopted throughout the United States so that the law varies little from state to state.

The advent of the corporate form of business organization, and the growth of commercial enterprises requiring substantially greater capital, have been accompanied by a decrease in the use of the partnership. While the partnership form affords many advantages over the operation of a business by a single entrepreneur, by uniting the capital and skills of its members and spreading the risks of loss, it cannot match the advantage of limitation of personal liability provided by incorporation. Notwithstanding the corporate advantages, a substantial volume of the nation's business continues to be carried on by partnerships.

Where activities of a business extend beyond one state or into foreign countries, it is often found that the restrictions imposed on foreign corporations, as well as tax considerations, make the partnership a preferable vehicle of operation. It is also found that many of the risks inherent in commercial transactions can be adequately covered by insurance and thus the advantages offered by incorporation are of less significance. The problems of taxation are another important consideration in determining whether incorporation is preferable to partnership operation. In many jurisdictions corporations pay taxes that are not levied against partnerships. In the past there were statutory prohibitions regarding the conduct of certain businesses in the corporate form, especially the professions, but these restrictions now have been removed by most states.

The tax advantage of the partnership permits the partners to deduct losses from their personal tax returns while shareholders in a corporation ordinarily cannot do so. This advantage has been minimized by widespread use of Subchapter S Corporations which permits the taxable income to flow through to the shareholders. Further, the use of limited liability companies, which also provide this tax benefit to the owners has minimized the use of partnerships for the gain of tax benefits.

A partnership results from an agreement, express or implied, between two or more competent parties to unite their property, money, skill or labor for the entering into a lawful business for profit. No particular form of contract is necessary to create a partnership. It need only be in writing if it comes within the provisions of the Statute of Frauds. (*See* Chapter 5 for details on what triggers compliance with the Statute of Frauds.) Like other contracts, the general rules regarding the creation, validity and discharge of the contract are applicable. The partnership may be formed for the purpose of carrying out a single transaction or it may be formed for the operation of a general business over a period of time.

It should be noted that there must be mutual assent by all the parties to form a partnership agreement, each person must give his consent; one cannot be made a partner by the act of another. A person may act, however, in such a manner with another that the law will not permit him to deny that a partnership relationship exists. For example, where a person permits his name to be employed by a partnership, so that persons doing business with the partnership will rely upon his ostensible membership in extending credit, such person will not be permitted thereafter to deny the existence of his membership in the partnership. The filing of a certificate of doing business under an assumed name by two or more persons may constitute *prima facie* evidence of a partnership. Where there is an actual partnership, third parties are entitled to rights against the partnership in dealing with it even though the existence of the partnership is unknown to them.

UNIFORM PARTNERSHIP ACTS

Today every state has adopted the Uniform Partnership Act. The act defines a partnership to be "an association of two or more persons to carry on as co-owners of a business for profit." Uniform Partnership Act § 6(1). Within the purview of this Act, in order to have a partnership it is necessary that the elements of this definition be found in all relationships. One element without the other cannot create a partnership liability. For example, the mere fact that one shares profits in an enterprise is not a conclusive test of a partnership, for it is frequent that profits are paid as compensation for services in other than partnership transactions. The Uniform Partnership Law recognizes this distinction and makes provision for it. It is therefore extremely important that a particular state's version of the Act be reviewed for any local variations or changes.

There are three possible kinds of partners in a partnership: general, limited and silent (also known as a dormant or secret partner). A general partner, as the term suggests, is one who is liable for the firm's obligations without limitation as to amount. Before such a partner may relieve himself of liability to creditors, in the event that he wishes to sever his relationship with the partnership, he must give notice of his withdrawal to all those with whom the partnership has dealt. Limited partners are those who contribute capital to the partnership and who are liable only to the extent of their contribution. Full partnership liability may not be fastened upon them. A silent partner is one who, although not publicly acknowledging the relationship, has by his actions placed himself in such position that he is regarded in law as a general partner and, consequently, is liable for all the firm's obligations.

State Statutes Apply

When a partnership is formed, in the absence of statutory restrictions, it may do business under any name that it wishes to assume. Here again there are many statutory provisions regarding the use of partnership names, such as the use of the name of one who is not a partner, the use of fictitious names and the use of the designation "& Company" or "& Co." where such designation does not represent an actual partner. In many states there are statutes requiring the filing of partnership certificates, which must set forth the names of individual partners, the firm name, place of business and similar information.

The property of the partnership consists of such property that is contributed to the firm by the individual partners and which thereafter may be acquired in the course of partnership transactions. Profits received from the partnership business become the partnership's property as do goods manufactured or other types of capital produced or acquired by the partnership in its operations.

At common law a partnership could not, as such, hold title to real estate but by statute, such as the Uniform Partnership Act, a partnership is permitted to own real property. If a partnership is not permitted to own real estate, property must be acquired in the individual names of all the partners or in the name of one partner who is deemed to hold the property in trust for the partnership. When the partnership acquires real estate it is deemed to be converted into personalty and is subject to partnership debts.

Partnership Contract

The partnership contract usually sets forth the partners' rights and duties and the extent of their liability. *See generally* Uniform Partnership Act §§ 15, 18-22. The partners in some jurisdictions are expressly declared to be trustees for each other with respect to partnership property, and in all jurisdictions the partners are required to deal in partnership affairs with the utmost good faith; each partner is entitled to full knowledge of all partnership affairs. Every partner is entitled to take part in the conduct and management of the firm's business in the absence of a contrary agreement of the parties which may assign certain duties to each of the partners. In the event that the partners differ about the management or conduct of the business, the will of the majority is controlling.

Upon each of the partners rests the duty of seeing that proper books are kept of the firm's affairs and that each partner is entitled to statements of account of partnership transactions. The partners are entitled to share equally in the profits of the business in the absence of an agreement which apportions the profits. Likewise, the partners must share equal liability for expenses and losses in the absence of a contrary agreement. If a partner contributes personal service to the partnership business, in the absence of a contrary agreement, he is entitled to compensation for such service in addition to his share of the profits. The law does not permit suit against a partnership by a partner or by the partnership against a partner. The proper course is to secure an accounting.

Each partner is deemed an agent for the partnership and as such each partner is empowered to enter into contracts which bind the partnership. In this respect the principles of the law of agency are applicable to partnership transactions. Ordinarily third parties are entitled to rely upon the general power of a partner to contract on behalf of the partnership, except where the character of the transaction is such that the person may have reason to believe that the partner is not acting within the scope of the partnership business or is exceeding his authority. Within the scope of partnership business are such matters as making contracts in the ordinary course of business; sales; purchases; payments and receipts of money; borrowing money, including mortgaging or pledging firm assets; signing negotiable instruments and hiring or discharging employees or agents. Where the partner attempts to do some act such as to dispose of the entire assets of the business, assign for the benefit of creditors, sell furniture and fixtures or confess judgment, he is probably acting beyond the scope of his authority and one dealing with him acts at his own risk if the partner is actually exceeding his authority. A partner cannot bind his copartners by a contract of guarantee or suretyship for some third person. Credit professionals who accept a guarantee, to which the partnership name is signed will be responsible for proving to a court that the partner who signed the partnership name actually had authority to do so.

The partnership is liable for all acts done or representations made by each partner in the course of partnership business. This liability is, in general, the same as the liability of a principal for acts and representations of his agent.

Partners Jointly Liable

General partners are usually held to be jointly liable for partnership obligations. Such liability may be altered by agreement. In general, it may be stated that each partner is personally liable to the full extent of the partnership debts. Creditors of the firm may resort to the property of the individual partners. With respect to the rights of creditors of an individual partner it may be stated that such creditors' rights are limited to the personal property of the partner and his proportionate interest in the partnership.

Approximately 10 states provide for joint and several liability rather than joint liability. The functional difference is that the creditor can pick and choose which partner or partners it pursues for payment of debts.

It should also be noted that under the Uniform Partnership Act, newly admitted partners are not liable for obligations incurred by the partnership prior to the admission of the new partner.

However, please remember that each state when adopting the UPA had the opportunity to modify it, and of course, the courts may have interpreted various provisions differently based upon the facts in the individual cases.

Dissolution of Partnerships

The dissolution of the partnership may be effected by agreement of the parties or through court proceedings or by reason of some occurrence that effects a dissolution.

Under the Uniform Partnership Law, dissolution of a partnership is defined to be a change in relationship of the partners caused by any partner ceasing to be associated in the carrying on, as distinguished from the winding up, of the business.

The causes of dissolution include:

1. Without violation of the agreement between the partners: (a) by the termination of the definite term or particular undertaking specified in the agreement; (b) by the express will of any partner when no definite term or particular undertaking is specified; (c) by the express will of all the partners who have not assigned

their interests or suffered them to be charged for their separate debts, either before or after the termination of any specified term or particular undertaking; or (d) by the bona fide expulsion of any partner from the business in accordance with such a power conferred by the agreement between the partners.

2. In contravention of the agreement between the partners, where the circumstances do not permit a dissolution under any other provision of this section, by the express will of any partner at any time. [Note that Georgia and Louisiana do not provide for unilateral dissolution of a partnership in contravention of a partnership agreement.]

3. By any event which makes it unlawful for the business of the partnership to be carried on or for the members to carry it on in partnership.

4. By the death of any partner.

5. By the bankruptcy of any partner or the partnership.

In addition to the foregoing causes of dissolution, a judicial dissolution may be decreed under the following circumstances:

1. On application by or for a partner the court shall decree a dissolution whenever (a) a partner has been declared mentally incompetent in any judicial proceeding or is shown to be of unsound mind; (b) a partner becomes in any other way incapable of performing his part of the partnership contract; (c) a partner has been guilty of such conduct as tends to affect prejudicially the carrying on of the business; (d) a partner willfully or persistently commits a breach of the partnership agreement, or otherwise so conducts himself in matters relating to the partnership business that it is not reasonably practicable to carry on the business in partnership with him; (e) the business of the partnership can only be carried on at a loss; or (f) other circumstances render a dissolution equitable.

2. On the application of a purchaser of a partner's interest: (a) after the termination of the specified term or particular undertaking; or (b) at any time if the partnership was a partnership at will when the interest was assigned or when the charging order was issued. It is important to note that dissolution does not effect a complete termination of the partnership, but that the partnership continues until the winding up of partnership affairs is completed.

Continuation of Business After Death of Partner

Although the death of a partner may terminate a partnership, it continues for some purposes long enough to enable the surviving partners to settle the partnership affairs and wind up the business. However, the partners may agree prior thereto that the death of one will not terminate the partnership or the will of a deceased partner may sanction the continuation of the partnership business. In the absence of agreement or will to the contrary, the partnership is dissolved and the partnership assets vest in the surviving partners as "trustees" for the purpose of settling the partnership affairs. After payment of all the firm's debts, the deceased partner's estate is entitled to a pro-rata share of the partnership assets depending upon the proportionate interest of the decedent in the partnership. If the partnership is continued, the estate of the deceased partner is liable to the extent of its interest in the partnership assets but not beyond this.

The death of a partner does not generally terminate existing contracts to which the firm is a party. However, in special cases, such as where the performance of personal services by the deceased partner was an essential part of the contract, his death may terminate it. The surviving partners take possession of the assets, have the sole right to collect and sue upon claims and may make new contracts for the winding up of the partnership business. Except where it is essential to winding up the business, the surviving partners cannot make new contracts or incur obligations binding on the firm or the deceased partner's estate unless authorized by the decedent's will or prior agreement. The partnership business may be continued for a short time in order to dispose of stock on hand and small purchases of additional stock may be made to render that on hand more saleable; existing contracts of the firm, in most cases, may be completed. Contracts beyond the scope of the surviving partners' authority as above bind the surviving partners personally but not the estate of the deceased partner. After dissolution a partner can bind the partnership by any act appropriate to the winding up of partnership affairs. Furthermore, the partnership is bound by any postdissolution transaction that would have bound the partnership if dissolution had not taken place, if the other party to the postdissolution transaction had been a creditor prior to the dissolution and had no knowledge of the dissolution or had not previously extended credit but knew of the partnership before its dissolution, had no knowledge or notice of the dissolution, and the dissolution had not been advertised in a local general circulation newspaper. No definite rule can be laid down about how long a period of time the business may be continued, as this will depend on the nature of the business and the work necessary to settle its affairs and wind up the partnership. The surviving partners may sell, mortgage or pledge the firm's assets for the purpose of raising money to pay the firm's debts or to secure the payment thereof.

Where the partnership assets are insufficient to pay its obligations, the creditors may have recourse to the property of the surviving partners and the estate of the deceased partner. There is conflict of authority about whether a creditor of an insolvent partnership is precluded from asserting a claim against the deceased partner's estate after the time for filing claims against the estate has expired. No general rule can be laid down about the terms on which creditors of the partnership and creditors of the deceased partner may share in assets of the deceased partner's estate if the assets of the firm are insufficient to pay all partnership creditors. There are conflicting decisions in the various states and in many states this subject is covered by statute.

LIMITED PARTNERSHIPS

Limited partnerships provide that only the general partner is personally liable for the debts of the partnership (as is the partnership itself), and the limited partners are not. This curtails the ability of a creditor to effect collection on a debt. Additionally, the general partner may be a corporation or another limited partnership, thus further insulating the partners from any individual liability. The limited partnership is subject to the contract which creates it.

A limited partnership is defined in the Uniform Limited Partnership Act § 1 as a partnership "having as members one or more general partners and one or more limited partners." A limited partner is one who contributes to the partnership capital and shares in its profits but who has no powers in the control of the business of the partnership and no personal liability for its debts. The extent of such partner's liability is the amount of his capital investment in the partnership, which, like all partnership property, is subject to claims of creditors. In all respects, except the relationship of the limited partner to the other members and to third persons, the limited partnership is substantially the same as a general partnership. The general partners retain the same powers and are subject to the same liabilities to creditors as in a general partnership.

Although it is expected that the use of the word "limited" in the name of the entity means that it is a limited partnership, that cannot be relied on universally. For example, in Michigan, "partnership associations" are authorized to be created by statute and are required to have "limited" as the last word in the name. However, these entities are not limited partnerships and their character is more in line with that of a quasi-corporation.

How Formed

Most states require the filing of a limited partnership certificate signed by all partners containing (1) firm name and principal place of business; (2) nature of business partnership will engage in; (3) names and addresses of partners, specifying which are general and which are limited partners; (4) amount of capital contributed by each limited partner; and (5) duration of partnership. The contribution of capital by limited partners is usually required to be wholly in cash and prior to the formation of the partnership. This requirement, however, varies from state to state. For example, in New York a limited partner may contribute "cash or other property, but not services." In Delaware the limited partner may contribute or give a promissory note to contribute, cash, property or services. In many states a general partner must file an affidavit stating that such contributions have been made. All the required papers are usually filed or recorded with the recording officer of the county in which the business is to be conducted and the certificate of partnership published for a specified number of times in a newspaper of general circulation in the locality.

Various state statutes contain provisions as to the use of firm name and partners' names so as to advise the public of the nature of the partnership. Usually the name of at least one general partner must appear in the firm name. In some states the partnership is required to display a sign in front of its place of business designating which of its partners are general and which are limited partners.

There are a number of distinctions between limited and general partnerships, including the following: the limited partnership continues only for the period of time mentioned in its certificate; the limited partner may not usually engage in management of the business of the firm; his interest in the partnership assets is limited to his capital investment; the limited partner's compensation is in the form of interest on his contribution and a proportion of the profits; he is not permitted to withdraw any part of his capital contribution to the firm during the partnership's existence; under most statutes the death of a limited partner does not terminate the partnership.

Relationship to Third Persons

The general partners in a limited partnership are subject to all the liabilities of partners in a general partnership and are jointly and severally liable for the partnership debts and obligations as if they were guarantors of the obligations of the partnership. The limited partners are not liable beyond the capital contributed to the firm and are not generally liable to creditors. Dealings between the firm and third parties are to be carried on by the general partners. Although a limited partner cannot usually bind the partnership by his contract, such contract may be ratified by the general partners. The general participation of a limited partner in conduct of the firm business can subject him to liability as a general partner. For example, in Tennessee a limited partner may be liable for the obligations of the limited partnership if "he takes part in the control of the business." The limited partner will also be subjected to personal liability for obligations incurred after the firm has altered its capital, membership or business. The withdrawal of his capital contribution, or part thereof, from the firm may subject the limited partner to liability of a general partner and to restoration of the capital so withdrawn, depending on the statutory provisions of each state. A limited partner is not liable for torts of general partners and agents of the firm to which he is not a party. A limited partner is personally liable as a general partner to any person whom he has induced to deal with the partnership on the representation that he is a general partner. A limited partner is ordinarily not a proper party to a suit against the partnership.

Upon insolvency the partnership's assets become a trust fund for payment of claims of creditors. The partnership may make an assignment for the benefit of creditors or file a petition in bankruptcy. After all the general creditors are paid, a limited partner may share in the firm assets on his claim for capital contribution and loans. In some states he is permitted to share in assets along with general creditors for loans made to the partnership above his capital contribution. An individual creditor of a limited partner can assert no claim against the partnership. Nor can his interest be the subject of attachment or execution. In other respects the insolvency of limited partnerships is substantially the same as that of a general partnership.

As with corporations, most states require that a foreign limited partnership shall register in the state before it conducts business there.

A limited partnership may be dissolved upon death or bankruptcy of a general partner, misconduct of a general partner, fraud practiced upon a limited partner or by expiration of the term for which partnership was organized. Dissolution may also be by the consent of all partners. The general partners are obliged to distribute assets and settle the partnership affairs.

LIMITED LIABILITY PARTNERSHIPS

A Limited Liability Partnership ("LLP" or "PLLP") is one form of a limited liability company. This type of limited liability company applies only to professionals who may practice as a general partnership without any limited partners.

Only two types of general partnerships are eligible to be LLPs:

1. Partnerships, at least one of whom is a professional authorized by law of that particular state to provide a professional service. This would typically be accountants, architects, attorneys, dentists, doctors or engineers.

2. Partnerships authorized by or holding a license, certificate, registration or permit issued by the licensing authority pursuant to the law of a particular state. This would typically include the professionals listed above but might also include land surveying services, landscape architectural services, social workers or educators.

Although variations may occur—state by state—generally the name of an LLP must contain the words "Registered Limited Liability Partnership" or "Limited Liability Partnership". Alternatively, the abbreviations "R.L.L.P.", "RLLP", "L.L.P." or "LLP" may be used.

The registration with the Secretary of State must be signed by one or more partners and must state:

1. The name of the registered LLP
2. The address of the principal office of the LLP
3. The profession or professions to be practiced by the LLP and that it is eligible to register as a registered LLP pursuant to the Act
4. A designation of the Department (or Secretary) of State as agent of the LLP upon whom process against it may be served and the post office address within or without this state to which the Department (or Secretary) of State should mail a copy of any process against it or served upon it
5. If the LLP is to have a registered agent, its name and address in that state
6. That the LLP is filing a registration for status as a registered LLP
7. If the registration of the LLP is to be effective on a date later than the time of filing, the date, not to exceed 60 days from the date of the filing, of the proposed effectiveness
8. If all or specified partners of the LLP are to be liable in their capacity as partners for all or specified debts, obligations, or liabilities of the LLP as authorized by the Act
9. Any others matters the partnership determines to include in the registration

JOINT VENTURES

Joint ventures are informal partnerships where there may or may not be an agreement between the venturers. In most instances, each of the joint venturers are personally liable for the debts of the venture. Because each joint venture is different and states regulate them differently, each one may be different. Credit grantors assume that if more than one individual or entity is involved in a transaction it will be deemed to be a "partnership." That is not the case. Joint ventures can be created by direct action or by operation of law when there is inaction. There are distinctions between joint ventures and partnerships that must be understood. More importantly, the credit grantor must be able to determine if credit is being extended to a joint venture as opposed to a partnership.

Joint ventures may be defined as contracts in which two or more persons (together constituting one party thereto), as contractors, jointly and severally bind themselves for their mutual benefit, to perform definite promises or obligations in a certain special transaction, their interests being separate and apart from and not joined with any other interests. More simply stated, a joint venture is an association of two or more entities to carry out a single business enterprise by combining their abilities and property (monetary or otherwise) to earn a profit.

The relationship of the joined parties in such contracts verges on partnership and very little difference actually exists. In fact, as the decisions reveal, it is quite apparent that the theory of the law of partnership is being applied in joint venture situations. For the purpose of the extension of credit, one should consider a joint venture no differently than a partnership, except that the credit grantor does not have the benefits of the strict liability imposed by the Uniform Partnership Act. Unless a credit grantor is very comfortable with the assets of the joint venture as being able to satisfy any indebtedness, because of the somewhat "loose" nature of the entity, it is critically important to receive by way of guarantee the written confirmation of assumption of indebtedness by each of the joint venturers. Absent this, a creditor can run the risk that the loosely defined joint venture will be so loose that there will be no responsible individual or individuals available to deal with credit problems that may exist in the future. Generally a joint venture as opposed to a partnership is organized for a specific or limited purpose. A joint venture is usually taxed as a partnership. However, if it has certain characteristics of an association, it may be taxed as a corporation.

A slight difference does exist, however, when one co-venturer attempts to bind the other in his dealings with third persons. Also, the joint venture covers but one particular transaction while a partnership may continue indefinitely for various kinds of transactions.

The difference between a joint venture and an ordinary contract is marked. The usual contract may be made between a buyer and seller, the latter of whom agrees and is able to deliver merchandise or to perform certain specified services. Joint contractors or venturers, on the other hand, agree to perform the contract as one collective party to the transaction by exercising their respective combined resources, often quite different in nature, while depending upon each of the others for the completion of the enterprise. Joint venturers are mutual fiduciaries.

Often the joint contractors do not realize the status of their relationship when they enter into the agreement and do not know that they are operating under and are controlled by the law relating to joint ventures, which is gradually being placed in a special category. Consequently, a contract, which is believed to be just an ordinary written statement of mutual promises, or an agreement of employment, or even a partnership, may be held to be a joint venture.

As a result, the status of the relationship of the promisors and their liabilities and obligations, which each assumes jointly as well as severally, becomes more important. A properly drawn contract of joint venture, therefore, will set forth the intent and will use appropriate words to bind the promisors to complete the whole of the obligations either together, or separately if one or the other fails to perform. In connection with these requirements a credit statement evidencing the ability of both parties to perform is a wise preliminary.

In most jurisdictions the words "we jointly and severally," "we, or either of us" or "I promise" (followed by the signatures of two or more promisors) mean what they say, but in other jurisdictions, where the influence of Roman laws still prevail, these expressions are not always so interpreted. It follows, therefore, that such expressions should be supported by additional words of explanation so that the joint and several obligations may be enforced and the contract fully completed regardless of subsequent events, including the insolvency or the death of one of the parties.

Such expressions as "we will undertake," "the directors promise" or "we promise" import only a joint liability and do not carry the joint and several feature which is so necessary in joint ventures as mentioned above.

Releasing one venturer from his obligations discharges all from liability in some jurisdictions. A well-drawn joint contract provides for this contingency.

The status of the joint venturers, as between themselves, is one of the most important features of the agreement. Is there in fact a joint venture, or is there merely a contract of employment between the parties, or is there a partnership relation?

Another element worthy of mention is the right of another person who deals with the joint venturer in good faith and without knowledge of any limitations upon his authority. There is a presumption that the venturer has been given the power to bind his associates by such contracts as are reasonably necessary to carry on the business in which they are presently engaged, and this is so even though they may have expressly agreed among themselves that they should not be so liable.

This is not the law, however, if commitments are made covering transactions outside the scope of the business of the venturers. A third person, under such conditions, deals with a joint venturer at his peril. While this feature resembles a partnership and is one of the similarities referred to above, there still exists a fine distinction between them because the contract covering joint ventures will (or should) define the scope of an explicit enterprise.

Refer to Chapter 27 for the following forms:

- Affidavit of Capital Contributions
- Agreement of Limited Partnership
- Certificate of Limited Partnership
- Partnership Agreement

3 Creation of Agreements with Agents and Principals

When dealing with a representative of a debtor-entity, most credit professionals assume that the person is authorized to speak for and on behalf of the debtor-entity. That is not necessarily the case. Conversely, a credit grantor may be bound by others acting for and on its behalf (such as salespeople and independent agents) where a similar issue may arise. Understanding who may or may not bind an entity or an individual to an agreement is essential to a credit professional's ability to create an agreement and impose liability for a breach of that agreement.

An agent is a person who represents or is authorized to represent another person in a transaction or transactions with third parties. The person represented is known as the "principal" and the person appointed is designated as "agent," "attorney," "broker," "proxy," "factor" or by some other similar term.

An agency relationship exists where the agent performs acts or undertakes obligations for the principal's benefit. In an agency relationship, the agent acts as a fiduciary in that the agent acts in trust for the benefit of the principal. Normally, a written agency contract will be created to outline the authority granted by the principal to the agent. However, a written agency contract generally does not need to be created for an agency relationship to exist.

Any competent person may appoint an agent to represent him, and any qualified and competent person may be appointed as agent of another. Agents may be either general, in which case they are authorized to assume entire charge of their principal's business, or special, in which event they are authorized to act only in a specific transaction or a limited amount of business.

The power and authority of an agent is limited normally by the terms of the agency contract. A person dealing with an agent in the absence of specific information as to the limitations of the agent's authority, or because charged with notice of such limitations by virtue of past transactions with the agent, may rely upon the agent's authority to bind his principal in all matters coming within the usual scope of the agent's agency relationship.

A traveling salesperson, in the absence of special circumstances, cannot be presumed to have authority to bind a company by the acceptance of an order for its product. The usual function is merely to solicit orders and forward them to the office of his employer, where they are subject to acceptance or rejection. The limit of a salesperson's usual authority has been consistently recognized by the courts, and the acts of the salesperson's employer subsequent to the receipt of the order usually determine whether or not the order has been so accepted as to bind the seller to deliver.

Likewise, a traveling salesperson has no authority to accept and receive payment on behalf of a principal, and in the absence of evidence about the extent of the salesperson's authority, a payment made to the agent will not discharge the debt unless the moneys are actually received by the principal.

HOW AGENTS ARE APPOINTED

While the agent's appointment does not have to be evidenced by writing, it is prudent to insist upon proof of the agent's authority in all transactions involving substantial amounts. A special agent is often appointed by means of a written power of attorney which specifically delineates the scope of the agent's authority. As a result, the special agent will have "actual" authority to act on behalf of the principal.

A person may, however, without authorization, act on behalf of a principal. The acceptance by the principal of the fruits of such person's performance ratifies such person's agency. If a duly appointed agent performs an unauthorized act, the principal on learning of it may either refuse to be bound by it, or may expressly or impliedly ratify it.

Even if an agent has no express authority from a principal, the principal's conduct or negligent conduct, may be such as to indicate that the agent has apparent authority. A third person dealing with the agent and relying on such apparent authority may hold the principal liable. For example, if P stands by and permits A, an unauthorized agent, to sell P's goods and makes no protest, but acquiesces in the transaction, P will be held to have appointed A his agent and will be bound by the transaction.

Circumstances may arise where it may be necessary for one party to act for the benefit of another. For example, an employee, knowing that a corporate document must be filed with a state agency on a specific date, may effectuate the filing of the document without first obtaining the consent or authorization of the employer. Under this and similar fact patterns, an agency by necessity will be created. Of course, upon the employer learning of the filing, the employer will most likely ratify the employee's actions.

A court may order one party to act for the benefit of another party or may determine that an agency relationship exists based upon certain evidentiary facts. In these circumstances, the court will effectively create an agency by operation of law.

Subagents

The authority of an agent is delegated and is subject to the principle that a delegated power may not be further delegated. Therefore, an agent may not, without express authority from the principal, delegate to subagents authority to make contracts on behalf of the principal.

Liability of Agent Where Principal Is Disclosed

In general, if, at the time of entering into an agreement with an agent, the third party knows of the principal, then the principal and not the agent will be liable to the third party for breach of the agreement.

Liability of Agent Where Principal Is Undisclosed

If the person who is in fact an agent for another conceals the fact of his agency and makes a contract in his own name, he renders himself personally liable, unless the principal instructed that his identity be kept secret because he knew the third party would not deal with him. But if the agent acted within his authority, the third party, upon discovering the identity of the principal may elect to hold the principal liable instead of the agent. This rule is, however, subject to the following exceptions:

1. An undisclosed principal cannot be bound if the contract made by the agent is in the form of a negotiable instrument or a sealed contract
2. If the principal, before his identity was disclosed, furnished the agent with the money due on the contract, the principal cannot be forced to pay twice. There are exceptions to this rule in certain industries. It is incumbent upon the credit grantor to become familiar with the customs, practices and case law affecting a particular industry
3. If the third party elects to bind the agent, he cannot thereafter proceed against the principal
4. If the contract expressly recites that there are no other parties to the agreement, then the principal will not be liable under the contract.

DUTIES OF AGENT

An agent owes a fiduciary duty to the principal and therefore must, in dealing with his principal, act within the scope of his authority and exercise utmost good faith as well as the requisite prudence, skill and diligence.

The agent must at all times act in the highest good faith with complete loyalty to the employer and may not, without the permission of the principal, act for either a conflicting interest or for oneself. Information received by the agent in the course of one's employment is confidential and may not be used by the agent for his own benefit. If one enters into a contract without actual or apparent authority from the principal or in excess of an existing authority, the agent is personally liable unless the principal is estopped to deny the authority, usually because the principal has received some benefit or subsequently ratifies the contract. The agent is also personally liable for any tortious conduct resulting in damages to a third party, whether within or outside the scope of his authority; the principal joins in this liability when the conduct is within the scope of authority of the agent.

EMPLOYEES AND INDEPENDENT CONTRACTORS

It is important to distinguish employees from independent contractors because employees are agents of their employers, but independent contractors are not. There are no uniform criteria by which one can easily differentiate between an employee who is an agent of an employer, and an independent contractor who is generally not an agent. If a business desires to engage or employ an independent contractor, this should be clearly stated in any agreement between them, although courts are willing to look beyond the written language of an agreement to determine what the arrangement actually is in substance. Additionally, steps should be taken to make sure that the public at large dealing with the independent contractor recognizes or is able to determine this status. However, the theory adopted by most jurisdictions to differentiate between an employee and an independent contractor is based upon whether the person is subject to, or free from, the control of the employer with respect to the details of the work. An employee is subject to the employer, who has the right to control his conduct with respect to the details of the matters entrusted to him. On the other hand, an independent contractor is a person who, in exercising his independence, agrees to do certain work according to his own methods without being subject to the control of the employer, except as to the product of his work. Accordingly, where an employer may prescribe what shall be done, but not how it shall be done or who shall do it, the person employed is generally an independent contractor and not an agent. Some factors examined to determine the extent of control would include whether the hiring party has the right to instruct the hired person about when, where and how work is to be performed, whether the relationship is a continuing one and which party may hire and pay assistants or other support staff for the hired person.

Although the existence of the relation of independent contractor and employer often excludes the relation of principal and agent, there are occasions when both relations exist at the same time with regard to different portions or phases of the work. A person may be an independent contractor as to certain work, and a mere agent as to other work for the same employer not embraced within the independent contract. It should also be noted that a person may be both an agent and an independent contractor by virtue of being an attorney, a broker or an auctioneer. These persons are agents, although as to their physical activities they are independent contractors, because they have the power to act for and bind the principal in business negotiations within the scope of their agency.

PROTECTING YOURSELF WHEN DOING BUSINESS WITH AN AGENT

When a credit grantor knows that he/she is dealing with an agent, the most prudent thing to do is to receive some writing which clearly indicates that the agent has the express authority to bind the principal. Naturally, if such binding would be in the normal course of the agent's business or profession, such a writing is not needed. However, when any question arises with respect to the authority of the agent to bind the principal, care should be taken at the initial stages of the transaction to make sure that there is adequate documentation. An example would be to have the credit grantor request the delivery of corporate minutes that approve the purported transaction and authorize the agent to act on behalf of the principal corporation by executing the applicable contract. In particular, credit grantors dealing with municipal corporations must be extremely cautious. Specific Municipal Corporation Laws may contain restrictions as to limits of authority as to whom may bind that corporation.

If a credit grantor has any concern about an agent's authority and an agreement is reached with the agent which purportedly binds the principal, it can be very productive to forward a conforming copy of the agreement to the principal with a cover letter indicating that the credit grantor is relying on the representations of the agent to bind the principal. By providing the cover letter and a conforming copy of the agreement to the principal, the silence of the principal may have ratified the agreement to which it is to be bound.

This is one area where common sense may also play an important role. When something looks to be "too good" or suspicious, a credit grantor should be wary and investigate further. It does little good to try to secure the authority of the principal after the fact, especially when the principal sees a way to extricate itself from any potential exposure and liability.

4 Dealing with the Party Using an Assumed or Fictitious Name

When considering extending credit to a new customer, a credit manager should be thinking ahead to collecting the account. Knowing the proper identity of the person or entity you are doing business with is critical in the event that a lawsuit must be filed. If suit is filed in the wrong name, or against an entity that does not exist, then any judgment obtained is of no value because it cannot be executed upon. Occasionally, persons or businesses operate under an assumed or fictitious name. A credit manager should not take for granted that a customer is revealing the name of the person or entity legally responsible for the debts of the business.

Most state legislatures have enacted statutes requiring the filing of a certificate setting forth the real names of persons transacting business under partnerships or assumed names. The purpose of such statutes is well expressed in the case of *Sagel v. Fylar*, 89 Conn. 293, 93 A. 1027, 1028 (1915):

> The remedial purpose of the statute manifestly was that the public should have ready means of information as to the personal or financial responsibility behind the assumed name. Its aim was the protection of those who might deal with, or give credit to, the fictitious entity. It obviously was not to provide a means by which persons having received a benefit from another should be enabled to retain it without compensation and to repudiate any agreement for compensation.

FORMS OF STATUTES

The format of these statutes is substantially similar, although there are important differences, particularly with respect to the penalty imposed for failure to comply. Summaries of the statutes appear below, and references thereto may be had for specific information. Generally, the law usually requires any person transacting business under a fictitious name or a designation not showing the names of the persons interested as partners in such business, to file in the office of the County Clerk or the Town Clerk, as the case may be, a certificate setting forth the name under which the business is to be conducted and the true or real name or names of the person or persons conducting or transacting such business with the post office address or addresses of such persons.

The mere fact that there is compliance with a fictitious or assumed name statute does not permit a creditor to necessarily deal with that business or entity under the assumed name. The law is designated to provide others with information. The law does not substitute the assumed or fictitious name for a real name. Corporations, partnerships, and other business entities and ventures must still use exact legal names on documents. The use of an assumed name on a contract or other document may cause its invalidity.

STATUTES USUALLY PENAL

Note: State legislatures will, on occasion, modify an area of law without clear delineation as to its content and context. As a result, even the changes which have been enacted prior to placement in the state's Code may be difficult to locate. As a result, the Editors urge all users of the *Manual* to use this publication only as a guide, and consult the latest codified version of the state's law for all recent changes.

The statutes are usually penal in their nature and may provide fines or imprisonment for violation. The following is a summary of the laws of the various states with respect to the violation of the statutes governing the use of fictitious or assumed names.

ALABAMA

No assumed name statute. Trade names are not registrable except as trademarks or service marks. Trade names are protected by state common law.

ALASKA

No statutory provisions.

ARIZONA

Persons failing to record a trade name cannot maintain any action based on any contract made or transaction had until the required certificate is recorded. STATUTE—AZ Rev. Stat., Section 44-1236.

ARKANSAS

Failure to file certificate of doing business under a name other than one's own is a statutory violation for each day not filed and subjects one to a fine not less than $25 and not to exceed $100. No provision regarding maintenance of actions. STATUTE—AR Code Ann., Section 4-70-202.

CALIFORNIA

No person or partnership required to file statement or assignee may maintain an action on account of contract made or transaction had under fictitious or partnership name, until statement filed and published. One who executes, files or publishes any such statement, knowing that it is false may be found guilty of a misdemeanor and is suspect to a penalty up to $1000. STATUTE—CA Bus. & Prof. Code, Sections 17918 and 17930.

COLORADO

Penalty for lack of compliance with recording statute is fine up to $500 and inability to prosecute suits for collection of debts, until filed. STATUTE—CO Rev. Stat., Sections 24-35-303, 304.

CONNECTICUT

Failure to comply results in fine not more than $500 or imprisonment for not more than one year. STATUTE—CT Gen. Stat., Section 35-1.

DELAWARE

Every person, and each and every person comprising such firm or association shall be fined not more than $100 or imprisonment not exceeding three months or both. STATUTE—DE Code Ann. 6, Section 3106.

DISTRICT OF COLUMBIA

No registration requirements.

FLORIDA

Noncompliance prohibits maintenance of suit in Florida courts and is a misdemeanor of the second degree. Violation does not impair the validity of contracts or other acts of such business and does not prevent such business from defending any action. STATUTE—FL Stat. 865.09.

GEORGIA

Noncompliance is a misdemeanor and noncomplying party to lawsuit may pay court costs but there is no other penalty. STATUTE—GA Code Ann., Sections 10-1-491, 493.

GUAM

No person or partnership required to file may maintain any action upon or on account of any contracts made, or transactions had, until certificate has been filed. STATUTE—GM Stat., Sect 26103.

HAWAII

No penalty provisions.

IDAHO

In case of failure to file, such person or persons may not maintain any suit in any state court, and such failure is *prima facie* evidence of fraud in securing credit. Conducting business without certificate is a misdemeanor. Damages in the amount of loss, attorneys' fees and costs may be awarded. STATUTE—ID Code, Section 53-509.

ILLINOIS

Persons not complying with statute are subject to fine and imprisonment and may be sued under assumed name. Violation is a class C misdemeanor. Each day of noncompliance is a separate offense. Such persons may be sued under assumed name. STATUTE—805 IL Comp. Stat. 405/5, 6.

INDIANA

Noncompliance is a class B infraction. STATUTE—IN Code, Section 23-15-1-3.

IOWA

It is unlawful to conduct business under trade name other than surname of each person owning business unless statement is filed. Violation is a simple misdemeanor. STATUTE—IA Code, Section 490.401.

KANSAS

No statutory provisions.

KENTUCKY

Fee of $25 to $100 and imprisonment up to 10 days or both may be imposed for any violation of trades name statute. Each day of continued violation constitutes a separate offense. STATUTE—KY Rev. Stat. Ann., Section 365.990.

LOUISIANA

Violation shall carry a fine of not less than $25 nor more than $100, or imprisonment for not less than 10 days nor more than 60 days, or both. Each day of noncompliance is a separate offense. STATUTE—LA Rev. Stat. Ann., Section 284.

MAINE

Failure to file certificate shall be punishable by a fine of $5 for each day in default. Continued use of assumed name may be enjoined upon suit by Attorney General or any person adversely affected by its use. STATUTE—ME Rev. Stat. Ann. Section 31.5, and 13A Section 307.

MARYLAND

Failure to file certificate renders owner liable to suit by any creditor in name under which business is conducted and all property possessed, used or acquired in business is liable to seizure and sale under execution. Willful execution and filing of false certificate punishable by fine of up to $1,000, imprisonment of up to one year or both. STATUTE—MD Code Ann., Corp. & Assns., Section 1-406.

MASSACHUSETTS

Violation is punishable by a fine of not more than $300 for each month during which such violation continues. STATUTE—MA Ann. Laws 110, Section 5.

MICHIGAN

One failing to file a certificate when required is guilty of a misdemeanor punishable by a fine of not less than $25 nor more than $100, by imprisonment not exceeding 30 days or both. Each day of noncompliance constitutes a separate offense. Violation does not constitute invalidity of a contract, though one failing to file cannot bring an action on contracts made under assumed name until compliance and requirement is met. STATUTE—MI Comp. Laws, Section 445.5.

MINNESOTA

If any business that has failed to file trade name commences civil action in state court, action stayed until certificate filed and defendant entitled to $250 abatement or costs. Plaintiff entitled to $250 costs where any such business defends against civil action. STATUTE—MN Stat., Section 333.06.

MISSISSIPPI

No requirement for registration of business names.

MISSOURI

Failure to file is a misdemeanor. STATUTE—MO Ann. Stat., Section 417.230.

MONTANA

May not maintain suit or action under such name. STATUTE—MT Code Ann., Section 30-13-215.

NEBRASKA

Any person who shall engage in or transact any business in the state under trade name without registering shall be guilty of a class V misdemeanor. Each day of noncompliance is a separate and distinct offense. Any business which knowingly makes false or fraudulent representations or declarations in procuring registration shall be liable to pay all damages sustained in consequence of such filing. STATUTE—NE Rev. Stat., Sections 87-220, 215.

NEVADA

Persons violating the requirement to file, or their assignees, cannot commence or maintain an action on any transaction or cause arising out of the business illegally conducted until the requisite certificate is filed. Such violation constitutes a misdemeanor. STATUTE—NV Rev. Stat., Sections 602.070, 090.

NEW HAMPSHIRE

Failure to register is a misdemeanor. STATUTE—NH Rev. Stat., Section 349:9.

NEW JERSEY

Failure to register is a misdemeanor, subject to a fine of between $200 and $500. Untimely filing subjects business to additional filing fees equal to the regular fee multiplied by years of noncompliance. Violation does not impair validity of contract or prohibit defensive actions, though a business may not maintain an action arising out of a contract or act in which it used such alternate name until certificate is filed. STATUTE—NJ Stat. Ann., Section 14A:2-2.1.

NEW MEXICO

No statutory provisions.

NEW YORK

Anyone who knowingly fails to comply may be guilty of a misdemeanor. Noncompliance prohibits maintenance of an action or proceeding on any contract or other action until certificate is filed. Failure to comply does not affect rights of third persons and does not limit liability of partners under partnership law. STATUTE—NY Gen. Bus. Law, Section 130.

NORTH CAROLINA

A violating business may be guilty of a class 3 misdemeanor and liable in amount of $50 to any person demanding the filing of certificate of business if the business fails to file within seven days after such demand. Violation does not prevent recovery in any civil action. STATUTE—NC Gen. Stat., Section 66-71.

NORTH DAKOTA

Penalty for not complying is that a partnership may not maintain an action on, or an account of, any contracts made or transactions had in partnership name, in any court of state until such certificate and publication are made. It is unlawful to transact business in the name of a person as a partner if such person is not interested in the firm. STATUTE—ND Cent. Code, Sections 45-11-08, 45-11-04.

OHIO

No person doing business under trade name or fictitious name may commence or maintain any action in such name in any court in Ohio or on account of any contracts or transactions in such name until it has complied with the statute. Actions may be commenced against user of fictitious or trade name whether or not such name has been registered. Criminal penalties for misuse of any registered article. STATUTE—OH Rev. Code Ann., Section 1329.10.

OKLAHOMA

Failure to comply precludes the partnership from maintaining any action on contracts made or transactions had in partnership name in any court of the state until compliance. STATUTE—OK Stat. 54, Section 83.

OREGON

Failure to register is punishable by civil penalty of up to $100; precludes suit or action on contract until business name is registered; Secretary of State may enjoin any transaction of business if assumed business name registration is not current. In any suit arising out of business conducted without proper registration, plaintiff may recover $500 or costs, including attorneys' fees, (sic) plaintiff incurred in ascertaining defendant's real name, whichever is greater. Plaintiff may recover this sum even if defendant prevails. STATUTE—OR Rev. Stat., Section 648.135.

PENNSYLVANIA

Failure to register fictitious name will preclude entity, successors and assigns from bringing suit on any contract until application filed and $500 penalty paid to Department of State; however, these provisions are inapplicable if substantial compliance in good faith with this or prior law. Noncompliance does not impair validity of contracts or other acts and does not prohibit such business from defending a suit. STATUTE—54 PA Cons. Stat. Ann., Section 331.

PUERTO RICO

No penalties.

RHODE ISLAND

Failure to comply subjects offender to fine of up to $500 or imprisonment not to exceed one year, or both. STATUTE—RI Gen. Laws, Section 6-1-4.

SOUTH CAROLINA

Registration requirement only applies to limited partnerships. Violation results in a fine of $1 and imprisonment for five days for each day of noncompliance. Each partner may be severally liable for violations. STATUTE—SC Code Ann., Sections 33-42-45, 39-13-40.

SOUTH DAKOTA

No action may be filed unless statement of partnership name is filed. Disability to maintain action may be removed at any time by filing statement. Those failing to file are guilty of a misdemeanor punishable by 30 days in jail or $200 fine, or both. STATUTE—SD Codified Laws, Sections 48-7-907, 22-6-2.

TENNESSEE

No penalty provision.

TEXAS

Maximum fine of $2,000 upon conviction for intentional violation of assumed name statutes. STATUTE—TX Bus. and Com. Code Ann., Section 36.26.

UTAH

Persons who have not complied shall not sue, prosecute, or maintain any action, suit, counterclaim, cross-complaint, or proceeding in any court in this state until the provisions have been complied with. Violator may be subject to penalty in the form of a late filing fee. STATUTE—UT Code Ann., Section 42-2-10.

VERMONT

Failure to register renders members liable to forfeiture of $10 and they may be enjoined from conducting business and without standing in court to enforce obligations. Fined not more than $100 by a superior court. Noncomplying members may be enjoined from conducting business and have no standing in court to enforce obligations. Violators can be fined not more than $100 by a superior court. STATUTE—VT Stat. Ann., Sections 1634, 1626.

VIRGINIA

Failure to register is a misdemeanor. STATUTE—VA Code Ann., Section 59.1-75.

WASHINGTON

Failure to file precludes maintaining suit within state and is *prima facie* evidence of fraud in securing credit. Failure to file does not impair validity of contract or act and does not prevent defense of suit within state. STATUTE—WA Rev. Code, Section 19.80.040.

WEST VIRGINIA

Any entity who willfully fails to file certificate is guilty of a misdemeanor and may be fined not less than $25 nor more than $100, imprisonment for maximum of 30 days or both. STATUTE—WV Code, Section 47-8-5.

WISCONSIN

Violation may result in a fine not more than $1,000 or imprisonment not more than one year. STATUTE—WI Stat., Section 134.17.

WYOMING

No penalty provisions.

EFFECT OF NONCOMPLIANCE ON CONTRACTS

State case law differs as to whether these statutes render unenforceable contracts made by persons or partnerships who have failed to comply with their terms, in the absence of specific statutory provision to that effect. The Supreme Court of Connecticut in *Sagel v. Fylar et al.* held that it was not the intention of the legislature to interfere with the rights and liabilities of the contracting parties, and that the expression of one form of penalty and silence as to any other makes it clear that no further penalty or consequence beyond the possibility of imprisonment was contemplated or intended: "We are of the opinion that the intent of the General Assembly was that the penalty expressed in the statute should be exclusive, and that contracts entered into in the course of a business carried on in disregard of the statute should not be either void or unenforceable." (93 A. 1027, at 1028.) A contract for the purchase and sale of a commodity not in itself either immoral or otherwise illegal is not, by failure of one of the parties to comply with the assumed name statute, prohibited or made unlawful. Such is the weight of authority, although there are decisions to the contrary in some states.

PARTNERSHIPS

If the partnership is conducted under an assumed name, and all but one of the partners withdraws, the partnership is thereby dissolved, and if the partnership continues to operate under the assumed name, a new certificate must be filed, unless the partnership agreement permits the firm to continue to use the existing name. Failure to file the required certificate is a violation of the statute and is punishable as provided by the law of the state where the business is conducted. As a matter or precaution, the retiring partner should personally notify every customer of the old partnership that he is no longer connected with the firm and is not to be held responsible for firm debts.

CORPORATIONS

It is generally accepted that a corporation will do business under the name set forth in its charter and that any change in such name will be effected in accordance with the provisions of the laws of the state of its incorporation. For competitive reasons, because a corporation may have a license to use a franchised or trade name, or for any other purposes, a corporation may hold itself out to the public using a fictitious or assumed name. Additionally, one corporation may take over the business of a prior corporation or partnership, and be given the contractual right to use the prior entity's business name. While in most states it is improper and illegal to use the terms "Inc.," "Co.," "Corp." and "Ltd." without being a corporation of that name, many corporations use these suffixes as part of their assumed or fictitious name, leading the unsuspecting business and credit professional to believe that this is the correct and legal name. It should be kept in mind that an agreement entered into on behalf of a corporation without its exact corporate name may be invalid.

SOLE PROPRIETORSHIPS

A sole proprietorship is a business form in which one person owns all the assets of the business. Generally, the sole proprietor is solely liable for all the debts of the business. For example, John Smith may operate a sole proprietorship using the name John Smith & Sons Construction. John Smith would be personally responsible for the debts of John Smith & Sons Construction. Experience demonstrates that sole proprietors are more likely to not file a proper fictitious name certificate. For this reason, credit managers are well advised to learn the proper name, address and social security number of a sole proprietor before extending credit to a sole proprietorship. Personal guarantees are a useful tool when dealing with a sole proprietor. Chapter 27 contains a form of guarantee which may be used in a sole proprietorship situation.

STATUTORY REGULATIONS

Set forth below, in addition to the requirements for partnerships and other business entities, are the statutory requirements of those states that regulate the use of fictitious or assumed names by corporations. The purpose of these statutes is to protect the public that deals with a corporation using an assumed name. The use of an assumed name under most statutes will not give a corporation any rights to that name comparable to the rights it has to its legal corporate name.

SUMMARY OF STATE LAWS GOVERNING ASSUMED NAMES

Note: State legislatures will, on occasion, modify an area of law without clear delineation as to its content and context. As a result, even the changes which have been enacted prior to placement in the state's code may be difficult to locate. As a result, the Editors urge all users of the *Manual* to use this publication only as a guide and consult the latest codified version of the state's law for all recent changes.

ALABAMA

No assumed name statute.

Corporations

The foregoing applies.

ALASKA

Application—A person conducting a business may register its name if the name is not the same as, or deceptively similar to, the name of a corporation authorized to transact business in the state or to a name that is already registered or reserved.

Where Filed—The owner of a business must file an application for registration with the Commissioner of Commerce. The application must contain his name and address, the name and address of the business and each party having an interest in it, and a statement that he is doing business and the nature of the business. Filing is effective until the close of the fifth year beginning with the year of initial registration.

Filing Fee—To be established by the Department of Commerce.

Corporations

Corporations may also register an assumed name. When a foreign corporation applying for a certificate of authority has a name the same as or deceptively similar to that of another registered corporation, it shall select an assumed name under which it elects to do business in the state.

ARIZONA

Application—Any person other than a partnership transacting business in this state under a fictitious name, or a designation not showing the name of the owner of the business or the name of the corporation doing such business. Every partnership transacting business in this state under a fictitious name or designation not showing the names of the persons interested as partners in the business. If a firm name contains surnames of all partners or is formed for the practice of law, or where commercial or banking partnership established and transacting business outside this state under a fictitious name, name may be used without filing a certificate. Exceptions also for limited partnerships which have filed partnership certificate and for partnerships engaged in the practice of public accounting. Any change in membership in partnership requires a new certificate.

Where Filed—For any person other than a partnership, certificate stating the name and address of the owner of the business and signed by the owner and acknowledged. If a corporation, the name and address of the corporation, signed by the statutory agent and acknowledged. If a partnership, certificate stating names of all members of the partnership and their place of residence signed and acknowledged by all partners. Certificates are to be filed with the recorder of the county where the place of business is situated.

Filing Fee—$10 for the first five pages, plus $1 for each additional page.

Effect on Contract—No action upon or on account of any contract made or transaction had can be maintained until certificate has been filed.

Corporations

The foregoing applies.

ARKANSAS

Application—Any person who conducts or transacts business in the state under an assumed name or under any designated name or style, corporate or otherwise, other than the real name of the individual conducting or transacting such business.

Where Filed—Certificate must be filed in Office of the County Clerk of counties in which such person conducts or transacts such business, or intends to do so, setting forth the name under which such business is, or is to be, conducted or transacted, and the full name or names of each person conducting or transacting the business, with the post office address of each. Certificate must be acknowledged in manner provided for conveyances of real estate. In the event of change of ownership, each person disposing of his interest must file certificate, setting forth fact of such withdrawal from or disposition of interest in such business.

Filing Fee—$1.

Penalty—Fine not less than $25 or more than $100. Each day of such violation is deemed a separate offense.

Corporations

Where Filed—Domestic corporations file with the Secretary of State and the County Clerk of the county where the corporation's registered office is located, foreign corporations file with the Secretary of State. In both cases, a form is provided by the Secretary of State, which form must indicate the fictitious name, the nature of the business to be transacted thereunder, the true corporate name, and address of the corporate office registered in the state of the applicant corporation.

Filing Fee—$25.

Penalty—No action may be brought on any contract, deed, instrument, etc., executed in the fictitious name until the corporation files and pays a civil penalty of $300. In addition, the Attorney General or any affected party may seek an injunction.

CALIFORNIA

Application—Every person, including individuals, partnerships, and other associations and corporations, who regularly transact business in this state for profit under a fictitious business name. Exceptions for nonprofit corporations and certain real estate investment trusts. The fictitious business name statement must be filed within 40 days after business is first transacted under the name.

Where Filed—A certificate must be filed with the Office of the Clerk of the county in which the principal place of business is situated. If there is no principal place of business in the state, then filing is made with the Office of the Clerk in Sacramento. Filing is effective for five years from the date certificate was filed.

Filing Fee—$10 for the first fictitious business name and $2 for each additional name filed on the same statement and doing business at the same location. For partnerships, $10 for filing a fictitious business name statement for one partner and $2 for each additional partner operating under the same fictitious business statement.

Publication Required—Within 30 days after filing, the certificate must be published once a week for four consecutive weeks in a newspaper published in the county where the business is carried on, and if there be none in such county, then in a newspaper in an adjoining county. Affidavit of publication must be filed with the County Clerk within 30 days after completion of publication.

Effect on Contract—No action upon or on account of any contract or contracts made or transactions had under a fictitious name, may be maintained in any court of the state until certificate has been filed and publication made.

Discontinuance—A statement of abandonment of use of fictitious business name may be filed and published upon ceasing to do business under the assumed name.

Corporations

The foregoing applies.

COLORADO

Application—Any person and general partnership or other business organization doing business in the state under any name other than the personal name of its owner or owners.

Where Filed—Affidavit may be filed with the county clerk and recorder of the county in which the business or trade is carried on and in which any real property owned by the claimant is located. Trade names must be registered with the Department of Revenue.

Filing Fee—Established by the Department of Revenue.

Penalty—Civil penalty of not more than $500, and inability to maintain any action on debts until person or organization registers.

Corporations and Limited Partnerships

The foregoing applies.

Where Filed—Secretary of State and register with the Department of Revenue.

CONNECTICUT

Application—Person conducting or transacting business under any assumed name, or any designation, name, or style, corporate or otherwise, other than the real name or names of the individual or individuals conducting or transacting the business.

Where Filed—Office of Town Clerk of town where business is conducted or transacted.

Filing Fee—$10 for the first page and $5 for each additional page.

Penalty—Fine not more than $500 or imprisonment of not more than one year. Failure to comply shall also be deemed to be an unfair or deceptive trade practice.

Effect on Contract—No statutory provision.

Corporations

The foregoing applies, but not to limited partnerships, provided a partnership certificate is filed.

DELAWARE

Application—Persons, firms, or associations engaged in prosecuting or transacting business by using any trade name or title, which does not disclose the given and surnames of such persons, or, in case of a firm or association, the given and surname of each and every person comprising said firm or association. Change of membership in partnership or firm must be registered within 10 days after change.

Where Filed—Office of Prothonotary of each county in which business is transacted.

Filing Fee—$15.

Penalty—Fine not more than $100 or imprisonment not exceeding three months or both.

Corporations

Corporations are specifically excluded from the statute.

DISTRICT OF COLUMBIA

For foreign corporations only.

FLORIDA

Application—Person or persons engaged in business under a fictitious name.

Where Filed—Registration must be made by filing a sworn statement with the Division of Corporations of the Department of State.

Publication Required—Registration may not be made until the person or persons desiring to engage in business under a fictitious name have advertised his or their intention to register fictitious name at least once a week for four consecutive weeks in a newspaper as defined by law in the county where the principal place of business of the applicant will be located.

Filing Fee—$50 for registration of a fictitious name.

Penalty—Neither the business nor the members nor those interested in doing such business may defend or maintain suit either as plaintiff or defendant, until law is complied with, and any person violating this law may be charged with a misdemeanor, and upon conviction be fined the sum of $500 or sentenced to imprisonment for 60 days, or both.

Corporations

The foregoing applies.

GEORGIA

Application—Every person, firm, or partnership, carrying on in the state any trade or business under any trade name or partnership name or other names, which do not disclose the individual ownership of the trade, business, or profession carried on under such name. Does not apply to persons practicing a profession under partnership name.

Where Filed—In the office of the Clerk of the Superior Court of the county where business is chiefly carried on. Notice of application giving names and addresses of each person, firm, or partnership to engage in business under such trade name or partnership name, must be published in the paper in which the sheriff's advertisements are printed once a week for two weeks. No person, firm, partnership already registered is required to file a new and amended statement of registration except in the event of a change of ownership.

When Filed—Before commencing business.

Effect on Contract—Statute declares contracts to be valid even though business name not registered.

Filing Fee—$8 in counties with populations over 550,000; the Clerk of the Superior Court may also charge an additional $4.

Penalty—Punishable as misdemeanor by a fine of $1,000 or one year imprisonment or both. For failure to register, court costs will be charged against any such person, firm, or corporations doing business under an assumed name, where a party to any action whether in tort or contract, but there is no other penalty.

Corporations

Domestic corporations must file with the office of the clerk of the Superior Court in the county of its legal domicile. The foregoing does not apply to corporations or limited partnerships doing business under that corporate name or limited partnership name which has been filed.

GUAM

Application—Every person and partnership transacting business in Guam under a fictitious name, or a designation not showing the names of the persons interested as partners in such business must file certificate stating the name in full and place of residence of such person and stating the names in full of all the members of such partnership and their places of residence.

Where Filed—With the Director of Revenue and Taxation of Guam.

HAWAII

Application—May be registered by single proprietor, partnership, or corporation.

Where Filed—In the Office of the Director of Commerce and Consumer Affairs.

Filing Fee—$50 for filing; a special handling fee of $20 for expediting registration of trade name.

IDAHO

Application—Any person or persons doing business in the state under any assumed or fictitious name, or under any designation, name or style, partnership, or otherwise, other than the true and real names of the person or persons conducting or transacting such business or having an interest therein. Does not apply to corporations, limited partnerships, or to general partnerships which include names of all partners.

Where Filed—Secretary of State.

Filing Fee—$20 for filing, $10 for renewal, $10 for amendment, cancellation is free.

Effect on Contract—Not invalid, but no suit may be maintained in state courts without proof of compliance. Failure to file is *prima facie* evidence of fraud in securing credit.

Penalty—Misdemeanor punishable by fine of $25 to $200.

Corporations

Corporations are excluded from the statute.

ILLINOIS

Application—No person or persons may conduct or transact business in the state under an assumed name, or under any designation, name, or style, corporate or otherwise, other than the real name or names of the individual or individuals conducting or transacting such business.

Where Filed—Office of the County Clerk of the county in which such person or persons conduct or transact or intend to conduct or transact such business and county of each new or additional place of business setting forth assumed name, a certificate setting forth the name under which the said business is, or is to be, conducted or transacted, and the true or real full name or names of the person or persons owning, conducting, or transacting the same, with the post office address or addresses of said person or persons and every address where the business is to be conducted or transacted in the county. All name and address changes must likewise be recorded.

Notice of the Filing—Must be published in a newspaper of general circulation published within the county in which the certificate is filed. Notice must be published once a week for three consecutive weeks. The first publication shall be within 15 days after the certificate is filed in the Office of the County Clerk. Proof of publication shall be filed with the County Clerk within 50 days from the date of filing the certificate. Upon receiving proof of publication, the Clerk shall issue a receipt to the person filing such certificate but no additional charge shall be assessed by the Clerk for giving such receipt. Unless proof of publication is made to the Clerk, the certificate of registration of the assumed name is void.

Filing Fee—$5.

Penalty—Any person or persons carrying on, conducting, or transacting business who fails to comply with the provisions of this act is guilty of a Class C misdemeanor and may be sued under assumed name.

Corporations

Application—Any corporation desiring to transact business under an assumed corporate name or names.

Where Filed—Office of the Secretary of State. Effective to the first day of the anniversary month of the corporation that falls within the next calendar year evenly divisible by five, from date of filing. If an application is filed within the two months immediately preceding the anniversary month of a corporation that falls into a calendar year divisible by five, the right shall be effective for another period described above.

Filing Fee—$20 plus $2.50 for each month or part thereof between the date of filing the application and the date of the renewal of the assumed corporate name. Renewal fee is $150 for each assumed corporate name.

Penalty—Violators shall be deemed guilty of an additional petty offense for each day of continued violation.

INDIANA

Application—Person or persons conducting or transacting business under any name, designation, or title other than the real name or names of the person or persons conducting or transacting such business, whether individually or as a firm or partnership.

Where Filed—Office of Recorder of county in which place or places of business or office or offices are situated; for corporations, limited liability companies or limited partnerships, a copy certified by county recorder must also be filed with Secretary of State.

Filing Fee—$6 for the first page, $2 for each additional page. If applicable, Secretary of State shall collect a fee of $30 ($26 if corporation is not for profit).

Penalty—Violation is a Class B infraction.

Effect on Contract—No statutory provisions.

Corporations

The foregoing applies. Does not apply to any church, lodge, or association, business of which is transacted by trustees under written instrument or declaration of trust that is recorded in the office of recorder where business is transacted.

IOWA

Application—Any person or copartnership conducting business under any trade name or any assumed name of any character other than the true surname of each person or persons holding or having any interest in such business. All name changes must be likewise recorded.

Where Filed—County Recorder of county in which business is to be conducted and Secretary of State.

Filing Fee—$5 per page or a fraction thereof.

Penalty—Single misdemeanor.

KANSAS

No statutory provisions.

KENTUCKY

Application—All persons carrying on business under an assumed name, including corporations and limited partnerships using assumed name. Certificate of withdrawal is necessary when discontinuing.

Where Filed—Office of Clerk of county or counties in which business is conducted under the assumed name; for corporation, partnership, or business trust, certificate of assumed name must also be filed with the Secretary of State.

Filing Fee—$20 for filing with Secretary of State; add $5 for filing each certificate with County Clerk.

Penalty—Fine not less than $25 nor more than $100, or imprisonment in county jail for not less than 10 or more than 30 days, or both. Each day business is continued in violation of the statute is deemed a separate offense.

Effect on Contract—No statutory provisions.

Corporations

The foregoing applies.

LOUISIANA

Application—Any person or persons conducting business in Louisiana under an assumed name, or under any designation, name, or style, corporate or otherwise, other than the real name or names of the individuals conducting the business.

Where Filed—Office of the Register of Conveyances in New Orleans or in the Office of the Clerk of the Court of the parish or parishes in which business is to be conducted.

Filing Fee—25 cents per copy filed.

Penalty—Misdemeanor, subject to fine of not less than $25 or more than $100, or imprisonment of not less than 10 days or more than 60 days, or both. Each day business is conducted in violation of statute is deemed a separate offense.

Effect on Contract—No statutory provisions. The only penalty affixed by the statute to its violation is making it a misdemeanor and subjecting the offender to a fine. Fraud having been committed would, of course, be a defense to an action on the contract.

Corporations

Corporations are specifically excluded from the statute.

MAINE

Application—Person or persons conducting or transacting business under any name, designation, or title other than the real name or names of the person or persons conducting or transacting such business, whether individually or as a firm or partnership. Does not apply to corporations.

Where Filed—Office of City or Town Clerk where business is to be carried on.

Filing Fee—$10.

Penalty—For failure to file certificate, $5 fine for each day in default. False oath to such certificate is perjury.

Remarks—Not permitted in any judicial proceedings to contradict statements in such certificate.

Corporations

Where Filed—Foreign and domestic corporations must file a statement with the Secretary of State. The statement must indicate the corporate name, the registered Maine office, notice of intention to use the assumed name, the assumed name itself, and the locations where it is to be used. A separate statement must be filed for each assumed name intended to be used.

Filing Fee—$105.

Penalty—The Attorney General or any affected party may seek an injunction.

MARYLAND

Application—Any person or persons engaged in a mercantile, trading, or manufacturing business, as an agent or trading under any designation, title, or name other than the person's own name.

Where Filed—Department of Assessment and Taxation.

Filing Fee—$10 plus $1 for each signature on the certificate.

Penalty—A civil penalty may be assessed of up to $50 per day, not to exceed $1,000 total. This is the penalty for the improper use of corporate identification.

Effect on Contract—No statutory provisions.

Corporations

The foregoing applies.

MASSACHUSETTS

Application—Any person or persons conducting business under any title other than the real name of the person conducting the same, or a partnership conducting business under any title not including the true surname of at least one partner, or a corporation conducting business under any other title than its true corporate name. Statements of withdrawal necessary if discontinuing or withdrawal.

Where Filed—Office of Clerk of every city or town in which place or places of business or office or offices are located.

Filing Fee—$1.

Penalty—Fine not more than $300 for each month during which violation continues.

Effect on Contract—Persons may sue and be sued even though they may not have complied with the requirements of the statute.

Corporations

Foregoing applies.

MICHIGAN

Application—Any person or persons, partnership or trust or other entity, carrying on, conducting, or transacting business under any assumed name or any designation, name, or style, other than the real name or names of the individual or individuals owning, conducting, or transacting such business. County Clerk furnishes form which must be completed and acknowledged.

Where Filed—Office of Clerk of county or counties in which business is owned, conducted, or transacted or an office or place of business maintained. Certificate to be filed in duplicate, before business is commenced, on form furnished by County Clerk. Filing is effective for five years and is required to be renewed prior to the expiration of each five-year period. County Clerk is authorized to reject any assumed name which is likely to mislead the public, or any assumed name already filed in the county or so nearly similar thereto as to lead to confusion or deception.

Filing Fee—$6, renewal fee $4. Different amount possible by ordinance in a charter county with a population of more than 2,000,000. $10 for the indexing and the filing of the certificates for the alphabetical index.

Penalty—Fine not less than $25 or more than $100, or imprisonment in county jail, not exceeding 30 days, or both. Each day business conducted in violation of law is deemed a separate offense.

Effect on Contract—Does not void contracts, but any person or persons failing to file a certificate are prohibited from bringing suit in any of the courts of the state in relation to any contracts or other matter made or done by such person or persons under an assumed name until after a full compliance with the statute.

Corporations

Where Filed—Domestic or foreign corporations must file a statement with the chief officer of the Department of Commerce or of any other agency or department authorized by law to administer the Business Corporation Act, or his designated agent, indicating both the true name and the fictitious name.

Effective for five years to December 31 of the fifth full calendar year. The same name may be assumed by two or more corporations which participate together in any partnership or joint venture.

Filing Fee—No provision.

Penalty—No provision.

MINNESOTA

Application—Any person carrying on or conducting a commercial business under any designation, name, or style which does not set forth the true name or names of every person interested in such business.

Where Filed—Office of the Secretary of State. Filing is generally effective for 10 years, unless renewed within six months of expiration of the 10-year period. Duplicity or similarity with a previously filed name is permitted.

Publication—The certificate must be published in a qualified newspaper, in the county in which the person has a principal or registered office, for two successive issues.

Filing Fee—$25, renewal $25.

Effect on Contract—In any civil action commenced in any court on account of any contract made by, or transaction had, on behalf of such business, defendant may set up as a defense that the certificate has not been filed and the action will thereupon be stayed until the certificate is filed.

Corporations

The foregoing applies.

MISSISSIPPI

No statutory provision.

MISSOURI

Application—Persons, partnership, associations, or corporations engaging in business under any name other than the true name of such persons, partnership, association, or corporation must file within five days after the beginning of the business.

Where Filed—Secretary of State within five days of beginning of such business.

Filing Fee—$2 to State Director of Revenue.

Penalty—Violation is a misdemeanor.

Corporations

The foregoing applies.

MONTANA

Application—Every person transacting business under a fictitious name or a designation not showing the names of the persons interested in such business. Secretary of State may not register business, other than corporation or limited partnership, with words "Corporation," "Company," "Incorporated," or "Limited" in name.

Where Filed—Office of the Secretary of State. Filing is effective for five years from date of registration.

Filing Fee—Set by Administrative Code.

Effect on Contract—No action can be maintained until certificate is filed and publication made.

Corporations

The foregoing applies.

NEBRASKA

Application—Every name under which any person shall do or transact business in this state, other than the true name of such person, is declared to be a "trade name." It is unlawful for any person to engage in or transact any business in the state under a trade name without first registering the same.

Where Registered—Trade name must be registered with the Secretary of State on a form supplied by the Secretary. The form must disclose: the name and address of the applicant and, if a corporation, the state of incorporation, the trade name, how long used in the state, and the nature of the business.

Filing Fee—$100, renewal fee is $100.

Penalty—Any person not excepted from the application of the law transacting business under a trade name without registration shall be deemed guilty of a Class V misdemeanor and fined not less than $10 or more than $100. Each day of violation constitutes a separate offense.

Corporations

The foregoing applies.

NEVADA

Application—Every person doing business, or intending to conduct a business, in the state under an assumed or fictitious name or designation which does not show the real name or names of the person or persons engaged or interested in such business. In addition, every change in membership of a general partnership. Filing must be no later than one month after commencement of business.

Where Filed—Office of County Clerk of each county in which business is carried on or is intended to be carried on.

Filing Fee—$15.

Penalty—Noncompliance is a misdemeanor.

Effect on Contract—No action may be commenced or maintained by any person doing business under an assumed or fictitious name, or by an assignee of such person, upon or on account of any contract made or transaction had under the assumed or fictitious name, or upon or on account of any cause of action arising or growing out of a business conducted under that name, unless before commencement of the action the required certificate has been filed.

Corporations

The foregoing applies.

NEW HAMPSHIRE

Application—Every sole proprietor doing business under any name other than his own, and every partnership, New Hampshire Investment Trust or association. Effective for five years after date of filing. In case of withdrawal or change or addition must file within 10 days.

Where Filed—Office of Secretary of State.

Filing Fee—$50.

Penalty—No action abated or writ of attachment affected by certificate.

Corporations

The foregoing applies.

NEW JERSEY

Application—Persons transacting business using the designation "and Company" or "& Co." as part of name; persons conducting or transacting business under assumed names, corporate or otherwise.

Where Filed—Office of Clerk of county or counties in which business is transacted together with a duplicate for filing in office of the Secretary of State.

Filing Fee—$50, plus an additional $5 for duplicate sent to Secretary of State.

Penalty—Violation is a misdemeanor.

Effect on Contract—Does not prevent recovery on executed contract by person who should have complied with statute but did not.

Corporations

Where Filed—A corporation need not file if it uses its true name in the transaction in such a manner as not to be deceptive as to its identity or if it has been authorized to do business in New Jersey under the alternate name. Otherwise, it must register a certificate with the Secretary of State. The certificate must indicate the true name, the jurisdiction and date of incorporation, the alternate name, the nature of business to be transacted thereunder, and the fact that the corporation had never done business under the alternate name in violation of the statute. Filing effective for five years from date of filing; may be renewed for five-year intervals.

Filing Fee—$25.

Penalty—Validity of contract not impaired but no corporation may maintain an action arising from a transaction conducted under an alternate name until it has filed. Upon such filing, the corporation shall pay the prescribed fee plus an amount equal to the fee multiplied by the number of years that it had illicitly used the trade name. Failure to file within 60 days of notice of an obligation to do so served by the Secretary of State subjects the corporation to a fine ranging from $200 to $500.

NEW MEXICO

Statute repealed.

NEW YORK

Application—No individual, partnership, corporation, or unincorporated association shall (a) carry on or conduct or transact business under any name or designation other than his real name, or (b) carry on or conduct or transact business as a member of a partnership, unless such person files a certificate setting forth the name or designation under which, and the address within the county at which, such business is conducted or transacted, the full name or names of the person or persons conducting or transacting the same, including the names of all partners, with the residence address of each such person, and the age of any infants. Must also file amended certificate if any changes, and certificate of discontinuance within 30 days. Law firms and private bankers authorized to engage in business under banking law are exempt from filing a certificate.

Where Filed—Office of Clerk of each county in which such business is done.

Filing Fee—For filing with Secretary of State (by corporation), $25. For filing with County Clerks, $25 ($100 within City of New York).

Penalty—Noncompliance or falsification of the certificate is a misdemeanor punishable by $1,000 fine, one year imprisonment, or both. In addition, no action may be maintained on a transaction made under an unregistered fictitious name until the statute has been complied with.

Effect on Contract—Failure to comply does not void contract.

Certificate to Be Displayed at Premises—A certified copy of the original certificate, or if an amended certificate has been filed, then of the most recent amended certificate filed, shall be displayed on each place the business for which filed is conducted.

Corporations

Where Filed—Corporations must file with the Secretary of State and furnish the following information: the true name, the fictitious name, the principal place of business in New York, the name of each county where business is to be conducted, the location within each county where business is to be conducted. Does not apply to limited partnerships who duly filed a certificate of continued use of firm name. Exceptions for corporation as a member of a partnership.

Filing Fee—$25 plus an additional fee for each county filing effected by the Secretary of State.

Penalty—Same as above.

Effect—Corporation is prohibited from maintaining any action or any contract, account, or transaction in New York Courts until filed.

NORTH CAROLINA

Application—Before any person or partnership (other than a limited partnership) or corporation engages in business in any county of the state under an assumed name, or any name other than the real name of the owner or owners or corporate name, a certificate must be filed setting forth the name under which the business is to be conducted and the name and address of the owner or owners. The certificate must be signed and acknowledged by the individual owner or by each member in a partnership or by an appropriate officer of a corporation. Whenever a partner withdraws from or a new partner joins a partnership, a new certificate must be filed. This requirement does not apply to a partnership engaged in the practice of certified public accountancy if it files with the State Board of Certified Public Accountant Examiners a listing of names and addresses of partners and such listing is available to public inspection.

Where Filed—The Office of the Register of Deeds of the county in which business is carried on. It is not necessary to file in any county where no place of business is maintained and where the only business done is the sale of goods by sample, by traveling agents or by mail.

Filing Fee—$6.

Penalty—Failure to file certificate constitutes a misdemeanor punishable by fine of not more than $50, or imprisonment for not more than 30 days. In addition, failure to file certificate within seven days after demand made by any person gives rise to a cause of action in favor of such person for collection of penalty of $50. Failure to comply with the statute does not affect rights in any civil action brought in the courts of this state.

Corporations

The foregoing applies.

NORTH DAKOTA

Application—Every partnership transacting business under a fictitious name or designation not showing the names of the persons interested as partners therein. Filing is effective for five years from date of registration.

Where Filed—With Secretary of State.

Filing Fee—$25 plus $3 for each partner over two, with a $250 maximum.

Effect on Contract—Persons failing to comply may not maintain an action on or account of any contracts made or transactions had in the partnership name until compliance, but may subsequently file and thereafter an action may be maintained on prior transactions and contracts.

Corporations

The foregoing applies. Does not apply to limited partnerships as long as they filed according to general rules or to commercial partnerships doing business outside the United States.

OHIO

Application—Every person, including various business organizations, who does business under a fictitious name must report the fictitious name to the Secretary of State, within 30 days after the first use of the name. The person may, if he wishes, register the trade name with the Secretary. The Secretary is not permitted to accept registration of any trade name that might mislead the public or that is not readily distinguished from other trade names.

Where Filed—Secretary of State.

Filing Fee—$20. Filing is effective for five years from date of registration. Renewal fee is $10.

Penalty—The Attorney General shall bring an action for an injunction upon the request of the Secretary of State.

Effect on Contract—No action can be commenced or maintained on or on account of any contracts made or transactions had in the partnership name until registration or submission of the report.

Corporations

The foregoing applies.

OKLAHOMA

Application—Partnership transacting business under a fictitious name, except a commercial or banking partnership established and transacting business within the United States.

Where Filed—County Clerk of county or subdivision where principal place of business is situated.

Publication—Published one day in a newspaper published in the county if there is one, and if there is none, then in a newspaper published in an adjoining county. Publication provisions shall not apply to limited partnerships which filed with Secretary of State.

Filing Fee—$5 for first page, $2 for each additional page.

Effect on Contract—Persons failing to comply may not maintain action on, or on account of, any contract made, or transactions had, in the partnership name until compliance. May file subsequently and thereafter action may be maintained on prior transactions and contracts.

Remarks—New certificate to be filed and new publication required whenever personnel or partnership changes.

Corporations

Where Filed—A report containing the trade name, the true name, the name and address of the corporation's registered agent in Oklahoma, the nature of the business to be conducted, and the address where the business is to be conducted must be filed with the Secretary of State.

Filing Fee—$10 for documents filed in office of Secretary of State.

Penalty—No action may be brought on a transaction made under an unregistered fictitious name. The Attorney General or an affected party may seek an injunction.

OREGON

Application—Each person who will carry on, conduct, or transact business under an assumed business name shall sign an application to register the assumed business name and shall submit the application to the Office of the Secretary of State. All of the persons who will carry on, conduct, or transact a single business under an assumed business name shall file a consolidated application to register the assumed name. The statute prescribes the materials to be contained in the application.

Filing Fee—$10 for each application for registration and $2 for each county designated for registration or renewal. Registration is effective for two years from date of registration, must be renewed 30 days before this. Renewal $10 and $2 per county.

Penalty—Fine not exceeding $100.

Corporations

The foregoing applies.

PENNSYLVANIA

Application—Any entity which either alone or in combination with any other entity conducts any business in the Commonwealth under or through any fictitious name. In case of withdrawal or for cancellation a filing is required. Every registrant shall decennially during the year 2000 and each year thereafter divisible by 10 file a report in the same manner as an application.

Where Filed—Department of State.

Filing Fee—$52.

Penalty—Civil penalty of $500, if there had not been substantial compliance in good faith.

Effect on Contract—No entity shall be permitted to maintain any action nor shall any action be maintained by any successor or assignee of such entity on any right, claim or demand arising out of a transaction until filed. The failure does not impair the validity of any contract.

Publication—An entity which includes an individual party shall officially publish in the county in which the principal officer place of business of the entity is, or in the case of a proposed entity is to be, located, notice of its intention to file or the filing of an application for registration of a fictitious name under the law. The notice may appear prior to or after the day upon which the application is filed in the department and shall be kept in the permanent records thereof.

Corporations

Application—Under the Fictitious Corporate Name Act, no corporation alone or in combination with any other entity may conduct business in Pennsylvania under any fictitious name unless such name is registered. A foreign corporation must be authorized to conduct business in Pennsylvania prior to filing application. Application for registration is to be on a form supplied or approved by the Secretary of the Commonwealth and contain the fictitious name, a statement concerning the character of the business to be conducted, the corporate name, state and date of incorporation, address of principal place of business and registered office in Pennsylvania, name and address of any other entity in combination with which the corporation will conduct such business. If the business is not a Pennsylvania corporation, give the address of its principal office in its domiciliary jurisdiction. The document must be signed by the president or vice president and the secretary or treasurer and the corporate seal shall be affixed thereto.

Where Filed—Office of Secretary of the Commonwealth.

Filing Fee—Original application for registration—$30 to Secretary of the Commonwealth, $10 to the Prothonotary, and local county fee.

Amendment for Purpose of Change of Address—$52.

Penalty—Civil penalty of $500 for failure to comply with statute.

Effect on Contract—Failure to register fictitious name does not impair or affect the validity of any contract but corporation cannot resort to the Pennsylvania courts to enforce agreement made by it under fictitious name until after compliance with statute. Affidavit of compliance must be filed with complaint.

Publication Required—Publication is required in the county in which the principal office or place of business of the entity is, or, in the case of a proposed entity, is to be located. Publication must be in two newspapers in the proper county, one of which shall be the legal newspaper, if any, designated by the rules of court for publication of legal notices or, if there is no legal newspaper, in two newspapers of general circulation in the county. If there is only one newspaper in the county, advertisement in that paper is sufficient.

Failure to Publish—It is provided that no legal proceedings or the like, in which notice is required to be given by official or legal advertising, will be binding upon an interested person unless the advertising is effected and proof of publication is filed of record in the matter or proceeding.

RHODE ISLAND

Application—Any person or persons who carry on or conduct business in the state under any assumed name, designation, or style other than the real name or names of such person or persons.

Where Filed—Office of Town or City Clerk in town or city in which business is conducted or transacted.

Filing Fee—$10

Penalty—Fine not exceeding $500 or imprisonment not exceeding one year.

Corporations

Application—Any corporation organized and existing under the laws of any state or territory of the United States which desires to transact business in the state under a fictitious name.

Where Filed—Secretary of State.

Filing Fee—$50.

Effect on Contracts—Suits on contracts may not be maintained until the corporation registers.

SOUTH CAROLINA

Repealed

SOUTH DAKOTA

Application—Persons or copartnerships transacting business for profit under a fictitious name or designation not showing names of persons interested in the business. Filing is effective for five years from date of filing. Any change must be filed.

Where Filed—Officer of the Register of Deeds of each county where the business is maintained.

Filing Fee—$5, $2 for each renewal.

Effect on Contract—No action on account of any contract can be maintained until the statute has been complied with.

Penalty—Class 2 misdemeanor.

Corporations

No provision.

TENNESSEE

Application—Corporations must file before they transact any business under an assumed name. Filing is effective for five years from date of filing.

Where Filed—Secretary of State.

Filing Fee—$10.

TEXAS

Application—Any individual who regularly conducts business in the State of Texas under an assumed name is required to comply with the law.

Where Filed—Unincorporated businesses: must file a certificate with the County Clerk in each county where a business premises is maintained or where business will be conducted. Certificate must be executed and acknowledged by each individual or agent whose name appears thereon and shall state the assumed name, the name and address of the individual, partners, or company, the jurisdiction under the laws of which the company was organized, incorporated or associated, the period (not to exceed 10 years) for which the name will be used, and a statement specifying the form of business (e.g., proprietorship, sole practitioner, joint venture, general partnership, etc.) to be conducted. Incorporated businesses: must file a certificate with the Secretary of State, and if required to maintain a registered office in this state, in the Office of the County Clerk in the county in which such office is located and of the county in which its principal office is located if not the same county where the registered office is located. If the corporation is not required to maintain a registered office, with the Secretary of State and in the Office of the County Clerk of the county in which its office is located, and if not incorporated under the laws of this state, in the Office of the County Clerk of the county in which its principal place of business in this state is located if not the same as its office. Certificate must be executed and acknowledged by an officer, representative, or attorney for the corporation and shall state the assumed name, the name of the corporation as stated in its articles of incorporation, the jurisdiction under the laws of which organized and address of its registered office in that jurisdiction, the period (not to exceed 10 years) for which the name will be used, and the form of corporation to be conducted. If required to maintain a registered office in this state, the address of such office and the name of its registered agent and the address of its principal office if not the same as that of its registered office in this state. If not required to maintain a registered office in this state, the office address in this state, and if not incorporated under the laws of this state, the address of its business in this state and its office address elsewhere, if any. Certificate for all corporations must include the county or counties where business is to be conducted under the assumed name.

Filing Fee—$2 for each certificate filed with the County Clerk plus a fee of 50 cents for each name to be indexed; $25 for filing with the Secretary of State, $10 for filing each abandonment of use of assumed name.

Penalty—Noncompliance does not affect the validity of any contract or prevent the defending of any action, but no action may be maintained by a party not complying with the act until the required certificate is filed. Court may award expenses including attorneys' fees incurred in locating and serving process to party bringing suit against noncomplying party. Intentional noncompliance is a misdemeanor punishable by a fine not exceeding $2,000.

Corporations

The foregoing applies.

UTAH

Application—Every person or persons conducting or transacting business in this state under an assumed name.

Where Filed—Division of Corporations and Commercial Code. Certificate must set forth the name of the business, the true name or names of the person or persons owning and the person or persons conducting such business, the location of the principal place of business, and the street address. Certificate shall be filed not later than 30 days after commencing to conduct or transact said business and is effective for three years from date of filing. Any change in persons or in the registered agent or office of business must be filed.

Penalty—Noncompliance is a bar to suit, and person may be subject to a late filing fee.

Effect—Person otherwise cannot sue, prosecute or maintain any action, suit, counterclaim, cross-complaint or proceeding in any court until in compliance with the statute.

Corporations

The foregoing applies. Chapter shall not apply to corporations duly organized under the laws of this state or any other state if they do business under their true corporate name.

VERMONT

Application—Persons doing business under any name other than their own; every copartnership or association of individuals, except corporations, doing business in the state: corporations doing business in the state under any name other than that of the corporation. Withdrawals must be filed within 30 days.

Where Filed—Secretary of State and Town Clerk of town where principal place of business is located, within 10 days after commencement of business.

Filing Fee—$20.

Penalty—Any person, partnership, association, or corporation carrying on business contrary to the statute may, upon complaint of the Secretary of State, be enjoined therefrom by a Superior Court. Failure to register also carries a fine of up to $100.

Effect on Contract—No person, copartnership, association, or corporation subject to this Act may institute any proceedings for the enforcement of any right or obligation unless it shall, prior to the commencement of the proceeding, have filed the certificate and paid the registration fee required by the statute.

Corporations

The foregoing applies.

VIRGINIA

Application—Any person, partnership, or corporation conducting or transacting business under an assumed or fictitious name. Release certificate is necessary if business is no longer conducted.

Where Filed—Office of Clerk of Court where deeds are recorded in the county or corporation wherein the business is to be conducted. Corporation must also file a copy in the Office of the Clerk of the State Corporation Commission.

Filing Fee—$10.

Penalty—Noncompliance is a misdemeanor; fine not exceeding $2,500, or confinement in jail for not more than one year, or both.

Effect on Contract—No action shall be maintained until filed.

Corporations

The foregoing applies.

WASHINGTON

Application—Any person or persons who carry on or conduct business in the state under any assumed name, designation, or style other than the real name of such person or persons.

Where Filed—Department of Licensing. Notice of cancellation and new registration necessary if change of person conducting business. Executed amendment shall be filed if there is a change in name or mailing address.

Filing Fee—$5.

Effect on Contract—No suit can be maintained in any of the courts of the state until party complies with statute. Failure to file does not prevent from defending any suit and does not impair validity of contract.

Corporations

The foregoing applies.

WEST VIRGINIA

Application—Person or persons conducting or transacting business under an assumed name or under any designation, name, or style other than the true name or names of those persons conducting such business.

Where Filed—Office of Clerk of County Commission of the county in which person maintains his principal place of business.

Filing Fee—$2.

Penalty—Noncompliance is a misdemeanor, punishable by fine of not less than $25 or more than $100, or by not more than 30 days in county jail, or both.

Corporations

Corporations, partnerships and associations required to register unless they file in office of Secretary of State. New certificate necessary if new assumed name.

WISCONSIN

Application—Any person or persons who engage in or advertise any mercantile or commission business under a name purporting or appearing to be a corporate name, with intent thereby to obtain credit, and which name does not disclose the real name or names of one or more of the persons engaged in said business.

Where Filed—Office of the Register of Deeds of the county wherein his or their principal place of business may be.

Filing Fee—$10 for the first page, $2 for each additional page.

Penalty—Noncompliance is a misdemeanor, punishable by a fine not to exceed $1,000 or by imprisonment in the county jail not more than one year.

WYOMING

No statutory provisions.

The following summary is a chart which focuses upon the specific citations of each state's law.

ASSUMED OR FICTITIOUS NAME STATUTES: CITES AND UPDATES

Note: Noncorporate information for each state is shown in normal black and white; corporate information is shaded. If a state does not list a corporate section, assume that the information provided for the noncorporate section is applicable to the corporate section as well.

State	Application	Where Filed	Fee	Penalty	Effect on Contracts	Changes or Remarks
ALABAMA	10.35.010, 10.35.020					There are no statutory provisions as yet for Alabama.
ALASKA		10.35.050	10.35.060		10.35.080	
	10.06.125	10.06.135	10.06.140			
ARIZONA	10-506, 29-102,	29-102, 44-1236 44-1236	10-122*		44-1236(D),	*Amended 2001 29-102(B)
ARKANSAS	4-70-201	4-70-203	4-70-206	4-70-202		
	4-27-404	4-27-404	4-27-122*	4-27-404		*Amended 2001
CALIFORNIA	§ 17910, § 17911	§ 17915	§ 17929	§ 17918		
COLORADO	7-71-101	7-71-101	24-21-104	24-35-303	75-115-102	
CONNECTICUT	§ 35-1	§ 35-1	§ 7-34A*	§ 35-1		*Amended 2001
DELAWARE	§ 6-3101, § 6-3104	§ 6-3101, § 6-3104	Rule 77	§ 6-3106		
DISTRICT OF COLUMBIA						No provisions.
FLORIDA	865.09	865.09.	865.09	865.09	865.09	
GEORGIA	10-1-490	10-1-490	15-6-77*	10-1-493	10-1-491	See also GA Stat. § 15-6-77.
GUAM	26101	26103				
HAWAII						No provisions.
IDAHO	53-501, 53-504	53-504	53-510	53-509		

ASSUMED OR FICTITIOUS NAME STATUTES: CITES AND UPDATES (Continued)

State	Application	Where Filed	Fee	Penalty	Effect on Contracts	Changes or Remarks
ILLINOIS	805 ILCS 405/1 805 ILCS 5/4.15	805 ILCS 405/1 805 ILCS 5/4.15	805 ILCS 405/3 805 ILCS 5/15/10(q)	805 ILCS 405/5	Valid even if corporation is not registered. See *Grody v. Scatone*, 96 N.E. 2d 97 (1951).	
INDIANA	23-15-1-1	23-15-1-1	23-15-1-1, 36-2-7-10	23-15-1-3		None
IOWA	547.1	547.1	547.3	547.4		Copy to be filed with the Secretary of State. *See* § 490.401.
KANSAS						No statutory provisions.
KENTUCKY	365.015*	365.015*	64.012	365.990		*Amended 2001
LOUISIANA	51:281 Exemptions 51:283	51:281	51:282	51:284		
MAINE	31 § 2 13-A-307	31 § 2 13-A-307	13-A-1401*	31 § 5 13-A-307		*Amended 2001
MARYLAND	CA § 1-406	CA § 1-406	CA § 1-406			
MASSACHUSETTS	110 § 5	110 § 5	262 § 34(20)	110 § 5	110 § 5	
MICHIGAN	445.1 450.1217	445.1 450.1217	445.1	445.5	445.5	
MINNESOTA	333.01	333.01	333.055	333.065	333.06	

State						Notes
MISSISSIPPI						No provisions.
MISSOURI	417.200	417.210	417.220	417.230		
MONTANA	30-13-203	30-13-204	30-13-217		30-13-215	
NEBRASKA	87-210	87-210	87-220	87-220		
NEVADA	602.010*	602.010		602.090	602.070	*Amended 2001
NEW HAMPSHIRE	349:1	349:5	349:7	349:9		
NEW JERSEY	56:1-2	56:1-2	56:1-3	56:1-4	56:1-2	
NEW MEXICO	14A:2-2.1	14A:2-2.1	14A:15-3	14A:2-2.1	14A:2-2.1	No provisions.
NEW YORK	Gen B § 130, 132	Gen B § 130	CPLR § 8021	Gen B § 130	Gen B § 130	
NORTH CAROLINA	§ 66-68	§ 66-68		§ 66-71		
NORTH DAKOTA	45-11-01	45-11-01	45-11-01	45-11-04	45-11-04	
OHIO	1329.01	1329.01	1329.01	1329.10	1329.10	
OKLAHOMA	18 § 1140, 54 § 81*	18 § 1140, 54 § 81	18 § 1142	54 § 81	54 § 81	*Amended 2001
OREGON	648.010	648.010	648.115	648.990	648.135	
PENNSYLVANIA	54 § 303	54 § 303	54 § 153	54 § 331	54 § 331	
RHODE ISLAND	6-1-1, 7-1.1-7.1	6-1-1	6-1-2	6-1-4	7-1.1-7.1	
SOUTH CAROLINA	33-4-101, 33-42-45	33-4-101, 33-42-45	33-4-102	39-13-40	33-42-45	
SOUTH DAKOTA	37-11-1	37-11-1	7-9-15(3)	37-11-1	37-11-5	
TENNESSEE	48-14-101	48-14-101	48-11-303			

ASSUMED OR FICTITIOUS NAME STATUTES: CITES AND UPDATES *(Continued)*

State	Application	Where Filed	Fee	Penalty	Effect on Contracts	Changes or Remarks
TEXAS	BC 36.10, 36.11	36.10. 36.11	36.15	36.26	36.25	
	36.11					
UTAH	42-2-5	42-2-5	42-2-7	42-2-10	42-2-10	
VERMONT	11 § 1623	11 § 1623	11 § 1625	11 § 1626		
VIRGINIA	59.1-69	59.1-69	59.1-70	59.1-75	59.1-76	
WASHINGTON	19.80.010	19.80.010	19.80.045			
WEST VIRGINIA	47-8-2	47-8-2		47-8-5		
	47-8-4	47-8-4		47-8-5		
WISCONSIN	134.17	134.17	134.17, 59.43(2)	134.17		
WYOMING						No provisions.

Note: Non-corporate information for each state is shown in normal black and white; corporate information is shaded. If a state does not list a corporate section, assume that the information provided for the non-corporate section is applicable to the corporate section as well.

5 Transactional Guide to the Formation, Performance and Enforcement of Contracts

Today's credit professionals negotiate terms of sale that result in the formation of commercial contracts. The intent is to provide the credit professional with the fundamentals of contract law to better understand, analyze and in certain circumstances, draft a contract.

In its broadest construction, a contract is an agreement between two or more parties that creates an obligation to perform an act, or refrain from performing an act. The Restatement (Second) of Contracts defines a contract as "a promise or set of promises for the breach of which the law gives a remedy, or the performance of which the law in some way recognizes a legal duty." This definition is indicative of common law. In many jurisdictions, states have adopted the common law; however, other states have adopted legislation that substantively alters the common law as it pertains to the sale of goods (e.g., Article 2 of the Uniform Commercial Code). Fortunately, a majority of contracts will adhere to hornbook principles that transcend all methods of analyzing contracts.

This chapter discusses common law principles, and when applicable, considers principles developed by Article 2 of the Uniform Commercial Code ("UCC"). The UCC is a collection of statutes intended to provide uniformity to commercial sales among the states, but generally does not extend to the service-related industry. The UCC is a model, and accordingly, states are permitted to adopt its provisions or make revisions to satisfy its unique commercial needs. Additionally, the interpretation of these statutes and official comments has led state courts to different rulings. Accordingly, the UCC is not entirely uniform and may vary state to state.

Although memorializing an agreement in writing often supports the existence of a contract, a majority of states do not require certain agreements to be written. A note of caution—oral agreements are often subject to statutes and principles of common law that construe oral agreements unenforceable. For example, the statute of frauds under the UCC, *inter alia*, renders an oral contract unenforceable if made for goods with a value greater than $5,000.00. The procedural and substantive traps that oral agreements present should place the credit professional on notice that a writing is often far superior than its oral counterpart.

The definitions of contract may be helpful; however, these definitions usually do not encompass the variety of legal issues that may be created by the formation and enforcement of a contract. Likewise, although the fundamental elements are susceptible to simplification, the enforcement of a contract may fail for a variety of legal reasons. The fundamental elements required to form a valid contract include:

1. Offer
2. Acceptance
3. Mutuality of Assent
4. Consideration

The absence of these fundamentals, or any other requirement created by statute or otherwise, may result in an unenforceable contract. Moreover, there are defenses to the formation of contract that, if applicable, may render a contract unenforceable. These defenses, *inter alia*, include lack of legal capacity, illegality of subject matter, unconscionability, fraud, duress or undue influence.

OFFER: INITIATING A CONTRACT

It is an axiom to contract law that each contract requires an offer and acceptance of that offer. The party initiating the offer is identified as the "offeror," whereas the party receiving the offer is identified as the "offeree." Once an offer is made, the offeree is empowered with a conditional power of acceptance for a specified period of time or until the offer has lapsed.

Communication of Offer

An offer to contract initiates contract formation. The Restatement (Second) of Contracts defines an offer to contract as "a manifestation of a willingness to enter into a bargain, so made as to justify another person in understanding that assent to that bargain is invited." The communication of an offer must show a present intent to contract. A mere statement of a party's intention to enter into negotiations is not an offer, and thus is not a valid contract. The communication of an offer is sufficient if the terms provide a basis of determining the existence of a breach and an appropriate remedy.

It is often phrased that the offeror is the "master of the offer." An offer becomes effective upon receipt and the offeree's knowledge that an offer has been made. Generally, an offer is not assignable to a third party, but is only acceptable by the offeree or class of offerees to whom it is directed. Moreover, as master of the offer, the offeror controls the time, place and form or mode of acceptance of the offer. Courts often employ an objective test, or "reasonableness" standard, to determine whether a communication rises to the level of an offer. Therefore, a communication will be construed as an offer if the offeree reasonably believes that the offeror intended to instill a power of acceptance.

Public "At Large" Offers

It is common practice for businesses to offer their goods and services to the public at large. Public offers are presented in the form of an advertisement, catalogue or price quote that may be interpreted by the layperson as an offer creating a power of acceptance. As a general rule, public offers are not construed as an offer because these communications lack clear and unequivocal terms, nor do public offers identify an offeree. Instead, the law classifies these communications as "invitations" to the general public to make an offer. Most often, businesses that make public offers will not be contractually bound.

Some courts review the circumstances surrounding public offers to determine whether a reasonable person would believe that the communication was a mere invitation soliciting an offer, or alternatively, an offer to the public. Accordingly, if a vendor intends to limit its exposure to the potential binding effect of a public offer, then it should provide a conspicuous disclaimer stating that the advertisement is a solicitation only, and that the terms and conditions may be changed without further notice. Absent such disclosure, the vendor may find itself the target of a lawsuit to enforce the offer.

Duration and Termination of an Offer

Once communicated, an offer remains outstanding until it is revoked, rejected or accepted. An offer may also terminate after a reasonable period of time has elapsed. Acceptance of an offer validates the contract. It is at this moment a contract exists. Alternatively, revocation and rejection extinguish the power of acceptance and the offer ceases to exist. The duration of an offer depends upon the circumstances and communications between the parties. For example, an offer may terminate at a time that is specified by the offer or after a reasonable period of time has lapsed. Moreover, the duration of an offer is dependent upon certain circumstances and acts that may terminate an offer as a matter of law.

REVOCATION AND TERMINATION

The revocation of an offer is effectuated by the offeror, usually at any time prior to acceptance. The effect of revocation is subject to two diverging bodies of law: the common law and the UCC. The common law provides the offeror broad revocation rights, allowing revocation at any time the offer is outstanding. There are two exceptions to common law revocation. First, the offeror may not revoke an offer that is filed under seal. Second, an offer involving an option contract may not be revoked (i.e., an agreement that the offeror will keep the offer open for a designated period of time). Alternatively, UCC § 2-205 limits revocation by disallowing a merchant to revoke a "firm offer" during the period stated. A firm offer is an offer that has been reduced to a signed writing. If the period is not specified, then the offer remains irrevocable and outstanding for a commercially reasonable period of time, defined as a period not to exceed three months.

There are additional requirements at common law to revoke an offer. Similar to communicating an offer, revocation requires that the offeree receive notice of the revocation. Although actual notice of revocation is sufficient, it is not necessary. Instead, any information may constitute notice of revocation if it leads the offeree to reasonably conclude that the offer has been withdrawn. For example, an offer to sell specific merchandise is revoked when the offeree learns that the merchandise has been sold to another purchaser. This may occur when the offeree learns that its competition has purchased the remaining widgets from the manufacturer, a previous offer made to the offeree to purchase the widgets is no longer valid. The notice of revocation for a public offer is even more liberal; the law presumes notice of revocation if notice is presented through the same medium in which the public offer was made. For example, an offer published in a newspaper to sell the remaining inventory of furniture to the first successful bidder may be revoked through the newspaper.

REJECTION AND TERMINATION

Although revocation serves to terminate the offer, there are other events that constitute rejection and termination of an offer, including an express rejection, counter-offer, lapse of time, death or incapacity, or nonoccurrence of a condition precedent. Once a rejection is received, the offer is terminated and cannot be revived. The express rejection of an offer needs no explanation, however, other modes of rejection are considered.

The Counter-Offer

A counter-offer has the qualities of a purported acceptance; however, it is conditional on the offeror's assent to additional or contradicting terms (collectively, "the proposed terms"). At common law, a counter-offer is construed as a rejection and terminates the preceding offer. The proposed terms effectually begin the contract process over such that the original offeror becomes the offeree with the conditional power to accept or reject the counter-offer.

There are two common law exceptions to the termination of an offer on receipt of a counter-offer. First, an offeree is entitled to clarify terms without jeopardizing the validity of the offer. Second, often known as an "inquiry," an offeree may suggest a new term without insisting on its inclusion. For example, an offer to sell a specified quantity of goods at a specific price is not rejected by a request for a quotation of a price on a different quantity; nor is an offer to sell rejected because the offeree inquires into receiving a greater quantity or an extension of the offered terms for a future contract.

Section 2-207 of the UCC also provides an exception to manage the complicated issue regarding the "battle of the forms." This exception provides that a contract between merchants is valid, even if the terms for offer and acceptance on standardized forms are not identical, unless acceptance is conditioned upon assent to the different terms. It is important to note that the UCC regulates the sale of goods only, and accordingly, does not extend to service contracts.

The Lapse of Time

The passage of time may also lead to the termination of an offer. If a reasonable period of time has lapsed prior to communicating an acceptance, then the offer is deemed rejected. There are two measurements of lapse. First, lapse occurs if the period of time is specified by the offer and the offeree failed to communicate an acceptance. Second, if not specified, an offer will lapse after a reasonable period of time. At common law, the determination of reasonableness is a question of fact that is dependent upon the circumstances, which include the intention of the parties, nature of the transaction, or type of property at issue. The UCC adopts a commercially reasonable standard, which is not to exceed three months. Therefore, an offer that involves perishable or seasonal goods may have a shorter lifespan than an offer involving goods that maintain a constant value.

Death, Insanity and Failure of Condition

An offer automatically terminates at the death, dissolution or insanity of the offeror or the offeree. Since termination is automatic, the parties do not need to be aware of the event. However, if an option contract is involved, then it may survive the death or insanity of a party. Additionally, the failure of a condition precedent acts to terminate the offer. For example, if parties are aware that the success of a business venture is dependent upon goods being shipped and received on time, then the failure to ship and receive the goods on time may result in the failure of a condition precedent. The provisions of a contract will not be construed as conditions precedent unless the language plainly requires such construction.

ACCEPTANCE: BRINGING LIFE TO THE CONTRACT

If the remaining requisites are satisfied, a contract is created once an offeree accepts an offer. Generally, the offeree must demonstrate a definite and clear intention to accept an offer, which must also be communicated to the offeror. The acceptance may be communicated in any manner or medium that is reasonable, unless a specific mode of acceptance is stated. Reasonable methods may include oral and written communications, performance or an act, and under certain circumstances, acceptance through the offeree's silence. If a specific mode of acceptance is stated, then the mirror-image rule applies, which requires an acceptance to conform to the prescribed mode contained in the offer. Otherwise, a non-conforming acceptance may be construed as a rejection and counter-offer. If there is a dispute, or the mode of acceptance is unreasonable, then modern courts are more willing to interpret an offer as inviting acceptance by any reasonable manner, and are less likely to interpret an offer as requiring a specific mode of acceptance

Similarly, the UCC establishes a liberal standard for acceptance of an offer. Section 2-206 permits acceptance "in any manner reasonable under the circumstances," which has been defined as a seasonable expression of acceptance or written confirmation within a reasonable period of time even if that acceptance contains terms additional to, or different from, the offer. Additionally, if a seller is in receipt of an order from the buyer, the seller may accept the order by promising to ship goods. Acceptance is also validated through the prompt shipment of conforming or non-conforming goods. Although little or no concerns arise with the shipment of conforming goods, some acceptance issues are raised with the shipment of non-conforming goods. If the non-conforming goods are shipped with a notice that the goods are supplied as a mere accommodation, then the shipment is a counter-offer that instills the power of acceptance in the buyer. Accordingly, the purchaser may accept the nonconforming goods "as is, or reject and return the goods. If the goods are shipped without such notice, then the shipment constitutes acceptance and breach of contract. The breach permits the purchaser to cover the goods and sue on breach for any difference that would have been realized had the shipment been conforming.

Unilateral and Bilateral Contracts

The acceptance of an offer creates a unilateral or bilateral contract. The favored presumption is that the parties intended to enter into a bilateral contract. Although the legal distinction is well settled, classification of a particular offer and acceptance may be difficult at times. At other times, the distinction is clear. For example, offers for sale usually result in the formation of a bilateral contract.

As defined, a unilateral contract is initiated when the offeror requests the offeree to act in return for a promise. The offer may be withdrawn at anytime, but acceptance occurs, and the offeror is bound once performance has commenced. It is often too difficult to determine whether an offeror requests an act or promise to perform an act. Accordingly, common law favors a presumption that the parties intended to enter into a bilateral contract since it fully protects both parties in the event of breach. Simply defined, a bilateral contract occurs if two parties exchange promises and is enforceable once the promises are exchanged.

There are many examples of unilateral and bilateral contract, one of which may be found in today's sales practices. For example, a unilateral contract is created when a purchaser does nothing more than submit an order, which as discussed above, constitutes an offer and invitation to accept. The seller may accept the order and execute a unilateral contract by delivering the goods to the purchaser. On the other hand, a bilateral contract is created when a purchaser and seller exchange promises, such as providing an order and accepting an order by promising to ship at a specified date. The important distinction is the communications and intentions of the parties.

Battle of the Forms

As stated above, a counter-offer constitutes a rejection and termination of the preceding offer. In exchange, a new offer is created. The UCC substantially modifies the common law to address the "battle of the forms," whereby parties submit different terms and conditions concerning the same subject matter. Section 2-207 provides that the proposal of additional or different terms by an offeree (collectively, the "proposed terms") does not constitute a rejection or a counter-offer. Instead, terms that are in agreement form a contract regardless of whether there are additional and conflicting terms. Therefore, the terms of the contract are terms that appear on the record of both parties and terms, whether in the record or not, to which both parties agree.

The status of the parties determines whether the proposed terms will be incorporated into the contract. In dealings between non-merchants, an acceptance with proposed terms does not invalidate the acceptance, unless it is conditioned upon the assent of the offeror to the proposed terms. Otherwise, the proposed terms may be incorporated if accepted by the offeror. In dealings between merchants, proposed and non-contradicting terms are automatically incorporated into the contract. There are three exceptions to automatic incorporation, including: (1) the offeror expressly limits the mode of acceptance to specific terms; (2) the offeror rejects the proposed terms within a reasonable time, often construed as 10 days; and (3) the proposed terms constitute a material alteration of the offer. The "material alteration" exception is defined broadly and results in frequent litigation. Furthermore, a majority of jurisdictions cancel contradicting terms, often referenced as the "knock out" rule.

The battle of the forms has led some businesses to specify language on its credit application to protect against an inadvertent acceptance of a counteroffer. Commercial transactions often involve the communication of quotes and proposals on the one hand (i.e., the offer), and a return on the other hand (i.e., the acceptance). These communications contain terms and conditions that are unique and favorable to the parties. It is a good practice to have favorable and readily available forms that address specific business concerns. A party should limit its quotes, proposals or purchase orders to the express terms and conditions affixed to the communication. For example, quotes issued by a seller should expressly state that the proposal is subject to the seller's terms and conditions, and that any acceptance by the purchaser is limited to same. Although not exhaustive, the following language may be considered for a credit application:

> No term or condition contained in any offer, counter-offer, acceptance, purchase order, invoice, writing or other communication to the seller shall be valid and binding upon the seller unless, at the seller's sole discretion, the seller provides a separate written statement indicating the terms and conditions that it will accept.

Likewise, if a party is accepting a proposal or confirming a purchase order, then an opportunity exists to modify the other party's terms and conditions. Moreover, in correspondence between contracting parties, a party should review correspondence to assure that it does not contain inaccurate descriptions or inaccurate terms of the contract. If inaccurate descriptions have been made, then a party should object as soon as practicable, or run the risk that the inaccuracies will materially alter the contract.

The Mailbox Rule

Generally, an offer or an acceptance is effective the moment that it is received. However, if an offer or acceptance is communicated through the mail, then different rules apply. This is known as the "Mailbox Rule," which renders acceptance effective upon dispatch, unless otherwise agreed to by the parties or provided by law. Several states adapted the Mailbox Rule acknowledging that acceptance is made as soon as the offeree has put the acceptance in the mail.

Originally, the Mailbox Rule was created to protect offerees against uncommunicated revocations, however, the purposes has expanded to provide the offeree a base to decide on whether to accept an offer. Accordingly, the Mailbox Rule has created a substantial amount of confusion over the effective date of an offer and acceptance under certain variations. The first variation occurs where the offeree sends an acceptance, but subsequently sends a rejection. In this scenario, the Mailbox Rule applies and a contract is created, unless the rejection arrives first and the offeror detrimentally relies on the rejection. The second variation occurs where the rejection is dispatched first and the acceptance is sent second. The Mailbox Rule does not apply and no contract exists, if the rejection is received first and the acceptance is received second. The third variation occurs where the offeror sends a revocation first, however, the offeree sends an acceptance prior to receipt of the revocation. The Mailbox Rule applies and a contract is created since revocation is effective upon receipt opposed to acceptance upon dispatch. Finally, if revocation is sent and received prior to the dispatch of an acceptance, then no contract is formed.

Absent the Mailbox Rule, an offeror may communicate the withdrawal of an offer to the offeree at any time prior to an act that constitutes acceptance. Since the law presumes the receipt of a properly mailed letter, parties should maintain an accurate record of outgoing and incoming mail that includes the date of mailing and the recipient's name and address. Additionally, incoming mail should be date stamped and logged. Undoubtedly, a recordkeeping system will assist if a dispute occurs involving the date and place of acceptance, revocation or other matters.

Facsimile Transmissions

Facsimile use has gained widespread support to validate an offer and acceptance, and to consummate a contract through the submission of the parties' signatures. Since transmittal of a document by facsimile is simultaneous, the offer is accepted as soon as it is transmitted. At first, the law did not recognize facsimile transmissions and construed the transmittal as a copy of the original. Although some jurisdictions remain uneasy concerning the adequacy of a facsimile transmission, other jurisdictions readily accept the same. Moreover, the evolution of facsimile has alleviated many concerns, including transmission proof sheets. At the very least, a party contemplating signatures by facsimile should include a provision that reads, "a facsimile copy of this agreement, acceptable at the sole discretion of [the party], shall have the same cause and effect of the original." In an abundance of caution, a party should request the receipt of the original as soon as practicable, often by overnight mail or courier service.

Electronic Transmissions

Many businesses are "going electronic" for a variety of reasons, including expedited payments, reduced customer discrepancies, lowered administrative costs and maintaining competition in the marketplace. Businesses are using the Internet for a myriad of credit and financial functions, including credit research and scoring, invoicing and payment collection. Additionally, access to credit applications, guarantees and other contracts has led to the "e-signature," an electronic or digital signature to consummate the contract. The e-signature taps modern technology to certify contracts through fingerprint readers, stylus pads and encrypted Asmart cards.

By the late 1990s, a majority of states accepted e-signatures as legally binding to certify commercial contracts. However, the lack of uniformity among the states forced Congress to enact the Electronic Signatures in Global and National Commerce Act (The "E-Sign Act"). The Federal Trade Commission is the federal agency responsible for regulating the E-Sign Act. The E-Sign Act utilizes the UCC's provisions that allow any symbol to constitute a signature if it is executed or adopted by a party with a present intention to authenticate a writing. The E-Sign Act creates a uniform and nationwide system that legally recognizes that a vendor may engage in e-credit transactions throughout the country. Additionally, statutes are being enacted to make greater use of electronic transmissions, including the Government Paperwork Elimination Act, the Uniform Electronic Transactions Act, the Uniform Computer Information Transactions Act (*See* Chapter 6 for a detailed discussion of UCITA), and the UNCITRAL Model Law.

The E-Sign Act permits a party to accept an e-signature to form a binding contract. For the credit professional, this may eliminate a customer's need to download an application and mail the completed application with a handwritten signature. Some of the relevant provisions of the E-Sign Act are: (1) parties to the contract decide on the form of digital signature technology to validate the contract; (2) businesses may use e-signatures on checks; (3) businesses must require parties to the contract to make at least two clicks of a computer to complete a deal; (4) the consumer decides whether to use an e-signature or handwritten signature; (5) cancellation and foreclosure notices must be sent on paper; (6) e-signatures on adoptions, wills, and product safety recalls are not allowed; and (7) records of e-contracts may be stored electronically.

A key issue confronting a party utilizing e-signatures is determining the most reliable way to certify an e-contract, authenticate e-signatures and reduce the risk of fraud and claims of unauthorized use of an e-signature. Technology to verify a person's identity is available. The most common is a "smart card" which looks like a credit card and stores digital information about the signer used to verify a party's identity. Efforts to address these concerns have improved exponentially. For example, a number of security companies now offer services to verify an e-signature. Undoubtedly, the advance of modern technology will tighten the noose on fraud and fuel the expansion of e-commerce through growing confidence in the marketplace. The electronic credit department will continue to expand.

Forming Contracts Electronically

The nature of the Internet allows people to access, store, manipulate and transmit information in a nanosecond. Speed and instantaneous transmission is one of the greatest attributes of the Internet and is exactly the feature that has the public hooked. Today, more and more people are making legally binding and enforceable contracts on the Internet. This new means of contract formation has raised a host of new challenges for the paper-based rules of law. With more contracts being formed on the Internet, businesses need to be aware of the many issues with forming contracts electronically.

Requirements for contract formation may differ from jurisdiction to jurisdiction, but in general, the same basic legal requirements that have been discussed in the previous sections must also be satisfied for a contract to be formed electronically. In almost all jurisdictions, there must be (1) an intention to create legal relations, (2) an offer from one party to another, (3) an acceptance of that offer, (4) an exchange of value or a "promise for a promise," and (5) a certainty of terms. Given the nature of the Internet, satisfying these requirements requires some acknowledgement by law.

For instance, the state legislature and the federal government have moved to adopt legislation that puts electric contracts on par with paper agreements and handwritten signatures. Both the Uniform Electronic Transactions Act, adopted by a majority of the states, and the Federal Electronic Signatures and National Commerce Act (E-sign, discussed in the previous section) provide that electronic records, signatures and contracts are not to be denied legal enforceability simply because they are in electronic form. Consequently, if laws require writings or signatures, electronic records and signatures satisfy those laws. Almost any means of communication that can be stored and later retrieved is considered a "record," the electronic world's equivalent of paper writing. Also, paper documents may be saved in electronic form and the original destroyed, so long as the electronic version accurately reflects the information in the original and remains accessible for future reference.

One of the most prevalent areas for companies to inadvertently enter into a contract is via e-mail, as e-mails can be perceived as a record and a method of contracting. For example, in a recently decided case, a set of back-and-forth e-mails was found to be a sufficient contract for purchase of real property. To avoid being bound by these sorts of interactions, companies should create policies regarding e-mail exchanges; as such, it may be necessary to add a disclaimer message that follows an employee's signature stating that the employee's company does not intend to be bound by the message in order to avoid formation of an unintended contract.

Contracts can also be formed by messages, transmitted between computers or other machines with any human involvement, so long as the parties have the intent to form a contract. Care must be taken in such cases since the terms of the contract will only be those that the equipment used to transmit them can take into account. Additional terms will not be recognized and often time will be ignored.

Guidelines recently published by a committee of the American Bar Association for the formation of valid electronic contracts strongly suggest that a party being asked to enter into a contract electronically be required to view the terms of the contract before agreeing to them. It is necessary that the terms of the contract be available for view more than once in order to permit comparison shopping. Also, the consumer must be given a clear choice between accepting and rejecting its terms. Concrete actions such as clicking on an icon marked "I agree" or "I accept" should be required in order to form the contract as opposed to ambiguous terms such as "continue," "submit" or "download." The fact that a party is being asked to enter into a biding contract and the consequences associated with entering that contract should also be made clear. In addition, the parties must be able to save and print a copy of the terms for their records. Lastly, parties should be required to agree to the terms of the contract before being given access to the goods or services covered by the agreement.

Silence or Inaction

As a general rule, silence or inaction does not constitute acceptance of an offer. This remains true regardless of whether the offeror states that silence will operate as a mode of acceptance. However, there is a limited set of circumstances that construes silence or inaction as a form of acceptance. First, silence will operate as a form of acceptance if an offeree receives goods or services with a reasonable opportunity to reject the service and knows that there is a reasonable expectation that the goods or services were offered for compensation. Second, silence operates as acceptance where the offeror has stated or gives the offeree reason to believe that assent may be manifested by silence or inaction, and the offeree intends to accept the offer.

At common law, courts have also been willing to review silence against a given set of circumstances. For example, the course of dealing between the parties may be a factor to determine whether silence is a valid form of acceptance. Often, these courts construe silence as creating an implied contract. However, a party relying on such construction should understand that it is a distant exception and applied infrequently. Nevertheless, if silence is at issue, it is a good idea to keep in mind the concepts that are traditionally associated with implied contracts, including estoppel, reliance and restitution.

Solicitations

The rank and file of today's businesses consist of employees that do not usually possess the requisite authority to bind a business. Rank and file employees include salespersons, independent contractors and similarly situated employees (collectively, the "unauthorized agents"), whereas the requisite authority to bind a business is usually delegated to mid-level to upper-level management or authorized credit departments (collectively, the "authorized agents"). Prior to acceptance, the authorized agents review the solicitations with sophisticated scrutiny to determine whether the solicitation should be accepted, and particularly, the creditworthiness of the purchaser.

Accordingly, preventative measures are necessary to ensure that a business is not bound by the acts or representations of unauthorized agents. These preventative measures should include express language on credit applications and other documents that acceptance of the solicitation is subject to a specified mode issued by an authorized agent. For example, the solicitation may include a statement that approval of the solicitation is based on the "express written acceptance of the seller." Additionally, a credit application or other document should state that all sales or transactions are subject to the terms and conditions that are approved at the seller's sole discretion. Furthermore, although acceptance may be accomplished by performance or any reasonable method, acceptance of a solicitation should be communicated in writing to avoid cancellations and dispute.

Acknowledgment of Receipt

Although less prominent during the previous years, many businesses have developed a custom to acknowledge the receipt of an order prior to its acceptance. If the seller intends to submit the acknowledgment as a receipt and acceptance, then it should clearly indicate its intention to bind the parties to contract. However, if the acknowledgment is not intended to form a contract, then it should conspicuously state the same. Otherwise, while the order is being processed and customer information reviewed, the purchaser may have a mistaken assumption that the order was received and accepted. To prevent confusion, the acknowledgment should clearly state that the order was received and in the process of review. Additionally, the language should clearly reserve the right of the seller to reject the order, which is simply an offer.

MUTUAL ASSENT OF THE PARTIES

An essential element of contract law is the mutual assent of the parties, often termed the "meeting of the minds." The courts apply an objective analysis to determine whether the outward manifestations of a party's assent are sufficient to create reasonable reliance in the other party. The courts impute an intention corresponding to the reasonable meaning of a person's words or acts to determine the position that a "reasonable person" would conclude from such manifestations. Accordingly, mental assent is not a requisite to contract and a party's state of mind is immaterial, if outward manifestations evidence assent to contract. Therefore, the law recognizes a contract based exclusively on the parties' communicated intentions.

Despite the objective standard, courts may review a party's subjective beliefs involving the formation of the contract. A court may engage in a subjective analysis if the terms of the contract are ambiguous and subject to different interpretations. For example, the parol evidence rule may provide terms to a contract that are not specifically stated, but explanation is required to understand the basis for the contract. Under certain circumstances, the language or circumstances of a contract may distort the intentions of the parties to the extent that mutual assent is not satisfied.

CONSIDERATION

Consideration is a fundamental element required to form a valid contract. Often a misunderstood concept, consideration does not always equate to monetary compensation. Instead, consideration has been construed broadly to include any right, interest or benefit accruing to one party, or some discernible detriment, loss or responsibility undertaken by the other. A familiar simplification describes consideration as the "bargained for exchange of promises."

Mutuality of Consideration

In its early development, a common cited maxim of consideration proposed that "both parties must be bound or neither will be." Most often, the bargained-for exchange consisted of exchanged promises. The consideration must be agreed upon, or implied such that each party must agree to a legal detriment bargained for by the other. Additionally, the consideration must induce the parties to contract. However, a party may have more than one motive to enter into contract. This is especially true when reviewed in the commercial context. Unless both parties have knowledge that the purported consideration is a pretext, then it is immaterial that the party's desire for consideration is incidental to other objectives. Today, the maxim has lost considerable leverage because modern courts and the UCC are more willing to find that consideration exists, despite whether a promise is voidable or unenforceable.

A requirement for the mutuality of consideration is further weakened by the UCC's treatment of output contracts. For example, in Section 2-306(1), the measurement of the quantity purchased or sold by the output of the seller, or the requirements of the buyer, is not deemed to be without mutuality of consideration. Further, Section 2-306(2) provides that an exclusive dealing arrangement is not without consideration, even if the party holding the exclusive right makes no express promise in return. Instead, the law merely imposes on that party a duty to exercise its best efforts to supply the merchandise.

Inadequacy of Consideration

The mere inadequacy of consideration will not void a contract. Ordinarily, courts will not inquire into the adequacy of consideration and view such inquiry as an unwise interference with the exercise of a party's judgment. Courts distinguish between the sufficiency of consideration and the adequacy of consideration. Generally, consideration is sufficient if the law recognizes it as having value, but courts refrain from assessing the comparative value of the exchanged promises (i.e., adequacy). The type of value assigned to consideration is an issue that the courts have struggled with over the course of time.

Listed below are circumstances where the "inadequacy" of consideration will render a contract unenforceable.

PRE-EXISTING LEGAL DUTY

The pre-existing legal duty rule states that a promise to do, or refrain from doing, something that a person already has a legal duty will not form the basis of valid consideration. A familiar example of a pre-existing legal duty is a credit arrangement where the customer has charged against an account and agrees to pay a lesser sum to satisfy the debt in full.

If the antecedent debt is liquidated (i.e., sum certain, no dispute), then payment of a lesser sum will fail for lack of consideration. Instead, the payment of a lesser sum will offset the amount due and the creditor is entitled to the remaining sum and can enforce payment on the balance. Accordingly, payment of a lesser sum than the balance must be accompanied by consideration (e.g., advanced payment).

If the balance is unliquidated and in dispute, then courts usually conclude that valid consideration for the discharge of debt exists. Therefore, if a purchaser alleges that shipped goods were defective or of lesser value, then discharge of the obligation to pay for the goods occurs after the payment and acceptance of an amount that the purchaser believed the goods were worth.

There are some notable exceptions to the pre-existing rule, especially concerning modification of an existing contract. First, if the modification is "fair and equitable" and the result of unanticipated circumstances, then a court may permit modification. An exception to the pre-existing duty rule finds valid consideration if there are "unanticipated circumstances." Unforeseen difficulties may arise during the course of its performance. For example, consider the circumstance where a manufacturer contracts with a vendor for the land shipment of widgets at a specified date. If the vendor requires the shipment to arrive the following day because demand had depleted the widgets on hand, then the increased costs to ship airfreight will not fail for lack of consideration. Second, if a party assumes additional duties, no matter how trivial, then a court may view the additional duties as a detriment. Section 2-209(1) of the UCC completely abolishes the pre-existing duty rule if the modification is in writing and proposed in good faith.

The pre-existing duty rule has some profound implications for the credit professional. For example, if a debt is liquidated, courts have rendered unenforceable a creditor's promise to accept a lesser amount paid on the debt as full satisfaction of an account. Moreover, a creditor's promise to permit a debtor additional time to pay outside of invoice terms may also be unenforceable. Section 3-311 has changed these common law rules. Under the UCC, if a debtor submits its payment under the caveat that the payment is "in full settlement" and the creditor cashes the check, then the UCC considers it an acceptance of the settlement, despite the creditor's protest.

PAST CONSIDERATION

Past consideration is similar to a pre-existing duty; however, it differs to the extent that the promise to perform is made in recognition of a benefit already received. Generally, "past consideration is no consideration." The rationale supporting this rule is that there must be a bargained for exchange of consideration to form a valid contract, which cannot occur if the consideration is based on a legal detriment or benefit that occurred in the past. Courts look to the facts and circumstances of a particular case, instead of the language of any agreement executed between the parties. For example, a previously entered contract will usually constitute past consideration in relation to a subsequent contract regarding the same subject matter.

NOMINAL CONSIDERATION

Nominal consideration does not constitute adequate consideration. Generally, nominal consideration consists of the exchange of unequal sums of money. Modern courts review nominal consideration with a focus on the level of bargaining between the parties. If bargaining is absent, then the courts will weigh the relative value of benefit and detriment to determine whether there was an adequacy of consideration.

MORAL OBLIGATION

A moral obligation does not constitute adequate consideration. Like other events that do not constitute adequate consideration, moral obligations lack a bargained for exchange. A moral obligation is a duty that one party owes and should perform to another party; however, there is no legal duty to perform. For example, if a creditor fails to pursue a cause of action against a debtor to recover a debt, then the debt may be barred by the applicable statute of limitations (i.e., time barred). The debt may not be recovered by law, but it subsists in morality. However, there are three exceptions, in which a moral obligation may constitute adequate consideration. The first follows the referenced example and finds adequacy of consideration where a debtor "reaffirms" his promise to pay a time-barred claim. The remaining exceptions find adequacy of consideration where a bankruptcy debtor promises to pay a discharged debt or a minor ratifies a contract after reaching the age of majority.

There are several other circumstances in which an event will not constitute valid consideration. A promise for a gift cannot be enforced if it is not based on consideration (i.e., when there is no benefit to the donor or no detriment to the donee). However, a promise for a gift may be enforced if the donee can demonstrate reliance on the promise through altering its position or if the gift has been fully executed (i.e., donative intent and delivery).

Illusory promises and altruistic acts also do not constitute adequate consideration. First, illusory promises are promises in which the promisor chooses whether to perform, but is under no legal duty to perform. For example, a party that wishes, wills or desires to perform an act or refrain from performance offers nothing more than an illusory promises that cannot be enforced. Furthermore, altruism, or an act done out of kindness, is not sufficient consideration to base a contract.

Modification of Contract Requires New Consideration

At common law, modification of a contract requires consideration. Generally, consideration will be valid if there is mutual assent between the parties to alter the terms of the contract. Accordingly, modification may be supported by additional consideration, mutual recision of the contract and replacement with a new contract (i.e., accord and satisfaction), and in a few states, modification is available if the parties agree in writing. In addition, modification is available where unanticipated circumstances occur and the parties are bound under a pre-existing duty.

Alternatively, under UCC § 2-209, no consideration is needed to modify a contract for the sale of goods. Additionally, the modification does not require a writing, unless its subject matter falls within the purview of the state's statute of frauds. Similarly, under UCC § 1-107, a cause of action for breach of contract can be discharged without consideration if a written waiver or renunciation is executed by the aggrieved party.

Substitute Consideration

If no consideration exists to support a contract, then substitutes for consideration need to be consulted. Generally, there are three types of substitute consideration, including promissory estoppel, pre-existing moral obligation and charitable subscriptions. First, as applied by modern courts, "promissory estoppel" will apply where the promisor should reasonably expect that its promise would induce the promisee to action, the promisee acts, and that such reliance was detrimental to the promisee. If promissory estoppel is applied, then a contract will be enforced to the extent to cure the injustice. Second, a minority of states provide that a pre-existing moral obligation will substitute for consideration. Under this theory, recovery will be permitted if a benefit is conferred, an expectation of payment is created and the benefiting party is unjustly enriched. The recovery is limited to restitution to prevent injustice. Finally, charitable subscriptions are not subject to the rules of consideration and are enforceable as a matter of law.

COVENANTS AND CONDITIONS

In formulating a contract, the parties attempt to reach an agreement on the covenants and conditions that will regulate performance under the contract and determine a breach. If there is a covenant to the contract, then there is an absolute duty to perform; otherwise, the failure to perform constitutes a breach. The determination of whether a covenant exists is based on the intent of the parties and language adopted by the contract. On the other hand, conditions are acts that have the effect of creating or extinguishing a duty to perform. Generally, conditions are created with use of phrases such as "on condition that," "provided that," "if, then," "subject to," and like phrases.

A condition may be express or implied. The determination that a condition is express requires strict compliance to the condition whereas only substantial compliance is required to satisfy an implied condition. An express condition is a condition that is agreed to between the parties. Alternatively, implied conditions are either "implied in fact" or "implied in law." Conditions that are implied in fact are determined based on "reasonableness," and include such conditions as good faith, cooperation and fair dealing. Conditions that are implied in law include conditions precedent (i.e., conditions creating a duty to perform), conditions concurrent (i.e., performance that must occur simultaneously), and conditions subsequent (i.e., conditions extinguishing a duty to perform). If a condition brings rise to a duty to perform, then the condition must be satisfied or excused to prevent a breach.

PAROL EVIDENCE RULE

If a contract is unambiguous, then it is deemed the final and complete expression of the parties' intent. If ambiguity exists, then the parties' intent may become an issue. The cornerstone of contract construction is to ascertain the intent of the parties. If an agreement is valid and unambiguous, then a court should refrain from any inquiry beyond the four corners of the document. An ambiguity exists where reasonable persons could disagree to the effect of a provision.

The parol evidence rule bars extrinsic evidence of any agreement that was made prior or contemporaneous to an agreement between the parties that was not reduced to writing. There is little, if any, deviation between the common law and the UCC. The purpose of the parol evidence rule is to provide fully integrated contracts with a degree of certainty and predictability. The rule applies to integrated, or in some instances, partially integrated contracts in which the parties intend the writing to be a final and complete expression of their agreement.

Although once a rigid rule of construction, courts have applied several exceptions that permit the evaluation of extrinsic evidence. Moreover, the rule does not bar all evidence of extrinsic agreement, but only agreements made, or intentions expressed prior to or contemporaneous with the execution of an unambiguous written agreement.

Integration: Total or Partial

As stated above, a contract must be integrated and in writing for a party to invoke the parol evidence rule. The parol evidence rule only applies to agreements that are integrated. It is important to note that the parol evidence rule bars any contradictory terms to a totally or partially integrated agreement.

TOTAL INTEGRATION

A totally integrated agreement is an agreement that addresses the entire understanding of the parties and includes all the terms and conditions agreed to between the parties. If an agreement is totally integrated, then courts employ a strict parol evidence rule that bars any evidence of prior or contemporaneous agreements or negotiations that may contradict or add to the totally integrated agreement.

Partial Integration

A partially integrated agreement is intended to be a final expression of the parties; however, it does not include all the details of the agreement. Partially integrated agreements supplement, but do not contradict, an original agreement. For example, if the original agreement is for the sale of goods, then a court will allow consistent additional terms unless it is determined that the original agreement was the exclusive agreement between the parties. Courts apply the parol evidence rule only to prior or contemporaneous agreements that contradict a partially integrated agreement.

To avoid partial integration of prior or contemporaneous agreements, parties may include an integration clause to exclude additional understandings or agreements not contained in the most recent agreement. An integration clause may include negative, collateral or antecedent agreements. An integration clause should be drafted to cancel all prior agreements, either oral or in writing, as applied to the final agreement.

Exceptions to the Parol Evidence Rule

The parol evidence rule is subject to certain exceptions that do not bar oral or written agreements executed prior to or contemporaneously to an integrated agreement.

Conditions Precedent

The parol evidence rule does not bar evidence that the parties orally agreed on a condition precedent to the enforceability of an agreement. For example, a vendor agrees to sell a buyer its entire inventory of widgets, provided that the corporate office approves. The vendor and buyer execute a sale agreement, but do not include the condition for approval. In most instances, a court would permit evidence of the oral requirement for approval.

Resolution of Ambiguity

The parol evidence rule does not bar extrinsic evidence to determine the parties' intentions and meaning of an ambiguous contract.

Integration and Intent

The parol evidence rule does not bar evidence to determine whether the parties intended the writing to be a final and complete, or in some instances a partial, statement of their agreement.

Consistent Additional and Supplemental Agreements

The parol evidence rule does not bar the enforcement of collateral or supplemental agreements that are consistent with the terms of the original agreement. In addition, the rule does not bar evidence to explain the parties' agreement, if the evidence does not vary or contradict the terms of the parties' agreement.

Fraud, Mistake and Invalidity

The existence of a fully integrated agreement does not bar a party from introducing extrinsic evidence that the agreement was the result of fraud, mistake, duress, illegality, an abuse of bargaining power or lack of consideration. If evidence exists to demonstrate that a valid contract does not exist, then the court will not permit the parol evidence rule to stand in its way.

Subsequent Agreements

The parol evidence rule does not bar subsequent agreements, despite whether the agreement contains contradictory terms.

UCC: Specific Exceptions for the Sale of Goods

Although the UCC codifies common law parol evidence rules, it incorporates three important additions. The UCC provides that integrated agreements may be explained or supplemented by evidence of the course of dealing or usage of trade (i.e., conduct of the parties concerning the agreement at issue), course of performance (i.e., conduct of the parties concerning past agreements), and the addition of consistent terms. Although the UCC permits explanation and supplementation, extrinsic evidence may never contradict the terms of an integrated agreement.

IMPORTANT TERMS AND CONDITIONS
FOR THE CREDIT PROFESSIONAL

The incorporation of contract provisions, other than provisions dealing with subject matter, is largely dependent on the parties' circumstances. However, certain clauses may be beneficial to add predictability in the event of a dispute, or may be required by law.

Jurisdiction Clauses and Venue Clauses

A prudent choice of law provision that includes a jurisdiction and venue clause may include the following language:

> [t]he Undersigned expressly provides irrevocable consent and agrees that all suits for breach of the Agreement, or for default in payment, or for any dispute arising hereunder, shall be subject to the laws of the State of Nantucket. The Undersigned hereby submits to the nonexclusive jurisdiction of the United States District Court for the State of Nantucket, or any Nantucket State Court sitting in Nantucket City for the purposes of any dispute arising under the Agreement or the transactions contemplated hereunder.

In addition, a party may wish to include a waiver to defenses of personal jurisdiction. For example, a waiver clause may include the following language, "[t]he Undersigned expressly waives any defenses to personal jurisdiction, including express waiver of forum non-conveniens objections."

Service Designations

More often, parties are including provisions that predetermine service of court documents and pleadings. For example, a party may include language that:

[a]ll writs, process and summonses in any such suit, action or proceeding brought in the State of Nantucket may be made upon the [designated party] (the "Process Agent"), presently located at [address], and the Guarantor hereby irrevocably appoints the Process Agent its true and lawful attorney-in-fact in its name, place and stead to accept, and use its best efforts to deliver a copy to the Undersigned of such service of any and all such writs, process and summonses, and agrees that the failure of the Process Agent to give any notice of any such service or process to the Undersigned shall not impair or affect the validity of such service or of any judgment based thereon.

The goal of choice of law provisions and service designations is to add certainty and predictability to contractual relations, even if such provisions are in contemplation of a party's or the parties' breach.

Force Majeure Clauses

The sufficiency of a contract's force majeure clause has received renewed interest in light of recent events. The catastrophic events of September 11 and the continued threat of terrorism, domestic and abroad, are a grim reminder that tragedy is unpredictable. These events only compound the common risk associated with a cycling domestic economy and unpredictable international markets. In the post-September 11 contractual setting, a party must contemplate common risks while preparing to allocate the risk of nonperformance to counter events that were once unimaginable.

Force majeure is a term used to describe a "superior force" event. The purpose of a force majeure clause is two-fold: it allocates risk and places the parties on notice of the events that may suspend or excuse performance. The essential condition of force majeure is the prevention of a party's performance that is caused by an unforeseen supervening event not within the control of either party. Typical force majeure events include Acts of God, superceding governmental authority, civil strife and labor disputes.

In drafting a force majeure clause, parties may rely on general clauses or specifically enumerate which events will constitute force majeure. For example, a general force majeure clause may consist of the following language:

[i]t shall not constitute a material breach, and neither party shall lose any rights hereunder or be liable to the other party for damages or losses, on account of failure of performance by the defaulting party, if the failure is the result of a natural disaster, national emergency, the act or omission of a third party or similar event outside of a party's control.

A prudent force majeure clause specifically enumerates the events that will prevent performance and entitle a party to suspend or excuse its performance. For example, a specific and contemporary force majeure clause may consist of the following language:

[n]either party shall lose any rights hereunder or be liable to the other party for damages or losses, except for payment obligations, on account of failure of performance by the defaulting party if the failure is the result of an Act of God (e.g., fire, flood, inclement weather, epidemic or earthquake); war or act of terrorism, including chemical or biological warfare; labor dispute, lockout, strike, embargo; governmental acts, orders, or restrictions; failure of suppliers or third persons; or any other reason where failure to perform is beyond the reasonable control, and is not caused by the negligence, intentional conduct or misconduct of the defaulting party, and the defaulting party has exercised all reasonable efforts to avoid or remedy such force majeure. The defaulting party must provide written notice of the force majeure event to the remaining parties within two (2) business days of such event.

In addition, force majeure clauses may include language that is industry specific. The construction industry, for example, may incorporate a clause to suspend or excuse performance if the failure to perform is caused by subcontractors, material-men or carriers.

Attorneys' Fees and Costs of Enforcement Clauses

A party may include a provision concerning the payment of attorneys' fees and costs. Generally, attorneys' fees and costs provisions award the prevailing party its reasonable attorneys' fees and costs associated with litigation. An attorneys' fees and costs provision is required if a party seeks recovery for fees and costs, unless there is an alternative statutory basis for recovery. Some contracts attempt to introduce unilateral attorneys' fees and costs provisions to designate a certain party to pay fees and costs despite the outcome of litigation. In a majority of jurisdictions, unilateral fees and cost provisions are deemed against public policy. Instead, unilateral provisions will be construed as a source of recovery for the prevailing party.

An attorneys' fees and costs provision may include the following language:

[t]he parties expressly agree that the prevailing party shall be entitled to payment of all attorneys' fees, collection costs and court fees, and any other expenses in connection with the enforcement of the terms and conditions of the Agreement.

A party may also incorporate an attorneys' fees and costs provision to designate a party to pay fees and costs that occur outside litigation including, costs associated with an amendment or modification.

Interest and Late Fees

A party may include an interest provision that provides for a predetermined percentage of interest if a party were to default on a payment obligation. If an interest clause is not provided in the agreement, then a court may, or may not, award interest from the date of the breach. If a court awards interest, then it is likely to be a lower percentage than can be negotiated between the parties. In addition to interest, a party may include a late fee or service charge on returned payments. An example of an interest clause may include:

[t]he interest charge shall equal the amount obtained by multiplying the delinquent balance by one and one-half percent (1.5%) per month or eighteen (18%) per annum by the expiration of the thirtieth (30) day, then every thirty (30) days

thereafter. A service charge of $25.00 will apply if a check or payment is returned for insufficient funds. [Party] shall not waive any additional remedies available under applicable state law for any check or payment returned by [Party's] bank for insufficient funds.

International Transactions and Currency

If the agreement involves an international transaction in which the specification of a currency and place of payment is of the essence, then it is prudent to include a transaction and currency provision:

[t]he payment obligations shall not be discharged by an amount paid in another currency or in another place whether pursuant to a judgment or otherwise, to the extent that the amount so paid on conversion to the currency specified herein (the "Contract Currency") and transfer to the place of payment does not yield the amount of the Contract Currency in the place of payment due hereunder.

Equal Credit Opportunity Act (ECOA)

If an agreement involves the extension of credit, then it is imperative to include a statement concerning a party's rights under the Federal Equal Credit Opportunity Act (the "ECOA"). Specifically, the creditor should include language that the ECOA prohibits creditors from discriminating against credit applicants based on race, color, religion, national origin, sex, marital status, age; because all or part of the applicant's income derives from any public assistance program; or because the applicant has in good faith exercised any right under the Consumer Credit Protection Act. In addition, the creditor should include a statement concerning the rights of a party if credit is denied. If a creditor denies credit then it should provide its address to allow the party to request a written statement of the specific reasons for denial.

Fair Credit Reporting Act (FCRA)

If an agreement involves an extension of credit, and a creditor intends to review a credit report of an individual applicant, then it is imperative for the creditor to request permission to obtain the report. The Federal Trade Commission (FTC) requires that a creditor obtain a written consent from the consumer stating that the consumer understands and permits the creditor to utilize outside credit reporting services to obtain information on the party. The statement should specifically state that the creditor is authorized under the Fair Credit Reporting Act to evaluate information for the purpose of extending credit. The statement should also state that the authorization will remain valid and enforceable until the party expressly revokes authorization in writing. A credit report may be any written or oral report communication bearing on a consumer's credit standing, credit capacity, character, general reputation, persona characteristics or mode of living. The credit report must either be used, expected to be used, or collected whole or in part, for a permissible purpose. The FTC provides no authority for a creditor to obtain a consumer report in connection with a credit application for any commercial purpose.

If the creditor fails to obtain authorization to pull a credit report and the report is pulled through the credit information provider, the creditor may be liable for violating the FCRA. Criminal penalties may also be assessed, including fines and imprisonment, against any person who knowingly and willfully obtains a consumer report under false pretense.

The FCRA requires that creditors provide notice if the creditor is denying credit, or otherwise taking adverse action with respect to the credit application, based upon the information provided by the credit report. This notice can be oral, in writing or electronic. The creditor is required to provide the name, address and telephone number of the consumer reporting agency. The creditor must notify the consumer of the consumer's right to obtain a free copy of the consumer report. Notice must also be provided of the consumer's right to dispute with the consumer reporting agency the accuracy or completeness of any information in the consumer report.

RULES OF CONSTRUCTION

An agreement, and its terms and conditions, are subject to several rules of construction. Some of the pertinent rules are discussed.

The Contract As a Whole

A contract should be construed as a whole to give effect to the intended meaning of each term and provision. This rule of construction permits the parties to extract the intended meaning of one provision and apply it to another provision that may be ambiguous.

Unreasonable and Unconscionable Provisions

Although a court will usually not inquire into the parties' intent, unreasonable provisions may be unenforceable. An agreement is unreasonable, *inter alia*, if it violates public policy or its subject matter is illegal. Moreover, a provision may be unconscionable, and accordingly, unenforceable if it is unusual or extraordinary and produces an unfair or unreasonable result.

Illegal and Exculpatory Provisions

An agreement may not require a party to perform an unlawful act. Agreements requiring the performance of an unlawful act are *per se* against public policy. In addition, certain states may not enforce exculpatory clauses that indemnify a party of its own negligence under the theory that such clauses are against public policy.

Specific and General Provisions

An agreement may incorporate both general and specific language. This rule of construction states that specific language is given precedence over general language because the specific mention of certain matters excludes matters mentioned only generally.

Ambiguity Is Construed Against the Drafter

If a provision is ambiguous, then it is construed against the drafter. However, this rule of construction is subject to the parties' intent and is usually invoked only in situations where the drafting party has unequal bargaining power.

DEFENSES TO CONTRACT FORMATION

Although a party or the parties may believe that a valid contract was formed, there are certain defenses that may render the contract unenforceable. These defenses include the failure of any one of the four essential elements to formation. Additional defenses include lack of legal capacity, illegality of subject matter or public policy, the statute of frauds, unconscionability, mistake, fraud, misrepresentation and undue influence.

If a defense to contract formation exists, then the contract may be void or voidable. A void contract is never enforceable because it was never a contract. For example, a usury contract is void from its inception even if all elements to form a contract exist. On the other hand, a voidable contract is a contract that one party is required to perform whereas the other party has the option to rescind the contract or continue with performance. In reviewing the defenses, consider whether the contract is void or voidable, and if voidable, which party has the ability to rescind or perform.

Lack of Capacity to Contract

As explained above, a contract requires a "meeting of the minds," which in turn, requires that the parties to possess the requisite capacity to contract. Generally, it is presumed that a person or entity has the capacity to comprehend and understand the terms and conditions of a contract. However, common law and statutory law define certain classes of persons that have limited capacity, or no capacity to enter into a contract. The lack of capacity renders a contract void or voidable by the incapacitated person. These persons and entities include: (1) infants and minors, (2) mentally disabled, (3) intoxicated, (4) corporations, agents, fiduciaries and other legal representatives.

INFANTS AND MINORS

At common law, a person remained a minor until 21 years; however, states have enacted statutes to establish the age of majority at 18 years. In some states, the age of majority may be less than 18 years, if the minor is emancipated by operation of law, marriage or military status. The contractual capacity of a minor depends on whether the contract was entered into for "necessities of life" or other goods or services that are not necessities. A minor possesses the absolute right to void a contract for the purchase of goods or services that are not necessary.

MENTALLY INCOMPETENT AND INTOXICATED PERSONS

Incompetence to enter a contract arises when mental disease or disorder hinders the person's capacity to understand the nature and consequences of the transaction, or a compulsion brought upon by mental incapacity causes the person to enter into the contract. Intoxication is treated on par with mental incompetency if the intoxication caused the person to not understand and appreciate the nature and consequences of the transaction. Similar to a minority contracting for necessities, an incompetent or intoxicated person contracting for necessities is responsible for the reasonable value of the contracted goods or services.

Generally, the contract of a mental incompetent or intoxicated person is voidable at the incompetent's election. The law recognizes the incapacitated party's right to rescind the contract if the other party can be returned to the *status quo*. Moreover, if the *status quo* cannot be restored and the contracting party is unaware of the incompetent's mental disease or disorder, then the power to void the transaction terminates to the extent that the contract has been executed, or the circumstances have changed such that voiding the transaction would be unjust.

CORPORATIONS, FIDUCIARIES AND LEGAL REPRESENTATIVES

The ability for a corporation to enter into contracts is dependent upon its articles of incorporation, bylaws and several statutory provisions. Similarly, statutes and instruments (e.g., will or trust) usually establish authority and limitations to contract for administrators, executors, trustees, committees and other legal representatives. Accordingly, it is necessary to examine these documents and statutes prior to engaging in a contract.

Illegality of Subject Matter

A contract requires legality of the subject matter, otherwise it is unenforceable. A contract is illegal if its formation or performance is forbidden by a civil or criminal statute, or when a penalty is imposed for doing an act agreed upon. Accordingly, contracts may not violate a statute, or a state or federal constitution.

In addition, courts have uniformly identified three categories of contracts that are unenforceable. First, usurious contracts are unenforceable since these contracts charge an interest rate in excess of a state's prescribed interest rate (e.g., loan-sharking). Second, contracts based on gambling or wagering (e.g., betting through a bookie) are unenforceable, absent state guidelines regulating these establishments. Third, contracts that violate public policy are also unenforceable. Although public policy may be viewed as a "catch-all," more often it is referenced if the contract is injurious to the peace, health, good order or established morals of society. Moreover, current trends in federal and state law have targeted certain business practices as illegal to the subject matter of a contract. These business practices include restraint of trade, price fixing and unfair trade practices.

The Statute of Frauds

THE STATUTE OF FRAUDS DEFINED

As stated in the introduction, an enforceable contract may be agreed to orally or reduced to writing. However, if a state's statute of frauds applies, then an oral contract is unenforceable. The statute of frauds is a collection of statutes that require a writing to enforce a contract. The purpose of the statute is to prevent perjured testimony to prove the existence of a contract. Although the states vary in their statutes, a general understanding of the statute of frauds requires a contract to be reduced to a writing and signed by the party to be charged. Some states strictly require a formalized contract whereas other states require some form of written evidence that is signed by the party to be charged (i.e., written memorandum evidencing the terms of the contract). Most states permit a collection of separate writings to constitute a contract; and the signature may be a handwritten or a mere symbol of the party. At a minimum, the writing should identify the parties, subject matter, and the essential terms of the contract. If the UCC is applicable, then the essential terms of the contract may be omitted so long as a quantity is identified.

Although states differ in their treatment of contracts under the statute of frauds, there are certain generalities that apply specifically to the commercial context. The contracts that require a writing include contracts for the sale of land, contracts to answer for the debt or duty of another, contracts that by their terms cannot be performed within one year, or contracts for the sale of goods greater than $5,000. Additionally, a majority of states require credit agreements and wage assignments to be in writing. The determination that a contract violates the statute of frauds renders the contract void or voidable dependent upon state law. However, despite the writing requirement, it is almost universal that the statute of frauds is no obstacle to recovery under a restitution of performances rendered as part of the agreed exchanged by a party not in default of the oral agreement.

Contracts for the Sale of Land

The statute of frauds applies to any interest in land.

Contracts to Answer for the Debt of Another

The promise to guarantee another person's debt: a guarantee exists where a party binds himself to another's obligation for a debt. The guarantee must relate to the same subject as the original obligation and may not impose a more onerous burden. If the statute of frauds has been adopted, then the guarantee must be in writing and signed by the party to be charged.

Contracts That Cannot Be Performed Within One Year

The statute of frauds applies to any contract that, by its terms, cannot be performed within a year from its inception. A contract that is enforceable under the statute of frauds is not rendered unenforceable merely because it is not capable of being performed within one year or any other applicable period after its making. The phrase "any other applicable period" recognizes that some state statutes apply to periods longer than one year. The focus of inquiry is "by the terms" of the contract. The common test is whether the performance called for by the contact necessarily extends beyond a year. If the contract forbids performance within one year, then it falls within the statute.

Contracts for the Sale of Goods Greater Than $5,000

The final contract that falls within the statute of frauds is a contract for the sale of goods greater than $5,000. Under UCC § 2-201, a contract for the sale of goods for a price of $5,000 or more is not enforceable unless there is a writing sufficient to indicate the sale of goods and signed by the party charged. Under the common law, the price of goods needs to be $500 or more for the statute of fraud to apply. Although a writing is required, it does not have to be precise and may omit or incorrectly state a term. There are exceptions to this rule. First, if the goods are specially manufactured for the buyer, then the contract is enforceable if manufacturing has commenced or a party has made commitments to procure the goods. Second, a party admits that a contract has been made such that the contract is enforceable to its stated quantity. Finally, if the payment for goods has been received or the goods have been accepted, then the statute no longer applies.

MODERN TRENDS INVOLVING THE WRITING REQUIREMENT: CREDIT AGREEMENTS AND
WAGE ASSIGNMENTS

An increasing number of states are adopting statutes requiring credit agreements to be in writing, however, these statutes generally manage large credit extensions as opposed to smaller consumer credit accounts. Additionally, a creditor may not enforce an assignment of wages unless there is a writing signed by the assignee and filed with the clerk of the court. A majority of states have adopted legislation to control the assignment of wages. The Federal Trade Commission has adopted the Consumer Credit Regulations that the assignment of wages is an unfair trade practice unless: (1) the assignment is revocable; (2) the assignment is a part of a payroll deduction plan; or (3) the assignment applies to wages already earned.

For example, the following states require a writing for a credit agreement to be enforceable: Alabama, Alaska, Arizona (for business loans in excess of $250,000), Arkansas (applies to agreements in excess of $10,000), California (applies to loan agreements in excess of $250,000), Colorado, Delaware (business loan agreements in excess of $100,000), Indiana, Kentucky, Maryland, Michigan, Mississippi, Nebraska (loan agreements in excess of $25,000), Nevada (business credit agreements in excess of $100,000 or if fee is in excess of $1,000), New Mexico (business agreements in excess of $25,000), Virginia (in excess of $25,000), Texas, Washington and West Virginia (for business or nonagricultural purposes in excess of $50,000). In North Dakota an agreement to alter the terms of repayment or forgiveness of a debt in the amount of $25,000 or more must be in writing.

In an effort to protect consumer rights, a majority of states are becoming "consumer friendly" with their legislation. For example, several states have enacted legislation requiring contracts to be written in "plain language" for an easy and comprehensible analysis by a layperson. For example, the California legislature adopted a statute requiring trade and businesses to provide an unexecuted Spanish language translation of an agreement, upon a party's request, prior to execution of an agreement. Generally, these agreements concern extensions for consumer credit (e.g., personal, family and household goods or services).

Unconscionable Contracts

A court may deny the enforcement of an unfair or oppressive contract if it is unconscionable. A contract is unconscionable if abuse occurred during the formation of the contract that cast a pall over the process. To determine whether a process was procedurally unconscionable, courts review the relative bargaining power of the parties, economic strength and alternative sources of supply.

A majority of courts are reluctant find that a contract is unconscionable and unenforceable. Instead, courts review the reasonableness and will bind a party to the benefit of their bargain if the terms are reasonable. Additionally, if a court determines that a part of the contract is unconscionable, then it may enforce the remainder of the contract, or limit the application of any unconscionable clause to avoid an unconscionable result.

Mistake

A contract requires a "meeting of the minds." However, no meeting of the minds occurs if one or both parties were mistaken about an element of the contract. A mistake does not automatically make a contract void or voidable. Instead, common law has attempted to develop rules to manage different types of mistakes. Unfortunately, there is no general doctrine or two like authorities that agree on a uniform classification or terminology. The following will discuss common mistake, mutual mistake and unilateral mistake.

COMMON MISTAKES

A common mistake is a mistake where both parties are induced to contract by an error on a fundamental element or basic assumption. This may occur under at least three situations, including the destruction of subject matter, identity of subject matter and a mistake in quality or price. First, the destruction of the subject matter prior to contract will result in a void contract. For example, if a contract is entered into between parties for the sale of specific goods that had already been sold or destroyed, then the contract is void. Second, if both parties are honestly mistaken as to the identity of the subject matter of the contract, then no contract exists. For example, if the parties contract to have a famous artist paint a portfolio, but the artist is incorrectly identified, then the contract is void. Third, under limited circumstances, a common mistake as to the quality of the subject matter that renders it essentially different than what it was believed to be may void a contract. For example, if both parties believe that the goods are worth $1 million, but instead the goods are worthless imitations. Generally, common mistakes void the contract from its inception, or deem a contract voidable, which may result in recision.

MUTUAL MISTAKES

A mutual mistake occurs where the parties have a common intention to contract, but it is induced by a mistake because both parties fail to understand each other. Additionally, a mutual mistake occurs where there is a mistake of fact by the parties to an agreement concerning the subject matter, identity of the parties, or if the mistake is induced by the fraud, misrepresentation, or other wrongful act of the other party. The mutual nature of the mistake expresses a thought of reciprocity and distinguishes it from a common mistake.

Generally, there are three requirements necessary for a party to void a contract based on mutual mistake. First, the mistake must be based on a basic assumption on which the parties contracted. Second, the mistake must materially effect the agreement on which the contract was made. Third, the party seeking to void the contract must not be assigned the risk.

If the parties misunderstand the intentions of the other, then the courts apply an objective test to assess whether a reasonable person would construe the agreement to mean what each party believed it to mean. If the test reveals that the contract is ambiguous, then the mutual mistake will result in a void contract since there is no meeting of the minds. However, if the test concludes that the contract could have only one meaning, then the parties are bound by their agreement. For example, if the seller quotes an incorrect price, and the purchaser innocently accepts, then the terms of the contract can have only one meaning and the parties are bound to the contract. However, if the purchaser knew that the price was improperly quoted, then no contract exists because the purchaser knew of the mistake. In this situation, the contract may be void, or restitution of the proper price would be appropriate to correct the injustice.

UNILATERAL MISTAKES

If only one party is mistaken, then the mistake is unilateral. There are several situations in which a unilateral mistake may arise. For example, unilateral mistakes may arise to the terms of a contract. If one party is mistaken as to the nature of the contract, and the other party is aware of the mistake, then the contract is void. The mistake must be to the terms of the contract and not a mere error in the judgment as to the quality of the subject matter. Accordingly, if there is no mistake as to the identity or existence of the subject matter of the contract and the parties have equal access to information, then mistakes concerning the attributes, quality or value of an item will not void a contract or absolve the parties of liability.

It is a long-standing principle of law that a party is bound by its signature to a document, regardless of whether the party read or understands the document. Accordingly, a party is bound to the contract if signed, despite whether it contains terms and conditions in which no agreement was reached. However, if the person was induced to sign the contract through fraud or misrepresentation, then the transaction may be voidable. For example, if a party misrepresents the nature of an instrument to induce the party to contract, then the deceived party may not be bound.

Fraud, Misrepresentation and Undue Influence

If either party defrauds the other into executing a contract, then the contract is voidable by the innocent party. Although courts have found it undesirable to formulate rigid definitions, there are two common classifications. First, actual fraud requires an intent to deceive the innocent party through trickery and design. Second, constructive fraud occurs where a party has breached a legal or equitable duty, which has the tendency to deceive others, violate public confidence or injure the public's interest. In either case, a fraudulent contract is voidable by the innocent party. If performance has already been rendered, then the innocent party may recover the property or value exchanged after the return of the consideration. This returns the parties to the status quo. Otherwise, the innocent party may perform on the contract and recover damages, if any.

A material misrepresentation of fact is a variance of fraud, and likewise, the contract is voidable by an innocent party. A misrepresentation is a party's manifestation to another by words or conduct that amounts to an assertion that does not align with the facts of a particular circumstance. Simply stated, a misrepresentation is an untrue statement of fact.

One question that often arises is the level of disclosure that is required between the parties prior to contract. A duty to disclose is rarely imposed on parties that deal with each other at arm's length. Generally, the parties are under no duty to disclose, unless required by statute (e.g., fiduciaries), prevent a misrepresentation, correct a mistake as to basic assumption, or correct a mistake as to the contents or effects of a writing. Moreover, a party does not have to disclose information that is readily available at a reasonable cost or information that can be acquired through ordinary inspection and inquiry.

The effect of undue influence may also render a contract voidable by the innocent party. Undue influence or duress occurs where one party overpowers the dominated party's free will to contract such that the dominated party does not voluntarily enter into the contract. The amount of force exhibited against the dominated party is short of actual force, but greater than mere advice. Accordingly, duress may occur where one party uses intimidation or threatens a person to enter a contract and the dominated party reasonably believes that the threat will be carried out. For example, in the commercial context, duress may occur where a creditor seeks to get paid on delinquent debt and threatens to withdraw services if payment is not received.

Satisfaction, Excuse and Discharge

If a condition creates a duty to perform, then the condition must be discharged to release the parties from the obligation. Discharge occurs when the parties have satisfied their obligations or the parties are released from their obligations to perform through the happening of an event, conduct of the parties or operation of law.

Satisfaction

Satisfaction occurs when a party completes performance, substantially performs or a court permits recovery on the completed sections of the contract. Complete performance satisfies a party's obligation under the contract. On the other hand, substantial performance may satisfy the obligation. Substantial performance satisfies an obligation only if the other party received a substantial portion of the bargain, the remaining portion is compensable and a great hardship would arise if denied recovery. For example, if a party completes the construction of a house, but fails to apply the paint, substantial performance (i.e., building the house) will permit recovery under contract for building the home whereas the other party will be compensated for the failure to paint.

A court may also divide a contract into sections and provide recovery on the completed sections of the contract. There are four necessary requirements to divide a contract into sections. First, the contract must be susceptible to division (e.g., divisible into two or more parts). Second, the contract must be susceptible to apportionment such that equivalent values can be assigned to each section. Third, the party not seeking division should receive a substantial portion of its bargain. Fourth, the parties did not intend the sections to be dependent upon one another. If a contract is divisible, then a party's performance requires performance of the corresponding duty of the other party (e.g., shipment of goods and payment for goods). If the contract is not divisible, then the non-breaching party has no duty under contract at all.

The UCC imposes its own rules governing substantial performance by a seller of goods. For example, UCC § 2-601 enlists a "perfect tender rule." The perfect tender rule states, excluding installment contracts, that if goods or tender of delivery fail in any respect to conform to the contract, then the buyer may reject or accept the goods in whole, or alternatively, may accept any commercial units and reject the rest. Accordingly, under the UCC, it does not matter whether the seller substantially performed if there is not a perfect tender. Although harsh in meaning, courts have softened the perfect tender rule by requiring substantial defects or allowing the seller to cure any defects that occurred.

Recision

The recision of a contract may be unilateral or mutual. Unilateral recision occurs where an innocent party is the victim of fraud, misrepresentation, duress, mistake or a breach by the other party. Under unilateral recision, the innocent party alone has the right to void the contract. On the other hand, mutual recision of a contract is permitted if the contract remains "executory" on both sides and the parties agree to cancel the entire contract. An executory contract is defined as a contract that is so far underperformed that failure of either party to complete performance would constitute a material breach, excusing performance of the other. The mutual agreement to rescind the contract constitutes valid consideration. Additionally, a majority of the states do not require mutual recision to be in writing.

Accord and Satisfaction or Substitute Agreements

Accord and satisfaction is a method of discharging a contract where one party agrees to provide, and the other party agrees to accept, substitute performance (the "accord") to discharge an existing duty (the "satisfaction"). For example, a debtor owes a creditor $100 in 30 days, the creditor will accept $105 in 60 days in discharge of the antecedent debt; if the parties agree, then a new contract is formed. It is important to note that accords are wholly executory in nature and do not extinguish the previous contractual duty. Instead, the discharge only occurs when the terms of the accord are performed, or upon the "satisfaction."

On the other hand, a substituted agreement is similar to an executory accord, but instead, the previous contract is extinguished immediately. To determine whether a new contract is an executory accord or a substituted agreement, it is necessary to review whether the previous agreement is disputed. If the previous agreement is disputed, then an agreement fixing a liquidated sum will be construed as a substituted agreement. However, if there is no dispute, then the presumption is that a new agreement is an executory accord that does not extinguish the previous contractual duty.

Substituted agreements have evolved from common law principles that encourage parties to settle a disputed debt without judicial intervention. Accordingly, tendering a full satisfaction check in discharge of a disputed obligation has a long common law tradition. Currently, UCC § 3-311 codifies the common law and provides for certain requirements for substituted agreements. Under the UCC, for the full satisfaction check to work in a discharge of a disputed obligation, the instrument must be tendered in good faith, and in full satisfaction of either an unliquidated claim or a bona fide dispute, accompanied by a conspicuous statement of full satisfaction, either on the instrument or in an accompanying written communication, and the claimants shall have obtained payment of the instrument. Under the UCC, good faith is defined as honesty in fact; thus a debtor's open refusal to pay a debt is not enough to establish a good faith dispute, rather the debtor must demonstrate a just basis for refusing to pay. In addition, before a check can create an accord and satisfaction, the party who presents the check must make clear, by appropriate and conspicuous wording, that cashing the check will be construed as settlement of all outstanding claims between the parties. Such notation can take the form of a debtor writing on the check, or accompanying voucher: "payment in full settlement of stated accounts" or "endorsement of the check constitutes a complete settlement of your claim" in conspicuous letters. Lastly, since the claimant must obtain payment of the instrument before a check can create accord and satisfaction, a creditor may require that, to be effective, any attempted accord and satisfaction must be sent to a particular office. Under the UCC, a party may avoid an accord and satisfaction by returning the money within 90 days. A party's bid to prevent a satisfaction by accepting the check but scratching out the restrictive endorsement and adding the words "without prejudice" is of no avail. Under the UCC, words of protest cannot change the legal effect of an accord and satisfaction once a check has been cashed and in effect it extinguishes any previous contractual duties between the parties.

Although similar, executory accords and substituted agreements have some differences. For instance, there is no requirement that an executory accord be in writing, even though the original agreement may have been subject to the statute of frauds, whereas however, in almost every state, substitute agreements must always be in writing. Additionally, the most noticeable difference is the manner in which a party must seek recovery under the two theories of discharge. If a party breaches an executory accord, then the other must sue on the original debt. However, if the party breaches the substitute agreement, then the other may bring suit directly under the agreement for damages.

Novation

A novation may also serve to discharge a party to a contract. Novation is a type of substituted contract where a party under the original contract adds a party that was not a party to the contract. The added party may exist as either an obligee or obligor. The requisites of a novation are a previous obligation, consent from all parties to a new contract, and extinguishment of the old contract in exchange for the new contract. For example, a novation may occur where the obligee of the original contract agrees to release the obligor from the contract after the duty owed is delegated to a third party. Novation is common to the commercial setting in two situations; first, the debt remains the same, but the debtor is new, and second, the debt remains the same and the creditor is new.

Impossibility, Impracticability and Frustration of Purpose

If the parties did not allocate the risk of a particular event, then the doctrines of impossibility, impracticability or frustration may apply.

The doctrine of impossibility applies where it is objectively impossible to perform a condition to a contract. Generally, impossibility occurs in three situations including the destruction of subject matter, failure of method of performance and the death or incapacity of a party. First, if the subject matter of the contract is specifically identified (e.g., merchandise), but prior to performance it is destroyed or unavailable, then the courts will discharge the parties from performance. Second, if performance of an essential condition other than the subject matter is impossible, then the parties may be discharged from the contract. For example, the impossibility of a condition occurs where the delivery of goods to the purchaser is dependent upon the seller receiving the goods from the supplier. The doctrine of impossibility will discharge the parties if the supplier breaches its contract with the seller or the supplier does not possess the subject matter of the contract. Third, if performance is required by an identified person or the contract depends upon a third party, then death or incapacity will result in the discharge of the parties.

Modern courts treat the doctrine of impracticability similar to impossibility. Generally, the distinction rests on the commercial reasonableness of a transaction and whether changed circumstances have made performance impracticable. A majority of impracticability cases are related to fixed-price contracts and cost increases that burden the seller. Extreme or unreasonable difficulty, expense or injury will render performance impracticable, but a mere increase in costs alone will not discharge a contract.

In sales contracts, the UCC must be referenced to determine whether a contract for the sale of goods is impossible or impracticable. UCC § 2-615 states that nondelivery or delay is not a seller's breach if performance has been made impracticable by the occurrence of an event that defeats a basic assumption of the contract. Accordingly, if the contract requires the delivery of goods that are identifiable and unique, then a contract will be deemed impossible to perform if the risk of loss had not already passed to the buyer (i.e., the seller delivered the goods). Alternatively, if a contract for goods does not identify the particular goods (e.g., inventory), then neither party will be discharged for impossibility, but instead the parties must assess which party assumed the risk of loss.

The doctrine of frustration of purpose applies where the purpose of the contract is destroyed by a supervening event. Courts are willing to apply frustration of purpose where the supervening event was not foreseeable and caused a total frustration of purpose. Frustration of purpose is distinct from impossibility since the party seeking discharge can still perform on the contract. However, the consideration for performance no longer holds its value. For example, a vendor rents space at the county fair to sell goods, but the fair is later cancelled. Although the space may be used, the vendor may be discharged from performance for frustration of purpose.

REMEDIES

Statute of Limitations

In every jurisdiction, a statute of limitations has been enacted to serve as a time bar to a cause of action. The statute of limitations requires a party to bring suit to enforce a contract, recover money damages, or for some other form of relief within a prescribed period of time. After the applicable time period expires, a party cannot assert a legal cause of action. Each state prescribes its own statute of limitations for various types of contracts, agreements and theories of recovery. Generally, the limitations period begins to run from the date that an event occurred that gave rise to a cause of action (e.g., date of breach).

There are two common exceptions that manipulate the limitations period. First, the statute of limitations may be "tolled" to extend the period of limitations under certain statutory provisions and common law theories (e.g., disabled party, continuing violations, parties in negotiation or agreement between the parties). After the removal of the disability or condition, the statute of limitations continues to run from the date that it was tolled. Second, if a debtor reaffirms a debt that is beyond the statute of limitations, then the limitations period will begin from the last date of reaffirmed.

Equitable Remedies

The law of contracts provides two classifications of remedies: equitable and legal. Equitable remedies include specific performance, injunctions, reformation and recision. First, specific performance is a remedy that requires a party to perform exactly as agreed to and stated in the contract. Specific performance is only provided where there is an inadequacy of alternative remedies (i.e., monetary damages are insufficient to compensate the injured party). Specific performance will almost never be provided in personal service and employment contracts. Generally, a contract for the sale of land is usually afforded specific performance because the law considers all land unique. However, goods and merchandise are usually compensable by a monetary award and specific performance is not available, unless the goods are unique or one-of-a-kind (e.g., original works of art).

Second, a court may reform a contract to represent the parties' original agreement. There are several reasons that may provide to the need for a reformation of the contract, including mistaken belief, fraud and simple drafting errors. Third, recision is also classified as an equitable remedy since it has the effect of returning the parties to the *status quo*. Finally, a court may provide an injunction against a party requiring the party to refrain from doing something, but this remedy has been limited in the contractual setting to employment contracts containing valid negative covenants (e.g., non-compete agreements).

Legal Remedies

EXPECTANCY DAMAGES

Expectation damages are the usual measure of damages for the breach of contract. The purpose of expectation damages is to put the non-breaching party in as good a position as it would have occupied had the other party performed the contract. Generally, expectation damages are equal to the value of the contract minus the benefits that the non-breaching party received from not having to complete performance. For example, a vendor contracts to supply two shipments of widgets for $200. After the first shipment, the vendor requests payment for $100, which the buyer refuses to provide. If the widgets cost the vendor $50 per shipment, then the vendor is entitled to the contract price of $200 minus completion cost of $50, or $150. Additionally, if the breach concerns defective performance, then the non-breaching party may be entitled to the cost of completion or a decrease in value of the property.

Although the above example is illustrative of common law expectancy damages, the UCC changes the common law rules in several respects dependent upon whether the seller or buyer breaches a contract for the sale of goods. First, if a seller breaches a sales contract by failing to deliver or delivering defective goods, then the buyer must usually attempt to cover the goods to receive consequential damages (i.e., damages not flowing directly from the act of a party). If the buyer fails to cover, then the buyer is only entitled to expectation damages only (e.g., contract price minus market price). However, if the buyer covers, then it is entitled to expectation damages and consequential damages. Second, if the buyer breaches a sales contract, then the seller may recover expectation damages (i.e., the difference between the contract price and the market price). Alternatively, the seller can elect to resell the goods and recover the difference between the contract price and the resale price. If neither remedy is adequate, the seller can recover lost profits.

RELIANCE DAMAGES

Reliance damages are designed to return the non-breaching party to the position that it would have occupied had the contract not been made. Reliance damages are recoverable when expectation damages are too uncertain or too speculative. For example, reliance damages usually apply in situations where it is difficult to determine lost profits or recovery is based on restitution. Generally, a party is permitted to recover expenses incurred in reliance on the contract, including expenditures made in preparation of performance minus any loss that the non-breaching party would have suffered had it performed. However, reliance damages are not awarded if the contract is within the statute of frauds, although reasonable compensation for past services may be recovered. In any event, a party may not recover more reliance damages than the amount of expectancy damages that it may have been awarded.

RESTITUTION

Although restitution is not a suit on contract, it is a remedy to prevent unjust enrichment. Generally, where one party has unjustly received a benefit at the expense of the other party, the value of that benefit may be restored to the injured party. Most often, a non-breaching party will seek restitution if it began performance, but the other party subsequently breached the contract. Although the common law favors a non-breaching party, a party in breach may also seek to recover the value of its services.

CONSEQUENTIAL DAMAGES

Generally, consequential damages or "special" damages are not awarded on a suit for breach of contract. There are two common law exceptions to this rule. First, if the damages are foreseeable as a normal result of a breach, then a court may award consequential damages. Second, if the damages are remote and unlikely, and if the breaching party had actual notice of the possibility of damages and the consequences, then consequential damages may be awarded. Additionally, the UCC permits consequential damages if a buyer attempts to "cover" goods after the seller's breach on a contract for the sale of goods.

OTHER CONSIDERATIONS

Signatures on the Contract

In order to execute and authenticate a contract, a signature is required to evidence the intention of the contracting party to be bound by the contract. There is no requirement for the signature to be handwritten, but rather, any mark, stamp or symbol will constitute valid authentication. Accordingly, a signature is valid even if it uses initials, abbreviations or a fictitious name, and may be executed on any part of the document. However, a party may require subscription of a document, which requires the contracting party to place its signature at the end or bottom of the document. Absent fraud or other wrongful acts, the party that signs a contract is conclusively presumed to understand its terms and conditions.

The broad construction of what constitutes a signature provides a flexible and expansive universe in which parties may contract. For example, if a party intends to enter into a contract but is unable to write, then its signature may be evidenced by a mark or symbol. A majority of states have enacted statutory provisions that outline the requirements for authentication of a contract in this manner. Generally, these statutes require the presence of two witnesses to affirm that the party was the signatory of the contract. Alternatively, if no witnesses are present, a party may affirm that it entered into the contract through a notary public or judicial officer. The ability to contract by mark or symbol has also opened the door to electronic transactions through the use of e-signatures to authenticate a contract.

The signature may also be provided by an authorized agent that is acting on behalf of a principal. The law only requires that an agent sign the principal's signature. Additionally, an agent may sign the principal's name and insert its own signature. For example, /s/ Principal "by" /s/ Agent. However, it is common for an agent to sign with its own signature and one of several caveats that may include "on account of," "on behalf of," or "at the request of."

A recurring trouble spot for most agents occurs when an agent signs a negotiable instrument (e.g., business check) on behalf of a corporation. Most often, the agent is attending to its normal duties and does not anticipate personal liability on a negotiable instrument. This is especially true where an agent believes that it is acting on behalf of the corporation and includes a designation such as "president," "agent," or "trustee." However, at common law these designations are considered mere descriptions and courts will hold the agent personally liable if the corporate name is not affixed to the instrument. Like common law, the UCC § 3-403 assigns personal liability against an authorized agent if the negotiable instrument does not contain the name of the person or entity represented, and additionally, fails to identify the agent's representative capacity. As a saving grace, some courts may introduce parol evidence to determine whether the agent was signing in a representative capacity, but such inquiry is strictly scrutinized due to the nature of negotiable instruments. Furthermore, even if a designation and corporate name are affixed to the instrument, an agent may be liable if acting as an officer or director of the corporation. The following is a suggested format to guide the agent in signing negotiable and other instruments:

ABC, Inc.

By:_____ /s/
      Signature

As:_____ /s/
      Signature

Acknowledgments on Instruments

Although "acknowledgment" lends itself to many meanings (e.g., acknowledgment of a time barred debt), acknowledgment used here means a party's formal declaration before an authorized official that it executed the instrument through its own free will and deed. To finalize an acknowledgment, the office provides a certificate stating that the instrument has been acknowledged. Acknowledgments are usually required prior to filing and recording formal instruments such as deeds, leases and agreements. The certificate of acknowledgment makes the instrument "self-proving," which permits its introduction into evidence without proof of signature. In a majority of states, acknowledgment is a creature of statute and any acknowledgment should strictly abide to the prescribed statutory requirements.

Contracts Under Seal

In centuries past, contracts were required to be filed "under seal" to signify the parties' consent to the terms of the document. The "under seal" requirement constituted the requisite consideration to form a binding contract. The evolution of common law and the expansion of commercial transactions have virtually eliminated the justifications for a contract to be filed "under seal." For example, the common law finds that a seal exists if the parties intended the effect of a seal, and UCC § 2-203 gives no added effect to a contract under seal to buy or sell goods. However, in some states it is still customary to file deeds, mortgages and other conveyances of real estate under seal. Additionally, some statutes provide a longer limitation period if a contract is filed under seal.

The Passing of Title

Perhaps one of the most complex issues is determining when title passes from the seller to the buyer. Adding to this complexity is the lack of uniformity among state common laws and the additional disparity between the common law and the UCC. Of course, the issue remains important since the determination of when title passes will determine which party is responsible for the risk of loss.

Under the common law, a majority of states conclude that the risk of loss or damage during the executory phase of the contract remains with the seller. Alternatively, the UCC manages the passing of title differently; it either provides rules for a specific problem, or it provides a "catch-all" provision. UCC § 2-401 provides a four requirement catch-all provision to determine questions of title. First, the goods must be identifiable under the contract for title to pass. Second, any retention in title by the seller of goods shipped or delivered is a security interest. Third, title passes to the buyer at the time and place in which the seller physically delivers the goods. For example, if delivery is required, then title passes once the seller delivers the goods to the buyer; alternatively, if shipping is required, then title passes the moment that the goods are shipped. The focus is on the transfer of goods, not the actual document evidencing title. Finally, if the buyer refuses goods after the title has passed, then the title and goods revert back to the seller so long as the rejection was timely.

Cash Terms and Expedited Credit Facilities

The seller and purchaser may agree to transact business on cash terms. Cash terms include, *inter alia*, the purchase of goods or services through currency, personal or business check, cashier's check, certified check or cash-on-delivery. The cash may be delivered beforehand, concurrently or immediately after the goods are delivered. Oftentimes, a seller will attempt to induce a buyer with "cash terms." However, the purported cash terms really constitute an expedited credit facility since the payment is postponed for a period of days. For example, "10 days same as cash." Whereas the seller retains a lien right in the goods on a cash terms transaction; the implication of a credit transaction is that the seller relinquishes all right and title to the goods and has no right to repossession.

Cash and Quality Discounts

In today's commercial transactions, invoices may display a variety of payment terms dependent upon the nature of the goods or services and the needs of the seller. The most common invoice is "net 30 days," which requires payment within 30 days of the issuance of the invoice. Often times, a seller may induce payment in a shorter period of time. For example, the terms on an invoice may be stated: "2% 10 days–net 30 days." If the payment is received within 10 days, then a 2% discount will apply to the invoice.

Some sellers may elect to use EOM, or "end of the month terms." EOM terms permit the buyer to wait until the end of the month before the payment or discount terms take effect. For example, an EOM invoice may read, "2% 10 days–net 30." A variant of EOM that some vendors use is "middle-of-the-month," or MOM, which has the same effect of EOM, but begins the fifteenth of the month instead of the end.

Other sellers may use "Prox" or "Ult" terms to manage payment on their invoices. "Prox" specifies a certain day of the month following the sale to provide payment terms and offer a cash discount. For example, a Prox invoice may read, "2% 10th prox–net 30th." Accordingly, if payment is received by the tenth of the following month, then the discount will apply, while the balance of the invoice is due on the thirtieth of the following month. Moreover, if the seller offers a "prox" discount date and a customer pays in advance of that date, then some contracts provide for an additional discount referred to as *ultimo* ("ult").

A less familiar practice is offering invoice terms based on the "Receipt of Goods" ("ROG") and "Arrival of Goods" ("AOG") invoice terms. Under these invoice terms, a discount is based on the time that the goods are received by the buyer or arrive at the buyer's location. For example, an invoice may offer terms of "2% 10 days ROG–net 30 days."

Additionally, a majority of buyers will bargain for the best price possible. Oftentimes, the seller will offer "quantity discounts" to induce the buyer to purchase more goods in exchange for a lesser price. As a general rule, discounts based on quantity are lawful if the discount represents a cost savings to the seller. However, under the Robinson-Patman Act, a quantity discount is unlawful if it has the effect of substantially lessening competition in interstate commerce.

Refer to Chapter 27 for the following forms:

- Agreement to Pay a Debt Contracted during Infancy
- Agreement to Revive a Debt Barred by Statute of Limitations
- Assignment of Wages Due and to Become Due
- Endorsement on Check Constituting Accord and Satisfaction
- General Form of Bill of Sale
- Installment Note
- Simple Loan Agreement (With Promissory Note)

6 An Overview of the Uniform Computer Information Transactions Act

The Industrial Age, characterized by huge factories and the mass production of goods, has given way to the Information Age, characterized by the dominance of the service sector and exemplified by the explosive growth of the software industry. Advances in technology have pushed beyond the limits of existing jurisprudence. Internet commerce alone raises issues regarding jurisdiction, conflict of laws and electronic contracting, all of which have the potential for inconsistent treatment by the various states.

The Uniform Computer Information Transaction Act (UCITA), provides a framework within which to conduct commerce in information technology products and services. The development of UCITA was driven by the realization that the primary body of uniform contract law in this country, the UCC Article 2 model based on the delivery of tangible goods, is ill-suited to address the issues that arise in the information and software industries. Transactions in the information and software industries typically involve a transfer of limited rights to access or use an intangible "product" rather than a complete transfer of ownership and physical delivery of a tangible good.

SCOPE OF UCITA

Determining the scope of UCITA proved to be one of the most difficult tasks for the National Conference of Commissioners on Uniform State Laws drafting committee. Rules that work well for software licensing may not work well for the sale of a book on a compact disk. Having different rules apply to the sale of a book, depending on whether the book is in print or on a compact disk, is hard to reconcile.

Included Transactions

UCITA applies to computer information transactions under UCITA § 103(a). A computer information transaction is defined as an agreement to create, modify, transfer or license computer information (UCITA § 102(11)).

Determining whether a transaction falls within the scope of UCITA requires a careful examination of the subject matter of the transaction. Not all transactions involving computerized information, however, will come within the scope of the act. For example, the purchase of a book is not a computer information transaction, even though the text of the book may be delivered in an electronic form over the Internet or on a diskette. Nor does it matter that the book was purchased electronically from an Internet bookstore. The subject matter of the transaction is the book, not the media on which it is delivered or the means by which it is purchased according to Official Comment 2, § 103.

Mixed Transactions

A primary motivation for creating UCITA was the recognition that there are fundamental differences between a computer information transaction and the sale of goods. In a mixed transaction, it is important to match each component of the transaction with an appropriate set of rules. In short, the parties expect UCC Article 2 rules to apply.

The expectations of the parties with regard to the software aspects of the transaction are quite different. The acquiring party anticipates receiving a contractual right to use the software, while the vendor expects to retain both ownership of the intellectual property rights in the software and associated obligations, such as the burden of defending the acquiring party against claims of infringement by third parties. The parties expect UCITA's rules to apply to the software aspect of the transaction.

In mixed transactions, the body of law which will apply depends on the subject matter under consideration. Parties to a mixed transaction may avoid confusion regarding whether and to what degree UCITA applies by agreeing to either opt-in or opt-out of UCITA under Section 104.

ELECTRONIC CONTRACTS

A number of states are presently considering a variety of statutes dealing with electronic signatures, digital signatures and electronic contracting. UCC Article 4A has been amended to facilitate electronic transactions. The Uniform Electronic Transaction Act (UETA) has been enacted in a number of states. At the federal level, the E-SIGN Act provides a framework for electronic contracting that is very similar to that in UETA. UCITA establishes a special framework for electronic contracts dealing with computer information.

Section 107(a) of the act provides that a record or signature shall not be denied legal effect solely on the grounds that it is accomplished electronically. Thus, a contract may be formed electronically where, in response to an offer communicated in an electronic message, an electronic message signifying acceptance is received. A contract may also be formed electronically when, in response to an offer, the offeree responds by either providing the requested information or by providing access to the requested information.

Nothing in the act requires that parties use electronic processes; the act simply provides that paper writings and electronic records will be treated as equivalents. UCITA also recognizes that parties may choose to use electronic agents to engage in certain types of commerce. According to UCITA § 107(d), a party who chooses to use an electronic agent will be bound by the acts of the agent, including agreements entered into by the agent, even if no individual was aware of, or reviewed the acts of the agent.

UCITA recognizes the use of attribution procedures as a crucial element of electronic contracting. Under UCITA § 212, the parties may agree to a particular attribution procedure or adopt one established by law, as long as the attribution procedure is commercially reasonable. Because the technology is developing very rapidly in this area of commerce, the drafting committee elected to leave the selection of an attribution procedure completely within the discretion of the parties. A party who seeks to defend a selected attribution procedure need only show that it was a commercially reasonable choice under the circumstances. Under Section 213(a) an electronic message is attributed to a person if it was the act of that person or his electronic agent or if the person is bound by the act or message under agency or other law.

Per UCITA § 213(a), a party relying on attribution of an electronic message bears the burden of establishing attribution. Factors to be considered in determining whether an act should be attributed to a person include the effectiveness of the attribution procedure being relied upon in light of the context of the electronic act. UCITA creates for consumers a layer of protection over and above the contract doctrine of mistake. A consumer who acts promptly will not be held responsible for an electronic message that the consumer did not intend to send in those situations where the automated system being used by the consumer fails to provide reasonable means to detect and correct such an error according to UCITA § 214. To avoid the mistake, the consumer must act promptly to put the other party back in the same position it would have been but for the mistake. For example, if the licensor delivers 11 copies of the computer game, the consumer must notify the other party promptly and either return the games or follow the reasonable instructions of the other party to destroy the unwanted copies.

CONTRACT TERMS

Under Article 2 it is possible for parties to enter into a binding agreement even though there is uncertainty with respect to particular terms, such as price and quantity. Similarly, under UCITA, parties may find themselves bound to a contract even though there is uncertainty regarding certain terms.

The basic approach under UCITA as seen in UCITA § 208(1), is to include in the contract all those terms set forth in a "record" to which the parties have "manifested assent." This approach upholds the basic tenet of commercial law that parties will be bound by the terms of the contracts they sign. A party may manifest assent in a number of ways. A party may take some affirmative step to manifest assent, such as by clicking on a box to indicate "I agree," another way to manifest assent is by signing, or "authenticating," a record. Yet another way to manifest assent is through conduct. A party cannot manifest assent to contract terms which the party has never had an opportunity to review. The issue of the timing and conditions under which a party is provided the opportunity to review a proposed contract was discussed at great length by the UCITA drafting committee. Retail customers acquiring software find themselves forced to pay for a product before breaking the plastic wrapper and discovering the details of a license agreement containing terms which they may not wish to accept. Conversely, software licensors in the retail marketplace, who attempt to protect their products from improper usage, copying or distribution, face the practical problem of providing lengthy, complex contract terms on the outside of their packaging.

Ordinarily, as noted in UCITA § 112(e)(1), an opportunity to review a record or term has been afforded when it is made available "in a manner that ought to call it to the attention of a reasonable person and permit review." In an online transaction, if the purchaser is directed to the location of the agreement and only allowed to proceed after having indicated "I agree" to the terms of the agreement, an opportunity to review has been afforded. In those situations where a party is not given an opportunity to review the terms of the agreement until after having made a commitment to the transaction, such as by paying or beginning performance, the party has an opportunity to review only, per UCITA § 112(e)(3), if there is an accompanying right to a return if the terms are unacceptable. The retail customer who only sees the terms of the license after paying will only be deemed to have received an opportunity to review if he is afforded a right of return if he deems the license terms unacceptable.

MASS MARKET CONCEPT

UCITA introduces to commercial law a new concept called "mass market." In § 102(45) the Act defines "mass market transaction" to include all covered transactions involving consumers as well as all other UCITA transactions conducted in a retail setting. The idea is that all persons who acquire computer information directed at the general public in small transactions in a retail market should be afforded similar protections. Whether a transaction falls within the mass market is determined by looking at three factors. The first consideration is the market in which the transaction occurs. Next is a consideration of the terms of the transaction. The third consideration is whether the information is of a type ordinarily marketed to the general public. "Mass market" does not include transactions intended for redistribution or public performance. Nor does it include transactions between businesses involving customized information. If the transaction includes terms that are not generally available to the public, it falls outside the mass market.

The general rule as stated in UCITA § 209(a) is that a party adopts the terms of a mass market license only if the party agrees to the license prior to or during the party's initial use of, or access to the information. A court may refuse to enforce terms which it deems unconscionable or in violation of fundamental public policy. A court may also refuse to enforce any term in a mass market license which conflicts with a term to which the parties to the license specifically agreed. Computer information transactions in the mass market often feature "shrink wrap" licenses, the terms of which are not available for review prior to purchase. Often, the license terms are available only after the information is accessed or installed. In those situations, the mass market licensee, who sees the license terms for the first time after making the purchase, and who does not agree to the license terms, is afforded special rights in addition to the right of return generally available under § 112. Licensors also receive special protections in mass market license transactions. A licensor under UCITA § 209(c) will not be bound by unacceptable terms proposed by a licensee which are available only after performance by the licensor.

PERFORMANCE

In a typical sale of goods transaction, performance of the agreement means that the seller must deliver goods and that the buyer must pay. In a computer information transaction, a party's duty of performance can be more complex. For example, a software licensor may be required not only to provide a program that functions as specified in the agreement, but also to provide training and support to the licensee. A party may refuse to accept a nonconforming performance. The concept of "refusal" under UCITA is analogous to the concept of "rejection" under UCC Article 2. See Official Comment 1, UCITA § 601. Because computer information is fundamentally different from goods, additional rules apply. If the license contained terms restricting the licensee's use of the information, such as "for noncommercial uses only," the licensee would not be permitted to install the nonconforming software on its business computers. Similarly, a licensee would not be allowed to ignore the intellectual property rights of the licensor even though the licensor may be in breach of the contract.

A party that tenders performance which conforms to the contract is entitled to acceptance by the other party. A party that accepts a performance is obligated to pay or render the consideration required by the contract.

WARRANTIES

Special rules apply to licensors who are merchants regularly dealing in computer information. Those licensors warrant that the information will be delivered free from rightful claims of others for infringement or misappropriation as noted in UCITA § 401(a). The warranty only extends to claims existing at the time of delivery to the licensee. The warranties provided in Section 401(c)(2) apply solely to informational rights arising under the laws of the United States or a State unless the agreement specifically provides otherwise. Grants of "worldwide" rights or the like are only valid to the extent that the rights are recognized under a treaty or international convention signed by both the United States and the particular country. The warranties under Section 401 may only be disclaimed or modified by specific language or by circumstances that give the licensee reason to know that the licensor is not making the warranties.

BREACH OF CONTRACT

Simply stated, a breach of contract under UCITA is a failure to comply with an obligation imposed by the contract or, in the absence of an agreement with respect to an element of performance, by UCITA itself. Section 701 establishes standards for determining breach and makes a distinction between material breach and non-material breach. UCITA follows the common law in distinguishing between material and non-material breaches. Subsection 701(a) points out that parties will need to look to intellectual property law to determine whether violation of a contractual use term is also an infringement or misappropriation of another's intellectual property rights.

REMEDIES

Section 807 provides the general rules for measurement of damages. Specific rules for calculating licensor's and licensee's damages are provided in Sections 808 and 809. The duty to mitigate is spelled out in Section 807(a). This rule is consistent with contract law generally. Section 807(b) also precludes recovery of damages which are speculative. Measurement of damages for improper disclosure of trade secret or other confidential information can be difficult. Subsection 807(c) provides that such damages may be measured by valuing the benefit obtained by the breaching party.

Where market value plays a role in calculating damages, UCITA § 807(d) provides that parties must look to market value at the time and place for performance.

Cancellation

Cancellation is the remedy whereby one party ends the contract based on breach. According to UCITA § 802(a) cancellation is permitted following a material breach and in situations where the agreement allows cancellation upon breach. Cancellation is an extreme remedy not normally permitted in the absence of a material breach. Cancellation is not effective per UCITA § 802(b) until the canceling party gives notice, unless the delay caused by giving notice would cause or threaten loss to the aggrieved party. It is only required that the notice be reasonable under the circumstances. No notice is required before cancellation of the right of access in an access contract.

Cancellation terminates the licensee's use rights, except where permitted for the limited purpose of mitigating damages, and discharges any executory obligations of the parties. Cancellation does not, however, alter a party's rights arising out of prior performance or as a result of the breach. *See* Official Comment 2, UCITA § 802.

An agreement between the parties that a contract may not be canceled is enforceable. A licensee might seek such a term in a redistribution agreement. A "no cancellation" term does not by itself prohibit resort to other remedies.

TERMINATION

For purposes of UCITA, termination means the end of a contract other than because of breach. Termination signifies the cessation of executory duties between the parties. Certain obligations, however, survive termination. On termination UCITA § 616(a) provides that all obligations that are still executory are discharged. Vested rights or remedies that have not been waived survive termination. A party who has received performance by the other party and therefore has an obligation to provide a reciprocal performance is not excused from that reciprocal performance by virtue of termination.

UCITA § 617(b) provides that an access agreement may be terminated without notice unless the access pertains to information provided by the licensee to the licensor.

In all other cases, a party may only terminate a computer information contract following reasonable notice of termination to the other party. A party may waive its right to notice of termination unless enforcement of the waiver would be unconscionable as authorized under UCITA § 617(c). The same subsection provides standards for notice of termination agreed upon by the parties will be enforceable unless the terms are unreasonable.

7 Uniform Commercial Code: An Overview

BACKGROUND AND INTRODUCTION

Although the movement toward uniform commercial laws is now more than a century old, some of the uniform laws still have not been adopted by every state. The National Conference of Commissioners on Uniform State Laws, whose first major project was the promulgation of the Negotiable Instruments Law in 1896 remains active today. The year 2001 realized the revisions to Article 9 of the Uniform Commercial Code being adopted by each state.

Revised Article 1 (general provisions including definitions) has been enacted in Alabama, Arkansas, Connecticut, Delaware, Hawaii, Idaho, Minnesota, Montana, Nebraska, Nevada, New Mexico, Oklahoma, Texas, U.S. Virgin Islands and Virginia. Revised Articles 3 and 4 have been adopted by Nevada and Texas. Revised Article 7 (Warehouse Receipts, Bills of Lading and other Documents of Title) has been enacted in Alabama, Connecticut, Delaware, Hawaii, Idaho, Maryland, Minnesota, Montana, Nebraska, Nevada, New Mexico, North Dakota, Texas and Virginia.

It should be kept in mind that frequently in the adoption of a uniform law, a state legislature might depart from the recommended provisions and adopt a statute with substantial variations or modifications. There are also occasions when it is necessary for the courts to interpret various uniform law provisions and such interpretations may vary among states.

In 1940, when the Conference met to consider amendments to the Uniform Sales Act in order to avoid conflict with a proposed Federal Sales Act, a proposal was made to abandon the piecemeal approach to codification of commercial law in favor of a single comprehensive statute. The suggestion was accepted and the Uniform Commercial Code (UCC or Code) was conceived.

In 1942 the American Law Institute and the Conference joined together in this undertaking and appointed an editorial board and numerous drafting committees composed of many nationally prominent judges, lawyers and law professors. The Corporation, Banking and Business Law sections of the American Bar Association worked with the editorial board and made numerous suggestions, which were incorporated into the Code. In 1952, the official text was approved by the two sponsoring organizations and by the House of Delegates of the American Bar Association.

Pennsylvania was the first state to adopt the Code, and Louisiana is the only state that has not adopted the Code in its entirety. Louisiana has never adopted Article 2 (Sales); Article 2A (Leases) and Article 6 (Bulk Transfers).

The basic premise on which the Uniform Commercial Code is based is that the personal property commercial transaction is a single subject of the law, notwithstanding its many facets, involving the sale of and payment for goods. There may be a contract for sale, the giving of a check for part of the purchase price and the acceptance of some form of security for the balance.

The basic objective of the Code is to bring all of these phases under one statute and to make the law simple, clear, modern and uniform. The Code treats these various phases under nine operative articles. These consist of:

Article 1:   General Provisions (including definitions)
Article 2:   Sales
Article 2A: Leases (personal property only)
Article 3:   Commercial Paper
Article 4:   Bank Deposits and Collections
Article 4A: Funds Transfers
Article 5:   Letters of Credit
Article 6:   Bulk Transfers
Article 7:   Warehouse Receipts, Bills of Lading and Other Documents of Title
Article 8:   Investment Securities
Article 9:   Secured Transactions

ARTICLE 1: GENERAL PROVISIONS[1]

To be consistent with a major objective of flexibility in order to permit adaptability to change and expansion of commercial practice through custom, usage and agreement of the parties, Article 1 contains several general policy pronouncements as a guide to the construction of sections throughout the Code. Section 1-102 expresses a noncontroversial preference for freedom of contract. This general language is at once compromised by policy considerations that preclude enforcement of such contract terms that would relieve a party of the obligation of good faith, due care and other specific exceptions. For example, the invalidity of a clause in a security contract which deprives the debtor of certain rights in the collateral upon default is found in Section 9-602.

The preference for liberal administration of remedies (§ 1-106) is another policy contained in the Code. This is, no doubt, a reaction against the tendency to restrict damages for breach, which is found in some court decisions. It is more specifically illustrated in the Code by Section 2-708, which permits a seller to include lost profits as part of damages against a breaching party.

In interstate commercial transactions, the parties to the transaction are authorized to designate in their contract the application of the law of a state having some reasonable relation to the contract. Subsection (2) provides an index to other sections of the Code that specify the applicable law to govern a specific type of commercial transaction.

Section 1-201 contains definitions that are used throughout the Code. Some definitions were in familiar usage in the commercial field; others are new or are defined in a revised or modified way.

ARTICLE 2: SALES

Article 2 was designed to replace the Uniform Sales Act. It modified many of the provisions in order to meet modern commercial needs and fill gaps of coverage that could not have been anticipated when that uniform act was drafted in 1906. Although about a dozen states had never enacted the Uniform Sales Act, the act was

---

[1] This section discusses current Article 1 in effect in 44 states.

essentially a codification of the common law and most of the provisions had been followed by the case decisions in those states.

Chapter 5, "Transactional Guide to the Formation, Performance and Enforcement of Contracts," contains a substantive discussion of Article 2 of the Uniform Commercial Code.

A novelty of this sales article of the Code is the attempt to stratify sales law by enacting separate rules where the parties to a sale are merchants as opposed to the casual or inexperienced buyer or seller. This is more apparent than real, however, since the term "merchant" is defined in Section 2-104(1) as "a person who deals in goods of the kind…involved in the transaction," which would include the great bulk of all sales transactions.

Formation of the Sales Contract

One area of sales law that was neither covered by the Uniform Sales Act nor treated separately from the general common law of contracts is the formation of a sales contract. The application of the usual rules of offer, acceptance and consideration has resulted in some uncommercial and unexpected results—at least results which are not expected by the businessperson who is not also an attorney. The Code makes sales contract law conform to commercial practice and understanding, at least regarding when merchants are bound by their agreements. Under Section 2-205, a written firm offer to buy or to sell goods is not revocable for a limited time (not to exceed three months) even though no consideration has passed. Under Section 2-207, an offer to buy goods may be accepted and a contract formed, even though the acceptance contains some minor additional or different terms; such additional terms will become part of the contract unless (a) acceptance is expressly conditioned on assent to the original terms, (b) the terms materially alter the contract, or (c) notification of objection to the additional terms has already been given or is sent within a reasonable time. Section 2-209 permits a good faith modification of an existing sales contract without additional consideration. However, Section 2-209(2) states that "a signed agreement which excludes modification or rescission except by a signed writing cannot be otherwise modified or rescinded." In authorizing the commercially expedient open-price agreements and output and requirement contracts, Sections 2-305 and 2-306 deliver the final death blow to the common-law objections of uncertainty and lack of mutuality.

Section 2-201 continues the application of the Statute of Frauds to sales contracts with some apparent reluctance, as evidenced by some liberalizing modifications. The amount of the purchase price creating the requirement of a writing is increased to $500. The language "some writing sufficient to indicate that a contract of sale has been made" rejects the strict early case law requirement of stating all material terms of the contract in a written memorandum. Where merchants make an oral contract and a confirmation of the conversation is sent by letter, the other party must object to the contents of the writing within 10 days. Thereafter, the contract may be proved by oral evidence and is not subject to the Statute of Frauds defense. Partial performance of an oral contract satisfies the Statute of Frauds only to the extent that goods or payment have actually been received.

Title Passing Concept

A much more significant aspect of Article 2 is the attempt to state the law without reference to what has been considered the central point in Anglo-American sales law for at least a century and a half—the location of title. Many of the controversies between buyer and seller have been answered by early common law decisions, and subsequently by the Uniform Sales Act, through a determination of the location of title to the goods that formed the subject matter of the sales transaction. It has been fictitiously supposed that the parties intended title to pass at some particular time. To compound the fiction, presumptions about when the parties intended the title to pass were invented; those presumptions now seem to approach the status of substantive rules of law. Having thus located title in either the buyer or seller, it appears to be a simple and certain matter to proceed from that point to resolve important questions such as the risk of loss, the right of the seller to maintain an action for the price (as distinguished from an action for damages), the buyer's right to have the goods, as well as matters not directly involved with sales law such as the tax upon the goods and the right of creditors and a trustee in bankruptcy of either the buyer or seller to reach the goods.

The drafters of Article 2 took the position that this "lump concept thinking" created many uncertain and unfair results since it is frequently difficult to predict when title passes or is even established. Furthermore, passing of title may have no logical relationship to the rights in question. The basic approach to determine questions of title is generally stated in Section 2-401 and encompasses four points:

1. Title cannot pass unless the goods can be identified
2. A security interest may be maintained even though title passes
3. Transfer of the goods is required for title to pass
4. Even though title has passed, the buyer may reject the goods and title reverts to the seller

Unless the specific provisions of Article 2 refer to the necessity of title passing, each provision of this Article applies with regard to the rights, obligations and remedies of a seller, buyer or third party.

Having thus de-emphasized title, specific rules provide solutions to specific problems. Thus, for example, on the recurring risk of loss problem, possession of the goods is the controlling factor and replaces the test of when title passes. However, where either party is in breach, the loss falls on the breaching party (§§ 2-509 and 2-510). Where the goods are to be shipped from the seller to buyer, possession, and thus risk of loss, passes to the buyer when the goods are delivered to the carrier. However, this is not the situation with a destination contract (e.g., "F.O.B., Columbia, South Carolina," where goods are to be shipped to the buyer in Columbia). In this case, possession and risk of loss pass to the buyer when the goods are tendered at their destination.

Furthermore, the seller's rights, upon breach by the buyer, to recover the contract price (and hold the goods for the buyer—the seller's equivalent of the buyer's action for specific performance) would not turn on the passage of title under the Code but on the more functional basis of whether the seller may be able to resell the goods (§ 2-709).

Where there are no specific provisions dealing with an issue regarding who bears the risk of loss, and title passing remains relevant, such as in determining the tax consequences or application of other public regulations, Section 2-401 prescribes the point in time when title passes. Generally, title passes when the seller completes his performance by delivery of the goods, or if there is to be no delivery of goods, when the documents of title are shipped, or if there is to be no shipment of goods, at the time and place of shipment; otherwise, title passes at the time and place of contracting. In no event, however, will title pass until the goods are identified to the contract, e.g., with respect to future goods, when they are designated by the seller as goods to which the contract refers (§ 2-501(b)).

Performance

Section 2-601 of the Code states that "if goods or the tender of delivery fail in any respect to conform to the contract" the buyer has the option to accept all of the goods, reject all of the goods or accept those goods which it is commercially reasonable to accept and reject the balance of the goods. This differs from "substantial performance" where delivery is to be made in installments. Section 2-612 provides that the buyer may reject any nonconforming installment "if the nonconformity substantially impairs the value of that installment." However, Section 2-612 also provides that unless the nonconformity impairs the value of the entire contract, the seller is entitled to "cure" the nonconformity and provide the buyer with adequate assurance that it will do so. This concept of "cure" is set forth in Section 2-508 whereby a seller is permitted to remedy a defective tender if he can do so within the time originally set for performance. Furthermore, the seller may cure after the time for performance has passed, if the "buyer rejects a nonconforming tender which the seller had reasonable grounds to believe would be acceptable." This latter provision is designed to relieve the seller from the "forced breach" advantage enjoyed by the buyer who could wait until the eleventh hour and reject the goods (usually for the real reason that due to a change in market conditions the contract is no longer attractive) because of some minor defect.

Section 2-605 requires a buyer to state the grounds for rejection where a defect in the tender could have been ascertained by reasonable inspection and could have been cured by the seller if stated seasonably. Failure on the part of the buyer to so particularize will preclude him from relying on the unstated defect to justify his rejection. With respect to other grounds of rejection (those not readily apparent or not so minor as to be cured), the merchant buyer, upon request from a merchant seller, must make a written final statement of all the defects on which he proposes to rely. Thereafter, the buyer is limited to the objections so stated.

Remedies for Breach

Where the seller fails to perform buyer has a right to "cover." Section 2-712 allows a buyer the alternative right to purchase substitute goods and recover from the seller the difference between the contract price and the cost of cover as an absolute measure of damages, provided the buyer purchases these substitute goods in a reasonable manner. Consistent with the right to cover, the buyer's alternative right to sue for damages is measured by the difference between the contract price and the market price at the time he learned of the breach (the time when he could have made a cover purchase), and not the market price at the time when the goods should have been delivered (§ 2-713). The buyer's right to specific performance is liberalized by Section 2-716. Thus, the buyer is entitled to specific performance not only when the goods are "unique" (the usual rule) but also "in other proper circumstances." This last phrase apparently permits the buyer to have the specific goods, for example, in an "output" or "requirements" contract where he is unable to cover even though the goods are not necessarily unique.

As in the case of the buyer's remedies, the seller's rights under the Code upon breach are similar to existing law but with some liberalizing modifications. The seller has the absolute right to resell the goods wrongfully refused by the buyer and to recover the difference between the resale price and the contract price, provided the resale is "commercially reasonable" (§ 2-706). Section 2-709 expressly permits the seller to recover any lost profits which he would have received had the buyer performed; case law, on the other hand, has been reluctant to allow a recovery of profits.

The seller's remedies in the event it is discovered that the buyer is insolvent are governed by Section 2-702. However, since the remedies provided under the Uniform Commercial Code are most often entwined with the remedies granted under the U.S. Bankruptcy Code, this remedy is treated separately. Chapter 15, "Reclamation, Stoppage in Transit, New Administrative Claim in Favor of Goods Suppliers, and Other Return of Goods Remedies," contains a thorough discussion of the seller's rights under each of these statutes.

Public policy restrictions are imposed on freedom of contract under Section 2-718; a liquidated damage clause upon breach is enforceable only where reasonable. A clause fixing unreasonably large liquidated damages is void as a penalty. An interesting balance between freedom of contract and the policy limitations in the Code is found in Section 2-725, which prescribes a four-year statute of limitations for actions on a sales contract which by agreement may be reduced to not less than one year, but which may not be extended.

The court, under the provisions of Section 2-302, may refuse to enforce a contract that it finds to be unconscionable or may strike out any unconscionable clauses and enforce the contract as if the stricken clause had never existed. Consequential damages may be limited or excluded by contract unless the limitation is unconscionable. The Code provides, however, that limitation of consequential damages for injury to the person in the case of consumer goods is *prima facie* unconscionable, but such a limitation where the loss is commercial is not (§ 2-719(3)).

Warranties

In dealing with the frequently litigated problem of sales warranties, the Code makes some changes from the common law and the Uniform Sales Act. Under Section 2-314 there is an implied warranty not only for the sale of goods where "the seller is a merchant with respect to goods of that kind" but also for the "serving for value of food or drink to be consumed either on the premises or elsewhere."

Section 2-318 provides three alternatives (states are to select one) regarding third-party beneficiaries of warranties. Under Alternative A, warranties, whether expressed or implied, are extended to any natural person who is in the family or household of the buyer, or who is a guest in the home of the buyer, if it is reasonable to expect that such person may use the goods, and who is injured by breach of the warranty. Alternatives B and C differ slightly by eliminating the reference to the family or household of the buyer. The references in these alternatives is, instead, to the person who is reasonably anticipated to use the goods and who is injured resulting from the breach of warranty. In all alternatives, the extension of the warranty to the respective third parties cannot be limited by any action of the seller. Consequently, with respect to the class of persons covered by the section, no privity of contract is required before an action can be commenced for breach of warranty.

Disclaimer of warranties is still permitted as a matter of freedom of contract, but with the condition that if in a written contract, the disclaimer must be conspicuous; to disclaim the implied warranty of merchantability the writing must mention the word "merchantability" (§ 2-316).

Aside from the provisions mentioned here, the Code is silent on the question of privity between the seller and buyer as a prerequisite for a breach of warranty claim. This highly controversial issue, where a buyer seeks to hold the manufacturer of the goods liable for defects that constitute a breach of the "contractual" warranty obligation, is left to the courts.

Battle of the Forms

Section 2-207 creates a concept known as the "battle of the forms." Because the concept of the formation of contract is somewhat flexible in today's business environment, there is no longer the structured single-document contract. The UCC provides that if a party to an agreement provides additional terms, they are to be construed as proposals for additions to the contract and they will become a part of the contract unless the offer expressly limits the acceptance to the terms of the offer, the additional terms materially alter it, or there has been notification of objection within a reasonable time.

This has created the environment where purchase orders will now contain very unusual terms, which will be construed as part of the contract if the vendor then ships following receipt of the purchase order. Since most vendors do not carefully review all of the fine print on a purchase order, this has led to serious problems with respect to additional terms being included in an agreement, many times to the surprise of the vendor.

By including a provision in an overall agreement of sale (such as a credit application that acts as a contract), which by its terms precludes additional terms unless agreed to in writing by the vendor, this can eliminate the battle of the forms. This is a significant and timely issue, which must be considered by all businesspeople.

ARTICLE 2A: LEASES

Scope

The Article applies to all leases, which are defined as the transfer of the right to possession and use of goods for a term in return for consideration (§§ 2A-102 and 103). Included within the scope of the Article are transactions as diverse as the lease of a hand tool for a few hours and the leverage lease of a complex line of industrial equipment.

A finance lease is also governed by the Article, which is defined as a lease in which the lessor does not manufacture or produce the goods and the lessor only acquires the goods in connection with the lease.

A lease is to be distinguished from a security interest, which is governed by Article 9 of the UCC and from a sale governed by Article 2.

The Article generally preserves the concept of freedom of contract except that there are special rules for consumer leases. If the law chosen by the parties to a consumer lease is that of a jurisdiction other than the jurisdiction in which the lessee resides, the choice of law is not enforceable (§ 2A-106).

If a court finds as a matter of law that a lease or clause is unconscionable at the time it was made, the court may refuse to enforce such lease or clause which is unconscionable. If a consumer lease has been induced by unconscionable conduct or if unconscionable conduct has occurred in the collection of a claim arising from the lease, a court can grant appropriate relief (§ 2A-108).

Construction of a Lease

The Article has its own statute of frauds provisions, which provide that a lease is not enforceable unless the total payments to be made, excluding payment for options to renew or buy, are less than $1,000 or there is a written agreement which describes the goods leased and the lease terms so that they are reasonably identified (§ 2A-201). A lease is not insufficient merely because it omits or incorrectly states an agreed-upon term. A lease is also enforceable if the goods are to be specially manufactured or maintained for the lessee and are not suitable for lease or sale to others in the ordinary course of business, or if a party admits that the lease was made or if the goods have been received and accepted by the lessee (§ 2A-201).

The same provisions regarding parol or extrinsic evidence exist in Article 2A which exist in Article 2. In other words, oral statements will only be permitted to clarify, explain or supplement a written lease agreement in excess of $1,000. But such written lease cannot be contradicted by anything other than a written and signed document (§ 2A-202).

A lease contract can be made in any manner that shows agreement between the parties. Even if one or more terms are omitted, a lease contract is valid if the parties so intend it (§ 2A-204). A written offer by a merchant to lease goods which gives assurance that it will be held open is firm and not revocable for lack of consideration during the time stated in the offer or for a reasonable time not to exceed three months (§ 2A-205).

An agreement to modify a lease needs no consideration to be binding (§ 2A-208). The benefit of a supplier's promise to the lessor under a supply contract and of all related warranties under such contract are extended to the lessee to the extent of the lessee's interest under a finance lease related to such supply contract (§ 2A-209).

The function of the lessor in a finance lease is very limited, since the lessee looks to the supplier of the goods for warranties and similar matters. The supplier and lessor can modify the supply contract unless the lessee has previously entered into a supply contract with the lessor.

Warranties

Promises made by a lessor to a lessee create a warranty that the goods will conform to the promises. Any description of the goods creates an express warranty that the goods will conform to the description, and any sample or model used creates a warranty that the goods will conform to the sample or model. To create an express warranty it is not necessary that any formal words be used (§ 2A-210). These warranties are the same as in Article 2 of the UCC.

There is a warranty in a lease that no person holds a claim to, or interest in, the goods which arose from an act or omission of the lessor that will interfere with the lessee's enjoyment of its leasehold interest (§ 2A-211). The section is modeled after § 2-312 of Article 2 of the UCC.

Except in a finance lease, there is an implied warranty of merchantability in a lease contract if the lessor is a merchant with respect to goods of that kind (§ 2A-212). In addition, there is an implied warranty of fitness for the particular purpose for which the goods are leased, provided that the lessor knows of such purpose at the time the lease is entered into and the lessee is relying thereon (§ 2A-213).

Subject to the provisions of § 2-202 on parol or extrinsic evidence, words or conduct may be used to create, negate or limit a warranty. To exclude or modify an implied warranty of merchantability, there must be a writing which must mention merchantability and be conspicuous. Modification of a warranty of fitness must also be in writing and be conspicuous. All implied warranties are excluded by expressions such as "as is" (§ 2A-214).

The official text proposes three alternatives with respect to third-party beneficiaries of express and implied warranties. Alternative A extends the warranties to any natural person who is in the family or household of the lessee or who is a guest in such home. Alternative B extends the warranty to any natural person who may reasonably be expected to use, consume, or be affected by the goods and who is injured in person by breach of the warranty. Neither Alternative A nor Alternative B displaces principles of common law or equity. Alternative C extends the warranty to any person who may reasonably be expected to use, consume or be affected by the goods and who is injured. The operation of this section may not be excluded, modified or limited with respect to injury to a person to whom the warranty extends (§ 2A-216).

A lessee obtains an insurable interest in leased goods when the goods are identified (even if nonconforming), and the lessee can reject them (§ 2A-218).

Except in the case of a finance lease, the risk of loss is retained by the lessor and does not pass to the lessee. In the case of a finance lease, risk of loss passes to the lessee (§ 2A-219).

Effect of a Lease Contract

A lease contract is effective and enforceable between the parties, except as is otherwise stated in Article 2A, against purchasers of the goods and against creditors of the parties. The effectiveness of the lease does not depend on any filing. Article 2A applies whether the lessor, lessee or a third party has possession or title (§ 2A-302).

Any interest of a lessee or a lessor under a lease contract may be transferred, unless the lease prohibits the transfer or the transfer materially changes the duty or materially increases the burden of risk imposed on the other party.

If goods are returned to a lessor, the lessor may subsequently lease such goods and the subsequent lessee will obtain the same leasehold interest in the goods that the lessor had (§ 2A-304). A lessee can transfer his interest in leased goods to a buyer or sublessee (§ 2A-305).

A person in the ordinary course of business who furnishes services or materials with respect to leased goods and who obtains a lien given by statute or rule of law upon such goods in the possession of the lessee, such lien takes priority over any interest of the lessor or lessee under the lease and the lien is enforceable (§ 2A-306).

A creditor of a lessee takes subject to the lease contract unless the creditor acquires a lien in the goods before the contract became enforceable or unless the creditor holds a security interest in the goods. A lessee in the ordinary course of business takes a leasehold interest free of a security interest in the goods created by the lessor even if there is a perfected security interest and the lessee knows of its existence. A lessee other than one in the ordinary course of business takes a leasehold interest free of a security interest to the extent that it secures future advances made after the secured party acquired knowledge of the lease, or more than 45 days after the lease becomes enforceable whichever first occurs (§ 2A-307).

A creditor of a lessor in possession of goods subject to a lease may treat the lease as void if, as against the creditor, retention of possession by the lessor is fraudulent under any statute or rule of law. However, retention of possession in good faith and in the current course of trade by the lessor for a commercially reasonably time after the lease becomes enforceable is not fraudulent (§ 2A-308).

Section 2A-309 establishes rights with respect to goods that become fixtures by being so related to real estate that an interest in them arises under real estate law. Section 2A-310 establishes the rights of the parties when goods become accessions that are installed in or affixed to other goods.

Performance of Lease Contract

A lease imposes an obligation on each party that the other's expectation of receiving due performance will not be impaired. If reasonable grounds for insecurity arise with respect to the performance of either party, the insecure party may demand in writing adequate assurance of due performance. Until the insecure party receives such assurance, if commercially reasonable, the insecure party may suspend any performance for which payment has not been received (§ 2A-401).

The reasonableness of grounds for insecurity and the adequacy of any assurances offered must be determined according to commercial standards. Acceptance of any nonconforming delivery or payment does not prejudice an aggrieved party's right to demand adequate assurance of future performance (§ 2A-401).

Section 2A-402 establishes the rights of a party on anticipatory repudiation, and Section 2A-403 governs retraction of anticipatory repudiation. If, without fault of any of the parties, the facilitation of delivery becomes commercially impractical but a commercially reasonable substitute is available, the substitute performance must be tendered and accepted (§ 2A-404).

Sections 2A-405 and 406 establish rules and procedures for excusing performance.

In the case of a finance lease that is not a consumer lease, the lessee's promises under the lease become irrevocable and independent upon the lessee's acceptance of the goods. This section requires the lessee to perform even if the lessor's performance is not in accordance with the lease contract (§ 2A-407).

General Default

A default is determined by the lease agreement and Article 2A. If either party is in default under the lease, the party seeking enforcement may obtain a judgment or otherwise enforce the lease by self-help or any available judicial or non-judicial procedure. Remedies are cumulative (§ 2A-501).

Except as otherwise provided in Article 2A or the lease the lessor or lessee in default is not entitled to notice of default or notice of enforcement from the other party to the lease agreement (§ 2A-502).

A lease may include rights or remedies for default in addition to or in substitution for those provided in Article 2A (§ 2A-503). A lease may also provide for liquidated damages but only in an amount or by a formula that is reasonable in light of the anticipated harm caused by the default (§ 2A-504).

Statute of Limitations

An action for default under a lease, including a breach of warranty or indemnity, must be commenced within four years after the cause of action accrued. The parties, however, may reduce the period of limitation to not less than one year (§ 2A-506).

Default by Lessor

Section 2A-508 establishes the lessee's remedies on default, which include canceling the lease, recovering so much of the rent and security that has been paid, and recovery of damages. The lessee may reject or accept the goods or any part thereof, but such rejection is ineffective unless it is done within a reasonable time (§ 2A-509).

If a lessor or supplier has no agent or place of business at the market of rejection, a merchant lessee after rejection of goods shall follow any reasonable instruction received from the lessor or the supplier with respect to the goods. In the absence of such instructions, a merchant lessee shall make reasonable effort to sell, lease, or otherwise dispose of the goods for the lessor's account. Absent instruction, a lessee has a duty to dispose of goods that speedily decline in value (§ 2A-511).

In rejecting goods a lessee's failure to state a particular defect that can be discovered by reasonable inspection precludes a lessee from relying on the defect to justify rejection or establish default (§ 2A-514). Acceptance of goods occurs after the lessee has had a reasonable opportunity to inspect the goods and the lessee acts with respect to the goods in a manner that signifies to the lessor or supplier that the goods are conforming, or that the lessee will retain them despite their nonconformity (§ 2A-515).

A lessee must pay rent for any goods accepted in accordance with the lease contract, with due allowance for goods rightfully rejected or not delivered (§ 2A-516).

After default by lessor under the lease, the lessee may cover by making in good faith and without unreasonable delay, a purchase or lease or contract to substitute goods for those due from the lessor (§ 2A-518).

Section 2A-519 establishes rules for lessee's damages for nondelivery repudiation, default and breach of warranty in regard to accepted goods. Damages are defined in Section 2A-520 as including incidental and consequential damages. Specific performance may be decreed if the goods are unique or in other appropriate circumstances (§ 2A-521).

Even if the goods have not been shipped, a lessee who has paid for a part or all of the rent and security for the goods may recover the goods if the lessor becomes insolvent within 10 days of receipt of the first installment of rent and security (§ 2A-522).

Default by Lessee

Section 2A-523 establishes the lessor's remedies, which include canceling the lease, withholding delivery, or recovering damages. If a lessor discovers the lessee to be insolvent, the lessor may refuse to deliver the goods, and if the lessee is in default, the lessor may take possession of the goods without judicial process provided no breach of the peace results (§ 2A-525). A lessor may stop goods in possession of a carrier if he discovers the lessee to be insolvent (§ 2A-526).

After default by a lessee, or after lessee refuses to deliver or take possession of goods, lessor may dispose of the goods concerned or the undelivered balance in good faith and without unreasonable delay (§ 2A-527).

A lessor's right to damages for nonacceptance or repudiation are established by Section 2A-528. After default by the lessee under a lease contract, the lessor may recover from the lessee damages for goods accepted by the lessee and for conforming goods lost or damaged within a commercially reasonable time; accrued and unpaid rent, the value of the lease and incidental damages (§ 2A-529).

Incidental damages to a lessor include any commercially reasonable charges, expenses or commissions in stopping delivery and the transportation, carrying or custody of goods after lessee's default (§ 2A-530).

ARTICLE 3: COMMERCIAL PAPER

Article 3 applies only to negotiable instruments. It does not apply to money, to payment orders governed by Article 4A or to securities governed by Article 8. Included in the coverage of this Article are negotiable instruments, notes, checks, certificates of deposit, money orders and drafts. The basic principle underlying Article 3 is ensuring that commercial paper is treated as a substitute for money; therefore, the "paper" must represent an unconditional promise to pay a definite amount at a definite time.

Chapter 9, "Negotiable Instruments: Notes, Checks, Drafts—How They Work— And Interest Rates," contains a substantive discussion of Article 3 of the Uniform Commercial Code. Only New York and South Carolina have not adopted Revised Article 3.

The following is a discussion of the version of UCC Article 3 in effect in New York and South Carolina. The other states have adopted later versions of Article 3.

Specific Requirements

A negotiable instrument is defined as an unconditional promise or order to pay a fixed amount of money, with or without interest or other charges described in the promise or order if specific requirements are met. The key to understanding negotiable instruments is to understand the explicit provisions of Section 3-104.

The negotiable instrument must:

(1) be payable to bearer or to order at the time it is issued or first comes into possession of a holder;
(2) be payable on demand or at a definite time; and
(3) not state any other undertaking or instruction by the person promising or ordering payment to do any act in addition to the payment of money.

In addition, Section 3-104 provides the various terms that are commonly heard by the credit professional, all of which are included in the definition of a negotiable instrument:

1. An "Instrument" means a negotiable instrument.
2. An instrument is a "note" if it is a promise and is a "draft" if it is an order. If an instrument falls within the definition of both "note" and "draft," a person entitled to enforce the instrument may treat it as either.

3. "Check" means (i) a draft, other than a documentary draft, payable on demand and drawn on a bank or (ii) a cashier's check or teller's check. An instrument may be a check even though it is described on its face by another term, such as "money order."

4. "Cashier's check" means a draft with respect to which the drawer and drawee are the same bank or branches of the same bank.

5. "Teller's check" means a draft drawn by a bank (i) on another bank, or (ii) payable at or through a bank.

6. "Traveler's check" means an instrument that (i) is payable on demand, (ii) is drawn on or payable at or through a bank, (iii) is designated by the term "traveler's check" or by a substantially similar term, and (iv) requires, as a condition to payment, a countersignature by a person whose specimen signature appears on the instrument.

7. "Certificate of deposit" means an instrument containing an acknowledgment by a bank that a sum of money has been received by the bank and a promise by the bank to repay the sum of money. A certificate of deposit is a note of the bank.

As can readily be understood, the essential element of commercial paper is that it can be transferred or negotiated. Negotiation is merely a type of transfer where the transferee becomes a holder. The negotiation of an order instrument is accomplished by an endorsement of the instrument while a bearer instrument is negotiated by mere delivery.

The policy of the Code, i.e., the facilitation of the use of commercial paper, is illustrated by Section 3-202, which provides that a negotiation is effective even if executed by an incompetent party or through fraud or illegality. Negotiations so obtained, however, may be rescinded. The implication is that commercial paper is equivalent to cash; the possession of the instrument enables it to be used for transactions.

Liability of Parties

Liability can arise in two contexts, contractually or by a warranty. Contractually, the liability of an endorser is set out in Section 3-415, which essentially provides that the endorser guarantees to pay the instrument upon dishonor and presentment. The effect of an improper endorsement is covered by Sections 3-404 and 3-405. In most cases, an improper endorsement is effective, and the loss is borne by the drawer of the check, rather than the payee. Thus, in the situation where the name of a payee is improperly supplied and subsequently indorsed, the check will be paid and the bank (payee) will not be liable.

The second class of liability exists by virtue of a warranty. Section 3-417 provides that the transferor of the instrument grants an implied warranty that (1) he has good title, (2) all signatures are genuine and authorized, (3) the instrument has not been altered, (4) no defense of any party is good against him, and (5) he has no knowledge of bankruptcy proceedings against the maker of the instrument. Violation of any of these warranties can impose liability upon the transferor.

The requirements of timely presentment to parties who are primarily liable (drawees, makers and acceptors) and notice of dishonor to parties who are secondary holders (indorsers) are conditions precedent to any right of action (§ 3-501). Section 3-508 defines when notice of dishonor must be given.

Discharge

Section 3-601 of the Code makes it clear that discharge from liability applies only to the parties to the instrument and not to the instrument itself and removes the implication that an act which constitutes a discharge may create a defense to a holder in due course. Section 3-603 permits the liability of any party to be discharged by payment to the holder, despite that party's knowledge of an adverse claim (thus preserving the payor's credit standing) unless the adverse claimant supplies indemnity. This does not apply, however, to a party who pays a holder who acquired the instrument by theft or who satisfies a holder where the instrument was "restrictively endorsed in a manner not consistent with the terms of such restrictive endorsement."

ARTICLE 4: BANK DEPOSITS AND COLLECTIONS

This Article deals with matters relating to dealings between banks and their customers, other banks and third parties. It covers such matters as deposits and collection of negotiable instruments, the relationship between a bank and its customers, and the dealings between banks. The scope of this Article encompasses practically every "item," which is broadly defined as "an instrument or a promise or order to pay money handled by a bank for collection or payment," that passes through banks for the purpose of presentment, payment, or collection (§ 4-104). The challenge faced by the credit professional today is for the credit professional to understand the juxtaposition of UCC Articles 3, 4 and 4A with the federal statutes such as the Electronic Fund Transfer Act, CFR Regulations J and CC.

The following is a discussion of the version of UCC Article 4 in effect in New York and South Carolina. The other states have adopted later versions of Article 4.

Final Payment of Checks

One of the most important problems in the bank collection process is the establishment of the precise time when a check is deemed to have been finally paid by the drawee bank. It is at that point that it is no longer possible for the drawer to stop payment; the drawer's account is charged with the amount of the check so that his creditors may not thereafter attach these funds on deposit. Additionally, the provisional credit to the account of the depositor of the check becomes irrevocable so that he may draw against that credit; drawers and endorsers of the check are discharged and the point of no return is reached so that the payor bank is accountable for the amount of the check.

Section 4-213 provides, that final payment occurs when the payor bank pays cash to the holder over the counter. This Section further fixes definite rules for time of payment in the more usual case when a check comes to the payor from a depository bank—either directly or through an intermediary bank or through a clearinghouse in the collection process. The usual practice in this case is for the payor bank to give provisional credit for the item at the time of receipt reserving the right to subsequently revoke that credit if it decides that the check should not be paid. Since time is of the essence, the payor bank will be deemed to have finally paid if it takes no action to revoke the provisional credit within the period prescribed by clearinghouse rules (in some instances, a matter of hours after receipt). When a check is sent through the mail to the payor bank, the Code requires a revocation of the provisional credit by the "midnight deadline." This is a term which, in most cases, will extend the time within which a bank must act to avoid final payment; it is defined in Section

4-104 as "midnight on [the] next banking day following the banking day on which [the payor bank] receives the item." "Midnight deadline" is also the presumed period of time within which a collecting or intermediary bank receiving a check in the collection process must act in presenting a check for payment, sending notice of dishonor, etc. The Code recognizes the current banking practice of fixing an afternoon hour of 2:00pm or later as a cutoff time after which items will be considered as being received on the next banking day for the purpose of computing the commencement of the "midnight deadline" (§ 4-108).

An alternative point of final payment, after which a check may not be returned, is the "posting" of the check by the payor, i.e., the mechanical act of debiting the drawer's account. The point of time after which a stop-payment order from the drawer or attachment of the account by the drawer's creditors is not effective is established as the time of "sight posting" the item to the account of the drawer (§ 4-303). The check does not actually have to be posted in order for there to be a final payment of a check. A bank may otherwise evidence its intention to pay the item. This is commonly referred to as "sight posting" (§ 4-303, Official Comment 3). In the collection process, this occurs when a clerk has placed the check in a stack to be sent to another office for final posting, and this alternative point is based on the practical difficulty of preventing the payment after this time.

Relationship between Payor Bank and Its Customer

Article 4 contains a number of rules, some of which modify or directly change existing law or settle areas of present uncertainty, governing the relationship between a payor bank and its customers. Section 4-402 recognizes the generally understood rule that a drawee bank has a duty to pay a check which is a proper order to pay, but modifies the damage rule for breach of this duty by limiting recovery to actual damages proved. When two or more checks are presented for payment at the same time and the account is insufficient to pay them all, the bank may pay in any order with impunity until the deposit is no longer sufficient to pay any one (§ 4-303). Present uncertainty about what constitutes effective stop-payment orders is removed by Section 4-403, which makes an oral order binding upon the bank for 14 days and a written order effective for six months. A bank's duty to its depositor with respect to a stale check presented for payment is clarified by Section 4-404, which provides that the bank may, but need not, pay a check which is presented more than six months after its date. The specific exception is a certified check. When the drawer of a check dies or is incompetent before the check is paid, the order to pay is still effective until the banks learn of the death or incompetence and may pay for 10 days after knowledge of death unless ordered to stop by a person claiming interest in the account (§ 4-405).

Section 4-406 incorporates the common-law duty of a depositor to examine his bank statements and items paid and notify the bank with reasonable promptness of a forgery of his signature on a check that has been paid or any alteration; failure to do so will preclude the depositor from asserting such irregularities. This section gives the drawer 30 days after the return of an item and statement to discover and notify the bank of a forgery or alteration; thereafter, the drawer is estopped from asserting any subsequent forgery or alteration by the same wrongdoer which was paid in good faith prior to notification of the bank. In all other cases, without regard to negligence, the customer has one year from the time the statement and items are made available to him to discover and report to the bank a forgery of his signature or an alteration.

ARTICLE 4A: FUNDS TRANSFERS

Scope

Article 4A applies to wholesale wire transfers, including those over CHIPS and Fedwire, and to automated clearinghouse ("ACH") credit entry transfers through a "bank" (i.e., a Federal Reserve Bank, commercial bank, savings and loan association, credit union or other entity engaged in the business of banking), but does not cover non-"bank" wire transfers. Checks, credit card sale drafts, ACH debit entries and other "debit" transfers are excluded from coverage.

One must look to the definitions of "payment order" and "funds transfer" found in Section 4A-103 and Section 4A-104 for a clearer understanding of what is covered by this statute. Prior to the drafting and passage of Article 4, there were no statutory provisions covering the technological advances which have been made.

The comments to Article 4A state that "in the drafting of Article 4A, a deliberate decision was made to write on a clean slate and to treat a funds transfer as a unique method of payment to be governed by unique rules that address the particular issues raised by this method of payment." Precise and detailed rules were established to assign responsibility, define behavioral norms, allocate risks and establish limits on liability, rather than to rely on broadly stated, flexible principles. In the drafting of these rules, a critical consideration was that the various parties to funds transfers need to be able to predict risk with certainty, to insure against risk, to adjust operational and security procedures, and to price funds transfer services appropriately.

Consumer electronic funds transfers subject to the federal Electronic Fund Transfer Act are expressly excluded from coverage so that, in general, the Article applies only to wholesale "credit" transfers. However, the federal Act excludes a number of categories of consumer electronic funds transfers from its coverage. Those excluded consumer transfers are subject to Article 4A.

Substantive Provisions

The following are the significant three areas covered by the Article, which has been enacted in all states, the District of Columbia and Puerto Rico.

1. Damages for late or improper transmittal of instructions with respect to a funds transfer (a "payment order") and for failure to transmit a payment order absent a contrary agreement, Article 4A relieves a bank from potential liability for consequential damages.
2. Allocation of liability between the originator of a payment order and the originator's bank for an unauthorized payment order, i.e., an order fraudulently initiated by an unauthorized employee or agent of the originator or by a third-party interloper. The rules provided by Article 4A for such allocation are complex. In general, however, protection is afforded a "bank" if it complies with a commercially reasonable procedure for providing security against unauthorized payment orders and that procedure has been agreed upon with the user of that institute's funds transfer services.
3. A beneficiary's bank may not recover a payment made to the beneficiary with respect to a funds transfer in the event of the insolvency of a prior bank involved in the transfer: except that an exception is made for ACH transfers in prescribed circumstances.

In addition to covering the parties' rights and obligations with respect to properly completed funds transfers and those involving various problem situations, the article also imposes various obligations on particular parties to a funds transfer. For example, it imposes a duty on the beneficiary's bank and, in some circumstances, a prior bank, to provide timely notice of rejection of a payment order, a duty on the beneficiary's bank to give notice to the beneficiary of receipt of a payment order within certain time limits, and a duty on an originator or other sender of a payment order to report unauthorized or erroneously issued orders.

The Article also deals with attachment and other legal process and injunction issues involving funds transfers subject to its provisions. It also contains a choice of law provision designed to validate a funds transfer system choice of law rule without the specific agreement of persons other than banks participating in the system. Systems such as CHIPS and ACH networks will presumably take advantage of that provision to select the law of a state which has enacted Article 4A.

ARTICLE 5: DOCUMENTARY LETTERS OF CREDIT

The commercial letter of credit has been employed principally in international trade where the foreign seller is willing to ship goods only on the credit of a known bank that promises to pay the purchase price upon the receipt of the bill of lading and other necessary documents. The customary documentary sale, whereby the seller sends the bill of lading with a draft drawn on the buyer to a bank in the buyer's town for collection, unlike the letter of credit, does not shift the risk of nonpayment from the seller to the bank.

Prior to the enactment of the Code, the law concerning letters of credit came from common law decisions, principally of New York, Massachusetts and California, where the bulk of foreign commerce is financed. Thus, Article 5 of the Code broke new ground in codifying the legal rules concerning this device. It also fostered the invention of the "standby" letter of credit as a means for banks to effectively guarantee the performance of their customers. Like commercial letters of credit, standby letters of credit are payable upon presentation of documents, but the documents do not necessarily have anything to do with a sale of goods. Rather they generally evidence non-performance with an underlying contract.

In order for a letter of credit to serve its essential risk-shifting function, the bank is legally divorced from matters relating to the underlying contract, such as the quantity and quality of the goods. Thus, under the Code, the issuing bank's liability to pay and its entitlement to reimbursement from its customer becomes absolute upon the receipt of the documents required (§ 5-108). If the bank is notified prior to payment that the documents are forged or there is fraud in the transaction between the buyer and seller, the bank is given an option to honor the draft or demand for payment unless the customer has obtained a court injunction against the issuer's exercise of its option (§ 5-109).

Sometimes, a bank will issue a straight letter of credit where the language "we engage with you" is used. In such form, the promise does not run to a purchaser of the draft as a holder in due course on the theory that the purchaser sees on the face that the promise runs only to the beneficiary. A letter of credit will often, however, be made negotiable, allowing documents to be negotiated to a holder in due course who may enforce the letter of credit against the issuer regardless of any fraud in the transaction or forgery of the document (§ 5-108).

In order to examine the documents properly and make sure that they comply with the letter of credit, the bank is given a "reasonable time" not to exceed the close of the seventh banking day following receipt of the documents to honor the draft. Failure to act within that time precludes the bank from asserting discrepancies in the documents, thus compelling payment except in the case of fraud or forgery (§ 5-108).

Upon wrongful dishonor under an irrevocable credit, the presenter may recover from the issuer the face amount of the draft, plus incidental damages recoverable by a seller under Article 2, less any amount realized from resale or other use of the subject matter of the transaction (§ 5-111).

A sample letter of credit can be found in Chapter 27.

ARTICLE 6: BULK TRANSFERS

Article 6 seeks to protect creditors of a merchant by voiding a bulk transfer of his merchandise out of the ordinary course of trade, unless the transferee gives notice of the contemplated transfer to all known creditors at least 10 days before he takes possession.

Coverage is extended under Section 6-102 to include business equipment, if it is made in connection with a bulk transfer of inventory. Also, a bulk sale at an auction under Section 6-108 expands existing coverage so that the auctioneer is charged with the responsibility similar to that of a transferee of other bulk sales, i.e., where the auctioneer knows the auction constitutes a bulk transfer he is personally liable to the creditors of the transferor for uncollected debts. Creditors must receive the requisite notice. And, the proceeds of sale of the assets must be utilized to pay creditors their pro rata distribution. The rights of the purchasers, however, are not affected. As long as the purchaser buys in good faith, that purchaser will not be deprived of the assets it has purchased.

For years, however, bulk sales resulted in litigation. In particular, the variances among the states dealing with the notification provisions often created hardships to the unknowing creditor. Additionally, the statute of limitations within which to pursue an action for fraudulent bulk transfer under the UCC is extremely short. Other state statutes provide better protections to the creditor that has not been paid.

In 1988, the National Conference of Commissioners on Uniform State Laws adopted a new Article 6 which provides two alternatives. The first alternative repeals the old Article 6 and the second alternative (also referred to as Alternative B) proposes adoption of a revised and expanded new Article 6.

The most important differences between the new article and the old one are:

1. The period of notice to be provided to creditors prior to the sale is extended from 10 days to 45 days.
2. In transactions involving more than 200 creditors, a system of central filing of the notice is provided in lieu of individual notices to each creditor.
3. The definition of property included within inventory in a covered transaction is expanded to encompass factory and office equipment and intangibles.
4. Sales of more than half of the inventory are covered by the new Article. The old statute applied to sales of a major portion of the inventory.
5. A schedule of distribution of proceeds is provided to be given to all creditors by the seller, which enables the creditors and the transferee to know the dis-

position of the proceeds of the sale. However, only the seller has the obligation to make payment and to distribute the proceeds.

6. In addition to declaring the transaction ineffective, a damaged creditor is entitled to money damages.

7. Personal liability is imposed on corporate officers in control who fail to distribute the proceeds of the sale in accordance with the schedule of distribution.

8. A penalty of twice the price of the transfer less amounts paid the seller or the creditor is imposed on the transferee for violation of the notice section of the Article.

9. The statute of limitations for actions under the Act is extended from six months to one year.

10. A good faith effort by the buyer to comply excuses noncompliance.

11. The Article is applicable only if the seller is going out of business and does not apply to bulk sales made while the seller is continuing in business.

12. No optional or mandatory section is included, comparable to the old Section 6-106, which provides that the transferee is to hold the proceeds of the sale to pay off creditors.

The original bulk sale law contained in Article 6 of the UCC was disfavored by business people almost from its inception. Even as the Commission on Uniform Laws was attempting to revise Article 6 so that it would be more acceptable to business people, many states were determined to repeal Article 6 in its entirety.

The states of Alabama, Alaska, Arkansas, Colorado, Connecticut, Delaware, Florida, Idaho, Illinois, Iowa, Kansas, Kentucky, Louisiana, Maine, Massachusetts, Michigan, Minnesota, Mississippi, Missouri, Montana, Nebraska, Nevada, New Hampshire, New Jersey, New Mexico, New York, North Dakota, Ohio, Oregon, Pennsylvania, Puerto Rico, Rhode Island, South Carolina, South Dakota, Tennessee, Texas, Utah, Vermont, Virgin Islands, Washington, West Virginia and Wyoming have repealed Article 6 and have adopted no revision nor any other replacement. Lousiana never adopted the original Article 6 nor has it adopted the 1989 revision. Arizona, Hawaii, Oklahoma, Utah and Virginia adopted the 1989 revision and later repealed it, currently having no Article 6.

The states of California, Indiana, and the District of Columbia adopted the 1989 Article 6 revisions - Alternative B. Maryland adopted its own independent body of law titled "Commercial Law."

Article 6: Bulk Sales Status

UCC Article 6
Alabama - repealed without adopting 1989 revision
Alaska - repealed without adopting 1989 revision
Arizona - adopted 1989 revision and then repealed it
Arkansas - repealed without adopting 1989 revision
California - §§ 6101 to 6111 - adopted 1989 revision
Colorado - repealed without adopting 1989 revision
Connecticut - repealed without adopting 1989 revision
Delaware - repealed without adopting 1989 revision
District of Columbia - adopted 1989 revision
Florida - repealed without adopting 1989 revision
Georgia - § 11-6-101 (old Article 6)

Hawaii - adopted 1989 revision and then repealed it
Idaho - repealed without adopting 1989 Revision
Illinois - repealed without adopting 1989 Revision
Indiana - adopted 1989 revision
Iowa - repealed without adopting 1989 revision
Kansas - repealed without adopting 1989 revision
Kentucky - repealed without adopting 1989 revision
Louisiana - repealed without adopting 1989 revision
Maine - repealed without adopting 1989 revision
Maryland - article = "Commercial Law"
Massachusetts - repealed without adopting 1989 revision
Michigan - repealed without adopting 1989 revision
Minnesota - repealed without adopting 1989 revision
Mississippi - repealed without adopting 1989 revision
Missouri - repealed without adopting 1989 revision
Montana - repealed without adopting 1989 revision
Nebraska - repealed without adopting 1989 revision
Nevada - repealed without adopting 1989 revision
New Hampshire - repealed without adopting 1989 revision
New Jersey - repealed without adopting 1989 revision
New Mexico - repealed without adopting 1989 revision
New York - repealed without adopting 1989 revision
North Carolina - repealed without adopting 1989 revision
North Dakota - repealed without adopting 1989 revision
Ohio - repealed without adopting 1989 revision
Oklahoma - adopted and later repealed 1989 revision
Oregon - repealed without adopting 1989 revision
Pennsylvania - repealed without adopting 1989 revision
Rhode Island - repealed without adopting 1989 revision
South Carolina - repealed without adopting 1989 revision
South Dakota - repealed without adopting 1989 revision
Tennessee - repealed without adopting 1989 revision
Texas - repealed without adopting 1989 revision
Utah - adopted 1989 revision and then repealed it
Vermont - repealed without adopting 1989 revision
Virgin Islands - repealed without adopting 1989 revision
Virginia - adopted 1989 revision and then repealed it
Washington - repealed without adopting 1989 revision
West Virginia - repealed without adopting 1989 revision
Wisconsin - Old Article 6
Wyoming - repealed without adopting 1989 revision

Article 6 includes bulk sales conducted by sellers whose principal business is the operation of a restaurant or tavern. Expansion of the scope of revised Article 6 is inconsistent with the recommendation that Article 6 be repealed. Nevertheless, the inclusion of restaurants and taverns within the scope of the revised Article as it is enacted in particular jurisdictions would not disturb the internal logic and structure of the revised Article.

ARTICLE 7: WAREHOUSE RECEIPTS, BILLS OF LADING AND OTHER DOCUMENTS OF TITLE[2]

Article 7 repeals and modernizes the half-century-old Uniform Warehouse Receipts Act (UWRA) and the Uniform Bills of Lading Act (UBLA) and integrates the statutory treatment of these documents. Some new coverage is included to cover modern shipping and the storage practices which were not contemplated by the original Uniform Acts, such as bonded storage required by federal or state statute and air bills and problems which arise under modern high-speed air or truck transportation. Of course, this state legislation does not affect federal legislation dealing with interstate shipments, such as the Federal Bills of Lading Act or the Federal Carriage of Goods by Sea Act.

As under the UWRA, a warehouse receipt, by definition, must be issued by a warehouse that does not include a person who stores his own goods (§ 7-201). An important exception to this is found in § 7-201(2), which treats a receipt as a warehouse receipt when issued by a non-warehouseman, including the owner of the goods, under a statute requiring a bond against withdrawal.

The essential terms of the warehouse receipts are similar to those under existing law, but the Code preserves the obligations of the issuer even though the document does not comply with the formal requirements (§ 7-202). Essential terms of a bill of lading provided by the UBLA are omitted from the Code, but federal regulation of the forms used in interstate commerce will continue to control.

An illustration of the Code's modernization of documents of title is the use of the "destination bill," which is designed to meet the problem of high-speed air transportation where the goods may arrive at the destination before the documents. This could be inconvenient where the carrier does not have storage facilities and could be even more serious where the goods are perishable. To meet this problem, Section 7-305 authorizes the carrier, upon receipt of the goods for shipment, to issue the bill at the destination point. (Of course, the carrier may not issue the bill until the goods are received.) Assuming the usual documentary sale, the bill would be issued to the buyer's bank, the seller would wire the bank a draft on the buyer, and the bank would endorse the bill to the buyer when he honors the draft.

Many of the familiar negotiable instruments rules apply where a document of title is negotiable and is taken by "due negotiation." A new requirement, however, is that negotiation must be in the "regular course of business or financing" in order for the transferee to take the instrument free of defenses and claims of ownership to which his transferor is subject. To qualify, the person making the transfer must be a person in the trade and the nature of the transaction must be a usual and ordinary transaction in which documents are transferred (§ 7-501).

A bona fide purchaser of an altered document of title may enforce it according to its original tenor. The same rule applies to the filling in of blanks in a bill of lading (§ 7-306), but a bona fide purchaser may treat as authorized the filling of a blank in a negotiable warehouse receipt (§ 7-208). This absolute liability imposed on a warehouseman for the unauthorized filling of blanks is in recognition of the dangerous practice of executing warehouse receipts in blank. It is often necessary for carriers to execute bills of lading in blank to be filled out by various employees, and thus the consequence of improper completion of bills carries no sanction.

---

[2] This section deals with current Article 7 in effect in 43 states.

ARTICLE 8: INVESTMENT SECURITIES

The Uniform Stock Transfer Act was the principal statutory law governing the transfer of certificates of stock as an investment security, prior to the Uniform Commercial Code. The Code repeals the Uniform Stock Transfer Act and replaces it with Article 8 which separates the law of investment securities from the short-term negotiable paper of Article 3. Article 8 extends statutory coverage to registered bonds and other types of investment paper not covered by any other uniform act. The matter of regulation of securities under the federal and state "blue sky law" is not dealt with by this article. The basic policies of free transferability and protection to a holder underlying the negotiable instruments law of securities are similar to those of Article 3, but without the formal prerequisites of negotiability required by the Negotiable Instruments Law and Article 3 of the Code. Thus, a bona fide purchaser of securities is similar to a holder in due course in negotiable instrument law, in that he takes free of defenses and adverse claims of ownership. Similar to the rule of forged commercial paper, no holder has a right against an issuer of a counterfeit security or one on which the validating signature is unauthorized. Under Section 8-205, however, an unauthorized signature is valid in favor of a good faith purchaser for value when it is of a person entrusted by the issuer with signing the security or an employee entrusted with handling the security. Section 8-206 follows the change in the law of commercial paper under Article 3, and protects a purchaser for value without notice of incorrectness from the defense of improper completion where blanks are left upon the issue of a security.

The purchaser of commercial paper after maturity is automatically subject to all defenses under Article 3. His counterpart, i.e., a purchaser of security under Section 8-203, will be deprived of the bona fide purchaser status only where he purchases more than two years after a call for redemption or exchange, or one year after such call if the funds or securities are available for delivery when due.

Section 8-104 prescribes a formula for adjusting the rights of a person entitled to issue against the issuer of an overissue of securities, for example, where a stock transfer agent issues the new certificate without the surrender of a certificate for a corresponding number of shares, creating an excess of the issuer's chartered allowance. The Code resolves this problem by compelling the issuer to purchase shares on the market to replace the overissue. If shares are not available from the market, the person entitled may obtain reimbursement at the price he or the last purchaser for value paid for the security, with interest from the date of demand.

ARTICLE 9: SECURED TRANSACTIONS

Article 9 of the Uniform Commercial Code has been completely revised. Each state adopted the Revised Article 9 by July 1, 2001. Because of the thorough revision, Chapter 10 entitled "Secured Transactions—A Step-by-Step Explanation" discusses this Article in depth. However, following is a brief overview of Article 9.

A credit grantor needs to be familiar with the law of secured transactions for two very important reasons. First, a credit grantor must satisfy all of the requirements of Article 9 in order to obtain a valid and perfected security interest in all of the collateral securing payment of its claim against its customer or the performance of the customer's obligations. Second, a credit grantor also must determine whether a secured creditor of its customer has satisfied all of the requirements for obtaining a perfected security interest that would confer upon it priority over junior secured and judgment creditors and a bankruptcy trustee.

The law of secured transactions for personal property and fixtures is contained in Article 9 of the UCC. UCC Article 9 contains the rules for obtaining a security interest in personal property and fixture collateral, perfecting a security interest in these assets that would grant the secured creditor a priority over a subsequent secured creditor, judgment creditor and bankruptcy trustee, and enforcing a security interest in these assets.

The current version of UCC Article 9 is a substantial revision of the prior version of Article 9. The revised version of Article 9 has been passed by and is currently in effect in all 50 states and the District of Columbia. The text of current Article 9 is contained in Appendix C.

The changes arising under current Article 9 are designed to accommodate new technologies and, in particular, electronic-based transactions that are becoming more prevalent. Current Article 9 has also expanded the scope of personal property assets that are now covered by the UCC and that were excluded under the prior version of Article 9 (hereinafter called "Old Article 9"). Current Article 9 also simplifies the requirements for filing UCC financing statements as a means for perfecting a security interest in most categories of personal property collateral and fixtures. Current Article 9 also provides additional methods for perfecting a security interest by control or possession. Finally current Article 9 provides a transition period for bringing UCC filings, filed under and in compliance with Old Article 9, into compliance with the new requirements of current Article 9.

You should understand the basic elements of Article 9. A security interest is an interest in personal property created by the debtor to secure repayment of a debt. A security interest is consensual and requires that the debtor authenticate a security agreement that describes the goods to be covered, known as the collateral. A security interest attaches when the security agreement is executed and the debtor acquires rights in the assets subject to the security interest. A security interest is perfected when the secured creditor either takes possession or control of the collateral or files a proper financing statement with the appropriate state authority. As a general rule, competing security interests have priority in the order they are perfected, or if all competing interests are unperfected, in the order in which they attached.

"Perfection" is the process of taking the legal steps necessary to ensure that a secured party's interest in collateral will withstand attack by competing secured creditors, judgment lien creditors, and a bankruptcy trustee. A security interest is said to be perfected when all the steps have been taken to assure it priority in the collateral described against all possible competing claimants. Generally, a security interest is perfected either through the taking of possession or control of the collateral or the filing of a financing statement under the UCC or both. In a limited number of cases, perfection is obtained through compliance with other state or federal law.

Perfection is important since it generally determines a creditor's priority to proceeds from the disposition of the collateral. Perfected security interests generally have priority from the date of perfection where the perfection was accomplished through filing, possession, control or some other means. Proper classification of the collateral into the appropriate category is essential since the proper means of perfection is based upon the classification of collateral.

Chapter 10 contains a chart that should assist creditors in determining the means of perfection applicable. *Also see* this chapter for a detailed discussion of these and other issues relating to Article 9 of the UCC.

ARTICLE 10: EFFECTIVE DATE AND REPEALER

This Article, which of necessity varies in the several states that have enacted the Code, provides the date as of which it became effective and the repeal of various Uniform Laws and other statutes which it supersedes.

ARTICLE 11: EFFECTIVE DATE AND TRANSITION PROVISIONS

This Article includes provisions that cover the transition from the original version of the Code and the subsequent changes which have been made.

Refer to Chapter 27 for the following form:

- Letter of Credit

8 Equipment Leasing

Equipment leasing has become a primary form of equipment financing. It is attractive for a number of reasons: title to the equipment remains with the lessor and the lessor is entitled to the benefits of ownership for tax purposes. The lessee may be able to avoid the risk of equipment obsolescence or may be able to lease the equipment for only the period of time it is needed. A lease of equipment may allow the lessee to avoid restrictions on balance sheet total debt imposed by its lender. A lease may also serve as a hedge against inflation or as a way to increase cash flow and preserve capital. Properly structuring an agreement for the use of equipment as a finance lease instead of a security agreement is an advantage for a number of reasons, but most importantly in the case of lessee bankruptcy.

The law governing equipment leases is based upon a number of sources. State property laws govern most issues of title and contract terms. Equipment leasing is influenced by the Bankruptcy Code and by state secured transactions laws. Because finance leases have significant parallels to sales contracts, Article 2 of the Uniform Commercial Code (Sales) has greatly influenced the law of equipment leases. The link was believed to be so strong that in the late 1980s and early 1990s, the National Conference of Commissioners on Uniform State Laws proposed Article 2A which specifically governs personal property leasing. There are also parallels with the provisions of Article 9 and these have been incorporated into Article 2A. As of September 2005, the District of Columbia, U.S. Virgin Islands and all states except Louisiana have adopted Article 2A and its 1990 Amendments with some variations. An overview of Article 2A is presented in Chapter 7 and Appendix C of this manual contains text from the 1990 version of Article 2A. The end of this chapter lists the state-by-state summary of laws and specific variations.

DEFINITION OF "FINANCE LEASE"

Currently, many transactions that would normally have been asset purchases are now either direct or financed leases. A direct lease is a two party agreement, one in which the manufacturer of the equipment maintains ownership and rents or leases the equipment to the end user. This is frequently used for smaller pieces of equipment. In a direct lease situation, the lessee generally maintains all rights directly against the lessor, including warranty claims. A finance lease involves three parties, the manufacturer of the equipment, the finance leasing company ("lessor") and the lessee or user of the equipment. To be a "finance lease," a lease must qualify as a finance lease under UCC Section 2A-103(1)(g). Section 103(1)(g) defines a finance lease as a lease in which the lessor (i) does not select, manufacture or supply the goods, (ii) acquires the goods or the right to possession and use of the goods in connection with the lease and leases the equipment directly to the lessee; and (iii) one of the following occurs:

(A) the lessee receives a copy of the contract by which the lessor acquired the goods or the right to possession and use of the goods before signing the lease contract;

(B) the lessee's approval of the contract by which the lessor acquired the goods or the right to possession and use of the goods is a condition to effectiveness of the lease contract;

(C) the lessee, before signing the lease contract, receives an accurate and complete statement designating the promises and warranties, and any disclaimers of warranties, limitations or modifications of remedies, or liquidated damages, including those of a third party, such as the manufacturer of the goods, provided to the lessor by the person supplying the goods in connection with or as part of the contract by which the lessor acquired the goods or the right to possession and use of the goods; or

(D) if the lease is not a consumer lease, the lessor, before the lessee signs the lease contract, informs the lessee in writing (1) of the identity of the person supplying the goods to the lessor, unless the lessee has selected that person and directed the lessor to acquire the goods or the right to possession and use of the goods from that person, (2) that the lessee is entitled under this Article to the promises and warranties, including those of any third party, provided to the lessor by the person supplying the goods in connection with or as part of the contract by which the lessor acquired the goods or the right to possession and use of the goods, and (3) that the lessee may communicate with the person supplying the goods to the lessor and receive an accurate and complete statement of those promises and warranties, including any disclaimers and limitations of them or of remedies.

GENERAL PROVISIONS FOUND IN FINANCE LEASE AGREEMENTS

The principal purpose of a finance lease is to allow the lessor to finance the purchase of the equipment without taking on the burden of ownership and the warranties and representations that are generally placed upon the owner of the equipment. The lessee must look to the manufacturer of the equipment for these representations and warranties. Typically finance leases contain certain provisions which emphasize the "incidents of ownership" held by the lessee. Included among these are the following:

- the lessor is in the business of financing
- the lease provides that the leased goods are acquired solely in connection with the lease
- the lessor has not selected, manufactured or supplied the leased equipment
- the lessor disclaims warranty and promissory liability
- the lessee bears the risk of loss
- the lease contains a "hell or high water" clause
- the lease contains a non-cancellation clause
- the lease contains an accelerated payment clause
- the lease contains a late payment clause
- the lessee is obligated to pay all taxes on the equipment
- the lessee is obligated to insure the equipment
- the lessor retains title to the equipment and to use markings on the equipment stating that it is owned by the lessor

- the lessee is prohibited from assigning the lease, subleasing the equipment
- the lessee is required to keep the leased equipment free and clear of all liens and encumbrances.

If the parties create an agreement which includes the provisions listed above, it is likely that the agreement will be considered a finance lease. If there is a dispute, the final determination will be made by the facts of each case.

PROTECTING FINANCE LESSOR'S INTEREST IN EQUIPMENT

Although the lessor under a finance lease retains title to the equipment, it is prudent for the finance lessor to provide notice to the world that it retains title to the equipment. The lessee may have provided a blanket lien to its lender which grants a lien on all assets, including equipment. Thus, if the finance lessor wants to make sure that the equipment subject to the lease is not confused with the equipment subject to the lender's blanket lien, a UCC Financing Statement should be filed with the proper office to insure that proper notice of the lessor's ownership interest is provided. This also provides protection to a bankruptcy trustee or other parties in the event the lessee becomes a bankruptcy debtor. In addition, the finance lessor should make sure the equipment is tagged to indicate it is subject to the finance lease and that title remains with the lessor.

Security Interest versus Finance Lease

The Uniform Commercial Code defines a security interest in Section 1-201(37) as an interest in personal property or fixtures which secures payment or performance of an obligation. In a secured loan transaction, title to the equipment is held by the borrower. The borrower grants a security interest in the equipment so that in the event of default, the secured creditor can foreclose on the equipment and liquidate it to repay the obligations of the borrower. Under the terms of a finance lease, the finance lessor does not hold a security interest but is the owner of the equipment.

Sometimes, however, the question of whether the lessor is a secured creditor or a lessor is more difficult to determine. This may become a crucial issue in a bankruptcy case. The determination will be made by the facts in each situation. Section 1-201(37) of the Uniform Commercial Code provides further insight into the facts which help make this determination. A security interest in personal property or fixtures is defined as an interest which secures payment or performance of an obligation. The rights that a lessor holds under Article 2A to retain or acquire possession of the equipment is not a security interest. Article 2A provides that a transaction creates a security interest, if the amount the lessee is to pay the lessor for possession and use of the goods is an obligation for the term of the lease not subject to termination by the lessee and:

- the original term of the lease is equal to or greater than the remaining economic life of the goods,
- the lessee is bound to renew the lease for the remaining economic life of the goods or is bound to become the owner of the goods,
- the lessee has an option to renew the lease for the remaining economic life of the goods for no additional consideration or nominal additional consideration upon compliance with the lease agreement, or

- the lessee has an option to become the owner of the goods for no additional consideration or nominal additional consideration upon compliance with the lease agreement.

Moreover, a transaction does not create a security interest merely because it provides that the present value of the lease payments is substantially equal to or is greater than the fair market value of the equipment at the beginning of the lease. The fact that the lessee assumes risk of loss does not necessarily create a security interest nor does the fact that the lessee has an option to renew the lease or to become the owner of the goods create a security interest. A security interest is created if the price to be paid for the equipment at the termination of the lease is truly nominal and the above conditions are met. Where the residual value is less than 15 percent of the contract amount, courts tend to interpret it as a conditional sale "disguised" as a lease. Where the residual value of the equipment is 15 percent or more, the courts tend to see it as a "true lease."

CONSIDERATIONS IN BANKRUPTCY CASES

Among the ins and outs of leases, the credit professional needs to know the rights of the lessor when a lessee becomes delinquent or defaults. Because of the special treatment of leases in the commercial world, the drafters of the Uniform Commercial Code crafted Article 2A to deal with lease rights and enforcement.

Without realizing it, the lessor may become a secured creditor. As we have seen elsewhere in this *Manual*, the perfection of a security interest requires certain other steps, including the filing of a financing statement (*see* Chapter 10). In the event the lessor becomes a "secured creditor" and the lessee or debtor files for bankruptcy, many of the protections afforded the creditor as a lessor, then disappear.

Here are just a few examples:

- Under a true lease covered by Article 2A, a creditor who has reason to feel insecure about the debtor's likelihood of meeting lease payment obligations has a right to demand "adequate assurance" of future performance by the debtor. No such safeguard for the creditor exists with conditional sales agreements governed by Revised Article 9.
- Because conditional sales are secured transactions subject to Revised Article 9, the creditor's disposition rights regarding the equipment is subject to extensive notice obligations: notice to the debtor, to any guarantors or other third persons affected by the debt, other lien creditors holding rights in the collateral and lien creditors who have given the creditor notice of their claims. No such notice requirements exist under true leases covered under Article 2A.
- Under Article 2A lease agreements, no particular warranties arise to third party purchasers upon disposition of the equipment. If Revised Article 9 governs the disposition of the equipment, then warranties of title and quiet enjoyment as well as warranties of fitness and merchantability will apply unless effectively discharged.
- Whether a company is creating lease arrangements or reviewing a customer's credit in relation to another creditor's "lease," it is important that the people responsible understand the differences between a finance lease and a security agreement. It is always easy to add a purchase option at the end of the lease term, but it may dramatically change the rights of the lessor/lender/creditor.

SUMMARY OF STATE LAWS

Note: State legislatures will, on occasion, modify an area of law without clear delineation as to its content and context. As a result, even the changes which have been enacted prior to placement in the state's Code may be difficult to locate. As a result, the Editors urge all users of the *Manual* to use this publication only as a guide, and to consult the latest codified version of the state's law for all recent changes. Another excellent source for monitoring amendments to the Uniform Commercial Code is the National Conference of Commissioners on Uniform State Laws. Current status of legislation can be found on its webpage, www.nccusl.org/update.

At present, only Louisiana has not adopted Article 2A of the UCC. The table at the end of this chapter lists the statutory citations for each state, as well as highlighting certain Article 2A provisions that are non-uniform.

ALABAMA

Criminal Actions and Fraud—Lessee's sale or conversion of leased property is considered theft. Failure of lessee to return property within seven days after lessor's notice of demand is *prima facie* evidence of intent to sell or convert leased property. Use of false or noncurrent identification to obtain lease of property subjects property to return on lessor's demand whether or not lease term has expired.

Specific Lease Legislation—Motor vehicles.

Miscellaneous—Third party trespass gives both lessor and lessee a cause of action. Lessor may terminate the lease when lessee permits a use contrary to agreement or does not make repairs within a reasonable time after request.

ALASKA

Criminal Actions and Fraud—Lessee's refusal to return leased property, or sale or conversion of leased property, subjects lessee to fines and/or imprisonment. Leasing property with intent to defraud gives rise to criminal action. Misrepresentation or impersonation in obtaining property is *prima facie* evidence of intent to defraud.

Specific Lease Legislation—Motor vehicles.

Miscellaneous—Banks under certain conditions are permitted to lease personal property.

ARIZONA

Criminal Actions and Fraud—Lessee's failure to return leased property within 72 hours of the time provided in lease agreement without notice to and permission of lessor subjects lessee to fines and/or imprisonment.

Specific Lease Legislation—Motor vehicles, motorcycles and boats.

ARKANSAS

Specific Lease Legislation—Aircraft and motor vehicles.

Miscellaneous—Banks under certain conditions are permitted to lease personal property.

CALIFORNIA

Criminal Actions and Fraud—Lessee's failure to return property within 20 days of written demand after lease's expiration creates a presumption of intent to commit theft by fraud. If lessor fails to make a written demand of return within 30 days of the lease's expiration, no such presumption will arise. Lessee's use of false identification creates presumption of intent to commit theft by fraud.

Specific Lease Legislation—Charter parties, boats and motor vehicles. Leases of motor vehicles for over four months for primarily personal, family or household purposes are covered by the California Vehicle Leasing Act.

COLORADO

Criminal Actions and Fraud—Lessee subject to criminal action for obtaining property by threat or deception, or without consent of owner. Also liable for failure to return leased property within 72 hours of expiration of lease.

Specific Lease Legislation—Motor vehicles.

UCCC Consumer Leases—Colorado has adopted the Uniform Consumer Credit Code which contains provisions concerning the leasing of personal property. The Code governs all consumer leases, which are defined as leases of goods that a lessor regularly engaged in the business of leasing makes to a person, other than an organization, who takes under the lease primarily for a personal, family, household or agricultural purpose and in which the amount payable under the lease does not exceed $25,000, and which is for a term exceeding four months. The definition does not include a lease made pursuant to a lender credit card or similar arrangement.

The Code affords the lessee protection by requiring the consumer lessor to disclose with respect to all consumer leases the following information: (a) a description of goods, (b) the amount of the down payment required, (c) the official fees, (d) taxes and other charges, (e) the types and amounts of insurance provided by the lessor, (f) the number, amount, and due dates of periodic payments including the total amount payable by lessee, (g) the conditions for premature termination by the lessee, and (h) the extent of lessee's liability at the end of the term. In addition to the disclosure requirements, the Code forbids all false or misleading advertising concerning the terms or conditions of credit with respect to consumer leases.

Other significant provisions of the Code are:

(1) In all consumer leases except those primarily for agricultural purposes, the assignee of the rights of the lessor is subject to all claims and defenses of the lessee against the lessor arising from the lease of goods. The claim or defense may be asserted against the assignee only to the extent of the amount owing to the assignee with respect to the lease of the goods to which the claim or defense arose at the time the assignee had written notice of the claim or defense.

(2) At the expiration of a consumer lease, other than one primarily for agricultural purposes, the lessee's liability is limited to twice the average monthly periodic payment, but this limitation does not apply to charges for damages to leased property or for other default.

(3) The lessor may not take a security interest (other than a security deposit) in the lessee's property to secure the debt arising from the lease. Nor may the lessor obtain an assignment of the lessee's earnings for payment of the debt.

(4) The lessor is prohibited from offering a rebate or other arrangements of value in consideration of lessee giving names of prospective buyers or lessees if the rebate or arrangement is contingent upon events subsequent to the time lessee agrees to lease. An agreement in violation of this provision renders the lease unenforceable, or the lessee has the option of keeping the goods already delivered without any obligation to pay for them.

(5) The lessee must continue to pay the lessor directly until adequate notice of an assignment is given.

(6) The lease may provide that the lessee pay reasonable attorneys' fees not in excess of 15 percent of the unpaid debt after default and referral to an attorney not in the employ of lessor. The court may also prescribe an additional fee.

(7) The lessee cannot authorize anyone to confess a judgment arising from the lease.

(8) Rights or benefits under the Code may not be waived, but any claim arising from the Code which is disputed in good faith may be settled by agreement.

(9) Discrimination by a consumer lessor in consumer leases solely because of race, creed, religion, color, sex, marital status, national origin or ancestry is prohibited in cases in which the aggregate of the original unpaid balances arising from all consumer leases from such consumer lessor for the previous calendar year is greater than or equal to one million dollars.

Rental Purchase Agreement Act has been adopted to protect consumers against unfair practices and to provide disclosure.

CONNECTICUT

Criminal Actions and Fraud—Any lessee under written agreement who places property beyond the control of the lessor, conceals it or aids in its concealment, refuses to return it, sells or encumbers it without the written consent of the lessor and without notifying the transferee of the lease is subject to fine and/or imprisonment. Use of a false name or failure to return leased property within 10 days of expiration of the lease or within five days after lessor's written demand, whichever is later, is *prima facie* evidence of a violation. Lessee is guilty of conversion on failure to return leased property within 10 days after lease terminates or 192 hours after notice from lessor demanding return of property.

Specific Lease Legislation—Motor vehicles and watercraft.

Miscellaneous—Banks may enter into leases of personal property acquired upon the specific request of and for the use of a prospective lessee.

DELAWARE

Criminal Actions and Fraud—Any lessee who intentionally, fraudulently or by false pretenses takes, destroys, converts, wrongfully withholds, or appropriates leased personal property is guilty of theft. Failure to make payment at the agreed rental rate for the full lease period, use of false identification, and failure to return lease property within 10 days of the end of the contract are all evidence of theft.

Specific Lease Legislation—Aircraft and motor vehicles.

Miscellaneous—A lessor's license is required annually of all those engaged in business as a lessor of tangible personal property, unless otherwise licensed as a retailer. According to *Collier v. Leedom Construction Co.*, 84 F. Supp. 348 (D.C. Del. 1949), a lessor has a duty to mitigate damages. When a lessee gives notice of discontinuation of use of the leased property before expiration of the term of the lease, the lessor is only entitled to damages if he can show that he could not use the property or find a user for it.

DISTRICT OF COLUMBIA

Specific Lease Legislation—Motor vehicles.

FLORIDA

Criminal Actions and Fraud—If lessee with intent to defraud lessor, takes possession of property by trick, deceit, or fraudulent or willful false representation he is guilty of theft. Failure to return or make arrangements to return property within 10 days of lessor's proper written notice following expiration of lease, or use of false or noncurrent identification is *prima facie* evidence of intent to commit larceny. Failure to return leased motor vehicle, aircraft, boat or boat motor within 72 hours of agreed return time and date is *prima facie* evidence of intent to commit larceny.

Specific Lease Legislation—Motor vehicles.

GEORGIA

Criminal Actions and Fraud—Lessee liable to criminal penalties for selling or converting property without lessor's consent, or for wrongfully neglecting or refusing to surrender property upon expiration of lease. Conversion by the lessee is presumed when he violates his agreement by disposing of any part of the property without the consent of the lessor, permits its concealment or removal, or refuses to surrender at end of lease.

Specific Lease Legislation—Boats and motor vehicles.

Miscellaneous—In the case of third party trespass, if the trespass interferes with possession, lessee has cause of action; if trespass injures property or interferes with property rights, lessor also has cause of action. Under certain conditions, banks are permitted to lease personal property. In foreclosure actions, the owner of the leased property in a consumer rental transaction may obtain a writ of possession in order to regain possession of leased property. When the writ is obtained, the leased property must be delivered to the owner and need not be levied upon.

HAWAII

Criminal Actions and Fraud—Lessee of personal property, other than a rental motor vehicle, who knowingly or intentionally fails to return property within 14 days after return date is guilty of a petty misdemeanor unless he gives notice that he will be unable to return property by that date and the owner gives permission to extend that date.

Specific Lease Legislation—Aircraft and motor vehicles.

IDAHO

Criminal Actions and Fraud—*Prima facie* evidence of lessee's intent to embezzle exists if lessee fails to return property within 10 days of lease expiration and within 48 hours after written notice by lessor. Use of false or noncurrent identification is also *prima facie* evidence of intent to embezzle.

Specific Lease Legislation—Aircraft and livestock.

UCCC Consumer Leases—Follows general pattern set for above for Colorado with the following changes: A consumer lease includes all such leases for amounts payable not over $45,000, which amount is subject to adjustment. Idaho has no clause concerning discrimination. Payment by lessee of reasonable attorneys' fees upon default is not limited to 15 percent of the unpaid debt upon default.

ILLINOIS

Criminal Actions and Fraud—Lessee's failure to return leased property within 30 days of lessor's demand after expiration of the lease is *prima facie* evidence of knowingly exerting of unauthorized control over property.

Specific Lease Legislation—Motor vehicles.

Miscellaneous—If money advanced for security on payment of rentals, such money shall be deposited in a separate bank account along with a copy of the agreement. Banks have the power to lease personal property.

INDIANA

Criminal Actions and Fraud—Lessee is guilty of theft for obtaining possession of property by deception or threat with the purpose of avoiding payment of rent. Purpose of avoiding rent payments is inferred from refusal to pay or absconding without payment or offer to pay.

Specific Lease Legislation—Motor vehicles, snowmobiles and off-road vehicles.

UCCC Consumer Leases—Follows general pattern set forth above for Colorado with the following changes: Indiana has no provisions concerning false or misleading advertising. An agreement by lessee not to assert claims or defenses against assignee is enforceable if assignment was in good faith for value, notice of assignment was given lessee, assignee is not related to assignor and notice of any claims or defenses of lessee is not given to assignee within 60 days after receiving notice of the assignment. A rebate arrangement in consideration of lessee giving names of prospective buyers or lessees is allowed if only contingent upon prospective buyers or lessees submitting to an interview or demonstration. Payment by lessee of reasonable attorney's fees upon default is not limited to 15 percent of the unpaid debt upon default.

Miscellaneous—Banks or trust companies may be lessors of personal property under certain circumstances. Personal property of an estate may be leased in accordance with provisions of a will, or under court order. A bank may become lessor of personal property at the request of a customer.

IOWA

Specific Lease Legislation—Boats and motor vehicles.

UCCC Consumer Leases—Follows the general pattern set forth above for Colorado with the following changes: A consumer lease includes credit card transactions. An agreement by lessee not to assert claims or defenses against assignee is enforceable if assignment was in good faith for value, notice of assignment was given lessee, assignee is not related to assignor and any claims or defenses of lessee are not provided to assignee within 30 days after receiving notice of the assignment. No attorneys' fees awarded lessor upon lessee's default.

KANSAS

Criminal Actions and Fraud—Use of false identification or failure to return property within 10 days of expiration, unless the property is returned within seven days of lessor's notice, is *prima facie* evidence of lessee's intent to deprive lessor of property.

Specific Lease Legislation—Motor vehicles.

Miscellaneous—Banks under certain circumstances are permitted to lease personal property.

UCCC Consumer Leases—Follows general pattern set forth above for Colorado with the following changes: No attorneys' fees awarded lessor upon lessee's default. Lessee may assert claims and defenses against lessor's assignee only if he gives notice when requested to do so by lessor or assignee.

KENTUCKY

Criminal Actions and Fraud—Lessee cannot remove personal property to another location or relinquish custody without giving 10 days' written notice to lessor. To do so is *prima facie* evidence of intent to defraud and lessee is liable for fine and/or imprisonment.

Specific Lease Legislation—Motor vehicles and watercrafts.

Miscellaneous—Banks may under certain circumstances lease personal property. Assignee of lease in all but credit card transactions is subject to same defenses of lessee against lessor except in cases defined by any federal agency having jurisdiction.

LOUISIANA

Criminal Actions and Fraud—Upon lessee's default, lessor has the option either to cancel the lease and exercise rights granted him thereunder, including recovery of liquidated damages and/or other damages, or to enforce his claim for all rentals and other amounts due before property is leased out again. Lessor has the right to a speedy hearing to obtain a judgment ordering the lessee to surrender possession of the leased property and to obtain a writ of possession ordering surrender and sequestration of possession of the leased property. Lessor may also cancel lease for unauthorized use by lessee.

Specific Lease Legislation—Motor vehicles and musical instruments.

Miscellaneous—There is a Louisiana Consumer Credit Code governing consumer transactions.

MAINE

Criminal Actions and Fraud—Lessee is guilty of misdemeanor for fraudulent conversion of leased property. Failure to return or account for property is *prima facie* evidence of intent to convert, but prosecution may be brought only if lessee fails to return goods within 10 days after lessor's written demand.

Specific Lease Legislation—Motor vehicles.

UCCC Consumer Leases—There is a Maine Consumer Credit Code governing consumer leases. *See* Colorado above for general provisions. In Maine, however, amount payable under lease cannot exceed $55,000 and there is no exception for consumer leases for agricultural purposes.

MARYLAND

Criminal Actions and Fraud—Failure to redeliver is *prima facie* evidence of conversion. Fines and/or imprisonment may be levied against lessee for secretion or sale of property with intent to defraud or for removal of property from location without lessor's consent with intent to defraud. A Maryland resident will not be prosecuted if he restores the property or accounts for it within 10 days of written demand.

Specific Lease Legislation—Aircraft, batteries and motor vehicles.

Miscellaneous—Banks under certain circumstances may lease personal property. Lease of personal property is covered under the Maryland Consumer Protection Act, protecting consumers against false or misleading advertising or representations.

MASSACHUSETTS

Criminal Actions and Fraud—Lessee criminally liable for conversion of leased personal property without consent of and notice to lessor. Lessee guilty of larceny if with intent to conceal property lessee fails to return property within 10 days of the expiration of the lease or rental agreement. Use of false identification or failure to return the leased or rented property within 30 days of notice shall be *prima facie* evidence of intent not to return.

Specific Lease Legislation—Motor vehicles, aircraft and consumer leases not exceeding $25,000.

Miscellaneous—Trust companies operating banking departments may lease personal property under certain conditions. The use of leased personal property in connection with illegal sale of liquor is subject to criminal penalties. Leases are among the transactions covered by the Massachusetts Retail Installment Sales and Service Law. Lessee may cancel a lease with notice within three days of its consummation if not executed at lessor's place of business. Lessor of personal property for household use must identify such property as new or used.

MICHIGAN

Criminal Actions and Fraud—Lessee is guilty of larceny if after lessor's notice he refuses or willfully neglects to return property with intent to defraud. If property is worth less than $100, lessee is guilty of a misdemeanor.

Specific Lease Legislation—Motor vehicles, motorcycles and snowmobiles.

Miscellaneous—Banks may under certain circumstances lease personal property.

MINNESOTA

Criminal Actions and Fraud—Lessee is liable for theft for conversion of leased property and subject to fine and/or imprisonment. Use of fictitious identification or failure to return property within five days of personal service or certified or registered mailing of the lessor's written demand is evidence to commit theft.

Specific Lease Legislation—Motor bicycles, aircraft and motor vehicles.

Miscellaneous—Banks under certain circumstances may lease personal property.

MISSISSIPPI

Criminal Actions and Fraud—Fraudulent appropriations of leased property past expiration date of lease is embezzlement by lessee.

Specific Lease Legislation—Motor vehicles.

Miscellaneous—Permit required for leasing dealers. (Note: When a lessee is injured due to a defect in the leased property of which he is aware, the lessor, even if negligent in duty of inspection, is relieved of liability. *Runnels v. Dixie Drive-It-Yourself System Jackson Co.*, 71 So.2d 453, 220 Miss. 678 (1954).

MISSOURI

Criminal Actions and Fraud—If lessee, with intent to steal, fails to return leased personal property, he shall be deemed guilty of stealing. It is *prima facie* evidence of intent to steal if lessee fails to return property within 10 days of lessor's demand following expiration of the lease.

Specific Lease Legislation—Watercraft.

MONTANA

Criminal Actions and Fraud—Lessee who converts property, removes it without lessor's consent, or purposely or knowingly fails to return it after lessor's demand shall be guilty of larceny if done with intent to deprive lessor of his interest in the property. Lessee must repair all deterioration resulting from his negligence or due to foreseeable use.

Specific Lease Legislation—Motor vehicles and watercraft.

NEBRASKA

Criminal Actions and Fraud—If lessee converts, fails or refuses to return, or removes leased personal property, other than a motor vehicle, outside of the state without permission of the lessor, he is guilty of theft. *Prima facie* evidence of theft exists if lessee uses false identification or refuses to return the leased property within 10 days of receipt of notice that lease has expired. This last sentence must be included in the lease to preserve a cause of action. Any person destroying or changing the serial numbers on leased manufactured goods is guilty of a misdemeanor.

Specific Lease Legislation—Motor vehicles, watercrafts and trucks/tractor trailers.

Miscellaneous—Mayor and city council of first or second class cities may lease personal property for purposes for which they could buy personal property. Banks under certain circumstances may lease personal property.

NEVADA

Criminal Actions and Fraud—Obtaining or retaining possession of leased property through misrepresentation or artifice is larceny. Failure to return property within 72 hours of lessor's demand following expiration of lease with intent to defraud is larceny. Failure to return property to place specified is *prima facie* evidence of intent to defraud or retain possession.

Specific Lease Legislation—Gaming equipment, railroads, motor vehicles, watercraft and aircraft.

NEW HAMPSHIRE

Criminal Actions and Fraud—If lessee fails to return property upon expiration of lease and refuses or willfully neglects to return the property on lessor's written demand, he is guilty of larceny. False identification and failure to return on written demand are *prima facie* evidence of intent to commit larceny. A person is guilty of theft if he intentionally fails to comply with the terms of a rental or lease agreement concerning the return of property, if such noncompliance constitutes a gross deviation from the agreement.

Specific Lease Legislation—Aircraft, motor vehicles and criminal provision regarding all propelled vehicles.

NEW JERSEY

Lessor's Statutory Obligations—None.

Specific Lease Legislation—Aircraft, motor vehicles and sanitation supplies.

NEW MEXICO

Criminal Actions and Fraud—Procuring lease with false identification subjects lessee to criminal penalties. Failure to return, according to specific written arrangements, with intent to defraud is a criminal violation. Failure to return within 72 hours after written demand creates presumption of intent to defraud.

Specific Lease Legislation—Motor vehicles and watercraft.

NEW YORK

Specific Lease Legislation—Aircraft and motor vehicles.

Miscellaneous—Under certain circumstances, banks and trust companies may lease personal property.

NORTH CAROLINA

Criminal Actions and Fraud—Willful or malicious damage, fraudulent conversion, subletting without lessor's consent, failure to return property at expiration of lease and misrepresentation with intent to defraud are misdemeanors punishable by fine and/or imprisonment. But if the value of the property fraudulently converted exceeds $400, the lessee is guilty of a felony. Intent to convert leased property is shown *prima facie* if lessee fails to return property within 10 days after expiration of lease and within 48 hours of lessor's written demand, or if lease was procured with false identification.

Specific Lease Legislation—Aircraft, livestock, motor vehicles, plus others covered in general leasing law.

NORTH DAKOTA

Lessor's Statutory Obligations—Lessor must secure lessee's quiet enjoyment, put property into condition fit for use for which it was let and repair deterioration not lessee's fault and not the result of normal use. If he fails to do this, lessee can expend and recover the necessary amounts. Lessor responsible for all expenses not natural or foreseeable.

Criminal Action and Fraud—Lessee must use ordinary care for preservation of property and may be held absolutely liable for safety of property or lessor may rescind lease. Lessee must bear all natural and foreseeable expenses.

Specific Lease Legislation—Aircraft and motor vehicles.

Miscellaneous—Banks under certain circumstances may lease personal property.

OHIO

Criminal Actions and Fraud—Lessee cannot lease any aircraft, motor vehicle, motorcycle, motorboat, sailboat, camper, trailer or horse and buggy with intent to defraud. *Prima facie* evidence of intent to defraud exists if lessee uses deception to hire one of above-mentioned properties, hires them knowing he cannot pay, absconds without payment, knowingly fails to pay or return property without a reasonable excuse, or knowingly fails to return the hired property without reasonable excuse. Violation is a misdemeanor, or felony for recidivism.

Specific Lease Legislation—Watercraft.

Miscellaneous—Banks under certain circumstances may lease personal property. "Consumer transactions" include leases whose purpose is primarily personal, family, or household and are governed by the Ohio retail installment sales law.

OKLAHOMA

Criminal Actions and Fraud—Lessee's fraudulent failure to return leased property within 10 days of lease's expiration or fraudulent secretion or appropriation of the property is embezzlement.

Specific Lease Legislation—Motor vehicles, oil and gas well equipment and watercraft.

Miscellaneous—Banks under certain circumstances may lease personal property.

UCCC Consumer Leases—Follows general pattern set forth above for Colorado with the following changes: A consumer lease includes such lease for amounts payable not over $45,000. Oklahoma forbids discrimination in leasing based upon sex or marital status. An agreement by lessee not to assert claims or defenses against assignee is enforceable if assignment was in good faith for value, notice of assignment given lessee, assignee not related to assignor, and notice of any claims or defenses of lessee is not given to assignee within 30 days after receiving notice of the assignment.

OREGON

Specific Lease Legislation—Aircraft, motor vehicles and watercraft.

PENNSYLVANIA

Criminal Actions and Fraud—A lessee of personal property is guilty of theft if he intentionally sells, secretes, destroys, converts to his own use, or otherwise disposes of the property. There is a presumption of theft if the person uses a false name and fails to return the property on time or fails to return the property within seven days after written demand is delivered by registered or certified mail to the lessee's last known address.

Specific Lease Legislation—Aircraft.

Miscellaneous—Savings banks are permitted under certain circumstances to lease personal property. Lessor may pursue civil action for theft of leased property.

RHODE ISLAND

Specific Lease Legislation—Horses and carriages, motor vehicles and watercraft.

SOUTH CAROLINA

Criminal Actions and Fraud—Lessee's willful and fraudulent failure to return leased property within 72 hours after lease's expiration or secretion or unauthorized use is larceny.

Specific Lease Legislation—Aircraft and watercraft.

UCCC Consumer Leases—Lease qualifying as a "consumer lease" is covered by South Carolina's Consumer Protection Code. *See* Colorado consumer credit code for general provisions.

SOUTH DAKOTA

Criminal Actions and Fraud—Any person who knowingly converts leased or rented personal property after having received a written demand sent by certified or registered mail to the lessee is guilty of theft. The defenses available to the lessee are: (1) at the time of the lease, lessee accurately stated name and address, (2) the failure to return was lawful, (3) the lessee failed to receive the written demand personally, and (4) the lessee returned the property and paid any added charges or damages to the leased property.

Specific Lease Legislation—Aircraft and watercraft.

Miscellaneous—Banks under certain conditions may lease personal property.

TENNESSEE

Criminal Actions and Fraud—Appropriation by lessee of lessor's property is larceny. Failure to return property with fraudulent intent within 10 days after lessor's written demand or use of false identification and failure to return property upon expiration of lease are both counts of larceny. Failure to return property within such time or use of false identification is *prima facie* evidence of intent to defraud.

Specific Lease Legislation—Aircraft, livestock and livery vehicles and watercraft.

Miscellaneous—Banks under certain conditions may lease personal property.

TEXAS

Specific Lease Legislation—Motor vehicles.

Miscellaneous—Banks under certain conditions may lease personal property.

UTAH

Specific Lease Legislation—Motor vehicles and watercraft.

UCCC Consumer Leases—The UCCC is not applicable to consumer leases; it is only applicable to consumer credit sales and consumer loans.

VERMONT

Criminal Actions and Fraud—Lessee's conversion of rental property, removal from state or failure to return as agreed subjects lessee to fine and/or imprisonment. Failure to return property within 72 hours of lessor's demand or within 15 days of expiration of lease or use of false identification is evidence of intent to commit larceny.

Specific Lease Legislation—Aircraft and watercraft.

VIRGINIA

Criminal Actions and Fraud—Willful injury to or unauthorized subletting of leased property is a misdemeanor. Lessee's conversion of leased property with intent to defraud, fraudulent removal of property from the state without lessor's permission, or failure to return property within 10 days of lease's expiration subjects lessee to penalties for larceny. Failure to return property within five or 10 days, depending on the property leased, of lessor's demand following expiration of lease is *prima facie* evidence of intent to defraud. Procuring rental property by use of false identification or misrepresentation with intent to defraud is a misdemeanor. Failure to pay rent, or absconding without payment, is *prima facie* evidence of intent to defraud at time of leasing.

Specific Lease Legislation—Motor vehicles, aircraft, livestock and watercraft.

Miscellaneous—Banks under certain conditions may lease personal property.

WASHINGTON

Criminal Actions and Fraud—Conversion or destruction and failure to return leased property within 10 days of lessor's notice of expiration of lease is a gross misdemeanor. Willful failure to return a leased motor vehicle worth more than $1,500 within five business days from receipt of the lessor's written demand therefor is a class C felony.

Specific Lease Legislation—Motor vehicles, motorcycles and dune buggies.

Miscellaneous—Lease transactions are regulated under a separate consumer leasing law.

WEST VIRGINIA

Specific Lease Legislation—Motor vehicles and watercraft.

Miscellaneous—Banks may under certain circumstances lease personal property. A lease qualifying as a "consumer lease" is governed by West Virginia's Consumer Credit Act.

WISCONSIN

Criminal Actions and Fraud—Failure to return lease property within 10 days of expiration of lease is a misdemeanor if property is valued under $500 and a felony if valued above $500.

Specific Lease Legislation—Motor vehicles, livestock.

UCCC Consumer Leases—Leases qualifying as "consumer leases" are governed by Wisconsin Consumer Act.

WYOMING

Specific Lease Legislation—Watercraft.

UCCC Consumer Leases—Follows general pattern set forth for Colorado with the following changes: A consumer lease includes all such leases payable in five or more installments. Wyoming has no provisions concerning discrimination in leases. An agreement by lessee not to assert claims or defenses against assignee is enforceable if assignment was in good faith for value, notice of assignment was given lessee, assignee is not related to assignor, and notice of any claims or defenses of lessee is not given to assignee within 45 days after receiving notice of the assignment. Wyoming allows an assignment of commissions or accounts receivable payable to lessee for payment of debts arising from consumer leases. Award of attorneys' fees is not limited to 15 percent of the unpaid debt.

Refer to Chapter 27 for the following forms:

- Lease of Personal Property
- Release of Lease of Personal Property

STATES ADOPTING ARTICLE 2A

STATE	CORRESPONDING STATE STATUTES BEGIN AT:	ADOPTS OPTIONAL LANGUAGE LIMITING TOTAL PAYMENTS FOR CONSUMER LEASES? (2A-103)	2A-103 MAXIMUM AMOUNT ($)	2A-216 ALTERNATIVE (A,B, or C)	OTHER NOTES
ALABAMA	7-2A-101	yes	100,000	B	
ALASKA	45.12.101	no	—	B	
ARIZONA	47-2A101	yes	25,000	A	Parties to the lease may determine the risk of loss by written agreement. (2A-219)
ARKANSAS	4-2A-101	yes	25,000	C	
CALIFORNIA	CA Coml 10101	no	—		1. Omits sections on Unconscionability (2A-108), Option to Accelerate at Will (2A-109), Seals (2A-203), and Third Party Beneficiaries of Express and Implied Warranties (2A-216). 2. 2A-307(4) contains no references to 45-day period. 3. 2A-308(2) (Special Rights of Creditors) omits section (a). 4. The time for perfection of the lessor's interest by a fixture filing is 20 days rather than 10. (2A-309(4)(a)) 5. 2A-309(9) omitted. 6. Parties may reduce the period of limitation to not less than one year only in a lease that is not a consumer lease. (2A-506)
COLORADO	4-2.5-101	yes	25,000	C	1. Liens upon goods given by statute or rule of law to one who furnishes services or materials for goods subject to a lease contract take priority only over interests of the party to the lease contract at whose instance the services or materials were furnished. (2A-306) 2. Statute of limitations is governed by section 13-80-101, CRS, which may not be varied by agreement of the parties. (2A-506) 3. 2A-518, 2A-519, 2A-527, and 2A-528 all allow for recovery of interest. 4. In the event of lessee's default, lessor has choice of present value or damages as provided in 2A-528(1). (2A-528(2)) 5. Colorado adds a section providing that a party to a lease contract, at its option, may, for the other party's default, recover any damages, determined in any reasonable manner, additional to or different from those provided as may be necessary to put the party in as good a position as if the other party had performed in accordance with the lease contract. (2A-506)
CONNECTICUT	42a-2a-101	no	—	B	
DELAWARE	2A-101	no	—	C	Effective October 1, 2002.

STATES ADOPTING ARTICLE 2A *(Continued)*

STATE	CORRESPONDING STATE STATUTES BEGIN AT:	ADOPTS OPTIONAL LANGUAGE LIMITING TOTAL PAYMENTS FOR CONSUMER LEASES? (2A-103)	2A-103 MAXIMUM AMOUNT ($)	2A-216 ALTERNATIVE (A,B, or C)	OTHER NOTES
D.C.	28:02A-0101	yes	25,000	C	
FLORIDA	680.101	*	*	*	
GEORGIA	11-2A-101	no	—	A	
HAWAII	490:2A-101	yes	25,000	C	
IDAHO	28-12-101	yes	25,000	A	
ILLINOIS	2A-101	yes	40,000	C	
INDIANA	26-1-2.1-101	yes	25,000	A	Indiana adds a non-Code section (26-1-3-103.5) stating that provisions of 2A which apply to a bank apply equally to any supervised financial organization which is authorized by state or federal law to permit persons to make withdrawals or payments from accounts by negotiable instruments.
IOWA	554.13101	yes	25,000	C	(none)
KANSAS	84-2A-101	yes	25,000	C	
KENTUCKY	335.2A-101	no	—	A	1. In an action in which the lessee claims unconscionability, if the court does not find unconscionability (Kentucky removes the requirement that the lessee brought an action the lessee knew to be groundless), the award of reasonable attorney's fees to the party against whom the claim was made is discretionary. (2A-108(4)(b)) 2. Dollar value in statute of frauds provision is $500. (2A-201(1)(a))
MAINE	2-1101	yes	25,000	C	In consumer leases that are not finance leases, the lessor's ability to modify or exclude any implied warranties or consumer's remedies for breach of those warranties is governed by 2-316(5). (2A-214)
MARYLAND	Md Coml 2A-101	no		A	1. 2A-104—Excludes consumer goods and motor vehicle transactions. 2. 2A-214—Limits disclaimer of warranties in consumer goods and motor vehicle transactions.
MASSACHUSETTS	440.280	no		***	2A-214—Excludes consumer leases from applicability of this section.
MICHIGAN	19.2A101	yes	25,000	A	

MINNESOTA	336.2A-101	yes	25,000	C	1. Minnesota's definition of finance lease does not conform to 1987 or 1990 official text of 2A-103(g)(iii). Minnesota's section reads: (3) either (i) the lessee receives a copy of the contract evidencing the lessor's purchase of the goods or a disclaimer statement on or before signing the lease contract, or (ii) the lessee's approval of the contract evidencing the lessor's purchase of the goods or a disclaimer statement is a condition to effectiveness of the lease contract. Disclaimer statement is defined as a written statement that is part of or separate from the lease contract that discloses all warranties and other rights provided to the lessee by the lessor and supplier in connection with the lease contract and informs the lessee in a conspicuous manner that there are no warranties or other rights provided to the lessee by the lessor and supplier other than those disclosed in the statement. 2. 1990 Amendment to 2A-104 not adopted. (Minnesota statute does not include wording on court decisions or statutes of the United States.) 3. In an action in which the lessee claims unconscionability with respect to a consumer lease, if the court finds unconscionability, the award of reasonable attorney's fees is discretionary rather than mandatory. (2A-108) 4. The court may award reasonable attorney's fees to the party against whom a claim of unconscionability is brought if the court does not find unconscionability (Minnesota removes the requirement that lessee has brought an action lessee knew to be groundless). (2A-108) 5. 2A-109(2) omitted. 6. Parties may reduce the period of limitation to not less than one year in the original lease contract only if the lease is not a consumer lease. (2A-506) 7. 2A-529(5) retains original (1987) language.[1] 8. 2A-532 is combined with 2A-529.
MISSISSIPPI	75-2A-101	yes	25,000	A	1. Certificate of title statute of the state, including but not limited to, those pertaining to motor vehicles in Chapter 21, Title 63, Mississippi Code of 1972. 2. 2A-201(1)(a)—$1,000. 3. 2A-407(3)—Validity of lease terms which make lessee's promise irrevocable and independent of acceptance not affected. 4. 2A-517(2) & (3)—Lessee may revoke acceptance of lot or commercial unit if lessor defaults under lease and default substantially impairs value of lot or unit.
MISSOURI	400.2A.101	yes	50,000	A	
MONTANA	30-2A-101	yes	25,000	A	
NEBRASKA	2A-101	yes	25,000	A	2A-529(5) retains original (1987) language.[1]
NEVADA	104A.2101	no	—	A	Parties may reduce the period of limitation to not less than one year only in a lease that is not a consumer lease.
NEW HAMPSHIRE	382-A:2-A-101	no	—	A	

STATES ADOPTING ARTICLE 2A *(Continued)*

STATE	CORRESPONDING STATE STATUTES BEGIN AT:	ADOPTS OPTIONAL LANGUAGE LIMITING TOTAL PAYMENTS FOR CONSUMER LEASES? (2A-103)	2A-103 MAXIMUM AMOUNT ($)	2A-216 ALTERNATIVE (A,B, or C)	OTHER NOTES
NEW JERSEY	12A:2A-101	no	—	A	
NEW MEXICO	55-2A-101	no	—	A	
NEW YORK	UCC-2-A-101	no	—	B	
NORTH CAROLINA	25-2A-101	yes	25,000	A	1. The term for a lease contract which is enforceable under 2A-201(4) may also be determined by evidence of the parties' intent. In the absence of such evidence, a reasonable lease term will be supplied. (2A-201(5)(c) 2. A lessee who has rightfully rejected goods, or justifiably revoked acceptance of the goods, shall account to the lessor for any excess over the amount of the lessee's security interest. (2A-508(5))
NORTH DAKOTA	41-02.1-01	yes	25,000	C	
OHIO	1310.01	no	—	C	Ohio does not provide that leases subject to 2A are also subject to consumer protection decisions of the courts. (2A-104)
OKLAHOMA	12A Section 2A-201	yes	45,000	A	
OREGON	72A.1010	yes	25,000	A	1. 2A-106(1) applies to residence of lessee or lessor. 2. To aid the court in determining unconscionability, the parties to the lease shall be afforded an opportunity to present evidence as to the commercial setting, purpose and effect of the lease. (2A-108) 3. It is reasonable to include a provision in the lease which states that damages in the event of the lessee's default and lessor's sale of the goods include, in addition to costs payable to third parties, any past due amounts plus the sum of the present value of future rentals, the lessor's costs of enforcing the lease, the lessor's reasonably predictable residual at expiration, reasonable compensation for any loss of tax benefits, or an equivalent amount, and any other damages suffered or to be suffered because of the lessee's default, less the net proceeds of sale. (2A-504) 4. By the original lease contract the parties may reduce the period of limitation to not less than two years. (2A-506) 5. Oregon adds a non-Code section (72A-5295), which provides as follows: "In addition to any other recovery permitted by any other law or chapter 2A, a lessor may recover from the lessee an amount that will fully compensate the lessor for any loss of or damage to the lessor's residual interest in the goods caused by the default of the lessee."

State	Citation				Notes
PENNSYLVANIA	2A101	yes	25,000	A	1. Pennsylvania does not provide that leases subject to 2A are also subject to consumer protection decisions of the courts. (2A-104). 2. Text of 2A-529(5) conforms to 1987 version.[1]
RHODE ISLAND	6A-2.1-101	no	—	C	
SOUTH CAROLINA	37-2A-101	yes	25,000	C	UCCC 37-2-101
SOUTH DAKOTA	57A-2A-101	*	*	*	*
TENNESSEE					Effective July 1, 1994.
TEXAS	2A.101	yes	25,000	**	1. This chapter does not apply to a transaction that creates an interest in or lease of real estate, except to the extent that provision is made for leases of fixtures. (2A-102) 2. Omits 2A-207, 2A-308(2)(a), 2A-311, 2A-407(3). 3. By the original lease contract, parties may not expand the period of limitation, but may reduce the period to not less than one year in the case of a consumer lease. (2A-506(1)) 4. A cause of action for indemnity accrues: (1) in the case of an indemnity against liability, when the act or omission on which the claim for indemnity is based is or should have been discovered by the indemnified party; or (2) in the case of an indemnity against loss or damage, when the person indemnified makes payment thereof. (2A-506(2)) 5. Omits 2A-511(2). 6. Adds subsections to 2A-512, providing that a merchant lessee is entitled to reimbursement for reasonable expenses for caring for and disposing of the goods; the lessee is held only to a good faith standard in complying with this section; and a purchaser who purchases in good faith from a lessee under this section takes the goods free of any rights of the lessor and supplier even though the lessee fails to comply with one or more of the requirements of this chapter. 7. 2A-529(5) retains 1987 official language.[1]
UTAH	70A-2a-101	no	—	A	1. $1,000 total dollar value in statute of frauds provision applies only to lease contracts that are not consumer leases. (2A-201(1)(a)) 2. There is no requirement that a signed lease agreement between merchants on a form supplied by a merchant excluding modification or rescission must be signed by the other party. (2A-208(2)) 3. A creditor of a lessor takes subject to the lease contract unless: (i) the creditor holds a security interest that attached and was perfected before the lease contract became enforceable; (ii) the lessee gave value and received delivery of the goods; or (iii) in the case of a purchase money security interest, the date that is 10 days after the date that the lessor received possession of the goods or the date that the lessee received possession of the goods, whichever is earlier.

STATES ADOPTING ARTICLE 2A (Continued)

The following notes (items 4–7) continue from the preceding page:

4. Omits 2A-308(2)(a).
5. A cause of action for indemnity accrues: (1) in the case of an indemnity against liability, when the act or omission on which the claim for indemnity is based is or should have been discovered by the indemnified party; or (2) in the case of an indemnity against loss or damage, when the person indemnified makes payment thereof. (2A-506(2))
6. 2A-516(3) does not contain language excepting consumer leases.
7. In the event of lessee's default, if a lessor elects to retain the goods or a lessor elects to dispose of the goods and the disposition is by lease agreement whether or not the lease agreement qualifies for treatment under 2A-527(2), the lessor may recover damages for a default of the type described in 2A-523. (2A-528)

STATE	CORRESPONDING STATE STATUTES BEGIN AT:	ADOPTS OPTIONAL LANGUAGE LIMITING TOTAL PAYMENTS FOR CONSUMER LEASES? (2A-103)	2A-103 MAXIMUM AMOUNT ($)	2A-216 ALTERNATIVE (A,B, or C)	OTHER NOTES
VERMONT	9A V.S.A.2A-101	no	—	B	2A-214—Excludes consumer leases from applicability of this section.
VIRGINIA	8.2A-101	no	—	***	
WASHINGTON	62A-2A-101	yes	25,000	A	1. Washington does not provide that leases subject to 2A are also subject to consumer protection decisions of the court. (2A-104(1)(c)) 2. The court shall allow a reasonable opportunity to present evidence to a lease or clause's commercial setting, purpose, and effect to aid the court in making a determination as to unconscionability. (2A-108(2)) 3. Omits 2A-108(3) and (4), 2A-109. 4. The time for perfection of the lessor's interest by a fixture filing is 20 days rather than 10. 2A-309(4)(a)
WEST VIRGINIA	42-2A-101	yes	25,000	A	The optional language of 2A-103 limiting consumer payments was not adopted.
WISCONSIN	411.101	yes	25,000	A	
WYOMING	34.1-2.A-101	yes	25,000	C	

* Florida's and South Dakota's versions of UCC 2A vary significantly from the 1991 version. See those states' statutes for details.
** Texas leaves the determination of validity of third-party beneficiaries of express and implied warranties to the courts.
*** Maryland and Virginia adopt language, similar to Alternative C, declaring that lack of "privity" between Plaintiff and Defendant is no defense.
¹ 1987 Official Version of 2A-529(5) reads as follows: "After a lessee has wrongfully rejected or revoked acceptance of goods, has failed to pay rent then due, or has repudiated, a lessor who is held not entitled to rent under this section must nevertheless be awarded damages for non-acceptance under Section 2A-527 or Section 2A-528."

9 Negotiable Instruments: Notes, Checks, Drafts—How They Work—and Interest Rates

Article 3 of the Uniform Commercial Code is the statutory law governing checks, promissory notes, drafts, trade acceptances and similar instruments. Article 4 of the Code governs bank deposits and collections that include the banker-depositor relationship and the responsibilities, obligations and liabilities of handling instruments. Article 5 of the Code governs letters of credit, an important commercial instrument.

In this chapter the general provisions of this law relating to negotiable instruments and letters of credit are summarized; trade and bank acceptances, judgment notes, attorneys' fees, negotiable instruments, checks for less than one dollar, checks marked "full payment" remitted in payment of an account, and interest and usury are treated and discussed.

Articles 3 and 4 of the Uniform Commercial Code have been adopted and are effective in the District of Columbia, the Virgin Islands and every state. The revisions of Articles 3 and 4 were a companion undertaking to the drafting of Article 4A on funds transfers. Both efforts were undertaken for the purpose of accommodating modern technologies and practices in payment systems and negotiable instruments. The revisions of Articles 3 and 4 were completed in 1990 and have been enacted in all states; however, the state of New York has not yet adopted the Revision. Article 5 was revised in 1995 and has been adopted in every state except Wisconsin, whose legislature introduced the Revision in 2002.

The original Article 3 (and Article 4) reflected a paper-based payment system. They did not adequately address the issues of responsibility and liability as they relate to modern technologies (such as truncation) and the procedures required by the current volume of checks and the Expedited Funds Availability Act. Also, other practices have arisen which are not accommodated within Article 3, such as variable rate notes and the question of "cash equivalency" of cashier's checks and money orders. The revised Article 3 accommodates changing practices and modern technologies, as well as the needs of a global business environment. The Revision as enacted in the different states varies in minor details to some extent, but the principal provisions are practically identical in all of the states. *See* Chapter 7 for a general discussion of the provisions of the Code. *See* Chapter 10 for more detailed information on Article 9 of the UCC.

Article 4 of the UCC deals with banking transactions, particularly as they may affect negotiable instruments as contained in Article 3 of the UCC. With the adoption of the Expedited Funds Availability Act and Regulations CC and J, a number of the provisions of old Article 4 were superseded by the federal statute and related regulations. Recently, an effort to revise Article 4 by including Regulation CC in the statute was abandoned. Elsewhere in this chapter there is a detailed discussion of the federal provisions. In Chapter 7, the section dealing with Article 4 of the

Uniform Commercial Code delineates those areas of the UCC that have been superseded by federal law. Unfortunately, this now requires the credit professional to be knowledgeable not only of the Uniform Commercial Code, but also of federal laws and regulatory enactments and their effect.

WHAT INSTRUMENTS ARE NEGOTIABLE

The importance to those interested in a transaction of determining whether an instrument is negotiable is based principally on the fact that the rights of transferees of negotiable paper are much more protected against defenses where the paper is in the hands of a bona fide holder in due course than the rights of transferees of non-negotiable instruments (i.e., assignees) who ordinarily are subject to the same defenses as may be interposed against the payee or transferor (i.e., assignor).

In order to be negotiable, Section 3-104(a) of the UCC provides that the instrument must be in writing; signed by the maker or drawer; contain an unconditional promise or order to pay a sum certain in money; be payable on demand or at a fixed date or a determinable future time; be payable to order or to bearer; and where addressed to a drawee, the drawee must be named or otherwise indicated therein with reasonable certainty.

Article 3 treats as negotiable an instrument which otherwise meets the definition of a negotiable instrument but does not contain an order. Thus, an instrument made payable to a person as opposed to payable to the order of a person can be a negotiable instrument. Under the former Article 3, "pay to" instruments were considered non-negotiable because of the absence of order language. Idaho, Louisiana, Mississippi, New York, Oregon, Tennessee and Virginia have enacted statutes which provide that negotiability is not destroyed by a promissory note with a variable rate of interest which is legal and readily ascertainable by an objective standard as compared to a fixed rate of interest (for example, "prime" plus two percent). These states provide that a variable rate of interest is a "stated rate of interest" as required for a note in order to be negotiable under the UCC. In some additional states variable rate interest notes may also be accepted by case law or common practice, but in other states a note with a variable rate of interest may destroy negotiability. Consequently, it is important to check applicable state law.

Pursuant to UCC § 3-104(e) and (f), if the instrument contains a *promise* to pay, it is a note; if it contains an *order* to pay, it is a draft; a draft drawn on a bank and payable on demand is a check. A "cashier's check" is defined as a check although it technically is a draft (the draft is drawn by a bank on itself, i.e., it is both drawer and drawee). *See* UCC § 3-104(g).

Negotiability is not affected by the want of a date, the failure to specify a consideration, the failure to specify the place where it is drawn or is payable, the fact that it has a seal or lacks a seal, or the fact that it designates a particular kind of currency or money in which payment is to be made. The Code under Sections 3-108 and 3-109 also expressly defines when an instrument is payable on demand, when payable to order and when payable to bearer.

Under the Code, "negotiation" requires transfer of possession of the instrument (delivery with) any necessary indorsement so that the transferee becomes a holder. A "holder" under UCC § 3-201 is a person in possession of an instrument which is drawn or indorsed to him or to his order or to bearer or in blank. Only a holder or one with rights of a holder can enforce an instrument according to UCC § 3-301. No consideration is necessary for a valid negotiation; however the payment of value is a requirement for a holder to qualify as a "holder in due course" (see UCC § 3-302(a)(2)), a status which affords greater rights than that of a mere holder.

A brief diversion for a moment is in order. The Code relentlessly spells indorsement with an "i." For a humorous explanation of why bankers routinely stamp checks "PEG" (prior endorsements guaranteed), *see Perini Corp. v. First Nat'l Bank*, 553 F.2d 398, 401 (fn. 1) (5th Cir. 1977).

Date. It has long been held that an instrument need not be dated to be negotiable; (UCC § 3-113) the materiality of a date is to be determined when the instrument is payable, but where dated, the date is *prima facie* the true date. When undated, the instrument is considered dated as of the time issued. UCC § 3-113(b). If the date is omitted, any holder may insert the true date. Ante-dating or post-dating does not invalidate the instrument or prevent the instrument from being negotiable unless done for an illegal or fraudulent purpose. The post-dating of a check does not prevent the instrument from being negotiated nor prevent the taker from becoming a holder or holder in due course, and does not preclude the drawee from paying the instrument prior to its stated date. If a drawee pays a post-dated check prior to its stated due date, the drawee merely cannot charge to the drawer's account the amount paid on the instrument until its date, as it is on that date when the item becomes properly payable *against* the drawer's account.

Nebraska amended the UCC to provide that a bank may charge the account of a customer with any item that is otherwise properly payable from that account even though payment is made before the date of the check, unless the customer has given notice to the bank of the post-dating and described the item with reasonable certainty.

Blanks. An incomplete instrument may be completed by the holder (the person in possession) consistent with authority granted therefor. Even where the instrument is completed not in accordance with the authority given, a bona fide holder in due course may recover on the instrument as completed. By signing an instrument with blanks, the drawer assumes the risk that the item will be completed improperly and, if it comes into the hands of a bona fide holder when completed, it may be enforced by the holder as completed.

Delivery. Delivery of an instrument is necessary to a negotiation and to make a binding contract. For example, if a drawer draws a check but never delivers it to the payee but the payee nevertheless obtains possession, the drawer has a defense to the claim of the payee on the instrument. A valid delivery will be presumed where the instrument is in the hands of a holder in due course.

RULES OF CONSTRUCTION

On occasion, an instrument will contain contradictory terms, usually the amount written in numbers is different than the amount written in words. Where an instrument contains contradictory terms, UCC § 3-114 provides that typewritten terms prevail over printed terms, handwritten terms prevail over both and words prevail over numbers. Unless an instrument provides that it is payable with interest, the Code considers the instrument as payable without interest (see UCC § 3-112(a)). Where the instrument provides that it is payable with interest, interest runs from the date of the item unless otherwise specified. If the instrument is ambiguous whether it is a draft or note, the holder may treat it as either. If it is not clear in what capacity a person intended to sign, the signer is deemed an indorser. The words "I promise to pay," where the instrument is signed by two or more, make them jointly and severally liable.

Persons Liable. Pursuant to UCC § 3-401(a) no person is liable on an instrument unless his signature appears thereon. A signature made by an agent authorized to sign by and for the principal will bind the principal. Unless the agent clearly indicates that he is signing in a representative capacity, he may also be held liable on the instrument to a holder in due course without knowledge of the agency.

Indorser before Delivery. A person placing his signature upon an instrument other than as a maker, drawer or acceptor is deemed an indorser and liable as such unless a contrary intention is clearly indicated by appropriate words. This settles a point about which there was conflict with many states holding such an indorser liable as a maker.

Consideration. A valuable consideration is presumed. An antecedent or preexisting debt is a sufficient consideration, and one having a lien on the instrument is deemed a holder for value.

Accommodation Party. A person who signs, with or without receiving any consideration for the purpose of lending his name (and credit) to some other party, is liable (as an indorser) to a holder for value, although such holder knew the party to be only an accommodation party.

Acceptance. Pursuant to UCC § 3-409, acceptance is necessary to charge the drawee of a check or payor of a draft. Acceptance is the drawee's signed engagement to pay the instrument. Presentment for acceptance, unless excused, is necessary in case of time drafts to fix their maturity; where presentment is stipulated for in the drafts; and where the draft is payable elsewhere than at the residence or place of business of the drawee. Acceptance must be in writing and signed by the drawee. Certification of a check is acceptance under UCC § 3-409(d). A bank's certification of its customer's check at the request of the holder results in the discharge of the drawer and indorsers because the certification represents the bank's agreement to pay. Where the drawer obtains certification before delivering the check to the payee, the drawer is not discharged and the drawer retains the right to direct the drawee to stop payment. Unless it has agreed otherwise, a drawee of a check has no obligation to accept, and failure or refusal to certify is not a dishonor. This is because an ordinary check is a demand item which calls for payment, not acceptance. A letter of credit may call for the presentation of a draft for acceptance, and the issuer "honors" a conforming presentation by acceptance of the draft and paying it at maturity. UCC § 5-102(a)(8)(ii). *See* Chapter 7 for more information on letters of credit. An ordinary check is not an assignment of funds in the hands of the drawee and is not an obligation of the drawee until it accepts the check. According to UCC § 3-408. Thus, if a drawee dishonors an ordinary check, whether rightfully or wrongfully, the payee or holder has no claim against the drawee; however, the drawer may have a claim for wrongful dishonor.

Under Article 3, presentment for payment must be made at a reasonable hour and may be on any day on which presentment for payment may be made. If made at a bank, presentment must be made during its banking day. If presentment is due on a day which is not a full business day, either because it is an official holiday or merely because of a practice to close for a full or a half day, the time for presentment is extended and presentment is due on the next and following full business day.

Bearer Instrument. Since a bearer instrument (i.e., an instrument made payable to cash, bearer or simply leaves blank the designation of payee) may be negotiated by delivery alone, Section 3-205 of the Uniform Commercial Code provides that a special indorsement made to a bearer instrument will change (convert) the instrument from a bearer instrument to one payable to the indorsee (i.e., an order instrument), who then may negotiate the item by further indorsement.

LIABILITY OF INDORSERS OF NEGOTIABLE INSTRUMENTS

Each indorsement to a negotiable instrument encompasses a separate obligation of the indorser, standing apart from that of the maker or any other indorser, to take up the instrument if it is dishonored and to reimburse subsequent transferees and the drawee or payor in the event of a breach of a transfer warranty or a presentment warranty. *See* UCC § 3-415, UCC §§ 3-416, 4-207, UCC §§ 3-417 and 4-208 respectively.

UCC §§ 3-205, 3-206 defines four types of indorsement: special, blank, anomalous and restrictive. As the Code makes clear, a "blank" or "general" indorsement consists merely of the signature of the payee and converts the instrument into a bearer instrument. A "special" indorsement names the person to whom the instrument is now made payable and who, alone, can further negotiate the instrument. An "anomalous" indorsement is made by a person who is not the holder, and typically reflects the indorsement of an accommodation party. A "restrictive" indorsement limits the person to whom the instrument is to be paid or the purpose for which the instrument can be further negotiated (i.e., for deposit at a named bank).

An indorser can disclaim the obligation to take up a dishonored instrument by indorsing "without recourse." By adding "without recourse" to his signature, the indorser disclaims liability on the instrument and cuts off his obligation to future indorsers and holders to pay on the instrument. Typically, such "without recourse" indorsements are found on notes rather than checks. (Transfer warranties on checks cannot be disclaimed because the warranties arise automatically by operation of law and run with the instrument. *See* UCC §§ 3-416(c), 4-207(d).) "Without recourse" indorsements also are used frequently on drafts being handled solely for collection purposes.

Warranties

Even the use of the words "without recourse," or words of similar import, however, cannot wholly relieve the indorser from all potential liability. Pursuant to Uniform Commercial Code Sections 3-416 and 3-417 (as to notes and drafts) and 4-207 and 4-208 (checks), every person who transfers an item for consideration or who obtains payment or acceptance makes certain warranties. As noted above, these warranties arise by operation of law and are made whether or not the transferor indorses the instrument.

The making of warranties is essential to foster and enhance negotiability. Subsequent takers and payors can rely on the warranties without having to make an independent determination of the propriety of all indorsements or the right of the prior party to transfer the instrument or demand payment.

The transfer and presentment warranties are similar. Sections 3-416 and 4-207 provide that by transferring an instrument for consideration, the transferor of an instrument (and as to checks, the customer and collecting bank) warrants to the transferee, and if the transfer is by indorsement, to any subsequent transferee that (a) the warrantor is entitled to enforce the instrument; (b) all signatures (while the Code's definition of "signature" includes indorsements, the warranties apply only to prior indorsements and not to the maker or drawer's signature) on the instrument are genuine or authorized; (c) the instrument has not been materially altered; (d) the instrument is not subject to a defense or claim in recoupment of any party which can be asserted against the warrantor; and (e) the warrantor has no knowledge of any insolvency proceeding commenced against the maker or acceptor or, as to unaccepted drafts, the drawer.

Similarly, pursuant to Sections 3-417 and 4-208, the person who obtains payment or acceptance of an instrument, and each prior transferor or collecting bank warrants, *inter alia*, that:

(1) he has a good title to the instrument or is authorized to obtain payment or acceptance on behalf of one who has a good title and the transfer is otherwise rightful;

(2) all signatures are genuine or authorized;

(3) the instrument has not been materially altered; and

(4) he has no knowledge that the signature of the maker or drawer is unauthorized.

In order for warranties to be made, however, the person making the warranties must receive a settlement or some other consideration and the person taking or paying the instrument must act in "good faith" (i.e., without knowledge of any claim or defect to the instrument). Thus, if A transfers an instrument to B, but B fails to give A any consideration for the instrument, A makes no transfer warranties to B. Or, if A transfers to B, and B pays consideration, no warranty is made to B if B, at the time it took the instrument, had knowledge of a defect otherwise warranted, for example, that an indorsement is unauthorized or that the item had been materially altered.

Both the transfer and presentment warranties exclude a specific warranty that the maker or drawer's signature is genuine or authorized and provide only that the warrantor warrants that he has no knowledge that the maker or drawer's signature is unauthorized. The theory is that an indorser is expected to warrant the signature of his prior indorser, the person with whom he has dealt, and by reliance on that prior indorser, all prior indorsements. No warranty is made as to the genuineness or authorization of the maker's or drawer's signature because the warrantor has not dealt with that party and, in any event, the drawee of a check is expected to know the signature of the drawer, its customer. Similarly, the payor or maker of a note or draft is expected to know his own signature and the instrument he purportedly made.

Liability for breach of warranty is limited to the amount of consideration received by the person breaching the warranty (i.e., the amount of the instrument), plus expenses related to the item, if any, and interest (on the amount paid from the date of payment). Expenses can be mailing charges, protest fees, etc. (UCC §§ 3-416(b), 3-417(b), 4-207(c), 4-208(b)). The black letter of the Code under UCC § 1-106(1) makes no specific provision for the recovery of attorneys' fees, which is consistent with the general policy of the Code to limit damages to compensation. Nevertheless, the phrase "expenses related to the item" has generated litigation of the question whether attorneys' fees may be considered as "expenses related to the item." The overwhelming weight of authority answers that question in the negative (see, e.g., *Lawyers' Fund for Client Protection v. Morgan Guaranty Trust Co.*, 259 A.D. 2d 598, 688 N.Y.S. 2d 159 (2nd Dept. 1999).

An indorser remains liable on his warranties even if the indorser's signature is obtained by fraud if the paper has passed into the hands of one who has no actual knowledge of a defect and who has accepted the paper in good faith, for value, and without notice that it is overdue, or has been dishonored, or of any defense against it.

The establishment of a breach of warranty, however, does not preclude the indorser or warrantor from establishing a defense. Some of these defenses are imposture (UCC § 3-404), employer responsibility for employee fraud (UCC § 3-405), contributory negligence (UCC § 3-406), and preclusion pursuant to Section 4-406.

Because each of these defenses (except employer responsibility for employee fraud) has a long jurisprudential history, all of these defenses are summarized.

The "impostor" or "fictitious payee" rule arises, for example, where A impersonates B and convinces the drawer or maker to make an instrument payable to B which the maker or drawer delivers to A thinking A is B. In such case, an indorsement in the name of B made by any person is deemed effective (i.e., as the indorsement of B). The rule is also typically seen in the so-called "padded payroll" cases where a dishonest bookkeeper adds the name of a fictitious employee to the payroll or induces the employer to write a check payable to a fictitious vendor, either actually existing or non-existing, who the employee intends to have no interest in the item. The dishonest employee then obtains the check, indorses it in the name of the named payee and collects it. The policy of the Code in such impostor cases is to validate the indorsement in the name of the named payee and place the loss on the drawer or maker of the instrument who dealt with the dishonest person and presumably was in the best position to prevent the fraud.

Employer responsibility for employee fraud (§ 3-405) is a new section. Its purpose is to expand the area of employer responsibility for loss caused by the dishonesty of an employee within its control, to whom the employer has granted authority with respect to items. The section includes the case of unauthorized indorsements made by an employee to checks made payable to the employer and to indorsements to checks issued by the employer.

For a Section 3-405 defense to be applicable it must be shown that the employer has entrusted responsibility with respect to checks to an employee (§ 3-405(b)). For example, employer entrusts bookkeeper with responsibility to receive checks made payable to the employer and process them for bookkeeping purposes and/or for deposit to employer's bank account. Bookkeeper indorses the item in name of employer then either deposits the check to his/her own account or to an account which the bookkeeper has established in the name of the employer or a similar name, or to a different name.

Or, bookkeeper has responsibility to control the distribution of instruments drawn by the employer (i.e., payroll checks, bill payment). Rather than remit the check to the vendor or employee, bookkeeper steals the check, indorses it in the name of the payee, then collects the instrument.

In these circumstances, the policy of the Code is to place the loss resulting from the dishonest acts of an employee on the employer because the employer put the employee in the position to steal, the employer is in the best position to implement safeguards to prevent employee fraud, and the employer can obtain fidelity insurance to cover loss.

The contributory negligence Section (§ 3-406) is a substantial modification of the same section number of the prior Code. Under the prior Code, a holder in due course or drawee who paid in good faith and in accordance with the reasonable commercial standards of its business had a complete defense to the claim of any person whose negligence substantially contributed to the making of a material alteration or unauthorized signature. That defense was preclusion—the person asserting the claim would be precluded from asserting the forgery or alteration.

For example, a drawer signs a check but leaves ample space for a dishonest person to change the amount of the item both in words and in numbers. The item is paid in an altered amount. Drawer sues drawee to recover the amount of the altered item which, it asserts, was improperly charged to its account. The drawee could defend on the ground that the drawer's negligence in leaving blanks substantially contributed to the alteration of the item and that, therefore, the drawer should be precluded from asserting the alteration against the drawee.

The prior section was ambiguous. For example, what was the difference in negligence contributing to the loss and negligence contributing to the making of an unauthorized signature? Second, what are "reasonable commercial standards" and how does one establish them? Third, the defense was all or nothing—a complete defense; even if the person asserting the claim may have been negligent to some extent, and that negligence contributed to the loss, the negligence may not suffice to provide a complete defense if the drawee's own negligence may have contributed to the loss.

Because the negligence defense was all or nothing, litigation was encouraged and settlement was discouraged. The revised § 3-406 seeks to strike a balance (and encourage resolution by settlement) by allocating the loss among the parties. It provides that a person whose failure to exercise ordinary care substantially contributes to an alteration or to the making of a forged signature can be precluded from asserting the claim against a person who takes or pays the instrument in good faith. It goes on to provide, however, that if the person subject to preclusion can show that the person asserting the preclusion itself failed to exercise ordinary care in taking or paying the instrument and that failure contributed to the loss, then in such case the loss will be allocated among the parties to the extent the failure of each to exercise ordinary care contributed to the loss.

Of significance, the revised § 3-406 eliminates the "reasonable commercial standards" provision of the prior version of Article 3.

The Article 3 defenses described above are not necessarily limited to claims asserted by the drawer or maker. For example, a drawer claims that its bank paid a check on a forged indorsement. The drawee elects to comply with the drawer's demand to recredit its account and then proceeds to sue the collecting bank for breach of warranty. In such case, the collecting bank can defend by proving any defense under Sections 3-404, 3-405 and 3-406. In addition, the collecting bank can assert any defense which the drawee could have asserted against the drawer under Section 4-406.

Revised § 4-406, as its predecessor of the same number, sets forth rules regarding the relationship between a customer and its bank regarding the rendering of statements of account, the customer's obligations to notify the bank of alleged improper payments and time limitations within which notification must be given.

In the early to mid 20th century, particularly for commercial accounts, banks did not provide by mail a monthly statement of account. Instead, the customer customarily would go to the bank to retrieve its statement of account and canceled items. It also was common for the customer to reconcile his statement of account in the bank, immediately after obtaining his statement and canceled checks. For these reasons, the law required the customer to notify the bank of any improper charges within a narrow time period—a reasonable time not exceeding 14 calendar days.

As the number of checking accounts, both commercial and personal, increased this customary practice became inconvenient for both customers and banks. Instead, banks adopted the practice of providing the statement of account and paid items by mail. With the advent of computers and other technological innovations, high volume check issuers often found it more convenient to receive check payment information in the form of magnetic tape, often delivered daily or weekly, or simply arranged with the bank for the customer to have computer access to its account online.

The predecessor to revised § 4-406 reflected both the old custom of holding a customer's statement for it and the "new" methods. It provided that when the bank sends to its customer a statement of account and items paid in good faith or held the statement and paid items pursuant to its customer's directions or otherwise made available the statement and items, the customer was obliged to exercise reasonable care and promptness to examine the statements and items and discover and report promptly to the bank any unauthorized signature or alteration to any paid item.

If the bank established that the customer failed to comply with these duties with respect to an item, the customer would be precluded from asserting against the bank (1) the unauthorized signature or alteration to the extent that the bank could establish that it suffered a loss thereby and (2) any unauthorized signature or alteration made by the same wrongdoer (i.e., repetitive forgeries) to any item paid in good faith by the bank after the first such item and statement was available to the customer for a reasonable period not exceeding 14 calendar days and before the customer notified the bank. However, these preclusions could be lost if the customer established that the bank failed to exercise ordinary care in paying the items.

The prior statute (§ 4-406(4)) also provided that, without regard to care or lack of care of either the customer or the bank, the customer must discover and report to the bank a forged signature or alteration within one year from the time the relevant statement and item is made available to the customer and discover and report unauthorized indorsements within three years of the making available of the relevant statement and item. If the customer failed to provide the bank with the required notice within the specified period, the customer would be precluded from asserting against the bank the unauthorized signature, indorsement or the alteration. Case law held that these one-year and three-year limits were not statutes of limitation but conditions precedent—substantive parts of the customer's case—to the bank's liability. As conditions precedent, they could not be waived and the bank neither had to plead nor prove the customer's failure to meet the time limits; rather, the customer had to plead and prove it met the time limits.

These statutory obligations and time periods can be modified by the agreements regulating the accounts. These agreements often were found in terms and conditions which were provided to the customer upon the opening of an account or were set forth in the bank's form of resolution (corporate, partnership, etc.) which the bank required the customer to provide in connection with the opening of an account. These agreements and rules typically shortened the reasonable time period for discovery and report both for single and repetitive forgeries, sometimes to a few days, and also shortened the one-year notification period for forgeries and alterations and the three-year notification period for unauthorized indorsements. These agreements have been upheld as permissible variations of the provisions of the Code and consistent with the rule of "freedom of contract." There are numerous decisions upholding the dismissal of a complaint by a bank customer for the customer's failure to comply with notification requirements contained in bank rules. If the customer is unwilling to accept the bank's terms and conditions, the customer is free either to negotiate other terms or take his business elsewhere.

Revised 4-406 continues the same structure as its predecessor with certain modifications. The new section reflects the modern bank practice of check truncation, the non-return of paid items (the originals or photocopies are retained by the drawee in order to save postage expense in mailing the items), and the provision of mini-copies (much like the practice of some credit card issuers). With respect to repetitive forgeries, the new section expands the maximum reasonable time period to 30 days from 14 days. Finally, the statute changes the preclusion rules with respect to repetitive forgeries. Now, if a preclusion is applicable due to the customer's breach of its duty to discover and report but the customer establishes that the bank failed to exercise ordinary care in paying an item and that failure substantially contributed to the loss, the loss is to be allocated among the customer and the bank as their relative degrees of failure to exercise ordinary care substantially contributed to the loss. Revised 4-406(f) and 4-111 relating generally to statutes of limitations continues the one-year and three-year notification rules set forth in prior 4-406(4).

The modern practice of not returning paid items reflects the reality that the amount of forged or altered checks paid as against all checks paid is *de minimis*, that the typical customer has little or no need for all of its paid checks, and the consequent saving in escalating postage costs results in a substantial reduction in the cost to the bank of maintaining checking accounts. Nevertheless many banks, either as a regular practice or by agreement with its customers, continue to return the original of all paid items with the account statement.

The Revision provides that the customer has an obligation to exercise reasonable care and promptness to reconcile its statement of account and paid checks returned with the statement (and if the checks are not returned with the statement, the bank has to provide sufficient information (i.e., item number, amount and date of payment) to allow the customer to identify the items paid. If the items are not returned with the statement, the person retaining the items (i.e., the drawee or remote truncation facility) must either retain the items or, if they are destroyed, have the capacity to provide legible copies for seven years. The customer has the right to request delivery of the original item. If such a request is made, the bank has a reasonable time to provide the original item or, if it has been destroyed or is not otherwise available, a legible copy.

The customer remains obliged to examine the statement and items provided to it and to determine and report the relevant facts promptly to the bank whether any item was altered or paid over an unauthorized signature of the drawer.

MULTIPLE PARTY (JOINT) CHECKS

Multiple party checks or drafts are a frequent source of litigation. Some cases result from confusion in the identification of the parties the drawer intends to receive payment. In other cases, typically seen in insurance drafts issued as a result of a claim loss, there are several payees—the broker, the insured, the loss payee, etc. Forged indorsement claims result when one of the payees, usually the one with no real interest in the instrument, collects it.

UCC § 3-110(d) provides a rule of construction where a check is made payable to the joint order of the payees (A and B) or in the alternative (A or B), and where a check is payable to two or more persons but is ambiguous whether the instrument is intended to be payable in the alternative or jointly (A and/or B or A/B).

Where an instrument is made payable to the joint order of two or more payees, it is payable to all of them, and may be negotiated or enforced only by all of them. Where an instrument is made payable to two or more payees in the alternative, it may be negotiated or enforced by either of them. Where an instrument is ambiguous whether it is payable jointly or in the alternative, the rule is that the instrument is payable in the alternative.

An ambiguous multi-party check typically includes a diagonal line ("/") separating the identification of the named payees. This diagonal line is referred to as a "virgule." The use of a virgule is considered the equivalent of using the word "or" which makes the instrument payable in the alternative.

As noted above, multiple payee checks can result in unauthorized indorsement claims. The drawer of the instrument may be unsure of the interests (or lack thereof) of the various payees, so as a protection to the drawer, it makes the instrument payable to everyone who might have an interest but delivers the instrument to only one person. For example, a check is issued to the order of a contractor and one or more materialmen. In the insurance loss draft situation, the carrier may deliver the instrument to the broker for delivery to the insureds (so the broker can show the insureds that he/she gave them service).

Assuming all of the payees are honorable, each will indorse the item and the party actually expected to receive the proceeds will do so. However, where one of the payees is not honorable, or the payees no longer are on speaking terms, one will inevitably take advantage of the situation. An illustration is the 1997 case of *Mouradian v. Astoria Federal Savings and Loan* which was decided under the prior version of the Code.

In that case, Astoria held a mortgage on a house jointly owned by Mr. and Mrs. Mouradian. The mortgage required the Mouradians to keep the house in good repair and immediately repair any portion of the house which became damaged.

Following a fire which damaged the house, the fire insuror issued its draft made payable to the joint order of Astoria, Mr. Mouradian and Mrs. Mouradian and sent the check to Astoria. This was perfectly appropriate as it allowed Astoria, the party in real interest, to control the disposition of the check.

Although the Mouradians were then in the midst of divorce proceedings, Astoria got both of them to indorse the draft which then was deposited to an escrow account established at Astoria. Astoria then issued three checks, each made payable to the joint order of Mr. and Mrs. Mouradian, and sent these checks to Mr. Mouradian. Mr. Mouradian forged his wife's indorsements, deposited the checks at other banks, and collected the proceeds which he alleged he used to pay materialmen and contractors he had hired to make repairs to the property (which was still jointly owned). Although there was evidence that a substantial portion of the proceeds of the three checks were used to repair the property, the exact amount which was used was not clear.

Mrs. Mouradian brought suit against all of the banks alleging that, because her indorsement to each check was unauthorized, and because each check was payable jointly to her and her husband, she was entitled to recover the face amount of each check for conversion.

The courts rejected the arguments raised by the banks that (1) the rule of absolute liability should not apply; and (2) the banks were entitled to a set-off because Mrs. Mouradian received the benefit of all or part of the proceeds in that the damaged property, of which she was a joint owner, was repaired through use of the proceeds.

The Court of Appeals held that the limited exception to the rule of absolute liability applies only where the non-indorsing payee actually received all or part of the proceeds. Since Mrs. Mouradian never actually received any part of the proceeds, and as she had no control over the disposition of the proceeds of the checks, the exception was not applicable. In short, the checks were hers to use as she saw fit and use of the proceeds, even to repair property of which she was an owner, could not be dictated by her husband, the forger. Further, general principles of equity were not available to displace the statutory rule of absolute liability.

The *Mouradian* decision gave Mrs. Mouradian the face amount of the instrument under former UCC § 3-419(2). Under Revised § 3-420(b), the measure of liability for conversion is only presumed to be the face amount of the instrument "but recovery may not exceed the amount of the plaintiff's interest in the instrument." Thus, as a joint payee of the three Astoria checks, Mrs. Mouradian's actual interest may have been more or less than half the amount of each check.

OTHER LIABILITY MATTERS

Since usury is a personal defense, (e.g., that a negotiable instrument is usurious as between the original parties (i.e., the maker and the payee)) it is not a defense which an indorser can successfully urge as against a person to or for whom he has indorsed the instrument or a holder seeking to enforce the instrument.

A bank on which a check is drawn is not bound, as against an indorser cashing the item, to detect the fact that the check may have been "raised" or otherwise altered because, as stated above, the drawee/payor is entitled to rely on the indorser's warranty that the item has not been materially altered. In either case where the indorser took an altered item, or the indorser altered the item after taking it, the payor is entitled to recover from the indorser the difference between the item as paid and as originally drawn (if raised) or the amount of the item if the item is materially altered in some other way (such as by changing the name of the original payee).

It should be noted, however, that the warranty against alterations, as with the warranties of title, apply only if the paper is in the precise form in which it left the hands of the indorser; that is to say, a payee or indorser breaches no warranty if the item is altered or an indorsement is forged after the indorser negotiates the item to a subsequent taker.

An accommodation indorser incurs liability as an indorser (or otherwise in the capacity in which he signs) even if he receives no consideration or direct value for his indorsement unless the indorsement unambiguously makes clear that the accommodation party is only guaranteeing collection rather than payment of the obligation. *See* UCC § 3-419(d).

Negotiation. The instrument may be negotiated by delivery if payable to bearer or by indorsement and delivery if payable to order. The indorsement must be written on the instrument or on a paper so firmly affixed or attached to the instrument so as to become a part of it. This attached piece of paper on which the indorsement is contained is called an "allonge." An indorsement may be made by either the mere signature (or mark) of the indorser without additional words, or it may be an indorsement to a particular person, or it may be qualified, as by adding the words "without recourse," or it may be conditional. Negotiation requires the indorsement of all named payees. Where an instrument is payable to the order of a partnership, any one partner having the authority to act for the other partners (i.e., a general partner) may indorse for the partnership. If the name of the payee is incorrectly designated or misspelled, the payee may indorse by that name and then add his proper signature or simply indorse in the correct name. Where the instrument is undated, the indorsement is presumed to have been made before the instrument was due and to have been made at the place where the instrument was dated. The holder may strike out unnecessary indorsements to his title. For example, payee A negotiates by indorsing and delivering the instrument to B. B indorses and delivers the note to C and C indorses and delivers to D. D indorses and delivers to B. B can strike out C's and D's indorsements because they are not necessary to establish his title to the instrument.

Holder in Due Course. This means a bona fide holder for value without notice of possible defenses and before maturity. *See* discussion under "Defenses" below.

COLLECTION

Presentation and Demand for Payment. In accordance with the UCC, presentation and demand for payment, unless waived, and the giving of notice of dishonor, are necessary to charge the drawer (except where there is no right to expect the drawer or acceptor to pay), or an indorser (except in the case of accommodation paper) (§§ 3-503(a) and 3-504(b)). Presentment must be made on the day the instrument falls due, except where the instrument is payable on demand, in which case presentment must be made within a reasonable time after the instrument is issued, except in case of a draft, in which case presentation made within a reasonable time after the last negotiation of the instrument is sufficient.

Presentment must be made at a reasonable hour on a business day. If the instrument is a draft payable at a bank, presentment must be made during banking hours. Delay in presentment is excused when caused by circumstances beyond the control of the holder. Presentment must be made to all parties primarily liable, except where they are partners.

"Stale" Checks. An uncertified check becomes overdue 90 days after its date. Credit professionals should note that by delaying the placement of a check into the bank collection process, the holder risks nonpayment under UCC § 3-304(a)(2). For example, during the delay period, the drawer may have stopped payment, or closed the account, or the account may become subject to restraint or levy. Under the UCC, a bank is under no obligation to a customer with a checking account to pay an uncertified check presented more than six months after its date, but it may pay such a check and charge the drawer's account if the bank acts in good faith (§ 4-402). In *Advanced Alloys, Inc. v. Sergeant Steel Corp.*, 72 Misc.2d 614, 340 N.Y.S.2d 266 (Civ. Ct. Queens County) revd., 79 Misc.2d 149, 360 N.Y.S.2d 142 (App. Term, 2nd Dept. 1973), a New York court held that a bank which makes payment of a stale check may charge the payment to the account of the drawer even though the drawer had filed a stop payment order, where the payment was made after the stop order had lapsed and the depositor had failed to renew it. On appeal, the Supreme Court reversed the summary judgment for the bank identifying as a factual issue whether the bank had acted with reasonable care. Some cases have held that a bank is not under any duty to inquire into its records regarding any prior stop orders or to inquire of its customer whether it still wants the item paid. It may be presumed that the customer's failure to renew the stop order or to simply close its account before presentation of the instrument, indicates that the customer's desire is that the item be paid.

Protest. A "protest" or "certificate of protest" is an affidavit, made by the person or entity to whom an item has been presented for payment, attesting to the facts of due presentment and dishonor (§ 3-505(b)). As to checks and drafts drawn on a bank, the certificate of protest will be made by a bank officer having knowledge of the relevant facts. For domestic checks and drafts, under the Code, formal protest is not necessary except where the holder requests it. However, protest is necessary, and is typically requested, with respect to drafts drawn or payable outside the United States. The person making the certificate of protest must be certain of the accuracy of the facts to which he/she is attesting as a certificate of protest often is used by the holder of the instrument as a basis for filing criminal bad check charges against the drawer of the instrument.

Notice of Dishonor. Unless waived, notice of dishonor ordinarily must be given to each drawer and indorser. Notice must be given *by a bank* before its midnight deadline—midnight of the next banking day after receipt of the item to be dishonored; any other person must be given notice by midnight after the third business day after the dishonor. Notice may be either written or oral, and delivered personally or by mail. Joint parties who are not partners must all be notified. If the person giving and the person receiving notice reside in the same place, notice must be given so that it will be received not later than the day following the day of maturity; if they reside in different places, it must be mailed in time to go by mail the day following the date of maturity, or if otherwise sent, must reach its destination as soon as if so mailed. A party receiving notice of dishonor need not forward it to antecedent parties before the next day. Deposit in an official mailbox is sufficient, and the sender is not responsible for any miscarriage of the mail. Waiver of "protest" includes waiver of notice of dishonor.

Time of Presentment. The time of presentment generally is the due date of the instrument or within a reasonable time thereof. Connecticut has adopted a statute that states that the maximum time limit permitted by a bank before it clears a check is four days if it is a check drawn on a bank within the state, and seven days if a check is drawn on an out-of-state bank. Rhode Island has a similar statute with the following time periods: items drawn on the same bank, one business day; items drawn on a local bank, two business days; items drawn on a bank in the state, four business days; items drawn on a bank in the Second Federal Reserve District, six business days; items drawn on any other bank in the United States, eight business days. The "availability" of funds with respect to a deposited check is set forth in Reg. CC's availability schedules.

DISCHARGE

Negotiable Instrument. The obligation of parties to an instrument is discharged by a proper payment, certification of the item for the holder, by intentional cancellation, by the principal debtor becoming the holder, or by any other act of the party entitled to enforce the instrument sufficient to discharge a simple contract for the payment of money (§§ 3-601 and 3-604). Persons secondarily liable, such as indorsers, are also discharged by the discharge of a prior party, by a valid tender of payment by a prior party, by a release of the principal debtor (unless the right of recourse is expressly reserved) or by an extension of the time of payment without the indorser's consent (§ 3-605). No discharge of any party is effective against a holder in due course unless he has notice of the discharge when he takes the instrument.

Demand before Suing the Maker. On a note payable on demand, demand before suing the maker is generally not necessary. It is necessary, however, in some states, but only on demand notes payable in property other than money.

ACCORD AND SATISFACTION

At common law, where A owed a debt to B but the amount of the debt was unliquidated (not agreed as to amount) or in dispute, the debt could be discharged by A's remittance, in good faith, and B's acceptance, of A's check in the amount A believes to be due if the check or accompanying wording indicates that the check is remitted in full settlement or discharge of B's claim. This methodology was known as an "accord and satisfaction" and the check was known as a "full payment" check.

The rule of accord and satisfaction required only that there be a legitimate dispute as to the amount owed and that the debtor remit the amount which he believed in good faith to be the amount owed in circumstances clearly showing that the remittance, if accepted, would be in full discharge of the debt. If the creditor accepted the debtor's tendered payment in those circumstances, the debt was discharged, even if the creditor struck the "full discharge" wording.

If, however, the debt or claim was fixed or liquidated in amount, and there was no genuine dispute as to how much was due, the debtor could not avoid his obligation by simply remitting less by tender of a supposed "full payment" check. In such case, the "full payment" wording could be ignored and the creditor could accept the tender as a partial payment. Of course, by accepting a full payment check the creditor runs the risk that a court may disagree with his view that his claim was liquidated. For example, a doctor bills a patient X dollars for services rendered and provides the patient with a detailed bill reflecting each service rendered and the amount of the charge for each service. The patient may not dispute that each service was rendered and the doctor's customary charge for the service but may dispute that a particular service was necessary or that service may have become necessary only because of some misfeasance of the doctor. In such circumstances, a court may well find that the amount of the claim was not liquidated.

These so-called "full payment" checks generated conflicting views among the commentators and a split of authority among the courts whether such an attempt to discharge a debt for less than the full amount claimed should be upheld. For an excellent discussion of the debate, *see* the collection of cases in *Horn Waterproofing Corp. v. Bushwick Iron & Steel Co.*, 66 N.Y.2d 321, 497 N.Y.S.2d 310 (1985). On the one hand, the law encouraged the resolution of disputes and, therefore, the tender and acceptance of a full payment check was treated as the entry by the parties into a new agreement which displaced their original agreement. On the other hand, it was argued that the debtor should not be permitted to get away with less than he owed, and the creditor should not be put into the position of having to reject money offered on a debt just to preserve his claim as to the remaining balance of his claim.

To accommodate these views, some courts recognized a modification of the common law rule of accord and satisfaction by means of a tendered full payment check. These courts held that the creditor could accept such a check but still preserve his rights by drawing a line through or scratching out the full payment wording or by accepting the check "under protest" or "with full reservation of rights" which would be written on the check, usually following the creditor's indorsement.

Section 1-207 of the original Code endorsed the latter view. It provided the creditor could indorse and accept the check under protest without entering into an accord and satisfaction.

The adoption of former Section 1-207, however, did not end the debate. Rather than simplify the law of negotiable instruments, recognition of the modification of the common law rule caused concern to mass billers, such as public utilities or credit card companies. Those entities typically established "lock box" arrangements with banks whereby customer remittances would go directly to a postal box which would be opened by bank employees in order to speed the collection of check remittances. These bank employees had no duty to review these remittances for accord and satisfaction wording. In addition, with the advent of widespread use of credit cards, and the dispute resolution procedures set forth in such laws as the Federal Fair Credit Billing Act, the continued wisdom underlying former Section 1-207 was called in question.

Revised § 3-311 preserves and encourages the effectiveness of common law accord and satisfaction by means of a full payment check but provides an exception for unintended accord and satisfaction as to "mass billers," and also permits a creditor to change his mind after having accepted a full payment check.

Revised § 3-111(a), (b) and (d) (and accompanying amendment to § 1-207) provide that if a debtor tenders in good faith an amount which he believes is due on an unliquidated claim, the amount of which is in bona fide dispute, in circumstances clearly indicating to the creditor that acceptance would be a full discharge of the claim, the creditor's acceptance, without reservation, of such a tender would effect a discharge of the claim. However, if the creditor is an "organization" which within a reasonable time prior to the tender notifies the debtor that communications (and remittances) regarding disputed debts are to be sent to a particular location, and the remittance is not sent to that location, acceptance of the tender does not result in a discharge.

Further, a creditor which is an organization and which did not provide the debtor with the foregoing notice, or is not an organization, can avert an accord and satisfaction (and preserve the creditor's claim as to the full amount said to be due) by returning to the debtor the amount tendered within 90 days of the payment of the debtor's "full payment" remittance.

DEFENSES

A "holder in due course" (§ 3-302) stands in a superior position with respect to defenses and claims to negotiable instruments than mere holders or transferees. A holder in due course generally takes free from legal or equitable claims (§ 3-306) while other parties do not. A legal claim would be one based upon ownership of the instrument or its proceeds; an equitable claim would be one in the nature of a lien. In discussing defenses available against a holder in due course, it is necessary to distinguish between real and personal defenses. Whereas both personal and real defenses may be asserted against mere holders and transferees, only real defenses are available as against holders in due course. UCC Section 3-305(a)(1) describes real defenses as follows:

(1) contractual incapacity by reason of infancy to the extent it is a defense on a simple contract;

(2) lack of legal capacity (i.e., the maker of the instrument was an adjudicated incompetent for whom a Committee or Guardian had been appointed at the time the instrument was made), duress, or illegality of the transaction which, under other law of the relevant jurisdiction, nullifies the obligation of the obligor;

(3) misrepresentation or fraud in the factum, described as tricking the issuer into signing the instrument while he was "excusably ignorant" of its contents; and

(4) discharge of the obligor in insolvency proceedings.

Personal defenses include all other defenses such as lack of consideration, fraud (misrepresentation) in the inducement, unconscionability and breach of warranty. Such defenses cannot be effectively asserted against a holder in due course, unless he was in privity with the defendant. Many states now provide that the holder in due course of a consumer's promissory note or other evidence of indebtedness delivered in connection with the sale of consumer goods is subject to all the defenses and claims of the consumer which would be available to the consumer in a simple contract action. In addition to the real defenses, a holder in due course may not enforce an instrument against a party whose signature was unauthorized (i.e., forged or made by an agent acting *ultra vires*), unless the party has ratified the signature or is precluded from disaffirming his signature. However, under the rules for "imposture" set forth above, a "forged" indorsement in the name of a payee is effective by a holder in due course as against a drawer or maker when an impostor has induced the maker or drawer to issue the instrument to him in the name of the payee; the person who signs on behalf of the maker or drawer never intended the payee to have an interest in the instrument; or the employee or agent of the maker or drawer has supplied the name of a payee, intending the payee to have no such interest.

Whether or not an unauthorized signature is effective against the person claiming the lack of authority, the signature is deemed to be that of the person who made it. Thus, in all cases, a person who in good faith pays the instrument or takes it for value may enforce it against the unauthorized signer. A material alteration is a defense except as against a good faith holder who may enforce payment according to the original tenor of the instrument. Alterations are material when they change a material obligation of a party to it such as the date, sum payable, time or place of payment, number of or relations of the parties, medium of payment, or add a place of payment, as well as any other change that alters the effect of the instrument. (But *see* earlier paragraph headed "Blanks.")

General Provisions As to Time. When the day or the last day for an act required or permitted to be done by the statute falls on Sunday or a holiday, the act may be done on the next succeeding secular or business day. Where an act is required to be done in a reasonable length of time, factors to be considered are the nature of the instrument, the usage of the trade or business (if any) with respect to the instrument, and the facts of the particular case.

Overdue Instruments. Provisions applicable to drafts apply to checks except where otherwise provided. A demand instrument becomes overdue at the earliest on the day after demand for payment is made; if the instrument is a check 90 days after its date; or if the instrument is not a check and is payable on demand it is overdue if it is outstanding for an unreasonably long period of time in the circumstances of the particular case. If the instrument is payable at a definite time and not payable in installments, it becomes overdue the day after the due date (§ 3-304).

VALIDITY OF STIPULATION FOR ATTORNEYS' FEES OR COLLECTION COSTS

There are four questions that are raised by the inclusion in a negotiable instrument of a stipulation for the payment of the costs of collection or of attorneys' fees, if the instrument is not paid at maturity or when due. They are:

1. Does such a stipulation affect the validity of the instrument itself?
2. Does such a stipulation destroy the negotiability of the instrument?

3. Is such a provision valid and enforceable?

4. What law governs the validity and enforceability of such a stipulation?

Effect upon the Instrument Itself. It seems to be universally conceded that such a stipulation does not destroy the validity of the instrument.

Effect upon Negotiability of the Instrument. One of the requirements of a negotiable instrument is that it must be payable in a "fixed amount of money" (§ 3-104(a)). Former § 3-106(1)(e) specifically provided that an instrument is payable in a "sum certain" even if it is payable with costs of collection or an attorney's fee or both upon default, but this provision was omitted in the revision of the Code. However, the omission does not affect the rule that the provision for the recovery of an attorney's fee and/or collection costs, if an action has to be brought to enforce the instrument, does not change the amount of the instrument and, therefore, does not affect the "sum certain" or "fixed amount of money" requirement.

Validity and Enforceability Stipulation. Upon the question of the *validity* of such stipulations, the UCC expressly provides that nothing within it validates any term which is otherwise illegal. The presence of the stipulation itself does not impair *negotiability*. The general rule, also known as the "American" rule, is that each party must bear his own legal fees unless the action is based upon a contract or a statute or other recognized cause of action which provides for the recovery of attorneys' fees to the successful party. The different states are in conflict with respect to the validity of stipulations in negotiable instruments for attorneys' fees, although the decided preponderance of opinion favors their validity. Where the question has been raised, it has generally been the opinion of the courts that there is no valid reason for distinguishing between such stipulations in mortgages and the same stipulations in negotiable instruments.

Whether a state's statutory law or decisional law recognizes the right to recover an attorney's fee, if so provided in the instrument, is separate from the issue whether a provision for the recovery of a fixed percentage of the instrument will be enforced. The question of enforceability of attorneys' fees provisions often is viewed in the context of the court's obligation to regulate the practice of the law. These questions typically arise where the stipulated percentage will result in an excessive fee (for example, 10 percent of a million dollar note where the attorney spent only a few hours and provided routine services). In such cases, the stipulated percentage may result in an unconscionable recovery. Whether or not a court will enforce the stipulated percentage, it will award what it determines to be a "reasonable" fee.

A study of the cases indicates that those states that have held valid stipulations for the payment of a specific percentage for attorneys' fees will likewise hold valid stipulations for the payment of a "reasonable fee" or of the "cost of collection." But it does not follow that where stipulations for "reasonable fees" or the "cost of collection" have been upheld, any given state will sustain a stipulation for the payment of a "specific percentage" for attorneys' fees. The question has not been decided in all states, and where the courts have not passed upon it, it is impossible to predict what the decision will be.

In *Citizens Nat'l Bank of Orange v. Waugh*, 78 F.2d 325 (4th Cir. 1935), the validity of a note containing a provision for the payment of a 10 percent attorney's fee for collection in case of default was sustained. The court, after holding that such a provision is not to be condemned as contrary to public policy, said:

Of course, if it should appear that a particular provision was used as a mere cloak for usury or that the provision was for so large an amount or was of such a character as to show an intention to provide a mere penalty for nonpayment, a different question would be presented, and it might well be condemned as in conflict with the well-settled policy of the law. But, where the provision is reasonable in amount and legal services are required and are actually rendered in the collection of the instrument, we can think of no consideration of public policy which should condemn it. In such case, it is properly viewed, not as a provision for additional interest exacted of the borrower for the use of the money, or as a provision for a penalty imposed upon him for breach of his contract, but as a provision for indemnifying the lender for the expense to which he may be put by reason of the borrower's default...The question is not a new one, but has been repeatedly before the courts; and the overwhelming weight of authority is in accordance with the view herein expressed....Id. at 329.

A stipulation for the payment of attorneys' fees, being in the nature of an indemnity agreement, has been interpreted so that the holder of the instrument can recover only such sums as have been reasonably expended. *See Citizens Nat'l Bank of Orange v. Waugh,* supra; *Taylor v. Continental Supply Co.,* 16 F.2d 578 (8th Cir. 1926); *Sarasota Publishing Co. v. E. C. Palmer & Co.,* 102 Fla. 303 (1931); *First Nat'l Bank of Eagle Lake v. Robinson,* 104 Texas 166 (1911); *Conway v. American Nat'l Bank of Danville,* 146 Va. 357 (1926).

A table on a summary of the law of each of the states on the question of attorneys' fees is contained in Appendix B.

What Law Governs the Validity and Enforceability of Such a Stipulation. It should be noted that the states which refuse to give effect to stipulations in negotiable instruments for the payment of attorneys' fees hold that such provisions render the contract usurious, or are attempts to enforce a penalty for breach of contract, or are contrary to public policy. In many states, provisions for the recovery of an increased rate of interest after default is upheld as a contractual provision providing for damages expressed by a specific formula and thus does not run afoul of usury laws. Such being the case, these states will usually not enforce such stipulations whether the contracts were made within their borders or elsewhere, even though such stipulations are valid at the place where the contract was made or at the place where the instrument was to be paid.

New York and Virginia have held that a stipulation for attorneys' fees valid in the state where the instrument is executed may be enforced in other states. The general rule, however, is that if such a provision is invalid in the state where suit is brought, such fees are not recoverable.

JUDGMENT NOTES

Judgment notes have been defined as promissory notes which contain a power or warrant of attorney whereby the holder of the note, or an attorney or any other person, named or unnamed, is authorized, after maturity of the note, to appear in a court having jurisdiction of the subject matter and confess judgment on the note against the maker for such amount as may be due thereon. These instruments are sometimes known as "*cognovit*" notes. Although cognovit notes are generally disfavored, they will be enforced, but courts will scrutinize such notes carefully to make sure the obligor was not taken advantage of and that all procedural requirements have been met.

Provision in a promissory note for a post-maturity confession of judgment does not affect negotiability. UCC § 3-104(a)(3)(ii). A Pennsylvania court, in a pre-Revision case, *Cheltenham Nat'l Bank v. Snelling*, 230 Pa. Super. 498, 326 A.2d 557 (1974), held that a note which contained a clause authorizing a confession of judgment "anytime before or after maturity" invalidated the negotiability of the note since it was not in accord with the requirements of (then) UCC § 3-112(1)(d) which authorized a confession only after default.

The hostility toward clauses authorizing confession judgments prior to maturity probably stemmed from the old Code requirement that the instrument contain an unconditional promise to pay at one definite time. In modern practice, a confession of judgment is used frequently to secure the obligor's obligation on the note. By entering the judgment by confession before maturity or default, the creditor or obligee may enhance its ability to collect on the obligation if the note is not paid when due. The limitations expressed in former § 3-104(1)(b) were not carried over into the revision. Thus, entry of a confession of judgment before maturity, if authorized by procedural law, is consistent with revised § 3-104(a)(3) which permits instruments to contain undertakings to secure payment, to confess judgment or waive "the benefit of any law intended for the advantage or protection of an obligor."

The constitutionality of judgment notes in certain consumer transactions is open to question. In *Swarb v. Lennox*, 405 U.S. 191 (1972), the Supreme Court declared that the Pennsylvania confession of a judgment process was unconstitutional as to a class of debtors with annual incomes of less than $10,000. But *see Jamerson and Wright v. Lennox*, 356 F. Supp. 1164 (E.D.Pa. 1972) where the court held that the plaintiffs were barred from asserting the general invalidity of confession of judgment clauses, aff'd, 414 U.S. 802 (1974). In *D. H. Overmeyer Co. v. Frick Co.*, 405 U.S. 174 (1972), the Supreme Court sustained a confession of judgment which had been willingly, knowingly and intelligently bargained for in a commercial situation.

Judgment notes frequently provide for the payment of costs and attorneys' fees as in the form referred to. It should be noted that the Retail Installment Sales Laws of many of the states contain provisions restricting the use of judgment notes and limiting attorneys' fees that may be imposed upon the debtor. A judgment note should be distinguished from a confession of judgment. The former is part of a promissory note and relates only thereto; the latter is a separate document applicable to any indebtedness. *See* discussion on confession of judgments in Chapter 16. As well, *see* the table in the Appendix B for state information on Validity of Judgment Notes and Stipulation for Attorney's Fee.

"TRADE" AND "BANK" ACCEPTANCES

A *trade acceptance* is a draft, order or bill of exchange drawn by the seller of merchandise upon the purchaser and accepted by the purchaser as payable at a certain definite time and place without qualifying conditions.

A *bank acceptance* is a written agreement on the part of a bank that it will pay at a certain definite time and place a draft drawn on it, usually by the seller of goods, such payment being for and on behalf of the purchaser of such goods.

A trade acceptance is to be filled out in accordance with the terms of sale—it is to be made for the amount of the invoice or statement, and the due date is the maturity of the account. If an invoice amounts to $100 on 30-day terms, the trade acceptance is made out for $100 due in 30 days. If the terms are 2%, 10 days, net

30 days, the customer has the option of discounting the invoice in 10 days or signing the 30-day acceptance.

The trade acceptance can be made to run for any length of time. The trade acceptance is created by the seller drawing on the buyer and the buyer's acceptance of the draft. The bank acceptance is created by the seller's drawing on a bank with which the buyer has previously made arrangements to accept such drafts as the seller might draw upon it and the bank's acceptance of the instrument.

Trade acceptances are created typically in sale of goods transactions and usually involve time drafts. These drafts are often handled on a collection basis pursuant to the Uniform Rules for Collection, ICC publication 522, promulgated by the International Chamber of Commerce.

An illustration of such a transaction is as follows: A in New York purchases hemp from B in Manila, for a price of $5,000 with payment to be made in four months (to allow A sufficient time to resell the goods and collect the resale price). B does not know A. B suggests that A enter into a credit relationship with A's bank (i.e., acceptance financing) by which the bank will accept drafts drawn on it for A's account up to the amount of $5,000. A makes this arrangement with his bank, notifies B, and B then forwards documents covering the shipment to A's bank and draws on the bank for the amount of the invoice. The bank, on receipt of the draft accompanied by bills of lading, insurance papers, etc., accepts the draft, payable in four months, thus giving to B a piece of negotiable paper bearing the acceptance of a well-known financial institution and readily convertible into cash. If the foreign seller had an acceptance bearing the name of A as acceptor, he might have difficulty in disposing of it because A's name was not known to foreign banks.

Sometimes the bank holds the bill of lading and, thereby, title to the goods shipped by B. It allows A to have the use of these goods, and may take a trust receipt for the goods as assurance that A will reimburse it for the amount of the acceptance. It will charge A a commission for its services in accepting B's drafts. Before the maturity date of the acceptance, A will have made arrangements to have funds on hand to meet the acceptance.

This example illustrates how, through the use of the acceptance, a transaction can be financed from its beginning to its end. B has the cash obtained from discounting the bank's acceptance long before the end of the four-month credit period. A has the goods for which the acceptance was given and has had an opportunity to dispose of them and thus obtain the funds necessary to liquidate the acceptance at its maturity date. The bank has financed the transaction by lending its credit to A for a period of four months, thus enabling A to make his profit on the original goods. This is placing the burden of financing business where it rightly belongs—with the banks.

In the above transaction it will be noted that neither A nor B had the sum of $5,000 tied up for the four-month credit period, as would have been the case under the open-account system. Under the open account, B would have had a charge against A on his books for four months—and he could not use the money represented by this charge until the maturity of the account. Or, if A were required to pay in advance for the goods, then A would have had the $5,000 tied up in merchandise until he had disposed of the goods.

The trade acceptance works in a similar manner. Suppose A in New York sells goods valued at $5,000 to B in Chicago, terms 2%, 10 days, net 60 days. Under the open-account system, if B did not discount the bill in 10 days, the entire amount ($5,000) would remain on A's books for 60 days. It would represent an asset of A's—but a frozen nonusable asset. And if there were many such accounts on A's books, regardless of the credit standing of the buyers, a considerable portion of A's capital would soon be tied up in open accounts receivable. But if a trade acceptance were issued by A and accepted by B, payable in 60 days, A would have available a negotiable instrument of the best type, which he might be able to present for discount at his bank and obtain cash forthwith instead of awaiting the expiration of the period of credit.

In using a trade acceptance, the creditor will do well to keep in mind the following points:

1. Don't sell to a customer merely because he is willing to sign an acceptance.
2. When you indorse an acceptance, you guarantee that it will be met at its maturity. Your bank will watch such paper—let it be good;
3. Don't use an acceptance form that bears qualifying phrases. The use of such phrases as "as per invoice of" or "as per invoice No." may render the acceptance nonnegotiable; and
4. Don't use an acceptance form that bears a provision for discount if paid on or before a certain date.

Legal Nature and Incidents of Trade Acceptances

Nature of Instrument. A trade acceptance is a special form of draft or bill of exchange drawn by the seller of goods on the purchaser and accepted by the purchaser. If properly drawn and executed, it is negotiable and is governed by the law with respect to negotiable instruments as set forth elsewhere in this chapter.

A trade acceptance differs from a promissory note in that *a trade acceptance is a draft drawn on a merchant by a merchant payable to order of a third person*, while a note is an instrument drawn *by a person to the order of another person*. Merely stamping on a promissory note such words as "This is a trade acceptance" will not change the two-party nature of the instrument.

Negotiability. A negotiable instrument must contain an unconditional promise or order. Revised UCC § 3-106(a) provides that a promise or order is unconditional unless (1) it states an express condition to payment (i.e., I promise to pay B if B sells me his watch) or (2) the promise or order is governed by another writing or (3) rights or obligations with respect to the promise or order are stated in another writing. A promise or order is unconditional even if there is a reference to another writing for a statement of rights with respect to collateral, prepayment or acceleration or because payment is limited to a particular fund or source.

Former § 3-105(1)(b), which provided that a promise or order was not made conditional if it contained a statement of the transaction "which gave rise to the instrument," was deleted from the Revision as unnecessary. Therefore, an acceptance containing the words: "The transaction which gives rise to this instrument is the purchase of goods by the acceptor from the drawer" remains a negotiable instrument.

Old cases, such as *Pierce, Butler & Pierce Mfg. Corp. v. Russell Boiler Works, Inc.*, 159 N.E. 625 (Mass. 1928), which held that the inclusion of a title retention clause in a trade acceptance rendered the acceptance nonnegotiable, are no longer good law. Rather than include such a statement in the acceptance, it may be more convenient simply to include a reference to the accompanying loan or security agreement for collateral rights.

As stated previously, inclusion in an instrument of a provision for the recovery of attorneys' fees and/or collection costs after default do not render the instrument nonnegotiable.

Right of a Bank to Charge Acceptance against Maker's Account. Revised Section 4-106 provides that if an item is made "payable at a bank" identified in the item, the item is equivalent to a draft drawn on the bank. If a draft names a non-bank drawee, and it is unclear whether the bank named in the item is a co-drawee or a collecting bank, the bank is deemed a collecting bank. The Revision resolves a conflict in prior law whether the "payable at" bank was a drawee or the location of the bank merely was the place where the item was payable.

The same Section 4-106 also carries forward the provision in former Section 3-120 that a "payable through" bank merely designates the named bank as a collecting bank and conveys no authorization to that bank to pay. Drafts which are expected to be handled through the banking system for collection, presentment and payment will name a "payable through" bank.

If the "payable at" bank is treated as a drawee, that bank must pay or dishonor within the time periods otherwise applicable to drawees under the Code. However, whether a named "payable at" bank was, or was expected to act as, a drawee, or was expected to be a collecting bank, may raise a factual issue.

For example, in *Whitehall Packing Co., Inc. v. First National City Bank*, 55 A.D.2d 675, 390 N.Y.S.2d 189 (2nd Dept.), *app. dismd.*, 41 N.Y.2d 804, 394 N.Y.S.2d 1027 (1976), Whitehall sold meat to a customer of the defendant bank. Whitehall drew drafts to its own order which it made payable at the defendant bank, and sent the draft to the bank with instructions to present the drafts to the buyer and collect them from it.

Although the bank attempted to collect from the buyer, the buyer never authorized the bank to remit. After more than 60 days had passed, Whitehall requested return of the drafts. It then sued the bank, contending that the bank was a drawee and was accountable for the amount of the drafts because the bank neither paid nor returned the drafts unpaid within the bank's midnight deadline. It was held that the collection letters accompanying the drafts raised an issue of fact whether the bank was intended to act as a drawee or as a collecting bank.

Necessity for Protest. Protest is not strictly necessary under current U.S. law. The acceptor is a primary obligor and is absolutely liable to pay whether the instrument be protested or not. Protest may be appropriate when the drawee resides outside the United States. Drafts drawn in or payable in foreign countries handled by banks for collection usually will require that nonpayment be protested.

Stopping Payment. The acceptor has the same right to stop payment of a trade acceptance as the maker of a check has to order payment stopped on a check. Every customer has the right to order his bank to stop payment on any item payable against the customer's account (provided the item has not previously been paid or accepted at the request of the holder).

Effect on Mechanics' Lien Rights. The law with respect to creating and enforcing mechanics' liens vary and should be consulted before any person takes any action or accepts an instrument affecting such a lien. It may be stated, as a general rule, subject to the important exceptions hereinafter noted, that a mechanics' lien claimant does not waive or forfeit his right to a lien by taking a trade acceptance of the owner or the contractor for what is due to him unless the parties have agreed that the acceptance shall have the effect of extinguishing the lien, or such intention can be otherwise established. The cases so holding are numerous, and it has been so held in the courts of a majority of states and the United States.

An old statement of the law is found in *Hopkins v. Forrester*, 39 Conn. 351, 354 (1872), as follows:

The lien...remains until the debt is paid or until it is satisfied or discharged or extinguished. The mere giving of promissory notes by the debtor is no payment. Such notes are evidence of debt and are securities for its payment, but surely a promise to pay, whether verbal or in writing, is not in itself payment. If, indeed, the plaintiff expressly agreed to receive the notes in satisfaction and discharge of his lien, he ought to be held to his agreement, but no such contract appears, express or implied, verbal or written.

In *Paddock v. Stout*, 121 Ill. 571 (1887), it was contended that the claimant had accepted notes in absolute payment of the debt and that the right to a mechanics' lien was therefore discharged. The court held: "By taking the note of the owner of the premises, who incurred the debt, the petitioner does not waive his lien. Such a note merely serves to liquidate the demand."

The courts are in accord upon the proposition that if there is an agreement to accept a note in absolute payment of the indebtedness, the right to a lien is waived, but it is not to be presumed that a note taken by a person entitled to a lien was taken as payment; even in those states where the acceptance of a negotiable promissory note is presumed, in the absence of any testimony or circumstance to the contrary, to be a payment of the indebtedness for which it was given, this presumption is overcome by the fact that the acceptance of a note in payment would deprive the creditor taking the note of the substantial benefit of some security.

Effect on Lien of Acceptance of a Promissory Note

If a trade acceptance or other negotiable instrument is accepted and the time of payment of such instrument extends beyond the period allowed by statute for enforcing the right to a mechanics' lien, it has been held that the taking of such a note evidences the intention of the claimant to rely upon the general credit of the maker and to waive his claim to a lien.

It was held in *Flenniken v. Liscoe*, 64 Minn. 269, 279 (Minn. 1896), that:

A special agreement inconsistent with the right to lien waives or destroys the lien. Plaintiff's lien was not destroyed because a promissory note was taken, but because the credit was extended to the defendant beyond the period within which an action to enforce a lien must be brought. If parties enter into a special contract, inconsistent with the existence of a lien, the statute was never intended so as to create or preserve the lien and thereby destroy the special contract.

The Supreme Court of Wisconsin in passing upon the same question held:

The preponderance of authority doubtless is to the effect that a mechanics' lien will be deemed waived either by taking therefor a promissory note maturing not until after the statutory time fixed for enforcing the lien, or by taking independent security. (*Phoenix Mfg. Co. v. McCormick Harvesting Company*, 111 Wis. 570, 87 N.W.458 (1901).)

However, Wisconsin law now changes the rule just stated so far as the effect of taking a new note or other evidence of indebtedness is concerned, regardless of the time of maturity of the note. Similar statutes will be found in other jurisdictions.

It is a condition precedent to the enforcement of a mechanics' lien, however, that a negotiable promissory note taken for the same indebtedness must be surrendered or otherwise accounted for before an action to foreclose the lien can be maintained. This was held in *Kankakee Coal Co. v. Crane Brothers Mfg. Co.*, 128 Ill. 627 (1889), where the court pointed out the injustice of permitting the mechanics' lien claimant, under such circumstances, to enforce his lien when the negotiable notes might, at the same time, be outstanding in the hands of a third person.

LETTERS OF CREDIT

Although not a negotiable instrument, letters of credit represent a useful and popular form of payment mechanism, particularly for international transactions. Letters of credit also are frequently used as escrow substitutes as well as assurances of payment.

A traditional letter of credit is essentially a sale by a bank (or other issuer) of its creditworthiness to its customer in favor of the bank's customer's customer, which permits the bank's customer to effect a business transaction. If the related agreement is a sale of goods, the credit provides the mechanism for the seller-beneficiary to be paid. A letter of credit also can be used as an escrow substitute (i.e., issuer is to deliver a work of art upon receipt of the beneficiary's written statement of payment) or as an assurance of payment (i.e., a credit used to support a financial obligation of the applicant to the beneficiary such as to secure a tenant's obligation to pay rent under a lease).

A letter of credit is uniquely a documentary instrument. It represents the independent obligation of the credit issuer to pay the beneficiary of the letter of credit upon the beneficiary's strict compliance with the documentary requirements of the letter of credit. Unless the letter of credit is a "clean" credit (one which requires the submission of a draft or demand for payment with no other documents, such as invoices, bills of lading, etc.), the beneficiary will be entitled to payment if he presents to the issuer the draft or demand for payment strictly complying with the payment conditions set forth in the letter of credit. The case of *Apex Oil Co. v. Archem Co.*, 770 F.2d 1353 (5th Cir. 1985) points out the confusion with defining a letter of credit by its intended purpose or use rather than by its character. Credits used as escrow substitutes or to support a money obligation are known as "standby" credits; credits used as the mechanism of payment of a commercial agreement are known as "payment" credits. Both payment credits and standby credits can be clean (non-documentary) or documentary, and whether a particular credit is one or the other is determined by the requirements for payment, not by the purpose for which the credit is being used.

The "independence" or "separate contracts" rule or principle, the bedrock of letters of credit, provides that the issuer's obligation is independent of the applicant's arrangement with the beneficiary. The issuer's obligation to pay is triggered solely by the beneficiary's tender of the required documents, irrespective of the beneficiary's performance or lack of performance of the related agreement with the applicant for the credit.

For example, if B sells goods to A with payment to come from a letter of credit which A causes its bank to issue, B will be entitled to payment if B submits the documents specified in the letter of credit even if A disputes the quality of B's performance under the sales contract. [Note, in limited circumstances, such as fraud of the beneficiary, A may be able to persuade a court to enjoin the issuing bank from honoring the beneficiary's demand for payment. As made clear by Revised UCC § 5-109, "fraud" is not a mere dispute over the quality of performance but involves conduct of the beneficiary which vitiates the purpose for which the credit was established.] B is not entitled to payment under the letter of credit if it fails to submit documents which comply strictly with the requirements of the credit even if B's performance of the related sales agreement was perfect. In this case, A still remains liable to pay B for the goods on the underlying agreement. B's failure to submit to the issuer strictly complying documents means only that B cannot obtain payment under the letter of credit (unless A and the issuing bank agree to waive the defects in B's documents or demand for payment).

A basic letter of credit transaction involves three parties: the buyer (applicant), the seller (beneficiary) and the buyer's bank (issuer). The buyer applies to his bank to issue a letter of credit in favor of the seller. The bank charges a small fee, usually a fraction of one percent of the amount of the letter of credit, for issuing the letter and it may also acquire a security interest in the goods. The bank then informs ("advises") or causes another entity (an "advising bank" which may be the issuer's correspondent or the beneficiary's bank) to inform the seller that a letter of credit (and its details) has been "established" in its favor, meaning that the seller's drafts or other required demand for honor will be honored against the letter when accompanied by the documents listed in the letter. After a seller ships the goods, he presents the bank with the required documents, usually a bill of lading, invoice and any other required documents specified in the letter. These documents, specified by the buyer, provide it with presumptive proof of the seller's performance of the contract. If the seller's documents comply strictly on their face with the requirements of the letter of credit, payment is made without any further inquiry.

First demand guarantees have been used for many years outside of the United States to secure financial obligations. These instruments required the issuer to pay upon receipt of a demand. Such instruments were not used in the United States due to laws and regulations precluding banks from issuing guarantees of the debts of other entities.

In the last few decades, some letters of credit have been utilized in the United States akin to first demand guarantees. Known as "standby" letters of credit, these instruments typically are expected to be drawn on only if the buyer fails to pay a money obligation (i.e., rent under a lease) or if the applicant defaults on another obligation (i.e., perform an improvement contract, such as a construction project). The applicant's purported default provides the beneficiary with the basis to demand payment under the credit. Although such standby credits may be used, in effect, as guarantees, they are not instruments of secondary liability—a letter of credit is the primary obligation of the issuing bank performable simply upon the beneficiary's satisfaction of the conditions requiring honor of the credit. Standby letters are used in many transactions: in sales, as backing for commercial paper, or as quasi-performance bonds.

In addition to the UCC provisions that govern letters of credit, the International Chamber of Commerce (ICC) also has promulgated certain rules of standard operational practices governing letters of credit. These rules are known as the Uniform Customs and Practice for Documentary Credits ("UCP"). A separate set of operational rules, the International Standby Practices (ISP98), intended to apply solely to standby letters of credit, also was adopted by the ICC. Although similar to the UCP, the ICC does include certain major variations. As with the UCP, any person using a letter of credit made subject to either the UCP or ISP98 should be knowledgeable of the rules which will govern the credit. Standby credits are now recognized in the UCP as true letters of credit.

In order to keep up with changes in banking and shipping practices, and changes in technology, the ICC has updated (revised) the UCP multiple times, on approximately a 10-year cycle. The current revision in effect was adopted in 1993 as ICC publication No. 500. There is no current revision project underway. However, in November 2001 the ICC adopted a set of definitions (the eUCP) to allow current UCP terminology to accommodate electronic (paperless) transactions. The eUCP became effective January 1, 2002.

It should be kept in mind that the UCP (and ISP98) are a promulgation of operational practices. They are not statutory law. However, if a credit specifically incorporates the UCP (or ISP98), the Code treats that incorporation as a permitted variation of the provisions of the Code (§ 5-116(c)) so that the UCP (or ISP) would govern rather than the UCC. However, the Code will still apply where a subject is not covered by the UCP, such as the fraud injunction provision, or where a provision of the UCP conflicts with a provision of the Code which the Code provides is a non-variable provision (see § 5-103(c) for a specification of such non-variable provisions).

Most credits are and have been issued subject to the UCP. As a consequence, a large body of case law has developed regarding the UCP. This well-defined body of law has added to the stability and certainty of letter of credit practice, and thus to the acceptability of letters of credit. By contrast, little or no case law has developed with respect to ISP98. Many standby credits are made subject to the UCP because of the many benefits which flow from a stable and defined body of law.

The Revision of Article 5, which was completed in 1995, not only harmonized the Code with the UCP and modernized the Code to reflect case law development, but also worked several substantive changes in the former Article 5.

CHECKS AND FUNDS AVAILABILITY

Introduction

In the "old" days, money managers from the individual consumer to the corporate treasurer had to deal with bank "hold" periods for deposited checks. While the UCC (then in effect, Section 4-213) provided that money (cash) deposited was available for withdrawal on the banking day following the day of deposit, and provisional credits for checks were deemed final and were available for withdrawal when the provisional settlement had become final and the bank had a reasonable time to learn that (generally, the third banking day after deposit) or, where the depositary also was the drawee and the item was finally paid, on the second banking day after the deposit.

This statutory availability schedule was routinely varied (extended) by banks through the terms and conditions which the banks made applicable to their accounts. The variations could be slight or, particularly with savings banks which, because they were not members of the Federal Reserve and local clearinghouses, and thus had to clear their deposited checks through commercial banks who were members, could be quite lengthy. While corporate depositors had more leverage, because of the nature of their banking relationships and size of their deposits, to extract short hold periods, most depositors simply had to go along with whatever hold period their bank imposed.

Banks justified their hold policies because of the inherent risks involved in the check collection process, which have been summarized in Clark & Clark, *Special*

Report - Regulation CC - Funds Availability and Check Collection, (Warren, Gorham & Lamont, 1988) at ¶1.01 (hereinafter "C&C") as follows: (1) the drawer insolvency risk (i.e., the drawer closes his account or the account has insufficient funds against which to pay the check); (2) the forgery risk (i.e., unauthorized signature or indorsement or alteration); (3) the kiting risk; and (4) the stop payment risk. In addition, the return check process was somewhat slow. Banks obviously were concerned in allowing a customer to withdraw a credit for a deposit before the bank knew for sure, or enough time had elapsed after the deposit that a bank could be reasonably sure, that the deposited item had been paid or returned unpaid.

The flip side, however, was that the incidents of returns were minimal, and that the banks themselves received prompt availability through the banking system. The net effect, then, of these lengthy hold periods was that the depositary usually had use of its depositors' money—a free loan—for nearly all of the hold period.

To be sure, these "free" loans helped to defray the banks' expense in maintaining deposit accounts and, as a consequence, consumer checking accounts were free. Nevertheless, there was substantial criticism of the fairness in permitting banks to use their depositors' funds interest free and justification for the haphazard hold periods (C&C, ¶1.02). The issue easily became a popular "consumerism" issue for politicians to champion.

While several states dealt with the issue on their own, it made sense to have one uniform policy—a federal statute (C&C, ¶1.03). Congress responded in 1987 with the enactment of the Expedited Funds Availability Act ("EFAA") (12 USC §§ 4001-4010). The EFAA delegated to the Board of Governors of the Federal Reserve System authority to adopt implementing regulations, which the it did with its promulgation of Regulation CC (12 CFR Part 229, *et seq.*) and Regulation J (12 CFR Part 210, *et seq.*).

Reg. CC and Reg. J dealt comprehensively with the entirety of the check collection and return process as well as with the process of funds transferred electronically. As such, these regulations supersede much of UCC Article 4. Of primary importance to depositors was Subpart B of Regulation CC. This Subpart provided for expedited funds availability in accordance with detailed schedules geared to the FED routing numbers of the depositary and drawee banks (i.e., local, non-local) and the type of item (ordinary check, cashier's check, etc.) being handled, specified the required disclosures to depositors of the bank's availability schedule, and provided for severe civil liability for noncompliance. Subpart A set forth general provisions and definitions. Subpart C set forth rules for the return of checks. The Regulation also contained appendices.

What a Credit Grantor Needs to Know

The most important implication of the EFAA is that it creates a definite schedule by which deposited funds must be made available to a depositor. Unlike other legislation, the Reg. CC rules apply irrespective of whether the depositor is a consumer or business entity. Therefore, every entity maintaining a deposit account should become familiar with its bank's published availability schedule.

NEXT-DAY AVAILABILITY

The following deposits will be made available for withdrawal not later than one business day after the banking day on which the deposit was made:

1. Cash deposits made in person to an employee of the depositary bank ("staffed teller station")
2. Deposits by an electronic payment
3. Deposits of U.S. Treasury checks in an account held by the payee of the check
4. Deposits of U.S. postal money orders in an account held by the payee of the money order, in person, and to an employee of the depositary bank
5. Deposits on checks drawn on a federal reserve bank or a federal home loan bank in an account held by the payee of the check, in person, and to an employee of the depositary bank
6. Deposits of checks drawn by a state or local government unit in an account held by the payee of the check, in a bank in the state of the governmental unit which issued the check, in person, and to an employee of depositary bank with a special deposit slip or envelope if so required by the depositary bank
7. Deposits of cashier's, certified, or teller's check in an account held by the payee of the check, in person, and to an employee of the depositary bank and with a special deposit slip or envelope if so required by the depositary bank
8. Deposits of check in a branch of the depository bank and drawn on the same or another branch of the same bank if both are located in the same state or check processing region ("on us" checks)
9. In addition, the lesser sum of $100 or the aggregate amount deposited on any one banking day to all accounts of the customer by check or checks not subject to next day availability under the categories listed above must be made available not later than the business day after the banking day on which the funds were deposited

Depositary banks are authorized to require the use of special deposit tickets as a condition to providing the customer with next-day availability. Many banks determine availability mechanically through computer reading of the MICR line along the bottom of the check that contains information as to the drawee's routing number. Thus a cashier's check of a California bank deposited at a New York bank would ordinarily receive five-day availability unless the deposit is handled on a special deposit slip.

Depositors also should note that, unless they agree otherwise with their banks, or the bank's policy is to afford more expedited availability than would otherwise apply, "mixed" deposits (i.e., deposit of checks which would otherwise have different availability) will be given the availability according to the longest availability of any of the deposited items.

It should be noted, with the exception of U.S. Treasury checks which are deposited to a proprietary ATM (i.e., the depositary's own ATM), and except as the depositary may agree otherwise, deposits to ATMs do not receive next-day availability because ATM deposits are not considered as being made to an employee of the bank.

It should also be noted that category 8 is very broad so long as the standards are met. In certain geographic areas where there are few dominant banks, it may be wise to have a deposit account in each of them to make the funds more readily available.

SECOND-DAY AVAILABILITY

The following deposits will be made available for withdrawal not later than the second business day after the banking day on which the deposit is made:

1. Cash deposits not made in person to an employee of the depositary bank
2. Deposits of the type described in categories 3 through 7 of the Next-Day Availability section that were not deposited in person to an employee of the depositary bank
3. Deposits of local checks

Category 2 covers deposits to ATMs that are proprietary to the depositary bank. Category 3 deals with checks that are drawn on banks other than the depositary bank.

FIVE-DAY AVAILABILITY

The following deposits will be made available for withdrawal not later than the fifth business day after the banking day on which the deposit was made subject to the exceptions mentioned below:

1. Deposits of non-local checks
2. Deposits at nonproprietary ATMs
3. Deposits of checks drawn on a Federal Reserve Bank, Federal Home Loan Bank, cashier's, certified or teller's check, state or local government check, an "on us" check if the check is a non-local check and is not otherwise entitled to next-day availability

Extensions. A bank may extend the period by one business day as it relates to five-day availabilities but must make $400 of the funds available for withdrawal not later than 5:00 p.m. on the business day they would normally be due. This sum is in addition to the $100 required to be made available under category 9 of the Next-Day Availability section. A depositary bank may also extend availability one day for certain deposits not otherwise entitled to one-day availability where (a) the deposit is made to a branch located in Alaska, Hawaii, Puerto Rico or the U.S. Virgin Islands and (b) the deposit is of a check drawn on or payable at or through a paying bank not located in the same state as the depositary.

EXCEPTIONS

Reg. CC provides for certain exceptions to the availability otherwise required to be given. These exceptions include generally deposits to new accounts (deposits to accounts established by a non-preexisting customer within the first 30 days after the account is opened); "large" deposits (i.e., deposits which, in the aggregate, exceed $5,000 on any banking day; redeposited checks; repeated overdrafts in the account; the depositary has a "reasonable doubt of collectability" of the deposited item (examples include post-dated checks, checks more than six months old, suspected kites, etc.); and emergency conditions.

If a bank uses one of these exceptions, it must generally give a written notice to the depositor of the exception that is being invoked at the time of the deposit.

LIABILITY ISSUES

The liability of a bank for failure to comply with the requirements of Subpart B (and related parts of Subpart A) is set forth in § 229.21 as follows: (1) actual damages sustained; (2) such additional amount as the court awards except that, in the case of an individual, liability shall be no less than $100 nor more than $1,000; and in respect of class actions, there is no minimum liability and maximum liability shall be the lesser of $500,000 or one percent of the net worth of the bank; and (4) costs and reasonable attorneys' fees. Additional rules are provided in determining the amount of any awards in class actions which include (1) the amount of any damages awarded; (2) the frequency and persistence of the bank's failure of compliance; (3) the resources of the bank; (4) the number of persons adversely affected by the bank's failure of compliance; and (5) the extent to which the failure of compliance was intentional.

Section 229.21(c) also provides banks with a "bona fide" error defense to liability. A bank will not be held liable for a failure of compliance if it demonstrates by a preponderance of the evidence that the violation was unintentional and resulted from bona fide error notwithstanding the maintenance of procedures reasonably adopted to avoid such errors. However, the bona fide error defense does not apply to claims arising under Subpart C (collection of checks and return items procedures) or to actions for wrongful dishonor (which are governed by Article 4 of the UCC).

Under the UCC, banks are required to act in good faith and exercise ordinary care. Section 4-103(e) provides that the measure of damages for failure to exercise ordinary care in handling an item is the amount of the item reduced by an amount that could not have been realized by the exercise of ordinary care (i.e., no harm—no foul) but if there is bad faith, damages include any other damages suffered as a proximate consequence. This is essentially the same as former Section 4-103(5).

For example, depositary misplaces a deposited check. The check is located five days after the deposit and is then presented to the drawee. The drawee returns the check unpaid for insufficient funds or stop order. If the evidence is that, had the depositary not lost the check it would have been presented to the drawee on the day after the deposit, but the drawer's account lacked sufficient available funds to pay the check on that day, or the stop payment order was already in effect, the check would not have been paid in any event. Hence, the depositary's liability for its failure to exercise ordinary care would be zero

Similarly, § 229.38 of Subpart C of Reg. CC provides that a bank shall act in good faith and exercise ordinary care in complying with Subpart C. A bank's failure to act in good faith or exercise ordinary care in complying with Subpart C may result in liability to the depositary bank, its customer, the owner of the check or another party to the check. The measure of damages for failure to exercise ordinary care is the amount of the loss (but not exceeding the amount of the check) reduced by the amount of loss the party incurred even had ordinary care been used. Where a bank fails to act in good faith under Subpart C, the bank may be liable for any other damages suffered as a proximate consequence. This subsection also provides that it does not affect a paying bank's liability to its customer under the UCC or other law.

Subpart C prescribes certain obligations for the return of items deposited as does the UCC. For example, the late return of an item can create liability on the drawee under UCC Article 4, FED Regulation J (12 CFR 210) and Reg. CC but Reg. CC's "expeditious return" provisions may have made the return timely under the Regulation. In such case, the party having the claim can proceed under either Reg. CC or UCC Article 4, but not both.

Section 229.38(c) of Subpart C provides for comparative negligence to apply in cases where a person or bank fails to exercise ordinary care or act in good faith in indorsing a check, accepting a returned check or notice of nonpayment, or otherwise. In such case, the damages incurred must be "diminished in proportion to the amount of negligence or bad faith attributable to that person." Aside from these two aspects of the EFAA, the majority of the law affects only the inner workings of a bank and its relations between itself and other banks. Thus, while other portions of the EFAA affect and/or preempt other portions of the UCC, these provisions do not affect the credit grantor on a day-to-day basis. All business people should be aware, however, that the EFAA represents a somewhat bold step by the federal government in its intrusion into state banking laws under the UCC, and the scope of the EFAA is likely to expand in the future. Thus, to be thorough, one should continuously check both the current UCC provisions and amendments/modifications to Reg. CC to see that other aspects of the UCC have not been preempted.

As a final note, "availability" simply is the right of a depositor to use ("avail") a credit given for a deposited item. If the depositor uses the deposit credit but his/her bank does not obtain final collection/payment of the item, the depositor is bound to reimburse the depositary for the credit used. A depositor's right to retain the benefit of the credit used is co-extensive with depositary's receipt of collection/payment of the item. If the depositary does not collect the item, the depositor is not entitled to retain the depositary's credit used or obtained.

STOPPING PAYMENT ON CHECKS

As a matter of policy, the UCC provides that a customer has the absolute right to order his/her bank to stop payment on any item payable for his/her account. Section 4-403 of the Code provides that any person authorized to draw on an account (a depositor, joint depositor, corporate officer with signing authority, etc.) may close the account or order the bank to stop payment of any item drawn on the account by providing the bank with a description of the item or account "with reasonable certainty" and provided further, that the bank has a reasonable opportunity to act on the order before the bank does any of the "four legals" (described in § 4-303) viz, accepts or certifies the item or pays the item in cash, settles for the item without having the right to revoke the settlement, completes the process of posting, or becomes accountable for the amount of the item (i.e., expiration of the time within which to return an item such that all provisional credits have become final (late return)).

Before the Revision of the UCC, a customer had no right to order a bank to stop payment on a cashier's or official check, certified check or teller's check with respect to the customer's account because those items represented primary obligations of the bank and were not payable for the customer's account. If a depositor withdrew money from his account and received a bank check therefor, or he received a bank check in remittance of a stock dividend, and then lost or misplaced the check, the customer had no right to direct the bank to stop payment on the item and issue a replacement because the bank remained responsible on the item to anyone who could be a holder in due course.

In such case, banks typically required the customer to post an indemnity bond in its favor, in at least twice the amount of the check, to induce it to issue a replacement; or the customer had to obtain a court order directing the bank not to pay, which also would require a bond, before the bank would issue a replacement.

Although the position taken by banks in these circumstances was supported by law and was entirely reasonable, the bonding requirement could cause hardship, particularly where the customer might not be able to obtain a bond. To ameliorate this hardship, the Code (§ 4-403(b)) provides that a remitter (i.e., the depositor who obtained the bank's check) or the payee may direct the issuing bank to stop payment if more than 90 days have passed since the check was issued by the bank, the bank has not done any of the "four legals," the customer provides a written stop order which describes the item with reasonable certainty, and provides an affidavit containing an averment that the item was lost or misplaced or is in the wrongful possession of an unknown person (i.e., a thief) or a person that cannot be found or is amenable to service of process.

Unless otherwise agreed by the bank, an oral stop order lapses after 14 days unless renewed; a written stop order lapses after six months, unless renewed (in writing). Renewals can continue to be made indefinitely. To avoid the possibility of the check being presented after the lapse of a stop order, the customer could simply close his account.

In the event a customer, payee or remitter claims that the bank paid a check notwithstanding an effective stop order or order to close the account, the Code (§ 4-403(c)) places the burden of establishing the fact and amount of the loss caused thereby on the claimant. In the event the payment of a check contrary to an effective stop payment order causes other checks to be dishonored, the loss from the improper payment may include damages for wrongful dishonor (§ 4-402) of the subsequent checks.

There was much litigation under the former Code and its predecessor, the Negotiable Instruments Law, regarding the sufficiency of the description of the check provided in the stop order which the customer intended not to be paid. In some cases, an otherwise accurate description failed because the amount was off by a penny (i.e., $192.01 instead of $192.02), or some of the digits were reversed (i.e., $192.01 instead of $192.10), or the check number was inaccurate (i.e., 102 instead of 1002).

In an era where checks were processed manually, an argument could be made that the bank should have known which check the customer wanted the bank not to pay notwithstanding the slight discrepancy. On the other hand, it was unfair to require the bank to guess at its peril and, after all, the customer was in the best position to know exactly which check he had issued and now wanted stopped. Further, the necessity for consistency and certainty in the law required a uniform policy and not a policy dependent on the particular facts of a case.

These cases often led to the cry that hard cases made bad law. However, as bank check operations became more and more computerized, exact description of every portion of the item to be stopped became unnecessary; indeed, it was only necessary for the correct check number to be given. This was because the computer read the MICR line which, in addition to the amount (which presumably was encoded accurately by the depositary) contained the check number. Thus, the computer would reject the item while in the process of payment merely by the check number.

Perhaps as a consequence of automation of check processing, the frequency of payment over stop payment order cases has been reduced to nearly zero.

CHECK 21

The Check Clearing for the 21st Century Act ("Check 21") became effective October 28, 2004. It is designed to make the system of moving checks through the banking and clearing system more efficient. This is accomplished by allowing banks to "truncate checks." That means, banks are allowed to stop the paper check and instead process the information on a check electronically. The paper check is stopped—taken out of circulation—by either destroying it or putting it into storage. Instead, an electronic copy of the check is made and used to move the check through the clearing system.

Before Check 21, banks had to receive permission from the customer to process a check electronically. That permission was most likely obtained from the customer when the customer opened the account. However, that permission extended only to the customer's bank. The customer could not give similar permission to all the other banks involved in the check clearing process.

Check 21 eliminates the need for permission to be given to the customer's bank and other banks in the process. This allows the information from paper checks to be captured electronically and that information moved electronically through the system.

If a customer or a bank wants to continue receiving paper checks, the Act also provides for something called a "substitute check." Under the Act, the substitute check takes on the status as a negotiable instrument and becomes the legal equivalent of the original check. It includes all the information contained on that original check.

The immediate result of Check 21 is that customers will no longer receive their cancelled checks back with their monthly bank statements. Another result is that checks should clear faster. Some believe that Check 21 will save the banks, and the system, money in processing by eliminating the need for transporting or storing the millions of checks that are written on a daily basis. Others warn that the cost of complying may offset any savings in transportation and storage—at least initially. Another expected benefit is the earlier identification of fraudulent checks as a result of the speed with which checks will be processed.

There are some practical effects of Check 21 that credit managers must take into account. When a customer claims payment was made, the credit manager must accept the substitute check as proper evidence of payment. According to the Act, courts, retailers, and services providers are all required to accept the substitute check as proof of payment in the same manner as they would accept the original. In order to ascertain if what the customer provides is in fact a substitute check, it must contain the following:

- An accurate representation of all the information on the front and bank of the original check
- A legend on the check that states: "This is a legal copy of your check. You can use it the same way you would use the original check."
- A cautionary note about substitute checks: Never accept a substitute check as original payment of an invoice.

One of the major results of Check 21 is the reduction in the "float". This is the period between when a check is written and when it clears the bank. Many consumers are concerned that because of the Act and its resultant faster clearing times, they will end up bouncing checks more frequently. From a credit manager's standpoint, the faster clearing process should have two significant benefits:

1. Funds will end up in the creditor's accounts faster thus increasing their cash balances
2. Problems with bounced checks will be known sooner

Some have expressed concern that both the original check and the substitute check might both be processed thus resulting in the account being hit twice for the same payment. Drafters of the Act and the banking community insist that this will be a very rare occurrence. However, should it happen, the writer of the check would need to submit a claim to the bank, thus making checking bank statements as soon as they are received even more important.

The process under the Act for re-crediting an account may cause some difficulty. The Act provides that banks re-credit consumers for amounts that are less than $2,500 within 10 business days if the bank can't prove the debit was valid. If the amount is greater than $2,500 (or the account has been opened for less than 30 days, is repeatedly overdrawn or the bank suspects fraud), the bank has 45 days to resolve and issue a re-credit. Some financial institutions have expressed concern that 10 days is not enough time to investigate and resolve issues, thus creating a situation that might be ripe for fraud. Financial institutions have been arguing for a change that would match the Uniform Commercial Code, which generally gives banks 30 days to re-credit.

The rules under the UCC remain important to credit managers. That's because all the re-credit provisions contained within Check 21 apply only to consumers and consumer accounts. The credit grantor, as an issuer of checks, needs to understand that their rights really haven't changed under the Check 21. Credit managers, when faced with a customer who claims that there was a double debit and that they are awaiting re-credit by their bank, must understand that re-credit and the time required may very well be different depending on whether the customer is a consumer or a business.

INTEREST AND USURY

The law of usury is an important and complicated aspect of the legitimate extension of commercial credit. Although the great bulk of usury limitations are contained in the various state laws, important exceptions have been created at the federal level. In some cases, a state may act to override the federal preemption with regard to certain insured loans and small business loans in the same manner in which it could override the federal preemption of mortgage loan and business and agricultural loan rates.

In addition to the complexity of the relationship between the federal and state usury laws, the credit manager must also be concerned with the diverse limitations of the state laws themselves. There are severe penalties for charging more than the legal rate of interest, including, in some states, not only forfeiture of all interest but also, forfeiture of the right to collect the principal of the obligation. Further, if the rate charged exceeds the criminal usury laws, criminal penalties may follow. (The reader should consult the table found in Appendix B.)

For example, a creditor in one state might prepare a promissory note which is perfectly valid in his own state, and send it to a debtor in another state for execution, only to find upon suit that the debtor might successfully set up usury as a complete defense. West Virginia permits the assignee of a consumer credit agreement executed by the debtor who is a resident of another state and a credit grantor from the other state to collect the finance charge provided by the original agreement even though such charge would be deemed usurious if the agreement had been executed in West Virginia.

Moreover, a contract may provide for the maximum lawful rate yet, because of other provisions, be held usurious. Thus, in *Cochran v. American Savings & Loan Assoc. of Houston*, 568 S.W.2d 672 (Tex. Ct. App. 1978), the court found a contract for the maximum interest usurious because interest was based on the 360-day rather than the 365-day year. However, in *Libowsky v. Lakeshore Commercial Finance Corp.*, 110 Wis. 2d 748, 331 N.W.2d 391 (1983), the court found that though the interest was calculated on a 360-day basis through a computer error, the lender was not liable since he lacked intent.

Because usury statutes are for the protection of the public, usurious agreements will not be enforced even if it was the borrower who set the rate. However, a limited exception to this rule has been recognized where the creditor acted "innocently" and borrower knowingly inserted a usurious interest rate with the intent of later asserting usury to avoid repayment.

It should be noted that the rate of interest that may be charged a corporation may be higher than the rate which may be charged to an individual. However, a guarantor of a corporate obligation would not be able to assert usury as a defense to an action on the guarantee so long as the rate charged on the corporate loan was legal. In some states, such as New York (*see* General Obligations Law § 5-521), corporations and individual guarantors of corporate loans are barred by statute from asserting the defense of usury.

There have been occasions where loans were, in form, made to corporations but were, in fact, made to the individual "guarantors" in order for the lender to avail itself of the higher rate allowed to be charged a corporation. In such event, the "loan" to the corporation is a subterfuge for a usurious loan to an individual and will not be enforced (e.g., *Schneider v. Phelps*, 41 N.Y.2d 238, 391 N.Y.S.2d 568 (1977)).

Service charges and interest charges after an obligation is due, if bona fide and not in violation of any specific statutory prohibition, have generally been held not to violate the usury laws (because they are not charges for the extension of credit), although the loan payments, when coupled with the amount charged for interest, may be in excess of the statutory rate.

In some states the parties may agree on any rate of interest, and in others they may agree on a rate above the legal rate, but within certain statutory limits. In some states where the parties are permitted to agree on a rate higher than the legal rate, it is not sufficient to print on the invoice such words as "Interest at rate of 1% a month charged on past due accounts," for the courts in some states have held that there must be a definite agreement in order to validate a rate of interest higher than the legal rate. To the contrary, the recent case of *Archer Mgmt. Services, Inc. v. Pennie & Edmonds*, 731 N.Y.S.2d 177 (1st Dept., 2001), the plaintiff provided in-house mail room services to a law firm. It sued the law firm, a partnership, to recover the amount of unpaid invoices plus interest at the rate of 1½ percent per month. That rate was printed on each invoice which stated that the rate would be applicable to overdue balances. The court held that the rate, which was never objected to by the defendant, became incorporated into the agreement of the parties, and thus was upheld as damages for breach of contract.

Statutes in several states expressly provide that the defense of usury cannot be raised against negotiable paper in the hands of one who takes it as a bona fide holder, for value before maturity. In many jurisdictions paper tainted with usury is declared void even in the hands of a bona fide purchaser.

Under laws of Connecticut, Hawaii, Kentucky, New Mexico, North Dakota and Vermont, the charging of usurious interest is a misdemeanor. In New York, interest charged in excess of 25 percent is deemed criminal usury and is a felony. In Texas, habitual offenders against the usury laws may be enjoined in the court.

The question of whether the law at the time the contract is made or at the time of payment applies has been answered differently by the courts of each state. In some states, such as Minnesota, the law at the time the contract was made controls.

Creditors, such as variable-rate lenders, who wish to avoid the usury laws have several alternatives: conduct transactions in a state which exempts from the usury laws that type of transaction desired; add a provision subjecting the transaction to the law of another jurisdiction more favorable to the transaction; or add a savings clause limiting the interest to a rate no higher than the law allows. The validity of the latter two provisions in a loan transaction will vary from state to state. The effect of such provisions in exempting loans from the usury laws must be determined before their use in each jurisdiction.

A draft or other form of negotiable instrument, valid at its inception and which has been once negotiated, may be sold at any discount that the holder sees fit. Where the sale of a draft is a mere loan, a rate of discount higher than the legal rate may be usurious. The usury statutes, it will be remembered, forbid only the loan or forbearance of money at more than the established rate of interest. The draft, having once been negotiated, becomes a chattel in the hands of the holder and may be sold for as low a price as the holder is willing to accept. Thus it is that a trade acceptance drawn by A and accepted by B may be taken to the bank by C and sold by or discounted at whatever price the bank will pay.

Where, however, a draft has been indorsed or otherwise guaranteed by the seller, the seller becomes contingently liable to pay to the purchaser, at a future day, a sum greater than that received with legal interest:

> As to the character and effect of such a transaction, the authorities present some four different views: (1) Some courts have held such a transaction clearly usurious, and that the usurious endorsee takes no rights against any of the parties to the instrument. (2) Others have held that while the transaction between the endorser and endorsee is usurious, the defense of usury is personal to the endorser and is not available to the prior parties. (3) A third view, while holding the transfer not usurious, limits the right of recovery against the vendor-endorser to the amount received by him with lawful interest, and gives the purchaser recourse against prior parties to the full amount of the obligation. (4) In other jurisdictions such a transaction is regarded as a valid sale of a chattel with a warranty of its soundness, and the purchaser is allowed to enforce the obligation to its full extent against his own endorser and all prior endorsers. 91 CJS *United States*, § 3 (1955).

If A made his promissory note to B's order, and were B to obtain possession of the note by theft, or in any other manner other than by delivery from A, or if A were to give his promissory note to B, without consideration, and B were to discount the note at more than the legal rate, the transaction in either event would have no valid inception and would constitute not a sale but a usurious loan. In all cases where the taker knows that the paper had no valid inception, the courts are in agreement in declaring the transaction usurious; but where the taker does not know that the paper had no prior inception, a different question arises, some states holding the loan usurious and the ignorance of the taker immaterial, while others have held to the contrary.

A distinction should be drawn between interest required to be made before maturity and a rate that is applicable after maturity. Interest payable prior to maturity is payable by virtue of the contract. That rate must be a legal rate. After maturity, any "interest" paid is considered damages for breach of contract, not a loan or forbearance of money, and therefore may exceed what would otherwise be a usurious rate.

Interest on Past-Due Accounts

As the cost of doing business mounts, businesses look for ways of reducing expenses. An economy used by some is to defer making payments to trade creditors, which enables cash resources to be used to pay more pressing obligations or avoid the need to borrow. Creditors consequently are often squeezed by the pressures of their own demanding creditors, which they are unable to meet because of slow-paying debtors. In response to these problems, more firms have begun to impose interest charges on past-due accounts.

The purpose of such charges is generally not to produce additional revenue, but to encourage customers to make timely payments of their bills. Sellers, therefore, generally charge a rate of interest on past due accounts which may be in excess of the prevailing commercial rate of interest so as to discourage purchasers from delaying payment. In doing so, however, sellers take the risk that a court may conclude that the interest charged is not for damages for breach of contract but illegal interest.

As noted, interest may be charged if there is an agreement permitting this to be done. The best place to include such a contractual provision is in a credit application, where the language can provide that the rate of interest shall be that which is charged from time to time by the creditor, but in no event shall it exceed the highest rate allowed by law. Placing a notation on an invoice or any other document not signed by the purchaser, especially if it is transmitted to the purchaser after the sale, may not provide the contractual basis permitting the interest or finance charge to be accrued or billed.

Most of the reported cases on this question involve promissory notes in which a fixed interest is agreed upon until maturity and thereafter the rate of interest is increased. The issue of the legality of a service charge on sales contracts has arisen less often. Presumably, however, the same principles would apply.

For example, in *Hayes v. First National Bank of Memphis*, 507 S.W.2d 701 (Ark. 1974), it was held that delinquency charges collected on an installment sales contract did not render the contract usurious. The court stated that since delinquency charges are avoidable by the borrower, they do not render a contract usurious unless the form is a sham. Similarly, in *Scientific Products v. Cyto Medical Laboratory, Inc.*, 457 F. Supp. 1373 (D. Conn. 1978), the defense of usury was held not applicable to interest charged after default in payment of a debt which arose out of a credit sale.

A minority of jurisdictions have declined to follow the majority rule and several states have modified it through statutory enactment.

Some jurisdictions have removed a maximum rate of interest on past-due accounts from the coverage of the usury laws by following the majority rule or, by way of legislation, permit charging interest at any rate agreed to by the parties, unless such rate is deemed unconscionably high. For example, a New Jersey court, in *Feller v. Architects Display Buildings*, 54 N.J. Super. 205 148 A.2d 634 (1959), held unenforceable as a penalty a contract clause that provided for an interest charge after maturity of ⅓ of one percent per day. The court deemed such rate to be unconscionably high and therefore unenforceable. With respect to another loan adjudicated in that case, in which interest at 19 percent per annum was charged, such interest was not deemed to be objectionable.

If the majority viewpoint does not obtain in any state, then the applicability of the usury law should be considered. Although many of the statutes speak of loans, this language has often been interpreted to apply to a transaction in which forbearance of collection of a debt is involved. Therefore, one cannot rely solely on the express language of the statute, but of course it always should be consulted first. *See London v. Toney*, 263 N.Y. 439, 91 A.L.R. 1100 (1934).

In considering this question one should also be aware of the substantial body of law in many of the states that holds there is no violation of the usury law if a higher price is charged in a credit sale than in a cash sale.

To determine whether a transaction is a true cash sale or credit sale (frequently called a time/price sale because a higher price is charged since payment is to be made at a later date), the following questions must be answered: On what amount is the sales tax charged? Is disclosure of the two different prices available made to the customer? Is there an express agreement by seller to finance the sale? Basically, there must be a bona fide difference in price between the cash and credit sale. The effort to transform a cash sale into a credit sale by merely adding thereon a service or interest charge has been unsuccessful in the courts. The problem was discussed in *State v. J.C. Penney & Co.*, 179 N.W.2d 641 (Wis. 1970), a case which involved a revolving retail credit. For purposes of commercial financing, the distinction between credit sales and cash sales is not of great significance since most commercial sales are with terms permitting delayed payment.

The following is a summary of the laws of each state as the law relates to maximum permissible interest rate on past-due accounts arising out of credit sales. The discussion of maximum interest rates in the various states deals only with commercial transactions; it does not deal with consumer sales, which are often governed by special statutes.

In Arkansas, Connecticut, Idaho, Michigan, New Jersey, New York, Tennessee, Washington and Wisconsin, creditors can charge interest on past-due accounts at a rate higher than permitted by the respective usury laws. The courts in these states have ruled that a provision *in a contract* by which a debtor agrees after maturity to pay interest at a higher rate than permitted by the usury laws is not deemed usurious, provided that the parties have no intent that the basic contractual obligation not be paid at maturity, and have not established the higher interest rate as a pretext to avoid the usury law.

Similarly, in Pennsylvania and Vermont, it is possible to charge interest on past-due accounts at a higher rate than permitted by the usury laws. The attorneys general of those states have each rendered an opinion to the effect that default charges are not subject to the usury laws as long as there has been no agreement to forbear collection of the overdue amounts in consideration of the additional payments.

On the other hand, courts in the states of Hawaii and Texas have held that damages due for delay in the performance of a debtor to pay money are called interest and subject to usury laws. It must be noted, in addition, that the federal preemption law is not applicable in Hawaii. Courts in Kentucky and Missouri also take the minority position, although the cases are very old. California courts have held that interest on past-due accounts is not subject to usury laws. The authority of such cases are, however, currently in doubt. Accordingly, creditors are advised to abide by the usury limitations of those states.

In Alaska, Delaware, Florida, Minnesota, Montana, North Carolina, Ohio and Rhode Island, the issue has not been specifically decided by courts nor by legislators. Hence, creditors are advised to abide by the usury limitations in those states. For state usury limitations on contracts, please refer to the table contained in Appendix B.

The statutes of Colorado, Indiana, Maine, Oklahoma, Utah and Wyoming provide that the parties may contract for payment by the buyer of any credit service charge for sales transactions that are not consumer credit sales or consumer-related sales.

In Arizona, Massachusetts, Nevada, New Hampshire, New Mexico, Oregon and South Dakota, parties may agree to interest at any rate. In the foregoing states, therefore, it is advisable for evidentiary purposes that a creditor obtain a written request from a customer specifying the rate at which late payments will be charged, even though a written agreement is not actually required.

The following is a summary of the governing law for the other states. When reviewing the information listed below, it is important to also look at the state statutes dealing with usury and the highest amount of interest permitted, as many states consider this type of finance charge to be nothing more than contractual interest.

Alabama—A vendor in credit sales may charge a maximum of two percent above the prime rate at the time the sales contract is executed. The prime rate is the average prime rate at the three largest New York City banks at close of business three days immediately preceding the date of the rate (maximum of 1¾ percent per month on first $750 or less, and 1½ percent per month on the excess).

District of Columbia—A corporation formed under the laws of the District of Columbia can agree to any interest rate.

Georgia—The late charge of not more than 1½ percent per month is permissible only if the account is overdue for 30 days or longer. This applies to all commercial customers, corporate or not.

Illinois—The statute provides that it is lawful to charge any rate of interest with respect to any credit transactions between a merchandise wholesaler and retailer. For business loans and loans to corporations, parties can agree to any interest rate.

Iowa—The parties may contract for payments by the buyer of any credit service charge for sales transactions that are not consumer credit sales or consumer-related sales.

Kansas—Under the Kansas statute the rate of interest for credit sales is not subject to the usury laws.

Louisiana—The damages due for delay in the performance of a debtor to pay money are called interest and are subject to usury laws. Charges assessed because of the nonpayment of the loan or any installment or part thereof after said loan or any installment of principal or interest thereof has become delinquent and is not timely paid, including cost of collecting and a reasonable attorneys' fees are not considered interest provided that such charges or the methods of fixing same are provided in writing in either the note or the mortgage securing same.

Maryland—A delinquency charge of up to five percent of the total amount owed is permissible for all customers, provided that the amount is at least 15 calendar days overdue. If the amount owed is greater than $5,000, or customer is a corporation, seller may charge interest at any rate.

Mississippi—Late payment charge, not exceeding $5 or four percent of the amount of any delinquency, whichever is greater, if contracted for in writing, shall not be considered a finance charge but no such charge shall be made unless such delinquency is more than 15 days past due.

Nebraska—Corporations and partnerships can be charged interest at any rate. For individuals as opposed to partnerships and corporations, a service charge of one percent per month is permissible provided the account is unpaid for 30 days following rendition of account.

North Dakota—Late charge of not more than 18 percent per year on all money due can be imposed from 30 days after the obligation of the debtor to pay has been incurred, provided that the creditor supplies the debtor with a monthly disclosure statement.

South Carolina—Corporations may be charged interest at any rate regardless of the amount of the account, so long as they have issued capital stock in an amount greater than $40,000.

Texas—Interest on past-due open accounts can only be charged 30 days after the due date at the maximum rate of six percent when no specified rate of interest is agreed upon in writing. Notice of interest in excess of six percent on invoices to debtor does not constitute an agreement in writing. Any attempt to collect interest in excess thereof results in forfeiture of principle and twice the interest charged, plus debtor's attorneys' fees.

Virginia—Late charges may be imposed at a rate not exceeding five percent of the overdue amount provided that the charge is specified in the contract between the lender or seller and debtor.

West Virginia—The interest rate limitations do not apply to loans or credit sales evidenced by notes. Usury limitations are not applicable to a debt that is incurred by a loan, installment sale, or other similar transaction, and is incurred for a business purpose.

Finance or Service Charges

In lieu of the term "interest" or "finance charge," the term "service charge" is often used. If the term is intended to apply to the charge for the extension of credit or forbearance for collection, then it has the same meaning as interest or finance charge and is subject to the same laws and regulations of usury and maximum interest rates. Otherwise, the term "service charge" may refer to charges for particular services rendered by a seller to the buyer, such as alteration of the product to fit the customer's requirements, delivery of merchandise, storage of merchandise, or charge for return or restocking of merchandise. For this type of charge, the usury laws would not apply. *See Cohen v. District of Columbia National Bank*, 382 F. Supp. 270 (D.D.C. 1974).

Mississippi, by statute, permits a late payment charge of $5 or four percent of the delinquency, provided debtor is 15 days late.

With respect to consumer loans other than consumer loans made pursuant to revolving credit accounts, West Virginia allows a lender to contract for a loan financing charge, so long as the charge does not exceed 18 percent per annum. The lender may receive a minimum loan finance charge of not more than $5 when the amount loaned does not exceed $75, or $7.50 when the amount exceeds $75.

A finance charge as a result of the regular discount of consumer contracts may be deemed an interest charge to the consumer in excess of the maximum legal rate of interest permitted by state law. This was the holding of a California court in *Glaire v. LaLanne-Paris Health Spas, Inc.*, 12 C.3d 915, 528 P.2d 357, 117 Cal. Rptr. 541 (1974).

The United States Court of Appeals for the Seventh Circuit has held that regulations promulgated under the Wisconsin Consumer Act, which impose maximum finance charges on Wisconsin residents by out-of-state companies, do not violate the U.S. Constitution. A Chicago mail order firm contended that Wisconsin should not determine the maximum rate the firm could charge under its revolving charge account plan for purchases by Wisconsin residents. The court, however, agreed that Wisconsin's interest in determining the maximum charges its residents had to pay was sufficient to avoid violation of due process. *Aldens, Inc. v. LaFollette*, 552 F.2d 745 (7th Cir. 1977).

Late charges imposed by an electric utility company were not deemed usurious under Tennessee law. *Ferguson v. Electric Power Bd. of Chattanooga, Tenn.*, 378 F. Supp. 787 (E.D. Tenn. 1974). In a case involving sale of fuel to a consumer in which a 1¼ percent monthly finance charge was made by the seller, the contention of the consumer that the finance charge was in excess of the maximum rate of the usury statute of Pennsylvania was rejected by the court. The restrictions under the usury statute, the court held, applied to loans or use of money, but not to sale of goods or furnishing of services. *Kressley v. Atlantic Richfield Company*, 230 Pa. Super. 710, 326 A.2d 418 (1974).

The following is a list of how various states have resolved the issue of whether a creditor can compound interest on revolving credit accounts:

Compounding of Interest Authorized: Michigan, Missouri, New Jersey, New York, Ohio, South Dakota and Wisconsin.

Compounding of Interest Probably Authorized: Colorado, District of Columbia, Idaho, Indiana, Iowa, Kansas, Kentucky, Maine, Maryland, Oklahoma, South Carolina, Texas, Utah, Virginia, Washington and Wyoming.

Compounding of Interest Prohibited: Arkansas, California, Georgia, Hawaii, Louisiana, Mississippi, North Dakota and Pennsylvania.

Compounding of Interest Probably Not Authorized: Alabama, Florida, Illinois, Oregon and Rhode Island.

No Provision or Judicial Decisions with Respect to Compounding of Interest: Alaska, Arizona, Connecticut, Delaware, Massachusetts, Minnesota, Montana, Nebraska, New Hampshire, Nevada, New Mexico, North Carolina, Puerto Rico, Tennessee, Vermont and West Virginia.

CALCULATION OF INTEREST

There are a number of alternative ways of calculating interest. These include the simple interest, add-on, and discount methods. Unless the parties agree to a different method, or such other method is the established custom, a reference to interest would be simple interest. The loan agreement also should specify how payments are to be allocated (i.e., first to accrued interest then to principal, etc.). The following is a brief description of the various methods:

1. Under the simple interest method, interest is charged only on the unpaid balance over the term the loan is outstanding. For example, in calculating the monthly payment for a loan of $1,000 made at six percent for one year, the monthly payment could be ¹⁄₁₂th of $1,000, plus interest of ½ of one percent on the remaining unpaid balance.

2. Under the discount method, the interest charge on the loan is deducted in advance from the proceeds at the time the loan is made. The borrower, however, repays the full face amount. For example, an individual borrowing $1,000 for one year at six percent has the interest charge of $60 deducted from

the proceeds of the loan at the time that the loan is made. The borrower gets only $940 and pays back $1,000 through the end of the year.

3. Under the add-on method, the interest charge on the loan is added to the face amount of the loan and the borrower pays back this larger amount rather than the principal. For example, if the borrower pays six percent on a $1,000 loan for one year, $60 is added to the principal. The borrower receives $1,000 initially, but repays $1,060.

In *American Timber & Trading Co. v. First Nat'l Bank of Oregon*, 511 F.2d 980 (9th Cir. 1973), an Oregon bank's method of computing interest by calculating the daily rate on the basis of a 360-day year and then applying that rate each day of a 365-day calendar year was held to violate the state's maximum interest rate statute.

In New Jersey, time periods are determined by statute; for purposes of interest, a day is determined to be 1/360 part of a year and a month to be 1/12 of a year.

In *Giventer v. Arnow*, 37 N.Y.2d 305, 372 N.Y.S.2d 63 (1974), plaintiff's demand for compound interest at the rate of 16 percent per annum (the note evidencing the loan stated interest at 7½ percent per annum, compounded quarterly) was held to be unenforceable as the rate was contrary to the usury law of New York (which at that time set a maximum rate of 7½ percent per annum).

National banks can seek the "most favored" rate prescribed by the laws of the state in which it is located, even if that rate is higher than the maximum rate permitted by the law of the state where the debtor is located (this is the reason why national banks establish subsidiaries in "high rate" states to issue credit cards). However, national banks are still obliged to comply with all other laws. A national bank in California has been held guilty of false and misleading advertising in quoting as a "per annum" rate, interest computed on the basis of a 360-day year. By using the 360-day calculation, the bank is actually collecting an annual interest rate greater than the advertised rate. 127 Cal. Rptr. 110, 544 P.2d 1310 (Calif. Sup. Ct. 1976).

Accommodation Paper

Where paper has been indorsed by A for the accommodation of B, there has been no valid negotiation of the paper and it falls into the class of paper which has had no legal inception; until it is negotiated for value, it cannot be discounted for more than the legal rate. Where the discounter is ignorant that the paper is accommodation paper, the conflict noted above occurs again; Alabama, Maryland, Massachusetts, New York, North Carolina, Ohio, South Carolina, and Texas hold that the transaction is usurious and Connecticut, Illinois, Iowa, Kansas, Louisiana, Minnesota, Pennsylvania, Tennessee, Virginia and Wisconsin among others holding the contrary.

In *Holmes v. State Bank*, 53 Minn. 350, the court said:

We are aware of the doctrine of the courts of New York and some other states, that accommodation paper in the hands of the payee cannot be the subject of a sale; 'that, to be the subject of a sale, the paper must have a pre-existing vitality'; that an accommodation note having, in fact, as against the maker, no validity and no legal inception, anyone who buys it of the payee takes the precise place of the payee in respect to the defense of usury, although he purchases in ignorance of its true character, and supposing it to be, as it appears on its face, business paper, and given for value; and hence when such a note is sold, even to a bona fide purchaser, at a discount greater than the legal rate of interest, the transaction is usurious. The same courts hold, as do all courts, that if a party buys of the payee an accommodation note for its face, he can recover on it, and that the fact that the maker received no consideration will be no defense; also, that after paper has had an inception, and has become live business paper, a person may buy at any discount he can get for it, without rendering the transaction usurious. We confess that these distinctions are altogether too refined to commend themselves to our judgment.

Refer to Chapter 27 for the following forms:

- A Form of Subordination Agreement
- Judgment Note
- Negotiable Promissory Note
- Series of Notes with Default Clauses

10

Secured Transactions: A Step-by-Step Explanation

This Chapter is dedicated to all of the heroes of 9/11/01, including those persons who sacrificed their lives to save countless other lives, and to all of the other persons who risk their lives every day to protect all of us.

AN OVERVIEW OF ARTICLE 9 OF THE UNIFORM COMMERCIAL CODE

A credit grantor needs to be familiar with the law of secured transactions. First, a credit grantor must satisfy all of the requirements of Article 9 of the Uniform Commercial Code ("UCC") in order to obtain a valid and perfected security interest in all of the collateral securing payment of its claim against its customer or the performance of the customer's obligations. A credit grantor also must determine whether a secured creditor of its customer has satisfied all of the requirements for obtaining a perfected security interest that would confer upon it priority over junior secured and judgment lien creditors and a bankruptcy trustee.

The law of secured transactions for personal property and fixtures is contained in Article 9 of the UCC. Article 9 contains the rules for obtaining a security interest in personal property and fixture collateral, perfecting a security interest in these assets that would grant the secured creditor a priority over a subsequent secured creditor, judgment lien creditor and bankruptcy trustee, and enforcing a security interest in these assets. The current version of UCC Article 9 is a substantial revision of the prior version of Article 9 ("Old Article 9"). The current version of Article 9 has been passed by and is currently in effect in all 50 states and the District of Columbia. The text of current Article 9 is contained in Appendix C. The changes arising under current Article 9 are designed to accommodate new technologies and, in particular, electronic-based transactions that are becoming more prevalent. Current Article 9 has also expanded the scope of personal property assets that are now covered by the UCC and that were excluded under Old Article 9. Current Article 9 simplifies the requirements for filing UCC financing statements as a means for perfecting a security interest in most categories of personal property collateral and fixtures. Current Article 9 also provides additional methods for perfecting a security interest by control or possession. Finally current Article 9 provides a transition period for bringing UCC filings, filed under and in compliance with Old Article 9, into compliance with the new requirements of current Article 9.

Article 9 excludes certain categories of property. Where the UCC does not apply, you must take other steps to create, perfect and enforce your security interests. The distinction between property subject to UCC Article 9 and property subject to other laws is critical. If the UCC provisions are followed in attempting to take or perfect a security interest in certain property subject to other law, no enforceable security interest will result.

However, a mortgage may create a security interest in certain types of personal property that become fixtures or are incorporated into structures on the real property.

Where you have any doubt as to what will become of the products you sell or finance, you should review the particular transaction with counsel to ensure that your security interests will be enforceable.

At the outset, we caution that there are numerous state variations in the basic UCC, civil procedure, and mechanics' lien laws that will require considerable care in conforming your practice to the necessary local variations. The following discussion is a review of the creation and enforcement of security interests in personal property. However, the general discussion will not apply in all states. To ensure that your system for the creation of security interests or your documentation for the particular transaction complies with applicable local law, it is suggested that you consult with counsel in establishing a system or creating a specific document. This particular discussion is also more generic than tailored to any specific state's version of the UCC. The drafters of Article 9 encouraged all states to pass the official text as a uniform statute. This chapter will focus on the official text of Article 9. However, certain states have passed Article 9 with some changes to the official text. Again it is suggested that the reader consult with counsel about a particular state's version of Article 9 to check for any variance from the official text.

BASIC COVERAGE OF THE UNIFORM COMMERCIAL CODE

While the UCC covers a transaction that is intended by the parties to create a security interest in personal property or fixtures to secure the future payment of the debt or performance of an obligation, certain types of personal property are specifically *excluded*. Unless one of the exceptions listed below applies, any transaction involving personal property is probably subject to the UCC. *In any case not excepted, you must comply with the UCC to create and perfect an enforceable security interest.*

If the transaction involves a security interest or lien on real estate, aircraft and certain vessels, wages, insurance claims that are not proceeds of UCC collateral, or consumer tort claims, the UCC does not apply. Motor vehicles present a special problem since creation of a security interest may be subject to the UCC, but perfection is subject to other law.

EXCEPTED TRANSACTIONS

Mechanics' Liens

Statutory mechanics', contractors', or similar liens are discussed in other sections of this book. *See generally* Chapter 12. These liens are created by state law for persons furnishing labor or materials in the construction of buildings, the repair of vehicles or equipment or the feeding of livestock. The nature and extent of mechanics' liens and other statutory laws is a subject of state law and may vary widely from one state to another. Such liens take precedence over security interests in the same property, including security interests under the UCC which attach before the work is done.

Aircraft, Ships and Motor Vehicles

Certain types of aircraft, barges, ocean-going ships and other means of conveyance registered by the federal government under federal law are excluded from the operation of UCC Article 9 to a limited extent. Likewise, certain motor vehicles titled under state law are partially excluded. Security interests in aircraft and barges are created under the UCC through the execution of a security agreement. The perfection of the security interest, however, is a question of federal law. Likewise, motor vehicles are subject to security interests created in a security agreement under the UCC, but generally perfected under the motor vehicle law of the state in which the vehicle is titled. In many states the notation of the security interest must be made on the vehicle's title issued by the state. Questions of the perfection of security interests in most vehicles should be referred to counsel.

Wages

The UCC expressly excludes the assignment of an individual's wages. This is rarely an issue in the commercial sale of goods and the granting of commercial credit.

Insurance Contracts

While the UCC Article 9 generally traces a security interest in goods into any casualty insurance proceeds, as a general rule, Article 9 does not apply to the transfer of, or assignment of any interests in an insurance policy itself. Thus, while you may take a security interest in goods and, thereby in most states automatically get a security interest in any proceeds if the goods are destroyed and covered by insurance, you cannot take a security interest in most insurance policies.

However, Article 9 of the UCC applies to healthcare insurance receivables. They include claims under health insurance policies of the debtor's patients.

THEORY OF THE UNIFORM COMMERCIAL CODE SECTIONS ON THE CREATION OF SECURITY INTERESTS IN PERSONAL PROPERTY

UCC Article 9 grants the parties a great deal of flexibility to tailor the creation of a security interest in many types of personal property to fit their particular transaction. The specific form of the security interest and its enforceability may be the subject of an agreement between the parties. In the absence of a specific contract setting out terms, the UCC provides specific remedies upon default. Moreover, a security interest may be limited to identified items of collateral or may be broad enough to cover all collateral of a particular kind or type then owned or thereafter acquired by the debtor. One of the most flexible features of the UCC grants the parties the right to create a security interest in property the debtor does not yet own or possess at the time that the security interest is created. This is the so-called "floating lien" of the UCC. A floating lien attaches to all of the debtor's property of a particular kind, properly described in the security agreement, even though the property of that kind is acquired long after the execution of the agreement. Property that is acquired thereafter is automatically covered and, is likewise automatically released from the lien as items are sold by the debtor in the ordinary course of business. Since the UCC has been in use now for over 40 years in most states, the concept of a floating lien is no longer a new one to most businesses. Most pre-UCC state law, however, did not specifically grant a floating lien on all types of inventory.

The UCC further permits a secured creditor to trace a security interest to the proceeds received by the debtor upon the disposition of the collateral. Indeed, under certain circumstances, you may trace proceeds of your collateral to the debtor's bank account, or the collateral itself may be traced into the hands of the person buying the property from the debtor unless the buyer is a good faith purchaser.

The UCC specifically replaces what used to be a bewildering array of security devices ranging from field warehousing to various types of factoring.

DEFINITIONS

Central to the concepts of the UCC are a wide variety of definitions. Many of the terms in the UCC are in common usage in many industries. However, the terminology of the UCC is very carefully defined within the Code itself and you should review the definitions contained in Articles 1 and 9 of the UCC to understand the balance of this discussion.

Most of the UCC definitions are standardized across the country. Occasionally specific definitions covering such things as fixtures are tailored by the state legislatures to cover common law definition that developed prior to the adoption of the UCC. If there is any question about a particular definition, you should review the UCC version in effect in the state in which the transaction will occur or in the state specified as the governing law under the parties' contract.

CLASSIFICATION OF COLLATERAL

The first step in undertaking a secured transaction is to review the classifications of personal property under the UCC. No matter how denominated in a particular industry, all collateral can be classified within one of the classifications under the UCC. For the most part you will be concerned with the types of property that will eventually become inventory or equipment in the hands of your purchaser (referred to here as the "debtor"). If the transaction is going to involve more than one type of collateral, greater care should be taken. Current Article 9 expands upon the categories of collateral covered under Old Article 9. Under Old Article 9, the categories of collateral included accounts, goods, such as inventory and equipment, instruments, investment property, such as securities and brokerage accounts, tangible chattel paper, documents, and a catchall category of intangible assets, called general intangibles.

Current Article 9 has expanded the definition of accounts to include assets categorized as general intangibles under Old Article 9. Under Old Article 9, an account was defined as the right to payment for goods sold or leased or for services rendered. Under current Article 9, accounts now include the right to payment arising from the sale, lease, license and other disposition of all types of tangible and intangible property. For instance, accounts include fees and royalties payable under intellectual property licenses, such as patent, trademark and copyright licenses, the right to lottery winnings, the right to payment under an installment real estate sales contract and manufacturers rebates.

Current Article 9 has also expanded the definition of accounts to include payment obligations not covered by or having an unclear status under Old Article 9. For instance, credit card receivables are now accounts under Article 9. Under Old Article 9, it was unclear whether credit card receivables were accounts, general intangibles or instruments.

Accounts now also include healthcare insurance receivables owing to healthcare providers. They are interests in claims under a policy of insurance evidencing a right to payment of money for providing healthcare goods and services. This is an expansion from Old Article 9 that did not cover insurance policies of any kind, except casualty insurance as proceeds of inventory or equipment collateral.

Current Article 9 has narrowed the scope of general intangibles since many rights to payment previously classified as general intangibles under Old Article 9 are now classified as accounts. Article 9 now has a new subcategory of general intangibles called payment intangibles where the obligor's principal obligation is the payment of money. Examples include loan agreements or commercial debt instruments that are usually sold or participated. General intangibles also include software consisting of a computer program and any supporting information in connection with a transaction relating to the program. For example, a retailer's inventory of disks containing computer programs for sale are general intangibles and not inventory. On the other hand, software consisting of a computer program embedded in goods and any supporting information provided in connection with a transaction relating to the program are goods with the program, considered part of the goods.

Current Article 9 has also expanded the definition of chattel paper to include electronic as well as tangible chattel paper. It also includes promissory notes as a subcategory of instruments.

Current Article 9 also includes several new categories of collateral that were excluded from Old Article 9. They include deposit accounts as original collateral, letter of credit rights and commercial tort claims.

A deposit account is a bank account, such as a demand, time, savings, passbook or similar account maintained with a bank. A security interest can now be granted in a deposit account as original collateral. Or, the security interest can attach to the sums on deposit in the account as proceeds of other collateral.

A letter of credit right is a right to payment or performance of a letter of credit. This does not include the right to make a drawing under a letter of credit which is reserved only to a letter of credit beneficiary.

A commercial tort claim is a tort claim in favor of an organization or in favor of an individual that arises in the course of the individual's business or profession. It does not include a personal injury or death claim.

Current Article 9 has also significantly expanded the definition of proceeds. Proceeds include whatever is realized from the sale, exchange, collection or other disposition of collateral. Proceeds also include rights arising from the lease or license of collateral, distributions on account of collateral and claims arising out of defects in or damage to collateral. Cash or stock dividends from pledged stock and claims against a third party for infringement of intellectual property collateral are likewise proceeds.

Under current Article 9, a security interest automatically continues in identifiable proceeds of the original collateral. Cash proceeds and other non-goods proceeds are identifiable to the extent the secured party identifies the proceeds by a method of tracing that is permitted under non-Article 9 law for commingled property of that type. Where the proceeds are goods that become commingled with other goods such that their identity is lost in the product or mass, identifiable proceeds include the entire product or mass.

Article 9 also includes "supporting obligations." They support payment or performance of other collateral, such as accounts. Where a creditor has a valid and perfected security interest in an account and payment of the account is secured by a letter of credit or guarantee, or other third party support, the latter is automatically subject to the creditor's security interest.

The collateral categories are mutually exclusive and a particular item of collateral cannot fall into two classifications or categories at the same time in the hands of one debtor. However, certain goods, depending upon whether they are being held for resale or for use by the debtor, may, under limited circumstances, fall into a different class. Proper classification is essential for determining the appropriate language to be used in a security agreement and financing statement as well as determining the proper method of perfecting the security interest through filing, control or possession.

DETERMINING PRIMARY USE OR PURPOSE

While the classification of certain types of collateral, such as accounts, does not change depending upon use, goods may be classified in several subcategories depending upon their primary use by the debtor.

The difficulty faced by most secured parties is that a particular good may be held by different individuals for different purposes or uses and, therefore, fall into different classes. Thus, as the same item is passed from hand to hand through the chain of commerce, it may change classification. For example, a computer in the hands of a wholesaler or retailer is inventory, but may become consumer goods when sold to an individual for home use, or equipment if sold to a physician for office use. Distinction in use is critical. A security agreement covering inventory would be ineffective if the debtor purchased the property for business use since the computer is no longer inventory. Likewise, a financing statement covering equipment would not be effective against the retailer holding the property as inventory for resale.

The classification of goods is usually obvious, except where a debtor uses machinery or other goods for more than one purpose. For example, a debtor operating a retail store selling equipment, but also using much of the equipment in a service business, will present special problems. The same item of goods that may be considered inventory if held for resale would be equipment if used by the debtor for repair of customers' purchases. If there is any question, a security agreement and financing statement should cover both classifications that the collateral may conceivably fall into. This may present special problems for manufacturers whose products would normally be purchased for resale. In such situations the purchaser may also have financing covering both inventory and equipment used in the operation of the business. The primary lender may have already perfected a security interest in all inventory and equipment. As discussed later in this chapter, the creation and perfection of a purchase money security interest in inventory and equipment requires extra steps to prime or come ahead of existing security interests.

If there is any question concerning the classification of collateral in a particular debtor's hands, counsel should review the documentation, including a comprehensive summary of all financing statements and other documents of record.

CREATION OF SECURITY INTERESTS: ANALYSIS OF A SAMPLE SECURITY AGREEMENT

Necessity for Security Agreement

The rules for the creation or attachment of a security interest under current Article 9 are largely the same as they were under Old Article 9. A secured creditor must satisfy all of the following requirements for the creation of a security interest: (a) the secured creditor provided value to the debtor; (b) the debtor has rights in the collateral and the power to transfer such rights to the secured party; and (c) there is a valid security agreement that describes the collateral in which the creditor is granted a security interest.

Article 9 liberalizes the requirements for a valid security agreement. A valid security agreement must contain a sufficient description of the collateral and be authenticated by the debtor. The term "authentication" is new to Article 9. Authentication includes a manual signature or the use of any electronic means by which the debtor as an authenticating party could be identified and the authenticity of the record can be established. A record is information that is inscribed on a tangible medium, such as on paper as a written security agreement, or which is stored on an electronic or other medium and is retrievable in perceptible form. Current technologies that qualify as a record include magnetic media, optical disks, digital voice message systems, electronic mail, auto tapes and photographic medium.

A security agreement must describe the collateral by item or type. The collateral may be identified as accounts, instruments, chattel paper, documents, investment property, inventory, equipment, and general intangibles. A supergeneric collateral description of "all personal property" or "all assets" of the debtor is not sufficient for a security agreement. For most assets, the security agreement could describe the collateral as all present and future collateral, a floating lien. This does not apply to commercial tort claims. When a security interest is granted in a commercial tort claim, the security agreement must contain a specific description of the claim. An adequate description would be "all claims arising out of the explosion at the debtor's chemical factory in Boston, Massachusetts on July 1, 2001."

Also, a security agreement must be an authenticated record. A security agreement signed by the debtor is an authenticated record. However, it is no longer necessary for a debtor to actually sign a security agreement for it to be valid and enforceable. Article 9 now is medium neutral. The parties will no longer have to rely on paper as long as they can demonstrate in some retrievable form that the debtor intended to grant a security interest in particular assets.

A security agreement could be a full-blown agreement. Or it could be contained in a purchase order or a confirmation, which contains the necessary security interest grant language, sufficiently describes the collateral and is authenticated by the debtor. A written security agreement is not necessary where a security interest in the collateral could be perfected by possession or control. Nevertheless, a secured party should insist upon a written security agreement for such collateral as additional proof of its security interest.

Most security interests are created through an agreement that contains standardized provisions and blanks for the necessary information. Nonstandard security agreements may be used if they are carefully reviewed to meet the minimum requirements of UCC Article 9. The security agreement (in Chapter 27) contains the necessary minimum legal language to create a simple security agreement.

Exception: Article 9 continues the sole exception under the UCC to the requirement of a written security agreement where the creditor has possession or control of the collateral, provided that the possession or control is with the agreement of the debtor. Obviously, since questions may arise as to whether the possession or control is with the permission and agreement of the debtor, better practice dictates that even in those situations where you take possession or control, you should obtain a written security agreement authenticated by the debtor.

CHECKLIST FOR SAMPLE SECURITY AGREEMENT

At a minimum any security agreement should contain the following:

Identification of Parties

A security agreement must contain a provision identifying both the debtor and the secured party. It also must contain the debtor's correct legal name. Mailing addresses are not required in the security agreement, but should be included.

Granting Clause

The law requires the use of the magic words "expressly grants security interest" in all present and future collateral described in the security agreement to secure all present and future indebtedness of the debtor to the secured party.

Collateral Description

The description of the collateral covered by the security interest created in the security agreement is the essence of the agreement. The form should either have a preprinted description of the collateral or provide a space for inserting a written description of the collateral and should contain language stating that the security interest attaches to all similar types of collateral now owned or subsequently acquired by the debtor as well as any proceeds generated by the disposition of the collateral and all supporting obligations relating to the collateral. An attachment listing the collateral may be used, but should be referred to in the agreement.

Debtor's Warranties, Covenants and Agreements

While the UCC gives the parties great latitude in creating documentation to suit their particular transaction, it does not require that the debtor warrant that it owns or has the right to grant a security interest in the collateral or that the agreement contain any specific events of default. However, a typical form of security agreement contains provisions setting out assorted warranties (such as that the debtor owns or has the right to grant a security interest in the collateral) and gives a comprehensive list of events of default, an acceleration clause and antiwaiver clause. The contract language in the sample agreement is typical. Additional provisions, such as a provision for obtaining insurance for inventory collateral or governing accounts receivable generated by the sale of the collateral, are also common.

INSTRUCTIONS FOR COMPLETION OF A SIMPLE SECURITY AGREEMENT FORM

Identity of the Parties

Generally, there are two groups of parties to any security agreement. The seller/creditor is the secured party and the buyer that is indebted to the seller, is the debtor. Most security agreement forms tend to eliminate excess verbiage by defining at the outset that the debtor includes certain individuals or entities and the secured party is referred to as the creditor. The sample security agreement (in Chapter 27) contains blanks at the top to identify the debtor and the secured party. Your name should go in the blank provided for the secured party, and the debtor's correct legal name or names should be inserted in the debtor blank. You should also include the debtor's mailing address even though it is not required. Note that the sample security agreement also contains a blank for reference to promissory notes or other debt instruments executed by the debtor. Insert the date of the promissory note, or other debt instrument evidencing the debtor's indebtedness to you in the blank provided.

Collateral Description

In the sample security agreement, you are given three or four lines to insert a description of the collateral. The proper completion of the collateral description portion of the security agreement is vital. Failure to properly describe the collateral may vitiate your effort to obtain a security interest. In preparing the form you should begin by using a collateral description identifying the goods subject to the security interest, either by type or category or by identifying the various individual items of collateral. If the blank provided is not long enough, you may add an extension sheet.

1. GENERAL RULE

If you are selling goods to the debtor on credit, the security agreement should include language such as the following: "All goods including all inventory now owned or hereafter acquired and including, but not limited to all widgets, sprockets, and springs."

You should avoid overly broad descriptions such as "all personal property," that is not an adequate description of collateral. You should also avoid overly detailed descriptions including serial numbers, which are prone to error. Virtually any description of the collateral covered is sufficient if it identifies the goods and other assets covered.

2. FIXTURES

Fixtures present special problems under the UCC since the boundary between the coverage of the UCC of personal property or goods is blurred in the case of fixtures that become permanently attached to real estate. Generally, fixtures are items of personal property that will be attached to real estate in some fashion. In some cases, machinery that would otherwise be classified as equipment may be treated as fixtures. If there is any question that you are dealing with a security interest in fixtures, great care should be taken to comply with applicable state law.

Moreover, most versions of the UCC require a special fixture filing with a legal description to properly perfect a security interest in fixtures. Thus, the description of the collateral in case of fixtures should include not only a reference to fixtures, but also identify the specific equipment to be affixed to the real estate and include an accurate legal description of the real property where the fixtures will be located. Note further that fixtures may be claimed by the lessor of the real estate, or the mortgagee of the real estate if attached after the lease or mortgage is executed. In many cases it will, therefore, be necessary to obtain a subordination agreement from the lessor or mortgagee.

3. ACCOUNTS AND GENERAL INTANGIBLES

Accounts and general intangibles are separate categories of collateral. A security interest in accounts should also reference general intangibles. For example: "All inventory and other goods held by the debtor for resale and all proceeds thereof, and all accounts, and general intangibles now owned or hereafter acquired."

Location of Debtor

The sample security agreement form includes the location of the debtor. For example, in the case of a corporation, limited liability company and limited partnership that should be the state of the company's organization and registration.

Location of Collateral

The sample security agreement form includes a provision for the location of collateral. Generally, reciting the collateral location is not necessary to create a security interest. However, a legal description of the location may be necessary to perfect a security interest in certain types of collateral, such as fixtures.

Authentication and Residence or Chief Business Address

A key requirement of the UCC for enforceability of a security interest is the debtor's authentication of a security agreement. Additionally, the debtor's correct legal name and residence or chief business address should be included in the security agreement. Space limitations do not permit an exhaustive discussion of name problems presented by trade names, "d/b/a's" or other fictitious names under which individuals, corporations, limited liability companies and partnerships may do business. *See in part* Chapter 4 for a general discussion of trade names. Moreover, the law of agency in the state in which the security interest is to be enforced will control the legal enforceability of signatures by an agent, officer or employee. The debtor should be identified by its full and correct legal name if an entity, and by an individual's full legal name. Nicknames of individuals are not recommended. If the debtor is a corporation, limited liability company or other registered organization, an officer employee or other authorized person must sign on behalf of the debtor and you must be satisfied that the particular individual has authorization to execute the documentation. If an agent is involved, similar authorization must be demonstrated. In any event, it is essential that you obtain a signature or other type of authentication on behalf of the debtor to enforce the security agreement. To ensure that a person has authority, a board of directors' or other governing body's resolution may be necessary.

Summary

You should understand the basic elements of Article 9: A *security interest* is an interest in personal property created by the *debtor* to secure repayment of a debt. A security interest is consensual and requires that the debtor *authenticate* a *security agreement* which describes the goods to be covered, known as the *collateral*. A security interest *attaches* when the security agreement is executed and the debtor acquires rights in the assets subject to the security interest. A security interest is *perfected* when the *secured creditor* either takes possession or control of the collateral or files a proper *financing statement* with the appropriate state authority. As a general rule, competing security interests have priority in the order they are perfected, or if all competing interests are unperfected, in the order in which they attached.

The balance of this discussion will focus on the perfection and enforcement of security interests. References are made throughout to the official text of the UCC. State variations are not specifically discussed. You must be sure that the local variations of the UCC in effect in the appropriate state are followed in creating your documentation.

PERFECTION: PRELIMINARY COMMENT

"Perfection" is the process of taking the legal steps necessary to ensure that a secured party's interest in collateral will withstand attack by competing secured creditors, judgment lien creditors and a bankruptcy trustee. A security interest is said to be perfected when all the steps have been taken to assure it priority in the collateral described against all possible competing claimants. Generally, a security interest is perfected either through the taking of possession or control of the collateral or the filing of a financing statement under the UCC or both. In a limited number of cases, perfection is obtained through compliance with other state or federal law.

Perfection is important since it generally determines a creditor's priority to proceeds from the disposition of the collateral. Perfected security interests generally have priority from the date of perfection where the perfection was accomplished through filing, possession, control or some other means. Proper classification of the collateral into the appropriate category is essential since the proper means of perfection is based upon the classification of collateral.

The following chart should assist creditors in determining the means of perfection applicable. The subsequent explanation should assist in perfecting a security interest.

PERFECTION METHODS BY TYPE OF COLLATERAL

TYPE OF COLLATERAL	METHOD OF PERFECTION METHOD OF PERFECTION UNDER ARTICLE 9	UNDER OLD ARTICLE 9
Accounts	Filing (9-310)	Filing
Agricultural Liens	Filing (9-310(a))	Outside UCC
Certified Securities	Possession or Filing (9-313(a))	Possession
Commercial Tort Claims	Filing (9-310)	Outside UCC
Deposit Accounts	Control (9-312(b)(1);9-314(a))	Outside UCC
Electronic Chattel Paper	Filing or Control (9-310; 9-312(a); 9-314(a))	None
General Intangibles	Filing	Filing
Goods	Possession or Filing (9-310; 9-313(a))	Possession or Filing
Healthcare Insurance Receivables	Filing (9-310)	Outside UCC
Instruments	Possession or Filing (9-312(a); 9-313(a))	Possession
Investment property (other than certificated securities)	Filing or Control (9-312(a); 9-314(a))	Filing or Control

(continued)

TYPE OF COLLATERAL	METHOD OF PERFECTION UNDER ARTICLE 9	METHOD OF PERFECTION UNDER OLD ARTICLE 9
Letter-of-Credit Rights	Control (9-312(b)(2); 9-314(a)	Possession
Money	Possession (9-312(b)(3); 9-313(a))	Possession
Negotiable Instruments	Possession or Filing (9-310; 9-312(a); 9-313(a))	Possession
Oil, Gas or Other Minerals Before Extraction	Filing (9-310)	Filing
Tangible Chattel Paper	Possession or Filing (9-312(a); 9-313(a))	Possession or Filing

PERFECTION BY POSSESSION

Security interests in most types of tangible collateral may be perfected by the secured party taking physical possession of the collateral. The question is, what constitutes possession? The courts have held generally that if a secured party has exclusive control of, access to, or the use of the collateral, it has possession of it. Thus, a negotiable instrument, such as a stock certificate in your safe, is in your possession. Similarly, inventory or equipment stored in a warehouse in your name is also in your possession. Special problems exist where goods are subject to a negotiable warehouse receipt. The secured party may take possession of the receipt or make an appropriate filing against documents, but it must perfect its interest in the receipt itself and not in the goods.

A security interest in money can be perfected only by possession and a security interest in goods and tangible chattel paper can be perfected by either filing or possession (although in the case of tangible chattel paper possession is better as discussed later). In a change from Old Article 9 where a security interest in instruments, certificated securities and negotiable documents was perfected only by possession, under current Article 9, a security interest in instruments, certificated securities and negotiable documents can be perfected by either possession or UCC filing. However, as more fully discussed later, possession is better.

Article 9 also deals with the way to perfect a security interest where a third party has possession of the collateral. Notice of the security interest to the third party alone will no longer be sufficient. Now the third party must acknowledge the security interest in an authenticated record that states that the third party is holding the collateral for the secured party's benefit.

PERFECTION BY CONTROL

A security interest in investment property may be perfected by UCC filing or control (although control is better). Investment property is governed by Article 8 of the UCC and includes securities and brokerage accounts. Control applies to situations where a secured party may not be in physical possession of the collateral but can still exercise a sufficient amount of power over the collateral to control it. This frequently requires that a third party having possession of the investment property collateral, such as a bank, broker or other financial institution, enter into an agreement with the secured party where the third party agrees to comply with the secured party's instructions concerning the disposition of the collateral without the debtor's consent.

A security interest in a deposit account and a letter of credit right can be perfected only by control and a security interest in electronic chattel paper can be perfected either by UCC filing or control, although as more fully discussed later control is better.

A secured party obtains control over a deposit account in a similar manner to obtaining control over investment property. Control over electronic chattel paper requires a unique "marking" of it. Control over a letter of credit right occurs when the secured party obtains the consent of the letter of credit issuer to the assignment of the proceeds of the letter of credit. However, there is automatic perfection of a security interest in a letter of credit right that is a supporting obligation of another category of collateral subject to a properly perfected security interest.

PERFECTION BY FILING

The most common method of perfecting a security interest under the UCC is through the filing of a UCC financing statement. To qualify as a financing statement, you must file a writing that meets all of the statutory requirements for a financing statement. The filing must be made with the proper authorities.

Moreover, you must continue your security interest to extend the validity of the perfection beyond the five-year period usually allowed.

NEW UCC FILING RULES

Current Article 9 has made extensive changes to the rules governing perfection by filing a UCC financing statement. These new rules are designed to simplify procedures for UCC filings, reduce the cost of compliance by UCC filing and reduce the risk of inadvertent errors.

Collateral Perfected by UCC Filing

Article 9 expands the categories of collateral where a security interest could be perfected by filing a UCC financing statement. A security interest in accounts, inventory, equipment and general intangibles could be perfected by filing a UCC financing statement. A secured party could also perfect a security interest in instruments, tangible chattel paper and negotiable documents by UCC filing, although perfection by possession is better. A secured party could also perfect a security interest in investment property and electronic chattel paper by UCC filing (although perfection by control is better).

Where to File a UCC Financing Statement

Perhaps the most significant change brought about by the revisions to Article 9 is the state in which a secured party is required to file a UCC financing statement to perfect a security interest by UCC filing. Under Old Article 9 this depended on the type of collateral. Where the collateral is tangible, such as inventory and equipment, the secured party had to file a UCC financing statement in the state where the collateral was physically located. Therefore, multiple state UCC filings were required for a retailer with inventory located in numerous states. There was always the potential for mistake or fraud where the secured party was not aware of the location of tangible collateral in a particular state and did not file a UCC there. Where the collateral is intangible, such as accounts and general intangibles, the secured creditor had to file a UCC in the state where the debtor's place of business is located and if there were multiple states where the debtor operated, the state where the debtor's chief executive office was located. This resulted in litigation where the debtor operated in more than one state and there was a question about the state of the debtor's chief executive office, or where the debtor moved its chief executive office after the UCC filing.

Current Article 9 substantially reduces the burden on a secured party by now requiring the filing of a UCC financing statement for all types of collateral where filing is permissible in the state where the debtor is located. A registered organization, such as a corporation, limited liability company and limited partnership, is located in the state where it is organized and registered. For example, a corporation is located in the state where it is incorporated. If a debtor is a corporation and it is incorporated in Delaware, its inventory is located in New Jersey and its chief executive office is located in New York, under current Article 9, a UCC financing statement must be filed only in Delaware. Under Old Article 9, UCC filings had to be made in New Jersey (the state where inventory is located) and in New York (where the debtor's chief executive office is located).

Where the debtor is an unregistered organization, such as a general partnership, it is located in the state where it has its place of business, and a UCC financing statement must be filed in that state. Where the debtor has a place of business in more than one state, it is deemed to be located in the state where it has its chief executive office, which is the state where a UCC must be filed.

Where the debtor is an individual, a UCC financing statement must be filed in the state of the debtor's principal residence. Where the debtor is a foreign entity that is located in a jurisdiction outside of the United States and the foreign jurisdiction does not provide for a public filing system that would enable a secured creditor to prevail over a subsequent lien creditor, the debtor is deemed to be located in the District of Columbia.

Article 9 now also simplifies the rules for filing a UCC financing statement in a particular state. Now it is necessary to file a UCC centrally in only one office in the state, usually with the Secretary of State for most categories of collateral. An exception continues for fixtures where local filings continue to be required.

The filing of a UCC financing statement is deemed completed upon presentation of a proper UCC and the tender of the necessary filing fee or the acceptance of the UCC by the filing officer. Follow-up should be done for actual receipt and filing of the UCC. A secured party may wish to conduct a UCC search immediately after submitting the UCC filing to confirm that the UCC was properly filed and indexed.

Contents of UCC Financing Statement

A UCC financing statement must now contain all of the following: (a) the debtor's correct legal name; (b) the name of the secured party or its representative; and (c) a description of the collateral. If a financing statement does not contain this information, it is ineffective and will not be accepted for filing. A financing statement should also contain the address of the debtor and secured party and the debtor's type and jurisdiction of organization and organizational identification number.

Name of Debtor

A UCC financing statement must contain the debtor's correct legal name. The use of a trade name for a debtor that is a registered entity (such as a corporation) is not acceptable and may not pass muster. The questions of whether an individual debtor's correct legal name must be used or whether a debtor may use his nickname or such debtor's nickname have engendered substantial litigation and should discourage identifying individual debtors by their nickname.

Article 9 also now has a new rule to determine when a mistake in the debtor's name renders a UCC ineffective. A UCC containing an incorrect legal name of the debtor will be effective if a computer search using the debtor's correct legal name and the state's standard search logic uncovers that UCC. On the other hand, that UCC will not be effective if a computer search using the debtor's correct legal name cannot find it.

Description of Collateral

Under Old Article 9, a UCC financing statement that contained a supergeneric description of collateral, such as "all assets" and "all personal property" was not effective. The UCC had to describe collateral by item or type. And to the extent the collateral description in the UCC was broader than that in the security agreement, the lender did not have a perfected security interest in the added collateral.

Under current Article 9, a UCC financing statement can contain a supergeneric "all asset" or "all personal property" description of collateral only if the description of collateral in the security agreement includes all categories of collateral or the security agreement otherwise authorizes it. However, the security agreement cannot contain such a supergeneric "all assets" or "all property" description of collateral. Also, the extent of the perfected security interest is limited to the collateral described in the security agreement.

Note that for fixtures, the UCC must contain a real estate description and the name of the record owner of the real estate where the debtor does not have an interest in the real property and should be filed in both the central location for personal property UCC filings and the real property records.

No Signature Requirement for UCC

Under Old Article 9, the debtor had to sign the UCC financing statement, unless the security agreement authorized the secured party to sign the debtor's name. Current Article 9 does not require the debtor to sign a UCC. The debtor's authentication of a security agreement that describes the collateral referred to in the UCC authorizes the secured party to file a UCC identifying such collateral. This will facilitate the electronic filing of UCCs and electronic UCC searches. As part of this rule, a secured party will have to obtain the debtor's authorization to pre-file a UCC where the debtor had not yet authenticated the security agreement.

Current UCC Financing Statement Forms

Article 9 contains a uniform UCC financing statement. A sample is included in Chapter 27. Virtually every state will now accept this uniform UCC form for filing. This is in contrast to the practice under Old Article 9 where each state had its own UCC financing statement form and many states would not accept any form other than the state's UCC form for filing.

Duration of UCC Financing Statement

In most states, Article 9 continues the rule that a UCC financing statement is effective for five years after the date of filing of the original UCC. Unless a continuation is timely filed, the perfected security interest lapses the day after the fifth anniversary of the original filing. The secured party must file a UCC continuation within six months prior to the fifth anniversary date of the original UCC filing. This is done by checking the continuation box on the uniform UCC Amendment form and noting the date, filing number and filing office of the original UCC that is being continued. A sample form of UCC Amendment is included in Chapter 27.

A continuation does not have to be signed. Once filed, the continuation continues the perfection of the UCC for an additional five years running from the end of the first five-year period and every succeeding five-year period and not five years from the date of the filing of the continuation.

Amendments to UCC Filings

Where a debtor changes its name so that an existing UCC financing statement is "seriously misleading," the secured party must file an amendment to the existing UCC to reflect the debtor's new name within four months of the name change. If this is done, the amendment relates back to the original UCC filing. If the secured party fails to do this, the UCC filing is no longer effective for assets acquired by the debtor after the four-month period.

The UCC also contemplates the filing of amendments to a UCC financing statement to cover additional items or types of collateral and to correct errors in or change the names and addresses of the debtor or secured party. Such amendments are effective only from the date of filing.

A secured party must use a UCC Amendment form for any amendment of an existing UCC financing statement: the UCC Amendment does not have to be signed; it must be authorized by the debtor's authentication of the security agreement. The Amendment refers to the original UCC filing by filing number, date and filing office and describes the change from the original UCC, such as a name change or change in collateral.

PRIORITY RULES

Article 9 continues the long-standing rule that the first secured party to file a UCC financing statement or otherwise perfect its security interest has priority over competing secured parties. However, there is an exception to this rule for certain categories of collateral: a later perfection by possession or control of the collateral has priority over an earlier perfection by UCC filing. For example, a security interest in an instrument that is perfected by possession has priority over a competing security interest that was previously perfected by a UCC filing. A security interest in tangible chattel paper that is perfected by possession also has priority over a competing security interest perfected by an earlier UCC filing, unless the latter security interest is legended on the chattel paper. And a security interest in either electronic chattel paper or investment property that is perfected by control has priority over a competing security interest that is perfected by an earlier UCC filing.

As a general rule, where two secured parties perfect by control, priority is determined by which secured party first obtains control. However, a depository bank's security interest or right of setoff with respect to a debtor's deposit account has priority over all other security interests in the account, whether such competing security interests are taken as original collateral or are proceeds of other collateral. And a security interest in favor of the debtor's securities intermediary perfected by control of the debtor's brokerage account always has priority over a competing security interest in the account perfected by control.

A security interest in a letter of credit right that is perfected by control has priority over a secured party's interest in letter of credit rights that was automatically perfected as a supporting obligation.

A buyer of goods, such as inventory, in the ordinary course of business, defeats a secured party that perfects by UCC filing. However, Article 9 now provides that an ordinary course buyer of goods takes the goods subject to the rights of a secured party that has possession of the goods. This rule overturns the decision of the New York Court of Appeals in *Tanbro Fabrics Corp. v. Deering Milliken, Inc.*

PURCHASE MONEY SECURITY INTERESTS

A purchase money security interest is a security interest granted to either a trade creditor in goods sold on credit terms to the debtor for the purchase price of its goods or a security interest granted to a third party lender in goods purchased by the debtor and paid for by loans or advances made by such lender. Assets subject to a purchase money security interest are usually goods, such as inventory or equipment. A purchase money security interest can also be granted in software. There can be no purchase money security interest in intangible collateral.

A nexus is required between the acquisition of the goods and the obligation to pay for them. A security interest does not qualify as a purchase money security interest if a debtor acquires property on unsecured credit terms and subsequently creates a security interest to secure the purchase price.

A purchase money security interest is granted superpriority status that has priority over existing perfected security interests where the secured party takes certain steps depending on the type of collateral. To obtain a purchase money security interest in collateral, other than livestock and inventory, such as a purchase money security interest in equipment, a secured party must have the debtor execute a security agreement containing the appropriate granting language in the collateral and file a UCC financing statement in the appropriate jurisdiction within 20 days after the debtor receives possession of the collateral. Where the purchase money collateral is inventory, the debtor must have executed or authenticated a security agreement identifying the purchase money inventory collateral; filed a UCC financing statement in the appropriate jurisdiction before the debtor had possession of the inventory; and notified all secured creditors with UCC filings in the same type of inventory that the secured party intends to take a purchase money security interest in the inventory within five years of the debtor's possession of the inventory. However, a secured party with a possessory purchase money security interest in inventory that has not been delivered to the debtor does not have to give advance notice to existing secured parties to achieve superpriority status. Finally, a purchase money financier of livestock must notify earlier filed secured parties as in the case of inventory.

Article 9 also expands the scope of a purchase money security interest in non-consumer transactions, adopting a "dual status" rule. A purchase money secured creditor does not lose its superpriority purchase money status in any of the following situations: (1) where the purchase money collateral also secures payment of other obligations; (2) the obligation secured by the purchase money collateral is also secured by other collateral; or (3) the purchase money obligation is refinanced.

A creditor that satisfies all of the requirements for a purchase money security has priority over an earlier filed security interest in the same collateral as after-acquired property. A superpriority purchase money security interest in goods other than inventory extends to all identifiable proceeds of the goods as to which the security interest is perfected. A purchase money security interest in inventory extends to identifiable cash proceeds received on or before delivery of the inventory and to chattel paper and instruments generated by the sale of the inventory if the secured party takes possession of or places a legend on the chattel paper or instruments. The superpriority status of a purchase money security interest in inventory does not extend to accounts arising from the sale of the inventory or to trade-ins. A purchase money security interest in inventory and equipment is subordinate to the security interest of a bank into which the cash proceeds of the collateral have been deposited.

Article 9 has created special priority rules for livestock financiers in proceeds of their purchase money collateral. A purchase money security interest in livestock extends to all proceeds, including accounts and all identifiable products in their unmanufactured states.

Finally Article 9 changes the priority rules for multiple purchase money security interests. A supplier's purchase money security interest for the purchase price of the collateral has priority over a third-party lender's purchase money security interest for an enabling loan. Multiple purchase money security interests asserted by third-party lenders having made enabling loans rank in order of UCC filing.

CONSIGNMENTS

Article 9 defines a consignment as a delivery of goods having a value of at least $1,000 to a merchant for sale provided the transaction does not create a security interest; the goods are not consumer goods immediately before delivery; and the merchant deals in goods of that kind under a name other than that of the consignor; is not an auctioneer and is not generally known by its creditors to be engaged substantially in selling the goods of others. This definition excludes consignments of consumer goods and consignments of small quantities of commercial goods (valued at less than $1,000). However, commercial consignments are not subject to Article 9 where the consignee is generally known by its creditors to be substantially engaged in selling the goods of others (which is difficult to prove).

A consignment is treated as a purchase money security interest in inventory. A consignor will have to follow the rules under Article 9 for the creation and perfection of security interests in inventory and the rules applicable to purchase money inventory security interests to obtain priority over existing floating inventory secured lenders.

MERGER/SUCCESSOR DEBTOR

Article 9 addresses a number of issues that arise when collateral is either transferred to a successor debtor or the original debtor merges with a third party. These issues are generally referred to as double debtor issues.

A filed UCC financing statement remains effective with respect to collateral transferred to a third party, unless the secured party consents to the transfer free of its security interest or the transfer is an ordinary course of sale to a good faith or bona fide purchaser. The secured party does not have to file a new UCC under the name of the transferee, unless the transferee is located (i.e., organized such as incorporated) in a different state. Where the transferee is located in another state, the original UCC will become ineffective as against the transferred collateral unless a new UCC is filed within one year of the transfer.

Where a successor of the original debtor is subject to an existing security agreement because of a merger with an existing debtor, a reincorporation of an existing debtor or after a transfer of collateral, and the successor is located (i.e. organized) in the same state as the original debtor, a UCC filed in the name of the original debtor will continue to be effective to perfect a security interest in assets acquired by the successor following the merger or transfer unless the UCC becomes seriously misleading. That would be the case where the name of the successor is not substantially the same as the name of the old debtor. Where the UCC becomes seriously misleading is when the secured party has four months to file a new UCC that names the successor as debtor. If the secured party does so, its security interest remains perfected in collateral acquired by the successor. Where the secured party fails to do so, its security interest will become unperfected in collateral that the successor acquires after the four-month period.

Where the successor or other new debtor is located (i.e., organized) in a different state than the original debtor, the UCC financing statement filed against the original debtor is no longer effective to perfect a security interest in collateral acquired by the successor or other new debtor immediately after the merger or other act that created the new debtor. The secured party must immediately file a new UCC in the name of the successor or other new debtor in the new state in order to continue the perfection of its security interest in collateral acquired by the debtor.

In a priority dispute between the secured party of the original debtor and the secured party of the successor or other new debtor, the original debtor's secured party will have priority in collateral transferred to the successor or other new debtor, even where the secured party of the successor or other new debtor was the first to file a UCC. However, the secured party of the successor or other new debtor will have priority in all new collateral acquired by that debtor.

PERFECTION OF SECURITY INTERESTS IN CERTAIN SPECIALIZED COLLATERAL

Security interests in certain assets are perfected through means other than a UCC filing. These assets include titled motor vehicles, aircraft, boats and most copyrights. The reader should consult with counsel concerning the requirements for perfecting a security interest in these types of assets.

DEFAULT AND ENFORCEMENT

Introduction and Definition of Default

Although a debtor's possible default may be the last thing you actually anticipate when you extend credit, your sales and security documentation must be prepared as if default were certain. The whole point of having a security interest in the debtor's assets is the secured party's ability to dispose of those assets toward payment of the debt if default occurs. That assumes, of course, that the secured party correctly assesses the value of its collateral, and the market available at the time of default. This section will outline, in generic fashion, possible events of default, the alternative steps to take to realize on collateral after default and the steps necessary to preserve a right to a deficiency judgment against the debtor, guarantors and other secondary obligors if the collateral is insufficient to pay the debt. It focuses on commercial transactions, rather than consumer transactions where the rules might be different.

Definition of Default

The UCC does not define the term "default," but gives the parties latitude in defining it in the security documentation. Unlike other provisions of the UCC, which generally define a term where the parties fail to do so, Article 9 makes no specific provision for a definition of default.

Even though the UCC does not require a definition of "default" in security documentation, it is generally advisable to do so. A secured party should define default in such a fashion as to cover most of the probable bases for the need to foreclose. A common definition of default in security documentation includes the following "events of default":

1. The debtor's failure to make any payment when due
2. The debtor's failure to satisfactorily insure the collateral
3. The debtor's refusal to allow an inspection of the collateral within a reasonable time after a request for inspection by the secured party
4. The debtor's failure to pay taxes on the collateral when due
5. The debtor's removal of the collateral permanently from the agreed location without the written approval of the secured party
6. The debtor's failure to periodically provide financial statements and other financial information
7. The debtor's sale of the collateral without the consent of the secured party
8. The debtor's death or incapacity
9. The debtor's cessation of business
10. The debtor's filing of bankruptcy or a filing of an involuntary bankruptcy against the debtor
11. The appointment of a receiver, conservator or trustee for the debtor's business and property or both
12. The debtor's assignment of assets for the benefit of creditors
13. The debtor's insolvency
14. The debtor's failure to make payments of debts to other secured creditors or to its lender
15. The secured party's determination that the prospect of repayment is impaired
16. The debtor's breach of the terms or covenants contained in any related agreement between the debtor and the secured party or any other secured lender
17. The destruction of, or substantial damage to, any of the collateral
18. The encumbrance, seizure or attachment of any of the collateral by the IRS or any other governmental entity, or by any judgment creditor

Assuming the debtor is in default, the secured party may pursue any of the following enforcement remedies.

Collection Rights

Under Article 9, following the debtor's default, the secured party may exercise collection rights with respect to intangible collateral, such as accounts and general intangibles, or to instruments or chattel paper. The secured party may notify an account debtor or other obligor to make payment directly to the secured party. The secured party could also compel the other obligor's performance of other obligations, such as enforcing warranties and obtaining injunctions regarding intellectual property rights. The secured party may also receive and apply funds in a deposit account over which it has control in reduction of its claim against the debtor.

Nonjudicial Repossession of Collateral

Article 9 permits a lender to take possession of the collateral upon default without any court action if it may do so peacefully. A good deal of case law has developed as to what constitutes peaceful nonjudicial repossession. Given the divergence of opinions in the several states, it is difficult to enunciate a rule that applies in every case. However, any nonjudicial attempt to repossess collateral that involves or threatens to result in the use of force by either the secured party or the debtor is probably improper and may result in the imposition of liability on the secured party. Recovery through stealth or deception, however, is permitted. When in doubt, you should consult counsel on your nonjudicial repossession rights.

The UCC specifically authorizes the secured party to place language in the security agreement requiring the debtor to assemble and deliver collateral to the secured party. In some cases it is impractical for a secured party to take possession of equipment or fixtures that are collateral.

Judicial Foreclosure of Article 9 Security Interests

A secured party may pursue judicial foreclosure in any court with jurisdiction over the parties. While federal jurisdiction may exist, generally foreclosures of Article 9 security interests take place in state court in the state where the collateral is located, unless the government is a party. It would be impractical to attempt to summarize the civil procedure of all states in which the UCC applies. Generally, the foreclosure process will involve the retention of counsel and the filing of a complaint or petition with the appropriate court and the payment of a filing fee. The pleadings filed with the appropriate court will seek the foreclosure of security interests in the property, the sale of the property and the distribution of proceeds to the secured party. If there is any amount unsatisfied after sale of the collateral, judgment will be entered against the debtor for the deficiency. If there is a surplus, after application of the proceeds to the sale expenses and the outstanding debt (and the attorney's fees of the secured party to the extent provided for by agreement and not precluded by law) the surplus must be distributed back to any junior secured creditors and then the debtor. In some cases you may be able to combine an Article 9 foreclosure action with a real estate foreclosure action where the collateral includes both personal and real property.

Disposition of Collateral after Default

Article 9 has clarified the rules governing a secured party's rights and obligations upon the disposition of collateral. A secured party may sell, lease, license or otherwise dispose of its collateral by public or private disposition and apply the proceeds in reduction of its secured claim. All subordinate interests in the collateral would be discharged by such disposition. Every aspect of the disposition must be commercially reasonable. A secured party's obligation to act in a commercially reasonable manner in disposing of its collateral cannot be waived by the debtor or guarantor or other secondary obligor.

As a general rule, a secured party must give advance notice of the disposition of collateral. That includes sending notice of the time and place of any public disposition, or reasonable authenticated notification of the time after which any private disposition of collateral will occur. However, no advance notice of disposition is required where the collateral is perishable or there is a threat of a quick decline in its value, or where the collateral is of a type that is customarily sold on a recognized market.

The secured party must send notice of the disposition of collateral to the debtor and all guarantors and other secondary obligors. The debtor and guarantors and other secondary obligors may waive their advance right to notice of disposition in an authenticated agreement following default. The secured party must also give notice to all secured parties and lienholders with an interest in the collateral that is disclosed on a search of the proper filing office within certain time parameters.

Article 9 creates a number of safe harbors as it relates to the secured party's obligation to give advance notice of disposition of its collateral. In a commercial transaction, 10 days advance notice of the disposition is deemed to be commercially reasonable. Notice of disposition of the collateral would also be deemed proper if it follows the form of notice provided in the statute. This notice can be found in Chapter 27.

Under Article 9, a secured party's realization of a low price from its disposition of collateral does not by itself render a disposition commercially unreasonable. However, a low price may prompt a court to carefully scrutinize all aspects of the disposition. And if a secured party or related party, or a guarantor or other secondary obligor acquires the collateral at a price that is significantly below the price that would have been realized from a disposition to an unrelated party, the secured party's deficiency claim would be reduced to reflect the higher price that would have been paid by such hypothetical unrelated party.

Article 9 also allows a secured party to receive noncash proceeds, such as a note, from the disposition of its collateral. The secured party does not have to apply any noncash proceeds, prior to their conversion to cash, toward the payment of its claim, unless a failure to do so would be commercially unreasonable. This enables the secured party to place a value on the noncash proceeds and apply an appropriate discount rate.

Article 9 affords a transferee of a disposition of collateral the benefit of any title, possession, quiet enjoyment and similar warranties (such as ordinary warranties arising from sales, or warranties of quality or fitness for a particular purpose) that would have accompanied the disposition of the asset by operation of non-Article 9 law had the disposition been under other circumstances. Article 9 also permits a secured party to disclaim or modify such warranties.

Finally under Article 9, a secured party may purchase collateral through a public disposition, such as a public auction. A secured party may not purchase collateral by private disposition, unless the collateral is of a kind customarily sold on a recognized market or subject to standard price quotations.

Strict Foreclosure

Under Article 9 strict foreclosure is another remedy available to a secured party following the debtor's default and involves the secured party's acceptance of its collateral in full or partial satisfaction of its secured claim. A strict foreclosure, like an ordinary foreclosure and disposition of collateral, discharges all subordinate interests in the collateral. This remedy is also available to a secured party in a commercial transaction even where the secured party does not have possession of its collateral.

As part of any full strict foreclosure, a secured party must send an authenticated notice to the debtor and all secured parties and other lienholders with a junior interest in the collateral where the secured party proposes to retain the collateral. If the secured party receives an objection from any of these parties within 20 days after sending the proposal, the secured party cannot retain the collateral. Otherwise, the secured party can retain its collateral in full satisfaction of its claim. The secured party's retention of its collateral over a long period without sending such notice does not give rise to a strict foreclosure.

Article 9 also now permits a secured party to retain collateral in partial satisfaction of its secured claim, a partial strict foreclosure. The debtor must consent to a partial strict foreclosure in a record authenticated after default. The proposal also must be sent to all guarantors and other secondary obligors as well as all junior secured parties and other lienholders with an interest in the collateral. If the secured party does not receive an objection within 20 days, the partial strict foreclosure can proceed; otherwise it cannot.

The debtor and guarantors and other secondary obligors can waive this notice requirement or agree to a secured party's retention of its collateral in full or partial satisfaction of its secured claim following the debtor's default.

Application of Proceeds of Disposition

Under Article 9, a secured party can apply the proceeds of the disposition of its collateral first toward payment of the expenses of disposition, including attorneys' fees and expenses, if provided for under the debtor's agreement with the secured party and not prohibited by law; and then toward the payment of the secured party's claim; then toward the payment of the claims of creditors with a junior lien in the collateral. Any remaining surplus proceeds would be paid to the debtor.

Accounting

Under Article 9, the secured party must account to the debtor for the distribution of the proceeds of the disposition of collateral and pay any surplus to the debtor.

Remedies

Article 9 adopts a rebuttable presumption rule where the secured party fails to comply with its provisions on the disposition of collateral. Where the secured party fails to comply with Article 9, there is a presumption that the value of its collateral equaled the amount of the secured claim, which eliminates its deficiency claim. However, this presumption is subject to rebuttal by the secured party.

ARTICLE 9'S TRANSITION RULES FOR OLD ARTICLE 9
SECURITY INTERESTS

Overview

Current Article 9 governs all secured transactions within its scope, even security interests created under Old Article 9. However, current Article 9 affords secured parties some time to take the necessary action to make sure that secured transactions entered into under Old Article 9 comply with current Article 9.

Transition Rule for UCC Filings under Old Article 9

A secured party is given a potentially longer period for UCC filings that comply with Old Article 9 but fail to comply with current Article 9. For example, a UCC that was filed in the correct jurisdiction under Old Article 9 (the state of the debtor's chief executive office for intangible collateral, such as accounts and general intangibles, and the state where tangible collateral was located, such as inventory and equipment) may not be filed in the correct jurisdiction (the state of the debtor's incorporation or organization) under current Article 9.

UCCs filed under and in compliance with Old Article 9 that do not comply with Article 9 will continue to be effective to perfect an Old Article 9 security interest until the earlier of the date that the UCC would otherwise lapse under Old Article 9 (in most states five years after the original filing, but check state law) or in most states, June 30, 2006. In order to continue perfection by UCC filing after these dates, the secured party must bring their UCCs into compliance with current Article 9 as more fully discussed below.

A UCC filed under Old Article 9 in the jurisdiction required under current Article 9 may be continued under Article 9 by checking the continuation box in a UCC Amendment form and including all of the information required in a continuation under Article 9. For example, a UCC was filed under Old Article 9 in the state where the debtor's chief executive office and all tangible collateral is located, and, therefore, was properly perfected under Old Article 9. That is also the state where the debtor is incorporated. The security interest is, therefore, properly perfected by the UCC filing under current Article 9. The secured party continues the perfection of the security interest under current Article 9 by filing a UCC Amendment/continuation with the appropriate central office within six months of the expiration of the UCC filing, just like under Old Article 9. The current Article 9 rules for continuations govern.

However, where the jurisdiction for filing a UCC under Old Article 9 is not the required jurisdiction for filing a UCC under current Article 9, a secured party must file an "in lieu financing statement" in the correct jurisdiction and filing office under Article 9. An "in lieu financing statement" looks like an ordinary UCC financing statement, must comply in all respects with Article 9's requirements for a UCC financing statement, and also must identify the existing UCC being continued by filing office, date of filing and the filing number of the original UCC and the most recent continuation, if any. The secured party can file an "in lieu financing statement" without the debtor's signature. A form of "in lieu financing statement" is included in Chapter 27.

The secured party can file an "in lieu financing statement" in the correct jurisdiction and filing office under Article 9 at any time prior to the lapse of the original Old Article 9 UCC filing but not later than an outside date, which in most states is

June 30, 2006. This can be done even before the normal six-month period prior to lapse for filing a continuation. The "in lieu financing statement" then has its own five-year term in most states, and unlike a continuation, is not dependent on the date of the original UCC filing.

If a secured party satisfies all of the requirements for an "in lieu financing statement," the perfection of its Old Article 9 security interest relates back to the date on which the UCC originally became effective for perfection under Old Article 9, provided the security interest was continuously perfected by UCC filing since then.

For example, a debtor is a Delaware corporation with its principal place of business in New York and its inventory located in New Jersey. The secured party filed UCCs under Old Article 9 on January 1, 2000 in the appropriate filing offices in New York (perfecting its security interest in the debtor's accounts and general intangibles) and in New Jersey (perfecting its security interest in inventory). The secured party must have filed an "in lieu financing statement" identifying each of the existing financing statements by filing number, filing office and date of filing with the Delaware Secretary of State by January 1, 2005 (at any time up to January 1, 2005) in order for perfection to relate back to the January 1, 2000 original UCC filing date.

Amendment of Old Article 9 UCC Financing Statements

A UCC financing statement filed under Old Article 9 may have to be amended under current Article 9. The amendment may become necessary in order to reflect the debtor's correct legal name, or a change in the description of collateral to reflect the changes brought about by current Article 9.

An amendment of a UCC financing statement filed under Old Article 9 must be filed in the jurisdiction and filing office required under current Article 9. Where the original UCC filed under Old Article 9 is in the same jurisdiction and filing office required under current Article 9, the secured party can amend the UCC by filing a UCC Amendment form that describes the change in that same office. However, where the original UCC to be amended is not filed in the jurisdiction and filing office required under current Article 9, the secured party must first file an "in lieu financing statement" in the required jurisdiction and filing office and then either include the amended information in the in lieu filing or then file a UCC Amendment form that reflects the changed information.

UCC Searches in Old Article 9 and Revised Article 9 Filing Jurisdictions

The transition period afforded by Article 9 gives secured parties until not later than June 30, 2006 in most states to bring their UCCs into compliance with current Article 9. Until then, UCCs that are filed in jurisdictions permitted under Old Article 9 may still be effective under current Article 9 to perfect a security interest created under Old Article 9. Therefore, for most states, until June 30, 2006, creditors should conduct UCC searches in both the jurisdictions and filing offices required under Old Article 9 and under current Article 9.

FIXTURES

Just as goods may be classified as equipment or inventory, depending upon their usage, goods that become associated with real estate may become fixtures or may remain equipment. Fixtures involve a hybrid situation where an item that is otherwise movable may become so associated with real estate as to be deemed part of the real estate. Obviously, the potential for litigation between the person providing the goods and the creditor with the mortgage on the real estate is enormous.

Generally, fixtures are a hybrid of personal property and real estate. Fixtures include, among other things: wall-to-wall carpeting, "built-in" air conditioners, "built-in" appliances such as dishwashers and stoves, restaurant equipment, milking equipment and commercial manufacturing equipment, to name a few.

Not only does the uncertainty with what constitutes fixtures generate potential litigation, but the conflict between an existing mortgage on real property and a security interest in the goods that may become fixtures also generates problems. Generally, the UCC defines goods as fixtures when they become so related to particular real estate that an interest in them arises under real estate law. Absent a familiarity with the applicable state law, however, it is difficult to predict exactly what might be a fixture and what might not. To cure the problem, a hybrid filing called a fixture filing is necessary. States have developed various tests to determine whether an item is a fixture. Generally, physical annexation to the real estate, the application or adaptation of the item to the use or purpose to which the realty is devoted, and the intention of the parties to make a permanent accession to the real estate are considered. Courts may consider many other factors, however. Generally, fixtures will be treated separately from other goods for security interest purposes.

CREATION OF SECURITY INTERESTS IN FIXTURES

The creation of security interests in fixtures still requires the security agreement describing the collateral and authenticated by the debtor. While no special language is required, the agreement must contain an adequate description of the collateral. No description of the location of the fixtures is required in the security agreement, but most lenders include one to facilitate preparation of the financing statement. The security agreement must then be authenticated by the debtor and identify the debtor.

The financing statement must identify the fixtures to be covered, must state that it covers fixture collateral and it must contain a legal description of the real estate. Further, the fixture filing must then be filed in the real estate records in the county in which the collateral is located as a part of the real estate record, and in the central office for UCC personal property filings. Alternatively, a mortgage identifying the fixtures may be executed and recorded.

Refer to Chapter 27 for the following forms:

- Disposition Notification for Commercial (or Consumer) Transaction after Default
- Security Agreement for Accounts Receivable
- Security Agreement under Article 9 of the Uniform Commercial Code
- Security Agreement for Equipment
- Simple Security Agreement
- UCC Financing Statement
- UCC Financing Statement Addendum
- UCC Financing Statement Amendment
- UCC Financing Statement Amendment Addendum
- UCC "In Lieu Financing Statement"

SPECIFIC UCC ARTICLE 9 REVISIONS AND/OR NEW TERMS

NEW OR REVISED ITEM OR TERM	OLD UCC ARTICLE 9	CURRENT ARTICLE 9
Accounts	"Account" means any right to payment for goods sold or leased or for services rendered which is not evidenced by an instrument or chattel paper, whether or not it has been earned by performance. All rights to payment earned or unearned under a charter or other contract involving the use or hire of a vessel and all rights incident to the charter or contract are accounts.	"Accounts" includes a wide variety of rights to payment arising out of the transfer of rights in tangible and intangible personal property, including credit card receivables, healthcare insurance receivables and license fees.
All Assets	N/A—This term on either the Security Agreement or the Financing Statement was too vague and broad to be of any use to the secured creditor.	Current Article 9 specifically provides that the Financing Statement sufficiently indicates the collateral that it covers if the financing statement provides a description of the collateral or an indication that the financing statement covers all assets or all personal property so long as this is consistent with the description of collateral in the Security Agreement. NOTE: this phrase "all assets" on a security agreement is insufficient.
Authenticate	N/A—An actual signature was required.	"Authenticate" means: (A) to sign; or (B) to execute or otherwise adopt a symbol, or encrypt or similarly process a record in whole or in part, with the present intent of the authenticating person to identify the person and adopt or accept a record.

SPECIFIC UCC ARTICLE 9 REVISIONS AND/OR NEW TERMS *(Continued)*

NEW OR REVISED ITEM OR TERM	OLD UCC ARTICLE 9	CURRENT ARTICLE 9
Consignment	Former Article 9 was questionable as to whether a transaction was a "sale on approval" or whether the transaction was a "sale or return." The States varied widely as to the requirements necessary to protect the interests of the owner of the goods. These ranged from a requirement to do nothing to a requirement to post a sign describing the goods as "consigned and not property of the vendor" to a requirement to file a UCC-1 Financing Statement for "Notification" purposes.	The definition of "security interest" now includes consignments. Under Current Article 9, a "consignment" means a transaction, regardless of its form, in which a person delivers goods to a merchant for the purpose of sale and: (A) The merchant deals in goods of that kind under a name other than the name of the person making delivery; is not an auctioneer; and is not generally known by its creditors to be substantially engaged in selling the goods of others (B) With respect to each delivery, the aggregate value of the goods is $1,000 or more at the time of delivery (C) The goods are not consumer goods immediately before delivery (D) The transaction does not create a security interest that secures an obligation
Filing Office	Each state had specific rules regarding the proper place for filing. The alternatives were as follows: • Central Filing (i.e., filing with the secretary of state in the state where the assets were located) • Local Filing (i.e., filing in the county where the assets were located) • Dual Filing (i.e., filing with the secretary of state and with the local filing officer	Each state will have the ability to designate its specific filing office. At present, it is anticipated the filing office will be either the office of the Secretary of State within each state or the office of a private party that maintains the state's filing system. Some states still provide for local filing.

Financing Statement Requisites	While many states used a "standard" UCC-1 Financing Statement Form, several states required their own specific form. The general information required to be included on the UCC-1 form was:
	• Name and address of debtor
	• Name and address of secured party
	• Description of collateral
	• Statement as to whether or not proceeds of collateral were included
	• Statement as to whether or not product of the collateral was included
	And there were also specific rules for financing statements that covered timber, minerals, crops, etc.
	The Debtor's signature was required, unless the security agreement specifically authorized the secured creditor to sign and file the financing statement on behalf of the debtor.
	A financing statement must provide the name of the debtor and the secured party and an indication of the collateral that it covers.
	Signature is not required. The elimination of the signature requirement has been done to facilitate paperless (electronic) filing.
Letter-of-Credit Rights	It was permissible to assign "letter of credit proceeds" as collateral under Article 5 of the UCC. However, perfection against such collateral under Articles 5 & 9 was confusing, oft overlooked and generally difficult.
	A Security Interest in "letter of credit rights" may be taken. However, a secured party still has no right to make a draw on the letter of credit. Article 5 will still control. And, a secured party can only perfect its lien on these letter of credit rights by control; however perfection is automatic where the letter of credit right is a supporting obligation.

SPECIFIC UCC ARTICLE 9 REVISIONS AND/OR NEW TERMS (Continued)

NEW OR REVISED ITEM OR TERM	OLD UCC ARTICLE 9	CURRENT ARTICLE 9
Location Definition	Where the debtor is located was virtually meaningless under the Old Article 9. What was more important is the location of the debtor's assets and principal place of business.	A debtor who is an individual is located at the individual's principal residence. A debtor that is an organization and has only one place of business is located at its place of business. A debtor that is an organization and has more than one place of business is located at its chief executive office. A registered organization that is organized under the law of a State is located in that State.
Name of Debtor	The statute provided that the exact registered name of the Debtor was to be used. An incorrect name, which disabled a party from finding the filing, would render the filing ineffective against subsequent competing parties. Frequently, UCC-1 Financing Statements were filed using the Debtor's trade name, often without negative consequences.	If the debtor is a registered organization (corp., LLC, etc.), the financing statement must provide the name of the debtor indicated on the public record of the debtor's jurisdiction of organization that shows the debtor to have been organized. A trade name is not needed and in fact, a trade name alone is insufficient.
Purchase Money Security Interests	A PMSI is a security interest taken by a seller of goods which protects the seller for the purchase price only with respect to the specific goods sold by the seller, or which protects the interest of the entity which supplies the funds to purchase the goods.	"Purchase money collateral" is defined as goods or software that secures a purchase-money obligation incurred with respect to that collateral. "Purchase money obligation" is defined as an obligation of an obligor incurred as all or part of the price of the collateral or for value given to enable the debtor to acquire rights in or the use of the collateral if the value is in fact so used.

11

Liens Affecting Personal Property

LIENS ON PERSONAL PROPERTY

In addition to mechanics' liens, which are liens only on real property, and in addition to rights of owners to bond the jobs which use payment bonds to eliminate the possibility of a lien on real estate, there are numerous liens against personal property which are available to a creditor. Real property is anything to do with an interest in land, while personal property is virtually anything else. As noted elsewhere in the Manual, personal property can be tangible or intangible, and for the purpose of attaching a security interest, may not have yet come into existence. This chapter will deal with the creation and existence of liens on personal property other than those created by Article 9 of the Uniform Commercial Code ("UCC") (see Chapter 10).

There are various other types of liens on personal property which can be available to creditors to satisfy unpaid debts or obligations. Unlike the concept of the security interest, which to a great degree is consistent throughout the UCC and may vary from state to state, each state has created liens on personal property which may be created and enforced only in that particular state.

Before detailing each state's statutory scheme for liens on personal property, this chapter will discuss the different types of liens on personal property. Since many liens on personal property are created by the common law and not by statute, two issues become of critical importance. First, do not assume that because there is no statutory authority for the creation of a lien, it is not available. As noted below, many times the common law has provided for the lien's creation in a particular state, yet no statute has been enacted to formalize it. Second, it is necessary to deal with competent legal counsel in a particular state to be advised of the non-statutory personal property liens that may be available. Because of the uniqueness of the development of state law, many times this analysis is critically important.

Importance of Liens When Extending Credit

Most business and credit professionals consider liens as an issue only when attempting to collect a debt, believing that the lien, when obtained, would be a useful tool for the collection process. However, the presence of liens should be considered a significant factor when extending or continuing credit.

As set forth below, there are numerous liens that can be obtained by governmental agencies and private parties. In each instance, the lien indicates that the property owner has failed to timely pay a debt. This is a factor which should be considered at the time of the extension or renewal of credit, as it has proven to be an extremely useful indicator of the debtor's ability to pay current obligations.

Unfortunately, mercantile and credit reporting agencies do not always have timely information concerning lien status. Thus, a credit report can be obtained which says nothing of liens, yet the debtor's ability to pay may be seriously impaired by the existence of one or more liens.

For a very nominal charge, a credit grantor can obtain a report which will be the result of a lien search in the locale of a debtor's place of business. Since all liens must be a matter of record in order to be effective, the absence of any liens can be considered conclusive for the date that the lien search has been effected.

There have been many surprised credit grantors who, after extending or continuing credit to a "good" customer, find the customer's business shut down due to the exercise of lien rights by a governmental authority or a private party. While a lien may arise at any time, periodic lien searches as part of a comprehensive credit evaluation process can prevent such surprises.

Statutory Liens and Common-Law Liens

Individual states may create or have created liens in two different manners. A statutory lien is one that is specifically referred to and created by a law of a particular state. In such an instance, the creation and extent of the lien is strictly limited to that provided by the statute. Additionally, the manner of the creation and enforcement of the lien can be effected only according to the statutory scheme.

There are, however, various other liens which have been created by common law. Common law is that area of the law that has developed outside of the statutory or legislative process, and, usually through the development of case law, has evolved over a considerable period of time. Many of the eastern states have common-law liens and other common-law principles that evolved from English common law, which was present prior to the Declaration of Independence.

The understanding and explanation of common-law liens cannot be set forth in material such as this. Since they are developed by court decisions (case law), they are not usually subject to any indexing or other quick means of identification. Should there be a question as to the existence of a common-law lien in a particular state, knowledgeable counsel should be consulted for such advice. Many times, however, a state legislature will take a common law lien and codify it by statute, at which point the strict language of the statute will control with respect to the particular lien on personal property.

Consensual and Nonconsensual Liens

The creation of a security interest is a clear example of the creation of a consensual lien. In that instance, the person or entity whose property is to be the subject of the security interest or lien will consent to the lien and the security agreement. Similarly, any writing which specifically grants a lien on personal property (or even real property) and is signed by the party whose property is to be affected by the lien will be considered a consensual lien.

Many liens on personal property are nonconsensual, and these are used, in most instances, for the recovery of the payment of a debt. Artisan's liens, garagemen's liens, liens for animals, etc., are not usually in the nature of a consensual lien. However, a creditor that expects to provide goods or services which will preserve, protect, maintain or enhance the value of personal property may, as part of the agreement for the work to be performed, create a consensual lien. In most instances, such a lien would be more in the nature of a security interest governed by Article 9 of the UCC, and the requirements of the UCC would be applicable. There are, however, instances where the creation of a consensual lien will not be subject to the security interest provisions.

Possessory and Nonpossessory Liens

A possessory lien is one in which the party claiming the lien has possession of the property which is to become or has become the subject of the lien, and that party will not relinquish possession of the property until the lien is satisfied. An example of a consensual lien of this nature would be the pledge of an asset at a pawn shop. An example of a nonconsensual lien of this nature would be a garagemen's lien. A nonpossessory lien is where the property sought to be the subject of the lien remains in the possession of its rightful owner, but can, in fact, by statutory or common law, become the subject of a lien.

For those creditors asserting a possessory lien, it is very important that they be aware of the statutory or common law principles which create such a lien. In most instances, the relinquishment of possession of the asset upon which the lien is to be imposed constitutes a waiver of that lien, even if there is a concurrent promise to pay. Absent a written agreement which creates a consensual lien (almost in the nature of a security interest), the possessory lien is lost when possession is surrendered.

Judicial and Nonjudicial Liens

A judicial lien is one in which it is necessary to go to court in order to have the lien created. A lien which is developed upon the enrolling of a judgment, a tax lien or similar lien is a judicial lien. A nonjudicial lien is one where the party asserting the lien may do so without the aid of a court proceeding or decree. Again, an artisan's lien, a garagemen's lien and liens for animals are examples of a nonjudicial lien.

Attention should be given to the fact that while a lien may be created as a nonjudicial lien without the need for a court decree, enforcement of the lien may, in many instances, require a court decree. Creditors seeking to assert a nonjudicial lien should carefully consult applicable law to determine if it is necessary to utilize the judicial process in order to take such action to satisfy the obligation which gave rise to the imposition of the lien.

Priority of Conflicting Liens

Once a lien on personal property has been established, the holder must recognize that the lien may be subordinate to another lien on the same asset. For instance, a garagemen's lien for the repair of a motor vehicle may be in conflict with a security interest granted in favor of the entity financing the purchase of the motor vehicle. This situation often results when one party is asserting a possessory, nonconsensual lien and the other party is asserting a nonpossessory, consensual lien.

Section 9-310 of the UCC determines the priority which may be applicable with respect to certain liens on personal property which are in conflict with security interests on the same asset. While this section is of some help to determine the rights of the conflicting lienors, there is no generalized principle that can be stated which will absolutely deal with conflicting liens on the same personal property. It is, therefore, important to review the statutory and common-law principles involving the types of liens created in order to determine the priority of the parties in the conflicting liens.

Liens Commonly Encountered

Consensual liens in property other than real estate are governed by Article 9 of the Uniform Commercial Code, which is discussed in Chapter 10. Similarly, judicial liens normally arise only as a result of court proceedings. The rest of this chapter, therefore, focuses on statutory liens. A specific type of statutory lien, the mechanics' liens, is discussed in detail in Chapter 12.

Most states, either by common law or by statute, provide for the creation of artisan's liens, garagemen's liens, liens for animals, hospital liens, innkeepers' liens, attorneys' liens, liens for performing services and other types of liens which do not involve the extension of commercial credit. A credit grantor in a particular industry (i.e., an owner of a hotel) should consult a particular state's statutory and common-law principles in order to determine what liens on personal property may be available, and the manner in which they are to be created, perfected and enforced.

In the materials listed below on a state-by-state basis, the Editors have chosen to highlight important or unusual types of liens which have been statutorily created by the individual states. Again, it should be noted that the following summary does not include common-law liens, and does not include the more traditional type of liens on personal property.

Landlords' Liens

Many states by statute give certain rights to landlords to permit them to establish a nonconsensual lien on property of a tenant in order secure payment for the renting or leasing of the particular premises. Creditors attempting to create any type of lien on personal property, including security interests, should be aware of the possibility that a landlord may claim a lien on the same assets.

For secured creditors who are attempting to gain a security interest in and to certain tangible personal property assets, care should be taken to determine if a particular state's laws gives the landlord a superior lien to that of the secured creditor. Additionally, creditors attempting to create any type of consensual or nonconsensual lien should pay careful attention to the fact that a landlords' lien may by statute be superior.

The secured creditor in obtaining a security interest and certainly any other creditor attempting to obtain a consensual lien should attempt to gain a waiver of a landlords' lien if there is any concern that such a landlords' lien could have priority in the same assets. It is a usual condition of doing business that a secured creditor will insist upon a waiver of the landlords' lien prior to advancing any funds. It is also surprising how many holders of liens on personal property are unaware of the possibility of landlords' liens, and find out too late that the lien on personal property is subject to a substantial claim for unpaid rent or breach of a lease. Unsecured creditors who will be selling a large amount of product to a customer which is to be stored at the customer's facility should also consider obtaining a waiver of a landlords' lien as a precondition of extending credit and delivery of the goods.

Following the section on liens of personal property on a state-by-state basis is a listing of landlords' liens. Since landlords' liens are all statutory liens, care should be taken in examining the particular provisions of a state's statute when a question of the possible priority of a conflicting lien may be important. It is always easier to deal with the situation before a problem develops than after the fact when it is first learned that the conflicting liens exist.

TAX LIENS

The United States Congress on behalf of federal taxes and each state legislature on behalf of individual states' taxes have enacted laws which create the mechanism for the imposition and enforcement of tax liens. The state or municipal tax liens may have different names, but each has the same effect—property of the taxpayer becomes subject to the lien of the governmental agency, irrespective of the fact that it may remain in the possession of the taxpayer without any other visible notice of the existence of the lien. Oftentimes, a creditor attempting to create, perfect, or enforce a lien on personal property will ignore the fact that there may be in existence prior, conflicting, or subsequent tax liens which must be considered in the perfection and enforcement process. The following is an explanation of the types of liens.

Federal Tax Liens

As a result of the Constitution's development of the U.S. Senate and House as the legislative arm of the government and especially passage of the Sixteenth Amendment, which created income taxation, the U.S. Congress has the authority to establish federal legislation dealing with the creation, perfection and enforcement of liens to ensure the payment of federal taxes. Of course, any such legislation is the law of the land and applicable in each state. Furthermore, because of the supremacy of the U.S. government, in most instances, the statutes involving federal tax liens will be superior to any tax liens created by the individual states. However, if the state lien is perfected first, it will have priority over the federal lien.

Because of provisions in the Fifth and Fourteenth Amendments which prohibit the taking of property without due process, a federal tax lien cannot by operation of law or otherwise become superior to a prior perfected lien in the same property. However, the development of the federal tax lien law has substantially and adversely affected the rights of secured and unsecured creditors. Under the appropriate legislation, if an arm of the U.S. government (such as the Internal Revenue Service) seeks to impose a lien, once that lien is appropriately recorded with the clerk of the court in the county (or city) where the property is located, there is in existence a lien in favor of the U.S. government on all of the property of the debtor located in that subdivision. Unlike other state statutes or the UCC, which requires a specific delineation of the assets to be covered by the lien, the possession of the property, a levy or any other activity which would put one on notice of the existence of the lien, the mere recording of the lien in the clerk's federal tax lien register is sufficient to create the lien. The development of the law in the United States frowns on "secret liens", but to many, the recordation of a federal tax lien is secret to them. However, the filing of the notice of a federal tax lien in the public record makes it just as public as an Article 9 lien for which a financing statement is filed.

The recordation of the federal tax lien affects any real or personal property, tangible or intangible, owned by the taxpayer. This includes real estate, tangible personal assets, insurance proceeds, accounts receivable, contract rights, deposits of monies and any other asset of the debtor taxpayer. As can be seen, the federal tax lien is much more expansive than most consensual and nonconsensual liens, and certainly more expansive than most other judicial liens.

The enforcement of a security interest or other personal property lien which is superior to a tax lien created difficulties for the IRS and other governmental agencies in that they had the belief that "games could be played" to deprive the U.S.

government of payment for the tax due. As a result, in 1966, Congress enacted the Federal Tax Lien Act which, although not directly affecting the priority of creditors, imposes certain rules and regulations concerning the enforcement of liens even if they are superior to a federal tax lien.

The Federal Tax Lien Act also provides certain protection for purchasers of assets from a business (or even from an individual) when there was no actual notice of the imposition and perfection of the lien. The concept is similar to the purchasing of an asset subject to a security interest when the sale is in the ordinary course of business from a dealer of the kind.

Of great importance, however, are the provisions of the Federal Tax Lien Act relating to the enforcement of liens and security interests where a federal tax lien comes into existence, either prior to or inferior to the lien or security interest sought to be enforced. The act requires specific notice to be given to the IRS or the appropriate governmental agency prior to any action being taken to sell or otherwise dispose of the property which is subject to the lien. Even though a secured creditor under the UCC or other lienholder may, by statutory or common law, have the absolute right to effect the disposition of the property subject to the lien, the Act provides substantial penalties if appropriate notice is not given to the IRS or the specific government agency holding the tax lien. There are very substantial penalties which can be imposed if the assets subject to a tax lien are liquidated without appropriate notice to the U.S. government, and this can eliminate the lienholder's right to receive the proceeds or the value of the collateral which is subject to a prior perfected and existing lien. The rules relating to the disposition of assets subject to a lien are technical and precise, and it is necessary for a creditor attempting to enforce a lien or security interest to use an attorney to comply with these provisions.

Too often, creditors fail to effect a review of the federal tax lien records affecting a particular debtor either prior to the creation of a lien or security interest, or prior to the enforcement of such a lien or security interest following default. Local NACM affiliates and other businesses provide inexpensive searches of the federal tax lien records in order to determine the existence of any such lien. Care should be taken to ensure that such a search is completed prior to any attempt to enforce a lien or security interest.

State Tax Liens

Like the federal tax lien, the laws of the individual states provide for the imposition of liens in favor of the states to collect unpaid income tax, withholding taxes, unemployment taxes, sales taxes, use taxes and the like. Because each state has a different tax scheme, it is important that each state's laws be reviewed if a question arises concerning the imposition or enforcement of a state tax lien.

Just as with a federal tax lien, a state tax lien cannot affect the priority of a properly perfected and existing prior lien. However, as with the federal tax lien, the states can establish procedures which require creditors to follow in order for their to be the enforcement of any lien where a state tax lien exists.

The methodology for establishing the state tax liens varies from state to state. In some states, a state tax lien is enrolled similar to a federal tax lien, and this constitutes a lien on all of the assets of the debtor taxpayer located in the particular subdivision. In other states, suits or other legal proceedings have to be commenced, and judgments or warrants need to be issued for the lien to be effective.

States also have enacted regulations with respect to the sale or disposition of property by a lienholder which is also subject to a state tax lien. Care must be taken to consult with appropriate local statutes prior to the liquidation of any assets which may be subject to a state tax lien.

STATE-BY-STATE LISTING OF LIENS ON PERSONAL PROPERTY

Note: State legislatures will, on occasion, modify an area of law without clear delineation as to its content and context. As a result, even the changes which have been enacted prior to placement in the state's Code may be difficult to locate. As a result, the Editors urge all users of the Manual to use this publication only as a guide, and consult the latest codified version of the state's law for all recent changes.

ALABAMA

Who May Claim—Owners of timber land or their assignees; operators of a public sawmill; keeper, owner or proprietor of a livery stable; owners of a cotton gin, peanut machine or pickler, or hay-baling machine or press, or plant for drying or processing planting seeds (hereinafter agricultural commodities processors).

In addition to other personal property liens, the owner of a self storage facility shall have a lien on all personal property stored within each leased space located at the self storage facility for rent, labor, or other charges, present or future, and for expenses reasonably incurred in enforcing the lien. Keepers of hotels, inns, boarding houses and restaurants shall have a lien on the goods and personal baggage of their guests and boarders to secure the payment of any money due from them for board and lodging.

Property Covered—Timber sold for the purposes of rafting, shipping, or manufacture; all lumber sawed by a sawmill under any contract with the owner; agricultural commodities processed under any contract with the owner of such commodities.

Extent of the Lien—Timber liens are for the stipulated price or value thereof. A sawmill operator's lien is for the amount agreed upon, or if none, for the reasonable or customary price of the sawing, as long as the lumber remains at the sawmill or in the sawmill owner's possession, and if removed without the knowledge and consent of that owner, the lien will follow the lumber.

An agricultural commodities processor's lien is for the toll or charge under any contract with the owner of the commodity whether the charge is expressed or implied. Livery stable keeper has lien on all stock kept and fed by him for payment of charges; he has right to keep stock for six months after notice of lien.

Duration of Lien—Where the process of attachment is authorized (see 7 below), suit must be commenced within six months after the demand becomes due.

The self storage facility lien attaches as of the date the personal property is brought to the self-service storage facility and continues so long as the owner retains possession and until the default is corrected, or a sale is conducted, or the property is otherwise disposed of to satisfy the lien.

Enforcement of Lien by Sale—Liens on lumber, agricultural commodities, baggage or goods of guests and borders, or livery stable stock if the charges due are not paid within 10 days after demand therefor, may be enforced, upon notice as described below, by sale of the lumber, stock or commodity to the highest bidder, for the payment of the expense of such sale and the charges due, and the residue paid to the owner of the property sold.

Notice of Sale—Ten days' notice of the time and place of sale must be given by advertisement in a newspaper published in the county in which the sawmill is located, the agricultural commodity processed, the hotel, inn, boarding house or restaurant is located; or in the county in which the stable, pasture or cattle, or livestock feed or fattening lot is located once a week for two successive weeks, or if there is no such paper, by posting the notice in two or more public places in the county; three places are required in the case of agricultural commodities liens and livery stable keeper liens.

Notice to perfected security interests under the Uniform Commercial Code, with the name of the occupant as debtor, is required before a sale when dealing with a self storage facility lien.

Enforcement of Lien by Attachment—Available if lumber, agricultural commodity or livery stock has been removed without the knowledge and consent of the lienor. Available on liens for timber removed without consent of the lienor and without payment, or when the claimant has good cause to believe that the timber is about to be removed.

Enforcement of Lien by Garnishment—Available for the enforcement of agricultural commodity liens.

Priority—A sawmill operator's lien is paramount to all others; an agricultural commodity processor's lien has priority over all other liens, mortgages, or encumbrances whether existing or not at the time of commencement of the processing or work except a landlord's lien. The self storage facility lien is superior to any other lien or security interest, except for any tax lien as otherwise provided by law.

ALASKA

Who May Claim—Common carriers or persons who, at the request of the owner or lawful possessor of personal property, carry, convey, or transport properties; persons who safely keep or store grain, wares, merchandise, and personal property at the request of the owner or lawful possessor; persons who perform, labor on, or assist in obtaining or securing timber, the owner of a tugboat or towboat which assists in towing lumber, the owner of a team or machine which hauls or assists in hauling lumber, the owner of a logging road over which timber is transported and delivered; a person who contributes to the preparation of fish or aquatic animals for food, fish, meal, fertilizer, oil, or other article of commerce by furnishing material or labor for it; persons employed as watchman have a lien upon the property for wages earned by him; persons who pasture or feed livestock or bestow labor, care, or attention thereupon; the operator of a hotel or boardinghouse has a lien upon, and may retain, all baggage and other property lawfully in the possession of a guest for all proper charges owed by the guest to the hotel or boardinghouse operator; an operator of a hospital in the state, a licensed special nurse in a hospital in the state, or a physician who furnishes service to a person who has a traumatic injury has a lien upon any sum awarded to the injured person.

Property Covered—Property transported by carrier or stored; timber and the product of a cannery, saltery, or other plant or establishment, and the plant or establishment itself; any sum awarded to the injured person or the personal representative of the injured person by judgment or obtained by a settlement or compromise.

How Claimed—Claims for timber liens must be sworn to and filed.

_____Claimant, v. _____

Notice is given by this claim that _____, residing at _____, State of Alaska claims a lien upon a _____ of _____, being about _____ in quantity, which were cut in _____ recording district, State of Alaska, and are now lying or being at _____, for labor performed and assistance provided in _____ said _____, that the name of the owner or reputed owner is _____; that _____ employed said _____ to perform the labor and provide the assistance upon the following terms and conditions, to wit -

That _____ agreed to pay the _____ for labor and assistance _____; that the contract has been faithfully performed and fully complied with on the part of _____, who performed labor and assisted in _____ for the period of _____; that the labor and assistance were so performed provided upon _____ between the ___ day of _____, and 45 days have not elapsed since that time; that the amount of the claimant's demand for the service is _____; that no part of the claim has been paid except _____; and there is now due and remaining unpaid on the claim paid except _____; and there is now due and remaining unpaid on the claim, after deducting all just credits and offsets, the sum of _____, and that _____ claims a lien in this amount upon the _____ and also claims a lien on all the _____ now owned by _____ in the recording district to secure payment for the work and labor in obtaining or securing the saw logs, spars, piles, cordwood, fuelwood, shingle bolts, or other timber herein this claim.

_____
(Signature)

State of Alaska
_____ Judicial District ss.

_____, being first duly sworn on oath says that the undersigned is _____ named in the foregoing claim of liens, has heard the claim read, knows the contents of the claim and believes the claim to be true.

_____
(Signature)

Subscribed and sworn to before me this ___ day of _____.

_____
(Signature)

A person claiming a fishpacker or processor claim must file a claim containing the following statement of: (1) the claimant's demand and the amount of the demand after deducting credits and offsets; (2) the name of the person by whom the claimant is employed or at whose request the material is furnished; (3) the terms and conditions of the contract of employment or under which the material was furnished; (4) a description of the property sufficient for identification on which the lien is claimed; and (5) the name of the owner or reputed owner thereof. The lien claim shall be verified by the oath of the lien claimant or someone on behalf of the lien claimant who has knowledge of the facts. If there is no express contract of employment or for furnishing the material the claim shall state the reasonable value of the work, labor or material.

A watchman's lien claim must contain a true statement of: (1) the demand and the amount of the demand after deducting all just credits and offsets; (2) the name of the person by whom the claimant is employed and a statement of the terms and conditions of the contract of employment; (3) a description of the property sufficient for identification on which the lien is claimed; and (4) the name of the owner or reputed owner of the property. The lien claim shall be verified by the oath of the claimant or someone on behalf of the lien claimant who has personal knowledge of the facts. If there is no express contract of employment the claim must state the reasonable value of the work or services.

Hospital liens are filed by filing a claim substantially in the following form:

NOTICE is hereby given that _____ has rendered services for hospitalization, physician services, or special nurses' services for _____, a person who was injured on the ___ day of _____ at _____ in the state, and the _____ (claimant) hereby claims a lien upon any money due or owing or any claim for compensation, damages, contribution, settlement, or judgment from _____ alleged to have caused the injuries and any other person liable for the injury or obligated to compensate the injured person on account of the injuries; the hospitalization, physician services, or special nurses' services were rendered to the injured person between the ___ day of _____ and _____:

General Description of Services Rendered and Statement of Amount Due

_____ and that 90 days have not elapsed since that time; that the claimant's demands for care and service is in the sum of $_____ and that no part of the demands has been paid, except $_____, and that there is now due and owing and remaining unpaid thereof, after deducting all credits and offsets, the sum of $_____, in which amount lien is hereby claimed.

United States of America
State of Alaska ss.
_____ Judicial District

I, _____, being first duly sworn on oath say: That I am _____ named in the foregoing claim of lien; that I have read the same and know the contents thereof and believe the same to be true.

_____

Subscribed and sworn to before me this ___ day of _____, 20___.

_____
Notary Public for Alaska

Where Filed—The Recorder's Office of the recording district where the property is located, where the cannery, saltery, or other plant is located, or where the timber is cut.

When to Be Filed—Within 90 days of the completion of the work or furnishing of material for fishpacker and processor's lien; within 60 days after completion of service or close of work for a timber lien; within 90 days after the completion of the services or the cessation of the labor for watchman's lien; within 90 days after the date of injury, or in no event later than 90 days after the discharge of the injured person from the hospital or the provision of the physician's services.

Extent of Lien—Carrier and storage liens are for the just reasonable charges. Timber liens are for the value of the work and services performed. Fish packer and processor's lien is for the value of service, work, or material furnished for the six months, or a shorter period, preceding the filing of a claim. Person claiming a Watchman's lien is only entitled to a lien for services or work for the nine months or a shorter period preceding the recording of the claim of lien. A watchman's lien binds all the right, title, and interest of the person at whose instance or request or for whom the work or services are performed, to the full extent of the interest that the person has at the commencement of the work or services for which the lien is claimed or that is subsequently acquired up to the time of the foreclosure of the lien, in the property where the work or services are performed. Hospital liens are to the extent of the amount due the hospital, nurse, or physician for the reasonable value of the service furnished before the date of judgment, settlement, or compromise, together with costs and reasonable attorney fees that the court allows, incurred in the enforcement of the lien. Hospital liens may not be allowed for hospitalization or the services of a physician or licensed special nurse furnished after a settlement is made by or on behalf of the person causing the injury unless the settlement is made within 20 days from the date of the injury. A lien is not allowed for necessary attorney fees, costs, and expenses incurred by the injured person in securing a settlement, compromise, or judgment.

Duration of Lien—Six months after notice of the lien is filed for record, unless suit is brought within that time, or if credit is given, within six months after the expiration of the credit; no lien may be carried in force for more than one year from the stopping of the work by an agreement to give credit.

Enforcement of Lien by Sale—If the just and reasonable charges of a carrier or person engaged in storage are not paid within three months after the service or food is furnished, the lienor may proceed to sell, at public auction, property sufficient to pay the charges and the expense of the sale, with the balance paid to the owner. A warehouseman is not authorized to sell more of the wool, wheat, oats, or other grain than is sufficient to pay charges due the warehouseman on the wool, wheat, oats, or other grain. If a hotel or boarding house lien is not satisfied within 60 days after the charges become due, the hotel or boardinghouse operator may proceed to sell the baggage or other property held under the lien at public auction.

Notice of Sale—Before the sale is made, notice of the sale shall be given to the debtor by registered letter directed to him at his last-known place of residence, if his residence is known, and also by posting notice of the sale in three public places in the recording district, one of which shall be at or near the front door of the post office nearest the place of sale, for 10 days before the day of sale. The notice shall contain a particular description of the article to be sold, the name of the owner or reputed owner, the amount due on the lien, and the time and place of said sale. Ten days before the sale the hotel or boardinghouse operator shall give notice of the time and place of sale by posting notice in three public places in the town or city where the hotel or boardinghouse is located and by mailing notice of the time and place to the owner of the baggage or other property at the place of residence as set out in the hotel or boardinghouse register. If the guest failed to register or to give sufficient address, the required notice shall be mailed to the guest at the city or town where the hotel or boardinghouse is located.

Priority—Timber and lumber liens are preferred liens and are prior to other liens. A sale or transfer of timber does not divest a lien on it. As between timber and lumber liens, those for work and labor are preferred. As between liens for work claimed by several laborers on the same timber, the claim or claims for work done or performed on the identical timber proceeded against, to the extent that the timber can be identified, are preferred as against the general claim of liens for work.

A fishpacker or processor or watchman's lien is preferred, prior, and superior to a mortgage, attachment, claim, or demand made or recorded in the recorder's office of the recording district where the property subject to the lien is located after: (1) the commencement of the work for which the lien is claimed; (2) the material is furnished for which the lien is claimed. A sale, transfer, mortgage, assignment, or attachment recorded after the commencement of the work or furnishing of the material does not postpone the lien. A fishpacker or processor lien is not prior or paramount to a valid prior lien for labor performed or material furnished in the construction, alteration, or repair of the houses, wharves, or other shore property.

ARIZONA

Who May Claim—Arizona allows liens for labor or material furnished on personal property. The lien applies to any article, implement, utensil or vehicle, except motor vehicles that are repaired or cleaned, glazed or washed by a carpenter, mechanic, artisan or other workman. The lien is possessory; the person shall have a lien on the item for the labor or material and may retain possession of it until the amount is fully paid.

Arizona law also provides several particular personal property liens.

Dry Cleaners' Liens. When any garment, wearing apparel or article is cleaned, pressed or washed by a dry cleaner or launderer, the dry cleaner or launderer shall have a lien on the item for the labor and may retain possession of it until the amount due is fully paid.

Garage or Repair Liens. Proprietors of garages, repair and service stations have lien rights on motor vehicles of every kind and aircraft, and the parts and accessories placed thereon for labor, materials, supply and storage. The lien is for the amount of the charges when that amount has been agreed to by the proprietor and the owner of the vehicle. The garagemen's lien shall not impair any other lien or conditional sale of record in place when the work started unless furnished with the consent and knowledge of the record lienor or vendor.

Aircraft. If a proprietor has a lien on an aircraft, the proprietor may relinquish possession of the aircraft and retain the lien by recording a lien with the county recorder of the county in which the labor or materials were provided within 30 days of relinquishing possession. In addition, the lien claimant may file a lien with the Federal Aviation Administration aircraft registry. The FAA lien shall comply with all requirements of federal law and shall: (a) accurately describe the aircraft; (b) list the amount due and the date the work was last furnished; (c) be signed by the claimant; and (d) be accompanied by the recording fee.

A lien recorded with a county recorder does not bind a purchaser of the aircraft without actual notice unless the lien has also been recorded with the FAA. The aircraft lien shall be foreclosed by an action in court.

Liens for Fabrication Work. Persons who fabricate patterns, molds, tools, dies or all other equipment or material furnished them by a customer shall have a lien on those items and all other equipment and material in their possession for the balance due for fabrication work which has been accepted by the customer.

Hotel, inn, boarding house, lodging house, apartment house and auto camp keepers shall have a lien upon the baggage and other property of their guests, boarders or lodgers, brought therein by their guests, boarders or lodgers, for charges due for accommodation, board, lodging or room rent and things furnished at the request of such guests, boarders or lodgers, with the right to possession of the baggage or other property until the charges are paid.

Foreclosure/Enforcement by Sale—Arizona law provides the following procedures for foreclosure of a possessory personal property lien if the applicable law does not include any other foreclosure provisions: (a) when possession of any property held under lien has continued for 20 days after the charges accrue and remain unpaid, the person holding the property may notify the owner, if the owner is in the county where the property is located, to pay the charges; (b) upon owner's failure within 10 days thereafter to pay the charges, the holder may sell it at public auction and apply the proceeds to payment of the charges with the balance of any proceeds to be paid to the owner; (c) if the owner's residence is not in the county where the property is located, the lienholder is not required to give the 10-day notice; (d) five days' notice of sale shall be given to the owner. If the owner's whereabouts are unknown, then notice shall be given by two publications in a newspaper published in the county; (e) if the person legally entitled to receive the balance is not known or has removed from the county, the holder shall pay the balance to the department of revenue. If the party, at any time within two years from the date of payment to the department of revenue, establishes his right to the money to the satisfaction of the director of the department of administration, it shall be paid to him. After two years, all unclaimed monies shall be deposited in the permanent state school fund; (f) a dry cleaner or launderer may foreclose its lien by private or public sale or by any manner determined by the dry cleaner or launderer, provided all of the following conditions exist: (1) the dry cleaner or launderer has posted on the premises, plainly visible to the article's owner, a poster (no less than 18 inches by 24 inches) notifying that the garment may be disposed of on or after 90 days if unclaimed; (2) the dry cleaner or launderer has imprinted a similar notice of the receipt given to the owner or agent; and (3) the item remains in the possession of the dry cleaner or launderer and the charges are unpaid for 90 days after the date the article is received to be cleaned, pressed or washed.

ARKANSAS

Who May Claim—The owner of a cotton gin or plant engaged in processing rice or other similar farm products; all keepers of livery, sale, or feed stables, or wagonyards; and the operator of a marina facility; any person, firm, or corporation engaged in the business of the storage of automobiles and other motor vehicles, whether the storage is the principal line of business or an incident to the regular business

In addition to other personal property liens, the owner of a self storage facility shall have a lien on all personal property stored within each leased space located at the self storage facility for rent, labor, or other charges, present or future, and for expenses reasonably incurred in enforcing the lien.

A practitioner, a nurse, a hospital, and an ambulance service provider shall each have a lien on any claim, right of action, and money to which the patient is entitled because of that injury, and to costs and attorney's fees incurred in enforcing that lien.

Property Covered—Cotton seed and baled cotton produced by cotton ginner; agricultural products of a rice processor or other similar farm products processor; any claim, right of action, and money to which the patient is entitled because of that injury, and to costs and attorney's fees incurred in enforcing that lien; all horses, mules, or other stock or property left in their charge to be kept, fed, sold, or otherwise cared for and sheltered; all personal property stored within each leased space at a marina facility for rent, labor, or other charges and for expenses reasonably incurred in its sale; the motor vehicle stored for the sums of money due for the storage.

Extent of Lien—The value of the service rendered and to be rendered by the practitioner, nurse, hospital, or ambulance service provider to a patient, at the express or implied request of that patient or of someone acting on his or her behalf, for the relief and cure of an injury suffered through the fault or neglect of someone other than the patient himself or herself; reasonable costs and charges for feeding, keeping, and otherwise taking care of all horses, mules, stock, or property.

Duration of Lien—A cotton ginner's lien must be enforced within six months after the cotton is ginned; a rice (or other similar farm product) processor's lien must be enforced within eight months after the agricultural product is processed.

Enforcement—Cotton, seed, rice, and other similar farm products may be held for 30 days unless the claim is sooner paid, and after that time may sell the same at the market price, at private sale, and from the proceeds pay his just debt, turning any residue over to the owner. Where the cotton, seed, rice, or other similar farm product is not in the ginner or processor's possession, he may enforce his claim in court. For livery stable keeper liens, stable or wagonyard keepers are authorized to keep possession of any horses, mules, or other stock or property until such reasonable charges are paid or tendered to them or their agents by the owner of the property or his or her agents. If the owners fail to pay the fixed charges provided for in the written contract, or otherwise breach their agreement, the person who has custody of the livestock may proceed to enforce his or her lien at any time after ten days from the date when the payment became delinquent or when the contract was breached, but at no time later than one year from the date of delinquency or of breach of contract. Any person, firm, or corporation having a lien for the storage of automobiles and retaining possession of the motor vehicle by virtue of the lien thereon for storage charges shall have the right to sell it for the satisfaction of the debt for which the motor vehicle was held.

Enforcement of Lien by Sale—The livery stable keeper lien may be enforced either by public sale or by suit filed in the circuit court of the county wherein the livestock on which the lien is attached is located, without regard as to the amount in controversy. The proceeds of the sale, after payment of the charges for the feeding, herding, pasturing, keeping, or ranching of the livestock, from the date when the lien became effective until the date of the sale, and all the expenses of the sale, including costs of publication, attorney's fees, and costs of public auctioneer, if any, shall, if the owners are absent or unknown, be deposited with the treasurer of the county where the sale takes place by the person making the sale. These net proceeds shall be paid to the persons entitled to them when they properly establish ownership in, or lien upon, the livestock, either by claim of title or by claim of valid lien.

Notice of Sale—Before any livestock shall be sold at public sale, without court action, if the names and addresses of the owners and if the name and address of the conditional sales vendor, mortgagor, or other prior lienholder are known, at least 20 days' notice of the sale shall be given them in writing, either by the sheriff serving the notice upon the owner and the lienholder or by registered or certified mail, return receipt requested.

In addition, a notice of the time and place of sale, containing a general description of the livestock, shall be published at least one time a week for a period of two weeks consecutively, in a newspaper of general circulation, if there is one published in the county where the livestock is kept and where the sale shall take place. If no newspaper is published in that county, five handbills containing the same information shall be posted in at least five public places in the township, the town, or the city where the sale shall take place. It shall be the duty of the person claiming the lien to cause the notices to be served, mailed, and published. Copies of the notice required by this section and proof of the publication or the posting of it, and an affidavit of the person causing the livestock to be sold to enforce his or her lien shall be filed and kept in the circuit clerk's office of the county where the sale takes place. Copies of it shall be received in evidence in all courts, if certified by the clerk.

Priority—Cotton ginner or rice or other similar farm product processor's lien is an absolute lien superior to all other prior liens. The livery stable keeper liens shall be first and prior to that of any conditional sale contract, recorded or filed chattel mortgage, or other encumbrance if the person feeding, herding, pasturing, keeping, or ranching the livestock complies with the statutory provisions and if the person also notifies the holder of the conditional sale contract, recorded or filed chattel mortgage, or other encumbrance about the existence of the written contract by the sheriff serving a written notice upon the lienholder, or by mailing a written notice to the lienholder by registered or certified mail, return receipt requested, that this person has entered into a written contract with the owners of the livestock to feed, herd, pasture, keep, or ranch them.

A marina facility lien attaches as of the date the lease or rental payment becomes delinquent and shall be superior to any other lien or security interest except the following: (1) a lien which is perfected and recorded in Arkansas in the name of the occupant, either in the county of the occupant's last known address or in the county where the marina facility is located, prior to the date the lease or rental payment becomes delinquent; (2) any tax lien; and (3) any lienholder with a perfected security interest in the property.

Judgments—Views from a municipal court do not attach to real estate unless or until they are filed and indexed in the judgment records of the Circuit Court where the real estate is located.

CALIFORNIA

California has a great number of nonconsensual statutory liens which can arise in unexpected ways to impair a party's position. Unanticipated statutory liens must be looked for when dealing with certain transactions and business. Of note, are jewelers that have a lien dependent upon possession for any account due for work or materials; repairmen, owners of self storage facilities and garages that have a lien against a vehicle in their possession for labor, services and materials; service providers that have a lien against property in their possession for services rendered. There are also agricultural laborer's liens, shipmaster's liens, seaman's liens, warehouseman's liens, timber man's liens, liens of aircraft workers and suppliers, liens of oil or gas leasehold workers, suppliers and other service providers. Last but not least is the "banker's lien" or "right of set-off".

Of particular importance, however, are the liens that a number of parties may have against the same agricultural property at the same point in time. Thought must be given to the priority of these liens even against the holder of a properly perfected Uniform Commercial Code security interest in the same property.

Who May Claim—Producers and transporters of farm products that sell such products grown and harvested by them to processors under contract, express or implied; carriers; sellers of livestock to meat packers in California.

Property Covered—Agricultural producer's lien is on the farm product sold and all processed or manufactured forms of such farm product. Carrier's lien is on the property transported, cared for, or preserved. Livestock lien is on livestock sold and identifiable proceeds.

Extent of Lien—Agricultural producer's lien is for the agreed price, or if none, for the value of the product as of the date of the delivery. Carrier's lien is for freightage and for services rendered at the request of the shipper or consignee, and for money advanced at the request of shipper or consignee to discharge a prior lien.

Duration of Lien—Agricultural producer's liens continue in effect for 60 days after delivery. After filing of notice, livestock lien is valid for five years.

Priority—Agricultural producer's lien is preferred to all other liens, claims, or encumbrances except labor claims for wages and salaries for personal services rendered to the processor after delivery. Livestock lien is superior to all other liens.

Limitations—No agricultural producer may have a lien on any farm product, or any manufactured or processed product derived from any farm product, that is hypothecated or pledged to a lender that advances new value to the processor and that has filed a statement in writing with the director. California sellers of livestock to meat packers now have a lien on the livestock and the identifiable proceeds for the purchase price or the unpaid value of the livestock. The lien is superior to all other liens but expires in 21 days unless notice is filed with the Secretary of State. One who provides feed or other materials to aid in raising poultry, fish, or for the production of eggs has a special lien on the proceeds of the sale of eggs, poultry, fish, or other products.

COLORADO

Who May Claim—Any ranchman, farmer, feeder, agistor, herder of cattle, livery stable keeper, veterinarian, or other person to whom horses, mules, asses, cattle, sheep, hogs, dogs, cats, or other domestic animals are entrusted for the purpose of feeding, herding, pasturing, keeping, ranching, boarding, or medical care shall have a lien; common carrier of goods or passengers; the owner of a self storage facility; harvesters; every hospital duly licensed by the department of public health and environment, which furnishes services to any person injured as the result of the negligence or other wrongful acts of another person and not covered by the provisions of the Workers' Compensation Act of Colorado.

Property Covered—Horses, mules, asses, cattle, sheep, hogs, dogs, cats, or other domestic animals; such personal property for his reasonable charges for the transportation, storage, or keeping; all personal property stored within each leased space located at the self storage facility; grain and other crops harvested for and on account of harvesting; all reasonable and necessary charges for hospital care, but not on any hospital charges incurred subsequent to any such judgment, settlement, or compromise.

Extent of Lien—The amount that may be due for such feeding, herding, pasturing, keeping, ranching, boarding, or medical care and for all costs incurred in enforcing such lien; rent, labor, or other charges, present or future, and for expenses reasonably incurred in enforcing the lien; a lien on grain or other crops shall be charged for at the prevailing price for a particular locality in which such grain or other crop is harvested; lien for all reasonable and necessary charges for hospital care upon the net amount payable to such injured person, his heirs, assigns, or legal representatives out of the total amount of any recovery or sum had or collected, or to be collected, whether by judgment, settlement, or compromise, by such person, his heirs, or legal representatives as damages on account of such injuries, not exceeding the net amount paid to such injured person, his heirs, assigns, or legal representatives.

Duration of Lien—A self storage facility lien attaches as of the date the personal property is brought to the self-service storage facility and continues so long as the owner retains possession and until the default is corrected, or a sale is conducted, or the property is otherwise disposed of to satisfy the lien.

Execution of Lien by Sale—After the occupant of a self storage facility has been in default continuously for a period of 30 days, the owner may begin enforcement action if the occupant has been notified in writing. Any sale or other disposition of the personal property shall be held at the self-service storage facility or at the nearest suitable place to where the personal property is held or stored. In the event of a sale, the owner may satisfy his lien from the proceeds of the sale, subject to the rights of any prior lienholder. The lien rights of such prior lienholder are automatically transferred to the proceeds of the sale. If the sale is made in good faith and is conducted in a reasonable manner, the owner shall not be subject to any surcharge for a deficiency in the amount of a prior secured lien but shall hold the balance, if any, for delivery to the occupant, lienholder, or other person in interest. If the occupant, lienholder, or other person in interest does not claim the balance of the proceeds within three years of the date of sale, it shall become the property of the owner without further recourse by the occupant, lienholder, or other person in interest.

Before any sale or other disposition of personal property for a self storage facility lien, the occupant may pay the amount necessary to satisfy the lien and the reasonable expenses incurred under this section and thereby redeem the personal property. Upon receipt of such payment, the owner shall return the personal property, and thereafter the owner shall have no liability to any person with respect to such personal property.

Notice of Sale—Notice of self storage facility lien shall be delivered in person or sent by certified mail to the last-known address of the occupant, and a copy of said notice shall, at the same time, be sent to the sheriff of the county where such self-service storage facility is located. Any lienholder with an interest in the property to be sold or otherwise disposed of, of whom the owner has knowledge either through the disclosure provision on the rental agreement or through finding a validly filed financing statement in the county where the self-service storage facility is located or in the county of the occupant's last-known address, or through other written notice, shall be included in the notice process. The notice shall include: (1) an itemized statement of the owner's claim showing the sum due at the time of the notice and the date when the sum became due; (2) a brief and general description of the personal property subject to the lien. Such description shall be reasonably adequate to permit the person notified to identify such property; except that any container including, but not limited to, a trunk, valise, or box that is locked, fastened, sealed, or tied in a manner which deters immediate access to its contents may be described as such without describing its contents; (3) a notification of denial of access to the personal property, if such denial is permitted under the terms of the rental agreement, which notification shall provide the name, street address, and telephone number of the owner or his designated agent whom the occupant may contact to respond to such notification; (4) a demand for payment within a specified time not less than 15 days after delivery of the notice; (5) a conspicuous statement that, unless the claim is paid within the time stated in the notice, the personal property will be advertised for sale or other disposition and will be sold or otherwise disposed of at a specified time and place.

After the expiration of the time given in the notice, an advertisement of the sale or other disposition shall be published once a week for two consecutive weeks in a newspaper of general circulation in the county where the self-service storage facility is located. The advertisement shall include: (1) a brief and general description of the personal property reasonably adequate to permit its identification; the address of the self-service storage facility and the number, if any, of the space where the personal property is located; and the name of the occupant and his last-known address; (2) the time, place, and manner of the sale or other disposition. The sale or other disposition shall take place not sooner than 15 days after the first publication; (3) if there is no newspaper of general circulation in the county where the self-service storage facility is located, the advertisement shall be posted at least 10 days before the date of the sale or other disposition in not less than six conspicuous places in the neighborhood where the self-service storage facility is located.

Every person intending to avail himself or herself of the benefits of a harvester's lien shall serve on the owner by certified or registered mail, return receipt requested, or by personal service, within 10 days after completing the harvesting, a notice that, within 20 days, a lien, shall be claimed, and, within said 20 days, such person shall file in the same locations for farm products and crops, a statement containing a just and true account of the amount due him or her for such harvesting, after allowing all just credits and offsets, and containing a correct description of the grain or other crops to be charged with such lien, the price agreed upon for such harvesting, the name of the person, firm, or corporation for whom such harvesting was performed, a legal description of the lands upon which said grain or other crops were raised, a description of the legal subdivision of land upon which said grain or other crops are stored and, if said grain or other crops are stored in a storage facility, the locality of the storage facility, which statement of facts shall be verified by affidavit of the person claiming such lien or his or her duly authorized agent or attorney having knowledge of the facts, and a copy of the notice of intent to file a lien and an affidavit of service or mailing thereof. Any immaterial error or mistake in the account or description of the grain or other crops or of the property upon which it was raised shall not invalidate such lien.

Notice of Lien—A hospital's lien shall take effect if, prior to any such judgment, settlement, or compromise, a written notice of lien containing the name and address of the injured person, the date of the accident, the name and location of the hospital, and the name of the person alleged to be liable to the injured person for the injuries received is filed by the hospital in the office of the secretary of state. Hospital liens properly recorded with the division of insurance shall be valid and enforceable without filing with the office of the secretary of state. Within 10 days after such filing, the hospital shall mail by certified mail, return receipt requested, a copy of said notice to such injured person at the last address provided to the hospital by such person, to his or her attorney, if known, to the persons alleged to be liable to such injured person for the injuries sustained, if known, and to the insurance carriers, if known, which have insured such persons alleged to be liable against such liability. If an action for damages on account of such injuries or death is pending, the requirements of notice contained in this section shall be satisfied by the filing of the said notice of lien in the pending action, with copies thereof to the attorneys of record for the parties thereto.

Priority—A lien for harvesting is not be prior to nor have precedence over any mortgage, encumbrance, security interest, or other valid lien upon the grain or other crops if such other mortgage, encumbrance, security interest, or valid lien attached or was filed prior to the filing of a lien. The lien of attorneys and counselors at law shall have precedence over and be senior to hospital liens.

When to Be Filed—Hospital liens are to be filed within one year after the date of payment to injured person, and the court shall allow a reasonable attorney's fee for the collection and enforcement of such lien.

CONNECTICUT

Who May Claim—Persons in the business of manufacturing, spinning, throwing, bleaching, mercerizing, printing, or finishing yarn or other goods made of cotton, wool, silk, linen, rayon, nylon, synthetic fibers, or artificial silk, or goods of which such materials form a component part; any person with a claim of at least $50 for work done, materials furnished, or expenses incurred in connection with the building, repairing, mooring, dockage, or storage of any vessel; each jeweler, watchmaker, silversmith or television and radio service dealer who alters, repairs or does any work on any article of personal property at the request of the owner or legal possessor of the property has a lien upon and may retain the possession of the article until the charges for the alteration, repairing or work have been paid; each person, firm, association and corporation engaged in the business of cleaning, laundering, repairing, dyeing, pressing or storing clothing, household goods, wearing apparel or other fabrics shall have a lien upon such clothing, household goods, wearing apparel or other fabrics for the amount due for such service until such amount is paid; the owner or keeper of any garage or other place where a motor vehicle is stored shall have a lien upon the same for such owner's or keeper's storage charges; any person who keeps and feeds any animals, including birds and fish; any hospital which is exempt from taxation, any ambulance owner, operator, association, partnership or corporation, or any hospital owned and operated by a municipality or the state, which furnished medical or other service or materials to any patient injured by reason of any accident not covered by the Workers' Compensation Act; any person who stores, cares for, maintains, repairs or furnishes any services, gasoline, accessories, materials or other supplies at the request of or with the consent of the owner, his agent or legal possessor of an aircraft has a lien.

Owners of self storage facilities will have a lien upon personal property located at the facilities for the amounts of any rent, labor, or charges incurred in relation to the property. Such liens will not have priority over other liens or security interests which attached or are perfected prior to default.

A warehouseman has a lien against the bailor on the goods covered by a warehouse receipt or on the proceeds thereof in his possession for charges for storage or transportation, including demurrage and terminal charges, insurance, labor, or charges present or future in relation to the goods, and for expenses necessary for preservation of the goods or reasonably incurred.

Property Covered—The goods and property of others which come into the possession of such a person for the purpose of being so processed. The proceeds of any accident and liability insurance policy issued by any company authorized to do business in this state.

Extent of Lien—This lien is for the amount of any debt due the lienor from the owner of the material by reason of any work performed or materials furnished in or about the processing of such goods or property, or other goods of such owner of which the lienor's possession has terminated. Proceeds which may be due such patient, either directly or indirectly, to the extent of the actual cost of such service and materials, provided such hospital or ambulance owner, operator, association, partnership or corporation, or, in the case of the state, the Department of Administrative Services, after the commencement of rendering of such service or providing of such materials and before payment by the insurance company.

The lienor shall be entitled to retain possession of the aircraft until payment of the amount of fees, expenses or charges for such storage, care, maintenance, repair or the furnishing of gasoline, accessories, materials or other supplies.

Enforcement by Sale—This lien may be enforced by public sale of the property after proper notice. The proceeds are applied to the payment of the amount of the lien and expenses of the sale, the balance to be paid to the owner. After 30 days of nonpayment by owner of animals, the keeper may sell such animals at public auction. If the amount due for such cleaning, laundering, repairing, dyeing or pressing is not paid within six months after it is due, the property subject to such lien, or so much thereof as is necessary to satisfy such lien, may be sold by the person, firm, association or corporation holding such lien at public or private sale for cash, and the proceeds of such sale, after payment of the expenses thereof, shall be applied upon the indebtedness, and any remainder shall be paid to the owner of such property.

If the debit arising from storing clothing, household goods, wearing apparel or other fabrics for which a lien is given is not paid within 12 months from the beginning of the storage period, the property subject to such lien, or so much thereof as is necessary to satisfy such lien, may be sold by the person, firm, association or corporation holding such lien at public or private sale for cash, and the proceeds of such sale applied to the expenses thereof, and to pay such debt, and the surplus, if any, shall be paid to the owner of such property.

Notice of Sale—No such sale shall be held by a jeweler, watchmaker, silversmith or television and radio service dealer until after 30 days' notice to the owner or legal possessor has been given by registered or certified mail at his last-known address, stating the time and place of sale. If the owner's or possessor's address is unknown, or if such registered or certified mail notice is returned, further notice shall be given by advertising the time and place of the sale in a newspaper having a substantial circulation in the locality where the sale is to take place at least 30 days in advance of the sale. Notice must be given to the owner of the animals of the time and place of such sale at least six days before such sale, and apply the proceeds to the payment of such debts, returning the surplus, if any, to such owner.

A lien on manufacturer's materials sale must have a notice of sale published at least once each week for two weeks preceding the date of such sale in some newspaper published in the county in which such goods or property is located, and by mailing, postage prepaid, a copy of such notice, at least five days before the date of such sale, to the owner or owners of such goods or property, addressed to such owner or owners' last-known residence or place of business. Before making sale for money due for cleaning, laundering, repairing, dyeing or pressing, the person, firm or corporation holding such lien shall give 30 days' written notice thereof by registered or certified mail sent to the last-known post-office address of such owner, and, in addition thereto, shall advertise the time and place thereof three times in a newspaper having a circulation in the community.

Before making sale for lien arising from storing clothing, household goods, wearing apparel or other fabrics the person, firm or corporation holding such lien shall give 30 days' written notice thereof by registered or certified mail sent to the last-known post-office address of such owner and, in addition thereto, shall advertise the time and place thereof three times in a newspaper having a circulation in the community, provided persons, firms, partnerships or corporations operating as warehouses or warehousemen shall not be affected by this section.

Notice of Lien—Written notice must be served upon the insurance company by registered or certified mail at its principal home office or any branch office, if the company issuing the policy is located within this state, and upon the Insurance Commissioner of this state by registered or certified mail, if the insurance company is located without the state. The notice shall be in duplicate and shall contain the name of the injured person, if known, the name of the company or companies issuing the policy and the amount expended and an estimate of the amount to be expended in the services rendered to or the materials provided for the patient.

Priority—Aircraft liens shall be superior to all other liens, except liens for taxes.

DELAWARE

Who May Claim—Owners of a threshing machine, corn picker, or hay baler; builders, owners, master, agents or consignees of a ship or vessel; any hotelkeeper, innkeeper, garage owner, auction service or other person who keeps a livery, boarding stable, garage, airport, marina or other establishment and, for price or reward at such livery, boarding stable, garage, airport, marina or other establishment, furnishes food or care for any horse or has the custody or care of any carriage, cart, wagon, sleigh, motor vehicle, trailer, moped, boat, airplane or other vehicle or any harness, robes or other equipment for the same or makes repairs, auctions, performs labor upon, furnishes services, supplies or materials for, stores, safekeeps or tows any carriage, cart, wagon, sleigh, motor vehicle, trailer, moped, boat, airplane or other vehicle or any harness, robes or other equipment for the same shall have a lien; every charitable association, corporation or other institution maintaining a hospital in this State, supported in whole or in part by private charity treating injured persons who may have, assert or maintain against any such other person or corporation for damages, compensation or other claim on account of such injuries; the owner of a self-service storage facility.

Property Covered—Wheat, corn, hay, or other grain threshed, picked, or baled by him with such machine; ships and vessels of all kinds built, repaired, fitted, furnished and supplied with necessities for navigation within this State; horse, carriage, cart, wagon, sleigh, motor vehicle, trailer, moped, boat, airplane or other vehicle, harness, robes or equipment; any and all claims or demands, all rights of action, suits, counterclaims of any person admitted to any such hospital and receiving treatment, care and maintenance therein which arise out of any personal injuries received in any such accident which any such injured person may have, assert or maintain against any such other person or corporation for damages, compensation or other claim on account of such injuries for the amount of the reasonable charges of such hospital for all medical treatment, care and nursing and maintenance of such injured person while in such hospital; all personal property located at a self-service storage facility.

How Claimed—A charitable association, corporation or other institution shall file in the office of the Prothonotary of the county in which such injuries shall have occurred a notice in writing, containing the names and addresses of the injured person, the date of the accident, the name and location of the hospital and, if then known, the name of the person alleged to be liable to such injured person by reason of the injuries received, prior to the payment of any moneys to such injured person or his legal representative by such person to such injured person. Copies of the notice shall be sent by registered mail by the hospital to such injured person and all parties in interest who are then known. Thereafter an affidavit by a competent person acting on behalf of such institution, setting forth such service, and all attempts to serve the same shall be filed in the office of the Prothonotary.

Extent of Lien—Work done or materials and supplies found or provided in the building, repairing, fitting, furnishing, supplying or equipping of a ship or vessel; to the extent of the full and true consideration paid or given to, or on behalf of, such injured person or his legal representative; for rent, labor or other charges, present or future, in relation to the personal property and for expenses necessary for its preservation or expenses reasonably incurred in its sale or other disposition.

Priority—Threshing machine owners have first lien. Where property subject to lien is sold upon any claim whatsoever, this claim shall be paid out of the proceeds of any such sale before any part of those proceeds are applied to any other claim. Liens held by garage owners or livery and stable keepers shall be superior to any lien, title or interest of any person who has a security interest by virtue of a conditional sales contract or a prior perfected security interest. Any person who stores or safekeeps any motor vehicle towed at the request of a party other than the owner of the vehicle may attain priority of lien as follows: (1) by providing notice by certified mail to a title holder of record within seven business days of the date upon which possession is taken; (2) by providing notice by certified mail to lienholders of record within seven business days of the date upon which possession is taken; and (3) by providing notice by telephone or in person to the appropriate police agency. The lien on self storage facility property is superior to any other lien or security interest, except liens or security interests secured by motor vehicles.

Duration of Lien—The lien on ships and vessels shall continue for and during the period of two years next after the work is done or the materials or supplies are furnished or provided to the ship or vessel and no longer.

Enforcement of Lien by Sale—If a garage owner or livery and stable keeper lienholder is not paid the amount due, and for which the lien is given within 30 days after the same or any part thereof became due, then the lienholder may proceed to sell the property, or so much thereof as may be necessary, to satisfy the lien and costs of sale if: (1) an authorization to conduct a lien sale has been issued; (2) a judgment has been entered in favor of the lienholder on the claim which gives rise to the lien; or (3) the owners and any secured parties of record or known lienholders of the property have signed, after the lien has arisen, a release of any interest in the property.

Notice of Sale—Prior to any sale by a garage owner or livery and stable keeper, the lienholder shall give at least 15 days' notice of the sale by handbills posted in five or more public places and by advertising in a newspaper published and/or circulated in the county in which the sale is to be held.

DISTRICT OF COLUMBIA

Who May Claim—All persons storing, repairing, or furnishing supplies of or concerning motor vehicles including trailers; all persons keeping or boarding any animals at livery within the District; every association, corporation, or other institution, and any agency of the United States or the District of Columbia, maintaining a hospital in the District of Columbia, which shall furnish medical or other service to any patient injured by reason of an accident causing injuries not covered by the Employees' Compensation Act or the Workmen's Compensation Act; operator of a storage facility.

Property Covered—Motor vehicles; any animals boarded at a livery; parts of a claim against another for damages on account of injuries by an injured party treated at a hospital, going or belonging to such patient, of any recovery or sum had or collected or to be collected by such patient, or by his heirs or personal representatives in the case of his death, whether by judgment or by settlement or compromise; all personal property stored within each leased space for rent, labor, or other charges.

Extent of Lien—The agreed or reasonable charges for such storage, repairs, and supplies when such charges are incurred by an owner or conditional vendee or chattel mortgagor (including a grantor of deed of trust in lieu of mortgage) of a motor vehicle; the amount of the reasonable and necessary charges of such hospital for the treatment, care, and maintenance of such patient in such hospital up to the date of payment of such damages; for expenses reasonably incurred in the sale of the personal property stored within a storage facility.

Priority—Motor vehicle liens shall have priority over every security interest and other lien, or right in, or to the vehicle except as hereinafter limited with respect to claims for storage.

Enforcement by Sale—If the amount due for a motor vehicle lien is not paid by the end of 30 days after the giving of notice, then the party entitled to such lien may proceed to sell the property so subject to lien at public auction; The sale of personal property stored at a storage facility shall be held at the self-service storage facility where the personal property is stored.

Notice of Sale—Notice of a motor vehicle lien sale must be given once a week for three successive weeks in some daily newspaper published in the District. Said advertisement shall set forth the date, time, and place of sale, which shall not be less than 15 days from date of the first publication of such notice, that the purpose of the sale is to satisfy a lien, the amount for which said lien is claimed, including storage to date of sale if allowable, the names of all interested parties, and a description of the chattel, including, in the case of vehicles, the make, type, year and model number, serial number and engine number, if any, and State or District license number and year.

Before conducting a sale of personal property at a storage facility, the operator of a storage facility shall: (1) notify the occupant of the default by regular mail at the occupant's last known address; (2) send a second notice of default by certified mail, return receipt requested, to the occupant at the occupant's last known address which includes: (a) a statement that the contents of the occupant's leased space are subject to the operator's lien; (b) a statement of the operator's claim, indicating the charges due on the date of the notice, the amount of any additional charges which shall become due before the date of sale, and the date those additional charges shall become due; (c) a demand for payment of the charges due within a specified time, not less than 14 days after the date that the notice was mailed; (d) a statement that unless the claim is paid within the time stated, the contents of the occupant's space will be sold at a specified time and place; and (e) The name, street address, and telephone number of the operator, or his designated agent, whom the occupant may contact to respond to the notice; and (3) at least three days before the sale, advertise the time, place, and terms of the sale in a newspaper of general circulation in the jurisdiction where the sale is to be held.

FLORIDA

Generally speaking, nonconsensual statutory liens arise under Florida law in connection with a contractual relationship between the owner of the property and a person who is providing materials or performing labor or a service. The lien is usually, but not always, established by possession and extinguished by the lack of possession. The list of these types of liens is long, but unlike other jurisdictions, these liens are contained in one section of the Florida statutes.

Who May Claim—Persons who furnish materials or labor to any of the following enterprises may have a statutory lien: newspapers, printers, hotels, logging or timber concerns, agricultural product producers or packers, including cotton, shipping or vessel maintenance, repair or construction, manufacturers using timber or other materials, railroads, telephone companies, any person who shall furnish corn, oats, hay, grain or other feed or feedstuffs or straw or bedding material to or upon the order of the owner, or the agent, bailee, lessee, or custodian of the owner, of any racehorse, polo pony or race dog. Interior designers and exterminators may also obtain a lien for their services as well as drillers on any oil or gas pipeline and veterinarians. Persons feeding or caring for the horse or other animal of another, including all keepers of livery, sale or feed or feed stables, for feeding or taking care of any horse or other animal put in their charge may also obtain a lien. Any person conducting or operating any hotel, apartment house, rooming-house, boardinghouse or tenement house where rooms or apartments are let for hire or rental on a transient basis may obtain a lien. Owners of stallions, jackasses or bulls. The owner, operator, or keeper of a mobile home park or recreational vehicle park for rent owing by, and for money or other property advanced to, any occupant thereof.

Property Covered—Usually, the lien attaches to the property either furnished or being worked upon or cared for; all the property including trunks, baggage, jewelry and wearing apparel, guns and sporting goods, furniture and furnishings and other personal property of any person which property is brought into or placed in any room or apartment of any hotel, apartment house, lodginghouse, roominghouse, boardinghouse or tenement house when such person shall occupy, on a transient basis; personal property upon who exterminator has performed pest control; upon the colt or calf of the get of said stallion, jackass or bull, and also upon the mare, jenny or cow served by said stallion, jackass or bull in breeding thereof for the sum stipulated to be paid for the service thereof; upon the goods, chattels, or other personal property of the occupant of a mobile home park or recreational vehicle park; any articles of furniture, including, but not limited to, desks, tables, lamps, area rugs, wall hangings, photographs, paintings or other works of art, or any items of furnishing furnished and upon all such articles manufactured or converted from such furnishing; The leasehold interest or that portion thereof covered by an assignment, farmout agreement, or operating agreement held by the operator, whichever shall be the lesser interest, held for oil or gas purposes or for any oil or gas pipeline for which the material or service was furnished or for which the labor was performed, and the appurtenances thereunto belonging as title thereto existed on the date such labor was first performed or such material or service was first furnished.

How Claimed—These liens on personal property are usually acquired by persons in privity with the owner against the purchasers and creditors without notice only while the lienor is in possession. Liens may be acquired by person not in privity with the owner only by delivery of notice to the owner, in writing, that the person to whom material has been furnished is indebted to the lienor by sum stated.

Duration of Lien—Liens against purchasers and creditors without notice continue as long as possession continues, not to exceed three months after furnishing of the material or as otherwise determined by appropriate legal proceedings; liens on personal property brought into hotels, apartment house, lodging house, roominghouse, boardinghouse or tenement shall continue and be in full force and effect for the amount payable for such occupancy until the same shall have been fully paid and discharged. Veterinarian liens shall remain valid and enforceable for a period of one year from the date the professional services were rendered, and such lien is to be enforced in the manner provided for the enforcement of other liens on personal property in this state. Racehorse liens shall remain valid and enforceable for a period of one year from the dates of the respective deliveries of such corn, oats, hay, grain, feed or feedstuffs, or straw; and such liens are to be enforced in the manner provided for the enforcement of other liens on personal property in this state.

Priority—Priority is established chronologically when liens attach to the property except for those liens which may have a statutory superpriority. Racehorse liens are superior to any and all claims, liens and mortgages, whether recorded or unrecorded, including, but not limited to, any lessor's or vendor's lien, and any chattel mortgage, which theretofore may have been or thereafter may be created against such racehorse, polo pony or race dog, and to the claims of any and all purchases thereof.

GEORGIA

Who May Claim—All those furnishing sawmills with timber, logs, provisions, other things necessary to carry on the work of the sawmill, and all those who haul stocks, logs, or lumber. The lien is for the amount of indebtedness and, if the price is not agreed on, the value of services. Pawnbrokers; jewelers; livery stable keepers; veterinarians; all persons, firms, or corporations engaged in the business of laundering, cleaning, tailoring, altering, repairing, or dyeing clothing, goods, wearing apparel, shoes, carpets, rugs, or other such articles; all persons, firms, or corporations engaged in the business of servicing or repairing bicycles, motor scooters, mopeds, motorcycles, lawn mowers, garden equipment, or other such related equipment; any person, firm, hospital authority, or corporation operating a hospital, nursing home, or physician practice or providing traumatic burn care medical practice in this state shall have a lien; every licensed veterinarian and every operator of a facility for boarding animals or pets. The owner or keeper of any stallion, jack, or blooded or imported bull or boar. Any person engaged in servicing or furnishing supplies or accessories for aircraft or providing contracts of indemnity for aircraft.

Owner of self storage facility has a lien for all personal property stored in the facility for rent, labor, or other charges incurred in relation to the property. Such liens will not have priority over liens perfected and recorded prior to the date of the rental agreement, tax liens, or liens and security interests disclosed in the rental agreement.

Property Covered—Sawmills and their products; material hauled; pledged goods pawned for the money advanced, interest, and pawnshop charge owed but not for other debts due to pawnbroker; the articles laundered, cleaned, tailored, altered, repaired, or dyed; the equipment serviced or repaired; any and all causes of action accruing to the person to whom the care was furnished or to the legal representative of such person on account of injuries giving rise to the causes of action and which necessitated the hospital, nursing home, physician practice, or provider of traumatic burn care medical practice care; each animal or pet treated, boarded, or cared for while in custody of a veterinarian or operator and under contract with the owner of the animal or pet for the payment of charges for the treatment, board, or care of the animal or pet. The offspring of any stallion, jack, or blooded or imported bull or boar for the service of the stallion, jack, or blooded or imported bull or boar for the period of one year from the birth of the offspring. Aircraft for any reasonable charges therefor, including charges for labor, for the use of tools, machinery, and equipment, and for all accessories, materials, fuel, oils, lubricants, earned premiums, and other supplies furnished in connection with the servicing or furnishing of supplies or accessories or providing contracts of indemnity for such aircraft.

Extent of Liens—Unpaid bills to veterinarians; livery stable keepers shall have a lien for their charges on the stock placed in their care for keeping; for materials furnished and work done, any jeweler or any other person, firm, or corporation engaged in the business of repairing watches, clocks, jewelry. Any persons, firms, or corporations shall have the right to retain possession of the equipment repaired by them until their charges have been paid; but, if any equipment is delivered to the person for whom the service or repair was performed without collecting the agreed price or reasonable value of servicing or repairing the equipment, the lien shall be lost upon the equipment so delivered. Veterinarian or operator of a facility shall have the right to retain the animal or pet until the charges are paid.

How Claimed—By affidavit showing all facts necessary to constitute a lien, and the amount claimed due.

Where Filed—Clerk of the Superior Court or, if the claim is under $100, the Justice of the Peace.

Duration of Lien—Liens must be prosecuted within one year after the debt comes due.

Priority—Sawmill liens are superior to all liens except those for taxes, labor, and those of which the lienor had actual notice before their debts were created. Among themselves these liens are ranked by the date on which the debts were created. Livery stable liens shall be superior to other liens except liens for taxes, special liens of landlords for rent, liens of laborers, and all general liens of which they had actual notice before the property claimed to be subject to lien came into their control

Enforcement by Foreclosure—Owners of self storage facilities may be able to enforce their liens without judicial intervention, but they must use a statutorily mandated form provided in the Georgia Code, Section 10-4-212, and the requirements specified therein. If the charges due for any services are not paid within 10 days after the demand therefor on the owner of the animal or pet or if the animal or pet is not picked up within 10 days after the demand therefor on the owner of the animal or pet, which demand shall be made in person or by registered or certified mail or statutory overnight delivery with return receipt requested and addressed to the owner at the address given when the animal or pet was delivered, the animal or pet shall be deemed to be abandoned and the licensed veterinarian or operator of a facility is authorized to dispose of the animal or pet in such manner as such veterinarian or operator shall determine. Such 10-day period will begin to run on the date the demand is postmarked or the date the verbal command is communicated in person and shall be noted on the veterinarian's or operator's file on the animal or pet. For purposes of this subsection, the term "dispose of" means selling the animal or pet at public or private sale, giving the animal or pet away, or turning the animal or pet over to any humane society or animal shelter or other such facility. Where no such shelter facility exists within a 50-mile radius of the veterinarian or operator of a facility's place of business and the veterinarian or operator has been unable to sell or give the animal away, then the veterinarian or operator is authorized to euthanize the animal in a humane manner. On the day of the disposal of the animal or pet, the veterinarian or operator of a facility shall notify the owner in person, by telephone, or by registered or certified mail or statutory overnight delivery with return receipt requested at the address given when the animal or pet was delivered, of the date of the disposal and the manner in which the animal was disposed.

Enforcement of Lien by Sale—All sales for jeweler liens shall be made at public auction before the courthouse door of the county where the person, firm, or corporation making the sale had its place of business at the time of receiving the article or articles to be sold and during the hours provided by law for holding sheriffs' sales. In order to satisfy the lien of the person, firm, or corporation performing the service or repair, whenever any bicycles, motor scooters, mopeds, motorcycles, lawn mowers, garden equipment, or such other related equipment remains in the possession of any person, firm, or corporation engaged in the business of servicing or repairing such equipment for a period of 60 days after the person, firm, or corporation has performed any services or repairs thereon without the agreed price or the reasonable value of the service or repair being paid, the equipment may be sold by the person, firm, or corporation having performed the service or repair.

Notice of Sale—Before any sale is made for a jeweler's lien, the person, firm, or corporation making the sale shall give 30 days' notice thereof by posting a notice of the sale before the courthouse door of the county in which the repairs were made. Such notice shall give the name of the owner of the article or articles so repaired, if known, and, if not known, the name of the person from whom the article or articles were received; a description of the article or articles to be sold; and the name of the person, firm, or corporation making the repairs and proposing to make such sale. The person, firm, or corporation shall also give written notice thereof by sending a registered or certified letter to the last known address of the owner of the article or articles or the person who left the article or articles for repairs advising such persons of the time and place of the sale, the description of the article or articles to be sold, and the amount claimed by the person, firm, or corporation for such repairs, including work done and materials furnished; and the amount so claimed for the repairs shall also be stated in the notice posted before the courthouse door.

Before any sale shall be made by all persons, firms, or corporations engaged in the business of laundering, cleaning, tailoring, altering, repairing, or dyeing clothing, goods, wearing apparel, shoes, carpets, rugs, or other such articles of, the person, firm, or corporation making the sale shall give 10 days' notice thereof by mail to the last known address of the owner if known, or otherwise to the last known address of the person from whom the goods were received. Such notice shall give the name of the owner of the goods, if known, and, if not known, the name of the person from whom the goods were received; a description of the goods to be sold; the time and place of the sale; the amount of the charges for which the goods or articles will be sold; and the name of the person, firm, or corporation having possession of the goods or articles and proposing to make the sale.

Before any sale shall be made, the person, firm, or corporation making the sale shall give 10 days' notice thereof by certified mail or statutory overnight delivery evidenced by return receipt to the last known address of the owner if known, or otherwise to the last known address of the person from whom the equipment was received. Such notice shall give the name of the owner of the equipment, if known, and, if not known, the name of the person from whom the equipment was received; a description of the equipment to be sold; the time and place of the sale; the amount of the charges for which the equipment will be sold; and the name of the person, firm, or corporation having possession of the equipment and proposing to make the sale. If such equipment is not claimed during the 10 days following the date that notice was mailed, the equipment may be sold.

HAWAII

Who May Claim—Whoever pastures, feeds, or shelters animals by virtue of a contract with or by the consent of the owner of the animals for a compensation agreed upon; any hospital which has furnished room, board, supplies, facilities, or accommodations to the injured person in connection with the care, or treatment of such injuries, and any dentist, doctor, physician, or surgeon who has treated the injured person for such injuries; every person to whom there has been or is delivered any article or lot of articles of wearing apparel or of household use for the purpose of laundering, cleaning, dyeing, or pressing thereof by such person, regardless of the process to be employed; person who makes, alters, or repairs any article of personal property at the request of the owner of the property; owner of a self storage facility.

Property Covered—Animals for pasturing, feeding, or sheltering to secure payment thereof with costs; judgment or the proceeds thereof for the agreed or reasonable value of the services performed or the agreed or reasonable value of the room, board, supplies, facilities, or accommodations furnished; any article or lot of articles of wearing apparel or of household use for the purpose of laundering, cleaning, dyeing, or pressing; all personal property stored within each leased space located at the self storage facility.

Extent of Lien—Person who makes, alters, or repairs any personal property shall have a lien on the property for the reasonable charges for the work done and materials furnished, excluding storage charges, and may retain possession of the property until the charges are paid. Lien on all personal property stored within each leased space located at the self storage facility for rent, labor, or other charges, present or future, and for expenses reasonably incurred in enforcing the lien.

Enforcement by Sale—If the owner of the animals, after demand and notice in writing that the lien will be enforced has been served upon the owner, fails to pay the amount due for the pasturing, feeding, or sheltering within 30 days, the holder of the lien may cause the animals to be sold at public auction. If a lien for any article or lot of articles of wearing apparel or of household use for the purpose of laundering, cleaning, dyeing, or pressing remains unsatisfied for a period of at least 90 days, the article or lot of articles may be sold. All articles received in one lot may be sold as one lot or as separate articles.

Notice of Sale—Notice of sale being given for 15 days by publication in a newspaper of general circulation in the county where the animals are pastured, fed, or sheltered. Notice of the time and place of sale shall be published in a newspaper of general circulation in the county where the articles or lots of articles to be sold have been delivered for laundering, cleaning, dyeing, or pressing, not less than five nor more than 10 days prior to the date of sale. The notice shall state the name of each person who delivered an article or lot of articles to be sold, if known, and shall state the amount of lien to be satisfied with respect to the article or lot of articles delivered by the person. As to the nature of the articles or lots of articles to be sold, the notice need merely state, in general terms, with reference to the articles or lots of articles collectively, that they are articles or lots of articles left for the purpose of laundering, cleaning, dyeing, or pressing.

Notice of Lien—Before satisfaction of judgment is docketed, the dentist, doctor, physician, surgeon, or hospital files in the office of the chief clerk of the circuit court of the circuit in which the judgment was recovered, or, in the case of a judgment recovered in a district court, in the office of the clerk of the district court of the circuit in which judgment was recovered, a notice setting forth the agreed or reasonable value of the services performed or the agreed or reasonable value of the room, board, supplies, facilities, or accommodations furnished

Foreclosure by Bailee—Whenever any lien has attached to any personal property in the possession of a bailee and is unsatisfied for the period of at least 60 days, and no other procedure is provided by law for the foreclosure of the lien, the bailee shall give public notice by publication for at least four issues of some newspaper published and circulating in the county where the bailee resides, which publication shall not be mor often than once per week. The notice shall particularly describe the personal property to be sold, the date and place of sale, the bailor's name, if known, and the nature and amount of lien to be satisfied. At the time and place named in the publication the property may be sold and the purchaser shall thereupon succeed to the bailor's title thereto. Out of the proceeds of sale the bailee may retain the amount of the lien, the cost of advertisement and sale, and other expenses incident to the sale. Any balance remaining which is not claimed by the owner of the property sold or the owner's legal representative within 30 days from the date of sale, shall be deposited by the bailee with the director of finance of the State to the credit of the owner and payable at any time to the owner or the owner's legal representatives; provided that the bailee may foreclose the lien in accordance with any written contract with the owner or by a civil action, and the proceedings shall be similar to proceedings to foreclose a mortgage of real property.

IDAHO

Who May Claim—Persons who perform labor on a farm, till land, or cultivate, harvest, thresh, or house crops; persons performing labor upon, or assisting in obtaining or securing saw logs, spars, piles, core wood, or other timber; manufacturing such into lumber or permitting another upon their timberland to cut such timber; persons rendering service for the protection, improvement, safekeeping, or carriage of personal property; agricultural commodity producer or dealer who sells an agricultural product, e.g., wheat, corn, oats, etc.; every individual, partnership, firm, association, corporation, institution or any governmental unit or combination or parts thereof maintaining and operating a hospital in this state; any person, firm or corporation, who makes, alters or repairs any article of personal property, at the request of the owner or person in legal possession thereof.

In addition to other personal property liens, the owner of a self storage facility shall have a lien on all personal property stored within each leased space located at the self storage facility for rent, labor, or other charges, present or future, and for expenses reasonably incurred in enforcing the lien.

Property Covered—Crops; saw logs, spars, piles, core wood or other timber or lumber; agricultural products; personal property protected, improved, stored, or carried. Any and all causes of action, suits, claims, counterclaims, or demands accruing to the person to whom such care, treatment, or maintenance was furnished, or to the legal representatives of such person, on account of injuries giving rise to such causes of action and which necessitated such hospital care, treatment and maintenance.

How Claimed—Agricultural and timber liens are claimed by filing a claim in substantially the following form:

_____ Claimant v. _____

Notice is hereby given that _____ of _____ County, State of Idaho, claims a lien upon a _____ of _____ being about _____ in quantity, which were cut in _____ County, State of Idaho, are marked thus _____, and are now lying in _____ for labor performed upon and assistance rendered in _____ said _____; that the name of the owner or reputed owner is _____; that _____ employed said _____ to perform such labor and render such assistance upon the following terms, to wit: The _____ agreed to pay the said _____ for such labor and assistance _____; that said contract has been faithfully performed and fully complied with on the part of said _____, who performed labor upon and assisted in _____ said _____ for the period of _____ that said labor and assistance were so performed and rendered upon said _____ between the ____ day of _____ and the ____ day of _____, and the rendition of said services was closed on the ____ day of _____ and _____ days have not elapsed since that time; that the amount of claimant's demand for said services is _____; that no part thereof has been paid except _____, and there is now due and unpaid thereon, after deducting all just credits and offsets, the sum of _____, in which amount he claims a lien upon said _____.

State of Idaho, _____ County, ss.: _____, being first duly sworn, on oath says that he is _____ named in the foregoing claim, has heard the same read and knows the contents thereof, and believes the same to be true _____.

Subscribed and sworn to before me this ____ day of, 20 ___.

Where Filed—With the county recorder of the county in which the agricultural work is performed, the timber cut, or the lumber manufactured.

When to Be Filed—Within 60 days after the close of the rendition of services or the close of work and labor. For agricultural commodity dealer lien, within 90 days after date of product sold or delivered, whichever occurs last.

Extent of Lien—Liens for labor or service related to timber or lumber are for work, labor, or purchase price for eight months preceding filing of claim. Hospital liens are for reasonable charges for hospital care, treatment and maintenance of an injured person.

Duration of Lien—Agricultural and timber liens are valid for six months.

Enforcement by Sale—Liens on personal property cared for by the lienor may, if not paid within 60 days after the work is done or service supplied, be enforced by sale of the property at public auction. The proceeds of the sale are applied to the discharge of the lien, and the remainder, if any, is paid over to the owner. If lien for alteration or repair of personal property is not paid within two (2) months after the work is done, the person, firm or corporation may proceed to sell the property at public auction.

Notice of Sale—Ten days' public notice by advertising in a newspaper published in the county where the property is situated or in which the work was done, or if there is no such paper, by posting notices in three of the most public places in the county, for 10 days previous to such sale.

Priority—Liens on crops are preferred and prior to any security interest therein. However, any interest in crops of a lessor of land for a share in the crop is not subject to such lien. Timber liens are prior to any other liens. No sale or transfer shall divest such lien and the lien will follow the property into any county in the state where notice is filed. A hotel keeper has a lien upon all baggage and other personal property of a guest for unpaid charges and for the cost of enforcing such lien including attorney's fees. A lien of a firm or corporation, who makes, alters or repairs any article of personal property, at the request of the owner or person in legal possession thereof, shall be superior and prior to any security interest in the same for his reasonable charges for work done and materials furnished.

ILLINOIS

Who May Claim—Attorneys; health care professionals and health care providers that render any service in the treatment, care, or maintenance of an injured person, except services rendered under the provisions of the Workers' Compensation Act or the Workers' Occupational Diseases Act; every person who, at the request of the owner or his authorized agent, shall shoe or cause to be shod by his employees any horse, mule, ox or other animal; hotel, inn and boarding house keepers; stable keepers; agisters and persons keeping, yarding, feeding or pasturing domestic animals; every person who, as owner or lessee of any threshing machine, clover huller, corn sheller or hay baler, threshes grain or seed, hulls clover, shells corn or presses hay or straw at the request of the owner, reputed owner, authorized agent of the owner or lawful possessor of such crops; every person, firm or corporation who has expended labor, skill or materials upon any chattel, or has furnished storage for said chattel, at the request of its owner, reputed owner, or authorized agent of the owner, or lawful possessor; all persons who may have furnished or who shall hereafter furnish to any railroad corporation now existing or hereafter to be organized under the laws of this State, any fuel, ties, material, supplies, or other article or thing necessary for the construction, maintenance, operation or repair of such roads, by contract with said corporation, or who shall have done and performed or shall hereafter do and perform any work or labor for such construction, maintenance, operation or repair by like contract; owner of a self-service storage facility; every owner of any stallion or jack kept for public service, who, at the request of the owner of any mare or jennet, or his authorized agent, shall cause such mare or jennet to be served by his stallion or jack.

Property Covered—All property that is furnished, improved or on which work has been done; attorneys have liens upon all claims, demands and causes of action, including all claims for unliquidated damages, which may be placed in their hands by their clients for suit or collection, or upon which suit or action has been instituted; all claims and causes of action of the injured person; the animal shod; the baggage and other valuables of their guests or boarders brought into such hotel, inn or boarding house by such guests or boarders; the horses, carriages and harness kept by stable keepers; the animals agistered, kept, yarded or fed; crops; all the property, real, personal and mixed, of said railroad corporation as against such railroad; all personal property located at a self-service storage facility; the mare or jennet served.

How Claimed—Generally, the method of making a claim is as simple as having possession or property. There are some instances however where the statute requires more. For example, liens on railroads are claimed by serving notice on the president or secretary of such railroad corporation, substantially as follows:

> To president (or secretary, as the case may be) of the _____: You are hereby notified that I am (or have been) employed by _____ as a laborer (or have furnished supplies, as the case may be) on or for the _____ and that I shall hold property of said railroad (or railway, as the case may be) company to secure my pay.

A copy of the contract between the original contractor and subcontractor, materialmen, or laborer, if any, should be attached to the notice. If neither the president nor the secretary of such railroad corporation reside or can be found in the county in which the subcontract was made or labor performed, lienor must file the notice in the office of the clerk of the circuit court.

To enforce liens, attorneys shall serve notice in writing, which service may be made by registered or certified mail, upon the party against whom their clients may have such suits, claims or causes of action, claiming such lien and stating therein the interest they have in such suits, claims, demands or causes of action.

When Claimed—Notice of claim, if required, will be determined by the specific statute. Notice of the claim of a railroad lien must be made within 20 days after the completion of the subcontract or labor.

Duration of Lien—A suit to enforce a railroad lien must be brought within six months after the contractor or laborer has completed the contract, or after the labor is performed or material furnished (three months for subcontractors). Chattel liens generally run for a period of one year. Duration of other liens is either determined by possession or by statute.

Priority—Railroad lien is preferred to all other subsequent liens. Generally, all liens discussed herein could have priority over a perfected UCC claim. A self-service storage facility lien shall be superior to any other lien or security interest except for a statutory lien or security interest which is perfected through filing and has been perfected, prior thereto, through proper filing.

INDIANA

Who May Claim—Persons engaged in repairing, storing, servicing, or furnishing supplies or accessories for motor vehicles, airplanes, construction machinery and equipment, boats and vessels, and farm machinery; transfermen, draymen, and all others involved in packing for shipment or storage, hauling or conveying articles of value, or erecting machinery and equipment; keeper of livery stable; owners or operators of machinery or tools used in threshing or hulling grain or seed, plowing, disking, or cultivating the land, or combining, picking, or baling of crops; persons engaged in the business of storing, warehousing, and forwarding goods, wares, and merchandise; a person who engages in the business of altering or repairing electronic home entertainment equipment; pawnbrokers for loan, interest, and charges; blacksmiths; persons engaged in cleaning, glazing, washing, alteration, repair, or furnishing any materials for any garment, clothing, or household goods; the owner or keeper of any hotel, inn, boarding, eating, or lodging house, or restaurant; hospitals and those providing emergency ambulance services to a patient whose illness or injury gives rise to a cause of action, suit or claim.

A fabricator has a possessory lien for dies, molds, forms, jigs, and patterns. A person who performs work upon watches, clocks or jewelry has a lien on such items.

In addition to other personal property liens, the owner of a self storage facility shall have a lien on all personal property stored within each leased space located at the self storage facility for rent, labor, or other charges that accrue in connection with the personal property under the rental agreement, expenses necessary for the preservation of the personal property, and for expenses reasonably incurred in enforcing the lien.

Property Covered—Motor vehicles, airplanes, or construction and farm equipment stored, serviced, or maintained; property transferred or packed and machinery and equipment erected; horses, mules, oxen or other animals which have been shod; livestock; boats or vessels; all goods, wares, and merchandise left with persons for storage, warehousing, or forwarding; electronic home entertainment equipment; clothing, garment, or household goods cleaned, glazed, washed, altered or repaired; baggage or other articles of value brought into a hotel, inn, boarding, eating, or lodging house, or restaurant.

Grain or seed so threshed or hulled, crops produced or prepared for market or storage by such plowing, disking, cultivating, combining, picking, or baling.

Hospitals and persons providing emergency ambulance services may obtain a lien on the patient's cause of action for the illness or injuries that necessitated the hospital or ambulance services, or in the case of the patient's death, may obtain a lien on the cause of action of the patient's legal representative. Hospitals may also obtain a lien on a patient's judgment for personal injuries.

How Claimed—By filing notice in writing of the intention to hold the lien which sets forth the amount claimed and gives a substantial description of the property in question. In addition, a lien on grain or crops must designate the person for whom such work was done, the location of such crops, and the date on which the work was done.

For a fabricator to claim a lien, the creditor must be in possession of the item claimed and give the customer against whom the claim is made written notice by mail or personal delivery to the owner's last known address which states that a lien is claimed for the damages set forth or attached for the amount due for fabrication work or other related services. The notice must include a demand for payment. If the lienholder is not paid within 60 days of this notice, it may sell the die, mold, form, jig, or pattern at auction if there is still possession of it, and the creditor must then give additional notice via certified mail to the customer and any person whose security interest is perfected by the filing of this notice. For liens for cleaning and other services on clothing and household goods, the lienholder may sell the clothing or household goods if the owner of such property has not paid for the lienholder's services for a period of 90 days if the lienholder notifies the owner of the time and place of sale. Innkeepers may enforce their liens on baggage if they have not been paid within 60 days of providing service by selling such baggage, provided the innkeeper gives the owner of the baggage 10 days' notice of the sale.

A person who performs work on a watch, clock or jewelry may sell the item upon which he holds the lien if the account remains unpaid 120 days after the work has been completed, provided that after the

120 days, the lienholder gives the owner notice, in writing, specifying the amount due, and informing him that the payment of the amount due within 30 days will entitle the owner to redemption of the property. If the owner does not redeem the property within the 30 days, the lienholder must give the owner notice again. If the property has not been redeemed within 15 days of the second notice, the lienholder may sell the property.

A hospital or provider of emergency ambulance services may obtain lien on a cause of action for personal injury or illness by filing a written statement. A hospital may obtain a lien on a patient's judgment for personal injury by entering its notice of intention to hold lien.

Before a lienholder on electronic home entertainment equipment may sell the equipment, the lienholder must, by certified mail, return receipt requested, notify the owner and any person whose security interest is perfected by filing concerning the following: (1) the lienholder's intention to sell the equipment 30 days after the owner's receipt of the notice; (2) a description of the equipment to be sold; (3) the time and place of the sale; (4) an itemized statement describing the value of labor and materials provided and for which the lienholder has not been paid.

Where Filed—The Recorder's Office of the county where the work or service was performed, or the material furnished. Blacksmith's liens are filed with the recorder of the county in which the owner of the animal resides. A hospital enters its notice of intention to hold lien on a patient's personal injury judgment upon the judgment docket where the judgment has been recorded and files its written statement for a lien on patient's cause of action with the recorder of the county in which the hospital is located.

When to Be Filed—Notice of liens on motor vehicles, airplanes, and machinery, and those on property transferred or packed and machinery erected must be filed within 60 days after labor is performed, or service or material furnished. Notice of liens on grain and crops must be filed within 30 days after the completion of plowing, disking, or cultivating and within 10 days after the completion of combining, picking, or baling. Notice of blacksmith's liens must be filed within 60 days after the shoeing of the animal.

In order to obtain a lien on a patient's cause of action for illness or personal injury, a hospital must file its written statement within 180 days after the patient is discharged from the hospital, and, within 10 days from the filing of the statement, mail a copy of the filed statement to each person claimed to be liable for the illness or injury, the attorney representing the patient and the Indiana Department of Insurance. The provider of emergency ambulance services may obtain a lien on a patient's cause of action for personal injury or illness by filing its written statement within 60 days after the provision of the services, and within 10 days from the filing of the statement, mailing a copy of the filed statement to each person claimed to be liable for the illness or injury and the attorney representing the patient.

Duration of Lien—Blacksmith's liens; three months. Lien of employee of corporation; six months. Transfer, moving and storage liens and liens for repairing storing or servicing motor vehicles, airplanes, machinery or equipment; one year after filing of notice of intention to hold lien. Hospital's lien on judgment for personal injuries; 10 years after judgment entered.

Priority—A lien on property transferred or packed, or machinery and equipment erected, has priority over all subsequent liens. A lien on personal property held by the owner of a self-service storage facility is superior to any other lien or security interest, except for liens or security interests perfected before any sale or other disposition of the personal property and any tax liens. A hospital's lien on a patient's judgment for personal injuries is inferior to all claims for attorney's fees, court costs, and all other expenses contracted or incurred in the recovery of claims or damages for personal injuries.

Comments—Where crops subject to lien are sold by the party for whom the work was done, such party must notify the purchaser that the account has not been paid, and the lien will shift from the crops to the purchase price thereof in the hands of the purchaser. Where such crops are sold with the consent and knowledge of the lienor, such lien will not attach to the crops or the purchase price unless the lienor personally notifies the purchaser of the lien.

Employee Liens—Employees of any corporation doing business in Indiana are entitled to hold a lien upon the corporate property of the corporation and the earnings of the corporation for all work and labor done and performed by the employees. This lien is acquired by filing in the recorder's office of the county where the corporation is located or doing business, notice of the employee's intention to hold a lien, setting forth the date of employment, the name of the corporation and the amount of the claim. This lien has priority over all liens created after the time the employee was employed by the corporation, except other employees' liens. The employee may enforce the lien within six months from the date such lien was acquired.

IOWA

Who May Claim—Operator of a machine for threshing, baling, or combining any kind of grain or seed, baling hay, straw, or other farm product, or mechanical husking and shelling of corn; livery and feed stable keepers, herders, feeders, keepers of stock and of places for the storage of motor vehicles, boats and boat motors, and engines; a lessor owning or operating a refrigerated locker plant; agricultural supply dealer; any person who renders any service or furnishes any material in the making, repairing, improving, or enhancing the value of any inanimate personal property, with the assent of the owner, express or implied; every lessor owning or operating a refrigerated locker plant or plants; a custom cattle feedlot operator; the owner or keeper of any stallion, bull or jack kept for public service, or any person, firm, or association which invokes pregnancy of animals for the public by means of artificial insemination; veterinarians; every association, corporation, county, or other institution, including a municipal corporation, maintaining a hospital in the state, which shall furnish medical or other service to any patient injured by reason of an accident not covered by the workers' compensation act; hotelkeepers.

In addition to other personal property liens, the owner of a self storage facility shall have a lien on all personal property stored within each leased space located at the self storage facility for rent, labor, or other charges, present or future, and for expenses reasonably incurred in enforcing the lien.

Property Covered—Grain and seed threshed, farm product baled, or corn shelled or husked; all property stored by livery and feed stable keepers, herders, feeders and keepers of stock, motor vehicles, boats, boat motors, and engines; all property of every kind in the possession of a refrigerator locker plant owner or operator; crops which are produced upon the land to which the agricultural chemical was applied, produced from the seed provided, or produced using the petroleum product provided; livestock consuming the feed; the cattle and the identifiable cash proceeds from the sale of the cattle for the amount of the contract price for the feed and care of the cattle at the custom cattle feedlot; the progeny of the stallion, bull, artificial insemination or jack; that part going or belonging to such patient of any recovery or sum had or collected or to be collected by such patient, or by the patient's heirs or personal representatives in the case of the patient's death, whether by judgment or by settlement or compromise; baggage of guest.

How Claimed—A thresherman, baler, or corn sheller's lien is preserved by filing an itemized and verified statement setting forth the services rendered, the number of bushels of grain threshed or corn shelled, the value of the services, the person for whom such services were rendered, and where such services were rendered.

Where Filed—In the office of the Secretary of State.

When to Be Filed—Within 10 days from the completion of the work for which the lien is claimed.

Enforcement by Sale—When charges for care of stock and storage of motor vehicles and boats are not paid, the lienholder may sell the stock and property at public auction after giving proper notice. The proceeds go to satisfy the charges and expenses of keeping the property, and the cost and expenses of the sale; the balance to be paid to the owner. The hotelkeeper shall retain the baggage upon which the hotelkeeper has a lien for a period of 90 days, at the expiration of which time, if such lien is not satisfied, the hotelkeeper may sell such baggage at public auction.

Notice of Sale—Proper notice consists of 10 days' written notice to the owner of the time and place of the sale if such owner is found within the county, and the posting of written notices in three public places in the township where the stock or property was kept or received. Hotelkeeper must give 10 days' notice of the time and place of sale in a newspaper of general circulation in the county where the hotel is situated, and also by mailing a copy of such notice addressed to said guest at the place of residence registered by the guest in the register of the hotel.

Duration of Lien—Proceedings to enforce a thresherman's, baler's, or cornsheller's lien must be brought within 30 days after the filing of the verified statement. A custom cattle feedlot operator lien terminates one year after the cattle have left the custom cattle feedlot. Hospital liens must be brought within one year of services provided.

Priority—A thresherman's, baler's, or cornsheller's lien is prior and superior to any landlords' lien. A lien in livestock feed shall have priority over an earlier perfected lien or security interest to the extent of the difference between the acquisition price of the livestock and the fair market value of the livestock at the time the lien attaches or the sale price of the livestock, whichever is greater. A landlord's lien that is perfected shall have priority over a conflicting agricultural supply dealer's lien and a harvester's lien that is perfected shall have priority over a conflicting agricultural supply dealer's lien. A custom feedlot operator lien is superior to and shall have priority over a conflicting lien or security interest in the cattle, including a lien or security interest that was perfected prior to the perfection of the custom cattle feedlot lien. However, a custom cattle feedlot lien shall not be superior to a veterinarian's lien, that is perfected as an agricultural lien. A veterinarian's lien that is perfected shall have priority over any conflicting security interest or lien in livestock treated by a veterinarian, regardless of when such security interest or lien is perfected. A lien for the care of stock and storage of motor vehicles, boats, boat motors, and engines is subject to all prior liens of record.

Notice of Enforcement—Must be filed with Secretary of State.

KANSAS

Who May Claim—Any person who at or with the owner's request or consent performs work, makes repairs or improvements or replaces, adds or installs equipment on any goods, personal property, chattels, horses, mules, wagons, buggies, automobiles, trucks, trailers, locomotives, railroad rolling stock, barges, aircraft, equipment of all kinds including but not limited to construction equipment, vehicles of all kinds, and farm implements of whatsoever kind; operators of threshing machines or persons engaged in the business of threshing and harvesting grain or grain crops; shucking, husking, or gathering corn for others under contract with the owners or mortgagees thereof; operators of broom corn seeders and balers, or hay balers or persons engaged in the business of seeding and baling broom corn and baling hay under contract with the owners or mortgagees thereof; keepers of livery stables, and all others engaged in feeding horses, cattle, hogs, or other livestock; any forwarding merchant, warehouse keeper, stage, express or railway company, hotelkeeper, carrier, or other bailee; any person doing any cleaning, pressing, glazing, washing, alteration, repair, or furnishing any materials or supplies for or upon any garment, clothing, wearing apparel, or household goods.

In addition to other personal property liens, the owner of a self storage facility shall have a lien on all personal property stored within each leased space located at the self storage facility for rent, labor, or other charges, present or future, and for expenses reasonably incurred in enforcing the lien.

Property Covered—All personal property worked on, repaired, or improved by lien claimant; horses, cattle, hogs, or other livestock that are kept and feed by livery stable; goods which may have remained in store or in the possession of a bailee; any materials or supplies for or upon any garment, clothing, wearing apparel, or household goods; grain and crops threshed and harvested and corn shucked, husked or gathered; broom corn or hay seeded or baled.

The lien extends to the full contract amount and the reasonable value of the services rendered, and includes the reasonable value of all material used in the performance of such services and the reasonable value of all equipment replaced, added or installed. A wrecker or towing service that renders service at the direction of a law enforcement officer or the owner has a first and prior lien on the motor vehicle in its possession for the amount of services rendered. Before the wrecking or towing service may sell the motor vehicle, it must: (1) request verification from the division of vehicles of the last registered owner or other lienholder not later than 60 days after taking possession of the motor vehicle; (2) by certified mail send a notice of sale to such registered owner and any lienholder; (3) publish where and when the sale shall take place; and (4) a description of the property to be sold.

How Claimed—Agricultural liens are claimed by filing a verified statement setting forth the name of the owner, kind of agricultural product, description of the land upon which such product was raised, the contract price, the date on which the work was done, the amount due, and the name of the claimant. Liens on other goods are claimed by filing under oath a statement of the items of the account and a description of the property on which the lien is claimed, with the name of the owner thereof.

Goods which have remained in store or in the possession of a bailee for six months or more, may proceed to sell such goods, or so much thereof as may be necessary to pay the amount of the lien and expenses: Provided, that such sale may be advertised and made by any carrier in any city of the first, second or third class through which its line runs, where, in the judgment of such carrier, the best price can be obtained for the property to be sold.

Any garment, clothing, wearing apparel, or household goods remaining in the possession of a person, firm, partnership, or corporation, on which cleaning, pressing, glazing, or washing has been done or upon which alterations or repairs have been made, or on which materials or supplies have been used or furnished, for a period of 90 days or more may after said cleaning, pressing, glazing or washing has been done or said alterations or repairs have been made or said materials or supplies have been used or furnished be sold to pay the reasonable or agreed charges and the cost of notifying the owner or owners provided, however, that the person, firm, partnership, or corporation to whom such charges are payable and owing shall first notify the owner or owners of the time and place of such sale; provided further, that property that is to be placed in storage after any of the services or labors mentioned herein, shall not be affected.

Where Filed—Agricultural liens are filed in the Office of the Register of Deeds of the county in which the work was done. Liens on other goods are filed in the Office of the Register of Deeds of the county in which the work was done, and in the county of the residence of the owner, if such is known to the claimant.

When to Be Filed—Agricultural liens must be filed within 15 days after completion of the work. In the case of threshing or harvesting, which has begun and been interrupted for more than five days, the statement must be filed within 15 days after the beginning of the interruption.

Liens on other goods in claimant's possession do not require filing. After parting with possession of said property, claimant may retain the lien by filing within 90 days. If lien claimant was never in possession of said property, he may retain said lien by filing within 90 days after the date upon which work was last performed, materials last furnished, or equipment was last replaced, added or installed.

Duration of Lien—For agricultural liens, 90 days after the filing of the statement. All other liens are valid as long as the lienor retains possession.

Priority—Agricultural liens are preferred to those of any prior security interest or encumbrance.

KENTUCKY

Who May Claim—Any person engaged in the business of selling, repairing, or furnishing accessories or supplies for any kind of equipment or machinery, including motors; any person performing work upon any watch, clock or jewelry; any person who cleans, presses, glazes, launders, alters, or repairs any wearing apparel or household goods; any person who keeps any wearing apparel or household goods in storage; any keeper of a hotel, inn, boarding house or house of private entertainment; any licensed keeper of a stallion, jack, or bull; any person who causes a molder to fabricate, cast, or otherwise make a die, mold, form, or pattern, or who provides a molder with a die, mold, form, or pattern, to manufacture, assemble, cast, fabricate, or otherwise make a product for a customer; veterinarians; and all persons, firms, and corporations engaged in the business of repairing radios, phonographs, automatic music instruments, refrigerators, televisions, electrical or electronic recording devices and all portable electric or electronic instruments or appliances. Any keepers and trainers of horses and other animals or persons furnishing labor or material on any horse, mule or other animal. Any warehouseman. Any person damaged shall have lien on the cattle committing the damage.

In addition to other personal property liens, the owner of a self storage facility shall have a lien on all personal property stored within each leased space located at the self storage facility for rent, labor, or other charges, present or future, and for expenses reasonably incurred in enforcing the lien.

Property Covered—Equipment, machinery, motors, watch, clock, or jewelry, wearing apparel or household goods; all baggage and other personal property owned and brought in by the person receiving board, nursing, care or attention from the landlord; any die, mold, form, or pattern in the possession of a molder and animals.

How Claimed—Filing sworn statement showing the amount and cost of materials furnished or labor performed. Lien is not dependent on possession. If the account for repairs of jewelry, clock or watch remains unpaid six months after completing the work, the person holding the lien may, upon 30 days' notice in writing to the owner specifying the amount due and informing the owner that the payment of the amount due within 30 days will entitle him to redeem the property, sell the article at public or bona fide private sale to satisfy the account. The notice may be served by mail directed to the owner's last known address, or, if the owner or his address is unknown, it may be published.

If a molder chooses to have all rights and title to any die, mold, form, or pattern transferred to the molder by operation of law, the molder shall send written notice by registered mail to the chief executive officer of the customer or, if the customer is not a business entity, to the customer, at the customer's last known address. The written notice shall indicate that the molder intends to terminate the customer's rights and title by having the rights and title transferred to the molder by operation of law. The notice shall include a statement of the customer's rights.

Where Filed—Office of the county clerk in the county where the owner resides or if a nonresident, in the county where the equipment is located.

When to Be Filed—Within three months of furnishing material or performing labor.

Enforcement of Lien by Sale—For stored property and motor vehicles, property may be sold if owner is in default of payment for over 45 days. Warehousemen may sell goods pursuant to law. The notice for household goods and wearing apparel sale of time and place of sale, when given, shall be by registered letter mailed to the last known address of the customer. The person sending the letter may do so anytime after an article has been held for at least 60 days, and the notice by registered letter shall specify that the article may be sold unless it is redeemed within 30 days from the date of the letter. If the reasonable or agreed charges have not been paid for a period of 12 months for the storage of household goods or wearing apparel article may be sold to pay the charges, after the owner has been notified of the time and place of sale.

Extent of Lien—For the reasonable or agreed charges for repairs, work done, accessories, parts, and supplies furnished. As against a holder of a mortgage or purchaser for value the lien shall not exceed the amount claimed in the statement. Lien on animals until fees are paid as well as possession on animal for keepers.

Contents of Lien Statement—Amount due the claimant, with all just credits and set-offs known to him, description of the property intended to be covered by the lien, subscribed and sworn to by the person claiming the lien.

Priority—Such lien is preferred to all subsequent mortgages or liens.

LOUISIANA

Who May Claim—Persons who furnish water to another for the purpose of assisting in growing or maturing a crop; threshermen, combinemen, and grain dryers; persons engaged in the business of hauling; persons providing money or supplies to enable another to deaden, cut, load, or transport any logs or to manufacture poles or cross ties; persons performing labor or services in deadening, cutting, loading, or transporting any logs, staves, poles or cross ties, or in manufacturing poles, cross ties, lumber, staves, hoops, boxes, shingles, doors, blinds, or window sashes; any person operating a garage or other place where automobiles or other machinery is repaired; any person who furnishes feed or medicines for a horse or horses, or any licensed veterinarian who furnishes medical services for a horse or horses, to or upon the order of the owner; any person conducting the business of cleaning carpets and rugs and storing them at his place of business after cleaning until delivery to the owner; any person who repaired, altered, dyed, cleaned, pressed, glazed or laundered any garment, clothing, wearing apparel or household goods; jewelers, jewelry manufacturers, watchmakers, and dealers; all managers, mechanics, or laborers employed in sugar refineries, sugar mills, or syrup mills; owners of private canals; a health care provider, hospital, or ambulance service that furnishes services or supplies to any injured person; marina owners.

In addition to other personal property liens, the owner of a self storage facility shall have a lien on all personal property stored within each leased space located at the self storage facility for rent, labor, or other charges, present or future, and for expenses reasonably incurred in enforcing the lien.

Property Covered—Crops to which water is furnished except where by agreement water is supplied for a share of the crop, in which case that share is unaffected by the lien; crops threshed, combined, or dried; property hauled; logs and products manufactured therefrom; horses which received the feed, medicine, or medical services; the carpets and rugs; any garment, clothing, wearing apparel or household goods which have been repaired, altered, dyed, cleaned, pressed, glazed or laundered; any goods, jewelry, gems, precious stones, watches, or any other article or articles usually handled, sold, or made by jewelers, jewelry manufacturers, watchmakers, and dealers; sugar, syrup, or molasses manufactured during the season by the refineries or mills; vessels; the net amount payable to the injured person, his heirs, or legal representatives, out of the total amount of any recovery or sum had, collected, or to be collected, whether by judgment or by settlement or compromise, from another person on account of such injuries, and on the net amount payable by any insurance company under any contract providing for indemnity or compensation to the injured person; property stored at a marina.

Extent of Lien—Lien for water supplied to crops is to secure the agreed compensation. Thresherman's, combinemen's, and grain dryer's lien is for services rendered. Carrier's lien is for the charges or labor performed in connection with hauling. Log liens are for the debt due for money advanced, or labor and services. Veterinarian liens are for the unpaid portion of the price of services. Garage keeper's liens are for the amount of the cost of repairs made, parts made or furnished, and labor performed. If estimate was given, then in order for amount of privilege to exceed the amount of estimate, authorization from owner must be secured. Carpet cleaning and storage lien is for services rendered. Sugar refineries, sugar mills, or syrup mills liens are for the payment of employees salaries or wages for a period of 30 days from the maturity of the debt. The owners of private canals within the state have a lien for the payment of the toll or canal fees. A health care provider, hospital, or ambulance service that furnishes services or supplies to any injured person shall have a privilege for the reasonable charges or fees of such health care provider, hospital, or ambulance service. A marina owner has a privilege on property stored at that marina for rent, labor, or other charges and for expenses reasonably incurred in the sale of that property.

Duration of Lien—A carrier's lien continues for a period of 180 days from the last day of hauling or performing labor. Log liens are effective for a period of 90 days from maturity of the debt. A veterinarian lien is effective for a period of six months from the dates of the respective deliveries. Garage keeper's liens are effective for a period of 180 days from the last day on which repairs were made, parts made or furnished or labor performed.

Priority—Thresherman's, combineman's, and grain dryer's lien is ranked as equal with the lien of a laborer and overseer, and above that of a lessor, a furnisher of supplies and money, a furnisher of water, a physician (not discussed herein), and pledges.

A lien for water supplied to crops is ranked equal to that of a furnisher of supplies and money and a physician, and below that of a laborer, thresherman, combineman, grain dryer, overseer, lessor, and pledges. Log liens are of concurrent rank. A veterinarian lien is superior to all claims, privileges, and mortgages, whether recorded or unrecorded, which theretofore may have been or thereafter may be created against such horse or horses, and to the claims of any and all purchasers thereof. The privilege of an attorney shall have precedence over the privilege on net proceeds collected from third party in favor of medical providers for services and supplies furnished injured persons.

Enforcement of Lien by Sale—Lien for cleaning or storage of rugs may be enforced by giving written notice to the person on whose account the goods are held, either by delivery in person or by registered letter addressed to his last known place of business or residence. This notice shall contain: (1) an itemized statement of the claim, showing the sum due at the time of the notice and the date or dates when it became due; (2) a demand, that the amount of the claim as stated in the notice, and of such further claim as shall accrue shall be paid on or before a day mentioned, not less than 10 days from the delivery of the notice if it is personally delivered, or from the time when the notice should reach its destination according to the due course of the mails, if the notice is sent by mail; (3) a statement that unless the claim is paid within the time specified, the goods will be sold.

Any garment, clothing, wearing apparel or household goods which have been repaired, altered, dyed, cleaned, pressed, glazed or laundered, which remain in the possession of a person for a period of 90 days or more, may be sold to pay reasonable or agreed charges, together with any costs or expenses provided for; provided, however, that the person to whom such charges are due and payable shall first notify the owner or owners of the proposed sale of the articles belonging to them and the amount of the charges due thereon, and provided, further, that no property that is to be placed in storage after any of the services or labors mentioned herein have been performed shall be subject to sale.

Whenever any goods, jewelry, gems, precious stones, watches, or any other article or articles usually handled, sold, or made by jewelers, jewelry manufacturers, watchmakers, and dealers are deposited with any person so engaged for repairing, cleaning, inspection, or appraisement, and are repaired, cleaned, inspected, or appraised and are not claimed by their owners within six months from the date of deposit, the person with whom they are deposited may offer by private sale any or all of the unclaimed goods for a price of not less than the amount due for the services, provided the goods are appraised at less than $10 by two sworn disinterested appraisers. The person with whom the goods are deposited shall first notify the apparent owner by registered mail at his last known address that the unclaimed goods are to be placed on sale. The notice shall be given at least 30 days prior to the sale and shall set forth the date, time, and place of the sale.

If a property owner is in default for a period of more than 180 days, a marina owner may enforce a privilege by selling the stored property at a commercially reasonable public sale for cash.

Notice of Lien—Notification of a marina owner's lien is satisfied by: (1) a written rental agreement signed by the property owner that includes a notice of the privilege created by this part; or (2) written notification of the privilege sent by the marina owner to the property owner. A marina owner who does not have a written rental agreement that includes a notice of the privilege may not initiate an enforcement action until 30 days after the written notice of a privilege is delivered to the property owner.

MAINE

Who May Claim—Persons who perform labor or furnish labor or wood for manufacturing and burning bricks for such labor and wood; persons who furnish corn or other grain or fruit for canning or preservation; persons who grow, harvest and sell potatoes; owners of stallions hired for service; persons who pasture, feed or shelter animals by virtue of a contract with or by consent of the owner; persons laboring in the cutting or harvesting of hay; persons pressing hay; persons or entities involved in the treatment or maintenance of an injured person; persons leasing or renting land; persons performing labor or services or furnishing labor, materials or services in laying out or construction of any road, path or walk, or in improving or beautifying any land in a manner commonly known as landscape gardening, by virtue of a contract with or by consent of the owner; persons performing labor in any tannery where leather of any kind is manufactured completely or partially; persons who labor at cutting, hauling, rafting or driving logs or lumber, or at cooking for persons engaged in such labor or in shoeing horses or oxen, or repairing property while thus employed; persons who labor at cutting, peeling or hauling hemlock bark, or cutting, yarding or hauling cordwood, or cutting peeling, yarding or hauling pulpwood or any wood used in the manufacture of pulpwood, or at cooking for persons engaged in such labor; persons laboring in the manufacture of last blocks, shovel handle blocks, railroad ties or ship knees, or is engaged in cooking for persons engaged in such labor, or cuts or furnishes wood for the manufacture of last blocks or shovel handle blocks, or furnishes a team for hauling of last blocks and shovel handle blocks or the lumber from which they are made, or for the hauling of railroad ties or ship knees; persons laboring at cutting, hauling or sawing shingle stave, lath, dowel or spool timber, or in the manufacture of shingle, stave, lath, dowel or spool timber, or at piling staves, laths, dowels or spool bars, or bunching shingles or dowels, or at cooking for persons engaged in such labor; persons who dig, haul or furnish rock for the manufacture of lime; persons who, under express contract fixing the price to be paid, sells, erects or furnishes any monument, tablet, headstone, vault, posts, curbing or other monumental work; banks or other entities engaged in leasing of safe deposit boxes; persons who perform labor by himself, or his employees in manufacturing or repairing the ironwork or woodwork of wagons, carts, sleighs and other vehicles, aircraft or component parts thereof, or parachutes, or so performing labor furnishes materials therefore or provides storage thereof by direction or consent of the owner; persons who perform labor or provide materials necessary for the repair of domestic vessels, or for the use of a wharf, dry dock or marina; person who furnish labor or materials for the building of a vessel; persons furnishing labor or materials in the making, altering, repairing or cleaning of any watch, clock, jewelry, electric motor, major and traffic appliance, small motor not to exceed 20 horsepower, radio, electronic equipment, musical instrument, furniture, photograph, artwork, sports equipment and photography equipment; and person furnishing labor or materials for the cleaning, repairing or pressing of clothes; whoever performs labor or furnishes labor or materials, including repair parts of machines used, or performs services as a surveyor, an architect or an engineer, or as a real estate licensee, or as an owner-renter, owner-lessor, or owner-supplier of equipment used in erecting, altering, moving or repairing a house, building or appurtenances, including any public building erected or owned by any city, town, county, school district or other municipal corporation, or in constructing, altering or repairing a wharf or pier, or any building thereon, including the surveying, clearing, grading, draining, excavating or landscaping of the ground adjacent to and upon which any such objects are constructed, or in selling any interest in land, improvements or structures, by virtue of a contract with or by consent of the owner.

Marinas, boatyards, and marine repair facilities may impose a lien for rent, storage, labor, or other charges. No lien may be imposed on a documented vessel subject to a perfected maritime lien.

Many of these liens have different rules covering duration, property covered, extent of the lien, and priority. Some examples will be given below, however, it is recommended that a person review the current statute regarding a specific lien, or obtain legal counsel to do so before utilizing a specific lien.

Property Covered—Brick lien is on bricks manufactured or burned. Canned goods lien is on the preserved article and everything with which it may have been mingled for its value when delivered, including the cans or other vessels and cases. Potato lien is on the product and all processed or manufactured forms of potatoes. Log driver's lien is on the logs or lumber driven. A marina lien is on the property stored at the property stored at the facility.

Extent of Lien—Brick lien is for the labor. Canned goods lien is for the value of the preserved article when delivered. Potato lien is for labor, care and expense in growing and harvesting the raw product. Log driver's lien is for the amount payable under the contract. A marina lien is for the rent, labor, or other charges and for expenses reasonably incurred in the sale of the property if necessary. Service fee for colts liens secure the payment of the service fee for the use of the stallion begetting the foal. Whoever pastures, feeds or shelters animals by virtue of a contract with or by consent of the owner has a lien thereon for the amount due for such pasturing, feeding or sheltering, and for necessary expenses incurred in the proper care of such animals and in payment of taxes assessed thereon, to secure payment thereof with costs.

Duration of Lien—Brick liens and canned goods liens continue for 30 days after such bricks are burned (provided they remain in the yard where stored) or such canned or preserved articles are delivered (and until shipped on board a vessel or laden in a car). Potato liens remain in effect until the producer receives payment in satisfaction of the total claim. Log driver's liens continue for 60 days after the logs or lumber arrive at the place of destination for sale or manufacture. For marina liens, if the property owner is in default for more than 90 days, the facility owner may enforce the lien by selling the stored property at a commercially reasonable public sale for cash, and only after notifying the property owner and allowing the property owner 30 days from delivery of the notification to cure the debt. Service fee for colts liens continue in force until the foal is six months old. Hay cutting lien continues for 30 days after the last of such services are performed.

Enforcement—These liens may be enforced by attachment or by suit in the Superior Court of the county where the claimant resides for a court ordered sale of the property. Buildings, lots, wharves and piers, labor and materials liens may be preserved and enforced by action against the debtor and owner of the property affected and all other parties interested therein, filed with the Superior Court or District Court Clerk in the county or division where the house, building or appurtenances, wharf, pier or building thereon, on which a lien is claimed, is situated, within 120 days after the last of the labor or services are performed or labor, materials or services are so furnished.

Priority—Brick liens take precedence over all other claims except attachments and encumbrances made to secure a similar lien. The potato producers lien takes precedence over all other claims except liens or security interests of financial institutions chartered by the Federal Government or by any state in the United States. Log drivers' liens take precedence over all other claims except liens for labor and stumpage.

Limitations—The potato producers' lien attached to the finished product shall be to the full extent of the agreed price, if any, or the unpaid balance of the agreed price of the raw product delivered to the processor. If there is no agreed price or a method of determining it which is agreed upon, the extent of the lien shall be the full value of the raw product as of the date of delivery and shall be determined by the commissioner upon notice and opportunity for hearing.

When a log driving contract is made with someone other than the owner of the logs or lumber, actual written notice must be given to the owner before work is begun, stating the terms of the contract. If the owner, at the time of notice or immediately thereafter, notifies the contractor that he will not be responsible for the amount payable under that contract, then the contractor will not have a lien on the logs or lumber driven.

MARYLAND

Who May Claim—All persons having custody of and providing service or material for an aircraft, boat or motor vehicle, mobile home and any airport operator. A park owner may claim a lien against a resident's mobile home if the park owner obtains a judgment against the resident under title 8A subtitle 17 of the real property article of the Annotated Code, and the resident fails to yield and render possession of the premises as ordered by the court. Any artisan who, with the consent of the owner, has possession of goods for repair, mending, improving, dry cleaning, laundering, or other work which includes storage of goods in the case of a dry cleaner or launderer; any owner or operator of a livery stable or other establishment who gives care or custody to any livestock; hotel keeper; any person who takes boarders or lodgers into his house; hospital which furnishes medical or other services to a patient injured in an accident not covered by the Maryland Workers' Compensation Act; veterinarians and commercial boarding kennel operators. In addition to other personal property liens, the owner of a self storage facility shall have a lien on all personal property stored within each leased space located at the self storage facility for rent, labor, or other charges, present or future, and for expenses reasonably incurred in enforcing the lien.

Property Covered—Aircraft, boats, mobile homes, motor vehicles; goods for repair, mending, improving, dry cleaning, laundering, or other work; livestock; the baggage or other property in the hotel which belong to or are under the control of a guest; the furniture or other property which the boarder or lodger has on the person's premises; 50 percent of the recovery or sum which the patient or, in case of death, the heirs or personal representative of the patient collect in judgment, settlement, or compromise of the patient's claim against another for damages on account of the injuries; animals serviced by veterinarian or boarded at kennel.

Extent of Lien—Aircraft liens are for inspection, maintenance, repair, servicing, rebuilding, storage, parking, handling, or tie-down; or parts, accessories, materials, or supplies. Airport owners have liens for landing fees, flight, or similar charge; boat and motor vehicle liens are for repair or rebuilding, storage, or parts and accessories. Mobile home liens are for a resident failing to yield and render possession of the property as defined in Section 1. Artisan liens are for the costs of the work done.

The owner or operator of a livery stable or other establishment who gives care or custody to any livestock has a lien on the livestock for any reasonable charge incurred for: (1) board and custody; (2) training; (3) veterinarians' and blacksmiths' services; and (4) other proper maintenance expenses.

A hotel keeper has a lien on the baggage or other property in the hotel which belong to or are under the control of a guest for any charge due or to become due to the hotel keeper for: (1) the price or value of food or accommodation; (2) the amount of any loan or advance; or (3) the amount provided by cashing a check, draft, or otherwise.

Any person who takes boarders or lodgers into his house has a lien on the furniture or other property which the boarder or lodger has on the person's premises for the contract price due or to become due for the room or board furnished.

The lien secures the reasonable and necessary charges of the hospital for treatment, care and maintenance provided to the patient. However, the charges secured may not exceed those allowed by the State Workers' Compensation Commission for medical services rendered to individuals coming under the Maryland Workers' Compensation Act.

Enforcement by Sale—Generally, if charges remain due and unpaid for 30 days, lienor in possession of the property subject to the lien may sell such property at public sale. The sale must be in a location convenient and accessible to the public between the hours of 10:00am and 6:00pm. The proceeds of the sale are applied first to the costs of holding the sale, second to the amount of the lien, and finally the remainder to the owner. For artisan liens, if the costs which give rise to the lien are due and unpaid 90 days after the work is completed or in the case of a dry cleaner or launderer goods are due to be retrieved from storage, the artisan may sell the goods to which the lien attaches at public or private sale. If the charges which give rise to the lien are unpaid 15 days after they become due, the hotel keeper may sell the property to which the lien attaches at public sale.

Notice of Sale—Notice of the time, place, and terms of the sale and a full description of the property must be published by the lienor once a week for the two weeks immediately preceding the sale, in one or more newspapers of general circulation in the county where the sale is to be held. In addition, the lienor must send the notice by registered or certified mail at least 10 days before the sale to the owner of the property, if the owner's address is known, or to general delivery at the post office of the city or county where the business of the lienor is located if the addresses of both the owner and the person who incurred the charges are unknown.

Notice of Lien—A lien is not effective under this subtitle unless, before payment of any money to the patient, his attorney, heirs, or personal representative as compensation for the injuries, the hospital: (1) files a notice of lien with the clerk of the circuit court of the county where the medical or other services were provided; and (2) sends a copy of the notice of lien and a statement of the date of its filing by registered or certified mail to the person alleged to be liable for the injuries received by the patient. The notice of lien shall be in writing and shall contain: (1) the name and address of the injured patient; (2) the date of the accident; (3) the name and location of the hospital; (4) the amount claimed; and (5) the name of the person alleged to be liable for the injuries received. The hospital also shall send a copy of the notice of lien by registered or certified mail to any insurance carrier known to insure the person alleged to be liable for the injuries received by the patient.

If the animal is not claimed and taken by the owner from the veterinarian or the boarding kennel within 10 days of the date the notice of readiness is given or posted, the owner forfeits his title to the animal and the veterinarian or the commercial boarding kennel operator may: (1) sell the animal at public sale, except for purposes of experimentation or vivisection; (2) turn the animal over to an animal welfare agency serving the county in which the animal is located or, if there is no animal welfare agency in that county, to the nearest animal welfare agency; or (3) turn the animal over to a responsible private individual in the county.

Comment—If the owner of the property disputes the charges, he may institute appropriate judicial proceedings, which stays execution of the lien until final determination of the dispute. The owner may also, if he disputes the charges, gain immediate repossession of the property by filing a corporate bond for double the amount of the charges claimed.

Priority—An aircraft lien is subject only to the rights of the holder of the bill of sale, contract of conditional sale, conveyance, a mortgage or assignment of mortgage, executed and recorded with the Federal Aviation Administration before the time the lien becomes effective. Boat, mobile home, and motor vehicle liens are subordinate only to a security interest perfected as required by law. A hospital's lien is subordinate only to an attorney's lien for professional services for collecting or obtaining damages.

MASSACHUSETTS

Who May Claim—Persons furnishing work, labor and materials in the spinning, throwing, manufacturing, bleaching, mercerizing, dyeing, printing, finishing, or otherwise processing of cotton, wool, silk, artificial silk or synthetic fibers, leather goods or hides, or goods of which such materials form a component part; and, in the processing of wood, metal, paper, paperboard, plastic and plastic compounds; and, in the processing of any material for use in electrical components.

In addition to other personal property liens, the owner of a self storage facility shall have a lien on all personal property stored within each leased space located at the self storage facility for rent, labor, or other charges, present or future, and for expenses reasonably incurred in enforcing the lien. Such lien shall be lost if operator voluntarily delivers or unjustifiably refuses to deliver goods.

An aircraft lien may be imposed within 60 days of last furnishing of labor or materials for the repair or alteration of an aircraft. The lien must be filed with the FAA registry within 60 days of last furnishing of labor, material or supplies. If a lien is filed after a third-party sale by a good faith purchaser unaware of the circumstances giving rise to the lien, it is non-enforceable. Special notice requirements exist.

In addition, various other liens are available over a wide spectrum, only illustrations of which follow: for the construction, launching or repair or storage of certain maritime vessels; garages for the storage and care of motor vehicles; persons maintaining manufactured housing communities; individuals who clean, press, wash, dye or repair clothing; persons who perform work on paintings and photographs; jewelers; persons having proper charges due them for pasturing, boarding or keeping horses or other domestic animals which are brought to their premises or placed in their care by or with the consent of the owners; persons, including but not limited to the commonwealth and any department, commission, division, agency, or branch thereof, maintaining public landing, parking, storage, and tie-down facilities for the landing, parking, storage, and tie-down of aircraft brought to their premises on an airport or placed in their care by or with the consent of the owners; molders.

Property Covered—Generally speaking, goods in the lienor's possession; in the case of persons maintaining manufactured housing the lien is on the house and the contents thereof; in the case of molders, dependent on possession, they have a lien on all dies, molds, forms, engraving plates, original art or patterns in their hands belonging to a customer.

Extent of Lien—What the lien will cover will be specified by the individual, specific relevant statute, providing or extending, generally to any unpaid balance of account for work, labor, and materials that were furnished in the course of such process. As for persons maintaining manufactured housing, the lien is for proper charges due them for such rental, facilities, storage and care, and any tax assessed by reason of such manufactured home having occupied a site in such manufactured housing community. Liens for maintenance of aircraft and associated facilities has a lien upon such aircraft for proper charges due them for the landing, parking, storage, and tie-down and care of the same. Molders have a lien for the balance due them from the customer for any manufacturing or fabrication work, and in the value of all material related to the work

Enforcement by Sale—Each lien will be enforced in accordance with the specific relevant statutory provision. As for molders, if the molder has not been paid the amount due within 60 days after the notice has been received by the customer, the molder may sell the die, mold, form, engraving plate, original art or pattern at a public auction. The sale may be subject to a customer's rights under federal patent or copyright law.

Notice of Sale—Each sale will be conducted in accordance with the specific relevant statutory provision. As for jeweler's liens, if any such account remains unpaid for one year after the completion of the work, the lienor may, upon 30 days' notice in writing to the owner specifying the amount due and informing him that payment of such amount within 30 days will entitle him to redeem the article or articles covered by such lien, sell the same at public or bona fide private sale to satisfy the account. The proceeds of the sale, after paying the expenses thereof, shall be applied in satisfaction of the indebtedness secured by such lien and the balance, if any, shall be paid over to the owner. Such notice may be served by mail, directed to the owner's last known address, or, if the owner or his address be unknown, it may be posted in two public places in the town where the property is located.

As for liens of persons working upon, or storing, articles of clothing or household goods, if any such account remains unpaid for 90 days after the completion of the work, or after the expiration of the agreed term of storage, if any, or in the absence of such agreement, after the expiration of 120 days from the date of storage, the lienor, upon notice in writing to the owner specifying the amount due and informing him that payment of such amount within 30 days will entitle him to redeem the article or articles covered by such lien, may, at the expiration of 30 days from the date of said notice, give said article or articles to a duly organized charitable corporation, or sell the same or any part thereof, at public or bona fide private sale to satisfy the account.

Before a molder may sell the die, mold, form, engraving plate, original art or pattern, the molder shall notify the customer by registered mail, return receipt requested. The notice shall include the following information: (1) the molder's intention to sell the die, mold, form, engraving plate, original art or pattern 30 days after the customer's receipt of the notice; (2) a description of the die, mold, form, engraving plate, original art or pattern to be sold; (3) the time and place of the sale; and (4) an itemized statement for the amount due.

Priority—The lien created for processors of certain goods and materials shall have priority over any title, lien, interest or encumbrance of any owner. Molder liens shall have priority over any title, lien, interest or encumbrance in the die, mold, form, engraving plate, original art or pattern.

MICHIGAN

Who May Claim—Garage keepers who furnish labor, material, or supplies to vehicles under contract, express or implied; any owner, part owner, or lessee of a hay press, threshing machine, huller, or similar machine, used for another person; any person who labors or provides any service in manufacturing lumber or shingles in or about any lumber or shingle mill; any person who shall shoe or cause to be shod by his employees, any horse, mule, ox or other animal.

In addition to other personal property liens, the owner of a self storage facility shall have a lien on all personal property stored within each leased space located at the self storage facility for rent, labor, or other charges, present or future, and for expenses reasonably incurred in enforcing the lien.

Property Covered—Vehicles stored, maintained, supplied, or repaired; hay, grain, or other vegetable product pressed, threshed, or hulled; lumber or shingles worked with or on; the animal shod; property stored at facility for storage, rent, labor, materials, supplies.

How Claimed—Liens for pressing, threshing, or hulling by filing a verified statement setting forth the name of the lienor; the amount, quantity and kind of hay or grain, seed, or vegetable product; the amount due over and above all legal setoffs; the name of the person for whom the work was done; and a description of the land upon which the hay, grain, seed, or product was grown and processed. Liens for lumber laborers must be filed by a verified statement.

If the garage keeper's lien is for an aircraft, and the amount due is not paid within 60 days after the last work or services performed, the claimant may file a claim of lien with the FAA aircraft registry.

If the charges due are not paid within 60 days of the filing of that claim, together with an itemized statement of the account being delivered to the registered owner of the aircraft by personal service or registered or certified mail to the last known address, the garage keeper may sell the aircraft at a public auction, provided it is not less than 20 days nor more than 60 days after the 60-day period, and not less than 20 days before the sale, the claimant gives written notice of the time and place of the sale to the FAA aircraft registry, and a lienholder as shown on their records, and the registered owner.

Any person desiring to secure the benefit of a horseshoeman lien shall, within 60 days after the shoeing of such horse, mule, ox or other animal, or in case he shall have shod such animal more than once within that time, then within 60 days after the date of the last shoeing, file with the register of deeds of the county in which such animal is, a statement made under oath by the claimant or someone in his or her behalf and a notice of his intention to claim a lien upon such animal for his charges for shoeing the same.

A facility owner shall notify a property owner and all prior lienholders of the lien created in this act before enforcing the lien. A property owner is notified if either of the following has occurred: (a) the property owner has signed a written storage agreement that includes a notice of the lien created in this act; (b) the facility owner has mailed written notification of the lien to the property owner and all prior lienholders.

Where Filed—The Office of the Register of Deeds of the county where the hay, grain, seed, or other product was pressed, threshed, or hulled. For lumber or laborers must be filed in the aforementioned office of the county where the labor was performed.

When to Be Filed—Pressing, threshing, or hulling liens must be claimed within 20 days after the work is completed.

Extent of Lien—A garage keeper's lien is for the proper charges due; a lumber labor lien is for the amount due for such services; a pressing, threshing, or hulling lien is for the agreed price, or if none, the value of services rendered, but the lien will not attach where the hay, grain, or product has passed into the hands of an innocent purchaser or dealer in the usual course of trade; a facility owner has a possessory lien on property stored at that facility for storage, rent, labor, materials, supplies, and other charges and for expenses reasonably incurred in the sale of that property

Enforcement by Sale—A garage keeper's lien, except for liens against aircraft (see Section 3 above), may be enforced by sale of the vehicle at public auction if the charges are not paid within 45 days after personal serving upon the owner of a claim of lien together with an itemized statement of the account. The sale must be held not less than 20 days or more than 60 days after the expiration of the 45-day period. If a property owner is in default for a period of more than 180 days, the facility owner may enforce the lien by selling the repaired or stored property at a commercially reasonable public sale.

Notice of Sale—Not less than 10 days' written notice of the time and place of the sale must be provided to the department of state and any lienholders shown on department records. Notice to the department and lienholders may be given by first-class mail. Notice to the owner must be certified mail to the last-known address of the owner.

Priority—A garage keeper's lien, insofar as it is for labor and materials furnished in making repairs, has priority over all other liens upon the vehicle. The lien becomes of no effect as against the holder of a chattel mortgage, conditional sales agreement, or other prior lien, by payment by the prior lienholder to the garage keeper of the amount of the lien, not exceeding $600 in the case of a ground vehicle, $200 in the case of watercraft. Such payment may then be added to the amount of the prior lien. The lumberman's lien has precedence over all other liens and claims. Horseshoeman lien shall take precedence of all other liens or claims thereon not duly recorded prior to recording claim of lien.

MINNESOTA

Who May Claim—Performers of manual labor or other personal service for hire in or in aid of cutting, saving, loading, peeling, hauling, rafting, etc.; any logs or timber; owners and operators of threshing machines, harvesters, clover hullers, corn picking machines, shellers, shredders, ensilage cutters, or hay bailers; owners of warehouse and self-service storage facilities; innkeepers; whoever stores, cares for or contributes to the value of personal property; any person, firm, or corporation operating a hospital in this state; any person, firm, or corporation involved in the following processes: repairs, alterations, dyeing, cleaning, pressing, or laundering; veterinarians; a person who produces an agricultural commodity, except grain and raw milk.

The owner of a self-service storage facility has a lien against the occupant on the personal property stored under a rental agreement in a storage space at the self-service storage facility, or on the proceeds of the personal property subject to the defaulting occupant's rental agreement in the owner's possession. The lien is for rent, labor, and other charges in relation to the personal property specified in the rental agreement that have become due and for expenses necessary for the preservation of the personal property or expenses reasonably incurred in the sale or other disposition of the personal property under law.

Property Covered—Logs and timber cut, loaded, hauled, etc.; grain, clover, corn, ensilage, and hay processed as described above; personal property held in warehouses and self storage facilities; any article of wearing apparel, bedding, linens, flatwork and household furnishings to be repaired, altered, dyed, cleaned, pressed, or laundered.

An agricultural lien is for the contract price or, if there is no contract the fair market value, of the agricultural commodity produced by the person and delivered to a buyer.

How Claimed—By filing a verified statement setting forth the lienor's address, the dates when service was begun and ended, the agreed compensation, amounts paid if any, amount due, and a description of the timber or crop.

Launderers may retain possession of said wearing apparel or garment until the amount due on the same for repairing, altering, dyeing, cleaning, pressing, or laundering by contract shall be fully paid off and discharged. In case no amount is agreed upon by contract, then said person, firm, or corporation shall retain possession of such wearing apparel or garment until all reasonable, customary, and usual compensation shall be paid in full.

Any unclaimed animal held by a veterinarian for more than 10 days after the completion of veterinary care and treatment requested by the owner or lawful possessor of said animal may be summarily sold by the veterinarian for the reasonable value of said animal.

Where Filed—Timber lien statements are filed with the Department of Natural Resources or, if no mark or description of such timber is filed with that office, then with the Court Administrator of the District Court of the county in which the labor or service was performed. Threshing and harvesting liens are filed with the register of deeds of the county in which the work was done. Storage and repair lien statements are filed under UCC Article 9.

When to Be Filed—Timber lien statements must be filed within 30 days after the termination of such labor or service; threshing and harvesting liens must be filed within 15 days after the work is completed; storage and repair liens must be filed within 60 days of losing possession.

Duration of Lien—A timber lien continues for 90 days after filing; a threshing or harvesting lien continues for six months after filing.

Enforcement/Enforcement by Sale—A timber lien may be enforced through process of attachment in a civil action in a District Court of any county or judicial district in which labor or service was performed or in which the Office of the Commissioner of Natural Resources (wherein the marks of the property are recorded) is located. A threshing or harvesting lien may be enforced by seizure and sale, authorized by a certified copy of the statement of so much grain, clover, corn, or hay covered by the lien as may be necessary to satisfy the claim; and reasonable costs and expenses. Liens on motor vehicles may be enforced by sale by the sheriff after 90 days, three weeks published notice is required before sale. Warehouse and self storage operators may enforced lien by foreclosure sale.

When possession of any of the articles of wearing apparel, bedding, linens, flatwork and household furnishings, has continued for 90 days after the charges accrue, and the charges so due have not been paid, it shall be the duty of the persons so holding said articles to notify the owner of these charges, by certified mail at the owner's last known address. On the owner's failure to pay these charges within 10 days after such notice has been given, the persons so holding said wearing apparel, bedding, linens, flatwork and household furnishings shall then be authorized to sell said wearing apparel, bedding, linens, flatwork and household furnishings. Said sale may be public or private and the proceeds of the same shall be applied toward the payment of the charges and any balance shall be paid over to the person entitled to the same. If the owner's residence is beyond the state, or is unknown, the person holding said wearing apparel, bedding, linens, flatwork and household furnishings shall not be required to give such notice before proceeding to sell.

As for veterinarian liens, written notice of the completion of care and treatment and written notice of the proposed sale of said animal shall be given to the owner or lawful possessor of said animal by certified mail. If the whereabouts of the owner or lawful possessor of the animal cannot be ascertained with reasonable diligence, a notice of the proposed sale shall be published in a legal newspaper circulated in the county where the animal is located at least 10 days preceding the sale. The notice shall state the amount due and the date, place and time of sale.

Priority—Timber liens are preferred to all other claims except those of the state and of the owner of the land from which the timber may have been unlawfully removed.

Threshing or harvesting liens are preferred to all other liens or encumbrances except those given for the seed from which the grain was grown. A hospital lien is subject to an attorney's lien. A lien on self storage facility property is superior to other security interests except those perfected before the date the lien attaches.

Extent of Lien—Any person, firm, or corporation operating a hospital in this state shall have a lien for the reasonable charges for hospital care of an injured person upon any and all causes of action accruing to the person to whom such care was furnished, or to the legal representatives of such person, on account of injuries giving rise to such causes of action and which necessitated such hospital care.

MISSISSIPPI

Statutory Liens on personal property in Mississippi include, but are not necessarily limited to, liens on: crops in favor of employers and employees producing them; lumber in favor of sawmill employees and shippers of timber; foals or calves in favor of owners of stud animals; watercraft in favor of materialmen and laborers; watercraft in favor of municipalities for dockage, wharfage, or anchorage fees; watches, jewelry, etc., left for over 90 days for repairs, etc.; manufactured goods in favor of materialmen and laborers; animals in favor of stable keepers; motor vehicles in favor of laborers and materialmen; renter's content in self storage facilities; amount due contractor in favor of laborers and materialmen; clothing in favor of laundry plant operators; motor vehicles in favor of those towing and storing them.

All references are to the Mississippi Code, 1972, as amended; surrounding statutes and cross references should be read prior to assertion of any lien to be sure that the creditor has a full understanding of all necessary procedures and notices.

MISSOURI

Missouri provides statutory liens for innkeepers, artisans and garagemen, locker plant operators, keepers and trainers of horses and other animals or persons furnishing labor or material on any horse, mule or other animal, plastic fabricators, and persons furnishing work or labor or certain materials to a railroad. Statutory liens for storing and repairing vehicles or equipment thereof include boats and other water transport craft as well as aircraft. A lien is also available for every person who furnishes labor or material on any vehicle or aircraft, or the parts or equipment thereof.

The holder of a repairmen's lien is entitled to court costs and attorneys' fees as part of the expenses incurred in obtaining title to the vehicles subject to the lien. Missouri also recognizes a common law possessory lien for repairs to motor vehicles.

In addition to other personal property liens, the owner of a self storage facility shall have a lien on all personal property stored within each leased space located at the self storage facility for rent, labor, or other charges, present or future, and for expenses reasonably incurred in enforcing the lien. A statutory warning is required in the rental agreement.

MONTANA

Who May Claim—Persons performing labor upon, or assisting in obtaining or securing, sawlogs, pilings, ties, cordwood, or other timber, or assisting in the manufacture of timber into lumber or shingles; persons who furnish seed to be sown or planted, or funds or means with which to purchase such seed, to another for use on lands owned, used, or occupied by that person; threshermen or swathers owning or operating threshing or swathing machines, and all owners of combine harvesters and threshers; persons who perform labor or services or furnish material in crop dusting or spraying for fertilization, weed disease or insect control have a lien in the grain or crops; physician, nurse, physical therapist, occupational therapist, chiropractor, dentist, psychologist, licensed social worker, licensed professional counselor, hospital, or ambulatory surgical facility; a rancher, farmer, agister, herder, hotelkeeper, livery, stablekeeper, or reproductive technology business to whom any horses, mules, cattle, sheep, hogs, or other stock are entrusted; every person who, while lawfully in possession of an article of personal property, renders any service to the owner or lawful claimant of the article by labor or skill employed for the making, repairing, protection, improvement, safekeeping, carriage, towing, or storage of the article or tows or stores the article as directed under authority of law.

Property Covered—Timber and lumber liens are on the timber for which labor or assistance was furnished and upon all other timber which, at the time of filing the lien, belonged to the person for whom labor or assistance was provided; and upon lumber for which labor or assistance was furnished while it remains at the mill where manufactured, or in the possession or under the control of the manufacturer; seed lien on the crop produced from the seed furnished and upon the seed or grain threshed therefrom; threshermen's, swathers' and combiners' liens are on the grain or other crops swathed, threshed, or cut; agister's lien on the stock entrusted; personal property repaired, protected, improved, towed or stored.

How Claimed—Timber and lumber liens are claimed by filing for record a claim containing the demand and the amount thereof, after deducting as nearly as possible all just credits and offsets, with the name of the person by whom claimant was employed, a statement of the terms and conditions of the contract, if any, and if not, a description of what the work is reasonably worth. It must also contain a sufficient description of the property to be charged. A statutory form is provided.

Seed liens are claimed by filing a verified written statement stating the kind and quantity of seed and grain furnished, its value, or the amount advanced therefor, the name of the person to whom furnished, and a description of the land.

Threshermen's, swathers', and combiners' liens are claimed by filing a notice that within 20 days a lien will be claimed, and within those 20 days filing a just and true account of the amount due containing a description of the grain or crop, the agreed price for services, the name of the person for whom services were performed, a description of the land where the crop was raised, a description of the legal subdivision of land upon which grain is stored, and a description of the elevator. If the grain or crop is being hauled directly from the machine to the elevator or other purchaser, notice of claim must be served on the elevatorman as other purchaser.

A physician, nurse, physical therapist, occupational therapist, chiropractor, dentist, psychologist, licensed social worker, licensed professional counselor, hospital, or ambulatory surgical facility claiming a lien shall serve written notice upon the person and upon the insurer, if any, against whom liability for injury, disease, counseling service, or death is asserted, stating the nature of the services, for whom and when rendered, the value of the services, and that a lien is claimed. A physician, nurse, physical therapist, occupational therapist, chiropractor, dentist, psychologist, licensed social worker, licensed professional counselor, hospital, or ambulatory surgical facility claiming a lien upon proceeds or payments payable by an insurer shall serve written notice upon the insurer against whom the lien is asserted, stating the nature of the services, for whom and when rendered, the value of the services, and that a lien is claimed.

If there is an express or implied contract for keeping, feeding, herding, pasturing, or ranching stock, a rancher, farmer, agister, herder, hotelkeeper, livery, stablekeeper, or reproductive technology business to whom any horses, mules, cattle, sheep, hogs, or other stock are entrusted has a lien upon the stock for the amount due for keeping, feeding, herding, pasturing, or ranching the stock or for providing a service and may retain possession of the stock until the sum due is paid.

Every person who, while lawfully in possession of an article of personal property, renders any service to the owner or lawful claimant of the article by labor or skill employed for the making, repairing, protection, improvement, safekeeping, carriage, towing, or storage of the article or tows or stores the article as directed under authority of law has a special lien on it. The lien is dependent on possession and is for the compensation, if any, that is due to the person from the owner or lawful claimant for the service and for material, if any, furnished in connection with the service. If the service is towing or storage, the lien is for the reasonable cost of the towing or storage.

If payment for such work, labor, feed, or services or material furnished is not made within 30 days after the performance or furnishing of the same, the person entitled to a lien under the provisions of this part may enforce said lien in the following manner: (1) he shall deliver to the sheriff or a constable of the county in which the property is located an affidavit of the amount of his claim against said property, a description of the property, and the name of the owner thereof or of the person at whose request the work, labor, or services were performed or the materials furnished; (2) upon receipt of such affidavit, the sheriff or constable shall proceed to advertise and sell at public auction so much of the property covered by said lien as will satisfy same; (3) before the sheriff or constable sells the property at public auction, he shall give notice of the sale to the owner or person at whose request the work, labor, or services were performed or the materials furnished: (a) notice to the owner must be given at least 10 days before the sale; (b) the notice must state: (i) the time and place of the sale; (ii) the amount of the claim against the property; (iii) a description of the property; (iv) the name of the owner or person who contracted for the services or materials; and (v) the name of the person claiming the lien; (c) the notice may be given by personal service or by mailing by certified mail a copy of the notice to the last-known post office address of the owner or person who contracted for the services or materials; (d) if the sheriff or constable is not able to effect personal service or service by mail because the location and mailing address of the owner or person who contracted for the services or materials are unknown, the sheriff or constable may give notice by posting notice of the sale in three public places in the county in which the property is located.

Where Filed—Timber and lumber lien claims are filed with the county in which the timber was cut or lumber manufactured. Seed liens claims are filed in the office of the county clerk and recorder of the county in which the seed or grain is to be planted or used. Notice of intention to claim a thresherman's, swather's, or combiner's lien is filed with the county clerk of the county in which the grain or crops were grown. The account claiming such lien is filed with the county clerk and recorder of that county.

When to Be Filed—Timber and lumber liens and seed liens must be filed within 30 days after the close of work or rendition of services, or after the seed, grain, or funds are furnished. Seed liens must be filed within 90 days. Notice of intention to claim a thresherman's, swather's, or combiner's lien must be filed within 30 days after the last service was rendered or labor performed.

Extent of Lien—Timber and lumber liens are for services and work rendered within the period of three months preceding the filing of the claim. Seed liens are for the payment of the amount or value of the seed grain or funds furnished, but may not exceed the purchase price of 700 bushels of the crop. Threshermen's, swathers', and combiners' liens are an account of the services rendered, and is charged for at the prevailing price for the particular locality in which the grain or crop is threshed, harvested, or combined. A hospital lien is for the value of services rendered and products provided for the diagnosis and treatment of medical conditions

Duration of Lien—Timber and lumber liens continue for eight months after the claim is filed. Action to enforce threshermen's, swathers', and combiners' liens must be brought within six months after filing of the lien.

Priority—Timber and lumber liens are preferred and prior to any other liens, and no sale will divest such liens. As between timber and lumber liens, liens for work and labor are preferred, and liens on logs which can be identified are preferred over general claims. Seed liens have priority over all other liens and encumbrances on the crops. Threshermen's, swathers', and combiners' liens are prior to and take precedence over any mortgage, encumbrance or other lien, except the lien for the seed furnished to produce the crop.

Special Statute—Montana has a statute providing for filing of a statement with the Secretary of State for agricultural liens.

NEBRASKA

Who May Claim—Owner or operator of any threshing machine or combine used to combine or hull grain or seed, any corn picker or husker, or any corn sheller; any person who furnishes fuel, oil, grease, or other petroleum product to another to be used in farm machinery in the production of any agricultural crop; frozen-food locker plant owners; any person who makes, alters, repairs, or in any way enhances the value of any vehicle, automobile, machinery, farm implement, or tool or shoes a horse or mule at the request of or with the consent of the owner; jewelers, silversmiths, or watch and clock repairers; physician, nurse, or hospital; A person who shall perform work or labor, or exert care or diligence, or who shall advance money or material upon personal property under a contract, expressed or implied, and who holds such property; veterinarians; persons performing cleaning, pressing, glazing, washing, alterations, or repairs; any person who furnishes gasoline, diesel fuel, tractor fuel, oil, grease, or other petroleum products to another to be used in farm machinery for power or lubricating purposes in the production of any agricultural crop; A person, including a firm or corporation, who contracts or agrees with another (1) to furnish any fertilizer, soil conditioner, or agricultural chemical, (2) to furnish machinery and equipment for the application of such products, or (3) to perform work or labor in the application of such products; any person, including any public power district, cooperative, firm, or corporation, who contracts or agrees to furnish (1) seed to be sown or planted or (2) electrical power or energy, or both, used in the production of crops; every owner, lessee, agent or manager of any stallion, jack or bull.

Property Covered—Grain seed or corn threshed, combined, hulled, picked, husked, or shelled; all crops produced by such machinery and owned by the person to whom petroleum products were furnished; the contents of each locker or space in the frozen-food locker plant; such vehicle, automobile, machinery, farm implement, tool, horse, or mule while in such person's possession for the reasonable or agreed charges for the work done or material furnished and shall have the right to retain such property until such charges are paid; all articles left or given to jewelers, silversmiths, or watch and clock repairers, for repairs, parts or work thereon; animals serviced by veterinarian; any garment, clothing, wearing apparel, or household goods on which cleaning, pressing, glazing, or washing has been done, upon which alterations or repairs have been made, or on which materials or supplies have been used or furnished; fertilizer and chemical liens cover such crops produced and owned by the person to whom such fuel or lubricant was furnished; all crops produced from the seed furnished or produced with the electrical power or energy furnished to secure the payment of the purchase price of the seed or the cost of the electrical power or energy used; upon any mare and her colt or upon any cow and her calf served by such stallion, jack or bull.

How Claimed—Threshing and petroleum products liens may be claimed by filing notice of lien setting forth the name of the person for whom work was done or petroleum products supplied, the amount of grain covered or petroleum furnished, the location of the grain or the land on which crops were grown, the amount due or claimed, the name of the person for whom the threshing was done and when, or the name of the claimant of a petroleum products lien.

Whenever any person employs a physician, nurse, or hospital to perform professional service or services of any nature, in the treatment of or in connection with an injury, and such injured person claims damages from the party causing the injury, such physician, nurse, or hospital, as the case may be, shall have a lien upon any sum awarded the injured person in judgment or obtained by settlement or compromise on the amount due for the usual and customary charges of such physician, nurse, or hospital applicable at the times services are performed, except that no such lien shall be valid against anyone coming under the Nebraska Workers' Compensation Act.

Person who shall perform work or labor, or exert care or diligence, or who shall advance money or material upon personal property under a contract, expressed or implied, and who holds such property for a period of ninety days, may dispose of the property by sale or other manner. Such disposition shall not occur until 30 days after the mailing of a written notice of the intended disposition by certified mail, return receipt requested, to the last-known address of the owner of the personal property to be disposed of, and to any lien or security interest holder of record.

Every such owner, lessee, agent or manager of such stallion, jack or bull desiring to perfect a lien upon any mare and her colt, or upon any cow and her calf, shall at any time after breeding any such animal to any such male, file with the county clerk of the county a verified notice of lien describing such animal with reasonable certainty, giving the name of the owner and his place of residence if known, and the name and residence of the person having the possession of such animal, the location of such animal, the terms of payment for such service, the amount thereof, the name of the male, the date of service, and the time or event when the same shall become due and payable and such other matters as to make the same more certain.

Where Claimed—The office of the county clerk where the threshing was done, the crop produced.

When to Be Filed—Within 30 days after the threshing, combining, hulling, picking, husking, or shelling is done; within six months after the fuel or lubricant is furnished.

Duration—Threshing and petroleum products liens must be enforced within 30 days after filing.

Enforcement by Sale—Frozen-food locker plant liens may be enforced by sale of the contents of the locker at public or private sale for its reasonable value. Proceeds in excess of the amount of the lien are paid to the locker-space renter. Garments upon which cleaning, pressing, glazing, washing, alterations or repairs has been done and have remained within the servicers possession for 90 days may be sold.

Notice of Sale—Ten days' written notice by registered mail to the renter of the locker. The person, firm, partnership, limited liability company, or corporation to whom such charges are payable and owing shall first notify the owner or owners of the time and place of such sale.

NEVADA

Who May Claim—Any person engaged in the business of buying and selling automobiles or airplanes, keeping a garage, airport, or place for the storage, repair, or maintenance of motor vehicles, airplanes, and trailers; keeping a trailer park; and in connection therewith stores, repairs, or furnishes service or supplies to any motor vehicle, airplane, or trailer; any person furnishing feed, pasture or otherwise boarding any animal or animals, at the request or with the consent of the owner or his representative; hospitals rendering care to injured persons; those providing towing or storage of a vessel; every person, firm or corporation engaged in cleaning, pressing, glazing or washing garments, clothing, wearing apparel or household goods for a price; persons selling ore to custom mills or reduction works; foundrymen and boilermakers on the mill, manufacturing or hoisting equipment for unpaid labor or materials; jewelers, watchmakers, carriers, and warehousemen.

Property Covered—Motor vehicles, aircraft, and trailers, and parts thereof; bullion product of mill or reduction works; labor, materials, services, freight and storage charges; the garments, clothing, wearing apparel or household goods upon which work was performed.

Extent of Lien—Lien on motor vehicles, aircraft, and trailers are for the sum due and all costs incurred in enforcing such lien. The lien of trailer park keeper may not exceed $300 or the amount due and unpaid for four months for rental and utilities, whichever is less. The lien is subordinate when the vehicle or aircraft is the subject of a secured transaction. A towing company has a lien on the vehicle for towing and storage charges for a period not exceeding 90 days. Any person furnishing feed, pasture or otherwise boarding any animal or animals, at the request or with the consent of the owner or his representative, has a lien upon the animal or animals, and may retain possession thereof until the sum due for the feed, pasture or board has been paid. Such a lien is subordinate only to such other liens of third persons as have been placed on record, as required by law, in the county where the feed, pasture or board was or is being furnished.

Whenever any person receives hospitalization on account of any injury, and he, or his personal representative after his death, claims damages from the person responsible for causing the injury, the hospital has a lien upon any sum awarded the injured person or his personal representative by judgment or obtained by a settlement or compromise to the extent of the amount due the hospital for the reasonable value of the hospitalization rendered before the date of judgment, settlement or compromise.

Vessel in this state is subject to a lien for wages due to persons employed, for work done or services rendered on board the vessel.

A person engaged in the business of buying or selling or keeping a shop or place for the storage, maintenance, keeping or repair of vessels or rental of spaces for vessels and who in connection therewith stores, maintains, keeps or repairs a vessel or furnishes accessories, facilities, services or supplies therefor, at the request or with the consent of the owner or his representative, or at the direction of any peace officer or other authorized person who orders the towing or storage of a vessel through any action permitted by law, has a lien upon the vessel or any part or parts thereof for the sum due for towing, storing, maintaining, keeping or repairing the vessel or for labor furnished thereon, or for furnishing accessories, facilities, services or supplies therefor, and for all costs incurred in enforcing the lien.

Launderer's liens include the amount of any account that may be due for the work done thereon, where such account is not paid for 90 days or more after completion of such work. The lien shall also include the value or agreed price, if any, of all materials furnished by the lienholder in connection with the work.

Enforcement by Sale—A motor vehicle, airplane, or trailer lien may be enforced by sale at auction of the property subject to the lien. The sale must be held where the lien was acquired, or if unsuitable, at the nearest suitable place. Jewelers and watchmakers: after one year if the account is unpaid, the lien claimant may sell the property.

Proceeds of the sale go first to the satisfaction of the lien, including the reasonable charges of notice, advertisement, and sale; and the balance goes to the person to whom the lien would have delivered the vehicle, airplane, or trailer.

Notice of Sale—Written notice of sale must be given to the person on whose account service was rendered, to any other person known to have an interest in the property to be sold, and where applicable, to the motor vehicle registration division of the Department of Motor Vehicles.

In case of enforcement of a lien for storage charges, the notice must include a statement of the claim, a description of the goods, a demand for full payment and a statement that the goods will be advertised for sale and sold at public auction unless payment is made in full before the time and date of the sale specified in the notice.

Notice must be given by delivery in person or by registered or certified letter addressed to the last-known place of business or abode of the person to be notified, and if no address is known, then addressed to that person at the place where the lien claimant has his place of business.

For jewelers and watchmakers notice and posting of sale is required, the owner has a right of redemption.

Before foreclosing the lien by sale, the person furnishing the feed, pasture or board shall mail a registered or certified letter to the owner, or purported owner, of the animal or animals, at the owner's, or purported owner's, last known address. The letter must demand payment of all money due for the feed, pasture or board, and must inform the owner that if payment is not made the lien will be foreclosed by sale. If payment is not made within 30 days from the date of mailing the registered or certified letter, the lien may be foreclosed by sale.

NEW HAMPSHIRE

Who May Claim—Persons who perform labor or furnish material or fuel to the amount of $15 or more for the making of brick under contract with the owner thereof or a contractor; persons furnishing labor or supplies to the amount of $15 or more for rafting, driving, cutting, hauling, sawing, or drawing wood, bark, lumber, or logs, or hauling supplies for such labor, under contract with the owner of the wood or a contractor; persons who maintain a public garage, public or private airport or hangar, or trailer court, for the parking, storage, or care of motor vehicles, aircraft, or house trailers, by or with consent of the owners; persons making advances of money to the owner or lawful possessor of logs, lumber, or pulpwood to finance cutting, hauling, yarding, piling, trucking, rafting, booming, driving, or towing; any person furnishing storage, labor, hauling, or transportation for any vessel, boat, or vessel or boat motor; perform labor or furnish materials to the amount of $15 or more for erecting or repairing a house or other building or appurtenances, or for building any dam, canal, sluiceway, well or bridge, or for consumption or use in the prosecution of such work, other than for a municipality; Any person keeping a boarder or lodger, not a mariner or seaman; a person to whom horses, cattle, sheep or other domestic animals shall be entrusted to be pastured or boarded; any person or carrier who transports animals; every individual, partnership, firm, association, corporation, institution or any governmental unit or combination or parts thereof maintaining and operating a hospital licensed in the state of New Hampshire which shall furnish medical or other service to any patient injured by reason of an accident not covered by the workers' compensation act or any home health care provider licensed under RSA 151 who furnishes medical or other services to any patient injured by reason of an accident not covered by the workers' compensation act; every person who maintains an establishment for cleaning, pressing, glazing, laundering, or dyeing, who shall place in storage, or do any work on, any article of personal property at the request of the owner or legal possessor of such property; every jeweler, watchmaker or silversmith; any person who maintains an establishment for repair on radio or television equipment; except to the extent otherwise provided by law, every person who shall repair, at the request of the owner, any article of personal property, the fair market value of which is not greater than $1,000; owners of self storage facilities; whoever, under contract with any person, sells or furnishes a monument, tablet, headstone, vault, post, curbing or other monumental work to be placed in a cemetery or at a grave.

Property Covered—Brick, the materials and fuel supplies to make same, and the kiln containing the brick; wood, bark, lumber, or logs transported or cut; motor vehicles, aircraft, or house trailers in the lienor's possession; logs, lumber, or pulpwood for which an advance was made and upon which lienor has caused his registered mark to be placed; boats, vessels, and boat and vessel motors stored, worked on, hauled, or transported; the baggage and effects of such boarder or lodger brought to the boarding or lodging house; equipment repaired; garments laundered, altered, or repaired; monument or grave furnished.

How Claimed—Brick and lumber subcontractors must give written notice to the owner, or a person in charge of the property, that they will claim the lien before furnishing the labor and material.

Extent of Lien—Brick and lumber liens are for labor and materials. Motor vehicle, aircraft, and trailer liens are for proper charges due. Lumber advance liens are for the advance and for all advances for two years after the date of making the advance. Boardinghouse liens are for all proper charges for boarders' fare and board or room rent. A person to whom horses, cattle, sheep or other domestic animals shall be entrusted to be pastured or boarded shall have a lien thereon for all proper charges due for such pasturing or board until the same shall be paid or tendered. Any person or carrier who transports animals shall have a lien upon such animals for food, care, and custody furnished, and shall not be liable for their detention. Every individual, partnership, firm, association, corporation, institution or any governmental unit or combination or parts thereof maintaining and operating a hospital licensed in the state of New Hampshire which shall furnish medical or other service to any patient injured by reason of an accident not covered by the workers' compensation act or any home health care provider licensed under RSA 151 who furnishes medical or other services to any patient injured by reason of an accident not covered by the workers' compensation act shall, if such injured patient shall assert or maintain a claim against another for damages on account of such injuries, have a lien upon that part going or belonging to such patient, or to the person responsible for the payment of such patient's bills, of any recovery or sum had or collected or to be collected by such patient or by the person responsible for the payment of such patient's bills, or by his heirs or personal representatives in the case of his death, whether by judgment or by settlement or compromise, to the amount of the reasonable and necessary charges of such hospital or home health care provider for the treatment, care and maintenance of such patient by the hospital or by the home health care provider up to the date of payment of such damages. Every person who maintains an establishment for cleaning, pressing, glazing, laundering, or dyeing, who shall place in storage, or do any work on, any article of personal property at the request of the owner or legal possessor of such property shall have a lien for such service, and may retain possession of such article until the charges for such work or storage have been paid.

Every jeweler, watchmaker or silversmith who shall alter, including manufacturing another article from, repair, or do any work on any article of personal property at the request of the owner or legal possessor of such property shall have a lien upon and may retain the possession of any such article until the charges for such alteration, repairing or other work have been paid.

Any person who maintains an establishment for repair on radio or television equipment, who shall at his establishment or repair shop alter, repair or do any work on any such equipment at the request of the owner or legal possessor of such property shall have a lien upon and may retain the possession of any such article until the charges for such alteration, repairing or other work have been paid.

Except to the extent otherwise provided by law, every person who shall repair, at the request of the owner, any article of personal property, the fair market value of which is not greater than $1,000, shall have a lien upon the property and may retain the possession of the article of property until the charges for such repair have been paid. Further, persons who repair articles of personal property shall provide notice that the owner of such personal property must disclose any prior lienholders having a security interest in such personal property at the time repairs are requested. The foregoing notice requirement may be satisfied either by sign or by express written notification at the time that a repair order is made.

Any owner of a self-service storage facility shall have a lien upon all personal property located at the self-service storage facility so long as the personal property shall remain in the possession of the owner, or, in accordance with any rental agreement or lease, shall have a lien for unpaid rent, charges, fees, or expenses due for storage, care, or sale of the personal property.

Whoever, under contract with any person, sells or furnishes a monument, tablet, headstone, vault, post, curbing or other monumental work to be placed in a cemetery or at a grave shall have a lien thereon to secure the payment for the same.

Duration of Lien—Brick and lumber liens exist for 120 days after services are performed or supplies furnished. Boat and vessel liens exist during lienor's possession, and once possession is relinquished, two years from the time the indebtedness became due and payable.

Enforcement by Sale—Persons having liens on personal property, where no time limit is limited for the payment of the debt or redemption of the property, may sell the property at auction. Before the sale the lienor must send a written inquiry to the Secretary of State and town clerk to ascertain if there is another lien on the property. If there is not, or if there is no response for 14 days, the lienor may proceed with the sale. If there is a lien, notice to that lienor must be provided.

From the proceeds the lienor may reimburse himself for his debt and the expenses incident to the sale. The balance, if any, must be paid to the owner on demand. When time is limited for payment or redemption of property, the property may be sold at any time after the expiration of the limited time. In the case of liens on motor vehicles, aircraft, boats, vessels, boat and vessel motors, and trailer, for care and storage, sale may be held after charges remain unpaid for 60 days.

If a launder's lien remains undischarged for a period of 60 days after work has been completed or after expiration of agreed terms of storage, if any, or in the absence of such agreement, after the expiration of 90 days from date of storage, the lienholder may give such article to a duly organized charitable corporation or sell such article at public or private sale.

Notice of Sale—Notice must be provided at least 14 days prior to the sale, by posting such notice in two or more public places in the town in which the property is located by serving such notice upon the owner, if a county resident, and, if the value of the property exceeds $100 by publishing the notice. The lienholder must also provide 14-day notice to other lienholders of record by certified mail return receipt requested. Any such lienholder of record shall be entitled to redeem the property prior to the sale by payment of the amount demanded by the claimant. In the case of boat and vessel liens, notice must be served on any holder of a security interest in such property stating time and place of sale, property to be sold, and amount of lien.

Enforcement by Attachment—Brick and lumber liens, and liens for lumber advances made, may be enforced by attachment.

Priority—Brick and lumber liens take precedence over all other claims except tax liens.

Liens for lumber advances take precedence over all claims except taxes, the lumber lien discussed above, and prior liens.

Boat and vessel liens are subordinate to all prior and subsequent perfected security interests and to the rights of subsequent purchasers for value without actual notice of such lien.

NEW JERSEY

Who May Claim—Persons operating hangers for the storage, maintenance, keeping, or repair of aircraft and who perform such services or supply materials for such aircraft; garage keepers who store, maintain, keep, repair, or furnish gasoline, accessories, or other supplies to motor vehicles; a processor who spins, manufactures, bleaches, dyes, finishes, dresses, or otherwise treats or processes linen, cotton, wool, real and artificial silk, yarn or goods, skins, pelts, furs, or hides, or products of which they form a part; film processors who furnish any work, supplies, or materials in connection with any motion picture film, or lend money in connection with such film or the production or distribution thereof; self-service storage facility owner who stores personal property; hospitals rendering, by way of treatment, care or maintenance after, to any person who shall have sustained personal injuries in an accident as a result of the negligence or alleged negligence of any other person; proprietor of any hotel, apartment hotel, inn or boarding house; every keeper of a livery stable; repairers of vessels; person furnishing or placing a monument in a cemetery; jewelers, watchmakers.

Property Covered—Aircraft or any part thereof; motor vehicle or any part thereof; any property of others coming into the hands of a cloth or fur processor; all motion picture films belonging to the owner of the film for which services or advance were furnished, and to all parties authorized with respect to such film; and the negatives and prints in the possession of the processor; any sum recovered by injured person treated at hospital; baggage, and other property belonging to any guest, or brought upon the premises by any guest, tenant, boarder or lodger; animals left to be cared for at livery stable; vessels; jewelry repaired.

Detention and Demand of Property—Owner or person entitled to possession of any aircraft or motor vehicle, upon learning of the detention of same by the lienor, may demand a statement of the amount due and owing. If such owner considers the amount excessive, he may offer what he considers reasonable and demand possession. If possession is refused, he may obtain possession by depositing the amount claimed with the clerk of any court of competent jurisdiction in the county where the aircraft or motor vehicle is situated, together with the fee to cover costs at Superior Court, low division, special civil part, or $60 in any other court. Lienor must then assert his claim in court, and if he fails to do so, may be liable for damages to the owner of the aircraft or motor vehicle.

Lienor of aircraft must file within 90 days after work performed or materials furnished. Statement must include the name of the person entitled to the lien, the owner of the aircraft, description of the aircraft, the amount for which a lien is claimed and date of work, etc.

The proprietor of any hotel, apartment hotel, inn or boarding house shall have a lien on all baggage, and other property belonging to any guest, or brought upon the premises by any guest, tenant, boarder or lodger, for the amount of his bill due to the proprietor thereof for the hire or rent of rooms, board, lodging, cash advanced or other accommodations furnished in said hotel, apartment hotel, inn or boarding house, and shall have the right, without process of law, to retain the same until the said amount of indebtedness is discharged.

Every keeper of a livery stable or boarding and exchange stable, shall have a lien on all animals left with him in livery, for board, sale or exchange and upon all carriages, wagons, sleighs and harness left with him for storage, sale or exchange for the amount due such proprietor for the board and keep of such animal and also for such storage, and shall have the right, without process of law, to retain the same until the amount of such indebtedness is discharged.

A debt contracted by an owner of a vessel within this State, shall be a continuing lien upon the vessel and her apparel until paid, for (1) labor performed or materials or articles furnished in this State for the building, repairing, fitting, furnishing or equipping the vessel in this State at the time when the same was performed or were furnished; (2) supplies, provisions and stores furnished within this State for the use of the vessel; or (3) towing, wharfage and drydockage of the vessel and the expenses of keeping the same in storage in port in water or on land, including expenses incurred in taking care of and employing persons to watch the vessel.

Enforcement by Sale—If no proceedings are taken for the repossession of aircraft detained, lienor may sell such aircraft at public auction after the expiration of 30 days from the date of detention. A cloth or fur processor's lien may be enforced by sale of the property at public auction after amount due has remained due and unpaid, in whole or in part, for two months. A film processor's lien may be enforced by sale of the film at public auction, at any time after the date on which the indebtedness became due and payable. Storage owner's lien may be satisfied by sale if amount due remains unpaid after demand. Property retained by the hotel, apartment hotel, inn or boarding house proprietor under this article may be sold at public auction.

If any money due for work done or materials furnished upon any watch, clock or jewelry shall remain unpaid for one year after the completion of said work or the furnishing of said materials, the lien claimant, having first given 30 days notice in writing to the owner specifying the amount due and informing him that payment of such amount within 30 days will entitle such owner to the return of the property in the custody of the lien claimant and that in default thereof the said property will be sold, may, if payment is not made within said period of 30 days, sell such watch, clock or jewelry at public sale to satisfy the amount due.

Notice of Sale—Notice of sale of aircraft or motor vehicle must be published for at least two weeks at least once each week, in a newspaper circulating in the municipality in which the aircraft or garage is located. Not less than five days' notice must be given by posting the notice in five public places in the municipality.

Notice of a cloth or fur processor's lien must comply with the above, and in addition a copy must be mailed to the owner, if known, at least five days before the sale, at his last-known post office address. Posted notice must be within 15 days before the sale.

Notice of a film processor's lien must comply with the requirements for aircraft and motor vehicle liens, and in addition 10 days' written notice must be provided to the owner or authorized party either by personal service or registered mail using the last-known address of such owner or authorized party.

Notice of self storage owner's lien must be published once a week for two consecutive weeks where the facility is located. Sale must be no sooner than 15 days after final publication.

Hotelkeepers and boardinghouse keepers must publish notice for three days in a newspaper circulating in the municipality wherein said hotel, apartment hotel, inn or boarding house is kept.

Priority—Aircraft liens are superior to all other liens, except tax liens. Garage keepers' liens are not superior to, nor affect, a lien, title, or interest held by virtue of a prior conditional sale or prior chattel mortgage properly recorded. Cloth and fur processors' liens are paramount to the title lien interest or encumbrance of the owner where the owner or representative consented or authorized the acquiring of possession by the lienor.

NEW MEXICO

Who May Claim—The following creditors have statutory liens on personal property: (a) liquor wholesalers; (b) innkeepers, livery stable keepers, agisters; (c) artisans and repairmen; (d) motor vehicle mechanics and parts salesmen; (e) blacksmiths (farriers); (f) common carriers; (g) hotels, motels, trailer courts, campgrounds; (h) motor vehicle garage owners, towers and wreckers; (i) launderers and dry cleaners; (j) aircraft repairers and servicers; (k) threshers; (l) agricultural harvesters; (m) agricultural producers; (n) credit unions; (o) warehousemen; (p) issuers of certified securities; (q) self storage facility owners; (r) lessors and agistors.

Property Covered—The personal property to which the liens of the foregoing creditors attaches is, respectively: liquor license of debtor; property and animals of persons for whom services and materials supplied; property produced or repaired; automobiles repaired or for which parts provided; animals shod; property transported and their bills of lading; property on premises of lienholder; vehicles stored, towed or on which wrecker service performed; items laundered or dry cleaned; aircraft repaired or services; grain threshed; agricultural products harvested; agricultural products delivered to processor; credit union shares, share accounts and deposits; stored goods or proceeds of the goods; certified securities; and self-stored property.

How Claimed—The foregoing liens which must be claimed are claimed as follows, respectively: (a), (g), and (h) lien is automatic on incurring debt; (b) and (i) posting on premises of lienholder; (c), (d), (e), (f), (o), and (q) possession; (j) possession and filing; (k) and (l) filing; (m) delivery of agricultural products to processor; (n) refusal to allow withdrawal; (p) legend on security document.

Where Filed—The foregoing liens which must be filed to be perfected must be filed in the following places, respectively: (j) county where aircraft based; (k) and (l) county where grain or other agricultural product grown.

When to Be Filed—The foregoing liens which must be filed, must be filed, respectively: (j) 90 days after labor, supplies, or services provided; (k) 10 days after threshing completed; (l) 21 days after harvest completed.

Loss of Lien—The foregoing liens which are susceptible to being lost, other than by the statute of limitations, can be lost, respectively: (b), (c), (d), (e), and (f) by voluntarily giving up possession of the liened property, except as to property delivered to the persons to whom labor, materials, or services were provided; (g), (h), (i), and (q) by voluntarily, and not induced by fraud, giving up possession of the liened property.

Enforcement—All liens may be enforced in the same manner as for foreclosure of security interest. When the property is in the possession or under the control of the lienor, he may, upon proper notice and demand, sell the property at public auction to the highest bidder for cash. Proceeds are to be applied to the cost of the sale and the satisfaction of the lien; and the residue, if any, is paid to the debtor. Reasonable attorneys' fees may be awarded to the lienor when litigation for foreclosure is employed.

Notice of Sale—Lienor may serve the lien debtor by delivery, or by certified or registered mail, return receipt requested, a written statement setting forth the indebtedness and the intent to sell the liened property if the debt is not paid. If the lien remains unpaid for 10 days thereafter, the lienor may advertise the sale and complete it 20 days thereafter. Where the liened property is a motor vehicle, it must be held another 14 days and if it is registered in a foreign jurisdiction or if the registration cannot be found in the New Mexico Department of Motor Vehicles, it must be held an additional 40 days after the 10 days' notice before sale.

Priority—Liens have priority as follows: (a) and (j) over all liens except those for taxes; (b), (e), (f), (g), (i), (l), and (m) over all, while in possession, and the liens for repairs and parts to automobiles continues for 30 days after delivery of possession induced by fraud; (k), (n), (o), (p), and (q) over all other liens.

NEW YORK

Who May Claim—Persons keeping a garage, hangar, a place for the storage, maintenance, keeping, or repair of motor vehicles, motor boats, or aircraft, and who in connection therewith performs such services or furnished gasoline or supplies, at the request or within the consent of the owner; persons who manufacture, spin, or throw silk into yarn or other goods; persons engaged in carting or trucking property; person operating motion picture film laboratories or in the business of developing, titling, storing, assembling, or reproducing such film. A person employed by a quarry, mine, yard, or dock may have a lien on the stone for the amount due or a person who labors on stone monuments, gravestones or cemetery structures may have a lien on the same for the amount due. Other artisans may have a lien on property for their work. A lien may be granted to persons who house or keep animals and to persons who provide stallion or bull stud services. Any person who shall perform any labor for a railroad corporation shall have a lien for the value of such labor.

In addition to other personal property liens, the owner of a self storage facility shall have a lien on all personal property stored within each leased space located at the self storage facility for rent, labor, or other charges, present or future, and for expenses reasonably incurred in enforcing the lien.

Property Covered—Generally speaking, the property covered is that which is the subject of the work preformed, the materials furnished, or both. For example, the claimants described above may claim a lien against motor vehicles, motorboats, or aircraft; goods and property of others in the possession of silk good manufacturers and throwsters; property carted or trucked by a truckman or drayman; positive prints printed in or in any way prepared, including distribution and exhibition rights, and other mortgagee or conditional vendee; railroad track, rolling stock, appurtenances, and land on which such property is situated.

NOTE: Liens for labor for railroad companies are claimed by filing a notice of such lien with the clerk of any county where such property is located. Specific mechanics' liens also require county filing and notice to the owner to have full force and effect.

Extent of Lien—Liens are generally for the amount due and owing.

Enforcement by Sale—Liens against personal property may, upon proper notice, be enforced by the sale of the property at a public auction to the highest bidder (*Sharrock v. Dell Buick-Cadillac, Inc.*, 45 N.Y. 2d 155, 408 N.Y.S.2d 39, 379 N.E.2d 1169 (1978), the New York Court of Appeals declared unconstitutional a provision of the lien law which permitted a garageman to conduct an ex parte of a bailed vehicle). The sale is held in the town where the lien was acquired. Proceeds of such sale are first used to satisfy the lien and expenses of advertisement and sale; the balance to be held by the lienor subject to the demands of the owner; and notice of such balance must be served on such owner. If balance is not claimed by the owner within 30 days from the day of the sale, it is deposited with the treasurer, financial administrator, or supervisor of the village, city, or town in which the sale was held.

Notice of Sale—The lienor must serve notice to the owner, and if not found in the county where the lien arose, then to the person for whose account the lien is held. If neither can be found in the county, or if the property is of a value under $100, notice may be served by mail to the owner's last-known residence or address, or if not known, to the last known residence or address of the person for whose account the lien is held. Similar notice is required for persons who have notified the lienor of an interest in the property. Such notice must state the nature of the debt, an itemized statement of claim, the time due, a description of the property and its estimated value, and the amount of the lien, and must require payment by a date not less than 10 days after service of notice, stating the time and place of the sale. After such time, notice of sale of property valued at $100 or more must be published once a week for two consecutive weeks in a newspaper published in the town or city where the sale is to be held. The sale may not be less than 15 days from the first publication. If there is no such newspaper, notice must be posted at least 10 days before the sale in at least six conspicuous places. Property of a value under $100 may be sold at bona fide private sale upon 20 days' posted notice.

NORTH CAROLINA

Who May Claim—Any person who tows, alters, repairs, stores, services, treats, or improves personal property, other than a motor vehicle, in the course of business under contract with the owner or legal possessor; any person who repairs, services, tows, or stores motor vehicles in the ordinary course of business under contract with the owner or legal possessor; any person who improves any textile goods in the ordinary course of business under contract with the owner or legal possessor; owner of a self storage facility.

Property Covered—The property towed, altered, repaired, stored, serviced, treated, or improved; the motor vehicle repaired, serviced, towed or stored; all textile goods of the owner in the claimant's possession for improvement; all personal property stored at a self storage facility.

Extent of Lien—Liens on personal property other than motor vehicles are for the lesser of the reasonable charges for services and materials, or contract price, or $100 if the lienor has dealt with a legal possessor not an owner. Motor vehicle liens are for reasonable charges. Textile liens are for the contract charges for improvement and any amount owed for improvement of goods relinquished. The owner of a self-service storage facility has a lien upon all personal property stored at the facility for rent, expenses necessary for the preservation of the personal property, and expenses reasonably incurred in the sale or other disposition of the personal property.

Duration of Lien—Liens arise when lienor acquires possession and become unenforceable when the lienor voluntarily relinquishes possession. Reacquisition of the property voluntarily relinquished does not reinstate the lien. Action to enforce lien for storage charge must be taken within 180 days following the commencement of storage; a lien for storage pursuant to an express contract may be enforced within 120 days of default.

Enforcement by Sale—If the charges remain unpaid for 30 days after maturity of the obligation, the lien may be enforced by public or private sale. If an owner, secured party, or other person claiming an interest in the property notifies the lienor, before the date of the private sale, that public sale is requested, enforcement must be by public sale. Proceeds of the sale are applied to payment of the expenses of the sale, satisfaction of the lien, and the surplus, if any, to the person entitled thereto.

If the rent and other charges for which a self storage facility lien is claimed under this Article remain unpaid or unsatisfied for 15 days following the maturity of the obligation to pay rent, the owner may enforce the lien by a public sale or other disposition of the property

Notice of Sale—At least 20 days prior to the date of the sale, notice of private or public sale must be made to the person holding legal title to the property if ascertainable, and to the person with whom the lienor dealt, if different, and to each secured party or person claiming interest in the property who is actually known to the lienor, by registered or certified mail. Notice must include the name and address of the lienor; the name of the title holder, and if not ascertainable, the person with whom the lienor dealt, a description of the property, the amount due, the place and time of sale, and a statement that recipient has 10 days to request a hearing. If the property is a motor vehicle that is required to be registered, notice must also be sent to the Commissioner of Motor Vehicles.

In addition, public sale must be advertised by posting a copy of the notice of sale at the courthouse door in the county in which the sale is to be held, and by publishing the notice of sale once per week for two consecutive weeks in a newspaper in general circulation in the same county.

In addition, the lienor may bring an action on the debt at any time following the maturity of the obligation, but failure to bring the action within 180 days from the beginning of the storage period constitutes a waiver of the right to collect storage charges which accrue after that period. A lien for storage pursuant to an express contract must be enforced within 120 days of default.

Priority—Liens have priority over perfected and unperfected security interests.

NORTH DAKOTA

Who May Claim—Agricultural processors including the owner or lessee of a threshing machine or combine; agricultural suppliers including persons furnishing or applying fertilizer, farm chemicals, or seed to another to be spread, sown, or planted; persons furnishing sugar beet seed for planting, or supplying insecticide or fertilizer, labor, materials, cash advances, or services necessary to the production, harvesting, or hauling of sugar beet crops; garage keeper or keeper of a place for the storage of motor vehicle who so stores or keeps motor vehicles at the request or with the consent of the owner or lawful possessor; any person to whom any animal is entrusted by the owner thereof for the purpose of feeding, herding, pasturing, or ranching; owners of self storage facilities; hospitals servicing injured persons whom have been harmed by another's neglect or fault; owner of a self storage facility .

Property Covered—Grain threshed or dried; crops produced from the fertilizer, chemicals, or seed furnished; sugar crop produced; motor vehicles stored or kept; animals entrusted; any claim awarded to injured persons; personal property stored at a self storage facility.

How Claimed—By filing a written verified statement of lien, a verified copy of the contract.

Filing a statement of a garage keeper's lien is necessary only where possession is relinquished. On a repairman's lien, or a lien by a farm equipment dealer, garage keeper, or aviation operator, if the cost of repair would exceed $1,000 or 25 percent of the value of the property in its repaired condition, whichever is greater, and the repairman, etc., intends to have the entire bill constitute a lien, the repairman, etc., shall give notice by registered mail to the owner of the estimated cost of repair, and the estimated value of the property in its repaired condition. If notice is not provided the lien is not valid in any amount in excess of $1,000 or 25 percent, whichever is greater.

A person claiming an agister's lien must serve notice within 10 days upon the holders of prior liens that the property has been entrusted, specifies which purpose, and the name of the person entrusting the property therefor. If the residence of the holder of the lien is unknown, or if the holder is not a resident of this state, the notice may be served by publication thereof in one issue of a newspaper published in the county in which the property is being kept.

Where Filed—Statements of the threshers' liens, fertilizer, chemical and seed liens, and garage owners' liens, and sugar beet contracts are filed in the Office of the Register of Deeds of the county in which the grain is threshed, the seed sown, the crops raised, or in which the motor vehicle owner resides or, if he is not a resident of the state, where the motor vehicle is stored.

When to Be Filed—A thresher's lien statement must be filed within 90 days after the processing is complete. Fertilizer, farm chemical and seed lien statements (including sugar beets) must be filed within 120 days after the supplies are furnished or the service is performed. Sugar beet contracts must be filed within 60 days after contract is entered into.

Extent of Lien—A thresher's lien is for the value of his services. A fertilizer, chemical, or seed lien is for the purchase price. A sugar beet lien is for the full amount due under the contract. A garage keeper's lien is for the reasonable charges for storage. An agister's lien is for the amount that may be due for feeding, herding, pasturing, or ranching. Any charitable association, corporation, or other institution maintaining a hospital in this state is entitled to a lien for the reasonable value of hospitalization services rendered to a person injured in any accident.

Priority—An agricultural processors', including threshers', lien has priority as to the crops and agricultural products covered thereby over all other liens. All agricultural suppliers' liens (including fertilizer and sugar beet liens) have priority over all liens except agricultural processors' liens. A sugar beet lien has priority over all other liens and encumbrances except crop production liens in favor of the federal or county government. A garage keeper's lien is subject and inferior only to mortgages and conditional sales contracts properly filed on or before the time when the property covered came into the possession of the lienor. An agister's lien has priority over all other liens on the property for 10 days after the receipt thereof, and thereafter has priority over all other liens on the property if the person to whom the property is entrusted serves notice. A self storage facility lien is superior to other security interests except those perfected before the date the lien attaches.

OHIO

Who May Claim—An artisan or repairman who furnishes material or performs labor for the building or repair of chattel property; a bailee for hire who performs services or provides materials with respect to any personal property; any person who boards an animal under contract with the owner; the owner of a self storage unit against the occupant on stored personal property.

Property Covered—Property improved, serviced, kept, stored, or otherwise fed or boarded.

How Claimed—A bailee's lien may be claimed by sending a certified written notice to the owner or legal possessor of the personal property; a lien upon animals is claimed by written demand to the owner or legal possessor; a repairman's lien arises by operation of law upon furnishing materials or performing labor for the building or repair of chattel property; a lien upon property contained in a self storage unit is claimed by certified notice to any party whom the owner of the unit has knowledge has an interest in the personal property.

Enforcement by Sale—A lien upon animals may be enforced by public sale upon 10 days' notice; a bailee may be enforced by sale upon posting in a conspicuous place that items left for more than 30 days after service has been provided may be sold in compliance with the law; a lien upon self-stored property may be enforced by public or private sale upon 10 days' notice.

Notice of Sale—Notice of sale must include the name of the owner and any other parties known to have an interest in the property, a description of the property, a description of the nature and reasonable value of the services provided, a demand for payment within a specified time period and the address and time where such public sale will occur or after what date such private sale will occur.

Priority—When a person in the ordinary course of business furnishes services or materials with respect to goods subject to a security interest, a lien upon goods in the possession of such person given by statute or rule of law for such materials or services takes priority over a perfected security interest unless the lien is statutory and the statute provides otherwise

OKLAHOMA

Who May Claim—*Possession.* Persons who, while in lawful possession of personal property, render service to the owner by furnishing material, labor or skill for the protection, improvement, safekeeping, towing, storage, or carriage thereof.

Nonpossession. Laborers, including blacksmiths, wheelwrights and horseshoers, without possession as long as title to property remains in the original owner.

Threshers. Persons who thresh or combine grain or seed for another.

Manufactured Home. Owner of real property upon which a manufactured home (owned by another) is located.

Owner of self storage facility.

Property Covered—Property protected, improved, kept, towed, stored, or carried; property that is production of labor; grain or seed threshed or combined; manufactured homes; property stored in self storage facility.

How Claimed—By possession. For nonpossession, persons must file statement of lien in county clerk's office within 60 days of last providing labor.

A thresher's lien may be claimed by filing verified written statement showing the amount, quantity, and kind of grain, the price agreed to for threshing or combining, the name of the person for whom work was done, and a description of the land. A verified account must be filed with the clerk of the district court of the county in which the debtor resides within 30 days of the completion of work.

Enforcement by Sale—*Possession.* Liens of persons rendering service to personal property in their possession may be enforced by sale of the property upon proper notice.

Nonpossession. Laborers without possession must enforce liens within eight months of work being completed.

Threshers. Enforce lien same as any secured party.

Manufactured Home. Possessors of manufactured homes enforce their liens the same as ordinary liens.

Notice of Sale—Notice of sale must include the name of the owner and other parties claiming interest in the property, a description of the property, nature of the services rendered, the time and place of the sale, and the name of the lienor. This notice must be posted in three public places in the county where the property is to be sold at least 10 days prior to the time of sale, and a copy must be mailed to the owner and other interested parties.

Priority—Possession. Liens of persons rendering services to personal property in their possession have priority over all others except innocent intervening purchasers without notice.

Nonpossession. Laborers without possession have priority over all others except innocent intervening purchasers without notice.

Threshers. A thresher's lien is subject to prior mortgage liens, unless the holder receives notice of the intention of threshing or combining the grain or seed and consented in writing, after which the mortgagee becomes jointly liable with the owner for the expenses of threshing or combining.

Manufactured Home. Liens of possessors of manufactured homes are subordinate to a creditor with a perfected security interest.

OREGON

Who May Claim—Persons performing labor upon or assisting in obtaining, securing, handling, or transporting sawlogs, spars, piles, cordwood, or other timber, or in manufacturing timber into lumber or other wood products; common carriers or persons who, at the owner's request, transport personal property from one place to another, and persons who store grain, merchandise, or personal property at the request of the owner or lawful possessor; hospitals providing care to those injured by neglect or doing of another; grain producers.

Property Covered—Timber lien is on the timber lumber or other wood product for which labor or assistance is furnished; any sum recovered by injured person in claim for injuries; any property stored in self storage facility; inventory of the purchaser of grain and proceeds received by the purchaser from the selling of the inventory; transportation and storage lien is on the property transported or stored.

How Claimed—A timber lien is claimed by filing a verified claim in substantially the following form:

_____, Claimant, v. _____, Defendant.

Notice is hereby given that _____ claims a lien upon (describing property), being about _____ more or less, which were (cut or manufactured) in _____ County, State of Oregon, are marked thus _____, are now lying in _____, for labor performed upon and assistance rendered in (cutting or manufacturing logs or lumber). That the name of the owner, or reputed owner, is _____; that _____ employed said _____ to perform such labor and render such assistance upon the following terms and conditions (state contract, if any, or reasonable value); that the contract has been faithfully performed and fully complied with on the part of _____, who performed labor upon and assisted in (cutting or manufacturing) for the period of _____; that said labor and assistance were so performed and rendered upon the property between the ____ day of _____, and the ____ day of _____, and the rendition of such services was closed on the ____ day of _____, and 30 days have not elapsed since that time; that the amount of the claimant's demand for the services is _____; that no part thereof has been paid (except _____), and there is now due and remaining unpaid thereon, after deducting all just credits and offsets, the sum of _____, in which amount he claims a lien upon such property.

State of Oregon } ss.
County of _____

I, _____, being first duly sworn, on oath say that I am the _____ named in the foregoing claim; that I have heard the same read, know the contents thereof, and believe the same to be true.

Subscribed and sworn to before me this ____ day of _____.

Transportation and storage liens are claimed by filing a verified notice of intention to so claim. This notice must state the name of the claimant, the name of the property owner, and a description of the property. A copy of the notice must be sent to the owner.

Where Filed—With the Recording Officer of the county in which the timber was cut or lumber manufactured, or where the property transported or stored is located.

When to Be Filed—Within 60 days after the close of rendition of services for timber or lumber or after the accrual of the transportation or storage claim.

Extent of Lien—Timber and lumber liens are for services, work, or labor done during the six months preceding the filing of notice of claim of lien. Transportation or storage lien may not extend to charges covering a period exceeding five months from the date the claim first began to accrue.

Enforcement—Transportation or storage liens are enforceable by suit, or by sale at public auction if the reasonable value of the property does not exceed $100.

Priority—Transportation and storage liens have preference over all other liens or encumbrances except a lien for herding animals.

PENNSYLVANIA

Who May Claim—Persons engaged in the business of manufacturing, spinning, or throwing cotton, wool, or silk into yarn or other goods, or dyeing cotton, wool, or silk yarns.

In addition to other personal property liens, the owner of a self storage facility shall have a lien on all personal property stored within each leased space located at the self storage facility for rent, labor, or other charges, present or future, and for expenses reasonably incurred in enforcing the lien.

Property Covered—Goods and property of others coming in the possession of such spinners, throwsters, and dyers for the purpose of being so manufactured, spun, thrown, or dyed.

Extent of Lien—The amount of the account due from the owner of the cotton, wool, or silk.

Enforcement—Lien may be enforced by levy and sale, upon 10 days' notice, if the lien has not been satisfied within 30 days, and the owner has not instituted a replevin suit.

PUERTO RICO

Who May Claim—(a) Those who construct, repair, preserve, or sell personal property in the possession of the debtor to the extent of the value of the same; (b) holders of a pledge in the possession of the creditor with regard to the property pledged, to the extent of its value; (c) those guaranteed by a security of goods or securities constituted in a public or commercial establishment concerning the security and for the value of the same; (d) those holders of credits for transportation, with regard to the goods transported, for the amount of said transportation, expenses and rates of carriage and preservation, until the time of the delivery and for a period of 30 days afterwards; (e) innkeepers, to the extent of expenses of boarding as to the personal property of the debtor remaining in the inn; (f) credits for seeds and expenses of cultivation and harvesting, advanced to the debtor, with regard to the fruits of the crops to which they were applied; (g) for costs incurred in unloading and lifting merchandise shipped to Puerto Rico, and for storage either before or after loading.

Duration—For transportation, loading, and storage, six months after charges incurred; innkeepers' lien, three years; for services rendered, three years. If the personal property, with regard to which the preference is allowed, has been surreptitiously removed, the creditor may claim it from the person who has the same, within the term of 30 days counted from the time it was so removed.

Perfection—Puerto Rico is a civil code jurisdiction, like Louisiana (albeit originally based on Spanish Civil Code). Majority of preferences cited indicate no formal perfection requirements outside of ordinary action for judicial sequestration or attachment. Innkeeper may sell personal property in custody after six months, upon notice.

Priority—Previously perfected factor's lien has priority and is superior to referenced liens (a) through (f). Lien for unloading of merchandise has priority over all prior liens except those for taxes.

Extent of Lien—Seller's lien not effective as against bona fide purchaser or pledgee.

RHODE ISLAND

Who May Claim—Processors in the business of spinning, manufacturing, dyeing, or otherwise treating or processing linen, cotton, wool, silk or artificial silk, yarn, or goods, or skins, pelts, furs, or hides, or goods of which any of these form a component part. An operator of dry dock storage facilities has a lien for rent due on all vessels and personal property thereon stored at dry dock storage facilities. The lien is lost if the vessel is voluntarily delivered.

Jeweler's, watchmakers, and silversmiths; molders; cleanser who shall launder, cleanse or store any article of apparel or other personal property at the request of the owner or legal possessor; keepers and feeders of animals.

In addition to other personal property liens, the owner of a self storage facility shall have a lien on all personal property stored within each leased space located at the self storage facility for rent, labor, or other charges, present or future, and for expenses reasonably incurred in enforcing the lien. The owner loses its lien on any personal property that it voluntarily delivers or that is unjustifiably refused delivery.

Property Covered—Property of others coming into the possession of processors.

Extent of Lien—The entire indebtedness of the person for whose account work was performed or materials furnished for the property in question or other property of such debtor.

Enforcement by Sale—When amount due remains unpaid on a spinning or processing claim, in whole or part, for two months after it becomes due and payable, lienor may sell the property subject to the lien at public auction. No more of the property may be sold, if easily separated, than is necessary to pay the lien and expenses of sale, and the balance, if any, is paid to those entitled thereto. If a vessel owner is in default for a period of more than 90 days, a facility operator may enforce a lien by selling the stored vessel at a commercially reasonable public sale for cash.

If the charge or charges remain unpaid for a period of at least six months the launderer or cleanser may sell the article at private or public sale or may dispose of the article in any other manner. After the six-month period has expired the owner and/or legal possessor of the article shall have no further right, title, or interest in and to the article.

The person keeping the animals may detain them until the debt is paid; and, if it is not paid within 30 days after it is due, he or she may sell the animals, or so many as necessary at public auction, upon giving written notice to the owner of the time and place of the sale at least six days before the sale.

Notice of Sale—*Spinning or Processing Claims.* Notice of sale on a spinning or processing claim must be published for two weeks prior to the day of sale, at least once each week, in a newspaper published in the county where the property is located, and a copy of the printed notice must be mailed to the owner, if known, at least five days before the day of sale if his address can be ascertained.

Dry-dock Facilities Claims. A vessel owner must be notified of a personal property lien before such a lien can be enforced. Notification is satisfied by a written storage agreement signed by the vessel owner that includes a notice of the lien; or written notification of the lien sent by the facility operator to the vessel owner. A facility operator who does not have a written storage agreement that includes a notice of the lien may not initiate an enforcement action until 30 days after the written notice of a lien is delivered to the vessel owner. Before conducting a sale of such vessel, the facility operator must also personally serve notice of default on the vessel owner if the vessel owner is a Rhode Island resident. If not, notice shall be by registered or certified mail. The operator must also provide a copy of the notice to each lien-holder of record. The notice must contain:

(1) a statement that the vessel is subject to a lien held by the facility operator;

(2) a statement of the operator's claim indicating the charges due on the date of the notice, the amount of any additional charges that will or may become due before the date of sale, and the date those additional charges will become due;

(3) a demand for payment of the charges due within a specified time not less than 40 days after the date that the notice is delivered;

(4) a statement that unless the claim is paid within the time stated, the vessel will be sold, specifying the time and place of the sale; and

(5) the name, street address, and telephone number of the facility operator or its agent, whom the vessel owner may contact to respond to the notice.

After the expiration of the 40-day period mentioned in (3) above, the operator shall publish an advertisement of the sale once a week for two consecutive weeks in a newspaper of general circulation in the area of the sale and the state of Rhode Island. This advertisement must include a general description of the vessel, the name of the owner, and the date, time and place of the sale. The date must be more than 15 days after the date of the first advertisement.

Priority—Lien is paramount to the title, lien, interest, or encumbrance of any owner unless such owner notifies the processor by registered or certified mail of such interest prior to the commencement of work and the creation of the lien.

SOUTH CAROLINA

Who May Claim—Laborers, subcontractors, materialmen, garagemen, boardinghouses, launderers; persons performing work and furnishing materials in manufacturing, bleaching, dyeing, or otherwise processing natural or man-made fibers, or goods of which such fibers form a component part; persons who service or furnish supplies or accessories for aircraft; boarders and keepers of animals; hospitals servicing persons injured by another persons neglect or actions; owners of a self storage facility.

Property Covered—Goods in the lienor's possession, storage and repair, boarding expenses, labor; any sum claimed by injured person; any property stored in a self storage facility.

Extent of Lien—Lien extends to any unpaid balance of account for work, labor, and materials furnished in the course of the processing described above, in respect of any other property of the same owner no longer in the lienor's possession.

Filing Notice—Lien on aircraft property or service is dissolved in 90 days unless the lienor files in the office of the register of mesne conveyances for the clerk of county in which the aircraft was located at the time the services were rendered.

Enforcement by Sale—For the lien on performing work or furnishing materials for processing of fibers, if any amount due remains unpaid for two months after it becomes due and payable, the lienor may sell the property at public auction. If the property is readily divisible, no more may be sold than is necessary to discharge the indebtedness and cover the expense of the sale. The balance of the proceeds, if any, is paid to the owner or person entitled thereto.

Notice of Sale—Notice of the time and place of the sale must be published once in each of two consecutive weeks in a newspaper published in the city or town, or if none, in the county, in which the property is situated, the last publication to be not less than five days before the sale; five days before the sale, notice must also be given by posting in five or more public places in the county, one of which must be in the town or city ward in which the property is situated, and sending by registered mail a copy of such notice to the owner, if his address can be ascertained.

Priority—The following expressly accord priority to liens on personal property to: laborers, subcontractors, and materialmen on money received by the building contractor; laborers and materialmen on ships or vessels for construction, repair or launching and provisions and stores; to employees of mining and manufacturing establishments on the output for salary and wages.

Liens prevail even over the perfected security interest, unless the statute creating the lien expressly provides otherwise. Therefore, to determine priority of South Carolina statutory liens and Article 9 perfected security interests; each section creating the lien must be reviewed.

SOUTH DAKOTA

Who May Claim—Persons furnishing wheat, oat, barley, rye, corn, flax, or potatoes (seedgrain) to be sown or planted on another's land; persons owning and operating threshing machines, combines, cornshellers, cornhuskers, cornshredders, silage cutters, seed hullers, balers, mowers, grinders, rakes on agricultural pulverizing machines; persons who, at the request or consent of the owner or lawful possessor, furnish services, materials, or facilities for the repair, storage, or maintenance of any personal property; persons who, while in lawful possession of personal property, render service to the owner by carriage.

Property Covered—A seedgrain lien is on the crop produced from the kind of seed furnished. Threshers' and processors' liens are on all grain or agricultural products threshed or processed. Persons furnishing service or material to personal property have a lien on such property. A carrier has a lien on the property carried.

Abandoned Property—For persons who furnish materials or facilities for the repair of personal property, such property, left for repair at a place of business shall be considered abandoned and may be sold if it is unclaimed by the owner for a period of 90 days after written notice of the intent to sell is given to the owner at the owner's last known address by certified mail. Such sale is subject to liens, mortgages, and other creditors' security interests properly filed or perfected before the date that the personal property came into the hands of the place of business.

How Claimed—Seedgrain liens and threshers' and processors' liens may be claimed by filing a written account of the claim. If the person furnishing services or material to personal property loses possession thereof, he may preserve his lien by filing notice of such lien in the same manner as the carrier's lien below.

Carriers may give public record notice of lien by filing a sworn, written statement of such lien. Before filing, a copy must be sent by registered or certified mail to the owner at his last-known post office address, and the post office receipt of such mailing is filed with the statement.

Where Filed—Seedgrain lien accounts are filed in the Office of the Register of Deeds in the county where the crop was produced and in the county of residence of the person who produced the crop, if he is a state resident.

Notice of lien on personal property by person furnishing service on material thereto is filed in the office of the register of deeds of the county where the property is located.

Carrier's lien statement is filed in the office of the register of deeds of the county where the property is located.

When to Be Filed—Notice of a lien on personal property by a person furnishing services or material thereto must be filed within 60 days after loss of possession.

Extent of Lien—Seedgrain lien is for payment for the seed furnished. Thresher's and processor's lien is for the value of services rendered. Lien of person rendering services or material for property is for the agreed price, if none, for the reasonable charge, dependent on possession or notice. Carrier's lien is for the compensation due him for his service, dependent on possession.

Enforcement by Sale—Subject to the right of adversely interested parties to require foreclosure by court action (except in the case of a carrier's lien), these liens may be satisfied by sale of the property at public auction.

Priority—Seedgrain lien, if filed within 10 days after the seedgrain is furnished, shall have preference in the order of filing, and shall have priority over all other liens and encumbrances except thresher's liens. Threshers' and processors' liens, if filed within 10 days after the threshing or processing is completed, have priority over all other liens and encumbrances. Liens of persons furnishing services or material to personal property are subject only to liens, mortgages, and conditional sales contracts properly filed on or before the time the property comes into the possession of the lien claimant.

Notice of Sale—A signed notice of sale including the names and addresses of the owner and all lien claimants, a description of the property and its location, the grounds on which lien is claimed, and the nature of default, the amount claimed and the time and place of the sale, must be mailed to the property owner and all other lien claimants, and published for at least one issue in a legal newspaper published in the county nearest the sale, or if none, by mailing and posting one copy on the bulletin board at the front of the courthouse, or if none, at the place where the circuit court was held in the county. This notice must be made at least 10 days before the date of sale.

Limitations on Sale—Lien of person furnishing services or material to personal property may be foreclosed any time after 60 days from the date of furnishing the last item. Sworn statement must be filed with Register of Deeds before foreclosure of lien.

TENNESSEE

Who May Claim—Cotton ginners; persons in the business of manufacturing, bleaching, mercerizing, dyeing, printing, or furnishing cotton, silk, or artificial silk, or goods of which they form a component part; typographers, printers, lithographers, photoengravers, electrotypers, stereotypers, book binders, and book manufacturers. One furnishing material or labor in any transportation industry has a lien on the property.

In addition to other personal property liens, the owner of a self storage facility shall have a lien on all personal property stored within each leased space located at the self storage facility for rent, labor, or other charges, present or future, and for expenses reasonably incurred in enforcing the lien; molders; marina owners; keepers of animals.

Property Covered—Cotton ginned and baled by cotton ginner; goods and property of others coming into the possession of textile processors; all plates, dies, molds, form, patterns, engravings, and materials of any sort prepared or supplied by the manufacturer or furnished by the customer to facilitate production, which remain in the custody of the manufacturer; a boat, its tackle and furnishings; animals.

How Claimed—Printers and binders wishing to enforce a lien must give notice of intention to claim lien, to the person for whom the work was done, by registered mail.

Extent of Lien—Cotton ginner's lien covers all ginning and baling charges. Textile processor's lien is for amounts due from the owners for freight advanced, processing performed, or materials furnished with respect to the same or other goods of the owner. Printers' and binders' liens are for amounts owing from the customer. Molder's liens are for the balance due them from such customer for any manufacturing or fabrication work. A keeper of animals lien extends for six months.

Duration of Lien—A cotton ginner's lien continues for six months after tolls and charges become due and payable. A textile processor's lien does not continue after the property has been transferred from the lienor. Printers' and binders' liens continue for 90 days from the giving of notice. The transportation, labor, or services lien is effective for 12 months.

Enforcement by Sale—Textile processors' liens may be enforced by sale at public auction when the amount due, in whole or part, remains unpaid for two months after the time it became due. Proceeds of the sale are applied to the payment of the lien and the expenses of the sale, and no more may be sold, if easily divided, than is necessary to pay such lien and expenses. The balance, if any, is paid to the owner entitled thereto.

Notice of Sale—Notice of the sale must be published for two preceding weeks, at least once in each week, in the county where the goods are located, and upon five days' notice of the sale set up in three or more public places in the same county, one of which is the town or the city, if any, in which the goods are located. A copy of the notice must be mailed to the owner, if his residence can be ascertained, at least five days before the day of the sale.

Priority—Cotton ginner's lien is second only to the landlords' or furnisher's lien. Printers' and binders' liens are subject to prior liens.

TEXAS

Who May Claim—Texas statutes grant liens to a long list of persons who provide either labor, materials or both to certain industries including artisans, stable keepers, stock breeders, garagemen, pasturers, mineral contractors or subcontractors, owners of self service storage facilities, persons who furnish supplies or materials or perform repairs or labor for or on account of a domestic vessel owned in whole or in part in the State of Texas, persons who repair, perform maintenance on, or provide fuel to an aircraft, and workers who provide service in an office, store, hotel, rooming house, boarding house, restaurant, shop, factory, mine, quarry or mill; on a farm; cutting preparing, hauling, or transporting logs or timber, or a means of transportation of logs or timber, or in construction/maintenance of a log/timber tram or railroad; owner or keeper of a stallion, jack, bull, or boar; agricultural producers.

Property Covered—Garments; offspring of breeding stock for the amount of the breeding fee; materials, machinery, or supplies furnished or hauled by the claimant, and the land leasehold, wells, and buildings; property tenant places in storage facility; motor vehicles; motorboats; vessels and its tackle, apparel, furniture and freight money; aircraft; offspring of a stallion, jack, bull, or boar; every agricultural crop, either in raw or processed form, that has been transferred or delivered by the agricultural producer and is in the possession of the contract purchaser.

How Claimed—Mineral contractor and subcontractor claims may be made by filing an affidavit as prescribed in statute with the county clerk in the county where the property is located within six months after accrual of the indebtedness and must be served on the property owner in writing within 10 days of this filing of the affidavit. Liens on aircraft may be made by filing with the Federal Aviation Administration Registry within 120 days of the last repair, maintenance, or fueling in the form and manner required by applicable federal law. Worker may secure the lien by serving a copy of the account on the employer and filing a verified affidavit with the county clerk in the county in which the work was performed.

Extent of Lien—For the amount claimed due or reasonable and usual compensation for the repair, maintenance and fuel. The lienholder may retain possession of the aircraft until the amount due is paid.

Duration of Lien—Lien for stock breeders may be enforced in the manner of a statutory landlords' lien and remains in effect for 10 months from the offspring's birth, but may not be enforced until after five months from birth.

UTAH

Who May Claim—Every ranchman, farmer, agistor, herder of cattle, tavern keeper or livery stable keeper to whom any domestic animals shall be entrusted for the purpose of feeding, herding or pasturing; every person who shall make, alter or repair, or bestow labor upon, any article of personal property at the request of the owner or other person entitled to possession; every laundry proprietor, person conducting a laundry business, dry cleaning establishment, proprietor and person conducting a dry cleaning establishment, shoe repair establishment proprietor and person conducting a shoe repair establishment.

In addition to other personal property liens, the owner of a self storage facility shall have a lien on all personal property within each leased space located at the self storage facility for rent, labor, or other charges, present or future, and for expenses reasonably incurred in enforcing the lien.

Property Covered—Entrusted domestic animals; articles of personal property made, altered, repaired, or bestowed labor upon; all personal property of customer in hands of launderer or shoe repairmen.

Extent of Lien—Liens on livestock are for the amount that may be due to farmer for such feeding, herding or pasturing, and is authorized to retain possession of such animals until such amount is paid. Repairmen may retain possession thereof until the amount so due is paid; provided such lien and right to possession shall be subject and subordinate to the rights and interests of any secured parties in such personal property unless such secured party has requested such person to make, alter or repair or bestow labor upon such property. Launderers and shoe repairmen have liens for the balance due him from such customer for laundry work, and for the balance due him for dry cleaning work, and for the balance due him for shoe repair work; but nothing in this section shall be construed to confer a lien in favor of a wholesale dry cleaner on materials received from a dry cleaning establishment proprietor or a person conducting a dry cleaning establishment.

Notice of Lien—Any garments, clothing, shoes, wearing apparel or household goods, remaining in the possession of a person, on which cleaning, pressing, glazing, laundry or washing or repair work has been done or upon which alterations or repairs have been made or on which materials or supplies have been used or furnished by said person holding possession thereof, for a period of 90 days or more after the completion of such services or labors, may be sold by said person holding possession, to pay the unpaid reasonable or agreed charges therefor and the costs of notifying the owner or owners as hereinafter provided; provided, however, that the person to whom such charges are payable and owing shall first notify the owner or owners of such property of the time and place of such sale; and provided further, that property that is to be placed in storage after any of the services or labors mentioned herein shall not be affected by the provisions of this subsection.

VERMONT

Who May Claim—Persons or entities who furnish materials or labor on personality, or realty, are owed wages, repair to ships, service of stallions or colts, for keeping or pasturing animals; persons who make, alter, launder, dry clean or repair an article of personal property.

Property Covered—All such property properly identified as the recipient of such labor and materials furnished or logs which it has caused its registered mark, mares of stallions and animals remaining in possession of pasture owner.

How Claimed—Persons or entities who rendered the benefits of material and labor to ownership, log owner, pastured animals or mare owner, or others of real or personal property, by filing notice of lien in town.

Where Claimed—Town clerk where goods are kept or debtor resides.

Extent of Lien—For the amount claimed due.

Duration of Lien—Ninety days for material and repair to real property and personal property and 30 days for other. Stallion liens shall continue in force until the colt is eight months old and may be enforced by attachment of such colt or mare at any time after the colt is four months old.

Enforcement—By filing a lawsuit and requesting a judicial attachment within 120 days.

Priority—Lien takes precedence over subsequent attaching creditors.

VIRGIN ISLANDS

Who May Claim—Any person who makes, alters, repairs, or bestows labor on any article of personal property at the request of the owner or lawful possessor thereof shall have a lien upon such property so made, altered, or repaired or upon which labor has been bestowed, for their just and reasonable charges for the labor they have performed and the material they have furnished, and such person may hold and retain possession of the same until such charges shall be paid.

Any person who (1) is a common carrier, or, at the request of the owner or lawful possessor of any personal property, carries, conveys, or transports the same from one place to another; (2) safely keeps or stores any grain, wares, merchandise, or personal property at the request of the owner or lawful possessor thereof; or (3) pastures or feeds any horses, cattle, hogs, sheep, or other livestock, or bestows any labor, care, or attention upon the same at the request of the owner or lawful possessor thereof shall have a lien upon such property for their just and reasonable charges for the labor, care, and attention they have bestowed and the food they have furnished, and they may retain possession of such property until such charges are paid.

Property Covered—The goods and property of others which come into possession of such a person for such purpose.

How Claimed—Claimant must file claim which shall be verified under oath. The claim shall contain: a statement of demand and the amount thereof, after deducting credits and offsets; the name of the party for whom such work was performed; statement of the terms of the contract, if any, or what such service or work is worth; and the description of the property to be charged with the lien.

Where Filed—Office of the Lieutenant Governor, Recorder of Deeds of the judicial district where the property is situated.

When to Be Filed—Within 30 days after the rendition of the service or after performing the work or labor.

Duration of Lien—Six months after claim is filed, unless civil action is commenced within that time.

Priority—Personal property liens are preferred liens and prior to any and all other liens.

Enforcement by Sale—Upon judgment in favor of the claimant, the court may order the property subject to the lien to be sold by the marshal. Upon motion, supported by affidavit, showing that the property is liable to loss or destruction, the court may order the property sold before judgment is rendered and the proceeds retained in the registry of the court until judgment is rendered.

Notice of Sale—Not less than 10 days prior to the day of sale of property on execution, a written or printed notice of the time and place of sale, particularly describing the property shall be: (1) posted in a public place in or near the office of the clerk of the court in the judicial district in which the sale is to take place; and (2) published in a newspaper which is published in the judicial district in which the sale is to take place.

VIRGINIA

Who May Claim—Persons furnishing railroad iron, engine, cars, fuel, and other supplies necessary to the operation of a railway, canal, or other transportation company; any person storing or repairing a motor vehicle.

Keepers of aircraft hangars or tie downs have a possessory lien. This must be filed with the Secretary of State and the FAA within 120 days. If the aircraft is subject to a chattel lien, it becomes nonpossessory.

In addition to other personal property liens, the owner of a self storage facility shall have a lien on all personal property stored within each leased space located at the self storage facility for rent, labor, or other charges, present or future, and for expenses reasonably incurred in enforcing the lien.

Property Covered—The franchises, gross earnings, and all real and personal property used in the operation of the company to whom supplies were furnished.

How Claimed—By filing a memorandum certified by affidavit of the amount and consideration of the claim and when due and payable.

Where Filed—In the clerk's office of the circuit court of the county or corporation court of the city in which the chief office in Virginia of the company against which the claim is located, or when that office is in Richmond, in the office of the chancery court of Richmond, or with the receiver, trustee, or assignee of such company.

When to Be Filed—Within 90 days after the last item of the bill becomes due and payable.

Extent of Lien—For the moneys due; lien for storing motor vehicles limited to extent of $150; lien for repairing motor vehicles limited to $300.

Enforcement—Lien may be enforced in a court of equity. The owner may give a bond and receive possession of the property.

Priority—Lien has priority over any amount due by the company for rents or royalties. No mortgage, deed of trust, sale, hypothecation, or conveyance executed may defeat or take precedence over this lien. Supply lien is subordinate to that allowed clerks, mechanics, foremen, superintendents, and laborers for services furnished to such company. Lien for repairing motor vehicle given priority with mechanics' liens over all other liens in the vehicle.

WASHINGTON

Who May Claim—Persons who perform labor or assist in obtaining or securing saw logs, or other timber, and manufacturing lumber, owners of tow boats used to tow logs and timber, and owners of logging teams or engines who haul logs and timber; persons, who, as warehousemen, commission merchants, carriers, or wharfingers, make advances for freight, transportation, wharfage, and storage of personal property; persons who prepare livestock products for market or who feed livestock; agisters; every person, firm or corporation who, as a commission merchant, carrier, wharfinger or storage warehouseman, shall make advances for freight, transportation, wharfage or storage upon the personal property of another, or shall carry or store such personal property; molders.

In addition to other personal property liens, the owner of a self storage facility shall have a lien on all personal property stored within each leased space located at the self storage facility for rent, labor, or other charges, present or future, and for expenses reasonably incurred in enforcing the lien. However, any lien on a motor vehicle or boat which has attached and is set forth in the title shall have priority over such a lien.

Property Covered—Agricultural lien is on the crops produced. Crop dusting lien is on the crops dusted or sprayed. Fertilizer, pesticide and weed-killer liens are on the crops on which such products are used. Timber lien is on the logs and timber for which service was performed, and on lumber still under the control of the manufacturer. Transportation and storage lien is for the personal property for which service was performed, still in the lienor's possession. Preparer or processor lien is for agricultural products delivered, inventory, and to accounts receivable. The horses, mules, cattle, or sheep, and upon the proceeds or accounts receivable from such animals. Personal property stored, transported or wharfed.

How Claimed—Agricultural liens must be claimed by filing a claim of lien, subscribed and verified under oath, to the effect that it is believed to be just. Preparer or processor lien must be claimed by filing a statement, signed and verified with description of lien, that amount claimed is bona fide and date payment was due.

For livestock liens, a notice must be posted where the animals are kept, with a copy to be provided to the owner and any lien creditor. The notice is only necessary if the amount is in excess of $1,500. The lien expires after 120 days.

Timber liens are claimed by filing a claim statement in substantially the following form:

_____, Claimant, v. _____

Notice is hereby given that _____ of _____ of _____, being about _____ in quantity, which were cut or manufactured in _____ County, State of Washington, are marked thus _____, and are now lying in _____, for labor performed upon and assistance rendered in _____ said _____; that _____ employed said _____ to perform such labor and render such assistance upon the following terms and conditions, to wit: The said _____ agreed to pay the said _____ for such labor and assistance _____; that said contract has been faithfully performed and fully complied with on the part of said _____, who performed labor upon and assisted in _____ said _____ for the period of _____; that said labor and assistance were so performed and rendered upon said between the ____ day of _____ and the ____ day of ; and the rendition of said service was closed on the ____ day of _____ and 60 days have not elapsed since that time; that the amount of claimant's demand for said service is _____; that no part thereof has been paid except _____, and there is now due and remaining unpaid thereon, after deducting all just credits and offsets, the sum of _____, in which amount he claims a lien upon said _____.

The said _____ also claims a lien on all said _____ now owned by said _____ of said county to secure payment for the work and labor performed in obtaining or securing the said logs, spars, piles, or other timber, lumber, or shingles herein described.

State of Washington, County of _____ ss. _____ being first duly sworn, on oath says that he is _____ named in the foregoing claim, has heard the same read, knows the contents thereof, and believes the same to be true.

Subscribed and sworn to before me this ____ day of _____.

Where Filed—Lien claims are filed with the county auditor of the county in which the crops were raised, or timber cut or lumber manufactured. Preparer or processor lien must be filed with the department of licensing.

When to Be Filed—Agricultural liens must be filed within 20 days after the cessation of work or within 20 days after payment is due for processor's liens. Timber liens must be filed within 60 days after timber is cut or lumber manufactured. Processor lien must be filed within 20 days of date payment due and remains unpaid.

Extent of Lien—Timber liens are for services rendered. Transportation and storage liens are for charges for advances, freight, transportation, wharfage, or storage. Preparer or processor lien is for the contract price, if any, or the fair market value of the products delivered. Agister liens are for amounts that may be due for the feeding, herding, pasturing, training, caring for, and ranching of the animals. For transportation liens, so long as the same remains in his possession, are for the charges for advances, freight, transportation, wharfage or storage

Duration of Lien—The processor lien extends for six months; the preparer lien is for 50 days after, unless suit to foreclose has been filed.

Enforcement by Sale—Lien on personal property transported or stored may be enforced by sale if the property subject to lien is in store and uncalled for with charges unpaid and due, for a period of 30 days after such charges became due.

Notice of Sale—Ten days must be given by posting written notice of the time and place of sale in three public places in the county where the sale is to take place.

Priority—Timber liens are preferred and are prior to any other liens. Processor or preparer lien has priority over all other liens, except for taxes or labor perfected before filing of the processor or preparer lien, if such lien is filed within 20 days.

WEST VIRGINIA

Who May Claim—Persons who, while in possession, make, alter, repair, store, or transport or in any way enhance the value of personal property; a person keeping a livery stable, or boarding stable for animals, or a garage or storage place for automobiles or other vehicles, or who boards, pastures, feeds or trains animals for hire; owner of any stallion, jack or bull, that is duly registered under the laws of the State of West Virginia; humane officer shall provide any neglected or abandoned animal with proper food, shelter and care; any citizen of the state; owner of a self storage facility.

Property Covered—The property for which service is rendered; foal of such stallion, jack or bull; such animal cared for; any domestic steamboat, steamer or vessel, propelled wholly or in part by steam, gas, fluid, naphtha, or electricity, which plies upon the navigable waters of this State, and which is registered in this State; personal property stored in self storage facility.

Extent of Lien—This lien is for the charges agreed upon, or if not agreed, for just and reasonable charges. A person keeping a livery stable, or boarding stable for animals, or a garage or storage place for automobiles or other vehicles, or who boards, pastures, feeds or trains animals for hire, has a lien upon such animals or vehicles for the sum due him for the care, boarding, pasturage, feeding, or training of such animals, or the care, keeping or storage of such vehicles, even though such animals or vehicles are permitted to be taken out of the possession of the one claiming such lien, if the contract between the owner and the person claiming such lien for keeping, boarding, pasturage, feeding, training or storage, has not been terminated at the time such animal or vehicle is taken out of such possession.

As for a stallion lien, such lien shall cease unless the person desiring to avail himself thereof shall, within six months from the birth of such foal or calf, file before some magistrate in the county in which such foal or calf may be, his own affidavit, or that of some credible person, stating the amount of his lien against such foal or calf and that such amount is due by contract, also a description of the foal or calf upon which such lien is claimed. Such affidavit shall be filed and preserved by such magistrate, for which service he shall receive any fee provided by law.

Humane officer has a lien for services provided to animal.

A citizen of this State shall have a lien upon any domestic steamboat, steamer or vessel, propelled wholly or in part by steam, gas, fluid, naphtha, or electricity, which plies upon the navigable waters of this State, and which is registered in this State, for all work and labor done upon such vessel, and for all materials, goods, wares and merchandise furnished such vessel by any such citizen.

The owner has a self-service storage lien on all personal property stored within each leased space for agreed rent, labor or other charges and for expenses reasonably incurred in its sale or destruction pursuant to this article. The self-service storage lien attaches as of the date the personal property is stored within each leased space and remains a lien until the occupant has satisfied the terms of the rental agreement.

Enforcement by Sale—This lien may be enforced by sale at auction in the county where lien was acquired, or, if unsuitable, at the nearest suitable place. Proceeds go to satisfy the lien, including seasonable charges for notice, advertisement, and sale; the balance, if any, is to be delivered on demand to the person to whom the lienor would have been bound or justified to deliver the goods.

Notice of Sale—The lienor must personally or by registered mail give notice to the person on whose account the goods are held to any other persons known to the lienor who claim an interest in the property. The notice should include an itemized statement of the claim, a description of the property, a demand for payment by a certain date, not less than 10 days from delivery of the notice, a statement that, unless paid, the property will be advertised and sold at a certain time and place. After the time specified for payment, advertisement of the sale must be published once a week for two consecutive weeks in a newspaper published in the place where the sale is to be held. The sale may not be less than 15 days after the first publication. If no such newspaper is published, the advertisement may be posted at least 10 days before the sale in not less than three conspicuous places including the premises where the property is held under lien.

Where the value of the property is less than $500, newspaper advertisement is not required, and the posting in these places is sufficient.

WISCONSIN

Who May Claim—Persons performing services in cutting, hauling, running, felling, piling, driving, rafting, booming, cutting, towing, sawing, peeling, or manufacturing, logs, timber, staves, pulpwood, cordwood, firewood, railroad ties, pilings, telegraph poles, telephone poles, fence posts, paving timber, tan or other barks, or in preparing wood for manufacturing charcoal; persons who thresh grain, cut, shred, husk, or shell corn, or bale hay and straw by machine for another.

Property Covered—Log liens are on the material to which labor or service is furnished.

Agricultural liens are on the grain threshed, the corn processed, or the straw or hay baled.

How Claimed—Log liens are claimed by filing a signed and verified petition setting forth the nature of the demand, the amount claimed, and a description of the property. To apply to an innocent purchaser for value, an agricultural lien must be filed.

Where Filed—Log liens are claimed in the office of the clerk of the circuit court of the county in which the services or some part thereof were performed.

Agricultural liens may be filed in the office of the Register of Deeds of the county where the services were performed.

When to Be Filed—Log liens must be filed within three months after last day of performing continuous services. Agricultural liens may be claimed within 15 days from the date of completion of service.

Extent of Lien—Log liens are for the amount owing for services. Agricultural liens are for the value of services to extent that the person contracting for such services has an interest in the property subject to the lien.

Duration of Lien—Action to enforce a log lien must be taken within four months after filing of petition. Agricultural liens may be foreclosed at any time within six months from the date of the last charge for services.

Enforcement by Sale—Agricultural liens may be enforced by sale at public auction. Proceeds are applied to the payment of services and the expense of seizure and sale, the residue being returned to the party entitled thereto.

Notice of Sale—Notice of sale must be not less than 10 nor more than 15 days from the date of taking possession of such grain, corn, straw, or hay. Notice is to be given personally and by posting in at least three public places in the town where the debtor resides or in the town where the sale is to be made and, if the debtor is a nonresident of the state, in the town where the grain, corn, straw, or hay, or part thereof, was threshed, processed, or baled.

WYOMING

Who May Claim—Persons who work upon, or furnish, or rent material or services for constructing, altering, digging, drilling, boring, operating, completing, or repairing any mine or quarry, under contract express or implied; persons performing work upon, or furnishing any material for the construction or repair of any ditch, canal, or reservoir under contract; threshermen, hay balers, and combiners operating such machines.

Property Covered—Mines, quarries, materials furnished, the land or leasehold, all other wells, buildings, and appurtenances located on the land or leasehold where the improvement is located; ditches, canals, reservoirs, right-of-way and water rights, and the land owned by the owner or proprietor for the reclamation of which the ditch, canal, or reservoir was constructed; grain, hay, or other crops threshed, baled, or combined.

How Claimed—Mine and quarry liens are claimed by filing notice setting forth the fact that claimant furnished the material, services or labor, the name of the party to whom furnished, the dates of such furnishing, the amount claimed, claimant's name and address, and a description of the premise to which the material, service or labor was furnished.

Ditch, canal, or reservoir liens are claimed by filing an account of the demand due in conformance with that required for a mechanics' lien to the extent possible.

Threshermen's, hay balers' and combiners' liens are claimed by filing an account of the amount due, containing a description of hay, grain, or other crop, the agreed price, a description of the land upon which crops, hay or grain were raised, a description of the legal subdivision of land upon which grain or hay, is stored, and, if stored in an elevator, the location of the elevator. Notice must be served on purchasers of grain, hay, or crops being hauled from the machine directly to the elevator or any purchaser.

Where Claimed—Mine and quarry liens, and threshermen's, hay balers', and combiners' liens are filed with the county clerk of the county in which the land, leasehold, or part thereof, is situated, or where the grain, hay, or crops were grown. Ditch, canal, or reservoir liens are filed in the same manner as mechanics' liens.

When to Be Claimed—Mine and quarry liens must be filed within six months after the last day when material or service was delivered or work done. Ditch, canal, or reservoir liens are filed in the same manner as mechanics' liens. Threshermen's, haybalers', and combiners' liens must be filed within 60 days after the last service was rendered or work done. With respect to an employee or subcontractor, after the last day work was performed at the direction of the employer.

Extent of Lien—Quarry and mine liens are for payment for services and material, including transportation and mileage charges, and interest from the date due.

Duration of Lien—Enforcement of mine and quarry liens must be commenced within six months after filing notice. Duration of ditch, canal, or reservoir liens is six months. Enforcement of the threshermen's, haybalers', and combiners' liens must be commenced within 60 days from the filing of the lien.

Priority—Mine and quarry liens attaching to materials, machinery and supplies and specific improvements are in preference to any prior lien or encumbrance or mortgage on the land or leasehold, provided that such liens, mortgages, or encumbrances on the land or leasehold existing at the inception of the lien are not affected.

Threshermen's, hay balers', and combiners' liens are prior to and have precedence over any mortgages, encumbrance, or other crops, except the lien for the seed furnished to grow the specific crop, if filed or of record.

SUMMARY OF STATE LAWS GOVERNING LANDLORDS' LIENS

Note: State legislatures will, on occasion, modify an area of law without clear delineation as to its content and context. As a result, even the changes which have been enacted prior to placement in the state's Code may be difficult to locate. As a result, the Editors urge all users of the Manual to use this publication only as a guide, and consult the latest codified version of the state's law for all recent changes.

ALABAMA

The landlord of any storehouse, dwelling house, or other building has a lien on the goods, furniture, and effects belonging to the tenant or subtenant for his rent, which is superior to all other liens except for taxes and crops bought on leased premises. Landlord has lien on livestock raised on leased land and on crops for current rent and advances.

ALASKA

No statutory provisions.

ARIZONA

Landlords' Liens for Rent. Under Arizona law, a landlord generally has a lien on all property of his tenant not exempt by law, placed upon or used on the leased premises, until the rent is paid. The landlords' lien does not apply to dwelling units.

The landlord may seize for rent any personal property of its tenant found on the premises. However, the personal property of any other person found on the premises shall not be subject to lien. If the tenant fails to allow the landlord to take possession of the tenant's property, the landlord may obtain possession of the property by an action to recover possession, and may hold or sell the property for the payment of the rent.

No Liens for Dwelling Units. Under Arizona's Residential Landlord and Tenant Act, which applies to the rental of "dwelling units," there is no lien or security interest on behalf of the landlord in a tenant's household goods.

ARKANSAS

Statutory provisions for farm landlords and on personal property left by tenant.

Every landlord shall have a lien upon the crop grown upon the demised premises in any year for rent that shall accrue for the year. In addition to the lien given by law to landlords, if any landlord, to enable his or her tenant or employee to make and gather the crop, shall advance the tenant or employee any necessary supplies, either of money, provisions, clothing, stock, or other necessary articles, the landlord shall have a lien upon the crop raised upon the premises for the value of the advances.

CALIFORNIA

No statutory provisions, except for hotels and boardinghouses.

COLORADO

A person renting to transients has a lien upon their personal property upon the premises for lodging and boarding services and all costs incurred in enforcing the lien. Such liens shall apply to the personal property of transient guests who rent temporary trailer space in any trailer court or auto court in this state. These provisions do not apply to motor vehicles owned by such transient guests parked on the premises of such hotel, motel, inn, or boardinghouse or to stolen property. Any person who rents furnished or unfurnished rooms or apartments for the housekeeping purposes of his tenants, as well as the keeper of a trailer court who rents trailer space, shall have a lien upon the tenant's personal property that is then on or in the rental premises. The value of the lien shall be for the amount of unpaid board, lodging, or rent, and for reasonable costs incurred in enforcing the lien, not including attorney fees. The lien shall be upon the household furniture, goods, appliances, and other personal property of the tenant and members of his household then being upon the rental premises, but exclusive of necessaries.

CONNECTICUT

When a special agreement has been made between the keeper of any boarding or lodging house and any person boarding or lodging at such house, regarding the price of such board or lodging, all the baggage and effects kept by such person at such house shall be subject to a lien in favor of the keeper of such house for all such sums as are at any time due him from such person for board or lodging; and such boardinghouse or lodging house keeper may detain such baggage and effects until such debt is paid; and, if it is not paid within 60 days after it is due, he may sell such property, or such part thereof as is necessary, and apply the proceeds to the payment of such debt.

Whenever the keeper of any hotel or inn receives into his hotel or inn any person as a boarder or lodger, he shall have a lien upon and right to detain the baggage and effects of such boarder or lodger; and such lien may be enforced in the manner hereinafter provided. At any time after 30 days after the person incurring any debt or obligation has left the hotel or inn wherein such debt or obligation was incurred, the debt or obligation being still due and unpaid, the proprietor of such hotel or inn may sell at public auction for cash at the office of such hotel or inn any baggage or property left at such hotel or inn and apply the avails of such sale toward the payment of such debt or obligation; provided such sale shall be advertised in a newspaper published or having a circulation in the town where such hotel or inn is situated three times, commencing at least five days before such sale; and, if the last usual place of abode of such debtor is known to or can reasonably be ascertained by such hotel keeper, notice of the time and place of sale shall be given him by mailing such notice to him in a registered or certified letter, postage paid, at such last usual place of abode at least five days before the time of sale. The proceeds of such sale, after deducting the amount due the proprietor of such hotel or inn and all expenses connected with such sale, shall be paid to the owner of the property or his legal representatives, if called for or claimed by him or them at any time within one year from the date of such sale, and, if such balance is not claimed or called for within said period, then it shall escheat to the state.

DELAWARE

Distress for rent has been abolished except pursuant to a rental agreement for a commercial unit. Liens also provided against crops for agricultural leases.

DISTRICT OF COLUMBIA

A landlord has a lien for his rent upon the tenant's personal chattels, on the premises, subject to execution for the debt. Lien to commence with the tenancy and continue for three months after the rent is due and until the termination of any action for the rent brought within said three months. Lien may be enforced by attachment, by judgment, by judgment execution, or by action against any purchaser of the chattels with notice of the liens.

FLORIDA

On residential property, landlord has lien for tenant's personal property on premises. On commercial property, landlord has lien for agricultural products and other property on premises.

GEORGIA

A landlord has a general lien upon the property of his debtor and a special lien for rent on crops grown on land rented from him subject to tax and laborers' liens. The special lien is superior to all liens except tax liens. The general lien is inferior to tax liens, but ranks with other liens and other general liens according to date, the date being from the time of levying a distress warrant.

HAWAII

No statutory provisions.

IDAHO

No statutory provisions except that hotel keepers have a lien for unpaid charges and attorneys' fees.

ILLINOIS

Lien on crops for rent due. Such lien is good for six months after expiration of the term and must be enforced by distraint. Lessor may enforce lien rights against sublessee or assignee.

INDIANA

A landlord holds a lien on crops for payment of rent in all cases where a tenant agrees to pay as rent a part of the crop raised on the leased premises, or rent in kind, or a cash rent. If the tenant fails to pay the rent when due, the lien may be enforced by sale of the crops, provided filing is made in the Recorder's office of the county in which the leased premises is located at any time 30 days prior to the maturity of the crop and during the year in which the crop is grown.

IOWA

A landlord shall have a lien for rent upon all crops grown upon the leased premises, and upon any other personal property of the tenant which has been used or kept thereon during the term and which is not exempt from execution.

KANSAS

The lessor of space for a mobile home site has a lien upon the mobile home for unpaid rent. Written notice of the lien must be posted on the home. The lien has priority over all other liens except prior perfected security interests. At any time following 30 days of the notice, the lessor may remove the mobile home, provided that it is unoccupied by the lessee. Any rent due for farming land shall be a lien on the crop growing or made on the premises or the animal occupying the pasture.

KENTUCKY

A landlord renting premises for farming or coal mining purposes shall have a lien on the produce of the premises rented and the fixtures, household furniture, and other personal property owned by the tenant, or under tenant, after possession is taken under the lease, but the lien shall not be for more than one year's rent due and to become due, nor for any rent which has been due for more than 11 months. Every other landlord shall have a lien on the fixtures, household furniture, and other personal property of the tenant or under tenant, from the time possession is taken under the lease, to secure the landlord in the payment of four months' rent due or to become due, but such lien shall not be effective for any rent which is past due for more than 120 days.

Statutes also provide for liens by innkeepers. Innkeepers may sell baggage or goods pursuant to law.

LOUISIANA

Lessor has a right of pledge of the lessee's movables which are found on the property for payment of his rent and other obligations of the lease. This includes the furniture of the lessee and the merchandise in the house or apartment. A privilege for rents of immovables exists on the crops of the year.

MAINE

No statutory provisions.

MARYLAND

Prior recorded security interest in all chattels in which tenant has an interest is exempt from distress for rent by the landlords' lien on crops. Otherwise no lien without distraint by action at law.

MASSACHUSETTS

Statutes only provide for liens by innkeeper.

MICHIGAN

No statutory provisions.

MINNESOTA

The remedy of distress for rent is abolished by statute on residential and commercial property in Minnesota. Landlords may obtain possession, but not unpaid rent, through an unlawful detainer action.

Innkeepers have alien on valuables, baggage or property of guests to secure payment of innkeeper charges. An innkeepers is enforced by suit and a judgment for charges; may hold possession by posting a bond; if the final judgment is not paid within 30 days, innkeeper may sell property.

Agricultural landlords may still assert a lien on crops on leased land by filing within 30 days of growing crops.

MISSISSIPPI

A landlord has a lien upon lessee's personal property located on leased land, except for stock of merchandise sold in the normal course of business, for payment of rent and may not be removed from land until rent is paid. Every landlord has a lien on the agricultural product of the leased premises. The lien on personal property is subordinate to prior perfected security interests; the agricultural lien is superior.

MISSOURI

Missouri has no landlords' lien except as to growing crops. Statute authorizes attachment of lessee's property for nonpayment of rent in cases where lessee is about to remove from the premises. The lien continues for eight months after rent becomes due and payable.

MONTANA

No statutory provisions, except for hotels and boardinghouses. Hotelmen and boardinghouse and lodginghouse keepers shall have a lien upon the baggage and other property of value brought into such hotel, inn, boardinghouse, or lodginghouse by such guest or boarder or lodger for his accommodation, board, or lodging and room rent and such extras as are furnished at his request, with the right of the possession of such baggage or other property of value until all such charges are paid. Nothing herein contained shall be construed to give a lien upon property sold on the installment plan, title to which is to remain in the vendor until final payment. Any hotelkeeper or innkeeper who shall have a lien upon any of the goods, baggage, or other chattel property of his guests may, at the expiration of six months from the date of the departure of such guest from such hotel or inn, sell and dispose of the same at public auction and to the highest bidder for cash or so much thereof as may be necessary to pay the sum due such hotelkeeper or innkeeper, together with the cost of storage, advertisement, and sale. Before proceeding to the sale of the property of any guest such hotelkeeper or innkeeper shall cause a notice of such sale, containing a description of the property to be sold and the time and place where such property will be sold, to be published once each week for two successive weeks in a newspaper published in the city or town in which such hotel or inn is situated but, if there be none, then in some newspaper published nearest such town or city and in case any balance arising from such sale shall not be claimed by the rightful owner within 30 days from the day of such sale, the same shall be paid into the treasury of the county in which such sale took place. If such balance be not claimed by the owner thereof or his legal representatives within 1 year thereafter, the same shall be paid into the school fund of such county.

NEBRASKA

No statutory provisions except for hotels, apartment houses, tourist camps, or rooming houses.

NEVADA

Nevada will recognize a commercial landlords' common law lien (right of distraint) on his tenant's property for unpaid lease obligations. No statutory provisions for liens on residential property. Nevada provides a hotel or motel owner with a lien on a guest's belongings for unpaid room rent. Surrender of the property probably waives the lien. The property must be sold at public auction no sooner than 30 days after default. The lien does not apply to tools of trade.

NEW HAMPSHIRE

No statutory provisions.

NEW JERSEY

Landlord has preferred claim for rent for not exceeding one year on goods of tenant located on the premises by execution or attachment thereof.

NEW MEXICO

Landlord has lien on property in leased premises for rent due or to become due. The lien shall not, however, attach where the premises rented is a household or dwelling. Lien on money, and value of tools, animals, provisions, supplies furnished by landlord where landlord of agricultural land.

NEW YORK

Apartment/hotel keeper has lien on property of guest on premises.

NORTH CAROLINA

A landlord has a lien upon crops; preferred against all other liens.

NORTH DAKOTA

The keeper of any inn or hotel or of any tourist camp, whether an individual, a partnership, a corporation, or a limited liability company, has a lien on the baggage and other property in and about such inn, hotel, or tourist camp belonging to or under the control of guests or boarders for the proper charges due from such guests for accommodation, board, and lodging, and for all money paid for or advanced to them not to exceed the sum of two hundred dollars, and for such other extras as are furnished at their request. The innkeeper, hotelkeeper, or tourist camp keeper has the right to detain the baggage and other property until the amount of such charges is paid, and such baggage and other property is exempt from attachment or execution until such innkeeper's lien and the cost of satisfying it are paid.

A landlord of a mobile home lot has a lien for accrued rents, storage, and removal relating to any mobile home left on the lot after the tenant has vacated the premises after an eviction or the expiration of the lease term. A lien under this section does not have priority over a prior perfected security interest in the property. A holder of a lien under this section may retain possession of the mobile home subject to the lien until the amount due is paid. A lienholder may sell a mobile home 30 days after the lienholder mails notice of the lien to the owner of the mobile home and secured parties of record. After the sale, the lienholder shall forward to the former owner any money resulting from the sale of the mobile home in excess of the amount owed to the lienholder for accrued rents, storage, and removal relating to the mobile home. If the location of the former mobile home owner is not known, any money from a sale in excess of the amount owed is presumed abandoned.

OHIO

No statutory provisions. Lease for nonresidential premises may provide for lien.

OKLAHOMA

Landlord has lien on personal property in rented premises that has reasonable relationship to amount owed. Landlord owed rent for farming land has lien on crops growing or made on premises; may recover from purchaser of crops with notice. Landlords in possession of personal property on their premises may enforce their lien by sale with proper notice. Notice to purchaser of crops. Landlords' lien on tenant's personal property is secondary to a claim of a prior holder of a chattel mortgage. Landlords' lien on crops is superior to a mortgage lien, but not to a laborers' lien.

OREGON

Landlord has a lien upon all personal property owned by a tenant, or occupant legally responsible for rent, brought upon the premises except for wearing apparel. Such lien is inferior to the lien of duly perfected security interests and purchase money security interests existing before personal property is brought upon the lease premises; lien on chattels owned by the tenant or occupant legally responsible for the rent includes instances of rental or lease of space in storage facilities to a person who has access to the space in order to store chattels for which no warehouse receipt, bill of lading, or other document of title is issued. The general exemption of wearing apparel from a landlords' lien does not apply in the case of such rentals or leases of storage space.

PENNSYLVANIA

The landlord may seize any personal property on the premises for rent due after judgment is obtained. In general, the property of strangers brought by tenant on the premises may be seized for rent prior to termination of lease. A landlord cannot levy or sell on distress for rent personal property which is leased or sold in any transaction in which a purchase money security interest is retained and written notice describing the property is placed upon the demised premises or within 10 days thereafter.

PUERTO RICO

A landlord has a "credit" or lien for rents and leases for one year with regard to the personal property of the lessee existing on the estate leased and on the fruits thereof. If the personal property, with regard to which the preference is allowed, has been surreptitiously removed, the creditor may claim it from the person who has the same, within the term of 30 days counted from the time it was so removed. An action to recover the payment of rents prescribes in five years.

RHODE ISLAND

Every hotelkeeper or innkeeper shall be entitled to a lien upon, and may detain, the baggage, goods, chattels, and property of a guest brought upon his or her premises for the proper charges due from the guest on account of his or her accommodation, board and lodging and for all extras furnished at the request of the guest, and for all moneys advanced or credit extended to the guest by the hotelkeeper or innkeeper. Any hotelkeeper or innkeeper who shall have a lien for accommodation, board and lodging or extras upon any baggage, goods, chattels, or property, or who, for a period of six months shall have in his or her custody any unclaimed trunk, box, valise, package or parcel, or other chattel property, may sell the property at public auction to the highest bidder for cash and out of the proceeds of the sale may retain the expense of storage, advertisement, and sale thereof, as well as the amount of lien, if any; provided, however, that not less than 15 days prior to the date of the sale, a notice designating the time and place of the sale, and containing a brief general description of the goods, baggage, or articles to be sold, shall be published in a newspaper published in the city or town in which the hotel or inn is situated, and if there is no newspaper published in the city or town, then in a newspaper published in the county where the hotel or inn is situated; and provided, further, that if the name and address of the guest or owner of the goods, baggage or articles appears on the records of the hotelkeeper or innkeeper, a copy of the published notice shall be mailed to the guest or owner at the address by registered or certified mail, postage prepaid, not less than 10 days prior to the date of the sale.

SOUTH CAROLINA

A landlord may enforce the collection of rent by distress, except for certain household articles. Distress lien is inferior to a recorded chattel mortgage, but the landlord may pay balance owing chattel mortgage and claim the property. Agricultural: A landlords' lien for rent.

SOUTH DAKOTA

Landlord has lien for handling and storing property having value in excess of $100 and left on residential premises.

TENNESSEE

A landlord and one controlling land by lease or otherwise shall have a lien on all crops grown on the land during the year for the payment of the rent for the year, whether the contract of rental be verbal or in writing, and this lien shall inure to the benefit of the assignee of the lienor. All keepers of hotels, boarding-houses, and lodging houses, whether licensed or not, shall have a lien on all furniture, baggage, wearing apparel, or other goods and chattels brought into any such hotel, boardinghouse, or lodginghouse, by any guest or patron of the same, to secure the payment by such guest of all sums due for board or lodging.

TEXAS

Landlord leasing residential or commercial property has lien on all nonexempt property of tenant on premises for rents due and to become due provided that, with respect to commercial property, in order to secure a lien for rents that are more than six months due the landlord files a verified statement with clerk of county where building is located. Property can be seized by landlord only if authorized by lease and no breach of peace occurs. A lien arises on property of tenant stored in a bonded warehouse for storage and moving charges. If property is removed and stored in a public warehouse under a writ of possession, the officer executing the writ must at execution deliver in person or by first-class mail to tenant's last known address written notice stating the complete address and telephone number of the location at which the property may be redeemed.

A landlord that leases agricultural land has a preference lien for rent that comes due and money and value of property furnished to a tenant to grow crops on the leased property and to gather, store, and prepare the crop for marketing. The lien exists so long as the crop is on the property and for one month after it is removed. If the crops are placed in a state-regulated warehouse, either public or bonded, before the 31st day after the removal, the lien exists while they are in the warehouse. A landlord may apply for a distress warrant in the Justice of the Peace Court.

UTAH

Landlord has a lien for rent due on all the property of the tenant not exempt from execution while in the building and for 30 days thereafter. Such lien has priority over all other liens except taxes, mortgages for purchase money and labor liens. In case of assignment for benefit of creditors, bankruptcy, or receivership, lien is limited to 90 days' rent prior thereto.

Every innkeeper, hotel keeper, boardinghouse or lodginghouse keeper shall have a lien on the baggage and other property in and about such inn belonging to or under control of his guests or boarders for the proper charges due him for their accommodation, board and lodging, for money paid for or advanced to them, and for such other extras as are furnished at their request. The innkeeper, hotel keeper, boarding-house or lodginghouse keeper may detain such baggage and other property until the amount of such charge is paid, and the baggage and other property shall not be exempt from attachment or execution until the hotel or boardinghouse keeper's lien and the costs of enforcing it are satisfied.

VERMONT

No statutory provisions.

VIRGIN ISLANDS

No statutory provisions, except for hotel keepers.

VIRGINIA

The landlord has a lien for six months' rent on tenant's or subtenant's property found on the premises in a city or town, and not more than 12 months' rent if land or premises are used for farming, or property which may have been removed from the premises not more than 30 days, unless another recorded lien is on the property.

WASHINGTON

Landlord has lien upon personal property of tenant used or kept upon premises for not more than two months' rent (exclusive of property in dwelling units). Landlord with a lien for rent effective for the term of a lease up to five years must file a statement evidencing the lien with the Department of Licensing. Conditional bill of sale or a mortgage has preference over landlords' liens. Landlords' liens on crops have priority over other encumbrances on such crops.

The keeper of any hotel, boarding house or lodging house, whether individual, partnership or corporation, has a lien upon, and may retain, all baggage, sample cases, and other property, lawfully in the possession of a guest, boarder, or lodger, brought upon the premises by such guest, boarder, or lodger, for the proper charges due from him or her, on account of his or her food, board, room rent, lodging and accommodation, and for such extras as are furnished at his or her request, and for all money and credit paid for or advanced to him or her; and for the costs of enforcing such lien; and said hotel keeper, inn keeper, lodging house keeper or boarding house keeper, shall have the right to retain and hold possession of such baggage, sample cases and other property until the amount of such charges and moneys be fully paid, and to sell such baggage, sample cases, or other property for the payment of such lien, charges and moneys; and such baggage, sample cases and property shall not be subject to attachment or execution until such lien and storage charges and the cost of satisfying such lien are fully satisfied

WEST VIRGINIA

Landlords' lien upon any goods of tenant found on premises or removed within 30 days has been held unconstitutional, except if preceded by prior notice and an opportunity to be heard.

The owner or keeper of any hotel, inn, lodginghouse, restaurant, eating house or boardinghouse shall have a lien upon and may retain possession of the baggage, luggage or other personal property of any kind, brought to such hotel, inn, lodginghouse, restaurant, eating house or boardinghouse by, or with the consent of, the owner thereof, for the amount of his lawful claim for lodging, board or other accommodations or facilities furnished by him at that time to such person bringing the same, or to any other person for whose charges the person so bringing such property is liable.

WISCONSIN

No statutory provisions except that landlord has a lien on personal property left on premises for reasonable costs of removal, storage, and disposal.

WYOMING

Any person leasing or renting space for a house trailer site shall have a lien on any house trailer thereon situated for unpaid lease or rental payments and for other unpaid charges due the lessor under the terms or conditions of any lease or rental agreement. The lien shall be effective after the lessee has defaulted in payments as provided in the written rental or lease agreement. Notice of the lien shall be given by the lessor by causing notice in writing to be posted conspicuously on the mobile home. The lien provided by this section shall have priority over all other liens except a previously perfected security interest in the mobile home. At any time after 30 days after notice is given the lessor may remove the house trailer from the leased or rented site and retain the lien as provided by this section. On removal, reasonable charges for the removal and storage may be assessed against the house trailer.

12 Mechanics' Liens

INTRODUCTION

Mechanics' liens are governed by specific statutory provisions in each of the 50 states and the District of Columbia to provide additional protection of payment for workers and suppliers who perform services to improve real or personal property. These laws vary from state to state and are often complex and technical. Mechanics' lien laws require strict compliance.

Anyone who supplies materials or services for the improvement of property needs to learn the basic rights afforded under applicable mechanics' lien law in each state. These laws can help a creditor obtain payment for materials and services by providing a lien on the improved property. These statutes are intended to pay contractors and material suppliers who contribute to the value of the owner's property by furnishing work or materials to a construction project where such materialmen would otherwise be left without recourse.

While the basic concept of the mechanics' lien is universal, every state has created a different statutory scheme to govern who is entitled to a lien, when and how a lien is to be filed or recorded, what information must be provided and what notices must be given and how to protect the lien rights afforded.

Common to all lien statuses is the requirement that a supplier seeking the benefits of the lien law must comply with the strict provisions of the law. This chapter is designed to provide a short synopsis of each state's requirements and is not intended to substitute for the advice and services of qualified legal counsel.

PRIVITY OF CONTRACT

"Privity of contract" exists between the parties to a contract. In the case of a mechanics' lien, the supplier of goods or services may not be in privity with the owner, but the law allows the materialman to impose a lien on the owner's property that has been improved by the goods or services.

The rights granted under mechanics' lien statutes are an exception to the legal principle of privity of contact. The parties to a contract are said to be in privity. The property owner is in privity with the general contractor; the general is in privity with those subcontractors (and only those) with whom the general has dealt directly, and so on down the chain of subcontractors and suppliers.

If there is a dispute between parties to one of these contracts, either one may bring suit to enforce the rights granted under the contract. However, there is no common-law right for an unpaid subcontractor or supplier to bring suit directly against the owner absent a direct contractual relationship with the owner. Where the owner, general contractor, or even a subcontractor fails or refuses to pay someone further down the chain for the work that has been done, a subcontractor or supplier's sole right or remedy may be against the general contractor or another subcontractor who has also not been paid.

The mechanics' lien statutes eliminate the need for privity for a subcontractor or supplier to act directly against the owner's property. Typically, these statutes do not award monetary damages (a money judgment directly against the owner), instead they create rights *in rem* against the owner's property. While it does not assure payment, the lien does allow the subcontractors and suppliers to look to the specific property of the owner in order to collect for work done to improve the owner's property.

Virtually all of the states permit a payment bond to be substituted for the right to file for a mechanics' lien. If a payment bond is posted by the owner or general contractor, a subcontractor's or supplier's rights extend to the bond, and not to the owner or the general contractor, as another exception to privity of contract, and the remedy is strictly limited to collection against the available proceeds on a bond.

HOW MECHANICS' LIENS WORK

The basic questions to determine whether a lien is proper are who is entitled to assert a lien, how it is filed or recorded and what notice is required. These basic issues are addressed more fully in the state-by-state compilation.

Those Entitled to Assert Liens

Contractors, subcontractors, material suppliers, equipment renters, workers, architects, engineers, surveyors and others who contribute services or materials to a construction project are typically entitled to enforce mechanics' lien claims for the value of their work.

To enforce a mechanics' lien, a claimant must prove that it supplied services or materials that were incorporated into the job or that it was employed by the owner, construction manager, architect, engineer, contractor or subcontractor of any tier.

Amount of Lien

Generally, a claimant asserting a mechanics' lien is entitled to the reasonable value of the services or materials supplied to the project or the contract price, whichever is less. In some states, the amount of the lien can be altered by the amount already paid by the owner or other limiting factors. In the event of court action, the prevailing party in mechanics' lien litigation typically recovers its costs of suit and, in some states, its attorneys' fees.

Notice of Lien

Many states now require that a supplier of goods or services provide a "notice to owner" prior to, or shortly after, the initial provision of goods or services. The failure to provide this notice to the owner prior to a particular job may totally defeat the mechanics' lien claim. Additionally, every state requires a notice (or claim) after there has been a failure to make a timely payment. The time limit is usually tied to the last date when the goods or services have been supplied to a particular job. The definition of "last date" varies by state, and is usually defined by court decisions rather than the statute itself. **There are very strict time limitations as to when notice must be given both before and after the supplying of goods and services. Additionally, there are equally strict limitations regarding who must be notified** of the possible assertion of a mechanics' lien claim. **Careful attention must be paid to these limitations.**

Filing of Lien

The form used to make a claim for a mechanics' lien itself is usually simple enough. Typically, the person signing on behalf of the claimant does so under penalty of perjury that the statements made in the claim are true. A claimant records the claim of lien in the county office (or, in some states, actually files a claim of lien in the county clerk's office), to create a lien of record. The title to the property is then subject to the claimant's mechanics' lien and persons taking title to the property are on notice that the claimant may have rights to the land (which may be superior to the person taking title).

The right to assert a mechanics' lien attaches to property immediately when a claimant has supplied services, equipment or materials to a project, creating a cloud on the title, because a claimant *might* record a claim of lien. Since the right exists prior to the deadline for filing or recording the actual lien, states have set relatively short periods of time within which a claimant is required to file its lien; this limits the period of uncertainty when claims might be filed.

Priority of Liens

Time. In many states, lien claims take priority not from the time when they are recorded, but from an earlier date. Such claims are said to "relate back" to the date provided by statute. In some states, liens relate back to the actual physical visible commencement of construction on the property. In those states, if construction work commences on a project on January 2, and a painting contractor starts work the following October and records a claim of lien in December, the claim of lien would take its priority from January 2. In other states, a claim of lien relates back to when the claimant first delivered work or materials to a project. In such a state, in our example, the claim of the painting contractor would take its priority from the commencement of painting work in October rather than from the commencement of construction work in January.

Seniority or Rank. In some states, a mechanics' lien is superior to all other liens except other mechanics' liens, ahead of construction loans, permanent mortgages and other similar loans even if the other liens are earlier, or more senior, than the lien. The mechanics' lien has significant value in this case, because the construction lender will usually satisfy the lien claim rather than face losing seniority. In other states, the mechanics' lien laws merely create rights in the owner's property subject to and subordinate to prior existing liens and subordinate to and behind all prior existing liens. Finally, in most states, all mechanics' lien claims on one project have the same priority no matter when the work was done or the claim recorded.

ENFORCEMENT OF MECHANICS' LIENS

Each state law provides the mechanism for enforcing a mechanics' lien once it has been obtained. A mechanics' lien usually does not have an infinite life span, and states typically require that a formal action be brought to enforce the lien within a specified period of time or else it will be lost.

After the filing procedure, a mechanics' lien claimant must proceed to enforce the claim against the owner's property. The necessary steps under most state laws to enforce the mechanics' lien after filing are beyond the scope of this survey. Briefly, though, these steps are typically (1) a legal proceeding against the contractor, owner or others to obtain judgment and, in most instances, filing a notice of *lis pendens*; (2) judgment of foreclosure, in which the court may also determine the priority of the mechanics' lien claim relative to other, competing liens or mortgages; and (3) an official sale of the owner's property to the highest bidder at public auction. Mechanics' lien holders should carefully consider the benefits of holding a sale of such property, because prior liens and expenses, along with a realistic appraisal of the auction price, will greatly effect the ultimate collection.

GLOSSARY

The following glossary of terms may be helpful in understanding lien process. Of course, the terminology and procedures will vary from state to state, with some required and other possibly not utilized at all.

Notice of Commencement. A notice of commencement or notice of contract is a document filed or recorded by the owner or general contractor to give notice that work has commenced. The proper filing or recording of this notice usually triggers a requirement that potential mechanics' lien claimants give a preliminary notice to the owner in order to preserve their rights under the mechanics' lien statute.

Preliminary Notice. A mechanics' lien claimant typically must give a preliminary notice to the property owner and others that work is beginning. The notice will inform the owner that the claimant is furnishing work or materials to the project and, if unpaid, reserves the right to record a claim of lien. The notice usually must disclose the name and address of the potential claimant, the type of work or materials being supplied, and sometimes includes an estimate of the value of the work or materials to be supplied. A claimant who fails to give the required preliminary notice within the time specified by statute may lose the right to claim a mechanics' lien, even if it is shown that the owner had actual knowledge that the claimant was supplying work or materials to the project, because the purpose of the notice is not to tell the owner that work is being performed, but to notify the owner that the claimant reserves the right to record a claim of lien.

Claim of Lien. The mechanics' lien claim is filed with the clerk or recorded in the county recorder's office. It usually includes the name of the claimant, the amount of the claim, and a description of the property where the project is located. The claim of lien must be filed or recorded promptly, usually 30 to 120 days after the completion of the work. Only the rare state allows a length of time as long as eight months to file the lien.

Notice of Completion. A notice of completion gives notice that the construction project has been completed and therefore potential lien claimants must act promptly to preserve their rights. The notice of completion usually must be recorded within a few days after the completion of the project and is used to reduce the time limit for recording a claim of lien.

Notice of Cessation. When a contractor walks off a job or is thrown off a job the owner may be permitted to file a notice of cessation to limit exposure to lien claims even though the job is not complete.

Foreclosure Suit. The foreclosure suit is the mechanism for preserving and establishing the lien. Typically, the suit must be filed in a short time and the claimant must prove it is entitled to assert a mechanics' lien claim. If the claimant fails to file suit or establish its claim, the court dissolves the lien.

Notice of Lis Pendens. A notice of *lis pendens* provides notice in the real estate records that the foreclosure has been commenced. It gives notice that anyone dealing with the property will take title subject to the outcome of the foreclosure suit.

Sheriff's Sale. The sheriff, under a court order, advertises the property for sale at public auction to the highest bidder to satisfy the lien. The highest bidder pays the sheriff, who distributes the purchase price to lien claimants, or as directed by the court.

CONTRACTUAL PROVISIONS PROHIBITING MECHANICS' LIENS

In some instances, an owner will attempt to provide by contract that no mechanics' liens may be imposed by a subcontractor or supplier. Such a provision may or may not be enforceable depending on the interpretation of the laws of a particular state and the facts and circumstances of the situation.

OTHER CONSIDERATIONS AND LIMITATIONS

Some states limit the owner's liability to a subcontractor or supplier to the unpaid portion of the original contract. If the owner has paid its general contractor a substantial portion of the contract price, the owner may be responsible only for a limited amount of the debt, even where the general contractor has not paid subcontractors and suppliers. These statutes are hardest on those subcontractors and suppliers providing goods and services at the end of the job (such as painting and landscaping suppliers and subcontractors) as opposed to those providing goods and services at the beginning of the job, because the owner may have paid a substantial portion of the contract price before the later suppliers even begin the job.

OTHER REMEDIES AVAILABLE TO SUBCONTRACTOR

Subcontractors and materialmen may have additional remedies in some states.

Stop Notices

Some states have created stop notice rights on private projects. While a mechanics' lien creates a security interest in real estate, a stop notice claim is a security interest in construction funds. Any person (e.g., owner, construction lender, insurance company, escrow) holding funds for the construction may be served with a stop notice. Parties with mechanics' lien rights also have stop notice rights. A stop notice must be served properly, usually by personal, certified or registered mail. The deadline for service of a stop notice is generally the same as the deadline for recording a claim of mechanics' lien. In some states, a stop notice may be given even before the work is completed or the materials supplied.

A stop notice expires unless a timely action to enforce it is filed in the proper court. The time limit for filing an action to enforce a stop notice is comparable to the period under the mechanics' lien laws. The stop notice establishes rights of the claimant higher in priority than the rights of the one holding the construction funds to utilize the funds in the construction loan account for the completion of the project. Service of a stop notice essentially effects a garnishment of construction funds. This means that the holder of the funds must set aside a sufficient amount to answer the stop notice claim, or ultimately be liable to the claimant if its claim is not satisfied.

Equitable Lien

In some cases, a subcontractor or materialman may be entitled to an equitable lien. This remedy available in equity generally arises when the subcontractor relies upon the representations of the one providing the funding for the construction project (e.g., the construction lender) and proceeds to render services or provide materials to the project. Where the subcontractor performed its work in reliance on the representation that construction funds existed, and that reliance was partly induced by the construction lender who confirmed the existence and amount of the construction loan account, the contractor may assert an *equitable lien* on the construction loan account under state law in favor of the subcontractor or supplier.

Claims against Payment Bond

In some instances, an owner may require the general contractor to provide a bond that guarantees that the general contractor will *pay* for all work required by the construction contract. The bond ensures that the general contractor will pay subcontractors and suppliers, and may create a right to payment for sub-subcontractors and their suppliers. Private bonds, however, can legally be limited in who is given the protection of the bond and in how much will be paid; the terms of the bond will determine whether a lien claimant can make a claim on the bond.

PUBLIC WORKS

Mechanics' liens generally deal with and involve private construction—i.e., nongovernmental construction. Federally owned public lands are, almost without exception, not subject to liens of this sort. Chapter 13, discusses mandatory payment bonds required when labor and materials supplied to projects owned by governments.

The Miller Act (40 USC § 270(a)) was enacted to require that general contractors on federal projects furnish payment bonds for the protection of those who supply work or materials to such projects. Amendments to The Miller Act effective in March, 2000 provide greater protection to subcontractors on federal projects. One change eliminated the cap on the penal sum of the bond which had been capped at $2.5 million. It requires that the bond at least equal the full dollar amount of the work to be performed under the subcontract. The contracting officer may require a greater bond but at least the subcontractor will be protected to at least the full value of the work performed. A second change eliminates the option for the subcontractor to waive rights under The Miller Act. Previously, some general contractors would require such a waiver from the subcontractor.

Most states have a "Little Miller Act" for the claims of laborers and material suppliers on state and local public works projects. Nevertheless, since each state has differing statutes, it is imperative for a potential lien claimant to check its particular state statute to determine whether or not a mechanics' lien will be necessary in connection with a public project which is owned by a state or local municipality as opposed to one owned by the federal government.

It should be noted that when mechanics' liens are permitted against public projects, the requirements for notification and filing will differ from those requirements on private projects.

In this chapter, the term "mechanics' lien" refers to the lien authorized by statute to attach to private land.

SUMMARY OF STATE LAWS GOVERNING MECHANICS' LIENS

The editors have attempted to verify that the synopsis of each state's statutes concerning mechanics' liens is up to date. Significant differences among the states regarding when the legislature is in session and when new laws are reported means that legislative changes may exist that are not listed here.

It is emphasized again that the material contained herein is only a summary of state laws. The statutory framework in each state is continually supplemented by judicial decisions, which are outside the scope of this work. The editors urge all users of the *Manual* to use it only as a guide, and read the latest state law for recent changes or consult with counsel to determine your rights.

ALABAMA

Who May Claim—Every mechanic, person, firm or corporation who does or performs any work or labor upon, or furnish any material, fixture, engine, boiler, waste disposal services and equipment or machinery for any building or improvement on land, or for repairing, altering or beautifying the same, under or by virtue of any contract with the owner or proprietor thereof, or his agent, architect, trustee, contractor or subcontractor, upon complying with the provisions of this division, shall have a lien therefor on such building or improvements, and on the land on which the same is situated. A lien is also granted to persons, firms, or corporations who perform work on, or furnish material for paving, gutter or other improvements in or on any public street or other public way, etc., such land.

How Claimed—It shall be the under or by virtue of any contract with the abutting land owner or proprietor, and if the amount involved exceeds $100. There is also a lien granted to persons, firms or corporations who rent or lease appliances, machinery or equipment to another for use in the construction of a building or improvement on land or in repairing, altering or beautifying the same or for use in clearing, excavating duty of every person entitled to such lien to file a statement in writing, verified by the oath of the person claiming the lien, or of some other person having knowledge of the facts.

Where Filed—Office of the Judge of Probate of the county in which the property upon which the lien is sought to be established is situated.

When to Be Filed—Every general contractor within six months, every journeyman and day laborer within 30 days and every other person entitled to such a lien within four months after the last item of work has been performed or the last item of material has been furnished.

Service of Prior Notice—Every person, except the original contractor, who may wish to avail himself of the provisions of this division, shall, before filing his statement in the Office of the Judge of Probate, give notice in writing to the owner or proprietor, or his agent, that he claims a lien on such building or improvement. But the provisions of this section shall not apply to the case of any material furnished for such building or improvement, of which the owner was notified in advance, as provided in paragraph 9 below.

Duration of Lien—Generally, any action for the enforcement of the lien must be commenced within six months after the maturity of the entire indebtedness secured thereby in the circuit court having jurisdiction in the county in which the property is situated.

Filing Fee—Fifteen cents per 100 words.

Contents of Statement of Lien—The verified statement must contain the amount of the demand secured by the lien, after all just credits have been given, a description of the property on which the lien is claimed in such a manner that same may be located or identified, and the name of the owner or proprietor. No error in amount or name of the owner shall affect the lien. Anyone other than the original contractor must first give written notice to the owner or proprietor or his agent that he claims a lien and shall state the amount, for what, and from whom it is owing. *See* paragraph 5 above. There is a statutory form for this verified statement.

Extent of Lien—The contractor's lien extends to all the right, title and interest of the owner or proprietor and to the extent in area of the entire lot or parcel of land in a city or town; or if not in a city or town, of one acre in addition to the land upon which the building or improvement is situated; or if employees of the contractor or persons furnishing material to him, the lien shall extend only to the amount of any unpaid balance due the contractor by the owner or proprietor at the time the notice required by paragraph 5 above is given unless he notifies the owner or proprietor before furnishing any material that he will furnish the contractor with certain materials at certain specified prices. If the owner does not disclaim responsibility for the price before the materials are used, the subcontractor or materialman shall have a lien for the full price regardless of whether the amount of the claim exceeds the unpaid balance due the contractor.

Priority of Lien—Such lien as to the land and buildings or improvements thereon, shall have priority over all other liens, mortgages or encumbrances created subsequent to the commencement of work on the building or improvement; and as to liens, mortgages or encumbrances created prior to the commencement of the work, the lien for such work shall have priority only against the building, or improvement, the product of such work which is an entirety, separable from the land, building or improvement subject to the prior lien, mortgage or encumbrance, and which can be removed therefrom without impairing the value or security of any prior lien, mortgage or encumbrance; and the person entitled to such lien may have it enforced, at any time prior to the foreclosure of such prior lien, mortgage or encumbrance, by a sale of such buildings or improvement under the provisions of this division and the purchaser may, within a reasonable time thereafter, remove the same. The separability and non-impairment requirements may create severe obstacles to recovery of a lien.

A mechanics' lien will be terminated if it is not enforced prior to foreclosure of an encumbrance having priority over the mechanics' lien.

Public Improvements—See Chapter 13.

Leased Land—A claimant may obtain a lien under a contract with a lessee in possession for building or improvement when the work is done in accordance with the terms of the unexpired lease. The lien-holder may avoid forfeiture upon the lessee's violation of the lease terms by paying rent to the lessor when due, or doing other acts which the lessee is bound to do. If the lien is enforced by sale, the claimant is entitled to reimbursement for any payments of rent or other pecuniary compensation to the lessor which should have been paid to the lessee.

Statutory Citation—Code of Alabama, Title 35, Chapter 11, Division 8, §§ 35-11-210 to 35-11-234.

ALASKA

Who May Claim—A person is entitled to a lien if he (1) performs labor upon real property at the request of the owner or his agent for the construction, alteration or repair of a building or improvement; (2) is a trustee of an employee benefit trust for the benefit of individuals performing labor on the building or improvement and has a direct contract with the owner or his agent for direct payments into the trust; (3) furnishes materials that are delivered to real property under a contract with the owner or his agent which are incorporated in the construction, alteration or repair of a building or improvement; (4) furnishes equipment that is delivered to real property under a contract with the owner or his agent that are incorporated in the construction, alteration or repair of a building or improvement; (5) performs services under a contract with the owner or his agent in connection with the preparation of plans, surveys or architectural or engineering plans or drawings for the construction, alteration or repair of a building or improvement, whether or not actually implemented on that property; or (6) is a general contractor.

How Claimed—A claimant may provide the owner with a written notice of right to lien before furnishing labor, material, service or equipment for a project, or the claimant will (1) bear the burden of proving that the owner knew of and consented to the furnishing of the labor, materials, service or equipment, and (2) bear the risk of not being notified of the completion date of the project and losing the ability to make a timely lien claim. The notice must be in writing, state that it is a notice of a right to assert a lien against real property for labor, materials, services or equipment furnished in connection with a project, and must contain a legal description sufficient for identification of the real property upon which the building or other improvement is located, the name of the owner, the name and address of the claimant, the name and address of the person with whom the claimant contracted, a general description of the labor, materials, services or equipment provided or to be provided, and a statement that the claimant may be entitled to record a claim of lien. In addition, the notice must contain the following statement in type no smaller than that used for the preceding information:

WARNING

Unless provision is made for payment of sums that may be due to the undersigned, your above property may be subject to foreclosure to satisfy those sums even though you may pay a prime contractor or other person for the labor, material, services, or equipment furnished by the undersigned.

In all cases, the claim of lien must be verified and contain the following information: (1) sufficient legal description of the real property concerned; (2) name of the owner; (3) name and address of the lien claimant; (4) name and address of the party with whom the claimant contracted; (5) general description of the labor, materials, services or equipment furnished for the construction, alteration or repair, and the contract price of the labor, materials, services or equipment; (6) amount due the claimant for the labor, materials, services or equipment; (7) date the last labor, materials, services or equipment was furnished; (8) lien shall be verified by the oath of the claimant or another person having knowledge of the fact and state.

Where Filed—Recorder of the recording district in which the land, building, or other improvement is located.

When to Be Filed—A notice of right to lien or a claim of lien may be recorded at any time after the claimant enters into a contract for or first furnishes labor, material, services or equipment in connection with the project. In no event may a lien claim be recorded more than 90 days after the claimant completes the construction contract or ceases to furnish labor, material, services or equipment for the construction, alteration, or repair of the owner's property.

An owner may reduce the time period for lien claims by giving at least five days' notice of his intent to record a notice of completion to persons who have given notice of right to lien or a stop-lending notice and then recording a statutory notice of completion not sooner than five days later. A claimant who has received the notice or who has not given notice of right to lien has 15 days from the recording of the notice of completion to record a claim of lien.

Duration of Lien—A lien is lost unless suit is brought in the superior court within six months after the claim has been filed. If an extension notice is recorded during the original six-month period, then suit must be brought within six months after the recording. A notice of extension must be recorded in the same recording office as the initial claim and contain the original recording date, book and page or instrument number of the initial claim of lien, and the balance owing.

Filing Fee—First page $10; each additional page $3; indexing each name over six, $2.

Extent of Lien—The building or improvement, along with the land upon which the building or other improvement is constructed, together with a convenient space about the building or other improvement or so much as is required for the convenient use and occupation of it if, at the time the work is started or the materials for the building or other improvements are first furnished, the land belongs to the person who causes the building or other improvement to be constructed, altered or repaired. If the person owns less than a fee simple estate in the land, then only the interest of the person in it is subject to the lien. No claimant may collect more than the amount due under the general contract.

Priority of Lien—A lien in favor of an individual actually performing original construction labor or the trustee of an employee benefit trust for such individuals has priority over prior recorded encumbrances. All other liens are subject to prior recorded encumbrances. Lien claims are awarded a priority of payment by classification among themselves: (1) individuals who provide labor other than prime or subcontractors; (2) trustees for employee benefit trusts for such individuals; (3) materialmen and subcontractors; (4) prime contractors other than general contractors and architects, engineers, surveyors and draftsman; (5) persons who perform services under a contract with the owner or the agent of the owner in connection with the preparation of plans, surveys or architectural or engineering plans or drawings for the construction, alteration or repair of a building or improvement, whether or not actually implemented on that property and prime contractors other than the general contractor.

Public Improvements—See Chapter 13.

Lien for Improvement of Oil or Gas Well—Work done at the instance of the owner gives rise to a lien upon a mine or mining claim, oil, gas or other well, so long as the property is in one mass and can be identified as being produced by the labor of the lienor.

Stop-Lending Notice—A claimant to whom payment is past due may give the construction lender a stop-lending notice. A copy must be given to the owner and to each prime contractor with or through whom the claimant or the claimant's debtor contracted. The notice must be verified by the claimant; instruct the lender to stop lending; state the claimant's name, address and telephone number; describe the labor, material, services or equipment furnished, and the name of the person to whom furnished; describe the real property improved and the name of the person believed to be the owner and the amount due and unpaid to the claimant. A stop-lending notice expires on the 91st day after it is received by the lender unless the claimant has commenced an action on the claim before that day, and the lender has received written notice of the action. In addition, a stop-lending notice may be revoked at any time in writing with the signature of the claimant. If the stop-lending notice expires or is revoked, there is no bank liability. The lender may make further disbursements by determining its statutory liability and setting aside the funds to cover that liability. A lender receiving a stop-lending notice or notice of right to lien for which it is not the lender must give written notice to the claimant within 10 days that it is not the lender.

Statutory Citation—Alaska Statute, Title 34, Chapter 34.35, §§ 34.35.050 to 34.35.120.

ARIZONA

Who May Claim—Except for an owner-occupied dwelling or when payment bond in lieu of lien recorded as per statute, every person who labors or furnishes professional services (holding a valid certificate of registration and has a written contract with the owner of the property or with an architect who has a written agreement with the owner of the property), materials, machinery, fixtures or tools to be used in the construction, alteration or repair of any building or other structure or improvement whatever, shall have a lien thereon for the work or labor done or professional services, materials, machinery, fixture or tools furnished, whether said work was done, or article furnished, at the instance of the owner of the building, structure or improvement, or his agent. Every contractor, subcontractor, architect, builder or other person having charge or control of the construction, alteration or repair, either in whole or in part, of any building, structure or improvement, is the agent of the owner and the owner shall be liable for the reasonable value of labor or materials furnished to his agent. A person furnishing professional services, material or labors on a lot in an incorporated city or town, or on any parcel of land not exceeding 160 acres in the aggregate or fills in or otherwise improves the lot or such parcel of land or an alley or street or proposed alley or street, within, in front of or adjoining such lot or parcel of land at the instance of the owner of the lot or parcel of land shall have a lien for the professional services or material furnished and labor performed. Right of lien is also given for labor or materials used in construction or repair of canals, ditches, aqueducts, bridges, fences, roads, excavations, railroads, etc., and in connection with mines and mining claims. Persons rendering professional services, defined as agricultural practice, engineering practice, or land survey practice, shall have mechanics' lien rights so long as such person holds a valid certificate of registration and has an agreement with the owner of the property. Also, a person required to be licensed as contractor who does not hold a valid license as required shall not have lien rights.

How Claimed—Every person entitled to a lien shall serve the owner or reputed owner, the original contractor or reputed contractor and the construction lender, if any, or reputed construction lender, if any, and the person with whom the claimant has contracted for the purchase of those items, with a written preliminary notice within 20 days after the claimant has first furnished labor, professional services, materials, machinery, fixtures or tools for the job site. Notice may be served by first class mail with certificate of mailing, registered or certified mail, addressed to the person to whom notice is to be given at his residence or business address. Within 10 days after receipt of a written request from any person or his agent intending to file a preliminary 20-day notice, which request shall identify the person, his address, the job site and the general nature of the person's labor, professional services, materials, machinery or tools to which the preliminary 20-day notice shall apply, or within 10 days of the receipt of a preliminary 20-day notice, the owner or other interested party shall furnish such person a written statement of: (1) legal description, subdivision plat, street address, location with respect to commonly known roads or other landmarks in the area, or any other description of the job site sufficient for identification; (2) name and address of the owner or reputed owner; (3) name and address of the original contractor or reputed contractor; (4) name and address of the construction lender, if any, or reputed construction lender; (5) if any payment bond in lieu of lien right has been recorded, a copy of the bond and the name and address of the surety company and bonding agent, if any, providing the payment bond.

Failure of the owner or other interested party to furnish the information required by this section does not excuse any claimant from timely giving a preliminary 20-day notice, but it does stop the owner from raising as a defense any inaccuracy of such information in a preliminary 20-day notice, provided the claimant's notice of lien otherwise complies with the provisions of this chapter. If the information is received by the claimant after the claimant has given a preliminary 20-day notice and the information contained in the 20-day notice is inaccurate, the claimant shall, within 30 days of the receipt of this information, serve an amended notice in the manner provided in this section. Such amended notice shall be considered as having been given at the same time as the original notice, except that the amended preliminary notice shall be effective only as to work performed, materials supplied or professional services rendered 20 days prior to the date of the amended preliminary notice or the date the original preliminary notice was served on the owner, whichever occurs first.

Any contractor, subcontractor or other person who is obligated by statute, contract or agreement to defend, remove, compromise or pay any claim of lien or action and who undertakes such activity has the rights of the owner and beneficial title holder against all persons concerning such activity, as specified in Sections 33-420 and 33-994.

If a payment bond in lieu of lien right has been recorded and the owner or other interested party fails to furnish a copy of the bond and the other interested party fails to furnish a copy of the bond and the other information as required by this section, the claimant shall retain lien rights to the extent precluded or prejudiced from asserting a claim against the bond as a direct result of not timely receiving a copy of the bond and the other information from the owner or other interested party.

Where Filed—With the County Recorder of the county in which the property or some part thereof is located.

When to Be Filed—Claimants must file within 120 days after completion, alteration or repair of building, structure or improvement. If Notice of Completion has been recorded, claimants have 60 days to file. Completion for lien purposes, depending on whether improvement is residential or commercial, is the earliest of: (a) 30 days after final inspection and acceptance by government body issuing building permit; or (b) cessation of labor for 60 consecutive days, except due to strike, shortage of materials or act of God.

Service of Copy of Notice—Upon the owner or owners of said building, structure or improvement, if he can be found within the county, within a reasonable time after recording.

Duration of Lien—Six months after the recording thereof in the County Recorder's office, unless suit is brought within such period to enforce the lien.

Filing Fee—$5 for the first five pages, $1 for each additional page, not to exceed $250.

Contents of Notice of Lien—(1) Legal description of the lands and improvements to be charged with the lien. (2) Name of the owner or reputed owner of the property, if known, and also the name of the person by whom the lienor was employed or to whom he furnished materials. (3) Statement of the terms, time given and conditions of his contract, if the same be oral, or a copy of the contract, if written. (4) Statement of the lienor's demand, after deducting all just credits and offsets. (5) Statement of date of completion of the building, structure, or improvement or any alteration or repair of the building, structure or improvement. Completion is defined as earlier of: (a) 30 days after final inspection and written final acceptance by government body issuing the building permit; or (b) cessation of labor for 60 consecutive days except due to strike, act of God or shortage of materials. (6) Date preliminary notice served, with copy of notice attached and required proof of mailing attached.

On multi-unit residential projects, each separate building is considered a separate work and the lien rights extend only from the time of work on that building.

Claim of lien must be made under oath by the claimant or by someone in his behalf who has knowledge of the facts.

The general contractor, supplier or subcontractor's 20-day preliminary notice must contain: (1) A general description of the labor, professional services, materials, machinery, fixtures or tools furnished or to be furnished, and an estimate of the total price thereof. If price exceeds estimate by 20 percent, new preliminary notice is required. (2) Name and address of the person furnishing such labor, professional services, materials, machinery, fixtures or tools. (3) Name of the person who contracted for purchase of such labor, professional services materials, machinery, fixtures or tools. (4) Legal description, subdivision plat, street address, location with respect to commonly known roads or other landmarks in the area or any other description of the job site sufficient for identification. (5) The following statement in bold-face type:

In accordance with Arizona Revised Statutes Section 33-992.01, this is not a lien, and this is not a reflection on the integrity of any contractor or subcontractor.

NOTICE TO PROPERTY OWNER

If bills are not paid in full for the labor, professional services, materials, machinery, fixtures or tools furnished or to be furnished, a mechanics' lien leading to the loss, through court foreclosure proceedings, of all or part of your property being improved may be placed against the property.

You may wish to protect yourself against the consequence by either:

1. **Requiring your contractor to furnish a conditional waiver and release pursuant to ARS Section 33-1008, subsection D, paragraphs 1 and 3 signed by the person or firm giving you this notice before you make payment to your contractor.**

2. **Requiring your contractor to furnish an unconditional waiver and release pursuant to ARS Section 33-1008, subsection D, paragraphs 2 and 4 signed by the person or firm giving you this notice after you make payment to your contractor.**

3. **Using any other method or device which is appropriate under the circumstances.**

Within 10 days of the receipt of this preliminary 20-day notice, the owner or other interested party is required to furnish all information necessary to correct any inaccuracies in the notice pursuant to Arizona Revised Statutes section 33-992.01, subsection I or lose as a defense any inaccuracy of that information.

Within 10 days of the receipt of this preliminary 20-day notice, if any payment bond has been recorded in compliance with Arizona Revised Statutes section 33-1003, the owner must provide a copy of the payment bond including the name and address of the surety company and bonding agent providing the payment bond to the person who has given the preliminary 20-day notice. In the event that the owner or other interested party fails to provide the bond information within that 10-day period, the claimant shall retain lien rights to the extent precluded or prejudiced from asserting a claim against the bond as a result of not timely receiving the bond information.

Dated: _____

_____
(Company name)

By: _____
(Signature)

_____
(Title)

If the notice is given later than 20 days, any lien cannot apply to labor, materials, machinery, fixtures or tools furnished beyond 20 days prior to the giving of notice. The notice may be served by delivering it personally, by leaving it at the residence or place of business of the person to be served with some person of suitable age and discretion residing or working there, or by first-class, registered or certified mail, postage prepaid, addressed to the person to whom notice is given at his residence or business address.

Extent of Lien—If land lies outside the limits of the recorded map or plat of a town site, an incorporated city or town, or a subdivision, the lien extends to and includes not exceeding 10 acres of land upon which the improvement is made and the labor performed. If land lies within said limits, the lien extends to and includes only the particular lot or lots upon which the improvement is made and the labor performed. The lien upon a mining claim extends to the whole of the claim and to the group of which said claim is a part, if the group is operated as one property.

Priority of Lien—These liens are preferred to all liens, mortgages or other encumbrances which shall have attached upon the property subsequent to the time the labor was commenced or the materials commenced to be furnished, except any mortgage or deed of trust that is given as security for a loan made by a construction lender as defined in Section 33-992.01(A)(1), if the mortgage or deed of trust is recorded within 10 days after labor was commenced or the materials commenced to be furnished. These liens are also preferred to all liens, mortgages or other encumbrances of which the lienholder has no actual or constructive notice at the time he commenced the labor or the furnishing of materials, except any mortgage or deed of trust that is given as security for a loan made by a construction lender as defined in Section 33-992.01(A)(1), if the mortgage or deed of trust is recorded within 10 days after labor was commenced or the materials commenced to be furnished. All liens of this character shall attach upon an equal footing, without reference to date of recording the notice and claim of lien and without reference to time or for forming such work and labor or furnishing the professional service or material. If a lien is foreclosed and the proceeds are insufficient to discharge all liens against the property without reference to the date of recording, the proceeds shall be prorated over the respective liens that have equal footing with the foreclosing lien.

Public Improvements—See Chapter 13.

Lien for Improvement of Oil or Gas Well—When separately owned property is embraced within one established drilling unit, and a pooling of interests is established, the owner drilling and operating for the benefit of others has a lien on the share of production from the unit accruing to the interest of each of the owners for the payment of his share of the expenses.

Separate and Different Provisions—Different provisions exist for dwelling units of single one family or single two family for residential purposes, if qualified as owner occupied. Liens only allowed for claimants having written, executed contracts with owner.

Statutory Citation—Arizona Revised Statutes, Chapter 7, Article 6, §§ 33-981 to 33-1008.

ARKANSAS

Who May Claim—Every contractor, subcontractor or material supplier as defined in the statute who supplies labor, services, material, fixtures, engines, boilers or machinery in the construction or repair of an improvement to real estate or any boat or vessel of any kind [see liens on personal property], by virtue of a contract with the owner, proprietor, contractor or subcontractor, or agent thereof, upon complying with the provisions of the code, shall have a lien upon the improvement and up to one acre of land upon which the improvement is located in order to secure payment, or to the extent of any number of acres of land upon which work has been done or improvements erected or repairs. The code defines contractor as one who deals directly with the person holding an interest in real estate, a subcontractor is defined as any person who supplies labor or services pursuant to a contract with contractor or to a first tier subcontractor and a material supplier is one who supplies materials, goods, fixtures or to a person in direct privity of contract with such person. The statute specifically requires a contractor or subcontractor to provide information sufficient to permit the lien to be filed.

How Claimed—By filing verified account, showing balance due after allowing all credits, describing the property (legal description) upon which the lien is claimed, and naming the person authorized to release the lien. Verified by affidavit.

Where Filed—Office of Clerk of the Circuit Court of county where property is situated.

When to Be Filed—Within 120 days after labor was performed or material furnished.

Service of Copy of Notice—While commercial projects, bonded projects, and direct sale contracts are supposed to be exempt under Arkansas law from the Pre-Construction Notice, until more case law is developed under the 1995 revisions to the Arkansas Materialmen's Lien Act, prudent parties in the construction process should consider every project as subject to the Pre-Construction Notice requirement and provide the notice required by Ark. Code Ann. §18-44-115(c). This Pre-Construction Notice to the owner must be provided in accordance with the statute, which notice must be provided prior to the performance of work. The notice may be effected by personal delivery or by certified mail. If the notice is given by personal delivery, there must be a signature of the owner or the owner's authorized agent. It is the obligation of the contractor to give the owner the notice, but any potential lien claimant may also give the notice in order to ensure that it is given. It is absolutely clear under Arkansas law that no lien may be asserted on residential property unless the owner has received this Pre-Construction Notice. The notice may be incorporated into the contract, affixed thereto, and shall be conspicuous and worded exactly as stated, in capital letters.

Assuming that a party on a commercial project does not provide the Pre-Construction Notice, in order to obtain and perfect a lien on commercial property, the lien claimant must strictly comply with statutorily required steps.

In order to assert the lien, within 75 days of the last date that labor was performed or materials were supplied to the project, a Notice to Owner and Contractor must be served on the property owner and the general contractor by either an officer authorized by law to serve process in civil actions or by registered mail, return receipt requested. The notice must contain a description of the labor or materials furnished, the amount due, the name and address of the person claiming the lien, the name and address of the person who has failed to pay the lien claimant, and a description of the job site sufficiently to identify it. The Notice to Owner and Contractor must duplicate statutory notice language that includes the following statement set out in boldface type:

Notice to property owner: If bills for labor, services, or materials used to construct an improvement to real estate are not paid in full, a construction lien may be placed against the property. This could result in the loss, through foreclosure proceedings, of all or part of your real estate being improved. This may occur even though you have paid your contractor in full. You may wish to protect yourself against this consequence by paying the above-named provider of labor, services, or materials directly, or making your check payable to the above-named provider and contractor jointly.

Next, in order to assert the lien, 10 days' notice must also be given to the owner or agent , and the notice must state the amount and the basis for the claim. The notice may be served by any officer authorized by law to serve process in civil actions, or by any person who would be a competent witness or by any form of mail addressed to the person served with the return receipt and delivery restricted to the addressee or the agent for the addressee. If delivery of a mailed notice is refused, the person holding the claim shall immediately mail to the owner or the owner's agent a copy of the notice by first class mail and may proceed to file a lien. Notice in cases where the owner is a nonresident of the county or state, where the owner has no agent in the county where the property is situated or where the owner conceals or absents themselves, should be filed with a recorder of deeds of the county where the property is situated.

Duration of Lien—Suit must be filed within 15 months from filing of lien.

Filing Fee—$8.

Contents of Pre-Construction Notice of Lien—As set forth above, the following Pre-Construction Notice must be provided to the owner in order to assert a claim. The notice must be exactly as prescribed below:

[Generally, this notice is required only with respect to the construction of or improvement to residential real estate containing four or fewer units, but as indicated above prudent parties on a commercial project will likewise give the Pre-Construction Notice.]

IMPORTANT NOTICE TO OWNER

I UNDERSTAND THAT EACH PERSON SUPPLYING MATERIAL OR FIXTURES IS ENTITLED TO A LIEN AGAINST PROPERTY IF NOT PAID IN FULL FOR MATERIALS USED TO IMPROVE THE PROPERTY EVEN THOUGH THE FULL CONTRACT PRICE MAY HAVE BEEN PAID TO THE CONTRACTOR. I REALIZE THAT THIS LIEN CAN BE ENFORCED BY THE SALE OF THE PROPERTY IF NECESSARY. I AM ALSO AWARE THAT PAYMENT MAY BE WITHHELD TO THE CONTRACTOR IN THE AMOUNT OF THE COST OF ANY MATERIALS OR LABOR NOT PAID FOR. I KNOW THAT IT IS ADVISABLE TO, AND I MAY, REQUIRE THE CONTRACTOR TO FURNISH TO ME A TRUE AND CORRECT FULL LIST OF ALL SUPPLIERS UNDER THE CONTRACT, AND I MAY CHECK WITH THEM TO DETERMINE IF ALL MATERIALS FURNISHED FOR THE PROPERTY HAVE BEEN PAID FOR. I MAY ALSO REQUIRE THE CONTRACTOR TO PRESENT LIEN WAIVERS BY ALL SUPPLIERS, STATING THAT THEY HAVE BEEN PAID IN FULL FOR SUPPLIES PROVIDED UNDER THE CONTRACT, BEFORE I PAY THE CONTRACTOR IN FULL. IF A SUPPLIER HAS NOT BEEN PAID, I MAY PAY THE SUPPLIER AND CONTRACTOR WITH A CHECK MADE PAYABLE TO THEM.

SIGNED: _____

_____
Address of Property

DATE: _____

—I HEREBY CERTIFY THAT THE SIGNATURE ABOVE IS THAT OF THE OWNER OR AGENT OF THE OWNER OF THE PROPERTY AT THE ADDRESS SET OUT ABOVE.

SIGNED: _____
Contractor

If a contractor supplies a performance and payment bond or if the transaction is a direct sale to the owner, the Pre-Construction Notice above shall not be applicable.

Extent of Lien—As stated above, the lien extends to all the right, title and interest of the owner for whose benefit the work was done. It includes the entire lot in any town, city or village, as well as the building or improvement made upon same. If not within a city, the lien extends to those areas on which work has been done or improvements erected. However, when prior liens exist, the property subject to the lien may include only the improvement. Where the improvement is on leased premises, the lien attaches to the improvement and to the leasehold term. Liens attach to the boats or vessels upon which work was done or material furnished.

Priority of Lien—The lien shall be preferred to all other encumbrances which may be attached to or upon such buildings, erections, improvements or boats, or the land, or either of them prior or subsequent to the commencement of such buildings or improvements, except where such prior lien, mortgage or other encumbrance was given to raise money for such buildings, erections or improvements. Any person enforcing such lien may have the building or improvement sold under execution. Lien for work performed or materials furnished to improve oil, gas and water wells, mines or quarries, or oil or gas pipelines is superior and paramount to any and all other subsequent liens or claims of any kind.

The liens for labor performed, material or fixtures furnished shall have equal priority toward each other without regard to the date of filing the account or lien, or the date when the particular labor or material was performed or furnished. All such liens shall date from the time that the construction or repair first commenced.

Lien for Improvement of Oil or Gas Well—Lien arises for performing labor or furnishing materials, machinery, or supplies for the construction, maintenance and repair of any oil, gas or water well; mine or quarry; or pipeline. Lien extends to the land, plant, building and appurtenances and is established in the same manner and the same time as a mechanics' lien. If labor or material is supplied to a leaseholder, the lien does not attach to the underlying fee title to the land. However, any lien, encumbrance or mortgage upon the land, or any leasehold interest, existing at the time of the inception of the lien for work or materials for oil, gas and water wells; mines or quarries; or oil or gas pipe lines shall not be affected by the oil, gas, water, mine or quarry lien.

Public Improvements—See Chapter 13.

Statutory Citation—Arkansas Code, Title 18, Subtitle 4, Chapter 44, §§ 18-44-101 to 18-44-135.

CALIFORNIA

Who May Claim—Mechanics, materialmen, subcontractors, lessors of equipment, artisans, architects, registered engineers, licensed land surveyors, machinists, builders, teamster and draymen, and all persons and laborers of every class performing labor upon or bestowing skill or other necessary services on, or furnishing materials or leasing equipment to be used or consumed in or furnishing appliances, teams or power, whether done or furnished at the instance of the owner or of any person acting by his authority or under him as contractor or otherwise, contributing to a work of improvement shall have a lien upon the property.

Twenty-Day Preliminary Notice Prerequisite to Claim—Every person, except one under direct contract with the owner or one performing actual labor of wages, must, as a necessary prerequisite to the validity of any claim of lien subsequently filed, cause to be given not later than 20 days after the claimant has first furnished labor, etc., a written preliminary notice to the owner or reputed owner and to the original contractor or reputed contractor and to the construction lender or reputed construction lender, if any. Failure to give the preliminary 20-day notice as specified will not preclude a claimant from giving notice later. Such later notice, however, will mean that a lien will be limited to labor, service, equipment or material furnished within 20 days prior to service of the late notice, and any time thereafter.

Contents of Preliminary Notice—(1) General description of the labor, service, equipment or materials furnished or to be furnished, and an estimate of the total price; (2) name and address of the person furnishing such labor, etc.; (3) name of the person who contracted for purchase of such labor, etc.; (4) description of the job site sufficient for identification; and (5) statement in boldface type that if bills are not paid in full for labor, etc., furnished, or to be furnished, the improved property may be subject to mechanics' liens. If an invoice for such materials contains the information required, a copy of such invoice shall be sufficient notice if properly served. Effective January 1, 2004, the form of notice is as follows and must be in boldface type:

NOTICE TO PROPERTY OWNER

If bills are not paid in full for the labor, services, equipment, or materials furnished or to be furnished, a mechanic's lien leading to the loss, through court foreclosure proceedings, of all or part of your property being so improved may be placed against the property even though you have paid your contractor in full. You may wish to protect yourself against this consequence by (1) requiring your contractor to furnish a signed release by the person or firm giving you this notice before making payment to your contractor, or (2) any other method or device that is appropriate under the circumstances. Other than residential homeowners of dwellings containing fewer than five units, private project owners must notify the original contractor and any lien claimant who has provided the owner with a preliminary 20-day lien notice in accordance with Section 3097 of the Civil Code that a notice of completion or notice of cessation has been recorded within 10 days of its recordation. Notice shall be by registered mail, certified mail, or first-class mail, evidenced by a certificate of mailing. Failure to notify will extend the deadlines to record a lien.

Service of Copy of Preliminary Notice—Service of the 20-day preliminary notice shall be by personal delivery, registered mail, or certified mail return receipt requested, upon the owner or reputed owner, original contractor or reputed original contractor, and construction lender or reputed construction lender.

Contents of Claim—Statement signed and verified by claimant or agent containing the following: (1) statement of demand after deducting credits and offsets; (2) name of owner or reputed owner; (3) statement of kind of labor, service equipment or materials furnished by the claimant; (4) name of person by whom claimant employed or to whom claimant furnished labor, service, equipment or materials; (5) description of the site sufficient for identification.

When to Be Recorded—(a) Every original contractor must file after completion of his contract and within 60 days after date owner files for record a notice of completion, or, if notice of completion is not filed by owner within 10 days after completion, the original contractor must file within 90 days after completion of contract. (b) Every person other than an original contractor must file his claim no later than 30 days after the date of filing of the owner's notice of completion or, if such notice of completion is not filed within 10 days after completion, the notice of claim must be filed within 90 days after the completion of such work of improvement. (c) If, after the commencement of a work of improvement, there shall be a cessation of labor for a continuous period of 60 days, all persons claiming lien rights shall within 90 days from the expiration of such 60-day period file their claims of lien, provided that if, after there shall be a cessation of labor thereon for a continuous period of 30 days or more, the owner files for record a notice of cessation; every original contractor must file within 60 days and every other person within 30 days after the date of filing of such notice of cessation.

Where Recorded—County Recorder of county in which the property or some part is situated.

Duration of Lien—No lien binds any property for a period of time longer than 90 days after the recording of the claim of lien, unless within that time, an action to foreclose the lien is commenced in a proper court. The action must be brought to trial within two years of commencement or the court may dismiss the lien.

Recording Fee—Varies from county to county.

Extent of Lien—The building, improvement or structure upon which labor is bestowed or materials furnished is subject to the lien, as is also the land upon which such building, etc., stands and as much ground around the same as is required for its use and occupation. Lien attaches to land improved by filling, grading or adding sidewalks, sewers and other improvements. The liens of subcontractors are direct liens and are not limited as to amount by contract price agreed upon between contractor and owner, but shall not exceed a reasonable value of the labor or materials furnished or the price agreed upon between the claimant and the person by whom employed. Filing of the contract with the County Recorder is equivalent to actual notice. The owner may limit his liability to subcontractors, etc., by filing the original contract and recording a payment bond for not less than 50% of the contract price. The owner's liability shall then be limited to the amount found to be due from the owner to the contractor, and the subcontractors shall look to the contractor and the sureties on his bond for any deficiency.

Forfeiture of Lien—Any claimant who willfully overstates its claim of lien shall forfeit the right to a mechanics' lien.

Any person who fails to file a stop notice after written demand from the owner shall forfeit the right to a mechanics' lien.

Priority of Lien—Liens (other than mechanics' liens with respect to site improvement) take priority over any lien, mortgage, deed of trust or other encumbrance which attached subsequent to time when the building, improvement or structure was commenced, work done or materials were commenced to be furnished; also to any lien, mortgage, deed of trust or other encumbrance of which the lienholder had no notice and which was unrecorded at the time building, improvement or structure was commenced, work done or the materials were commenced to be furnished.

Waiver of Lien Rights—Any provision in a subcontractor's or material supplier's contract to the effect that the subcontractor or material supplier waives its future lien or other collateral rights is void by statute (Civil Code 3262); and all subsequent lien releases must substantially conform to the forms set forth in the statute to be enforceable. The statute sets forth four distinct forms of release, each to be used in a different situation. They are: (i) a form for a conditional release to be given in return for a partial or progress payment, (ii) form for an unconditional release given in return for a partial or progress payment, (iii) a form for a conditional release to be effective when the final payment is received, and (iv) an unconditional release to be given after final payment has been received.

Notice Requirements of Owner Filing Notice of Completion or Notice of Cessation—The owner of a private work of improvement shall notify the original contractor, and any claimant other than the original contractor who has provided a Preliminary 20-Day Notice in accordance with Section 3097, that a notice of completion or notice of cessation has been recorded. The notice shall be sent within 10 days after recordation of the notice of completion or notice of cessation. Notification shall be sent by registered or certified mail, or by first-class mail, evidenced by a certificate of mailing. Failure to give notice to a contractor or claimant within 10 days of recording the notice of completion or notice of cessation shall extend the period of time in which that contractor or claimant may file a mechanics' lien or stop notice to 90 days beyond the date that a notice of completion or notice of cessation has been recorded. The sole liability for failing to give notice shall be the extension of the period of time in which that contractor or claimant may file a mechanics' lien or stop notice. "Owner" means a person who has an interest in real property, or the person's successor in interest on the date a notice of completion or notice of cessation from labor is filed for record, who causes a building, improvement, or structure, to be constructed, altered, or repaired on the property. If the property is owned by two or more persons as joint tenants or tenants in common, any one or more of the co-tenants may be deemed to be the "owner" within the meaning of this section. However, "owner" does not include a person who occupies the real property as a personal residence and the dwelling contains not more than four residential units, nor does it include a person who has a security interest in the property or obtains an interest pursuant to a transfer described in subdivision (b), (c), or (d) of Section 1102.2 of the California Civil Code.

Public Improvements—See Chapter 13.

Stop Notice, Private Work—A stop notice may be served on the owner of, and/or the construction lender by anyone entitled to a lien other than the original contractor for, a work of private improvement. The time periods for serving the stop notice and the 20-day pre-lien notice requirements are the same as for the mechanics' lien. The time period for filing suit to enforce a stop notice is 90 days from the last day to record the mechanics' lien, or it ceases to be effective. A stop notice served on the construction lender must be accompanied by a corporate surety bond, or an undertaking signed by two individual sureties, in one and a half times the amount sought to be withheld to be enforceable. Claimant can make written request of construction lender for election not to withhold funds pursuant to bonded stop notice by virtue of Payment Bond having been recorded. Stop notice and mechanics' lien rights are separate and distinct. Any person who shall fail to serve such a stop notice after a written demand therefore from the owner shall forfeit the right to a mechanics' lien.

Forfeiture of Stop Notice—Any person who willfully gives a false stop notice or bonded stop notice forfeits all right to participate in the pro rata distribution of such money.

Lien for Improvement of Oil or Gas Well—Labor or materials for the drilling or operating of oil or gas wells give rise to liens on the leasehold and appurtenances, all materials and fixtures owned by the lessee, all oil and gas produced, and the proceeds thereof. Lien is claimed by filing verified statement in the office of the County Recorder for the county where property is located within six months after the date on which labor was performed or material furnished and extends for six months after recording.

Statutory Citation—Civil Code §§ 3081.1 through and including 3267.

COLORADO

Who May Claim—All persons supplying equipment, materials, machinery, tools or labor to be used in the construction, alteration or repair of any structure, or to make an improvement upon the land itself is eligible to claim a mechanics' lien. Second tier suppliers (suppliers to first tier suppliers) are not entitled to a lien. Architects, engineers, draftsman and artisans who have furnished designs, plans, plats, maps, specifications, drawing, estimates of cost, surveys or superintendence, or who have rendered other professional or skilled service, or bestowed labor in whole or in part, describing or illustrating or superintending such structure or work done, shall have a mechanics' lien. An affirmative defense is available to owners who pay the prime contractor the full contract amount plus change orders for work performed by the subcontractor and/or supplier on single family residences that are occupied as the owner's primary residence.

No one is entitled to a mechanics' lien if a performance and a labor and materials payment bond, each equal to 150 percent of the contract price, have been executed by the principal contractor and one or more corporate sureties authorized and qualified to do business in the state. A notice of such bond must be filed with the County Clerk and Recorder of the county where the project is located prior to the commencement of any work on the project. The principal contractor must also post a notice on the property stating the bond has been filed and must make copies of the bond available to any subcontractors, materialmen, or laborers upon request.

How Claimed—By timely recording a verified Statement of Lien; by timely filing a lien foreclosure suit; and by timely recording notice of commencement of action (lis pendens) with the Clerk and Recorder no later than six months after the last labor is performed, materials furnished, or completion of the construction project, whichever is later.

A contract with a contractor which exceeds $500 must be in writing and a copy or memorandum thereof containing the names of all parties to the contract, a description of the property and of the character of the work to be done, the amount to be paid, and a schedule of payments shall be filed by the owner or reputed owner in the office of the County Recorder where the property is located before the work is commenced. If not so filed, the labor and materials furnished by all persons shall be deemed to have been done and furnished at the issuance of the owner and such persons shall have a lien for the value thereof.

Notice of Intent to Lien—A Notice of Intent to Lien must be served by personal service or by registered mail or certified mail, return receipt requested, upon the owner or reputed owner of the property or his agent and the principal or prime contractor or his agent at least 10 days before the filing of the Lien Statement with the County Clerk and Recorder. An affidavit of such service or mailing shall be filed for record with the Statement of Lien and shall constitute proof of service.

The notice for repair or construction of residential property shall be in at least 10-point bold-faced type, if printed, or in capital letters, if typewritten, shall identify the contractor by name and address, and shall state substantially as follows:

IMPORTANT NOTICE TO OWNERS: UNDER COLORADO LAW, SUPPLIERS, SUBCONTRACTORS OR OTHER PERSONS PROVIDING LABOR OR MATERIALS FOR WORK ON YOUR RESIDENTIAL PROPERTY MAY HAVE A RIGHT TO COLLECT THEIR MONEY FROM YOU BY FILING A LIEN AGAINST YOUR PROPERTY. A LIEN CAN BE FILED AGAINST YOUR RESIDENCE WHEN A SUPPLIER, SUBCONTRACTOR, OR OTHER PERSON IS NOT PAID BY YOUR CONTRACTOR FOR HIS LABOR OR MATERIALS. HOWEVER, IN ACCORDANCE WITH THE

COLORADO GENERAL MECHANICS' LIEN LAW, SECTIONS 38-22-102(3.5) AND 38-22-113(4), COLORADO REVISED STATUTES, YOU HAVE AN AFFIRMATIVE DEFENSE IN ANY ACTION TO ENFORCE A LIEN IF YOU OR SOME PERSON ACTING ON YOUR BEHALF HAS PAID YOUR CONTRACTOR AND SATISFIED YOUR LEGAL OBLIGATIONS.

YOU MAY ALSO WANT TO DISCUSS WITH YOUR CONTRACTOR, YOUR ATTORNEY, OR YOUR LENDER POSSIBLE PRECAUTIONS, INCLUDING THE USE OF LIEN WAIVERS OR REQUIRING THAT EVERY CHECK ISSUED BY YOU OR ON YOUR BEHALF IS MADE PAYABLE TO THE CONTRACTOR, THE SUBCONTRACTOR, AND THE SUPPLIER FOR AVOID-ING DOUBLE PAYMENTS IF YOUR PROPERTY DOES NOT SATISFY THE REQUIREMENTS OF SECTIONS 38-22-102(3.5) AND 38-22-113(4), COLORADO REVISED STATUTES.

YOU SHOULD TAKE WHATEVER STEPS NECESSARY TO PROTECT YOUR PROPERTY.

This provision does not apply when a building permit is issued for new residential construction or for residential property containing more than four living units.

Recording Lien Statement/Time Limits for Recording a Lien Statement—(a) Laborers (not furnishing materials)—no later than two months after improvement is concluded. (b) All others (including general contractors, subcontractors, and suppliers)—No later than four months after the last day on which the labor is performed or the material furnished by the claimant.

Notice Extending Time—A claimant can obtain an extension of time allowed for filing a lien by, within the time allowed for filing a lien, filing a notice with the Office of the County Clerk and Recorder in the county where the property is located containing the following information: (1) address or legal description of the property or other description that will identify the property; (2) name of the person with whom contracted; and (3) name of the claimant, plus his address and telephone number.

Filing this notice will extend the time for filing a lien claim to four months after completion of the structure or other improvement, or six months after filing a Notice of Intent, whichever comes first. Discontinuance of all labor, work, services or furnishing of materials on a structure for a three-month period constitutes abandonment. Once there has been abandonment, the building will be considered completed and the time limits for foreclosure of a lien will start to run.

Where Lien Is Recorded—Office of the County Clerk and Recorder in the county where the property, or the principal part thereof, to be affected by the lien is situated.

Duration of Lien—Unless, within six months, action is commenced to enforce the lien and a notice stating that such action has been commenced is filed at the office of the county clerk and recorder of the county in which the property is located, the lien is void. If construction continues more than a year after filing a Lien Statement, a lien claimant has to file an affidavit that the construction has not yet been completed with the Clerk and Recorder within 30 days after the first anniversary date of the filing of the Lien Statement and each year thereafter until the construction is concluded or unless foreclosure has been previously commenced.

Recording Fee—$5 per standard size page.

Contents of Lien—(1) Name of owner or reputed owner or, if not known, a statement to that effect; (2) name of person claiming lien; (3) name of principal contractor if lien claim by subcontractor; (4) description of property to be charged; (5) statement of the amount due or owing such claimant; (6) statement must be signed and sworn to by claimant or his agent; (7) affidavit of service of notice of intent to file lien statement to owner or reputed owner and principal contractor at least 10 days prior to recording lien statement.

Extent of Lien—The right or interest of the owner or person claiming an interest in the land, including landlord or vendor, is subject to liens for labor and material. Lien extends to the interests of the owner for the entire contract price and attaches to the property, structure or improvement unless such owner or person within five days after obtaining notice of erection, repair or other improvement, personally gives written notice to all persons performing labor or furnishing skills, that the interest shall not be subject to any lien or within five days of the aforementioned notice, gives notice by posting and keeping posted a written notice to the effect mentioned above in some conspicuous place on the land or building or other improvement which is subject to the work.

Priority of Lien—Claimant's lien takes effect as of the date when any work was commenced on the structure on a contract between the owner and first contractor. It has first priority over any encumbrances thereafter recorded, and unrecorded encumbrances of which claimant had no actual notice. No lien, except those claimed by laborers or mechanics filed more than two months after completion, will encumber the interests of any bona fide purchaser of real property, the principal improvement on which is a single- or double-family dwelling, except if purchaser had knowledge that the lien was filed prior to conveyance, or notice is filed. As between lien claimants, liens extend for the benefit of (1) day laborers; (2) subcontractors and materialmen; (3) other principal contractors. However, mechanics' liens do not have priority as to the improvements over a pre-existing deed of trust if the deed of trust is recorded prior to the recording of the mechanics' lien and the loan proceeds are used for construction purposes.

Trust Funds—All funds disbursed to any contractor or subcontractor under any building, construction, remodeling contract or construction project, shall be held in trust for payment of subcontractors, material suppliers or laborers who have a lien or may have a lien. Contractors and subcontractors are required to maintain separate records for each project, but not separate bank accounts.

Public Improvements—See Chapter 13.

Statutory Citation—Colorado Statutes, §§ 38-22-101 to 38-22-133.

Special Warning—For *bona fide* purchasers of single or double family residences: notice of extension must be filed within one month of the conveyance of the property; a lien statement must be filed within two months of the conveyance of the property.

CONNECTICUT

Who May Claim—Any person having a claim for more than $10 for materials furnished or services rendered in the construction, raising, removal or repair of any building, or any of its appurtenances or improvement of any lot or plot of land, by virtue of an agreement with or by consent of the owner of the land upon which the building is erected or has been moved, or his agent. Any person having a claim for more than $10 for materials furnished or services rendered in the construction, raising, removal or repair of any real property, and the claim is by virtue of an agreement with or by consent of the lessee of the real property or of some person having authority from or rightfully acting for such lessee in procuring the materials or labor, then the leasehold interest in such real property is subject to the payment of the claim.

How Claimed—(a) *Contractors*. Person performing services or furnishing materials within 90 days after he has ceased to do so must lodge with the Town Clerk of the town in which the building, lot or plot of land is situated, a certificate in writing, subscribed and sworn to by the claimant, describing the premises, the amount claimed, the name of the person against whom the lien is being filed, the date of commencement of the work or furnishing of the materials and stating that the amount claimed is justly due. Within the same time, or prior to the lodging of the certificate, but no later than 30 days after the lodging of the certificate, the contractor must also serve a true and attested copy of the certificate on the owner of the building, lot or plot as provided in section (b).

(b) *Subcontractors*. All persons, except the original contractor and a subcontractor, whose contract with the original contractor is in writing, must within 90 days after ceasing to furnish materials or render services, give written notice to the owner of the building and to the original (principal) contractor that they have furnished materials or rendered services or commenced to do so and that they intend to claim a lien therefor on the building, lot or plot of land. This notice must be served on the owner by leaving at his residence a copy thereof. Where the owner resides out of town, the notice may be served on his agent or may be mailed by registered or certified mail to the owner. If the copy is returned unclaimed, notice must be given by publication. When there are two or more owners, such notice must be served upon each owner. No lien is valid, unless within 90 days after he has ceased to furnish materials or render services, the person claiming the lien lodges with the Town Clerk of the town in which the building, lot or plot of land is situated a certificate in writing, subscribed and sworn to by the claimant, describing the premises, the amount claimed, the name of the person against whom the lien is being filed and the date of the commencement of the performance of services or furnishing materials, and stating that the amount claimed is justly due. A copy of the lien must be served in accordance with the same procedure as a notice of lien. Contractor shall be entitled to copy of notice provided that within 15 days after commencing the construction, contractor files with the Town Clerk an affidavit which contains the name under which he conducts business, his business address and a description of the property. The statute contains specific provisions for service of notice on owner depending on whether or not he resides in the same town as the property is located.

Where Recorded—Town Clerk of town in which building is situated.

When to Be Recorded—Within 90 days after the contractor shall have ceased to perform services or furnish materials, he shall lodge with the Town Clerk of the town in which the building, lot or plot of land was situated, a certificate in writing in accordance with the statute, which certificate shall be recorded by the Town Clerk with deeds of land and within the same time or prior to the lodging of such certificate but not later than 30 days after lodging such certificate, serve a true and attested copy of such certificate upon the owner of such building, lot or plot of land.

Duration of Lien—No lien shall continue in force for longer than one year after such lien has been perfected, unless the party claiming such lien commences an action to foreclose the same by complaint, crossclaim or counterclaim, and records a notice of lis pendens on the land records of the town in which the lien is recorded within one year from date such lien was filed or within 60 days of any final disposition of an appeal.

Recording Fee—$10 for the first page. $5 for each subsequent page or fractional part thereof.

Contents of Lien Certificate—(1) Description of premises; (2) amount claimed as a lien thereon; (3) date of commencement and date of termination of performance of services or furnishing of materials; (4) statement that amount claimed is justly due, as nearly as the same can be ascertained; (5) name of the person against whom the lien is being filed, and subscribed and sworn to by the claimant.

Extent of Lien—The lien attaches to the building or the appurtenances to the extent of the amount which the owner agreed to pay. It includes and attaches to the land upon which such building or appurtenances or any lot or plot of land are located.

Priority of Lien—Mechanics' liens take precedence over any other encumbrance originating after the commencement of the services or the furnishing of any materials. If a lien exists in favor of two or more persons on the same building for the same work, no one person has precedence over the other except as described below. Where the united claims of several claimants exceed the price agreed upon to be paid by the owner, then the claimants other than the original contractor are paid in full first, if the price is sufficient, or if not, the amount is apportioned between them in proportion to the amount due them respectively. If an encumbrance other than a mechanics' lien be filed for record during the time of construction and existing inchoate mechanics' liens do not waive priority to it, all mechanics' liens originating prior to the filing of such encumbrance for record shall take precedence over such encumbrance, but mechanics' liens for materials or services originating after the filing of said other encumbrance shall be subject thereto.

Public Improvements—See Chapter 13.

Statutory Citation—General Statutes of Connecticut, Title 49, Chapter 847, §§ 49-32a to 49-92f.

DELAWARE

Who May Claim—Any person having performed work or labor or furnished material to an amount exceeding $25 in or for the erection, alteration, or repair of any structure, in pursuance of any contract, express or implied, with the owner of such house, building, or structure, or with his agent. Where work or labor is performed on a house, building, bridge, or structure in any amount less than $100, person performing labor may obtain lien. Liens cover work and materials performed and furnished in gas fitting, plumbing, paving, paperhanging, placing iron works, and machinery of every kind in mills and factories. Liens also extend to architects and corporations. Work or materials for a building, house, or structure may be furnished under oral contract but for improvement to land alone must be written contract. No lien can be obtained on residential property if the owner has made full payment to the contractor with whom he contracted and received verified and notarized statement from contractor that all claims have been paid, or received a waiver of mechanics' lien; if owner has not made full payment, lien can only be obtained for balance due to be paid *pro rata* on any claimants who perfect lien. The statute prohibits as a matter of public policy an owner, developer, general contractor, or construction manager from requiring that mechanics' liens be waived as a condition of submitting a bid or entering into a contract to perform labor or supply materials to a structure. Labor or materials performed or furnished in the construction, alteration, furnishing, rigging, launching, or repairing of any ship or vessel may be subject to a lien.

How Claimed—By filing statement of claim in writing.

Where Filed—An amount exceeding $25 must be filed in the office of the Prothonotary in county where such structure is located. Statement of claim for labor in any amount less than $100 may be filed with the Justice of the Peace of the county where the property is situated.

When to Be Filed—(a) *Contractors*. A contractor who (1) has made his contract directly with the owner or reputed owner of any structure and (2) has furnished both labor and material in and for such structure, or have provided construction management services in connection with the furnishing of such labor and material, in order to enforce the lien, shall file a statement of claim within 180 days after the completion of the structure. A statement of claim is deemed timely if it is filed within 180 days of any of the following: (a) date of purported completion of all the work called for by the contract as provided by the contract if such date has been agreed to in the contract itself; (b) date when the statute of limitation commences to run in relation to the particular phase or segment of work performed pursuant to the contract, to which phase or segment of the work the statement of claim relates, where such date for such phase or segment has been specifically provided for in the contract itself; (c) date when the statute of limitations commences to run in relation to the contract itself where such date has been specifically provided for in the contract itself; (d) date when payment of 90 percent of the contract price, including the value of any work done pursuant to contract modifications or change orders, have been received by the contractor; (e) date when the contractor submits his final invoice to the owner or reputed owner of such structure; (f) with respect to a structure for which a certificate of occupancy must be issued, the date when such certificate is issued; (g) date when the structure has been accepted, as provided in the contract, by the owner or reputed owner, or such other representative designated by the owner or reputed owner for this purpose, and issues a certificate of completion; or (h) the date when permanent financing for the structure is completed.

(b) *Subcontractors and Others.* All other claimants shall file their claim within 120 days of the last delivery or completion of work, defined as (1) date final payment is due or (2) date final payment is made to the contractor with whom the claimant contracted who is in privity with the owner.

Duration of Lien—Statement of claim must be filed within 30 days of the 90-day period after completion of the structure.

Recording Fee—$10 for issuing a mechanics' lien; this includes $6.50 for issuing writ of scire facias.

Contents of Lien Certificate—(1) Name of the claimant; (2) name of the owner, or reputed owner; (3) name of the contractor, and the party with whom claimant dealt; (4) amount or sum claimed to be due, the nature and kind of labor or material with bill of particulars annexed; (5) time when the work and labor or furnishing of materials was commenced; (6) time when the work was finished, with the contractor identifying the completion date and the event which is relied upon as completion and the subcontractor identifying what event is relied upon as the completion of the work; (7) location of the structure with description sufficient to identify it; (8) that the labor was done and materials furnished on the credit of the property; (9) amount claimed and that the amount has not been paid; (10) amount claimant claims to be due on each structure; and (11) time of recording of a first mortgage, or a conveyance in the nature of a first mortgage, upon such structure which is granted to secure an existing indebtedness or future advances provided at least 50 percent of the loan proceeds are used for the payment of labor or materials, or both.

Extent of the Lien—The lien attaches to the building and the land upon which the work was rendered or material furnished.

Priority of Lien—Any judgment obtained upon such claims becomes a lien on such property and upon the ground upon which same is situated and relates back to the day when such work and labor was begun or furnishing of material was commenced or the time immediately following the time of recording of a first mortgage, or conveyance in the nature of a first mortgage, upon such structure which is granted to secure an existing indebtedness or future advances provided at least 50 percent of the loan proceeds are used for the payment of labor or materials, or both, for such structure, whichever shall last occur. If proceeds of estate are not sufficient to pay all liens in full, proceeds are divided ratably without priority to preference.

Public Improvements—See Chapter 13.

Statutory Citation—Delaware Code, Title 25, Part II, Chapter 27, §§ 2701 to 2737.

DISTRICT OF COLUMBIA

Who May Claim—Contractor, subcontractor, materialman or laborer directly employed by the original contractor. Claimant must have a contract with the owner or general contractor to have lien rights.

How Claimed—By filing notice of intention to hold lien on property.

Where Filed and Fee—Recorder of Deeds, 515 D Street NW, Washington, DC 20001. Filing fee is $20.

When to Be Filed—During construction or within 90 days after completion of building whether the claim is due or not.

Service of Copy of Notice—A subcontractor or other person employed by the contractor, besides filing a notice with the Recorder of Deeds of the District of Columbia must serve the owner of the property upon which the lien is claimed, by leaving a copy with the owner or his agent, if the owner or agent is a resident of the District, or if neither can be found, by posting the notice on the premises.

Contents of Notice of Lien—(1) Name and address of the contractor; (2) Name and address of the property owner; (3) Description of labor and/or materials; (4) Name of party against whose interest a lien is claimed and the amount claimed; (5) Legal description of property. Form supplied by Recorder of Deeds should be used. In addition, claimants need the following documents when filing the Notice of Lien. These documents are not filed with the Notice but are presented to the Clerk for review in accepting the Notice for recording: (a) a copy of the work agreement signed by all parties; (b) a valid residential home improvement contractor's license issued by the District of Columbia Department of Consumer and Regulatory Affairs; (c) a certificate of good standing issued by the District of Columbia Department of Consumer and Regulatory affairs within the past two years, if applicable; (d) a certificate or statement of good standing from the District of Columbia Office of Tax and Revenue, including the contractor's federal and local tax identification numbers.

Extent of Lien—Lien attaches to building erected, improved, added to or repaired, and the lot of ground used in connection therewith to the extent of the right, title and interest at the time existing of the owner.

Duration of Lien—Any person entitled to a lien must commence suit within 180 days after filing of the notice or from the completion of the building improvement or repairs or within three months after the claim is due if not due when the other time limits expire.

Subcontractors, Materialmen, etc.—The owner has a defense of payment. All subcontractor liens are limited to the amount to become due to the general contractor and are subject to the terms and conditions of the general contract except any waiver of liens in the general contract. If the general contractor is entitled to recover nothing, the liens are not enforceable at all. Subcontractors are entitled to request information from the owner concerning the contract and status of accounts between the owner and general contractor. If the owner fails or refuses to provide this information, the owner can lose the defense of payment to the subcontractor lien.

Priority of Lien—Lien preferred to all judgments, mortgages, deeds of trusts, liens and conveyances recorded after commencement of work, except mortgages or deeds of trust given to purchase land recorded within 10 days from date of acknowledgment. Lien has priority over all loan advances made after the lien is filed and has priority over contracts to purchase the land after the lien is filed. The lien of subcontractor who has given notice to the owner is preferred to the lien of the general contractor.

Public Improvements—See Chapter 13.

Statutory Citation—District of Columbia Code, Division VII, Property, Title 40 Liens, Chapter 3, §§ 40-301.01 to 303.20.

FLORIDA

Who May Claim—(a) *Persons in Privity with Owner.* A general contractor, subcontractors, sub-subcontractors, materialmen, or laborer ("Lienor") or professional lienors have a lien on the real property improved for any money that is owed to him for labor, services, materials or other items required by, or furnished and incorporated and for specially fabricated material, whether or not they are incorporated in accordance with, the direct contract and for unpaid finance charge due under the lienor's contract.

(b) *Persons Not in Privity with Owner.* A lienor who, as a subcontractor, sub-subcontractor, laborer, materialman or professional lienor not in privity with the owner, commences to furnish labor, services or materials to an improvement and who thereafter becomes in privity with the owner shall have a lien for any money that is owed to him for the labor, services or materials furnished and incorporated into the property. A laborer, either of whom is not in privity with the owner, or a laborer, subcontractor or a sub-subcontractor who complies with provisions of the law and is subject to its limitations, has a lien on the real property improved for any money that is owed to him for labor, services or materials furnished in accordance with this contract and with the direct contract and for any unpaid finance charges due under the lienor's contract. A laborer or materialman or subcontractor or sub-subcontractor who complies with the provisions of this part and is subject to the limitations thereof, also has a lien on the owner's real property for labor, services or materials furnished to improve public property if the improvement of the public property is furnished in accordance with this contract and with the direct contract. The total amount of all liens allowed under this part for furnishing labor, services or material conveyed by any certain direct contract must not exceed the amount of the contract price fixed by the direct contract.

Any persons who perform services as architects, engineers, geotechnical engineers, landscape architects, interior designers, or surveyors and mappers ("professional lienors"), subject to compliance with limits imposed by the law, has a lien on the real property improved for any money that is owed for services used in connection with improving the real property or for services used in supervising any portion for the work of improving the real property. A professional lienor's lien attaches at of the time of recording. Nobody can claim a lien as a contractor, subcontractor or sub-subcontractor unless they are appropriately licensed in the jurisdiction in which the work is performed.

How Claimed—As a prerequisite to perfecting and recording a claim of lien, all claimants not in privity with the owner, except professional lienors, must serve a notice on the owner in the form described below. A sub-subcontractor or a materialman to a subcontractor must serve a copy of the notice on the contractor as a prerequisite to perfecting or recording a claim of lien. A materialman to a sub-subcontractor must serve a copy of the notice to owner on the contractor as a prerequisite for perfecting a lien and recording a claim of lien. A materialman to a sub-subcontractor shall serve the notice to owner on the subcontractor if the materialman knows the name and address of the subcontractor. The notice must be received by the owner before recommencing, or not later than 45 days after commencing, to furnish labor services or materials, but, in any event, before the date of the owner's disbursement of the final payment after the contractor has furnished the affidavit required by law. The notice must be served regardless of the method of payments by the owner, whether proper or improper, and does not give the lienor serving the notice any priority over other lienors in the same category. The serving of the notice does not dispense with the requirement of recording of the claim of lien. The notice is not a lien, cloud or encumbrance on the real property nor actual or constructive notice of it.

In addition to the requirements above, for the purpose of perfecting a lien, every lienor, including laborers, professional lienors and persons in privity, shall record a claim of lien which is substantially in the following form:

WARNING!

THIS LEGAL DOCUMENT REFLECTS THAT A CONSTRUCTION LIEN HAS BEEN PLACED ON THE REAL PROPERTY LISTED HEREIN. UNLESS THE OWNER OF SUCH PROPERTY TAKES ACTION TO SHORTEN THE TIME PERIOD, THIS LIEN MAY REMAIN VALID FOR ONE YEAR FROM THE DATE OF RECORDING, AND SHALL EXPIRE AND BECOME NULL AND VOID THEREAFTER UNLESS LEGAL PROCEEDINGS HAVE BEEN COMMENCED TO FORECLOSE OR DISCHARGE THIS LIEN.

CLAIM OF LIEN

State of _____

County of _____

Before me, the undersigned notary public, personally appeared _____, who was duly sworn and says that she or he is (the lienor herein) (the agent of the lienor herein _____), whose address is _____; and that in accordance with a contract with _____, lienor furnished labor, services, or materials consisting of _____ on the following described real property in _____ County, Florida:

(Legal description of real property) owned by _____ of a total value of $_____, of which there remains unpaid $_____, and furnished the first of the items on (month day, year), and the last of the items on (month day, year); and (if the lien is claimed by one not in privity with the owner) that the lienor served her or his notice to owner on (month day, year), by _____; and (if required) that the lienor served copies of the notice on the contractor on (month day, year), by _____ and on the subcontractor, _____, on (month day, year), by _____.

(Signature)

Sworn to (or affirmed) and subscribed before me this _____ day of (month year), by (name of person making statement)

(Signature of Notary Public - State of Florida)
(Print, Type, or Stamp Commissioned Name of Notary Public)
Personally Known OR Produced Identification: _____
Type of Identification Produced: _____

Notice to Owner—One not in privity with owner must provide a notice to owner substantially in the following form, including all of the warnings included herein:

WARNING! FLORIDA'S CONSTRUCTION LIEN LAW ALLOWS SOME UNPAID CONTRACTORS, SUBCONTRACTORS, AND MATERIAL SUPPLIERS TO FILE LIENS AGAINST YOUR PROPERTY EVEN IF YOU HAVE MADE PAYMENT IN FULL.

UNDER FLORIDA LAW, YOUR FAILURE TO MAKE SURE THAT WE ARE PAID MAY RESULT IN A LIEN AGAINST YOUR PROPERTY AND YOUR PAYING TWICE.

TO AVOID A LIEN AND PAYING TWICE, YOU MUST OBTAIN A WRITTEN RELEASE FROM US EVERY TIME YOU PAY YOUR CONTRACTOR.

NOTICE TO OWNER

To: (Owner's name and address)

The undersigned hereby informs you that he has furnished or is furnishing services or materials as follows:

(General description or services or materials) for the improvement of the real property identified as (property description) under an order given by _____.

Florida law prescribes the serving of this notice and restricts your right to make payments under your contract in accordance with Section 713.06, Florida Statutes.

IMPORTANT INFORMATION FOR YOUR PROTECTION

Under Florida's laws, those who work on your property or provide materials and are not paid have a right to enforce their claim for payment against your property. This claim is known as a construction lien.

If your contractor fails to pay subcontractors or material suppliers or neglects to make other legally required payments, the people who are owed money may look to your property for payment, EVEN IF YOU HAVE PAID YOUR CONTRACTOR IN FULL.

PROTECT YOURSELF:

—RECOGNIZE that this Notice to Owner may result in a lien against your property unless all those supplying a Notice to Owner have been paid.

—LEARN more about the Construction Lien Law, Chapter 713, Part I, Florida Statutes, and the meaning of this notice by contacting an attorney or the Florida Department of Business and Professional Regulation.

(Lienor's Signature)
(Lienor's Name)
(Lienor's Address)

Copies to: (Those persons listed in Section 713.06(2)(a) and (b), Florida Statutes)

If a copy of such notice is served on lender to owner and lender pays contractor after receipt of notice, lender shall make proper payments as specified. Failure to do so renders the lender liable to owner for all damages suffered.

The notice to owner may be combined with a notice to contractor under § 713.23 or § 255.05 for private or public bonded jobs and thus entitled "Notice to Owner/Notice to Contractor".

The notice to owner must be served on the Owner, and must be delivered to the Owner by certified mail, return receipt requested, overnight or second-day delivery with proof of delivery, and delivery by hand delivery to the persons designated, if any, and to the place and address designated in the Notice of Commencement and if none of these methods are available, by posting on the job. It must also be served on the General Contractor if the lienor is not in privity with the General Contractor.

In each claim of lien, the owner under the direct contract must be the same person for all lots, parcels or tracts of land against which a single claim of lien is recorded.

Notice of Commencement—Except for an improvement that is exempt because the work consists solely of subdivision improvements or the total contract is less than $2,500, an owner or authorized agent before actually commencing to improve any real property, or recommencing completion of any improvement after default or abandonment, whether or not a project has a payment bond, shall record a notice of commencement with the clerk's office and forthwith post either a certified copy thereof of a notarized statement that the notice of the commencement has been filed for recording along with a copy.

The notice of commencement must be in substantially the following form:

Permit No. _____ Tax Folio No. _____

NOTICE OF COMMENCEMENT

State of _____
County of _____

The undersigned hereby gives notice that improvement will be made to certain real property, and in accordance with Chapter 713, Florida Statues, the following information is provided in this Notice of Commencement.

1. Description of property: (legal description of property, and street address, if available).
2. General description of improvement:
3. Owner information:

      a. Name and address:
      b. Interest in property:
      c. Name and address of fee simple title holder (if different than owner):
4. Contractor (name and address):
      a. Phone number:
      b. Fax number: (optional, if service by fax is acceptable)
5. Surety:
      a. Name and address:
      b. Phone number:
      c. Fax number: (optional, if service by fax is acceptable)
      d. Amount of bond: $_____
6. Lender: (name and address)
      a. Phone number:
      b. Fax number: (optional, if service by fax is acceptable)
7. Persons within the State of Florida designated by owner upon whom notices or other documents may be served provided by Section 713.13(1)(a)(7), Florida Statutes.
      a. Name and address:
      b. Phone number:
      c. Fax number: (optional, if service by fax is acceptable).
8. In addition to himself, owner designates _____ of _____ to receive a copy of the lienor's notice as provided by Section 713.13(1)(b), Florida Statues.
      a. Phone number:
      b. Fax number: (optional, if service by fax is acceptable)
9. Expiration date of notice of commencement (the expiration date is one year from the date of recording unless a different date is specified):

(Signature of Owner)

Sworn to (or affirmed) and subscribed before me this _____ day of (month, year), by (name of person making statement).

Signature of Notary Public State of Florida
Print, type, or stamp commissioned name of Notary Public
Personally known _____ or produced identification
Type of identification produced: _____
Notary public _____

A copy of any statutory bond must be attached to the Notice of Commencement at the time of recordation. The failure to attach a copy of the bond to the Notice of Commencement when the notice is recorded negates the exemption provided in section 713.02(6) and liens will attach to the real property. However, if such a bond exists but is not recorded, the bond may be used as a transfer bond.

The Notice of Commencement is effective upon recording. The owner must sign the Notice of Commencement and no one else may be permitted to sign in his stead. If the improvement described in the Notice of Commencement is not actually commenced within 90 days after the recording thereof, such notice is void and of no further effect.

The recording of a Notice of Commencement does not constitute a lien, cloud or encumbrance on real property, but gives constructive notice that claims of lien under this part may be recorded and may take priority. This does not apply to an owner who is constructing only subdivision improvements.

Unless otherwise provided in the Notice of Commencement, a Notice of Commencement is not effectual in law or equity against a conveyance, transfer to mortgage of, or lien on the real property described in the notice, or against creditors or subsequent purchasers for a valuable consideration, after one year after the date of recording and notice of commencement.

The certified copy of the Notice of Commencement must contain the name and address of the owner, the name and address of the contractor, and the location or address of the property being improved. The issuing shall verify this information is consistent with the building permit application. The issuing authority shall provide the recording information on the certified copy of the recorded Notice of Commencement upon request.

An owner may request from the contractor a list of all subcontractors and suppliers who have any contract with the contractor to furnish materials or perform any services to improve the real property. The contractor must furnish the information with 30 days of the owner's request or forfeits the right to file a lien. The list furnished does not qualify as a notice to owner.

Where Filed—Public records of the county in which the real property is situated. If property is situated in two or more counties, record in each county.

When to Be Filed—During the progress of the work, but not later than 90 days after the final furnishing of the labor or services or materials by the lienor, provided, if the original contractor defaults or contract is terminated before completion of construction, no claim for a lien attaching prior to such default shall be recorded after 90 days from the date of such default or 90 days after the final performance of labor or services or furnishing of materials, whichever occurs first. Copies of claim of lien must be served upon owner, within 15 days of recording. The time for recording a claim of lien is measured from the last day of furnishing labor, services, or material by the lienor and shall not be measured by any other standard.

Duration of Lien—No lien shall continue for a longer period than one year after the claim of lien has been recorded, unless a foreclosure action to enforce the lien is commenced within that time. The continuation of the lien effected by the commencement of the action shall be good against creditors or subsequent purchasers for a valuable consideration and without notice unless a notice of *lis pendens* is recorded. Owner can shorten to 60 days by filing notice of contest of lien, prior to 20 days by serving an Order to Show Cause Why the Lien Should Not be Discharged.

Fee for Recording—The fee for recording, indexing and filing any instrument varies from county to county. You should consult the Clerk of the Court for applicable recording fees.

Extent of Lien—Liens shall extend to, and only to, the right, title and interest of the person who contracts for the improvement, as such right, title and interest exists at the commencement of the improvement is thereafter acquired in the real property. The lien may attach to the fee even if the "owner" is a tenant if the landlord required the improvements in the Lease. *See below.*

Priority of Lien—All liens shall have priority over any conveyance, encumbrance or demand not recorded against the real property prior to the time lien attached or the Notice of Commencement, if one is recorded. Liens shall have preference in the following order: (1) laborers, (2) all persons other than the contractor, and (3) contractor. All liens relate back to the date of recording of the Notice of Commencement. Should total contract amount be less than all claims, all liens in a class must be allowed their full amounts before any liens of a subsequent class are allowed; if amount is insufficient for class, *pro rata* share will be paid, if the owner has made proper payments. Proper payments require the owner to obtain a release of lien from all lienors giving notice as the time of payment. Professional lienors, such as architects and engineers have priority of a lien as of the dates of the recording of the lien.

Remarks—If a husband and wife, who are not separate and not living apart from each other, own priority individually or together, the husband or wife who contracts shall be deemed to be the agent of the other to the extent of subjecting the right, title or interest of the other in said property to liens, unless such other shall within 10 days after learning of such contract notify the contractor and file, with the Circuit Court of the county in which the property is situated, written notice of his or her objection thereof. Any lienor may release his property from a lien thereon by filing a bond in the amount of the final bill with the clerk of the Circuit Court.

Limitations on Lessors—If a lease expressly provides that interest of lessor shall not be subject to liens for improvements, lessee shall notify contractor making the improvements, and the knowing or willful failure of lessee to provide such notice to contractor shall render contract between lessee and contractor voidable at option of contractor.

Interest of lessor shall not be subject to lien for improvements made by lessee if: (1) lease prohibits such liability and lease or short form is recorded; or (2) all leases of lessor prohibit liabilities for improvements and a notice recorded in office of public records where property located which notice states name of lessor and legal description of property or contains specific language in lease prohibiting such liability and a statement that all leases for the property contain such a clause; and (3) the lessee is a mobile home owner who is leasing a mobile home lot in a mobile home park from the lessor.

Lien for Improvement of Oil or Gas Well—Extends to the leasehold interest held for oil or gas purposes or for any oil or gas pipeline except that neither the land itself, apart from the rights granted under an oil and gas lease, nor any material interest, nor any royalty interest is subject to such liens. Lien also extends to materials and fixtures owned by the interest holder and any oil or gas produced. Lien is perfected in the same manner as a construction lien and exists for one year.

Public Improvements—See Chapter 13.

Statutory Citation—Florida Statutes, Chapter 713, §§ 713.001 to 713.37; 255.05.

GEORGIA

Who May Claim—The following persons shall each have a special lien on the real estate, factories, railroads and other property for which they furnish labor, service or materials at the instance of the owner, contractor or some person acting for the owner or contractor: (1) all mechanics of every sort who have taken no personal security for work done and material furnished in building, repairing or improving any real estate of their employers; (2) all contractors, all subcontractors and all materialmen furnishing material to subcontractors, and all laborers furnishing labor to subcontractors, materialmen and persons furnishing material for the improvement of real estate; (3) all registered architects furnishing plans, drawings, designs or other architectural services on or with respect to any real estate; (4) all registered foresters performing or furnishing services on or with respect to any real estate; (5) all registered land surveyors and registered professional engineers performing or furnishing services on or with respect to any real estate; (6) all contractors, all subcontractors and materialmen furnishing material to subcontractors, and all laborers furnishing labor for subcontractors for building factories, furnishing material for factories or furnishing machinery for factories; (7) all machinists and manufacturers of machinery, including corporations engaged in such business, who may furnish or put up any mill or other machinery in any county or who may repair the same; (8) all contractors to build railroads; and (9) suppliers who rent tools, appliances, machinery or equipment for the improvement of real estate.

How Claimed—Substantial compliance by the claimant of the lien with the contract is necessary. Claimant must file a claim of lien within three months after the completion of the work or furnishing of architectural services, or furnishing or performance of surveying or engineering services, or within three months after such material or machinery is furnished. Copy of claim must be served by certified or registered mail on owner or contractor as agent for owner.

If the owner files a Notice of Commencement for the project, a lien claimant who is not in privity of contract with the general contractor is barred unless the claimant serves a Notice to Contractor (see paragraph 8) within 30 days of the claimant beginning work on the project.

Where Recorded—In Office of Clerk of Superior Court of the county where property is located.

When to Be Recorded—Within three months after completion of work or furnishing machinery or materials. An optional preliminary notice may be filed within 30 days of delivery of any material or labor.

Service of Copy of Notice—Must send copy of preliminary notice to contractor on the property named in the notice or to the owner of the property, if filed, within seven days. Notice of lien required to be sent to owner or contractor, as agent of the owner, by registered or certified mail.

Duration of Lien—Lien lost unless an action is commenced within 12 months from the time claim becomes due and payable against the contractor with whom the claimant dealt for the amount of the claim. Within 14 days after filing the action, the party claiming the lien shall also file under oath with the Clerk of the Superior Court of the county wherein the subject lien was filed, a notice identifying the court wherein the action is brought, the style and number of the action, including the names of all parties thereto, the date of the filing of the action and the book and page number of the records of the county wherein the subject lien is recorded. Failure to bring action and to file such notice within the time required shall extinguish the subject claim of lien and render the same unenforceable. Before a subcontractor, laborer or materialman can obtain a judgment establishing a lien against a property owner, he must first obtain judgment. If contractor or subcontractor absconds, dies or removes from state during this 12-month period so that personal service cannot be made, or he is in bankruptcy, or no final judgment can be obtained by reason of death or bankruptcy, then the lienor need not obtain a judgment as a prerequisite to enforcing a lien against the property improved by the contractor.

Recording Fee—$5 for the filing of each preliminary notice. $5.00 for the filing of the lien for the first page; $2 for each additional page.

Contents of Notice of Lien—Statute provides for claim to be in substance as follows:

"A. B., a mechanic, contractor, subcontractor, materialman, machinist, manufacturer, registered architect, registered forester, registered land surveyor, registered professional engineer or other person (as the case may be), claims a lien in the amount of (specify the amount claimed) on the house, factory, mill, machinery or railroad (as the case may be), and the premises or real estate on which it is erected or built, of C. D. (describing the house, premises, real estate, or railroad) for satisfaction of a claim which became due on (specify the date the claim was due) for building, repairing, improving or furnishing material (or whatever the claim may be)."

Notice of Contractor shall set forth the name, address and telephone number of the person providing labor, services or materials; the name and address of each person at whose instance the labor, services or materials are being furnished; the name of the project and location of the project set forth in the Notice of Commencement; and a description of the labor, services or materials being provided and, if known, the contract price or anticipated value of the labor, services or materials to be provided or the amount claimed to be due, if any.

Extent of Lien—Liens attach to the real estate, factories, buildings, etc., erected, improved or repaired, for the amount of work done or material furnished or value of services performed but in no event shall the aggregate amount of liens exceed the contract price for the improvements made or services performed.

Preliminary Notice of Right to File a Lien—Within 30 days of providing any materials or labor a claimant may file a preliminary notice of right to file a lien with the Clerk of the Superior Court in the county where the property is located. The notice should provide the name, address and telephone number of the potential lien claimant, state name and address of contractor or other person at whose instance the labor, services or materials were furnished, state name of owner of the real estate and a description of the property against which the lien may be claimed and a general description of the labor, services or materials furnished or to be furnished. Within seven days of filing the notice, a copy of the notice must be sent to the owner of the property or the contractor by registered or certified mail. The filing of the preliminary notice is not a prerequisite or substitute to filing a claim of lien. Filing the preliminary notice protects the claimant from losing lien rights by a contractors filing affidavit indicating claimant's waiver of lien rights.

Priority of Lien—As among themselves, mechanics' liens rank according to date of filing (but are of the same date when declared and filed for record within three months after the work is done or before that time), but are inferior to liens for taxes, to the general and special liens of laborers, to the general lien of landlords for rent when a distress warrant is issued out and levied and to other general liens, when actual notice of the general lien of landlords and others has been communicated before the work was done or materials or services furnished; but the lien shall be superior to other liens not here excepted.

Public Improvements—See Chapter 13.

Waiver—Lien rights cannot be waived prior to providing the labor and materials. Waivers can be interim for partial payment or unconditional for final payment and must follow the forms contained in the statute.

Statutory Citation—Official Code of Georgia, §§ 44-14-360 to 44-14-366.

HAWAII

Who May Claim—Any person or association furnishing labor or material to be used in the improvement of real property, including persons rendering professional services of planning or supervision. A person advancing cash only is not entitled to lien.

How Claimed—Any person claiming a lien shall apply in a special proceeding to the Circuit Court of the circuit where the property is situated. Such application shall be accompanied by a written notice of lien setting forth the alleged facts upon which the lien is claimed. The application and notice shall be returnable not less than three nor more than 10 days after service. On the return, day a hearing shall be held by the court to determine if probable cause exists to attach a lien to the property. Any person to whom notice is required to be given shall be permitted to offer testimony and documentary evidence on the issue of whether probable cause exists to permit the lien to attach. If the person who contracted for the improvement from which the requested lien arises claims a setoff against the lienor or if any person to whom notice is required to be given otherwise disputes the amount of the requested lien, the court shall hear and receive all admissible evidence offered and shall only permit the attachment of a lien in the net amount which the court determines is the reasonable probable outcome of any such dispute. The return day hearing may be continued at the order of the court so that the entire controversy need not be determined on the originally scheduled return day. The lien shall not attach to the property until the court finds probable cause exists and so orders. No such order shall be entered before the application and notice have been served on the party contracting for the improvement, the general contractor and the owner of the property, and they were given an opportunity to appear at the hearing.

Where Filed—With the Clerk of the Circuit Court where the property is located.

When to Be Filed—The application and notice shall be filed not later than 45 days after the date of filing of the affidavit of publication of notice of completion of the improvement against which it is filed. The affidavit is filed in the Office of the Clerk of the Circuit Court of the county in which the improvement is located and a record is there available for public inspection. Where title to the property involved, or any portion thereof, is registered in the land court and the lien is not claimed solely against the lessees' interest in one or more leasehold time share interests as described in Section 501-20, it shall be incumbent upon the lienor to file a certified copy of the Order Directing Lien to Attach in the office of the Assistant Registrar of the land court within seven days after the entry thereof in order to preserve his rights against subsequent encumbrancers and purchasers of the property. If no notice of completion is filed, the date of completion is deemed to be one year after the work was performed.

Service of Copy of Application and Notice—Must be served upon owner of property and any person with an interest therein and persons who contracted for the improvements. If any such person cannot be served, notice may be given such person by posting same on the improvement. If the fee title to the land is held in joint or common ownership or as an estate by the entirety, service upon one of the owners of the application and notice shall be deemed service upon all of the owners.

Duration of Lien—Lien continues for three months after the entry of order directing the lien to attach. Unless suit is commenced within that time to enforce it, it expires at the end of such three-month period.

Filing Fee—$105.00

Contents of Application for Lien—The amount of the claim, the labor or material furnished, a description of the property and any other matter necessary to a clear understanding of the claim. Names of the parties who contracted for the improvement, the name of the general contractor, the names of the owners of the property and the name of any person with an interest therein. It may, but need not, specify the name of the mortgagee and the surety for the general contractor. If the claim has been assigned, the name of the assignor.

Extent of the Lien—Lien for the price agreed to be paid (if the price does not exceed the value of the labor and materials) or if the price exceeds the value thereof or if no price is agreed upon by the contracting parties, for the fair and reasonable value thereof, upon the improvement as well as upon the interest of the owner of the improvement in the real property on which the same is situated.

Priority of Lien—Mechanics' liens have priority over all other liens except liens in favor of the government and mortgages, liens or judgments recorded or filed prior to the time of the visible commencement of operation. Mortgages recorded subsequent to the visible commencement of operations and before the date of completion have priority over mechanics' liens provided such mortgages secure advances made for the purpose of paying for the improvement and recite that the purpose of the mortgage is to secure moneys advanced for the purpose of paying for the improvement in whole or in part. Mechanics' liens rank equally in priority with each other, irrespective of the date of filing or date of attachment except laborers' wage liens which have priority up to $300 over other liens.

Exceptions—(a) In connection with the repair or improvements on property which prior to such repair and improvements was used primarily for dwelling purposes, no lien shall exist either for the furnishing of materials to a general contractor or his subcontractor either of whom is required to be licensed but is not, or if unreasonable advancement of credit was given by the furnisher or the materials to the general contractor or subcontractor. Whether there is reasonable advancement of credit is to be determined by the Circuit Judge at a hearing on the matter. If the furnisher of materials has secured a credit application form from the general contractor or subcontractor to whom the materials were furnished or has reasonably inquired into the credit status of the general contractor or subcontractor, the advancement of credit by the furnisher of materials shall be *prima facie* reasonable. The credit application shall be current and shall include at least the following information: name, address, type of business, date business started, contractor's license number, bonding companies generally used, banks used, list of current creditors, balance sheet, total of outstanding construction contracts, incompleted portion of all contracts, names of partners and co-venturers. Corporate applications should also include names of officers, authorized capital and paid-in capital.

(b) No general contractor or his subcontractor or the subcontractor's subcontractor shall have lien rights unless such contractor or subcontractor was licensed under Chapter 444 Hawaii Revised statutes when the improvements to the real property were made or performed.

(c) All real property owned or held by the Hawaii Housing Authority is exempt from mechanics' liens.

(d) No lien may attach to the common elements of a condominium for work performance after substantial completion of the project and the recordation of the first conveyance or lease of an apartment therein or to an individual apartment therein unless contracted for or consented to by the owner of such apartment.

Public Improvements—See Chapter 13.

Statutory Citation—Hawaii Revised Statutes, Division 3, Title 28, Chapter 507, §§ 507-41 to 507-49.

IDAHO

Who May Claim—Every person, otherwise unsecured in whole or in part, performing labor upon, or furnishing materials to be used in the construction, alteration or repair of any mining claim, building, wharf, bridge, ditch, dike, flume, tunnel, fence, machinery, railroad, wagon road, aqueduct to create hydraulic power or any other structure, or who grades in, fills in, levels, surfaces or otherwise improves any land, or who performs labor in any mine or mining claim, and every professional engineer or licensed surveyor under contract who prepares or furnishes designs, plans, plats, maps, specifications, drawings, surveys, estimates of cost, on-site observation or supervision, or who renders any other professional service whatsoever for which he is legally authorized to perform in connection with any land or building development or improvement, or to establish boundaries has a lien upon the same for the work or labor done or professional services or materials, whether done or furnished at the instance of the owner of the building or other improvement or his agent. For the purposes of the statute, every contractor, subcontractor, architect, builder or any other person having charge of any mining claim (except the lessee or lessees of any mining claim) or of the construction, alteration or repair, in whole or in part, of any building or other improvement, shall be held to be the agent of the owner. General contractors on residential property must make certain disclosures to the owner prior to entering a contract (see §45-525 for full particulars).

How Claimed—Any person claiming a lien pursuant to the provisions of this chapter must, within 90 days after the completion of the labor or services or furnishing of materials or the cessation of the labor or services or furnishing of materials for any cause, file for record a lien claim.

Where Recorded—In the office of the County Recorder of the county where the property or some part thereof is located.

When to Be Recorded—Within 90 days after the completion of the labor or services or furnishing of materials or the cessation of labor or services or furnishing of materials for any cause.

Service of Copy of Notice—A true and correct copy of the claim of lien shall be served on the owner or reputed owner of the property either by delivering a copy thereof to the owner or reputed owner personally or by mailing a copy thereof by certified mail to the owner or reputed owner at his last known address. Such delivery of mailing shall be made no later than five business days following the filing of said claim of lien.

Duration of Lien—For six months after claim has been filed, unless proceedings commenced within said time to enforce lien and a lis pendens has been recorded. If a payment on account is made or an extension of credit is given with an expiration date, and endorsed on the record of the lien, the six-month period runs after the date of such payment of expiration of the extension. The lien on a final judgment obtained in the action expires five years after the judgment becomes final.

Recording Fee—$3 per page.

Contents of Lien Certificate—Must state the amount of demand after deducting all just credits and offsets, with the name of the owner, or reputed owner, if known, and also the name of the person by whom he was employed or to whom he furnished the materials and also a description of the property to be charged with the lien, sufficient for identification, which claim must be verified by the oath of the claimant, his agent or attorney, to the effect that the affiant believes the same to be just.

Extent of Lien—Lien attaches to building, improvement or structure, together with land on which same is situated or so much as may be required for the convenient use and occupation thereof, if at the commencement of the work the land belonged to the person causing the construction or improvement. If such person owns less than a fee simple, only his interest therein is subject to such lien.

Priority of Lien—Mechanics' liens take precedence over any other encumbrance which attached after work or materials commenced to be furnished; also to any other encumbrance of which lienholder had no notice and which was unrecorded at commencement of work. Rank of the liens as follows: (1) all laborers, other than contractors or subcontractors; (2) all materialmen, other than contractors or subcontractors; (3) subcontractors; (4) original contractor; (5) all professional engineers and licensed surveyors.

Public Improvements—See Chapter 13.

Statutory Citation—Idaho Statutes, Title 45, §§ 45-501 to 45-525.

ILLINOIS

Who May Claim—Any person who contracts with the owner of a lot or tract of land or his agent for the improving, altering, repairing or ornamenting of any house, building, walk, fence or improvement, or filling, sodding, excavating or landscaping, raising, lowering or removing house, or to perform services as architect, professional or structural engineer or land surveyor, or to drill a water well or to furnish labor or services as superintendent, timekeeper, realty management services, mechanic, laborer or otherwise, or furnish material, fixtures, apparatus or machinery, is entitled to a lien for the same. Every mechanic, workman or other person who furnishes materials, apparatus, machinery or fixtures or performs labor for the contractor is also entitled to a lien for the value thereof. Laborers and miners working and developing coal mines also may be lien holders. Any agreement to waive any right to enforce or claim any lien where the agreement is in anticipation of and in consideration for the awarding of a contract or subcontract is against public policy and is unenforceable.

Any person furnishing services, labor or material for the erection of a building or structure, or improvement by mistake upon land owed by anyone other than the party contracting as owner, shall have a lien for such services.

Any architect, contractor, subcontractor, materialman or other person furnishing services, labor or material for the purpose of in constructing, building, altering, repairing or ornamenting a boat, barge or other watercraft or mobile home, shall have a lien on such property, enforced in the same manner as a lien on real property.

How Claimed—(a) *Contractors.* The contractor must give to the owner and owner must require, before any money is paid to the contractor, a statement in writing, under oath or verified by affidavit, of the names and addresses of all parties furnishing materials and labor and the amount due to each. Failure of contractor to furnish statement has been held not to preclude him from enforcing his lien by suit. Each contractor shall provide each owner, either as part of the contract or as part of the printed statement, the following:

THE LAW REQUIRES THAT THE CONTRACTOR SHALL SUBMIT A SWORN STATEMENT OF PERSONS FURNISHING MATERIALS AND LABOR BEFORE ANY PAYMENTS ARE REQUIRED TO BE MADE TO THE CONTRACTOR.

If printed in the contract, the statement shall be set in type at least the same size as the largest type used in the body of the contract and must be boldfaced.

(b) *Subcontractors.* Subcontractor (including mechanics, laborers, materialmen, etc.) must within 90 days after completion of work or final delivery of materials serve a written notice of his claim and the amount due on the owner, his agent, architect or superintendent. Where Torrens system of registration is in use, notice must be filed in the office of the Registrar of Titles in the county in which the land or lot is situated. This notice is not required where a contractor has given the sworn statement to the owner as set forth in (a) above. If owner, architect, superintendent, or agent cannot be found in the county where improvement is located, or does not reside therein, the subcontractor may file notice with the office of the recorder.

Subcontractors who furnish materials or labor for existing owner-occupied single-family residence must notify occupant or his agent at the residence within 60 days from first furnishing labor or materials, that he is supplying labor or materials. The notice must contain: (1) the name and address of the subcontractor or materialman; (2) the date work was started or the delivery of materials, the type of work done and to be done, or the type of materials delivered and to be delivered; and (3) the name of the contractor requesting the work. Notice given after 60 days will preserve the lien only to the extent that the owner has not been prejudiced by payments made prior to receipt of the notice. Notice must also contain the following warning:

NOTICE TO OWNER

THE SUBCONTRACTOR PROVIDING THIS NOTICE HAS PERFORMED WORK FOR OR DELIVERED MATERIAL TO YOUR HOME IMPROVEMENT CONTRACTOR. THESE SERVICES OR MATERIALS ARE BEING USED IN THE IMPROVEMENTS TO YOUR RESIDENCE AND ENTITLE THE SUBCONTRACTOR TO FILE A LIEN AGAINST YOUR RESIDENCE, IF THE SERVICES OR MATERIALS ARE NOT PAID FOR BY YOUR HOME IMPROVEMENT CONTRACTOR. A LIEN WAIVER WILL BE PROVIDED TO YOUR CONTRACTOR WHEN THE SUBCONTRACTOR IS PAID, AND YOU ARE URGED TO REQUEST THIS WAIVER FROM YOUR CONTRACTOR WHEN PAYING FOR YOUR HOME IMPROVEMENTS.

Where Filed—A claim of lien must be filed with the office of the recorder in the county in which the property is situated. Where the land is registered under the Torrens system, the notice of the subcontractor must be filed in the office of the Registrar of Titles of the county in which the property is situated.

When to Be Filed—As against third persons, the contractor must within four months after completion of his contract either file suit to enforce lien or file a claim of lien. Subcontractors must serve notice upon the owner within 90 days after completion of extra work, and if filing of notice is necessary, filing must be effected within the same period. A contractor's lien as against the owner is valid if filed at any time after the contract is made and within two years after the completion of the contract or extra work or furnishing extra materials. Upon written demand of the owner, a person claiming a lien can, within 30 days after such demand is served, be required to commence suit to enforce lien or else lien is forfeited.

Service of Copy of Notice—Subcontractor must give written notice by registered or certified mail, return receipt requested, with delivery limited to addressee only or by personally delivering the written notice to the legal owner of record, with a copy to lender.

Duration of Lien—Suit to enforce the lien must be commenced within two years after completion of contract or extra work or furnishing of extra material.

Filing Fee—$12 first four pages, plus $1 for each additional page and $1 for each additional document number therein noted.

Contents of Notice of Lien—If by a contractor the suit or notice shall show the following: (1) name of owner; (2) brief statement of contract; (3) balance due after deducting credits; (4) description of property subject to lien; (5) verification of claimant by himself or herself or his agent or employee.

Where notice is served by a subcontractor on owner, it shall show the following: (1) name of owner; (2) name of contractor; (3) brief statement of subcontract; (4) description of property subject to lien; (5) amount due or to become due. If service cannot be made upon owner, then notice must be filed with Clerk of the Circuit Court, and it must be verified.

Extent of Lien—The lien attaches to the whole of the lot or tract of land upon which the property is situated and to the adjoining lots used in connection with the same together with interest at 10 percent per annum on amount due from due date. It extends to an estate in fee for life, for years, or any other estate, right of redemption or other interests which the owner may have at the time of contract or subsequently arise. Subcontractor's liens are limited to the value of service rendered and materials furnished on the same property, as contractor, material, fixtures, apparatus, machinery and on money due or to become due from the owner under the original contract. The owner cannot be compelled to pay a greater amount than the price fixed in the original contract, in the absence of fraud or a violation of the right of subcontractors.

Priority of Lien—No encumbrance upon land created before or after the making of the contract under the Mechanics' Lien Act shall operate upon the building erected or materials furnished until a lien in favor of persons having done work or furnished material is satisfied. All previous encumbrances are preferred to the extent of the value of the land at the time of making of the contract, and the lien creditor is preferred to the value of the improvements. As between different contractors, no preference is given to the one whose contract was made first, except the claim of any person for wages by him personally performed is a preferred lien. The contractor's lien is superior to any right of dower if the owner of the dower interest had knowledge of the improvement and gave no written notice of his or her objection. A subcontractor has no right to bring a civil action against either owner or contractor until he furnishes a statement of the persons furnishing material and labor, and the lien of such subcontractor shall be subject to the liens of all other creditors.

Public Improvements—See Chapter 13.

Lien for Improvement of Oil or Gas Well—Liens exist for any person who perform labor or furnishes material under contract with owner of land. Liens also exist for any persons who perform for a subcontractor. Lien extends to the whole of the land or leasehold, appurtenances, materials furnished, all oil and gas wells and oil and gas produced and their proceeds; it does not extend to underlying fee or royalty interest. If the claim under contract with owner, must file a lien within four months; if claim under subcontract, within three months. Such lien is created, perfected and enforced in the same manner as mechanics' liens. Any lien which extends to oil or gas or the proceeds of the sale of oil or gas is ineffective against any purchaser or pipeline carrier until written notice of the claim is given.

Waiver—An agreement to waive any right to enforce or claim any lien in anticipation of or in consideration for the awarding of a contract or subcontract for real estate improvements is against public policy and unenforceable.

Construction Trust Funds—Any owner, contractor, subcontractor or supplier of any tier who requests or requires the execution and delivery of waiver of mechanics lien by any person who furnishes labor, services or materials for the improvement of a lot or tract of land in exchange for payment of the promise of payment, shall hold in trust the unpaid sums subject to the waiver of mechanics lien, as trustee for the person who furnished the labor, services or materials.

Statutory Citation—Illinois Compiled Statutes, Chapter 770, §§ 60/0.01 to 60/39.0.

INDIANA

Who May Claim—Contractors, subcontractors, mechanics, journeymen, laborers, materialmen, lessors of construction and other equipment and tools, and all persons performing labor or furnishing materials or machinery for certain improvements to real property. Registered engineers, land surveyors and architects may also secure and enforce the same lien. Material suppliers to material suppliers are generally considered too remote to file mechanics' liens.

How Claimed—By filing a sworn statement in duplicate of intention to hold a lien upon the property for the amount claimed within 90 days after performing labor or furnishing materials or machinery, unless the work was for a single- or double-family dwelling ("Class 2 Structures"), when the notice time is 60 days. The statement must specifically set forth (a) the amount claimed; (b) the name and address of the claimant and the name of the owner or owners; (c) the latest address of the owner as shown on the property tax records of the county; and (d) the legal description with street and number, if any. The legal description is sufficient if it is substantially as set forth in the latest entry of the county auditor's transfer books at the time of filing notice. The recorder charges $2 for mailing a copy of such statement to each owner. The statement can be verified and filed on behalf of claimant by a licensed Indiana attorney in good standing.

Where Filed—In the office of the Recorder of the county where the land is located.

When to Be Filed—Within 90 days after last performing the labor or furnishing the material for commercial projects and utilities; 60 days for residential construction ("Class 2 Structures").

Service of Copy of Notice—A duplicate copy of the notice of intention to hold a mechanics' lien is forwarded to each owner by the county Recorder.

Duration of Lien—One year from receipt of the notice by the county Recorder's office or, if credit was given by written agreement, one year from the expiration of such credit. Suit must be filed within one year; the owner can shorten the time to 30 days by making written demand.

Filing Fee—$11 for the first page and one mailing, $2 for each additional page and/or additional mailing to owner.

Contents of Notice—Statement must set forth the amount claimed, name and address of claimant, name and address of owner and a legal description of the lot of land, including street and number, if any, where the improvement may stand.

Extent of Lien—The lien extends to the building, erection or improvement, including the land where it is situated, to the extent of all the right, title and interest of the owner. The lien extends to and includes leasehold interest and mortgaged lands.

Priority of Lien—Mechanics' liens take precedence over all other subsequent encumbrances, except other mechanics' liens, as all mechanics' liens are on a parity with each other, regardless of recording date. Lien claimants are paid in proportion to the amount due each, where proceeds are insufficient. The construction mortgage of a lender has priority over liens recorded after the mortgage for any funds actually utilized on the liened project; this does not apply to liens on Class 2 structures or utilities.

Public Improvements—See Chapter 13.

Remarks—No lien can be acquired for labor, machinery or materials supplied to a contractor, subcontractor or mechanic for the *alteration or repair of an owner-occupied single- or double-family dwelling* unless notice of such delivery or work and of the existence of lien rights is submitted to the owner within 30 days of the first delivery to or labor performed for the owner of the land where the material, labor or machinery was delivered. Similarly, a person intending to claim a lien for material, labor and machinery sold to a contractor, subcontractor and mechanic for the *original construction of a single- or double-family dwelling* for intended occupancy by the owner of the real estate must furnish the owner a written notice of such delivery or labor, the existence of lien rights within 60 days after the date of the first delivery or labor performed, and file a copy of the written notice in the recorder's office within the same 60-day period. The furnishing of such notice is a condition precedent to the right of acquiring a lien upon such property. A lien for material or labor in original construction shall not be valid without notice against an innocent purchaser for value of a single- or double-family dwelling for occupancy by the purchaser, unless notice of intention to hold such lien be recorded prior to the recording of the deed by which the purchaser takes title.

No-Lien Contracts—Indiana has eliminated much of the statute which permitted the owner and general contractor to enter into a no-lien contract which cut off the lien rights of all subcontractors and materialmen for commercial projects. These clauses are now limited to residential home construction, Class 2 structures and work for public utilities.

Statutory Citation—Indiana Code, Title 32, Article 28, §§ 32-28-3-1 to 32-28-3-18.

IOWA

Who May Claim—Any person who shall furnish any materials, machinery or fixtures or labor for, or perform any labor upon, any building or land for improvement, alteration or repair thereof, including those engaged in the construction or repair of any work of internal or external improvement, and those engaged in improving any land by virtue of any contract with the owner, his agent, trustee, contractor or subcontractor. If materials are rented by a person to the owner, the owner's agent, trustee, contractor or subcontractor, the person shall have a lien upon such building, improvement or land to secure payment for the material rental. The lien is for the reasonable rental value during the period of actual use of the material and any reasonable periods of nonuse of the material taken in account in the rental agreement.

Delivery of material to the job site creates a presumption that the material was used in the course of improvements; this presumption does not exist for claims against payment bonds.

How Claimed—By filing verified statement of account showing time when material was furnished or labor performed, and when completed, with a correct description of the property charged with lien and the name and last known address of the owner of the property.

Where Filed—With the Clerk of the District Court of the county in which property is situated.

When to Be Filed—By principal contractor and by subcontractor within 90 days from the date the last labor was performed or the last material furnished. If a subcontractor's lien is filed after this period, written notice must be immediately served upon the owner, agent or trustee upon the filing of the lien. Subcontractor liens perfected after the lapse of the 90-day period may be enforced only to the extent of the balance due from the owner to the contractor at time of service of notice of claim. The lien of a subcontractor is not enforceable against an owner-occupied dwelling, except to the extent of the amount owed to the principal contractor at the time the subcontractor serves a written notice of the claim on the owner.

A person furnishing labor or materials to a subcontractor must (1) send notice to the principal contractor in writing containing the name, mailing address and telephone number of the person furnishing the labor or materials, and the name of the subcontractor to whom the labor or material were furnished, within 30 days of first furnishing labor or materials for which a lien claim may be made; (2) provide a certified statement that this notice was provided.

Duration of Lien—Suit must be filed within two years from the expiration of 90 days from filing the claim. The owner may serve a demand that suit be filed within 30 days.

Filing Fee—$10.

Contents of Notice of Lien—Name of claimant, name of party charged with lien, the amount, the description of property charged, itemized statement of account showing dates furnished and when completed. Must be verified.

Extent of Lien—Lien attaches to the building or improvement and includes entire land upon which situated to the extent of the interest of the person for whose benefit work performed or material furnished. Liens also attach to leasehold interests. Where the lien is for work or material furnished in the construction, repair or equipment of any railroad, canal, viaduct or other similar improvement, it attaches to the erections, excavations, embankments, bridges, road beds, rolling stock and other equipment and to all land upon which such improvements may be situated, except an easement or right of way. However, the Iowa Supreme Court has recently clarified that the judgment arising out of a mechanic's lien foreclosure is not a personal judgment against the owner such that a garnishment could be placed against the owner.

Notices on Owner-Occupied Works—(a) *Contractor*. An original contractor who enters into a contract for an owner-occupied dwelling, and who has contracted or will contract with a subcontractor to provide labor or furnish material for the dwelling, shall provide the owner with a copy of the contract and shall include the following notice in any written contract with the owner:

"Persons or companies furnishing labor or materials for the improvement of real property may enforce a lien upon the improved property if they are not paid for their contributions, even if the parties have no direct contractual relationship with the owner."

If there is no written contract between the original contractor and the owner, the original contractor must within 10 days of commencing work on a dwelling provide written notice to the dwelling owner stating the name and address of all subcontractors the contractor intends to use for construction and that the subcontractors or suppliers may have lien rights in the event they are not paid for their labor or material. The notice of subcontractors used in the construction of a dwelling must be updated. The original contractor who fails to provide notice under this section is not entitled to lien remedies as they pertain to any labor performed or material furnished by a subcontractor not included in the notice. Supplier to subcontractor must give notice to prime contractor within 30 days of delivery to protect his lien rights.

(b) *Subcontractor*. Subcontractors on owner-occupied projects may only lien for the amount due after the owner receives a notice with the name of the owner, the address of the property charged with the lien, the name, address and telephone number of the lien claimant, and the following statement:

"The person named in this notice is providing labor or materials or both in connection with improvements to your residence or real property. Chapter 572 of the Code of Iowa will permit the enforcement of a lien against this property to secure payment for labor and materials supplied. Your are not required to pay more to the person claiming the lien than the amount of money due from you to the person with whom you contracted to perform the improvements. You should not make further payments to your contractor until the contractor presents you with a waiver of the lien claimed by the person named in this notice. If you have any questions regarding this notice you should call the person named in this notice at the phone number listed in the notice or contact an attorney. You should obtain answers to your questions before you make any payments to the contractor."

Priority of Lien—Mechanics' liens have priority over each other according to the order of filing. They take priority over garnishments of the owner without regard to date of filing of lien claim. Mechanics' liens shall be preferred to all others which may attach to or upon any building or improvement and to the land upon which it is situated, except liens of record prior to the time of original commencement of work or improvements. However, construction mortgage liens shall be preferred to all mechanics' liens of claimants who commenced their particular work or improvement subsequent to the date of the recording of the construction mortgage lien.

Public Improvements—See Chapter 13.

Lien for Improvement of Oil or Gas Well—The mechanics' lien statute is applicable to labor and materials furnished in connection with gas and oil wells or pipelines. Liens do not attach to realty, but only to lease, wells, buildings, appurtenances and pipelines.

Statutory Citation—Code of Iowa, Title XIV, Subtitle 3, Chapter 572, §§ 572.1 to 572.33.

KANSAS

Who May Claim—Any person furnishing labor, equipment, material or supplies used or consumed in the improvement of real property under a contact with the owner or trustee, agent or spouse of the owner.

How Claimed—(a) *Contractor*. Contractor shall file a verified statement showing the name of the owner, the name and address sufficient for service of process of the claimant, a description of the real property and a reasonably itemized statement and the amount of the claim.

(b) *Subcontractor*. Subcontractors shall file within three months a statement setting forth the name of the contractor, the supplier's affidavit that the warning statement was properly given (if required) and a notice of intent to perform (if required).

(c) *Residential Subcontractor*. Claimant, except if claim is for less than $250, must give a written warning statement to the owner of residential property (residential property is defined as owner-occupied preexisting structure of two-family units or less) containing substantially the following:

"Notice to owner: (name of supplier or subcontractor) is a supplier or subcontractor providing materials or labor on Job No. _____ at (residence address) under an agreement with (name of contractor). Kansas law will allow this supplier or subcontractor to file a lien against your property for materials or labor not paid for by your contractor unless you have a waiver of lien signed by this supplier or subcontractor. If you receive a notice of filing of a lien statement by this supplier or subcontractor, you may withhold from your contractor the amount claimed until the dispute is settled."

(d) *Notice of Intent to Perform*. A lien for the furnishing of labor, equipment, materials or supplies for the construction of new residential property may be claimed after the passage of title to such new residential property to a good faith purchaser for value only if the claimant has filed a notice of intent to perform prior to the recording of the deed effecting passage of title to such new residential property. Such notice shall be filed in the office of the Clerk of the District Court of the county where the property is located.

The notice of intent to perform shall contain substantially the following statement:

NOTICE OF INTENT TO PERFORM

I (name of supplier, subcontractor or contractor) of (address of supplier, subcontractor or contractor) do hereby give public notice that I am a supplier, subcontractor or contractor or other person providing materials or labor on property owned by (name of property owner) and having legal description as follows:

Where Filed—Office of Clerk of District Court of the county in which the land is located.

When to Be Filed—Contractor's statement shall be filed within four months after the last material furnished or labor performed. Subcontractor must file three months from last material furnished or last labor performed.

Service of Copy of Notice—Only subcontractor (furnishing labor or material) need serve on owner written notice of filing aforesaid statement. Upon filing, the clerk of the district court shall enter the filing in the general index. The claimant shall (1) serve a copy of the lien statement personally upon any one owner and any party obligated to pay the lien, for service within the state; or (2) outside the state, mail a copy of the lien to any one owner of the property and to any party obligated to pay; or (3) if the address of any one owner of such party is unknown and cannot be ascertained with reasonable diligence, post a copy of the lien statement in a conspicuous place on the premises. Service is deemed made if proven that the person received notice.

Duration of Lien—One year from filing lien, but where promissory note given one year from maturity.

Filing Fee—$5 for filing lien or notice of intent to perform.

Contents of Notice of Lien—See paragraph 2 above.

Extent of Lien—A mechanics' lien attaches to the property improved for labor, equipment, material or supplies furnished, and for the cost of transporting the same.

The owner of any land affected by such lien shall not become liable to any subcontractor for any greater amount than he contracted to pay the original contractor; except for payments to the contractor made prior to the expiration of the three-month period for filing lien claims provided no warning statement is required. If a warning is required, owner's liability extends to any payment made subsequent to the receipt of the warning statement.

Priority of Lien—Liens (for labor and material under contract) shall be preferred to all other encumbrances attaching to such property subsequent to the commencement of the furnishing of labor, equipment, material or supplies at the site of the property. When two or more liens attach to the same improvement, priority is accorded to the earliest unsatisfied lien.

Public Improvements—See Chapter 13.

Lien for Improvement of Oil or Gas Well—Lien claimed must be filed with the Clerk of the District Court of the county where the land is located within six months after the material or labor was furnished or performed. Such liens are preferred to all other liens and suit shall be brought within six months from filing.

Assignments—All claims for mechanics' liens and rights of action to recover are assignable.

Statutory Citation—Kansas Statutes, Chapter 60, §§ 60-1101 to 60-1109.

KENTUCKY

Who May Claim—Any person performing labor or furnishing material for erecting, altering or repairing any house, building or other structure, or for any fixture or machinery therein or for excavating or in any manner for improving real estate, by contract with or the written consent of owner, contractor, subcontractor, architect or authorized agent. A person who performs labor or furnishes materials to a lessee relating to oil, gas or other minerals shall have a lien on the leasehold for the entire interest of the lessee.

How Claimed—(a) *Contractor*. The claimant must file a statement of lien in the office of the County Clerk of the county in which the building is situated, within six months after he ceases to perform labor or furnish materials. The statement shall require the name and address of the claimant, the amount due, a description of the property sufficiently accurate to identify it, the name of the owner, if known, and whether the materials were furnished or the labor performed by the contract with the owner or with a contractor or subcontractor. If claimant is a corporation, name and address of process server must be included. This information must be included in claim of subcontractor.

(b) *Subcontractor*. Such person must notify the owner, or his authorized agent, in writing within 75 days for claims less than $1,000 and 120 days for claims more than $1,000 after the last item of the material or labor is furnished, of his intention to hold his property liable and the amount for which he will claim a lien. For owner-occupied single- or double-family dwellings, such written notice must be given to the owner-occupant or his authorized agent within 75 days after the last item of labor or material is furnished. No lien can be obtained if such owner occupant has, prior to receipt of the notice, paid contractor, subcontractor or architect. In order that such lien shall take precedence over a mortgage, lease or bona fide conveyance for value with notice duly recorded, the person claiming the lien must, before the recording of such other instruments, have filed in the Clerk's office of the County Court of the county wherein he shall have performed or furnished, or expects to perform or furnish, labor and materials, a statement that he furnished the same or expects to do so and the amount thereof in full. Such notice may be mailed to the last known address of the owner or his agent. Unless the claimant files a statement in the office of the Clerk of the County Court of the county in which the property is situated within six months after he ceases to perform labor or furnish materials, the lien is deemed dissolved.

Where Filed—In County Clerk's office.

When to Be Filed—Within six months after the claimant ceases to perform labor or furnish materials.

Service of Copy of Notice—Copy of mechanics' lien statement must be sent to the owner within seven days of filing.

Duration of Lien—Expires in one year from the filing date if no suit brought to enforce lien; where debtor dies within year, period extended another six months after qualification of personal representative.

Filing Fee—$8 with the County Clerk's office.

Contents of Notice of Lien—The name and address of the claimant (or, if claimant is a corporation, name and address of the corporation's process agent), statement of amount due, with all just credits and setoffs known to him, description of property sufficiently accurate to identify, name of owner, if known, and whether the labor was performed or materials were furnished by contract with owner, contractor or subcontractor and subscribed and sworn to by person claiming or someone on his behalf.

Extent of Lien—The lien of a principal contractor attaches to the extent of the interest of the owner in the house, building or other structure and the land upon which the same is situated; the lien of a subcontractor, materialman or laborer attaches to the same extent, but in no case may the liens be for a greater amount in the aggregate than the contract price under the original contract. Lienor entitled to interest at legal rate.

Priority of Lien—The liens are superior to any mortgage or encumbrance created subsequent to the beginning of the labor or the furnishing of materials and relate back and take effect from the time of the commencement of the labor or the furnishing of materials. The lien shall not take precedence over mortgages or other contract liens or bona fide conveyances or value without notice.

Public Improvements—See Chapter 13.

Statutory Citation—Kentucky Revised Statutes, Chapter 376, §§ 376.010 to 376.260.

LOUISIANA

Who May Claim—The following persons have a privilege (lien) on an immovable to secure the following obligations of the owner arising out of work on the immovable: (1) contractors for the price of their work; (2) laborers or employees of the owner for the price of work performed at the site of the immovable; (3) sellers for the price of movables sold to the owner that become component parts of the immovable or are consumed at the site of the immovable or are consumed in machinery or equipment used at the site of the immovable; (4) lessors for the rent of movables used at the site of the immovable and leased to the owner by written contract; (5) registered or certified surveyors or engineers or licensed architects employed by the owner for the price of professional services rendered in connection with a work that is undertaken by the owner.

The following persons have a claim against the owner and a claim against the contractor to secure payment: (1) subcontractors, for the price of their work; (2) laborers or employees of the contractor or a subcontractor for the price of work performed at the site of the immovable; (3) sellers for the price of movables sold to the contractor or a subcontractor that become component parts of the immovable or are consumed at the site of the immovable or are consumed in machinery or equipment used at the site of the immovable; (4) lessors for the rent of movables used at the site of the immovable and leased to the contractor or a subcontractor by written contract; (5) registered or certified surveyors or engineers or licensed architects or their professional subconsultants for the price of professional services rendered in connection with the work that is undertaken by the contractor or subcontractor.

The contract must be reduced to writing and signed by the parties, and a written notice of the contract must be recorded in the office of the Clerk of Court or the Recorder of Mortgages of the parish where the work is to be executed before the date on which the work is to commence. The notice must contain a legal property description and the name of the project, identification of the parties and their mailing addresses, price of the work or method for calculating it, when payment is to be made and a general description of the work to be done. The owner must require the contractor to give a bond with good and sufficient surety. The amount of the bond must be the amount of the contract, if the contract does not exceed $10,000; between $10,000 and $100,000 the amount of the bond must be 50 percent of the contract, but in no event less than $10,000. For contracts over $100,000, but not in excess of $1,000,000, the bond must be 33a percent of the contract, but in no event less than $50,000, and for contracts exceeding $1,000,000 the bond must be 25 percent of the amount of the contract but not less than $333,333. The bond must be attached to and recorded with the contract.

If an unpaid seller of movables has not sent notice of nonpayment to the general contractor and the owner, then the seller loses the right to file a lien.

How Claimed—(a) *Contractors.* Contract must be recorded before the date fixed on which the work is to commence. Where no written contract was entered into or notice of written contract not recorded and owner or agent has filed an affidavit that work has been completed, a claim must be recorded in the office of the Recorder of Mortgages in the parish where the work was done within 60 days after the date of the affidavit of completion, or if no affidavit of completion was filed, within 60 days after the date of termination or substantial completion or abandonment of the work. A general contractor shall not have claim if the contract exceeds $25,000 unless a notice of contract is timely filed. Architects, engineers and surveyors must record lien no later than 60 days after registry of notice, acceptance of notice or substantial completion of work. A statement of claim or lien shall be in writing, signed by the person asserting the claim or representative, identify the property, by legal descriptions, name the project and set forth the amount and nature of the claim. *See* §4852 for the form Notice of Lien Rights for residential home improvements.

(b) *Subcontractors*. Subcontractors, materialmen and laborers must serve personally on the owner, or by certified or registered mail, a sworn detailed statement of claim and must file same for record in Office of the Recorder of Mortgages in the parish in which the work was done, all within 30 days after registry in the Office of the Recorder of notice of termination. If no contract has been entered into or the notice of contract has not been recorded, claimant must record a copy of his estimate or an affidavit of his claim within 60 days after the substantial completion or abandonment of the work or after filing of the affidavit of completion of owner in the Office of the Recorder of Mortgages. The seller of moveables sold for use or consumption in work on an immovable for residential purposes, if a notice of contract is not filed, shall file a statement of claim or privilege within 70 days after (a) the filing of a notice of termination of the work; or (b) the substantial completion or abandonment of the work, if notice of termination is not filed.

(c) *Material Suppliers*. Material suppliers without privity of contract with the owner, where a Notice of Contract has been filed, must send a Notice of Nonpayment to both the owner and the general contractor within 75 days of the last day of the month in which the materials were provided or the end of the statutory lien period, whichever comes first; the return receipt indicating that notice was delivered satisfies this requirement.

Written notice of a contract between a general contractor and an owner shall: (1) be signed by the owner and the contractor; (2) contain the legal description of the immovable property upon which the work is to be performed and the name of the project; (3) identify the parties and give their mailing addresses; (4) state the price of the work or describe the method by which the price is to be calculated and give an estimate; (5) state when payment of the price is to be made; and (6) describe in general terms the work to be done. Any person who may be entitled to lien rights on residential property shall be furnished with a copy of the notice upon request.

Where Recorded—In the Office of the Clerk of Court or Recorder of Mortgages of the parish in which the property is located.

Recording Fee—$2 (varies in some areas).

Extent of Lien—The lien attaches to the land and improvements in the amount of the claim and interest and the cost of recording the lien.

Duration of Lien—One year from date of filing, unless proceedings are begun.

Personal Liability of Owners—If bond furnished by contractor is insufficient in amount or has not a proper and solvent surety, or if no bond has been furnished and recorded but the notice of contract has been timely recorded, the owner is personally liable to subcontractors, laborers and materialmen who recorded and served their claims as above provided.

Priority of Lien—The privileges rank among themselves and as to other mortgages and privileges in the following order of priority: (1) privileges for *ad valorem* taxes or local assessments for public improvements against the property are first in rank; (2) privileges granted to laborers and employees rank next and equally with each other; (3) bona fide mortgages or vendor's privileges that are effective as to third persons before the privileges here discussed are effective rank next and in accordance with their respective rank as to each other; (4) privileges granted to sellers, lessors and subcontractors rank next and equally with each other; (5) privileges granted to contractors, surveyors, engineers and architects rank next and equally with each other; (6) other mortgages or privileges rank next and in accordance with their respective rank as to each other.

Public Improvements—See Chapter 13.

Lien for Improvement of Oil or Gas Well—Persons performing labor or services in connection with the drilling or operation of any oil, gas or water well acquire liens on the oil or gas produced from the well, proceeds, the wells, lease, rigs, machinery and other structures on the property by filing a notice of claim in the mortgage records of the parish where the property is located within 180 days from the last day of performance. Lien is for the amounts due for work performed plus costs of recording and 10 percent of attorney's fees if necessary to enforce collection.

Bonds—Any interested party may file a bond for a maximum of 125 percent of the principal amount of the claim asserted. If the recorder of mortgage finds the bond adequate, he may then cancel the statement of claim or privilege. Any party who files a bond or other security to guarantee payment shall give notice by certified mail of the posting of such bond to the owner of the immovable, the holder of the lien and the contractor.

Miscellaneous—A supplier of movables claiming a mechanics' lien must provide the owner of the property with a notice of nonpayment at least 10 days before filing the statement of claim, if the immovable was used for residential purposes. Also, such a seller has 70 days instead of 60 days in which to file the statement of claim after the filing of the notice of termination or substantial completion or abandonment of the work.

Statutory Citation—Louisiana Statutes, Title 9, §§ 9:4801 to 9:4855.

MAINE

Who May Claim—Whoever performs labor or furnishes labor or materials or performs services as an architect, surveyor or engineer, or as a real estate licensee, or as an owner-renter, owner-lessor or owner-supplier of equipment used in erecting, altering, moving or repairing a house or building or appurtenances including any public building erected or owned by any city, town, county, school district or other municipal corporations, or in constructing, altering, repairing a wharf or pier or any building thereon, by contract with or by consent of owner, has a lien thereon and on the land on which it stands.

How Claimed—Maine mechanic's lien law was significantly amended as of 9/17/05. Maine law now requires all contractors or suppliers, even those with a direct contract with the owner, to file a Notice of Lien in the registry of deeds in the county where the project is located within 90 days after the date of last work or materials supplied. Maine's mechanic's lien law does not distinguish between the various tiers of contractors, subcontractors and suppliers. The Notice of Lien must provide the amount due, sufficiently describe the property and its owner(s), and be under oath. A copy of the Notice of Lien must be provided to the owner(s) by ordinary mail; a post office certificate of mailing is conclusive proof of receipt. A real estate licensee must additionally send by certified mail, return receipt requested, a copy of the Notice of Lien to the bona fide purchaser for value. To perfect the claim of lien, a lienor must file within 120 days of the date of the last labor, services or materials being provided, a complaint in the county or district court division in which the construction project is located. Within 60 days of filing the complaint, in order to be effective against bona fide purchasers for value, either (1) a certificate from the clerk of court must be filed in the registry of deeds for the county where the real estate is located; or (2) an affidavit from the claimant/claimant's attorney must be filed in the registry of deeds for the county where the real estate is located; or (3) an attested copy of the lien complaint must be filed in the registry of deeds for the county where the real estate is located. Failure to file any one of these three alternatives will not invalidate the lien but will render the lien ineffective against a bona fide purchaser for value. A bona fide purchaser takes the property free of any mechanic's lien unless the lienor has filed a notice of lien in the registry of deeds; this notice must be renewed every 120 days if work is ongoing. An owner can prevent a mechanic's lien by giving written notice to the person providing the materials or labor that the owner will not be responsible for the labor, materials or services. Residential property owners cannot be required to pay twice for a subcontractor's services unless the subcontractor has first provided the residential property owner with written notice of the work performed or served a lien complaint on the owner. The lien may also be enforced by attachment in actions commenced within 180 days in any court having jurisdiction where the property on which is lien is claimed is situated.

Where Filed—The notice of lien is filed in the registry of deeds in the county in which the project is located. The lien complaint is filed in the county or district court division in which the construction project is located.

When to Be Filed—All Notices of Liens must be filed within 90 days after the date of last work or materials supplied. All complaints to foreclose liens must be filed no later than 30 days thereafter or no later than 120 days after the date of last work or materials supplied.

Service of Copy of Notice—If labor, material or service was not performed or furnished by contract with the owner, this lien is enforceable against the property only to the extent of the balance due from the owner to the person with whom he contracted; however, this defense is available only with respect to sums paid by a residential property owner prior to commencement of action to enforce the lien or written notice from the claimant to the owner, including a warning that if owner fails to assure that claimant is paid before further payment to the contractor, the owner may be required to pay twice.

Duration of Lien—Action to enforce must be brought within 120 days after the last of the labor is performed or materials furnished. Where owner dies or is adjudicated bankrupt within said 120 days, action may be commenced within 90 days after adjudication or after notice is given of appointment of an executor or administrator.

Contents of Notice of Lien—A true statement of amount due lienor with all just credits with description of property and names of owners if known, and supported by oath of lienor or someone in his behalf.

Extent of Lien—Owner's right, title and interest in building or improvement covered and the land upon which it stands. Where owner has no legal interest in the land, then lien attaches to the building or other structure. A bona fide purchaser for value of the property takes free and clear of any liens which have not yet been filed.

Priority of Lien—If labor or materials provided under contract with or with consent of owner (which includes, under Maine law, a mortgage holder), the lien has priority over the property interest of the owner. If the lienor can show knowledge of the nature and the extent of work being performed on the mortgaged premises by the mortgage holder, then the lien has priority over that mortgage. In the event the property is sold and the aggregate amount of the mechanics' liens exceeds the proceeds from the sale, the proceeds are shared on a pro rata basis among the successful lienors.

Public Improvements—See Chapter 13.

Statutory Citation—Maine Statutes, Title 10, Part 7, 10 §§ 3251 to 3269.

MARYLAND

Who May Claim—Any person may claim a lien for work done and material furnished without regard to the amount of the claim. If a project is not new construction, the building must be repaired rebuilt or improved to the extent of 15% of its value if the owner ordered the work or 25% of its value if a tenant ordered the work. The statute includes wells, swimming pools, fencing, sod or seeding, landscaping, grading, filling, paving or the leasing of equipment, with or without an operator. If the owner contracts for the installation of waterlines, sanitary sewers, storm drains or streets to service all lots in a development, each lot is subject to a pro rata lien.

How Claimed—All claimants must file a petition (lawsuit) to establish a lien. If claimant's contract is with any person other than owner, the claimant must also give notice to the owner.

Service of Notice—If claimant's contract is with any person other than owner, notice must be served upon owner within 120 days after doing the work or furnishing the materials. The following notice is sufficient:

NOTICE TO OWNER OR OWNER'S AGENT OF INTENTION TO CLAIM A LIEN

(Insert subcontractor) did work or furnished material for or about the building generally designated or briefly described as _____ . The total amount earned under the subcontractor's undertaking to the date hereof is $_____ of which $_____ is due and unpaid as of the date hereof. The work done or the materials provided under the subcontract were as follows: (Insert brief description of the work done and materials furnished, the time when the work was done or the materials furnished and the name of the person for whom the work was done or to whom the materials were furnished.) I do solemnly declare and affirm under the penalties of perjury that the contents of the foregoing notice are true to the best of the affiant's knowledge, information and belief. [Signature line needed]

The notice must be given by registered or certified mail, return receipt requested, or personally delivered to the owner by the claimant or his agent. If there is more than one owner, then the notice is sufficient if received by any owner. If the notice cannot be given on account of the absence of the owner or other causes, the subcontractor or his agent, in the presence of a competent witness and within the 120 days, may place the notice on the door or other front part of the building. Notice by posting is sufficient in all cases where the owner of the property has died and the successors in title do not appear on the public records of the county.

Filing Fee—There is no fee for service of notice, except postage. There is a fee for filing petition to establish lien.

When Petition to Be Filed—Within 180 days of completion of work or delivery of material by the claimant.

Where Petition Filed—The Clerk of Circuit Court of the county in which the building is situated.

Contents of Petition to Establish Lien—Name and address of claimant, name and address of owner, nature or kind of work done or the kind and amount of materials furnished, name of person for whom work was done or materials furnished, amount or sum claimed to be due less any credit recognized by the claimant, a description of the land including a statement whether part of the land is located in another county, a description adequate to identify the building, the amounts claimed on each building if a lien is sought against several buildings or separate parcels and an affidavit setting forth facts establishing the lien. The petition must state that the project was new construction or that the improvement increased the value of the property 15% in the case of owner ordered improvements or 25% in the case of tenant ordered improvements. The petition must attach copies of all documents that constitute the basis of the lien claim. If the claimant's contract is with any person other than owner, the petition must also include facts showing that timely notice has been given to the owner.

Extent of Lien—The lien extends to the land covered by the building and so much adjacent thereto as may be necessary for the ordinary and useful purposes of the building. Where a building is commenced and not finished, the lien attaches to the extent of the work done or materials furnished. A lien may attach to a leasehold to the extent of the interest of the lessee. "Building" includes any unit of a nonresidential building that is leased or separately sold as a unit.

Subcontractors, Materialmen, etc.—The owner has no defense of payment, except an owner erecting a single family dwelling on his own land for his own residence. Otherwise, the owner has the burden of seeing that all subcontractors and suppliers are paid.

Priority of Lien—Lien preferred to all judgments, mortgages, deeds of trusts, liens and conveyances recorded after establishment of lien by the court. The claimant has no lien rights, however, until establishment of lien by the court. Lien proceedings are subject to a bankruptcy stay or preference proceeding. No lien can be established if the property has been conveyed or the owner has entered into a contract of sale with a bona fide purchaser for value, prior to the establishment of a lien.

Waiver—An executory contract may not waive mechanics' lien rights. A "pay when paid" provision in an executory contract does not waive mechanics' lien rights.

Public Improvements—See Chapter 13.

Statutory Citation—Code of Maryland Real Property, Title 9, §§ 9-101 to 9-304.

MASSACHUSETTS

Who May Claim—(a) *Contractor.* A person entering into a written contract with the owner of land for the whole or any part of the erection, alteration, repair or removal of a building or structure upon land or other improvement to real property, or for furnishing material or rental equipment, appliances or tools thereof, shall have a lien upon said building or structure and upon the interest of the owner in said lot of land as appears of record at the date when notice of said contract is filed or recorded in the Registry of Deeds for the county or district where such land lies, to secure the payment of all labor and materials which shall be furnished by virtue of said contract.

(b) *Subcontractor.* A person who, subsequent to the date of the original contract, furnishes labor or material, or both labor and material, or performs labor under a written contract with a contractor or furnishes subcontractor construction management services, rental equipment, appliances or tools, or with a subcontractor of such contractor, shall have a lien to secure the payment of all labor and material which he is to furnish or has furnished upon the building or structure and upon the interest of the owner, as appears of record at the time of such filing in the lot of land on which said building or structure is situated upon filing a notice of contract and giving actual notice to the owner of such filing. Such lien shall in no event exceed the amount due or to become due under the original contract when notice of the filing of the subcontract is given by the subcontractor to the owner.

(c) *Personal Labor.* A person to whom a debt is due for personal labor performed in the erection, alteration, repair or removal of a building or structure upon land or an improvement or alteration to real property, by virtue of an agreement with, or by consent of, the owner of such building or structure, or of a person having authority from or rightfully acting for such owner in procuring or furnishing such labor, shall have a lien upon such building or structure and upon the interest of the owner thereof in the lot of land upon which it is situated, for not more than 30 days of work actually performed during the 90 days next, prior to his filing a statement as described in section 8 below. A person shall include an assignee, agent, authorized representative or third party beneficiary to whom amounts are due or for whose benefit amounts are computed or due for.

How Claimed—(a) *Contractor.* The contractor must sign and file in the Registry of Deeds for the county or district where the land lies a notice of contract in substantially the following form:

Notice is hereby given that by virtue of a written contract, dated _____, between _____, owner, and _____, contractor, said contractor is to furnish or has furnished labor and material or rental equipment, appliances or tools for the erection, alteration, repair or removal of a building structure or other improvement on a lot of land or other interest in real property described as follows: (insert description).

(b) *Subcontractor.* The subcontractor must sign and file in the Registry of Deeds for the county or district where the land lies a notice of his contract substantially in the following form:

Notice is hereby given that by virtue of a written contract dated _____, between _____, contractor, (or subcontractor), and _____ said _____ is to furnish or has furnished labor or material, or both labor and material, or is to furnish or has furnished rental equipment, appliances or tools in the erection, alteration, repair or removal of a building, structure or other improvement of real property by _____ contractor, for _____, owner on a lot of land or other interest in real property described as follows: (insert description)

As of the date of this notice, an account of said contract is as follows:

1. Contract price $_____
2. Agreed change orders $_____
   (indicate whether addition or subtraction)
3. Pending change orders $_____
   (indicate whether addition or subtraction)
4. Disputed claims $_____
   (indicate whether addition or subtraction)
5. Payments received $_____

The regular mailing address of the party recording or filing this notice is as follows:_____.

(c) *Second Tier Subcontractor.* A lien by a second tier subcontractor shall not exceed the amount due or to become due under the subcontract between the original contractor and the subcontractor whose work includes the work of the person claiming the lien as of the date such person files his notice of contract, unless the person claiming the lien has, within 30 days of commencement of his performance, given written notice of identification by certified mail, return receipt requested, to the original contractor in substantially the following form:

NOTICE OF IDENTIFICATION

Notice is hereby given to _____, as contractor, that _____, as subcontractor/vendor, has entered into a written contract with _____ to furnish labor or materials, or labor and materials, or rental equipment, appliances or tools to a certain construction project located at (Street Address), (Town or City), Massachusetts. The amount or estimated amount of said contract is $_____. (No amount need be stated for contracts for the rental of equipment, appliances or tools).

Where Recorded—Registry of Deeds for the County and District where the land is located. If registered land is included with unregistered land in any such notice or other instrument, an attested copy thereof shall be filed with an assistant recorder and registered.

When Notice Must Be Recorded—*Applicable to Both Contractors and Subcontractors.* At any time after execution of the written contract whether or not the date for performance stated in such written contract has passed and whether or not the work under such contract has been performed, but not later than the earliest of: (i) 60 days after filing or recording the notice of substantial completion under section two A; or (ii) 90 days after filing or recording of the notice of termination under section two B; or (iii) 90 days after the last day a person entitled to enforce a lien under section two or anyone claiming by, through or under him performed or furnished labor or materials or both labor and materials to the project or furnished rental equipment, appliances or tools.

Statement of Account—(a) *Contractor and Subcontractor.* Liens under sections two (general contractors) and four (subcontractors) shall be dissolved unless the contractor, subcontractor, or some person claiming by, through or under them, shall, not later than the *earliest* of: (i) 90 days after the filing or recording of the notice of substantial completion under section two A; (ii) 120 days after the filing or recording of the notice of termination under section two B; or (iii) 120 days after the last day a person, entitled to enforce a lien under section two or anyone claiming by, through, or under him, performed or furnished labor or material or both labor and materials or furnished rental equipment, appliances or tools, file or record in the registry of deeds in the county or district where the land lies a statement, giving a just and true account of the amount due or to become due him, with all just credits, a brief description of the property, and the names of the owners set forth in the notice of contract.

(b) *Personal Labor.* A lien shall be dissolved unless a like statement, giving the names of the owners of record at the time the work was performed or at the time of filing the statement, is filed within the 90 days provided in section 1(c) above.

Enforcement Action; Errors—The lien shall be dissolved unless a civil action to enforce it is commenced within 90 days after the filing of the statement of account. The validity of the lien shall not be affected by an inaccuracy in the description of the property to which it attaches if the description is sufficient to identify the property, or by an inaccuracy in stating the amount due for labor or material unless it is shown that the person filing the statement has willfully and knowingly claimed more than is due him.

Extent of Lien—The lien extends to the building or structure and upon the interest of the owner in said lot of land as appears of record at the date when notice of said contract is filed or recorded. If the person for whom the labor has been performed or with whom the original contract has been entered into for the whole or any part of the erection, alteration, repair or removal of a building or structure upon land, or for furnishing material therefor, has an estate less than a fee simple in the land or if the property is subject to a mortgage or other encumbrance, the lien shall bind such person's whole estate and interest in the property.

Priority of Lien—(a) *Mortgages.* No lien for personal labor shall avail against such a mortgage unless the work or labor performed is in the erection, alteration, repair or removal of a building or structure which erection, alteration, repair or removal was actually begun prior to the recording of the mortgage. No liens filed by subcontractors or contractors shall avail as against a mortgage actually existing and duly registered or recorded to the extent of the amount actually advanced or unconditionally committed prior to the filing or recording in the registry of deeds of the notice of contract. No liens filed by subcontractors or contractors shall avail as against a purchaser other than the owner who entered into the written contract on which the lien is based, whose deed was duly registered or recorded prior to the filing of such notice of contract.

(b) *Attachments.* The rights of an attaching creditor shall not prevail as against a lien for personal labor nor against the claim of a subcontractor or contractor where notice or notices of contract have been filed or recorded in the registry of deeds prior to the recording of the attachment. An attachment recorded prior to the filing or recording of the notice of contract shall prevail against a lien, other than for personal labor, to the extent of the value of the buildings and land as they were at the time when the labor was commenced or the material furnished for which the lien is claimed.

Public Property—No lien shall attach to any land, building or structure thereon owned by the Commonwealth or by a county, city, town, water or fire district.

Void Agreements—A covenant, promise, agreement of understanding in, or in connection with or collateral to, a contract or agreement relative to the construction, alteration, repair or maintenance of a building, structure, appurtenance and appliance or other improvement to real property, including moving, demolition and excavating connected therewith, purporting to bar the filing of a notice of contract or the taking of any steps to enforce a lien as set forth in this chapter is against public policy and is void and unenforceable. Partial lien waivers by contractors are permitted if the form provided in the statute is followed.

Statutory Citation—Massachusetts General Laws, Chapter 254, §§ 1 to 33.

MICHIGAN

Who May Claim—Each contractor, subcontractor, supplier or laborer who provides an improvement to real property has a right to a construction lien upon the interest of the owner or lessee who contracted for the improvement to the real property.

How Claimed—By recording a claim of lien in the Office of the Register of Deeds for each county where the real property to which the improvement was made is located within 90 days after the lien claimant's last furnishing of labor or material for the improvement. A claim of lien shall be valid only as to the real property described in the claim of lien and located within the county where the claim of lien has been recorded.

Notice of Commencement—(a) *Actual Physical Improvements to Real Property.* Before the commencement of any actual physical improvement to real property, the owner or lessee contracting for the improvements shall record a notice of commencement along with a notice of furnishing (below) with the Register of Deeds for the county in which the property is located, a copy of which is as follows:

NOTICE OF COMMENCEMENT

STATE OF MICHIGAN

County of _____ } ss.

(Name of owner, lessee, or agent) being duly sworn verifies the truth and accuracy of the contents of this notice and says that he or she is authorized by the contracting (owner) (lessee) to execute this Notice of Commencement and that the person contracting for improvement to the following described real property is (description of property) whose address is (address) and whose interest in said real property is that of (interest) and that the DESIGNEE of said contracting party is (contracting party) whose address is (address)and that the real property to be improved is situated in the (location) of (name) County, State of Michigan and described as follows: (insert description) and that the fee owner of said real property is (name of fee owner) of (address of fee owner) and that the general contractor, if any is (name of person with whom you have contracted) of (address of general contractor to provide substantially all the improvements to the property) and deponent further says and gives notice as follows:

TO LIEN CLAIMANTS AND SUBSEQUENT PURCHASERS

Take notice that work is about to commence on an improvement to the real property described in this instrument. A person having a construction lien may preserve the lien by providing a notice of furnishing to the above-named designee and the general contractor, if any, and by timely recording a claim of lien, in accordance with law.

A person having a construction lien arising by virtue of work performed on this improvement should refer to the name of the owner or lessee and the legal description appearing in this notice. A person subsequently acquiring an interest in the land described is not required to be named in a claim of lien.

A copy of this notice with an attached form for notice of furnishing may be obtained upon making a written request by certified mail to the above named owner or lessee, the designee or the person with whom you have contracted.

Subscribed and sworn to before me, this _____ day of (month), 20__.

_____
(Owner, Lessee, or Agent)

Name and business address of the person who drafted this instrument:

_____

_____   _____ County, Michigan
(Notary Public)   My Commission Expires: _____, 20__.

A copy of the notice of commencement must be posted and kept posted in a conspicuous place on the real property described in the notice and must be furnished to each subcontractor, supplier or laborer upon demand.

The owner, lessee or signee shall provide a copy of the notice of commencement to the general contractor, if any. Failure to do so shall render the owner or lessee liable to the general contractor for all actual expenses sustained by the general contractor in obtaining the information otherwise provided by the notice of commencement. In addition, a contractor or subcontractor who has been provided with a notice of commencement from the owner, lessee, contractor or subcontractor must furnish a copy of the notice in addition to a blank notice of furnishing form within 10 days of a written request by a subcontractor, supplier or laborer who has a direct contact with the contractor or subcontractor. When an owner or lessee fails to record a Notice of Commencement, this failure serves to extend the time within which a subcontractor or supplier must serve a Notice of Furnishing, until 20 days after the Notice of Commencement is actually provided; 30 days for laborers. Thus, where no Notice of Commencement is ever recorded, a Notice of Furnishing may properly be served up to the day a lien is recorded. Part (a) does not apply to improvements to residential structures.

(b) *Improvements to Residential Structures.* An owner or lessee contracting for an improvement to a residential structure shall prepare and provide a notice of commencement to a contractor, subcontractor, supplier or laborer. The notice shall contain the following: (1) the legal description of the real property on which the improvement is to be made; (2) the name, address and capacity of the owner or lessee of the real property contracting for the improvement; (3) the name and address of the fee owner of the real property, if the person contracting for the improvement is a land contract vendee or lessee; (4) the name and address of the owner's or lessee's designee; (5) the name and address of the general contractor, if any; (6) the following caption below the line for the general contractor's name and address "(the name of the person with whom you have contracted to provide substantially all of the improvements to the property)"; (7) the name and address of the person preparing the notice; (8) an affidavit of the owner or lessee or the agent of the owner or lessee which verifies the notice; and (9) the following statement in boldface type on the front of the form:

WARNING THE HOMEOWNER

Michigan law requires you to do the following: (1) complete and return this form to the person who asked for it within 10 days after the date of the postmark on the request; (2) if you do not complete and return this form within 10 days, you may have to pay the expenses incurred in getting the information; (3) if you do not live at the site of the improvement, you must post a copy of this form in a conspicuous place at that site.

You are not required to but should do the following: (1) complete and post a copy of this form at a place where the improvement is being made, even if you live there; (2) make and keep a copy of this form for your own records. In addition, the notice of commencement must contain the following statement:

Take notice that the work is about to commence on an improvement to the real property described in this instrument. A person having a construction lien may preserve the lien by providing a notice of furnishing to the above-named designee and the general contractor, if any, and by timely recording a claim of lien, in accordance with law.

A person having a construction lien arising by virtue of work performed on this improvement should refer to the name of the owner or lessee and the legal description appearing in this notice. A person subsequently acquiring an interest in the land described is not required to be named in a claim of lien.

A copy of this notice with an attached form for notice of furnishing may be obtained upon making a written request by certified mail to the above-named owner or lessee, the designee, or the person with whom you have contracted.

Each copy of the notice of commencement shall have a blank notice of furnishing (see below) form attached to it. The blank form shall be easily detachable from the copy of the notice and need not be recorded.

A contractor or subcontractor is not entitled to any payment and may not file any action to enforce the lien unless he provides the owner with a sworn statement as to those with whom he/she has contracted relative to the improvement.

A claim of lien shall be in the following form. Also, an owner must, and a contractor may be required to provide a notice of commencement and, or, for contractors, subcontractors and laborers, a notice of furnishing. *See* sections 3 and 4 below.

CLAIM OF LIEN

Notice is hereby given that on the _____ day of (month), (year), (name)(address) first provided labor or material for an improvement to: (legal description from Notice of Commencement), the (owner) (lessee) of which property is: (name of owner or lessee from Notice of Commencement)

The last day of providing the labor or material was the _____ day of (month), (year).

TO BE COMPLETED BY A LIEN CLAIMANT WHO IS A CONTRACTOR, SUBCONTRACTOR, OR SUPPLIER

The lien claimant's contract amount, including extras, is $_____. The lien claimant has received payment thereon in the total amount of $_____, and therefore claims a construction lien upon the above-described real property in the amount of $_____.

TO BE COMPLETED BY A LIEN CLAIMANT WHO IS A LABORER

The lien claimant's hourly rate, including fringe benefits and withholdings, is $_____. There is due and owing to or on behalf of the laborer the sum of $_____ for which the laborer claims a construction lien upon the above-described real property.

TO BE COMPLETED IF CLAIM OF LIEN HAS BEEN ASSIGNED

The claim of lien having been assigned, this claim of lien is made by (name of assignee), as assignee thereof.

_____
(Lien claimant)

By _____
(Signature of lien claimant, agent or attorney)

_____
(Address of party signing claim of lien)

Date _____

STATE OF MICHIGAN   }
                          } ss.
County of _____   }

Subscribed and sworn to before me this _____ day of _____, 20___.

_____
(Owner, Lessee, or Agent)

Name and business address of the person who drafted this instrument:

_____

_____   _____ County, Michigan
(Notary Public)

                                        My Commission Expires: _____, 20__

Notice of Furnishing—During performance, a subcontractor or materialman must serve notice of furnishing by certified mail (return receipt requested) to the owner and general contractor, if any, within 20 days after first furnishing labor or materials. Failure of a lien claimant to provide the notice of furnishing within the specified time will not defeat the right to the lien but it may reduce the value of the lien by the amount that the owner or lessee paid for the work prior to receipt of notice, if such payments have been made in reliance on a contractor's sworn statement or waiver of lien. A notice of furnishing is as follows:

NOTICE OF FURNISHING

To: (name of designee [or owner or lessee] from notice of commencement)
(address from notice of commencement)

Please take notice that the undersigned is furnishing to (name of owner and general contractor)certain labor or (name and address of other contracting party) material for (describe type of work) in connection with the improvement to the real property described in the Notice of Commencement recorded in liber _____, on page _____, (name of county) records, or _____ (a copy of which is attached hereto).

WARNING TO OWNER: THIS NOTICE IS REQUIRED BY THE MICHIGAN CONSTRUCTION LIEN ACT. IF YOU HAVE QUESTIONS ABOUT YOUR RIGHTS AND DUTIES UNDER THIS ACT, YOU SHOULD CONTACT AN ATTORNEY TO PROTECT YOU FROM THE POSSIBILITY OF PAYING TWICE FOR THE IMPROVEMENTS TO YOUR PROPERTY.

                                        (name and address of lien claimant)

Date:_____   by: (name and capacity of party signing for lien claimant)

                                        (address of party signing)

A contractor or subcontractor is not entitled to any payment and may not file any action to enforce the lien unless he provides the owner with a sworn statement as to those with whom he/she has contracted relative to the improvement.

A laborer who contracts to provide an improvement to real property shall provide a notice of furnishing to the designee and the general contractor, if any, as named in the notice of commencement, either personally or by mail, within 30 days after wages were contractually due but were unpaid. In addition, such laborer shall provide such notice at the address shown on the notice of commencement, either personally or by certified mail, by the fifth day of the second month following the month in which fringe benefits or withholdings from wages were contractually due but were unpaid. Failure of a laborer to provide the notice within the specified time will defeat the lien for the wages or benefits or withholdings for which the notice was due but will not defeat the right to a construction lien.

Foreclosing the Lien—An action to enforce a construction lien through foreclosure shall be brought in the circuit court for the county where the real property described in the claim of lien is located. Arbitrators may also have the authority to decide the validity of a construction lien but do not have the legal authority to order that the property be sold to satisfy the construction lien.

Notice of Lis Pendens—At the time of commencing an action for the enforcement of a construction lien through foreclosure, the plaintiff shall record a Notice of Lis Pendens with respect to the action in the office of the register of deeds for the county in which the real property involved in the action is located. The Notice of Lis Pendens, once filed, is effective for three years from the date of filing and may be extended for a maximum of three additional years. Upon the completion of a lien foreclosure lawsuit, a Release of Lis Pendens must be recorded with the Register of Deeds.

Discharging the Lien—A claim of lien may be discharged upon payment of the lien amount, the filing of a cash or surety bond in an amount of twice the lien amount, with the county clerk where the property is located. The claimant is required to provide a Discharge of Construction Lien and if a Notice of Lis

Pendens was filed, a Release of Lis Pendens. Within 10 days of receiving the bond, the county clerk must notify all lien claimants who then have an additional 10 days within which to file any objections as to the adequacy or sufficiency of the bond. An administrative process may also be followed to obtain a discharge of lien. If a foreclosure action is not commenced within one year of the date of recording the lien, any interested person may provide an affidavit to the county clerk stating when the lien was recorded and the identity of the lien claimant; whereupon the clerk must provide a certification as to whether or not a foreclosure action had been commenced and if not, provide a certification to that effect, after the recording of which the claim of lien has no effect.

Homeowner Construction Lien Recovery Fund—Developers or other persons not intending to reside in the building under construction, upon completion, are not entitled to participate in the Fund. The Fund was established in 1982 to provide a means of redress to homeowners, subcontractors, suppliers and laborers in the event that all debts owed on a home building or remodeling project are not paid by the licensed contractor. Unpaid subcontractors, suppliers or laborers may present their claims to the Fund. Every licensed residential builder, electrical contractor, plumbing contractor and mechanical contractor is required to contribute into the Fund.

Michigan Builder's Trust Fund Act—Building contract funds paid by any person to a contractor or by such a person or contractor to a subcontractor, is considered to be a trust fund for the benefit of the person making the payment, contractors, laborers, subcontractors or materialmen, and the contractor or subcontractor is considered the trustee of all funds so paid to him for building construction purposes. There may be criminal, civil and personal liability for any contractor which misuses funds intended for subcontractors or suppliers.

Where Recorded—Office of the Register of Deeds for each county where the real property to which the improvement was made is located. Within 15 days after recording, a copy of the recorded claim of lien must be served upon the owner and/or designee personally or by certified mail, returned receipt requested.

When to Be Filed—Contractor must file claim of lien within 90 days after last furnishing of labor or material, must serve on owner within 15 days thereafter. Subcontractor must also file claim of lien within 90 days and must serve lien on owner within 15 days of recording.

Duration of Lien—One year after recording unless action to foreclose is begun within that period of time.

Extent of Lien—The lien attaches to the entire interest of the owner or lessee who contracted for the improvement, including any subsequently acquired legal or equitable interest. The lien applies only to private property; public property is not subject to construction liens. The sum of the construction liens cannot exceed the amount which the owner or lessee agreed to pay the person with whom he or she contracted for the improvement, as modified by any and all additions, deletions and any other amendments, and less payments made by or on behalf of the owner or lessee, pursuant to either sworn statement or waiver of lien in accordance with the act.

Priority of Lien—As between lien claimants themselves, valid liens shall have equal priority. The liens take priority over all garnishments made after commencement of the first actual physical improvement. They take priority over all other liens or encumbrances given or recorded subsequent to the first actual physical improvement. However, such liens are subject to prior recorded encumbrances.

Public Improvements—See Chapter 13.

Lien for Improvement of Oil or Gas Well—Lien extends to the oil and gas leasehold, oil or gas well, lease, pipeline, buildings, fixtures and any things of value furnished. Lien must be recorded in the office of Register of Deeds in the county where the property is located within six months from the date on which the last material was furnished or labor performed. Must be enforced within one year or lien will expire.

Statutory Citation—§§ 570.1101 to 570.1305.

MINNESOTA

Who May Claim—Anyone contributing to the improvement of real estate by performing labor or furnishing skill, material or machinery, including the erection, alteration, repair or removal of any building, fixture, bridge, wharf, fence or other structure thereon or for grading, filling in or excavating, clearing, grubbing, first breaking, furnishing and placing soil or sod, or for furnishing and planting of trees, shrubs or plant materials, or for labor performed in placing soil or sod, or for labor performed in planting trees, shrubs or plant materials, or digging or repairing any mine, ditch, drain, etc., or performing engineering, architectural or land surveying services; whether under a contract with the owner thereof, or agent, contractor or subcontractor. Separate provisions for liens on logs and agricultural production input and timber.

How Claimed—By recording lien statement and serving on or mailing by certified mail to the owner a copy of the lien statement.

Where Filed—County Recorder or, if registered land, with the Register of Titles, of county where real estate is situated or if made upon railway, telephone, telegraph, or electric line, with the Secretary of State.

When to Be Filed—Within 120 days from furnishing of last item of work, labor or materials.

General Contractor's Notice—Every person who enters into a contract with the owner for the improvement of real property and who has contracted or will contract with subcontractors or materialmen to provide labor, skill or materials for the improvement shall include in any written contract with the owner the notice required in this subdivision and shall provide the owner with a copy of the written contract. If no written contract for the improvement is entered into, the notice must be prepared separately and delivered personally or by certified mail to the owner or the owner's authorized agent within 10 days after the work of improvement is agreed upon. The notice, whether included in a written contract or separately given, must be in at least 10-point bold type, if printed, or in capital letters, if typewritten and must state as follows:

Any person or company supplying labor or materials for this improvement to your property may file a lien against your property if that person or company is not paid for the contributions.

Under Minnesota law you have the right to pay persons who supplied labor or materials for improvement directly and deduct this amount from our contract price, or withhold the amounts due them from us until 120 days after completion of the improvement unless we give you a waiver signed by persons who supplied any labor or material for the improvement and who gave you timely notice. A person who fails to provide the notice shall not have the lien and remedy provided by these statutes.

However, there are numerous exceptions to the requirement of this notice. The notice required in sections 5, 6 and 7 is not required in connection with an improvement to real property which is not in agricultural use and which is wholly or partially nonresidential in use if the work or improvement:

a. is to provide or add more than 5,000 total usable square feet of floor space;
b. is an improvement to real property where the existing property contains more than 5,000 total usable total square feet of floor space;
c. is an improvement to real property which contains more than 5,000 square feet and does not involve the construction of a new building or an addition to or the improvement of an existing building;
d. there will not be any contract with other subcontractors or suppliers;
e. the property is wholly residential and provides more than four family units;
f. the contractor is managed or controlled by substantially the same persons who manage or control the property owner;
g. the contractor is the property owner;
h. the contractor is a corporation and the property owner is an officer or controlling shareholder of that corporation;
i. the property owner is a corporation and the contractor is an officer or controlling shareholder of that corporation;
j. the contractor and the property owner are both corporations managed or controlled by essentially the same persons.

Lien Claimant's Notice—Every subcontractor must, as a prerequisite to the validity of any claim or lien, give the owner or his authorized agent, by personal delivery or by certified mail not later than 45 days after the lien claimant has first furnished labor, skills, or materials for the improvement, a written notice in at least 10-point bold type which shall state:

This notice is to advise you of your rights under Minnesota law in connection with the improvement to your property.

Any person or company supplying labor or materials for this improvement may file a lien against your property if that person or company is not paid for the contributions.

We (insert name and address of subcontractor) have been hired by your contractor (insert name of your contractor) to provide (insert type of service) or (insert material) for this improvement. To the best of our knowledge, our estimated charges will be (insert value of service or material).

If we are not paid by your contractor, we can file a claim against your property for the price of our services.

You have the right to pay us directly and deduct this amount from the contract price, or withhold the amount due us from your contractor until 120 days after completion of the improvement unless your contractor gives you a lien waiver signed by me (us).

We may not file a lien if you paid your contractor in full before receiving this notice.

A person entitled to a lien does not lose the right to the lien for failure to strictly comply with this subdivision if a good faith effort is made to comply, unless the owner or another lien claimant proves damage as a direct result of the failure to comply.

However, there are numerous exceptions to the requirement of this notice if the work or improvement:

(a) is to provide or add more than 5,000 total usable square feet of floor space;

(b) is an improvement to real property where the existing property contains more than 5,000 total usable square feet of floor space;

(c) is an improvement to real property which contains more than 5,000 square feet and does not involve the construction of a new building or an addition to or the improvement of an existing building;

(d) the property is not agricultural and is wholly or partially nonresidential;

(e) the property is wholly residential and provides more than four family units;

(f) the lien claimant is managed or controlled by substantially the same persons who manage or control the property owner.

Please note that it is important that the Lien Claimant's Notice should be provided as soon as possible after commencing work (but not later than 45 days after the claimant's first item of labor, skill or material is furnished to the improvement). Minnesota law provides that the total amount of all liens on an owner's property will be reduced by payments made by the owner to the contractor prior to receipt of the lien claimants' notices. This implies that a lien claimant will be barred from asserting all or a portion of its lien claim if the owner pays the general contractor before it receives a Lien Claimant's Notice.

Foreclosing the Lien—A mechanic's lien foreclosure action along with a Notice of Lis Pendens must be filed within one year of the last item of labor, skill or material furnished to improve the property. This is done by filing an action in the district court in the county in which the improved property is located and by filing a Notice of Lis Pendens with the county recorder or the Registrar of Titles depending on whether the improved property is abstract or torrens. The successful lien foreclosure action is culminated by the initiation of a sheriff's sale of the property. The priority of the lien compared to other interests will be determined in the foreclosure sale.

Discharge of Lien—An owner of property against which a lien has been filed may start an action to quiet title in district court or apply to have the property released from the lien, by giving 10 days' notice to the lien claimant of its intention to apply in court for a release of the lien. The judge will require the owner to deposit an appropriate sum of money or bond, against which the lien claimant shall have the same right of lien as it would have had against the property.

Attorney's Fees and Interest—Attorney's fees and interest may be awarded to a successful lien claimant.

Trust Funds—Payments received by a person contributing to the improvement of real property shall be held in trust by that person for the benefit of those who have furnished the labor, materials, skill or machinery contributing to the improvements and are not subject to garnishment, execution, levy or attachment. There may be civil or criminal penalties imposed on those contractors who fail to pass on the owner's payments to subcontractors and suppliers.

Request for Information—A subcontractor or materialman may ask a contractor for the name and address of the owner of real estate for which it has provided labor, skill and materials, and the contractor shall provide the same within 10 days.

Duration of Lien—The lien shall cease at the end of 120 days after the doing of the last of the work or furnishing of materials unless the lien statement is filed and statutory notice of *lis pendens* given within that time. No lien shall be enforced unless the holder shall assert it within one year after the date of the last item of his claim as set forth in the recorded lien statement.

Contents of Notice of Lien—(1) Notice of intention to claim a lien and amount thereof; (2) nature of claim; (3) name of claimant and person for whom work, labor or materials were performed or furnished; (4) dates of first and last items of furnishing or performing work, labor, etc.; (5) description of premises to be charged; (6) name of owner of property to best of lien claimant's information and belief at time of making statement; (7) post office address of claimant; (8) that copy of statement of notice was mailed; (9) that the subcontractor notice, if required, was given.

Extent of Lien—The lien shall extend to all the interest and title of the owner in and to the premises improved not exceeding 80 acres, or in the case of homestead agricultural land, 40 acres.

With respect to any contract or improvement for which notice is not required to be given the amount of the lien shall be as follows: (a) if the contribution is made under a contract with the owner and for an agreed price, the lien as against him shall be for the sum so agreed upon; (b) in all other cases it shall be for the reasonable value of the work done and of the skill, material, and machinery furnished.

With respect to any contract or improvement as to which notice is required, the amount of the lien shall be as follows: If the contribution is made under a contract with the owner and for an agreed price, the lien against him shall be for the agreed upon sum. In all other cases it shall be for the reasonable value of the work done and of the skill, material and machinery furnished. Provided, however, the total sum of all items shall not exceed the total of the contract price plus the contract price or reasonable value of any additional contract or contracts between the owner and the contractor less the total of the following: (a) payments made by the owner or his agent to the contractor prior to receiving any notice; (b) payment authorized by law made by the owner or his agent to discharge any liens or claims; (c) payments made by the owner or his agent pursuant to presentation of valid lien waivers from persons or companies contributing to the improvement where previously given the required notice.

Owner May Withhold Payment—Owner may withhold from his contractor so much of the contract price as may be necessary to meet the demands of all persons other than the contractor having a lien upon the premises for labor, skill or material furnished for the improvement and in which the contractor is liable and he may pay and discharge all such liens and deduct the cost thereof from the contract price. No owner is required to pay his contractor until the expiration of 120 days from the completion of the improvement except to the extent that the contractor shall furnish to the owner waivers of claims for mechanics' liens signed by persons who furnished labor, skill or material for the improvement and given the notice required by statute. As against a bona fide purchaser, mortgagee or encumberor without actual or record notice, no lien shall attach prior to the actual and visible beginning of the improvement on the ground.

Priority of Lien—All liens attach and take effect from the time the first item of material or labor is furnished upon the premises for the beginning of the improvement and shall be preferred to any mortgage or other encumbrance not then of record unless the lien holder had actual notice thereof.

Public Improvements—See Chapter 13.

Statutory Citation—Minnesota Statutes, Chapter 514, §§ 514.01 to 514.18.

MISSISSIPPI

Who May Claim—Architects, engineers, surveyors, laborers, water well drillers, materialmen or contractors for labor done, materials furnished or services rendered in the erection, construction, alteration or repair of structures, fixed machinery and fixtures, railroad embankment, and subdivided property. The lien exists only in favor of the person employed, or with whom the contract is made to perform such labor or furnish such materials and services, and when the contract is made by the owner, or by the owner's agent, representative, guardian or tenant, authorized, either expressly or impliedly, by the owner of the property upon which the lien is claimed. Laborers, subcontractors or material suppliers who have furnished materials or labor to a contractor or master workman for the construction, alteration or repair of any house, structure, fixture, boat, railroad or railroad embankment who have not been paid for their labor, services or materials have no direct lien rights in the owner's property, but may stop payment of sums due the contractor from the owner. If the claim is determined to be valid and the owner fails to withhold from the amount due the contractor the amount claimed, the laborer, subcontractor or material supplier may obtain a judgment against the owner for the amount claimed and said judgment constitutes a lien on the property of the owner. In any case, the owner will not be liable for an amount greater than the amount contracted for originally with the contractor.

How Claimed—Lien rights take effect as to purchaser/encumbrancers for valuable consideration without notice of the lien, only from the time of commencing suit to enforce the lien, or from the time of recordation of the contract under which the lien arose, or a notice of lien, in the Notice of Construction Lien Book in the office of the Clerk of the Chancery Court of the county in which the property is situated; if the lien relates to a railroad or a railroad embankment, the notice must be recorded in the office of the Chancery Clerk where the work was performed. Laborers, subcontractors and material suppliers providing labor or materials to a contractor or master workman as described above may bind sums due the contractor from the owner by giving written notice to the owner of the amount due. When the written Stop Payment Notice is given, any amount that may be due upon the date of the service of the notice to the owner will be bound in his hands for the payment in full. If contract funds are insufficient at that point, funds will be due pro rata to the claimants having lawfully given notice. If, however, the notices are received after all sums have been paid out by the owner in good faith, the owner has no further obligation to laborers and materialmen. At the point suit is filed to foreclose the lien, all other interested parties will be made parties to the suit and summonsed into court to protect their rights. At that point, the owner may pay into court the amount admitted to be due on the contract or sufficient to pay the sums claimed.

When to Be Filed—There is no specified time for recording the contract or notice of lien. However, if the amount of the lien exceeds $200, suits to enforce a lien or a stop payment right must be filed within 12 months from the time the debt became due.

Where Filed—With the Clerk of the Chancery Court.

Duration of Lien—If the amount of the lien exceeds $200, suit must be commenced within 12 months from the time when the money became due and payable.

Contents of Notice of Lien—The notice filed in the Notice of Construction Lien Book must describe the property involved, the name of the lienor or lienors, the date of the filing, if and where suit is filed and if and where the contract is filed or recorded. Any laborer, materialman or architect entitled to a lien or to bind funds due a contractor by an owner, also has the right to record his claim in the *lis pendens* record maintained by the office of the Chancery Clerk in the county where the land is situated, provided the claimant (i) reduces his claim to a writing showing the basis of his claim, all the parties affected by the lien, a description of the property subject to the lien and the rights claimed in the property, and (ii) gives the owner a copy of the notice in person or by certified mail. The lienor must attach an affidavit that notice has been given the owner and the date and manner thereof.

Extent of Lien—If the house, building, structure or fixture for which the labor or materials were supplied is in a city, town or village, the lien extends to and covers the entire lot of land on which it stands; if not in a city, town or village, the lien extends to and covers up to one acre of land on which the structure is standing. If the structure is a railroad or railroad embankment, the lien extends to the entire roadbed and right of way, depots and other buildings used or connected therewith. If the structure is a water well, the lien extends only to the pumps, pipes, equipment therein and water well appurtenances. If the structure is a rented structure and the work or services or materials are provided at the instance of a tenant, guardian or other person who is not the owner of the land, only the estate of the tenant in the house, building, structure or fixture can be subject to the lien unless the labor, services and materials and work are done with the written consent of the owner. If the services are upon a whole subdivision, the lien extends to and covers the entire subdivision; but if only a part of the land is subdivided, then the lien extends only to that portion of the subdivision upon which the work was done or materials were furnished.

Priority of Lien—Liens arising out of the same transaction are concurrent; if arising out of different transactions, they take precedence in order of filing of contract or commencing suit.

The lien shall take effect as to purchasers/encumbrancers for a valuable consideration without notice thereof only from the time of commencement of suit to enforce the lien, or from the time of filing the contract under which the lien arose. The lien of a deed of trust securing a construction loan has priority over the lien only to the extent that the funds disbursed actually went into the construction or to the extent that the lender used reasonable diligence in disbursing the proceeds of the construction loan.

Requirement of Written Contract—The knowledge and consent of the owner to the contract in question are considered to be sufficient. There is no requirement that the contract be in writing.

Assignments and Transfers—By statute, no contractor has the right to assign, transfer or dispose of, in any way, the contract or the proceeds of the contract to the detriment or prejudice of the subcontractors, laborers and materialmen.

Public Improvements—See Chapter 13.

Statutory Citation—Mississippi Code, Title 85, §§ 85-7-131 to 85-7-265.

MISSOURI

Mechanics' and Materialmen's Lien, Who May Assert; Extent of Lien—Any person who shall do or perform any work or labor upon, or furnish any material, fixtures, engine, boiler or machinery for any building, erection or improvements upon land, or for repairing the same, or furnish and plant trees, shrubs, bushes or other plants or provides any type of landscaping goods or services or who installs outdoor irrigation systems under or by virtue of any contract with the owner or proprietor thereof, or his agent, trustee, contractor or subcontractor, or without a contract if ordered by a city, town, village or county having a charter form of government to abate the conditions that caused a structure on that property to be deemed a dangerous building under local ordinances pursuant to section 67.410, R.S.Mo, upon complying with the provisions of sections 429.010 to 429.340, shall have for his work or labor done, or materials, fixtures, engine, boiler, machinery, trees, shrubs, bushes or other plants furnished, or any type of landscaping goods or services provided, a lien upon such building, erection or improvements, and upon the land belonging to such owner or proprietor on which the same are situated, to the extent of three acres; or if such building, erection or improvements be upon any lot of land in any town, city or village, or if such building, erection or improvements be upon any lot of land in any town, city or village, or if such building, erection or improvements be for manufacturing, industrial or commercial purposes and not within any city, town or village, then such lien shall be upon such building, erection or improvements, and the lot, tract or parcel of land upon which the same are situated, and not limited to the extent of three acres, to secure the payment of such work or labor done, or materials, fixtures, engine, boiler, machinery, trees, shrubs, bushes or other plants or any type of landscaping goods or services furnished, or outdoor irrigation systems installed; except that if such building, erection or improvements be not within the limits of any city, town or village, then such lien shall be also upon the land to the extent necessary to provide a roadway for ingress to and egress from the lot, tract or parcel of land upon which said building, erection or improvements are situated, not to exceed 40 feet in width, to the nearest public road or highway. Such lien shall be enforceable only against the property of the original purchaser of such plants unless the lien is filed against the property prior to the conveyance of such property to a third person.

Mandatory Notice Requirements—The timing of the required notice depends upon whether a claimant is the prime contractor or subcontractor and whether the property in question is residential or commercial in character. A subcontractor/supplier must give the owner written notice of the subcontractor's/supplier's intention to file a lien 10 days before filing the lien, in addition to requiring the general contractor obtain the written consent of the owner to a possible lien, prior to the start of work. The general contractor, on residential property, as a condition precedent to a valid mechanic's lien, must give notice to the owner prior to the receiving payment from the owner in any form (a) either at the time of execution of the contract; (b) when the materials are delivered; (c) when the work is commenced; or (d) delivered with the first invoice:

NOTICE TO OWNER

FAILURE OF THIS CONTRACTOR TO PAY THOSE PERSONS SUPPLYING MATERIAL CAN RESULT IN THE FILING OF A MECHANIC'S LIEN ON THE PROPERTY WHICH IS THE SUBJECT OF THIS CONTRACT PURSUANT TO CHAPTER 429, R.S.MO. TO AVOID THIS RESULT YOU MAY ASK THIS CONTRACTOR FOR "LIEN WAIVERS" FROM ALL PERSONS SUPPLYING MATERIAL OR SERVICES FOR THE WORK DESCRIBED IN THIS CONTRACT. FAILURE TO SECURE LIEN WAIVERS MAY RESULT IN YOUR PAYING FOR LABOR AND MATERIAL TWICE. 429.012 R.S.Mo.

Consent of Owner—With regard to the improvement, repair or remodeling of owner-occupied residential property of four units or less, no person, other than an original contractor, shall have a lien for work performed unless the owner of the property has signed a written consent to be liable in the event the subcontractor's or supplier's charges are not paid. The consent must appear in 10-point bold print and be signed separately from any other notice and agreement and must provide as follows:

CONSENT OF OWNER

CONSENT IS HEREBY GIVEN FOR FILING OF MECHANICS' LIENS BY ANY PERSON WHO SUPPLIES MATERIALS OR SERVICES FOR THE WORK DESCRIBED IN THIS CONTRACT ON THE PROPERTY ON WHICH IT IS LOCATED IF HE IS NOT PAID.

Every original contractor shall retain a copy of the Notice to Owner described below and any consent signed by an owner and shall furnish a copy to any person performing work or labor or furnishing material, fixtures, engines, boilers or machinery upon their request for such copy of the notice or consent. It shall be a condition precedent to the creation, existence or validity of any lien by anyone other than an original contractor that a copy of the consent, signed by an owner, be attached to the recording of a claim of lien. The signature of one or more of the owners shall be binding upon all owners. In the absence of a consent, full payment of the amount due under a contract to the contractor shall be a complete defense to all liens filed by any person performing work or labor or furnishing material, fixtures, engines, boilers or machinery. Partial payment to the contractor shall only act as an offset to the extent of such payment.

How Claimed—By filing a just and true account of demand. Every person except original contractor must give 10 days' notice before filing lien, to the owner.

Where Filed—Office of Clerk of Circuit Court in County where property is situated.

When to Be Filed—Within six months after indebtedness shall have accrued.

Service of Copy of Notice—All persons, other than original contractor, shall give 10 days' notice in the form of a Notice of Intent to File Mechanic's Lien Statement before filing lien to owner, owners or agents. Service must be verified by affidavit of the person so serving. Service of this 10-day notice must be filed no less than 10 days prior to the expiration of the six-month period, or the lien will be untimely. All parties with a recorded interest in the property should be served and the notice should be filed with the county recorder's office. Notice to be served by an officer or person who would be a competent witness.

Duration of Lien—For six months after filing of lien. Lien lapses unless suit is filed within that time.

Contents of Lien—Just and true account of demand, description of the property upon which lien is intended to apply, name of owner and contractor, verified under oath. A claimant other than an original contractor must set forth an itemized statement of the labor and materials. The "Consent of Owner" referred to in paragraph 2 above, if applicable, must be filed with lien.

Priority of Lien—When a Deed of Trust is given and recorded to secure a construction loan, in which the lender is involved in construction disbursement, the mechanics' lien claim is given priority as to the improvements and the land. The lien shall attach to the buildings, erections or improvements in preference to any prior lien or encumbrance or mortgage upon the land. The lien for work and materials shall be preferred to all other encumbrances which may be attached to the buildings, bridges or other improvements, or the ground, subsequent to the commencement of such buildings or improvements.

Public Improvements—See Chapter 13.

Lien for Improvement of Oil or Gas Well—Person to whom another is indebted for expenses incurred in drilling and operating a well or a drilling unit with pooled interests may place a lien to secure payment of amount due by recording an affidavit setting forth amount due and interest of debtor in production in office of Recorder of Deeds in county where property is located.

Notice to Owner—Every original contractor shall provide to the person with whom the contract is made prior to receiving payment in any form of any kind from such person either (a) at the time of the execution of the contract, (b) when the materials are delivered, (c) when the work is commenced, or (d) delivered with the first invoice, a written notice which shall include the following disclosure language in 10-point bold type:

NOTICE TO OWNER

Failure of this contractor to pay those persons supplying material or services to complete this contract can result in the filing of a mechanics' lien on the property which is the subject of this contract pursuant to chapter 429, R.S.Mo. To avoid this result you may ask this contractor for "lien waivers" from all persons supplying material or services for the work described in this contract. Failure to secure lien waivers may result in your paying for labor and material twice.

Service of notice is a condition precedent to the creation and valid existence of a mechanics' lien in favor of an original contractor. The notice is not required when performing work for a builder-developer of new residences if the buyer has title insurance protecting him from mechanics' liens issued by a title insurance company registered in Missouri. Any original contractor who fails to provide the notice is guilty of a misdemeanor and can be fined.

Design Professionals, Commercial Real Estate Brokers, Certified Appraisers and Title Companies— Architects and engineers licensed in Missouri, providing services on a project where there has been actual physical improvements made to the property, and where those services are directly related to those actual physical improvements, are entitled to a mechanic's lien under a separate Missouri statute, 429.015.1. There are some differences in how to perfect the lien. Real estate brokers, certified appraisers and title companies may also assert liens against property being sold under certain circumstances, but only after satisfying various and detailed statutory provisions.

Statutory Citation—Missouri Statutes, Title XXVII, Chapter 429, §§ 429.005 to 429.360.

MONTANA

Who May Claim—Any person who furnishes services or materials pursuant to a real estate improvement contract, including alteration of the surface by excavation; construction or installation on, above or below the surface of land; demolition, repair, remodeling or removal of a structure previously constructed or installed; seeding, sodding or other landscape operations; surface of subsurface testing, boring or analysis; and preparation of plans, surveys or architectural or engineering plans or drawings for any change in the physical condition of the real estate, regardless of whether they are used to produce a change in the physical condition of the real estate; may claim a construction lien to secure the payment of his contract price. Real estate improvement contract does not include a contract for the mining or removal of timber, minerals, gravel, soil, sod or things growing on the land or a similar contract on which the activity is primarily for the purpose of making the materials available for sale or use; or a contract for the planting, cultivation or harvesting of crops or for the preparation of the soil for planting of crops.

A lien for furnishing materials arises only if the materials are supplied with the intent that they be used in the course of construction of or incorporated into the improvement in connection with which the lien arises; and that intent can be shown by a contract of sale, a delivery order, delivery to the site by the lien claimant or at his direction, or by other evidence; and the materials are: (1) incorporated in the improvement or consumed as normal wastage in construction operations; (2) specifically fabricated for incorporation into the improvement and not readily resalable in the ordinary course of the fabricator's business, even though the materials are not actually incorporated into the improvement; (3) used for the construction or operation of machinery or equipment used in the course of construction and not remaining in the improvement, subject to diminution by the salvage value of those materials; or (4) tools, appliances or machinery used on the particular improvement.

A mechanics' lien has been renamed a construction lien.

How Claimed—By filing claim in writing. Subcontractor must provide an owner with notice of rights and advise owner of possibility that a construction lien may be filed; statutory form is provided.

Where Filed—County Clerk of county where property is situated.

Notice of Completion—Montana law allows an owner to file and publish a Notice of Completion, which starts the running of the timeframe for filing a Claim of Lien. The timeframe for filing a Claim of Lien is not later than 90 days after the final provision of materials or services for the project, or after the owner files a Notice of Completion.

When to Be Filed—Within 90 days from the date of last work performed or material furnished or owner files a notice of completion. With respect to real estate improvement contracts, notice of right to claim a lien must be filed within five days after the date on which the notice of right to claim a lien is given to the contracting owner. Notice of right to claim must be given to the contracting owner within 20 days after the date that services or materials are furnished. The period is 45 days if construction is financed by a regulated lender. This does not apply to owner occupied residences. This copy must be filed five business days after the date on which the notice of the right to claim a lien is given to contracting owner. The notice of completion and affidavit must set forth the date when the work or improvement was completed or the date on which cessation from labor occurred first and the period of its duration; the name and address of the owner; a description of the property sufficient for identification; the nature of the title, if any, of the person signing the notice, and the name of the contractor, if any. The notice must be verified by the owner or his agent and a copy published once each week for three successive weeks in a newspaper of general circulation in the county where the land on which the work or improvement was performed is situated. A lien must then be filed within 90 days immediately following the first publication of the notice of completion. For the purpose of filing a notice of completion, "completion of any work or improvement" constitutes the following: (1) the written acceptance by the owner, his agent or his representative of the building, improvement or structure; (2) the cessation from labor for 30 days upon any building, improvement or structure, or the alteration, addition to or repair thereof. In the event of untimely notice, the claimant is entitled only to a lien for the services or materials furnished within the 20-day or 45-day period, whichever is applicable, preceding the date on which the notice is provided.

Discharging the Lien—At any time before a lien foreclosure action is filed, the owner may file a bond in an amount equal to one and one-half times the amount of the lien with the Clerk of the District Court in the county where the liened property is located. Once a lien foreclosure action has been started, the lien may not be transferred to a bond.

Exemptions to Preliminary Statutory Notice Requirements—(a) a person furnishing services or materials directly to the owner at the owner's request; (b) a wage earner or laborer performing personal labor for a person furnishing any service or material pursuant to a real estate improvement contract; (c) a person furnishing services or materials pursuant to a real estate improvement contract that relates to a dwelling for five or more families; and (d) a person furnishing services or materials pursuant to a real estate improvement contract that relates to an improvement that is partly or wholly commercial in character.

Service of Copy of Notice—Service shall be made by personal service on each owner or by mailing a copy of the lien by certified or registered mail with return receipt requested to each owner's last known address. A copy of the notice must be filed with the Clerk and Recorder of the county in which the improved real property is located. The notice must be filed not later than five business days after the date on which the Notice of the Right to Claim a Lien is given to the contracting owner. In filing the lien, the lien claimant must certify to the County Clerk and Recorder that a copy of the lien has been served upon each owner of record and attach this certification to the lien document. The certification shall identify whether service of the lien on the property owner of record has been made personally by delivery of certified or registered mail.

Duration of Lien—One year from date of filing of lien, with a right to file a one-year continuation of the lien.

Contents of Preliminary Notice of Right to Claim a Lien/Notice of Lien—(a) *Notice of a Right to Claim a Lien.* The preliminary notice must contain the following information and be in substantially the following form:

NOTICE OF THE RIGHT TO CLAIM A LIEN

WARNING: READ THIS NOTICE. PROTECT YOURSELF FROM PAYING ANY CONTRACTOR OR SUPPLIER TWICE FOR THE SAME SERVICE.

To: (Owner)   Date of mailing: _____
   (Owner's address)

This is to inform you that (name of subcontractor or material supplier) has begun to provide (description of services or materials) ordered by (contractor) for improvements to property you own. The property is located at (property address).

A lien may be claimed for all services and materials furnished to you if this notice is given to you within 20 days after the date on which the services or materials described are first furnished to you. If the notice is not given within that time, a lien is enforceable for only the services or materials furnished within the 20-day period before the date on which the notice is given. However, if a regulated lender has provided the funds for the services or materials described in this notice, the notice may be given 45 days after the date the service or materials are first furnished to you. If the notice is not given within that time, a lien is enforceable for only the services or materials furnished within the 45-day period before the date the notice is given.

Even if you or your mortgage lender have made full payment to the contractor who ordered these services or materials, your property may still be subject to a lien unless the subcontractor or material supplier providing this notice is paid. THIS IS NOT A LIEN. It is a notice sent to you for your protection in compliance with the construction lien laws of the state of Montana.

This notice has been sent to you by:

(Name)
(Address)   IF YOU HAVE ANY QUESTIONS ABOUT
(Telephone)   THIS NOTICE PLEASE CALL US.

IMPORTANT INFORMATION ON REVERSE SIDE

IMPORTANT INFORMATION FOR YOUR PROTECTION

Under Montana's laws, those who work on your property or provide materials and are not paid have a right to enforce their claim for payment against your property. This claim is known as a construction lien.

If your contractor fails to pay subcontractors or material suppliers or neglects to make other legally required payments, the people who are owed money may look to your property for payment, even if you have paid your contractor in full.

The law states that all people hired by a contractor to provide you with services or materials are required to give you a notice of the right to lien to let you know what they have provided.

WAYS TO PROTECT YOURSELF ARE:

—RECOGNIZE that this notice of delivery of services or materials may result in a lien against your property unless all those supplying a notice of the right to lien have been paid.

—LEARN more about the construction lien laws and the meaning of this notice by contacting an attorney or the firm sending this notice.

—WHEN PAYING YOUR CONTRACTOR for services or materials, you may make checks payable jointly to the contractor and the firm furnishing services or materials for which you have received a notice of the right to lien.

—OBTAIN EVIDENCE that all firms from whom you have received a notice of the right to lien have been paid or have waived the right to claim a lien against your property.

—CONSULT AN ATTORNEY, a professional escrow company or your mortgage lender. Lien is effective for one year from filing. Thereafter it lapses unless prior to expiration of one-year period claimant files a one-year continuation of notice. Such continuation must contain clerk and recorder file number; date of original filing, name of person to whom notice originally given.

(b) *Contents of Lien Notice.* The form for the lien is as follows:

CONSTRUCTION LIEN

I, (name and address of person claiming the construction lien), claim a construction lien pursuant to Title 71, chapter 3, of the Montana Code Annotated.

I claim this lien against (give sufficient description of the real property against which the lien is claimed to identify it). The contracting owner is (name of the person who owns the real estate and name of the person who entered into the contract to improve it).

At the request of (name and address of party with whom person claiming the lien contracted to furnish services or materials), I provided the following: (description of the services or materials provided). The amount remaining unpaid is (amount unpaid; if no amount was fixed by the contract, give your good faith estimate of the amount and identify it as an estimate).

I first furnished these services or materials on (date) and last furnished services or materials on (date; if the date has not yet arrived, insert an estimate of the date on which services or materials will be last furnished and identify the date as an estimate).

I gave notice of the right to claim a lien as required by 71-3-531 on (date) to (name of contracting owner). [If it is not required to give a notice of the right to claim a lien, state the reason it is not required.]

The Notice of the Right to Claim a Lien, when properly filed, is valid for a period of one year from the date of the filing. The notice lapses upon the expiration of that one-year period, unless the lien claimant files with the Clerk and Recorder a one-year Continuation of the Notice of the Right to Claim a Lien prior to the date on which the first notice will lapse. If a Notice of the Right to Claim a Lien is required, a construction lien claim may not be asserted unless there is an unexpired Notice of the Right to Claim a Lien or an unexpired Continuation Notice, properly filed with the Clerk and Recorder at the time the lien claimant files the construction lien. The Continuation Notice must contain certain required information: (a) the Clerk and Recorder's file number of the notice; (b) the date on which the notice originally was filed; and (c) the name of the person to whom the original notice was given.

Extent of Lien—A construction lien extends to the interest of the contracting owner in the real estate, as the interest exists at the commencement of work or is thereafter acquired in the real estate, subject to the following provisions: (1) if an improvement is located wholly on one or more platted lots belonging to the contracting owner, the lien applies to the improvement and to the lots on which the improvement is located; (2) if an improvement is not located wholly on one or more platted lots, the lien applies to the improvement and to the smallest identifiable tract or parcel of land on which the improvement is located; (3) if the improvement is to leased premises, the lien attaches to the improvement and to the leasehold term; (4) if a contracting owner contracts for improvements on real estate not owned by him as part of an improvement on his real estate or for the purpose of directly benefiting his real estate, there is a lien against the contracting owner's real estate being improved or directly benefited in favor of persons furnishing services or materials to the same extent as if the improvement had been on the contracting owner's real estate.

Priority of Lien—A construction lien has priority over any other interest, lien, mortgage or encumbrance that may attach to the building, structure or improvement or on the real property on which the building, structure or improvement is located and which is filed after the construction lien attaches. An interest, lien, mortgage or encumbrance that is filed before the construction lien attaches has priority over a construction lien, provided that the value of the work or improvement is not severable, or provided that prior interest was not taken to secure advances for the purpose of paying for the particular real estate improvement being liened. There is equal priority between or among construction lien claimants who contribute to the same real estate improvement project, regardless of the date on which each lien claimant first contributed services or materials and regardless of the date on which he filed his notice of lien. When the proceeds of a foreclosure sale are not sufficient to pay all construction lien claimants in full, each claimant will receive a *pro rata* share of the proceeds based on the amount of his respective lien. Construction liens attaching at different times have priority in the order of attachment.

Lien Foreclosure Action—A legal action must be filed within two years from the date of the filing of the construction lien. If successful, the lien claimant may recover lien recording and filing fees, as well as a reasonable attorneys' fee.

Public Improvements—See Chapter 13.

Lien for Improvement of Oil or Gas Well—Liens are created and perfected in the same manner as mechanics' liens except that filing statement must be within six months of completion of work.

Statutory Citation—Montana Statutes, Title 71, Chapter 3, §§ 71-3-521 to 71-3-563.

NEBRASKA

Who May Claim—Any person who furnishes services or materials pursuant to a real estate improvement contract. This includes: (1) altering the surface by excavating, filling, grading or changing a bank or flood plain of a body of water; (2) construction or installation on, above or below the surface of the land; (3) demolition, renovation, repair or removal of an existing structure or installation; (4) seeding, sodding or other landscaping; (5) surface or subsurface testing, boring or analyzing; and (6) architectural or engineering plans, drawings, surveys or preparation thereof regardless if actually used incident to producing a change in the real estate.

How Claimed—A claimant may record a lien which shall be signed by the claimant and state: (a) real estate subject to the lien, with a description thereof sufficient for identification; (b) name of the person against whose interest in the real estate a lien is claimed; (c) name and address of the claimant; (d) name and address of the person with whom the claimant contracted; (e) general description of the services performed or to be performed or materials furnished or to be furnished for the improvement and the contract price thereof; (f) amount unpaid, whether or not due, to the claimant for the services or materials, or if no amount is fixed by the contract, a good faith estimate of the amount designated as an estimate; and (g) time the last services or materials were furnished or if that time has not yet occurred, an estimate of the time.

Where Recorded—Register of Deeds of county where land is situated.

When to Be Recorded—Not later than 120 days after materials or services are last furnished. If the owner is a Protected Party, the claimant must send a copy of a recorded lien to the contracting owner within 10 days of recording.

Notices—(a) *Notice of Commencement*. Must be signed by contracting owner and denominated notice of commencement. It must state the real estate being or intended to be improved or directly benefitted, with a description sufficient for identification; the name and address of the contracting owner, his or her interest in the real estate and the name and address of the fee simple title holder, if other than the contracting owner; and that if after the notice of commencement is recorded a lien is recorded as to an improvement covered by the notice of commencement, the lien has priority from the time the notice of commencement is recorded. The notice of commencement may state its duration, but if a duration is stated of less than six months from the time of recording, the duration of the notice is six months. If no duration is stated, the duration is one year after recording. The duration can be extended by a continuation statement.

(b) *Notice to Protected Owner*. In cases of residential real estate, the contractor after entering into a contract may give notice of lien liability to the contracting Protected Owner, which notice shall be in writing, state that it is a notice of a right to assert a lien and contain the following information: name and address of the claimant; name and address of the person with whom contracted; name of owner; general description of materials and services provided; description of the property; statement that the claimant has recorded a lien and date of record or statement that claimant is entitled to record a lien, for the amount unpaid to the claimant for services or materials, whether or not due, or if no amount is fixed by the contract, a good faith estimate of the amount designated as an estimate. The statement must also contain the following warning in boldface type, in type no smaller than that provided for the other portions of the notice:

Warning: If you did not contract with the person giving this notice, any future payments you make in connection with this project may subject you to double liability.

Duration of Lien—Lien is enforceable for two years from date of filing or one year if a bond is provided. If owner demands that lienor commence suit within 30 days, lien will lapse unless lienor does so or records an affidavit that the contract price is not yet due.

Filing Fee—$5 per page.

Extent of Lien—(1) If at the time a construction lien is recorded there is a recorded notice of commencement covering the improvement pursuant to which the lien arises, the lien is on the contracting owner's real estate described in the notice of commencement.

(2) If at the time a construction lien is recorded there is no recorded notice of commencement covering the improvement pursuant to which the lien arises, the lien is on the contracting owner's real estate being improved or directly benefited.

For a subcontractor a lien is for the amount unpaid under claimant's contract.

Priority of Lien—Liens attaching at the same time have equal priority. Liens attaching at different times have priority in order of attachment. A claimant who records a notice of commencement after he or she has recorded a lien has only equal priority with claimants who record a lien while the notice of commencement is effective.

Lien for Improvement of Oil or Gas Well—Lien is accorded to any person furnishing material or services under contract of the owner of any leasehold interest or owner of any pipeline for digging, drilling, operating or repairing of wells, or the construction of any pipeline. The lien extends to the leasehold interest on materials and fixtures of the owner, oil and gas wells located on the leasehold interest, and oil or gas produced therefrom and the proceeds thereof, and the pipeline. Lien is not effective against the oil or gas until written notice of claim is given to the purchaser. Verified lien statement must be filed within four months after date of furnishing last material or services in Office of Clerk of county in which land is situated. Action to enforce lien must be brought within two years after date of filing.

Public Improvements—See Chapter 13.

Statutory Citation—Nebraska Statutes, Chapter 52, §§ 52-110 to 52-304.

NEVADA

Who May Claim—Every person who performs labor upon or furnishes material of the value of $500 or more to be used in the construction, alteration or repair of any building or other structure is entitled to assert a claim of lien upon the property and buildings. In addition to those lien rights, all miners, laborers and others who work or perform labor in the amount of $500 or more upon any mine or upon any shaft or tunnel or other excavation have a lien upon the mine. If a license is required to do the work, however, only a contractor licensed pursuant to Nevada Statute, an employee of such contractor, or a person who furnishes material to be used in the project may have a lien as described above.

In any case where a mechanics' lien attaches to any of the foregoing buildings or structures it also attaches to the land on which the building or structure stands provided that, at the commencement of the work or the furnishing of the materials for the same, the land belonged to the person who caused the building or structure to be constructed, altered or repaired. If the owner's interest is less than a fee simple, the lien attaches to whatever interest the owner has.

Any person who at the request of the owner of any lot in any incorporated town, grades, fills or improves it, or the street in front of or adjoining it, has a lien on the lot for the value of his labor and materials.

Notice of Intention to Claim a Lien—Anyone other than a person who performs only labor, in order to claim a lien, in addition to recording the lien claim must within 31 days after the first delivery of material or performance of work deliver, in person or by certified mail, to the owner or person whose name appears as owner on the building permit a notice of materials supplied or of work or services performed. A general contractor, or other person who contracts directly with the owner or sells material directly to the owner, is not required to give such notice. Prior to execution of a construction contract, a contractor must inform the owner that he may receive notices of materials supplied or services performed.

How Claimed—By filing a notice of lien. In addition, a subcontractor must send a copy of notice of materials supplied or of work or services performed to the general contractor by certified mail or deliver in person.

Where Filed—County Recorder of the county where the property or some part of it is situated.

When to Be Filed—Every person claiming a lien shall record his notice of lien not later than 90 days after the completion of the work or improvement; or 90 days after the last delivery of material; or 90 days after last performance of labor, whichever is last to expire. However, if owner files a notice of completion, lienor must record within 40 days after the owner's recording.

Service of Notice—In addition to the recording, a copy of the notice of lien must be served upon the owner within 30 days after recording by personal delivery, certified mail, or if there is no address for the owner by additional means set out in §108.227. Subcontractors must also deliver a copy of the notice of lien to the prime contractor.

Duration of Lien—Foreclosure proceedings must be commenced within six months after filing; this requirement may be extended by an agreement to extend such time filed within six months.

Recording Fee—First page $7, each additional page $1.

Contents of Lien Claim—The notice of lien must be in substantially the following form:

Assessors Parcel Numbers

NOTICE OF LIEN

The undersigned claims a lien upon property described in this notice for work, materials, or equipment furnished for the improvement of the property:

(1) The total amount of the original contract is: $_____

(2) The total amount of all charges and additions if any is: $_____

(3) The total amount of all payments received to date is: $_____

(4) The amount of the lien, after deducting all just credits and offsets is: $_____

(5) The name of the owner, if known, of the property is: _____

(6) The name of the person by whom the lien claimant was employed or to whom the lien claimant furnished work, materials or equipment is: _____

(7) A brief statement of the terms of payment of the lien claimant's contract is: _____

(8) A description of the property to be charged with the lien is: _____

_____
(Print name of Lien Claimant)

By: _____
(Authorized Signature)

State of _____ }
                         } ss.
County of _____ }

_____ (print name), being first duly sworn on oath according to law, deposes and says: I have read the foregoing Notice of Lien, know the contents thereof and state that the same is true of my own knowledge, except those matters stated upon information and belief, and as to those matters, I believe them to be true.

_____
(Authorized Signature of Lien Claimant)

[Notary Seal]

Priority of Lien—*Liens Against Property Rank in Priority As Between Themselves As Follows:* (1) labor; (2) material suppliers; (3) the subcontractors, architects, land surveyors, geologists and engineers if they have performed their services under contract with the general contractor; (4) the original contractors, architects, land surveyors, geologists and engineers if they have not performed their services under contract with a general contractor, and all other persons other than original contractors, subcontractors, architects, land surveyors, geologists and engineers;

Priorities As Between Mechanics' and Other Liens. Mechanics' liens are preferred to any lien, mortgage or other encumbrance which may have attached after the time the building, improvement or structure was commenced, or of which the lienholder had no notice and the notice was not recorded at the time when the building, improvement, or structure was commenced.

Notice of Completion—The owner may record a notice of completion and must deliver a copy in person or by certified mail to the general contractor.

Public Improvements—See Chapter 13.

Statutory Citation—Nevada Statutes, Chapter 108, §§ 108.221 to 108.246.

NEW HAMPSHIRE

Who May Claim—Any person performing labor or furnishing materials, by himself or others, to the amount of $15 or more for erecting or repairing a house or other building or appurtenance, or for building any dam, canal, bridge, sluiceway or well, other than for a municipality. Special statute covering building, logging and work on railroad properties and brick work, by virtue of a contract with the owner.

How Claimed—The subcontractor must give notice to owner before starting the work and must furnish a statement of work done or material furnished every 30 days thereafter, to the owner.

Notice of Lien—Principal contractor, no notice of lien is required; subcontractor, notice must be given to owner before starting work and a statement furnished to him every 30 days.

Duration of Lien—120 days after services are performed, or material furnished.

Filing Fee—No statutory provision.

Contents of Notice of Lien—Notice in writing that subcontractor shall claim a lien for services to be performed.

Extent of Lien—Covers land and buildings. Subcontractor's lien is limited to the sum due contractor by the owner at the time notice of lien is given to the owner.

Priority of Lien—Perfected lien has priority over all claims except liens on account of taxes. Among lienholders, liens take precedence in the order of their perfecting except for liens acquired in performance of a contract existing when the attachment was made, or was necessary to preserve the property, in which case they share pro rata. A "perfected lien" is one in which an attachment has been made claiming a lien within 90 days of finishing the work. Bona fide purchaser who records prior to attachment has priority; no priority over construction mortgage where funds have been properly disbursed.

Public Improvements—See Chapter 13.

Statutory Citation—New Hampshire Statutes, Title XLI, Chapter 447, §§ 447:1 to 447:14.

NEW JERSEY

Who May Claim—Any contractor (including any licensed architect, engineer or land surveyor who is not a salaried employee of the contractor or the owner), subcontractor or supplier who provides work, services, material or equipment pursuant to a written contract, shall be entitled to a lien. No lien shall attach for materials that have been furnished or delivered subject to a security agreement which has been entered into pursuant to Chapter 9 of Title 12A of the New Jersey Statutes.

How Claimed—A lien claim shall be signed, acknowledged and verified by oath of the claimant or, in the case of a partnership or corporation, a partner or duly authorized officer thereof.

Where Filed—County Clerk of the county in which real property to be improved is situated.

When to Be Filed—No later than 90 days following the date the last work, services, material or equipment was provided for which payment is claimed. Warranty or other service calls or work, materials or equipment provided after completion or termination of a claimant's contract shall not be used to determine the last day that work, services, material or equipment was provided.

Contents of Lien Claim—There is a statutory form provided.

Service of Copy of Lien Claim—Within 10 business days following the filing of a lien claim, the claimant shall, by personal service or registered or certified mail, return receipt requested, postage prepaid, serve or mail a copy of the lien claim as prescribed in the Mechanics' Lien Act to the last known business address or place of residence of the owner and, if any, of the contractor and the subcontractor, against whom the claim is asserted.

Duration of Lien—Action to enforce the lien must be brought within one year of the date of the last provision of work, services, material or equipment, payment for which the lien claim was filed; or within 30 days following receipt of written notice, by personal service or certified mail, return receipt requested, from the owner requiring the claimant to commence an action to establish the lien claim.

Filing Fee—$4.50 for each lien claim.

Extent of Lien—The lien extends to the value of the work or services performed, or materials or equipment furnished in accordance with the contract price. The lien shall attach to the interest of the owner in the real property. Liens for the following improvements shall attach to real property only in the manner described: (a) for improvements involving a dock, wharf, pier, bulkhead, return, jetty, piling, groin, boardwalk or pipeline above, on or below lands under waters within the State's jurisdiction, the lien shall be on the improvements together with the contracting owner's interest in the lots of land in front of or upon which the improvements are constructed and any interest of the contracting owner of the land in the land or waters in front of the land; (b) for improvements involving removal of a building or structure or part of a building or structure from its situs and its relocation on other land, the lien shall be on the contracting owner's interest in the improved real property on which the building or structure has been relocated; (c) for improvements involving excavation, drainage, dredging, landfill, irrigation work, construction of banks, making of channels, grading, filling, landscaping or the planting of any shrubs, trees or other nursery products, the lien shall be on the land to which the improvements are made, and shall not be upon the adjoining lands directly or indirectly benefited from the improvements.

Priority of Lien—In the event of the creation, conveyance, lease or mortgage of an estate or interest in real property to which improvements have been made that are subject to the lien provision of the Mechanics' Liens Act, a lien claim validly filed shall have priority over any prior creation, conveyance, lease or mortgage of an estate or interest in real property, only if the claimant has filed with the county clerk prior to that creation, conveyance, lease or mortgage, a Notice of Unpaid Balance and Right to File Lien (statutory form provided). No lien claim shall attach to the estate or interest acquired by a bona fide purchaser first recorded or lodged for record; nor shall a lien claim enjoy priority over any mortgage, judgment or other lien first recorded, lodged for record, filed or docketed. All claims established by judgment shall be ordered *pro rata*.

Residential Construction Contracts—The filing of a lien for work, services, materials or equipment furnished pursuant to a residential construction contract (defined as any written contract between a buyer and a seller for the purchase of a one- or two-family dwelling or any portion of the dwelling, which shall include residential units in condominiums, any residential unit in a housing cooperative, any residential unit contained in a fee simple townhouse development, any residential unit contained in a horizontal property regime and any residential unit contained in a planned unit development) is subject to additional statutory requirements.

Statutory Citation—New Jersey Permanent Statutes, Title 2A, §§ 44A-1 to 45-5.

NEW MEXICO

Who May Claim—Every person performing labor, including services of a surveyor, upon providing or hauling equipment, tools or machinery for, or furnishing materials for the construction, alteration or repair of any mine, building, wharf, bridge, ditch, flume, tunnel, fence, machinery, railroad, road or aqueduct to create hydraulic power or any other structure, or who performs labor in any mining claim, has a lien upon the same for the work or labor done or materials furnished by each respectively, whether done or furnished at the instance of the owner of the building or improvement or his agent, and every contractor, subcontractor, architect, builder or other person having charge in whole or in part shall be held to be the agent of the owner. A contractor may not file a mechanics' lien, if not licensed under the construction industries licensing law.

How Claimed—By filing verified lien claim.

Where Filed—County Clerk of the county where property or some part thereof is situated.

When to Be Filed—An original contractor is given 120 days after the completion of his contract to file said lien. Every other person must file his notice of lien within 90 days after the completion of any building or completion of any alteration or repair thereof, or the performance of any labor in a mining claim.

Payment by the owner or his successor in interest to any person entitled to payment of all and any amounts due and owing for any labor or materials furnished or other actions, the performance of which could give rise to a lien to be performed upon a residential site shall discharge all such liens unless prior to payment any person who is entitled to such lien has filed for record his lien as stated above. Person intending to claim a mechanics' lien must provide notice to the owner or the original contractor within 60 days of furnishing work or materials; not required for claims of $5,000 or less or residential units of four or less. Person can elect to give the notice later, but effective date of the lien is changed to 30 days prior to date notice given. Notice must contain description of the property, name, address and phone number of the claimant and name and address of the person with whom claimant contracted.

Duration of Lien—No lien remains valid for a longer period than two years after the claim of lien has been filed unless proceedings have been commenced in a court of competent jurisdiction within that time to enforce the lien.

Filing Fee—$1.75. Where instrument contains more than 700 words in description of property, an additional charge of 25 cents is made for each 100 words. If instrument is photocopied, fee is $5 for first page and $2 for each additional page.

Contents of Notice—(1) Statement of demands after deducting all just credits and offsets; (2) name of owner or reputed owner, if known; (3) names of persons by whom he was employed or to whom he furnished materials; (4) statement of terms, time given and condition of contract; (5) description of property to be charged with the lien sufficient for identification; (6) claim must be verified by oath of claimant or of some other person on his behalf.

Extent of Lien—Lien extends to building, structure or improvement and the land on which situated, together with a convenient space about the same or so much as may be required for the convenient use and occupation of the same. To the extent of the right, title and interest of the person who caused such building, structure or improvement to be erected, repaired, etc. Liability is limited to the amount contracted to be paid to the original contractor.

Contractor Liable for Liens of Subcontractor—The contractor shall be entitled to recover upon a lien filed by him only such amount as is due pursuant to the terms of the contract, less the amount of claims of subcontractors who have filed liens.

Upon notice of the pendency of any action on the lien of a subcontractor, the owner may withhold the amount due principal contractor. If a judgment be obtained against the owner including costs, such total sum may be charged against the amount due the contractor, or he may be sued for difference, if he has already been paid.

Priority of Lien—Lien takes preference over any lien, mortgage or other encumbrance which attaches subsequent to the time when the building, improvement or structure was commenced, work done or materials were commenced to be furnished; also to any lien, mortgage or other encumbrance of which the lien holder has no notice, and which was unrecorded at the time the building, improvement or structure was commenced, work done or materials were commenced to be furnished.

Where different liens are asserted against the same property, the rank of preference is as follows: (1) all persons other than contractor or subcontractor; (2) subcontractor; (3) original contractors.

Public Improvements—See Chapter 13.

Lien for Improvement of Oil or Gas Well—Every person who performs labor or furnishes or hauls material, equipment, tools, etc., in digging, drilling, completing, maintaining, operating and repairing oil or gas well, or pipeline, or equipment in connection therewith, shall have a lien upon the land, leasehold, pipeline, buildings and equipment thereon, and the materials, tools, etc., so furnished, and the oil and gas well. Lien does not extend to the underlying fee or royalty interest unless expressly provided by contract. Verified claim must be filed by original contractor within 210 days, and by other lien claimant within 180 days after furnishing last material or last labor with the Clerk of the county in which property is located. Proceedings to enforce lien must be instituted within one year from date of filing.

Statutory Citation—New Mexico Territorial Laws, Chapter 48, §§ 48-2-1 to 48-2-19; 48-2A-1 to 48-2A-12.

NEW YORK

Who May Claim—Contractor, subcontractor, laborer, trust fund to which benefits and wage supplements are due or payable for the benefit of such laborers, materialman, landscape gardener, nurseryman or person or corporation selling fruit or ornamental trees, roses, shrubbery, vines and small fruit, who performs labor or furnishes materials for the improvement of real property, with the consent, or at the request, of the owner thereof, or of his agent, contractor or subcontractor. Where the contract for an improvement is made with a husband or wife and the property belongs to the other or both, the husband or wife contracting shall also be presumed to be the agent of the other, unless such other having knowledge of the improvement shall, within 10 days after learning of the contract, give the contractor written notice of his or her refusal to consent to the improvement. Materials actually manufactured for but not delivered to the real property shall also be deemed to be materials furnished. Lien also for person who performs labor for a railroad corporation for value of such labor upon the railroad track, rolling stock and appurtenances and upon the land upon which they are situated.

The term "improvement" includes the demolition, erection, alteration or repair of any structure upon, connected with, or beneath the surface of any real property and any work done upon such property or materials furnished for its permanent improvement, including work done or materials furnished in equipping any such structure with chandeliers, brackets or other fixtures or apparatus for supplying gas or electric light; the drawing by an architect or engineer or surveyor of plans or specifications or survey which are prepared for or used in connection with such improvement; the value of materials actually manufactured for but not delivered to the real property; the reasonable rental value for the period of actual use of machinery, tools and equipment and the value of compressed gases furnished for welding or cutting; the value of fuel and lubricants consumed by machinery operating on the improvement, or by motor vehicles owned, operated or controlled by the owner, or a contractor or subcontractor while engaged exclusively in the transportation of materials to or from the improvement for the purposes thereof; and the performance of real estate brokerage services in obtaining a lessee for a term of more than three years where property not to be used for residential purposes.

How Claimed—By filing notice of lien.

Where Filed—County Clerk of county where property is situated. Where property is situated in more than one county, file in each county where part of property is situated. If the Clerk maintains a block index, the notice filed shall contain the number of every block on the land map of the county which is affected. Notice of lien on railroad property filed in any county where railroad is situated.

When to Be Filed—At any time during progress of work and furnishing of materials, or within eight months after completion of contract, or final performance of work, or final furnishing of materials, dating from last item of work or materials furnished (four months for single-family dwelling) except where lien by real estate broker, notice may be filed only after performance of brokerage services.

Service of Copy of Notice—A copy of the notice must be served or left at last known place of residence in city or town where property is situated or sent by certified mail either simultaneously or within 30 days after filing the notice of lien to the owner, contractor or subcontractor. Affidavit of service of the notice of lien must be filed in the County Clerk's Office in which the property is situated within 35 days after the notice of lien is filed. Failure to do so shall terminate the notice as a lien. Any lienor who fails to serve such copy is liable for the attorneys' fees, costs, and expenses incurred in obtaining the copy.

Duration of Lien—One year after notice has been filed, unless within that time an action is commenced to foreclose the lien and notice of the pendency of the action is filed in the county in which the lien was filed. Before a mechanics' lien expires in New York for non-prosecution, a one-year extension may be obtained by a filing with the County Clerk. Additional extensions may then be obtained by means of a court order, and, if the property is a single family dwelling, a court order is required in all instances.

Filing Fee—$15 for filing or recording a notice of pendency of action or a notice of attachment; within the city of New York, $35.

Contents of Notice of Lien—(1) Name and residence of lienor; and if lienor is a partnership or corporation, business address of such firm or corporation, names of partners and principal place of business, and if a foreign corporation, its principal place of business within the state; (2) name and address of lienor's attorney, if any; (3) name of owner of property and owner's interest therein; (4) name of person by whom lienor was employed, or to whom he furnished or is to furnish materials, or if lienor is a contractor or subcontractor, person with whom contract was made; (5) labor performed or materials furnished and agreed price or value thereof, or materials actually manufactured for but not delivered to the real property and the agreed price or value thereof; (6) amount unpaid to lienor for such labor or materials; (7) time when first and last items of work were performed and materials were furnished; (8) property subject to the lien, with a description and, if in a city or village, its location by street and number, if known; (9) verification by lienor or his agent to effect that statements therein contained are true to his knowledge, except as to the matters therein stated to be alleged on information and belief, and as to those matters on which he believes them to be true.

Extent of Lien—Owner's right, title or interest in the real property and improvements existing at or after the time of filing notice of lien. Extends to an interest assigned for the benefit of creditors where the assignment was within 30 days prior to the filing. Lien cannot exceed amount earned and unpaid on contract at time of filing notice or any sum subsequently earned thereon. Owner's liability may not exceed, by reason of all liens filed, a sum greater than the value or agreed price of the labor and materials remaining unpaid at the time of filing notices.

Insurance Proceeds Liable for Demands—In the event that an improvement on which a lien is claimed is destroyed by fire or other casualty and insurance proceeds paid to the owner for such loss or casualty, the owner is entitled to reimbursement for premiums paid, after which the balance is subject to the lien as realty would have been. If insurance is payable to contractor after he reimburses himself for premiums paid, contractor must pay balance to laborers and materialmen to whom he is liable as if payments made to him under the contract.

Priority of Lien—(1) A lien for material furnished or labor performed in the improvement of real property has priority over a conveyance, mortgage, judgment or other claim against such property not recorded, docketed or filed at the time of the filing of the notice of lien; over advances made upon any mortgage or other encumbrance thereon after such filing; and over the claim of a creditor who has not furnished materials or performed labor upon such property, if such property has been assigned by the owner by a general assignment for the benefit of creditors, within 30 days before the filing of either of such notices; and also over an attachment issued or a money judgment recovered upon a claim, which, in whole or in part, was not for material furnished, labor performed or monies advanced for the improvement of such real property; and over any claim or lien acquired in any proceedings upon such judgment. Such liens also have priority over advances made upon a contract by an owner for an improvement of real property which contains an option of purchase to the contractor, his successor or assigns to purchase the property, if such advances were made after the time when the labor began or the first item of material was furnished, as stated in the notice of lien. If several buildings are erected, demolished, altered or repaired, or several pieces or parcels of real property are improved, under one contract, and there are conflicting liens thereon, each lienor has priority upon the particular building or premises where his labor is performed or his materials are used. Persons have no priority on account of the time of filing their respective notices of liens, but all liens are on a parity except that laborers, subcontractors and materialmen are preferred over contractors.

(2) When a building loan mortgage is delivered and recorded, the lien has priority over advances made on the building loan mortgage after the filing of the notice of lien; but such building loan mortgage, whenever recorded, to the extent of advances made before the filing of such notice of lien, has priority over the lien, provided it or the building loan contract contains a covenant by the mortgagee to receive and hold advances thereunder as trust funds for payment of the costs of the improvement, and provided the building loan contract is filed. No mortgage recorded subsequent to the commencement of the improvement and before the expiration of four months after the completion thereof shall have priority over liens thereafter filed unless it contains such covenant.

(3) Every such building loan mortgage and every mortgage recorded subsequent to the commencement of the improvement and before the expiration of four months after the completion of the improvement shall contain a similar covenant by the mortgagor that he will receive the advances secured thereby as a trust fund to be applied first for the purpose of paying the cost of improvement, and that he will apply the same first to the payment of the cost of improvement before using any part of the total of the same for any other purpose, provided, however, that if the party executing the building loan contract is not the owner of the fee but is the party to whom such advances are to be made, a building loan contract executed and filed pursuant to this chapter shall contain the said covenant by such party executing such building loan contract, in place of the covenant by the mortgagor in the building loan mortgage. Nothing in the statute is to be considered as imposing upon the lender any obligation to see to the proper application of such advances by the owner.

(4) No instrument of conveyance recorded subsequent to the commencement of the improvement, and before the expiration of four months after the completion thereof, is valid as against liens filed within four months from the recording of such conveyance, unless the instrument contains a covenant by the grantor that he will receive the consideration for such conveyance as a trust fund to be applied first for the purpose of paying the cost of the improvement and that he will apply the same first to the payment of the cost of the improvement before using any part of the total of the same for any other purpose. Nothing in the statute is to be construed as imposing upon the grantee any obligation to see to the proper application of such consideration by the grantor. Does not apply to a deed given by a referee or other person appointed by the court for the sole purpose of a selling real property, or to the consideration received by a grantor who, pursuant to a written agreement entered into and duly recorded prior to the commencement of the improvement, conveys to the person making such improvement, the land upon which such improvement is made. However, such a conveyance is subject to liens filed prior thereto. Section does not apply to mortgages taken by Home Owners Loan Corp.

Waiver of Lien—Notwithstanding the provisions of any other law, any contract, agreement, or understanding whereby the right to file or enforce any lien is waived, shall be void as against public policy and wholly unenforceable. This shall not preclude a requirement for a written waiver of the right to file a mechanics' lien executed and delivered by a contractor, subcontractor, material supplier or laborer simultaneously with or after payment for the labor performed or the materials furnished has been made to such contractor, subcontractor, materialman or laborer. Nor shall this section be applicable to a written agreement to subordinate, release or satisfy all or part of such a lien made after a notice of lien has been filed.

Assignments of Contracts and Orders to Be Filed—Assignments of contracts for the improvement of real property; orders drawn by contractors upon owners of real property for the payment of money; orders drawn by subcontractors upon contractors or subcontractors for such payments; orders drawn by an owner upon the maker of a building loan; and assignments of money due and to grow due on a building loan contract, must be filed within 10 days after the date of such assignment of contract, or such assignment of moneys or such order in the office of the County Clerk of the county where the realty is situated. Unfiled assignments and orders are absolutely void as against subsequent assignees in good faith and for a valuable consideration whose assignments and orders are first duly recorded.

Public Improvements—See Chapter 13.

Lien for Improvement of Oil or Gas Well—Under lien law real property includes all oil or gas wells and structures and fixtures connected therewith, and any lease of oil lands or other right to operate for the production of oil or gas upon such lands.

Statutory Citation—NY Lien Law §§ 3 to 39-c, Article 2.

NORTH CAROLINA

Who May Claim—Any person who performs or furnishes labor or furnishes materials, professional design or surveying services pursuant to a contract, either express or implied, or any person who furnishes rental equipment to or with the owner of real property for the making of improvement thereon. A Notice of Lien may also be claimed by a subcontractor on funds owed the contractor (see paragraph 6). The subcontractor may enforce the lien of the contractor against the owner of real property to the extent of his claim. Waiver of right to file or claim a lien is against public policy and is unenforceable.

Where Filed—Office of the Clerk of the Superior Court in each county wherein the real property subject to the claim is located. A subcontractor perfects a lien upon the giving of notice in writing to obligor; effective upon receipt (see paragraph 6).

When Notice Filed—Notice of lien shall be filed at any time after maturity of the obligation but not later than 120 days after the last furnishing of labor or materials by persons claiming them.

Contents of Notice of Claim of Lien—The contents of a lien claim must be in substantially the following form: (1) name and address of the person claiming the lien; (2) name and address of the record owner of the real property claimed to be subject to the lien at the time the claim of lien is filed; (3) description of the real property upon which the lien is claimed: street address, tax lot and block number, reference to recorded instrument, or any other description of real property is sufficient, whether or not it is specific, if it reasonably identifies what is described; (4) name and address of the person with whom the claimant contracted for the furnishing of labor or materials; (5) date upon which labor or materials were first furnished upon said property by the claimant; (6) general description of the labor performed or materials furnished and the amount claimed therefor; and (7) date upon which labor or materials were last furnished upon said property by the claimant.

Filing Fee—$4 for the first page and 25 cents per page for each additional page.

Notice to Obligor—Subcontractors rights are by subrogation of the claims, enforced by a Notice to the party with whom the claimant contracted. Notice of lien must be sent by subcontractor for labor or materials to the obligor and sending of such notice perfects the lien. Upon receipt of such notice, the obligor is under a duty to retain the funds subject to the lien. If, after receipt of notice, the obligor makes any payment to a contractor or subcontractor against whom the lien is claimed, the lien shall continue on the funds in the hands of the contractor or subcontractor who receives the payment and in addition the obligor shall be personally liable. A subcontractor can enforce any contractor's lien against owner. Upon the filing of the notice, a claim of lien and commencement of an action by subcontractor, no action of the contractor shall be effective to prejudice the rights of the subcontractor without his written consent.

Contents of Notice to Obligor—The notice must contain the following: (1) the name and address of person claiming the lien; (2) a general description of the real property improved; (3) the name and address of the person with whom the lien claimant contracted to improve real property; (4) the name and address of each person against or through whom subrogation rights are claimed (5) a general description of the contract and the person against whose interest the lien is claimed; and (6) the amount claimed by the lien claimant under his contract. A statutory form is provided for subcontractors giving notice of claim of lien.

Extent of Lien—Lien extends to the improvement and to the lot or tract on which improvement is situated and to extent of interest of owner. Lien secures payment of all debts owing for labor done or material furnished pursuant to the contract. A subcontractor's lien extends to the funds owed its contractor or to the person with whom it dealt.

Duration of Lien—A timely claim of lien must be perfected by filing a civil action to enforce the lien within 180 days after the last furnishing of labor or materials at the site of improvement. Either the civil action or a *lis pendens* referencing the civil action must be filed in the county where the lien is filed. An action to enforce the lien may be instituted in any county in which the lien is filed. Such action may not be commenced later than 180 days after the last furnishing of labor or materials at the site of the improvement.

Priority of Lien—Liens of general contractors are entitled to priority in accordance with time of the filing of notice. Exemptions of personal and real property shall not be construed as to prevent a laborer's lien for work done and performed for the person claiming such exemption, or a mechanics' lien for work done on the premises. Subcontractor's liens perfected by notice to the obligor have priority over all interest including garnishment, attachment, levy and judgment. If the amount due the contractor by the owner is not sufficient to pay in full the laborer, mechanic or artisan for his labor and the person furnishing materials, owner must distribute amount pro rata among several claimants.

Public Improvements—See Chapter 13.

Statutory Citation—General Statutes of North Carolina, Chapter 44A, Article 2, Part 1, §§ 44A-7 to 44A-23.

NORTH DAKOTA

Who May Claim—Any person who improves real estate by the contribution of labor, skill or materials, whether under contract with the owner of such real estate, or at the instance of any agent, trustee, contractor or subcontractor of such owner, shall have a lien upon the improvement, and upon the land on which it is situated or to which it may be removed, for the price or value of such contribution. "Improve" includes performing architectural services, construction staking, engineering and surveying, mapping and soil testing services. Liens also exist upon railroad property and in favor of miners.

How Claimed—A contractor must keep an itemized account thereof separate and apart from all other items of account against the purchaser; serve a written notice by registered or certified mail upon owner demanding payment of such account and notify him that unless payment is made within 15 days of mailing a lien will be perfected; and record a verified notice of intention to claim a lien. The notice of intention to claim lien shall contain the following: (1) name of the person in possession of the land; (2) description of the property to be charged with the lien; (3) date of the contract; and (4) that a mechanics' lien against the building, improvement, or premises will be perfected according to law unless the account has been paid.

A claimant may serve upon the owner, at any time, a notice of his claim. The owner, within 15 days after completion of the contract, may demand the claimant to furnish an itemized and verified account, the amount due and his name and address. The demand must contain a provision informing the person holding the lien that if suit is not commenced within 30 days, the person holding the lien forfeits the lien.

Where Filed—Recorder of the County in county where land, building or improvement is situated.

When to Be Filed—Every person desiring to perfect his lien shall file with the Recorder of the County in which the property is situated, within 90 days after all the contribution is done, or if the property is used in the exploration for or the production of oil and gas, within six months, after all his contribution is done a mechanics' lien describing the property and stating the amount due. Failure to file within 90 days shall not defeat lien except as to purchasers or encumbrancers in good faith and for value whose rights accrue after the 90 days and before any claim for lien is filed, and as against the owner to the extent of the amount paid to a contractor after the expiration of the 90 days and before filing of the account.

Duration of Lien—Suit to enforce lien must be commenced within 30 days after written demand of the owner, his agent or contractor. In any event action must be instituted within three years after the date of recording of the verified notice of intention to claim a mechanics' lien. Notice of suit must be given to the owner before suit is filed; 20 days notice is sent by mail, 10 days if served personally.

Filing Fee—The fee for recording the notice of intention to claim a lien is $7 for the first page and $3 for each additional page.

Extent of Lien—The lien attaches from the time the first item of material or labor is furnished. It covers the agreed contract price, otherwise, the reasonable value of the work done. The entire land upon which the building or improvement situated is subject to the lien to the extent of the landowner's right, title and interest. When the interest owned in land by the owner of the building or other improvement for which the lien is claimed is only a leasehold interest, the forfeiture of the lease will not impair the lien so far as it applies to the buildings or improvements, but the improvements may be sold to satisfy the lien and may be removed by the purchaser within 30 days after the sale.

Priority of Lien—Mechanics' liens are preferred to any mortgage or other encumbrance not then of record, unless the lienholder had actual notice thereof. Mechanics' liens shall have priority in the following order: (1) for manual labor; (2) for materials; (3) subcontractors other than manual laborers; and (4) original contractors. Liens for manual labor filed within 90-day period share pro rata; those filed thereafter shall have priority in order of filing; liens for materials have priority in order of the filing of notices of intention.

Improvements Not Authorized by Owner—Any person who has not authorized the same may protect his interest from such liens by serving upon person doing work, etc., within five days after he has knowledge thereof, a written notice that the improvement is not being made at his instance, or by posting like notice and keeping the same posted, in a conspicuous place on the premises. As against a lessor, no lien is given for repairs made by or at the instance of his lessee, unless the lessor shall have actual or constructive notice thereof and not object thereto.

Public Improvements—See Chapter 13.

Lien for Improvement of Oil or Gas Well—Such liens are created, perfected and enforced in the same manner as mechanics' liens, except that filing must be made within six months of performing labor or furnishing materials.

Statutory Citation—North Dakota Century Code, Title 35, Chapter 35-27, §§ 35-27-01 to 35-27-28.

OHIO

Who May Claim—Every person who performs work or labor upon or furnishes material in furtherance of any improvement undertaken by virtue of a contract, express or implied, with the owner, part owner or lessee of any interest in real estate, or his authorized agent, and every person who as a subcontractor, laborer or materialman, performs any labor or work or furnishes any material to an original contractor or any subcontractor, in carrying forward, performing or completing any improvement, has a lien to secure the payment therefore upon the improvement and all interests that the owner, part owner, or lessee may have or subsequently acquire in the land or leasehold to which the improvement was made or removed.

Private Residential Projects. No original contractor, subcontractor, materialman or laborer has a lien to secure payment for labor or work performed or materials furnished by him, in connection with a home construction contract between the original contractor and the owner, part owner or lessee in connection with a dwelling or residential unit of condominium property, that is the subject of a home purchase contract, if the owner, part owner or lessee paid the original contractor in full or if the purchaser has paid in full for the amount of the home construction or home purchase contract price, and the payment was made prior to the owner's, part owner's or lessee's receipt of a copy of an affidavit of mechanics' lien pursuant to Section 1311.07 of the Ohio Revised Code.

How Claimed—Prior to the performance of any labor or work or the furnishing of any materials for an improvement on real property which may give rise to a mechanics' lien, the owner, part owner or lessee who contracts for the labor, work or materials shall record in the office of the county recorder a notice of commencement. Every subcontractor or materialman who performs work or labor or furnishes material for an improvement must serve a notice of furnishing on the original contractor to preserve his lien rights if a notice of commencement has been filed within 21 days of first performing labor or furnishing materials.

To claim a lien, claimant must make and file for record an Affidavit for Mechanics' Lien and serve a copy of it on the owner.

Where Filed—Office of the county recorder in the counties in which the improved property is located.

When to Be Filed—If the lien arises in connection with a one- or two-family dwelling or in connection with a residential unit of condominium property, affidavit must be filed within 60 days from the date on which the last labor or work was performed or material was furnished by the person claiming the lien. If the lien is in connection with work done on an oil or gas well, affidavit must be filed within 120 days from the date on which the last labor or work was performed or material was furnished. If the lien is for any other type of work, affidavit must be filed within 75 days from the date on which the last of the labor or work was performed or material was furnished by the person claiming the lien.

Contents of Affidavit. (1) Amount due over and above all legal setoffs; (2) description of the property to be charged with the lien; (3) name and address of the person to or for whom the labor or work was performed or material was furnished; (4) name of the owner, part owner or lessee, if known; (5) name and address of the lien claimant; and (6) first and last dates that the lien claimant performed any labor or work or furnished any material to the improvement giving rise to his lien. The affidavit may be verified before any person authorized to administer oaths, whether for the owner, part owner, lessee, lien claimant, or an interested other party. There is a statutory form for the affidavit.

Service of Copy of Affidavit. Claimant shall serve a copy of the affidavit on the owner, part owner or lessee of the improved property or his designee, within 30 days after filing the affidavit. If the affidavit cannot be properly served, the claimant shall post the copy in some conspicuous place on the premises of the improved property within 10 days after the expiration of the 30 days.

Contents of Notice of Commencement. Subcontractors and materialmen must serve notice of furnishing within 21 days after the date that the subcontractor or materialman first performed labor or furnished materials on the site of the public improvement, or be limited to amounts owed or labor and work performed and material furnished during and after the 21 days immediately preceding service of the notice of furnishing. So subcontractor who is in direct privity of contract with the principal contractor need provide this notice with the following contents: (1) legal description of the real property on which the improvement is to be made; (2) brief description of the improvement to be performed; (3) name, address and capacity of the owner, part owner or lessee of the real property contracting for the improvement; (4) name and address of the fee owner of the real property, if the person contracting for the improvement is a land contract vendee or lessee; (5) name and address of the owner's, part owner's or lessee's designee, if any; (6) name and address of all original contractors; (7) date the owner, part owner or lessee first executed a contract with an original contractor for the improvement; (8) name and address of all lending institutions which provide financing for the improvements, if any; (9) name and address of all sureties on any bond which guarantee payment of the original contractor's obligations under the contract for the improvement, if any; (10) name and address of the person preparing the notice; (11) affidavit of the owner, part owner or lessee or the agent of the owner, part owner or lessee which verifies the notice; and (12) the following statement: "To Lien Claimants and Subsequent Purchasers: Take notice that labor or work is about to begin on or materials are about to be furnished for an improvement to the real property described in this instrument. A person having a mechanics' lien may preserve the lien by providing a notice of furnishing to the above-named designee and his original contractor, if any, and by timely recording an affidavit pursuant to Section 1311.06 of Revised Code. A copy of this notice may be obtained upon making a written request by certified mail to the above-named owner, part owner, lessee, designee or person with whom you have contracted."

Extent of Lien—Liens extend to the improvement and all interests that the owner, part owner or lessee may have or subsequently acquire in the land or leasehold to which the improvement was made or removed.

Duration of Lien—Liens for labor or work performed or materials furnished prior to the recording of the notice of commencement are effective from the date the first visible work or labor is performed or the first materials are furnished by the original contractor, subcontractor, materialman or laborer at the site of improvement. Liens for labor or work performed or materials furnished after the recording of a notice of commencement are effective from the date of the recording of the notice of commencement. Liens continue in force for six years after an affidavit is filed in the office of the county recorder. If an action is brought to enforce the lien within that time, the lien continues in force until final adjudication thereof. The owner may serve a Notice to Commence Suit; suit must be commenced within 60 days.

Priority of Lien—If several liens are obtained by several persons upon the same improvement, they have no priority among themselves, except as follows: Liens for which the effective date is the date the first visible work or labor is performed or the first materials are furnished (i.e., liens for labor performed or materials furnished prior to recording of a notice of commencement), have priority over all other liens except those claimed by laborers. Liens filed by laborers have priority over all other liens whether the labor or work was performed before or after the recording of notice of commencement. Liens for work performed or materials furnished after the recording of a notice of commencement shall be preferred to all other titles, liens, or encumbrances which may attach to or upon such improvement or to or upon the land upon which it is situated, which either are given or recorded subsequent to the recording of the notice of commencement. The lien of a subcontractor is superior to any already taken or to be taken by the original contractor in respect of the same labor, work or material, and the liens of laborers, materialmen and subcontractors to an original contractor or subcontractor indebted to them in respect of such labor, work or material.

Statutory Citation—Ohio Statutes, Title 13, Chapter 11, §§ 1311.01 to 1311.38.

OKLAHOMA

Who May Claim—Any person who shall perform labor or furnish material for the erection, alteration or repair of any building, improvement or structure, or who shall furnish material and perform labor in putting up any fixtures, or who shall plant any trees, vines, plants or hedges, or who shall furnish labor, or material for buildings, or repairs any fence, footwalk or sidewalk, shall have lien upon the land upon which such buildings or improvements are made and upon such buildings and appurtenances. Miners and other employees in or about mines have lien on machinery, equipment, income, leases, etc., for payment for work done.

Any person claiming a lien shall file in the office of the county clerk in the county in which the land or property is located, a statement containing: the amount claimed and items thereof, as nearly as practicable, the names of the owners, the contractor, the claimant and the legal description of the property, subject to such lien and verified by affidavit. Such statement by the original contractor shall be filed within four months after the date upon which labor was last performed; subcontractors have 90 days.

How Claimed—(a) *Original Contractor.* Any person claiming a lien as aforesaid shall file in the office of the county clerk of the county in which the land is situated a statement setting forth the amount claimed and the items thereof as nearly as practicable, the names of the owner, the contractor, the claimant, and a legal description of the property subject to the lien, verified by affidavit.

(b) *Subcontractors.* By filing with the county clerk of the county in which the land is situated, within 90 days after the date upon which material or equipment used on said land was last furnished or labor last performed under such subcontract, a statement, verified by affidavit, setting forth the amount due from the contractor to the claimant, and the items thereof, as nearly as practicable, the name of the owner, the name of the contractor, the name of the claimant, and a legal description of the property upon which a lien is claimed.

In addition, a lien cannot attach to an owner-occupied dwelling unless the original contractor, subcontractor, laborer or materialman gives the owner notice of his rights before the first performance of labor or furnishing materials (see section 8). The owner of equipment leased or rented must give written notice to the owner of the property that the equipment used was leased or rented. Within one business day after filing of lien statement, notice of such lien shall be mailed to owner by certified mail return receipt requested.

Pre-Lien Notice—A subcontractor or supplier has 75 days after supplying labor, materials, service or equipment to give written notice of a claim to the general contractor and property owner to the last known address or original contractor and owner of the property by hand delivery with confirmation receipt, certified mail, return receipt requested, or by fax or e-mail. Notice must contain a statement that it is a pre-lien notice, the complete name, address and telephone number of subcontractor or supplier, date of supply of material, equipment or service, description of such, name and last known address of person requesting material, address or legal description of property, statement that the dollar amount of material, etc. exceeds $2500, and signature of the representative of claimant company. Notice requirement does not apply to single-family homes or residential projects of four or fewer units or a claim total of less than $2500.

Where Recorded—In the office of the County Clerk in the county where the land is situated.

When to Be Recorded—Original contractor has four months after the date upon which the material was last furnished or labor last performed, within which to file his statement for a lien; subcontractors, 90 days. Both contractors and subcontractors must serve notice of filing on the owner within one business day after the date of the filing of the lien statement.

Duration of Lien—Suit must be commenced within one year from date of filing lien claim.

Filing Fee—$10 for the recording and filing of mechanics' or materialmen's liens and the release thereof; $2 for each additional page, $8 for preparing and mailing notice of lien.

Notice of Lien—County Clerk shall mail notice of lien to owner of property on which lien attaches. The notice shall contain date of filing, name and address of party claiming lien, the person against whom the claim is made and the owner of the property, a legal description of the property and the amount claimed. Within one business day of filing the claim of lien, a notice of such lien shall be mailed by certified mail, return receipt requested to the owner of the property on which the lien attached. The claimant shall furnish the County Clerk with the last known mailing address of the person against whom the claim is made and of the owner.

Contents of Notice of Lien—Statement setting forth amount claimed and items thereof, name of the owner, the contractor and claimant, and description of the property subject to the lien, verified by affidavit. In addition, a lien cannot attach to an owner-occupied dwelling unless prior to first performance the contractor, subcontractor, laborer or materialman provides a written notice with the following language:

NOTICE TO OWNER

YOU ARE HEREBY NOTIFIED THAT THE ANY PERSON PERFORMING LABOR ON YOUR PROPERTY OR FURNISHING MATERIALS FOR THE CONSTRUCTION, REPAIR OR IMPROVEMENT OF YOUR PROPERTY WILL BE ENTITLED TO A LIEN AGAINST YOUR PROPERTY IF HE IS NOT PAID IN FULL, EVEN THOUGH YOU MAY HAVE PAID THE FULL CONTRACT PRICE TO YOUR CONTRACTOR. THIS COULD RESULT IN YOUR PAYING FOR LABOR AND MATERIALS TWICE. THIS LIEN CAN BE ENFORCED BY THE SALE OF YOUR PROPERTY. TO AVOID THIS RESULT, YOU MAY DEMAND FROM YOUR CONTRACTOR LIEN WAIVERS FROM ALL PERSONS PERFORMING LABOR OR FURNISHING MATERIALS FOR THE WORK ON YOUR PROPERTY. YOU MAY WITHHOLD PAYMENT TO THE CONTRACTOR IN THE AMOUNT OF ANY UNPAID CLAIMS FOR LABOR OR MATERIALS. YOU ALSO HAVE THE RIGHT TO DEMAND FROM YOUR CONTRACTOR A COMPLETE LIST OF ALL LABORERS AND MATERIAL SUPPLIERS UNDER YOUR CONTRACT, AND THE RIGHT TO DETERMINE FROM THEM IF THEY HAVE BEEN PAID FOR LABOR PERFORMED AND MATERIALS FURNISHED.

Extent of Lien—Lien is upon the whole of the tract or piece of land, the buildings and appurtenances. If the title to the land is not in the person with whom contract was made, lien shall be allowed on the buildings and improvements separate from the real estate. The owner shall not be liable for a subcontractor's lien for an amount greater than he contracted to pay the original contractor.

Priority of Lien—Such lien shall be preferred to all other liens or encumbrances which may attach to or upon such land, building or improvements subsequent to the commencement of such building or furnishing or putting up fixtures or machinery.

Public Improvements—See Chapter 13.

Lien for Improvement of Oil or Gas Well—A lien exists for anyone contracting to perform labor or services, or furnish material, machinery and oil well supplies used in the digging, drilling, torpedoing, operating, completing or repairing of any oil or gas well. The lien extends to the whole leasehold including the proceeds from sale of the oil or gas. The lien has priority as to all other encumbrances obtained subsequent to the commencement of the furnishing or putting up of the material or supplies. The lien will follow the property and be enforceable against the property wherever it may be found. Filing of a lien statement will constitute constructive notice of the lien to third parties. No lien on the proceeds from the sale of oil or gas produced shall be effective against any purchaser of such oil or gas until a copy of the statement of lien has been delivered to such purchaser by registered or certified mail. Notice of such lien is given and filed in same manner as mechanics' liens. Liens for oil and gas wells are limited to the leasehold estate; they do not affect any other interest in the real property involved. However, if the owner also owns a working interest in a well located thereon, the lien attaches the working interest. Contractor and subcontractor each have 180 days to file lien from date of last work or supply of materials; one year from filing date to file suit.

Statutory Citation—Oklahoma State Statutes, Title 42, §§ 42-141 to 42-180.

OREGON

Who May Claim—(1) Any person performing labor upon, transporting or furnishing any material to be used in, or renting equipment used in the construction of any improvement, which includes any building, wharf, bridge, ditch, flume, reservoir, well, tunnel, fence, street, sidewalk, machinery, aqueduct and all other structures and superstructures, whenever it can be made applicable thereto, ORS 87.005(5), shall have a lien upon the improvement for the labor, transportation, or material furnished or equipment rented at the instance of the owner of the improvement or the owner's construction agent. (2) Any person who engages in or rents equipment for the preparation of a lot or parcel of land, or improves or rents equipment for the improvement of a street or road adjoining a lot or parcel of land at the request of the owner of the lot or parcel, shall have a lien upon the land for work done and materials furnished or equipment rented. (3) The lien for rented equipment is limited to the reasonable rental value of the equipment notwithstanding the terms of the underlying rental agreement. (4) Trustees of an employee benefit plan shall have a lien upon the improvement for the amount of contributions, due to labor performed on that improvement, required to be paid by agreement or otherwise into a fund of the employee benefit plan. (5) An architect, landscape architect, land surveyor or registered engineer who, at the request of the owner or an agent of the owner, prepares plans, drawings or specifications that are intended for use in or to facilitate the construction of an improvement or who supervises the construction shall have a lien upon the land and structures necessary for the use of the plans, drawings, or specifications so provided or supervision performed. (6) A landscape architect, land surveyor or other person who prepares plans, drawings, surveys or specifications that are used for the landscaping or preparation of a lot or parcel of land or who supervises the landscaping or preparation shall have a lien upon the land for the plans, drawings, surveys or specifications used or supervision performed.

How Claimed—Except when material or labor described in (1) to (3), (5) and (6) above is furnished at the request of the owner, a person furnishing any materials or labor for which a lien may be claimed shall give a notice of the right to lien to the owner of the site. The notice may be given at any time during the progress of the improvement, but it only protects the right to claim a lien on those materials and that labor provided after a date which is eight days, not including Saturday, Sunday or holidays, before the notice is delivered or mailed. No right to claim a lien under (5) or (6) above exists for any services provided for an owner-occupied residence at the request of an agent of the owner. The notice must include the following information and must be in substantially the following form:

NOTICE OF THE RIGHT TO A LIEN

WARNING: READ THIS NOTICE. PROTECT YOURSELF FROM PAYING ANY CONTRACTOR OR SUPPLIER TWICE FOR THE SAME SERVICE.

To: (Owner)   Date of mailing: _____
    (Owner's address)

This is to inform you that (name of subcontractor or material supplier) has begun to provide (description of materials, equipment, labor, or services) ordered by (contractor) for improvements to property you own. The property is located at (address of property).

A lien may be claimed for all materials, equipment, labor, and services furnished after a date that is eight days (not including Saturdays, Sundays and other holidays as defined in O.R.S. 187.010) before this notice was mailed to you.

Even if you or your mortgage lender have made full payment to the contractor who ordered these materials or services, your property may still be subject to a lien unless the supplier providing this notice is paid. THIS IS NOT A LIEN. It is a notice sent to you for your protection in compliance with the construction lien laws of the State of Oregon.

This notice has been sent to you by:

(Name)
(Address)   IF YOU HAVE ANY QUESTIONS ABOUT
(Telephone)   THIS NOTICE, PLEASE CALL US.

IMPORTANT INFORMATION ON REVERSE SIDE

IMPORTANT INFORMATION FOR YOUR PROTECTION

Under Oregon's laws, those who work on your property or provide labor, equipment, services or materials and are not paid have a right to enforce their claim for payment against your property. This claim is known as a construction lien.

If your contractor fails to pay subcontractors, material suppliers, rental equipment suppliers, service providers or laborers or neglects to make other legally required payments, the people who are owed money can look to your property for payment, *even if you have paid your contractor in full.*

The law states that all people hired by a contractor to provide you with materials, equipment, labor or services must give you a notice of right to a lien to let you know what they have provided.

WAYS TO PROTECT YOURSELF ARE:

—RECOGNIZE that this notice of right to a lien may result in a lien against your property unless all those supplying a notice of the right to lien have been paid.

—LEARN more about the lien laws and the meaning of this notice by contacting the Builders Board, an attorney or the firm sending this notice.

—ASK for a statement of the labor, equipment, services or materials provided to your property from each party that sends you a notice of right to a lien.

—WHEN paying your contractor for materials, labor, equipment or services, you may make checks payable jointly to the contractor and the firm furnishing materials, equipment, labor or services for which you have received a notice of the right to a lien.

OR use one of the methods suggested in the "Information Notice to Owners." If you have not received such a notice, contact the Builders Board.

—GET EVIDENCE that all firms from whom you have received a notice of the right to a lien have been paid or have waived the right to claim a lien against your property.

—CONSULT AN ATTORNEY, a professional escrow company, or your mortgage lender.

Where Filed—Recording Officer in county or counties where such property is located.

When to Be Filed—Every person claiming a lien, or having performed labor or furnished any materials or rented equipment in the construction of an improvement, or preparation of lot or parcel of land, or improvement of street or road adjoining lot or parcel at the request of the owner, shall perfect the lien not later than 75 days after such person has ceased to provide such labor or equipment or furnish materials, or 75 days after completion of construction, whichever is earlier. Every other person claiming a lien shall perfect the lien not later than 75 days after the completion of construction. A person filing a claim for a lien shall deliver to the owner and to the mortgagee not later than 20 days after the date of filing a notice in writing that the claim has been filed. A copy of the claim of lien shall be attached to the notice.

Duration of Lien—120 days unless suit commenced; or if credit is given, and the terms stated in the claim of lien, within 120 days after expiration of credit term but no longer than two years from date claim for lien is filed. Notice of intent to foreclose must be provided 10 days before suit is instituted.

Filing Fee—$5 for the first page; $5 for each additional page.

Contents of Lien Claim—Lien claim must contain: (1) true statement of demand, after credits and deductions; (2) name of owner or reputed owner, if known; (3) name of person by whom claimant was employed or to whom claimant furnished materials, labor or equipment; (4) description of the property, including address. The claim must be verified on oath by the claimant or another person having a knowledge of the facts.

Extent of Lien—Lien applies to land upon which any improvement is constructed together with any such space as may be required for the convenient use and occupation thereof to be determined by the court at the time of the foreclosure of the lien. If the person who caused the improvement to be constructed had less than absolute ownership, then only his interest in the land shall be subject to the lien.

Priority of Lien—Lien takes priority over any lien, mortgage (except purchase money mortgages or duly perfected security interest and purchase money security interest), or other encumbrance not recorded or filed at time the improvement was commenced, or materials were commenced to be furnished. To enforce a lien the improvement may be sold separately from the land. If proceeds of sale are insufficient to pay all claimants, the payments shall be made to each class pro rata. A lien for materials and supplies shall have priority over any recorded mortgage on land or buildings if the person supplying the materials, not later than eight days not including Saturdays, Sundays or holidays after date of delivery, delivers a notice of the supply to the mortgagee. Unless the mortgage or trust deed is given to secure a loan made to finance an alteration or repair, a lien for the alteration or repair of an improvement commenced and made subsequent to the date of record of a mortgage or trust deed on the improvement or on the site shall not take precedence over the mortgage or trust deed. Suits to enforce a lien shall have preference on the calendar of the court over any other civil suit, except suits to which the state is a party, and shall be tried without unnecessary delay.

Public Improvements—See Chapter 13.

Statutory Citation—Oregon Revised Statutes, Chapter 87, §§ 87.001 to 88.093.

PENNSYLVANIA

Who May Claim—Contractors and subcontractors are entitled to a lien for all debts due for labor or materials furnished in the erection or construction, or the alteration or repair of an improvement, provided that the amount of the claim exceeds $500.

How Claimed—Every claimant must file a claim with the Prothonotary of the county where improvement located and serve notice of filing upon the owner within one month after filing. A subcontractor in privity with the contractor must give a written notice to the property owner, prior to filing a mechanic's lien, in accordance with the Notice to Owner provisions set forth below. The notices that are required to be given by a subcontractor depend on whether the project involves new construction, or merely alteration or repair of an existing improvement.

Where Filed—The claim must be filed with the Prothonotary of the county where the improvement is located. Where the improvement is located in more than one county, the claim may be filed in any one or more said counties but shall be effective only as to the part of the property in the county in which it has been filed.

When to Be Filed—Claim must be filed within four months after the claimant last supplied labor and/or material to the job site property.

Notice to Owner—Notice of intention to file a claim must only be given by a subcontractor.

(a) *Preliminary Notice.* In the case of an alteration or repair of an existing improvement, the subcontractor's preliminary notice of intent to file mechanic's lien claim shall be given to the owner, agent of the owner and to the general contractor on or before the date of completion of his work in the following form: (1) name of the subcontractor and the contractor; (2) general description of the property against which the claim is to be filed; (3) amount due or to become due; (4) statement of intention to file a claim therefore.

(b) *Formal Notice.* No claim by a subcontractor shall be valid unless, at least 30 days before the claim is filed, the subcontractor gives to the owner a formal written notice of the intention to file a claim. The formal notice shall state: (1) name of the party claimant; (2) name of the person with whom contracted; (3) amount claimed to be due; (4) general nature and character of the labor or materials furnished; (5) date of completion of the work for which the claim is made; (6) brief description sufficient to identify the property subject to the lien; and (7) date on which preliminary notice of intention to file a claim was given and a copy thereof. Both the Preliminary Notice and the Formal Notice are required in projects involving alteration or repair of an existing improvement. Only the Formal Notice is required in projects involving new construction of an improvement.

The notice may consist of a copy of the claim intended to be filed, together with a statement that the claimant intends to file the original or a counterpart thereof. Notice provided in this section may be served by first-class mail, registered or certified mail, on the owner or the owner's agent by an adult in the same manner as a writ of summons in assumpsit, or if service cannot be so made, then by posting upon a conspicuous public part of the improvement.

(c) *Notice of Fact of Filing Claim*. Notice of filing of the claim must be given by all claimants whether contractors or subcontractors. Notice of filing must be served upon the owner within one month after filing, giving the court term and number of date of filing of the claim.

An affidavit of service of notice or the acceptance of service must be filed within 20 days after such service setting forth the date and manner of service. Failure to serve such notice or file the affidavit within the time specified shall be sufficient grounds for striking off the claim.

(d) *Rule by Owner*. After completion of the work by a subcontractor, any owner or contractor may file a rule or rules in the court in which the claim may be filed requiring the party named to file his claim within 30 days after notice of the rule. Failure to file the claim within such period shall defeat the right to do so. If subcontractor files as a result of the rule, no notice of intention to file is required. Where a claim is filed by a subcontractor, owner may give written notice thereof to a subcontractor.

Contents of the Claim—The claim of lien must state: (1) name of the party claimant and whether he files as contractor or subcontractor; (2) name and address of the owner or reputed owner; (3) date of completion of the claimant's work; (4) if filed by subcontractor, the name of the person with whom he contracted and the dates on which preliminary notice, if required, and of formal notice of intention to file a claim were given; (5) if filed by a contractor under a contract or contracts for an agreed sum, an identification of the contract and a general statement of the kind and character of the labor or materials furnished; (6) in all other cases than that set forth in clause (5) of this section, a detailed statement of the kind and character of the labor or materials furnished or both and the prices charged for each thereof; (7) amount or sum claimed to be due; and (8) such description of the improvement and of the property claimed to be subject to the lien as may be reasonably necessary to identify them.

Duration of Lien—An action to obtain a judgment must be commenced within two years from date of filing of lien unless time extended in writing by owner. A verdict must be recovered or judgment entered within five years from date of filing claim.

Filing Fee—Varies from county to county.

Extent of Lien—Every improvement and the estate or title of the owner in the property is subject to the lien. Claimant may maintain a lien against the owner in fee or any other person having any estate or interest in the property who by agreement, express or implied, contracts for the erection or alteration of the property. If the subcontractor has actual knowledge of the total contract price between the owner and contractor before he began work, his lien will be limited to the unpaid balance to the contractor or a *pro rata* portion thereof.

Priority of Lien—Liens filed take effect and have priority: (1) in the case of an improvement, as of the date of the visible commencement of the improvement, and (2) in the case of alteration or repair of an improvement, as of the date of filing of the claim.

Waiver of Liens—The contractor may enter into an agreement with the owner waiving the right of the contractor and of all persons under him to file or maintain a mechanics' lien claim. Such an agreement is binding upon a subcontractor, provided such subcontractor has had actual notice thereof before he has furnished any labor or material, or a signed copy of said waiver has been filed in the office of the Prothonotary of the Court of Common Pleas of the county or counties where the structure or other improvement is situated prior to the commencement of the work upon the ground, or within 10 days after the execution of the principal contract, or not less than 10 days prior to the contract with the claimant. Such a waiver of lien is indexed by the prothonotary.

Public Improvements—See Chapter 13.

Statutory Citation—Pennsylvania Consolidated Statutes, Title 49, §§ 49-1101 to 1902.

RHODE ISLAND

Who May Claim—Any person who constructs, erects, alters or repairs any building, canal, turnpike, railroad or other improvement with the consent of the owner, tenant or lessee (but not of the state) for all work done and for materials furnished, including architectural and engineering work. Providing materials includes rental or lease of equipment.

A covenant, promise, agreement of understanding in, or in connection with, or collateral to a contract or agreement relative to the construction, alteration, repair or maintenance of a building, structure, appurtenance and appliance, including moving, demolition and excavating connected therewith, purporting to bar the filing of a notice of contract or the taking of any steps to enforce a lien is against public policy and is void and unenforceable.

How Claimed—By serving and filing a notice of intention to claim a lien.

Where Filed—In the records of land evidence in the city or town in which the land is located.

When to File—Within 120 days after the doing of work or furnishing of materials.

Service of Copy of Notice—A copy of the notice must be served not later than 120 days after furnishing work or materials by certified or registered mail with return receipt requested, addressed to the last known address of the owner or lessee or, if not known, to the address of the land. If the notice is returned undelivered, it must be filed with its envelope within 30 days after the return and in no event more than 120 days after the mailing. It is sufficient to describe the realty by metes and bounds and street address, by recitation of the taxing authority's assessor's plat and lost designation and street address or by recitation of the book and page of the mortgage and street address.

Contents of Notice of Intention—The notice of intention shall contain the name of the owner of record of the land or if the lien is claimed against the interest of the lessee, the name of the lessee, the mailing address of the owner or lessee (name and address to be located in upper lefthand corner), general description of the land, a general description of the work to be done or of the materials to be furnished, the approximate value of the materials and work performed, the name and address of the person for whom directly the work has been done or the materials furnished, the name and address of the person mailing such notice, a statement that the person mailing said notice has not been paid for said work done or materials furnished or both and a statement that the sender may perfect all liens claimed or that could be claimed by filing the notice of intention within 120 days after doing the work or furnishing of the materials. The filing of the notice perfects the lien on work done 120 days before the mailing of the notice and thereafter for 120 days, but not for work done before the 120-day period. The statement must be executed under oath and state that the claimant has not been paid. A statutory form is provided.

Duration of Lien—A petition to enforce the lien must be commenced within 120 days of the date the notice of intention was recorded. A *lis pendens* must be filed, and the petition must be filed within seven days of the *lis pendens*.

Filing Fee—$8 for filing notice of intention to claim a lien and renewals.

Priority of Lien—All liens receive distribution *pro rata*. Liens are senior to any subsequently recorded encumbrances, but junior to prior recorded encumbrances.

Extent of Lien—Lien improvement and land on which situated; when contract with husband of owner consent in writing of both husband and wife required.

Public Improvements—See Chapter 13.

Statutory Citation—General Laws of Rhode Island, Title 34, Chapter 34-28, §§ 34-28-1 to 34-28-37.

SOUTH CAROLINA

Who May Claim—Any contractor, subcontractor, laborer or materialman who furnishes labor or materials used in the erection or repair of any structure upon real estate with the consent or at the request of the owner thereof, or of his agent, contractor or subcontractor, doing land surveying, providing private security guard services at the site, preparing plans, preparations, drawings and specifications for improvement to the site, gradings, pruning, well borings, etc. Lien also available to one who rents tools, appliances, machinery or equipment for use in building or structure. Lien for materials includes flooring, floor coverings and wallpaper.

How Claimed—By serving upon the owner or the person in possession and filing sworn statement of account describing property covered and naming the owner or owners thereof. If neither the owner nor the person in possession can be located after a diligent search, verified by a sheriff's affidavit, the statement shall be considered delivered when filed along with the affidavit.

Where Filed—In the office of the Register of Deeds or Clerk of the court of the county where property is situated.

When to Be Filed—At any time after payment is due and within 90 days after the party claiming the lien ceases to labor or to furnish labor or materials for such building or structure.

Notice of Commencement. The owner or contractor in privity with the owner may file a notice of commencement within 30 days of beginning work on the project.

Notice to Contractor. If notice of commencement is filed, no subcontractor or supplier to a subcontractor not in privity with the contractor can file a lien unless it has first filed a notice of furnishing labor or materials; this notice must be given by certified or registered mail not later than 60 days after the last day of work.

Service of Copy of Notice—Copy of notice must be served upon owner or, if owner cannot be found, upon person in possession, or filed with the clerk as specified above in section 2.

Duration of Lien—Unless a suit for enforcing the lien is commenced and a notice of pendency of the action is filed, within six months after person desiring to avail himself thereof ceases to labor on or to furnish labor or material for such building or structure, the lien shall be dissolved.

Filing Fee—$6; additional page, $1; satisfaction of lien, $5.

Contents of Notice of Lien—A statement of a just and true account of the amount due with all just credits given, together with a description of the property intended to be covered by the lien, sufficiently accurate for identification, with the name of the owner or owners of the property, if known, which certificate shall be subscribed and sworn to by the person claiming the lien, or by someone in his behalf, and proof of mailing to the owner of the copy of the lien.

Extent of Lien—The lien shall extend to the building or structure and the interest of the owner thereof and the land or place upon which the same is situated. A subcontractor's lien shall in no event exceed the amount due by the owner under the contract for construction. The lien covers the value of the lienor's work and materials. The prevailing party may recover attorneys' fees.

Priority of Lien—Lien of laborer, mechanic, subcontractor or materialman is subject to existing liens of which he had actual or constructive notice. The liens of laborer, materialman and subcontractor take precedence over the lien of the principal contractor. Mortgage recorded at date of contract is prior to lien, but as to future advances, if the mortgagee has been served with a lien, the lien prevails.

Miscellaneous—Owner is required to pay contractor or subcontractor within 21 days of request for payment of work completed or service provided. Contractor shall pay subcontractor within seven days of receipt of payment from owner.

Public Improvements—See Chapter 13.

Statutory Citation—Code of Laws of South Carolina, Title 29, §§ 29-5-10 to 29-5-430; 29-6-10 to 29-6-60; 29-7-10 to 29-7-30.

SOUTH DAKOTA

Who May Claim—Whoever furnishes skill, labor, services or materials for the improvement, development or operation of any building, fixture, bridge, fence or other structure or public utility or mine or well. Liens also to persons furnishing services, skills, labor, parts, materials, etc., for the alteration, repair, storage, etc., of personal property.

An owner may protect his property against liens for unauthorized improvements by serving upon persons doing the work, within five days after knowledge thereof, written notice that improvement was not made at his instance, or by posting such notice in a conspicuous place on the premises.

How Claimed—By filing verified statement of some person shown by such verification to have knowledge of facts stated. Contractor files a brief statement of the nature of his contract, which statement constitutes his notice of lien. In addition, subcontractor must serve notice of his claim on the owner.

Where Filed—With the Clerk of Court or Register of Deeds in the county or counties where the real property is situated.

When to Be Filed—Subcontractors, materialmen and laborers must file within 120 days after doing the last of such work or furnishing the last item of such skill, material or machinery. Persons other than original contractor may serve upon owner at any time notice of claim. Owner within 15 days after completion of the contract may require person having such lien to furnish him with an itemized and verified account of the claim, the amount thereof, and his name and address. No action shall be commenced or enforcement of the lien until 10 days after this statement is furnished. Before filing lien with Register of Deeds, claimant must mail to the property owner, at his last known address by registered or certified mail, a copy of the lien statement, and receipt for mailing must be attached to the lien statement and filed in the Office of the Register of Deeds.

Service of Copy of Notice—Notice must be served by registered or certified mail prior to filing. Filed statement must be accompanied by post office receipt. Owner may demand written itemized account within 15 days after the contract is completed. Owner may then pay claim or claimant may proceed to enforce his lien upon the expiration of 10 days after furnishing such statement.

Duration of Lien—Action to establish the same must be instituted within six years after the date of the last item of the claim as set forth in the filed lien statement; provided that upon written demand of the owner, his agent or contractor served on the person holding the lien, requiring him to commence suit to enforce such lien, suit shall be commenced within 30 days thereafter or the lien shall be forfeited. At the time suit is filed, a notice must be recorded in the deed records.

Filing Fee—$3.

Contents of Statement of Lien—(1) Notice of intention to claim and hold a lien and the amount thereof; (2) that such amount is due and owing to the claimant for labor performed or for skill, material or machinery furnished and for what improvement the same was done or supplied; (3) names and addresses of the claimant and of the person for or to whom performed or furnished; (4) dates when the first and last items of the claimant's contribution to the improvement were made; (5) name of the owner thereof at the time of making such statement according to the best information then had; (6) description of the premises to be charged, identifying same with reasonable certainty; and (7) itemized statement of account upon which lien is claimed.

Extent of Lien—If work or materials made under contract with owner for an agreed price, lien shall be for the sum agreed on plus cost of any additional material or work agreed on, otherwise for the reasonable value of work done. Lien shall not extend or affect any right in any homestead otherwise except by law.

Priority of Lien—The liens shall, as against the owner of the land, attach and take effect from the time the first item of material or labor is furnished upon the premises by the lien claimant, and shall be preferred to any mortgage or other encumbrance not then of record, unless the lienholder had actual notice thereof. As against a bona fide purchaser, mortgagor or encumbrancer without notice, however, no lien shall be attached prior to the actual and visible beginning of the improvement of the grounds, but a person having a contract for such improvement may file with the Register of Deeds of the county within which the premises are situated, a brief statement of the nature of such contract, which statement shall be notice of his lien for the contract price or value of the contribution of such improvement thereafter made by him or at his instance.

Public Improvements—See Chapter 13.

Lien for Improvement of Oil or Gas Well—The mechanics' lien laws are equally applicable to oil and gas wells.

Statutory Citation—South Dakota Codified Laws, Title 44, §§ 44-9-1 to 44-9-49; 44-9A-1 to 44-9A-5.

TENNESSEE

Who May Claim—Every mechanic, person, firm or corporation who shall do or perform any work, or labor upon or furnish any material, fixture, engine, boiler, waste disposal services and equipment, machinery for any building or improvement on land, or for repairing, altering or beautifying the same, or the placement of sewer or drainage lines or other underground utility lines or work in preparation therefore, and for the erection of temporary security fencing under or by virtue of any contract with the owner or proprietor thereof, or his or her agent, architect, trustee, contractor or subcontractor, upon complying with the provisions of this division, shall have a lien therefore on such building or improvements and on the land on which the same is situated, to the extent in ownership of all the right, title and interest therein of the owner or proprietor, and to the extent in area of the entire lot or parcel of land in a city or town; or, if not in a city or town, of one acre in addition to the land upon which the building or improvement is situated; or, if employees of the contractor or persons furnishing material to him or her, the lien shall extend only to the amount of any unpaid balance due the contractor by the owner or proprietor, and the employees and materialmen shall also have a lien on the unpaid balance. It is against public policy for any contract to waive anyone's right to file a mechanic's lien.

How Claimed—Original contractor and furnisher must bring suit within one year after completion of the work. Subcontractor, furnisher or laborer employed by original contractor, must serve on owner written notice of nonpayment within 90 days after the last day of the month within which work, services or materials were provided which sets forth amount due, name and address of claimant, general description of the work, services or materials provided, the last date the claimant performed work or provided the services or materials and a description of the real property. Subcontractor cannot claim mechanics' lien against residential real property consisting of one or two dwelling units in which owner resides or intends to reside as principal place of residence. Notice of nonpayment requirement does not apply to one-to four-family residential units. Within 90 days after the work is completed, or the contract of the laborer, furnisher or other person shall expire, or such person is discharged, such person shall notify the owner in writing that the lien is claimed. Suit must be brought within 90 days to enforce lien of subcontractor, laborer, and materialman.

Where Filed—Abstracts and notices of completion must be filed with the Register of Deeds in the county where the real property or any affected part thereof is located.

When to Be Filed—The subcontractor, furnisher or laborer employed by original contractor may file suit to enforce claim for lien at any time within 90 days after notice to owner.

Service of Copy of Notice—Tennessee's Truth in Construction and Consumer Protection Act of 1975 requires any contractor who is about to enter into a contract, either written or oral, for improving real property with the owner or owners thereof, prior to commencing the improvement of said real property or making of the contract, to deliver by registered mail or otherwise, to the owner or owners of the real property to be improved, written notice.

Time of Attachment of Lien—Liens shall relate to and take effect from the time of the visible commencement of operations, excluding, however, demolition, surveying, excavating, clearing, filling or grading and the delivery of materials therefor. If there be a cessation of all operations at the site of the improvement for more than 90 days, any lien for labor of any nature performed or for materials of any nature furnished after the visible resumption of operations shall relate to and take effect only from said visible resumption of operations. Upon completion of the job, the owner may file a notice of completion; if filed, lien claimants who have not previously recorded their contract must send notice of nonpayment by certified mail. On one to four-family residential projects, claimants have 10 days to send the notice; on other projects, the notice must be sent within 30 days.

Duration of Lien—The mechanic, founder or machinist under contract with owner has lien for one year after the work is finished or materials are furnished and until the decision of any suit brought within that time. The lien in favor of the subcontractor, laborer or furnisher employed by original contract extends for period of 90 days after notice to the owner. If suit is brought in a court of general sessions, after judgment is obtained and within 20 days an abstract thereof must be registered to constitute a lien. Owner of property against which lien has been filed can, before entry of judgment enforcing the lien, discharge the lien by posting a bond for double the amount thereof.

Filing Fee—For registration of abstract (requisite to precedence of the lien) or notice of completion, $8, plus $4 per page for each additional page over two.

Contents of Abstract—As a requisite to precedence of the lien, a sworn statement of the amount due and/or approximating that to accrue for such work, labor or materials, and a reasonably certain description of the premises, shall be filed with the county register.

Extent of Lien—The claims secured by lien for work and labor done and materials furnished shall in no case exceed the amount agreed to be paid by the owner in the owner's contract with the original contractor, except if before furnishing any material, the contractor shall notify the owner or his or her agent in writing that certain specified material will be furnished by him or her to the contractor or subcontractor for use in the building or improvements on the land, the furnisher of the materials shall have a lien for the full price thereof as specified in the notice to owner. Lien attaches to building, fixtures or improvements as well as land upon which same are situated.

Priority of Lien—Provided that an abstract is recorded, lienor takes precedence over all other encumbrances originating after commencement of operations. Liens of all laborers shall be on a parity one with another, and shall have preference over all other liens. All other liens shall be on parity with one another and shall be settled *pro rata*. Prior mortgagee may consent to liens taking priority either expressly or by failure to object thereto within 10 days of receiving notice of same.

Public Improvements—See Chapter 13.

Liens for Improvement of Wells or Equipment—Lien to persons who have drilled a well by contract with owner or authorized agent against tract of land for all labor, materials and equipment used or furnished by driller. Lien is effective for two years after completion of well or after furnishing pump or other apparatus unless sooner discharged by payment in full.

Miscellaneous—Requires a contractor who is about to enter into a contract involving real property to deliver to the owner written notice that a lien may be imposed against the property. Upon completion of the contract or improvement and upon the receipt of the contract price, the contractor shall deliver to the owner a notice providing that the contractor agrees to pay all subcontractors for services, labor or materials no later than 10 days from the date a bill is rendered for such services, labor or materials; that the owner has accepted the work and paid for it in full and that the contractor agrees to hold the owner harmless against any liens, claims or suits by others in connection with the work. In the event the contractor fails to comply with the act, he shall be guilty of a class B misdemeanor.

Notice of Completion—Upon completion of work owner may register in office of Register of Deeds a Notice of Completion, or require contractor to do same. Thereafter, lien rights of claimant are lost unless claimant gives written notice, within 10 days for residential projects and 30 days in the case of commercial projects, of the filing of the Notice of Completion to addressee.

Escrow Account for Retainage—Retainage can be required to be deposited into an escrow account. Said escrow provision cannot be waived.

Statutory Citation—Tennessee Code, Title 66, Chapter 11, §§ 66-11-101 to 66-11-208.

TEXAS

Who May Claim—Any person, including architects, engineers, or surveyors, who performs labor, furnishes specially fabricated material, even if not delivered, or furnishes labor or materials under contract with the owner, the owner's agent, contractor or subcontractor for construction or repair of a house, building, or improvement, for the construction or repair of levees or embankments, for the reclamation of overflow lands, or for the construction or repair of any railroad, may claim a lien. The word "improvement" includes: (a) abutting sidewalks and streets and utilities in or on those sidewalks and streets; (b) clearing, grubbing, draining, or fencing of land; (c) wells, cisterns, tanks, reservoirs, or artificial lakes or pools made for supplying or storing water; (d) pumps, siphons, and windmills or other machinery or apparatuses used for raising water for stock, domestic use, or irrigation; and (e) planting orchard trees, grubbing out orchards and replacing trees, and pruning of orchard trees. Additionally, any person who provides labor, material, or other supplies for the installation of landscaping for a house, building, or improvement, or provides labor or materials for the demolition of a structure on real property under a written contract with the owner or owner's agent may claim a lien.

How to Claim—If the claimant has a direct contractual relationship with the owner, then the only step required to perfect a lien claim is that claimant must file an affidavit claiming lien with the county clerk of the county in which the property is located by the 15th day of the fourth calendar month after the day on which the indebtedness accrues. A person who files an affidavit must send a copy of the affidavit by registered or certified mail to the owner or reputed owner not later than the fifth day after the affidavit is filed with the county clerk. If the claimant does not have a direct contractual relationship with the owner, but contracted with the original contractor, then in addition to filing the lien affidavit, the claimant must also give notice to the owner or reputed owner, with a copy to the original contractor, of the unpaid balance not later than the 15th day of the third month following each month in which all or part of the claimant's labor was performed or material was delivered. This notice is commonly referred to as a "fund trapping" notice and must state "that if the claim remains unpaid, the owner may be personally liable and the owner's property may be subjected to a lien unless the owner withholds payments from the contractor for payment of the claim, or the claim is otherwise paid or settled." If the claimant is a second tier subcontractor or below, i.e., does not have a direct contractual relationship with the original contractor, then in addition to filing the lien affidavit and sending the fund trapping notice, the claimant must also give notice to the original contractor of the unpaid balance not later than the 15th day of the second month following each month in which all or part of the claimant's labor was performed or material was delivered. This notice is commonly called the "preliminary notice". All notices must be sent by registered or certified mail.

Where to File—The lien affidavit must be filed with the County Clerk of the county in which the property is located.

When to File—The affidavit must be filed not later than the 15th day of the fourth calendar month after the day on which the indebtedness accrues. Indebtedness to an original contractor accrues on the last day of the month in which a written declaration by the original contractor or the owner is received by the other party to the contract stating that the original contract has been terminated, or on the last day of the month in which the original contract has been completed, finally settled, or abandoned. Indebtedness to a subcontractor accrues on the last day of the last month in which labor was performed or material furnished.

However, for derivative claimants the preliminary notice and fund trapping notice discussed above are conditions precedent to the enforceability of the lien. For deadlines for mailing the fund trapping notice and preliminary notice, *see* section 2 above.

Notice Required—In addition to the fund trapping notice and preliminary notice outlined in section 2 above, the following notices may also be necessary.

(a) *Notice for Contractual Retainage Claim.* If an agreement providing for retainage exists, written notice must be given to the owner or reputed owner not later than the 15th day of the second month following the first delivery of materials or the performance of labor by the claimant after the claimant has agreed to the contractual retainage. If the agreement is with a subcontractor, the claimant must also give notice within that time to the original contractor. The notice must state the sum to be retained, the due dates if known, and generally indicate the nature of the agreement, and must be sent by certified or registered mail. A lien for retainage may not be a greater amount than the amount specified to be retained in the contract between the claimant and contractor.

(b) *Notice for Specially Fabricated Items.* If the claim is based on specially fabricated items, notice to owner must be given not later than the 15th day of the second month after the month in which the claimant receives and accepts the order for the material. The notice must state that the order was received and accepted, and the price of the order. In cases where indebtedness was incurred by one other than an original contractor, claimant must also give notice to the original contractor.

Duration of Lien—Suit must be filed within two years after the last day a claimant may file the lien affidavit, or within one year after completion, termination, or abandonment of the work under the original contract, whichever is later. For claims arising from a residential construction project, suit must be filed within one year after the last day the lien claimant may file a lien affidavit. Where a surety bond is filed to indemnify against a lien claim on private improvements, the claimant must sue on the bond within one year after the claim is perfected. If the bond is not recorded at the time the lien is filed, the claimant must sue on the bond within two years following perfection of a claim.

Filing Fee—The filing fee varies from county to county and depends upon the length of the affidavit and attachments to be recorded.

Contents of Statement of Lien—The affidavit claiming a lien must contain the following: (1) a sworn statement of the amount of the claim; (2) the name and last known address of the owner or reputed owner; (3) a general statement of the kind of work done and materials furnished by the claimant, and, for a claimant other than an original contractor, a statement of each month in which work was done and materials furnished for which payment is requested; (4) the name and last known address of the person by whom the claimant was employed or to whom the claimant furnished the materials of labor; (5) the name and last known address of the original contractor; (6) a description, legally sufficient for identification, of the property sought to be charged with the lien; (7) the claimant's name, mailing address, and, if different, physical address; and (8) for a claimant other than the original contractor, a statement identifying the date each notice of the claim was sent to the owner and the method by which the notice was sent.

The affidavit must "substantially comply" with the statutory requirements to perfect a lien. The affidavit is not required to set forth individual items of work done, or material furnished or specially fabricated. The affidavit may use any abbreviations or symbols customary in the trade.

Demand for Payment—If an owner has received proper notice of a claim, and is authorized to withhold funds, the claimant may then proceed to make a demand for payment of the funds withheld. A copy of the demand must be sent to the original contractor, who may give written notice to the owner that he disputes the claim. If the original contractor does not dispute the claim within 30 days after it receives the demand, the owner must then pay the claim. The demand may accompany the original notice of nonpayment, but may not be made after the expiration of the time within which a claimant may secure a lien.

Extent of Lien—The lien secures payment for (1) the labor done or material furnished for the construction or repair; (2) the specially fabricated material, even if the material has not been delivered or incorporated into the construction or repair, less its fair salvage value; or (3) the preparation of a plan or plat by an architect, engineer, or surveyor. However, the amount of a lien claimed by a subcontractor may not exceed (1) an amount equal to the proportion of the total subcontract price equal to the sum of the labor performed, materials furnished, or materials specially fabricated, plus reasonable overhead costs incurred, and proportionate profit margin bears to the total subcontract price; minus (2) the sum of previous payments received by the claimant on the subcontract. The lien extends to the house, building, fixtures, or improvements, the land reclaimed from overflow, or the railroad and all of its properties, and to each lot of land necessarily connected or reclaimed. The lien does not extend to abutting sidewalks, streets, and utilities that are public property. The time of inception of the lien relates back to the commencement of construction of improvements or delivery of materials to the land on which the improvements are to be located and in which the materials are to be used.

Priorities—A mechanic's lien attaches to the house, building, improvements, or railroad property in preference to any prior lien, encumbrance, or mortgage on the land on which it is located, and the person enforcing the lien may have the house, building, improvement, or any piece of the railroad property sold separately. However, the mechanic's lien does not affect any lien, encumbrance, or mortgage on the land or improvement at the time of the inception of the mechanic's lien, and the holder of the lien, encumbrance, or mortgage need not be made a party to a suit to foreclose the mechanic's lien. Subcontractor, laborers, and materialmen who have a mechanic's lien have preference over other creditors of the original contractor. Except as is otherwise provided, mechanic's liens are on equal footing without reference to date of filing the lien affidavit. If the proceeds are insufficient to pay all in full, the lien claimants shall share *pro rata*.

Retainage—During the progress of work under an original contract for which a mechanic's lien may be claimed and for 30 days after the work is completed, the owner shall retain: (1) 10 percent of the contract price of the work to the owner; or (2) 10 percent of the value of the work, measured by the proportion that the work done bears to the work to be done, using the contract price or, if there is no contract price, using the reasonable value of the completed work. The retained funds secure the payment of contractors who perform labor, furnish material, or furnish specially fabricated material for any contractor, subcontractor, agent or receiver in the performance of the work. A claimant has a lien on the retained funds if the claimant: (1) sends the required notices; and (2) files an affidavit claiming a lien not later than the 30th day after the work is completed, the 30th day after the original contract is terminated, or the 30th day after the original contractor abandons performance under the original contract, whichever is earliest. Not later than the 10th day after the date an original contract is terminated or the original contractor abandons performance under the original contract, the owner is required to give notice to each subcontractor who, before the date of termination or abandonment, has: (1) given notice to the owner of an unpaid claim; or (2) sent to the owner by certified or registered mail a written request for notice of termination or abandonment. The owner's notice must contain: (1) the name and address of the owner; (2) the name and address of the original contractor; (3) a description, legally sufficient for identification, of the real property on which the improvements are located; (4) a general description of the improvements agreed to be furnished under the original contract; (5) a statement that the original contract has been terminated or that performance under the contract has been abandoned; (6) the date of the termination or abandonment; and (7) a conspicuous statement that a claimant may not have a lien on the retained funds unless the claimant files an affidavit claiming a lien not later than the 30th day after the date of the termination or abandonment. An owner's notice of termination is not required for residential construction projects.

Public Improvements—See Chapter regarding Texas Public Project Bond Laws.

Liens for Improvement of Gas and Oil Wells—A mineral contractor or subcontractor has a lien to secure payment for labor or services related to the mineral activities. "Mineral contractor" means a person who performs labor or furnishes or hauls material, machinery, or supplies used in mineral activities under an express or implied contract with a mineral property owner. "Mineral property owner" means an owner of land, an oil, gas, or other mineral leasehold, or an oil or gas pipeline right-of-way. "Mineral activities" means digging, drilling, torpedoing, operating, completing, maintaining, or repairing an oil, gas, or water well, an oil or gas pipeline, or a mine or quarry. The lien extends to the material, machinery, and supplies furnished, and to the land, leasehold, oil or gas well for which the labor performed or the material was supplied, and the buildings and appurtenances on this property. However, a lien created by performing labor or furnishing materials for a lease holder does not attach to the fee title in the property. To claim a lien, not later than six months after the day the indebtedness accrues, a person claiming the lien must file an affidavit with the county clerk of the county in which the property is located. However, not later than the 10th day before the affidavit is filed, a mineral subcontractor claiming lien must serve on the property owner written notice that the lien is claimed.

Lien on Homestead—In addition to the substantive requirements for a lien affidavit discussed above, an affidavit claiming lien on homestead property must contain the following notice conspicuously printed, stamped, or typed in a size equal to at least 10-point boldface or computer equivalent, at the top of the page:

NOTICE: THIS IS NOT A LIEN, THIS IS ONLY AN AFFIDAVIT CLAIMING A LIEN.
TX Prop. Code Ann. § 53.254.

To claim a lien on a residential construction project the lien affidavit must be filed not later than the 15th day of the third calendar month after the day on which the indebtedness accrues, which is one month earlier than a standard lien affidavit.

For a lien on a homestead to be valid, notice must be provided to the owner not later than the 15th day of the second month following each month in which all or part of the claimant's labor was performed or material delivered, and in addition to the fund trapping language discussed above, the notice must include the following additional language:

"If a subcontractor or supplier who furnishes materials or performs labor for construction of improvement on your property is not paid, your property may be subject to a lien for the unpaid amount if: (1) after receiving notice of the unpaid claim from the claimant, you fail to withhold payment to your contractor that is sufficient to cover the unpaid claim until the dispute is resolved; or (2) during construction and for 30 days after completion of construction, you fail to retain 10% of the contract price or 10% of the value of the work performed by your contractor.

If you have complied with the law regarding the 10% retainage and you have withheld payment to the contractor sufficient to cover any written notice of claim and have paid that amount, if any, to the claimant, any lien claim filed on your property by a subcontractor or supplier, other than a person who contracted directly with you, will not be a valid lien on your property. In addition, except for the required 10% retainage, you are not liable to a subcontractor before you received written notice of the claim."

Affidavit of Completion—An owner may file an affidavit of completion with the county clerk of the county in which the property is located. A copy of this affidavit must be sent by certified or registered mail to original contractor not later than the date the affidavit is filed and to each claimant who sends a notice of lien liability to the owner not later than the date the affidavit is filed or the 10th day after the date the owner receives the notice of lien liability, whichever is later. A copy must also be sent to each person who provides labor or materials and who furnishes the owner with a written request for a copy.

Discharge—Mechanics' lien may be discharged by recording a release of lien signed by claimant, failure to initiate suit on time, recording final judgment providing for discharge, or by bonding around the lien.

Governing Statutes—Texas Property Code §§ 53.001 to 53.260, 56.001 to 56.045.

UTAH

Who May Claim—Contractors, subcontractors and all persons performing any services or furnishing or renting any materials or equipment used in the construction, alteration or improvement of any building or structure or improvement to any premises in any manner, or persons who shall do work or furnish materials for prospecting, development, preservation or working of any mining claim, mine, quarry, oil or gas well, or deposit. Licensed architects and engineers and artisans may all have lien for value of service or labor performed or materials furnished for the value thereof. A person otherwise entitled to file a lien upon an owner-occupied residence and the real property associated with it who provides qualified services under an agreement as a subcontractor, shall be barred after January 1, 1995, from maintaining a lien upon that residence and real property or recovering a judgment in any civil action against the owner or the owner-occupied residence to recover monies owed for said services provided by that person if: (a) the owner of the residence or the owner's agent entered a written agreement with an original contractor, electrician, or plumber for the performance of qualified services, to obtain the performance of a qualified service by others, or for the supervision of the performance by others of the services in construction on that residence; and (b) construction on that residence is performed pursuant to a building permit issued by the local jurisdiction in which the residence is located, if required; and (c) the owner has paid the original contractor, electrician or plumber with whom the owner had a written agreement in accord with its terms and the original contractor, electrician or plumber subsequently failed to pay the claimant or subcontractor who contracted with the original owner failed to pay the claimant or a subcontractor who contracted with the subcontractor failed to pay the claimant.

How Claimed—By filing a claim containing a notice of intention to hold and claim a lien.

Where Filed—With County Recorder in county in which property or some part is located.

When to Be Filed—Within 90 days from the date of the final completion of the original contract.

Notice of Commencement and Preliminary Notice—Within 15 days of the issuance of the building permit, or commencement of physical construction where no building permit is issued, the owner, lender, surety or other interested person shall file a notice of commencement, which shall include: (1) name and address of the owner of the project or improvement; (2) name and address of the original contractor; (3) name and address of the surety providing any payment bond for the project or improvement, or if none exists, a statement that a payment bond was not required for the work being done; (4) the project address if the project can be reasonably identified by address or the name and general description of the project if it cannot; (5) a general description of the project; (6) the lot or parcel number, and any subdivision, development or other project name, of the real property.

A subcontractor or supplier must file a preliminary notice within 20 days of commencement of its own work, which notice shall include: (1) the name, address and telephone number of the person furnishing the labor or materials, (2) the name and address of the person who contracted with the claimant, (3) the name of the record or reputed owner of the project, (4) the name of the original contractor under which the claimant is performing the work, and (5) the address of the project or a description of the location of the project.

Service of Copy of Notice—Within 30 days after filing notice of lien, the lien claimant shall deliver or mail by certified mail to either the reputed owner or record owner of the real property a copy of the said notice of lien. Where the record owner's current address is not readily available, the copy of the claim may be mailed to the last known address of the record owner using for such purpose the names and addresses appearing on the last completed real property assessment rolls of the county where the affected property is located. Failure to deliver or mail the notice of lien to the reputed owner or record owner shall prevent the lien claimant from collection of costs and attorneys' fees against the reputed owner or record owner in an action to enforce the lien.

If suit is filed to enforce a lien on residential real property, the claimant must also serve to the owner a notice, instructions and forms relating to the Residence Lien Restriction and Lien Recovery Fund Act.

Duration of Lien—Must be enforced by filing an action within 180 days of the date of filing the notice of claim of lien and by filing a *lis pendens*.

Filing Fee—$10 plus $2 for each added page in excess of one. If more than one description, $1 for each.

Contents of Notice of Lien—A statement of lien shall include: (1) the name of the reputed owner of the property, if known, or if not known, the name of record owner, (2) the name of the person by whom the claimant was employed, or to whom he furnished the material, (3) the time when the first and last labors were performed, or the first and last equipment or materials were furnished, (4) a description of the property sufficient for identification, (5) the name, address and current phone number of the lien claimant, (6) the amount of the lien claim, (7) signature of the lien claimant or his authorized agent and (8) an acknowledgment or certificate as required by Chapter 3, Title 57.

Extent of Lien—Lien shall extend only to such interests as the owner or lessee may have in the real estate. Subcontractors' liens shall extend to the full contract price, but if at the time of commencement to do the work or furnish materials, owner has paid upon the contract, any portion of the contract price, either in money or property, the lien of the contractor shall extend only to such unpaid balance, and the lien of any subcontractor having notice of such payment shall be limited to the unpaid balance of the contract price. No part of the contract price shall by the terms of any contract be made payable nor shall the same or any part thereof be paid in advance of the commencement of the work for the purpose of defeating the lien law. Lien shall extend to so much of the land on which the improvement is situated as may be necessary for its convenient use and occupation, and if the improvement shall occupy two or more lots or other subdivisions of land, they shall be deemed as one lot and the lien shall attach all machinery and other fixtures used in connection with such improvement.

Priorities—Such a lien is prior to an attachment, levy or garnishment by the original contractor and is preferred to encumbrance that may have attached to the land subsequent to the commencement of the building—or any unrecorded encumbrance. Lien of principal contractor is inferior to the other mechanics' liens; among the latter there is no priority.

Public Improvements—See UCA 63-56-38 and Chapter 13.

Bond—In the case of a private construction contract involving more than $2,000, the owner must require from the contractor a bond equal to the contract price running to the owner and conditioned for the payment of the amounts contracted. An owner, failing to demand and receive such bond, is held personally liable to materialmen and subcontractors for debts of contractor.

Liens for Improvement of Oil or Gas Wells—Contractors, subcontractors and all persons performing work upon, or furnishing materials or equipment for, any production unit under contract with the owner, his agent or contractor must file a notice of lien within 180 days after the last day work was performed, or material or equipment was furnished, by the lien claimant. Preliminary notice to the owner or operator within 20 days of commencement of work is required for all subcontractors on material or equipment suppliers. Service of copy of notice is done in accordance with paragraph 5 above. To enforce the liens, the lien claimant shall institute an action within 180 days of the date of filing of the notice of lien, and shall, within 10 working days after commencement of the action, file a *lis pendens* with the County Recorder of each county in which the lien is recorded. Lien claimant's interest extends to the owner's production unit and access rights, pipelines, buildings, wells and oil tanks located on the property, as well as the ore, minerals, oil or gas substances in the ground or in storage. The owner of an interest in the production unit shall not be subject to a lien if he gives timely written notice in recordable form filed with the County Recorder of the county where the production unit is located stating that he will not be responsible for work performed or materials or equipment furnished.

Statutory Citation—Utah Code, Title 38, §§ 38-1-1 to 38-1-37.

VERMONT

Who May Claim—A person who is proceeding pursuant to a contract or agreement for erecting, repairing, moving or altering improvements to real property, or for furnishing materials or labor therefore has a lien; and a person who performs labor or furnishes material in the above-named works, under an agreement with an agent, the contractor or subcontractor of the owner shall have a lien.

How Claimed—Claimant must file signed written memorandum. Notice of such memorandum must be given by materialmen and laborers to the owner or his agent that the mechanic will claim a lien for labor to be performed or materials to be furnished.

Where Filed—Town Clerk of town in which real estate is situated.

When to Be Filed—Within 180 days from time payment becomes due.

Service of Copy of Notice—Required of materialmen and laborers.

Duration of Lien—Suit must be filed within 180 days of filing the notice, if payment was due at the time of the filing; if payment was not yet due at the time of the filing, suit must be filed within 180 days of the time payment becomes due.

Filing Fee—$6 per page.

Contents of Statement of Lien—An example of sufficient contents would be a description of the building or improvement, assertion of a lien thereon, amount claimed and that it is for such indebtedness as specified by Vermont Statute Section 1921, person to whom and from whom it is due and the latter's interest in the building or improvement.

Extent of Lien—Not to exceed the amount due at the time when lien is asserted or to become due by virtue of such contract or agreement. Lien attaches to project and lot of land on which it is situated. Within five months after judgment being entered, the claimant may foreclose by filing a certified copy of the judgment.

Priority of Lien—Does not take precedence over a mortgage given by the owner upon such building, etc., as security for the payment of money loaned and to be used by said owner in payment of the expenses of the same. Does not take precedence over a deed or conveyance to the extent that consideration has been given before record of lien. If several mechanics' liens are asserted, they shall be paid pro rata.

Public Improvements—See Chapter 13.

Statutory Citation—Vermont Statutes, Title 9, §§ 1921 to 1928.

VIRGINIA

Who May Claim—All persons performing labor or furnishing materials, including general contractors, subcontractors and sub-subcontractors. The statute includes storage tanks, dispensing equipment, wells, excavations, sidewalks, driveways, pavements, parking lots, retaining walls, curb and/or gutter, breakwater, water system, drainage structure, filtering systems (including septic or waste disposal systems), swimming pools, surveying, grading, clearing, earth moving, shrubbery, sod, sand, gravel, brick and the rental or use value of equipment. Any person providing labor or materials for site development improvements or for streets, sanitary sewers or water lines for the purpose of providing access of service to the individual lots in a development shall have a *pro rata* lien on each individual lot in the development, provided that the claimant files a Memorandum of Disclosure in the land records prior to the sale of such lot, setting forth a full disclosure of the nature of the lien to be claimed, the amount claimed against each lot and a description of the development. Special provisions also exist for liens on condominiums.

How Claimed—All claimants must file a Memorandum of Mechanics' Lien and later a suit to enforce the Mechanics' Lien. Some claimants on residential projects must also give a preliminary notice.

Where Filed—The Memorandum of Mechanics' Lien is filed in the land records of the Circuit Court Clerk's office of county or city in which property is located.

When to Be Filed—Any time after work is commenced or material furnished, but not later than 90 days after the last day of the month in which the claimant last performed work or furnished material and in no event later than 90 days after the improvement is completed.

Service of Copy of Notice—All claimants must also give notice of the mechanics' lien by certified mail to owner of property and any general contractor in the form required by statute. General contractor must also file with their memorandum of lien a certification that a copy was sent to the owner's last known address.

Preliminary Notice—For single- or double-family residences, the owner can identify a Mechanics' Lien Agent (MLA) in the building permit, in which case all claimants are also required to give notice to the Mechanics' Lien Agent (MLA) by certified mail within 30 days of beginning supply of labor or materials. The MLA notice must contain: (i) The name, mailing address and telephone number of the person (or company) sending the Notice; (ii) The building permit number; (iii) a description of the property as shown on the building permit; (iv) a statement that the person filing such Notice seeks payment for labor performed or material furnished.

Duration of Lien—Suit to enforce the mechanics' lien must be filed with six months from time memorandum of lien was recorded, or 60 days from the time the building, structure or railroad was completed or work terminated, whichever last occurs.

Filing Fee—$19 for up to four pages and $1 for each additional page for Memorandum of Mechanics' Lien.

Contents of Lien Memorandum—The memorandum contents are: (1) name and address of the owner; (2) name of the general contractor, if any; (3) name and address of the claimant; (4) type of materials or service furnished; (5) amount claimed; (6) type of structure on which the work was performed; (7) brief description and location of the property; (8) date from which interest is claimed and (9) a statement declaring the intention to claim the benefit of the lien. Any number of such memoranda may be filed, but no memorandum may include sums due for labor or materials furnished more than 150 days prior to the last day on which labor was performed or material furnished to the job preceding the filing. However, any memorandum may include retainages of up to 10% of the contract price or sums not yet due because of a "pay when paid" contract clause. Any person who, with intent to mislead, includes in the memorandum work not performed upon, or materials not furnished for the property described in the memorandum, forfeits any right to this lien.

Extent of Lien—Upon the buildings or structures, and so much land therewith as shall be necessary for the convenient use and enjoyment thereof. If a tenant or contract purchaser ordered the work, the lien extends only to the extent of the interest of the tenant or contract purchaser.

Subcontractors, Materialmen, etc.—The owner has a defense of payment. A subcontractor may not perfect a lien for an amount greater than the amount that the owner is, or shall thereafter become, indebted to the general contractor. A sub-subcontractor cannot perfect a lien for an amount greater than the amount the subcontractor could perfect a lien. A subcontractor or sub-subcontractor may be able to avoid a defense of payment and create personal liability on the owner and/or the general contractor by providing a Virginia Code 43-11 notice to the owner and/or the general contractor before furnishing labor or material and then providing a statement of account verified by affidavit within 30 days after the building or structure is completed. However, an owner always has priority to deductions allowed in an agreement because of the failure or refusal of the general contractor to comply with his contract.

Priority of Lien—Lien preferred to all judgments, mortgages, deeds of trusts, liens and conveyances recorded after commencement of work and to all loan advances made after commencement of work. Subcontractor liens have priority over general contractor liens, and the lien of a person performing labor or furnishing materials for a subcontractor shall be preferred to a subcontractor lien. Manual laborers are preferred to other lienors for labor performed during last 30 days of work. If owner is compelled to finish his own structure, the amount so expended shall have priority over all mechanics' liens. No lien upon land created after work commenced or materials were furnished shall operate on the land or the new building until the mechanics' lien is satisfied.

Public Improvements—See Chapter 13.

Waiver—The right to file or enforce a mechanics' lien may be waived at any time by the person entitled to the lien.

Statutory Citation—Code of Virginia, Title 43, Chapter 1, §§ 43-1 to 43-71.

WASHINGTON

Who May Claim—Any person furnishing labor, professional services, materials or equipment for the improvement of real property shall have a lien upon the improvement for the contract price of labor, professional services, materials or equipment furnished at the instance of the owner, or the agent or construction agent of the owner.

How Claimed—By giving notice to owner that claim may be filed and by filing notice of claim of lien.

Recording/Time/Contents of Lien—Every person claiming a lien shall file for recording, in the county where the subject property is located, a notice of claim of lien not later than 90 days after the person has ceased to furnish labor, professional services, materials or equipment or the last date on which employee benefit contributions were due.

When to Be Filed—Within 90 days from the date of cessation of performance of labor, furnishing material or supplying equipment. Liens for supply of agricultural materials must be filed after commencement of delivery of materials and products, but before commencement of the harvest of the crops.

Notices/Exceptions—(1) Every person furnishing professional services, materials or equipment for the improvement of real property who is not in privity with the owner shall give the owner or reputed owner and prime contractor notice in writing of the right to claim a lien. The notice may be given at any time but only protects the right to claim a lien for professional services, materials or equipment supplied after the date which is 60 days before: (a) mailing the notice by certified or registered mail to the owner or reputed owner; or (b) delivering or serving the notice personally upon the owner or reputed owner and obtaining evidence of delivery in the form of a receipt or other acknowledgment signed by the owner or reputed owner or an affidavit of service.

In the case of new construction of a single-family residence, the notice of a right to claim a lien may be given at any time but only protects the right to claim a lien for professional services, materials or equipment supplied after a date which is 10 days before the notice is given as described in this subsection.

(2) Notices of a right to claim a lien shall not be required of: (a) persons who contract directly with the owner or the owner's common-law agent; (b) laborers whose claim of lien is based solely on performing labor; or (c) subcontractors who contract for the improvement of real property directly with the prime contractor.

(3) Persons who furnish professional services, materials or equipment in connection with the repair, alteration or remodel of an existing owner-occupied single-family residence or appurtenant garage: (a) who contract directly with the owner-occupier or their common-law agent shall not be required to send a written notice of the right to claim a lien and shall have a lien for the full amount due under their contract, as provided in RCW 60.04.021; of this act; or (b) who do not contract directly with the owner-occupier or their common-law agent shall give notice of the right to claim a lien to the owner-occupier. Liens of persons who do not contract directly with the owner-occupier may only be satisfied from amounts not yet paid to the prime contractor by the owner at the time the notice described in this section is received, regardless of whether amounts not yet paid to the prime contractor are due.

Contents of Notice—The notice required shall include but not be limited to the following information and shall substantially be in the following form, using lowercase and uppercase 10-point type where appropriate.

NOTICE TO OWNER

IMPORTANT: READ BOTH SIDES OF THIS NOTICE CAREFULLY.
PROTECT YOURSELF FROM PAYING TWICE.

To:_____   Date:_____

RE:_____ (description of property: street address or general location)

From:_____

AT THE REQUEST OF: (Name of person placing the order)

THIS IS NOT A LIEN: This notice is sent to you to tell you who is providing professional services, materials or equipment for the improvement of your property and to advise you of the rights of these persons and your responsibilities. Also take note that laborers on your project may claim a lien without sending you a notice.

OWNER/OCCUPIER OF EXISTING RESIDENTIAL PROPERTY

Under Washington law, those who work on or provide materials for the repair, remodel or alteration of your owner-occupied principal residence and who are not paid, have a right to enforce their claim for payment against your property. This claim is known as a construction lien.

The law limits the amount that a lien claimant can claim against your property. Claims may only be made against that portion of the contract you have not yet paid to your prime contractor as of the time you received this notice. Review the back of this notice for more information and ways to avoid lien claims.

COMMERCIAL AND/OR NEW RESIDENTIAL PROPERTY

We have or will be providing labor, materials, professional services or equipment for the improvement of your commercial or new residential project. In the event you or your contractor fail to pay us, we may file a lien against your property. A lien may be claimed for all materials, equipment and professional services furnished after a date that is 60 days before this notice was given to you, unless the improvement to your property is the construction of a new single-family residence, then 10 days before this notice was mailed to you.

(Sender)
(Address)
(Telephone)

Brief description of professional services, materials or equipment provided or to be provided:

IMPORTANT INFORMATION FOR YOUR PROTECTION

This notice is sent to inform you that we have or will provide materials, professional services or equipment for the repair, remodel or alteration of your property. We expect to be paid by the person who ordered our services, but if we are not paid, we have the right to enforce our claim by filing a construction lien against your property.

—LEARN more about the lien laws and the meaning of this notice by discussing with your contractor, suppliers, Department of Labor and Industries, the firm sending you this notice, your lender or your attorney.

—COMMON METHODS TO AVOID CONSTRUCTION LIENS: There are several methods available to protect your property from construction liens. The following are two of the more commonly used methods.

—DUAL PAYCHECKS (Joint Checks): When paying your contractor for services or materials, you may make checks payable jointly to the contractor and the firms furnishing you this notice.

—LIEN RELEASES: You may require your contractor to provide lien releases signed by all the suppliers and subcontractors from whom you have received this notice. If they cannot obtain lien releases because you have not paid them, you may use the dual payee check method to protect yourself.

YOU SHOULD TAKE WHATEVER STEPS YOU BELIEVE NECESSARY TO PROTECT YOUR PROPERTY FROM LIENS.

YOUR PRIME CONTRACTOR AND YOUR CONSTRUCTION LENDER ARE REQUIRED BY LAW TO GIVE YOU WRITTEN INFORMATION ABOUT LIEN CLAIMS. IF YOU HAVE NOT RECEIVED IT, ASK THEM FOR IT.

Contractor Registration—A contractor or subcontractor required to be registered under chapter 18.27 RCW or licensed under chapter 19.28 RCW, or otherwise required to be registered or licensed by law, shall be deemed the construction agent of the owner for the purpose of establishing the lien created by this chapter only if so registered or licensed.

Duration—No lien binds the property subject to the lien for a longer period than eight calendar months after the claim of lien has been recorded unless an action is filed by the lien claimant within that time in the superior court in the county where the subject property is located to enforce the lien, and service is made upon the owner of the subject property within 90 days of the date of filing the action; or, if credit is given and the terms are stated in the claim of lien, then eight calendar months after the expiration of such credit; and in case the action is not prosecuted to judgment within two years after the commencement, the court may dismiss the action for want of prosecution, and the dismissal of the action or a judgment rendered thereon that no lien exists shall constitute a cancellation of the lien. This is a period of limitation, which shall be tolled by the filing of any petition seeking protection under USC Title 11 by an owner of any property subject to the lien established by this chapter.

Filing Fee—$5 for first page, $1 for each additional page, plus a $2 surcharge.

Contents of Statement of Lien—The notice of claim of lien: (1) Shall state in substance and effect: (a) name, phone number and address of the claimant; (b) first and last date on which the labor, professional services, materials or equipment was furnished or employee benefit contributions were due; (c) name of the person indebted to the claimant; (d) street address, legal description or other description reasonably calculated to identify, for a person familiar with the area, the location of the real property to be charged with the lien; (e) name of the owner or reputed owner of the property, if known, and if not known, that fact shall be stated; and (f) principal amount for which the lien is claimed.

(2) Shall be signed by the claimant or some person authorized to act on his or her behalf who shall affirmatively state they have read the notice of claim of lien and believe the notice of claim of lien to be true and correct under penalty of perjury, and shall be acknowledged. If the lien has been assigned, the name of the assignee shall be stated. Where an action to foreclose the lien has been commenced such notice of claim of lien may be amended as pleadings may be by order of the court insofar as the interests of third parties are not adversely affected by such amendment. A claim of lien substantially in the following form shall be sufficient:

_____, claimant, v. _____, name of person indebted to claimant.

Notice is hereby given that the person named below claims a lien pursuant to chapter 64.04 RCW. In support of this lien the following information is submitted:

1. NAME OF LIEN CLAIMANT:
    TELEPHONE NUMBER:
    ADDRESS:

2. DATE ON WHICH THE CLAIMANT BEGAN TO PERFORM LABOR, PROVIDE PROFES-SIONAL SERVICES, SUPPLY MATERIAL OR EQUIPMENT OR THE DATE ON WHICH EMPLOYEE BENEFIT CONTRIBUTIONS BECAME DUE
3. NAME OF PERSON INDEBTED TO THE CLAIMANT:
4. DESCRIPTION OF THE PROPERTY AGAINST WHICH A LIEN IS CLAIMED (Street address, legal description or other information that will reasonably describe the property):
5. NAME OF THE OWNER OR REPUTED OWNER (If not known state "unknown"):
6. THE LAST DATE ON WHICH LABOR WAS PERFORMED; PROFESSIONAL SERVICES WERE FURNISHED; CONTRIBUTIONS TO AN EMPLOYEE BENEFIT PLAN WERE DUE; OR MATERIAL, OR EQUIPMENT WAS FURNISHED:
7. PRINCIPAL AMOUNT FOR WHICH THE LIEN IS CLAIMED IS:
8. IF THE CLAIMANT IS THE ASSIGNEE OF THIS CLAIM SO STATE HERE:

(Claimant)
(Phone number, address, city and state of claimant)

STATE OF WASHINGTON
⎫
⎬ ss.
⎭
COUNTY OF _____

_____, being sworn, says: I am the claimant (or attorney of the claimant, or administrator, representative, or agent of the trustees of an employee benefit plan) above named; I have read of heard the foregoing claim, read and know the contents thereof, and believe the same to be true and correct and that the claim of lien is not frivolous and is made with reasonable cause, and is not clearly excessive under penalty of perjury.

(Signature)
Subscribed and sworn to before me this _____ day of _____, 20___.

Property Subject to Lien—The lot, tract or parcel of land which is improved is subject to a lien to the extent of the interest of the owner at whose instance, directly or through a common-law or construction agent, the labor, professional services, equipment or materials were furnished, as the court deems appropriate for satisfaction of the lien. If, for any reason, the title or interest in the land upon which the improvement is situated cannot be subjected to the lien, the court in order to satisfy the lien may order the sale and removal of the improvement which is subject to the lien, from the land.

Priority of Lien—The claim of lien created by this chapter upon any lot or parcel of land shall be prior to any lien, mortgage, deed of trust or other encumbrance which attached to the land after or was unrecorded at the time of commencement of labor or professional services or first delivery of materials or equipment by the lien claimant.

(1) In every case in which different construction liens are claimed against the same property, the court shall declare the rank of such lien or class of liens, which liens shall be in the following order: (a) liens for the performance of labor; (b) liens for contributions owed to employee benefit plans; (c) liens for furnishing material, supplies or equipment; (d) liens for subcontractors, including but not limited to their labor and materials; and (e) liens for prime contractors, or for professional services.

(2) The proceeds of the sale of property must be applied to each lien or class of liens in order of its rank and, in an action brought to foreclose a lien, *pro rata* among each claimant in each separate priority class. A personal judgment may be rendered against any party personally liable for any debt for which the lien is claimed. If the lien is established, the judgment shall provide for the enforcement thereof upon the property liable as in the case of foreclosure of judgment liens. The amount realized by such enforcement of the lien shall be credited upon the proper personal judgment. The deficiency, if any, remaining unsatisfied, shall stand as a personal judgment and may be collected by execution against any party liable therefor.

(3) The court may allow the prevailing party in the action, whether plaintiff or defendant, as part of the costs of the action, the moneys paid for recording the notice of costs of title report, bond costs and attorneys' fees and necessary expenses incurred by the attorney in the superior court, court of appeals, supreme court or arbitration, as the court or arbitrator deems reasonable. Such costs shall have the priority of the class of lien to which they are related, as established by subsection (1) of this section.

Real property against which a lien is enforced may be ordered sold by the court and the proceeds deposited into the registry of the clerk of the court, pending further determination respecting distribution of the proceeds of the sale.

Release of Lien Rights—Upon payment and acceptance of the amount due to the lien claimant and upon demand of the owner or the person making payment, the lien claimant shall immediately prepare and execute a release of all lien rights for which payment has been made, and deliver the release to the person making payment. In any suit to compel deliverance of the release thereafter in which the court determines the delay was unjustified, the court shall, in addition to ordering the deliverance of the release, award the costs of the action including reasonable attorneys' fees and any damages.

Public Improvements—See Chapter 13.

Remarks—Where there is not a payment bond of at least 50 percent of the amount of construction financing, lien claimants who have not received payments for labor or materials previously furnished within five days after the date required by the contract or purchase order may within 35 days of the date required for payment file a written notice with the lender, with a copy to the owner and appropriate general contractor, stating the sums due and to become due for which a potential lien claimant may claim a lien. After receipt of such notice the lender shall withhold from the next and subsequent draws the percentage thereof equal to that percentage of completion which is attributable to the potential lien claimant. Such sums, however, shall not be disbursed by the lender except by written agreement of claimant, owner and general contractor or an order of the court.

Statutory Citation—Revised Code of Washington, Title 60, Chapter 60.04, §§ 60.04.011 to 60.04.904.

WEST VIRGINIA

Who May Claim—Every person, workman, artisan, mechanic, laborer or other person who shall erect, build, construct, alter, remove or repair any building or other structure or other improvement appurtenant to any such building or other structure, or alters or improves the real property in which a building or structure strands, under and by virtue of a contract with the owner or his authorized agent. Architects, engineers and landscape architects are included within such definition.

How Claimed—If contract made with owner, by recording notice in the Office of the Clerk of the County Court [County Commission] of the county wherein such property is situated; if contract made with contractor or subcontractor, by serving notice on the owner or his authorized agent within 75 days and recording in County Clerk's office within 100 days.

Where Filed—In the Office of the Clerk of the County Commission where the property is situated.

When to Be Filed—Within 100 days of the last work performed by Claimant, subject to the notice requirements set out above.

Service of Copy of Notice—On the owner, when the material or labor was furnished by a subcontractor within 75 days after completion of subcontract. If the owner cannot be served, notice is sufficient by publication and posting.

Duration of Lien—Suit in chancery must be brought within six months after the filing of the notice such lien shall be discharged, but a suit commenced by any person having such lien shall for the purpose of preserving the same, inure to the benefit of all other persons having a lien under this chapter on the same property, and such persons may intervene in such suit for the purpose of enforcing their liens, in the same manner as in other chancery suits.

Filing Fee—$1.50 and $1 per page in excess of two.

Contents of Statement of Lien—Description of property and the improvements thereon as well as amount due. The statutory language is found at §38-2-9.

Extent of Lien—Lien extends to interest of owner in the improvement and the land on which same is situated.

Priority of Lien—Deeds of trust made subsequent to commencement of work or furnishing material are inferior to mechanics' lien. The lien of the contractor is inferior to that of the subcontractor, and those for labor and materials, and the lien of the contractor and subcontractor is inferior to mechanics' liens for labor and materials. Otherwise, there is no priority among liens.

Public Improvements—See Chapter 13.

Statutory Citation—West Virginia Code, Chapter 38, §§ 38-2-1 to 38-2-39; 38-12-1 to 38-12-13.

WISCONSIN

Who May Claim—Every person who performs any work or procures its performance or furnishes any labor or furnishes any labor materials, plans or specifications for the improvement of land, including any building, structure, fixture, demolition, erection, alteration, excavation, filling, grading, tiling, planting, clearing or landscaping which is built, erected, made or done on or to land for its permanent benefit. Prime contractor is a person, other than laborer, including an architect, professional engineer or surveyor employed by the owner, who enters into a contract with an owner or an owner acting as his own general contractor. Despite owner's payment bond, unless contract between owner and contractor contains a provision for payment by prime contractor of all claims for labor and materials and the prime contractor posts a bond issued by a surety company licensed in the state, a subcontractor's lien rights are effective. Where a payment bond is provided in conformance with the statute, special notice and limitations provisions apply.

How Claimed—A construction lien does not exist and no action to enforce it can be maintained unless (1) claim for lien is properly filed; (2) written notice of intent to file a lien claim is properly served on the owner; (3) for prime contractors only, a written notice about the lien law, either as part of the contract or separately stated is given to the owner; and (4) for subcontractors only, duplicate written notices of participation in the project served on the owner, unless special exemptions apply.

(a) *Claim for Lien.* The claim for lien must have attached a copy of the notice of intent to file a lien claim and a copy of any prime contractor's notice about the lien law or subcontractor's notice of participation. The claim must contain a statement of the contract or demand upon which it is founded, the name of the person against whom the demand is claimed, the name of the claimant and any assignee, the last date of the performance of any labor or the furnishing of any materials, a legal description of the property against which the lien is claimed, a statement of the amount claimed and all other material facts. Claim must be signed by claimant or attorney.

(b) *Notice of Intent to File.* The notice of intent to file must be served on the owner personally or by registered mail, return receipt requested, at least 30 days before filing of the claim for lien. The written notice is required whether or not the claimant has given the written notice about the lien law or participation. The notice of intent to file must briefly describe the nature of the claim, its amounts, and the land and improvements to which it relates.

(c) *Notice by Prime Contractor about Lien Law.* Every prime contractor who has contracted or will contract with any subcontractors or materialmen for the improvement must include in any written contract with the owner or if an oral contract, prepared separately and serve personally or by registered mail on the owner within 10 days after the first labor or materials are furnished the following notice printed in at least eight-point boldface type, or in capital letters, if typewritten, in substantially the following form:

"As required by the Wisconsin construction lien law, builder hereby notifies owner that persons or companies furnishing labor or materials for the construction on owner's land may have lien rights on owner's land and buildings if not paid. Those entitled to lien rights, in addition to the undersigned builder, are those who contract directly with the owner or those who give the owner notice within 60 days after they first furnish labor or materials for the construction. Accordingly, owner probably will receive notices from those who furnish labor or materials for the construction, and should give a copy of each notice received to mortgage lender, if any. Builder agrees to cooperate with the owner and his lender, if any, to see that all potential lien claimants are duly paid."

If any prime contractor required to give the notice about lien law fails to do so as required, the prime contractor will not have a lien unless the contractor pays all of the contractor's obligations to subcontractors and materialmen in respect to the work of improvement within the time limits for notice of intent to file and filing of claim for lien and until the time for notice by subcontractors, materialmen, or laborers [see paragraph (d) below] has elapsed and no subcontractor, materialman or laborer has given notice.

(d) *Notice by Subcontractor, Materialmen or Laborers.* Every person other than a prime contractor must, within 60 days after furnishing the first labor or materials, serve two signed copies on the owner either by personal service or by registered mail, return receipt requested. The owner must provide a copy of the notice within 10 days after receipt to any mortgage lender providing funds for the construction of the improvement. The notice must be in substantially the following language:

"As part of your construction contract, your contractor or builder has already advised you that those who furnish labor or materials for the work will be notifying you. The undersigned first furnished labor or materials on (give date) for the improvement now under construction on your real estate at (give legal description, street address or other clear description). Please give your mortgage lender an extra copy of this notice within 10 days after you receive this, so your lender, too, will know that the undersigned is included in the job."

The failure to give this notice prohibits the acquisition of a lien except in those instances identified in subparagraph (c) above as exceptions to the notice about the lien law.

Any subcontractor who serves a late but otherwise proper notice of participation personally or by registered mail on the owner shall have a lien for any labor or materials furnished after the late notice is actually received by the owner. There are also special provisions relating to theft by contractor available to subcontractors where the prime contractor has received payment by the owner but has not paid the subcontractor. Where the nonpaying contractor or subcontractor is a corporation, the misappropriation is also deemed theft by any officers, directors or agents of the corporation responsible for the misappropriation.

(e) *Exceptions to Notice Requirements.* In the following instances the notice about the lien law need not be given: (1) by any laborer or mechanic employed by any prime contractor or subcontractor; (2) by any lien claimant who has contracted directly with the owner for the work or materials furnished, unless the claimant is a prime contractor; (3) by any lien claimant furnishing labor or materials for an improvement in any case where more than four-family living units are to be provided or added by such work of improvement which is wholly residential in character, or in any case where more than 10,000 total usable square feet of floor space is to be provided or added by such work of improvement; (4) by any prime contractor who is an owner of the land to be improved, by any corporate prime contractor of which an owner of the land is an officer or controlling shareholder, by any prime contractor who is an officer or controlling shareholder of a corporation which is an owner of the land, or by any corporate prime contractor managed or controlled by substantially the same persons who manage or control a corporation which is an owner of the land; and (5) by any lien claimant, other than a prime contractor, who furnishes labor or materials for an improvement on a project on which the prime contractor is not required to give notice under this section.

Where Filed—The claim for lien must be filed in Office of Clerk of the Circuit Court for the county in which the real estate is situated.

When to Be Filed—Lien claim must be filed within six months from date last labor or materials performed or furnished by lien claimant.

Duration of Lien—Action to foreclose must be commenced within two years from date of filing such claim for lien.

Filing Fee—$5.

Extent of Lien—Lien attaches upon the interest of the owner, in and to the land. Lien extends to all contiguous land of the owner, but if improvement is located wholly on one or more platted lots belonging to the owner, the lien applies only to the lots on which the improvement is located.

Priority of Lien—Take precedence over any other encumbrances except tax and special assessment liens originated after visible commencement of service or furnishing materials. When new construction is the principal improvement involved, commencement is deemed to occur no earlier than the beginning of substantial excavation for the foundations, footings or base of the new construction, except where the new construction is to be added to a substantial existing structure, in which case the commencement is the time of the beginning of substantial excavation or the time of the beginning of substantial preparation of the existing structure to receive the added new construction, whichever is earlier. Also prior to any unrecorded mortgage given before commencement of such services, etc., of which mortgage person claiming lien has no notice. An exception to general priority rules is that recorded mortgages of state savings and loan associations and federal savings and loan associations have priority over all liens filed subsequent to the recording of such mortgages.

Public Improvements—See Chapter 13.

Statutory Citation—Wisconsin Statutes, Chapter 779, §§ 779.01 to 779.17.

WYOMING

Who May Claim—Every person performing any work on or furnishing any materials or plans for any building or any improvement upon land shall have a lien upon the building or improvements and upon the land of the owner on which they are situated.

How Claimed—A lien claimant must file a lien statement with the County Clerk, sworn to before a notary public. Notice must be given of the lien to the last known owner by certified mail promptly after lien statement is filed.

Where Filed—Office of County Clerk of proper county.

When to Be Filed—Every contractor shall file his lien statement within 120 days, and every other person within 90 days: (1) after the last day when work was performed or materials furnished under contract; (2) from the date the work was substantially completed or substantial completion of the contract to furnish materials, whichever is earlier; or (3) with respect to an employee or subcontractor, after the last day he performed work at the direction of his employer or contractor. The parties may agree to extend the time for filing for up to twice the otherwise applicable time limit. The agreement must be acknowledged before a notary public and signed by the owner, the contractor and any other parties to the contract and it shall be filed with and recorded by the county clerk in the same manner as lien statements.

Service of Copy of Notice—All persons must give written notice of their claim, its amount and from whom it is due, to the owner or his agent 10 days prior to filing the lien statement.

Duration of Lien—Duration 180 days after filing lien, unless action commenced.

Filing Fee—$5.

Contents of Statement of Lien—(1) Name and address of the person seeking to enforce the lien; (2) amount claimed to be due and owing; (3) name and address of the person against whose property the lien is filed; (4) itemized list setting forth and describing materials delivered or work performed; (5) name of the person against whom the lien claim is made; (6) date when labor was last performed or services were last rendered or the date when the project was substantially completed; (7) legal description of the premises where the materials were furnished or upon which the work was performed; and (8) copy of the contract, if available.

Extent of Lien—Upon buildings or improvements and the land belonging to owner upon which same is erected to the extent of one acre, or if such improvements cover more than one acre, the lien shall extend to the additional land covered thereby. If the land subject to a lien is located in any city, town, or subdivision, the lien shall extend to the entire lot upon which the building or improvement is located.

Notice of Right to Claim Lien—Prime contractor shall post a construction site notice saying that any subcontractor or materialman shall give notice to prime contractor of right to claim a lien and that failure to do so waives right to a lien. Applies only if prime contractor's contract is for $50,000 or more. Any subcontractor or materialman who may claim a lien must give notice to prime contractor within 60 days of furnishing services or materials and shall be sent by certified mail or delivered to and receipted by the prime contractor or his agent. Notice must state that it is a notice of a right to claim a lien, and contain subcontractor's or materialman's name, address, phone number, contact person, name and address of vendor and description of services or material provided.

Notice to Owner—Every prime contractor or subcontractor shall give to the owner or the owner's agent, within 30 days of providing any materials or services, a written notice which shall include the following language in 10-point bold type:

NOTICE TO OWNER

FAILURE OF THIS PRIME CONTRACTOR OR SUBCONTRACTOR TO PAY THOSE PERSONS SUPPLYING MATERIALS OR SERVICES TO COMPLETE THIS CONTRACT CAN RESULT IN THE FILING OF A MECHANICS' LIEN ON THE PROPERTY WHICH IS THE SUBJECT OF THIS CONTRACT PURSUANT TO W.S. 29-2-101 THROUGH 29-2-110. TO AVOID THIS RESULT, WHEN PAYING FOR LABOR AND MATERIALS YOU MAY ASK THIS PRIME CONTRACTOR OR SUBCONTRACTOR FOR "LIEN WAIVERS" FROM ALL PERSONS SUPPLYING MATERIALS OR SERVICES FOR THE WORK DESCRIBED IN THE CONTRACT. FAILURE TO SECURE LIEN WAIVERS MAY RESULT IN YOUR PAYING FOR LABOR AND MATERIALS TWICE.

This notice must be given of the job in question if the property is: (a) an existing single-family dwelling unit; (b) a residence constructed by the owner or under a contract entered into by the owner prior to its occupancy as a primary residence; or (c) a single-family, owner-occupied dwelling unit, including a residence constructed and sold for occupancy as a primary residence.

This notice shall not be required for a developer or builder of multiple residences.

Priority of Lien—Liens are on equal footing without reference to date of filing. A perfected lien has priority over any subsequent lien, security interest or mortgage, but is subordinated to liens perfected prior to the commencement of any construction work or repairs.

Public Improvements—See Chapter 13.

Liens for Improvement of Oil or Gas Wells—Wyoming statutes specify certain procedures for liens against specific types of property which may be in addition to or different from the above. A list of these specific types of liens is as follows: (1) mines, quarries, oil, gas or other wells; (2) labor and materials on ditches, canals and reservoirs; (3) owners and operators of harvesting machines; (4) Uniform Federal Tax Lien Registration Act; and (5) personal property, breeders and house trailers.

Statutory Citation—Wyoming Statutes, Title 29, §§ 29-1-201 to 29-1-311; 29-2-101 to 29-2-111.

Refer to Chapter 27 for the following forms:

- Satisfaction of Mechanics' Liens
- Waiver of Right to File Mechanics' Lien

13 Construction Bonds on Public Projects

During the New Deal, the federal government initiated massive public construction projects. Problems arose when subcontractors and suppliers went unpaid because of defaulting or unscrupulous general contractors working with government agencies. Attempts by suppliers to protect their rights under lien laws ran contrary to the principle of sovereign immunity granted to the United States.

In 1935, Congress passed the Miller Act, which completely eliminated the right of a subcontractor or supplier to impose any form of mechanics' lien or other encumbrance against federal public works projects. The primary purpose of the Miller Act, however, was to protect subcontractors who supplied material and labor to federal public works projects by providing an alternative, and usually superior remedy to the assertion of mechanics' liens. Under the Miller Act, a payment bond must be provided by the principal or general contractor on every federal contract to protect the right of payment for those supplying materials or services to the federal project. With few exceptions not pertinent here, all federal public construction projects are subject to the provisions of the Miller Act.

In the states, suppliers encountered some of the same difficulties with state, county, municipal, and other local projects that created the need for the Miller Act. Where payments by the general contractor were not made, the state and local authorities which owned the project sought to insulate themselves from mechanics' liens by suppliers and subcontractors as the federal government had. Early efforts by states to declare sovereign immunity to eliminate a mechanics' lien were met with constitutional challenges.

Following the success of the Miller Act for federal projects, the states then began enacting what came to be known as "Little Miller Acts." These Little Miller Acts are modeled after the federal Miller Act and state courts have generally held that the Little Miller Acts are to be interpreted in conformity with the federal statute.

The Little Miller Acts also require the principal or general contractor to post a payment bond as a condition of awarding the contract. This payment bond takes the place of any right of a supplier or subcontractor to assert a mechanics' or other type of lien. Since the substantive rights of the suppliers and subcontractors were not being adversely affected, and, in fact, in many instances they were being enhanced, public policy and constitutional protections permitted the elimination of the right to claim a mechanics' lien on state and municipally funded public projects. Since each state's statute is somewhat different, suppliers and subcontractors attempting to rely on the provisions of the state legislation should be careful to understand any unique or particular provisions contained in a particular state's law.

PERFORMANCE BONDS AND PRIVATE BONDS

The Miller Act and the state statutes discussed here address bonds taken to assure payment to the suppliers and materialmen. Many states also have statutes requiring performance bonds. These are separate bonds by which the general contractors assure that the work will be done. These performance bonds are outside the scope of this chapter.

Similarly, this chapter does not address private bonds, which may provide payment protection for suppliers even where there is no contractual relationship between the owner and the subcontractor or supplier. Since private bonds are not usually regulated by statute, they may take any form. However, some of the qualities of a private payment bond also apply to public payment bonds.

When payment bonds have been made available for a particular project, whether it is governmental or private, the owner is able to substitute the right to assert a mechanics' lien with the right to make a claim against the bond. It is always valuable to know, as a credit grantor, whether there are bonds on a construction project. The terms of the bond can materially affect (positively or negatively) the supplier's rights with respect to payment.

It must be remembered that bonds are obligations of third parties not related to the debtor-creditor relationship that exists. A bond is additional security, like having a third-party guarantee, but like a guarantee, it has conditions which must be met to obtain the payment protections granted. In private bonds, and frequently on public bond projects, the creditor, as a third-party beneficiary, is bound by the terms of the contract created by the bond, even though the creditor is not a party to this contract. Therefore, it is very important that credit grantors not rely on generalities or oral representations when dealing with bonds, but rather review the actual terms of the bonds to make sure that any reliance is justified, and that any compliance is strictly in accordance with the terms of the agreement.

Payment bonds may have provisions limiting the time in which a claim may be asserted. They may also have additional restrictive periods during which litigation may be filed and prosecuted. Again, it is important that if a credit grantor intends to rely on a payment bond, a copy of the bond should be obtained; careful attention should be paid to the requirements for giving notice, the type of notice, the documentation to be presented and other time limitations, including the limitation period by which litigation must be commenced.

THE MILLER ACT

The Miller Act sets out the terms and conditions governing bonds and claims on bonds for federal projects. The following sections discuss specific provisions of the Miller Act along with some of the case law which was developed to apply to the Act.

Obtaining Copies of Payment Bonds

Under the Miller Act, a subcontractor or supplier has the legal right to obtain a copy of the bond which secures a federal construction project. The department or agency is required to provide a certified copy of the bond upon payment of a fee and receipt of an affidavit that the claimant has supplied labor or materials for such work and payment has not been made. The agency is only required to give a copy of the bond after there has been default; however, suppliers and subcontractors should attempt to secure a copy of the bond during the process of negotiating the underlying contract or as soon as possible thereafter.

What Materials and Labor Can Be Reimbursed

A subcontractor or supplier may recover the value of the labor and material furnished for the construction, alteration or repair of any public building or public work of the United States. Labor includes on-site supervisory work of a project manager if he did or might have been called upon to do some on-site work in the regular course of the job.

The general test for whether a particular part or item of equipment is covered by the bond is whether the item was or will be consumed by performance of the work at the job-site. The cost of renting equipment for a job has been held to constitute the supplying of goods and transportation costs relating to moving materials to a job-site has also been held to be reimbursable.

MAKING A CLAIM UNDER THE MILLER ACT

Remote Suppliers and Subcontractors Do Not Have the Right to Recover

The Miller Act limits the right to make a claim and file a lawsuit to those suppliers and subcontractors who deal directly with the prime contractor and to those suppliers who, lacking any contractual relationship with the general contractor, have a direct contractual relationship with a subcontractor. A supplier to another supplier who then sells goods to the general contractor has no claim, nor does anyone whose relationship to the general contractor is more remote than a second-tier subcontractor.

90-Day Notice of Intent to Seek Recovery

Any supplier having a contractual relationship with a subcontractor, but not a contractual relationship with the principal or general contractor, can only recover if a notice is given to the contractor within 90 days from the date on which the last material supplied to the job or the last labor furnished on which a claim is being made. A supplier or subcontractor having a direct contractual relationship with the general contractor does *not* need to give the 90-day notice.

TO WHOM/WHICH ENTITY NOTICE SHOULD BE GIVEN

Claimants must give the 90-day notice only to the principal or general contractor; notice does not have to be given to the surety (the bonding company). However, the surety is the only necessary party in a lawsuit raising a Miller Act claim, so it is a good practice to give the 90-day notice to the surety as well. Notice to any subcontractor with whom the claimant has dealt, and to the government or agency may speed resolution of the claim (even where there is no right to sue on the bond).

CONDITION PRECEDENT TO THE RIGHT TO SUE

Providing proper notice is a condition precedent to the right to sue. If the proper notice is not provided, claimants do *not* have the right to sue. The 90-day limitation is strict, and applies to goods supplied and services performed under the terms of the original contract or any approved modifications.

START OF THE 90-DAY PERIOD

The 90-day period begins to run on the date materials or labor were last supplied. It is important that a supplier not allow the 90-day period to pass, while discussing payment or payment terms without the 90-day notice being sent. Even where the contractor promises (or even delivers) payments, once the ninetieth day passes, the claimant loses all rights, absent some form of fraud (which is difficult to prove).

NOTICE MUST BE RECEIVED

The majority of courts have ruled that notice *must* be received within the 90-day period and the date that the notice was sent by putting it in the mail, does not constitute giving notice under the Miller Act.

CONTENT OF THE 90-DAY NOTICE

The notice must state with specificity the amount due. It must also identify the subcontractor in default that received materials or labor. The notice must inform the general contractor that payment is being sought from the general contractor, in other words, that the supplier is looking to the general contractor for payment. Some of the case law suggests a formal demand is required; other cases suggest the demand can be express or implied. Merely sending open invoices to the general contractor will not be sufficient to comply with the notice requirement of the Miller Act. Even where the principal contractor admits knowledge of the claim, the failure to give the statutory notice legally bars the claim.

SERVICE OF THE 90-DAY NOTICE

The notice must be served by registered mail, return receipt requested.

JURISDICTIONAL REQUIREMENTS

Where the initial construction contract is private and the government or its agent is not actually a contracting party, courts have generally declined to find jurisdiction even when the construction project itself has been carried out for a public purpose or been funded by public revenues.

Filing a Lawsuit on the Bond

A subcontractor may sue on the payment bond for the balance unpaid at the time of institution of the suit. The suit must be brought in the name of the United States for the claimants use. Generally, the only necessary party defendant to the suit is the surety, as the issuer of the payment bond. The claimant need not join the general contractor (or subcontractor) which was actually furnished with the labor or material to recover; however, most sureties have an agreement by the general contractor to indemnify the surety for losses on the bond, so the general contractor will almost always have financial interest in the case (and should be included if they can be properly brought into that court.)

Deadline for Filing Lawsuit on the Bond

The statute of limitations contained in the Miller Act provides that a suit must be brought within one year after the last day on which materials were supplied or labor was performed. The provisions requiring a suit to be brought within one year are not waived or modified merely because there is an arbitration clause in any of the agreements involving the project.

Where to File the Lawsuit

The suit must be brought in U.S. District Court in the district in which the contract was to be performed.

CONSTRUCTION BONDS ON STATE AND LOCAL PUBLIC PROJECTS

As with the Miller Act, those suppliers seeking to secure payment based upon a payment bond for a state or local project must strictly comply with the statute which creates the bonding requirement. In many instances, these state statutes parallel and may even be identical to the Miller Act. However, there are significant differences which require a review of the state law prior to delivery of goods or services in reliance on the bond as the ultimate form of payment.

While the state statutes in many instances deal with state, county, municipal, or political subdivision's repair, construction, or development of any public building, public work, highway, bridge, sewer project, water project, or the like, careful attention must be paid to determine if a particular job is covered by a state's bond law. Do not hesitate to contact the state contracting officer to determine in advance if the project is covered by the law, or subject to some other provision which will require some type of payment bond to ensure payment to subcontractors and suppliers.

STATE-BY-STATE REVIEW OF PUBLIC PROJECT BOND LAWS

Note: State legislatures will on occasion modify an area of law without clear delineation as to its content and context. As a result, even the changes which have been enacted, prior to placement in the state's code, may be difficult to locate. As a result, the Editors urge all users of this *Manual* only as a guide, and consult the latest codified version of the state's law, and applicable case law, for all recent changes.

ALABAMA

Amount of Bond—Not less than 50% of the contract price.

Labor and Material Covered—All labor, supplies and materials used in connection with the public works contract.

Notice Required—Written notice to the surety of the amount claimed to be due and the nature of the claim shall be sent by registered or certified mail.

Time for Suit—Claimant may institute an action upon the additional bond any time after 45 days after the written notice to the surety but such suit must be commenced not later than one year from the date of final settlement of the contract.

Contracts Excluded—Less than $50,000.

Penalty for Failure to Take Bond—No special statutory provision.

ALASKA

Amount of Bond—One-half of the contract price where the total amount payable by the terms of the contract is not more than $1,000,000; 40% of the contract price whenever the total amount payable by the terms of the contract is more than $1,000,000 but not more than $5,000,000; whenever the total amount payable by the terms of the contract is more than $5,000,000 the payment bond is in the sum of $2,500,000.

Labor and Material Covered—Labor and material furnished for the construction, alteration, or repair of any public building or public work of the state.

Notice Required—No notice is required by a person having a contractual relationship, express or implied with the principal contractor. Any person having a direct contractual relationship with a subcontractor but no contractual relationship, express or implied, with the principal contractor must give written notice to the contractor within 90 days from the date on which such person performed the last of the labor or furnished or supplied the last of the material for which the claim is made, stating with substantial accuracy the amount claimed and the name of the party to whom the material was furnished or for whom the labor was performed. Such notice shall be served by mailing it by registered mail, postage prepaid, in an envelope addressed to the contractor at any place where he maintains an office or conducts his business or his residence, or in any manner in which a peace officer is authorized to serve summons.

Time for Suit—Any time after the expiration of 90 days after the day on which the last of the labor was performed or material was furnished for which the claim is made, but such suit must be commenced within one year after the date of final settlement of the contract.

Contracts Excluded—Under $100,000.

Penalty for Failure to Take Bond—No special statutory provision.

ARIZONA

Performance bond and payment bond amount equal the full contract amount.

Amount of Bond—100% of the contract price solely for the protection of claimants supplying labor or material to the contractor or his subcontractors in the prosecution of the work provided for in contracts for the construction, alteration, or repair of the public work.

Labor and Material Covered—Labor or material furnished in the prosecution of the work provided for in such contract.

Notice Required—None for a subcontractor having a contract with the general contractor; otherwise, if a subcontractor is unpaid for 90 days after labor performed or materials supplied, and a written preliminary 20-day notice has been given, then upon giving to the contractor written notice within 90 days from the date the labor was performed or materials supplied, which notice states with substantial accuracy the amount claimed and the name of the party to whom the material was furnished or for whom the labor was supplied, the claimant can then sue on the bond. Such notice must be served by registered or certified mail.

Time for Suit—No suit can be commenced within 90 days from the date on which the last of the labor was performed or material furnished. Suit must be commenced within one year of the date on which the last of the labor was performed or material furnished for which the claim is being made.

Contracts Excluded—No express statutory provision.

Penalty for Failure to Take Bond—No statutory provision.

ARKANSAS

In Arkansas, special bond statutes are passed because contractors cannot create a lien against a public property when working for a public entity. Arkansas has passed two statutes concerning bonds. The first act was passed in 1911, and is codified under the Mechanics' and Materialmen's Liens section Act of the Arkansas Code. The second act was passed in 1929 and is in the Public Property/Public Works section of the Arkansas Code. These two statutes do not require two separate bonds, and have been interpreted to be one whole statute by the Arkansas courts. *See Berry Asphalt Co. v. Western Surety Co.*, 223 Ark. 344, 266 S.W.2d 835 (1954).

Amount of Bond—A sum equal to the amount of the contract on all public works.

Labor and Material Covered—All labor and material furnished in the prosecution of the contract to execute and deliver the contract, except Arkansas Highway and Transportation Department contracts. The statute covers all surety bonds required by the State and provides that these bonds shall be liable on all claims for labor and materials entering into the construction, or necessary to or used in the course of construction of the public improvements.

Notice Required—No special statutory provision.

Time for Suit—No action shall be brought on the bond after six months from the final payment on the job, unless it is a project on which the Arkansas State Building Services approves final payment on the state contract, in which case the suit must be filed within 12 months from the date that Arkansas State Building Services approves final payment. To avoid controversy, bond claimants should follow the six month statute of limitations.

Statutory Bonds v. Common Law Bonds—The Arkansas courts distinguish statutory bonds and common law bonds in determining the applicable statute of limitations. If a bond provides greater coverage than that set out in A.C.A. § 22-9-401, then the bond is a common law bond not covered by statute, then a bond claimant is not bound by the one-year limitation. *United States Fidelity and Guaranty Co. v. Little Rock Quarry Co.*, 309 Ark. 269, 830 S.W.2d 362 (1992).

Contracts Excluded—Under $20,000.

Penalty for Failure to Take Bond—No special statutory provision.

Surety Company—The bonds must be made by surety companies authorized to do business in Arkansas, and must be executed by a resident agent or nonresident agent licensed by the Insurance Commissioner to represent the surety company executing the bond.

Bond from a Particular Source—It is a Class A misdemeanor for any person to require a bidder or contractor to purchase a surety bond from a particular insurance.

CALIFORNIA

Amount of Bond—100% on the total amount payable by the terms of the contract.

Labor and Material Covered—Any materials, provisions, provender or other supplies, power or teams, used in, upon, for or about the performance of the work contracted to be done, or for any work or labor thereon of any kind, or for amounts due under the Unemployment Insurance Code with respect to work or labor performed under the contract, or for any amounts required to be deducted, withheld and paid over to the Employment Development Board from the wages of employees of the contractor and his subcontractors.

Notice Required—A claimant must give the 20-day preliminary notice, or give written notice to the surety or bond principal within 15 days after the recording of the notice of completion, or 75 days after completion if no notice was filed. A claimant must give stop notice by registered or certified mail, or by personal delivery, to public agency disbursement officer or contracting officer within 30 days after the recording of a notice of completion or notice of cessation. If no notice is recorded, stop notice must be given within 90 days after completion or cessation.

Preliminary Notice—Claimant must give notice to the contractor and public agency within 20 days of first furnishing labor or materials. Notice must be in exact form as prescribe by statute, which contains specific warning to owners in the prescribed format.

Time for Suit—Claimant must file suit not later than six months from the time within he is entitled to file a stop notice. The stop notice must be filed within 30 days of the recordation of the notice of completion or cessation or, if no such notice is filed, within 90 days after actual completion or cessation of work.

Contracts Excluded—Under $25,000.

Penalty for Failure to Take Bond—Unless the contractor's bond is filed and duly approved, no claim in favor of the contractor arising under the contract shall be audited, allowed or paid.

COLORADO

Amount of Bond—Set by owner, but not less than one-half of the contract price.

Labor and Material Covered—Labor, materials, team hire, sustenance, provisions, provender or other supplies used or consumed by contractor or his subcontractor in or about the performance of the public work. Second tier material suppliers (material suppliers to a material supplier) do not have protection under the Colorado public works act. The claimant should carefully read to the terms and conditions of the payment bond to determine if there is coverage.

Notice Required—Person furnishing labor or material to contractor or subcontractor, at any time up to and including the time of final settlement for the work contracted to be done, which final settlement shall be duly advertised at least 10 days prior thereto in the county or counties where the work was contracted for and wherein such work was performed, may file, with the official awarding the contract, a verified statement of the amount due and unpaid, whereupon such official shall withhold payments from contractor sufficient to ensure the payment of such claim, until the same has been paid or the claim has been properly withdrawn. However, such funds shall not be withheld longer than 90 days following the date fixed for final settlement, unless an action is commenced within that time to enforce such unpaid claim and notice thereof is filed with the public body by whom the contract was awarded.

Time for Suit—Within six months after the completion of the public work, or the time limitation set forth in the bond if greater than six months after completion of the project.

Contracts Excluded—Under $50,000.

Penalty for Failure to Take Bond—Unless such bond is executed, delivered and filed, no claim in favor of the contractor arising under such contract shall be audited, allowed or paid.

Special Provisions—Notwithstanding the monetary qualification, the governing body of any county, city, town or school district determining it to be in the best interest of the county, city, town or school district may require the execution of a penal bond for any contract of $50,000 or less.

CONNECTICUT

Amount of Bond—A bond in the amount of the contract is required.

Labor and Material Covered—Labor and materials in the prosecution of the work provided for in contract for the construction, alteration or repair of any public building or public work of the state or any subdivision thereof. The word "material" includes the rental of equipment used in the prosecution of such work.

Notice Required—Every person who has furnished labor or material in the prosecution of the work provided for in such contract in respect of which a payment bond is furnished and who has not been paid in full therefore before the expiration of a period of 60 days after the day on which the last of the labor was done or performed by him or for material which was furnished or supplied by him for which the claim is made may enforce the right to payment under the bond by serving a written notice of claim within 180 days from the date when such person performed the last of the labor or furnished the last of the material for which claim is made, on the surety that issued the bond and a copy of the notice on the principal contractor. The notice shall state with substantial accuracy the amount claimed, name of the party for whom labor was performed or to whom materials were furnished and a detailed description of the bonded public project involved. Within 90 days after service of the notice of claim, the surety must pay the claim or such amount which is not disputed in good faith and must notify the claimant as to any unpaid portion for which liability is denied. Notices shall be served by registered mail or certified mail, postage prepaid, in envelopes addressed to any office at which the surety, principal or claimant conducts his business, or in any manner in which civil process may be served.

Time for Suit—No suit may be commenced after the expiration of one year after the day on which the last of the labor was performed or material was supplied by the claimant.

Contracts Excluded—Under $50,000.

Penalty for Failure to Take Bond—Unless such bond is executed, delivered and filed, no claim in favor of the contractor arising under such contract shall be audited, allowed or paid.

DELAWARE

Amount of Bond—100% of the contract price.

Labor and Material Covered—Every person furnishing material or performing labor under the contract may maintain an action thereon for the recovery of such sum as may be due from the contractor. "Material" is defined to mean materials, equipment, tools, supplies or any other personal property but does not include electric, gas, water, telephone or similar utilities.

Notice Required—No special statutory provision.

Time for Suit—Suit must be brought within three years of completion of the work. However, the contract can provide that no suit be commenced within one year following the completion of the work.

Contracts Excluded—A special state body, the Contracting and Purchasing Advisory Council, sets the threshold amount for "large public works" where bonds are required.

Penalty for Failure to Take Bond—No special statutory provision.

DISTRICT OF COLUMBIA

Amount of Bond—One-half of the total amount payable by the terms of the prime contract.

Labor and Material Covered—Labor or material furnished to the prime contractor or a subcontractor in performance of work in the prime contract, including lessors of equipment.

Notice Required—No notice is required by a person having a contract with the prime contractor. Any person having a contract with a subcontractor must give written notice to the prime contractor within 90 days from the date on which the claimant performed the last of the labor or furnished the last of the material for which the claim is made, stating with substantial accuracy the amount claimed and the name of the party to whom the material was furnished or for whom the labor was performed. Such notice shall be served in person or by mailing the same by certified or registered mail, postage prepaid, in an envelope addressed to the contractor at any place he maintains an office or conducts his business, or his residence.

Time for Suit—Suit must be instituted more than 90 days after the last day of labor or material for which claim is made, but within one year from the date final labor was performed or the material was supplied.

Contracts Excluded—Procurement regulations may waive bonds for contracts of $100,000 or less.

Penalty for Failure to Take Bond—No special statutory provision.

Statutory Citation—District of Columbia Code, Title 2 Government Administration, Chapter 3, §§ 2-305.01 to 2-305.08.

FLORIDA

Amount of Bond—In an amount equal to the contract price.

Labor and Material Covered—Labor, material and supplies used directly or indirectly in the prosecution of the work by contractors, subcontractors, sub-subcontractors, laborers, materialmen and professional lienors.

Notice Required—A claimant, except a laborer, who is not in privity with the contractor shall, within 45 days after beginning to furnish labor, material or supplies for the prosecution of such work, furnish the contractor with a notice that he intends to look to the bond for protection. A claimant who is or is not in privity with the contractor and who has not received payment for his labor, material or supplies, shall within 90 days after performance of the labor or after complete delivery of all the materials and supplies, deliver to the contractor and the surety written notice of the performance of the labor or delivery of the material and supplies and of the nonpayment and amount of nonpayment.

Time for Suit—No action or suit shall be instituted or prosecuted against the contractor or against the surety on the bond required by the statute after one year from the performance of the labor or completion of delivery of the materials or supplies.

Contracts Excluded—The threshold for exemption from the bond requirement is $100,000. Contracts under $200,000 may be exempted.

Penalty for Failure to Take Bond—No special statutory provision.

GEORGIA

Amount of Bond—Not less than the contract price.

Labor and Material Covered—All persons supplying labor or material used in the prosecution of the work.

Notice Required—No notice required if there is a direct contractual relationship with the general contractor. Those not under direct contract with the general contractor must give written notice of claim within 90 days after the date on which the last of the labor was performed or the last of the materials furnished.

If the owner, agent of the owner, or general contractor files a Notice of Commencement within 15 days of beginning the project, a lien claimant who does not have a direct contractual relationship with the general contractor is barred unless the claimant serves a Notice to Contractor within 30 days of the claimant beginning work on the project.

Time for Suit—All suits must be brought within one year after the completion of the project and acceptance by the public authority.

Contracts Excluded—Less than $100.000. However, public authority may require bond when the contract price is less than $100,000. Less than $50,000 for DOT projects.

Penalty for Failure to Take Bond—No special statutory provision.

HAWAII

Amount of Bond—Equal to 100% of the contract price.

Labor and Material Covered—All labor and materials furnished to the contractor and used in the prosecution of the work provided for in such contract.

Notice Required—Written notice shall be served by registered or certified mail to contractor and surety within 90 days from the date on which the person did or performed the last labor or furnished or supplied the last of the material for which claim is made, stating with substantial accuracy the amount claimed and the name of the party to whom the material was furnished or supplied or for whom the labor was done or performed. The notice shall be served to the contractor and surety at any place they maintain an office or conduct their business or in any manner authorized by law to serve summons.

Time for Suit—Every suit instituted on a payment bond shall be brought within one year after the last labor was performed or material supplied for the work provided in the contract.

Contracts Excluded—Contracts $25,000 and under for construction projects.

Penalty for Failure to Take Bond—No special statutory provision.

IDAHO

Amount of Bond—An amount to be fixed by the contracting body but in no event less than 85% of the contract amount.

Labor and Material Covered—Construction, alteration or repair of any public building or public work or improvement in the state of Idaho or any political subdivision, public authority or public instrumentality thereof, including the renting or leasing of equipment.

Notice Required—No notice is required by a person having a contractual relationship, express or implied, with the principal contractor. Any person having a direct contractual relationship with a subcontractor but no contractual relationship, express or implied, with the principal contractor must give written notice to the contractor within 90 days from the date on which such claimant performed the last of the labor or furnished or supplied the last of the material or equipment for which such claim is made, stating with substantial accuracy the amount claimed and the name of the person to whom the material was furnished or supplied or for whom the labor was done or performed. Each notice shall be served by mailing the same by registered or certified mail, postage prepaid, in an envelope addressed to the contractor at any place he maintains an office or conducts his business or at his residence.

Time for Suit—No such suit shall be commenced after the expiration of one year from the date on which claimant performed the last of the labor or furnished or supplied the last of the material or equipment for which such suit is brought except that if the claimant is a subcontractor of the contractor no such suit shall be commenced after the expiration of one year from the date on which final payment under the subcontract became due.

Contracts Excluded—No special statutory provision.

Penalty for Failure to Take Bond—Any public body subject to this statute who fails or neglects to obtain the required payment bond shall, upon demand, itself make prompt payment to all persons who have supplied materials or performed labor in the prosecution of the work under the contract, and if such creditor has a direct right of action upon his account against such public body in any court having jurisdiction in any county in which the contract was to be performed and executed, which action must be commenced within one year after the furnishing of materials or labor.

ILLINOIS

Amount of Bond—Shall be fixed by such officials, boards, commissions, commissioners or agents awarding the contract in an amount equal to or greater than 110% of bid.

Labor and Material Covered—Material used in such work and for all labor performed in such work, whether by subcontractor or otherwise.

Notice Required—Every person furnishing material or performing labor, either as an individual or as a subcontractor for any contractor with the state or any political subdivision thereof, has a right to sue on the bond provided, however, that any person having a claim for labor or material as aforesaid shall have no such right of action unless he shall have filed verified notice of claim with the officer, board, bureau or department awarding the contract within 180 days after the date of the last item of work or the furnishing of the last item of materials and files a copy of the notice with the contractor within 10 days after filing the notice with the officer.

The claim shall be verified and shall contain (1) the name and address of the claimant; the business address of the claimant within the state of Illinois, and if the claimant be a foreign corporation having no place of business within the state of Illinois, the notice shall state the principal place of business of said corporation, and in the case of a partnership the notice shall state the name and residence of each of the partners; (2) the name of the contractor for the government; (3) the name of the person, firm or corporation by whom the claimant was employed or to whom he or it furnished materials; (4) the amount of the claim; (5) a brief description of public improvement sufficient for identification.

Time for Suit—No action shall be brought on the bond until the expiration of 120 days after the date of the last item of work or the furnishing of the last item of materials, except where the final settlement between the public body and the contractor shall have been made prior to the expiration of the 120-day period "in which case action may be taken immediately following such final settlement." No action of any kind can be brought later than six months after the acceptance by the State or political subdivision thereof, of the building project or work.

Contract Excluded—Under $5,000.

Penalty for Failure to Take Bond—No special statutory provision.

INDIANA

Types of Projects—In Indiana there are four different public works statutes: Title 4 for State of Indiana ownership projects like state prisons; Title 5 for other state projects like state supported universities; Title 8 for state highways, bridges and rest stops; and Title 36 for local government projects, including public schools.

Amount of Bond—Total contract price. Each of the four statutes requires a bond for the total contract price if the project is required to be bonded.

Labor and Material Covered—Any labor or services performed or materials furnished or services rendered in the construction, erection, alteration or repair of any public building; work or improvement of any nature or character, however, under Title 36 projects, lessors of equipment to a subcontractor are not covered.

Notice Required—Title 4: To impound contract proceeds, a Verified Claim in writing, stating the amount due and owing to the claimant must be filed with the Public Works Division of the Indiana Department of Administration within 60 days after the last labor performed, last materials furnished, or last services rendered. To make a claim under the bond, a Verified Claim must be given to the surety and the Public Works Division must be notified that the surety has been given the Verified Claim.

Title 5: To make a claim against the retainages, a Verified Statement of Claim, setting forth the amount due and owing, the name of the subcontractor, when the work was performed or materials furnished, must be filed in duplicate with the public agency that is administering the contract within 60 days after the last work or services performed on or last item of materials furnished to the project by the claimant. To make a claim against the bond, a Duplicate Verified Statement must be filed with the appropriate state agency within 60 days after any claimant has worked on the project setting forth the same information as required in the Verified Statement of Claim.

Title 8: To claim against the contract proceeds, a Triplicate Verified Itemized Statement must be filed with the Department of Transportation. This must be in writing, verified, contain an itemized statement of the amount due, identify the claimant by name and address, identify the contractor for whom the work was performed, set forth the dates including the last date on which the work was performed, describe the work and the costs thereof, and attach an itemized statements or invoices. This should be filed in triplicate within 60 days of the last labor performed or materials furnished and in all events within 30 days after final acceptance of the project. To claim against the bond, the claimant must file a statement of the amount due and owing with the surety on the bond. The statement of the amount due and owing must be furnished to the surety within one year after acceptance of the labor, materials or services by DOT. The surety must be given 60 days to respond, after which suit may commence on the bond.

Title 36: To claim against retainages, file a Verified Claim, containing the project by name and address, the amount due and owing, the contractual relationship between the claimant and the subcontractor or general contractor, the date upon which the last work was performed or materials furnished, and in the case of local road, street, or bridge projects, the signature of an official responsible for the project verifying quantity or weight of materials furnished. This Verified Claim is filed with the public agency. To claim against the bond, file a signed duplicate statement with the governing body setting forth the same information as the Verified Claim within 60 days after the last labor or materials were furnished to the project by any contractor on the project.

Time for Suit—Title 4: Claimant may not file suit against the contractor's surety on the payment bond until 30 days after filing the Verified Claim with the Public Works Division. Unless the bond provides a greater period of time, all suits must be brought against the surety on the payment bond under Title 4 within one year after final settlement with the contractor.

Title 5 and Title 36: If a Verified Statement is filed, suit cannot be brought against the surety on the payment bond until the expiration of 30 days after the filing of the Verified Duplicate Statement with the governing body. Must commence suit within 60 days after final completion and acceptance of the public works project by the public agency which by case law interpretation is generally the "substantial completion date."

Title 8: If the triplicate notice is filed with DOT as against retainages, then the DOT is required upon receipt to withhold from the retainages a sum equal to the amount of the claim. The prime contractor is given 20 days within which to give written notice to DOT of allowing or rejecting the claim. If the claim is rejected in whole or in part, the DOT is to give immediate notice of the contractor's action by registered mail to the claimant. Within 90 days after receiving notice of a rejection from DOT, the claimant must take two procedural steps to perfect its claim. First, it must commence an action against the contractor or surety in a court of competent jurisdiction. Second, once the lawsuit has been filed, the claimant must obtain a certificate from the clerk stating that the action has been filed, date filed and identify the parties to the action. The claimant must file a certificate with the DOT within a 90-day period. If a claim is made as against the bond only, and not retainages, then after the surety is given 60 days to respond, suit must be filed 18 months from the date of final acceptance of the project.

Contracts Excluded—Title 4: Bonds required for projects in excess of $150,000.

Title 5: Requires a bond on all projects, except for state universities or Title 5 projects only if taxpayer monies in excess of $25,000 are expended.

Title 8: Requires a bond for all projects, but the commissioner may waive the bond requirements for projects less than $100,000.

Title 36: Requires a bond for projects in excess of $100,000.

Penalty for Failure to Take Bond—No special statutory provision.

IOWA

Amount of Bond—Not less than 75% of the contract price, excepting that, in contracts where no part of the contract price is paid until after the completion of the public improvement, the amount of the bond may be fixed at not less than 25% of the contract price.

Labor and Material Covered—Labor performed or material, services or transportation furnished in the construction of a public improvement under a contract with the principal contractor or with subcontractors, except those furnishing materials to a subcontractor.

Notice Required—To principal contractor. No part of the unpaid fund due the contractor shall be retained on claims for material furnished other than material ordered by the general contractor or the authorized agent thereof unless such claims are supported by a certified statement that the general contractor has been notified within 30 days after the materials are furnished, or by itemized invoices rendered to the contractor during the progress of the work, of the amount, kind and value of the material furnished for use upon said public improvement.

To government. Claims must be filed no later than 30 days after completion and final acceptance of the project, or at any time if no action is pending and the full contract price has not been paid.

To municipality. Claims must be filed no later than 30 days to the officer charged by law to issue warrants in payment of the public improvement, to include an itemized written statement of claim. In case of highway improvements for the county, claims shall be filed with the county auditor of the county letting the contract. In case of contracts for improvements on the farm-to-market highway system paid from farm-to-market funds, claims shall be filed with the auditor of the state department of transportation.

Time for Suit—Any time after the expiration of 30 days and not later than 60 days following the completion and final acceptance of the public improvement. Claims may be filed with the proper officer at any time before the expiration of 30 days immediately following the completion and final acceptance of the improvement, and at any time after said 30-day period if the public corporation has not paid the full contract price and no action is pending to adjudicate rights in and to the unpaid portion of the contract price.

Contracts Excluded—Public improvement contracts under $25,000. No minimum for other contracts.

Penalty for Failure to Take Bond—Bond mandatory.

KANSAS

Amount of Bond—Not less than the sum total of the contract.

Labor and Material Covered—All supplies, materials or labor furnished, used or consumed in connection with or in or about the construction of said public improvements or in making such public improvements.

Notice Required—No special statutory provision, except in connection with the improvement of highways.

Time for Suit—On bonds other than state highway bonds, no action shall be brought on the bond after six months from the completion of the public improvement. On bonds given in connection with the construction, improvement, reconstruction, and maintenance of the state highway system, no action may be brought after one year from the completion of the contract.

Contracts Excluded—Under $100,000.

Penalty for Failure to Take Bond—No special statutory provision.

KENTUCKY

Amount of Bond—A payment bond in the amount of 100% of the contract price.

Labor and Material Covered—All persons supplying labor and material to the contractor or his subcontractors for the performance of the work provided for in the contract.

Notice Required—Within 60 days of the last day of the month in which materials were provided, the claimant must file a statement in writing verified by affidavit, setting for the amount due, the date on which work was last performed, and the name of the public improvement upon which it is claimed. The statement shall be filed in the county clerk's office of the county in which the seat of government of the owner is located.

Time for Suit—This also is not specified in the statute. Kentucky's general statute of limitations includes civil actions on bonds in the class of procedures which must be initiated within 15 years after cause of action has accrued. However, the Kentucky courts have allowed the surety to a shorter period in the bond.

Contracts Excluded—Under $25,000.

Penalty for Failure to Take Bond—No special provisions.

LOUISIANA

Amount of Bond—Not less than 50% of the contract price. Such recordation preserves the privileges on the structure and on the land on which it is situated in favor of every contractor, subcontractor, laborer, furnisher of material, machinery or fixtures, etc., as their interest may arise. The owner of such work shall require of every such contractor a surety bond as follows. For all contracts not exceeding $10,000 the amount of the bond shall be the amount of the contract. If the contract is over $10,000 but does not exceed $100,000, the penal sum of the bond must be not less than 50% of the amount of the contract but not less than $10,000 in any event. If the contract is over $100,000 but does not exceed $1,000,000, the bond shall be not less than one-third of the amount of the contract; and if the contract exceeds $1,000,000, the bond shall be not less than one-fourth on the amount of the contract. The bond is required to be attached to and recorded with the contract and the bond is required to be conditioned for the faithful performance of the contract and payment of all subcontractors, laborers and furnishers of material, machinery and fixtures jointly as their interest may appear.

Labor and Material Covered—Any person to whom money is due pursuant to a contract with a contractor or subcontractor for doing work, performing labor or furnishing materials or supplies for the construction, alteration, or repair of any public works, or for transporting and delivering such materials or supplies to the site of the job by a for-hire carrier, or for furnishing oil, gas, electricity or other materials or works, including persons to whom money is due for the lease or rental of movable property used at the site and including any architect or consulting engineer engaged by the contractor or subcontractor in connection with the building of any public work.

Notice Required—Any person having a direct contractual relationship with a subcontractor but not contractual relationship with a contractor shall have a right of action against the contractor or the surety on the bond furnished by the contractor, he shall record his claim or give written notice to said contractor within 45 days from the recordation of the notice of acceptance by the owner of the work or notice by the owner of default, stating with substantial accuracy the amount claimed and the name of the party to whom the material was furnished or supplied or for whom the labor or service was done or performed. Such notice shall be served by mailing the same by registered or certified mail, postage prepaid, in an envelope addressed to the contractor at any place he maintains an office in the state of Louisiana.

To municipality. Any person to whom money is due for doing work, performing labor or furnishing materials and supplies for use in machines used in the construction, alteration or repair of any public works, excluding persons to whom money is due for the lease or rental of movable property, may, after the maturity of his claim and within 45 days after the recordation of acceptance of the work by the governing authority or notice of default of the contractor or subcontractor, file a sworn statement of the amount due him with the governing authority having the work done and recorded in the Office of the Recorder of Mortgages for the parish in which the work is done. Notice of filing of a bond must be by certified mail to public entity, claimant and contractor.

To assert a claim, a lessor of movables shall deliver a copy of lease to owner, not more than 10 days after movables are placed at site.

Time for Suit—Within one year from the registry of acceptance of the work or notice of default of the contractor.

Contracts Excluded—Under $25,000.

Penalty for Failure to Take Bond—When an awarding authority makes final payment to the contractor without deducting the total amount of all outstanding claims so served on it or without obtaining a bond from the contractor to cover the total amount of all outstanding claims, the awarding authority shall become liable for the amount of these claims.

MAINE

Amount of Bond—100% of the contract price.

Labor and Material Covered—Labor or material supplied to the contractor or his subcontractor in the prosecution of the work provided for in the contract for the construction, alteration, or repair of any public building or other public improvement or public work including highways awarded to any person by the state or by any political subdivision or quasi municipal corporation or by any public authority. The term "material" includes rental of equipment.

Notice Required—No notice is required by a claimant having a contractual relationship, express or implied, with the principal contractor. A claimant having a direct contractual relationship with a subcontractor of the contractor but no contractual relationship, express or implied, with such contractor shall not have the right of action upon such payment bond unless he shall have given written notice to such contractor within 90 days from the date on which such claimant performed the last of the labor or furnished or supplied the last of the material for which such claim is made, stating with substantial accuracy the amount claimed and the name of the party to whom the material was furnished or supplied or for whom the labor was done or performed. Such notice shall be served by registered or certified mail, postage prepaid, in an envelope addressed to the contractor at any place he maintains an office or conducts his business or at his residence.

Time for Suit—No suit shall be commenced prior to 90 days from the date on which claimant furnished the last of the labor or material for which such claim is made and no action may be commenced after the expiration of one year from the date on which the last of the labor was performed or material was supplied for the payment of which such action is brought. Every action shall be brought in the county in which the principal or surety has its principal place of business.

Contracts Excluded—Under $100,000.

Penalty for Failure to Take Bond—No special statutory provision.

Statutory Citation—14 M.R.S.A. §871.

MARYLAND

Amount of Bond—50% of the total amount payable under the prime contract.

Labor and Material Covered—For the protection of all persons supplying labor and material to the contractor, a subcontractor or a sub-subcontractor in the prosecution of the work provided for in the contract.

Notice Required—No notice is required by a person having a contract with the prime contractor. Any claimant having a contract with a subcontractor, or with any sub-subcontractor must give written notice to the prime contractor within 90 days from the date on which the claimant performed the last of the labor or furnished the last of the material for which such claim is made, stating with substantial accuracy the amount claimed and the name of the party to whom the material was furnished, or for whom the labor was performed. Such notice shall be served by mailing certified mail to the contractor at the contractor's residence or a place where the contractor has an office or does business.

Time for Suit—Suit must be instituted more than 90 days after the day on which the claimant last supplied labor or materials for which the claim is made, but no more than one year after the public body finally accepts the work performed under the contract.

Contracts Excluded—Under $100,000, except in the case of highways.

Penalty for Failure to Take Bond—No special statutory provision, except in the Transportation Code. The Controller shall furnish a certified copy of a payment bond to a person who submits an affidavit that the person has supplied labor or materials for which payment has not been made.

Waiver—An executory contract may not waive payment bond rights. A "pay when paid" provision in an executory contract does not waive payment bond rights.

MASSACHUSETTS

Amount of Bond—A bond in the amount of not less than one-half of the total contact price shall be obtained.

Labor and Material Covered—All subcontractors and materialmen.

Notice Required—A claimant having a contractual relationship with a subcontractor, but not with the general contractor, must give notice of a claim in writing to the general contractor within 65 days after the day on which the claimant last performed labor or furnished labor, materials, equipment, appliances or transportation, stating with substantial accuracy the amount claimed, the name of the party for whom such labor was performed or such labor, materials, equipment, appliances or transportation was furnished.

To make a claim covering specially fabricated material the claimant must give the contractor principal written notice of the placement of the order and the amount thereof not later than 20 days after receiving the final approval in writing for the use of the material. The notices shall be served by mailing a sworn statement by registered or certified mail postage prepaid in an envelope addressed to the contractor principal at any place at which the contractor principal maintains an office or conducts his business, or at the contractor principal's residence, or in any manner in which civil process may be served.

Time for Suit—Within one year after the day such claimant last performed the labor or furnished the labor, materials, equipment, appliances or transportation included in his claim, and by prosecuting the claim thereunder by trial in the superior court to final adjudication.

Contracts Excluded—Statute requires that bond must be furnished where the amount of the contract is more than $5,000 in the case of the Commonwealth and more than $2,000 in the case of a contract with a county, city, town, district or other political subdivision.

Penalty for Failure to Take Bond—No special statutory provision.

MICHIGAN

Amount of Bond—An amount fixed by the government unit to not less than 25% of the contract price.

Labor and Material Covered—Labor, material, or both used or reasonably required for use in the performance of the contract, including that part of water, gas, power, light, heat, oil, gasoline, telephone service or rental of equipment directly applicable to the contract. A separate statute (MCL 570.101 et seq.) covers State highway projects.

Notice Required—No notice is required by a claimant having a contractual relationship with the principal contractor. A claimant not having a direct contractual relationship with the principal contractor does not have a right of action upon the payment bond unless: (a) claimant has within 30 days after furnishing the first of such material or performing the first of such labor served on the principal contractor a written notice which shall inform the principal of the nature of the materials being furnished or to be furnished or labor being performed or to be performed and identifying the party contracting for such labor or material and the site for the performance of such work or the delivery of such materials; and (b) claimant has given written notice to the contractor and the governmental unit involved within 90 days from the date on which the claimant performed the last of the labor or furnished or supplied the last of the material for which the claim was made, stating with substantial accuracy the amount claimed and the name of the party to whom the material was furnished or supplied or for whom the labor was done or performed.

Each notice shall be served by mailing the same by certified mail, postage prepaid, in an envelope addressed to the principal contractor, the governmental unit involved, at any place at which said parties maintain a business or residence.

Time for Suit—Within one year after final payment was made to the principal contractor. An action instituted on the payment bond shall be brought only in the appropriate court in the political subdivision in which the contract was to be performed.

Contracts Excluded—Under $50,000.

Penalty for Failure to Take Bond—No special statutory provision.

Statutory Citation—MCL 129.201 et seq.; MCL 570.101 et seq.

MINNESOTA

Amount of Bond—The amount shall be not less than the contract price.

Labor and Material Covered—Claims of all persons doing work or furnishing skill, tools, machinery or materials, or insurance premiums, or sales or wage tax, under or for the purpose of such contract.

Notice Required—In the event of a claim on a payment bond by a person furnishing labor and materials, no action shall be maintained unless, within 120 days after completion, delivery or provision by the person of its last item of work, the person serves a written notice of claim personally or by certified mail upon the surety that issued the bond and the contractor on whose behalf the bond was issued at their addresses as specified in the bond. The notice must specify the nature and amount of the claim and the date the claimant furnished its last item of labor or materials for the public work.

Time for Suit—No action shall be maintained unless begun within one year after the date of the last work by the claimant on the public project as stated in its notice of claim.

Contracts Excluded—Under $75,000.

Penalty for Failure to Take Bond—If the bond is taken, the corporation or body for which work is done under the contract shall not be liable to any person furnishing labor, skill, or material to the contractor, and for any loss resulting to them from such failure.

MISSISSIPPI

Amount of Bond—Not less than the contract price.

Labor and Material Covered—All persons supplying labor or material used in the prosecution of the work. However, Mississippi's Little Miller Act does not require protection for materialmen of materialmen, and for subcontractors below the sub-sub level, although the bond itself may include such protection.

Notice Required—Persons having a direct contractual relationship with a subcontractor but not the contractor must give written notice to the contractor by hand delivery or certified mail within a 90-day period after the date on which the last of the labor was performed by him or the last of the materials was furnished by him.

Time for Suit—All suits must be brought within one year after the performance and final settlement of the contract or within one year after abandonment by the contractor. The period does not begin to run, however, until the obligee publishes a notice in a newspaper published in a county in which the contract or some part thereof was performed, or in a newspaper having a general circulation in such a county.

Suit by subcontractors and materialmen may not be instituted until after (1) complete performance of the contract, (2) final settlement thereof, (3) the public body has published notice thereof in some newspaper published in the county or, if there be none, then in some newspaper having a general circulation therein.

Suit must be commenced within one year after performance and final settlement of the contract and not later, provided that, if the contractor quits or abandons the contract before its completion, suit may be instituted by any such claimant on said bond and shall be commenced within one year after such abandonment and not later.

Contracts Excluded—Whenever a contract is less than $25,000, the owners may elect to make a lump sum payment at the end of the job. In such cases, a performance bond is not required.

Penalty for Failure to Take Bond—No special statutory provision.

Statutory Citation—Mississippi's Little Miller Act appears at §§ 31-5-51 to 57; Miss. Code Ann. (1972).

MISSOURI

Amount of Bond—No special statutory provision, except in the case of county building contracts, which is 110% of the amount to be given for erecting the building.

Labor and Material Covered—Material, lubricants, oil, gasoline, grain, hay, feed, coal and coke, repairs to machinery, groceries and foodstuffs, equipment and tools, consumed or used in connection with the construction of the public improvement and all insurance premiums, both compensation and all other kinds of insurance, on said work and for labor performed in such work, whether by subcontractor or otherwise.

Notice Required—No special statutory provision, the terms of the bond will typically be enforced.

Time for Suit—No special statutory provision except in specific municipalities, most notably St. Louis, where suit must be brought within 90 days of completion of the work.

Contracts Excluded—Under $25,000.

Penalty for Failure to Take Bond—No special statutory provision.

MONTANA

Amount of Bond—Full contract price for state contracts. The amount may be fixed by municipal ordinance, but in no event shall the penal sum be less than 25% of the contract price.

Labor and Material Covered—Provender, materials, supplies, provisions or goods supplied and performed or labor furnished in the prosecution of the public work.

Notice Required—Not later than 30 days after the date of the first delivery of the provender, material, supplies or provisions to any subcontractor or agent of any person, firm or corporation having a subcontract with respect to the prosecution of said public work, delivered or sent by registered mail to the contractor. This notice must contain the name of the subcontractor or agent ordering or to whom the same was furnished and state that such contractor or his bond will be held for the same. No suit or action shall be maintained in any court against the contractor or his bond to recover for such provender, provisions, material or supplies or any part thereof unless such notice shall have been given.

No right of action shall be had on the bond unless within 90 days from and after the completion of the contract and the acceptance of the work by the public officials the claimant shall present to and file with the public body a notice in writing substantially in the form as required by the statute.

Time for Suit—No special statutory provision. In the case where a settlement procedure is provided by a contracting agency, all actions authorized thereunder must be commenced within one year after a final decision has been rendered pursuant to such settlement procedure; and in the case where no settlement procedure is provided by the contracting agency, the action must be commenced by the contractor within one year after the cause of action has arisen.

Contracts Excluded—A school district may waive their requirements of these bonds for contracts under $7,500. Other state or governmental authorities may waive their requirements for under $50,000.

Penalty for Failure to Take Bond—The municipal corporation is liable to the persons intended to be protected by the bond to the full extent and for the full amount of all the debts so contracted by any subcontractor as well as the contractor.

Statutory Citation—Montana Code, Title 18, Chapters 1 through 11.

NEBRASKA

Amount of Bond—The amount of the bond on a public structure or improvement to which the mechanics' lien laws do not apply shall be not less than the contract price.

Labor and Material Covered—Labor performed, materials furnished and rental of equipment actually used in the erecting, furnishing or repairing of public building, bridge, highway or other public structures or improvements for the state of Nebraska or any political subdivision thereof.

Notice Required—Any person having direct contractual relationship with a subcontractor, but no contractual relationship, express or implied, with the contractor furnishing said bond, shall have a right of action upon the bond upon giving written notice to the contractor within four months from the date on which such person did or performed the last of the labor or furnished or supplied the last of the material for which such claim is made, stating with substantial accuracy the amount claimed and the name of the party to whom the material was furnished or supplied or for whom the labor was done or performed. Such notice shall be served by registered or certified mail, postage prepaid, in an envelope directed to the contractor at any place where he maintains an office or conducts his business, or his residence or in any other manner in which a notice may be served.

Time for Suit—No suit shall be commenced after the expiration of one year after the time of final settlement of the principal contract.

Contracts Excluded—Any project bid which has a total cost of $5,000 or less, or state projects if less than $15,000.

Penalty for Failure to Take Bond—No special statutory provision.

NEVADA

Amount of Bond—The payment bond shall be not less than 50% of the contract price.

Labor and Material Covered—Labor performed or materials furnished in the prosecution of the work.

Notice Required—To principal contractor. No notice is required by a claimant having a contractual relationship, expressed or implied, with the principal contractor. Any claimant who has a direct contractual relationship with any subcontractor of the contractor who gave such payment bond, but no contractual relationship, expressed or implied, with such contractor, may bring an action on the payment bond, only: (a) if he has, within 30 days after furnishing the first of such materials or performing the first of such labor, served on the contractor a written notice which shall inform the latter of the nature of the materials being furnished or to be furnished, or the labor performed or to be performed, and identifying the person contracting for such labor or materials and the site for the performance of such labor or materials; and (b) after giving written notice to such contractor within 90 days from the date on which the claimant performed the last of the labor or furnished the last of the materials for which he claims payment.

Each written notice shall state with substantial accuracy the amount claimed and the name of the person for whom the work was performed or the material supplied, and shall be served by being sent by registered mail, postage prepaid, in an envelope addressed to such contractor at any place in which he maintains an office or conducts business, or at his residence.

Time for Suit—A period commencing 90 days after the date on which claimant performed the last of the labor or furnished the last of the material for which he claims payment but no such action may be commenced after the expiration of one year from the date on which the claimant performed the last of the labor or furnished the last of the material for the payment of which such action is brought.

Contracts Excluded—Under $35,000.

Penalty for Failure to Take Bond—No statutory provision.

NEW HAMPSHIRE

Amount of Bond—At least 100% of the contract price or of the estimated cost of the work if no aggregate price is agreed upon.

Labor and Material Covered—All labor performed or furnished, all equipment hired including trucks, all material used, fuels, lubricants, power, tools, hardware and supplies purchased by the principal contractor and used in carrying out said contract, and for labor and parts furnished upon the order of the contractor for the repair of equipment used in carrying out said contract.

Notice Required—In order to obtain the benefit of such bond any person, firm or corporation having any claim for labor performed, materials, machinery, tools or equipment furnished as aforesaid, shall within 90 days after the completion and acceptance of the project by the contracting party, file in the Office of the Secretary of State, if the state is a contracting party, or with the Department of Public Works and Highways, if the state is a party to said contract by or through said department, or in the Office of the Clerk of the Superior Court for the county within which the contract shall be principally performed, if any political subdivision of the state is a contracting party, a statement of the claim; a copy of which shall forthwith be sent by mail by the office where it is filed to the principal and surety.

Time for Suit—One year after filing of claim as above.

Contracts Excluded—Generally those under $25,000.

Penalty for Failure to Take Bond—No statutory provision.

NEW JERSEY

Amount of Bond—At least 100% of the contract price.

Labor and Material Covered—All labor performed or materials, provisions, provender or other supplies, or teams, fuels, oils, implements or machinery used or consumed in, upon, for, or about the construction, alteration or repair of any public building or other public work or improvement.

Notice Required—Any person who does not have a direct contract with the contractor furnishing the bond shall provide the contractor with written notice via certified mail, prior to furnishing work, that such person is a beneficiary under the bond. Failure to give notice limits the claimant to "the benefits available" from the date on which notice is given.

Time for Suit—No suit shall be brought against the sureties on said bond until after the expiration of 90 days from the date last materials or labor were provided, but within one year of the same date of last furnishing of materials and labor.

Contracts Excluded—The state may waive the bond requirements on contracts for its public works not in excess of $200,000. In addition, a public body may waive the bond requirements on contracts for public works at the expense of a county, municipality, or school district, not in excess of $100,000.

Penalty for Failure to Take Bond—No special statutory provision.

NEW MEXICO

Amount of Bond—100% of the contract price, but in its discretion, the state purchasing agent or central purchasing office may reduce this amount under certain circumstances, but in no case can the amount be less than 50% of the contract price.

Labor and Material Covered—All just claims for labor performed, and materials and supplies furnished, upon or for the work of construction, alteration, improvement or repair of any public buildings, structure or highway or for any public work, furnished under the original contract or under any subcontract.

Notice Required—Any person having a direct contractual relationship with a subcontractor but no contractual relation, express or implied, with the principal contractor, must give written notice to the contractor within 90 days from the date on which such person performed the last of the labor or furnished or supplied the last of the material for which the claim is made, stating with substantial accuracy the amount claimed and the name of the party to whom the material was furnished or supplied or for whom the labor was done or performed. Such notice shall be served by mailing the same by registered mail, postage prepaid, in an envelope addressed to the contractor at any place he maintains an office or conducts his business, or his residence, or in any manner in which the service of summons in civil process is authorized by law.

Time for Suit—No suit on the bond may be commenced after the expiration of one year from the date of final settlement of the contract. Claimant in such suit shall notify the public body of the beginning of the action, stating the amount claimed and no judgment shall be entered in such action within 30 days after giving such notice.

Contracts Excluded—$25,000 or under at sole discretion of state agency.

Penalty for Failure to Take Bond—No special statutory provision.

NEW YORK

Amount of Bond—No special statutory provision.

Labor and Material Covered—Labor or material furnished to the contractor or his subcontractors in the prosecution of the work provided for in a contract for the prosecution of a public improvement for the State of New York.

Notice Required—No notice is required by a person having a direct contractual relationship with the principal contractor. Any person having a direct contractual relationship with a subcontractor of the contractor furnishing the payment bond but no contractual relationship, express or implied, with the principal contractor, must give written notice to the contractor within 120 days from the date on which the last of the labor was performed or the last of the material was furnished for which his claim was made, stating with substantial accuracy the amount claimed and the name of the party to whom the material was furnished or for whom the labor was performed. The notice shall be served by delivering the same personally to the contractor or by mailing the same by registered mail, postage prepaid, in an envelope addressed to the contractor at any place where he maintains an office or conducts his business or at his residence, provided, however, that where such notice is actually received by the contractor by other means, such notice shall be deemed sufficient.

Time for Suit—No action on a payment bond shall be commenced after the expiration of one year from the date on which final payment under the claimant's subcontract became due.

Contracts Excluded—Payment bond may be waived for public works contracts for less than $50,000 or where the contract is not subject to the multiple contract award requirements of Section 135 of the State Finance Law, waiving the bonds is in the public interest and the aggregate amount of the contract is less than $200,000.

Penalty for Failure to Take Bond—No special statutory provision.

NORTH CAROLINA

Amount of Bond—100% of the contract price.

Labor and Material Covered—All materials furnished or labor performed in the prosecution of the public work, whether or not the labor or materials enter into or become a component part of the public improvement, including gas, power, light, heat, oil, gasoline, telephone services and rental of equipment or the reasonable value of the use of equipment directly utilized in the performance of the public work.

Notice Required—Any claimant who has a direct contractual relationship with any subcontractor but has no contractual relationship, express or implied, with the contractor must give written notice to the contractor within 120 days from the date on which the claimant performed the last of the labor or furnished the last of the materials for which he claims payment stating with substantial accuracy the amount claimed and the name of the person for whom the work was performed or to whom the material was furnished. This notice is required to be served by registered or certified mail, postage prepaid, in an envelope addressed to such contractor at any place where his office is regularly maintained for the transaction of business or served in any manner provided by law for the service of summons.

Time for Suit—At any time after the expiration of 90 days after claimant performed the last of the labor or furnished the last of the material for which he claims payment, but no such suit may be commenced after the expiration of the "longer period of one year from the day on which the last of the labor was performed or material was furnished by the claimant, or one year from the day on which final settlement was made with the contractor."

Contracts Excluded—Under $300,000.

Penalty for Failure to Take Bond—Designated official who fails to require the bonds guilty of a Class 1 misdemeanor.

NORTH DAKOTA

Amount of Bond—100% of contract price, plus interest.

Labor and Material Covered—Materials including supplies used for machinery and equipment performed, furnished and used in performance of the contract including all demands of subcontractors.

Notice Required—Any person having a direct contractual relationship with a subcontractor but no contractual relationship with the contractor furnishing the bond shall not have a right of action against the bond unless he has given written notice to the contractor within 90 days from the date on which the person completed his contribution, stating with substantial accuracy the amount claimed and the name of the person for whom the contribution was performed. Each notice shall be served by registered or certified mail, postage prepaid, in an envelope addressed to the contractor at any place he maintains an office, conducts his business, or has a residence.

Time for Suit—Suit must be commenced within one year of final completion and acceptance of the project.

Contracts Excluded—Under $100,000.

Penalty for Failure to Take Bond—Any officer and the members of any board who shall fail to take a bond before entering into such a public contract shall be personally liable for all such bills, claims and demands which are not paid within 30 days after the completion of the work.

OHIO

Amount of Bond—Contract price.

Labor and Material Covered—All labor performed or materials furnished in carrying forward, performing, or completing a contract for the construction, demolition, alteration, repair or reconstruction of any public improvement.

Notice Required—At any time after furnishing labor or material, but not later than 90 days after the acceptance of the public improvement by the duly authorized board or officer, claimant shall furnish surety a statement of the amount due. Subcontractors and materialmen must serve notice of furnishing within 21 days after the date that the subcontractor or materialman first performed labor or furnished materials on the site of the public improvement, or be limited to amounts owed or labor and work performed and material furnished during and after the 21 days immediately preceding service of the notice of furnishing. No subcontractor who is in direct privity of contract with the principal contractor need provide this notice.

Time for Suit—No suit shall be brought against the surety until after 60 days after the furnishing of the statement, but suit must be commenced not later than one year from date of acceptance of the public improvement.

Contracts Excluded—No specific statutory provision.

Penalty for Failure to Take Bond—No special statutory provision.

OKLAHOMA

Amount of Bond—100% of the contract amount.

Labor and Material Covered—All indebtedness by contractor or his subcontractors for labor and materials and repairs to and parts for equipment used and consumed in the performance of said contract.

Notice Required—Any person having direct contractual relationship with a subcontractor performing work on said contract but no contractual relationship expressed or implied with contractor furnishing said payment bond must give written notice to the contractor and surety on said payment bond within 90 days from the date on which said person did or performed the last of the labor or furnished or supplied the last of the material or parts for which such claim is made stating with substantial accuracy the amount claimed and the names of the parties to whom the material or parts were supplied or for whom the labor was done or performed. Such notice is required to be served by registered or certified mail, postage prepaid, in an envelope addressed to the contractor at any place he maintains an office or conducts his business together with a copy thereof to the surety or sureties on said payment bond.

Time for Suit—No action shall be brought on said payment bond after one year from the date on which the last of the labor was performed or materials or parts furnished for which such claim is made.

Contracts Excluded—Under $25,000.
Penalty for Failure to Take Bond—No special statutory provisions.

OREGON

Amount of Bond—Bond shall be equal to contract price except for forest road contracts (bond amount determined by county court, ORS 376.340), certain bridge contracts (50% of contract amount) and certain water district contracts (an amount to insure the completion of the work).

Labor and Material Covered—All persons supplying labor or materials to the contractor or his subcontractor for prosecution of the work provided in the contract (including lower tier subcontractors and suppliers to a subcontractor at any level); a person furnishing or providing medical, surgical or hospital care to the employees of a contractor of a contract made with a public body or the subcontractor; all contributions due the State Industrial Accident Fund and the State Unemployment Compensation Fund from the contractor or his subcontractor, in connection with the performance of the contract, shall promptly be made; and all sums required to be deducted from the wages of employees of the contractor and his subcontractor pursuant to the Oregon Revised Statutes shall be paid over to the State Tax Commission.

Notice Required—Any person claiming to have supplied labor or material, including any person having a direct relationship with the contractor furnishing the bond, a subcontractor or an assignee of such person, or a person claiming monies due the State Accident Insurance Fund, the State Department of Employment Trust Fund, or the Department of Revenue in connection with the performance of the contract has a right of action on the bond, cashier's check, or certified check only if he or his assignee has not been paid in full and has presented and filed a Notice of Claim to the contractor and the Secretary of State or Clerk of other public entity before the expiration of 120 days after the person last provided labor or furnished material or 150 days for claims for contribution to employee benefit plans.

Such notice must be in writing addressed to the appropriate public body and setting forth information such as the name of the claimant; a brief description of the labor or material performed or furnished and the name of the person who performed or furnished labor or material; if the claim is for other than labor or materials, a brief description of the claim; the amount of the claim and the name of the principal and surety or sureties upon the bond and a brief description of the work involved for which the bond was issued; and to whom materials and labor were supplied. The notice shall be signed by the person making the claim or giving the notice.

The notice shall be in substantially the following form:

To: (name of the contractor and the name of the state agency or public body)

Notice hereby is given that the undersigned (name of the claimant) has a claim for (insert a brief description of the labor or materials performed or furnished and the person by whom performed or furnished; if the claim is for other than labor or materials, insert a brief description of the claim) in the sum of (amount) dollars against the bond taken from (name of the principal and, if known, the surety or sureties upon the bond) for the work of (insert a brief description of the work concerning which the bond was taken). Such material or labor was supplied to (name of the contractor or subcontractor).

Signature:

The notice of claim must be sent by registered or certified mail or hand delivered no later than 120 days after the person last provided labor or furnished materials. The notice may be sent or delivered to the contractor at any place the contractor maintains an office or conducts business, or at the residence of the contractor.

A person who has made such claim, or his assignee, may institute an action on the contractor's bond.

Time for Suit—A claimant may institute an action on the contractor's bond not later than two years after the person last provided labor or materials or two years after the worker listed in the commissioners' notice of claim last provided labor.

Contracts Excluded—The Public Contract Review Board or the local contract review board may exempt certain contracts, both security and bond.

Penalty for Failure to Take Bond—The state of Oregon and the officers authorizing the contract are jointly liable for the labor and material used in the prosecution of any work under the contract, and for claims due the State Industrial Accident Fund, the State Unemployment Compensation Trust Fund, and the State Tax Commission, if the contract was entered into with the state of Oregon and the state neglected to require the execution of a bond, cashier's check, or certified check. The public body and the officers authorizing the contract are jointly liable if the contract was entered into on behalf of a public body other than the state.

Statutory Citation—Oregon Revised Statutes, Chapter 279, §§ 279.526 to 279.542. For public contracts first advertised, or if not advertised then entered into, on or after March 1, 2005, the effective statutes have been renumbered Oregon Revised Statutes, Chapter 279C, §§ 279C.600 to 279C.625.

PENNSYLVANIA

Amount of Bond—100% of the contract price.

Labor and Material Covered—All labor or materials supplied to the prime contractor to whom the contract was awarded or to any of his subcontractors in the prosecution of the work provided for in such contract whether or not the material furnished or labor performed enters into and becomes a component part of the public building or other public work or public improvement including highway work. "Labor or materials" includes public utility services and reasonable rental of equipment, but only for the periods when equipment rented is actually used at the site. Materials supplied by a material supplier to another material supplier are not covered by the bond. Note: Under the Commonwealth Procurement Code, once a contractor has made payment to the subcontractor according to the provisions of the Code, future claims for payment against the contractor or its surety by parties owed payment from the subcontractor which has been paid, are barred.

Notice Required—A claimant who has a direct contractual relationship with any subcontractor of the prime contractor who gave a payment bond but has no contractual relationship, with such prime contractor may bring an action on the payment bond only if he has given written notice to such contractor within 90 days from the date on which the claimant performed the last of the labor or furnished the last of the materials for which he claims payment, stating with substantial accuracy the amount claimed and the name of the person for whom the work was performed or to whom the material was furnished.

Notice shall be served by registered or certified mail, postage prepaid, in an envelope addressed to the contractor at any place where his office is regularly maintained for the transaction of business or served in any manner in which legal process may be served.

To municipality. Duplicate copy of financial security to be filed with contracting agency.

Time for Suit—An action upon any payment or performance bond must be commenced after the expiration of 90 days, but within one year, after performance.

Contracts Excluded—Under $10,000.

Penalty for Failure to Take Bond—No statutory provisions.

PUERTO RICO

Amount of Bond—The Commonwealth of Puerto Rico requires a payment bond for not less than one-half the contract amount. The penal sum of the payment bond required by various Authorities in Puerto Rico varies in amount

Labor and Material Covered—The payment bond required by the Commonwealth of Puerto Rico from every contractor who is awarded a contract for the construction, reconstruction, enlargement, alteration or preparation of any public work covers: (a) the payment to the workers and employees for the contractor, of the salaries and wages earned by them in their work; and (b) the payment, to the persons selling, supplying or delivering equipment, tools and material for the work of the price or value of the materials, equipment and tools supplied, sold or delivered.

Notice Required—The law of Puerto Rico applicable to bonds taken by the Commonwealth of Puerto Rico first reads that every person who has worked as a worker or employee on or who has supplied, sold or delivered materials, equipment and tools for work and who has not been paid, in whole or in part, his salaries or wages or the price of the materials, equipment and tools sold, delivered or supplied for the work shall have the right to file suit on the bond without necessity for previous notice for recovery of any amount, which may for such reason be owing him.

It also reads: "Any person or persons who have a direct contractual relationship with a subcontractor on the work and who have or do not have an expressed or implied contractual relationship with the contractor on the work, who has posted the bond, may institute action against the contractor, the bond of the contractor, the bondsmen of the contractor, or against any of said bondsmen, for the recovery of any part of: (a) any amount which may be owed them by the subcontractor for salaries or wages they have earned as employees or workers of the subcontractor on the work; and (b) any amount which may be owed them by reason of their having supplied, sold or delivered materials, equipment and tools for the subcontractor on the work.

Suppliers or sellers of materials, equipment and tools to the subcontractor shall be obligated, before instituting action against the contractor, his bond or his bondsmen, to notify the contractor by registered mail of their claim. At the expiration of 30 days from the mailing of said notice they may institute the action herein authorized.

Workers and employees of the subcontractor may institute action at any time without previous notice to the contractor of their claim."

Time for Suit—Cannot be filed until after 30 days from the date of mailing of notice to the contractor before instituting suit on the contractor's public work bonds. Suit must instituted by all claimants within six months after final acceptance of the work by the Commonwealth of Puerto Rico.

Contracts Excluded—No special statutory provision.

Penalty for Failure to Take Bond—No special statutory provision.

RHODE ISLAND

Amount of Bond—Not less than 50% and not more than 100% of the contract price.

Labor and Material Covered—All labor performed or materials and equipment furnished.

Notice Required—Any person having a direct contract with a subcontractor but no express or implied contract with the contractor furnishing the bond shall only have a right of action upon giving written notice to the contractor within 90 days of the date on which the person furnished or performed the last labor, materials or supplies. The notice must state with substantial accuracy the amount claimed and the name of the party to whom the labor or materials was furnished. The notice shall be served by mailing via certified mail, postage prepaid, in an envelope addressed to the contractor at any place he or she maintains an office or conducts his or her business or his or her residence.

Time for Suit—Any time after the expiration of 90 days after the day which the last of the labor was furnished or performed or material or equipment was furnished or supplied by any person claiming, but within two years, or under the maximum time limit as contained within any labor or material payment bond required under § 37-12-1, whichever period is longer.

In any suit brought under this chapter, such personal notice of the pendency of the suit as the court may order shall be given to all known creditors or persons claiming to be such under the bond as shall not have entered their appearances in the suit. In addition, the notice of pendency must be published in some newspaper in the state of general circulation in the city or town where the work in the contract was carried out. Such publication shall be once a week for three consecutive weeks in such form as is ordered by the court. These notice requirements may, however, be waived by the court.

Contracts Excluded—Any public road or portion thereof or any bridge in which the contract price shall be in excess of $50,000 shall be required to furnish a bond; no exclusion provided for other projects.

Penalty for Failure to Take Bond—No express statutory provision.

SOUTH CAROLINA

Amount of Bond—For public highway construction contracts, a performance bond for 100% of the contract and in no case less than $10,000; payment bond not less than 50% of the contract. For other public improvement contracts, a performance and payment bond, both equal to 100% of the contract price.

Labor and Material Covered—Labor and material supplied in the prosecution of the work.

Notice Required—No notice is required by a claimant having a contractual relationship, expressed or implied, with the principal contractor. However, any claimant having a direct contractual relationship with a subcontractor but no contractual relationship, expressed or implied, with the contractor must give written notice to contractor within 90 days from the date on which claimant did or performed the last of the labor or furnished or supplied the last of the material for which the claim is made stating with substantial accuracy the amount claimed and the name of the party to whom material was furnished or supplied or for whom labor was done or performed.

Time for Suit—In no event, may suit be commenced more than one year after the final settlement of the contract with respect to highway work. As to all other state construction, suit must be brought within one year after plaintiff last supplied materials or labor.

Contracts Excluded—Under $10,000 (highway work). In the case of other public improvement contracts valued at $100,000 or less, the using agency may waive the bond requirements providing the using agency has protected the state.

Penalty for Failure to Take Bond—No special statutory provision.

SOUTH DAKOTA

Amount of Bond—Not less than contract price.

Labor and Material Covered—Labor and material used in the prosecution of the work provided for in the public contract.

Notice Required—Anytime after the completion of any work or improvement for any public body the contractor may issue notice stating that the improvement has been completed and that all subcontractors or persons furnishing any item of labor, service, skill, material, shipment or supplies for any subcontractor must file their claims with the contractor within 120 days after the first publication of such notice. Assuming that the labor is proper (there are specific requirements concerning notice), the claim by any subcontractor or any other person will be barred as a claim or lien against the public body and contractor if such claim is not filed within 120 days from the date of first publication. If notice is not timely, all claims, setoffs or counterclaims will be barred as to the public body or contractor or surety.

Time for Suit—If no suit is brought by the public corporation within six months of the completion and final settlement of the contract, any person furnishing the contractor with labor or material shall, on proper application therefore, be provided with a certified copy of the contract and surety. Such person shall be permitted to bring suit in the name of the public corporation for his use and benefit against the contractor and surety from whom he has not received payment. If suit is instituted against the surety of the contractor, it may not be commenced until six months after the complete performance of the contract and final settlement thereof. Any suit commenced more than one year thereafter shall be barred. Personal notice of the pendency of such suit must be given to all known creditors and, in addition thereto, notice shall be given by publication in some newspaper of general circulation published in the county where the contract is being performed for at least three successive weeks, the last publication to be at least three months before the time limited for suit.

Contracts Excluded—The state may waive the bond requirement on contracts of less than $50,000.

Penalty for Failure to Take Bond—The public corporation shall be liable to pay all persons who have performed labor or furnished material that entered into the public building the value of the work or material, and an action may be maintained therefore, provided same is commenced within 90 days from the acceptance of the work for which the same is claimed.

TENNESSEE

Amount of Bond—Bond shall be 25% of the contract price on all contracts in excess of $100,000.

Labor and Material Covered—Labor or material furnished to a contractor or to any immediate or remote subcontractor under him.

Notice Required—The person furnishing labor and/or material shall, after such labor or material is furnished, within 90 days after the completion of such public work, give written notice to either the contractor or the public official who had charge of the letting of the contract, by return-receipt registered mail or by personal delivery, such written notice to set forth the nature and itemized account of the material furnished or labor done, balance due therefore, and a description of the property improved; provided that, in the case of public work undertaken by a municipality, the required notice or statements so mailed or delivered to the mayor thereof shall be deemed sufficient; in the case of public work by any county, the required notice or statements so mailed or delivered to the Chairman of the County Court of such county shall be deemed sufficient; in the case of public work by the state, the required notice so mailed or delivered to the governor shall be deemed sufficient.

The statute pertaining to highways provides that the performance of a highway contract shall not be finally accepted until the general contractor has satisfied the Highway Department that all materials "used by him, his subcontractors, or his agents" have been paid for and until "laborers and other employees working for him, his subcontractors, or his agents" have been paid. The Highway Department is required to take the initiative and advertise in the county where the work was done 30 days prior to final settlement. Such advertisement must state the date of the proposed final settlement and notify claimants to file notice with the Department not less than 30 days after the last published notice.

The Highway Commissioner is required to withhold, for a period of 60 days after the date of the last advertisement, sufficient funds to pay all claims so filed. If a claimant brings suit against the contractor within such 60-day period, the Highway Department pays such retained fund into court, otherwise to the contractor.

Time for Suit—Action shall be brought or claims so filed within six months following the completion of such public work or the furnishing of such labor or materials.

Under the Highway Code all actions on bonds furnished under the Highway Code shall be commenced after the expiration of one year following the date of the first publication of the notice required to be published in some newspaper in the county where the work was done, etc.; that settlement is about to be made, notifying all claimants to file notice of their claims with the department.

Contracts Excluded—Under $100,000.

Penalty for Failure to Take Bond—Public officer who fails to obtain the bond is guilty of a misdemeanor. No similar counterpart in Highway Code. The Highway Commissioner is required to withhold, for a period of 60 days after the date of the last advertisement, sufficient funds to pay all claims so filed. If a claimant brings suit against the contractor within such 60-day period, the Highway Department pays such retained fund into court, otherwise to the contractor.

Time for Suit—Action shall be brought or claims so filed within six months following the completion of such public work or the furnishing of such labor or materials.

Under the Highway Code all actions on bonds furnished under the Highway Code shall be commenced after the expiration of one year following the date of the first publication of the notice required to be published in some newspaper in the county where the work was done, etc.; that settlement is about to be made, notifying all claimants to file notice of their claims with the department.

Contracts Excluded—Under $100,000.

Penalty for Failure to Take Bond—Public officer who fails to obtain the bond is guilty of a misdemeanor. No similar counterpart in Highway Code.

TEXAS

Amount of Payment Bond—An amount equal to the amount of the prime contract.

Labor and Material Covered—All public work labor or material supplied to the project is covered. Id. "Public work labor" means labor used directly to carry out a public work. "Public work material" means: (1) material used, or ordered and delivered for use, directly to carry out a public work; (2) specially fabricated material, which is material ordered by a prime contractor or subcontractor, that is specially fabricated for use in a public work and reasonably unsuitable for another use; (3) reasonable rental and actual running repair costs for construction equipment used, or reasonably required and delivered for use, directly to carry out work at the project site; or (4) power, water, fuel, and lubricants used, or ordered and delivered for use, to carry out a public work.

Notice Required—A claimant must mail to the prime contractor and the surety written notice of the claim on or before the 15th day of the third month after each month in which any of the claimed labor was performed or any of the claimed material was delivered. The notice must be accompanied by a sworn statement of account that states in substance that the amount claimed is just and correct, and all just and lawful offsets, payments, and credits known to the claimant have been allowed. The statement of account shall include the amount of any retainage applicable to the account that has not become due under the terms of the public work contract between the claimant and the prime contractor or between the claimant and a subcontractor.

Notice of Claim When Written Agreement Does Not Exist. When no written agreement exists between the claimant and the prime contractor or between the claimant and a subcontractor, the bond claim notice must contain additional information including, the name of the party for whom the public work labor was performed or to whom the public work material was delivered, the approximate date of performance or delivery, a description of the public work labor or material for reasonable identification, and the amount due. The claimant shall generally itemize the claim and include with it copies of documents, invoices or orders that reasonably identify the public work labor performed or public work material delivered for which the claim is made, the job, and the destination of delivery.

Notice of Claim for Multiple Items of Labor or Material. When the claim is for multiple items of public work labor or material to be paid on a lump sum basis, the notice must describe the labor or material in a manner that reasonably identifies the labor or material, state the name of the party for whom the labor was performed or to whom the material was delivered, state the approximate date of performance or delivery, state whether the contract is written or oral, state the amount of the contract, and state the amount claimed.

Notice of Claim for Unpaid Labor or Material Under Written Unit Price Agreement. Where a claimant who is a subcontractor or materialman to the prime contractor or to a subcontractor has a written unit price agreement that is wholly or partially completed, notice is sufficient, if claimant attaches to the sworn statement of account a list of units and unit prices as fixed by his contract, and a statement of those completed and partially completed units.

Additional Notice Required for Claimant Without Direct Contractual Relationship with Prime Contractor. A claimant that does not have a direct contractual relationship with the prime contractor must mail the prime contractor written notice of a claim on or before the 15th day of the second month after each month in which the labor was performed or the material was delivered. A copy of the statement sent to a subcontractor is sufficient notice. Additionally, a claimant without a direct contractual relationship with the prime contractor who contracts to specially fabricate materials must mail to the prime contractor written notice that the order for specially fabricated material has been received and accepted on or before the 15th day of the second month after the receipt and acceptance of the order.

Retainage. Retainage, as defined in the statute, means the part of the payments under a public work contract that are not required to be paid within the month after the month in which the labor is performed or material delivered.

Notice Required for Retainage Claim. To recover on a claim for retainage, a claimant whose contract provides for retainage must mail written notice of the claim for retainage to the prime contractor and the surety on or before the 90th day after the date of the final completion of the public work contract. The notice must state the amount of the contract, any amount paid, and the outstanding balance. If the claimant does not have a direct contractual relationship with the prime contractor, the claimant must provide the prime contractor notice that the subcontract provides for retainage and the general nature of the retainage required. This notice must be provided on or before the 15th day of the second month after the date of the beginning of the delivery of public work labor or material under the contract.

Notwithstanding the above, notice for a retainage claim is not required if the amount claimed is part of a prior claim made for payments other than retainage.

Time for Suit—Suit on a payment bond may be filed if the claim is not paid before the 61st day after the date the notice of claim is mailed. No suit may be brought on the payment bond after the expiration of one year after the date the notice of claim is mailed.

Contracts Excluded—A payment bond is not required for a construction contract for less than $25,000.

Penalty for Failure to Provide Bond—If the payment bond is not furnished, the governmental entity is subject to the same liability that a surety would have if the surety had issued the payment bond, and the governmental entity had required the bond to be provided. Under these circumstances, the claimant should provide the governmental entity with notice as if the governmental entity were the surety in the same manner discussed above.

Governing Statutes—Chapter 2253 Texas Government Code titled Public Work Performance and Payment Bonds.

UTAH

Amount of Bond—A payment bond must be in an amount equal to 100% of the contract amount.

Labor and Material Covered—Labor and material supplied to the contractor or his subcontractors in the prosecution of the public work.

Notice Required—No notice is required by a claimant having a contractual relationship expressed or implied with the principal contractor. Second tier claimants are required to give "preliminary notice" to the principal of their claim.

Time for Suit—A period commencing 90 days after the date on which claimant performed the last of the labor or furnished the last of the material for which he claims payment to one year after the date of last work performed or material supplied.

Contracts Excluded—Under $2000 for payment bonds.

Penalty for Failure to Take Bond—If the state or a political subdivision fails to obtain a payment bond, it shall, upon demand by a person who has furnished labor or supplied materials to the contractor or subcontractor for the work provided for in a contract promptly make payment to that person. That person shall have a direct right of action against the state or the political subdivision upon giving written notice to the state or political subdivision within 90 days from the date on which such person performed the last of the labor or supplied the last of the material for which claim is made. The person shall state in the notice a designation of the construction project and its location, the amount claimed, and the name of the party for whom the labor was performed or to whom the material was supplied. The notice shall be served by registered or certified mail, postage prepaid, on the state agency or political subdivision that is a party to the contract. No such action may be commenced after the expiration of one year after the day on which the last of the labor was performed or material was supplied by such person.

VERMONT

Amount of Bond—The penal sum of the additional bond is to be in such an amount as the Highway Board shall direct.

Labor and Material Covered—All creditors of the contractor for materials, merchandise, labor, rent or hire of vehicles, power shovels, rollers, concrete-mixers, tools and other appliances, professional services, premiums and other services used or employed in carrying on the work, and is further conditioned for the payment of taxes, both state and municipal, and contributions to the State Commissioner of Employment and Training accruing during the term of performance of said contract.

Notice Required—The claimant must file with the secretary a sworn statement of his claim within 90 days after the final acceptance of the project by the state of Vermont or within 90 days from the time such taxes or contributions to the Vermont Commissioner of Employment and Training are due and payable.

Time for Suit—Within one year after filing his claim with the Commissioner of Highways, claimant must institute suit on the bond, with notice and summons to the contractor, the surety and the secretary to enforce such claim, or must intervene in a suit theretofore instituted.

Contracts Excluded—Non-highway projects.

Penalty for Failure to Take Bond—No special statutory provision.

VIRGINIA

Amount of Bond—Payment bonds in the sum of the prime contract amount required on all public construction contracts exceeding $100,000.

Labor and Material Covered—Labor performed and material furnished to the prime contractor or to a subcontractor in furtherance of the work in the prime contract, including public utility services and equipment rented.

Notice Required—No notice is required by a person having a contract with the prime contractor. Claimant having a contract with a subcontractor must give written notice of the bond claim to the prime contractor within 180 days from the date on which the claimant performed the last labor or furnished the last material for which he claims payment, stating with substantial accuracy the amount claimed and the name of the party to whom the work was performed or to whom the material was furnished. Such notice shall be served by registered or certified mail, postage prepaid, to the contractor at any place where his office is regularly maintained for the transaction of business. The 180-day time limit does not apply to claims for retainages. A claimant having a contract with a subcontractor required by the prime contractor to have a subcontractor payment bond is allowed to bring an action on the subcontractor's payment bond, but may not bring an action on the prime contractor's payment bond.

Time for Suit—Suit must be instituted more than 90 days after the last day labor or material was supplied for which payment is claimed, but within one year after the day on which the claimant last performed labor or last furnished materials.

Contracts Excluded—Contracts of $100,000 or less, unless required by a public body.

Penalty for Failure to Take Bond—No special statutory provision.

Waiver—A waiver of bond rights is void unless in writing and signed after the supply of labor or material.

WASHINGTON

Amount of Bond—Full contract price, except in cases of cities and towns, in which case the municipality may, by general ordinance, fix and determine the amount of the bond, provided same shall not be less than 25% of contract price.

Labor and Material Covered—All laborers, mechanics', subcontractors and materialmen, and all persons who shall supply such person or persons with provisions or supplies for the carrying on, prosecution, or doing of any public work.

Notice Required by Suppliers. Every person, firm or corporation furnishing materials, supplies or provisions shall, not later than 10 days after the date of the first delivery of such materials, supplies or provisions to any subcontractor or agent of any person, firm, or corporation having a subcontract for the construction, performance, carrying on, prosecution, or doing of such work, deliver or mail to the contractor a notice in writing, stating, in substance and effect, that such person, firm or corporation has commenced to deliver materials, supplies or provisions for use thereon, with the name of the subcontractor or agent ordering or to whom the same is furnished, and that such contractor and his bond will be held for the payment of the same. No suit may be maintained in any court against the contractor or his bond to recover for such material, supplies, or provisions or any part thereof unless this notice has been given.

Generally. Creditor shall not have any right of action on the bond unless, within 30 days from and after the completion of the contract with an acceptance of the work by the executive action of the municipal officers, the creditor shall present to and file with such public official a notice in writing in substance of claim. This notice must be signed by the person or corporation making the claim or giving the notice, and, after being presented and filed, the notice becomes a public record.

Time for Suit—No special statutory provision for suit against payment bond.

Contracts Excluded—In cases of contracts of $25,000 or less, the public entity may retain 50% of the contract amount in lieu of bond.

Penalty for Failure to Take Bond—Municipality is liable to all persons authorized to sue on the bond to the full extent and for the full amount of all debts due them by the contractor.

WEST VIRGINIA

Amount of Bond—In contracts for the construction, alteration or repair of public buildings other than school edifices, penal sum equal at least to the reasonable cost of the materials, machinery, equipment and labor required for the completion of said contract. In the case of highway work, in such penal sum as the State Road Commissioner shall require, but not to exceed the contract price. A bond in double the amount of the contract price is required in connection with contracts for the building or repair of school property. With respect to school construction, boards shall require all persons contracting for the building or repairing of school property, where the contract exceeds $100, to execute a bond, with approved security, in the amount of the contract price.

Labor and Material Covered—All materials, machinery, equipment and labor delivered to the contractor for use in the erection, construction, improvement, alteration or repair of any public building used or to be used for public purposes.

Notice Required—No special statutory provision.

Time for Suit—No special statutory provision.

Contracts Excluded—No special statutory provision.

Penalty for Failure to Take Bond—No special statutory provision.

WISCONSIN

Amount of Bond—Not less than contract price.

Labor and Material Covered—All labor or material furnished, used, or consumed in making a public improvement or performing a public work where the claimant has a direct contract with the prime contractor or with any subcontractor of the prime contractor.

Notice Required—A subcontractor or supplier may only maintain an action if the claimant has, within 60 days after the first provision of labor or materials, notified the prime contractor in writing that the claimant has or will provide labor and materials on the project. Written notice of claim to Public Authority and contractor prior to funds being paid to contractor. If contractor does not dispute within 30 days, the claim must be paid upon demand.

Time for Suit—No later than one year after the completion of the work under the contract.

Contracts Excluded—All contracts with state for amounts less than $10,000, but not more than $100,000.

Penalty for Failure to Take Bond—No special statutory provision.

WYOMING

Amount of Bond—Not less than one-half of the contract price, except where such price exceeds $100,000, in which case the bond shall be in such amount as the appropriate officer, agency or governing body deems sufficient.

Labor and Material Covered—All work, labor, material or goods of any kind which were used in the execution of the contract concerning any public building or other public structure.

Notice Required—Subcontractors or materialmen on projects of $50,000 or more must give written notice to the general contractor of his rights under the bond within 60 days of first providing labor or materials. If this notice is not given, all rights under the payment bonds are waived.

Time for Suit—Suit must be brought within one year after the date of the first publication of notice of final payment of the contract. Any person entitled to protection of the bond shall notify the obligee named in the bond at the beginning of his suit and shall include in said notice the names of the parties, a description of the guarantee and the amount and nature of his claim.

Contracts Excluded—$7,500 or under.

Penalty for Failure to Take Bond—None.

14 Trust Fund Laws and Agreements

INTRODUCTION TO TRUSTS

Let's suppose your last will and testament for you and your spouse creates a trust for the benefit of your children. If you and your spouse are killed in an accident, all of your money goes into a trust fund for the health, education and welfare of your children. Let's suppose your brother is set up as the trustee of that trust fund. Your brother, as trustee, has the discretion to use the trust fund to purchase groceries, buy clothing, take the family on vacation, pay a portion of the mortgage, and pay for tuition for your children.

If your trustee brother later becomes insolvent and files bankruptcy, many of your trustee brother's creditors may try to attach the trust fund. They would argue that your trustee brother had the discretion to use trust funds whenever he thought it was appropriate for the children. Your brother wrote checks off of the trust fund account monthly for any variety of household expenses. Will your brother's creditors be able to attach this trust fund?

No, the creditor should fail in this attempt. The money does not belong to your bankrupt brother-trustee. The money still belongs to your children as "beneficiaries." Your brother has only "legal" title. Your children have "beneficial" or "equitable" title to the trust fund.

Some states have trust fund "statutes" or laws to protect owners, general contractors, subcontractors and suppliers in the construction industry, including Maryland, New York, New Jersey, Illinois, Minnesota, Wisconsin and Michigan. Summaries of the state laws are provided below. A creditor in the construction industry should consult the *Construction Law Survival Manual*, published by NACM for a 50-state survey of trust fund laws protecting construction labor and material suppliers in many states. In general, when a general contractor receives payment from the construction project owner, the general contractor holds funds in trust for the benefit of the subcontractors and suppliers. Subcontractors then hold funds in trust for their suppliers and sub-subcontractors.

The federal government has also enacted the Perishable Agricultural Commodities Act (PACA), which creates a statutory trust to protect unpaid sellers of perishable agricultural commodities. Produce sellers must carefully follow some basic procedures, including limits on payment terms and a notice on all invoices. However, the trust will then apply to all sales in the United States. *See below* for further discussion on PACA.

In some state trust fund laws, the officers and directors of a company holding trust funds are also personally liable to make sure that trust funds get to the proper subcontractor and supplier beneficiaries. This works very much like personal liability for federal "941" income withholding taxes. In addition to having special status if the trustee contractor files bankruptcy, the trust beneficiary may also have a personal guarantee from the officers and directors of the bankrupt debtor.

In the event of bankruptcy, the trust funds held for the benefit of others do not become a part of the bankruptcy estate. These funds always belong to the beneficiary. The trustee is merely "holding" the beneficiary's money. The creditor may need to get appropriate bankruptcy orders, but may be entitled to payment directly from an owner, general contractor or from the bankruptcy estate by bankruptcy court order. This concept can also be a very important defense to a preference claim in bankruptcy.

Since a debtor-trustee is never the owner of trust funds, it is also impossible for the debtor to sell or give away trust property or grant a security interest in trust property. The trustee could not give away or sell trust property, since a trustee does not have title (does not own) to the trust property. The beneficiary of the trust could claim ownership of the trust property, even in the hands of third parties. By the same token, a trustee cannot grant an effective security interest in trust property.

Even without trust fund laws, it is possible to create a trust fund relationship by agreement. This works just like a bank trust fund or the trust fund for the children. It is possible to add trust language to a contract, joint check agreement, or credit agreement with just a few sentences.

Construction trust fund statutes were created to protect various players in the construction industry from impecunious or dishonest contractors. The beneficiaries of the trust are often lower tier subcontractors or suppliers that generate the trust fund by supplying labor and materials to a construction project. If poor management or dishonesty causes a contractor to become insolvent, receivables on construction projects will often go to the bankrupt's secured creditors, banks or will be shared pro rata with all of the bankrupt's general unsecured creditors. In any event, the lower tiered subcontractor or supplier will receive little or nothing in the absence of mechanics' lien or payment bond rights.

The primary motivation to create many trust fund statutes, however, has been the desire to protect owners and general contractors. Many states have no "defense of payment" to their mechanics' lien (see Chapter 12). In other words, an owner can be required to pay for a project twice, if a general or subcontractor fails to properly pass funds on. In some such states, the trust fund statute was in large part created to protect owners. The personal liability feature of the trust fund statute particularly would motivate contractors to protect owners from double liability and make sure funds went to subs and suppliers.

Similarly, general contractors on public projects normally are required to provide payment bonds that can also create double liability for general contractors. Generally, there is no "defense of payment" on a payment bond. On federal projects, general contractors are liable to second tier subcontractors. This means a general contractor can pay its obligations to subcontractors in full and then still be liable to pay for the same labor and materials again to a sub-subcontractor. The general contractor may not have even been aware of lower tier subs and suppliers on the project. The New Jersey Trust Fund Statute, for example, is applicable only to public projects and was created in part to protect general contractors on public projects (*Universal Bonding Insurance Company v. Gittens and Sprinkle Enterprises, Inc.*, 960 F.2d 966 (3rd Cir. 1992)).

Some state bond laws ("Little Miller Act") actually provide protection to *third*-tier sub-subcontractors. This puts general contractors in a particularly risky position. It is difficult to police funds paid to direct subcontractors, much less sub-subcontractors. General contractors require subcontractor payment bonds, but this generates higher costs for subcontractors, general contractors and ultimately owners. Some subcontractors also have insufficient bonding capacity, taking many potential bidders out of contention. General contractors can and should carefully police claim waivers from lower tiered subcontractors and suppliers. This also generates higher administrative costs, however, and is not always practical. It may be impossible where there is exposure to third-tier subcontractors and suppliers.

For all these reasons, some states such as Maryland and New Jersey, created trust fund statutes applicable to projects with Little Miller Act contracts and/or mechanics' lien rights. While trust fund statutes certainly protect lower tier creditor-beneficiaries, protection for owners and general contractors from double liability is often a primary motivation.

All of the same players will want consensual trust fund agreements, if there is no trust fund statute for protection. Material suppliers would certainly want a trust fund provision in their credit agreement or quote before supplying. Lower tier subcontractors have a similar interest.

Owners will also want trust fund provisions in their general contracts. This is particularly true in states, such as Maryland or Pennsylvania, with no defense of payment to the mechanics' lien. Trust fund provisions will help preserve and protect funds for subs and suppliers, protecting owners from dual liability. Consensual trust fund provisions can also protect the owner or general contractor from completion costs in the event of contractor abandonment and insolvency. General contractors should require these trust fund provisions in all subcontracts. These documents already contractually require subcontractors to complete projects and pay for all labor and materials. There is no real additional cost to either party in modifying this language to create a trust relationship.

Who is the loser in a trust fund relationship? The trustee's liability for breach of a trust relationship duplicates contract liability. Personal liability of officers and directors under trust fund laws and the potential for punitive or treble damages may add additional liability (see Personal Liability of Officers and Directors below). If a materials supplier can sue a customer under a credit agreement, what does it add to sue the customer for breach of trust? The real difference comes in the event of insolvency and the trust beneficiary's relationship with third parties, with whom there is no contract.

Bankruptcy or insolvency is not a battle between the creditor and the debtor that breached a contract. The debtor is gone and is out of business. Even in a Chapter 11 Reorganization, the stockholders of the corporation normally change. The "bad guy" is gone. Bankruptcy is generally a "battle between innocents." All participants deserve to be paid in full, the question becomes who will bear the cost of the debtor's insolvency?

Secured creditors have a preferred position in bankruptcy. Article 9 of the Uniform Commercial Code allows a creditor to obtain a first priority lien on a debtor's accounts receivable. In bankruptcy, all moneys still owed to the debtor will go to this secured creditor, unless there are superior security interests, such as a mechanics' lien or payment bond. This result can seem very unfair. Material suppliers and lower tier subcontractors may remain unpaid. Owners and general contractors may face double liability to pay them. It is the labor and materials that generated this receivable, which would not otherwise exist. Why should the secured creditor have first priority to this receivable? The secured creditor is also an innocent that has lost money, but this is quite arguably different money. The secured lender is often a bank that lent money for general operations. This receivable was created by the labor and/or materials supplied by a different creditor.

If secured creditors do not consume all assets in bankruptcy, any remainder goes to general unsecured creditors. All these creditors are certainly innocent and in a similarly vulnerable position. At the same time, however, it is arguable that these general unsecured creditors also did not generate this particular receivable. In any event the owner, general contractors, subs, suppliers and the general unsecured creditors of the insolvent debtor are all innocents competing for limited assets.

TRUST FUND THEORY

Most of the theory behind trust fund laws and trust fund agreements are the same. As courts began to deal with new trust fund laws in the last couple of decades, the courts understandably looked for guidance to the older and well-established case law regarding traditional trust arrangements. Since a trust fund law is created from scratch by a legislature, the exact wording of a trust fund law can vary. These differences in wording can result in operational differences. Some states, for example, create personal liability for officers and directors. Accordingly, the case law on conventional trust arrangements tends to be the same from state to state, but can still have differences.

Comparison with Security Interest

Security is the conventional method by which creditors establish priority, including voluntary security interests in accounts receivable, vehicles, real estate, or equipment. Mechanics' lien laws can also help a creditor establish priority over a certain receivable. If the creditor can establish mechanics' lien rights, the receivable from that property owner is not shared with general unsecured creditors. The mechanics' lien claimant can claim priority over that entire receivable and avoid general unsecured creditor status.

Trust fund laws or agreements are theoretically different from security interests. Technically, the trust beneficiary is not a secured creditor, but is something even better instead. If there is a trust, the receivable is simply not property of the estate. The debtor does not own this property and cannot grant a security interest in this property. The debtor is simply "holding" the beneficiary's property.

You may be familiar with a "contract for deed" or an "installment contract" in a real estate sale. In this arrangement, the debtor makes payments each month for several years. When the payments are complete the seller then deeds the property to the buyer. The debtor does not "own" the property until he is finished making payments. This same transaction could be structured as a mortgage where the seller deeds the property now and takes back a security interest. If the debtor defaults on the loan, the creditor must foreclose on the security property. It is safer for the creditor, if the debtor never owns the property.

Comparison with Contract Rights

You could logically wonder what advantage a trust fund relationship has over a contract or credit agreement. If your debtor-buyer does not pay for labor or materials supplied, the contract provides the right to sue and obtain judgment for the balance due. What does it add to be able to sue the debtor-trustee for "breach of trust"?

A trust fund law or agreement may not give you any better remedy *against your debtor* than your contract rights. The real difference is in the quality of the remedy against third parties. First the trust fund agreement, if properly worded, may allow a creditor to collect directly from property owners or other third parties. This would be similar to rights of collection under a UCC-1.

Even more important, however, are the creditor-beneficiary's rights against third parties in the event of bankruptcy. Bankruptcy is actually a battle between creditors over the limited assets available for distribution. A creditor always wants to identify a receivable somewhere and establish an absolute right to collect the entire receivable and not share it with any other creditors. A creditor accomplishes this, for example, in a mechanics' lien proceeding. The other creditors in the bankruptcy estate will always argue that this receivable should go into the general pot to be shared by all of the general unsecured creditors.

A trust fund relationship is a mechanism to claim exclusive ownership of this one receivable from a property owner or a general contractor. This is similar to the advantage in establishing a mechanics' lien right, but it is not actually a security interest. It also has no specific timeline and can be less expensive. If the debtor has agreed to a trust fund agreement, the receivable never becomes property of the debtor-trustee. It is always the creditor's property and there is no need to share it with any other creditor.

As between the creditor-beneficiary and the debtor-trustee, the trust fund relationship does not add anything, unless you are dealing with a trust fund law that creates personal liability for officers and directors. The biggest difference in trust fund laws and agreements will be in the relationship between the creditor-beneficiary and the debtor's other creditors in an insolvency situation.

Tracing and Identifying Funds in Debtor's Possession

The creditor-beneficiary will normally have the "burden of proof" to properly trace funds. Money is very "fungible." One dollar looks the same as another. In order to establish ownership over a particular fund of money a creditor-beneficiary must be able to prove that those particular dollars are the trust fund dollars. The creditor-beneficiary must prove not only that it has a right to funds generally, but a superior right over secured creditors and other claimants to these particular funds.

In tracing funds, the creditor-beneficiary does get help from a legal presumption that the debtor-trustee will spend his own money before the debtor-trustee spends trust funds. When trust funds are "commingled" or mixed with the debtor-trustee's funds in a bank account, the law will presume that the debtor-trustee is honest and will avoid misappropriating trust funds. The creditor-beneficiary will need bank records to show that a trust fund received from a certain construction project was deposited in a certain bank account. If the balance in that bank account never drops below the amount of the trust fund, then the law will assume that the trust fund is still intact in that bank account. The creditor-beneficiary has successfully traced and identified the trust fund.

Once a commingled account goes into a negative balance, however, the funds lose their identity and tracing becomes impossible. This is called the lowest intermediate balance test. This is a legal fiction that says that when trust funds have been traced into a general bank account, the creditor-beneficiary can successfully identify funds if the balance of the account has always equaled or exceeded the amount of the trust fund. However, if all monies are withdrawn, the trust fund is lost, even if new monies are later deposited into the account. If the account balance remains positive, but the balance drops lower than the amount of the trust fund, then the trust fund is considered dissipated or lost to that extent, unless the creditor-beneficiary can prove the debtor-trustee intended to replace the trust funds with the later deposits.

A few courts have extended the legal fiction to assume that a debtor-trustee will always replace trust funds at the earliest opportunity. In other words, as long as there is sufficient money currently in the bank account where trust funds were originally deposited, this will be sufficient tracing for some courts.

Commingling Funds

Most trust fund laws allow a debtor-trustee to "commingle" funds. This means that it is not necessary to keep the trust funds in a separate bank account. The debtor-trustee does not need to separately account for trust funds, but must make sure that funds received on a construction project are eventually paid to all subcontractors and suppliers that helped generate the fund. PACA also creates a non-segregated trust that can be mixed with other debtor funds.

Accordingly, trust funds go into the debtor-trustee's regular bank account. The trust fund is mixed with trust funds belonging to other creditor-beneficiaries and funds belonging to the debtor. This makes banking and accounting easier for the debtor-trustee, but also creates problems for the creditor-beneficiary in identifying or tracing funds.

Of course, it would be possible to prohibit commingling in any voluntary trust fund agreement. Where a creditor has a strong bargaining position, a creditor could require a separate bank account for all proceeds coming from a particular construction project. This would certainly aid the creditor in collecting trust funds and eliminate the need to trace funds. However, this is not a requirement under most trust fund laws.

Collecting Trust Funds Directly from Project Owner or Upstream Contractor

One important difference between a simple contract relationship and a trust fund relationship may be the creditor-beneficiary's ability to collect from "third parties" (someone other than the debtor-trustee). For example, a creditor-beneficiary may be able to collect directly from a construction project owner or general contractor.

In other situations, trust funds may go through or past the debtor-trustee to other third parties. The debtor may use the trust funds to pay another creditor, may give the money away to a family member or spend it on luxury items. A secured creditor of the debtor-trustee might actually seize or garnish the trust funds. This is discussed below under "Involuntary Trustees."

The wording of a trust fund law in any particular state may control whether a creditor-beneficiary has direct collection rights against an owner or general contractor. The Maryland Trust Fund Statute, for example, states "any moneys *paid* under a contract by an owner to a contractor…shall be held in trust." If the money has not yet been paid, it is arguable whether a trust exists.

Under the New Jersey Trust Fund Statute, there is no trust until the money is "paid" by the owner. In other words, there is no trust in money held by the owner and a creditor-beneficiary has no claim against an owner. Wisconsin courts on a trust fund law with similar language have ruled that there is no trust until the fund is paid to a general contractor. A secured creditor of the debtor-trustee could win this battle over a trust fund claimant in an attempt to collect money from an owner.

Similarly, the wording of a consensual trust fund agreement could also control whether the creditor-beneficiary had collection rights from third parties. A secured creditor can include collection rights in a security agreement. Article 9 of the Uniform Commercial Code also gives a secured creditor the right to collect accounts receivable of the debtor. Presumably a creditor-beneficiary could include the same type of language in a consensual trust fund agreement.

In the historic general law of trusts, a beneficiary always had the ability to collect a trust fund that could be traced and identified (*Williams v. Dickinson County Bank*, 175 Va 359 (1940)). The wording of some state trust fund statutes also (explicitly or implicitly) allows collection rights against a project owner or upstream contractor. The Maryland Trust Fund Statute, for example, seems to provide a different status for owners or general contractors when it states:

> MD Real Property Code 9-201(a): *Moneys to Be Held in Trust*. "Any moneys paid under a contract by an owner to a contractor, or by the owner or contractor to a subcontractor for work done or materials furnished, or both, for or about a building by any subcontractor shall be held in trust by the contractor or subcontractor, as trustee, for those subcontractors who did work or furnished materials..."

The language of this trust fund law seems to allow a sub-subcontractor to collect directly from a general contractor. Other courts faced with similar wording have allowed such direct collection rights.

As a practical matter, a trust relationship may aid a creditor-beneficiary tremendously, even if there is technically no right to sue a stakeholder (owner or general contractor) directly. Owners and general contractors are normally supportive of getting the payment to lower tiered subcontractors and suppliers. Owners often fear mechanics' lien rights. In addition, a debtor-trustee will not normally contest the debt and may begrudgingly allow a joint check or direct payment. In addition, priority battles often occur when a debtor is insolvent or has gone out of business. The competition is often between creditors. An owner or general contractor will normally prefer to pay a subcontractor that supplied labor and materials to the project, rather than a bank that has a security interest in the debtor-trustee's accounts receivable.

In any event, a notice or demand letter reciting a trust fund law or agreement will often help obtain direct payment from an owner or general contractor.

Involuntary Trustees

A trustee cannot convey good title to trust property, because he has no good title. The creditor-beneficiary is always the true owner of a trust fund. If a thief steals your car and then "sells" it, you still own the car and can recover it. The thief could not grant an ownership interest in the car, because the thief had no good title to convey.

What if the debtor-trustee has received the trust fund and then paid it over to another creditor, friend or family member? The creditor-beneficiary may need to collect directly from such a third party as an "involuntary trustee." This person did not agree to be a trustee, but could be required to act as trustee nonetheless.

A trustee cannot give trust property away. Many of the involuntary trustee cases come down to whether the recipient was a "bona fide purchaser," that is someone who paid good money for the property without knowledge of the breach of trust. If the recipient of the money did not pay for it, they cannot be a bona fide purchaser and must return the money to the beneficiary.

Under a PACA trust, courts seem to allow a creditor-beneficiary to collect from a debtor's bank in possession of trust funds (*Overton Distribs., Inc. v. Heritage Bank*, 340 F.3d 361 (6th Cir. 2003)). The creditor-beneficiary may need to trace funds and show that the bank is in possession of funds that came from a produce sale covered by PACA. It is not entirely clear whether the federal courts will require proof of knowledge by the bank of the trust.

Generally, the involuntary trustee status may be imposed only on a recipient that did not pay for the property or one who *knowingly* receives trust funds, or any of its parts. The beneficiary has a right that no person shall knowingly aid the trustee in committing a breach of his duties. There is no dispute on this principle, but there can be difficulties deciding whether certain conduct amounts to a participation in a breach of trust. If a third party helps or takes part with the trustee in a breach of trust, a creditor-beneficiary may be able to trace the trust property and make a claim against the involuntary trustee.

There are two elements for wrongful participation in a breach of trust:

1. An act or omission which furthers or completes the breach of trust by the trustee; and
2. Knowledge at the time that the transaction amounted to a breach of trust.

Many of the involuntary trustee cases will come down to the quality of the involuntary trustee's knowledge that their receipt of the money was a breach of trust. A third person has notice of a breach of trust not only when they have actual knowledge, but also when they should know of the trust. An involuntary trustee knows facts that would lead a reasonably intelligent and diligent person to inquire whether they are receiving funds from a trustee committing a breach of trust.

If a creditor-beneficiary cannot prove involuntary trustee status, then the trust is probably broken when the money leaves the hands of the debtor-trustee. Although there is no strict deadline in enforcing trust fund rights, this provides a practical deadline. It may be important to enforce trust fund rights while the trustee still has the money. This may not be long.

Trustee Cannot Grant Security Interest in Trust Funds

Secured creditors of the debtor-trustee cannot obtain a security interest in trust funds. Just as a trustee cannot convey good title by selling or giving away trust property, a trustee also cannot grant a security interest in property it does not own. This is true even if the secured creditor has a "super priority" security interest in a bankruptcy proceeding.

Setoff Rights

What if the trust funds are in a bank account and the debtor-trust owes the bank money on an unrelated transaction? It would seem that if a trustee cannot grant a valid security interest in a trust fund, then a bank in this situation also could not have setoff rights. However, at least one case describes this as a "minority rule," not followed by most courts.

The United States Court of Appeals for the 6th Circuit has stated that the majority rule is that a bank may setoff obligations to the bank against a bank account, where the bank "has no knowledge of the interest of a third party in an account" (*Federal Insurance Company v. Fifth Third Bank*, 867 F.2d. 330, 334-335 (6th Cir.

1989)). This majority rule still has a "no knowledge" requirement, similar to the involuntary trustee status described above. In other words, a bank still could not setoff obligations if the bank had reason to know that the funds in the bank account were trust funds.

The United States Court of Appeals for the 6th Circuit went on to observe, however, that Ohio follows the minority rule, also termed the "equitable rule," which states that a bank, even without express or implied knowledge of a trust cannot apply trust funds against funds that the trustee owes the bank, "where such lack of knowledge has not resulted in any change in the bank's position." In other words, if the bank has relied somehow on the existence of funds in the bank account, without knowledge of the trust, the bank may still be able to setoff.

In short, a bank or other third party's ability to setoff will be based on factors very similar to those used to determine whether a third party can be an involuntary trustee. It will depend namely on the quality of the third party's knowledge of the existence of the trust.

If an owner or other upstream contractor wished to setoff obligations, however, the situation would seem to be different. Suppose a general contractor received funds from an owner for labor and materials supplied. These would constitute trust funds under most state trust fund laws. If the general contractor had backcharges against a subcontractor for defective work, however, that subcontractor probably could not enforce trust fund rights to rise above its contract obligations. In other words, the subcontractor-beneficiary could not force the general contractor to pay more than the subcontractor would be owed under the subcontract agreement.

What if a supplier to the subcontractor tried to assert trust fund rights? The backcharges against the subcontractor had nothing to do with defects in the supplier's material. Could the supplier force the general contractor to pay more than the subcontractor could?

A review of the banking industry case law discussed above would indicate that the general contractor could not offset in this situation. A general contractor doing business in a state with a trust fund statute would probably have actual knowledge of the trust fund relationships. At the same time, this situation does seem different than that of the third-party secured bank.

Personal Liability of Officers and Directors

Individual shareholders, officers, or directors of a corporation who are in position to control PACA trust assets and who breach their fiduciary duty to preserve those assets may be held personally liable.

In some states, the construction industry trust fund statute makes officers, directors or managing agents personally liable for misuse of trust funds. There are specific provisions for personal liability in some state codes. The possibility of personal liability is an important protection for subcontractors and suppliers who would otherwise have no remedy when a corporation went out of business. This concept of personal liability for trust funds seems similar to the personal liability attaching to officers and directors for failure to account for Internal Revenue Cost Section 941 taxes. This personal liability does make individuals take their duties seriously for withholding taxes.

New York's Lien Law establishes a trust fund for the protection of subcontractors and suppliers, as well as personal liability for the misappropriation of such trust funds. The statute provides:

Any trustee of a trust arising under this article [Article 3-A], and any officer, director or agent of such trustee, who applies or consents to the application of trust funds received by the trust as money or an instrument of the payment of money for any purpose other than the trust purposes of that trust, as defined in section seventy-one, is guilty of larceny and punishable as provided in the penal law... (New York State Consolidated Laws, Article 3-A § 79-a)

Under the Maryland Trust Fund Statute, personal liability can attach to "any officer, director or managing agent of any contractor or subcontractor...." A "managing agent" means an employee of a contractor or subcontractor who is responsible for the direction over, or control of, money held in trust.

Under the Maryland Trust Fund Statute, any officer, director or managing agent "who knowingly retains or uses the monies held in trust...for any purpose other than to pay those subcontractors for whom the monies are held in trust, shall be personally liable to any person damaged by the action."

The potential for personal liability is very helpful, but does have its shortcomings. For example, contractors are usually allowed to "commingle" funds. In other words, it is not necessary to keep the trust funds in separate accounts. Most general contractors are working on several projects. Funds are entering and leaving the general contractor's bank account for many purposes. If a general contractor can show that all funds leaving the account were used to pay subcontractors and suppliers on *some* construction project then it is unlikely that a court will hold any individual officer or director personally liable, especially if all contract funds had been devoted to legitimate business debts and expenses and the defendant had invested a large amount of his own money in an unsuccessful attempt to keep the corporation in business. The court may require some sort of bad faith by the defendant. This means that the defendant must have acted dishonestly or at least with reckless indifference.

As a practical matter, a contractor will usually be "robbing Peter to pay Paul" for a long time prior to insolvency. A claimant may not be able to establish personal liability, unless there is a blatant case where an individual officer used funds for personal reasons.

ABILITY TO DISCHARGE IN BANKRUPTCY

Once a corporation goes out of business, its creditors may seek to establish personal liability on the corporate officers and directors pursuant to a trust fund statute. Those corporate officers, directors or managing agents may personally file bankruptcy soon thereafter. Can personal liability under a trust fund statute be discharged in bankruptcy? In other words, will a personal bankruptcy get rid of personal liability under a trust fund statute?

Under the Bankruptcy Code, an individual cannot get a discharge from any debt obtained by false pretenses, a false representation, or actual fraud (11 USC § 523(a)(2)(A)). In order to avoid discharge, a creditor must prove:

1. The debtor made a representation,
2. At the time, the debtor knew the representations were false,
3. The debtor made the representations with the intention and purpose of deceiving the creditor,
4. The creditor relied on such representation, and
5. The creditor sustained loss and damage as the proximate result of the representations.

This standard required under the Bankruptcy Code may be more than is required by a state trust fund statute. State law would control what is necessary to obtain a personal judgment against an officer, director or managing agent. If that individual becomes insolvent and files bankruptcy, however, the Bankruptcy Code determines whether or not the debt will be discharged in bankruptcy.

Many trust fund statutes or agreements also create "fiduciary responsibility" for officers, directors or managing agents. Debts arising from a breach of fiduciary duty can also be nondischargeable under the Bankruptcy Code. To avoid a bankruptcy discharge on this type of debt, the claimant must prove:

1. The existence of a trust,
2. That the debtor was a fiduciary of that trust,
3. Fraud or defalcation by the debtor while acting as a fiduciary of the trust.

Defalcation means a willful neglect of duty. Defalcation in bankruptcy requires more than negligence, though less than fraud. A claimant must show more than mere negligence.

Whether there would be individual liability for breach of fiduciary duty should depend on whether a trust fund statute or agreement makes the individual officer or director a trustee, as opposed to only the corporation being a trustee. For example, the Maryland Trust Fund Statute now states, "an officer, director or managing agent of a contractor or subcontractor who has direction over or control of money held by trust…is a trustee for the purpose of paying the money to the subcontractors who are entitled to it."

Punitive and Treble Damages

If a creditor can prove actual fraud by a trustee or fiduciary, then it should be possible to obtain punitive damages in addition to compensatory damages.

To prove actual fraud, a claimant would have to produce clear and convincing evidence of the five elements discussed above to avoid bankruptcy discharge. If a creditor can prove these five elements by clear and convincing evidence, the claimant should be entitled to punitive damages under either a trust fund statute or any type of voluntary or contractual trust agreement.

The same should be true if a claimant can prove breach of trust or breach of fiduciary duty as discussed above. Under many state's law, punitive damages may be awarded for breach of a fiduciary duty. Some states require proof of conduct that is willful or wanton and in reckless disregard of rights.

Some states also have special laws allowing for recovery of triple damages for fraudulent activity. These treble damage laws may be applicable to a trust fund statute.

Insolvency Protections and Bankruptcy

A federal bankruptcy court cannot circumvent a legislature's determination that produce sellers or public construction contractors and suppliers require special protection. Federal bankruptcy law will recognize and enforce the property right created by state or federal law. Federal bankruptcy law does not determine whether a trust exists. Other law establishes a trust relationship, either through a trust fund statute or any type of voluntary trust agreement. A creditor will need to look at the state law where the transactions occurred (or PACA), therefore, to determine the result once a debtor files bankruptcy.

A trust will have important implications in a bankruptcy. The trust fund is simply not "property of the estate." The United States Supreme Court has stated that Congress plainly excluded property of others held by the debtor in trust at the time of filing the bankruptcy petition. The debtor or bankruptcy trustee has no real interest in trust funds. The trustee holds only bare legal and not equitable title. Courts have consistently found that funds are not property of the bankruptcy estate, if covered by construction industry or PACA trust fund statutes.

Without a trust relationship, this fund would be an asset of the debtor. The fund would either be property of the debtor in its bank account or in an account receivable from an owner or general contractor. The general rule is that this "property of the estate" would go into the general pot to be shared by all general unsecured creditors. Insolvency or bankruptcy is no longer a battle between the debtor and creditor. It is a battle between creditors over the limited assets available for distribution.

A creditor always wants to identify a receivable somewhere and establish that the creditor has an absolute right to collect the entire receivable and does not need to share it with any other creditors. A creditor can accomplish this, for example, in a mechanics' lien proceeding. If a creditor establishes valid mechanics' lien rights, this particular receivable does not go into the general pot to be shared with other creditors. The mechanics' lien claimant can keep the entire receivable. Similarly, a bank may have a blanket security interest and UCC financing statement covering all accounts receivable of the debtor. If this security interest proves to be valid, then this secured creditor can collect these receivables and does not need to share.

A trust fund relationship is a mechanism by which a creditor can claim exclusive ownership of one receivable. Technically, this is not a security interest and a trust fund claimant is not a secured creditor. Instead, the trust fund creditor is something even better. The receivable is simply not property of the estate. The debtor does not own this property and is simply "holding" the beneficiary's property.

This distinction has some similarities with a "contract for deed" or "installment contract" in a real estate sale. In this arrangement, the debtor makes payments each month for several years. When the payments are complete, the seller then deeds the property to the buyer. The debtor does not "own" the property until he is finished making payments. This same transaction could be structured as a mortgage where the seller deeds the property now and takes back a mortgage. It is safer for the creditor, however, if the debtor never owns the property until the debt is paid in full. The creditor will not need to "foreclose," because the creditor still owns the property. The debtor is simply in breach of contract and loses its rights under the contract.

Similarly, a trust fund is not property of the estate, whether the money is sitting in the debtor's bank account or held by a property owner. A trust fund creditor-beneficiary will prevail over a secured creditor claiming priority over a trust fund receivable. A trust fund creditor-beneficiary may be able to collect funds directly from an owner or a general contractor, force a debtor in bankruptcy to release funds, assert personal liability on officers or directors under a trust fund law, and may have defenses against future preference litigation.

COLLECTING TRUST FUNDS DIRECTLY FROM THIRD PARTIES

As discussed above, a creditor-beneficiary may be able to collect trust funds directly from a general contractor or up-stream contractor. In one bankruptcy court case, a sub-subcontractor obtained payment directly from a general contractor. The bankruptcy trustee failed in an attempt to force the creditor-beneficiary to repay the money to the bankruptcy court. The bankruptcy trustee unsuccessfully argued that the sub-subcontractor was effectively collecting on the debtor's account receivable, diminishing the value of the bankruptcy estate. The court dismissed that argument as purely theoretical. The pool of funds from which the unsecured creditors may recover was not diminished.

Collecting Trust Funds Directly from Bankruptcy Estate

The pool of funds available to the debtor and its reorganization or to all creditors for payment of claims is not diminished if the debtor pays the trust beneficiaries. The trust funds would have to be held and managed by the debtor-trustee for the benefit of the beneficiaries only. If trust funds were paid into the bankruptcy estate, the debtor's sole permissible administrative act would be to pay over or endorse the sums due to the beneficial owners of the trust property.

Personal Liability of Officers and Directors

As discussed above, some state trust fund laws create personal liability for the officers, directors or managing agents of corporations in the construction industry. This statutory personal liability is similar to having a personal guarantee from an officer or director. If the corporation is in bankruptcy, a creditor can no longer sue the corporation. The creditor is free to pursue the personal guarantor, however, unless the personal guarantor files bankruptcy.

If an individual guarantor files bankruptcy, they will normally get a discharge from contract debts arising from guarantees. As discussed above, however, individuals may not be able to get a discharge from trust fund obligations (*see above*). This ability to pursue individuals, even in bankruptcy, can be an important weapon for a creditor in bankruptcy.

Bankruptcy Preference Protections

A debtor-contractor has a property right in trust funds only if there is a balance remaining after all the trust beneficiaries have been paid. In other words, a contractor receiving payment must pay the supplier on the contract first, before taking its profit. The bankruptcy trustee has no right to appropriate trust funds for the benefit of general creditors. In other words, trust funds received by a creditor-beneficiary cannot be a preference and do not have to be repaid to the bankruptcy estate. Bankruptcy law simply does not authorize a trustee to distribute other people's money amongst a bankrupt's creditors.

Accordingly, a creditor receiving a preference repayment demand or lawsuit should investigate whether a trust fund agreement existed in a contract or credit agreement. If not, a state trust fund law may provide an effective defense to the preference action. Trust fund claims do not have short notice deadlines, as do mechanics' lien or payment bond claims. This is one advantage to trust fund claims. In other words, even if a creditor took no action to enforce trust fund rights and even if the creditor was never aware of the trust funds rights, there may still be an effective defense to a future preference action.

TRUST FUND LAWS

The workings of trust fund laws vary from the federal PACA law and from state to state in construction industry statutes, just as the wording of negotiated trust fund agreements can vary. The wording of a particular state statute can vary the general discussions above regarding trust fund rights. Particular differences from state to state can be whether personal liability exists for officers and directors, what type of construction project is covered by the trust fund law, and how far the benefits of the trust may extend. Other features of trust fund law do not arise from specific statute wording, but are derived from the general common law of trusts. These features will tend to be the same from state to state, unless a state legislature has enacted a specific law to the contrary. These features would generally include a claimant's need to trace funds, a trustee's inability to convey good title or a security interest in trust funds and the bankruptcy implications.

A creditor in the construction industry should consult the *Construction Law Survival Manual*, published by NACM, for a 50-state survey of trust fund laws protecting construction labor and material suppliers in many states.

PERISHABLE AGRICULTURAL COMMODITIES ACT (PACA)

The Perishable Agricultural Commodities Act (PACA), 7 U.S.C. §§ 499a-499t, creates a statutory trust to protect unpaid sellers of perishable agricultural products ("produce"). This is a federal law, so it applies to all such produce sales in the United States. Because produce needs to be sold quickly, "sellers of perishable commodities are often placed in the position of being unsecured creditors of companies whose creditworthiness the seller is unable to verify" (*Endico Potatoes, Inc. v. CIT Group/Factoring, Inc.*, 67 F.3d 1063, 1067 (2d Cir. 1995)). The trust protects the sellers against financing arrangements made by merchants, dealers, or brokers who give lenders a security interest in the commodities or the receivables or proceeds from the sale of the commodities. This gives the claims of PACA sellers priority over the secured creditors of the buyer.

The PACA statute and the federal regulations lay out the steps that a produce seller must take to come within PACA's protection. Under all circumstances, the seller must give the buyer written notice of the seller's intention to preserve its trust benefits. Sellers are allowed to provide this notice on the invoices given to the buyer or the notice can be sent separately from the invoices, as long as it is sent within 30 days after the expiration of payment terms. If the seller and the buyer use the default payment terms provided in the regulations ("within 10 days after the day on which the produce is accepted"), this notice of intent to preserve benefits is all that is necessary. On the other hand, if the parties agree to payment terms greater than 10 days after acceptance (but it cannot be more than 30 days after acceptance) this agreement must be in writing. The seller must also disclose these non-statutory payment terms "on invoices, accountings, and other documents relating to the transaction."

Thirty days is the maximum allowable payment term under PACA regulations. This limitation exists because the statute is intended to protect only those produce sellers making short-term credit arrangements.

Courts seem to consistently deny the benefits of the trust to sellers that do not follow these procedures strictly, including sellers that have credit agreements allowing more than 30 days' time or sellers that fail to accurately disclose the terms of payment on invoices.

If a seller does follow the relatively simply procedures, however, there are impressive benefits. The seller can assert a superior claim to the proceeds from the sale of its produce that were acquired by a bank from the customer. When a party establishes an interest in a PACA trust, the trust proceeds are separate from a PACA trustee's bankruptcy estate.

TRUST FUND AGREEMENTS

All parties generally have freedom of contract. A supplier or subcontractor could simply refuse to supply labor or materials if some "unrelated" secured creditor would have first priority to the resulting receivable. An owner or general contractor could refuse to award a contract, if a contractor refused to hold completion costs in trust. Logically, there is no reason why a potentially insolvent contractor and its bank couldn't decide between themselves that the bank will have first priority to all receivables. Trust fund statutes are created as a matter of public policy to protect owners and grant first priority to suppliers and subcontractors. A consensual trust fund agreement comes to the same result. Owners and general contractors, as well as lower tier subcontractors and suppliers, can simply refuse to do business unless their contracts include trust fund provisions.

Based on court case law on public trust fund statutes, consensual trust provisions in contracts enable owners, contractors and suppliers to "trump" or preserve priority over a debtor's secured lenders and avoid general unsecured creditor status in bankruptcy. Consensual trust fund provisions in commercial contracts seem to be a fairly new idea. As a result, there is little court case law providing direct guidance. There is much more case law on the workings of trust fund statutes, both in state and federal bankruptcy courts. These cases provide guidance on the operation of wording in various trust fund provisions, which language could be duplicated in contracts. This case law also describes the relationship between trustees, beneficiaries, secured lenders, and other third parties.

There is also a great deal of case law regarding trust agreements historically. Trusts have existed for centuries in connection with estate planning, protection of assets, real estate development and other commercial purposes. There is no doubt that consensual trust agreements have a significant legal status. It is only their use in commercial contracts that is at all new or uncertain. It is fairly clear, for example, that no specific form or wording is required for a consensual trust agreement. It is the intent of the parties that is controlling. A long document with various provisions is unnecessary. If it is clear that the creator of the trust (settlor) intended to create a trust and did not intend the trustee to take ownership of the property, then a trust exists. The language can be quite short as long as the intent is clear.

It seems clear that there are no public policy or fairness objections to consensual trust fund agreements. Many state legislatures have decided to inject involuntary trust relationships into construction contracts to promote justice and fairness. It would seem that the same relationship created by agreement also promotes justice and should be protected by the law.

Protective Provisions for Owners and General Contractors

There is some significant case law in support of consensual trust agreements in commercial contracts. One case before the United States Court of Appeals involved a general contract that stated:

All monies paid on account to any contractor for materials or labor *shall be regarded as fund [sic] in his trust for payment of any and all obligations relating to this contract* and no such amount of monies shall be permitted to accrue to the contractor until all such obligations are satisfied. Evidence satisfactory to the state may be required to show that all current obligations relating to this work are satisfied before releasing any payment due on the work. Before payment of the final estimate, each contractor shall file an affidavit with the state, stating that the monetary obligations [sic] relating to lienable items in connection with the work have been fulfilled. (*Federal Insurance Company v. Fifth Third Bank*, 867 F.2d. 330, 332 (6th Cir. 1989))

One party to the lawsuit asserted that the contractor agreed in this contractual provision to hold as trustee all progress payments received from the state.

Notice that this contract provision is similar to provisions in many construction contracts, requiring the contractor to promptly pay for all labor and materials on receipt of payment, providing affidavits of payment and avoiding liens. The difference was in the first sentence alone, which used the word "trust." The Federal Court of Appeals reviewed historic trust law, including the need to show that a trust was clearly intended. The court decided that an express trust was formed by this contract provision and decided that the subcontractors and suppliers that should have received the money had priority over the bank with a recorded security interest in the receivable. The bank, which actually already had possession of the deposit, was required to return the money. The bank was not allowed to setoff the deposit against money the bank was owed by the same debtor.

In another case, a subcontract provided:

All sums tentatively earned by Subcontractor by the partial or complete performance of the Subcontract Work and any balance of unearned Subcontract price if and when paid by Owner to Contractor, shall constitute a fund for the purpose of (a) full and timely completion of the Subcontract Work and fulfillment of all Subcontract requirements, (b) payment of any backcharges or claims due Contractor, from Subcontractor, based upon this Subcontract or otherwise, and (c) payment to the sub-subcontractor, workers, design professionals, material and service suppliers of Subcontractor, and others who have valid and enforceable mechanics' lien claims or valid and enforceable bond claims (if project is bonded). *Such Tentative earning shall not be due or payable to Subcontractor…or anyone else claiming in Subcontractor's…place and stead, including but not limited to a Trustee in bankruptcy or receiver, until and unless such Subcontract Work is fully and satisfactorily completed, all Subcontract requirements are fulfilled, Contractor and such persons are fully paid and satisfied and the provisions…below are fully satisfied. Subcontractor agrees to promptly pay all sub-subcontractors, workers, vendors and suppliers* of Subcontractor and to provide Contractor with each application for periodic progress payments, and the final payment, such lien waivers of proof of such payment as Contractor may require. At any time, Contractor may demand additional written evidence of Subcontractor's capability to perform and of such payments to such persons be Subcontractor. Subcontractor declares that all funds received by Subcontractor from Contractor hereunder shall be deemed to be held by Subcontractor in *trust* for the benefit of those furnishing work, labor, materials, services, equipment, etc. to or through Subcontractor for the Subcontract Work. (*In re Marrs-Winn Co. Inc.*, 103 F.3d 584, 591 (7th Cir. 1996))

This contract provision also contains common agreements to promptly pay all sub-subcontractors, provide lien waivers and proof of payment. The Federal 7th Circuit Court of Appeals found that this contract provision created a trust. Notice that this subcontract provision also created a trust agreement to protect the general contractor against completion costs for failure to complete the subcontract. This subcontract provision would seem to be very beneficial for any general contractor. After the subcontractor filed a bankruptcy, this general contractor was able to enforce this trust fund agreement even against a secured lender that had a bankruptcy court approved "super priority" security interest in all property of the debtor. The secured lender was forced to return to the general contractor funds it had seized from a bank account.

The language quoted above seems to provide a good model for trust language to protect an owner or general contractor in a contract. This would help protect payment to subcontractors and suppliers in the event of bankruptcy and protect the owner or general contractor from double liability under mechanics' lien law or payment bonds. In the event of insolvency, this language should also help an owner or general contractor recover the costs of completing a project.

Protections for Suppliers and Subcontractors

Lower tier subcontractors and suppliers also have opportunities to create trusts. It would be preferable to get a "three party" agreement, with the endorsement of the owner (or general contractor). This is helpful as a practical matter. If the owner (or general contractor) has approved the arrangement, they can help make sure money flows to the creditor-beneficiary. This will probably also help ensure that an enforceable trust exists.

Owners or general contractors may resist this arrangement, as joint check agreements are often resisted. It is respectfully suggested to owners and contractors, however, that trust fund relationships have all the advantages described above for general contractors and owners.

It is often best to create a trust relationship in the form of a "joint check agreement," because the players on the construction project are familiar and hopefully comfortable with this concept. The "joint check" provisions are also helpful procedures to follow to make sure that trust funds get to the creditor-beneficiary. Fairly minor changes are necessary to a "standard" joint check agreement in order to create a trust agreement. Suggested language for a Trust Fund Joint Check Agreement would be:

AGREEMENT

In consideration of the sum of one dollar cash in hand paid and the supply of labor and/or materials by Seller on the Project, the receipt and sufficiency of which is hereby acknowledged _____ owner or general contractor ("Owner/G.C."), _____ (Seller) and _____ contractor or Seller's customer ("Contractor") and _____ ("Seller"), agree as follows:

1. All checks issued by Owner/G.C. to Contractor for (all labor or materials supplied) or (only for the Seller's sales price of material supplied by Seller) on the _____ construction project ("Project") shall be made jointly payable to Contractor and Seller and shall be promptly delivered to

Seller. Owner/G.C. may rely on any written notice provided by Seller, stating the total current indebtedness of Contractor to Seller and limiting any obligation under this Agreement for any current requisition. Contractor appoints Seller its attorney in fact to sign or endorse on behalf of Contractor all checks received from Owner/G.C.

2. Contractor agrees that all funds owed to Contractor from anyone or received by Contractor to the extent those funds result from the labor or materials supplied by Seller shall be held in trust for the benefit of Seller ("Trust Funds"). **Contractor agrees it has no interest in Trust Funds held by anyone and to promptly account for and pay to Seller all such Trust Funds. Customer irrevocably assigns to Seller any interest it may have in its Trust Fund account receivable.**

3. Seller agrees to supply labor and/or materials to the Project in accordance with Seller's contract.

4. This Agreement is not in payment of obligations of Contractor to Seller and will not affect Seller's rights to withdraw or refuse further credit, or Seller's rights to any payment bond, mechanics' lien, trust fund or other legal rights.

It should also be possible to create trust agreements in contracts, proposals, or quotes. Consult the *Construction Law Survival Manual*, published by NACM for ready to use contracts, proposals, or quotes and credit agreements containing trust fund agreements.

It is advantageous, at least as a practical matter, to get the agreement of the person that will issue payment to the debtor. This should not be legally necessary, however, to create a trust. A creditor could simply refuse to supply labor or material unless the debtor agreed to hold resultant funds in trust. The operative trust language, shown above, can be included in any contract, proposal, or quote as follows:

Contractor agrees that all funds owed to Contractor from anyone or received by Contractor to the extent those funds result from the labor or materials supplied by Seller shall be held in trust for the benefit of Seller ("Trust Funds"). Contractor agrees it has no interest in Trust Funds held by anyone and to promptly account for and pay to Seller all such Trust Funds.

It may also be possible to include this language in a blanket credit agreement for all transactions. It would be preferable, however, to have the provision in a separate contract for each project.

Expansions of this language could include the right to collect funds directly from third parties, such as owners or general contractors. A trustee could also agree that there is no need to trace particular funds from particular projects and agree that whatever money is left in a bank account are trust funds. These provisions are probably enforceable against the trustee. They may not, however, be enforceable against third parties holding the money. Nonetheless, it may help convince a fund holder to voluntarily cooperate. It may be possible and is preferable to get the stakeholder (owner or general contractor) to agree to these provisions by endorsing the contract, by separate letter agreement, or by joint check agreement.

It may be helpful to get a trustee to agree to act "without compensation." In some states, the trustee may otherwise have a claim to a percentage of the trust fund as compensation for acting as trustee.

Trust fund agreements have significant advantages for lower-tiered subcontractors and suppliers. They should be easy to sell as creating no additional cost to the debtor. There is no filing fee and no deadline compared to mechanics' lien or bond litigation.

This trust fund language creates a relationship that should work just like the trust fund laws. The debtor-trustee agrees that all funds received are held in trust, to the extent funds result from labor or materials supplied. If the debtor-trustee files bankruptcy, these funds will not be property of the bankruptcy estate. The creditor-beneficiary will not need to share with the general unsecured creditors and should be able to keep these funds as the trust beneficiary.

Trust fund laws or agreements are one way that a vendor can gain priority over a customer's bank that has a blanket security interest on receivables. This also makes sense. The creditor-beneficiary is essentially saying that it will not provide the value of labor and materials if some other lender will have priority over the receivable that is generated by the labor and materials provided. A creditor can refuse to supply labor or materials unless it will have absolute first priority to the value provided. This absolute first priority is a trust fund agreement.

Trust fund agreements would seem to be a simple, cheap and unobtrusive way for a creditor to protect itself from insolvencies. Trust fund laws have now been around for a few decades. There is a growing body of case law explaining the protections of a trust fund law against blanket security interests or preference litigation. Conventional, voluntary trusts, such as trust funds for children, have also been around for centuries. There is a great deal of court case law explaining the workings and protections of such consensual trust agreements.

By reviewing the case law on consensual trust agreements and the newer case law on trust fund laws, you can get a good picture of how a court should view trust fund arrangements in a conventional vendor-buyer relationship in the construction industry or in any other sale of goods or services. It is important to keep in mind, however, that the use of trust fund arrangements in a traditional debtor-creditor commercial transaction is an innovation that has not yet been tested in the courts.

15 Reclamation, Stoppage in Transit, New Administrative Claim in Favor of Goods Suppliers, and Other Return of Goods Remedies

GROUNDS FOR RECLAMATION

State Law

Reclamation is the seller's right to require an insolvent buyer to return goods purchased on credit. The seller's right of reclamation arises under Section 2-702 of the Uniform Commercial Code (UCC), the uniform state law enacted in all 50 states. Under state law, a seller could reclaim goods delivered to a buyer if the seller satisfies all of the following conditions:

(a) the goods were shipped on credit;
(b) the buyer was insolvent at the time it received the goods;
(c) the seller demands return of the goods within 10 days of the buyer's receipt of the goods; and
(d) the buyer was in possession of the goods when the seller made its reclamation demand.

State law grants a reclaiming creditor an unlimited period of time in which to make its reclamation demand in one particular circumstance. This occurs where the buyer provided a written misrepresentation of solvency to the seller within three months of the seller's delivery of the goods. A buyer may provide a written misrepresentation of solvency in a balance sheet or other type of financial statement, in a letter addressed to the seller, or even in financial information disseminated to a trade or credit association.

Under state law (§ 2-702(3) of the UCC), the seller's right of reclamation is subject to the rights of a buyer in the ordinary course of business or other good faith purchaser. For example, the buyer's sale of goods in the ordinary course of the buyer's business prior to the reclamation demand will defeat the seller's right of reclamation. Reclamation may also fail if the goods the seller is seeking to reclaim are not identifiable or have been converted into a different form prior to the demand.

Impact of Buyer's Bankruptcy Filing

The seller's right of reclamation continues where the buyer becomes the subject of a bankruptcy case and notwithstanding the automatic stay that arises upon the filing of the case. Section 546(c) of the Bankruptcy Code permits the seller to reclaim goods if it satisfies all of the requirements for reclamation under Section 2-702 of the UCC. The seller is also subject to all of the defenses to reclamation available to the buyer under state law. However, there are additional requirements in

Section 546(c) not found in state law which must be followed in order for the seller to be granted an allowed reclamation claim in the buyer's bankruptcy case.

First, Section 546(c) requires a written reclamation demand. Section 2-702 of the UCC is silent on this point and may permit an oral reclamation demand. It is always recommended that a seller seeking reclamation of its goods make a written reclamation demand. At least one court held that a seller may be subject to preference risk where the buyer returned goods pre-petition during the 90-day preference period in response to an oral reclamation demand.

Other requirements for reclamation depend on whether the bankruptcy case was filed prior to, or on and after, October 17, 2005, the effective date of the Bankruptcy Abuse Prevention and Consumer Protection Act of 2005. Section 546(c) contains different reclamation rules for bankruptcy cases filed before, or on and after, October 17, 2005. The version of Section 546(c) that governs bankruptcy cases filed prior to October 17, 2005 (Old Section 546(c)) requires that the seller makes a written reclamation demand within 10 (and sometimes 20) days after the buyer's receipt of the goods. The version of Section 546(c) that governs bankruptcy cases filed on or after October 17, 2005 (New Section 546(c)) expands the reclamation reachback period to 45 days. The UCC provision that eliminates the 10-day state law notice where the buyer makes a written misrepresentation of solvency to the seller does not apply when the buyer is the subject of a bankruptcy case.

There are other differences between Section 546(c) of the Bankruptcy Code and Section 2-702 of the UCC. Section 546(c) is limited to sales in the ordinary course of the seller's business. The UCC is silent on this point and may permit the exercise of reclamation rights with respect to goods that were the subject of a non-ordinary course sale, such as a bulk sale. As more fully discussed later, it is more difficult for the reclaiming seller to prove the buyer's insolvency in a bankruptcy case than under state law. Finally, under state law if the reclaiming seller proves all of the elements of a reclamation claim, the seller is entitled to return of the goods. As more fully discussed later, Old Section 546(c) establishes alternative remedies, instead of the buyer's return of goods, to the reclaiming seller. These remedies include an administrative claim in the amount of the allowed reclamation claim or a replacement lien that secures payment of any allowed reclamation claim. New Section 546(c) just provides a return of goods for a successful reclaiming seller.

RECLAMATION DEMAND

Section 546(c) of the Bankruptcy Code requires a written reclamation demand. Although there is no magic to drafting an adequate reclamation demand letter, the demand should follow the following guidelines:

(1) the letter should state that it is a demand for reclamation under applicable state law;

(2) the letter should identify the goods that are the subject of the reclamation claim and include a listing of the invoices making up the claim;

(3) the letter should demand an inventory of the reclamation goods on hand at the time of the demand and the buyer's segregation of the goods until arrangements could be made for their return; and

(4) the demand should be addressed to the correct company. While a demand addressed to a corporate buyer includes all of buyer's divisions, the demand does not include goods held by the buyer's subsidiaries or affiliates. The

reclaiming seller must send a separate written reclamation demand to each subsidiary or affiliate of the buyer that is obligated to pay for and/or received the goods.

A recommended form of reclamation demand where the buyer is the subject of a bankruptcy case can be found in Chapter 27.

TIMING REQUIREMENTS FOR A RECLAMATION DEMAND

Reclamation Demand Time Period—Old Section 546(c)

Section 546(c) of the Bankruptcy Code requires the reclaiming seller to make a written reclamation demand before 10 days after buyer's receipt of the goods. If this 10-day period expires after the commencement of the buyer's bankruptcy case, the reclaiming seller is entitled to an extra 10 days (or before 20 days after the buyer's receipt of the goods) to send its written reclamation demand. In other words, the reclaiming seller has a 20-day reclamation period for goods that the buyer received during the 10-day period prior to its bankruptcy filing. If the 10-day period expires prior to the commencement of the case, the additional 10-day grace period does not apply and the seller's reclamation claim is limited to goods that the buyer received within 10 days of the demand. There is not an absolute 20-day period for reclamation of goods in every case!

For example, let us assume that the reclaiming seller shipped goods that the buyer received on December 1 and December 3 and the buyer filed its bankruptcy petition on December 12. For the goods that the buyer received on December 1, the reclaiming seller must make its reclamation demand not later than December 11. Since the goods were received more than 10 days before the commencement of the buyer's bankruptcy case, the reclaiming seller cannot take advantage of the longer 20-day reclamation period. For the goods that the buyer received on December 3, which the buyer had received within 10 days of the commencement of its bankruptcy case, the reclaiming seller is entitled to a 20-day reclamation period, and must make its demand not later than December 23.

Reclamation Demand Time Period—New Section 546(c)

New Section 546(c) expands the reclamation reachback period from the 10-day, or sometimes 20-day, period under Old Section 546(c) to an expanded 45-day period. An unpaid seller can reclaim goods it had sold on credit to a buyer in the ordinary course of the seller's business that the buyer had received within 45 days of the buyer's bankruptcy filing. The seller's reclamation rights are contingent upon the seller sending a written reclamation demand, and complying with all of the other requirements that exist under Old Section 546(c), not later than 45 days after the buyer's receipt of such goods. The seller is also given up to 20 days after the bankruptcy filing to send its reclamation demand when the 45-day reclamation demand period expires after the bankruptcy filing (i.e., for goods received within 45 days of bankruptcy).

Computing the Reclamation Demand Time Period

In computing the time period for making a reclamation demand, the seller must consider three issues:

1. When did the buyer receive the goods?
2. What is the proper method for computing the time period for making the demand?
3. When is the reclamation demand deemed to be made?

WHAT CONSTITUTES RECEIPT OF THE GOODS

The time period for making a reclamation demand is measured from the date that the buyer received the goods. The Bankruptcy Code does not define the term "receipt." The UCC (§ 2-103(1)(c)) defines receipt of goods as "taking physical possession of them." The courts have generally held that the buyer received goods when the buyer or a third-party bailee of the buyer (but not a common carrier) takes physical possession of the goods. Neither passage of title or risk of loss to the buyer, nor the seller's FOB delivery of goods to a carrier has any bearing on when the buyer received the goods.

METHOD FOR COMPUTING RECLAMATION DEMAND TIME PERIOD

In calculating the time period for making a reclamation demand, the seller should begin counting forward starting on the day after the buyer received the goods. If the last day of the time period falls on a Saturday, Sunday, or holiday, the period in which the reclamation demand must be made may be extended until the next business day. This may expand the period for making a demand by an additional day or two or more.

WHEN IS THE RECLAMATION DEMAND MADE?

To compute the period for making a demand, the reclaiming seller must determine when it made the demand. Neither Section 2-702 of the UCC nor Section 546(c) of the Bankruptcy Code indicates when a reclamation demand is made. Most courts have adopted the "Dispatch Rule," in which the reclamation demand would be deemed made when the seller mails or otherwise dispatches the demand. This is contingent upon the seller's showing that the method of communicating the demand was "commercially reasonable." The courts could alternatively adopt a "Receipt Rule" where the reclamation demand is deemed made on the date the buyer received the demand. The courts adopting the "Dispatch Rule" may also hold that the reclaiming creditor could reclaim only goods on hand on the date the buyer received the demand.

Reclaiming sellers prefer the "Dispatch Rule" as establishing the earliest possible date for the reclamation demand and maximizing any potential reclamation claim. Buyers prefer the "Receipt Rule" as setting the latest possible date for the reclamation demand and minimizing any potential reclamation claim.

In view of the lack of statutory guidance on this issue and the possibility that a court could apply the "Receipt Rule," a reclaiming seller should send its reclamation demand by hand, facsimile, electronic mail, or other means to ensure that the buyer receives the demand on the day it was sent. A seller that mails its reclamation demand risks the erosion or loss of its reclamation claim if the court follows the "Receipt Rule." Regardless of the mode of dispatch that a reclaiming seller uses, the seller should obtain confirmation of the date and time of the buyer's receipt of the demand.

INSOLVENCY

Another condition that the reclaiming seller must satisfy is the buyer's insolvency when the buyer received the goods. The Bankruptcy Code adopts the balance sheet definition of insolvency. Under this test, the buyer is insolvent if its debts exceed the fair market value of its assets. The UCC defines insolvency as either based on the balance sheet test or an "equity" test. According to the equity test, the buyer is insolvent when it has ceased to pay its debts in the ordinary course of business or is unable to pay its debts as they become due. Which definition of insolvency, balance sheet, or equity, is applied, would be critical to the seller's ability to prove its right to reclaim its goods. The equity test for insolvency may be easier to satisfy than a balance sheet test. It is conceivable that the buyer could be insolvent under an equity test because it is not paying its debts in the ordinary course of its business or is unable to pay its debts as they mature and yet be solvent under a balance sheet definition.

Most courts have applied the balance sheet definition of insolvency where the buyer is the subject of a bankruptcy case. A few bankruptcy courts have adopted the more easily satisfied equity definition of solvency.

BUYER'S POSSESSION OF RECLAMATION GOODS AT THE TIME OF DEMAND

A seller seeking to reclaim goods has the burden of proving that the buyer was in possession of identifiable goods when the seller made its reclamation demand. If, at the time of the demand, the buyer was no longer in possession of the goods or the goods were no longer identifiable, the seller may lose its reclamation rights. For example, if the seller sells and delivers 1,000 red dresses to the buyer, makes a timely reclamation demand for return of these dresses, but before the demand, the buyer sold 500 of the dresses to its customers, the seller would be able to recover only 500 of the dresses. At least one court has gone as far as to hold that the goods also had to be on hand when the buyer filed bankruptcy.

Goods that the seller is seeking to reclaim, in addition to being in the buyer's possession, should also be identifiable when the demand is made. Goods that have been altered or processed, such as the conversion of raw materials into a final product, may no longer be subject to reclamation. Likewise, issues of identifiability have been raised where fungible goods (like oil) that the reclaiming seller sold to the buyer are mixed with similar goods supplied by third parties. Most courts have not required that the reclaiming seller identify fungible goods sold to the buyer. The seller must trace its goods into an identifiable mass and show that the mass contains goods of like kind and grade to the reclaiming seller's goods and that the mass is subject to the buyer's control. Some courts have also required a first in–first out approach in determining whether the seller's goods were on hand at the time of the demand.

Since the buyer must be in possession of the goods that are the subject of the seller's reclamation demand, the seller should send its demand as quickly as possible and make every effort for expedited delivery of the demand to ensure prompt receipt by the buyer. Every day the seller fails to make its demand, the buyer may sell, transfer, process, or otherwise alter or incorporate the goods into manufactured goods, thereby cutting off the seller's reclamation rights.

If possible, the reclaiming seller should also follow up its demand with an immediate visit to the buyer's premises and perform an inspection of the goods the seller is seeking to reclaim. At a minimum, the seller should obtain a written statement from the buyer indicating what goods were on hand at the time the buyer received the demand. Absent such information, the seller will be unable to prove the buyer's possession of the goods at the time of the demand, which is necessary to prove the seller's reclamation claim.

Although New Section 546(c) has created an increased 45-day reachback period for reclamation claims, it is likely that the reclaiming seller still has the burden of proving the goods subject to reclamation were in the debtor's possession at the time of the demand. The debtor's sale, consumption or processing of the goods prior to the demand presumably still wipes out reclamation rights, notwithstanding the longer 45-day reclamation time period.

PRIORITY OF DEBTOR'S SECURED CREDITOR
OVER RECLAIMING SELLER

Old Section 546(c)

The seller may lose its reclamation claim if all of the buyer's inventory is subject to a prior perfected security interest. That is because Section 2-702(3) of the UCC subjects the seller's right of reclamation to the rights of a good faith purchaser. Since a creditor with a perfected security interest in inventory is considered a good faith purchaser, virtually all reported court decisions hold that a secured creditor's interest in the buyer's inventory is superior to the seller's reclamation claim. Nevertheless, the seller may have some reclamation remedies that would not be defeated by an existing perfected security interest in the buyer's inventory.

A majority of the courts have denied the seller relief on its reclamation claim until the existing perfected inventory lienholder's claim has been either paid in full or released, or where the proceeds of reclamation goods are paid to the lienholder. These courts reason that under state law, a seller's reclamation rights have no value where there is an undersecured inventory lienholder. The seller should not be entitled to greater relief on its reclamation claim in bankruptcy when the seller would not be entitled to any reclamation relief under state law. Otherwise, the seller would fare better in bankruptcy than it would under state law.

A minority of courts dealing with Old Section 546(c) have denied reclamation of the seller's goods where there is an existing perfected inventory lien, but granted the seller an administration claim or replacement lien based upon the value of the goods. This relief has been granted without considering whether there is sufficient equity in the lienholder's collateral to pay the lienholder's claim. These courts reason that under UCC Section 2-702(3), a seller's reclamation rights are "subject to" and not extinguished by an existing perfected security interest in the buyer's inventory. Where the seller satisfies all the requirements of Bankruptcy Code Section 546(c), the seller should be entitled to reclamation of its goods. If the court refuses to approve reclamation of the goods due to an existing perfected inventory lien, the court must grant the seller alternative relief in the form of an administration claim or replacement lien.

A few older court decisions dealing with Old Section 546(c) have held that a perfected inventory lien extinguishes the reclaiming seller's right of reclamation. These courts deny the seller any relief, including an administration claim or a replacement lien. Since a lender or other creditor with a perfected inventory lien is a good faith purchaser under Section 2-702(3) of the UCC, the seller's reclamation claim is subject to the existing inventory lien. Since a reclaiming creditor cannot exercise its reclamation rights where there is an existing perfected inventory lien, the lien extinguishes all reclamation rights. The existence of a prior perfected inventory lien renders the reclamation claim valueless under state law and, therefore, equally valueless in bankruptcy.

A few courts have held that a seller's right of reclamation is superior to a prior perfected security interest in the goods. Since these decisions are rather dated, it is questionable whether they remain good law.

New Section 546(c)

Under New Section 546(c), a seller's reclamation rights are subject to the prior rights of a creditor with a security interest in the goods. This change ratifies the consensus view of the courts that have similarly held reclamation rights are subject to the prior rights of a secured creditor with a security interest in the debtor's inventory. Therefore, creditors seeking to enforce their expanded reclamation rights under New Section 546(c) must continue to deal with adverse court decisions under Old Section 546(c) that have effectively rendered reclamation rights valueless where the debtor has an outstanding floating inventory secured claim.

PROPERLY ENFORCING A RECLAMATION CLAIM

Unfortunately, more often than not, a reclaiming seller will send a timely reclamation demand and satisfy all of the other requirements for reclaiming its goods and then take a wait and see attitude. This could result in the loss of its reclamation claim. The seller could enforce its reclamation claim in state court by commencing suit for recovery of the reclamation goods. That lawsuit would be stayed by the buyer's bankruptcy filing and the Bankruptcy Code's Section 362 automatic stay. Following the commencement of the buyer's bankruptcy case the seller can enforce its reclamation claim by commencing a lawsuit for reclamation of the goods in the bankruptcy court. The seller could also move for injunctive relief compelling the buyer's production of records concerning the goods, granting the seller immediate access to inspect the goods and preventing the buyer from selling the goods. The seller's filing of a proof of claim on account of the reclamation claim may not be sufficient to recover on the claim.

Some courts require the reclaiming seller to initiate a reclamation lawsuit as soon as possible. These courts have denied the reclamation claim where the seller failed to act diligently to enforce its claim, in particular, where the goods were sold or an intervening lender was granted a security interest in the goods following the demand. Other courts have refused to penalize the reclaiming seller where the seller failed to diligently commence a lawsuit to enforce its reclamation claim.

A reclaiming seller's best course of action is to commence a reclamation lawsuit shortly after making its demand. This will force the buyer to immediately address the seller's reclamation claim and avoid the argument that the seller waived its reclamation claim by sitting on its rights. However, creditors with small reclamation claims may not wish to spend the legal fees that may be needed to prosecute a reclamation lawsuit. These creditors may forego filing a lawsuit and file a proof of administrative claim with the bankruptcy court. This may pass muster with those courts that follow the more relaxed approach of not requiring a creditor to diligently commence suit to enforce its reclamation claim. However, a seller that just files a proof of claim on account of its reclamation claim runs the risk that the bankruptcy court will deny the reclamation claim based upon the seller's failure to diligently commence a lawsuit to enforce the claim.

REMEDIES AVAILABLE TO SUCCESSFUL RECLAMATION CREDITOR

Old Section 546(c)

Where the seller has taken all of the necessary steps to enforce its reclamation claim, the bankruptcy court may direct the buyer to return the goods to the seller; direct the buyer to immediately pay for the goods; grant the seller a security interest in the buyer's assets to secure payment of the claim; or grant the seller an administrative claim.

Where the court grants the seller an administrative claim or a substitute secured claim or directs the buyer's immediate payment of the reclamation claim, the court must determine the amount of the claim. Many courts look to the invoice price of the goods. A few courts have relied upon the sales price that the buyer received from its resale of the goods in the ordinary course of its business or based on a commercially reasonable sale of the goods.

Where payment of an allowed reclamation claim is deferred, the seller could also argue that it is entitled to interest on its claim. Most courts that have addressed this issue have denied the reclaiming seller interest on its claim. Nevertheless, there is a minority view that has allowed interest on the claim.

New Section 546(c)

Where the seller takes all the necessary steps to enforce its reclamation claim, its sole remedy is the return of the goods under new Section 546(c). The alternative remedies available to a successful reclaiming seller under Old Section 546(c), a replacement lien in the debtor's assets and/or an allowed administrative priority claim in the amount of the reclamation claim, have been eliminated in New Section 546(c). It remains to be seen whether the actual return of the goods is the reclaiming seller's sole remedy. This might lead to more cases where the debtor is directed to pay for the goods. Or alternatively, since reclamation rights under New Section 546(c) are expressly subject to the rights of a secured inventory lender in the goods, the reclaiming seller may be left with no remedy.

GLOBAL RECLAMATION PROGRAMS

Sometimes debtors' and creditors' committees have agreed to global reclamation programs in Chapter 11 cases. These programs provide a far more expeditious and less expensive means of resolving reclamation claims than would occur following the prosecution of a reclamation litigation in the bankruptcy court. While there may be no one-size-fits-all program, many of the programs share similar reconciliation mechanisms that have made it much easier for reclaiming sellers to realize upon their reclamation claims.

Most global reclamation programs provide a mechanism for reconciling reclamation claims. The programs usually require the buyer to provide reclaiming sellers notice of the amount of the reclamation claim. The buyer and each reclaiming seller are then provided a fixed time period to exchange documentation and negotiate a settlement of the reclamation claim. In the absence of an agreement by the conclusion of the reconciliation period, the buyer or seller must file a motion for resolution of the reclamation claim with the bankruptcy court and the court then resolves the dispute.

Global reclamation programs have varied on the disposition of various defenses to reclamation claims. Some programs have waived the requirement that the reclaiming creditor prove insolvency and the buyer's possession of the goods even where litigation is necessary to resolve disputed reclamation claims. Other programs have waived these requirements and reclamation defenses only for resolved reclamation claims while preserving these requirements and defenses for litigated reclamation claims. Other programs preserved these requirements and all reclamation defenses for all purposes. The terms of these programs should be carefully reviewed as they might allow a debtor or secured lender to challenge reclamation claims even after the amount of the claim had been agreed to between the debtor and reclaiming creditor.

Global reclamation programs have also established a uniform treatment of allowed reclamation claims. Treatment has ranged from the partial or full cash payment of allowed reclamation claims to the allowance of the reclamation claim as an administrative priority claim and payment of this claim at the end of the case. Some programs provide alternative treatment for allowed reclamation claims depending upon the seller's willingness to extend credit to the buyer. Partial or full cash payments have been provided to those sellers that agree to extend credit either on the same terms they had offered the buyer during the year (or some other period) prior to the Chapter 11 or based on "mutually agreeable" credit terms, with the balance of the seller's allowed reclamation claim treated as an administrative claim. Those sellers that refuse to extend acceptable credit terms to the buyer but still wish to participate in the program were granted an administrative priority claim payable ahead of the claims of general unsecured creditors.

Reclamation creditors might be granted the right to forego the benefits of the buyer's reclamation program and independently pursue their reclamation remedies in the bankruptcy court. However, that is the exception rather than the rule. Most programs bar litigation until passage of the time period set by the program for reconciling reclamation claims.

NEW ADMINISTRATIVE CLAIM IN FAVOR OF SELLERS OF GOODS

New Section 546(c)(2) grants an unpaid seller of goods a safety net where the unpaid seller fails to satisfy the requirements for obtaining relief on its reclamation claim. The safety net is in the form of a newly created administrative priority claim under Section 503(b)(9) of the Bankruptcy Code.

Suppliers of goods (but not services) are granted an administrative expense claim for the value of all goods received by the buyer within 20 days of bankruptcy. This has the effect of elevating all or a portion of an unpaid goods supplier's claim from a low priority general unsecured claim to a higher priority administrative expense claim. An unpaid seller of goods seeking to obtain administrative priority status must also prove that the goods were sold to the buyer in the ordinary course of the buyer's business and must obtain bankruptcy court approval for allowance and payment of the administrative claim.

This new administrative claim affords unpaid sellers of goods valuable new leverage in bankruptcy cases. It amounts to a step up in priority for that portion of the trade creditor's claim for the value of goods received by the buyer within 20 days of bankruptcy. A trade creditor is also no longer subject to all of the requirements and limitations that make pursuing reclamation claims costly and risky. For instance, a trade creditor does not have to send a written reclamation demand or prove the buyer's insolvency or that the goods were in the buyer's possession and not otherwise sold, consumed or otherwise commingled with other like goods of the buyer. The reclaiming creditor is also not subject to loss of its reclamation rights where the buyer has an outstanding secured inventory loan claim. While a secured inventory creditor still retains priority over the newly created administrative claim in favor of suppliers of goods, suppliers will still be entitled to payment of their administrative claim if the buyer has sufficient available unencumbered assets to pay administrative expense claims.

Trade creditors must seek bankruptcy court approval for allowance and payment of this new administrative expense claim. An aggressive trade creditor can even challenge the buyer's financing arrangement with its secured lender that does not provide for payment of these administrative expense claims or for a carveout from the lender's collateral to secure payment of these claims.

The new administrative claim in favor of suppliers of goods is not risk-free and might engender litigation over the following questions:

(1) How does the unpaid seller determine the value of the goods subject to this new administrative claim? Presumably the seller will claim value based upon the invoice amount of the goods, but a debtor or trustee might argue a lesser value.

(2) What is the meaning of the term "receipt" for determining the amount of the administrative claim? Will the UCC definition of "receipt"—the buyer's taking actual physical possession of the goods—govern?

(3) How quickly must the creditor act to obtain allowance and payment of the administrative claim? Do creditors that sit on their rights risk losing this claim?

(4) When is an allowed administrative claim in favor of a supplier of goods entitled to payment? Sections 546(c)(2) and 503(b)(9) are silent on the timing of payment of the claim. Time will tell whether coordinated action by trade creditors will impact the timing of payment of the claim. Obviously, quicker payment lessens the risk of an unsuccessful Chapter 11 and an administratively insolvent estate and reduced payment on, or nonpayment of, the administrative claim.

(5) Will a goods supplier that could assert the new administrative claim be kept off an unsecured creditors' committee?

SELLER'S RIGHT TO STOP DELIVERY

Where the seller has not shipped goods purchased by a buyer and discovers that the buyer has filed a bankruptcy petition or is otherwise insolvent, the seller could stop delivery of the goods. Under Section 2-702(1) of the UCC, the seller could refuse delivery until the buyer pays for the goods and all outstanding invoices due under the same contract. This converts the seller's payment terms from credit to cash on or before delivery.

Where the seller's goods are being held by a carrier, warehouse, or other third-party bailee, and the buyer is insolvent or files a bankruptcy petition, the seller can also stop delivery of the goods and the seller's right of stoppage in transit is not affected by passage of title or risk of loss to the buyer. Under Sections 2-702(1), 2-703 and 2-705 of the UCC, a seller seeking to stop delivery of its goods must give notice to the carrier, warehouse, or other bailee. The seller should also give notice of the stoppage to the buyer. This notice should be in writing.

The seller's right of stoppage in transit is cut off by the occurrence of any of the following events:

(1) the buyer's receipt of the goods;
(2) the third-party bailee's acknowledgment that it is holding the goods for the buyer, and in the case of a carrier, such acknowledgment consists of either reshipping the goods according to the buyer's instructions or holding the goods as the buyer's warehouseman; or
(3) negotiation to the buyer of a negotiable document of title such as a bill of lading or warehouse receipt.

Section 546(c) of the Bankruptcy Code also preserves the seller's right to stop goods in transit (or stop delivery of goods in the seller's possession) after the commencement of the buyer's bankruptcy case to the same extent that it preserves the seller's right to reclaim goods previously delivered to the buyer. The seller's stoppage of goods in transit (or refusal to deliver goods in the seller's possession) also does not violate the automatic stay and does not give rise to an avoidable preference. The seller's stoppage of delivery rights may also have priority over the rights of the buyer's secured lender, a clear advantage over the seller's right of reclamation.

GROUNDS FOR RETURNING GOODS SHIPPED PRE-PETITION

Section 546(g)*, which is the operative law for cases filed prior to October 17, 2005, deals with the buyer's return of goods shipped pre-petition on credit terms. (Due to a drafting error, Section 546 contains two subsections designated as "(g)." To address this, the subsection dealing with return of goods was assigned the asterisk "*".) Section 546(g)* allows the buyer to return goods that a seller/creditor had shipped to the buyer on credit terms before the commencement of the bankruptcy case in exchange for an offset equal to the invoice price of the returned goods. The buyer's ability to obtain relief under Section 546(g)* for the return of goods that a seller had shipped prior to the commencement of the bankruptcy case is conditioned upon the satisfaction of all of the following conditions:

(1) the seller must consent to the return and to reduce its pre-petition claim by an amount equal to the invoice value of the returned goods;
(2) the buyer must move for bankruptcy court approval of the return of goods within 120 days of the commencement of the case; and
(3) the court must approve the buyer's return of goods after finding that the return is in the best interests of the bankruptcy estate.

The bankruptcy court in the *Federated Department Stores* Chapter 11 case considered the following factors in determining whether a return of goods is in the best interest of the buyer's bankruptcy estate:

1. Get rid of unsalable seasonable or perishable merchandise
2. Open up credit lines with vendors
3. Provide access to fresh merchandise
4. Free shelf space for more profitable lines
5. Maintain the up-to-date image of the company
6. Prevent stigmatizing the company as a discounter
7. Obviate the need to rent storage space
8. Prevent violation of restrictive debt covenants regarding volume of inventory
9. Allow maintenance of internal buying policies

A buyer that can offset the full invoice value of the returns against the seller's pre-petition claim may realize a greater recovery than the buyer would otherwise realize from a liquidation sale of the goods. In addition, in the publishing, print, and music industries, in which the finished product has a short shelf life, the return of goods in exchange for a full invoice credit is a normal part of industry practice. In a bankruptcy case a return of goods would enable the buyer to return old, damaged, or otherwise unsalable goods in exchange for a reduction of its pre-petition unsecured debt by the invoice value of the returns. The return also benefits each creditor/seller receiving the return. The seller/creditor obtains some immediate recovery on its unsecured claim without the delay usually associated with the completion of the bankruptcy case.

A return for full credit against the seller/creditor's pre-petition claim is particularly valuable where the finished product is sold with return rights to the original seller. The return takes the product out of the market and eliminates the risk that a subsequent purchaser of the goods could return the product to the original seller for full credit. This minimizes the risk that the buyer would conduct an auction or other distress sales of the goods at a substantial discount off the original invoice price of the goods to purchasers who would then return the product to the original seller for credit based on the original invoice price of the goods.

The operative return of goods provision for cases filed on or after October 17, 2005 is Section 546(h). New Section 546(h) is identical to Section 546(g)*, except that under New Section 546(h), returns of goods would be subject to the prior rights of the debtor's secured inventory creditor.

SECURED INVENTORY LENDER'S RESPONSE
TO RETURN PROGRAM

The buyer's lender with a blanket security interest in the buyer's inventory may be the most significant roadblock to the implementation of a return of goods program. Section 546(g)* is silent on whether the buyer could return goods to its vendors free and clear of an inventory lien. New Section 546(h) makes a debtor's return of goods subject to a prior inventory security interest. A court would not authorize the return of goods free and clear of an inventory lien unless the buyer's secured creditor consents or is protected. Vendors would certainly not participate in a return of goods program if the returns were subject to liens. Any return of goods program should, therefore, provide that returns are free and clear of liens and security interests.

It is likely that inventory lienholders will demand that any return of goods program include a provision for replacement inventory that would be subject to the lender's security interest. This would prevent the diminution of the lender's inventory collateral. The program could condition vendors' participation to their agreement to provide post-petition trade credit of an equivalent invoice amount to the invoice amount of the returns. Vendors extending such post-petition trade credit would have a claim entitled to treatment as a priority administrative claim payable ahead of the claims of general unsecured creditors. For example, an unsecured creditor with a $100,000 unsecured claim who wished to participate in such a goods return program could accept the return of its goods with an invoice value of up to $100,000 and reduce its pre-petition claim by the invoice amount of the returns to zero. In exchange, the creditor would be obligated to extend a post-petition line of credit to the debtor in an amount totaling at least up to $100,000 for which the creditor would be granted an administrative claim. This would permit the debtor to replace old inventory with new inventory which would satisfy the debtor's inventory lender. A creditor participating in the returns program would also benefit by converting a lower priority unsecured claim to a higher priority administrative claim and thereby increase the likelihood of payment of the creditor's claim without any increase in credit risk.

EXAMPLES OF RETURN OF GOODS PROGRAMS

Return of goods programs have been implemented in the Chapter 11 cases of distributors and retailers in the publishing and print industries. In the liquidating Chapter 11 case of *Golden Lee Book Distributors Inc.*, in the U.S. Bankruptcy Court for the Eastern District of New York, the creditors' committee successfully pushed for a return of books program. This program provided for the return of goods to publishers and other creditors in exchange for a reduction of their claims by the invoice value of the returns. There was no lender with a blanket inventory security interest to object to the program. The program also benefited a sufficient number of unsecured creditors that no disgruntled group of creditors objected to the program.

A more sophisticated return of goods program was developed in the liquidating Chapter 11 case of *Pacific Pipeline Inc.* in the U.S. Bankruptcy Court for the Western District of Washington. While there was a secured creditor with a security interest in all of the debtor's accounts and inventory, the lender's claim was paid from the debtor's accounts receivable collections. The lender, therefore, did not object to the return program. However, a group of unsecured creditors who could not participate in the program demanded that the program provide some benefit to non-participating creditors. The creditors' committee in *Pacific Pipeline* developed a return program that guaranteed nonparticipating creditors a cash recovery equivalent to the distribution those creditors would have received in the event the returns and all other inventory of Pacific Pipeline had been sold in one or more liquidation sales. These guaranteed that cash payments to nonparticipating creditors were funded by creditors participating in the program and obtaining return of their product. Each participating creditor agreed to accept returns of its product in exchange for a reduction of its pre-petition claim by the invoice value of the returns. Participating creditors were also required to pay a cash fee in an amount equal to 10 percent of the invoice price of the returns to that creditor. The cash was then escrowed and nonparticipating creditors were entitled to receive a priority cash distribution in an amount equal to the sum they would have received under a liquidating Chapter 11 plan following a liquidation sale of all the debtor's inventory. In an out of court liquidation by Moving Books, a small book distributor located in Seattle, Washington, the debtor successfully implemented a return of books program which provided identical treatment for participating and nonparticipating creditors as the returns program in *Pacific Pipeline*.

A return of goods program was also approved in the Chapter 11 case of *Lauriat's, Inc.*, a Chapter 11 case in the U.S. Bankruptcy Court for the District of Massachusetts. Lauriat's, an operator of bookstores in New England and the Mid-Atlantic states, had a secured lender with a blanket security interest in all the Lauriat's inventory. Lauriat's lender opposed any book return program that provided for return of goods to the debtor's creditors without the debtor obtaining replacement inventory as additional collateral for the lender. In order to accommodate the lender, Lauriat's book return program required participating creditors to extend a post-petition line of credit to Lauriat's. Participants accepted returns and reduced their pre-petition claims by approximately the invoice value of the returns. In exchange for the returns, participating creditors agreed to extend a post-petition line of credit to the debtor in the amount of at least the amount of the returns credited in reduction of their pre-petition claims. Participating creditors have been granted junior superpriority administrative claims for unpaid claims under their post-petition lines of credit which are payable after payment of the claims of Lauriat's secured creditors and payment of a portion of the allowed fees of Lauriat's and the creditors' committee's professionals. The participants' superpriority claims would be payable ahead of other Chapter 11 administrative creditors and all general unsecured and lower-level priority claims. Credit terms on such post-petition lines of credit have been fixed at net 30-day terms with an end of the month payment. The obligation of each participant to continue to extend credit to Lauriat's would terminate upon a payment default that is not timely cured, the declaration of a default under Lauriat's debtor in possession financing facility or the filing of a motion to either convert Lauriat's Chapter 11 case to a Chapter 7 or appoint a Chapter 11 trustee. This program enabled Lauriat's to return stale non-saleable inventory to its suppliers and obtain new readily saleable inventory on credit terms.

A return of goods program was adopted in the Chapter 11 liquidation of Jay Garment Corporation pending in the U.S. Bankruptcy Court for the Northern District of Indiana. Jay Garment was a manufacturer of jeans and other related apparel and a contractor for other apparel manufacturers. The creditors' committee had pushed for the adoption of a program involving the return of fabric and other raw materials provided by certain of the debtor's larger vendors. As a result of the program, unsecured claims were reduced by the invoice value of the returns, $800,000, to approximately $1.7 million. This reduced the pool of unsecured claims that would share in the cash proceeds of the debtor's assets and has enabled the debtor to nearly double the cash distribution to unsecured creditors to approximately 80 percent of claims. The far less attractive alternative was a nominal recovery from a fire sale of the debtor's raw material and fabric and no reduction of unsecured claims. This scenario would have yielded unsecured creditors a far smaller distribution on their claims.

A return of goods program was also part of a program approved in the Chapter 11 case of *Barry's Jewelers, Inc.*, in the U.S. Bankruptcy Court, Central District of California. Barry's operated approximately 130 specialty jewelry stores in 18 states. The program provided for the return of pre-petition merchandise shipped by participating vendors as a credit against their pre-petition claims. Barry's agreed to return merchandise delivered prior to the Chapter 11 filing with an invoice value equal to at least 75 percent of the participating vendor's pre-petition claim against Barry's.

The invoice value of the returned goods was applied in reduction of the vendor's pre-petition claim against Barry's.

In order to participate in the global program, each participating vendor executed a trade financing agreement. The vendor agreed that for at least one year, it would provide post-petition trade credit to Barry's on a minimum, very favorable 90-day terms in an amount equal to at least 2½ times the value of the pre-petition merchandise returned to the vendor. The minimum credit commitment would terminate on the earlier of one year or the occurrence of an event of default. In exchange for a participating vendor's extension of post-petition credit to Barry's, the vendor would share in a $2 million cash trade trust established under the program, enjoy the benefit of a $4 million subordination of the security interest of Barry's secured bondholders, and receive a super-priority administrative claim, payable ahead of all other administrative claims for all unpaid post-petition trade payables in excess of $6 million.

Return of goods programs have also been approved in the following Chapter 11 cases: *In re Alliance Entertainment Corp.* and *In re Caldor, Inc.* in the U.S. Bankruptcy Court, Southern District of New York; *In re Strawberries, Inc.*, *In re CM Holdings, Inc.*, *Camelot Music Inc.* and *In re Wherehouse Entertainment Inc.* in the U.S. Bankruptcy Court in Delaware; and *Sher Distributing Company* in the U.S. Bankruptcy Court, District of New Jersey.

16 Steps in the Collection Process

Collection of past-due accounts is an important function of a credit professional. This chapter seeks to advise the financial professional (CFO, Treasurer, Controller, Credit Manager) about the component elements of collection so that the professional can be aware of errors and omissions in the development and maintenance of systems and programs for collection of accounts.

This chapter is designed with the commercial account, rather than those involving consumer transactions, in mind. However, a number of the concepts contained in this discussion affect both commercial and consumer accounts. More importantly, the line between commercial and consumer is not always clear, such as when an individual guarantees a business debt. Therefore, purely consumer laws and regulations have not been excluded from this chapter.

The importance of collections and the methods used will vary according to the business in which they are used. In some lines of industry, the amounts uncollected after expiration of the "term" dates are but a small fraction of the total monthly accounts receivable. In other lines the "past due" items frequently represent the margin between profit and loss. Within this broad range, the liquidation of accounts is accomplished in three ways: (1) by correspondence, (2) by collection bureaus, or (3) by lawsuits. Special phases of these three methods will be discussed in the following pages.

The slogan used for a number of years by the National Association of Credit Management, "*Poor Information*, Not Poor Judgment, Is the Cause of Most Credit Losses," certainly has a direct bearing upon collection operations.

Credit is defined as one's "confidence or trustworthiness in a person or company to honor and repay debt." A business that sells its merchandise without regard to the creditworthiness of the purchaser would soon be in financial difficulty.

In these days of close competition and advanced business methods, businesses realize that only when accounts receivable are paid may profits be computed. To coin an old phrase, "It's not money in the bank until it's in your bank account." The credit and collection departments of a business should be regarded just as importantly as the sales and production departments. For any business that fails to collect its receivables will soon perish.

Part I: Pre-Litigation

COLLECTION METHODS

There is an increasing amount of government regulation, both federal and state, dealing with the collection of delinquent accounts, even those that are commercial in nature. Failure to comply with the legal requirements, can subject the creditor to substantial damages and penalties.

There is also a growing trend by consumer groups and others to recommend that debtors record all collection calls to create an accurate record of the alleged harassment calls by collectors. Note: one-party recordings of conversations maybe in violation of certain State laws. They are also "set-ups" whereby the debtor baits and lures the caller into an argument or to lose his or her temper and/or use profane or obscene language, not knowing they are being recorded.

Before placing an account in the hands of an attorney and taking the debtor to court, credit managers will (or should) exhaust all other courteous collection remedies at their disposal that do not require litigation: personal contact with the debtor by telephone, fax and e-mail communication; collection letters; and, perhaps, the intervention of a collection agency.

Although it is frequently said that any legal means may be used to collect a debt, courts and state legislatures are becoming more strict in their views as to what "means" may be employed. Many expedients which may appear to be of value in bringing an obstinate debtor into line may also subject the creditor to possible liability for extortion, libel or invasion of the right of privacy, or be deemed harassment or in violation of fair debt collection laws. In pursuing these various methods, therefore, discretion should be the watchword. Retention of a collection agency does not relieve the creditor of liability for wrongful acts of the agent in seeking to make the collection.

Extortion

The term extortion generally means "to gain by wrongful methods, to obtain in an unlawful manner, to compel payment by means of threats of injury to person, property or reputation." It is also "an attempt by threat to collect money which is not legally due, and may bring a criminal penalty as well as civil liability." Nevertheless, the attempt to collect money that is legally due by sending a collection letter calculated to harass the debtor and to coerce payment of the claim may be actionable. In *Barnett v. Collection Service Co.*, 214 Iowa 1303, 242 N.W. 25 (1932), a widow who was dunned for a coal bill amounting to about $28 by a series of letters, which included threats to expose her to her employer as a delinquent debtor, was allowed damages for the mental anguish she suffered.

While the threat to do what one has a legal right to do, such as to sue if a just debt is not paid, may not ordinarily result in liability, a threat of bankruptcy, criminal prosecution, or to render an unfavorable credit report to the members of a credit association, intended to coerce payment of the account may render one liable. In *Clark v. Associated Retail Credit Men*, 165 F.2d 62 (D.C. Cir. 1939), the debtor was allowed to recover for physical injuries resulting from mental stress that the court found had been intentionally inflicted by the creditor when it wrote to the debtor threatening suit and an unfavorable credit rating among the members of its credit association if the debt was not paid.

Don'ts for Collection Letters

By far the greatest risk which the creditor may run in pursuing various non-legal collection methods will be that of incurring liability for libel. The publication of matter which will tend to disgrace or degrade the debtor or to hold one up to public hatred, contempt or ridicule, or deprive one of public confidence and esteem, may bring one afoul of the law of libel.

Publication means the communication of the defamatory matter to some third person. If communicated solely to the person it concerns, it is not actionable. On the other hand, a letter, although addressed to the debtor, sent in such a way that it is likely to be opened and read by a third person may result in a publication. The sending of a fax or e-mail necessarily results in publication because the fax cannot be sent without the reading of the communication by some agent or employee of the recipient company. Likewise, e-mail is not deemed private if in the workplace an employer may read same. In general, matter that falsely imputes a criminal act or moral turpitude or tends to injure the person defamed in his business is regarded as libelous per se and no special showing of damages need be made in order to allow recovery.

Libel Per Se

The distinction between words which will give rise to an action for libel without any showing of special damage and those which are not actionable unless some specific injury is shown to have resulted depends largely upon whether or not they are such that a court may presume as a matter of law that they will tend to degrade or disgrace or hold one up to public hatred, contempt, or ridicule. To charge another with fraud or dishonesty is libelous per se. A written charge that one is guilty of falsehood, or implying want of veracity, is usually libelous per se.

In the cases involving publication of credit information in which recovery has been allowed to one not engaged in business without any showing of special damages, it has been on the theory that the publications involved necessarily imputed dishonesty and want of credit depriving the debtor of public confidence and esteem and holding him up to public hatred, contempt and ridicule. Statutes dealing with restrictions on the disclosure of credit information are treated differently by the courts than libel or defamation statutes. A cause of action for defamation or libel is complete upon publication; the victim need not show any damage to his reputation. On the other hand, credit information disclosure statutes require a showing that the debtor's reputation was in fact damaged.

While the truth of the matter published is ordinarily a complete defense to an action for libel, it should be borne in mind that while the words themselves may state no more than the truth, the manner of publication may impute insolvency, bankruptcy or want of credit so as to make the whole thereof libelous. It may be said that the resort to unusual collection methods necessarily implies that the debtor is not amenable to the ordinary means of collection and is therefore not worthy of credit. Among the various devices which have brought creditors afoul of the law of libel are the listing of the debtor's name in a list of delinquent accounts, placarding, envelopes and postcards addressed to the debtor on which there appear words or symbols indicating that the addressee is a delinquent debtor and advertising the debt for sale. When one is a member of an industry group affiliated with NACM, the appropriate interchange of delinquent account information is protected from any action for libel, assuming that the information provided is true and correct. Outside of the protected credit interchange, the publication of information concerning delinquent accounts is very dangerous.

If the publication of libel about a public figure appears in a newspaper, magazine or other medium of general circulation, there may be no liability on the part of the newspaper, absent malice, based on the constitutional protection of freedom of the press. *See New York Times v. Sullivan*, 376 U.S. 254 (1964).

The United States Supreme Court, however, held in *Greenmoss Builders, Inc. v. Dun & Bradstreet*, 105 S.Ct. 2939 (1985) that Dun & Bradstreet was liable for punitive damages as a result of issuing an erroneous credit report which stated that the subject of the report had filed bankruptcy. Under Vermont law, where the case arose, a jury can impose punitive damages absent proof of any malice on the part of the issuer of the false credit report. The qualified privilege which most states recognize, and which permits a bona fide error to be made in a credit report issued by a credit reporting agency, did not exist in Vermont. The argument that Dun & Bradstreet was denied its freedom of speech by imposition of punitive damages was rejected by the Supreme Court. The court held that the doctrine of *New York Times v. Sullivan* did not apply to issues of private concern, such as credit reporting, and applied only to issues of public concern.

Prohibited Collection Practices

Although a creditor has the right to demand payment from the debtor, it may not engage in conduct that is illegal or unlawful. Many states have adopted statutes that proscribe certain practices as illegal and improper. In addition, there are numerous judicial decisions based on common-law principles that condemn improper collection practices.

The Federal Communications Commission released a public notice (70-609) reminding creditors that it is a violation of the telephone company's tariff to use the telephone (including voice, fax and e-mail) to frighten, torment or harass another. Practices which come within the scope of this prohibition are:

1. Calls to debtors at odd hours of the day or night
2. Repeated calls
3. Calls making threats to friends, neighbors, relatives and children
4. Calls falsely asserting that credit ratings will be hurt
5. Calls stating that legal process is about to be served
6. Calls demanding payment for amounts not owed
7. Calls to place of employment
8. Calls after a debtor demands the calls stop
9. Calls after a claim cannot be verified or substantiated
10. Numerous faxes and e-mails, may also qualify

A creditor who is in this class may be subject to having his telephone service or Internet service disconnected or may be subject to fines or imprisonment in violation of state or federal statutes and civil damages.

Some of the practices condemned by state laws are:

1. Threats of violence or other criminal means to cause harm to the person, property or reputation of the debtor
2. False accusation of fraud
3. Threat to sell or assign the claim, resulting in a loss of any defense by the debtor
4. Threat of arrest
5. Use of profane or obscene language
6. Telephone calls that do not disclose the identity of the caller
7. Unreasonable publicity concerning the indebtedness

8. Use of any fraudulent, deceptive or misleading representations in seeking to collect claims such as, that the debt collector represents an official agency
9. Use of any unfair or unconscionable means to collect claims, including the collection from the consumer of all or any part of the debt collector's fee or charges

It is a crime under federal law, 18 USC § 712, in the collection of private debts or obligations to use or employ in any communication or correspondence the words national, federal or United States or the initials U.S. in a manner reasonably calculated to convey a false impression that such communication is from a department, agency or bureau or in any manner represents the United States.

Postal Laws

In addition to incurring liability for libel, the mailing of postal cards or letters upon the outside cover of which there appears matter tending to reflect upon the character of the addressee may violate the postal laws. In the United States Criminal Code, such matter is declared to be non-mailable and to deposit it or to cause it to be deposited for mailing or delivery may subject one to a fine of not more than $1,000 or imprisonment for not more than one year, or both, under 18 USC § 1718. The Postal Service has ruled that cards indicating that the addressee is being dunned for an account that is past due were non-mailable under this provision. It has been held that postal cards threatening suit or other legal action, such as garnishment and attachment, fall within the ban. Cards bearing respectful requests for the settlement of credit accounts or that give notice when an account will be due do not fall within this prohibition.

Privilege

While the foregoing cases and principles seem to condemn any publication of credit information which may be damaging to a debtor, the interchange of such information among creditors having mutual interests to protect has been deemed to be privileged and hence does not fall within the condemnation of the law. Many cases have established the rule that the good faith interchange of credit information among persons interested therein and seeking the information as a guide in the conduct of their own affairs is privileged and not actionable. However, this may change with the growing and evolving laws relative to privacy.

Invasion of the Right of Privacy

Although, as indicated above, the truth of the matter published, if not published in such a manner as to carry with it the imputation of dishonesty, insolvency or want of credit, may be a defense to an action for libel, the same is not true of an action based upon an *invasion of the right of privacy*, which may be broadly defined as the giving of publicity, selling information and sharing information as to the private affairs, such as:

1. Purchasing habits
2. Health data
3. Personal financial data
4. Personal data of individuals without their permission

The private financial data (debts and assets), personal and family purchase data and personal health data are among the growing areas to be protected. The right to be free from such undue publicity is a growing concern addressed by both state and federal legislatures.

The Right to Privacy must be distinguished from other types of litigation which might be brought under the same or similar facts, such as a suit for malicious prosecution; a suit for extortion, libel or slander; or a suit for false imprisonment.

Many of the cases which have considered the question have been influenced by such factors as whether the creditor was motivated by malice, whether the debt was due and truly owed and whether the action of the creditor involved a public disclosure of the indebtedness. However, the better view is that if a right to privacy exists, the motive of the party violating it is not of any consequence in establishing liability.

Section 652(A) of the Restatement of Torts proposes that a violation of the right to privacy has occurred when there is:

(a) unreasonable intrusion upon the seclusion of another;
(b) appropriation of the other's name or likeness;
(c) unreasonable publicity given to the other's private life; or
(d) publicity which unreasonably places the other in a false light before the public.

It should be noted that since the turn of the millennium, the new media of communications in cyberspace, i.e., the Internet and developing technologies are changing traditional definitions of privacy. Numerous laws regulating privacy are being introduced in state and federal legislatures on a regular basis and new laws and regulations are being adopted at a rapid pace.

It is generally recognized in debt collection cases that the mere threat, institution or prosecution of a legal action as a method of debt collection does not constitute an actionable invasion of privacy, at least in the absence of malice. Accordingly, a creditor has the right to pursue his debtor in a lawful manner and persuade him to make payment. However, the manner in which the threat of legal action to collect the debt is used, may subject some collectors to fines and penalties in violations of law, at least where such threat or use of legal process is not attended by undue harassment, malice or other oppressive circumstances. Such acts may under certain conditions violate the FTC Guide Against Debt Collection Deceptions or a local law regulating debt collection practices. Notwithstanding, a creditor may always resort to the courts to enforce his rights.

In *Rugg v. McCarty*, 173 Colo. 70, 476 P.2d 753 (1973), a creditor repeatedly harassed a sick debtor with numerous telephone calls and threats of garnishment proceedings against her, notwithstanding the fact that the creditor did not have a judgment against the debtor. In addition, the creditor sent a letter to her employer inquiring how many garnishments would be tolerated. Based on these facts the court found that there was a violation of the debtor's right to privacy and gave judgment against the creditor. The court stated:

When unreasonable action in pursuing a debtor is taken, which foreseeably will probably result in extreme mental anguish, embarrassment, humiliation or mental suffering and injury to a person possessed of ordinary sensibilities, under the same or similar circumstances, then such conduct falls within the forbidden area and a claim for invasion of privacy may be asserted.

Gramm-Leach-Bliley Act

The Gramm-Leach-Bliley Act ("GLB") has been one of the most misunderstood and confusing laws for businesses. Since its enactment in 1999, many businesses have complied with its demands without knowing why. For a large number of businesses, compliance has seemed easier than trying to understand whether they are supposed to comply with GLB in the first place.

The GLB contains important provisions designed to protect the privacy of sensitive personal information about individuals. Protection is primarily provided through required notices that indicate what and how information is shared with others, along with the chance to "opt out" of such sharing.

Even though its apparent intent was focused upon consumer transactions with banks, insurance companies and securities firms, the reach of GLB is actually quite broad. This is because of the definition of "financial institution," taken from a 1956 law called the Bank Holding Company Act, which looks at the activities in which a business engages. If, for example, the activities of a particular business involved brokering or servicing loans, leasing or appraising real or personal property, check guarantee, collection agency, credit bureau and real estate settlement services, courier services for banking instruments, the business is a "financial institution" for purposes of GLB. Note that the examples given are far from exhaustive of the activities that define financial institution.

Information protected by GLB includes information (1) a consumer provides to you to obtain a financial product or service; (2) about a consumer resulting from any transaction involving a financial product or service; or (3) you otherwise obtain about a consumer in connection with providing a financial product or service to that consumer. Examples would include information on credit or other applications, account balances or purchase information. Information that indicates the person is or has been your customer is also protected, as are lists, descriptions or other groupings concerning consumers and derived from protected information that the business itself creates and shares.

Unfortunately, the regulations are not very helpful in identifying who a "nonaffiliated third party" would be. Suffice it to say, however, that if the person with whom a financial institution plans to share information is not an employee or someone jointly employed by the financial institution and an entity that is clearly its affiliate, then the sharing of information is probably with a "nonaffiliated third party."

GLB applies only to transactions with consumers, that is, individuals who obtain a financial product or service that is to be used primarily for personal, family or household purposes. Caution is required, however, because there could be a consumer transaction hidden in what appears to be completely commercial, such as when you require a personal guarantee on a loan.

The type of notice required by GLB depends on whether a consumer becomes your customer, meaning there is a continuing relationship between the consumer and the financial institution.

If a customer relationship has been established, the financial institution must give the customer notice of its policies on privacy and information sharing not later than the time that the customer relationship is established and annually thereafter. The customer must also be advised of the opportunity to "opt out," that is, to tell the financial institution not to share the information. The notice itself must describe:

- the categories of nonpublic personal information the financial institution collects and discloses;

- the categories of affiliates and nonaffiliated third parties with which information is shared;
- the categories of nonpublic personal information about former customers that are disclosed and the parties, affiliated and nonaffiliated, to which disclosures are made;
- an explanation of the consumer's right to opt out of the disclosures made, including the method(s) by which the opt out right may be exercised; and
- the financial institution's policies and practices with respect to protecting the confidentiality and security of nonpublic personal information.

The notice must also indicate that the financial institution makes other disclosures as required (e.g., by court order) or permitted (e.g., reporting information to a credit bureau) by law.

The description of the "opt out" right must clearly and conspicuously: (1) state that the financial institution discloses nonpublic personal information to nonaffiliated third parties, or reserves the right to do so; (2) inform the consumer of the right to opt out; and (3) provide a reasonable opportunity by which that right may be exercised.

Even if the consumer transaction has not resulted in a customer relationship, compliance with GLB is nevertheless required. The difference concerns the timing and content of the required notice. The notice must be provided to the consumer prior to disclosure by the financial institution of nonpublic personal information. A "short form" notice is permitted, which is less specific than the notice required for customers, but it must clearly and conspicuously state that the financial institution's privacy notice is available on request and provide an explanation of the reasonable means by which the consumer may obtain the notice.

Private Debt Collectors

The American Jobs Creation Act, H.R. 4520 was signed into law in October 2004. The Act permits the use of private debt collection professionals ("private professionals") by the Internal Revenue Service to contact taxpayers for the collection of outstanding taxes. These private professionals also have the authority to offer installment payment plans to taxpayers. However, a limitation of a five-year repayment plan is imposed. The financial information of the taxpayer is provided to the private professional. The private professionals are regulated in the same manner as employees of the Internal Revenue Service. Specifically, the private professionals are prohibited from having contracts with taxpayers, providing quality assurance services, and composing debt collection notices. The United States is not liable for any act or omission of any private professional while collecting.

PROMPT PAY LEGISLATION FOR SOME TRANSACTIONS WITH THE GOVERNMENT

Federal Prompt Payment Act

The federal law, Public Law 97-177, was enacted on May 21, 1982. It requires all federal agencies to pay for goods or services by the date specified in the contract or, in the absence of a contract date, 30-days after receipt of a proper invoice or delivery of goods or completion of services, whichever is later. Meat or meat food products are to be paid for within seven days and perishable agricultural commodities within 10 days.

Federal agencies are required to notify vendors within seven days if the vendor's invoice is incorrect or if, for any reason, payment cannot be made within the 30-day period.

Interest must be paid if a check is not issued according to the following schedule: for meat or meat food products, on the third day after the seven-day payment period; for perishable agricultural commodities, on the fifth day after the 10-day period; and for any other item, on the 15th day after the 30-day payment period.

The interest rate is determined in January and July by the Secretary of the Treasury under Section 12 of the Contract Disputes Act of 1978 (41 USC 611), therefore, changing every six months. The obligation to pay interest begins on the 31st day.

In 1988, the Federal Prompt Payment Act was amended. The following is a summary of the major provisions of the amendment:

- Federal agencies are limited to seven days for acceptance of goods or services
- Federal agencies must review all invoices promptly, but not later than seven days after receipt
- A definition of a receipt of invoice is provided
- Grace periods are eliminated
- Interest penalties are to be paid without request or invoice
- Failure by a federal agency to pay an interest penalty within 10 days subjects an agency to an additional penalty
- Late payment of an interest penalty must be explained in an accompanying notice that states the amount of the penalty, the rate of interest, and the period for which such interest is computed
- Specified time for taking offered discounts is defined
- Partial payment for partial delivery is to be required by regulations to be issued unless prohibited by contract
- The United States Postal Service is subject to the Prompt Payment Act
- Ensures payments of interest on progress payments made after the 14-day period required by the statute
- Contractors with federal agencies are required to include in contracts with their subcontractors clauses requiring the prime contractor to pay subcontractor within seven days or pay a penalty
- Benefits of prompt pay are extended to subcontractors in federal construction projects
- Prompt Pay Act is extended to farmers
- Federal government is required to pay for dairy and other products within 10 days
- Unavailability of funds does not excuse an agency from obligation to pay promptly
- Office of Small and Disadvantaged Business in each agency is given the authority to assist small and disadvantaged businesses in getting bills paid promptly

In 1999, the Federal Prompt Payment Act was again amended. The revisions focused primarily on increasing the use of electronic commerce and conforming to the Debt Collection Improvement Act of 1996.

Beginning January 2, 1999, the Debt Collection Improvement Act required the majority of Federal payments, with the exception of tax refunds, to be made by electronic funds transfers. Therefore, the Federal Prompt Payment Act was amended to require vendors to include (i) electronic funds transfer information and (ii) Taxpayer Identification Numbers as part of a proper invoice.

If the vendor does not include the electronic funds transfer information and a Taxpayer Identification Number on its invoice, late interest penalties do not apply. There are exceptions. For example, if an agency requires the submission of electronic funds transfer information prior to awarding a contract, then the requirement of it appearing on the invoice is waived. There are also waivers that apply in certain limited circumstances, like a hardship waiver for sole proprietors.

Changes were also made in interest calculation. The Renegotiation Board Rate, established for interest payments under the Contract Dispute Act of 1978, is now used to calculate interest payments under the Federal Prompt Payment Act. The interest is still computed from the day after the payment is due through the payment date. However, if the payment and interest remain unpaid after a 30-day period, the interest is added to the principal. New interest accrues monthly on the principal and unpaid interest. The rate is based upon private commercial rates for new loans maturing in approximately five years. It is still adjusted every six months and is announced on or about the first of January and July each year. More information on the calculation of interest can be obtained at http://www.fms.treas.gov/prompt/ppinterest.html.

The amended Federal Prompt Payment Act authorizes accelerated payments for invoices under $2,500, payments to small businesses, and payments related to military deployments, emergencies and disasters. It also provides guidance to Federal agencies on when to make credit card payments. A spreadsheet to calculate when an agency should make a credit card payment can be obtained at http://www.fms.treas.gov/prompt/formulas.html.

More information regarding the Federal Prompt Payment Act can be found at http://www.fms.treas.gov/prompt/.

State Prompt Pay Statutes

Many states have enacted statutes similar to the Federal Prompt Pay Act, requiring state agencies to pay bills on time.

On page 16–13 is a chart of those states that have enacted such legislation and a summary of the salient features of such legislation.

In addition to the state prompt pay statutes listed on the chart dealing with government debts and obligations, several states have created prompt pay statutes for private construction. This is a very effective alternative to mechanics' lien situations, and may be the forerunner of nationwide legislation on state-by-state basis, hopefully in a uniform manner. The prompt pay legislation of those states with respect to private construction are summarized as follows:

Arizona—A prime contractor is required to pay a subcontractor within 14 days of receipt of each progress payment, unless the parties have otherwise agreed to in writing. Contractors will be assessed a late penalty of 1 percent of the amount due per month, or a higher rate as agreed by the contractor and the subcontractor in writing. This requires the subcontractor to pay close attention to the contract itself to make sure that the applicable provisions are not waived.

A subcontractor is required to pay its subcontractors and suppliers within 14 days of receipt of payment from the prime contractor. If payment is delayed, the subcontractor will be obligated to pay its subcontractors interest at the rate of 1 percent per month, or a higher rate as agreed to in the subcontract. In this situation, the third-tier and lower subcontractors cannot waive the late payment, but can be required to take a lower interest rate if agreed in the contract.

California—A prime contractor is required to pay a subcontractor within 10 days of receipt of each progress payment, unless otherwise agreed to in writing. In the event that there is a good faith dispute over any portion of the amount due, the amount withheld may not exceed 150 percent of the disputed amount. Contractors will be assessed a late penalty of 2 percent of the amount due per month until payment is made. If there is court action concerning an amount wrongfully withheld, the prevailing party will be entitled to attorneys' fees and costs.

Connecticut—Note: An agreement between sub and sub-sub did not give rise to contractual relationship with surety under Little Miller Act. *Connecticut Elec. Equipment Co., Inc. v. United States Fidelity and Guar. Co.*, 2002 WL 653312 Conn. Super. (2002).

Georgia—When a contractor has performed in accordance with the provisions of a contract, the owner shall pay the contractor within 15 days of receipt by the owner or the owner's representative of any payment requested based upon work completed or service provided under the contract.

When all conditions precedent to payment have been satisfied by a subcontractor, the contractor shall pay to the subcontractor and each subcontractor shall pay to its subcontractors within 10 days of receipt of each periodic or final payment, provided, however, that the subcontractor has provided reasonable assurance of continued performance, including, but not limited to a payment in performance bond.

Interest begins accruing at the rate of 1 percent per month after nonpayment beginning on the 16th day for the contractor and on the 11th day for subcontractors.

A payroll company does not qualify under the Little Miller Act because providing administrative services is not considered providing labor. *Gulf Ins. Co. v. GFA Group, Inc.*, 251 GA App 539 (Ga. App. Div. 2001).

Kansas—A construction owner must pay contractor within 30 days of receiving proper invoice for undisputed, completed work. A contractor must pay subcontractors within seven business days of being paid by owner. The subcontractor has seven days from payment by contractor to pay material suppliers. Contractors and subcontractors have the right to suspend performance when undisputed payments are more than 14 days late. Contractor must give to owner, and subcontractor to contractor, at least seven days' written notice to before such suspension. Contractor or subcontractor may take claim to court in the county where real property is located. Owners may be charged 18 percent per annum for construction bills 31 or more days past due.

Louisiana—When a contractor receives payment from the owner for work completed, it is required to pay its subcontractors promptly. If the contractor fails to pay its subcontractors within 14 days of receipt of payment from the owner, the contractor must pay an interest penalty of 0.5 percent of the amount due *per day* beginning on the 15th day after payment was due. The total penalty may not exceed 15 percent of the outstanding balance due. The contractor is liable for reasonable attorneys' fees that the subcontractor incurs while trying to collect payment. These payment provisions apply to all tiers of subcontractors.

Maryland—If the contract does not provide for a specific date of payment, the owner is then required to pay the contractor by the earlier of 30 days after the date on which the occupancy permit is granted, or 30 days after the owner takes possession of the project. If the contract does provide for a specific date of payment, the owner must pay the contractor within seven days of this date.

Subcontractors must be paid by the contractor within seven days of payment by the owner. The payment provision of the statute applies to all tiers of subcontractors. If a contractor or subcontractor is not paid promptly, the court may grant whatever relief it deems necessary and appropriate under the circumstances, including issuing an injunction to prevent future violations of the statute. The court may also award the prevailing party prejudgment interest on the amount due and owning. The court may also award attorneys' fees to the prevailing party if the court decides that payment was withheld in bad faith.

New Mexico—Even though the Contract between General Contractor and leasing contractor was invalid, the leasing contractor is still protected by Little Miller Act. *Eastland Financial Services v. Mendoza*, 43 P.3d 375 (N.M.App. 2002).

New York—Now need only one notice for entire contract and not one notice per late invoice. *Specialty Products & Insulation Co. v. St. Paul Fire & Marine Ins. Co.*, 731 N.Y.S.2d 284 (N.Y.A.D. 3 Dept. 2001).

Nevada—The owner must pay its contractor within 30 days after acceptance of completed work by the owner. Unless otherwise provided in the construction contract, any amount that remains unpaid after the 30-day time period will accrue interest at a rate equal to the lowest daily prime rate at the three largest United States banking institutions on the date the contract is executed plus 2 percent. The contractor is required to make payments to its subcontractors including any interest within 15 days after it receives payment from the owner.

North Carolina—The contractor is required to pay its subcontractors within seven days of receipt by the contractor of each periodic or final payment. If the contractor makes a late payment, the contractor will pay to the subcontractor an interest penalty of 1 percent per month. These payment provisions apply to all tiers of subcontractors.

Ohio—If the subcontractor or materialmen request payment in time to allow the general contractor to include in its pay request to the owner, the general contractor is required to pay the subcontractor within 10 days after receiving payment from the owner. If the general contractor fails to comply, it shall have to pay 18 percent interest beginning on the 11th day after receipt of payment from the owner.

Pennsylvania—When a subcontractor has performed in accordance with the provisions of the contract, a contractor shall pay to the subcontractor and each subcontractor shall in turn pay its subcontractors the full or proportional amount received for each such subcontractor's work and materials, based upon work completed or service provided under the subcontract 14 days after the receipt of each progress or final payment or 14 days after receipt of the subcontractor's invoice, whichever is later. Payment shall be made unless it is being withheld for good faith claims. In the case of such good faith claims, the contractor or subcontractor must notify the subcontractor or supplier and the owner of the reason for the good faith claim within seven calendar days of the date after receipt of notice of the deficiency item. (PA ST 8 PS § 194).

South Carolina—A private owner must pay the general contractor within 21 days of a proper invoice. The contractor is then required to pay its subcontractors within seven days of receipt of payment by the owner. This payment provision applies to all tiers of subcontractors. If a payment is paid late, it must include an interest penalty of 1 percent a month. No interest is due unless the person being charged interest has been notified of the requirements of the interest penalty on late payments. It is therefore absolutely imperative that suppliers and subcontractors be aware of this provision, and so notify the general contractor.

The owner must pay the contractor no later than the 45th day after receiving a proper written payment request for properly performed work or suitably stored materials. A contractor who receives prompt payment from the owner must pay each of its subcontractors for properly performed work or suitably stored materials, including interest, if any, no later than the seventh day after the day that the contractor receives the owner's payment. The subcontractors must in turn pay the sub-subcontractors in the same manner within seven days of receiving payment from the contractor.

Any unpaid amount begins to accrue interest on the day after the date on which the payment becomes due at the rate of 1.5 percent each month. The interest stops accruing on the earlier of the dates on which the payment is delivered, the payment is mailed (if payment is mailed and delivery occurs within three days) or the date court judgment is entered. If a good faith dispute exists, no more than 110 percent of the difference between the obligee claims is due and the amount the obligor claims due may be held. A person may bring an action to enforce the person's right to prompt payment, and the court may award costs and reasonable attorneys' fees as the court determines is equitable or just.

2000 Amendment extends right to sue to persons furnishing rental equipment and give remote claimants a right of action. (SC ST § 57-5-1660)

Virginia—Note: Amendments pending (c.556, c.643, c.682) VA ST § 2.2-4337.

Washington—Supplier of temporary personnel to subcontractor is not a proper claimant under Little Miller Act. *Better Financial Solutions, Inc. v. Transtech Electric, Inc.*, 2002 WL 1746752 (Wash. App. Div. 1, 2002).

(Continued on p. 16–19)

PROMPT PAY STATUTES*

Note: State legislatures will, on occasion, modify an area of law without clear delineation as to its content and context. As a result, even the changes which have been enacted prior to placement in the state's Code may be difficult to locate. As a result, the Editors urge all users of the *Manual* to use this publication only as a guide, and consult the latest codified version of the state's law for all recent changes.

State	Limitations	Interest	Time Limits	Coverage for Subcontractors	Other Remarks
Alabama		Legal amount set by state	30 days		
Alaska	Construction contracts	1.5% per month 10.5% per year	30 days		The law restricts the taking of early payment discounts to payments made within specified discount period.
Arizona		10.0% per year	30 days	All public contracts	
Arkansas	Construction contracts	8.0% per year	Architects—5 working days. State Agency, Board, Commission, or Institution—5 working days. State Building Service—2 days. Department of Finance—5 days.		
California 1982 statute 1983 statute	Small business Nonprofit public benefit corporations	0.25% per day 0.25% per day	30 days		
1986 statute		1% above rate accrued June 30 of prior by pooled money investment account—not to exceed 15% per year.			

PROMPT PAY STATUTES *(Continued)*

State	Limitations	Interest	Time Limits	Coverage for Subcontractors	Other Remarks
1987 statute		1% above rate accrued June 30 of prior by pooled money investment account—not to exceed 15% per year.			
Colorado		1.0% per month	45 days		
Connecticut		1.0% per month	45 days	All public contracts	
Delaware		Not to exceed 12.0% per year	30 days		
District of Columbia		Minimum of 1.0% per month	30 days		
Florida		1.0% per month	30 days	All public contracts	
Georgia[1]		None	30 days		
Hawaii 1988 statute		12%	45 days		
1983 statute	Subcontractor	None	10 days		
Idaho		10% per month	45 days		
Illinois 1984 statute	Local governments	2.0% per month	60 days		and then 60 days to pay.
1985 statute		1.0% per month	60 days		
Indiana 1988 statute	Highway contracts	1% per month	35 days		
1983 statute	Road or street contracts	12.0% per month	180 days		

State	Rate	Days	Type	Notes
Iowa	1.0% per month	60 days	All public contracts	
Kansas	1.5% per month	30 days		
Kentucky	1.0% per month	30 days		
Louisiana	.05% per day	90 days	Construction contracts	
Maine	Current rate charged by a business concern.	25 days		
Maryland	12.0% per year	30 days		Interest to be assessed after 45 days
Massachusetts	Rate set semi-annually by Commissioner of Administration on January 1 or July 1 of each year. Legal discount rate charged by Federal Reserve Bank of Boston.	45 days		
1988 statute	Construction	Progress payments within 15 days (124 days for Commonwealth).		
Michigan 1984 statute	0.75% per month	15 days after public agency has received funds to make progress payment.		
Minnesota 1984 statute	1.0% per month	30 days		
1985 statute	1.5% per month	30 days		
Mississippi	1.5% per month	30 days	Construction contracts	45 days for agencies; authorized to pay checks.

PROMPT PAY STATUTES *(Continued)*

State	Limitations	Interest	Time Limits	Coverage for Subcontractors	Other Remarks
Missouri		3 percentage points above prime	45 days		Interest retroactive to 30 days.
Montana		0.05% per day	30 days		
Nebraska		14.0% per year	45 days		
Nevada	Construction contracts	Rate equal to that quoted by 3 financial institutions paid on 90-day certificate of deposit.	Within reasonable time	Construction contracts (except public works and residential building).	Not more than 90% may be paid until at least 50% work completed.
New Hampshire		No statute			
New Jersey		Rate specified by State Treasurer. 11.0%	25 days		35 days to submit invoice, 25 days to pay.
New Mexico 1989 statute		1.5% per month	60 days	Yes, under separate statute	
1987 statute	Applies to work contracts		21 days	None	
New York		Corporate tax rate	30 days		Public authorities not required to pay interest less than $100. Contractor who fails to pay subcontractor within 15 calendar days is liable for interest at rate in effect on date of payment.

State		Interest Rate	Period	Applicability	Notes
North Carolina	Construction contracts	1.0% per month	45 days	Construction contracts	Does not apply to Dept. of Transportation.
North Dakota		1.75% per month	45 days	All public contracts	
Ohio		Rate set by the Tax Commissioner.	45 days		
Oklahoma		Annual interest rate set by the State Treasurer based on the average of the interest rate for 30 day time deposits of state funds during the last calendar quarter of last preceding fiscal year.	45 days		Interest begins to accrue the 31st day.
Oregon		8.0% per year	45 days		
Pennsylvania		Interest rate computed by the Secretary of Revenue based on interest payments on overdue taxes or the refund of taxes.	30 days	Construction contracts exceeding $50,000.	Interest begins to accrue the 31st day.
Rhode Island		Prime rate	30 days	Limited to materialmen	
South Carolina		15.0% per year	30 days		
South Dakota		1.5% per month	30 days	All public contracts	
Tennessee		1.5% per month	30 days	All public contracts	
Texas		1.0% per month	30 days	All public contracts	Vendors are required to pay subcontractors and subcontractors' suppliers within 10 days.

PROMPT PAY STATUTES (Continued)

State	Limitations	Interest	Time Limits	Coverage for Subcontractors	Other Remarks
Utah		15.5% per year	60 days	All public contracts	Vendors are required to pay subcontractors and subcontractors' suppliers within 30 days.
Vermont		No statute[2]			
Virginia 1984 statute		Same as discounted 90-day U.S. Treasury bill rate	30 days	Yes	Local governments must pay within 45 days.
1985 statute		Prime rate.	30 days		
Washington		1.0% per month	30 days		
West Virginia		6.0% per year	90 days		150 days for Department of Highways.
Wisconsin		Rate charged by state for delinquent taxes.	45 days		After 2-year period 45-day period is reduced to 30 days.
Wyoming		1.5% per month	45 days		

* The editors thank the Coalition for Prompt Pay which prepared the report on which this chart is based.

[1] By Executive Order

[2] Vermont has prompt pay statute that applies to private owners of real estate and contractors which requires payment within 20 days after billing.

(Continued from p. 16–12)

DEBT POOLING PLANS

Debt pooling is where efforts are made to work with a financially distressed business debtor to try to fully or partially satisfy all of the claims on an equal basis. Various states have very strict laws as to what may or may not be done with respect to debt pooling, even though it may be in the best interests of all parties.

Credit grantors, sometimes with the assistance of a third party, may with the best of intentions intend to create an environment to assist a troubled business debtor in satisfying its debts. Unfortunately, most creditors are unaware of various state laws that create civil and criminal penalties for this practice unless carried on in the manner prescribed by that state's laws. Before attempting any debt pooling or consolidation plan for a debtor, one must review applicable state law to make sure that the best of intentions do not turn into a disaster.

Often when a debtor is delinquent in the payment of an account because of financial difficulties, there will be numerous other creditors also pressing their respective claims. In order to minimize the harassment by his creditors, the debtor may pay in full or make partial payments to those who press the hardest, as the exigencies of the situation seem to demand. In other cases a more practical solution will be found in making pro rata payments to all the creditors at periodic intervals. This may be done in accordance with an agreement among creditors and the debtor and through the utilization of the services of an attorney or a trade association.

To an individual burdened with debt who is just one step ahead of the bill collector and threatened with repossession of his automobile and other personal property purchased on the installment plan, or the threat of litigation to recover other obligations, there is now available the services of various companies which offer to relieve his burdens by budgeting his income and satisfying his creditors. These services are operated under various names and offer "common law workouts," "debt adjustment," "prorating," "debt lumping," "budget planning," or "debt pooling." Regardless of the name, the usual procedure is to advise the debtor with respect to budgeting his income, making provision for the periodic payment to the agency of amounts that are then distributed to the various creditors after deduction of the agency's servicing charges. In principle, such debt adjustment appears to be unobjectionable and provides a valuable service to both the debtor and creditors.

Evils and abuses have arisen, however, including excessive charges for services, failure to make payments to creditors, and the offering of unauthorized legal advice. In numerous cases, the action of unscrupulous agencies has been to increase rather than diminish the burdens and obligations of the debtor. As a result, legislation has been enacted in a number of states outlawing such debt adjustment practices.

Most states have previously enacted legislation on the subject, some of those have been repealed and it is likely that similar legislation may be in doubt as to passage in the near future by other states. Historically, the statutes have approached the problem in three ways:

1. Engaging in the business of debt adjustment as defined in the statute is prohibited and fines and/or imprisonment are imposed for violation of the statute
2. Debt adjustment as defined by the statute is held to constitute the practice of law, and unauthorized persons engaging in such activities are subject to the penalties provided for unlawful practice

3. Provision is made for the licensing of persons conducting a debt adjustment service and statutory restrictions govern the methods of operation

However, there appears to be a rise in the number of businesses assisting debtors in negotiation, compromise and arrangement of payment plans, where the debtor makes the payments directly to the cooperating creditors or their agents. Many advertise these "workout" services on radio, television and the Internet. These new businesses have yet to be challenged.

Debt Pooling and Trade Association Practices

While the debt adjustment legislation serves a useful purpose in curbing the abuses previously noted, it has caused serious concern among trade associations and credit managers. They are fearful that loosely drawn legislation may unintentionally restrict or prohibit procedures that have been legitimately utilized for years in protecting creditors and assisting debtors in temporary financial difficulties. It has been found advantageous to both creditor and debtor in many instances, in order to avoid the expense and consequences of bankruptcy or other insolvency proceedings, to enter into voluntary agreements for the composition or extension of payment of debts. Historically, under such arrangements the services of an individual or of a board of trade or adjustment bureau may be utilized as a trustee, as a creditors' committee secretary, or as an agency to perform the necessary services in connection with the payment and distribution to creditors. Appropriate compensation was part of the cost for such services.

It has not generally been the intention of legislators to interfere with such legitimate business practices that ostensibly appear to be closely related to the debt pooling services previously described. In practice, many new independent companies are performing substantially the same service nationwide, without much regulation.

The adjustment bureau or trade association acts for the creditor group and is compensated for the services it renders in such capacity, as distinguished from being compensated by the debtor for the solving of his financial problems and staying off his creditors, together with the furnishing of incidental legal services. **Note:** the new debt adjusters are paid by the debtor to compromise debt and formulate a payment schedule.

Historically, it was not the intention of legislators to prohibit or restrict the legitimate activities of trade and credit associations, but was intended to limit their methods of operations, so they did not inadvertently transgress the letter of the law. The credit professional should also note that future legislation does not seem likely and may loosen current restrictions, in an effort to assist in the adjustment of debt.

Since a trade or credit association acts as the agent of one or more principals in attempting to adjust or pool debts, each of the creditors will be held responsible for actions taken by the trade or credit association on their behalf, whether specifically authorized or not. It is, therefore, very important that creditors deal only with recognized trade or credit groups, such as NACM affiliates, or recognized and bonded mercantile collection or adjustment companies and agencies.

The following extracts from the various statutes will indicate that extreme caution must be used in drawing agreements and in the practices of trade associations, which are to be compensated for services rendered in debt adjustments between debtor and creditors. It is important to note that even where it is not specifically stated, attorneys, banks, judicial officers and nonprofit organizations are exempted from the statutory restriction or licensing requirements. Also, many states permit collection agencies to so operate, frequently requiring a license or permit.

Alabama—No person as a service or for a fee shall engage in business of selling, issuing or otherwise dispersing checks or receiving money as agent for obligors for purpose of paying such obligors' bills, accounts, etc., without first obtaining a license and otherwise complying with statute. License fee is $250 and bond is required in a minimum amount of $5,000 for individual and $10,000 for corporation with $50,000 maximum. Violation of the statute is a misdemeanor punishable by a fine of $100-$500 or up to 12 months' imprisonment or both. Code of AL, §§ 8-7-3, 8-7-7, 8-7-9 and 8-7-15.

Alaska—There is no statute prohibiting debt pooling nor any statute regulating the practice.

Arizona—No person may engage in the business of a debt management company without the license required. Annual license fee is $500 first year and $500 thereafter. Statute provides specific procedures and regulations with which licensee must comply. ARS, §§ 6-703, 6-702 and 6-126.

Arkansas—Debt adjusting is a misdemeanor punishable by fine of not less than $500 or more than $1,000 or by imprisonment of not more than one year or both. Debt adjusting is the practice of acting for a consideration as an intermediary between a debtor and his creditors for the purpose of settling, compounding or otherwise altering the terms of payment of any debt or contracting to collect a certain amount of money from the debtor periodically and distribute among the debtor's creditors. Attorneys, banks, employers and nonprofit organizations are not debt adjusters even if they perform these services. ASA, §§ 5-63-301 through 5-63-305.

California—No person shall engage in the business, for compensation, of receiving money as agent of an obligor for the purpose of paying bills, invoices or accounts of such obligor, or acting as a prorater, without first obtaining a license. Merchant-owned credit associations and others are exempted. Limits are placed on the charges that may be received by a prorater commencing with 12 percent on the first $5,000. Other limitations are placed upon the practices and procedures of those engaged in such prorating. Detailed provisions are also made with respect to the form of contract between a prorater and a debtor. A semiannual accounting to the debtor is required. CA FC, §§ 12100 and 12200.

Colorado—No individual or corporation shall engage in the business of debt management without a license, except attorneys, banks, judicial officers and others who do so in the regular course of their businesses and professions. Debt management is the planning and management of the financial affairs of a debtor for a fee and receiving money for distribution to creditors. Violation of the statute is a misdemeanor punishable by a fine of no more than $1,000 or imprisonment up to six months or both. CRS, §§ 12-20-103 and 12-20-112.

Connecticut—Debt adjustment is receiving, for a fee, money for the purpose of distributing it among the creditors of the debtor. Engaging in debt adjustment without a license is punishable by a fine of not more than $1,000 or imprisonment for not more than one year or both for each violation. Each day on which a person engages in debt adjustment without a license is a separate violation. CT GS, § 36a-655.

Delaware—Debt adjusting is a Class B misdemeanor. Debt adjusting is making any contract with a debtor whereby the debtor pays a certain amount of money periodically to the person engaged in the debt adjusting business who for a consideration distributes the same among creditors. 11 DE Code, § 910.

Florida—The practice of "budget planning" is prohibited except as practiced by an attorney admitted to the state bar. Violation of the statute is a misdemeanor. FL Statutes, §§ 59.10 through 559.13.

Georgia—It is a misdemeanor to engage in the debt adjustment business except in the case of attorneys. Debt adjustment is defined as "providing services to debtors in the management of their debts and contracting with a debtor for a fee to: (1) effect the adjustment, compromise or discharge of any account, note or other indebtedness, of the debtor; or (2) receive from the debtor and disburse to his creditors any money or other thing of value." OCGA, §§ 18-5-1 and 18-5-4.

Hawaii—Debt adjusting is engaging for a profit in a business by acting as an intermediary between a debtor and his creditors for the purpose of settling, compromising or in any way altering the terms of payments of any debts and distributing property or making payment to creditors of the debtor. Debt adjusting is a misdemeanor punishable by a fine of not more than $500 or imprisonment of not more than six months, or both. HRS, §§ 446-1 and 446-2.

Idaho—The statute does not prohibit debt adjustment or similar practices. It does require the licensing of collection agencies and bureaus and persons engaging in the business of receiving money from debtors for application to, or prorating of, any creditor or creditors of such debtor, for compensation or otherwise. Licensee shall pay an initial examination fee of $20, post a $5,000 bond, and pay an annual permit fee of $50.

Operation of a collection agency without a permit, failure to keep separate trust accounts for creditors' funds, and failure to keep the records required constitute a felony, punishable by up to $5,000 fine or five years' confinement, or both. Equitable relief is available in addition to fine or punishment. ID Code, §§ 26-2223, 26-2232, 26-2238 and 26-2239.

Illinois—The statute does not prohibit debt adjustment or similar practices. It does require the licensing of collection agencies and bureaus and control procedures for debt adjustment. Licensee shall post a bond up to $7,500 running to the state of Illinois for the use of the state and of anyone who may have a cause of action against licensee. Violation of the statute is a Class B misdemeanor and is punishable by a fine of up to $500 or up to six months in jail, or both. Any contract of financial planning made by an unlicensed person shall be null and void and of no legal effect. Unlicensed practice of debt adjustment is a public nuisance and may be enjoined by the state in addition to the above penalties. Detailed provisions are also made with respect to the form of contract required, fees and charges and remittance of funds to the creditor.

Illinois also has a statute permitting nonprofit corporations to be organized for the purpose of giving credit advice and accepting wage assignments for the payment of creditors for individuals earning less than $10,000 per year. 225 ILCAS 425/2.02 through 2.09.

Indiana—Statute does not prohibit debt adjustment practices.

Iowa—Debt management is the planning in management of the affairs of a debtor for the purpose of distributing the same to his creditors. Debt managers must obtain licenses and post a bond in the amount of $10,000, which can be raised to $25,000. Engaging in debt management without a license is a misdemeanor. Remittance of funds must be made within 45 days after initial receipt of funds and within 30 days thereafter. Licensee may not act as a collection agent for the same account without disclosure to both debtor and creditor or collect fees from both debtor and creditor. IA Code, § 533A.

Kansas—Prior law prohibiting debt adjusting has been repealed. KSA, § 21-4402.

Kentucky—Debt adjusting is a misdemeanor punishable by a fine of $500 or imprisonment up to 60 days, or both. The court has the power to enjoin debt adjusting activities and appoint a receiver. Those exempt from the statute include creditors of the debtor or any person acting without compensation for services rendered in adjusting debts. KRS, §§ 380.010, 380.020, 380.030 and 380.990.

Louisiana—Prior law prohibiting debt adjusting has been repealed.

Maine—Prior law prohibiting budget planning has been repealed.

Maryland—Debt adjusting is prohibited. Violation of the statute is a misdemeanor punishable by a fine of up to $500 or up to six months in jail, or both. Among those exempt from the statute are certified public accountants, bona fide trade associations in the course of arranging adjustment of debts with business establishments and nonprofit organizations provided no fee or charge is imposed. Annotated Code, Article 27, § 79A.

Massachusetts—Debt adjusting practices by those not authorized to practice law in the state is a misdemeanor and is punishable by a fine of up to $500 or imprisonment up to six months, or both. Nonprofit credit counseling service corporations are exempt. MA AL, Chapter 221, § 46d.

Michigan—The statute requires licensing of persons engaged in debt management. The statute contains detailed provisions concerning company records and other activities of the licensees. A surety bond in the amount of $5,000 must be furnished with the application for a license. Violation of the statute is a felony punishable by a fine of up to $5,000 or imprisonment up to two years, or both. MSA, § 23.630.

Minnesota—The statute does not prohibit debt adjustment or similar practices. It does require the licensing of collection agencies and bureaus and control procedures for debt adjustment. The licensee is required to actively seek the consent of all creditors to the plan of distribution set forth in the contract with the debtor. A contract made by an unlicensed person renders the contract null and void and the debtor can recover all fees paid including reasonable attorneys' fees. In addition to revocation/suspension of license, violation of the statute is punishable by a fine of up to $10,000. Annual license fee is $100 and minimum bond of $5,000 is required. Other detailed provisions are made with respect to contract form, accounting and prohibited acts. MN Statutes, §§ 332.31 through 332.37.

Mississippi—Debt adjustment is prohibited except by the following: lawyers, banks, title insurers, judicial officers, nonprofit religious or charitable organizations in connection with counseling services, certified public accountants, employers for employees, and bona fide trade or mercantile associations in the course of arrangements of debts with business establishments. Debt adjusting is contracting for a fee to provide services of budget management, debt pooling or debt management. Violation of the statute is punishable by a penalty of up to $500 or up to six months in jail, or both. MCA, §§ 85-9-1, 85-9-3 and 85-9-5.

Missouri—The practice of debt adjusting is prohibited and violation constitutes a misdemeanor. The Circuit Court has the power to enjoin such activity and appoint a receiver. Among those exempt from the statute are creditors or agents of the creditors of the debtor whose services in adjusting the debtor's debts are rendered without cost to the debtor, employer of the debtor, and one who arranges for or makes a loan to the debtor, and who, with the debtor's authority, acts as adjuster of the debtor's debts in the disbursements of the proceeds of the loan without compensation for such adjusting services rendered. RS MO, §§ 425.020, 425.030 and 425.040.

Montana—Substantially same as Mississippi. Exemptions same as Missouri's. MCA, §§ 31-3-202 and 31-3-203.

Nebraska—Debt management is the planning in management of the affairs of a debtor for the purpose of distributing the same to his creditors. A debtor is defined as a wage earner. Remittances to creditor must be made within 15 days after receipt of any funds, seven days if received in cash. In no case may licensee retain funds for greater than 35 days. RRS NE, §§ 69-1201 through 69-1215.

Nevada—The statute requires licensing of persons engaged in debt management. Annual license fee is $100 to $200 and bond of $10,000 is required. Remittance must be made to creditors within 10 days of receipt of funds. Detailed provisions are also made with respect to schedule of fees, contract form, prohibited practices and other guidelines which must be complied with. Engaging in the business of debt adjusting without a license is a misdemeanor. NRSA, §§ 676.040 through 676.130.

New Hampshire—Under the law a debt adjuster must be licensed and must post a bond of $10,000 or greater depending on the discretion of the Commissioner of Banks. Provisions are also made with respect to separate accounts, record keeping, budget analysis and prohibited acts. Violation of the statute is a misdemeanor for an individual and a felony for corporations. RSA, § 399-D.

New Jersey—Prior statute prohibiting debt adjusting has been repealed.

New Mexico—Statute is substantially the same as Missouri's. NMSA, § 56-2.

New York—Budget planning is a misdemeanor punishable by a $500 fine and imprisonment for not more than six months. Budget planning is defined as "the making of a contract with a particular debtor whereby the debtor agrees to pay a sum of money periodically to the person engaged in the budget planning, who shall distribute the same among certain specified creditors in accordance with a plan agreed upon, and the debtor further agrees to pay such person any valuable consideration for such services or any other services rendered in connection therewith." Attorneys, however, are permitted to engage in this practice. NYCLS Gen. Bus., §§ 455 through 457.

North Carolina—The statute prohibits the practice of debt adjusting or the attempt thereof and violation constitutes a misdemeanor punishable in the discretion of the court but in any case no more than $500 or six months' imprisonment, or both. The Solicitor may bring an action in the Superior Court to enjoin any person from acting or attempting to act as a debt adjuster. The exceptions are similar to those in the statute. NCGS, §§ 14.423 through 14.426.

North Dakota—Debt adjustment is prohibited except as practiced by those exempted. NDCC, §§ 13-06-01 through 13-06-03.

Ohio—Statute is substantially the same as Georgia's. Violation is a misdemeanor, unless party licensed under local law, punishable by a fine between $50 and $1,000 and between 30 days and six months in jail, or both. ORCA, §§ 4710.01 through 4710.99.

Oklahoma—Debt pooling is defined as making a contract with a particular debtor whereby the debtor agrees to pay a sum or sums of money periodically to the person engaged in the debt pooling who shall distribute the same among certain specified creditors in accordance with a plan agreed upon, and the debtor further agrees to pay such person any valuable consideration for such services or for any other services rendered in connection therewith. Penalty for engaging in the debt adjustment business is a fine of $100-$500, or imprisonment up to 30 days, or both. 24 OK St., §§ 16 through 18.

Oregon—The statute requires licensing of persons before engaging in the business of debt consolidation. Such persons must pay an annual license fee and post a $10,000 bond. Penalty of $100 fine or 30 days in prison for practicing without a license. Other violations are punishable by $500 fine or six months' imprisonment or both for individual and $1,000 for corporation in addition to individual penalties. Other provisions govern maximum fees, records, and audits of the company. ORS, §§ 697.005, 697.042, 697.087 and 697.095.

Pennsylvania—Prior law prohibiting practice of debt pooling has been repealed.

Rhode Island—The practice of debt pooling is prohibited. This restriction does not apply to attorneys. Penalty is $200 for each offense. RIGS, §§ 5-66-1 through 5-66-5.

South Carolina—Statute is substantially the same as Virginia's. SCCA, § 40-5-370.

South Dakota—The furnishing of advice to a debtor in connection with debt pooling where the debtor deposits funds for the purpose of distributing them among creditors shall be deemed a practice of law. Any person who violates this shall be guilty of a misdemeanor. SDCL, § 22-47.

Tennessee—Debt adjusting is prohibited. A violation of the law is punishable by a fine of up to $1,000 or imprisonment for up to 11 months and 29 days, or both. Attorneys, banks, title insurers and abstract companies doing escrow businesses, judicial officers, nonprofit organizations rendering services for not over $10 per month per debtor, and employers for their employees are exempt. TCA, § 39-14-142.

Texas—Statute provides that contract whereby a debtor deposits, periodically or otherwise, a specified sum of money with any person, firm, corporation or association for distribution among creditors, for which the debtor pays a valuable consideration, is debt pooling and is void, and persons engaging in the business of debt pooling are guilty of a misdemeanor. Attorneys are exempt. Statute provides for the establishment of nonprofit debt counseling services under the "Consumer Debt Counseling and Education Act." TFC, §§ 394.101 through 394.104.

Utah—Prior law requiring licensing of debt managers has been repealed.

Vermont—Statute is similar to Iowa. A violation of the statute is punishable by a fine of up to $500 and up to two years in prison.

Virginia—Statute provides that "the furnishing of advice or services for compensation to a debtor in connection with a debt pooling plan, pursuant to which the debtor deposits funds for the purpose of distributing them among his creditors, shall be deemed to be the practice of law" and is punishable as a misdemeanor. Statute does not apply to attorneys licensed to practice in state. VCA, § 54.1-3905.

Washington—Debt adjusting is the managing, counseling, settling, adjusting, prorating or liquidating the indebtedness of a debtor or receiving funds for the purpose of distributing said funds among creditors. Debt adjustors must obtain licenses and post a bond in the amount of $10,000, which may be raised in the discretion of the director of the Department of Licensing. A violation of the Debt Adjustment Law is a misdemeanor. Disbursement must be made to creditors within five days upon demand of debtor and no later than 30 days within receipt of funds. Fees charged may not exceed 15 percent of total debt. Other provisions are made with respect to contract form, duties to be performed, investigations, accounting and prohibited practices. Violation of the statute constitutes an unfair or deceptive act or practice in the conduct of trade or commerce. RCW, §§ 18.28.010 through 18.28.220.

West Virginia—It is unlawful to solicit debt pooling and unlawful to charge (as a service charge or otherwise) greater than 2 percent of the money deposited. This percentage restriction does not apply to attorneys. Penalty for violation of the statute is a fine of between $100 and $250 or from 30 to 60 days in jail. WVC, § 61.10.23.

Wisconsin—Statute requires licensing of "adjustment service companies" who are in the business of prorating the income of a debtor to his creditor(s), or of assuming the obligations of any debtor by purchasing the accounts he may have with general creditors, in return for which the principal receives a service charge or other consideration. Annual license fees are $200 plus a $200 investigative fee depending on the population of the city in which the business is located and licensee is required to post bond up to $5,000. Violation of the statute is punishable by fine of no more than $500 or up to 90 days in jail or both. WI Stat., § 218.03.

Wyoming—Statute is substantially the same as Georgia's. Misdemeanor punishable by a fine up to $100 and up to six months in jail or both. WY Stat., §§ 33-14-101 through 33-14-103.

Part II: Litigation

COLLECTION BY SUIT

It should be remembered that an attorney hired for the collection of an overdue account is the agent of the creditor, even if the attorney is initially engaged by a collection agency. Thus, should the attorney act in a manner inconsistent with appropriate legal standards, Fair Debt Collection Practices (state or federal), ethical standards, or contract, the creditor may be liable as the principal for the attorney acting as its agent. Always make sure that an attorney engaged to represent you has provided the appropriate references so you can be certain that problems will not arise if the attorney attempts to act in an improper manner.

When an account is placed in the hands of an attorney for collection, with instructions to commence suit, he should be furnished, electronically or in hard copies in triplicate, the following: credit application, any contracts, purchase orders, confirmations, correspondences (especially noting disputes or promises to pay), copy of the debtor's checks (bank information), invoices, statements of account, ledger cards, proofs of delivery, terms of sale, nature of merchandise or services rendered and the amount to be collected.

Two of the most important and often ignored elements of information are: (i) debtor's full name and (ii) its business nature. In the absence of credit applications and/or purchase orders, the name on the account may often be different than the actual name of the debtor. For example, "R&J Painting and Decorating Co., Inc.," may be recorded by the credit grantor as "R&J Painting," or "Integrated Strategic Technologies Company, Ltd.," may be recorded by the credit grantor as "Integrated Strategies" or "is.com." Unless the collection attorney conducts a due diligence investigation, such as an inquiry with the secretary of state's office, or other search, which takes time and may incur costs, the wrong party or worse, the wrong name may be used in a suit, that may ultimately render a subsequent judgment useless and uncollectible, as debtor's assets may be held in its proper name, such as bank accounts, real estate or vehicles' titles, while the judgment is in a different name.

The debtor's business nature, that is, whether it is a proprietorship, partnership, corporation, limited liability partnership or corporation, may be overlooked. This information is vital for the proper designation of a named party to a suit. Often a name of a division or trade name is mistakenly used instead of the proper name of the debtor, for example, your local McDonald's may in fact be "123 Main Corporation trading as McDonald's."

Upon receipt of these papers, the attorney will be in a position to commence the action by naming the proper party in the complaint and causing service of process upon the correct debtor by a summons or such other process as may be required by the law of the state in which the action is to be commenced, together with a statement of the account or such other papers as may be required by law.

After service of process, the debtor is allowed by the laws of all states a certain time period in which to answer or respond to the allegations of the complaint, and the answer may assert defenses to plaintiff's claim, including a denial of the allegations of the complaint or any special defenses such as the expiration of the statute of limitations. In addition, the debtor may claim an offset or may counterclaim, which is an independent or new cause of action by the defendant against the plaintiff. This new action by the defendant may constitute a defense and may necessitate the filing of a reply by the plaintiff, or under the laws of some jurisdictions may be deemed to be denied without the necessity of any further pleading by the plaintiff.

Security for Costs

It is customary, when a claim is placed in the hands of an attorney for suit, for the attorney to request a payment or deposit for costs and expenses, or security for costs. In most states, at the time of commencement of suit it is necessary for the attorney to incur certain expenses or pay into court various fees. Although the nature of these charges and the amounts thereof vary in different states and in the different courts in the several states, the following are some of the items for which advance payment may be requested: service of process, filing fees, premiums on court bonds, posting security for costs (particularly where plaintiff is a nonresident), trial fees, jury fees and charges for taxation of costs and entry of judgment.

If an action is placed in the hands of an attorney for suit, his request for security for costs or advance for disbursements should be promptly complied with, not only to facilitate prompt proceedings against the debtor, but also because in many states it is improper for the attorney to advance fees or expenses of litigation for his client.

Collection Fees

To avoid any problem, it is advisable for a creditor to establish the rates that may be charged by an attorney in a collection matter at the time the matter is referred. Each attorney and creditor must make their own arrangements. In addition to the attorney's fee, there is usually a suit fee, which is what the court charges for the commencement of litigation.

Need for Full Information

When the pleadings by all parties have been filed with the court and served upon each other, then the issues raised through the allegations of both the plaintiff's Complaint, (the first party to start suit) and the defendant's Answer to the Complaint, (the party defending) constitute the total of all legal and factual matters to be determined by the judge or jury.

Each party is entitled to conduct discovery, i.e., each can obtain information to prosecute or defend a suit by serving the other party with a variety of discovery demands. Discovery demands include Interrogatories (a series of written questions to be answered under oath), Requests for Admissions (a series of written fact questions to be admitted or denied), Requests for Production of Documents (a demand for the production of a particular documents), and Requests for Depositions (a demand for the production of a particular person to appear in person and give sworn testimony to oral questions). While the various methods of discovery may vary slightly among the jurisdictions, they are authorized by the rules for the state or federal court where the case was brought. All discovery has a common purpose, i.e., to permit each party the opportunity to examine under oath the strengths and weaknesses of the other party's case, which will narrow the issues to be determined at trial or encourage the parties to reach an amicable settlement.

Prudent credit professionals keep in mind the necessity of gathering together all of the information needed either by their collection bureau or by the attorney who is instructed to file suit, so that time will not be wasted in writing back and forth to obtain complete data.

A credit grantor should maintain and retain a record of all communications and transactions it has with its customers in the ordinary course of business.

It would be a wise plan to begin to collect such data after the account reaches the delinquency stage. Thus, there will be no delay in presenting the support documentation to the attorney, once the decision is reached to force collections by a suit. It is important to send the collection bureau or attorney all information, including a record of conversations with the debtor, about the account that would have any bearing on a case in court, such as, statements that the goods or services were acceptable or that his business is experiencing "cash flow" problems. Collection attorneys frequently are faced with a Counterclaim, (a cross suit by the defendant for damages), when they go to court to try a collection case. The credit professional may be in for an unpleasant surprise if his company has neglected to maintain detailed records of all transactions with the debtor in the ordinary course of business or has failed to forward completed records to the attorney.

Another important benefit of having all of the documents delivered to the attorney is that after an Answer is filed, the attorney may file a motion for summary judgment. Under this motion, an affidavit of the creditor is submitted along with the documentation, and the motion states that there is no genuine dispute as to any matter of fact, and the creditor is entitled to a judgment as a matter of law based upon the documentation and the facts stated in the affidavit. This requires the debtor to come forward with specific allegations of fact that deny that the obligation is due. The mere denial of the indebtedness will not be sufficient in most states to defeat a motion for summary judgment. If sufficient facts are not stated in opposition to the motion, the creditor will be given a summary judgment at that point. If facts are stated which are sufficient to defeat the motion for summary judgment, it permits the creditor to identify the areas of dispute in order to be prepared for the trial.

Of course, obtaining a judgment does not automatically put the funds in the creditor's bank account. Information about the debtor's assets including bank accounts will be needed to turn the judgment into cash.

Lost Documents in Suits

The loss or destruction of an original document on which a claim is based, or which is necessary for proof of the claim, is not necessarily fatal to the successful prosecution of the suit.

The original document is, of course, the best evidence, and no substitute for the original document will be accepted if the document itself can be produced. But if it can be proved that the original document has been lost or destroyed, secondary evidence of the contents of the document is admissible.

Such secondary evidence may be a copy of the missing paper or, if no copy exists, the contents of the instrument may be proved by the oral testimony of witnesses who are familiar with its terms and provisions.

The general rule is that a copy of the missing document must be used if obtainable, and only on proof that neither the original document nor a copy is accessible may oral testimony be admitted. Failure to produce the original document must in all cases be satisfactorily explained. With the advent of sophisticated copying equipment and document storage and retrieval mechanisms, electronic data basis, courts have become more liberal in admitting photocopies or microfilm copies of documents, and electronic data so long as there is a witness available who will testify that the copy is a complete and correct duplicate of the original, with the original having been kept in the ordinary course of business.

Confession of Judgment

Confessions of judgment (or cognovits) are provisions in a note, guarantee or other agreement that permit the holder to have a judgment automatically entered upon the other party's default. Confessions of judgment are allowed only in certain states, and in order to receive the benefits, strict compliance with the laws is required.

A practice in some jurisdictions is to obtain a confession of judgment from the debtor upon the sale of merchandise or loan of money. The confession is a security device which assures creditors of an easy means of entering a judgment without the necessity of going to trial. Since a confession of judgment can usually be entered without any notice of suit to the debtor, this practice has become subject to criticism as violative of constitutional rights of due process (notice and opportunity to be heard).

If a confession of judgment is used as a security device in consumer transactions, the creditor should be certain that the execution of the confession meets the requirements of the Truth in Lending Act, which requires adequate disclosure to the debtor of the meaning of the document.

Under recent Federal Trade Commission rules, use of a confession of judgment is deemed an unfair consumer practice.

The following is a brief summary of the laws of the various states on the question.

STATE LAWS ON CONFESSIONS OF JUDGMENT

Alabama—Invalid before suit. § 8-9-11.

Alaska—Authorized. § 09.30.050 and .060.

Arizona—Only after maturity of note. § 44-143.

Arkansas—Court appearance needed. §§ 16-65-301 to 304.

California—1979 Amendment to handle U.S. Const. Amend. 14 concerns. Subsection (b) added—Attorney for debtor must file certificate with confession of judgment. CCP § 1132 and 1133.

Colorado—Void in consumer transactions. § 5-2-415.

Connecticut—Void in installment contracts. § 36A-775.

Delaware—Authorized with warrant of attorney. 10 § 2306.

District of Columbia—Void in consumer transactions. § 28-3804.

Florida—Void. § 55.05.

Georgia—OK only after action is commenced. § 9-12-18.

Hawaii—Invalid in a credit sale contract. § 476-15.

Idaho—Void in consumer transactions. § 28-43-305.

Illinois—Void in consumer transactions. 735 ILCS 5/2-1301.

Indiana—Void in consumer transactions and before suit. § 24-4.5-2-415.

Iowa—Void in consumer transactions before default. Most have verified statement in commercial transactions. § 537.3306.

Kansas—Void in consumer transactions. § 16a-3-306.

Kentucky—Void. § 288.580.

Louisiana—Valid after maturity of debt. 9 § 3590.

Maine—Void in consumer transactions. 9-A § 3-306.

Maryland—Not allowed in consumer loans and defined as an unfair or deceptive trade practice. CL 12-311 & 13-301.

Massachusetts—Provision in a contract for confession of judgment is void; however, the other parts of the contract are still effective. 231 § 13A.

Michigan—Valid in separate instrument. Void in consumer transactions. §§ 600.2906 and 19.416(114).

Minnesota—Valid with signed, verified separate statement. § 325G.16.

Mississippi—Void. § 11-7-187.

Missouri—Void in rental and credit contracts. §§ 511.070, 407.662 and 408.560.

Montana—Provision in a contract is void. §§ 28-2-709 and 27-9-101.

Nebraska—Prohibited for banks and in rental purchase agreements. §§ 25-906, 8-447 and 8-823.

Nevada—Valid with signed, verified statement. §§ 17.090 and 17.100.

New Hampshire—Cannot appear in loan contract. §§ 515:2 and 399A:5.

New Jersey—Not valid if contained in the body of a contract. 2A:16-9.

New Mexico—Void. §§ 39-1-18 and 39-1-9.

New York—Need affidavit of debtor. Invalid on installment contracts of $1500 or less for consumer transactions. CPLR §§ 3201 and 3218.

North Carolina—Valid in separate instrument. Void in consumer transactions. §§ 53-181, 1A-1.R68.1.

North Dakota—Void in consumer credit transactions and loans. Valid in separate, verified statement. § 13-03.12, 13-03.16 and § 68.

Ohio—Confession of Judgments. Invalid UNLESS: Statutory warning appears on the instrument evidencing indebtedness. Must appear directly above or below the space or spaces provided for the signature of the makers in such type size or distinctive marking that it appears more clearly and conspicuously than anything else on the document. Applies to promissory notes, bonds, security agreements, leases, contracts or other evidence of indebtedness. §§ 1303.11 and 2323.13 et seq.

Oklahoma—Void in consumer transactions. Need attorney warrant for others. 14A § 3-407 and § 2-415; 12 § 689-695.

Oregon—Void in consumer transactions and rental agreements. All others must be acknowledged by the debtor. § 90.245 and ORCP 73.

Pennsylvania—Void in consumer credit transactions. RCP 2950.

Puerto Rico—Does not affect negotiability of instrument. 19 LPRA § 6.

Rhode Island—Valid except for money lenders and loan brokers. 6A-312 and DCR 58(b).

South Carolina—Void to licensee and in consumer credit transactions. Valid in separate, verified statement. §§ 34-29-170, 37-2-415 and 15-350-15.380.

South Dakota—Void in lease purchase agreements. Valid in separate, verified statement. §§ 21-26-1 and 54-6A-6.

Tennessee—Void in rental-purchase consumer transactions. §§ 47-18-606 and 25-2-101.

Texas—Void before action and in consumer transactions. TX CIV STAT 5069-3.20.

Utah—Need signed verified agreement. Void in consumer transactions. § 78-22-3 and 70C-2-201.

Vermont—Must be in writing. Void in consumer transactions. T.8 § 2229 and 12-4671-12-4672.

Virginia—Not valid with consumer loans. §§ 6.1-283, 8.01-426 et seq.

Washington—Need signed, verified statement. § 4.60.010.

West Virginia—May be confessed in a suit. Void in consumer transactions. § 56-6-30.

Wisconsin—Void. §§ 806.25 and 422.405.

Wyoming—Void in consumer transactions. § §40-14-249.

Jurisdiction

Before suit against a defaulting debtor is initiated, a creditor should determine whether the court selected (whether at the state or federal level) can obtain jurisdiction over the "person" of the debtor or can entertain the "subject matter" of the suit.

A debtor who is a domiciliary of a state is subject to the jurisdiction of the courts of such state, no matter where process of service is effectuated, whether within or without the state. The traditional bases for a court's jurisdiction over a nondomiciliary are in *personam*, *in rem* and *quasi in rem*.

IN PERSONAM (PERSONAL JURISDICTION)

The most obvious form of *in personam* jurisdiction is the defendant's actual physical "presence" within the state. Such jurisdiction permits entry of a judgment for any amount of money, subject to any limitation inherent in the court's power. If a summons is delivered to a person while he is physically present in a state, even if traveling through the state, he is subject to the jurisdiction of the court of that state. A state court establishes *in personam* jurisdiction over a partnership if any one partner is domiciled or is personally served while present in the state. Also, the partnership is considered "present," and subject to the jurisdiction of the court of the state, if it is "doing business" in the state. A corporate officer, unlike a partner in a partnership, is not responsible for the debts of the business he works for; notwithstanding, service upon a corporate officer may result in jurisdiction over the corporation. A court has jurisdiction over a corporation when the corporation is "doing business" in the state. For a discussion of what constitutes "doing business," *see* Chapter 1.

In 1945, in the landmark case of *International Shoe Co. v. Washington*, 326 U.S. 310 (1945), the United States Supreme Court stressed that if the claims sued on were connected with activities conducted within the state, the state may exercise *in personam* jurisdiction over the defendant, no matter where served with process, in a suit on those claims. This came to be known as "long-arm" jurisdiction. It allows a state to exercise extraterritorial jurisdiction over a non-domiciliary based upon contracts he had with the state if the claim arose from those contracts. In recent years the courts have taken jurisdiction over parties and corporations who have caused their product or services to enter the state within the "stream of commerce." Some courts have imposed jurisdiction upon parties whose websites have been accessed by their citizens.

IN REM

In rem jurisdiction is a method upon which the defendant's property is seized within the state to compel the defendant to personally submit to the court's jurisdiction, or the subject property may be forfeited. Generally, it is exercised when personal jurisdiction is unavailable. When the debtor's real or personal property, including debts owed to him (e.g., the debtor's accounts receivable), is in a state where the courts can acquire jurisdiction; such jurisdiction will affect only the debtor's interest in the property.

QUASI IN REM

If a person seeks a money judgment against an individual over whom *in personam* jurisdiction cannot be obtained, the doctrine of *quasi in rem* jurisdiction allows attachment of any property of the non-domiciliary that happens to be in the state for use as a jurisdictional basis. Unlike *in rem* jurisdiction, the property forming the basis of the *quasi in rem* jurisdiction need not be the subject of the litigation.

Part III: Post-Judgment

STEPS IN EXECUTION

Attachment

Certain provisional remedies pending determination of a lawsuit are available to a creditor pursuant to which the property of a defendant may be impounded by an officer of the court, and held to await the outcome of the suit. The remedy most frequently available to a creditor for this purpose is an attachment against the debtor's property.

The word "attachment" has been defined as a method whereby a debtor's property, real or personal, or any interest therein, capable of being taken under a levy of execution, is placed in the custody of the law to secure the interests of the creditor, pending the termination of the cause. That is to say, the writ of attachment is a provisional remedy by which a defendant's property is taken out of his control, during the pendency of an action, so that he is thereby prevented from so disposing of it as to place it beyond the reach of the plaintiff in case the plaintiff is successful in the action.

In the majority of states, the writ of attachment is auxiliary to certain classes of actions only, and the statutes specify in detail not only the classes of actions in which the writ may be issued, but also the peculiar circumstances and relationships which must exist in such actions before the writ will issue. In these jurisdictions, therefore, attachment proceedings are of a highly technical nature, and the requirements of the law must be strictly complied with or the attachment will be vacated at the instance of the defendant.

An examination of the statutes shows that attachment may issue in most states in actions on contract, express or implied, and in some states in any civil action. The grounds on which a writ of attachment may be obtained are different in practically every state, but the most usual grounds are:

- The debtor is a nonresident or a foreign corporation
- The defendant has absconded from the jurisdiction or conceals or hides himself
- The debtor has done so or is about to remove, conceal, assign or dispose of his property to defraud creditors

In these jurisdictions also, it is generally necessary for the attaching creditor to put up a bond for the payment of any damages which his attachment may occasion. The debtor can then usually release the property by filing a counter bond in the same sum.

Garnishment

Where a third person holds property or is indebted to the defendant, proceedings by way of "garnishment" may, in most jurisdictions, be invoked to procure a judgment directly against the third person to reach the property of the defendant.

Garnishment is a proceeding by which the plaintiff in an action seeks to reach the property of the defendant by calling into court some third party who has such property in its possession or who is indebted to defendant. The purpose of the remedy is to apply a debt due a defendant from a third person to the extinguishment of a judgment or claim against such defendant.

Garnishment exists in one form or another in practically all the states. In Massachusetts, New Hampshire, Maine and Vermont, the remedy is called a "trustee process." In Montana, garnishment is by attachment. In Pennsylvania and New Jersey, it is known as "judgment execution."

In all cases the remedy of garnishment is essentially statutory, and the statutes must be consulted to determine under what conditions it can be applied. In many states, garnishment proceedings are limited to actions on contract and are not permitted in actions in tort, though in other jurisdictions this distinction is not made and the various actions are specifically stated in the statute.

Garnishment procedures differ among the jurisdictions. In some states it is permitted only after an execution against the original debtor has been returned unsatisfied; in other states it serves as an aid to a writ of attachment, and becomes effective by the simple expedient of serving a copy of the writ of attachment upon the person in whose hands the plaintiff believes there is money or property belonging to the defendant. In several states the garnishment statutes compel the garnishee (i.e., the third person in possession of the defendant's property) to answer upon oath as to the amount of its indebtedness to the principal debtor or the property in its possession, and in some jurisdictions to appear in court at the trial of the action to answer to the plaintiff as to the amount of the defendant's property which it possesses. If the property claimed by the plaintiff to be in the possession of the garnishee is an unliquidated or uncertain sum, it usually cannot be subjected to the plaintiff's claim. The reason for this is that the statutes limit the process to "debts."

It will be seen therefore that the terminology of the various statutes is important in determining what claims or demands are or are not so unliquidated or contingent as to be beyond the reach of the process.

Garnishment is open to anyone not expressly denied the remedy by the terms of a statute whether an individual or a corporation. It is founded upon a subsisting right of action by the defendant against the garnishee, and after service of the writ upon the garnishee or trustee, as the case may be, such person can pay his indebtedness to the principal defendant only at his peril.

Wage Garnishments

The term "garnishment" is often applied to the legal process by which the employer of a debtor is served with process requiring him to make payment of the debtor's wages, directly to the judgment creditor. This process is known by many names in the various states, such as wage garnishment, income execution and attachment of wages.

Federal law on wage garnishments became effective July 1, 1970 (Title III of the Consumer Credit Protection Act, the federal statute that governs many transactions with consumer debtors including credit granting and debt collection, *see* Chapter 22). Under the federal law, the amount of weekly wages subject to garnishment is limited to the lesser of 25 percent of the disposable earnings of the debtor, or the amount by which the weekly disposable earnings exceed 30 times the hourly wage. However, in the event that a state wage garnishment law is more beneficial to the debtor or is substantially similar to the federal law, then the Secretary of Labor can exempt such state from coverage by the federal law.

In Arizona, Colorado, Delaware, District of Columbia, Hawaii, Indiana, Kansas, Maine, Michigan, Minnesota, Montana, New Jersey, New York, North Dakota,

Oregon, Tennessee, Vermont and Wyoming (wage assignment only), it is unlawful for an employer to dismiss his employee because of the issuance of a garnishment process. The Federal Consumer Protection Act and many state statutes also prohibit discharge of an employee because of a single garnishment proceeding against him.

The following states have statutes prohibiting discharging an employee because of a single garnishment proceeding against him or her: Alaska, California, Colorado, Georgia, Hawaii, Illinois, Indiana, Iowa, Kansas, Kentucky, Louisiana, Maine, Maryland, Missouri, Nebraska, Ohio, Utah, Virginia and Wisconsin.

In the following states, discharging an employee because of a garnishment arising out of consumer credit transaction is prohibited:

- Idaho, South Carolina, West Virginia (rent-to-own transactions) and Wisconsin
- Connecticut: discharge, discipline or suspension is prohibited unless more than seven garnishments in a year
- Oklahoma: discharge because of garnishment in connection with consumer credit transactions is prohibited unless there are more than two garnishments in a year
- Vermont: discharge because of garnishment is prohibited unless there are five garnishments within a year
- Washington: discharge prohibited unless three garnishments within the year

The U.S. Supreme Court in *Sniadach v. Family Finance Corp. of Bay View*, 395 U.S. 337 (1969), held unconstitutional a Wisconsin statute that permitted garnishment of wages prior to the entry of a judgment establishing the debt. The rationale of the opinion was that the property of the debtor, i.e., his wages, was being taken without due process of law since there had been no adjudication that the debt was valid and owing prior to the forced payment to the creditor by wage garnishment. Prejudgment garnishment proceedings therefore should not be used. The fact that the debtor does not reside within the state in which the creditor has his business does not necessarily mean that judgment cannot be obtained within the creditor's home state. Under the long-arm statutes previously mentioned in this chapter, a court may be able to obtain jurisdiction over a debtor by other than personal service of process in the event that the debtor has "transacted business" within the state, committed a tort within the state, or owns real property within the state. The *Sniadach* decision has cast into doubt all prejudgment remedies, and many states have revised their legislation to conform to the new requirements of federal law. For example, California, Nevada, New Hampshire and Rhode Island have amended their prejudgment procedures.

Connecticut, by statute, provides a procedure by which an application to the court is required for an order and summons in those cases in which a prejudgment remedy is sought and thereafter a hearing is held on the application. The act applies to consumer as well as commercial transactions except in commercial transactions in which the debtor has executed a prior waiver as provided for in the statute. It is recommended that in Connecticut as a matter of routine procedure, commercial creditors obtain a written waiver for debtors. Similarly, Kansas has changed its law relating to garnishment providing that garnishment may be ordered only by a judge, not a clerk of the court.

Judgment

A creditor faced with a recalcitrant debtor may have no choice but to commence a civil action against that debtor in order to recover the amount which is allegedly due and owing. If the creditor is successful in such civil action, the court will award a "judgment" in the creditor's favor, i.e., a decree that the creditor as a matter of law is entitled to a sum certain plus post judgment interest from the debtor. Such a decree is given the "full force and effect" by all other states. A judgment does not guarantee, however, that the creditor will be able to recover from the debtor the sum of money which was awarded by the judgment, and indeed a substantial number of judgments recovered remain uncollectible. Thus, where payment of a judgment is not immediately made, the judgment creditor should be acutely aware of its post-judgment collection rights.

A judgment of the courts of any state is the best evidence of indebtedness and can be made the basis of an action in any other state between the same parties to enforce the original judgment. For example, a creditor obtaining a judgment in New York may obtain from the clerk of the court or the county clerk an exemplified copy of the judgment, duly certified by the clerk of the court and by a judge, and with this in hand the creditor may bring an action in any other state setting forth that the judgment was obtained against the defendant and was obtained in the courts of New York. The only defense to such an action would be that the New York court did not have the jurisdiction of the defendant or of the subject matter.

If a judgment is obtained in one county within a given state and it is desired to have an execution issued against property in another county of the same state, it is usually necessary to obtain from the county clerk, the clerk of the court, or other appropriate officer of the court or county in which the judgment was filed or docketed, a transcript of judgment. This transcript can usually be filed in any other county within the state and an execution issued thereon exactly as though the judgment had originally been rendered in the latter county.

The United States Constitution provides that judgments of the courts of any state shall be entitled to full faith and credit by the courts of any other state within the United States.

A growing number of states have adopted the Uniform Judgment Act whereby a foreign judgment, (one awarded in a sister state) can be docketed within its courts system without the necessity of commencing another suit and service of process to gain recognition, the creditor would need only to file a transcript of the judgment in the state.

Execution and Levy

The enforcement of judgments by execution and levy is statutory and thus varies from state to state.

An "execution" is an order, decree or writ of the court directing a sheriff or other officer to seize the defendant's property to satisfy a judgment. A "levy" is the process by which the sheriff or other court officer acquires "legal custody," i.e., actual or constructive possession and control over the property that is to satisfy the judgment. Generally, a writ of execution is required to be issued by the clerk of the court that rendered the judgment. The issuance of the writ is a ministerial act and thus does not require either a hearing or separate court order in most jurisdictions. Some state statutes provide that specific periods of time must elapse after a judgment is rendered before an execution may issue. These time limits vary greatly among states, and in some instances between different courts of the same state and, therefore, local rules should always be consulted.

The issuance of the execution is generally done at the application of the judgment creditor, but some states, including Minnesota, require the clerk to issue the execution automatically upon the entry of the judgment.

A writ of execution is generally directed to the sheriff, marshal, or constable or other authorized official of the county within which the debtor's property is situated. The execution directs this official to levy upon, i.e., take into legal custody, the debtor's property described in the writ and to sell same at a public sale, after giving the debtor sufficient notice, and apply the net proceeds to satisfy the judgment, and in the event that a surplus occurs, return any surplus to the debtor.

It is important to note that just as the time at which the lien status accrues is important in determining the priority to be accorded various competing judgment creditors, it is equally important that execution and levy upon a judgment be made in a timely manner. As the time for execution and levy varies from state to state, a judgment creditor should always consult local statutes for the time limit applicable to the enforcement of its judgment.

Supplementary Proceedings

Where a judgment debtor fails to satisfy a judgment upon demand of the sheriff, marshal or constable, or where the officer has been unable to find property upon which to levy, or the execution has been returned unsatisfied, the judgment creditor may resort to proceedings supplementary to execution in an effort to collect the debt. Supplementary proceedings are governed by statute in all jurisdictions where they are available, and differ in accordance with the statutory provisions. The statutes usually provide that the judgment creditor may, by order or subpoena, direct the judgment debtor or others who may have knowledge of property or assets of the debtor to appear before the court or a referee for examination, under oath, by the judgment creditor. The examination in supplementary proceedings is used by attorneys to ferret out fraudulent transfers of the debtor's property and concealed assets.

In addition to supplementary proceedings where a subpoena must be first obtained, the discovery rules in many states permit the use of interrogatories in aid of execution and depositions in aid of execution in order to find assets that may be subject to execution and levy. If such procedures are used promptly after judgment, personal service on the defendant may be eliminated, with service made upon the attorney for the defendant. A comprehensive set of interrogatories is a very cost-efficient and effective method to determine the nature and extent of a judgment debtor's assets and other liens and claims.

Judgment Liens

The vast majority of states have enacted legislation that accord to judgments the status of "liens." This lien status provides an otherwise unsecured judgment creditor with a priority over all subsequent judgment lien creditors, as well as any and all unsecured creditors. Therefore, where it becomes necessary to compel the sale of a debtor's property in order to satisfy the claims of his creditors, the proceeds realized by the sale of this property will be applied in satisfaction of the claim of the creditor whose judgment was first to attain the status of a lien. Thus, while a judgment establishes the right of the creditor to a fixed sum of money from the debtor, it is the lien status acquired by or flowing from that judgment which provides the creditor with security and priority over any and all subsequent judgment lien creditors and subsequent and prior consensual lien creditors. Under UCC Section 9-401, a debtor's rights in collateral can generally be transferred by judgment lien, attachment, levy, or garnishment notwithstanding an existing security agreement even if the agreement prohibits such a transfer. Of course, secured creditors' rights cannot be extinguished by any transfer of the debtor.

Since judgment liens are purely creatures of statute, the point in time at which lien status accrues, the scope of the lien, and the means of enforcing the lien vary from state to state.

While the majority view holds that a judgment does not acquire the status of lien with respect to a judgment debtor's real property until it has been duly filed or docketed with the clerk of the county within which the debtor's realty is situated, many state statutes adhere to the view that a judgment becomes a lien upon real property as soon as it is rendered by a court of record. Among the states adhering to the latter view are Arkansas, Delaware, Indiana, Kansas, Maryland, Missouri, New Jersey and Wyoming. In other jurisdictions, such as Colorado, Kentucky, Maine, Michigan, New Hampshire and Rhode Island, statutes provide that a judgment does not acquire the status of lien, with respect to the judgment debtor's real estate, until execution and levy are actually had against the debtor's property.

As noted earlier, the point in time at which a judgment actually acquires the status of a "lien" is important in determining priority among competing judgment creditors. Therefore, in those states in which the docketing of a judgment creates a lien upon the debtor's realty, the first creditor to docket his judgment is given priority over all subsequently docketed judgments as well as all unsecured creditors. Thus, where several creditors have docketed judgments at various times, the proceeds realized from the sale of the debtor's property will be paid to the creditor who was first to have his judgment docketed, i.e., "first in time, first in right." Once this senior judgment lien creditor is satisfied, the proceeds of the sale of the debtor's property may be applied toward the satisfaction of the claims of subsequent judgment lien creditors according to the order in which the judgments were docketed.

In those states that adhere to the rule that a judgment becomes a lien upon the debtor's real property as soon as it is rendered, priority among judgment lien creditors depends upon the order in time in which the judgments were rendered. Thus, the creditor whose judgment was first rendered has priority over all subsequent judgment creditors. In Georgia, however, all judgment liens obtained in damage actions arising from a common disaster or occurrence are equal in rank or priority regardless of the date upon which the judgment was rendered provided the judgment creditor had commenced its action within 12 months from the date of the common disaster.

Once a judgment acquires the status of a lien upon the judgment debtor's realty, any subsequent transfer of ownership of that real property is subject to the preexisting lien. Thus, where a creditor has obtained a judgment lien upon the debtor's real property, any subsequent transfer of ownership of such property is subject to the lien. The creditor, however, may not use its lien status against the proceeds acquired by the debtor as a result of this subsequent sale. Rather, the judgment lien creditor's recourse is solely and exclusively to the land. Therefore, even though title to the judgment debtor's property has passed to another, the preexisting judgment lien entitles the creditor to execute and levy against the real property.

While the time of the accrual of lien status varies greatly from state to state, there seems to be general agreement among the states with respect to the scope of judgment liens. In almost every state a judgment lien operates only with respect to the debtor's real property. It is only in Alabama, Georgia and Mississippi that judgment liens apply to both real and personal property. The statutes of an overwhelming majority of states provide that a judgment does not become a lien with respect to a judgment debtor's personal property until such time as a writ is issued, or levy is actually made upon the property by the county sheriff or another appropriate official.

Moreover, there seems to be universal agreement among the states that a judgment lien operates as a "general lien," effective upon all of the judgment debtor's real property situated within the county wherein the judgment was rendered or docketed. Thus, the lien acquired by a judgment creditor does not attach to a specific parcel of the debtor's realty, to the exclusion of all other real property holdings.

In order for the judgment creditor to obtain a lien on property in a different county from that within which the judgment was rendered or docketed, generally it is necessary that the creditor file a transcript of the judgment in the county in which the property is located. State law governs such requirements.

Creditors should be aware that all states have either homestead and/or personal property exemption laws that exempt certain real and personal property from levy and execution from judgment creditors.

Thus, it is apparent that the rendering of a judgment, or even the acquisition of a judgment lien, is by no means the final step in the collection process. It is only through the enforcement of the judgment that the creditor is finally able to satisfy its claim. As with the acquisition of lien status, jurisdictions vary greatly with respect to the proper method of enforcing judgments. Generally, the preferred method of enforcing a judgment is by execution and levy. However, a few states, including West Virginia, allow for the enforcement of a judgment only by way of an action upon the judgment, while several states allow judgment creditors to choose between these two methods of enforcement. These latter states include: Connecticut, Massachusetts, Mississippi, Montana, Nebraska, North Carolina and Wisconsin.

The following list sets forth how a creditor can obtain a judgment lien on real property of the debtor in each of the states.

How Lien Status is Achieved

Alabama—Judgment of court of record acquires lien status with respect to judgment debtor's property once judgment is registered with clerk of the county within which debtor's property is situated. Lien is effective against all of judgment debtor's property, both real and personal. Lien effective for 10 years. § 6-9-211.

Alaska—Judgment of any court becomes a lien when filed with recorder of the district within which debtor's real property is situated. Lien affects real property owned by judgment debtor when judgment is recorded or thereafter acquired but before lien expires. Lien effective for 10 years. § 9.30.010.

Arizona—Judgment rendered by court of record becomes lien when abstract of judgment, certified by clerk of the rendering court, is filed and recorded in office of county recorder. A recorded judgment becomes a lien against all the judgment debtor's real property situated within that county except exempt property. Lien effective for five years from date of judgment. § 33-964.

Arkansas—Judgments and decrees of circuit and chancery courts are liens on real estate of judgment debtors from time judgment or decree is rendered. Lien applies only to debtor's real estate situated within county wherein judgment or decree was rendered. To extend lien to real property in another county, certified copy of judgment or decree must be filed in the Office of the Circuit Clerk of that county. Lien effective for three years, with liens on realty effective for 10 years. §§ 16-65-117 and 16-65-501.

California—Judgment of court of record becomes a lien once abstract of judgment, certified by the clerk of the recording court, is recorded with the county recorder. Once recorded, judgment lien applies to all debtor's real property situated within that county, whether owned by the judgment debtor at that time or acquired thereafter. Lien effective for 10 years. §§ 697.310 to 697.410.

Colorado—Judgment becomes lien on judgment debtor's real property once a transcript of judgment, certified by the clerk of rendering court, is filed with the office of county recorder. The lien applies to real property situated within the county in which the judgment is filed. Lien effective for six years from entry of judgment. § 13-52-102.

Connecticut—Mere rendering of judgment does not constitute a lien unless creditor attached debtor's property during course of action. If personal property was attached by creditor, judgment lien effective for 60 days following rendition of final judgment. If real property was attached, lien continues for four months following judgment. Lien may be recorded in town clerk's office in any town where real property is situated. Lien effective for 20 years. §§ 52-328 and 52-380(a).

Delaware—Judgment of Superior Court constitutes a lien on judgment debtor's real property situated within the county from date of entry of the judgment. Judgments of Common Pleas Court and Justice of the Peace become liens on real property once transcripts of such judgments are filed in Superior Court. Lien effective for 10 years. § 10-4711.

District of Columbia—Final judgments or decrees of District Court or Superior Court become liens from date judgment is filed and recorded with office of recorder of deeds. Lien applies to all judgment debtor's freehold and leasehold interests in real property. Lien effective for 12 years. §§ 15-102 through 15-103.

Florida—Judgment or decree becomes lien on the debtor's real property once certified copy of judgment is recorded in lien record of county wherein debtor's real property is situated. Lien is effective for seven years, but may be extended up to a 20-year period. §§ 55.081 and 55.10.

Georgia—Judgment becomes lien once it is entered on the general execution docket. Judgment liens take priority according to date entered upon said execution docket, and are effective against all of the judgment debtor's property, both real and personal, situated within the county wherein judgment is entered upon execution docket. Lien effective for seven years. § 9-12-60 and §§ 9-12-80 through 9-12-81.

Hawaii—Judgment or decree becomes lien upon real property once copy of judgment, certified by clerk of rendering court, is recorded with the Bureau of Conveyances. § 636-3.

Idaho—Judgment becomes a lien when abstract is recorded with clerk of the county in which property is situated. Once recorded, judgment lien applies to all judgment debtor's real property within that county. Lien effective for five years. § 10-1110.

Illinois—Judgment becomes a lien with respect to real property registered under Land Titles ("Torrens") Act once it is filed with registrar of titles and entered upon register. With respect to land not registered under Torrens Act, judgment becomes a lien when filed with recorder of deeds for county within which property is situated. Lien effective for seven years; may be extended for additional seven years. ILCS 735-5/12-101 through 735-5/12-104, 765-35/1, 765-35/85 and 765-35/86.

Indiana—Judgment of court of record becomes a lien on all judgment debtor's real property situated within the county wherein judgment was rendered. Judgment becomes a lien against judgment debtor's real property situated elsewhere only upon filing of transcript with clerk of the appropriate county. Lien effective for 10 years. §§ 33-17-2-3 and 34-1-45-2.

Iowa—Judgment of District Court becomes a lien from date judgment is entered upon docket and lien index. Lien extends to all judgment debtor's real property situated within the county in which judgment was entered. With respect to real estate located outside such county, judgment becomes a lien once transcript of judgment is filed in the district court of the county within which such real estate is located. Lien effective for 10 years. §§ 624.23 through 624.26.

Kansas—Upon rendition, a judgment of District Court is a lien on all debtor's real estate situated within the county. Lien effective from time petition stating claim against debtor was filed; however, under no circumstances may the lien take effect more than four months before entry of judgment. Judgment becomes a lien on debtor's real property situated outside the county once attested copy of journal entry of judgment is filed with Clerk of District Court for the county in which debtor's real property is located. § 60-2202.

Kentucky—Judgments are not liens against any of judgment debtor's property. In order to obtain a lien, judgment creditor must deliver writ of execution to the proper public officer. Once writ is delivered to this officer, the creditor has a lien on all of the judgment debtor's property, whether real or personal. In order to preserve lien against subsequent purchasers or lessees of judgment debtor's real property, a memorandum of the lien should be filed with the county clerk of the county within which the property is situated. § 426.120.

Louisiana—Judgment is not a lien on debtor's real property until recorded with recorder of mortgages for the parish within which the property is situated. Once recorded, lien becomes effective against all debtor's real estate within that parish. Lien effective for 10 years. §§ 3322 and 3547.

Maine—Judgment is not a lien on debtor's property. In order to obtain a lien, creditor must have attached debtor's property while action was pending. Attachment may proceed only pursuant to court order, and such order may only be entered after a hearing on notice to debtor and upon a finding by the court that creditor is reasonably likely to recover judgment in an amount equal to, or greater than, the value of the property sought to be attached.

Maryland—Judgment of Circuit Court is lien on debtor's real property within the county wherein judgment was rendered. Lien is effective from date of judgment. Judgment may become a lien on debtor's realty located outside of the county by filing certified copy of docket entry with clerk of the county wherein the realty is situated. Lien effective for 12 years. §§ 2-622 through 2-625 and § 11-402.

Massachusetts—Judgment is not a lien; however, judgment becomes a lien against all of debtor's real property once recorded with registry of deeds. Judgment may be sued on in civil action. C. 184, § 17, C. 185, § 86 and C. 185, § 88.

Michigan—Judgment is not a lien on debtor's real property until notice of levy has been recorded in the office of the register of deeds for the county wherein the realty is situated. Thus, upon obtaining judgment, creditor should obtain a writ of execution and have same delivered to the appropriate officer for levy. Real property is bound by the lien from the time of levy, but no levy upon real estate is effective against subsequent bona fide purchasers unless notice of levy is recorded. Lien effective for 10 years. §§ 600.6012(27a.6012) and 600.6051(27a.6051).

Minnesota—Judgment of District or County Court becomes a lien once it is entered and docketed by the clerk of that court. Lien is effective upon all debtor's real property within the county, whether owned by the debtor at the time the judgment is docketed or acquired thereafter. Lien effective for 10 years. §§ 487.23 and 558.090.

Mississippi—Judgment becomes a lien against debtor's real and personal property once recorded in the office of the clerk of the Circuit Court of the county within which the property is situated. Lien effective for seven years from judgment or decree. §§ 11-7-191, 11-7-195 and 15-1-51.

Missouri—Judgment is a lien upon the debtor's real property from the day judgment is rendered. Lien applies to all of the debtor's real property within the county in which judgment was rendered. Judgment becomes a lien on real property located elsewhere once a transcript is filed with the circuit clerk of the county where it is located. Lien effective for 10 years. §§ 74.09, 511.350 and 511.424.

Montana—Judgment becomes a lien once it is docketed, and is effective against all debtor's real property within the county. The clerk of the court is required to docket a judgment immediately upon entry thereof. Lien effective for six years and can be extended upon application to court in certain circumstances. §§ 25-9-301, 25-9-302 and 25-31-914.

Nebraska—Judgment of District Court is lien upon debtor's real property situated within the county from the time it is rendered. Judgment becomes lien on real property located in other counties once transcript is filed in office of the clerk of the district court of that county. Lien effective for five years. §§ 25-1303, 25-1504 and 25-1515.

Nevada—Judgment becomes a lien only upon filing of a certified transcript of the original docket, abstract, or copy of judgment with the county recorder for the county within which the debtor's real property is located. Lien is generally effective for six years from the date of the original docketing. § 17.150.

New Hampshire—No lien is created by rendition, entry or docketing of a judgment. However, if creditor attached debtor's property when suit commenced, the lien created by that attachment continues from the time judgment is rendered for 60 days upon personal property and six years upon real property. C.511 § 55.

New Jersey—Judgments (except special civil and municipal court judgments) create qualified liens upon debtor's real property from time judgment is entered upon the court's minutes. Entry of judgment creates a lien upon realty that gives creditor priority over subsequent deeds and mortgages. However, subsequent judgment creditor who executes and levies upon real property acquires priority over prior judgment creditors who fail to levy. Lien effective for 20 years. 2A, C.16 § 1, 2A, C.17 § 3, 2A and C.17 § 39.

New Mexico—Judgment is a lien on debtor's real property from date upon which a certified transcript is filed with the county clerk of the county within which the property is located. Lien effective for 14 years. § 39-1-6.

New York—Judgment becomes a lien upon debtor's real property once it is docketed by the clerk of the county within which the debtor's real property is situated. Lien effective for 10 years. §§ 5203 and 5235. Judgment becomes a lien upon debtor's personal property only once a notice of levy is issued pursuant to an execution delivered to the appropriate sheriff or marshal. CPLR § 5202 and 5232.

North Carolina—Judgment of Superior Court is a lien upon debtor's real property situated within county in which judgment is docketed. Transcript filed with county clerk in any county where debtor has realty will be a lien upon that property. Lien effective for 10 years from entry of judgment. §§ 1-47, 1-234 and 1-235.

North Dakota—Judgment becomes a lien once it is docketed by the clerk of the court. Lien is effective upon all debtor's real property except homestead, then owned or thereafter acquired, which is located within the county in which the judgment is docketed. Judgment becomes a lien upon debtor's real property located in another county once a transcript is filed in that county. Lien effective for 10 years. §§ 28-20-13 and 28-20-21.

Ohio—Judgment of court of general jurisdiction is lien upon real property once a certificate of the judgment is filed with the clerk of the Common Pleas Court for the county wherein the land is situated. Judgment does not become a lien against registered land until a certified copy of the judgment is filed with the Office of the County Recorder. Lien status may also be obtained upon debtor's real property via seizure under execution. Lien effective for five years. §§ 2329.02 through 2329.05.

Oklahoma—Judgment of court of record becomes a lien on a debtor's real property except homestead after a certified copy of judgment is filed with the county clerk of the county wherein the property is situated. However, unless execution is issued and levied upon within one year following the judgment, the creditor's priority is lost as against subsequent judgment creditors. Lien effective for five years. §§ 12-706, 12-735, 12-770 and 16-5.

Oregon—Judgments of Circuit or County Courts are liens upon debtor's real property situated within those counties wherein the judgment, or a transcript thereof, is docketed. Lien applies to property then owned or thereafter acquired by the debtor. Lien effective for 10 years. §§ 18.350 and 18.360.

Pennsylvania—Judgment of court of record is a lien once it is entered and indexed. Lien applies to all debtor's real property located within that judicial district. Lien created by entry and indexing of judgment applies only to real property which is then owned by the debtor. Creditor may obtain lien upon debtor's property acquired thereafter by execution and levy. Lien effective for five years. §§ 12-883, 42-1722 and 42-4303.

Rhode Island—Judgment is not a lien upon debtor's property until execution is levied. First creditor to levy upon execution is entitled to have his claim satisfied before all creditors who levy thereafter.

South Carolina—Judgment becomes a lien from the time it is entered. Lien is effective upon all of the debtor's real property located within the county wherein the judgment is entered, or a transcript thereof is filed. Lien effective for 10 years. § 15-35-810.

South Dakota—Judgment of court of record is a lien once it is docketed, and applies to all of debtor's real property except homestead situated within the county in which the judgment is docketed, or a transcript thereof is filed. Lien effective for 10 years. §§ 15-16-5 through 15-16-7.

Tennessee—Judgment of court of record, General Session Court or Justice of Peace over $500, becomes a lien once certified copy of the judgment is registered in the county wherein the debtor's real property is situated. Lien is effective for 10 years. Lien extends to lands acquired after its inception and continues for one year. § 25-5-101.

Texas—Lien is created once an abstract of a judgment is recorded with the county clerk of county wherein the debtor's real property is located. Lien extends to real property then owned or thereafter acquired by debtor. Lien effective for 10 years. Prop. Code § 52.001 & Civ. P. Rem. Code § 34.001.

Utah—Judgment of District Court is a lien when judgment is recorded in Registry of Judgments of District Court of county where property is located. Lien applies to all of the debtor's real property within the county wherein the judgment is recorded. Lien effective for eight years. §§ 78-22-1 and 78-22-15.

Vermont—Judgment does not become a lien until it is recorded in the county wherein the judgment debtor's real property is located. Once recorded, judgment may constitute a lien on any real property of judgment debtor. Lien is effective for eight years. 12-2901, VRCP 81b.

Virginia—Judgment becomes a lien once it is recorded on the judgment lien docket in the county clerk's office, and is effective upon all of debtor's real property situated within that county. Lien extends to real property acquired by debtor before or after the judgment is docketed. Lien effective for 20 years. § 8-01-458 et seq.

Washington—Judgment of the Superior Court, and those judgments of District Court which are filed with the Superior Court, are liens upon all debtor's real property situated within the county in which the judgment was rendered. Lien is effective from time judgment is entered. Lien becomes effective upon real property, except homestead located in another county once a certified transcript of the judgment is filed with the county clerk of that county. Lien effective for 10 years. §§ 4.56.190 through 4.56.200 and 4.55.210.

West Virginia—Lien is created against the real property of a judgment debtor once a judgment against that debtor is entered. However, this lien is not effective against subsequent bona fide purchasers unless docketed by the Clerk of the County Commission for the county wherein the real property is situated. Lien effective for 10 years. C.38, Art. 3, § 6-8.

Wisconsin—Judgment of court of record is a lien on real property, except homestead from the time the judgment is rendered, provided judgment is properly docketed thereafter. Lien effective for 10 years. § 806.15.

Wyoming—Judgment becomes a lien upon the debtor's real property situated within the county in which the judgment was rendered from the time the judgment is entered. Judgment is not a lien on debtor's real property located in other counties until such property is seized in execution. Lien effective for five years. §§ 1-17-302 through 1-17-307.

Enforcement of Foreign and Federal Judgments

Unless a state has adopted the Uniform Enforcement of Foreign Judgments Act, the judgment of one state cannot be automatically enforced in another state despite the constitutional requirement that "full faith and credit" be given to the judgments of sister states; it is necessary that a new suit on the judgment be commenced against the debtor. Although proof of liability will be easier, there still is the attendant expense and delay of a new suit. Under the Uniform Enforcement of Foreign Judgments Act, however, the judgment creditor is required only to file an authenticated copy of the foreign judgment along with proof of service with the clerk of the court of the state in which enforcement is sought, and advise the debtor thereof. The judgment so filed has the same effect as a judgment issuing out of the state of the court in which the judgment was entered, and all local enforcement proceedings are available to execute the judgment. The Uniform Act does not apply to judgments of foreign countries. Enforcement of such judgments depends on state law and generally a suit on the judgment is required.

The following states have enacted the Uniform Act: Alabama, Alaska, Arizona, Arkansas, Colorado, Connecticut, Delaware, Georgia, Hawaii, Idaho, Illinois, Iowa, Kansas, Kentucky, Louisiana, Maine, Maryland, Minnesota, Mississippi, Missouri, Montana, New Mexico, Nebraska, Nevada, New Jersey, New York, North Dakota, Ohio, Oklahoma, Oregon, Pennsylvania, Rhode Island, South Dakota, Tennessee, Texas, Utah, Virginia, Washington, West Virginia, Wisconsin and Wyoming.

Under Rule 69(a) of the Federal Rules of Civil Procedure, a federal judgment can be enforced by use of the legal procedures authorized by the state law of the state within which is located the federal court that issued the judgment.

Statutory Repossession (Replevin)

Almost all states have adopted some form of statutory repossession procedures by which personal property wrongfully taken or held can be recovered. Such procedures are designated in some states as replevin actions. These statutes are in addition to UCC provisions authorizing a secured creditor to repossess collateral or an equipment/vehicle lessor to repossess its property. The procedures of each state are different and legal counsel should be consulted before any such proceeding is initiated.

The essence of the remedy of replevin is the recovery of a chattel, such as vehicles, equipment or other assets, by one who has a general or a special property interest in the thing taken or detained. Obviously, a plaintiff with no title and with no right to possession has no right to take the property in dispute by replevin from the possession of another, no matter how defective the latter's title may be. To recover in replevin, the plaintiff must show a title or possessory right superior to that of the defendant.

Creditors are most frequently confronted with the problem of replevin in equipment and vehicle leases, conditional sale and chattel mortgage contracts. Upon completion of a sale of goods in which both title and possession have passed to the buyer, the seller has no right to maintain a replevin action. It is only when the sale is made on conditions which are to be performed by the buyer, the failure of performance (payment) of which prevents title passing, or in the case of leasing, the lessee only secures use and possession of the asset, not title which remains in the lessor, that replevin will lie.

In the case of conditional sales and chattel mortgage contracts, the right to possession is ordinarily in the buyer and mortgagor respectively. The usual provision in the contract is that upon default in the performance of the agreement, the right to possession shall vest in the conditional vendor, or mortgagee, subject to rules and regulations which are usually provided in the statutes of the various states. The requirements of these state laws differ. Some permit replevin upon default regardless of the amount of money paid on the contract; others permit replevin without accounting to the buyer or mortgagor only in the event that less than half of the contract price is paid; finally, some states prescribe limitation on the right to replevin when more than half of the contract price is paid. These provisions are sometimes derived from the common law and, most frequently, from the statutes passed regulating such transactions.

In *Fuentes v. Shevin*, 407 U.S. 67 (1972), the United States Supreme Court, in two companion cases, considered the statutes of Pennsylvania and Florida, which permitted a creditor to obtain a writ of replevin to recover property wrongfully detained by a debtor, without any requirement of prior notice to the debtor or of a judicial hearing. Both cases were factually similar in that the debtors had purchased consumer goods from their respective creditors on installment plans. The documents executed at the time of sale provided that the creditors could recover the property in the event of a default in payment.

The cases arose under similar factual situations. The plaintiffs borrowed relatively small sums of money from banks issuing promissory notes and pledging personal property as security. The security agreement provided that in the event of default the secured party was entitled to take possession of the property. On the occasion of the default by the debtors, the creditors did proceed to recover the property. Repossession was accomplished by the basic remedy of self-help pursuant to former UCC § 9-503 (§ 9-609 under the 2000 revision to Article 9) which provides: "Unless otherwise agreed a secured party has on default the right to take possession of the collateral...[and] may proceed without judicial process if this can be done without breach of the peace...."

The court held that both statutes were constitutionally defective in not providing notice and an opportunity to be heard prior to the taking of the debtors' property by the creditors. The fact that a hearing could be held after the property had been recovered was not sufficient to cure the defect, nor was the requirement that a bond be posted an adequate substitute for the prior hearing. The court saw no meaningful distinction between the household goods in question in the case before it and the matter of wage assignments which it had considered in the *Sniadach* case.

Section § 9-609 of the Uniform Commercial Code gives a secured party the right to take possession of the security upon default of the debtor without judicial process if this can be done without a breach of the peace.

Many of the problems of conditional sales contracts have been avoided by the growing number of the equipment lessor industry, where a finance company enters into a contract to finance the lessee use and possession of the equipment and the lessor retains title ownership. *See* Article 2A of the Uniform Commercial Code.

Satisfactions of Judgments

Almost all states have statutory requirements which provide that a satisfaction must be filed by a creditor if a debtor satisfies the indebtedness, whether voluntarily or through judgment enforcement proceedings.

The requirements vary from state to state. For example, in California and Virginia, a creditor must file a satisfaction of judgment within 30 days of receipt of payment in full, while Arkansas and Florida require that a satisfaction be filed within 60 days. Some states, e.g., California and Illinois, require that a satisfaction be filed within a certain amount of time upon written demand by the debtor after payment in full.

The form of the satisfaction may be statutorily prescribed, such as in California, District of Columbia, Florida, Michigan, New Jersey, New Mexico and North Dakota; or the creditor may be required to merely make an entry of satisfaction upon the judgment record, such as in Alabama and Iowa. Other states, e.g., Ohio, Oklahoma, Oregon, South Dakota, Wisconsin and Wyoming, provide suggested forms of satisfactions.

Creditors must be certain to check the appropriate law in the state where the original judgment was entered as well as the law in each state where an authenticated copy of the judgment was filed.

LIMITATIONS OF ACTIONS

Each state provides for statutes of limitations limiting when a suit may be brought on a cause of action. The Uniform Commercial Code contains statutes of limitations for the areas that it covers. It is very important that every business professional understand that limitations vary completely from state to state, and in almost every instance, an action brought outside of the statute of limitations will be dismissed. Too often, creditors do not move quickly enough in order to try to collect a delinquent account or to assert a claim. Different states have different statutes of limitations, and within a state, there are different statutes of limitations for different types of actions. Once the statute of limitations has passed, a claim may be totally barred.

Statutes of limitations are concerned with the period of time within which an action may be brought to enforce a legal right. Their purpose is to compel the commencement of litigation within a prescribed time, not only because the law looks with suspicion upon stale claims but also because of the difficulty of proof after passing of time with loss of documents and other evidence, failure of memory and death or removal of witnesses from the jurisdiction.

The statutes are matters of adjective or evidentiary law and not of a substantive character. The defense that the statutory number of years has elapsed since the particular cause of action accrued must be affirmatively pleaded after the commencement of an action, for otherwise the statute is deemed waived and a recovery may be had in spite of the staleness of the claim. On the other hand, the pleading of the statute affords a complete and perfect defense to the action regardless of its merits and the certainty of proof that may be adduced to support it.

The time limitations prescribed in each state vary with the type of action, the longest period being generally that for actions on instruments under seal and the shortest for actions on oral contracts or open accounts. Where difficulty of proof is the greatest, the statutory period is the shortest.

Many statutes provide that the limitations can be tolled or suspended in the event a defendant is out of the state or resides within the state under a false name. In addition, some statutes provide that the statute be extended if during the period of limitations the plaintiff is either an infant or an incompetent or in prison for a term of years. The period of limitations is often also extended in the event that the liable party fraudulently concealed the existence of the cause of action on which the claim is based. Should the claimant die prior to the running of the statute, the limitation often will not terminate—if the claim survives—until a stated time after claimant's death, such as four months in Hawaii.

When Statute Begins to Run

The period of limitation begins to run from the date that a cause of action first accrues, which is a matter determined by state law. It is at times difficult, however, to determine at what precise time this occurs. Some examples are set forth as follows:

Contracts in General. A cause of action accrues when either party first breaches a term of the contract. Where time of performance under the contract is fixed, the cause will accrue upon the termination of such period. Where no time is specified in the contract, an action for failure to perform may be brought after a reasonable time has elapsed during which performance might have been made. Where either party announces his intention not to comply with his contractual obligation, a cause of action arises for anticipatory breach of contract at that time.

Sales on Accounts. Compute time from entry of last item in the account.

Contracts of Sale. An action for the purchase price accrues at time of delivery unless the parties have agreed upon a different date for payment.

Broker's Contract. Compensation is due upon completion of services and statute runs from that date.

Factor's Contract. The weight of authority holds that the statute does not commence running against a consignor until the factor has rendered an account or instructions have been given to remit, or a demand for an account is made and not complied with.

Breach of Warranty. Ordinarily, a warranty relating to a present condition is breached at the date contract is made; but if the warranty relates to a future event, such as production capacity of a particular machine over a period of time, a cause of action does not arise until the event occurs.

Guarantee Contracts. Where the contract is one of indemnity or guarantee of collection, a cause of action does not accrue against the guarantor until the creditor has exhausted his remedies against the principal debtor. But where the contract is one of absolute guarantee of payment, the cause accrues and statute begins to run from the time the obligation of the principal debtor first becomes due.

Sureties, Endorsers and Other Accommodating Parties. May maintain an action against their principal only after full payment of the principal's obligation and the statute runs in favor of the principal from the time of such payment.

Bills and Notes. A cause of action accrues to the holder, and the time limitations begin to run from the date that a demand may first be made for payment. If a time note, the demand may not be made until the dates of maturity. If a demand note, it may be made at once.

Secured Debt. It is a general rule that taking of collateral will not affect the running of the statute on the debt itself.

What Law Governs

Where the parties live in different states, and where the contract sued upon was made in a third, the question arises: which statute of limitations will control? The place of contracting and domicile of the parties are not determinative, and it has been held that an action may be maintained although the statute has run against the claim in the state where the contract was made or where the parties reside. The place where the action is brought will determine whether the claim is timely asserted according to the laws of that jurisdiction. It is provided by statute in some states, however, that an action may not be maintained in such state where the cause of action was barred by the statute of the state where the cause of action arose.

Part Payment, Acknowledgment of Debt and New Promise

In most jurisdictions part payment, acknowledgment of the debt or new promise will toll the running of the statute of limitations or revive a barred debt and the statute will commence to run again from the date of the last payment, the date of acknowledgment of the obligation or promise to pay.

The table beginning on page 16–47 summarizes the law on the subject.

Limitations of Actions on Judgments

When an action is brought and judgment is entered against one of the parties to such action, the judgment is effective for a period of years ranging from one to 20 depending on the state statutes and the court rendering the judgment, i.e., whether a court of record or not, and whether the judgment is a domestic or foreign judgment. The table of statutes of limitations on page 16–52 sets forth these periods of limitations in the various states.

A court of record is generally a court taking and keeping a permanent record. It may be stated generally, however, that courts of the Justice of the Peace and in some cases municipal courts are not courts of record. Other civil courts in most jurisdictions are courts of record. Most states have longer statutes of limitations for judgments of courts of record than for judgments of courts not of record.

A foreign judgment is a judgment secured in another jurisdiction from the one in which suit thereon is brought. Thus, in the state of New York, every judgment secured in any other state of the United States or foreign country is a foreign judgment. It should be noted that although each of the states is required to give full faith and credit to the judgments of sister states, the judgment creditor usually may not avail himself of the remedies provided in one state for enforcement of a judgment secured in another without reducing his claim to judgment in the former state. This is done by bringing suit in one state on the judgment secured in the other. A domestic judgment is a judgment secured in the same state in which suit thereon is brought. In many states the statute of limitation for domestic judgments is longer than that for foreign judgments.

TENANTS BY THE ENTIRETIES

A Tenancy by the Entireties is where, under state common law or statutory law, a husband and wife can own property jointly and indivisibly with rights of survivorship, i.e., together where it will pass to the other upon the death of one. Additionally, in those states that have a "strict" tenancy by the entireties, a creditor of one spouse may not reach the assets that are held by both spouses as tenants by the entireties.

With more emphasis being placed upon the use of personal guarantees and the need for appropriate security for credit extension, credit grantors are utilizing guarantees of principals of an entity with increasing frequency. It has always been the concept that a personal guarantee appears to ensure that the guarantors will do everything they can to make sure that the principal obligor pays the debt.

The term "guarantee," unfortunately, can be a misnomer because a guarantor's liability on a debt is not an assurance that the debt will be satisfied. Individual guarantors may avail themselves of exemption statutes and may be able to remove valuable property, such as real estate, from the reach of their creditors. It is therefore important to understand the overall concept of exemptions, but especially the "tenancy by the entireties."

Historical Context

The concept of tenants by the entireties originated in England around the time of the Norman conquest. Applicable only to married couples, the tenancy by the entireties protects one spouse from the unauthorized acts of the other by providing that a creditor of one spouse may not reach the assets held by them as tenants by the entireties. In other words, both spouses own the whole of the entireties property and so it is not possible for the creditor of one spouse to take the property in satisfaction of a debt without also taking the lawful property of the nondebtor spouse.

This concept was part of the English common law, before there were statutes codifying it, but is simply a variation of the "law of the land." When the original 13 colonies were established in the "New World," the original colonies adopted, in many aspects, the then-existing English common law, including the concept of the tenancy by the entireties.

As the population moved south and west, various new states chose to either adopt English common law principles or to create statutes in their place. Please keep in mind that when the common law is adopted, there is no legislative act by a state or local government, but, instead, it is simply "adopted" into the law of the state. This creates some difficulty for the legal purist, as there is no hard and fast law that may be reviewed by the courts or otherwise to determine the exact extent of the provision. Furthermore, since it is beyond legislative enactment, it becomes subject to judicial determination to establish the parameters of its effectiveness.

As will be seen from the accompanying chart, most of the states in the eastern part of the United States still have a form of tenancy by the entireties, while states in the west have opted for either community property or the absence of tenancy by the entireties.

(Continued on p. 16–59)

STATES' LAWS ON TOLLING OF STATUTE AND REVIVING OF EXPIRED DEBT

Note: State legislatures will, on occasion, modify an area of law without clear delineation as to its content and context. As a result, even the changes which have been enacted prior to placement in the state's Code may be difficult to locate. As a result, the Editors urge all users of the Manual to use this publication only as a guide, and consult the latest codified version of the state's law for all recent changes.

X = Statutory Authority; C = Authority based on Case Law; Statutory Citations

State	Tolling of Statute			Reviving of Barred Debt		
	Part Payment	Written Acknowledgment	Written Promise	Part Payment	Written Acknowledgment	Written Promise
AL	C 161 SO. 486			X 6-2-16		
AK	X 9.10.210	X 9.10.200	X 9.10.200		X 9.10.200	X 9.10.200
AZ	X 12-508	X 12-508	X 12-508		X 12-508	X 12-508
AR	X	X 18-49-101	X 18-49-101	X	X 18-49-101	X 18-49-101
CA	X C.C.P. 360	X C.C.P. 360	X C.C.P. 360	X C.C.P. 360	X C.C.P. 360	X C.C.P. 360
CO	X 13-80-113; 13-80-114; 13-80-116		X 13-80-113; 13-80-114; 13-80-116	X 13-80-113; 13-80-114; 13-80-116		X 13-80-113; 13-80-114; 13-80-116
CT	C (But see: 57-1-76 which states that these actions will be governed by the common law.)	C (But see: 57-1-76 which states that these actions will be governed by the common law.)	C (But see: 57-1-76 which states that these actions will be governed by the common law.)	C (But see: 57-1-76 which states that these actions will be governed by the common law.)	C (But see: 57-1-76 which states that these actions will be governed by the common law.)	C (But see: 57-1-76 which states that these actions will be governed by the common law.)

STATES' LAWS ON TOLLING OF STATUTE AND REVIVING OF EXPIRED DEBT (Continued)

X = Statutory Authority; C = Authority based on Case Law; Statutory Citations

State	Tolling of Statute			Reviving of Barred Debt		
	Part Payment	Written Acknowledgment	Written Promise	Part Payment	Written Acknowledgment	Written Promise
DE		C 43 A. 166	C 43 A. 166		C 43 A. 166	C 43 A. 166
DC	C 1 APP.DC 123	X 28-3504	X 28-3504	C 1 APP.DC 123	X 28-3504	X 28-3504
FL	X 95.01	C 483 SO.2D 833	C 483 SO.2D 833		X 95.04	X 95.04
GA		X 93-110	X 93-110		X¹ 93-114,-115	X¹ 93-114,-115
HI	C			C	C	C
ID	X	X	X	X	X	X
IL	X 735-5/13-216		X 735-5/13-216	X 735-5/13-216		X 735-5/13-216
IN	C 186 NE. 908	X 16 34-1-2-10	X 16 34-1-2-10	X 186 NE. 908	X 16 34-1-2-10	X 16 34-1-2-10
IA		C 614.11	C 614.11		X 614.11	X 614.11
KS	X 60-520	X 60-520	X 60-520	X 60-520	X 60-520	X 60-520
KY	C 186 SW.2D 797	C 172 SW.2D 457	C 172 SW.2D 457		C 10 SW.2D 1095 & 147 SW.2D 70 (both a written acknowledgment and a new promise are necessary to revive debt.)	C 10 SW.2D 1095 & 147 SW.2D 70 (both a written acknowledgment and a new promise are necessary to revive debt.)

LA	X[2] T.9 §5807	X[2] CC3503	X[2] CC3503			X CC 2278
ME	X T.14 §§ 860, 863	X T.14 §§ 860, 863	X T.14 §§ 860, 863	X T.14 §§ 860, 863	X T.14 §§ 860, 863	X T.14 §§ 860, 863
MD	C[3] 7 A.2D 186	C[3] 7 A.2D 186	C[3] 7 A.2D 186	C[3] 7 A.2D 186	C[3] 7 A.2D 186	C[3] 7 A.2D 186
MA	X 260 § 14	X 260 § 13	X 260 § 13	X 260 § 14	X 260 § 13	X 260 § 13
MI	NO	PROVISIONS	EXIST	C	X MSA 27A.5866 MCLA 600.5866	X MSA 27A.5866 MCLA 600.5866
MN	X 514.17	X 514.17	X 514.17	X 514.17	X 514.17	X 514.17
MS	X	X	X	NO	PROVISIONS	EXIST
MO	C 188 SW.2D 84	X 516.320	X 516.320	X 516.320	X 516.320	X 516.320
MT	X 27-2-409	X 27-2-409	X 27-2-409	NO	PROVISIONS	EXIST
NE	X 25-216	X 25-216	X 25-216	X 25-216	X 25-216	X 25-216
NV	X 11.200	X 11.390	X 11.390	X 11.390 11.200		X 11.390 11.200
NH	C	C	C	C	C	C

STATES' LAWS ON TOLLING OF STATUTE AND REVIVING OF EXPIRED DEBT (Continued)

X = Statutory Authority; C = Authority based on Case Law; Statutory Citations

State	Tolling of Statute			Reviving of Barred Debt		
	Part Payment	Written Acknowledgment	Written Promise	Part Payment	Written Acknowledgment	Written Promise
NJ	C 20 A.2D 609	C 20 A.2D 609	C 20 A.2D 609	C 20 A.2D 609	C 20 A.2D 609	C 20 A.2D 609
NM	X 37-1-16	X 37-1-16	X 37-1-16	X 37-1-16	X 37-1-16	X 37-1-16
NY	X G.O.L. §17-101	X G.O.L. §17-101	X G.O.L. §17-101	X G.O.L. §17-101	X G.O.L. §17-101	X G.O.L. §17-101
NC	X 1-26	X 1-26	X 1-26	C 45 SE.2D 51		X 1-26
ND	X 28-01-36	X 28-01-36	X 28-01-36	X 28-01-36	X 28-01-36	X 28-01-36
OH	X 2305.08	X 2305.08	X 2305.08	X 2305.08	X 2305.08	X 2305.08
OK	X 12-101	X 12-101	X 12-101	C 149 P. 878	C 149 P. 878	C 149 P. 878
OR	X 12.240	X & C 12.240 298 P.2D 1000	C 298 P.2D 1000	X 12.230,.240 Must also contain, in writing, new promise to pay or written acknow.; no revival otherwise.	X 12.230,.240 Only revives debt if included with part payment	X 12.230,.240 Only revives debt if included with part payment
PA	C 19 A.2D 61	C 19 A.2D 61	C 19 A.2D 61	C 57 A.2D 915	C 57 A.2D 915	C 57 A.2D 915

State						
RI	C 141 A. 307	C 141 A. 307	C 141 A. 307	C 141 A. 307	C 141 A. 307	C 141 A. 307
SC	X 15-3-120	X 15-3-120	X 15-3-120	X 15-3-120	X 15-3-120	X 15-3-120
SD	C 28 NW.2D 881	X 15-2-29	X 15-2-29	C 28 NW.2D 881	C 28 NW.2D 881	C 28 NW.2D
TN	C 588 SW.2D 542	C 588 SW.2D 542	C 588 SW.2D 542	C 588 SW.2D 542	C 588 SW.2D 542	C 588 SW.2D 542
TX					X 16.065	
UT	X 78-12-44	X 78-12-44	X 78-12-44	X 78-12-44	X 78-12-44	X 78-12-44
VT	X¹ 12-592	X¹ 12-592	X¹ 12-591	X¹ 12-592		X¹ 12-591
VA		X 5-32	X 5-32	NO	STATUTORY	PROVISIONS
WA	X 4.16.270	X 4.16.280	X 4.16.280	X 4.16.270	X 4.16.280	X 4.16.280
WV	C 332 SE.2D 589	X C.55, ART.2,§8	X C.55, ART.2,§8	C 332 SE.2D 589	X C.55, ART.2,§8	X C.55, ART.2,§8
WI	X 893.45 through 893.49	X 893.45 through 893.49	X 893.45 through 893.49	X 893.45 through 893.49	X 893.45 through 893.49	X 893.45 through 893.49
WY	X 1-3-119	X 1-3-119	X 1-3-119	X 1-3-119 see also: 270 P. 174	X 1-3-119 see also: 270 P. 174	X 1-3-119 see also: 270 P. 174

¹ Removes the bar or revives the debt, only as to the payor or the promisee; has no effect on other joint obligors.

² Any such action of a single debtor interrupts prescription (or revives debt) as to all joint obligors.

³ Revives or tolls for 3 years.

LIMITATIONS FOR CIVIL ACTIONS

Note: Some state statutes allow renewal/revival of the limitation period, or contain provisions for real property. These are not denoted in the table below. Please seek counsel.

In the first row of text for each state, figures indicate the limitation in number of years; letters or asterisks (*) indicate a corresponding footnote at end of table. The second row of text for each state refers to the corresponding statutory citation for each column.

Other: W=Written; O=Oral;

Daggers (†) denote that the citation is identical to the column immediately to its left.

State	Promissory Notes	Open Accounts	Instruments and Contracts Under Seal	Ordinary Contracts	Domestic Judgments in Courts of Record	Domestic Judgments in Courts Not of Record	Foreign Judgments in Courts of Record	Foreign Judgments in Courts Not of Record
AL	6(e) 6-2-34	3(a) 6-2-37	10 6-2-33	6(a) 6-2-34	20 6-2-32	20 †	6 †	20 †
AK	6 09.10.50	6(a) †	10 09.10.40	6(a) 09.10.50	10 09.10.40	6 †	10 †	10 09.10.100
AZ	6(b) 12.548	3(a) 12.543	6(b) 12.548	6-W, 3-O(a) †-W, 12.543-O	4 12.550	4 †	4 or (d) 12.544	4 or (d) †
AR	5 16-56-111	3(a) 16-56-105	5 16-56-111	5-W, 3-O(a) †-W, 16-56-105-O	10 16-56-114	10 †	10 †	10 †
CA	4 CCP § 337	4(a) †	4 †	4-W, 2-O(a) †-W, CCP § 339-O	10 CCP § 337.5	10 †	10 †	10 †
CO	6 13-80-103.5	6(a) †	6(a)(c) †	6(a)(c) †	20 †	6 †	6 †	6 †
CT	6 52-576	6(a) †	6-W, 3-O(a) †	6-W, 3-O(a) 52-576-W, 52-581-O	20(ff) 52-598	20(ff) †	20 †	20 †
DE	6 10 § 8109	3(a) 10 § 8106	3-O †	3(a) †	No prov. None	No prov. †	No prov. †	No prov. †

State								
DC	3 12-301	3(a) †	12 †	3(a) †	12 15-101	3 †	(d) 12-307	(d) †
FL	5 95.11	4(a) †	4 †	5-W, 4-O(a) †	20 †	5 †	5 †	5 †
GA	6 9-3-24	4(a) 9-3-25	20 9-3-23	6-W, 4-O(a) 9-3-24-W, 9-3-26-O	7(e) 9-12-60	7(e) †	5 9-3-20	5 †
HI	6 657-1	6(a) †	6(a) †	6(a) †	10 657-5	10 †	4 657-6	4 †
ID	5 5-216	4(a) 5-217	5 5-216	5-W, 4-O(a) †-W, 5-217-O	6 5-215	6 †	6 †	6 †
IL	10 735 ILCS 5/13-206	5(a) 735 ILCS 5/13-205	10(f) 735 ILCS 5/13-206	10-W, 5-O(a) †-W, 735 ILCS-O 5/13-205	7 735 ILCS 5/12-108	7 †	7 †	7 †
IN	10(y) 34-11-2-9	6(a) 34-11-2-7	10 34-11-1-2	10-W(y), 6-O 34-11-2-7-O, 34-11-2-11-W	10(v) 34-11-1-2	10(v) †	10(v) †	10(v) †
IA	10 614.1	5(a) †	10 †	10-W, 5-O(a) †	20(ee) 614.3	10 614.1	20 614.3	10 614.1
KS	5 60-511	3(a) 60-512	5 60-511	5-W, 3-O(a) †-W, 60-512-O	60-2403	Kept alive by execution every 5 years †		No prov. †
KY	15(h) 413.090	5(a)(i) 413.120	15 413.090	15-W, 5-O(a) †-W, 413.120-O	15 413.090	15 †	15 †	15 †
LA	5 CC § 3498	3 CC § 3494	5 CC § 3498	5-O, 10-W	10(dd) CC § 3501	10(dd) †	10(dd) †	10(dd) †
ME	6(j) 14 § 752	6(a) †	20(a) 14 § 751	6(a) 14 § 752-W, 14 § 752-O	20(v) 14 § 751	6(k)(v) 14 § 752	20 14 § 751	6 14 § 752

LIMITATIONS FOR CIVIL ACTIONS (Continued)

In the first row of text for each state, figures indicate the limitation in number of years; letters or asterisks (*) indicate a corresponding footnote at end of table. The second row of text for each state refers to the corresponding statutory citation for each column.

Other: W=Written; O=Oral;

Daggers (†) denote that column is identical to the column immediately to its left.

State	Promissory Notes	Open Accounts	Instruments and Contracts Under Seal	Ordinary Contracts	Domestic Judgments in Courts of Record	Domestic Judgments in Courts Not of Record	Foreign Judgments in Courts of Record	Foreign Judgments in Courts Not of Record
MD	3(a) CJ 5-101	3(a) †	12 CJ 5-102	3(a) CJ 5-101-W, †-O	12 CJ 5-101	12 †	12 †	12 †
MA	6(l) 260 § 2	6(a) †	20 260 § 1	6(a) 260 § 2-W, †-O	20(v) 260 § 1	6 260 § 2	20(v) 260 § 1	6 260 § 2
MI	6(a) 600.5813	6(a) †	6(a) †	6(a) †	10 600.5809	6 †	10 †	6 †
MN	6(a)(cc) 541.05	6(a)(cc) †	6 †	6(a)(cc) †	10 541.04	10 †	10 †	10 †
MS	3 15-1-49	3 †	3 †	3-W, 3-O(a) †-W, 15-1-29-O	7 15-1-43	3 15-1-49	7(m) 15-1-45	3 15-1-49
MO	10-W, 5(a) 516.110	5 516.120	10-W, 5(a) 516.110	10-W, 5-O(a) †	10 †	5 516.120	10 516.110	5 516.120
MT	8 27-2-202	5(a) †	8 †	8-W, 5-O(a) †	10 27-2-201	10 †	10 †	10 †
NE	5 25-205	4(a) 25-206	5 25-205	5-W, 4-O(a) †-W, 25-206-O	Kept alive by execution every five years 25-205	†	5 †	5 †

	UNABLE	TO	LOCATE	STATUTE	REFER			
NV	6 11.190	4(a)(aa) †	6 †	6-W, 4-O(a) †	6(aa) †	6 †	6 †	6 †
NH	3 508:4	3(a) †	20 508:5	3(a) 508:4-W, †-O	20 508:5	20 †	20 †	20 †
NJ	6 2A:14-1	6(a) †	16¹ 2A:14-4	6(a) 2A:14-1-W, †-O	20 2A:14-5	20(d) †	20(d) †	20(d) †
NM	6 37-1-3	4(a) 37-1-4	6 37-1-3	6-W, 4-O(a) †-W, 37-1-4-O	14 37-1-2	6 37-1-3	14 37-1-2	6 37-1-3
NY	6(a) CPLR § 213	6(a) †	6(a) †	6(a) †	20 CPLR § 211	20(v) †	20(v) †	20(v) †
NC	3 1-52	3(a) †	10 1-47	3(a) 1-52-W, †-O	10 1-47	10 †	10 †	10 †
ND	6(a) 28-01-16	6(a) †	6(c) †	6(a) †	10 28-01-15	10 †	10 †	10 †
OH	15 2305.06	15W(a) †	15 †	15-W, 6-O(a) †-W, 2305.07-O	21 2325.18	21 †	15 †	15 †
OK	5 12 § 95	3(a) †	5 †	5-W, 3-O(a) †	Kept alive by execution or garnishment summons every five years †	3 †	3 †	3 †
OR	6 12.080	6(a) †	6 †	6(a) †	10 12.070	10 †	10 †	10 †
PA	4* 42 § 5525	6(a) †	20 42 § 5529	6-W, 4-O 42 § 5227-W, 42 § 5525-O	6 42 § 5527	6 †	6 †	6 †
PR	15	3	15	15-W	15	15	15	15

LIMITATIONS FOR CIVIL ACTIONS *(Continued)*

In the first row of text for each state, figures indicate the limitation in number of years; letters or asterisks (*) indicate a corresponding footnote at end of table. The second row of text for each state refers to the corresponding statutory citation for each column.

Other: W=Written; O=Oral;

Daggers (†) denote that column is identical to the column immediately to its left.

State	Promissory Notes	Open Accounts	Instruments and Contracts Under Seal	Ordinary Contracts	Domestic Judgments in Courts of Record	Domestic Judgments in Courts Not of Record	Foreign Judgments in Courts of Record	Foreign Judgments in Courts Not of Record
RI	10 9-1-13	10 †	20 9-1-17	10 9-1-13-W, †-O	20 9-1-17	10 9-1-13	20 9-1-17	10 9-1-13
SC	3 15-3-530	3(a) †	20(gg) †	3(a) †	10 †	10 †	10 †	10 †
SD	6 15-2-13	6(a) †	20 15-2-6	6(a) 15-2-13-W, †-O	20 15-2-6	20 †	10 15-2-8	10 †
TN	6 28-3-109	6(a) †	6(a) †	6(a) †	10 28-3-110	10 †	10 †	10 †
TX	4 16.004	4(a) †	4 †	4(a) †	10 16.066	10 †	10 †	10 †
UT	6 78-12-23	4(a) 78-12-25	6 78-12-23	6-W, 4-O(a) †	8 78-12-22	8 †	8 †	8 †
VT	6(bb) 12 § 511	6(a) †	8 12 § 507	6(a) 12 § 511-W, †-O	8(bb) 12 § 506	6 12 § 511	8(bb) 12 § 506	6 12 § 511

VA	5 / 8.01-246	3(a) / †	5-W, 3-O(a) / †	20 / †	20 / 8.01-251	20 / †	10 / 8.01-252	10 / †
WA	6 / 4.16.040	3(a) / 4.16.080	6-W, 3-O(a) / 4.16.080	10 / †	10 / 4.16.20	10 / †	10 / †	10 / †
WV	10 / 55-2-6	5(a) / †	10-W, 5-O(a) / †	10 / †	10 / †	10 / †	10 / 55-2-13	10 / †
WI	6(a) / 893.436	6(a)* / †	6(a) / †	6 / 893.42	20 / 893.40	6 / 893.42	20 / 893.40	6 / 893.42
WY	10 / 1-3-105	8(a) / †	10-W, 8-O(a) / †	5(q) / 1-17-307	5(q) / †	5(q) / †	5 / †	5 / †

*Where the note is payable on demand, the time is computed from the later of the demand on any payment of principal or interest on the instrument.

†Note: An action founded upon an instrument under seal by a merchant or bank, finance company, or other financial institutions in New Jersey must be commenced within six years after the cause of action accrues.

(a) Uniform Commercial Code § 2-725 provides a four-year statute of limitations as to *sales* contracts. The parties may by original agreement reduce the period of limitation to not less than one year, but they may not extend it.

(b) Instruments executed without the state, four years.

(c) Contracts affected real property, 10 years.

(d) Suit may be brought on a foreign judgment unless statue of limitations has run against it in the jurisdiction where it was entered.

(e) Judgments are dormant seven years after rendition if no execution, or seven years after execution or seven years after written notice of public effort to enforce is filed with the clerk.

(f) Vendor's lien, mortgage, 20 years.

(g) Contract to convey land, 15 years; contract for payment of money, 10 years.

(h) If note has been placed on the footing of a bill of exchange, five years.

(i) An action on a merchant's account must be instituted within five years from January 1 following the dates or time of delivery of the articles charged in the account.

(j) If attested by witnesses, 20 years.

(k) Judgments of Trial Justices Courts, 20 years.

(l) If note attested by witness and action brought by original payee or executor or administrator, 20 years.

(m) If debtor resided in Mississippi when foreign judgment was rendered, then it is barred in three years.

(n) Held by case law to be 20 years.

(o) If note attested by witnesses, 21 years.

(p) If action accrues outside the state, 10 years.

(q) May be revived within 21 years after it becomes dormant.

(r) As provided in state giving judgment.

(s) May be revived once by filing a transcript of the judgment before the limitation expires, action may be brought within seven years after revival.

(t) 15 years written accounts.

LIMITATIONS FOR CIVIL ACTIONS *(Continued)*

(u)   An action on a sealed instrument entered into before August 13, 1965, must be commenced within 10 years.

(v)   Presumption of payment arises after 20 years.

(w)   Except as provided in Maine UCC Section 2-725.

(x)   Special limitations apply to counterclaims.

(y)   Six years Oral, 10 years Money, 15 years Realty, 20 years other than money.

(z)   An action on a merchant's account must be commenced within five years of the next January 1st succeeding the date of delivery.

(aa)   Nevada limitation periods apply unless further limited by UCC.

(bb)   If a promissory note was witnessed—21 years.

(cc)   Except where Uniform Commercial Code otherwise applies.

(dd)   Foreign judgments unenforceable in foreign state are unenforceable in Louisiana.

(ee)   No judgment in an action for foreclosure of a real estate mortgage or deed of trust or for rent or judgment of credits assigned by a receiver of a closed bank when assignee is not a trustee for creditors or depositors shall be enforced and no execution thereon given for other than as a set-off or counterclaim after two years from the entry thereof. The judgment may not be renewed except by voluntary written stipulation of the parties.

(ff)   Ten years small claims.

(gg)   Six years for sealed notes and personal bonds for payment of money.

(Continued from p. 16–46)

Joint Tenants versus Tenants by the Entireties

Many people become confused in thinking that in those states where there is tenancy by the entireties, joint tenancy or joint tenancy with the right of survivorship constitute the same thing. This is not correct. Joint tenancy means that the two or more individuals who own an asset as joint tenants provide that in the event of the death of any one of them, that person's interest automatically transfers to the other individual(s) who may be a joint tenant. Virtually any co-owners of property, including married couples, may be joint tenants.

Tenancy by the entireties, by contrast, can only be between husband and wife. Although each shares the right of survivorship in the same manner as with a joint tenancy, a tenancy by the entireties specifically insulates the property from creditor execution where only one spouse is indebted to the creditor.

How It Works

Any type of real estate and most every kind of personal property (except perhaps clothing, jewelry and IRAs) can be held as tenants by the entireties. In some states, when a husband and wife own a piece of real property, the law presumes that the property is held as tenants by the entireties, even if nothing is said in the deed. In these states as well, it is almost boilerplate to insert in a deed that the property is owned as tenants by the entireties where the owners are married.

With respect to real property, the creation of the tenancy by the entireties is either by specific language in the deed or by legal presumption. With respect to personal property, there needs to be something in writing that evidences an attempt on the part of the parties for the entireties to be created. Unlike real property, the mere fact that assets are owned by husband and wife does not presumably create a tenancy by the entireties.

With respect to any type of account (such as bank accounts, certificates of deposit, brokerage accounts, etc.), there must be an indication in the documentation creating the account to the effect that it is held as tenants by the entireties. As stated above, there is no presumption in favor of such tenancy, so that if there is no specific language in the title of the account with the term "tenants by the entireties," it will generally be held as joint tenants. With respect to stock certificates, motor vehicle titles and other assets that are evidenced by a certificate, the term "tenants by the entireties" or the abbreviation "TEN-ENT" must be on the face of the certificate or title. With respect to other personal property, there is less structure to how the tenancy by the entireties is to be established and proved, but there must be something in writing in order to establish the intent of the married couple to create the ownership as tenants by the entireties.

When an asset is held as tenants by the entireties, as noted above, a creditor of one spouse may not reach such an asset. This must be reviewed in connection with exemptions, as property held as tenants by the entireties is effectively exempt from execution by creditors of one spouse. Thus, when relying on a personal guarantee, note or other evidence of debt by one spouse (without the other being an obligor), the collectability of that obligation will turn on the availability of nonexempt assets, which specifically excludes from execution assets held as tenants by the entireties.

A decision in 2002 by the United States Supreme Court has limited to some extent the absolute protection afforded tenants by the entireties. In *United States v. Craft,*

535 U.S. 274 (2002), the Court looked at the various rights held by the husband in his real property, which was held as a tenancy by the entireties with his wife, including the right to sell the property with his wife's consent and receive one-half of the proceeds. These rights were held to be "property" or "rights to property" as defined by federal tax lien law, which was intended to have a very broad sweep. Therefore, according to the Court, the tax lien of the United States could properly attach to the property even though only the husband was liable for the underlying tax debt.

There is a common misconception that one needs to file a bankruptcy in order to invoke the exemption created by tenants by the entireties. That is not correct. In those states where tenancy by the entireties is permitted and enforced, the exemption of the asset from execution by a creditor of just one of the spouses is equally applicable to exempt the asset from collection by a judgment or other lien creditor, just as if it were an exempt asset in bankruptcy. As a result, in states where tenancy by the entireties exists and there may also be substantial other exemptions for debtors, they may never have to file a bankruptcy proceeding in order to avail themselves of the exemptions as creditors will be unable to effect a collection.

Tenancy by the Entireties in Bankruptcy

Section 522 of the Bankruptcy Code provides that any interest in property in which the debtor had, immediately before the commencement of the bankruptcy case, as an interest as a tenant by the entirety or joint tenant is exempt in bankruptcy *to the extent that such interest is exempt from process under applicable non-bankruptcy law.* This means that if a creditor may not reach an asset by virtue of a state law, that law will carry through in the bankruptcy case and the asset will be exempt.

This does not mean that entireties property is absolutely immune. In addition to the limitation expressed in the *United States v. Craft,* decision discussed above, a tenancy by the entireties may be defeated if fraudulently created. That is, if just one spouse holds title to property, or both spouses are joint or co-tenants, but the interest is transferred to a tenancy by the entireties on the eve of bankruptcy, the transfer might be avoidable if it was done with the intent to evade creditors.

There is also case law in bankruptcy to the effect that if there is even just one creditor of both spouses and one spouse files a bankruptcy case, the existence of that one creditor will defeat the tenancy by the entireties with respect to all creditors in the bankruptcy case. It therefore is incumbent upon the credit grantor to monitor bankruptcy cases where there are large debts outstanding and a claim of valuable assets as being exempt. It should be kept in mind, however, that assets which are held as tenants by the entireties may also be out of creditors' reach for other reasons such as a homestead exemption. In such a situation, even if the tenancy by the entireties were to be defeated, the primary residence held as tenants by the entireties may be fully or partially exempt by virtue of the status of the property as homestead, although a fraudulent transfer might also defeat the debtor's attempt to claim an exemption in the homestead.

State-by-State Analysis

Unlike other areas of the *Manual,* the following chart should be used as a starting point to determine the applicability of tenancy by the entireties in a particular state. Since in many instances there is no statute involved, but rather common law principles enunciated by case law, counsel in that particular state should be consulted to determine the full extent of the tenancy by the entireties, if it exists at all.

TENANCY BY THE ENTIRETIES

State	Recognized? (Y/N)	Citations	Comments	Authority Type—[C]ase, [S]tatute, or [B]oth
AL	N	101 SO.663		C
AK	Y	34.15.120-.140		S
AZ	Y	71 P.2D 791		
		33-431(c)		B
AR	Y	18-12-401		S
CA	N	299 P.2D 281		C
CO	N	163 P. 76		C
CT	Y	11 CONN 337		C
DE	Y	68 A. 450		C
DC	Y	45 § 216		S
FL	Y	63 SO. 822; 689.14		B
GA	N	44-6-190(a)		S
HI	Y	509-1		S
ID	N	55-104	Statute lists allowed tenancies; entireties is not among them.	S
IL	Y	765 ILCS 1005/lc; (76/1(c))		S
IN	Y	IC 32-1-2-33		S
IA	N	207 NW 369		C
KS	N	96 P.140	Abolished May 20, 1891.	C
KY	Y	KRS 381.050	Must be expressly created.	S
LA	N		French Civil System does not have analogous concept.	
ME	N	33 A. 652		C
MD	Y	67 A.2D 258		C
MA	Y	C. 184 § 7	Must be married.	S
MI	Y	MCLA §§ 554.43-.45; MSA §§ 26.43-45		S
MN	N	500.01		S
MS	N	89-1-1		S
MO	Y	442.450		S
MT	N	§§ 70-1-306 through 70-1		S
NE	N	84 NW 92		C
NV	N	111.060 through 111.064	Abolished by implication.	S
NH	N	C. 477 § 18	Creates joint tenancy instead.	S
NJ	Y	TIT.46, C.3, §§ 17.2 & 17.3		S
NM	N	47-1-36	Community property state—creation of joint tenancy is OK.	S
NY	Y	EPTL § 6-2.2(b-d)		S
NC	Y	41-2		S
ND	N	47-02-05		S

TENANCY BY THE ENTIRETIES *(Continued)*

State	Recognized? (Y/N)	Citations	Comments	Authority Type— [C]ase, [S]tatute, or [B]oth
OH	N	5302.21	Only those created prior to 4/4/85 are recognized.	S
OK	Y	60-74	Must be married.	S
OR	Y	541 P.2D 460		C
PA	Y	161 A. 898		C
PR	N		Concept does not translate into Spanish, therefore no corresponding provisions.	Info obtained from Mar-Hub Law Digest
RI	Y	25 A.2D 354		C
SC	N	NO REFERENCE		Info obtained from Mar-Hub Law Digest
SD	N	18 N.W.2D 284		C
TN	Y	36-3-505 & 66-1-109		S
TX	N	PROB.C. § 46		S
UT	N	57-1-5		S
VT	Y	27-2		S
VI	Y	28-7		S
VA	Y	55-20-21		S
WI	N	282 NW 585	*BUT SEE* 766.605— Husband and wife take homestead as survivorship marital property unless document or marital property agreement expresses different intent.	B
WY	Y	34-1-140		S

EXEMPTIONS

Homestead and Personal Property

Exemptions permit individuals to protect certain of their assets from attachment by their creditors. Exemptions are not available to partnerships, joint ventures, limited liability companies or corporations. However, individuals who participate in or have ownership interests in a partnership, joint venture, limited liability company or corporation may exempt their personal assets. The issue of exemptions becomes important in considering the value of a personal guarantee or the collectability of a claim against a sole proprietor, or a guarantor of a business debt.

The theory of exemptions is so deeply ingrained in the body politic as a natural right that legislatures are willing to keep laws on the statute books which admittedly do great injustice to creditors. The courts, in many cases, tend to give a liberal construction to those laws or constitutional provisions if, as is often the case, exemptions are named in the state constitution.

The table at the end of this chapter is presented with realization of the limitations inherent in a summary of laws so arranged. The provisions of nearly every state go into much detail, naming in many instances a long list, mainly household articles, which are exempt.

However, since the average creditor is more interested in the value of the exemptions (both homestead and personal), the lists of the personal exemptions do not play an important role in the majority of decisions made, as the value of the exempt personal property is usually not large. Homestead exemptions play a significant role, however since the equity in one person's homestead may be substantial. All or a portion of that equity may be protected by a homestead exemption. These homestead exemptions vary greatly from state to state. A creditor seeking to enforce a judgment should carefully check the applicable state law.

In many states, a debtor is required to file for a homestead exemption or take some other action before he is entitled to claim it. Therefore, in the event a creditor is confronted with a debtor claiming a homestead exemption, the creditor should ascertain whether the debtor has complied with state requirements as to filing the exemption. Beginning on p. 16–66 is a table of states that require a debtor to file a statement claiming exemption.

In some states, before a creditor can proceed to levy against a *homestead* property with a value in excess of that permitted by law, he must fulfill certain statutory requirements. For instance, in Colorado the creditor must file an affidavit showing the description of the property, the name of the claimant of the homestead, the fair market value of the property, that no previous execution arising out of the same judgment has been levied upon the property and attach the affidavit of a professionally qualified independent appraiser.

The list below indicates how exempt property can be waived in each state. It is important to note that the list does not deal with the situation where an individual attempts to waive his exemption in advance of sale or levy, i.e., by agreement or executory contract. In most states this is void as against public policy. It also violates the rules of the Federal Trade Commission. In this list the abbreviation "PPE" stands for Personal Property Exemption and "HE" stands for Homestead Exemption.

WAIVER OF EXEMPTIONS

Alabama—PPE—Waiver must be in writing but cannot waive exemption as to certain cooking utensils, furniture, etc. HE—Waiver must be signed by both husband and wife, and witnessed.

Alaska—PPE—Waiver is not prohibited. HE—Exemption can only be waived if there is knowledge of the right and the intention to relinquish it.

Arizona—PPE and HE—Waiver of exemption rights is void and unenforceable except process used to enforce security interest or obtain possession of leased property and when done with notice.

Arkansas—PPE and HE can both be waived, but not in advance. Must be executed by both spouses.

California—PPE and HE.

Colorado—Stipulation in note waiving right of exemption void as against public policy.

Connecticut—Contractual or other prior waiver of exemption; other than by failure to claim exemption is void. HE—No waiver legislation.

Delaware—PPE may be waived by husband and wife jointly. HE—No waiver legislation.

District of Columbia—PPE cannot be waived. HE—No waiver legislation.

Florida—No general waiver of PPE, but specific liens may be created against which exemption may not be claimed. HE can be waived only by abandonment or alienation and waiver in promissory note or mortgage is unenforceable.

Georgia—PPE and HE—Waiver effective, but not as to wearing apparel or household furniture and provisions up to $300 in value.

Hawaii—No special statute or cases dealing with waiver of exemptions.

Idaho—PPE—Can be waived and exemption of earnings is automatically waived for failing to file claim for exemption. HE—Can also be waived or released.

Illinois—PPE—Can be waived. HE—Can be waived but wife is not bound unless she joins therein.

Indiana—PPE—Can be waived. HE—No waiver legislation.

Iowa—All exemptions can be waived except as to those for unemployment compensation and old age assistance.

Kansas—PPE—Can be waived by chattel mortgage if signed by husband and wife. HE—Cannot be waived.

Kentucky—PPE—Can be waived, but not in advance. HE—Waiver must be joined in by both husband and wife and must be in writing.

Louisiana—PPE and HE—Waivers must be in writing and the latter must be signed by the wife if any.

Maine—PPE—Can be waived. HE—May be waived. If married, joinder of husband and wife necessary. HE—Can be released by deed and joinder of wife.

Maryland—PPE—Can be waived by a writing entered on the court docket. HE—No waiver legislation.

Massachusetts—PPE and HE—Can be waived, the latter requiring the wife's written joinder.

Michigan—PPE—Waiver can be express or implied. HE—No specific statutes, but waiver of exemption is indicated.

Minnesota—All PPE except wages can be waived. HE—Cannot be waived except by writing signed by the husband and wife creating a specific charge on the homestead.

Mississippi—PPE—Can be waived by contract creating a lien thereon and any exemption is waived by failure to claim it. General waivers of exemptions in advance not enforceable. HE—Cannot be waived except by an instrument which conveys real property.

Missouri—PPE—Is waived unless claimed. HE—Can be waived, and if a wife exists, she must sign and acknowledge the waiver.

Montana—PPE—May be waived. HE—Is permitted if specific and executed by claimant and spouse, if any.

Nebraska—Both PPE and HE permitted to be waived under case law.

Nevada—HE—Can be waived by written abandonment, signed, acknowledged and recorded, or by conveyance or mortgage executed by husband and wife. PPE—No statutory or case law as to waiver.

New Hampshire—PPE—May be waived by agreement or by conduct as can HE. The latter must be executed by the husband and wife with the formalities of a land conveyance.

New Jersey—PPE—Can be waived. HE—No statutory provisions as waiver of exemption.

New Mexico—PPE—May be waived as can HE.

New York—Both PPE and HE can be waived by executing and acknowledging a notice of waiver and recording it. As a general rule the exemption cannot be waived by contract.

North Carolina—PPE—Constitutional exemptions cannot be waived except in certain limited situations. HE waivers are regarded with disfavor and will usually not be enforced.

North Dakota—PPE—May not be waived in advance. HE—May be waived by head of family.

Ohio—Here as in many other states the exemption, by statute, cannot be waived in advance, but a waiver upon levy or sale of the property is valid.

Oklahoma—Both PPE and HE can be waived.

Oregon—PPE can be waived. HE—No statutory provision.

Pennsylvania—PPE—May not be waived by express or implied contract. HE—No waiver legislation.

Rhode Island—PPE—May be waived. HE—No exemption.

South Carolina—There are no cases or statutes dealing with the waiver of PPE. HE—Can be waived only if executed by both the husband and wife.

South Dakota—PPE—Can be waived here in advance. Exemptions not waived by failure to claim. HE—May be waived in advance, but failure to claim is not a waiver.

Tennessee—PPE—Cannot be waived. HE—Waiver must be joined by husband and wife.

Texas—PPE—Can be waived. Any personal property exemption is waived by failure to claim it. HE—Can be waived by alienation or encumbrance. Failure to plead exemption can operate as a waiver.

Utah—Both PPE and HE can be waived if the waiver is joined in by both spouses but may not be waived in advance.

Vermont—PPE—Can be waived by turning property over to levying officer. HE—Can be waived if both husband and wife join in.

Virginia—All of the PPE except wages and certain household furniture can be waived. HE—Can be waived by a writing.

Washington—Both exemptions can be waived. HE—Waiver must be joined in by the wife.

West Virginia—Both the PPE and HE may be waived, but in the latter the wife must join. Waiver may not be made by executory contract.

Wisconsin—Both PPE and HE may be waived and failure to claim the latter may result in a waiver.

Wyoming—No statutory provisions. HE—Can be waived only by acknowledged instrument specifically releasing homestead.

Exemptions in Bankruptcy

The Bankruptcy Reform Act of 1978, as amended from time to time, including the last substantive set of amendments in 1994 is commonly called The Bankruptcy Code. Section 522 of the Bankruptcy Code sets forth the exemptions that may be claimed by a debtor filing a personal bankruptcy petition. The Bankruptcy Code permits a debtor to choose the exemptions given under federal law in the Bankruptcy Code or the exemptions under state law. In many instances, the homestead exemption granted by a particular state exceeds the federal real property exemption and the debtor will clearly choose the more favorable exemption statute. Certain states, however, mandate that a debtor residing in that state and filing a personal bankruptcy petition, may only use the state permitted exemptions and not the federal exemptions.

The Bankruptcy Abuse Prevention and Consumer Protection Act of 2005 ("BAPCPA") (discussed fully in Chapter 19) includes substantial changes in the area of exemptions. Those portions of BAPCPA which relate to exemptions is included here.

The definition of retirement funds that may be exempted has been broadened and clarified. Those funds contained "in a fund or account that is exempt from taxation under Section 401, 403, 408, 408A, 414, 457 or 501(a) of the Internal Revenue Code of 1096 are now exempt under BAPCPA.

The types of property which can be claimed as a homestead had been expanded to include:

- real or personal property that the debtor or dependent of the debtor uses as a residence;
- a cooperative that owns property that the debtor or a dependent of the debtor uses as a residence;
- a burial plot for the debtor or a dependent of the debtor; or
- real or personal property that the debtor or a dependent of the debtor claims as a homestead.

Each of these homestead exemptions will be reduced by the value of any asset disposed of within 10 years prior to the filing of a debtor's bankruptcy with the intent to delay, hinder or defraud creditors, unless that property would have been eligible for exemption at the time it was transferred.

While a debtor may still choose state exemptions over the federal exemptions, a debtor choosing its state exemption is now subject to a limitation of $125,000 for its homestead acquired within 1215 days prior to the filing of his bankruptcy petition.

In addition, a debtor will be bound by this $125,000 limitation on exemptions if:

(A)　the court determines, after notice and a hearing, that the debtor has been convicted of a felony (as defined in Section 3156 of Title 18), which under the circumstances, demonstrates that the filing of the case was an abuse of the provisions of this title; or

(B)　the debtor owes a debt arising from:

　　(i)　any violation of the Federal securities laws (as defined in Section 3(a)(47) of the Securities Exchange Act of 1934), any State securities laws, or any regulation or order issued under Federal securities laws or State securities laws;

　　(ii)　fraud, deceit, or manipulation in a fiduciary capacity or in connection with the purchase or sale of any security registered under Section 12 or 15(d) of the Securities Exchange Act of 1934 or under Section 6 of the Securities Act of 1933;

　　(iii)　any civil remedy under Section 1964 of Title 18; or

　　(iv)　any criminal act, intentional tort, or willful or reckless misconduct that caused serious physical injury or death to another individual in the preceding five years.

Formerly, a debtor had to reside in a state for 180 days in order to claim that state's exemptions. BAPCPA has expanded that residency requirement to 730 days before a debtor may claim that state's exemptions. If the debtor has not resided in a state for 730 days, then the state where the debtor resided for the previous 180 days will be used.

STATES WHICH REQUIRE DEBTOR TO FILE WRITTEN STATEMENT CLAIMING PERSONAL EXEMPTION AND HOMESTEAD EXEMPTION

State	Personal Property Exemption	Homestead Exemption
Alabama	Yes	Yes
Alaska	No	No
Arizona	No	Yes
Arkansas	Yes	No
California	No	Yes
Colorado	No	No[1]
Connecticut	No	No
Delaware	Yes	No
District of Columbia	Yes	Yes
Florida	Yes	Yes
Georgia	Yes	Yes
Hawaii	No	No
Idaho	Yes	No

STATES WHICH REQUIRE DEBTOR TO FILE WRITTEN STATEMENT
CLAIMING PERSONAL EXEMPTION AND HOMESTEAD EXEMPTION
(Continued)

State	Personal Property Exemption	Homestead Exemption
Illinois	Yes	No
Indiana	Yes	Yes
Iowa	No	Yes
Kansas	No	Yes[2]
Kentucky	No	No
Louisiana	No	No
Maine	No	Yes
Maryland	No	No
Massachusetts	No	No
Michigan	No	No[12]
Minnesota	No	Yes[3]
Mississippi	No	No
Missouri	Yes	No
Montana	No	Yes
Nebraska	Yes[4]	No[5]
Nevada	No	Yes
New Hampshire	No[6]	Yes
New Jersey	No	Yes[3]
New Mexico	Yes	Yes
New York	No	Yes
North Carolina	No	Yes
North Dakota	Yes	Yes[11]
Ohio	Repealed	Yes[13]
Oklahoma	No	Yes
Oregon	No[7]	Yes
Pennsylvania	No	No
Rhode Island	No[14]	No
South Carolina	No	Yes
South Dakota	Yes[8]	No
Tennessee	No[15]	No
Texas	No	No
Utah	No	Yes
Vermont	No	No
Virginia	No	Yes
Washington	No[9]	Yes
West Virginia	No	No formal procedure
Wisconsin	Yes	Yes
Wyoming	No[2]	No

[1] Although written claim of valid homestead exemption is not required, better practice dictates filing a claim with clerk of court of record where writ was issued. Filing should be within 10 days after property levied upon or taken into possession by officer (15 Colo. 223).

[2] If homestead not selected or set apart, notice in writing must be sent to court.

[3] If owner removes from homestead for more than six consecutive months, homestead exemption is lost unless within that time he files with registrar of deeds of county in which homestead lies.

[4] If additional personal property exemption is taken in lieu of homestead exemption, debtor must file inventory list under oath.

[5] On levy of execution, debtor must notify officer as to property claimed as homestead. Judgment creditor may file verified petition that the property claimed exceeds the statutory amount of exemption.

[6] In event exempt property is levied upon, exemption must be claimed or it is lost and consent to the levy will be implied from nonaction.

[7] Exempt property must be selected by the debtor or his agent before levy or sale. Otherwise, exemptions are waived.

[8] Absolute exemptions are not waived by failure to claim them. Debtor may claim his additional exemptions at any time up to five days after notice of such levy. Such claim is made by service of the claim on creditor and officer and filing the same with the court.

[9] Debtor must deliver verified list of property claimed as exempt to officers making levy.

[10] No general statutory provisions of filing on claim exemptions. However, if wages are garnished, exemption must be claimed in court where wages are garnished.

[11] Bankruptcy Court's finding of homestead exemption is a declaration of homestead and copy of bankrupt's discharge of bankruptcy may be filed to constitute notice.

[12] If area occupied exceeds limitation, officer levying execution notifies debtor to elect homestead, and in default of such election, officer can maintain execution.

[13] Certain articles are absolutely exempt while others must be selected by debtor in order to be exempted.

[14] Privilege is personal to debtor and can only be claimed by debtor.

[15] $4,000 exemption must be claimed by filing with court a list, under oath, of claimed exemptions and value thereof.

Exemptions on Insurance

In a number of states, special provisions of exemption on moneys received from insurance policies have been passed. The following summary shows the main features of these insurance exemptions for each state and the District of Columbia.

Alabama—Proceeds and avails of life insurance in favor of a person other than himself, exempt as against creditors, except amount of premiums paid with intent to defraud creditors. Benefits from fraternal societies exempt.

Alaska—Proceeds of life insurance policies in favor of a person other than himself and beneficiaries' certificates are exempt to $5,000. Proceeds of disability insurance are exempt from liability for the debts of the insured and from the debts of the beneficiary.

Arizona—Money arising from fire or other insurance upon property exempt from sale on execution. All money received by or payable to surviving wife or child on life of deceased husband or father up to $20,000.

Arkansas—Insurance proceeds from life, health, accident and disability policies paid or payable to state residents are exempt to $500 constitutional limitation.

California—Proceeds of life, disability or health insurance, if annual premiums do not exceed $500, exempt, and if premiums exceed said sum, a like exemption in the same proportion to the benefits accruing out of insurance, that $500 bears to whole annual premiums paid. But where debts are incurred by a beneficiary of a health or disability policy or by his wife or family for necessaries, benefits to $1,000 are exempt.

Colorado—Proceeds of life insurance to the extent of $5,000. Proceeds of any claims for personal injuries or loss, destruction or damage of property; also avails of any fire or casualty insurance. Group life insurance exempt. Proceeds of health, accident, or disability 70 percent exempt for head of family; 35 percent for single person.

Connecticut—Life insurance, when beneficiary is other than the insured, unless secured with intent to defraud creditors. Insurance on property which is itself subject to exemption.

All benefits allowed by any association of persons in this state toward the support of any of its members incapacitated by sickness or infirmity from attending to their usual business shall be exempt and not liable to be taken by foreign attachment or execution; and all moneys due the debtor from any insurance company upon policies issued for insurance upon property, either real or personal, which is exempt from attachment and execution shall, in like manner, be exempt to the same extent as the property so insured.

Delaware—Substantially the same as Alabama.

District of Columbia—Proceeds of life insurance and disability insurance are exempt as are proceeds of life insurance except as to premiums paid to defraud creditors.

Florida—Substantially the same as Alabama. No provision with respect to fraternal benefits. Proceeds of disability insurance unless same was taken out for benefit of creditors.

Georgia—Substantially the same as Alabama.

Hawaii—All proceeds payable because of the death of the insured and the aggregate net cash value of any and all life and endowment policies and annuity contracts payable to a husband or wife, child, parent or other dependent are exempt from execution, attachment, garnishment or other process for debts or liabilities of the insured. Proceeds from disability insurance are also exempt.

Idaho—Proceeds of life insurance policies exempt to an amount reasonably necessary for support. Proceeds of group insurance are exempt.

Illinois—Substantially the same as Alabama as well as insurance on homestead if loss occurs.

Indiana—Substantially the same as Alabama.

Iowa—Proceeds of life insurance and accident policies payable to husband, wife or children of the insured are exempt. Proceeds of policies of life insurance and accident insurance payable to surviving widow are exempt from all debts of the beneficiary contracted prior to the death of the insured, but not exceeding $15,000. Fraternal benefits exempt.

Kansas—Substantially the same as Alabama.

Kentucky—Substantially the same as Alabama and in addition includes proceeds of casualty insurance.

Louisiana—Proceeds of life, health and accident insurance except debt secured by pledge of the policy. Fraternal benefits exempt.

Maine—Substantially the same as Alabama.

Maryland—Proceeds including cash surrender and loan values, where policy is made for benefit, or assigned to spouse, children or dependent relative are exempt. Fraternal benefits exempt. Maximum of $500.

Massachusetts—Life endowment and group annuity contract. Funds of certain relief societies are exempt. Disability insurance benefits liable only for necessities contracted for after accrual of benefits and up to $35 per week.

Michigan—Life insurance contract may exempt proceeds of policy from execution or liability to any creditor of the insured.

Minnesota—Moneys arising from fire and other insurance on exempt property, exempt; life insurance proceeds payable to surviving wife or child upon the life of a deceased husband or father exempt, not exceeding $20,000 which shall be increased by $5,000 for each dependent of the surviving spouse or child. When insurance is effected in favor of another, the beneficiary is entitled to proceeds as against creditors and representatives of the person effecting the same. Fraternal benefits exempt.

Mississippi—Life insurance proceeds exempt not exceeding $50,000. Proceeds of life insurance policy not exceeding $5,000 payable to executor or administrator of insured passes to the heirs or legatees free of all liability for the debts of the decedent except premiums paid on the policy by anyone other than the insured for debts due for expenses of last illness and for burial. If deceased was insured for the benefit of his heirs or legatees and they shall collect the insurance, the sum collected is to be deducted from the $5,000 and the excess of the latter only is exempt; fraternal benefits exempt. Proceeds of insurance on property, real and personal, are exempt as well as income from disability insurance.

Missouri—Life insurance payable to the wife of the insured is exempt from the husband's debts, but where premiums were paid out of husband's funds, insurance representing excess of premiums over $500 annually insure to benefit of his creditors. Fraternal benefits exempt.

Montana—Life insurance benefits exempt, if annual premiums do not exceed $500. Proceeds of bail insurance exempt. Proceeds of accident insurance exempt. Fraternal benefits exempt.

Nebraska—All proceeds of life insurance unless a written assignment to the contrary has been obtained by the claimant. Any loan value in excess of $5,000 of an unmatured life insurance contract is not exempted.

Nevada—Life insurance exempt to the extent of amount purchased by annual premium of $1,000. If it exceeds $1,000, a like exemption shall exist which shall bear the same proportion to the proceeds accruing that the $1,000 bears to the whole annual premium.

New Hampshire—Benefits of life insurance payable to a married woman are exempt as to her and to her children. Policies of life or endowment insurance effected upon any person upon his own life or life of another, in favor of a third person having insurable interest, is exempt in the hands of the beneficiary against creditors and representatives of the person effecting the same. Fraternal benefits exempt as are insurance proceeds on exempt property.

New Jersey—Proceeds and avails of life insurance in favor of a person other than himself, exempt as against creditors, except amount of premiums paid with intent to defraud creditors. Benefits from fraternal societies exempt as well as an exemption for disability and health insurance proceeds.

New Mexico—Cash surrender value of life insurance policies are exempt as well as proceeds of health and disability insurance. The proceeds of a life insurance policy are exempt except by special contract or arrangement, to be made in writing. Fraternal benefits exempt.

New York—Substantially the same as Alabama. Annuities exempt except as to excess over amount necessary for education and support. Certain accident benefits are also exempt.

North Carolina—Proceeds from an insurance policy that insures the life of a husband is exempt if it is for the sole use and benefit of his wife or children or both. Proceeds from group life insurance payable to an employee are exempt.

North Dakota—Insurance on exempt property not exceeding the amount of exemption is exempt. Cash surrender value of life insurance policies payable to wife or children or any relative of insured dependent or liable to be dependent upon him for claims of support is exempt from creditors of the insured. Avails of a life insurance policy payable by any mutual aid or benevolent society when made payable to the personal representatives of the deceased, his heirs, or estate upon the death of a member of such society, or of such assured, are not subject to the debts of the decedent except by such contract. Fraternal benefits exempt.

Ohio—Life endowment, insurance or annuity payable to dependent together with their proceeds. Policies of group insurance and proceeds are exempt from claims against employee.

Oklahoma—Substantially the same as Alabama.

Oregon—Substantially the same as Alabama.

Pennsylvania—Where the proceeds of a policy of life insurance are retained by the company at maturity or otherwise, pursuant to an agreement, or by the terms of the policy the same may not be alienated or assigned, if prohibited by the terms of the policy or agreement, and if the policy or agreement so provides, no payments on interest or principal shall be subject to the debts, contracts or engagements of the beneficiary. Any policy or contract of insurance or annuity whereby the insured or the purchaser of the annuity is the beneficiary or annuitant, not exceeding in income thereof $100 per month, is exempt from the claims of creditors. Life insurance, etc., for the benefit of wife or children or dependent relative of the insured is exempt from the claims of creditors of the insured. Proceeds of accident and disability insurance are exempt. Fraternal benefits exempt.

Rhode Island—Substantially the same as Alabama including proceeds of accident and sickness insurance.

South Carolina—Proceeds of life insurance policies for the benefit of any married woman, or heirs and children, or heirs and children of her husband, are exempt from the claims of the husband's creditors and representatives, to the extent of the insurance proceeds not exceeding $25,000. Fraternal benefits exempt.

South Dakota—Proceeds of life insurance to the extent of $10,000 insured to the use of the husband or wife and children of the insured, free and clear of the claims of the insured's creditors, and of the creditors of the surviving husband, wife or children. Proceeds of endowment policies payable to the insured to an amount of $10,000 are exempt. Insurance payable to surviving widow, husband or minor child or children, payable upon insured's death to the order of his assigns, estate, executor or administrator, not exceeding $10,000, insured to the use of the surviving widow, husband, minor child or children are not subject to the debts of the decedent or of the beneficiaries. Fraternal benefits exempt.

Tennessee—Proceeds of life, health and disability insurance exempt. Cash surrender value and proceeds of life insurance payable to or for benefit of wife and children are exempt. Net amount payable on life insurance or annuity contract for benefit of, or assigned to, insured's wife, children or dependent relative is exempt, even if insured could have changed contract beneficiary.

Texas—Cash surrender value of any life insurance policy which has been in force more than two years is exempt, provided the beneficiary is a member of the family of the insured. If members of the insured's family are only partially the beneficiaries, the policies are exempt to the extent of their beneficiary interest. Fraternal benefits exempt as are health and accident benefits. Life endowment and group annuity are exempt under certain conditions. Money or benefits to be paid or rendered to an insured or any beneficiary under any policy of insurance issued by a life, health or accident insurance company are exempt, as are mutual or fraternal insurance and employer programs of annuity, except premiums payable on such policy or a debt of the insured secured by a pledge thereof.

Utah—Life insurance exempt to the extent reasonably necessary for support. Insurance upon a homestead is exempt. Fraternal benefits exempt. Unmatured life insurance contracts are exempt up to value of $1,500.

Vermont—Proceeds of life insurance not exceeding $10,000, where right is reserved to charge the beneficiary if payable to householder as head of family. Installments on health or accident insurance are exempt. The proceeds of fire insurance on exempt property are exempt as are proceeds of health insurance up to $200 per month.

Virginia—Fraternal benefits exempt as well as proceeds of life insurance up to $10,000 and installment payments on health and accident insurance. Fraternal benefits exempt.

Washington—Proceeds of life and disability insurance and annuities exempt under certain specified conditions. Proceeds or avails of accident and health insurance exempt from the debts of the assured and any debt of the beneficiary existing at the time the policy is made available for his use. Fire insurance is exempt to extent of exemption of property destroyed.

West Virginia—Substantially the same as Alabama.

Wisconsin—Substantially the same as Alabama except that the exemption attaches only to benefits not exceeding $5,000 where the insured pays the premiums. Proceeds from disability insurance not to exceed $150 per month. Fire insurance upon exempt property including homestead is exempt.

Wyoming—Proceeds of life insurance payable to person other than the insured or person effectuating insurance, or executor or administrator of person effecting insurance, are payable to such person free of all claims of creditors.

SERVICEMEMBERS' RELIEF ACT OF 2003

The Servicemembers' Civil Relief Act of 2003 ("SCRA"), Pub. L. No. 108-189, 117 Stat. 2835, signed into law on December 19, 2003, made major revisions to the Soldiers' and Sailors' Civil Relief Act of 1940. The purpose of SCRA is to temporarily suspend judicial and administrative proceedings and transactions adverse to servicemen during their military service. SCRA does not, however, apply to criminal proceedings. The changes made by SCRA are detailed in the following paragraphs. However, for the full and complete details of SCRA one should consult the Act itself.

SCRA extended protection to persons secondarily liable. Now, whenever a court stays the enforcement of an obligation; the prosecution of a civil suit; the entry or enforcement of an order, writ, judgment, or decree; or the performance of any other act, the court may likewise stay a surety, guarantor, endorser, accommodation maker, comaker or other person who is primarily or secondarily subject to the obligation, the performance of which is stayed. Similarly, when a court sets aside a judgment pursuant to SCRA, it may also set aside the judgment as to a surety, guarantor, endorser, accommodation maker, comaker or other person who is primarily or secondarily liable. Furthermore, a bail bond may not be enforced during the principal's military service when his service prevents the surety from obtaining the attendance of the principal.

Citizens serving with allied forces, reservists, inductees and in some cases dependents of a servicemember are now covered under SCRA.

Any waiver of the rights provided under SCRA must be in writing and be a separate instrument from the obligation, and execution of such waiver must occur after one enters military service. Any modification, termination or cancellation of a contract, lease or bailment; or an obligation secured by a mortgage, trust, deed or lien must be received in written form to be valid. Furthermore, the repossession, retention, foreclosure, sale, forfeiture or taking possession of property that is a security for any obligation or was purchased under a contract, lease or bailment must also be received in writing.

The exercise of a servicemember's rights under SCRA may not affect his future financial transactions. In particular, relief sought under SCRA may not itself result in the following:

1. A determination by a lender or other person that the servicemember is unable to pay the civil obligation or liability in accordance with its terms
2. A denial or revocation of credit by the creditor
3. A change by the creditor in the terms of an existing credit arrangement
4. A refusal by the creditor to grant credit to the servicemember in substantially the amount or on substantially the terms requested
5. An adverse report relating to the creditworthiness of the servicemember by or to a person engaged in the practice of assembling or evaluating consumer credit information
6. A refusal by an insurer to insure the servicemember
7. An annotation in a servicemember's record by a creditor or a person engaged in the practice of assembling or evaluating consumer credit information, identifying the servicemember as a member of the National Guard or a reserve component
8. A change in the terms offered or conditions required for the issuance of insurance

Before judgment is entered in any civil action, plaintiffs must file an affidavit of non-military service. The affidavit must set forth whether or not the defendant is in military service or that the plaintiff is unable to determine whether or not the defendant is in military service. In the event the court cannot determine if the defendant is in military service, the court may require the plaintiff to file a bond to indemnify the defendant against any loss or damage. If the defendant appears to be in military service, the court must appoint an attorney to represent the defendant before a judgment may be entered.

A minimal 90-day stay of proceedings will be granted for any action covered by SCRA. An application to vacate or set aside any judgment must be filed within 90 days of a servicemember's termination from military service. The setting aside of a default judgment under SCRA will not impair a right acquired by a bona fide purchaser for value. Fines and or penalties are prohibited from occurring under any contract when proceedings are stayed under SCRA. Plaintiffs may proceed against codefendants of a servicemember who are not in the military and not covered under SCRA with court approval.

The period of a servicemember's service may not be included in the tolling of statutes of limitations or any period for the redemption of real property. However, this exemption does not apply to Internal Revenue Laws.

The SCRA limits the maximum interest on debts incurred by a service member before military service to 6 percent.

Under SCRA, a landlord may not evict a servicemember or the dependents of a servicemember from the member's primary residence for which the monthly rent does not exceed $2,400 during a period of military service.

Contracts entered into by a servicemember before entering military service for the purchase of property (real or personal) or the lease or bailment of such property may not be terminated for a breach of terms occurring before or during the member's military service, nor may the property be repossessed for such a breach without a court order.

A court order is needed for the enforcement of any lien for storage, repair or cleaning of property during any period of military service and for the 90 days thereafter. Courts may also stay proceedings to foreclose or enforce liens when a servicemember's ability to comply was materially affected by military service.

Under SCRA, an insurer of a life insurance contract may not: (1) decrease the amount of coverage or require the payment of an additional amount of premiums if the insured engages in military service (except increases in premiums in individual term insurance based upon age); or (2) limit coverage for any activity required by military service. However, the policy must be in force at least 180 days before the date of the servicemember's entry into military service. The insured must apply in writing for this protection. The rights and protections are limited to life insurance coverage not to exceed $250,000 or an amount equal to the servicemember's group life insurance maximum limit. During the period the policy is protected under SCRA, dividends or other monetary benefits may not be paid to an insured or used to purchase dividend additions without the approval of the Secretary of Veterans Affairs. If such approval is not obtained, the dividends or benefits shall be added to the value of the policy to be used as a credit when final settlement is made with the insurer. While a policy is protected, the cash value, loan value, withdrawal of dividend accumulation, unearned premiums, or other value of similar character may not be available to the insured without the approval of the Secretary. Furthermore, the right of the insured to change a beneficiary designation or select an optional settlement for a beneficiary shall not be affected by these provisions. If a policy matures as a result of death or otherwise during the period of protection, the insurance company, in making settlement, shall deduct from the insurance proceeds the amount of the unpaid premiums guaranteed under SCRA together with interest due at the rate fixed in the policy for policy loans; and said deductions shall be reported by the insurer to the Secretary of Veterans Affairs.

Payment of premiums, and interest which become due on a policy under the protection period are guaranteed by the United States. If the amount guaranteed is not paid to the insurer before the period of insurance protection expires, the amount due shall be treated by the insurer as a policy loan on the policy. If, at the expiration of insurance protection period, the cash surrender value of a policy is less than the amount due to pay premiums and interest on premiums on the policy, the policy shall terminate and the United States shall pay the insurer the difference between the amount due and the cash surrender value. Said debt shall be payable to the United States by the insured on whose policy payment was made. Such amount may be collected by the United States, either as an offset from any amount due the insured by the United States or as otherwise authorized by law, and shall not be dischargeable in bankruptcy.

A civil or administrative action for damages based upon alleged professional negligence or other professional liability of a servicemember whose professional liability insurance coverage has been suspended is stayed until the end of the period of the suspension. Any stay shall toll any statutory period of limitation on the commencement of such action.

If a servicemember dies during the period of the suspension of coverage, the requirement for the grant or continuance of a stay in any civil or administrative action against such servicemember terminates on the date of the death.

If a tax or assessment becomes due during a servicemember's military service, the personal property or real property occupied for dwelling, business or for agricultural purposes may not be sold to enforce collection of such tax or assessment. A court may stay a proceeding to enforce collection of such tax or sale of such property during a period of military service and for 180 days after the termination of the servicemember from military service. When protected property is sold to enforce the collection of a tax, a servicemember has the right to redeem or commence an action to redeem the property.

Rights to public lands acquired by a servicemember before military service shall not be forfeited as a result of being absent from the land or by failing to begin or complete any work or improvements to the land during the period of service or 180 days thereafter.

The collection of income tax on the income of a servicemember falling due before or during military service shall be deferred for the length of service plus 180 days thereafter if a servicemember's ability to pay is materially affected by military service. Furthermore the running of the statute of limitations for these actions is suspended during the length of service and for 270 days thereafter. Servicemembers can neither lose nor acquire a residence or domicile for purposes of taxation with respect to the person, personal property or income of the servicemember by reason of being absent or present in any tax jurisdiction of the United States solely in compliance with military orders.

Under SCRA, any Certificate signed by the Secretary concerned is *prima facie* evidence as to any of the following facts stated in the certificate: (1) that a person named is, is not, has been, or has not been in military service; (2) the time and the place the person entered military service; (3) the person's residence at the time the person entered military service; (4) the rank, branch and unit of military service of the person upon entry; (5) the inclusive dates of the person's military service; (6) the monthly pay received by the person at the date of the certificate's issuance; (7) the time and place of the person's termination of, or release from, military service, or the person's death during military service.

The reinstatement of healthcare insurance coverage for the health or physical condition of a servicemember is not subject to an exclusion or a waiting period, if: (1) the condition arose before or during the period of such service; (2) an exclusion or a waiting period would not have been imposed for the condition during the period of coverage; and (3) if the condition relates to the servicemember and the condition has not been determined by the Secretary of Veterans Affairs to be a disability incurred or aggravated in the line of duty. An application for reinstatement must be filed not later than 120 days after the date of the termination of or release from military service.

ENFORCEABILITY OF ARBITRATION CLAUSES

While arbitration may be an appropriate vehicle for the prompt resolution of claims, there are times when a party to a dispute would rather have the case decided by a court of law with or without a jury. Careful attention needs to be paid to the "fine print" in purchase orders or other types of agreements where an arbitration clause may be included. One should not be surprised when arbitration is invoked as it can become not only embarrassing, but also time consuming and expensive. Arbitration clauses will usually be enforced, even if a business person has failed to see it in an agreement.

Commercial arbitration agreements today are recognized by statute by the Federal Arbitration Act, 9 USC § 1, et seq., and in all states. However, the extent to which these agreements are enforceable differs widely. In overruling the common law, many statutes distinguish between agreements to submit pending disputes to arbitration and agreements to arbitrate unknown disputes which might arise in the future. Most laws provide that all agreements to arbitrate, whether of pending or future controversies, are valid, irrevocable and enforceable. NACM has established a popular program for binding arbitration of commercial disputes. In existing disputes, however, many statutes require that the agreement be made a rule of court before it becomes irrevocable and enforceable.

As a rule, arbitration clauses do not bind the parties absent an express bilateral agreement such as in a credit application. A proposal in contract negotiations to resolve disputes by arbitration has been held under the UCC to constitute a material alteration under UCC 2-207(2), which will be binding only if expressly accepted by the other side.

Generally, in order for an arbitration award to be enforced, it must be confirmed by judicial proceedings in the state in which it was rendered. A problem may arise, however, in connection with enforcement of an arbitrator's award rendered under the laws of a sister state. In most cases, out-of-state awards can be enforced only by obtaining a confirming judgment in the state in which the award was originally entered. This judgment can then be executed in the desired state by virtue of the full faith and credit provision of the federal Constitution.

It will be convenient, therefore, for purposes of comparison, to divide the states into two groups. The breakdown will be based upon those states which have by statute or judicial law changed the common law rule of revocability which permitted either party to an arbitration agreement to terminate it at will at any time prior to the rendition of an award.

The first group of states to be discussed includes those in which there is specific authority by statute or judicial ruling holding an arbitration clause in a commercial contract to be valid, irrevocable and enforceable. The first 44 states and the District of Columbia listed below, as well as the United States, have statutes that reverse the common law rule of revocability and make written promises to arbitrate specifically enforceable. Most of these states have adopted the Uniform Arbitration Act, and in some states with modifications, generally to provide that it does not apply to certain contracts. Some states have not adopted the Uniform Arbitration Act, but have similar statutory provisions.

Connecticut and Texas have each adopted a statute providing for international commercial arbitration.

The 44 states and the District of Columbia and federal law in Group I are shown below with brief reference to applicable statutes and court decisions:

Group I

Alaska—AK Statutes § 09.43.010.

Arizona—RSA § 12-1517. Uniform Arbitration Act adopted a written arbitration agreement is enforceable and irrevocable. No application to employer-employee disputes.

Arkansas—ASA, §§ 16-108-201 through 16-108-224. The Act, originally passed in 1969, applied only to construction and manufacturing contracts. Now it applies to everything but excludes personal injury, tort, employer-employee disputes and insurance matters.

California—CPC § 1281. Written agreement to arbitrate enforceable and irrevocable.

Colorado—Rule 109, West CO RSA. §§ 13-22-201 through §§ 13-22-223, Uniform Arbitration Act adopted.

Connecticut—GSR § 52-408 through § 52-423.

Delaware—Code, Title 10, Chap. 5 §§ 5701-5728 (1972). Uniform Arbitration Act adopted, but does apply to collective bargaining, labor contracts with public and private employers.

District of Columbia—DC Code 1981, §§ 16-4301 through 16-4319. Uniform Arbitration Act adopted.

Florida—West's FSA §§ 682.01 through 682.22. Uniform Arbitration Act adopted.

Georgia—§§ 9-9-1 et seq. "Georgia Arbitration Act" (1988). A written agreement to submit any existing controversy to arbitration or a provision in a written contract to submit any controversy thereafter arising to arbitration to enforceable. This act does not apply to collective bargaining agreements between employers and labor unions, to any contract of insurance, to any loan agreement or consumer financing agreement in which the amount of indebtedness is $25,000 or less at the time of execution, to any contract for the purchase of consumer goods, and to certain other contracts.

Hawaii—Rev. Laws of HI 1967, Chap. 658-1 et seq. Provision in a written contract to arbitrate is enforceable and irrevocable. Either party is entitled to jury trial.

Idaho—§§ 7-901 through 7-922. Uniform Arbitration Act adopted.

Illinois—IRS Chapter 710, 5/1 et seq.

Indiana—West's AIC 34-57-2-1 to 34-57-2-22. Uniform Arbitration Act adopted.

Iowa—ICA §§ 679A.1 through 679A.19. Uniform Arbitration Act.

Kansas—KSA §§ 5-401 through 5-422. Uniform Arbitration Act adopted, but existing statutes not repealed.

Kentucky—KRS §§ 417.045 through 417.240. (1984) Uniform Arbitration Act with some modifications adopted. There is no application to employer-employee agreements and insurance contracts.

Louisiana—RSA §§ 9:4201 through 9:4217. A written agreement to submit a controversy to arbitration is enforceable and irrevocable.

Maine—§§ 5927 through 5949. (1967) Uniform Arbitration Act adopted.

Maryland—Courts Art. §§ 3-201 through 3-234. Uniform Arbitration Act adopted. Unless not expressly provided by parties, Uniform Act does not apply to arbitration agreements between employers and employees.

Massachusetts—MGLA c. 251, §§ 1 through 19. Uniform Arbitration Act adopted.

Michigan—MCLA §§ 600.5001 through 600.5035. Uniform Arbitration Act adopted.

Minnesota—MSA §§ 572.08 through 572.30. Uniform Arbitration Act adopted.

Mississippi—MCA, §§ 11-15-1 through 11-15-37; 11-15-101 through 11-15-143. Parties can agree in advance to arbitrate disputes and the agreement can be binding.

Missouri—§§ 435.350 through 435.470. Uniform Arbitration Act adopted.

Montana—MCA §§ 27-5-111 through 27-5-324. Uniform Arbitration Act adopted. It is applicable to employer-employee agreements if the agreement so specifies. It is not applicable to personal injury actions based on tort or contract, contracts for real property or services where the total consideration is $5,000 or less, insurance contracts and worker's compensation claims.

Nebraska—§§ 25.2601 through 2622. Uniform Arbitration Act adopted. Not applicable to personal injury claims based on tort, claims under Nebraska Fair Employment Practices Act, insurance contracts and certain other agreements.

Nevada—NRS 38.015 through 38.205. Uniform Arbitration Act adopted. It applies to employer-employee disputes unless otherwise provided in the agreement.

New Jersey—RS § 2A-24-1. Arbitration clause does not operate so as to deprive party of ancillary relief, short of arbitrable matters, by the court unless provision in contract specifically excludes it. *Pyramid Electric Co. v. Staklinski*, 61 N.J. Super. 278, 160 A.2d 505 (1960).

New Mexico—NMSA 1978, §§ 44-7-1 through 44-7-22. Uniform Arbitration Act adopted. It applies to employer-employee disputes unless otherwise provided in the agreement.

North Carolina—GS §§ 1-567.1 through 1-567.20. Uniform Arbitration Act adopted. Not applicable to employer-employee agreements unless agreement so provides.

North Dakota—NDCC §§ 32-29.2-01 through 32-29.2-20. Uniform Arbitration Act adopted. It applies to employer-employee disputes unless otherwise provided in the agreement.

Oklahoma—15 OSA §§ 801 through 818. Uniform Arbitration Act adopted. Not applicable to employer-employee agreements or insurance contracts, except when insurer and insured are both insurance companies.

Oregon—36.00 through 36.365. Contract to arbitrate current dispute, or provision in written contract to settle by arbitration controversy thereafter arising, based on contract or its breach, is valid, irrevocable and enforceable if arbitration is held in Oregon.

Pennsylvania—42 PCSA §§ 7301 through 7320, Uniform Arbitration Act adopted despite the existence of a modern arbitration statute, Pennsylvania courts have held that arbitration proceeds at common law unless the agreement itself provides that the statute governs or a municipal authority is involved. *John A. Robbins Co. v. Airportels, Inc.*, 418 Pa. 257, 210 A.2d 896 (1965), *Wingate Construction Co. v. Schweizer Dipple, Inc.*, 419 Pa. 74, 213 A.2d 275 (1965), *La Vale Plaza Inc. v. R.S. Noonan, Inc.*, 378 F.2d 569 (3rd Cir. 1967).

Rhode Island—GLA 10-3-2 et seq.: Rhode Island Gen. Laws 37-16-1 et al., known as "The Public Works Arbitration Act," says that any construction contract for a public works project executed in 1962 or thereafter may contain a provision concerning arbitration of disputes and that any such contract executed on or after July 1, 1967, involving a sum of $10,000 or more must contain a clause providing arbitration for disputes and claims arising out of or concerning the performance of interpretation of the contract. School teachers have also been included under this act.

South Carolina—Uniform Arbitration Act § 1 (1978) §§ 15-48-10 through 15-48-240. Not applicable to employer-employee agreements unless the agreement so specifies. Not applicable to pre-agreement between doctor and patient and attorney and client or any claim arising out of personal injury (based on contract or tort) or any insurance contract.

South Dakota—Comp. Laws §§ 21-25A-1 through 38 (Supp. 1978). Not applicable to insurance contracts.

Tennessee—TCA §§ 29-5-301 through 29-5-320. Uniform Arbitration Act adopted.

Texas—TCPR §§171.001 through 172.175. Not applicable for employer-employee contracts, agreement for property services where the total consideration is not more than $50,000, not applicable to personal injury claims or worker's compensation claims.

Utah—78-31a-1 through 20. Uniform Arbitration Act has been adopted as "Utah Arbitration Act."

Vermont—12 VSA §§ 5651 through 5681. Not applicable to labor disputes or insurance contracts.

Virginia—§§ 8.01-581.01 through 8.01-581.016. Applicable to employer-employee agreements.

Washington—WRCA §§ 7.04.010 through 7.04.220. Not applicable to employer-employee agreements.

Wisconsin—WI Statutes, §§ 1-36-101 through 1-36-119. Applicable to employer-employee agreements unless otherwise provided.

Wyoming—§§ 1-36-101 through 1-36-119. Uniform Arbitration Act in substance adopted.

United States—9 USC §§ 1 through 4. For a discussion of the Federal Arbitration Act, *see Bernhardt v. Polygraphic Co. of America*, 350 U.S. 198 (1956), and *Prima Paint Corp. v. Flood & Conklin*, 388 U.S. 395 (1967).

Group II

The following two states, designated Group II, have statutes which provide essentially that agreements only to arbitrate existing controversies are valid.

Alabama—Code of AL, §§ 6-6-1 through 6-6-16. Agreements to arbitrate existing disputes valid; and future disputes as to amount only. *Moss v. W. K. Upchurch*, 278 Ala. 615, 179 So. 2d 741 (1965).

West Virginia—WVC §§ 55-10-1 through 55-10-4, Official Code of 1931, covers agreements to arbitrate existing controversies. Although a contract to submit future differences to arbitration is not binding, where a contract for future arbitration of controversies has become executed in respect to any pertinent matter of difference between the parties, the award is binding. *Hughes v. National Fuel Co.*, 121 W.Va. 392, 3 S.E.2d 621 (1939). Statutory procedure is not exclusive but is supplementary to that already existing at common law. *United Fuel Gas Co. v. Columbian Fuel Corp.*, 165 F.2d 746 (4th Cir. 1948).

NEW LAWS AND TRENDS

Many states including California, Illinois, Louisiana, Michigan, New Jersey and New York, among others, have recently enacted Data Breach Notification Laws, which require businesses and state agencies to notify consumers when there is a security breach of their personal information.

These statutes require various notification to consumers by various media, such as, writing, telephone, e-mail in certain cases, when "unauthorized acquisition or acquisition without valid authorization" of private information that "compromises the security, confidentiality, or integrity of personal information" occurs.

These laws address "private/personal information," such as any information concerning a natural person's name, identification, or account number, personal marks, or other items that can be used to identify such natural person in conjunction with one or more data elements including: social security, driver's license, or credit card numbers, bank account information, or other financial account numbers with codes or passwords allowing access.

The definition as to the Data Holding Entity being regulated varies from state to state and may include concurrent notification to various state offices in addition to the account holders involved.

Currently there is no uniformity amongst the states. Many state laws vary greatly in the following areas:

- *Limits in scope of the release relative to unencrypted data.* Various laws have different risk threshold provisions that allow a covered entity to avoid disclosure if there is little risk of harm to individuals as the result of a breach.
- *Notification provisions.* Some laws may create the potential for "over-notification" and desensitization. Some contain various safe harbors from notification for a covered entity with its own consumer breach notification policy that is at least as strong as the State's. Others provide a safe harbor or exemption for entities that are governed by federal regulators and already are subject to data security and consumer notification requirements of federal laws, such as GLB or the Health Insurance Portability and Accountability Act (HIPAA).

Some state laws provide a substitute notice provision at various levels of persons involved; e.g., if there are more than 500,000 names or if the cost of notifying individual consumers would exceed a certain dollar value, such as $250,000, then consumers can be notified by alternate means, including e-mail, if their e-mail addresses are known, and by posting announcements in statewide media and on the entity's website.

It is clear that Federal Legislation would be appropriate to create uniformity. Currently the Senate Banking Committee and the Judiciary Committee are working on data security breach notification legislation. Whatever finally emerges will hopefully be fairly comprehensive and include not only data security, notification to consumers in cases of security breaches, fraud alerts; but also include the regulation of data brokers (specifically attempting to provide "transparency" by giving consumers the right to examine data broker's records and allow them to correct inaccuracies); as well as access to and use of social security numbers.

FACTA Disposal Rule

On June 1, 2005, a new rule became effective requiring businesses and individuals to take appropriate measures when disposing of personal information obtained from consumer credit reports.

This new amendment to the Fair and Accurate Credit Transactions Act of 2003 covers personal or financial information and may include social security numbers, banking information, addresses or telephone numbers, to name a few.

The rule applies to small and large businesses and includes any entity that has or obtains the kind of information which must be properly discarded. The acceptable methods of disposal include burning, pulverizing, or shredding of papers containing consumer report information so that the information cannot be read or reconstructed; destruction or erasure of electronic files or media containing consumer report information so that the information cannot be read or reconstructed. Further, due diligence in hiring a document destruction contractor to dispose of this type of material is mandated.

Refer to Chapter 27 for the following forms:

- Agreement to Revive a Debt Barred by Statute of Limitations
- Arbitration Clause for Domestic Trade Contracts
- Arbitration Clause for Foreign Trade Contracts
- Compromise Agreement (General)
- Endorsement on Check Constituting Accord and Satisfaction
- Proof of Claim with Power of Attorney

EXECUTION EXEMPTIONS[1]

Note: State legislatures will, on occasion, modify an area of law without clear delineation as to its content and context. As a result, even the changes which have been enacted prior to placement in the state's Code may be difficult to locate. As a result, the Editors urge all users of the *Manual* to use this publication only as a guide, and consult the latest codified version of the state's law for all recent changes.

STATE	HOMESTEAD		PERSONAL PROPERTY[3]		WAGES[2]
	AMOUNT	WHO MAY CLAIM	AMOUNT	WHO MAY CLAIM	
Alabama	Area 160 acres. Value $5,000.	Any resident.	Personal property to $3,000 and necessary family clothing, family portraits, and books. Personal property in the custody of a trustee in bankruptcy is exempt to the bankrupt and cannot be garnished. Insurance for benefit of wife and children to extent of premium of $1,000 per year, pension and retirement plans, disability and debts benefits that constitute a qualified trust under the Internal Revenue Code.	Any resident.	Of laborers or employees who are residents of the state in an amount equal to 75% of wages. On judgments based on consumer transactions, lesser of 25% of disposable earnings for week, or twice amount of disposable earnings each week equal to 30 times. "Disposable earnings" means earnings remaining after deductions required by law; periodic payments pursuant to pension, retirement, or disability programs are not "disposable earnings."
Alaska	Area 160 acres in country; ¼ acre in town or city, laid off in blocks or lots. Value not in excess of $67,500. For trailer or mobile home the exemption is $12,000. Homestead to value of $8000 held by tenants by entirety is not liable for debts of either or both tenants, except by special agreement.	Any resident or dependent who owns and uses same as his actual abode. Owner or owner's spouse, agent, or attorney.	$3,750 of personal property, clothing, and household goods; $1,250 of pets; $1,250 of jewelry; $3,500 of tools; $3,750 of automobile, if value does not exceed $25,000.	Any resident.	75% of weekly net income or $402.50 whichever is more.
Arizona	Residence and land of debtor, equity interest in apartment, not to exceed $150,000 in value, mobile home and land on which it is located not to exceed $150,000 in value. Claim for exemption must be filed in office of County Recorder.	Any person 18 or over married or single who resides in state.	Property must be designated by debtor. Household goods, up to $4,000; cash, $150; clothing, $500; motor vehicle, $5,000; and miscellaneous articles. Money received by surviving spouse or child upon life of deceased spouse or parent not exceeding $20,000.	Every family.	One-half of earnings for 30 days prior to levy when necessary for use of family. 25% of disposable earnings or 30 times the federal minimum hourly wage, whichever is less.
Arkansas	Unlimited value of residence, or real or personal property used as residence, to $800 if single; $1250 if married, subject to certain liens. 160 aces and up to $2,500 in country for homesteads of 80 acres or more; 1 acre and up to $2,500 in city.	Resident married or head of family (surviving spouse and dependent minor children).	Not head of family: Specific articles as selected not exceeding value of $200 in addition to wearing apparel. Head of family: Articles to value of $500 besides clothes. Exemption does not apply to debts in payment of articles for which purchase price is claimed.	Resident who is not married or head of family. Married or head of family.	Constitutional exemption: *Single person*—$200 including personal property other than wearing apparel. *Head of family*—$500 including personal property other than wearing apparel. *Laborers and mechanics*—Wages for 60 days exempt provided statement is filed that said wages plus personal property holdings are less than constitutional exemption. First $25 a week net wages absolutely exempt. Wages may be garnished for support of children under 18.

State	Homestead Exemption		Personal Property Exemption		Wages Exemption
California	By any head of a family, , $75,000; if single, $50,000; by any person 55 or older not exceeding $150,000 in cash value. If a person is 65 years of age or physically or mentally disabled and unable to work, the limit is $150,000. Dwelling includes mobile home, a condominium or can be a dwelling situated on property leased for a period of 30 years or more. Debtors may claim exemption for a dwelling house which has not been declared a homestead but in which debtor or his family actually resides and which could be selected as a homestead pursuant to law.	Resident head of family. By any other resident.	Numerous necessary articles for their business, trade, calling, profession, etc., up to $6,075 if only used by one spouse and $12,150 if used by both; household furniture, equipment and clothing is usually exempt; jewelry, $6,075; and art. Motor vehicle, $2,300. Residents are entitled to an exemption on proceeds from disability, death, retirement, pension, and unemployment insurance plans, and the like whether government sponsored or paid pursuant to private programs.	Any person. Farmers, mechanics, miners, truckmen, professional men, etc.	Greater of (1) 75% of disposable earnings for work week; or (2) amount each week equal to 30 times federal minimum hourly wage. No exemption for 50% of judgment debtor's earnings minus wage assignment amount under support order. All paid earnings are exempt if prior to payment to employee, they were subject to an earnings withholding order or wage assignment for support. That portion of debtor's earnings proven necessary for support of himself or family unless debt incurred for personal services, the order is for delinquent support, or the order is for state tax liability.
Colorado	No limitation on area. Homestead occupied as home exempt to $45,000 in excess of any liens or encumbrances. Word "homestead" must be entered on margin of record title. A house trailer or coach is exempt if used as residence. Mobile home is exempt to $6000.	Householder, head of family, or deceased debtor's spouse or child.	Necessary wearing apparel to the extent of $750 per person; watches, jewelry, and articles of adornment $500 per person; library, family pictures, and school books to the extent of $750; burial sites; household goods to the extent of $1,500 in value; provisions and fuel on hand to the extent of $300; livestock not exceeding $3,000 and horses, mules, carts, machinery not exceeding $2,000; pensions; stock in trade, supplies, fixtures, tools of business not exceeding $1500; motor vehicle not exceeding $1000; library of a professional person not exceeding $1500; life insurance policies to the extent of $50,000; aggregate value of all items excepted shall be limited to $12,500.	Single resident or head of family.	75% of earnings due head of family and 40% of earnings due a single person or an amount each week equal to 30 times federal minimum hourly wage; also subject to UCCC provisions.
Connecticut	Occupied. Residence and land of debtor up to the market value of $75,000.	Resident.	Certain specific articles such as apparel, household furniture, ERISA benefits and IRAs entirely exempt, and other articles up to designated values. One motor vehicle to $1,500.	Resident.	Greater of 75% of disposable earnings for work week or twice disposable earnings for week up to an amount equal to 40 times the higher of the minimum hourly wage under the Fair Labor Standards Act or the full minimum fair wage under state labor law.
Delaware	No homestead exemption.		Total exemptions for husband and wife may not exceed $10,000; single person, $5,000.	Any resident. Any resident being head of family.	Exemption of 85% of wages. Wages or salary are exempt from garnishment for 60 days from date of default on a contract or installment account.

EXECUTION EXEMPTIONS *(Continued)*

STATE	HOMESTEAD		PERSONAL PROPERTY		WAGES
	AMOUNT	WHO MAY CLAIM	AMOUNT	WHO MAY CLAIM	
District of Columbia	Real property used as residence by debtor.	Head of family or householder.	Implements and tools of trade to extent of $1,625; household furnishings, goods, clothing, books, animals to the aggregate value of $8,625; family pictures/library, $400. Burial plot is exempt. Motor vehicle $2,750.	Resident head of family or householder. All persons.	Greater of 75% of disposable earnings per week or amount of disposable earnings per week equal to 30 times Federal minimum hourly wage. *Withholding by Garnishee-Employer*—90% of first $200 of gross wages payable in a month, 80% of gross wages payable in a month in excess of $200 and under $500. *Debtor Principal Support of Family*—$200 each month of earnings other than wages of resident or non-resident earning major portion of livelihood in D.C. exempt for two months preceding issuance of writ. *Debtor Not Principal Support of Family*—$60 each month is exempt. Support judgments 50% of gross wages exempt.
Florida	Totally exempt except; 160 acres in country, ½ acre in city. No limit on value may be claimed by recording declaration of homestead or after levy and before sale by ratifying officer who is to sell, in writing of claim of homestead. Interest in 98-year lease qualifies for homestead exemption.	Only $1,000 of personal property exempt. Head of family residing in state. Surviving tenant by the entirety or spouse of the owner.	$1,000 of personal property is exempt. Pensions and some benefits are exempt.	Head of family residing in state.	Entire wages of the head of family when wages are due for personal labor or services of such person. Amount exempt is exclusive of payroll deductions for taxes. Courts may limit exception for alimony or child support.
Georgia	Real property, including co-op to $10,000; unused homestead may be applied to any property. A couple may double the real property amount.	Head of family or aged or infirm person or one having care of dependent minor of any age.	Value $5,000, real or personal or both set apart by petition. Purchase money debt enforceable against. (Either this exemption or homestead exemption may be claimed but not both.) Certain IRA, pension and retirement funds.	Head of family or aged or infirm person or one having care of dependent female of any age.	Greater of 75% of disposable earnings per week or amount by which disposable earnings exceed 30 times the federal minimum hourly wage. General exemption ineffective against support orders and alimony decree where garnishment based on such judgment, a maximum of 50% of disposable earnings subject to garnishment.
Hawaii	An interest in one parcel of property owned by head of family or person 65 years or older may not exceed $30,000; when owned by any other person may not exceed $20,000 as determined by assessed valuation.	Any person.	Various specified articles of personal property. (The exemption does not apply, however, to execution on a judgment recovered for the purchase price of such goods as on a foreclosure of a security agreement or other encumbrancing instrument on the goods.)	Any resident.	95% of first $100, 90% of next $100, and 80% of wages in excess of $2,000 per month, or equivalent per week. Whether then or thereafter to become owing.

State	Homestead	Persons Entitled	Personal Property	Persons Entitled	Wages
Idaho	$50,000 in excess of mortgage. Exemption is confined to dwelling house and land on which it is situated. Declaration must be executed and recorded.	Family. By any other person.	Burial plot, necessary health aids, public assistance benefits, health benefits—100% exemption; if necessary for support: income of various types and some assets—100% exemption; necessary furnishings and appliances, personal clothing, books, musical instruments, animals, family portraits, one firearm, and heirlooms—value not to exceed $4000; personal jewelry—value not to exceed $250; implements, professional books, tools of the trade—value not to exceed $1,000; one motor vehicle—value not to exceed $1500; various other types of property.	Any person.	Greater of 75% of disposable earnings for workweek or amount each week equal to 30 times federal minimum hourly wage. Married woman's wages are exempt from garnishment for husband's debt. For judgments arising from debt on consumer credit sale, greater of (1) 75% of disposable earnings for workweek; or (2) amount each week equal to 40 times federal minimum hourly wage. Support orders: Maximum is 50% if other child or a spouse, 40% if not.
Illinois	$7,500 in land with buildings, owned or leased, occupied as residence. A couple may double the exemption.	Resident and householder	Wearing apparel, Bible, school books, family pictures, military pensions for one year. $2,000 in any other property. $1,200 in motor vehicle, $750 in implements, professional books, or tools of trade.	Any person.	Weekly disposable wages not in excess of 40 times federal minimum hourly wage.
Indiana	Personal or family residence, $7,500; other real estate or tangible personal property $4,000. In no event shall total exemptions exceed $10,000. Wife can claim one-third of any real estate owned by husband.	Resident householder. Where a husband and wife are each conducting a separate and distinct business each may have the full exemption of $1,000.	Tangible personal property, along with other non-residential personal property, not to exceed $10,000. Intangible personal property, including choses in action (but excluding debts owing, and income owing) up to $100 tort claims.	Debtor residing in state. Where a husband and wife are each conducting a separate and distinct business out of their own individual funds may claim separate exemption.	UCCC provides exemption for 75% of disposable earnings per week or the amount in excess of 30 times the federal minimum hourly wage, whichever is greater. The following provisions have not been repealed by the UCCC and appear to be in conflict with it: Householder exemption not exceeding $25. In *Mims v. Consumer Credit Corp.*, (Ind. Sup. Ct., March 13, 1974), the court held that statute most beneficial to householder would be enforced. Exemptions are inapplicable to alimony, support orders and wages earned by nonresidents within the state. For support orders: Maximum is 50% if a spouse or other child, 40% if not.
Iowa	If within city or town plot must not exceed one-half acre, otherwise not more than 40 acres, but if in either case value is less than $500, it may be enlarged to reach that amount. Exceptions: Homestead liable for deficiency remaining after exhausting all other nonexempt property where debt is contracted prior to acquisition of homestead; by written contract stipulating that homestead shall be liable; also, for debts incurred for work done or material furnished exclusively for the improvement of homestead; also, if no survivor or issue, for payment of debts to which it might at that time be subject if it had never been held as a homestead.	Resident, head of family, husband, or wife.	Extensive exemptions not exceeding $5,000 in aggregate, including: wearing apparel, $1,000; household furnishings/goods, $2,000; books/pictures/paintings, $1,000; life insurance, $10,000; health aids, burial plot; some retirement benefits; a combination of musical instruments, motor vehicle and tax refunds not exceeding $1,000. Tools of trade, $10,000. Also provisions for farming exemptions.	Resident, head of family. Nonresident or unmarried resident not head of family.	75% of disposable earnings for week or amount by which disposable earnings for week exceed 30 times federal minimum hourly wage, whichever is greater. Except for child support orders, maximum amount that can be garnished in any year is $250 for each creditor. For consumer credit debt, exemption is greater of 75% of disposable weekly earnings, or 40 times federal hourly minimum wage. Debtor earning less than $12,000 per year—maximum sum permitted to be executed is $250.

EXECUTION EXEMPTIONS *(Continued)*

STATE	HOMESTEAD AMOUNT	HOMESTEAD WHO MAY CLAIM	PERSONAL PROPERTY AMOUNT	PERSONAL PROPERTY WHO MAY CLAIM	WAGES
Kansas	160 acres, farm; one acre in city, occupied as residence. No limitation in homestead value.	Any resident.	Head of household: (1) furnishing and supplies, including food and clothing for a period of one year; (2) one means of conveyance; (3) family burial plot; (4) equipment or other means of production necessary in carrying on a trade, business, occupation, or profession not to exceed $7,500; (5) jewelry not exceeding $1,000 in value.	Any resident.	75% of disposable earnings for week or amount by which disposable earnings exceed 30 times federal minimum hourly wage, whichever is greater. For support orders: 40% of weekly disposable earnings or 50% if debtor is supporting a spouse or child not involved in the support order. Amounts withheld pursuant to an order of withholding for support may not exceed the maximums set by the Federal Consumer Credit Protection Act.
Kentucky	$5,000 including improvements, unless liability existed before purchase of land. Property or the erections on the improvements thereon. Mortgage on homestead, release or waiver must be in writing and signed also by wife and recorded.	Householder.	Many articles, household goods, wearing apparel, etc., not to exceed $3,000 in value, tools, equipment and livestock of a person engaged in farming, not to exceed $3,000, certain payments; money or property for alimony or support; mechanic's tools, livestock not to exceed $3,000 in value; one motor vehicle not to exceed $2,500 in value. Pension and retirement plans, disability and benefits death.	Individual debtor.	Greater of 75% of disposable income per week or 30 times federal minimum hourly wage. Exemptions inapplicable to support and bankruptcy orders and state and federal taxes.
Louisiana	$25,000 not over 200 acres. Exemption may be waived. Claim must be in writing and recorded in parish where homestead is situated. A couple may double the exemption.	Resident with family or other dependents.	Certain articles specified in statute, such as musical instruments and household pets, clothing, tools of a trade other articles.	Householder.	75% of disposable earnings for any week, but not less than 30 times the federal minimum wage in effect when the wages are payable. For child and spouse support, 50% of disposable earnings. Loans with interest in excess of 10%—lender cannot use garnishment.
Maine	Principal residence up to $35,000 or $70,000 if minor dependents are residing with debtor, or if debtor is 60 years of age or older.	Householder and spouse.	Motor vehicle $5,000; clothing, furniture, appliances, and similar items, the debtor's interest not to exceed $200 in any particular item that is held for personal, family, or household use; jewelry not to exceed $750, tools of trade not to exceed $5000.	Resident.	Greater of 75% of disposable earnings for week or amount by which disposable earnings exceed 30 times federal minimum hourly wage. 75% of weekly disposable earnings or 40 times the hourly wage in consumer transactions. Wages due debtor for wife's or minor child's personal service are exempt. Trustee process—100% of wages exempt. Support orders: Maximum of 50% if another child or a spouse, 40% if not. Exemptions do not apply to court-ordered support orders in Chapter 13 bankruptcy cases, state or federal taxes.
Maryland	None. $5,500 total in unrestricted exemptions which may be applied to a residence.	Debtor.	$1,000 in household goods, clothing, and other items kept for household, personal, or family use; $6,000 in real or personal property; personal property not to exceed $5,000 for practice of any trade or profession.	Bona fide residents.	$145 multiplied by the number of weeks in which such wages due were earned or 75% of such wages, whichever is greater. Except that in Caroline, Worcester, Kent, and Queen Anne counties exemption for any workweek shall be greater of 75% of wages due or 30 times federal minimum hourly wage. Any medical insurance payment deducted from employee's wages by employer.

State	Homestead Exemption		Personal Property Exemption		Wages
Massachusetts	$500,000; elderly and/or disabled persons: $500,000 in value of land and buildings. Must be established by deed or declaration and recorded. Exemptions do not apply to taxes, debts contracted prior to acquisition of homestead, purchase money and support orders.	Householder, including holder of possessory interest by lease, or otherwise, provided the estate serves as the principal residence of the debtor and the debtor has a family.	Many articles. Household furniture not exceeding $3,000 in value. Materials and stock necessary for carrying on trade or business, value of $500. Cash savings or deposits not to exceed $80. An automobile necessary for personal transportation or to secure or maintain employment, not exceeding $700.	Debtor.	Up to $125. Trustee process.—Wages for personal labor or services earned but not paid exempted from attachment to amount of $125 per week. Exemption of $125 of personal income which is not otherwise exempt by law. $100 per week in pension is exempt.
Michigan	$3,500 in lot, if in city, and not exceeding 40 acres in extent, if in country or one lot if in city.	Resident citizen.	As to householders: certain articles, household goods, amounting to $1,000. As to businessmen: tools, implements, stock in trade necessary to carry on business, $1,000. Partners' right in specific partnership property is not subject to attachment or execution except on a claim against the partnership. When partnership debt there is no exemption under the laws.	Resident citizen.	No statutory provision.
Minnesota	160 acres in country, in village or city ½ acre with improvements. No limitation in value. House owned and occupied by debtor and land on which such house is situated are exempt but only a total of 160 acres in country; ½ acre in village or city; a mobile home actually inhabited by debtor is exempt. $200,000, if homestead is used primarily for agriculture purposes $500,000.	Resident.	Farm machines and implements and livestock produce and standing crops not exceeding $13,000 in value; tools and stock of a trade or business not exceeding $5,000 in value; clothes, household furniture, etc., not exceeding $4,500 in value; one motor vehicle to the extent of a value not exceeding $2,000; other specific articles; a mobile home, the earnings of a minor child of any debtor by reason of any liability of any such debtor not contracted for the special benefit of said child. Nothing exempt from execution or attachment in action for balance of purchase price thereof. Judgment for the unpaid balance of agricultural property owed by a farm debtor does not attach to real or personal property acquired by farmer after judgment is entered.	Resident.	Greater of 75% of disposable earnings or 40 times the federal minimum hourly wage.
Mississippi	$75,000 in value and not exceeding 160 acres if outside city, town or village. Homestead can be house or apartment or condominium. Homestead exemption is denied under certain circumstances where portions of property are rented or used for other commercial purposes. Homestead is subject to liens; up to $30,000 in insurance proceeds covering homestead are exempt if buildings are destroyed; proceeds from sale of property are exempt.	Citizen householder. Husband or wife, widow or widower over 60 years of age not occupying homestead.	Tangible personal property not exceeding $10,000, selected by debtor; proceeds of insurance on property and proceeds of sale of property; income from disability insurance; pension, stock bonuses, profit sharing plans and annuities.	Any person.	After a 30-day grace period, the greater of 75% of disposable earnings or the amount equal to 30 times the minimum hourly federal wage law. Exemptions not applicable to taxes, pensions.

EXECUTION EXEMPTIONS *(Continued)*

STATE	HOMESTEAD		PERSONAL PROPERTY		WAGES
	AMOUNT	WHO MAY CLAIM	AMOUNT	WHO MAY CLAIM	
Missouri	$15,000 in value in dwelling house and land; a mobile home used as a residence not exceeding $1,000 in value is exempt.	Debtor.	Household furnishings and clothes to $3,000. If head of family, may also select any other property to be exempt from execution up to $850 in value. Jewelry not to exceed $500, except wedding ring for $1,500; any other property of any kind not to exceed $3000; tools of trade not to exceed $3000; motor vehicle, $3,000.	Head of family. Non-head of family.	Greatest of (1) 75% percent of disposable weekly earnings, (2) weekly amount equal to 30 times federal minimum hourly wage, or (3) 90% of disposable weekly earnings for resident head of family. Exemptions inapplicable to debtors about to leave the state, support orders, bankruptcy court order under Chapter 13, and alimony and any debt due for federal or state tax.
Montana	Not exceeding $100,000 assessed valuation on 320 acres of agricultural land, one acre outside city, or ¼ acre in city, and dwelling house or mobile home thereon.	Resident.	One automobile or truck value of $2,500. Professional libraries. Minor entitled to $1,000. Property of either spouse can be selected for exemption. Only wearing apparel to unmarried person under 60 years. Certain health and retirement benefits; child support; and burial plot for debtor and his family are exempt without limitation. Judgment debtor's interest not to exceed $4,500 in aggregate value, to the extent of a value not to exceed $600 in any item of property; household furnishings, appliances, jewelry, wearing apparel, books, firearms, other sporting goods, animals, feed crops, and musical instruments; $3,000 in value in any books or tools of the trade; $4,000 in value in any unmatured life insurance contract owned by him.	Resident.	Maximum part of the aggregate disposable earnings subject to garnishment may not exceed the lesser of the amount by which his disposable earnings for the week exceed 30 times the federal minimum wage or 25% of his disposable earnings for that week except that garnishment may not exceed 50% of the debtor's disposable earnings for one week if the debtor is supporting his spouse or dependent child or 60% of the debtor's disposable income if he is not supporting a spouse or dependent child. The latter amounts may be 55% and 65% if the garnishment is to enforce an order of support.
Nebraska	$12,500, consisting of dwelling in which claimant lives and its appurtenances, not over 160 acres in country; two adjoining lots in city.	Debtor.	Personal possessions of debtor and family; necessary wearing apparel of debtor and family; kitchen utensils and household furniture selected by debtor to $1,500. Debtors without homestead may exempt $2,500 in personal property except for wages; equipment or tools not exceeding $1,500; provisions for debtor and family necessary for six months' support; and fuel necessary for six months' support. All articles intended to be exempt shall be chosen by debtor, his agent or legal rep.; pension of soldier and sailor and property purchased therewith $2,000; life insurance on policies not payable to executor or administrator of insured or his beneficiary in an amount paid for by annual premium not exceeding $500.	Any resident debtor.	Greatest of 75% of disposable earnings or amount equal to 30 times federal minimum hourly wage or 85% of disposable earnings if wage earner is head of family. Exemptions are inapplicable bankruptcy court orders and taxes. For support orders, subject to maximum set forth above, $5 per month.

State					
Nevada	Land with house or mobile home with or without land of value not exceeding $200,000, but does not apply to claim for purchase price, taxes on property or lien of mortgage or deed of trust created by and with the consent of the husband and wife.	Any head of family or husband or wife or single person.	Private libraries over $1,500; family fixtures and keepsakes; necessary household goods, appliances and furniture not over $3,000; farm trucks, farm stocks, farm tools, supplies, and seed not over $4,500; professional libraries, office equipment supplies, tools, instruments, and materials used to carry on the trade not over $4,500; one vehicle not over $1,000 or the creditor is paid an amount equal to any excess above that amount; all arms, uniforms required by law to be kept by debtor plus one gun selected by debtor; all monies growing out of any life insurance if annual premium paid not over $1,000.	Debtor.	The amount by which disposable earnings exceed 75% of disposable earnings for any pay period or 30 times the minimum hourly federal wage law. Exemption does not apply to support orders, bankruptcy court orders and state and federal tax debts.
New Hampshire	$100,000 if owned and occupied as dwelling.	Debtor, wife, and children of debtor.	Household furniture $3,500; necessary wearing apparel; tools in trade to value of $5,000; stove; refrigerator; provisions and fuel to value of $400, one automobile to the value of $4,000, jewelry to value of $500. Also miscellaneous property set forth in statute.	Debtor.	Wages for labor performed after service of writ; wages for labor performed before service exempt unless action founded on debt on judgment issued by state court. In such case wages equal to 50 times federal minimum hourly wage are exempt. Special exemption for small loan law debts. 50% of disposable earnings subject to child support order for weekly, monthly, or other pay period. Exemptions inapplicable to tax obligations.
New Jersey	No statutory provisions.		Personal property, value $1,000, and wearing apparel except for a debt incurred in the purchase thereof. Life insurance is exempt.	Debtor.	Minimum exemption of $48 per week; 90% exemption if earnings are $7,500 per year or less. If earnings are more than $7,500 reduced exemption percentage by order of court.
New Mexico	$30,000 in land or dwelling if debtor owns, leases or purchases the dwelling and is married, widowed or supporting another person; jointly owned property entitles each owner to $30,000 exemption; exemption is subject to certain liens; exemption does not apply to taxes, garnishment and recorded liens of mortgages.	Husband and wife or widow or widower living with unmarried daughter or minor son or person supporting himself.	Wearing apparel, household goods under certain values. $500 real or personal property exclusive of articles specified if debtor has no homestead, unless debt is for necessities or for manual labor. Resident not having household has additional exemption of $1,000 of personal property. One motor vehicle up to $4,000, clothing, furniture, tools of trade of $1,500. Books and jewelry in amount of $2,500. Personal property used as security under UCC is not exempt; exemptions are not applicable to taxes or garnishment.	Resident. There are some minor differences for a non-head of household.	Greater of 75% of debtor's disposable earnings or of excess of 40 times federal minimum hourly wage rate. Disposable earnings is that part of debtor's salary remaining after deduction of amounts required to be withheld by law. For child support, 50% of disposable earnings during any pay period.

EXECUTION EXEMPTIONS *(Continued)*

STATE	HOMESTEAD		PERSONAL PROPERTY		WAGES
	WHO MAY CLAIM	AMOUNT	AMOUNT	WHO MAY CLAIM	
New York	Resident householder or woman, principal residence only.	Lot of land with dwelling, a mobile home, shares of stock in cooperative apartment corporation or condominium owned and occupied as a principal residence not to exceed $50,000 in value above liens and encumbrances. No exemption from judgments recovered for purchase price of homestead or for taxes or assessments. Security deposit for rental of realty used as residence of debtor or his family, and utility services deposits are exempt; proceeds from a judgment sale of homestead property are exempt for one year.	All wearing apparel, household goods, television set, tools, implements to the value of $600. Certain other articles; motor vehicle up to $2,400 Keogh and pension plans but not IRAs and certain other health and retirement benefits. Active family burial plot not exceeding ¼ acre.	Debtor.	Income execution cannot exceed lesser of 25% of disposable earnings or amount by which disposable earnings exceed 30 times the minimum wage, also subject to deduction for alimony, support, or maintenance.
North Carolina	Resident.	Property used as a residence not to exceed $10,000 in value; exemption inapplicable to taxes and purchase money mortgage. Property held in tenancy by the entireties exempt from the debts of one spouse.	Articles of personal property not to exceed $3,500 plus $750 for each dependent not to exceed $3,000; one motor vehicle up to $1,500; implements, professional books or tools of the trade up to $750; life insurance, certain compensations; exemption inapplicable to taxes and purchase money.	Resident.	Earnings for personal services for 60 days preceding levy if necessary for support of family. For support orders, exemptions are inapplicable up to 40% of monthly disposable earnings.
North Dakota	Resident.	Resident land and dwelling house with improvements not to exceed $80,000 over and above liens; proceeds of sale of homestead exempt.	Head of a family, money or personal property, $5,000; single person, money or personal property, $2,500. Absolute exemptions include: all wearing apparel and clothing of the debtor and his family; one year's provisions and fuel and crops raised by him on an area not to exceed 160 acres occupied as his homestead; family pictures; a pew or other seating in a house of worship; lots in a burial ground; the family Bible and all school books not to exceed $100 in value; all insurance benefits resulting from insurance covering any or all of the absolute exemptions; any housetrailer or mobile home occupied by the debtor or his family. Resident in addition to other exemptions may select: (1) in lieu of homestead exemption $7,500; (2) motor vehicle exemption not to exceed $1,500; (3) life insurance policy not to exceed $7,500.	Head of a family or single person, resident or nonresident.	Greater of 75% of debtor's disposable earnings or of excess of 40 times federal minimum hourly wage rate. 100% of earnings for personal services within 60 days can be exempted by judge upon affidavit of need for support of family: maximum amount subject to garnishment reduced by 20% for each dependent residing with debtor.

State	Real/Homestead Exemption		Personal Property Exemption		Wage Exemption
Ohio	Property used as residence up to $5000. Property held in tenancy by entirety exempt from the debt of one spouse.	Resident.	Certain specified articles, including wearing apparel, $200 per item; tools and implements for carrying out profession, trade, or business to $750. Motor vehicle up to $1000 in value. $400 in cash. Life insurance is exempt with use of specific clause.	Resident.	Of earnings owed debtor for services rendered within 30 days before attachment, process, judgment, or order, the greater of: (1) if paid weekly, 30 times federal minimum hourly wage; if paid biweekly, 60 times minimum hourly wage; if paid semimonthly, 65 times minimum hourly wage; if paid monthly, 130 times minimum hourly wage; or (2) 75% of disposable earnings. If creditor notified in writing that debtor has entered into a debt-scheduling agreement unless creditor gives 15 days written notice of objection, creditor may not garnish. Garnishment allowed if debtor more than 45 days overdue on plan or plan terminated.
Oklahoma	Principal residence.	Resident.	Household and kitchen furniture, books and pictures are exempt. Wearing apparel up to aggregate value of $4,000. Motor vehicle of a value not to exceed $7,500 as well as mobile homes used as residences. Tools of trade or husbandry, $10,000.	All persons.	75% of all earnings for personal or professional services earned during the 90 days before execution. Garnishment to satisfy child support order may, in certain cases, extend to 50% of disposable earnings. Earnings for personal services are 100% exempt from garnishment prior to trial court judgment with statutory exceptions. Debtor may exempt a larger percentage on a showing of hardship.
Oregon	Not over $25,000 or $33,000 for two debtors and not exceeding one block in any town or city laid off into blocks and lots; not exceeding 160 acres elsewhere. In case of mobile home, $23,000 one debtor, $30,000 two debtors. Proceeds of sale exempt for one year if to be used to purchase another homestead. Homestead is subject to certain liens.	Resident householder.	Books, pictures, musical instruments to $600; wearing apparel, jewelry, and other personal items to $1800; household goods, furniture, and radio $800; domestic animals to $1000; tools, library, etc., necessary to carry on trade of profession except for payment of debt, contracted to assist in carrying on trade or profession to $3000; vehicle to $1700; other specific exemptions. No article is exempt from execution on judgment recovered for its purchase price.	Householder.	Greater of 75% of individual disposable earnings for week; or $170.
Pennsylvania	None. Property held in tenancy by entirety may be exempt from debts of one spouse.		$300 in real or personal property, sewing machines, wearing apparel, other specified articles including retirement funds and accounts and certain leased articles are exempt. Exemptions inapplicable to claims for support.	Resident.	100% of all wages in hands of employer; does not apply to support orders, board for four weeks or less or student loan obligations.
Rhode Island	None. $200,000 in land and buildings for an owner or owners of a home.	Debtor.	Wearing apparel, household goods to value of $1,000, tools used in trade to value of $500; certain personal property of a housekeeper not exceeding $1,000; certain farm animals; burial plot.	Resident.	Wages due not exceeding $50, social welfare payments. Wages due to any seaman; $50 of holding in a consumer cooperative association. The active wages of any debtor payable from any employer where debtor has been object of relief from state federal or municipal corporation for period of one year after relief. Wages due to the wife and minor children of any debtor.

EXECUTION EXEMPTIONS (Continued)

STATE	HOMESTEAD		PERSONAL PROPERTY		WAGES
	AMOUNT	WHO MAY CLAIM	AMOUNT	WHO MAY CLAIM	
South Carolina	$5000 in real property that debtor uses as a residence, in a cooperative association that owns property that the debtor uses as a residence or in a burial plot. Couples may double the amount.	Debtor.	Personal property to $2,500; $1,200 in one motor vehicle; $500 in jewelry; $750 in implements, tools of trade or professional books; $1,000 in cash for debtors without homestead.	Head of family. Persons not head of family.	100% of earnings for personal service earned within 60 days. Garnishment prohibited with respect to debt arising from a consumer credit transaction.
South Dakota	A homestead is absolutely exempt. If the property is sold, then the proceeds up to $30,000 will be exempt for one year from receipt thereof, proceeds exemptions unlimited if debtor is 70 years or older and married spouse of third person, otherwise exemption is limited to $170,000.	Head of family, or in case he fails to claim, any member of the family over 14 years of age.	$4,000 to head of family. $2,000 to person not head of family in addition to absolute exemptions; i.e., books to $200, wearing apparel, provisions, and fuel for one year. Both of the above are in addition to what are known as absolute exemptions. Exemption inapplicable to child and spousal support obligations.	Debtor, his agent or attorney, head of family, or, in case of his failure to do so, by any member of his family over the age of 14 years.	Lesser of 25% of disposable earnings or amount by which disposable earnings for week exceed 40 times federal minimum hourly wage less $25 per week for each dependent.
Tennessee	$5,000. No limitation in area. Property jointly owned by debtors $7,500. Exemption inapplicable to taxes and debts for improvements on homestead. Specific exemptions for the elderly.	Resident.	Personal property up to $4,000 in aggregate. Residents are entitled to absolute exemption on necessary and proper wearing apparel of debtor and his family, family portraits, Bible, and school books. Implements, professional books to tools of the trade not to exceed $750.	All persons who are bona fide citizens and permanent residents of Tennessee.	Greater of 75% of disposable earnings per week or amount by which disposable earnings exceed 30 times the federal minimum hourly wage (does not apply to child support orders or to alimony to unmarried spouse); additional $2.50 per week exemption for each resident, dependent child under 16. Does not apply to taxes and alimony or child support.
Texas	Absolutely exempt. Limitations on amount of land: Homestead for a family, if not in a city, town, or village, not more than 200 acres; in a city, town, or village lot or lots not to exceed 10 acres; burial lot. Exemption does not apply to purchase money of homestead and taxes due on homestead.	Head of family or single adult person.	Personal property not to exceed an aggregate fair market value of $30,000 for each single adult person and $60,000 for a family which can include the following; furnishings of a home; all the following: tools, equipment, books used in trade or profession, wearing apparel, firearms, athletic and sporting equipment; a two, three or four wheeled vehicle for each member of the family with a driver's license, or who relies on another person to operate the vehicle; numerous farm animals and pets. Right to the assets, vested or not, under stock bonus, pension profit-sharing, annuity, or similar programs including retirement plan for self-employed individual are exempt. Exemption inapplicable to debts secured by a lien on property or due for rents on advances from a landlord to the tenant not exceeding $500.	Every family and single person.	100% of current wages for personal services.

State	Homestead Exemption		Personal and Other Property Exemptions		Wages Exempt from Garnishment
Utah	Homestead not exceeding one acre, used as primary residence not exceeding $20,000; if jointly owned, $40,000.	Single person or husband or wife when claimant is married.	Specified items such as burial plot, furniture, clothing and sufficient provisions for 12 months are exempt. Tools or implements of trade to $3,500 and motor vehicles used in business up to $2,500.	Single person or husband or wife when claimant is married.	Garnishment of weekly earnings cannot exceed greater of 75% of weekly earnings or 30 times federal minimum hourly wage for that week.
Vermont	The homestead of a natural person consisting of a dwelling house, outbuildings and the land used in connection therewith, not exceeding $75,000 in value, and owned and used or kept by such person as a homestead together with the rents, issues, profits, and products thereof.	Housekeeper or head of a family.	Specified articles and benefits. Not to exceed $2,500 for motor vehicle; $5000 household furnishings; $500 jewelry; $5000 trade books or tools.	Resident.	75% of disposable earnings for week or excess of 30 times federal minimum hourly wage whichever is greater. Different formula for child support orders. If consumer credit debt, 85% of the debtor's weekly disposable earnings, or 40 times the federal minimum wage, whichever is greater.
Virginia	An estate not in excess of $5,000 comprised of personal and real property of the debtor, to be selected by him. $500 additional for each dependent. Veterans with at least 40% disability are entitled to extra $2,000 exemption. Profits derived from the homestead are exempt; homestead is subject to certain liens.	Resident householder or head of family.	In addition to the $5000 estate, enumerated articles such as the family Bible, wedding rings, wearing apparel, furniture, etc. Exemption inapplicable to all taxes and purchase money of property therein mentioned. Motor vehicle not to exceed $2000.	Resident householder or head of family.	75% of disposable earnings for that week or of excess of 30 times federal minimum hourly wage, whichever is greater. For support orders: 40% of weekly disposable earnings or 50% if debtor is supporting a spouse or dependent child not involved in the support order. Exemption is reduced by 5% if garnishment is necessary to enforce a support order issued more than 12 weeks prior to the beginning of the work week. Exemptions inapplicable to support orders and more than 12 weeks prior to the beginning of the work week. Exemptions inapplicable to support orders and bankruptcy court orders. Debtor must be served with notice of how to claim exemption from garnishment.
Washington	Not exceeding $40,000 in case of land, mobile homes and improvements, or $15,000 in personal property. Not exempt from claims of mechanic's, laborer's, or materialmen's liens or from mortgages and child support; exemption does not apply to certain bankruptcy cases.	Each person or family.	Household furniture and utensils, $1,500. $500 of other goods (no more than $100 in cash), wearing apparel, but not to exceed $1000 in value of furs, jewelry, and personal items. Many specially enumerated articles. Pension and life insurance also exempt. Private libraries not to exceed $1,500. Provisions and fuel for an individual for three months. To each individual or as community property of spouses maintaining a single household: Two motor vehicles; farm trucks, stock, tools, and seed not to exceed $5,000. Exemption does not apply to certain bankruptcy cases.	Householder in case of household furniture. Beneficiary in case of pensions and life insurance.	The greater part of 30 times the state hourly minimum wage or of 75% of the disposable earnings of the defendant is exempt from garnishment. Disposable earnings means that part of the earnings remaining after deduction of the amounts required by law to be withheld. Child support order: 50% if debtor is supporting spouse or dependent child, 40% if not supporting spouse or child.

EXECUTION EXEMPTIONS *(Continued)*

STATE	HOMESTEAD		PERSONAL PROPERTY		WAGES
	AMOUNT	WHO MAY CLAIM	AMOUNT	WHO MAY CLAIM	
West Virginia	$25,000 for property used as residence or for burial plot.	Husbands, parents, or infants of deceased or insane parents.	Household goods, furnishings, clothing, appliances, animals, etc. not to exceed $8,000; jewelry, $1,000; $800 in property; working tools of trade, $1,000; motor vehicle, $2,400; some benefits.	Resident and head of family only.	80% of wages due or to become due within one year after issuance of execution or 30 times federal minimum hourly wage. For consumer credit debts, 80% of disposable earnings for week or 30 times federal hourly minimum wage.
Wisconsin	Property occupied or with intent to occupy to $40,000; sale proceeds exempt for two years from sale if obtaining another home is planned.	Resident. Homestead must be occupied by him or her. $40,000 for household.	Automobiles used and kept for purpose of carrying on debtor's business to value of $1,200 burial plots, business and farm property, child support payments, consumer goods not to exceed $7,500; like insurance, retirement benefits, deposit of accounts to a value of $1000.	Resident. Mechanic, artisan, or laborer.	Greater of 75% of debtor's disposable earnings or of excess of 30 times federal minimum hourly wage rate. Disposable earnings means that part of earnings after deduction of amounts required by law to be withheld.
Wyoming	$10,000. House and lot or lots in city, on farm consisting of any number of acres within the value limitation, or house trailer or movable home. Must be occupied by owner or his family. Exemption does not apply to taxes and to purchase money of said premises. Mobile home value not to exceed $6,000.	Householder, being head of family and every resident 60 years or over whether head of family or not. Widow, husband, or minor child entitled to homestead on death of owner, subject to debts of deceased.	Bible, pictures, school books, lot in cemetery, furniture, provisions, household articles, value $2,000, clothing value $1,000. Tools, teams, implements, stock in trade to carry on business not over $2,000 and library, instruments and implements, $2,000. Motor vehicle, $2,400. Veterans' benefits, black lung benefits, aid to families with dependent children and general assistance payments, retirement benefits, worker's compensation benefits, unemployment compensation benefits.	Head of family or person 60 years or over residing in state. Every resident. Professional men.	Judgments on consumer credit sales, home or loan; greater of 75% of disposable earnings or excess over 30 times federal minimum hourly wage. Otherwise, 25% of earnings for personal services within 60 days before levy if necessary for use of resident family. For support orders, 35% of the income.

[1] Bankruptcy and execution exemptions may differ.

[2] Title III of the Federal Consumer Credit Protection Act exempts from garnishment the greater of 75% of disposable earnings per work week or an amount each week equal to 30 times the federal minimum hourly wage. The exemption does not apply to support orders or orders of any court of bankruptcy. The statute does not provide that an employee cannot be discharged because his earnings have been subjected to garnishment for one indebtedness.

[3] Personal property exemptions for the various states can be lengthy. This is only a partial listing of what may be available.

17 Bad Check Laws

Each state has laws with respect to the issuing of checks that are returned unpaid. This chapter discusses *civil* and *criminal* statutes pertaining to the passing of checks that are dishonored by the bank where the account is maintained. It is very important for the credit professional to distinguish between civil and criminal remedies. While many who receive bad checks think "it is a crime," careful consideration should be given before utilizing the criminal statutes. First and foremost, the filing of a criminal complaint and proceeding with criminal prosecution will not necessarily get you paid. Additionally, most states have very strict laws as to utilization of criminal proceedings for civil purposes. As well, most prosecutors and judicial officials are very hesitant about utilizing the criminal process in the bad check area, especially when it is perceived that the criminal court is being used in an effort to collect the bad check. *Civil remedies should always be considered first.* Finally, the credit grantor must realize that a district attorney's office may be too busy to consider handling a bad check prosecution.

In a world that runs on credit and paper, bad checks are a growing problem and all states have criminal statutes dealing with check fraud. While statutes differ in details, they are essentially the same in principle: a maker who issues, and the holder who negotiates a check knowing that there are insufficient funds or credit to honor it are guilty of a crime and may be subject to civil or criminal penalties. Most of the statutes provide that in any prosecution, proof that a check, draft or order was made or delivered, and that payment of the same was refused by the drawee because of lack of funds or credit, establishes a *prima facie* case of intent to defraud and of knowledge of insufficient funds in, or credit with, the bank.

NATURE OF THE CRIME

While the maker or holder may be able to overcome the effect of the statute, it makes prosecution of check fraud cases much easier. Unfortunately, there is little evidence that criminal prosecution is a serious deterrent to check fraud. While some state constitutions prohibit imprisonment on account of debt, the constitutionality of bad check laws has been long settled. Most courts that have had to deal with constitutional challenges have treated bad check laws as a form of fraud or theft. As noted above, appropriate consideration should be given to the civil remedies that are available prior to the utilization of criminal prosecutorial procedures. Check fraud takes a number of forms. Bad check laws deal primarily with individuals who pass checks without sufficient funds (NSF checks) or upon closed accounts. Other, more elaborate check frauds include check kiting schemes which involve multiple accounts, and various types of forgery, where a legitimate check is stolen and the endorsements forged. One may also encounter schemes where an employee uses legitimate business checks of the employer to pay personal expenses. While all schemes are subject to criminal penalties, this section will focus only on the problems of bad or NSF checks.

Criminal law generally treats check fraud crimes as either misdemeanors or felonies. A misdemeanor is a less serious crime, usually punishable by up to one year in jail and a fine. A felony is a serious offense usually punishable by more than one year in prison and a substantial fine. Each bad check is a separate offense. In reality, prosecutors view check fraud as a less serious problem than drug dealing, bank robbery, assault or murder and may not be willing to prosecute every case. Moreover, there is little evidence that the threat of prosecution has any deterrent effect.

INTENT TO DEFRAUD AND KNOWLEDGE OF INSUFFICIENT FUNDS AS NECESSARY ELEMENTS

Generally, NSF check laws expressly provide that intent to defraud is a necessary element of the offense. The making, drawing, uttering or delivering of any check, draft or order for the payment of money upon any bank or other depository, knowing at the time of such making, drawing, uttering or delivering that the maker or drawer has not sufficient funds in or credit with such bank or other depository, for the payment of such check, draft or order in full upon its presentation is fraudulent. Rarely does a drawer of a check publicly state that he or she intended to defraud the payee. Therefore, the simple making, drawing, uttering or delivering of such check, draft or order is, under most of the statutes, *prima facie* evidence of intent to defraud. The word "credit" as used in the bad check laws means an arrangement or understanding with the bank or depository for the payment of such check, draft or order. Without a provision that giving the NSF check is *prima facie* evidence of fraudulent intent it would be virtually impossible to prosecute bad check cases.

The words "with intent to defraud" as used in the statutes do not mean that the payee need have been actually defrauded. The intention to defraud is sufficient. The majority of the statutes provide in effect that failure to pay the check, draft or order within a specified number of days after demand is presumptive evidence of intent to defraud and of knowledge of insufficient funds in, or credit with, the bank for the payment of the same. These presumptions of fraudulent intent and of knowledge of insufficient funds are not conclusive, but are rebuttable. Where the evidence introduced by the state in prosecuting an alleged offender against the statute is rebutted by contrary evidence which makes it appear that the maker of the check was not motivated by an intent to defraud in making, drawing, uttering or delivering the instrument, the presumption is overcome. Further, the presumption is overcome where the maker pays the check within any statutory grace period. For example, in some states, the time period establishing *prima facie* evidence of fraudulent intend is different than the grace period allowed to pay a debt before prosecution can be sought. As well, not all states presume intent. In California, for instance, intent to defraud must be affirmatively proved by the prosecution. Although it can be proved by circumstantial evidence, the presumption of law is insufficient. The drawer must also have knowledge of insufficient funds or credit.

In those states where an intent to defraud is presumed, knowledge of insufficient funds, which is a necessary element in proving the intent to defraud, is also presumed. The presumption may arise at the time of the making of the check, although it usually arises upon the notice of nonpayment. When the payee has agreed to hold the check for a period of time, there is a question of fact as to whether the check was issued with the required intent to defraud. With the payor claiming innocence, it will be difficult for the credit grantor to prove the intent existed.

A number of states provide that the presumption of intent to defraud is rebutted upon the payment, after receipt of notice by the maker, of the amount of the check plus a service charge within the grace period as provided by statute.

TIME WITHIN WHICH CHECK MAY BE MADE GOOD

The person who makes, draws, utters or delivers a bad check is given a period of time specified in the statute within which to "make good" after receiving a certain prescribed notice that the check has been dishonored. Under some statutes, prosecution cannot be commenced until the expiration of the time allowed; in other states, the statutes provide that prosecution is dismissed if the check is made good within the time specified; and in other states, if the check is made good within the time specified, the presumption that the check was given with fraudulent intent and with knowledge of insufficient funds does not attach. In the following state-by-state summary of laws, the number of days within which a bad check and any additional fees must be paid to avoid prosecution is listed. Where the time period establishing *prima facie* evidence of fraudulent intent differs, it is noted. Also listed is the maximum service charge amount (or fee) allowable by law.

Many times, after dishonored checks have been issued, the maker files for protection under one of the chapters of the Bankruptcy Code. The filing of a bankruptcy petition invokes the automatic stay which enjoins any civil action to attempt to collect a debt or to recover property from the debtor. The bankruptcy filing will stop all civil efforts to collect on a bad check. With respect to criminal prosecutions, this is a much more complicated area. Section 362(b) of the Bankruptcy Code lists the areas where the automatic stay does not apply, and criminal prosecutions is one of them. However, a number of courts have held that a criminal prosecution on a bad check is nothing more than an attempt to collect the debt, and the bankruptcy courts have enjoined the creditor from proceeding. Because Section 362 permits the bankruptcy court to impose damages for violation of the automatic stay, care should be taken if a criminal prosecution is pending and a bankruptcy is filed, so that competent counsel is able to review the issues and determine whether the stay will affect the criminal proceedings. While a creditor may not necessarily be directly involved in the prosecution of the criminal proceeding, a creditor must be certain to alert counsel regarding the bankruptcy proceeding so that there will not be an accidental violation of the automatic stay by the creditor.

CHECKS IN PAYMENT OF PREEXISTING DEBTS

Bank checks are not payment in most cases until they are paid; giving a check for payment on a note or open account does not extinguish the debt. Generally, therefore, the giving of a bad check to pay a note or open account does not fall within the bad check law. The account creditor or note holder can simply sue on the note. What this means is that most bad check laws clearly provide for civil or criminal prosecution for a check given on a COD purchase. However, if the check is in payment of an antecedent debt, such as one on an open account, the individual laws must be reviewed to determine the applicability, if any, to the check being held.

STOPPING PAYMENT ON CHECKS

The bad check laws do not apply where an individual stops payment on a check issued on an account with sufficient funds. However, if it can be proved that the issuer gave the check, intending at the time to stop the check, the bad check law may apply.

POSTDATED CHECKS

The Uniform Commercial Code, Section 3-104(f), defines a check as "a draft, other than a documentary draft, payable on demand and drawn on a bank…" A postdated check, since it is not payable on demand, does not satisfy this definition. Consequently, it has generally been held by most states that the giving of a post-dated check does not constitute a present fraud nor is it within the scope of the "bad check laws."

TO WHOM STATUTES APPLY

The various statutes usually apply to "any person who shall make, or draw, or utter or deliver any check, etc.," and therefore apply not only to the maker, but to anyone who passes a bad check with fraudulent intent, even though the check be that of a third person. It may apply to one who, with intent to defraud, endorses and transfers a worthless check.

HOW TO TAKE ADVANTAGE OF THE STATUTE

If a check is returned, you may have to give a written notice to the maker and a demand that the check be made good within the number of days specified in the statute. A notice is required in most states, and where required should be served personally upon the maker of the check. If the check is not made good after demand, you may refer the matter to the prosecuting attorney in your district. The title of the prosecutor will vary (i.e., State's Attorney, District Attorney, County Attorney, etc.). The prosecutor has discretion to refuse to prosecute, however. In referring a check for prosecution, you should forward a legible copy of the NSF check (keep the original in a safe place) together with any demand letter(s) and other correspondence relating to the check. You should also include the names and addresses of any necessary witnesses.

CIVIL PENALTIES

The credit grantor should resort to its available civil remedies in order to recover payment and costs of bad checks. Credit grantors must also note that statutes, which govern the civil remedies available to credit grantors to recover on bad checks, may overlap among two or three different sets of statutes within the state. Therefore, in seeking its remedy, the credit grantor must seek advice as to the pertinent statute in affect at a particular time.

CRIMINAL PENALTIES

The prudent credit professional should utilize the criminal statutes only where the true intent of its utilization is punishment as opposed to utilizing the system to try to collect on the bad check. In fact, some states contain statutes that will punish the creditor who attempts to utilize criminal prosecution as a means to collect the debt on the bad check. As states are becoming more conscious of the severity of the problem, the civil statutes are becoming increasingly "user friendly," and the need to resort to criminal sanctions is being curtailed. In addition to many of the same elements listed for civil penalties, the criminal statutes require additional elements before the case can be sustained. It must be remembered that under our form of jurisprudence in the United States, in a criminal action, the burden of proof is upon the state and a defendant is presumed to be innocent unless proven guilty beyond a reasonable doubt. As will be noted below, this burden of proof is substantially higher than that necessary to be able to prevail in a civil case. Strict compliance with the laws is necessary. The elements that are necessary in addition to the civil elements are the following:

Necessity of Damage

A number of states have held that it is not necessary that the payee be actually defrauded as a result of the bad check, but that the intent to defraud is sufficient. This means that even if one ultimately receives payment for the dishonored check, the intent to issue the worthless check was there at the beginning and the criminal action may be pursued. The corollary to this principle is that once a complaint is initiated to begin a criminal proceeding, it may not necessarily be able to be withdrawn just because the check is made good. The creditor must also realize that courts, both criminal and civil, will want to ascertain actual damages in order to assess punishment. If payment has been made and there is no remaining damage the court will consider this in its final decision.

Sufficiency of Notice of Nonpayment

Most of the statutes provide that the failure to make the check good within a certain number of days after receipt of written notice of nonpayment shall be *prima facie* evidence of intent to defraud and of knowledge of insufficient funds to cover the check. As with the civil statutes set forth above, many states require the written notice to the issuer of the check before any criminal action may be taken. The notice needs to be sent by mail in the method prescribed by statute. The letter or notice should identify the check by reference to the names of the maker and the payee, the amount, the date of check and the number of the check. The notice or letter should also demand payment for the check since the purpose is to give the maker an opportunity to make good on the transaction. Reference to the civil and/or criminal statute may help further in clearly identifying the purpose of the notice.

Rules of Evidence

In most states, the attempt to defraud and the knowledge of insufficient funds are presumed by the laws. The rationale is that one is charged with knowledge as to the sufficiency of funds in an account prior to the issuance of a check, and that the issuance of a check where there are insufficient funds to cover it (with or without knowledge) further presumes the intent necessary for a criminal act.

Since the criminal laws vary differently from state to state, it is important to review each state's evidence rules before pursuing a course to proceed with a criminal complaint. In this instance, a conversation with the office of the local prosecutor, especially if there are prosecutors assigned to commercial crimes, may be helpful in the preparation of the materials. It must be remembered that the more that the credit professional is able to "spoon feed" to the prosecutor, the more likely the case will be accepted and investigation will then ensue.

An important note to remember is that some states provide that if the payee of the check knows or has reason to know that the check may not be good when it was issued (the maker asks the payee to hold the check for several days), the court may not find the requisite intent, and the burden of proof will not have been met.

When contemplating the type of action to be brought, the credit professional should compare the elements of the civil and criminal penalties contained in the following listing. Keep in mind that the mere prosecution or even conviction in a criminal action will not necessarily provide repayment or restitution. There is something to be said, though, for letting the business community in a particular area know that a particular business entity or credit department will not do anything when confronted with a clear case of criminal intent with respect to bad checks.

STATE-BY-STATE LISTING OF BAD CHECK LAWS

Note: State legislatures will, on occasion, modify an area of law without clear delineation as to its content and context. As a result, even the changes which have been enacted prior to placement in the state's Code may be difficult to locate. As a result, the Editors urge all users of the *Manual* to use this publication only as a guide, and consult the latest codified version of the state's law for all recent changes.

ALABAMA
Service Charge—$30.
Evidence for Prosecution—If debt is not paid within 10 days from receipt of notice of nonpayment.
Civil Penalty—Greater of $10 or actual bank charges. May recover damages, including attorney fees, as determined by jury or court..
Criminal Penalty—Misdemeanor.
Statutory Citation—Sections § 6-5-285, 8-8-15, 12-17-224 and 13A-9-13.1.

ALASKA
Service Charge—$30.
Evidence for Prosecution—If debt is not paid within 15 days from the date notice of dishonor is deposited as first class mail.
Civil Penalty—$100 or three times the amount of the check, whichever is greater, but not to exceed amount of check by more than $1,000.
Criminal Penalty—Misdemeanor if less than $500, otherwise a felony.
Statutory Citation—Sections 09.68.115 and 11.46.280.

ARIZONA
Service Charge—$25.
Evidence for Prosecution—If debt is not paid within 12 days from mailing date, return receipt requested, of notice of nonpayment.
Civil Penalty—$50 or two times the amount of the check, whichever is greater, plus costs and attorney fees as the court may allow.
Criminal Penalty—Misdemeanor.
Statutory Citation—ARS § 44-6852, 12-671, 13-1807 and 13-1809.

ARKANSAS
Service Charge—$25.
Evidence for Prosecution—If debt is not paid within 10 days of receipt of notice of nonpayment by certified mail, return receipt requested.

Civil Penalty—Two times the amount of the check, but in no case less than $50, a collection fee, interest and attorney and court fees.

Criminal Penalty—Misdemeanor if less than $200, otherwise a felony.

Statutory Citation—Sections 4-60-103, 5-37-304 and 5-37-307.

CALIFORNIA

Service Charge—$25 for the first check, $35 for each subsequent.

Evidence for Prosecution—If debt is not paid within 30 days from mailing date of notice of nonpayment by certified mail.

Civil Penalty—Liable for the amount of the check, minus any partial payments, and damages equal to three times that amount, which shall not be less than $100 nor more than $1500.

Criminal Penalty—Felony in all amounts, unless deemed a misdemeanor by the court.

Statutory Citation—CC § 476A and 1719.

COLORADO

Service Charge—Greater of $30 or 20% of check amount.

Evidence for Prosecution—If debt is not paid within 15 days from mailing date of notice of nonpayment by certified mail, return receipt requested.

Civil Penalty—Three times the amount of the check but not less than $100, plus costs of collection.

Criminal Penalty—Misdemeanor if less than $500, otherwise a felony.

Statutory Citation—CRS § 13-21-109, 18-5-205 and 18-5-512.

CONNECTICUT

Service Charge—$30.

Evidence for Prosecution—If debt is not paid within 30 days from presentation and the issuer fails to make good within eight days after receiving notice of nonpayment by certified and first class mail.

Civil Penalty—Appropriate damages determined by the court. For a check drawn on a non-existent account, the amount of awarded damages may be the face amount of the check or $750, whichever is less. For NSF checks, the amount may be the face amount of the check or $400, whichever is less.

Criminal Penalty—Misdemeanor if less than $1,000, otherwise a felony.

Statutory Citation—Sections § 52-565A and 53A-128.

DELAWARE

Service Charge—$25.

Evidence for Prosecution—If debt is not paid within 10 days of receipt of notice of refusal.

Civil Penalty—$100 or three times the amount of the check not to exceed $500.

Criminal Penalty—Misdemeanor if less than $1,000, otherwise a felony.

Statutory Citation—Sections 11 § 900 and 11 § 4206.

DISTRICT OF COLUMBIA

Service Charge—$25, $15 for checks made payable to governmental offices.

Evidence for Prosecution—If debt is not paid within five days after personally receiving notice that check has not been paid.

Civil Penalty—Amount of check.

Criminal Penalty—Misdemeanor if less than $100, otherwise a felony.

Statutory Citation—DC 22-1510.

FLORIDA

Service Charge—Fees start at $25 if face value does not exceed $50.

Evidence for Prosecution—If debt is not paid within 30 days from date of receipt of notice to tender payment by registered or certified mail, or by first class mail supported by affidavit.

Civil Penalty—Three times the amount of the check, but in no case less than $50, together with the amount of the check, a service charge, court costs, reasonable attorney fees, and incurred bank fees.

Criminal Penalty—Misdemeanor if less than $50, otherwise a felony.

Statutory Citation—Sections 68.065 and 832.07.

GEORGIA

Service Charge—$30 or 5% of face amount, whichever is greater.

Evidence for Prosecution—If debt is not paid within 10 days of receipt of notice, by certified or overnight mail, to tender payment.

Civil Penalty—Two times the amount of the check, but in no case more than $500, plus any court costs.

Criminal Penalty—Misdemeanor if less than $500, otherwise a felony.

Statutory Citation—Sections 13-6-15 and 16-9-20.

GUAM

Service Charge—$35.

Evidence for Prosecution—If debt is not paid within 30 days of written demand delivered personally, or by certified mail to the maker.

Civil Penalty—Three times the amount of check, but in no case less than $50 nor more than $750, plus reasonable attorneys' fees.

Criminal Penalty—Misdemeanor for all amounts.

Statutory Citation—Sections § 4630, 6104 and 6105.

HAWAII

Service Charge—$30.

Evidence for Prosecution—If debt is not paid within 10 days after actual receipt of notice of dishonor by certified mail.

Civil Penalty—$100 or three times the amount of the check, whichever is greater, not to exceed $500.

Criminal Penalty—Misdemeanor for all amounts.

Statutory Citation—Sections § 490:3-503, 490:3-506.5 and 708-857.

IDAHO

Service Charge—$20.

Evidence for Prosecution—If debt is not paid within 15 days of receipt of written notice by certified mail, or regular mail supported by affidavit.

Civil Penalty—Amount of check and $100 or three times the amount of the check, whichever is greater, not to exceed $500.

Criminal Penalty—Misdemeanor for all amounts.

Statutory Citation—Section 1-2301A.

ILLINOIS

Service Charge—$25, or for all costs and expenses, including reasonable attorneys' fees to collect the check.

Evidence for Prosecution—If debt is not paid within 30 days of the delivery and acceptance of demand for payment by certified mail and first class mail; or attempted delivery with notation of refusal.

Civil Penalty—$100 or three times the amount of the check, whichever is greater, not to exceed $1,500, plus attorneys' fees and court costs.

Criminal Penalty—Misdemeanor for all amounts for first offense.

Statutory Citation—720 ILCS 5/17-1a and 810 ILCS 5/3-806.

INDIANA

Service Charge—$20 or 5%, whichever is greater, not to exceed $250.

Evidence for Prosecution—Depends on knowledge and conditions of NSF. Either, if debt is not paid within 10 days of mailing of written notice, or if not paid within 30 days after the date of certified mailing.

Civil Penalty—Three times the amount of check, not to exceed $500.

Criminal Penalty—Misdemeanor for all amounts, felony if amount was at least $2,500 and the property acquired was a motor vehicle.

Statutory Citation—IC 26-2-7-3, 26-2-7-6 and 35-43-5-5.

IOWA

Service Charge—$30.

Evidence for Prosecution—If debt is not paid within 30 days of receipt of written demand by certified mail, personal service, or regular mail supported by affidavit.

Civil Penalty—Three times the amount of the check not to exceed more than $500 the amount of the check.

Criminal Penalty—Misdemeanor if $1000 or less, otherwise a felony.

Statutory Citation—Sections 554.3512, 554.3513 and 714.1

KANSAS

Service Charge—$30.

Evidence for Prosecution—If debt is not paid within 14 days of mailing of written demand by certified mail first class mail.

Civil Penalty—$100 or three times the amount of the check but not to exceed the amount of the check by more than $500; plus court and reasonable attorneys' fees.

Criminal Penalty—Misdemeanor if less than $500, otherwise a felony.

Statutory Citation—Sections 21.3707 and 60.2610.

KENTUCKY

Service Charge—$25.

Evidence for Prosecution—If debt is not paid within 10 days after receipt of notice.

Civil Penalty—None.

Criminal Penalty—Misdemeanor if less than $300, otherwise a felony.

Statutory Citation—Section 514.040.

LOUISIANA

Service Charge—$25 or 5%, whichever is greater.

Evidence for Prosecution—If debt is not paid within 15 days of receipt of notice by certified or registered mail.

Civil Penalty—Twice the amount of the check, but in no case less than $100 plus attorneys' fees and court costs.

Criminal Penalty—Misdemeanor if less than $100, otherwise a felony.

Statutory Citation—LRS 9:2782 and 14.71.

MAINE

Service Charge—$25.

Evidence for Prosecution—If debt is not paid within 10 days of receipt of notice by certified mail.

Civil Penalty—Amount of the check plus court costs, processing charges and interest. Court may also award reasonable attorneys' fees and assess a civil penalty of $50.

Criminal Penalty—Repealed.

Statutory Citation—Sections 14 § 6071.

MARYLAND

Service Charge—$35.

Evidence for Prosecution—If debt is not paid within 30 days of notice of nonpayment by certified mail, or first class mail supported by affidavit.

Civil Penalty—Amount of check plus up to two times the amount of the check, but not more than $1,000.

Criminal Penalty—Misdemeanor if less than $500, otherwise a felony.

Statutory Citation—Sections (gcr) § 8-106 and (gcl) § 15-802.

MASSACHUSETTS

Service Charge—$25.

Evidence for Prosecution—If debt is not paid within 30 days after receiving notice of nonpayment by certified mail, return receipt requested. *Prima facie* evidence if not paid within two days of receipt of notice.

Civil Penalty—Amount of check plus damages determined by the court, but in no event less than $100 or more than $500.

Criminal Penalty—Misdemeanor if less than $100, otherwise a felony.

Statutory Citation—Sections § 93.40A and 266.37.

MICHIGAN

Service Charge—$25.

Evidence for Prosecution—If debt is not paid within 30 days of receipt of notice by certified mail.

Civil Penalty—May be liable for double damages in amount of not less than $50, but not more than $500 plus costs up to $250.

Criminal Penalty—Misdemeanor if less than $50.

Statutory Citation—MSA 445.1856, 27A.2952 and 750.131a.

MINNESOTA

Service Charge—$30, or actual costs of collection not to exceed $30.

Evidence for Prosecution—If debt is not paid within 30 days after receipt of notice by certified mail. *Prima facie* evidence if not paid within five business days or receipt of notice.

Civil Penalty—Up to $100 or the value of the check, whichever is greater, interest at the rate payable on judgments and reasonable attorneys' fees.

Criminal Penalty—Misdemeanor for all amounts.

Statutory Citation—Sections § 604.113 and 609.535.

MISSISSIPPI

Service Charge—$40.

Evidence for Prosecution—If debt is not paid within 15 days of receipt of notice.

Civil Penalty—Amount of check plus additional charges depending on amount of check beginning at $30 and a maximum of 25% of check if check is over $200.

Criminal Penalty—Misdemeanor if less than $100, otherwise a felony.

Statutory Citation—Sections § 11-7-12, 97-19-55, 97-19-57 and 97-19-67.

MISSOURI

Service Charge—$25.

Evidence for Prosecution—With knowledge of NSF, if debt is not paid within 10 days of receipt of notice by certified mail. Otherwise, if not paid within 30 days of receipt of notice.

Civil Penalty—Amount of check plus attorney fees and $100 or up to three times the amount of check, whichever is greater.

Criminal Penalty—Misdemeanor if less than $500, otherwise a felony.

Statutory Citation—Sections 570.120 and 570.123.

MONTANA

Service Charge—$30.

Evidence for Prosecution—If debt is not paid within 10 days of receipt of notice. *Prima facie* evidence if not paid within five days of receipt of notice.

Civil Penalty—Must be an amount equal to the service charge plus the greater of $100 or three times the amount of check, not to exceed the amount of check by more than $500.

Criminal Penalty—Misdemeanor if less than $300, otherwise a felony.

Statutory Citation—MCA 27-1-717 and 45-6-316.

NEBRASKA

Service Charge—$30.

Evidence for Prosecution—If debt is not paid within 10 days of receipt of notice, return receipt requested.

Civil Penalty—$10, plus any reasonable handling fee imposed by the bank.

Criminal Penalty—Misdemeanor if less than $500, otherwise a felony.

Statutory Citation—Sections 28-611.

NEVADA

Service Charge—$25.

Evidence for Prosecution—If debt is not paid within 30 days of receipt of notice by certified mail. *Prima facie* evidence if not paid within five days of receipt of notice.

Civil Penalty—Three times the amount of the check, but not less than $100, nor more than $500.

Criminal Penalty—Misdemeanor if less than $250, otherwise a felony.

Statutory Citation—NRS 41-620, 205.130, 205.132, 597.960 and 604.162.

NEW HAMPSHIRE

Service Charge—$30.

Evidence for Prosecution—If debt is not paid within 14 days of receipt of notice of nonpayment by certified or registered mail, return receipt requested.

Civil Penalty—Court, service and collection costs. Failure to pay within allotted time may result in a $10 per day fee up to $500 until paid.

Criminal Penalty—Misdemeanor if less than $1000, otherwise a felony.

Statutory Citation—Sections 55 § 544-B and 62 § 638:4.

NEW JERSEY

Service Charge—$20.

Evidence for Prosecution—If debt is not paid within 35 days of receipt of notice by certified mail.

Civil Penalty—Liable for attorneys' fees, court fees, mailing fees for notice and damages equal to $100 or three times the amount of the check, whichever is greater, not to exceed $500 than the amount of the check.

Criminal Penalty—Misdemeanor if less than $200, otherwise a felony.

Statutory Citation—Sections 2A:32A-1, 2C:21-5 and 40:5-18(c).

NEW MEXICO

Service Charge—$20.

Evidence for Prosecution—If debt is not paid within 10 days of receipt of notice by certified mail, return receipt requested.

Civil Penalty—$100 or three times the amount of check, whichever is greater, not to exceed $500.

Criminal Penalty—Misdemeanor if less than $25, otherwise a felony.

Statutory Citation—Sections 55 § 544-B, 56 § 14:1 and 62 § 638:4.

NEW YORK

Service Charge—$20.

Evidence for Prosecution—If debt is not paid within 30 days following mailing date by first-class mail of second notice.

Civil Penalty—If reason for bad check is no existing bank account, damages can be two times the amount of the check or $750, whichever is less. If reason is NSF, damages can be two times the amount of the check or $400, whichever is less.

Criminal Penalty—Misdemeanor for all amounts.

Statutory Citation—Sections 24A:11.104 and 40:190.05.

NORTH CAROLINA

Service Charge—$25.

Evidence for Prosecution—If debt is not paid within 30 days of receipt of second notice by certified mail.

Civil Penalty—Three times the amount of check, not to be less than $100 or exceeding $500, in addition to amount of check, and processing and bank fees.

Criminal Penalty—Misdemeanor if $2000 or less, otherwise a felony.

Statutory Citation—Sections § 6-21.3, 14-107 and 25-3-506.

NORTH DAKOTA

Service Charge—$25.

Evidence for Prosecution—If debt is not paid within 10 days of receipt of notice, return receipt requested or first class mail supported by affidavit.

Civil Penalty—The lessor of $200 or three times the amount of check.

Criminal Penalty—Misdemeanor if over $50, felony if over $500.

Statutory Citation—Section 6-08-16.

OHIO

Service Charge—$30 or 10%, whichever is greater.

Evidence for Prosecution—If debt is not paid within 10 days of receipt of notice by certified mail.

Civil Penalty—$200 or three times the amount of the check, all bank fees, court costs and attorneys' fees.

Criminal Penalty—Misdemeanor if less than $500, otherwise a felony.

Statutory Citation—Sections 2307.61A and 2913.11.

OKLAHOMA

Service Charge—$30.

Evidence for Prosecution—If debt is not paid within five days from date check is presented for payment. (Applies to both business and personal checks.)

Civil Penalty—An amount not to exceed $5000.

Criminal Penalty—Misdemeanor if less than $500, otherwise a felony.

Statutory Citation—Sections T.12 14 § 937, § 21-1541.1 and 68 § 218.1.

OREGON

Service Charge—$25.

Evidence for Prosecution—If debt is not paid within 30 days from date of receipt of notice of nonpayment. *Prima facie* evidence if not paid within 10 days from receipt of notice.

Civil Penalty—$100 or three times the amount of the check, whichever is greater but not to exceed $500, and reasonable attorneys' fees.

Criminal Penalty—Misdemeanor if less than $75, otherwise a felony.

Statutory Citation—Sections 30.701 and 165.065.

PENNSYLVANIA

Service Charge—$25.

Evidence for Prosecution—If debt is not paid within 10 days from date of receipt of notice by certified or registered mail.

Civil Penalty—$100 or three times the amount of the check but not to exceed $500 the value of the check, whichever is greater.

Criminal Penalty—Misdemeanor if less than $75,000, otherwise a felony.

Statutory Citation—Sections 18 § 4105 and 42 § 8304.

PUERTO RICO

Service Charge—$25.

Evidence for Prosecution—Refusal of bank to pay the check because of NSF, 15 days after receipt of notice.

Civil Penalty—Not less than two times the amount of the check.

Criminal Penalty—Misdemeanor for all amounts.

Statutory Citation—Sections T.33 s1851-54.

RHODE ISLAND

Service Charge—$25.

Evidence for Prosecution—If debt is not paid within 30 days of receipt of notice by certified mail, return receipt requested. *Prima facie* evidence if not paid within seven days of receipt of notice.

Civil Penalty—Amount of check, collection fee, and an amount equal to three times the amount of the check, but in no case less than $200 and in no case more than $1000.

Criminal Penalty—Misdemeanor if less than $1000, but may be charged a felony if over $100.

Statutory Citation—Sections § 6-42-3 and 19-9-24.

SOUTH CAROLINA

Service Charge—$30.

Evidence for Prosecution—If debt is not paid within 10 days of receipt of notice by certified mail.

Civil Penalty—The lessor of $500 or three times the amount of the check. May also be entitled to court costs and reasonable attorneys' fees.

Criminal Penalty—Felony if over $5000.

Statutory Citation—Sections 34-11-70a, 34-11-75 and 34-11-90.

SOUTH DAKOTA

Service Charge—$30.

Evidence for Prosecution—If debt is not paid within 30 days of receipt of notice by certified mail.

Civil Penalty—All reasonable costs and expenses of collection.

Criminal Penalty—Misdemeanor if less than $500, otherwise a felony. Action is limited to six months from date of notice of dishonor.

Statutory Citation—Sections § 21-1-14, 22-41-1 and 22-41-3.

TENNESSEE

Service Charge—$20.

Evidence for Prosecution—If debt is not paid within 10 days of receipt of notice by certified mail, return receipt requested, notice being sent within 30 days from date of nonpayment.

Civil Penalty—If fraudulent intent, three times the amount of the check, not to exceed $500, otherwise 10% interest per annum, service charges, court costs and attorneys' fees.

Criminal Penalty—Misdemeanor if less than $500, otherwise a felony.

Statutory Citation—Sections 39-14-105, 39-14-121 and 47-29-101.

TEXAS

Service Charge—$25.

Evidence for Prosecution—If debt is not paid within 10 days of receipt of notice by certified mail, return receipt requested. Notice of dishonor must be given within 30 days from date dishonor occurred.

Civil Penalty—None.

Criminal Penalty—Felony if over $1500.

Statutory Citation—Penal Code Sections § 31.03, 32.41 and 132.9022.

UTAH

Service Charge—$20.

Evidence for Prosecution—If debt is not paid within 15 days of the date notice is mailed.

Civil Penalty—Interest; all costs of collection including court costs and reasonable attorneys' fees equal to the greater of $100 or three times the check amount, not to exceed the check amount plus $500.

Criminal Penalty—Misdemeanor if less than $1000, otherwise a felony.

Statutory Citation—Sections 7-15-1 and 76-6-505.

VERMONT

Service Charge—$25.

Evidence for Prosecution—If debt is not paid within 30 days of receipt of notice by certified mail. *Prima facie* evidence if not paid within 10 days of receipt of notice.

Civil Penalty—Court costs, costs of service, the amount of the check, bank fees, interest, attorneys' fees and damages in the amount of $50.

Criminal Penalty—Misdemeanor for all amounts.

Statutory Citation—Titles 9:57 § 2311 and 13:47 § 2022.

VIRGINIA

Service Charge—$35.

Evidence for Prosecution—If debt is not paid within 30 days of receipt of notice by certified mail. *Prima facie* evidence if not paid within five days of receipt of notice, by certified or registered mail.

Civil Penalty—Three times the amount of the check, up to a maximum amount of $250, in addition to the amount of the check, legal interest from the date of the check, service fee and processing fee, and attorney fees if awarded by court.

Criminal Penalty—Misdemeanor if less than $200, otherwise a felony.

Statutory Citation—Sections § 8.01-27.1 and § 18.2-181 through 18.2-183.

WASHINGTON

Service Charge—$30.

Evidence for Prosecution—If debt is not paid within 20 days of receipt of notice by certified mail. *Prima facie* evidence if not paid within 15 days of receipt of notice.

Civil Penalty—Lesser of three times the amount of the check and reasonable attorneys' fees or $300.

Criminal Penalty—Misdemeanor for all amounts.

Statutory Citation—Section § 62A.3-515.

WEST VIRGINIA

Service Charge—$15.

Evidence for Prosecution—If debt is not paid within 30 days of receipt of notice by certified mail or regular mail supported by affidavit.

Civil Penalty—$500 or the amount of the check, whichever is less, plus reasonable costs incurred in filing the action.

Criminal Penalty—Misdemeanor if less than $500, otherwise a felony.

Statutory Citation—Sections § 55-16-1 and § 61-3-39.

WISCONSIN

Service Charge—$30.

Evidence for Prosecution—If debt is not paid within 20 days of receipt of notice by certified mail. *Prima facie* evidence if not paid within five days of receipt of notice.

Civil Penalty—Three times the amount of the check and all actual costs of legal action, including attorneys' fees, not to exceed $500.

Criminal Penalty—Misdemeanor if $2500 or less, otherwise a felony.

Statutory Citation—Sections 943.24 and 943.245.

WYOMING

Service Charge—$30.

Evidence for Prosecution—If debt is not paid within 30 days of receipt of written demand by certified mail. *Prima facie* evidence if not paid within five days of receipt of notice delivered personally or sent to address shown on check.

Civil Penalty—Three times the amount of the check, but in no case less than $100, collection fees, and court costs. Attorney fees may also be awarded.

Criminal Penalty—Misdemeanor if less than $1000, otherwise a felony.

Statutory Citation—Sections 1-1-115, 6-3-702 and 6-3-703.

18 Claims against Decedents' Estates

The moment credit is extended, an individual debtor is created. That individual may either be the obligor of a personal debt or the guarantor of the debt of a corporate entity. In the event that the individual should die with a debt of any sort in their name, the only method for the creditor to recover from the decedent is through the decedent's probate estate. If the situation is such that there is more than one obligor or guarantor, the surviving individuals are not relieved from their obligations and may still be pursued for collection of the debt. It is very important to note that, in those situations, the creditor must protect its interest by also pursuing the decedent's estate as that may be the most likely source for recovery.

The probate codes of each state—and each county within each state—are very precise, and the statutes of limitations very strict. As a result, when dealing with decedents' estates, creditors must be vigilant and very careful not to miss filing deadlines because if they do, they may be forever barred from recovery of the debt owed to them.

The manner and process for presentment of claims against a decedent's estate run the gamut from simple to complex. In some jurisdictions, it is the customary procedure for the executor, personal representative, or administrator of a solvent estate to pay estate administration expenses, funeral expenses, and the decedent's debts without the requirement of a formal claim, but that is not the norm. When the local procedures become more complex, the claim is disputed, or the estate is insolvent, it is recommended that creditors be represented by legal counsel for the filing of claims, attending hearings and negotiating settlements.

The summary presented below contains brief statements of the requirements and guidelines of the probate codes of each of the several states with respect to the presentation and filing of claims against the estates of deceased persons as well as the deadline for filing a civil lawsuit against the estate in the event that the creditor's claim is wrongfully rejected. The term "representative" as used below refers to the executor, personal representative, or administrator of the estate. Where a deceased person dies "testate," or leaving a will, "letters testamentary" are issued to the executor or representative named therein. If the decedent dies "intestate," or leaving no will, an administrator rather than an executor is appointed and "letters of administration" are issued.

It is the duty of the representative to take possession of, and sometimes liquidate, the assets of the decedent; pay the expenses of administration, the funeral, and the claims of creditors; and dispose of the balance of the estate in accordance with the decedent's will, or in accordance with the local statutes governing the distribution of decedents' estates. Unless the decedent's will provides that the executor shall not be required to file a bond, the executor must file a bond in an amount ordered by the court. In the case of an administrator, a bond is always required. In some states, the representative is required to either publish the time for presentment of creditor claims in the legal news of the county in which the decedent resided or send actual notice to known creditors advising them of the deadline and procedure for presentment of their claims into the estate. In some states, no such notice is required. Instead, creditors must file their claims within a time prescribed by statute after the date of the decedent's death. In all states, if the creditor misses the deadline for presentment of claims, they may be forever barred from recovery of the debt owed to them.

SUMMARY OF STATE LAWS GOVERNING CLAIMS AGAINST ESTATES

Note: State legislatures will, on occasion, modify an area of law without clear delineation as to its content and context. As a result, even the changes which have been enacted prior to placement in the state's Code may be difficult to locate. As a result, the Editors urge all users of the *Manual* to use this publication only as a guide, and consult the latest codified version of the state's law for all recent changes.

ALABAMA

Time for Filing—Within six months after grant of letters of administration or letters testamentary are issued or within five months from the date of first publication of notice to creditors of appointment or will be forever barred from recovery. Creditors who are known or easily ascertainable by the personal representative must be sent notice and given 30 days after receipt of actual notice within which to present a claim.

Where Filed—Probate Court of the county in which the decedent resided.

Must Claim Be Sworn To?—Yes.

Remarks—If estate is insolvent, claim must be filed within six months after declaration of insolvency.

Rejection—Upon receipt of rejection, the creditor must request a hearing from the Court.

Statutory Citation—Section 43-2-350.

ALASKA

Time for Presentment—Within four months after date of the first publication of notice to creditors or within three years after decedent's death if notice to creditors has not been published. For claims against decedent's estate, which arise at or after the death of the decedent, claims must be presented within four months after performance of contract by personal representative or four months after claim arises.

Where Presented—To representative or to Clerk of Court.

Must Claim Be Sworn To?—No.

Rejection—Creditor must file suit within 60 days of receipt of the rejection.

Statutory Citation—Sections 13.16.460 and 13.16.465.

ARIZONA

Time for Filing—Claims arising before death must be presented within four months from first publication or actual notice to known creditors, or within two years of decedent's death if no notice was published. Claims arising at or after death must be presented within four months after performance by personal representative is due if based on a contract with him or four months after claim arises. The statute does not provide for any extension of time for creditors who did not receive notice by virtue of being out of state.

Where Filed—Presented to representative for allowance or rejection.

Must Claim Be Sworn To?—No particular form of proof of claim is required.

Rejection—Creditor must file suit within 60 days of mailing of notice of rejection.

Statutory Citation—Sections 14-3802 and 14-3804.

ARKANSAS

Time for Filing—Within three months from the date of the first publication of the notice or forever barred. Within two years of the date of death if an estate was opened but no notice was given. If no notice was published, claims are barred at the end of five years of decedent's death. Claims for injury or death caused by negligence of decedent shall be filed within six months.

Where Filed—Presented to representative or filed with the court.

Must Claim Be Sworn To?—Yes. Affidavit must state nature and amount of claim, that nothing has been paid, that there are no offsets, and that the sum demanded is justly due.

Rejection—Court shall set the deadline for the filing of a suit on rejection of creditor's claim.

Statutory Citation—Sections 28-50-101, 28-50-103 and 28-50-104.

CALIFORNIA

Time for Filing—Within four months after letters are issued to a general personal representative or 60 days after date actual notice of administration is given to creditors provided such notice is timely. If no notice is given, within one year from the date of death of the decedent. Court can extend time under special circumstances.

Where Filed—With Clerk of the Court that issued letters. Copy must also be mailed to personal representative.

Must Claim Be Sworn To?—Yes, must be verified and supported by an affidavit showing that the amount is justly due, that no payments have been made which are not credited, and that there are no offsets.

Remarks—If claim is allowed it must be presented to the Judge of the Superior Court for his approval and must be filed with the court within 30 days thereafter.

Rejection—When claim is rejected by either the court or the representative, the creditor must, under penalty of being barred, bring suit within 90 days of receipt of the rejection.

Statutory Citation—Probate Sections 9100, 9150, 9151 and 9250.

COLORADO

Time for Filing—Within four months after the date of the first publication of notice to creditors or such other time set forth in publication. Within 60 days of actual notice that is mailed or delivered to the creditor. Within one year after decedent's death if notice has not been published. Claims arising at or after death must be presented within four months after performance by personal representative is due or four months after claim arises.

Where Filed—Presented to representative or filed with Clerk of Court.

Must Claim Be Sworn To?—No particular form of proof of claim is required.

Rejection—The creditor has 60 days from the date of the rejection within which to petition for allowance.

Statutory Citation—Sections 15-12-801 and 15-12-804.

CONNECTICUT

Time for Filing—The deadline for claims is stated in the notice published by the representative and is usually not less than three months or more than 12 months from the time of granting of the order. In cases of an insolvent estate, the creditor has 120 days from date of determination of insolvency to present claims or be forever barred.

Where Filed—Presented to the representative, or if fiduciary resides outside the jurisdiction, claims may be filed with the Judge of the Probate Court in the county where the estate has been filed.

Must Claim Be Sworn To?—Yes, if requested by the representative or probate court. Affidavit must state nature and amount of claim, that nothing has been paid, that there are no offsets, and that the sum demanded is justly due.

Rejection—Claim is forever barred if suit is not brought within 60 days after notice of rejection.

Statutory Citation—Sections 45a-354 and 45a-358.

DELAWARE

Time for Filing—Within eight months of decedent's death, whether or not notice was given, no exceptions. Claims arising at or after death must be presented within six months after claim arises or after performance by representative is due. Claims based on bond secured by mortgage must be presented within eight months.

Where Filed—With representative or with Register of Wills or presented by commencing a proceeding against personal representative in any court in which he is subject to jurisdiction.

Must Claim Be Sworn To?—No. Basis of claim must be indicated with name and address of claimant and amount claimed.

Rejection—Any claim rejected by the representative will be forever barred unless suit is filed within 90 days of receipt of the rejection.

Statutory Citation—Title 12 Section 2102 and Title 12 Section 2104.

DISTRICT OF COLUMBIA

Time for Filing—Claims must be presented within six months after date of first publication of notice of appointment. Suit may be brought to recover amount due even though no claim was filed, subject to general three-year statute of limitation, provided that the representative has not distributed the assets of the estate.

Where Filed—Presented by mail or delivery, receipt requested, to the representative and entered upon claims docket of the Register of Wills or to Register with copy to representative.

Must Claim Be Sworn To?—Yes, with statement that the account as stated is true and just, that no part of the claim has been paid, and that all credits have been made.

Rejection—Creditor has 60 days from the date of the rejection to file suit.

Statutory Citation—Sections 20-903 and 20-905.

FLORIDA

Time for Filing—Within three months from the first publication of notice to creditors or within 30 days after date of service of actual notice to creditor. If no notice was published then within two years after the decedent's death or forever barred.

Where Filed—With the Clerk of Court who will serve a copy to the representative.

Must Claim Be Sworn To?—Yes, must be verified.

Remarks—Objection to claims may be filed within four months from the first publication of notice to creditors. The court may extend the time for filing objections for good cause shown.

Rejection—If an objection is filed, the claimant has 30 days from such service within which to bring suit.

Statutory Citation—Sections 733.702, 733.703 and 733.710.

GEORGIA

Time for Filing—Within three months from date of publication of last notice. If filed thereafter, creditor loses right to equal participation with claims that were filed within the deadline. Representative must give four weeks' notice within which to present claims.

Where Filed—With representative.

Must Claim Be Sworn To?—Verification is not required, but some courts will demand it.

Remarks—No suit to recover a debt may be commenced against representative until six months after his qualification.

Rejection—There is no deadline stated in the statute.

Statutory Citation—Sections 53-7-41 and 53-7-42.

GUAM

Time for Filing—Within 60 days from publication or service of first notice to creditor.

Where Filed—With the representative or sent to the decedent's address.

Must Claim Be Sworn To?—Yes.

Remarks—The personal representative is required to investigate the identities of creditors. Creditors' written notices of debt, if timely, are treated as claims if subsequently perfected.

Statutory Citation—Probate Sections 700 and 2503.

HAWAII

Time for Filing—Claims are forever barred if not presented by creditors within four months after the first publication of notice by representative or 60 days of actual notice sent to known creditors. If no notice is given, claims must be filed within two years of the date of death of the decedent. Claims arising at or after death must be presented within four months after performance by representative, any other claims within four months after claim arises.

Where Filed—With representative and Clerk of Court.

Must Claim Be Sworn To?—There is no statutory form of proof of claim. It is advisable that claims be itemized and an affidavit attached stating that the claim is due and unpaid and that there are no offsets or counterclaims thereto.

Remarks—Secured creditors may foreclose on security held without filing a claim.

Rejection—Creditor must file suit within 90 days of receipt of the rejection.

Statutory Citation—Sections 560:3-801, 560:3-803 and 560:3-804.

IDAHO

Time for Filing—Within four months after the first publication of notice or within 60 days after mailing or delivery of actual notice, whichever is later. Claim will be forever barred within two years after the decedent's death whether or not notice has been published.

Where Filed—With representative and Clerk of Court.

Must Claim Be Sworn To?—No.

Rejection—If claim is rejected, suit must be brought within 60 days after date of rejection, if claim is due; if not due, then within two months after becoming due, otherwise claim is barred. Representative or court may order an extension of the period, but in no event shall the extension run beyond the applicable statute of limitations.

Statutory Citation—Sections 15-3-801/803 and 15-3-804.

ILLINOIS

Time for Filing—Within six months after the date of first publication of notice or within three months after receipt of actual notice.

Where Filed—With Probate Court administering the estate or with representative.

Must Claim Be Sworn To?—Yes. When based on contract, an affidavit must accompany the claim and must state that claim is just and unpaid after allowing all credits, deductions, and setoffs.

Remarks—If an additional list of inventory is filed, not covering previously inventoried property, and the Clerk of Court publishes notice of a new claim date, all claims not filed before such date are barred as to such additional property. All claims filed on or before such date share pro rata in additional property according to the classification of the claims.

Rejection—Creditor must file suit within 60 days of receipt of the rejection.

Statutory Citation—Sections 755 ILCS 5/18-2 and 755 ILCS 5/18-3.

INDIANA

Time for Filing—Within five months after first published notice to creditors or three months after the court has revoked probate of will if claimant was named as beneficiary in will, whichever is later, or within nine months after the date of death.

Where Filed—In Office of Clerk where estate proceedings are pending.

Must Claim Be Sworn To?—Yes. An affidavit must be attached to the claim stating that it is justly due and wholly unpaid after deducting all credits, setoffs, and deductions.

Rejection—No deadline is specified in the statute.

Statutory Citation—Sections 29-1-14-1 and 29-1-14-2.

IOWA

Time for Filing—Within four months after the date of the second publication of notice to creditors, or one month after service of actual notice by ordinary mail to known creditor, whichever is later, or forever barred.

Where Filed—Filed with the Clerk of the District Court of county in which estate is being administered. Court will serve a copy to the representative.

Must Claim Be Sworn To?—Yes. If founded on written instrument, it must be attached; if upon account, an itemized copy showing the balance should be attached.

Rejection—Creditor has 20 days from the date of the rejection within which to request a hearing.

Statutory Citation—Sections 633.410 and 633.418.

KANSAS

Time for Filing—Within four months from the date of first published notice to creditors as long as the first publication is within six months from the decedent's date of death, or forever barred.

Where Filed—With the Probate Court. If claimed amount is under $5000, it may be allowed by representative without filing with Court.

Must Claim Be Sworn To?—Yes. Claims must be verified.

Rejection—There is no deadline. Creditor must just file suit upon rejection.

Statutory Citation—Sections 59-2236 and 59-2237.

KENTUCKY

Time for Filing—Within six months after appointment of personal representative. If no personal representative is appointed, then two years after decedent's death.

Where Filed—With representative.

Must Claim Be Sworn To?—Yes. Representative may pay claim without verification when he is satisfied the estate is solvent and that claim is just and owing. Otherwise, claim must be sworn to.

Remarks—If debt is on a written contract, nothing further than affidavit of claimant required. If upon an account, in addition to claimant's affidavit, that of a disinterested person is required.

Rejection—Creditor has 60 days from the date of rejection within which to petition the Court for allowance.

Statutory Citation—Sections 396.011, 396.015 and 396.026.

LOUISIANA

Time for Filing—Within three years from the date of the last activity such as the last payment or date of last purchase. Representative must file an account every 12 months. Claims are passed upon and allowed at that time.

Where Filed—With representative.

Must Claim Be Sworn To?—No, except for specific purposes.

Rejection—There is no deadline. Creditor must just file suit upon rejection.

Statutory Citation—CCP T.3 Articles 3241 and 3245.

MAINE

Time for Filing—Within four months after the date of first publication of the notice or within 60 days from receipt of actual notice, whichever is later. If no notice is given, then nine months after death of decedent or forever barred. Claims arising at or after death must be presented within four months after the performance by representative is due, all other claims within four months after they arise.

Where Filed—With representative or Clerk of the Court.

Must Claim Be Sworn To?—No.

Rejection—Creditor has 60 days from receipt of rejection within which to file suit.

Statutory Citation—Title 18A, Sections 3-801, 3-803 and 3-804.

MARYLAND

Time for Filing—Within two months after required mailing or delivery of notice of appointment of representative or six months of decedent's death, whichever is earlier. Suit against the estate must be commenced within six months after appointment unless decedent was covered by insurance, in which case the statute of limitations for the particular action governs. Six-month limitation period extended if first published more than 20 days after appointment.

Where Filed—With representative or Register of Wills with a copy sent to representative.

Remarks—Suit against the estate must be commenced within six months after appointment unless decedent was covered by insurance, in which case the statute of limitations for the particular action governs. Six-month limitation period extended if first published more than 20 days after appointment.

Must Claim Be Sworn To?—No.

Rejection—The creditor has 60 days from the date of the rejection within which to petition for allowance.

Statutory Citation—ET Sections 8-103 and 8-104.

MASSACHUSETTS

Time for Filing—Within four months date of receipt of actual notice or, if no notice given, within one year of date of death. If representative, after end of six-month period after death, has no notice of demand sufficient to warrant his representing the estate as insolvent, he may pay debts of estate and is not personally liable for demands of creditors of which he had no notice.

Where Filed—With representative.

Rejection—No deadline specified.

Must Claim Be Sworn To?—No, but preferable practice.

Statutory Citation—Title II, Chapter 198.

MICHIGAN

Time for Filing—Within four months from date of publication or one month from date of actual notice to the creditor, whichever is later. If no notice is given, within three years from the decedent's date of death.

Where Filed—With court, and copy must be served on fiduciary.

Must Claim Be Sworn To?—No.

Remarks—Creditor may, within 18 months after last date to file claims and before estate is closed, file application to file claim and application shall be granted not more than one month thereafter, upon payment of costs. After the 18 months, the court may permit a claim to be filed for special cause.

Rejection—Creditor has 60 days from date of rejection within which to file suit.

Statutory Citation—Sections 700.3801 and 700.3803.

MINNESOTA

Time for Filing—Within four months after the date of publication of the Clerk of Court's notice to creditors or within one month of actual notice sent to the creditor, whichever is later. If notice is not published, within one year after the decedent's death.

Where Filed—In the Probate Court or sent to the personal representative.

Must Claim Be Sworn To?—No, if sent to personal representative. If filed with court, *see* local court rules.

Rejection—Creditor has 60 days from date of rejection within which to file suit.

Statutory Citation—Section 524.3-803 and 524.3-804.

MISSISSIPPI

Time for Filing—Within 90 days from the first publication of notice to creditors. If no estate opened, within three years of the decedent's date of death.

Where Filed—With Clerk of the Chancery Court.

Must Claim Be Sworn To?—Yes, must be duly verified and attached to claim.

Remarks—Before clerk will accept claims, affidavit of claim must be probated and registered. The affidavit of creditor must be attached to the written evidence of the indebtedness. Such affidavit must state that the claim is just, correct, and owing from the deceased, that it is not usurious, and that no part of it has been paid.

Rejection—Creditor has 90 days from date of rejection within which to file suit.

Statutory Citation—Sections 91-7-149 and 91-7-151.

MISSOURI

Time for Filing—Claims must be filed within six months after the first published notice of letters testamentary or of administration or within two months of receipt of actual notice to the creditor, whichever is later.

Where Filed—With the Probate Court.

Must Claim Be Sworn To?—Yes.

Remarks—Claim must be served on representative in writing stating the nature and amount of claim with a copy of the written evidence of indebtedness.

Rejection—The Court will set a hearing on the rejections.

Statutory Citation—Sections 473.360 and 473.380.

MONTANA

Time for Filing—Within one year from date of death if notice has not been published. Personal representative may give written notice to creditors to present claims within four months from date of publication or 30 days from date of mailing of notice. Claims that arise at or after death must be filed within four months after performance by representative is due if based on a contract with the representative, any other claim within four months after it arises.

Where Filed—With representative by mail, return receipt requested, or with the Clerk of Court.

Must Claim Be Sworn To?—No.

Rejection—Creditor has 60 days from date of rejection within which to file suit.

Statutory Citation—Sections 72-3-801, 72-3-803 and 72-3-804.

NEBRASKA

Time for Filing—Within two months of first publication of notice, or three years if notice was not given. Claims that arise at or after death must be filed within four months after performance by representative is due if based on a contract with the representative, any other claim within four months after it arises.

Where Filed—Clerk of the Probate Court.

Must Claim Be Sworn To?—Yes.

Remarks—If claim is not presented within stipulated time, it shall be forever barred unless good cause is shown.

Rejection—Creditor has 60 days from date of rejection within which to file suit.

Statutory Citation—Sections 30-2485 and 30-2486.

NEVADA

Time for Filing—Within 90 days from date of first publication of notice to creditors or of mailing of actual notice to creditors for claims against the deceased. If no notice is given, then anytime before the filing of the final account.

Where Filed—Clerk of Court.

Must Claim Be Sworn To?—Yes. If claim is for $250 or more, an affidavit must state that the amount is justly due (or date it will be due), that no payments have been made thereon which are not credited, and that there are no offsets to the same.

Rejection—Creditor has 60 days from date of rejection within which to file suit. Claim will not be barred if claimant can prove that he did not receive notice.

Statutory Citation—Sections 147.040, 147.070 and 147.130.

NEW HAMPSHIRE

Time for Filing—Within six months from grant of letters. If estate is insolvent, no presentation is required and notice sent to representative by registered mail stating nature and amount of claim is sufficient.

Where Filed—Presented to representative.

Must Claim Be Sworn To?—At discretion of representative.

Rejection—Creditor has 30 days from date of rejection within which to file suit.

Statutory Citation—Sections 556:1, 556:2 and 554:24.

NEW JERSEY

Time for Filing—Within six months after entry of order of publication to creditors by the Superior Court or surrogate.

Where Filed—Presented to representative.

Must Claim Be Sworn To?—Yes, with statement of amount and particulars of claim.

Rejection—Creditor has 90 days from date of rejection within which to file suit.

Statutory Citation—Sections 3B-22-4 and 3B-22-8.

NEW MEXICO

Time for Filing—Within two months of the date of first publication of notice of appointment of executor or administrator or within one year of the decedent's death if notice to creditors has not been published. Claims arising at or after death based on a contract with personal representative must be presented within four months after performance by representative is due, any other claim within four months after it arises.

Where Filed—With District Court or representative.

Must Claim Be Sworn To?—No.

Rejection—Creditor has 60 days from date of rejection within which to file suit.

Statutory Citation—Sections 45-3-801, 45-3-803 and 45-3-804.

NEW YORK

Time for Filing—Claims should be presented to fiduciary on or before date fixed in the notice to creditors or, if no notice is published, within seven months from the date of the issue of letters.

Where Filed—With the representative at the location stated in the notice.

Must Claim Be Sworn To?—The fiduciary may require the claimant to present proof by affidavit with satisfactory vouchers and affidavit stating the claim is justly due, that no payments have been made thereon, and that there are no offsets against the same to the knowledge of the claimant.

Rejection—Creditor has 60 days from date of rejection within which to file suit.

Statutory Citation—Title 59A Sections 1801 and 1803.

NORTH CAROLINA

Time for Filing—Within time specified in general notice to creditors, but it must be at least three months from the day of first publication or posting of notice or 90 days after actual notice, whichever is later. Claims arising at or after death must be presented within six months after performance by representative is due if based on contract with him, all other claims within six months after claim arises, except certain claims covered by insurance.

Where Filed—With representative or Clerk of Superior Court.

Must Claim Be Sworn To?—Within discretion of representative or collector.

Remarks—Claim must contain name and address of claimant, amount claimed, and basis of the claim. Upon failure to file within six months, creditor may recover from the representative if he still has funds; if not, he may proceed against the heirs.

Rejection—Creditor has 90 days from date of rejection within which to file suit.

Statutory Citation—Sections 28A-14-1, 28A-19-1 and 28A-19-3.

NORTH DAKOTA

Time for Filing—Within three months after the date of the first publication of notice to creditors. Within three years after decedent's death if no notice is published. Claims at or after death based on contract with representative or collector must be presented within four months after which performance is due, all other claims within three months after they arise.

Where Filed—Present to personal representative or file with Clerk of Court.

Must Claim Be Sworn To?—No, if filed with personal representative. If filed with Clerk of Court, consult local court rules. County rules may require that the claim be verified.

Rejection—Creditor has 60 days from date of rejection within which to file suit.

Statutory Citation—Sections 30.1-19-3 and 30.1-19-4.

OHIO

Time for Filing—Within six months from date of death of the decedent for deaths on or after April 8, 2004. Within one year from date of death of the decedent for deaths before April 8, 2004, or forever barred. Executor or administrator can shorten notice period by giving notice to creditor to file claim within 30 days.

Where Filed—With representative and Probate Court in the county where the decedent resided.

Must Claim Be Sworn To?—If representative so requires, affidavit must state that such claim is justly due, that no payments have been made thereon, and that there are no offsets against the same.

Rejection—Creditor has 60 days from date of rejection within which to file suit.

Statutory Citation—Sections 2117.06 and 2117.07.

OKLAHOMA

Time for Filing—Claims have to be presented by the presentment date stated in the notice to creditors. The presentment date shall be a date certain which is at least two months following the date said notice is filed. The first publication of said notice shall appear on or before the tenth day after the filing of said notice. For claimants who are out of state and who do not receive actual notice, the claim may be presented at any time before a final decree of distribution is entered. The claimant may prove by affidavit that he had no notice by reason of being out of state and that a copy of the notice was not mailed to such claimant.

Where Filed—Presented at place specified in notice to the representative.

Must Claim Be Sworn To?—No form for proof of claim is prescribed by statute; but claimant must, if requested by executor or administrator, file with clerk vouchers or proofs in support of his claim.

Rejection—Creditor has 45 days from date of rejection within which to file suit.

Statutory Citation—Title 58 Sections 331 and 332.

OREGON

Time for Filing—Within four months of date of first publication or within 30 days of receipt of actual notice to the creditor. Claims presented within four months after date of first publication of notice have priority. If notice is published, claims not presented before expiration of 12 months after date of first publication or before date personal representative files his final account, whichever occurs first, are barred from payment. If no notice is published to interested persons, claims are barred after two years after death if not statute-barred before.

Where Filed—Presented to representative.

Must Claim Be Sworn To?—No.

Rejection—Creditor has 30 days from date of rejection within which to file suit.

Statutory Citation—Section 115.005.

PENNSYLVANIA

Time for Filing—Within one year from date of death of the decedent or by the call for the audit of the account of the representative, whichever is first.

Where Filed—With representative or the attorney of record.

Must Claim Be Sworn To?—It is not necessary that a claim be verified, but it must be presented and proved in Orphans' Court at audit of account, unless admitted by representative.

Rejection—Nothing is stated in the statute.

Statutory Citation—Title 20 Sections 3383 and 3384.

RHODE ISLAND

Time for Filing—Within six months from first publication of notice to creditors.

Where Filed—In the office of the Probate Court together with affidavit that copy was delivered by hand or registered mail, return receipt requested, to representative or his attorney.

Must Claim Be Sworn To?—No form for proof of claim is prescribed by statute but claimant must, if requested by executor or administrator, file with Clerk affidavit in support of his claim.

Remarks—For sufficient cause shown, the Probate Court may permit a claim to be filed after six months.

Rejection—A hearing will be set with the Commissioner 30-60 days after the date of the filing of the rejection.

Statutory Citation—Sections 33-11-4, 33-11-5 and 33-11-7.

SOUTH CAROLINA

Time for Filing—Within eight months after first publication of notice or within 60 days of actual notice to the creditor, whichever is earlier. Within one year if no notice has been published.

Where Filed—With representative and Probate Clerk.

Must Claim Be Sworn To?—No.

Rejection—Creditor has 30 days from date of rejection within which to file suit.

Statutory Citation—Sections 62-3-801, 62-3-803 and 62-3-804.

SOUTH DAKOTA

Time for Filing—Within four months from time of first publication of notice or within 60 days after mailing of actual notice. In any event, claims are barred if not filed within three years of date of death.

Where Filed—Claims must be filed with clerk of court where proceedings are pending; a copy thereof must be mailed to the representative.

Must Claim Be Sworn To?—Yes.

Remarks—Suit on claim must be commenced no more than 60 days after personal representative has mailed notice of disallowance except for claims that are not due or are contingent, in which event extension may be obtained from court. It is acceptable for the creditor to proceed against the personal representative in any court where the personal representative may be subject to jurisdiction. A petition for allowance may also be filed.

Rejection—Creditor has 60 days from date of rejection within which to file suit.

Statutory Citation—Sections 29A-3-801, 29A-3-803 and 29A-3-804.

TENNESSEE

Time for Filing—Claims must be filed within six months after the first publication or posting. If creditor receives actual notice less than 60 days before expiration of the six-month period or after expiration of the six-month period, such creditor's claim is barred unless filed within 60 days from date of receipt of actual notice. In any event, claims are barred if not filed within 12 months after decedent's date of death.

Where Filed—Triplicate copies of claim to be filed with Clerk of Court in which estate is being administered.

Must Claim Be Sworn To?—Claim must be verified by affidavit of creditor stating that the claim is a correct, just, and valid obligation of the estate and that no payment or security has been received except as indicated therein.

Rejection—Trial by jury may be requested to determine the validity of the claim.

Statutory Citation—Sections 30.2-306, 30.2-307 and 30.2-310.

TEXAS

Time for Filing—A claim may be presented to the personal representative at any time before the estate is closed if suit on the claim has not been barred by the general statute of limitations. If a claim of an unsecured creditor for money is not presented within four months after the date of receipt of the notice, the claim is forever barred.

Where Filed—Presented to the representative or Clerk of Court.

Must Claim Be Sworn To?—Yes.

Rejection—Creditor has 90 days from date of rejection within which to file suit.

Statutory Citation—Probate Code Sections 294, 298 and 301.

UTAH

Time for Filing—Within three months after the first publication of notice to creditors or within 60 days of actual notice to the creditor, or forever barred. Within three years if no notice has been published. Claims arising at or after death must be presented within three months after performance by representative is due, if based on a contract with him all other claims within three months after they arise.

Where Filed—Presented to representative, representative's attorney of record or Clerk of Court.

Must Claim Be Sworn To?—No.

Rejection—Creditor has 90 days from date of rejection within which to file suit.

Statutory Citation—Sections 75-3-801 and 75-3-803.

VERMONT

Time for Filing—Claims must be filed within four months of first publication of notice. If no notice is published, then within three years of decedent's date of death. Claims arising at or after death must be filed within four months of date of death.

Where Filed—With representative and Probate Court.

Must Claim Be Sworn To?—No.

Rejection—Creditor has 60 days from date of rejection to petition for allowance.

Statutory Citation—Title 14 Sections 1203 and 1204.

VIRGIN ISLANDS

Time for Filing—Within six months of date of first publication. Claims not presented within six months are not barred, but cannot be paid until properly presented claims are satisfied.

Where Filed—With representative.

Must Claim Be Sworn To?—Yes. Claims should include an affidavit.

Statutory Citation—Title 15 Sections 391, 392 and 393.

VIRGINIA

Time for Filing—Within one year of date of death of decedent.

Where Filed—With court-appointed Commissioner of Accounts.

Must Claim Be Sworn To?—No form prescribed but claim should be in writing.

Rejection—Creditor must file exceptions with the Court upon receipt of rejection.

Statutory Citation—Sections 64.1-171 and 64.1-173.

WASHINGTON

Time for Filing—Within four months after the first publication of notice to creditors or date of filing copy of notice or within 30 days after giving actual notice to creditor, whichever is later. If no notice is given, within 18 months after the date of death of the decedent.

Where Filed—Presented to representative who must endorse on claim his allowance or rejection. Claim is then filed with court.

Must Claim Be Sworn To?—Claims need not be supported by an affidavit. The statement should include that the claim is correct, that the amount is justly due, that no payments have been made thereon, and that there are no offsets to the same.

Rejection—Creditor has 30 days from date of rejection within which to file suit.

Statutory Citation—Sections 11.40.30, 11.40.51 and 11.40.100.

WEST VIRGINIA

Time for Filing—Commissioner appointed by court must publish notice to file claims, which time will not be more than 30 days after the date of the first publication of notice to creditors. Notice to creditors shall not be less than two months nor more than three months from date of death of the decedent. Claimant who had no actual knowledge of notice and presented his claim after such time limit may participate only in surplus, if any, remaining after payment of claims presented in time.

Where Filed—With the Probate Court.

Must Claim Be Sworn To?—No particular form is prescribed except that claims must be itemized and accompanied by proper vouchers with statement of character of claim in full detail.

Rejection—Creditor has 30 days from date of rejection within which to file suit.

Statutory Citation—Sections 44.2-1.

WISCONSIN

Time for Filing—Within three months from date of first publication or 30 days from date of actual notice to creditors. If no notice given, within one year from date of death of decedent.

Where Filed—Verified claims, in court of the county of defendant's domicile, or if nonresident, in any county in which property is located and with representative.

Must Claim Be Sworn To?—Yes.

Remarks—Time to file claims may be extended for good cause, but not beyond two years from date of appointment of executor or administrator.

Rejection—Hearing may be requested by the creditor upon receipt of rejection.

Statutory Citation—Sections 859.01, 859.02 and 859.13.

WYOMING

Time for Filing—Claims must be filed within three months after first publication of notice or within 30 days after mailing of notice to owner, whichever date is later.

Where Filed—In duplicate with Clerk of Court.

Must Claim Be Sworn To?—Yes.

Rejection—Creditor has 30 days from date of rejection within which to file suit.

Statutory Citation—Sections 2-7-701, 2-7-703 and 2-7-704.

A Creditor's Guide to the Bankruptcy Process

STRUCTURE OF THE BANKRUPTCY CODE

Bankruptcy law presently in effect in the United States is referred to as the United States Bankruptcy Code. It is found in Title 11 of the United States Code and is referred to as "11 USC § ____." All references in this text to "11 USC § ____" are references to the Bankruptcy Code. The Bankruptcy Code was first adopted in 1978 and became effective October 1, 1979. The Bankruptcy Code has been amended from time to time since October 1, 1979. The Bankruptcy Abuse Prevention and Consumer Protection Act of 2002 has amended and modified the Bankruptcy Code in a greater manner than any of the prior law changes.

The Bankruptcy Code as revised by the Bankruptcy Abuse Prevention and Consumer Protection Act (hereinafter referred to as "BAPCPA"), contains the most substantive changes made since the original 1979 enactment. The reader must understand that although BAPCPA, itself, contains numerous titles and sections, all the permanent changes are referenced in the Bankruptcy Code. One of major revisions made by the BAPCPA is the addition of a new Chapter 15 to the Bankruptcy Code, entitled "Ancillary and Cross-Border Cases." Further, Title X of the BAPCPA, entitled "Protection of Family Farmers and Family Fisherman" has added substantive changes to the Bankruptcy Code.

The Code itself is broken down into nine chapters. The first three chapters, Chapters 1, 3 and 5, contain administrative provisions that apply in all cases under the Code. For example, the mechanics for filing a petition for relief, the provisions for compensation of professionals and the general definitions are all found in the first three chapters and apply in all chapters. The remaining five chapters, Chapters 7, 9, 11, 12 and 13, are the operative chapters under which the various types of bankruptcies are filed. Chapter 15 has been added to manage the many cases that are being filed with U.S. and foreign nation counterparts. Chapter 7 is a liquidation bankruptcy in which a trustee is appointed by the United States Trustee, or in rare cases, elected by creditors, to liquidate nonexempt assets. Chapter 9 is the municipal reorganization chapter that is seldom used. Chapter 11 is the reorganization chapter. Chapters 12 and 13 are specialized reorganization chapters for family farmers, fisherman and wage earners (including individuals who may operate small businesses as sole proprietorships and who otherwise qualify under the debt limits).

The following is a summary of the Bankruptcy Code chapters followed by detailed explanation of Bankruptcy Code chapter, sections, and changes that are most pertinent to commercial credit grantors.

Chapter 1
Code Sections 101 to 110—General Provisions and Definitions

Chapter 3—Case Administration
Code Sections 301 to 307—Commencement of the Case
Code Sections 321 to 331—Officers of the Estate
Code Sections 341 to 350—Administration of the Case
Code Sections 361 to 366—Administrative Powers

Chapter 5—Creditor, Debtor and the Estate
Code Sections 501 to 510—Creditors and Claims
Code Sections 521 to 525—Debtor's Duties and Benefits
Code Sections 541 to 560—The Estate and Avoidance Powers

Chapter 7—Liquidation
Code Sections 701 to 707—Officers of the Case
Code Sections 721 to 728—Collection, Liquidation and Distribution of the Estate
Code Sections 741 to 752—Stock Broker Liquidations
Code Sections 761 to 766—Commodity Broker Liquidations

Chapter 9—Adjustment of Debts of a Municipality
Code Sections 901 to 904—General Provisions
Code Sections 921 to 930—Administration
Code Sections 941 to 946—The Plan

Chapter 11—Reorganization
Code Sections 1101 to 1114—Officers and Administration
Code Sections 1121 to 1129—The Plan
Code Sections 1141 to 1146—Post-Confirmation Matters
Code Sections 1161 to 1174—Railroad Reorganizations

Chapter 12—Adjustment of Debts of a Family Farmer or Fisherman with
Regular Annual Income
Code Sections 1201 to 1208—Officers, Administration and the Estate
Code Sections 1221 to 1231—The Plan

Chapter 13—Adjustment of Debts of an Individual with Regular Income
Code Sections 1301 to 1307—Officers, Administration and the Estate
Code Sections 1321 to 1330—The Plan

Chapter 15—Ancillary and Cross-Border Cases
Code Sections 1501 to 1508—Purpose, Scope and General Provisions
Code Sections 1509 to 1514—Access of Foreign Representatives and Creditors
to Court
Code Sections 1515 to 1524—Recognition of a Foreign Proceeding and Relief
Code Sections 1525 to 1527—Cooperation with Foreign Courts and Foreign
Representatives
Code Sections 1528 to 1532—Concurrent Proceedings

Bankruptcy practice runs on deadlines. You must file in a timely manner your proof of claim, objections to discharge, complaints to determine dischargeability, objections to sales and objections to confirmation of plans. If you understand nothing else about bankruptcy practice, you must understand that failure to comply with the Code's deadlines may dramatically affect your rights.

FEDERAL RULES OF BANKRUPTCY PROCEDURE

To complement the provisions of the Bankruptcy Code, Congress provided for the adoption of rules of procedure relating to bankruptcy cases. The Federal Rules of Bankruptcy Procedure are the result. The Bankruptcy Rules govern how bankruptcy cases are to proceed. While a credit grantor is not required to understand all of the rules, if one acts outside of or in contravention to the rules, sanctions may be imposed by the Court, default or summary judgments may be entered, and rights lost. It is very important that a creditor in a bankruptcy proceeding either fully understands the rules or seeks competent advice.

References in this text to "Fed. R. Bankr. P." are to the Federal Rules of Bankruptcy Procedure. The rules are broken down into 10 chapters and contain a number of deadlines and other regulations governing pleadings in the Bankruptcy Court. The Federal Rules of Bankruptcy Procedure also provide for the bankruptcy courts and the United States District Courts to adopt specific local rules. Most courts have adopted local rules governing such matters as the filing of pleadings and the establishment of trial dockets and motion practice. If there is a conflict between the provisions of the Bankruptcy Code itself and the various applicable rules, the Bankruptcy Code will control. Knowledge of the rules is essential to meeting deadlines. Your library should include a current copy of the rules and a copy of the local rules of any bankruptcy court where you may file papers.

One of the most important changes to the rules of procedure with respect to the Bankruptcy Code has been the implementation of electronic filing throughout all bankruptcy courts within the United States. With the enactment of BAPCPA, even those courts that had not previously enacted electronic filing, have now done so.

It is also important for credit grantors to realize that with the enactment of the BAPCPA, it was impossible to have permanent rules adopted as fast as the BAPCPA became effective. Accordingly, the Judicial Conference has issued a set of Interim Rules that are anticipated to be adopted by each individual bankruptcy court.

AUTOMATIC STAY

Upon the filing of a bankruptcy petition, the Bankruptcy Code imposes a type of injunction, referred to as the automatic stay, which bars creditors' enforcement actions against the debtor or assets of the debtor. 11 USC § 362. The automatic stay is imposed to further one of the Bankruptcy Code's principal goals of ensuring a fair distribution of the debtor's nonexempt, unencumbered assets among creditors. While creditors generally view the automatic stay as an infringement on their rights, it is actually designed to protect them. Without the automatic stay it would be possible for a creditor to conceal or seize assets of the estate even postpetition.

Once the filing of the petition has imposed the automatic stay, any action to collect the debt from the debtor or the debtor's property is prohibited. Note that the automatic stay is in force, even without notice to creditors and in certain limited circumstances in Chapters 12 and 13, and also protects consumer codebtors and guarantors until a stay is lifted. Any action that violates the automatic stay may be set aside by the bankruptcy court. The court may also impose penalties. A violation of the automatic stay is contempt of court and may be punished by an award of damages and attorneys' fees against the person violating the automatic stay. Of particular interest to unsecured creditors is the fact that the automatic stay bars actions by governmental units such as the IRS and prevents the postpetition seizure of assets to satisfy IRS claims. The IRS and other tax authorities may continue tax assessments and audits and may demand filing of tax returns without violating the stay, but it may not impose a lien on the debtor's property.

The automatic stay specifically prohibits the setoff of mutual debts without an appropriate court order. This, for instance, prevents a bank from seizing the debtor's deposits upon the filing of the bankruptcy, although the bank may retain a lien on any deposits. In a trade debt situation, the automatic stay would prevent you from offsetting any credits or returns that you may owe the debtor against the debtor's debt, unless bankruptcy court approval is sought and obtained. The automatic stay will generally not, however, prevent you from exercising rights under the UCC to stop goods in transit before delivery to the debtor or to demand reclamation of goods under UCC 2-702.

In order to lift the automatic stay, a creditor must file a motion for relief from the automatic stay. The creditor must pay a filing fee unless the debtor or the trustee stipulates to the relief. Check with the appropriate clerk of court to confirm the current fee. Additionally, the website for the Judiciary home page www.uscourts.gov provides links to the Bankruptcy Courts, many of which post all of the filing fees as set by the Federal Judiciary Law. Motions for relief are generally handled on a notice and hearing basis. In routine Chapter 7 consumer cases there is rarely a hearing. In a complicated Chapter 11 case, however, relief from the automatic stay is one of the first major battles in the reorganization process.

As an unsecured creditor or a member of an unsecured creditors' committee, you and your counsel will be concerned that any relief from the stay does not adversely affect the ability of the debtor to reorganize. Since most motions for relief are heard on a notice and hearing basis, you may wish to consult counsel upon receiving a copy of the notice to determine whether any objection is necessary or appropriate.

The BAPCPA has amended the automatic stay provisions to deal with the abuse of serial bankruptcy filings. It limits the availability of the automatic stay when a debtor refiles a bankruptcy following the dismissal of a prior bankruptcy.

First, when an individual debtor files a bankruptcy case under Chapter 7, 11 or 13, within one year after dismissal of a prior bankruptcy case, the automatic stay terminates within 30 days of the later bankruptcy case. This does not apply where the debtor's prior case was dismissed as a result of the debtor's inability to comply with the "means test."

The debtor could have the bankruptcy court extend the automatic stay beyond the initial 30-day period if the court finds the later filing was in good faith. However, a bankruptcy case is presumed to have been filed in bad faith if (1) there was a prior bankruptcy case where the debtor had failed to (a) file schedules or other documents as required by the Bankruptcy Code or Rules or court order; (b) provide adequate protection as directed by the court; or (c) perform under a confirmed plan; (2) there has not been a substantial change in the debtor's financial or personal affairs or any other reason to conclude that the case will not be concluded, if Chapter 7, with a discharge and if Chapter 11 or 13, with a confirmed plan that will be fully performed; or (3) as to any creditor who had filed a lift stay motion that was pending or granted in the prior case. The debtor can rebut any such presumed bad faith bankruptcy filing by the difficult to prove clear and convincing evidence standard.

If an individual debtor had filed two or more Chapter 7, 11 or 13 cases during the year preceding the debtor's bankruptcy filing, the automatic stay will not apply in the debtor's subsequently filed bankruptcy case, unless the prior cases were dismissed because the debtor had failed the "means test." The debtor could have the stay reimposed by moving for court approval within 30 days of the later filing and proving the filing was in good faith. Similar presumptions of bad faith apply here too.

Further, the automatic stay with respect to the debtor's real property could be terminated if the court finds that the bankruptcy filing was part of a scheme to hinder, delay, or defraud the debtor's mortgage creditors by either transferring ownership of the property or filing multiple bankruptcy cases involving the property. If the mortgage creditors record the order terminating the stay as to the real property under state law, that order would be effective for two years following entry of the order and would apply to subsequent bankruptcy cases affecting the real property. The debtor could obtain relief from the order in a subsequent case by showing good cause or changed circumstances.

Finally, there are specific exceptions to the general rules of an automatic stay in small business cases. The automatic stay does not apply in a case in which the debtor has a small business case pending at the time a petition is filed. And, the automatic stay does not apply if the debtor was a debtor in a small business case that was dismissed or confirmed within two years from the filing of a subsequent petition. Likewise if the debtor is an entity that acquired substantially its assets or business from a small business debtor, the automatic stay does not apply unless the entity can prove that it acquired these assets or business in good faith and not merely to have the automatic stay imposed.

ADMINISTRATION OF A TYPICAL CHAPTER 7 CASE

While a detailed discussion of Chapter 7 is beyond the scope of this text, the basic elements of a Chapter 7 need to be understood, particularly to fully understand and appreciate the alternatives available in reorganizations under Chapter 11. Chapter 7, also referred to as "straight bankruptcy" or "liquidation," is by far the most common type of bankruptcy filing in the United States. The overwhelming majority of cases filed in Bankruptcy Court are in Chapter 7. Generally, most of them are consumer cases.

Bankruptcy Abuse

With the passage of the BAPCPA, an individual, with predominantly consumer debts, filing a Chapter 7 proceeding must pass what has commonly become known as the "means test." This test takes into consideration the debtor's currently monthly income, which is defined as:

1. The average monthly income from all sources that the debtor receives (or in a joint case the debtor and the debtor's spouse receive) without regard to whether such income is taxable income, derived during the six-month period ending on the last day of the calendar month immediately preceding the date of the filing of the debtor's petition; or in the event the debtor does not file the requisite schedule of current income now required, then the date on which current income is determined by the court for purposes of this section

2. Current monthly income includes any amount paid by a third-party on a regular basis for the household expenses of the debtor or the debtor's dependents, but excludes:

    a. Social Security benefits,

    b. payments to victims of war crimes or crimes against humanity on account of their status as victims of such crimes, and

    c. payments to victims of international terrorism on account of their status as victims of such terrorism.

In determining this "means test," the debtor's current monthly income is reduced by certain monthly expenses. Those necessary monthly expenses are divided into two categories. The first set of expenses is rigid and shall include:

1. Applicable monthly expense amounts specified under the National Standards and Local Standards, plus
2. Actual monthly expenses for the debtor, his dependents and his spouse (if a joint case and unless the spouse is also a dependent) for categories specified by the Internal Revenue Service for the area in which the debtor resides. If the debtor demonstrates necessity, then an additional allowance for food and clothing as categorized by the National Standards issued by the Internal Revenue Service
3. Reasonably necessary expenses for health insurance, disability insurance, health savings account expenses for the debtor, the spouse of the debtor and the debtor's dependents
4. Reasonably necessary expenses to maintain the safety of the debtor and his family from family violence as identified in section 309 of the Family Violence Prevention and Services Act or other federal law

The second set of expenses is permissive and may include, if applicable:

1. The continuation of actual expenses paid by the debtor that are reasonable and necessary for care and support of an elderly, chronically ill, or disabled household member or member of the debtor's immediate family (including parents, grandparents, siblings, children, and grandchildren of the debtor, the dependents of the debtor, and the spouse of the debtor in a joint case who is not a dependent) and who is unable to pay for such reasonable and necessary expenses
2. The actual administrative expenses of administering a Chapter 13 plan, if the debtor is eligible for Chapter 13, up to 10 percent of the projected plan payments, as set forth in schedules established by the Executive Office for the United States Trustee
3. The actual expenses, for each dependent under 18 years of age, up to $1,500 per year per child, to attend a private or elementary school if the debtor provides documentation of the expenses and can establish that the expenses are reasonable and necessary and not already included in any of the rigid expenses described above
4. The actual expenses for housing and utilities, in excess of the local standards for housing and utilities if the debtor provides documentation of the actual expenses and can establish that the expenses are reasonable and necessary

In order to determine whether there is bankruptcy abuse, the debtor's monthly income, after the allowed expenses as delineated above is multiplied by 60. Substantial abuse will be found to exist if the resulting monthly income of the debtor is:

(1) not less than the lesser of 25 percent of the debtor's nonpriority unsecured claims in the case, or $6,000, whichever is greater; or
(2) $10,000.

There is provision for the debtor's average monthly payments on account of secured debts to be calculated as the sum of:

(1) the total of all amounts scheduled as contractually due to secured creditors in each of the 60 months following the date of the petition; and
(2) any additional payments to secured creditors necessary for a Chapter 13 debtor to maintain possession of:
    (a) the debtor's primary residence
    (b) the debtor's motor vehicle
    (c) other property of the debtor necessary for the support of the debtor and his dependents, which property serves as collateral to secured creditors.

These sums are then divided by 60. Further debtor's expenses for payment of all priority claims, including child support and alimony are calculated as the total of those debts divided by 60.

In order to overcome a presumption of abuse, an individual debtor may show special circumstances that justify additional expenses or adjustments to his current monthly income for which there is no reasonable alternative. These special circumstances can be proven by documentation evidencing the expense or adjustment to income, and a detailed explanation as to the special circumstances that make such expense or adjustment to income necessary and reasonable. The Congressional Report* states that these special circumstances may include a serious medical condition, or a call to active duty in the United States Armed Forces to the extent such special circumstances justify additional expenses or adjustments of current monthly income for which there is no reasonable alternative.

In the vast majority of the cases there are no assets for administration and the case is closed shortly after the § 341 meeting. Again, practice varies from one part of the country to another, but generally the United States Trustee will approve a no asset report and the court will close the case within 180 days of the filing of the case. In the cases in which there are assets for distribution, the trustee will generally take possession of them through agents and begin making arrangements for their liquidation.

The trustee will generally liquidate assets through a notice and sale procedure. The trustee will give notice of the intended sale to all creditors, listing the assets to be sold and specifying the terms of sale, whether private sale, auction, etc. You will have an opportunity to object to the proposed sale, but must file the objection before the date specified in the notice of sale. Generally, the sale will be free and clear of liens so that the purchaser takes clear title to the property. If you have a security interest in the property, your concern will be to ensure that your security interest is recognized and that the trustee intends to distribute the proceeds to you.

---

* The "Congressional Report refers to the text from House Report 109-031 Bankruptcy Abuse Prevention and Consumer Protection Act of 2005, Which has been reproduced herein with the report's footnotes omitted.

Chapter 7 Trustees

In all cases under Chapter 7, a trustee is appointed whose primary responsibility is to take possession of any nonexempt assets and sell them for the benefit of creditors. Ninety-five percent of the cases involve no distributable assets. Even in a majority of the business cases, most of the assets are fully encumbered and there is nothing for the trustee to sell for the benefit of the estate.

In a typical Chapter 7 case, after the debtor has filed the bankruptcy petition and paid the filing fee, the United States Trustee appoints an interim trustee. The exception is North Carolina and Alabama where the Bankruptcy Court makes the appointment. Generally, the trustee will be an attorney or an accountant with experience in bankruptcy. The United States Trustee is required by statute to maintain a panel of private trustees to serve in bankruptcy cases in those districts for which the United States Trustee is responsible. Trustees are appointed to the panel after an FBI background investigation and credit check. Typically, the trustees are selected at random from the panel of trustees to handle a particular case. Occasionally, a case will have substantial assets or involve the operation of a business and require special expertise. Only then will the United States Trustee consider going outside the panel and select a businessperson to serve as trustee.

The interim trustee's first duty is to review the file and take possession of any assets that are unencumbered and subject to immediate depreciation.

The second duty for the interim trustee is to preside at the § 341 meeting of creditors. Occasionally, at the § 341 meeting creditors elect a new trustee under 11 USC § 702. The process for electing a trustee is somewhat arcane. To be eligible to vote, a creditor must hold an allowable, undisputed, liquidated, unsecured claim. Further, the creditor may not have a materially adverse interest and may not be an insider. Generally, it is necessary to file a proof of claim before participating in an election. The interim trustee must conduct the election at the § 341 meeting if creditors eligible to vote and who hold at least 20 percent of all of the undisputed unsecured claims request an election. Creditors then vote their claims and, if at least 20 percent of the allowed claims vote in the election and a candidate for trustee receives a majority of those votes cast, that person is elected as trustee. It is extremely rare that creditors will choose to elect a Chapter 7 trustee.

DUTIES OF A TRUSTEE

A trustee, whether elected or otherwise, has certain duties that are specified in 11 USC § 704. These duties have been expanded by the BAPCPA. Generally, the trustee must sell any unencumbered, nonexempt assets of the estate and account for the proceeds to creditors. The trustee must investigate the financial affairs of the debtor, examine proofs of claim and object to their allowance, if a purpose would be served, and, oppose the discharge of the debtor, if advisable. The trustee also investigates possible claims for preference recovery and fraudulent transfer. Most trustees will carefully scrutinize a secured creditors' documentation to determine whether there is any possibility for avoiding the security interests claimed under the trustee's avoidance and strong arm powers. *See* 11 USC §§ 544, 547 and 548 and the discussion of the trustee's powers below. On occasion the trustee may be authorized to operate the business of the debtor on a limited basis.

Some of the new areas in which the trustee has new duties imposed by the BAPCPA are where a debtor:

- Owes a domestic support obligation
- Is a health care business
- Served as the administrator of an employee benefit plan

Specifically, with respect to individual Chapter 7 proceedings, a Chapter 7 trustee must, within 10 days after the date of the first meeting of creditors, file with the court a statement as to whether the debtor's case would be presumed to be an abuse under section 707(b). If such statement is filed, then within 30 days after filing said statement, the Chapter 7 trustee must either file a motion to dismiss or convert the Chapter 7 proceeding to one under Chapter 11 or 13.

Distribution of Assets

The distribution of assets in a bankruptcy estate is governed by the provisions of the Bankruptcy Code based upon the type of claim that is held by the creditor and the order of distribution entered by the court. Oftentimes, creditors do not file a proper proof of claim where they are entitled to secured or priority status, and, as such, do not receive a maximum distribution. Understanding the types of claims and the distribution method is very important.

Eventually, the trustee will wind down all of the litigation, resolve all objections to claims and be prepared to distribute the funds. The trustee will file a final report with the court and, with the approval of the United States Trustee, seek to close the case. Procedures again vary from one part of the country to another, but generally notice will be given of a final hearing on the case or an opportunity to request a final hearing. If a hearing is scheduled, generally the trustee must appear before the court will award fees. In most cases, however, trustees notice out the intended distribution of the estate assets, including payment of their fees, and, if no objection is filed within the deadline established by the court, no final hearing is held and the distribution is approved as noticed. If you wish to object to the intended distribution or the requested fees and expenses, you should file a written objection with the court within the deadline established in the notice. Note that the objection must reach the court prior to the deadline.

The trustees are required to satisfy claims in a particular order. Under 11 USC § 507, administrative expenses of the estate have priority over all claims of creditors. Thereafter, certain creditors who hold wage, retirement, consumer deposit and tax claims are paid in the order specified in that section before any distribution is made to general unsecured creditors. Finally, tax claims have a priority, and quite often the tax claims will absorb any funds remaining after the other priorities are satisfied, leaving nothing for the unsecured creditors.

It is not uncommon for the trustee to overlook a claim or simply omit a claim from an intended distribution. If you have filed a proof of claim and you are not listed as one of the potential distributees, you must file an objection and review the case with the trustee to determine why your claim, as filed, was not included in the distribution. If you do not object, the court may approve the distribution without payment to you.

TRUSTEE'S COMPENSATION

Chapter 7 trustees are paid compensation per each case handled. 11 USC § 330. In addition, the court will usually allow the Chapter 7 trustee to receive a percentage of the assets distributed to creditors. 11 USC § 326. Maximum fees for Chapter

7 trustees and Chapter 11 trustees may not exceed 25 percent of the first $5,000, 10 percent of any amount in excess of $5,000, but not in excess of $50,000, 5 percent on any amount in excess of $50,000 and but not in excess of $1,000,000, and 3 percent of any amount in excess of $1,000,000. Note that these fee caps are the statutory *maximums* the court may approve in any case. Monies turned over to the debtor and to secured creditors from the sale of property subject to liens are not subject to the trustee's fees. The compensation is generally considered inadequate. Particularly in the no asset cases where the trustee receives only the statutory fee, the $60 is insufficient to cover the trustee's costs and time in reviewing the file, conducting the § 341 meeting and filing reports with the United States Trustee and the court. This has become truer than ever with the increased duties of the trustee imposed by the BAPCPA. The tendency, therefore, is for the court to award the maximum compensation possible in the asset cases.

Trustees are entitled to reimbursement of expenses from the estate. The type of expenses reimbursed will vary from fees for lawyers, accountants and realtors to the cost of preparing assets for sale, costs of sale notices and virtually all other expenses necessary to the administrative process. Trustees are not entitled to recover office overhead, however. It is routine practice for the trustees in most districts to employ themselves as attorneys for the trustee at the expense of the estate. Some courts have suggested that this raises a conflict of interest since the trustee is not getting independent legal advice. Generally, the trustee will not be compensated for work done in the capacity of trustee, but only for legal work or other professional work on behalf of the estate.

Before the court can award fees and expenses, the court must give you notice of the intended payment to the trustee and the professionals involved. You have an opportunity to object to the compensation and expenses and should do so within the deadlines set out in the notice of the request for compensation.

COMPLAINTS ABOUT THE TRUSTEE

Even in those cases where the trustee is an attorney, the trustee cannot give you legal advice on your claim or disputes with the debtor. The trustee is a fiduciary and holds the estate for all creditors. Thus, do not expect a trustee to respond to specific legal questions about how you should proceed. Moreover, the trustee generally will not respond to requests for information in no asset cases. Many of the trustees handle dozens, if not hundreds, of cases in any given year, and simply putting postage on repeated requests for information would exhaust the fees paid to the trustee.

If you have concerns about the trustee's handling of a particular case, you may wish to retain counsel to object to the trustee's final report and bring the complaints before the court in that fashion. Other, less formal complaints about a trustee's handling of a particular case or cases in general should be directed to the United States Trustee for the district in which the case is pending. The United States Trustee has general supervisory authority over the Chapter 7 trustees and regularly audits Chapter 7 trustees in their handling of cases. A locator for the United States Trustees is found in Chapter 26. While the United States Trustee will discuss a particular trustee with you, he or she will not give you legal advice on pursuing claims against an estate or against a trustee.

Trade Creditors' Primary Concerns

Prompt Administration of the Estate

One of your primary concerns in any Chapter 7 case will be the prompt and efficient liquidation of the bankruptcy estate. In most cases simply monitoring the notices of sale and eventually the notice of distribution will be sufficient. There will be cases, however, in which you have information about the estate or the conduct of the debtor's business, which would be of use to the trustee in recovering funds. At the same time, if the debtor's assets include inventory or raw materials that you have sold to the debtor, you may be able to repurchase your products from the estate more efficiently rather than having the trustee sell the inventory or materials to the general market.

Your first decision, therefore, will relate to your involvement in the case. You may simply choose to file a claim (after consulting counsel) and await the distribution. You may, however, wish to contact the trustee and furnish information about possible fraudulent or preferential transfers, the value of inventory being held by the debtor, or other information that will assist the trustee in recovering assets for the benefit of creditors.

Exemptions and Estate Planning

Trade creditors of businesses are finding themselves more often encountering a situation in which you have a claim against an individual. These cases will arise where your debtor is a guarantor or a sole proprietor of a business. You will, therefore, need to review the exemptions that the individual is claiming, and you may possibly need to determine whether the debtor has converted property that should be available to satisfy your claim into exempt property. The Bankruptcy Code permits the states to allow individual debtors to claim either state or federal exemptions in an effort to give the debtor a fresh start after bankruptcy. The Code further contemplates that the debtor may convert nonexempt assets into exempt assets as part of the debtor's estate planning prebankruptcy. Creditors are given an opportunity to object to the debtor's exemptions, but must file the objection within 30 days of the conclusion of the § 341 meeting. In order to make a decision on an objection, you must be familiar with the exemption laws that apply in the state where the individual debtor is a resident and have some knowledge of the debtor's assets. Since an objection will generally require the assistance of counsel and because the time deadline is so short, you should review the case as soon as you receive notice to determine whether you intend to object to the exemptions claimed by the debtor.

Homestead Exemptions

The BAPCPA has changed the Bankruptcy Code substantially in the area of homestead exemptions. First, the definition of homestead has been clarified to create a consistency throughout the country. A homestead is defined as:

- real or personal property that the debtor or dependent of the debtor uses as a residence;
- a cooperative that owns property that the debtor or a dependent of the debtor uses as a residence;
- a burial plot for the debtor or a dependent of the debtor; or

- real or personal property that the debtor or a dependent of the debtor claims as a homestead.

For those debtors who choose state exemptions, the homestead exemption is limited to no more than $125,000 in value that the debtor has acquired during the 1215-day period preceding the filing of the petition. (*See* Chapter 16 for a fuller discussion of exemptions, including homestead exemptions.)

DISCHARGE LITIGATION

The Bankruptcy Code offers the honest debtor a new financial start through a discharge. Only individuals are granted a discharge. In certain circumstances, specific debts are not discharged or a dishonest individual may be denied a discharge completely. In those isolated instances in which you are dealing with an *individual* debtor who has filed a Chapter 7, you may wish to review the case for a possible objection to discharge under § 727 or to dispute the dischargeability of the debt owed you under § 523. The Bankruptcy Code allows creditors to object to the discharge or to determine nondischargeability if, among other things, the debtor has committed fraud in connection with the bankruptcy case or in connection with the extension of the credit. Any objection to discharge and most complaints to determine dischargeability in Chapter 7 must be filed within 60 days of the § 341 meeting specified in the initial notice of the bankruptcy filing. The BAPCPA has expanded the bases under which a debtor can be denied a discharge. For example, an individual debtor who is guilty of securities fraud will not receive a discharge. Certain consumer debts or cash advances that are extensions of consumer debt are presumed to be nondischargeable. Domestic support obligations are exempt from discharge. For the general trade creditor, the kinds of debts for which a discharge might be refused, remain those that may have been incurred through fraud or through a false financial statement. In those cases, you need to review the case very promptly with counsel or the opportunity to object may be lost.

FILING A PROOF OF CLAIM

In a Chapter 7 bankruptcy, a creditor must file a proof of claim to participate in the distribution of estate assets. The Official Proof of Claim form (Form B10) has been amended as of October 2005. Official Form 10 and instructions for the filing of a proof of claim are discussed below. Before filing a claim, you should review with counsel any claim that the debtor may have against you. The filing of a proof of claim has been held to waive a creditor's right to a jury trial on certain preference and fraudulent transfer actions and is generally considered to be sufficient to submit the creditor to the jurisdiction of the bankruptcy court for other purposes. Unless you are satisfied that the debtor has no potential claim for fraudulent or preferential transfer or otherwise against you, you should discuss the filing of a claim with counsel.

CHAPTER 11 REORGANIZATION PROCESS

A detailed analysis of Chapter 11 problems is beyond the scope of this text. The following is a general summary of Chapter 11.

Debtor in Possession

Upon filing a Chapter 11 petition under the Bankruptcy Code, the debtor continues to operate the business as a debtor in possession with the protection of the automatic stay. You will see the debtor referred to as the "debtor in possession," the "debtor," or occasionally as the "trustee." Chapter 11 of the Bankruptcy Code uses the term "trustee" even though the debtor normally continues the operation of its business as debtor in possession. An actual trustee is only appointed by court order. The debtor in possession, however, has the status of a trustee in that the debtor must manage the assets of the estate for the benefit of creditors. The debtor also has the powers of the trustee, such as the strong arm powers and the preferential and fraudulent transfer avoidance powers discussed below. There is a provision, however, for the appointment of a trustee to operate the business under 11 USC § 1104. *See below.*

DEBTOR IN POSSESSION REPORTING

The debtor in possession is required to make periodic reports to the United States Trustee and the bankruptcy court. Those reports will generally be made available to interested creditors and the creditors' committee. The reports, which are standardized by the Office of the United States Trustee, include a balance sheet, a cash flow statement and statement of any unpaid liabilities for postpetition expenses, such as insurance, inventory, etc. Often the debtor will be permitted to continue to use prepetition financial statements that may require some deciphering. You may want to review the reports to determine the salaries of the officers and other information. The reports may demonstrate that the debtor is continuing to lose money.

AUTHORITY TO OPERATE BUSINESS

The debtor in possession's broad authority to conduct the business includes ordinary course of business asset sales without specific court order. Thus, if the debtor is in the business of manufacturing and selling widgets, the debtor will normally continue to manufacture and sell widgets just as it did before the bankruptcy case was filed and the automatic stay went into effect. Only if the debtor intends to sell assets outside the ordinary course of business is specific notice to creditors and possible court approval required.

For example, if the debtor, a widget manufacturer, intended to sell most of its manufacturing equipment or its real estate, it would have to apply to the court for approval and give notice to creditors of the proposed sale because such a sale would not ordinarily be part of its business. You may assume that absent a request for intervention by the creditors, the creditors' committee or the stockholders, the debtor will continue in operation of its business subject to the general supervision of the court and overview by the United States Trustee and the creditors' committee (if one exists).

As will be discussed in greater detail to follow, in most Chapter 11 cases the debtor is given the exclusive right to file a plan of reorganization for the first 120 days after the filing of the petition for relief. In small business cases and certain single asset cases filed under the Bankruptcy Reform Act of 1994, the plan must be filed within 100 days and 90 days, respectively (*see below*). While its power may be restricted or modified by court order, the debtor, at least initially, remains in possession of the business, operates it in the ordinary course of that particular type of business, and initially has the exclusive right to propose a plan of reorganization.

Debtors in possession will seek unsecured trade credit during the Chapter 11 proceeding from the debtor's vendors. Oftentimes, these vendors will be told that "the court guaranteed the debt" or "it is a number one priority" in payment. The court does not guarantee any debt. An obligation of the debtor in possession is a first administrative priority, but as an unsecured obligation. If the secured debts are greater than the value of the assets securing them, or if the estate is administratively insolvent (the administrative debts are more than the assets), administrative expense creditors will not be paid in full. Creditors should consider a debtor in possession a new customer, and consider the extension of trade credit as they would with any new customer. If the debtor in possession has arranged for a line of credit or cash availability, then it certainly may be appropriate to extend credit. Absent this, vendors should be wary and not compound the loss in the bankruptcy case.

Creditors' Committee

FORMATION OF THE CREDITORS' COMMITTEE

Under Chapter 11, the United States Trustee is required to attempt to appoint a creditors' committee of unsecured creditors willing to serve. The well-known presumption in favor of the seven largest unsecured creditors being appointed to the creditors' committee no longer holds true in every case. 11 USC § 1102(b)(1). Creditors willing to serve do not necessarily hold the largest claims, and sometimes an active creditors' network exists that results in the formation of a creditors' committee even before a bankruptcy is filed. The Bankruptcy Code specifically authorizes the United States Trustee to approve and appoint a prepetition committee if it is appropriately representative. Creditors' committees are appointed in fewer cases simply because creditors are unwilling to serve. On the other hand, the BAPCPA, discussed below, now provides for the appointment of a small business creditor to a creditors' committee if the creditor holds a claim, the aggregate of which is disproportionately large, in comparison to the annual gross income of that creditor.

In most instances, the United States Trustee will contact the 20 largest unsecured creditors from the list filed with the petition for relief by the debtor and solicit their input on the appointment of a committee. In many large cases, the United States Trustee is now notifying the 30 or 40 largest unsecured creditors to ascertain their interest in serving on a creditors' committee. If you are interested in appointment to the committee and hold a substantial claim, you should contact the United States Trustee supervising the case. You should also return any solicitation form sent by the United States Trustee in order to be considered for membership on the committee.

The United States Trustee will normally file a formal pleading with the court stating the names and addresses of the particular creditors appointed to serve on the committee.

COMMITTEE'S FIDUCIARY DUTY

If you are considering potential membership in the creditors' committee, you should remember that the committee has a fiduciary duty to represent all creditors rather than the specific interest of the individual creditor appointed to the committee. Generally, the committee must act through its members and all members must act in a fashion that is in the best interest of all creditors and not in the interest of a specific creditor or a small group of creditors.

CONSIDERATIONS FOR MEMBERS

Membership in the committee not only gives you an opportunity to help shape the direction of the case and have input on what a plan of reorganization may provide, it is also a good way to gather information about the debtor. The committee will generally be provided with reports concerning the debtor's operation as they are filed with the United States Trustee as well as reports from its professionals.

COMMITTEE GOVERNANCE

Just how the committee calls and controls its meetings, votes on issues presented, and otherwise governs its actions is not the subject of any statutory provision or rule. Most committees meet on an ad hoc basis when everyone is available and take action by a majority vote. Some committees have elaborate bylaws governing the calling of meetings, quorum, expenses, etc. While elaborate bylaws may be appropriate in a large case, they may hinder the quick action necessary in some of the smaller cases. You should decide on a case-by-case basis what rules, if any, are appropriate.

EMPLOYMENT OF PROFESSIONALS

The Bankruptcy Code specifically allows official creditors' committees to retain counsel, accountants, and other professionals at the expense of the estate. 11 USC § 1103(a). Note, however, that the professional fees are an administrative expense and are paid before any distribution is made to creditors. Generally, the committee will vote to retain a particular attorney, accountant, or other professional and submit an application to the court for approval of the employment of the professional. The application must have been submitted and approved by the court before the professional can be paid any compensation from the bankruptcy estate. 11 USC §§ 327, 328. Generally, individual members of the committee are not liable for the fees of professionals unless they separately contract with the individual professional. Thus, simply being on the creditors' committee does not obligate you to pay the fees of the professional. You may, however, agree to guarantee payment of those fees.

COMMITTEE'S RELATIONSHIP WITH THE DEBTOR IN POSSESSION

The committee's relationship with the debtor in possession is often a complicated one since there are no specific statutory or regulatory guidelines defining the role of the committee in the day-to-day operations of the business. *See* 11 USC § 1103(c). For the most part the relationship will depend upon the size and complexity of the case and the knowledge of both the officers of the debtor and the members of the committee. The committee's involvement may range from objecting to salaries paid to insiders, to active pursuit of preferential and fraudulent transfers on behalf of all creditors, to the filing of a plan. Certainly, the committee should be involved in negotiations on any proposed plan of reorganization.

In some respects the committee's relationship to the debtor is similar to that of an advisory board of directors that cannot directly instruct the debtor or the debtor's officers to take action in the operation of the business, but it may make suggestions and, if those suggestions are not considered, may bring the issue before the court for ruling. Normally, the court will not substitute its business judgment for that of the debtor's officers, however. At least in theory, the existing board of the debtor in possession continues to govern the actions of the debtor provided those actions are in the best interests of all creditors. The situation is more difficult with the sole proprietorship or closely controlled corporation. There the officers may also be the shareholders and directors of the corporation or the sole proprietor of the business, and their individual interests may actually conflict with those of the creditors. Even in a large reorganization the officers often seem more interested in preserving their salaries and perks than paying creditors.

Generally, the committee's chief weapon will be its ability to object to motions for which the debtor seeks court approval and recommend or oppose confirmation of a proposed plan of reorganization. Creditors will be much more willing to accept and approve a plan of reorganization that is supported by the creditors' committee. Likewise, a plan that has been rejected by the committee and against which the committee actively campaigns is more likely to fail. *See below* for a discussion of potential plans and the voting process.

PURSUIT OF TRANSFERS

Often, the committee will find itself in the position of pursuing, subject to court approval, fraudulent or preferential transfer actions, even against its own members. For a variety of reasons the debtor may refuse to pursue fraudulent or preferential transfer actions against essential suppliers, insiders, family members or other individuals or entities that are closely related to the debtor. The pursuit of the preferential or fraudulent transfer may also be used as a negotiating tactic to offset a claim asserted against the debtor.

AVOIDANCE ACTIONS

Equally as frequent, the committee may ask the court for authority to pursue an avoidance action against a secured creditor whose claim is not properly perfected. Particularly in the tumultuous period leading to the filing of the bankruptcy petition, creditors often do not properly perfect their security interests. In that case the debtor may have good reason for not wanting to pursue the avoidance action. The committee may bring the action to either create assets for the unsecured estate or as a negotiating tactic in the formulation of a plan.

NEGOTIATIONS ON THE PLAN OF REORGANIZATION

Perhaps the primary role that a creditors' committee can play in any Chapter 11 case proceeding is providing input in negotiations toward the formulation of a plan of reorganization. In the negotiation process, the committee's primary weapon is its ability to object to the plan proposed by the debtor and to oppose confirmation of the plan, both through the solicitation of votes against the plan and litigation of the confirmability of the plan after the solicitation of votes. *See below.*

COMMITTEE INTERACTION WITH TRUSTEE

The committee, as well as other parties in interest, may seek the appointment of an examiner or a trustee in any case. The United States Trustee appoints an interim trustee, after consultation with the parties upon order of the court. If a party in interest so requests within 30 days of the entry of the court order directing appointment of a trustee, the United States Trustee must convene a meeting of creditors for the purpose of electing a trustee in the case (except in a railroad proceeding). This provision will give creditors considerable leverage in selection of the trustee. The request for an election should be in writing and filed as a pleading with the court and served by mail on the interim trustee, the United States Trustee and such other parties in interest as the court may order. The United States Trustee will then pick a date for the meeting of creditors. It is not clear whether the United States Trustee or the party requesting the election will be required to give notice of the meeting. At the meeting, the election will be conducted according to 11 USC § 702, which requires that creditors holding at least 20 percent in amount of the undisputed, liquidated and unsecured claims actually vote in the election. A candidate must be "disinterested," that is the potential trustee must not represent any party in interest and may not hold any interest adverse to the estate. If no trustee is elected under 11 USC § 702, the interim trustee apparently continues in office.

CAVEAT: In many cases the prompt appointment, and qualification of a trustee is critical to safeguarding the assets. Since an election demand might slow down the process, creditors should consider carefully the effect of making a demand.

Once the trustee is appointed, the committee's relationship with the debtor and role in the case may change significantly. The debtor is no longer the debtor in possession, but has been supplanted by the trustee. The trustee becomes the overall manager of the business even though the trustee may not personally operate the business on a day-to-day basis. The trustee can control the hiring and firing of staff to operate the business, effect changes in the business operation itself, and continue to operate the business absent a court order limiting the trustee's authority. Although many parties consider the appointment of a trustee as a sure sign that the bankruptcy is headed for liquidation, the appointment of a trustee may be the only way to get control of certain expenses and sales of assets for the benefit of all creditors. Once selected, the trustee becomes a fiduciary for all creditors and must consider the interests of all creditors and other parties in interest, whether secured, unsecured, or otherwise. While a trustee will generally act as a caretaker to conserve the business assets pending the proposal and confirmation of a plan, a trustee may propose a plan and submit it to creditors.

BAPCPA CHANGES CONCERNING COMMITTEES

Under BAPCPA, Section 1102(a) of the Bankruptcy Code has been modified to increase the bankruptcy court's powers relative to committees. The court will now have the power to determine any disputes with respect to membership on a committee. At the request of an interested party or parties, and after notice and a hearing, the bankruptcy court can direct the United States Trustee to add a creditor to the committee or otherwise change the size or composition of the committee to ensure adequate representation of creditors.

The change also specifically allows the United States Trustee to add a small business concern to a creditors' committee if the court determines that the small business' claim is of the kind represented by the committee and is disproportionately large when compared to the creditor's annual gross revenue. A "small business concern" is defined as "independently owned and operated" and "not dominant in its field of operation." 15 USC 9632(a)—Small Business Act. This is designed to enable small businesses to play a larger role in Chapter 11 cases, in contrast to pre-BAPCPA Chapter 11 cases where most small businesses frequently have claims too small to be eligible to serve on a committee. If you are a small business and wish to serve on a creditors' committee, you should write to the United States Trustee and request appointment. Otherwise, your only recourse is to move for a court order directing your appointment to the committee.

In addition, the creditors' committee must provide creditors, who hold claims of the kind represented by that committee and who are not appointed to the committee, access to information about the debtor in the committee's possession. A disgruntled creditor who does not obtain information requested from the committee can also obtain a court order directing the committee to provide the information. This raises confidentiality issues since the committee usually holds nonpublic information about the debtor and its business. The committee is foisted into the middle between a debtor who would be reluctant to provide nonpublic information because of the risk that a non-member creditor will force its disclosure, and the creditor seeking the information.

The committee is also required to solicit and receive comments from those creditors holding claims of the kind represented by that committee and who are not committee members.

The statute is silent about what information a committee must provide to non-member creditors whose interests the committee represents. The action a committee must take to solicit comments from creditors is also unclear. It is anticipated that committee counsel will establish procedures to provide information about the debtor to, and solicit comments from, creditors. That might include establishing a web page or otherwise communicating with creditors to provide information and solicit comments. The committee might also seek court approval of these procedures in order to protect the committee and its members and professionals from litigation risk.

Committee members will also now be precluded from being reimbursed the legal and other fees they may incur as a result of their membership on the committee. Existing case law is not clear whether committee members are entitled to administrative expense claims for fees associated with professional services (i.e., legal and accounting) that were rendered to such member in connection with service on the committee.

KEY PROBLEMS IN REORGANIZATION

Overview

The Bankruptcy Code also affords creditors the right to notice on many actions affecting the operation of the business and the assets of the bankruptcy estate. In particular, unsecured creditors are entitled to notice, at least through a committee, of many actions that may have the effect of diminishing the assets available for the unsecured creditors. Thus, while the bankruptcy petition in one respect bars the immediate dismemberment of the debtor, it creates a number of problems for all of the parties that must be dealt with almost immediately. They range from the use of cash and assets subject to existing security interests to the assumption and rejection of existing leases and contracts. This section will deal briefly with some of the key postpetition problems and some of the practical and legal problems inherent in dealing with them. As always, this list is not exhaustive. Virtually every case has its unique aspects and it is impossible to enumerate all of the problems that you will encounter immediately after the filing of the bankruptcy petition.

Cash Collateral

Just as the Bankruptcy Code's automatic stay prohibits the creditor from seizing its collateral through judicial or other action, the Code also limits the extent to which a debtor can use "cash collateral," or cash generated through the sale of inventory or the collection of receivables subject to a prepetition lien. Cash collateral encompasses any cash assets in the hands of the debtor at the time of the petition that are subject to a valid and properly perfected security interest. 11 USC § 363(a). Included in the definition of security interest for these purposes is the right to offset a bank account against any obligations of the debtor. While accounts receivable and funds generated from the sale of assets or services by the debtor are the most common examples, virtually any cash that is the identifiable proceeds of a prepetition asset subject to a valid security interest is subject to the rules on cash collateral. If the accounts receivable or inventory, or both, are subject to valid prepetition security interests, the debtor may not use those cash proceeds without (1) the express permission of the creditor holding the security interest; or (2) a court order allowing the use. 11 USC § 363(c)(2). Cash collateral may include rent and payment for lodging. The court order allowing the use of cash collateral may not be entered unless the creditor is afforded "adequate protection" for the use of its collateral. Generally, of course, the creditor will be granted a security interest in the replacement inventory purchased with its cash collateral.

Procedurally, before the debtor and the secured lender can enter into an agreement for the use of cash collateral, the debtor must give notice to all parties in interest of the proposed agreement and its terms and conditions. 11 USC § 363, Fed. R. Bankr. P. 2002, 4001. Moreover, no *final* order can be entered earlier than 15 days after the service of a motion for use of cash collateral. This prevents a debtor and creditor from tying up the estate without notice the day the petition is filed. Quite often, filing results in a frantic scramble to round up cash to pay salaries, payroll, utilities and key suppliers, among other things. Since creditors do not learn of the bankruptcy filing for some time, the Bankruptcy Code requires that the debtor give notice to either the creditors' committee, if one has properly been formed, or the 20 largest unsecured creditors as well as any other parties claiming a security interest in the receivables, anyone claiming a lien on the real estate, the United States Trustee, the IRS, and several other government agencies. Fed. R. Bankr. P. 4001. Failure to give the proper notice to the largest unsecured creditors prior to approval of an agreement between the debtor and a secured creditor concerning the use of cash allows the court to subsequently set aside the agreement and avoid any liens created in the agreement. The court may, on an emergency basis, allow the debtor to use receivables for the minimum necessary operating expenses for the first 15 days of the case. However, until the court holds a final hearing, it may not enter a final cash collateral order approving the debtor's agreement with the secured creditor as to the validity of its security interest and the lien on the unencumbered real estate. The final hearing may not take place less than 15 days after the notice is given. This will give you, as an unsecured creditor or a member of the committee, an opportunity to review not only the bank's documentation for defects, but also give the committee a chance to hire counsel and make the necessary objections.

Postpetition Credit

Postpetition credit is one of the major problems in any reorganization case. While the Bankruptcy Code and the Federal Rules of Bankruptcy Procedure require that any postpetition *secured* credit obtained have court approval before it can become effective, certain types of unsecured postpetition credit do not require notice or court approval. 11 USC § 364, Fed. R. Bankr. P. 4001.

Beyond requiring that the parties give notice and an opportunity to object to the proposed postpetition credit (whether secured or unsecured), the court does not regulate in any detail the terms under which credit can be obtained to continue the operation of the debtor in possession. Generally speaking, the notice of any postpetition credit requested by the debtor must contain a summary of the terms, the amount of the credit, and the proposed creditor. More often than not a prepetition secured creditor will extend postpetition credit to keep the debtor afloat to preserve the value of inventory and receivables. The difficulty is that the postpetition credit may come at the expense of the unsecured creditors if the postpetition credit is secured by a lien on the remaining unencumbered assets of the debtor. Thus, as an unsecured creditor, you will want to examine, and if necessary, oppose any proposed postpetition credit. At the same time, if you are continuing to sell inventory or services to the debtor on a postpetition basis, you should understand your rights against the estate in the event of liquidation.

Assumption or Rejection of Executory Contracts and Leases

One of the more complicated issues in any major bankruptcy case will involve the assumption or rejection of executory contracts and unexpired leases under 11 USC § 365. This enables a trustee or debtor in possession to take advantage of favorable executory contracts and leases and shed burdensome and unprofitable agreements. This section permits the debtor, with court approval, to "assume or reject" an executory contract or an unexpired lease.

The Bankruptcy Code does not define an executory contract. An executory contract has been defined by the Courts to include contracts on which performance remains due to some extent on both sides. An alternative definition includes contracts under which the obligations of other parties are so unperformed that the failure of either party to complete performance would constitute a mutual breach excusing the other from performance.

As a general rule, in Chapter 11 cases, Section 365 does not contain any deadline for assumption or rejection of executory contracts or personal property leases. However, Section 365 contains a deadline with respect to nonresidential real property (i.e., commercial) leases under which the debtor is a tenant.

Prior to the BAPCPA, the debtor must assume nonresidential real property leases within 60 days of the petition or the lease is deemed rejected, although the court may extend that time if necessary upon application of the lessor or the debtor, which is routinely granted. 11 USC § 365(d)(1). Any claim arising from the rejection of the lease is limited to the greater of one year's rent or 15 percent of the remaining lease price. 11 USC § 502(b)(6).

The importance of this rather esoteric area in the bankruptcy law is that the timely assumption of the lease may generate a valuable asset since the debtor may sublease or sell the lease tenancy to a purchaser who can take advantage of the favorable rates provided in the lease with the debtor. Moreover, if the debtor is a retailing business with multiple locations and is seeking to cut back and restructure the business on a smaller scale, the ability to reject unexpired leases on store locations may be essential. Likewise, however, if the restructuring includes closing stores which are leased at a favorable rate, the debtor may be able to generate cash for unsecured creditors or for continued operations by assuming the lease and assigning it to a purchaser.

The BAPCPA modifies Section 365(d)(4) to provide that a debtor must assume or reject an unexpired lease of nonresidential real property by the earlier of: (i) 120 days from the date of the commencement of the bankruptcy case; and (ii) the date of confirmation of a plan. The debtor's failure to assume or reject a lease by such date will result in the lease being deemed rejected. A court may extend the 120-day deadline for up to one additional 90-day period, upon motion of the debtor, for cause shown, which is generally satisfied. This extension must be granted prior to the expiration of the original 120-day period. The court may only grant subsequent extensions upon the prior written consent of the lessor for each such extension.

The bankruptcy court no longer has the authority to grant extensions of time to assume or reject a nonresidential real property lease outside the 210-day period absent the lessor's written agreement. This will greatly expand a lessor's ability to force a debtor to decide early in a case whether to assume or reject commercial leases by denying the court any discretion to extend the debtor's time to assume or reject the lease after the maximum 210-day period, without the lessor's written consent. This could make it far more difficult for a debtor, particularly a retail debtor, to reorganize, forcing the debtor to make a premature decision to either (a) assume burdensome leases, that would require the debtor to pay unpaid prepetition rent charges, and, if later rejected, could saddle the estate with substantial administrative debt, or (b) reject valuable leases.

A new Section 503(b)(7) caps the landlord's administrative expense claim related to a nonresidential real property lease that is assumed under Section 365 and subsequently rejected. The amount of the allowed administrative claim arising from the debtor's rejection of a previously assumed nonresidential real property lease is equal to all monetary obligations due (excluding those relating to failure to operate or a penalty provision) for a period of two years following the later of: (i) the date of rejection of the lease; or (ii) the date of actual turnover of the premises. This administrative claim cannot be subject to reduction or setoff for any reason, except for amounts actually received or to be received from a nondebtor entity. The lessor's claim for the balance of rejection damages beyond this two-year period will be treated as a general unsecured claim subject to the cap contained in Section 502(b)(6). This is in contrast to pre-BAPCPA Section 365(g)(2), where all sums due under an assumed and subsequently rejected lease could be granted an administrative priority status.

Also under new Section 365(p), when a personal property lease is rejected or not timely assumed, the leased property is no longer property of the estate and no longer subject to the automatic stay. This change enables a personal property lessor to repossess the leased equipment without the necessity for obtaining a court order lifting the automatic stay.

Expanded Rights for Utilities

Prior to the BAPCPA, Section 366 of the Bankruptcy Code allowed utilities to alter, refuse or discontinue service to a debtor, unless the debtor provides adequate assurance of payment of the utilities' charges. The courts have generally held that adequate assurance of payment does not require a debtor to pay additional cash deposits to utilities. A significant number of courts have considered a debtor's payment history prior to the commencement of the bankruptcy case, as well as any security deposits held by the utility providers. Often courts have found that a debtor provided adequate assurance of payment through an existing cash deposit, the liquidity provided by a debtor's Chapter 11 financing arrangement with its lender, and the administrative expense claim a utility is entitled to for providing postpetition service.

The BAPCPA overrules this entire line of cases and affords utility providers far greater protections. A utility will be permitted to alter, refuse or discontinue service, after 20 or 30 days (there is an inconsistency in Section 366) from the commencement of a Chapter 11 bankruptcy case if the utility does not receive adequate assurance of payment. Section 366 is modified to require a debtor to provide its utilities "assurance of payment" of their postpetition charges in exchange for the utilities' continued service. "Assurance of payment" will now require: (i) a cash deposit; (ii) a letter of credit; (iii) a certificate of deposit; (iv) a surety bond; (v) a prepayment of utility consumption; or (vi) another form of security agreed to by the utility and the debtor. An administrative expense claim does not constitute adequate assurance of payment. These changes will likely force debtors to increase cash payments to utilities.

The court may order modification of the amount of the cash deposit or other assurance of payment to a debtor's utilities. In making a determination of the adequacy of such payment, the court may not consider: (i) the absence of security before the commencement of the bankruptcy case; (ii) the debtor's timely payments to the utility prior to the commencement of the bankruptcy case; or (iii) the availability of an administrative expense priority.

Section 366 also allows a utility to recover or setoff any security deposit held by the utility prior to the commencement of the debtor's Chapter 11 case, against the utility's prepetition claim against the debtor, without notice or order of the court.

Conversion/Dismissal of a Chapter 11 Case

The BAPCPA modifies Section 1112(b) by expanding the grounds that a court can rely upon to dismiss a Chapter 11 case or convert a Chapter 11 case to a case under Chapter 7. A court is required to convert or dismiss a case (whichever is in the best interest of the estate) if a movant establishes "cause." The amended Section 1112(b) provides a non-exhaustive list of 16 factors that may be a basis for finding "cause." These are:

i.   substantial or continuing loss to, or diminution of, the estate and the absence of a reasonable likelihood of rehabilitation;

ii.   gross mismanagement of the estate;

iii.   failure to maintain appropriate insurance that poses a risk to the estate or to the public;

iv.   unauthorized use of cash collateral substantially harmful to one or more creditors;

v.   failure to comply with an order of the court;

vi.   unexcused failure to timely satisfy any filing or reporting requirement established by this title or by any rule applicable to a case under this chapter;

vii.   failure to attend the meeting of creditors convened under Section 341(a) or an examination ordered under Rule 2004 of the Federal Rules of Bankruptcy Procedure without good cause shown by the debtor;

viii. failure to timely provide information or attend meetings reasonably requested by the United States Trustee (or the bankruptcy administrator, if any);

ix. failure to timely pay taxes owed after the commencement of the bankruptcy or to file tax returns due thereafter;

x. failure to file a disclosure statement, or to file or confirm a plan, within the time fixed by the Bankruptcy Code or by order of the court;

xi. failure to pay any fees or charges required under Chapter 123 of Title 28;

xii. revocation of an order of confirmation under Section 1144 of the Bankruptcy Code;

xiii. inability to effectuate substantial consummation of a confirmed plan;

xiv. material default by the debtor with respect to a confirmed plan;

xv. termination of a confirmed plan by reason of the occurrence of a condition specified in the plan; and

xvi. failure of the debtor to pay any domestic support obligation that first becomes payable after the date of the filing of the bankruptcy case.

The additional grounds for cause under the BAPCPA appear to be easier to satisfy than the grounds for conversion or dismissal prior to the BAPCPA. By way of an example, one of the grounds for cause under the BAPCPA, the debtor's failure to file a disclosure statement or to file or confirm a plan within the time fixed by the Bankruptcy Code or by court order, might be easier to satisfy than the old standard of the debtor's inability to effectuate a plan.

If the movant does establish cause, the court may only deny a motion to convert or dismiss the case if the debtor, or another party in interest, objects and establishes: (i) there is a reasonable likelihood that a plan will be confirmed within applicable timeframes; (ii) the grounds for granting the relief include an act or omission for which there exists a reasonable justification; and (iii) such act or omission will be cured in a reasonable time, and the court identifies unusual circumstances (not defined in the statute) showing that conversion or dismissal is not in the best interests of creditors and the estate. However, where the grounds of "cause" is the substantial and continuing loss or diminution of the estate and the absence of a reasonable likelihood of rehabilitation, the court cannot deny dismissal or conversion. This is a far more difficult burden of proof for debtors to satisfy to overcome a conversion/dismissal motion.

Section 1112 also expedites the disposition of conversion/dismissal motions. It requires the court to commence a hearing on a motion to convert or dismiss a Chapter 11 case not later than 30 days after the date the motion is filed. The court must decide the motion within 15 days after the commencement of the hearing. However, the court could delay the hearing and ruling if: (i) the movant expressly consents to the continuance for a specific time; or (ii) compelling circumstances (not defined in the statute) prevent the court from meeting these time requirements.

Motions for a Trustee or Examiner

PRELIMINARY COMMENT

As a general rule, the debtor remains in possession and operates the debtor's business under Chapter 11. The Code provides, however, for the appointment (and, in some cases, the election) of a trustee or an examiner for cause pursuant to 11 USC § 1104.

APPOINTMENT OF A TRUSTEE OR EXAMINER

Prior to the BAPCPA, the appointment of a trustee was an extraordinary remedy justified only for cause. Under 11 USC § 1104, cause is broadly defined as including (but is not limited to) pre- or postpetition fraud by management, dishonesty or gross mismanagement. The basis for appointment of a trustee has been the subject of a great deal of case law, and it is difficult to set out a single, clear rule. If you believe that "cause" exists for appointment of a trustee, you should consult counsel early in the case. An examiner may be appointed for similar reasons, but generally will not operate a business.

The BAPCPA has modified Section 1104(a) to include additional grounds for a court to direct the United States Trustee to appoint a Chapter 11 trustee. The court could order appointment if grounds exist to convert or dismiss the Chapter 11 case under Section 1112, and the court determines that the appointment of a trustee is in the best interests of creditors and the estate.

The grounds for conversion or dismissal under Section 1112 have been expanded and now include:

(i)   substantial or continuing loss to or diminution of the estate and the absence of a reasonable likelihood of rehabilitation;

(ii)   gross mismanagement of the estate;

(iii)   failure to maintain appropriate insurance that poses a risk to the estate or to the public;

(iv)   unauthorized use of cash collateral substantially harmful to one or more creditors;

(v)   failure to comply with an order of the court;

(vi)   unexcused failure to satisfy timely any filing or reporting requirement established by this title or by any rule applicable to a case under this chapter;

(vii)   failure to attend the meeting of creditors convened under Section 341(a) or an examination ordered under Rule 2004 of the Federal Rules of Bankruptcy Procedure without good cause shown by the debtor;

(viii) failure to timely provide information or attend meetings reasonably requested by the United States Trustee (or the bankruptcy administrator, if any);

(ix)   failure to timely pay taxes owed after the commencement of the bankruptcy or to file tax returns due thereafter;

(x)   failure to file a disclosure statement, or to file or confirm a plan, within the time fixed by the Bankruptcy Code or by order of the court;

(xi)   failure to pay any fees or charges required under Chapter 123 of Title 28;

(xii)   revocation of an order of confirmation under Section 1144 of the Bankruptcy Code;

(xiii) inability to effectuate substantial consummation of a confirmed plan;

(xiv)   material default by the debtor with respect to a confirmed plan;

(xv)   termination of a confirmed plan by reason of the occurrence of a condition specified in the plan; and

(xvi)   failure of the debtor to pay any domestic support obligation that first becomes payable after the date of the filing of the bankruptcy case.

Section 1104 has also been modified to require the United States Trustee to move for the appointment of a Chapter 11 trustee if there are reasonable grounds to suspect that: (i) current members of the debtor's governing body; (ii) the debtor's CEO or CFO; or (iii) the members of the governing body who selected the debtor's CEO or CFO participated in actual fraud, dishonesty or criminal conduct in the management of the debtor or the debtor's public financial reporting. This requirement is new and is in response to cases like Enron, WorldCom and Adelphia, where allegations of fraud by prepetition management were raised.

Section 1104 also requires that the United States Trustee file a report certifying the election of a Chapter 11 trustee at a meeting of creditors. The newly elected trustee is deemed appointed, and any interim trustee's appointment is deemed terminated, upon such filing. The bankruptcy court shall resolve any election disputes.

Note that creditors may request that the United States Trustee convene a meeting of creditors for the purpose of electing a disinterested person trustee. There is no provision for electing an examiner. A creditor desiring an election must file a written request for one within 30 days of the entry of an order directing the appointment of a trustee. Thereafter, the United States Trustee must convene a meeting of creditors and conduct the election. If creditors holding at least 20 percent in amount of the fixed, liquidated, undisputed, unsecured claims in the case vote, the disinterested nominee receiving a majority of the votes in the election becomes the trustee. Presumably, in those cases where the creditors holding the necessary minimum amount do not vote, the appointed trustee remains trustee.

TRUSTEES' DUTIES AND POWERS

A trustee has all of the powers of a Chapter 7 trustee and, in addition, may continue to operate the business if, in the trustee's judgment, the business should be operated. In effect, the trustee becomes like a new board of directors in a large case, directing management in the continued operation of the business. In a smaller case the trustee may actually take over the business and run it personally. Generally that is not practical, however, since the trustee may lack the time or the specific experience necessary to run the debtor's business. The trustee is a fiduciary who acts for the benefit of all creditors in a case, whether secured or unsecured, and must also consider the interest of equity security interest holders. A Chapter 11 trustee may employ counsel, accountants, and other professionals and take virtually any action necessary to preserve and protect the assets of the estate and operate the business. The courts will rarely interfere with a trustee's business judgment on continued operation of the business or the sale of specific assets pending the reorganization plan. Occasionally, however, a court will limit a trustee's ability to sell certain assets pending the proposal of a plan of reorganization.

As will be discussed below in the section on plans, the appointment of a trustee terminates the debtor's exclusive right to propose a plan of reorganization and a trustee or any party in interest may, thereafter, propose a plan of reorganization.

THE EXAMINER

The Bankruptcy Code authorizes the court to direct the appointment of an examiner as an alternative to the appointment of a trustee where cause exists where the unsecured debts of the company exceed 5,000,000, or under BAPCPA where there are grounds for dismissal or conversion of the case and the appointment is in the best interest of the estate. Often, the court will direct the appointment of an examiner where it is not satisfied that the expense of a trustee is warranted, but feels the creditors are entitled to an objective analysis of the debtor's assets and operation.

In theory, an examiner is an objective reviewer of the financial and legal condition of the debtor. An examiner is required to make a report on the debtor's business, but may not operate the business or interfere in the operation of the business by the debtor in possession. Anyone appointed as an examiner is barred from serving as a trustee in the case if the court later directs the appointment of a trustee. The process for appointment of an examiner is the same as that of a trustee: The court directs the appointment and the United States Trustee, after appropriate consultation with the parties, makes the appointment. There is, however, no provision for election of an examiner in any case.

In many cases an examiner is a less expensive alternative to the appointment of a trustee since an examiner does not operate the business and is not entitled to a fee based on distributions from the business while the examiner is in control. In practice most examiners are attorneys, accountants or business people with experience in the industry in which the debtor operates. Generally, an examiner is compensated on an hourly basis based on time spent. An examiner may, with court approval, employ other professionals such as an attorney or an accountant.

TACTICAL CONSIDERATIONS

A creditor should not lightly seek the appointment of a trustee or examiner because of expense to the estate of both in the litigation over the appointment and, if appointed, the trustee's or examiner's fees and expenses. The courts are not anxious to appoint trustees, particularly in the more complex and unusual cases. For example, a trustee can rarely be found to operate a farming operation, and it is, therefore, simply impractical to have the court order that the case proceed under the direction of a trustee.

A major drawback to the appointment of a trustee from an unsecured creditor's point of view is the trustee's compensation scheme. The fees requested are an administrative expense that is paid ahead of unsecured claims in the bankruptcy case.

Under the Bankruptcy Code, a trustee appointed by the United States Trustee in a Chapter 11 case is entitled to compensation based upon distributions to creditors in the bankruptcy case. In a major case, the trustee's fees can be substantial since they are assessed as a percentage of the gross expenditures of the estate. The maximum compensation is an upper limit on what the court may award. In some cases the courts will cut the requested compensation, based upon the amount of time the trustee actually had to spend on the case.

Before the trustee can be paid, the trustee must apply to the court and give notice to creditors of the intended request. The court may approve the request on an interim or on a final basis if no one objects.

PLANS OF REORGANIZATION

Overview

Given the ever-increasing number of Chapter 11 filings, an observer might assume that Chapter 11 is some sort of panacea for all the ills of debtors, large and small. During the past 10 years, many large businesses have been filing Chapter 11s to eliminate executory leases or union contracts. The fact still exists, that few

Chapter 11 cases actually result in confirmation of a plan. The vast majority of cases are converted to Chapter 7 or are dismissed.

There are very few reliable statistics on the percentage of cases in which a plan has actually been confirmed and the case passes out of the bankruptcy court while still in Chapter 11 mode. It is now estimated that between 25 and 30 percent of all Chapter 11 cases result in some sort of plan. The percentage, however, may vary from district to district, depending upon the attitude of the court toward the reorganization process, the sophistication of the bankruptcy bar, and financial conditions in the region. Statistics about plan confirmation, conversion to Chapter 7, and the like, are not terribly helpful because they do not properly indicate whether Chapter 11 is a "success." For example, a confirmed plan that revests the owners who so mismanaged the business that bankruptcy became necessary may not be terribly good for creditors. Similarly, a liquidating Chapter 11, or conversion of a Chapter 11 case to Chapter 7, may not signify failure because liquidation may present the most viable opportunity for creditors to be paid. From the standpoint of the trade creditor, the debate is purely academic because your ability to be paid stems from the statutory language of the Code itself, not from spirited debate over the value of Chapter 11.

The confirmation of a plan is the goal of the reorganization process. Proposing and confirming a plan can be difficult and time consuming even in a relatively simple case. "Prepackaged" plans have been proposed in some cases in which the parties have generally agreed on the terms and conditions of the plan, exchanged the necessary financial information, and solicited acceptances from creditors prior to the petition for relief. The prepackaged plan works only if there has been complete and candid prepetition disclosure in a genuine effort to work the case out. The prepackaged plans are an illustration that the bankruptcy process need not take the months or years that many debtors and creditors have come to expect. The bankruptcy process, in fact, works better if a plan is proposed early on and a genuine effort is made to consider the interests of all parties.

The Bankruptcy Code provides a very broad framework on what must be contained in a plan. The statutory requirements are sufficiently general that they fit all types of cases. At the heart of the statutory scheme is the requirement that the plan classify claims and equity security interests and provide for their treatment. The plan must also provide for the execution of the plan, which generally requires a detailed description of how the debtor will be liquidated or reorganized and specific provisions for treatment of claims. Generally, in implementing the plan, a proposal may provide for the retention or sale of property, the merger of the debtor or virtually any other effort at liquidation or reorganization necessary to conclude the case. Quite often, reorganization cases are filed to either renegotiate or reinstate mortgages or other secured and unsecured debt instruments. If the requisite majority of creditors does not accept a plan, it may be crammed down. Cramdown is the process by which a plan is confirmed over the objections of creditors or shareholders to the provisions of the plan. The process is neither simple nor as successful as debtors' attorneys would have creditors think. Unless the plan provides for full payment of all unsecured claims with interest over a relatively short period of time, cramdown is going to be rarely possible over the objections of unsecured creditors.

Many debtors (or debtors' officers) seem to think that Chapter 11 permits them to force creditors to accept virtually any treatment so long as it is better than the treatment they would receive in liquidation. That simply is not the case. You need to study the cramdown provisions since cramdown will be the major threat in negotiating the terms of a plan. The Bankruptcy Code includes a number of terms that must be considered before you can understand the provisions of the Code itself.

Unless you choose to propose a plan to creditors in a particular case, a process that is complicated by creditors' lack of access to much of the information necessary, your primary concern will be the terms and conditions of the plan proposed by the debtor. Avoid the temptation to reject the plan simply because it was proposed by the debtor. Also, do not focus your energies on the plan that you might propose if given the chance.

Potential Plan Proponents

DEBTOR'S EXCLUSIVE PERIOD

In cases filed prior to or after the BAPCPA, the debtor in possession is given the exclusive right to file a plan of reorganization for the first 120 days following the petition for relief. 11 USC § 1121. During the exclusive period only the debtor in possession may file a reorganization plan and have it considered by creditors. The court may shorten or extend that period after notice to creditors. While theoretically another party could propose a plan during the exclusivity period, it could not be submitted to creditors. Once that exclusive period has expired or has been terminated by the court, or a trustee has been appointed, virtually any party in interest in the case may file a plan. The debtor's exclusive period may be extended by court order if an application for the extension is made within the exclusive period itself. Practice varies from one part of the country to another. Some courts will routinely allow the debtor an extension of time to file a plan if it appears that progress is being made in the case. Other courts routinely refuse to extend the exclusive period on the theory that it puts more pressure on the debtor to bring the case to a successful conclusion as quickly as possible. You will have to review with counsel the court's recent rulings on the extension of the exclusive period.

The exclusive period terminates 120 days after the petition for relief is filed unless the court extends it, which is routinely what courts have granted. It may also be terminated by court order on application of one of the parties in interest, and it automatically terminates upon the appointment of a trustee. Many courts will consider a motion to require the debtor to file a plan by a particular time or to terminate the exclusive period early in the case. Generally, a showing that the debtor is not actively pursuing a plan of reorganization or has no reasonable likelihood of reorganizing is necessary to terminate the exclusive period. Once the debtor's exclusive period has expired or has been terminated by the court, virtually *any* party in interest in the case can propose a plan. The debtor still retains the right to propose a plan of reorganization even though the debtor's exclusive period has expired.

The BAPCPA amends Section 1121(d) by: setting a deadline for the exclusive time periods afforded to the debtor to file and solicit acceptances of a Chapter 11 plan. A debtor's exclusive right to file a Chapter 11 plan cannot be extended more than 18 months following the commencement of the bankruptcy case; and its exclusive right to solicit acceptances of a Chapter 11 plan cannot be extended more than 20 months after filing. These deadlines are absolute and cannot be further extended by the court.

Any exclusivity extensions beyond the original 120 days are not automatic. The court can extend those times only if:

(A) the debtor, after notice to parties in interest, demonstrates by a preponderance of the evidence that it is more likely than not that the court will confirm a plan within a reasonable period of time;

(B) a new deadline is imposed at the time the extension is granted; and

(C) the order extending the time is signed before the existing deadline has expired.

Another absolute deadline imposed by the BAPCPA is that a plan and disclosure statement shall be filed no later than 300 days after the original Chapter 11 filing date.

NON-DEBTOR POTENTIAL PLAN PROPONENTS

Often, the failure to propose a plan is due to some conflict among the debtor's shareholders, partners, or officers if the debtor is a partnership or a corporation. In this situation the courts have held that the corporate officers and board of directors may propose a plan on behalf of the debtor. Shareholders are also parties in interest and, therefore, may propose a plan, but the plan may not be proposed on behalf of the debtor. Similarly, any partner in a partnership may propose a plan of reorganization. Remember, however, that in a limited partnership case setting, the confirmation of a plan proposed by the limited partners may have substantial other legal consequences for the limited partners.

The creditors' committee may propose a plan of reorganization and often does as a negotiating tactic to bring the debtor to the bargaining table. Often, the debtor's proposed plan is unrealistic or proposes to retain management with which the creditors are unwilling to work.

An individual creditor may propose a plan of reorganization. Unless the creditor has a substantial claim or is seeking to acquire the debtor's assets through what is essentially a hostile takeover plan, the expense and effort necessary to propose a plan may not be worthwhile for the individual creditor. There is increasing interest on behalf of outsiders to use the Chapter 11 process as a method of acquiring either the debtor's assets or the debtor as an entity itself. Since the Bankruptcy Code does not specifically address the issue of a hostile takeover in the guise of a reorganization plan, the courts are still evolving the procedural and substantive rules that a plan proponent must meet in such a circumstance. Further, since the Bankruptcy Code does not specifically regulate the process for the acquisition of claims, if the potential plan proponent is not actually a creditor in the case, the proponent must acquire a claim to become a party in interest to propose a plan. This has led to further litigation over the circumstances over which a noncreditor may purchase claims in an effort to become a party in interest to propose a plan of reorganization. Note, however, that not all persons interested in acquiring claims are doing so in an effort to be in a position to propose a plan of reorganization. In many of the larger cases that involve publicly traded debt instruments, a regular market has sprung up that permits the purchase and sale of those debt instruments of a corporate entity in a Chapter 11 reorganization. Obviously, trading in claims in a bankruptcy reorganization is, at best, somewhat speculative.

Plan Contents: Claims Classification and Treatment of Claims

OVERVIEW

The heart of any plan of reorganization is the classification and treatment of claims and interests. One of the first steps will be determining what assets will be available in the event of liquidation, which will essentially set the floor for any plan payment to creditors and what other assets might be recoverable for the benefit of unsecured creditors to create a pool of assets for potential distribution to creditors.

Definition and Priorities of Claims

The statutory definition of the term "claim" in the Bankruptcy Code includes either a right to payment or a right to some equitable remedy such as injunctive relief in the event of a breach of contract. The claim need not have matured at the time of the filing of the petition and it may be disputed or contingent.

Within the broad concept of claim, there are a number of categories. Creditors holding liens on assets of the estate are secured creditors. 11 USC § 502. All other claims are unsecured. *Under*secured claims, where the value of the collateral is less than the amount of the claim held by the creditor, are partially secured and partially unsecured. Unsecured creditors are further broken down into priority claims that are entitled under the Bankruptcy Code to satisfaction from any unencumbered assets of the estate ahead of general unsecured claims. Certain types of claims are afforded priority in the assets of the debtor's estate under § 507 of the Bankruptcy Code. Administrative expenses, including claims for goods delivered or services rendered to the debtor on an unsecured basis postpetition have the first priority. These claims must be satisfied in full before distribution is made to any other lower priority creditor. Various other claims entitled to lower priority status (which must be paid in full before nonpriority unsecured creditors) include certain postpetition unsecured claims against an involuntary debtor; claims for wages, salaries, commissions, vacation, severance and sick leave pay earned immediately prior to the bankruptcy; contributions to an employee benefit plan; certain claims of farmers for grain stored or fish delivered to a processing facility; certain consumer deposits and tax claims. Priority claims that are limited in amount are usually indexed for inflation and will increase every three years. In classifying and providing for the treatment of claims in a bankruptcy reorganization, you must consider both their status as secured or unsecured claims and any priority status that they may have.

Classification and Treatment of Claims in a Plan

The heart of any plan of reorganization will be the classification of claims and the provisions for treatment for each class of claims. In the simplest possible case—with a single fully secured creditor, a number of trade creditors with no priority unsecured claims, and a single stockholder—a liquidation plan might provide a class for the secured creditor, a class for the unsecured trade creditors, and an interest class for the single stockholder. The plan will provide for liquidation of the assets, satisfaction of the secured claim from the proceeds of any collateral, and the distribution of the balance to the unsecured creditors. In the unlikely event that there is any surplus after the satisfaction of all unsecured claims, the balance will be distributed to the stockholder.

The voting requirements of the Code require that at least one impaired class accept the plan before the court can consider it for confirmation. This often leads to some amazing hairsplitting by counsel for a proponent of a plan in an effort to create an impaired class likely to vote for the plan.

Secured Creditors

Classification

The classification of secured creditors in a reorganization case is straightforward. As a general rule, the courts require that each secured creditor be placed in a separate class. However, if several secured creditors have liens with equal priority against the same collateral, they may be placed in a single class. For example, assume that the debtor's real estate is subject to a first, a second and a third mortgage. Assume that the value of the collateral is less than the total of the first and second claims. The first mortgage would be placed in a class and treated as fully secured; the second mortgage would be placed in a separate class and treated as partially secured and partially unsecured; the third mortgage would be relegated to unsecured status to be treated with other unsecured claims. In the unlikely event that a number of creditors have separate claims all secured by the same assets with an equal priority, those creditors would be placed in a single class. In designating the classes, the proponent must consider the legal rights of the creditors and the value of their collateral.

Treatment of Secured Creditors

The potential treatment of secured creditors will depend upon the value of their collateral. If the value equals or exceeds the amount of the claim, the proponent of the plan may surrender the collateral in full satisfaction of the claim. In other cases the debtor will wish to retain the collateral and reamortize the debt. This may include an extension of the debt beyond the existing maturity date or a rewriting of the terms of the debt including interest rate. Reamortization of the debt is particularly attractive where the debtor originally agreed to a relatively short term with a substantial balloon obligation, which the debtor now cannot refinance because of the value of the collateral or the condition of the local economy. In many situations the debtor will then propose a plan that calls for retention of the collateral, preservation of the creditor's lien on the collateral, and reamortization of the balance due at a reduced interest rate. Of course, any change in the terms of the repayment impairs the claim and requires that the creditor accept the proposed treatment or that the court confirm the plan under the cramdown rules. Litigation often ensues over the interest rate and the term of the paydown.

Another alternative is for the debtor to cure the default in the existing mortgage, if the terms of the existing mortgage are at less than current market rate. Generally, the plan will provide for the debtor to retain the collateral and make contract payments on the existing mortgage according to its terms, and an additional payment to cure any default. Often, the creditor will object that the mortgage is at a rate that is below the current market rate or that the period the debtor proposes for the cure of the default is too long. While the cure and reinstatement of the mortgage is more often a feature of consumer reorganization under Chapter 13, it does occur in Chapter 11 where the debtor wants to retain collateral, particularly if it has equity, but has fallen behind on an otherwise favorable mortgage.

Yet another option is for the debtor to sell the collateral, use the proceeds in the reorganization effort, and provide the creditor with a lien on other assets. A variation of this treatment involves sale of part of the creditor's collateral with the creditor retaining a lien on the unsold assets, but not receiving the sale proceeds. The value of the remaining assets must exceed the amount of the creditor's claim so that it remains fully secured. Assume, for example, that the debtor owns real estate that is no longer essential for the reorganization effort, but needs cash to generate a payment to unsecured creditors. Creditors secured by the real estate that is to be sold may be offered a second lien on assets to be retained and periodic payments to amortize the outstanding obligation as a replacement for the lien on the real estate.

Obviously, from the secured creditor's point of view, it is less interested in payments over a period of time from an often-shaky reorganized debtor than it is in the proceeds of its collateral. This, of course, can lead to some valuation and treatment battles, but the option exists to provide a secured creditor with a replacement lien and sell the property for the benefit of the estate.

Finally, of course, the plan may provide for an orderly liquidation of the creditor's collateral over a period of time, with the proceeds being used to pay part of the administrative expenses and to satisfy the claim of the secured creditor. This type of treatment has been quite common in real estate reorganizations where the market has slumped sharply. For example, assume that the debtor owns a number of undeveloped lots. The secured creditor and the estate generally might benefit from an orderly liquidation of the lots over a long period of time rather than suddenly dumping them on the market, which would have the effect of depressing the price. The plan may provide for the continued operation of the debtor with ongoing sales and the sales proceeds used to pay the operating expenses of the debtor with the net proceeds being paid to the creditor.

Another form of liquidation may simply provide for an auction sale to be conducted after the confirmation of the plan. The proceeds would be applied first to the sale expenses and then to the lien holder's claim. The debtor would distribute any surplus to, first, priority unsecured creditors, and then what's remaining to nonpriority unsecured creditors pro rata. The unsecured creditor's concern in these situations is the timing of the sale. While dumping a large quantity of personal property of a particular type or a large amount of real estate on a particular market at once might depress the price, the other problem is the cost of debtor's continued operation during the liquidation process.

Potential Objections to Classification or Treatment of Secured Creditors

The creditors' committee or an individual creditor may potentially object to the classification or treatment of a secured creditor if it adversely affects the payment to unsecured creditors. If the debtor's officers or insiders have guaranteed payment of a particular debt, they may be inclined to treat that creditor as fully secured even where the collateral is worth less than the debt. Likewise, they are less likely to use the debtor in possession's strong arm powers to avoid an improperly perfected security interest. Therefore, the first step in the unsecured creditor's review of a plan will be to review the validity of a purportedly secured creditor's security interest and raise any objections as to the validity, extent, etc., of that security interest. This will require legal assistance since the defects in any given security agreement or mortgage are not often readily apparent. The creditor should also be cognizant that an order approving financing or the debtor's use of cash collateral might set deadlines for asserting such claims.

Unsecured creditors may also want to review the interest rate offered secured creditors under the plan. The Bankruptcy Code generally mandates a market interest rate for reamortized debt. The contract interest rate may be substantially higher than the market rate at the time of confirmation.

Unsecured Creditors

Classification of Unsecured Claims

If the classification and treatment of creditors and claims is the heart of any plan of reorganization, the most important part from an unsecured creditor's point of view is the classification and treatment of unsecured claims. At least one impaired class of creditors (determined without counting the votes of insiders) must accept a plan before it is eligible for confirmation under the cramdown rules of 11 USC § 1129(b). A proponent must design one class of impaired claimants that is likely to accept the plan. This often leads to some interesting attempts at gerrymandering to ensure that one hostile creditor (generally the unsecured deficiency claim of a major undersecured creditor) is lumped together with friendly trade creditors in such a fashion that trade creditors' votes control the class and accept the plan. Conversely, the debtor may occasionally propose a plan that separates the trade creditors from the unsecured deficiency claim in an effort to generate the necessary accepting impaired class.

The rules for classification of unsecured creditors are always evolving. The Bankruptcy Code specifically mandates that all claims of a similar nature in a single class be given the same treatment. The courts have struggled with classification of claims and there appear to be three general theories that have evolved to this point including: (1) the single class theory; (2) the factual basis for classification theory; and (3) the administrative ease class theory. As a general rule, courts will approve any plan that places all unsecured creditors in a single class. Some courts have approved a classification of unsecured creditors in different classes so long as there is a rational legal or factual basis for the distinction.

From a practical point of view, the lumping of all unsecured creditors into a single large class can create substantial problems for the plan proponent at the confirmation stage. Acceptance requires that at least one-half in number and two-thirds in amount of the claims in that class that vote to actually accept the plan. Thus, a holder of a single large claim equaling or exceeding one-third of the claims *voting* on the plan may veto the plan even if all other creditors in that class accept. In a small to medium-size case, this may give the holder of a large deficiency claim considerable leverage in negotiating the plan. In other situations, it may give veto power to the holders of a large number of small claims. Since more than one-half in number (and two-thirds in dollar amount) of the claims voting in the class must accept, the single large claim can block the plan, but cannot force other claimholders to accept. For example, assume that the debtor owes the bank $500,000 secured by a lien on property having a value of $400,000. The bank holds a $400,000 secured claim and an unsecured deficiency claim in the amount of $100,000. The debtor proposes a plan of reorganization that provides for payment of 10 cents on the dollar to unsecured creditors and the reamortization of the secured claim over a 30-year period at 6 percent interest. The debtor also owes trade creditors $200,000. Approximately 30 creditors hold the trade debt. The plan is put to a vote and the bank votes its entire $100,000 deficiency against the plan. Twenty of the unsecured trade creditors holding claims totaling $150,000 vote in favor of the plan. While the plan may be confirmable under certain limited circumstances under the cramdown rules, the unsecured class proposed here has not accepted the plan since the bank voted $100,000 of its claim against the plan. The $100,000 is more than one-third of the $250,000 actually voting on the plan.

Conversely, if only the bank had voted for the plan, but 20 of the unsecured creditors voted *against* it, irrespective of the total of unsecured claims voting against the plan, only one creditor voted for the plan and 20 creditors voted against the plan and, therefore, the class is deemed to have rejected the plan. Again, while there may be an avenue for confirmation under 11 USC § 1129(b), the class itself has rejected the plan under these circumstances.

A number of courts have, however, approved plans with separate classification of groups of unsecured creditors based upon their relationship to the debtor or some other factual basis that relates to the operation of the case. In some respects the separate classification rules have developed from the Chapter 13 case law. Under Chapter 13 the courts have generally approved separate classification and treatment of creditors essential to the individual debtor's continued well being and worth. For example, Chapter 13 cases fairly routinely approve a separate class for physicians or other health care providers treating the debtor postpetition. The theory is that if the unpaid doctor refuses to provide treatment, the debtor will be unable to continue work and make payments under the plan. Some courts have, likewise, allowed separate Chapter 11 treatment for trade creditors who will continue to do business with the debtor on a postpetition basis.

For example, if manufacturer Y supplies an essential subassembly or raw material for the debtor's products, manufacturer Y's prepetition claim might be placed in a separate class since without their assent and continued delivery of the essential products, the debtor's reorganization will not succeed. The courts have also approved separate classification and treatment for priority claimants such as employee claims and tax claims. The case law in this is still evolving and each case will have to be separately considered. If you are dealing with a plan that classifies unsecured creditors into multiple classes with separate and more favorable treatment for some classes than others, you may wish to consider an objection to the classification of creditors. Normally, the objection will have to be filed before the confirmation hearing at the latest.

Conversely, if you are dealing with a large group of creditors holding different types of unsecured claims, and you wish to propose a plan, you may be able to come up with a factual basis for splitting the unsecured claims into different classes for treatment and voting purposes. Most courts accept such separate treatment if there is a factual basis for the separate classification.

Finally, the Code specifically permits the proponent of a plan to propose an administrative class of small claims for distribution purposes, which will be treated separately. This is known as a "convenience class." The object is to provide a cash out option for creditors willing to take a fixed amount on their claim for a multitude of small claims. Typically, the class will provide for a percentage payment on all claims under $500 or $1,000. The idea is to eliminate substantial bookkeeping expenses that may be necessary to make larger payments to the multitude of small claims. In some middle to small cases, proponents have attempted to manipulate the convenience class by setting the amount of the convenience class cutoff high enough to include all of the trade creditors, but exclude the holders of unsecured deficiency claims. For example, in a typical single asset case involving an apartment building or other project where the sole asset of the case is the building, the debtor, in proposing a plan, may provide for a convenience class of all claims under $10,000. The dollar figure would be chosen to include all trade class claims, but exclude the holder of the undersecured claim against the building. This virtually guarantees that the trade creditors will accept the plan. The plan may still be confirmed under

11 USC 1129(b) under certain limited circumstances (discussed below) because the convenience class has accepted. The confirmation requirements often lead to negotiations between the creditors over both classification and treatment issues. Again, the case law in this area is still developing, but a consensus seems to be building that so long as the proponent of the plan (whether the debtor or someone else) has a rational basis in fact for the segregation of creditors into different classes, then the classification scheme may be approved.

TREATMENT OF UNSECURED CLAIMS

The concepts of classification and treatment of unsecured claims are very closely interwoven. As mentioned above, some courts have held that even though a proponent of a plan may separately classify different types of unsecured creditors, they must all be treated the same in the plan. (This makes little sense because separate treatment is often the key to voting on the plan.) Generally, however, the courts have not taken such a narrow view and the evolving rule seems to be that separate classification and treatment are possible, as long as there is a rational factual basis for the separate classification and treatment.

The treatment provision of the plan of reorganization tells you what you will receive under the plan as proposed. Depending upon the type of plan proposed, the plan language will detail what, if anything, will be distributed to creditors on account of their claims in that class. Generally, the treatment and the plan will be dictated by the requirements of the confirmation process discussed below.

There is no typical Chapter 11 plan, and plans fall into a variety of general types. Plans range from full payment immediately or over a period of years to a zero percent payment to unsecured creditors. Plans are generally classified as "compromise plans" if they provide for less than full payment, and as "extension plans" if they provide for full payment with or without interest over a period of time. Some plans, commonly referred to as "pot plans," call for some of the debtor's assets to be set aside for liquidation and distribution to unsecured creditors. A creditor's primary concern is to understand the amount of payment of its claim. A plan may provide for no payment to general unsecured creditors. The unsecured creditors are wiped out and the debtor's assets liquidated and the proceeds paid to secured and priority creditors. From a general unsecured creditor's point of view, a plan providing for no payment is confirmable only if there is no equity in the assets, whether based on liquidation or going concern value, and if the debtor's stockholders or owners will retain no interest in the business after confirmation. *See* the confirmation discussion that follows. Generally, a plan that wipes out the unsecured creditors also wipes out equity holders.

Partial payment plans fall into a variety of categories. These plans generally provide for cash payment of a certain percentage of unsecured claims either upon confirmation or in periodic payments over a period of years. From a tactical point of view, of course, the proffer of an immediate 15 or 20 percent cash payment is generally going to be received more favorably by creditors than a payment of the same amount over a period of time. Thus, the amount and the timing of the payment will be key negotiation points in the formulation of the plan.

The formulation of the percentage to be paid to unsecured creditors will largely depend upon the assets of the bankruptcy estate. This often leads to disputes over valuation methods. Generally, a liquidation value is placed on the debtor's assets based upon the net distribution to unsecured creditors in the event of a *forced sale* of the business. If this involves inventory or work in progress of a small manufacturer, the liquidation value of the complete inventory may be substantially less than the cost value on the company's books. Likewise, depending on the local economy, the sale of both real and personal property at auction may bring substantially less than the same property would if the business is sold as a going concern. Thus, a creditors' committee will often place a going concern value on the business in the negotiations and may even try to locate a potential buyer for the whole business. An offer to purchase the business assets as a going concern is a strong bargaining position in dealing with a debtor or secured creditor in plan negotiations.

The courts will look to the plan provisions to determine the appropriate valuation method. If the debtor proposes to retain the business and continue the operation with the shareholders or principals retaining an equity interest, the court will generally require a going concern value in setting the minimum distribution to unsecured creditors. On the other hand, if the plan provides for liquidation of the assets, whether over a period of time or through an immediate auction, the court will generally accept a liquidation valuation.

In evaluating a proposed plan, you should compare what is being offered with what might be achieved through a reasonable liquidation process. The liquidation value is the floor; if the plan offers more than you would receive in a liquidation under Chapter 7, you must then evaluate whether the plan is confirmable.

While under optimum conditions, a debtor might be sold as a going concern for a value sufficient to satisfy all creditors, which rarely occurs in the bankruptcy context. Unless you know of a buyer who is willing to pay a going concern value for the debtor's business, you should very carefully consider what the proponent of the plan offers. That offer, of course, should be compared with the minimum dividend that would be payable in the event of a complete and quick liquidation of the debtor's assets through auction. However, if the liquidation dividend exceeds what is being offered, the plan is not confirmable. On the other hand some debtors will take the position that if they are offering more than what would be obtained in liquidation, the plan can be confirmed even if the creditors reject it. This is not always the case. *See* the confirmation discussion below. As a general rule, it will be difficult to obtain court approval of a plan which allows shareholders to retain their stock if rejected by unsecured creditors, even if the plan pays a dividend equal to or greater than the liquidation value.

A pot plan involves the setting aside of some of the debtor's assets for distribution to unsecured creditors. Often, the valuation of those assets is speculative. The assets may consist of an interest in litigation or specific properties. In limited cases a secured creditor or someone else will put up a specific amount for distribution to unsecured creditors pro rata based on their claims. These are "pot plans" since the proponent is putting up a "pot" of assets for distribution to unsecured creditors. The amount of assets distributed to the pot will be divided pro rata among all allowed unsecured claims.

Since the value of the assets to be placed in the pot and the total amount of allowed claims are often uncertain, it is difficult to calculate the distribution to unsecured creditors. In many cases, the total amount of the unsecured claims either has not been determined or is the subject of litigation at the time the plan is proposed.

Pot plans are most often proposed where the proponent is willing to put up a fund in return for the unsecured creditors accepting the plan. In certain circumstances there may be tax advantages to maintaining the corporate entity of a debtor in possession through the bankruptcy process. For instance, a debtor's loss will carry forward and other tax attributes may be preserved and used to shelter postpetition income. While a discussion of those tax advantages is beyond the scope of this work, they may figure prominently in the reorganization negotiations between the parties.

Just as the uncertainties as to the valuation of the assets and the amount of class claims make evaluation of a proposed pot plan difficult for creditors, those same uncertainties make it difficult for the court to approve confirmation. If creditors reject the proposed plan, the court must find that the liquidation value is actually being paid to unsecured creditors. The plan proponent may not be able to convince the court that that is true.

Full payment or extension plans are rarely proposed, but are always an option. A simple extension of the existing unsecured debt over some period of time is always an option. This is particularly attractive where the debtor has suffered a setback in a start-up business, but has a viable operation that will, over a period of time, generate sufficient cash flow to pay back the debts. A full payment plan, of course, depends upon the viability of the business. Often, the debtors are overly optimistic about future cash flow. In evaluating a proposed extension plan, you will want to consider whether there is any interest to be paid on your claim and the true viability of the debtor's business. Again, the payment over a period of time, with or without interest, must be compared with the liquidation value of the debtor's business. If, in liquidation the debtor would generate sufficient assets to pay all claims, the debtor will be required to pay interest on all claims.

In a limited number of cases, the debtor or other proponent will offer a stock distribution or a "debt for equity swap." In this situation, you will be asked to give up your claim against the debtor in return for stock in the corporation or in a new corporation to be formed to take over the assets of the debtor. Some regulated lenders may not be permitted to hold the stock in a business. Other creditors may not wish to hold the stock. The value of the stock may be virtually nil since there may be no market for it. On the other hand, in the K-Mart Chapter 11 proceeding, unsecured creditors were given stock for their unsecured claims. Those who held on to the stock found themselves receiving substantial returns as the stock value increased dramatically following confirmation of the K-Mart Chapter 11. Nevertheless, distribution of stock may create substantial securities law problems for the proponent and for you. While the discussion of the securities problems is generally beyond the scope of this work, you may want to consider the advisability of owning, along with many other creditors, a small piece of the new debtor where there may be little chance of selling the stock aside from potential securities problems.

A stock distribution or debt for equity swap plan presents few drafting problems and the only points for negotiation are the value to be placed on the stock for purposes of the swap. Since the Bankruptcy Code expressly prohibits the issuance of nonvoting stock, any stock issued must be voting stock. This will lead to some interesting control questions once the debtor is reorganized. Since a debt for equity swap plan will generally identify the initial board of directors and their terms, you may find yourself owning stock in a business controlled either by other creditors or indirectly by management, which can continue its prepetition ways.

A variation on a debt for equity swap plan is a two-step proposition in which someone interested in acquiring the debtor's operation proposes a stock distribution or debt for equity swap and then, at the same time, offers to acquire the newly issued stock at a discount from the former creditors.

Depending on the complexities of the case all of the above options may be included in a single plan. For example, creditors may be offered an opportunity to cash out their claims or accept issuance of stock in return for their claims. They may be offered the alternative of partial payment of their claim on the effective date of the plan. Since protracted litigation is rarely in anyone's interest in these circumstances, your consideration of any proposed plan ought to be limited to a review of what is offered against what might be achieved in liquidation or if you were to propose some other plan. All too often, creditors will see greater value in the debtor than actually exists and will reject a partial payment plan, forcing the company into liquidation. Once the liquidation is complete, of course, there may not be enough to satisfy priority and administrative claims.

Interest Classification and Treatment

Any plan of reorganization must provide for the classification of any interests held by equity security holders and for their treatment. Equity security holders include stockholders in a corporation and limited partners in a limited partnership. The Bankruptcy Code does not deal very well with a sole proprietorship business even though the sole proprietor has an ownership interest in the assets akin to, but distinctly different from, that of a stockholder. A sole proprietorship business would be an individual Chapter 11 or 13. In a sole proprietorship, partnership, or a corporate plan, the plan must specifically classify the ownership interest and provide for treatment. That treatment will vary depending upon the type of plan. As a general rule, however, equity holders are last in line for any payment, or other distribution, and a plan must be accepted by creditors or pay them in full before equity holders receive or retain anything.

Provision for Execution of Plan

At the very least a plan should provide how the assets, claims, and interests will be treated and any sale, liquidation, or restructuring provided in the plan will be accomplished. Generally, any administrative expenses must be paid in full upon confirmation. If the plan provides for restructuring, the transfer of assets, issuance of stock, and payments to creditors must be carefully detailed. If a liquidation of assets is contemplated, provision for conduct of the sale, payment of expenses, and distribution of the net proceeds must be carefully set out. Above all, a plan should establish clear deadlines for all sales, transfers and distributions.

The greatest danger from a creditor's point of view is that a liquidating plan will not specify the means of liquidation of assets and the dates for payments to creditors. Thus, for example, a liquidation plan for a company with substantial real estate might allow the debtor six months to sell the real estate through a broker and then provide for an auction to be held within a certain period thereafter if the broker is unsuccessful in locating buyers. The plan may specify a minimum auction price, the maximum expenses to be incurred in connection with the auction and other details of the auction. It should also detail the distribution of the proceeds from the auction. Similarly, a cash out plan should provide, in detail, how claims will be determined and a date for payment of the dividend on unsecured claims.

Other Plan Provisions

A plan may contain a variety of optional provisions, again depending upon the type of plan and its acceptance by creditors. A typical liquidating plan or pot plan will provide for the creation of a liquidating trust and the appointment of a trustee or other administrator to handle the assets to be liquidated and distributed to creditors, the prosecution of claims against third parties and the adjudication of claims against the estate.

A plan may further provide for the vesting of all of the debtor's assets in a new entity subject to existing security interests. It may provide for the retention of the right to pursue preference and other actions by the newly formed entity. Some plans have provided for specific limits on management salary and restricted a debtor's right to make capital purchases pending payments to unsecured creditors. Still other plans have limited management perquisites pending the payout to creditors. Generally, a plan will provide for the retention of jurisdiction by the bankruptcy court to resolve disputes concerning interpretation of the plan and to hear preference actions retained by the debtor.

You should be aware of one restriction on plan provisions that the courts have generally upheld: A plan may not discharge guarantors who are not themselves in bankruptcy unless the creditor holding the guaranty specifically approves that provision. If, for example, you hold a guarantee of a principal of the business, the plan may not discharge your guarantee claim against the principal simply by so stating in the plan *if you object*. The courts that have considered the issue have generally held that the bankruptcy court does not have jurisdiction to discharge a guarantee executed by a nondebtor in favor of a creditor. However, at least one court has upheld such a provision where the creditor did not object to the confirmation of the plan.

MANDATORY DISCLOSURE

Preliminary Comment

Fundamental to the Chapter 11 process is the statutory requirement that a proponent of a plan make disclosure of certain information in conjunction with the solicitation of the votes on the plan. While the disclosure requirements may vary considerably depending upon the proponent of the plan and the plan's provisions, before the plan can be submitted to creditors for solicitation of votes and formal confirmation, the proponent must submit to the court a disclosure statement for approval. 11 USC § 1125. The parties in interest are given an opportunity to object to the disclosure statement submitted.

The courts have made every effort to avoid rigidly structuring the disclosure process with strict disclosure requirements on the theory that the amount of disclosure required should reflect the complexity of the plan. The disclosure process can, however, be overly cumbersome and expensive for the smaller debtors. The BAPCPA now includes specific mandates and leniencies for small business. The Small Business provisions of the BAPCPA will be explained separately, below. However, in some courts an accelerated Chapter 11 process has been informally approved where the disclosure statement is approved at the same hearing as the confirmation hearing.

A final preliminary comment: Getting embroiled in protracted litigation over the sufficiency of the information disclosed by the proponent of the plan is counterproductive. Not only does it cost the estate money for fees and expenses, it may also delay a vote on a plan which otherwise might not be confirmable. Moreover, it may delay the confirmation of a plan that is dependent upon speedy execution for distribution of any assets to creditors. Many courts actively discourage objections to the disclosure statement unless the disclosure statement is patently inadequate. Much of the risk is placed on the proponent of the plan because the court will refuse to confirm a plan that is accompanied by an inaccurate or inadequate disclosure statement. Your counsel should be familiar with the particular judge's requirements for disclosure and object only if those requirements are not met.

Disclosure Statement

Before a proponent of a plan can solicit votes from creditors and seek confirmation thereof, the disclosure statement must be submitted to the court and approved. 11 USC § 1125. Occasionally, a proponent will file a plan and then, as a delaying tactic, withhold the filing of a disclosure statement. Generally, however, a plan and disclosure statement are filed in close proximity to each other and are interrelated. Indeed, in some of the simpler cases, the courts have approved combined plans and disclosure statements.

The first step in the approval process after the filing of the plan and the disclosure statement is to give notice to creditors that the disclosure statement has been filed and set for hearing. Not all creditors will receive a copy of the plan and disclosure statement unless they request one. Only the creditors' committee and the major secured creditors will receive copies automatically. If you are not on the committee, you must contact the debtor's lawyer and request a copy. The request should be in writing. The court will set a hearing date at least 25 days after the mailing of the notice of the filing of the disclosure statement. Creditors will be given an objection deadline. For the most part, if the case involves experienced counsel, the disclosure statement hearing will be perfunctory and counsel and the court will quickly approve the disclosure statement. Again, it is often counterproductive to file detailed objections to the disclosure statement since that merely delays resolution of the case.

The BAPCPA amends Section 1125(a)(1) to require that a bankruptcy court must take into account the complexity of the case, the benefit of additional information to creditors and other parties in interest, and the costs associated with providing any additional information when the court considers the adequacy of information contained in the disclosure statement. The disclosure statement must also discuss the potential federal tax consequences of the Chapter 11 plan to the debtor, any successor of the debtor, and a hypothetical investor typical of the holders of claims or interests in the case that would enable such a hypothetical investor of the relevant class to make an informed judgment about the plan.

Section 1111(b) Election

Certain *under*secured nonrecourse creditors are given the opportunity under 11 USC § 1111(b) to elect to have their undersecured claim treated as though it were fully secured. An election to be treated under § 1111(b) means that an undersecured creditor is treated as fully secured for confirmation purposes. If you are presented with a § 1111(b) election, you should consult counsel about a response.

Solicitation of Acceptances and Rejections

Only after the court has approved the disclosure statement may anyone solicit rejections or acceptances of a plan by creditors and other parties in interest. Often, the creditors' committee will oppose or support confirmation and assist in solicitation of acceptances or rejections by sending a letter to the parties soliciting either acceptance or rejection of the plan. Great care should be taken, however, if you solicit rejections of a plan that you do not inject information into the solicitation letter that either has not been approved by the court or goes beyond the disclosure materials. Before soliciting acceptances or rejections of a particular plan you should consult counsel.

The BAPCPA adds a new Section 1125(g) to permit an entity to solicit acceptances or rejections of a plan from a holder of a claim or interest if the holder of such claim or interest was solicited before commencement of the bankruptcy case in a manner that complied with applicable non-bankruptcy law, and to continue soliciting acceptances subsequent to the bankruptcy filing. This provision provides explicit statutory authority for a party to solicit acceptances or rejections prior to and after a bankruptcy case being filed, as is frequently done in a "prepackaged" Chapter 11 case. This represents a change from Section 1125 pre-BAPCPA that precluded the continued postpetition solicitation of acceptances or rejections of a prepetition prepackaged plan unless accompanied by a court-approved disclosure statement.

VOTING PROCESS

Majorities Required

The voting process is relatively simple. Each creditor or interest holder with a claim in a particular class is asked to return a formal ballot either accepting or rejecting the plan. Only those plan ballots actually returned are counted in determining whether the plan is accepted or rejected. A class of creditors is deemed to have accepted the plan if those holding at least two-thirds in amount and one-half in number of the allowed claims in the class *actually voting* accept the plan. 11 USC § 1126. Conversely, a class is deemed to have rejected the plan if *either* more than one-third in amount or more than one-half in number of the allowed claims actually voting on the plan reject it. However, the Code allows the bankruptcy court to strike any vote that is procured in bad faith or not in accordance with the Bankruptcy Code. For example, a ballot cast against the plan in return for payment by an opponent is in bad faith and not in accordance with the plan.

As you can see, creditors holding a substantial percentage of the unsecured claims or other claims in a particular class have a strong negotiating position in that their rejection may cause the class to reject the plan. Quite often, the unsecured creditors' committee, which normally represents the largest unsecured creditors, will hold a substantial percentage of the unsecured claims. The committee's acceptance or rejection of the plan may be key to the confirmation process. As will be discussed below, the debtor or other proponent must obtain the necessary majorities in each class or go through the cramdown procedure under 11 USC § 1129(b).

Procedure

BALLOTS AND VOTING

The proposed plan is sent out to the creditors with an accompanying form ballot. Generally, ballots must be returned to the court or the plan proponent by a particular deadline. If you intend to vote on a plan you must return your ballot in a timely fashion. Allow extra time for returning your ballot by mail, as ballots received after the deadline, even though they may have been mailed prior to the deadline, are not counted.

After the deadline, counsel for the proponent prepares and files a certificate of voting from summarizing the ballots in court file or returned to counsel. Generally, copies of the ballots will be attached to the certificate of voting, which will list and total all ballots cast in each class. Note that even if the committee is actively soliciting rejections, the ballots must still be returned to the court or the proponent of the plan rather than to the committee, unless the court orders otherwise. The certificate of voting should list all ballots, whether late or disputed, and leave it to the court to resolve any disputes over the result.

CLAIMS OBJECTIONS

Occasionally, in an effort to affect the voting, the proponent or the debtor will object to a particular claim and ask that the court to disallow it for voting purposes. Usually, the basis for the disallowance is that the claim is in some way disputed, contingent or unliquidated. Most objections to a particular claim are purely a tactical effort to disenfranchise a particular creditor during the voting on the plan.

If you hold a claim and receive such an objection, you will need the assistance of counsel to respond in a timely fashion. Generally, you have to respond to the objection and request a hearing before a deadline or appear at a hearing prior to the confirmation hearing for a preliminary ruling by the court on the objection. Failure to respond in a timely manner may result in disallowance of your claim.

ALTERNATE PLANS

Occasionally, competing plans will be submitted to creditors simultaneously. The better practice is to have the competing plans submitted with a joint ballot with a blank for creditors to express their preference for one plan over the other. The case law suggests that the court should confirm the plan preferred by a majority of creditors if both plans are, in fact, confirmable.

CONFIRMATION PROCESS

Procedure

Despite its apparent intricacy, the confirmation process is relatively straightforward. If no objections are lodged to the confirmation of the plan and creditors in the necessary quantity and amount accept the plan, the confirmation hearing is often a very perfunctory process and the plan is confirmed.

The process begins with the filing of the plan and disclosure statement. Once the disclosure statement is approved as containing the necessary information (described above), a notice of a confirmation hearing is mailed to all creditors together with a copy of the plan and disclosure statement. A court may direct the plan proponent to mail out both the plan and disclosure statement and combine the hearings thereon. This will shorten the process. A copy of the plan and the disclosure statement will be mailed to each creditor entitled to vote on the plan, with the notice of the confirmation hearing and a ballot for voting. The notice will identify the proponent of the plan and set out deadlines for filing objections and for returning the ballot and specifying the person or entity to receive the ballots. The ballots will be returned either to the court or to the attorney for the proponent of the plan, depending upon the practice in the local court. In voting on the plan you should follow the directions contained in the notice of the confirmation hearing on the return of the ballot. Ballots must be timely received to be counted.

Generally, any objections to confirmation must be filed a week or so before the confirmation hearing set out in the notice. The objections to confirmation should set out, in detail, the bases for the objection by the party in interest. An objection will generally require the assistance of counsel.

Some courts accelerate the process by combining the confirmation hearing and the disclosure statement hearings, especially in the smaller cases, and that will be the norm in small business Chapter 11's under BAPCPA. The court first reviews the disclosure statement and, if it is acceptable, then turns to the confirmation of the plan. If there are errors in the disclosure statement, it will have to be corrected and resent. This may cut out some 30 to 45 days in the confirmation process.

Preconfirmation Modification

In a complex case, it is not uncommon for the debtor or other proponent to submit preconfirmation modifications to the plan, even up to the time of the confirmation hearing. The Code specifically permits modification of the plan up until the time of that hearing. Unless the proposed modifications require revoting, the modifications can be included in the plan as confirmed at the confirmation hearing. Typically, such last-minute modifications affect a single unsecured or secured class. The plan does not need to be resubmitted to creditors for a general vote if the modification improves the treatment for a particular class or does not affect all classes.

The BAPCPA adds a new Section 1127(f) that requires any modification of a Chapter 11 plan prior to confirmation to satisfy Sections 1121 through 1128 and the plan confirmation requirements of Section 1129. It further provides that the modified plan shall become the plan only after there has been disclosure as the court may direct under Section 1125, notice and a hearing on the modification, and court approval of the modification.

Procedure at Confirmation Hearing

The procedure at a confirmation hearing is generally routine. However, if objections are filed and depending on the complexity of the case, the confirmation hearing may become extremely complicated. 11 USC § 1129(a) sets forth the criteria that must be established in order for a plan to be confirmed. The confirmation hearing always begins with a requirement that debtor's counsel present a certificate regarding the voting by creditors on the plan. Counsel for the proponent (which may be an entity other than the debtor) will be asked to place the results of the voting into the record. This recitation is necessary to establish the fact that at least one class of impaired creditors has accepted the plan. Once that fact has been established, the court then turns to the confirmation requirements set forth in § 1129 of the Bankruptcy Code.

In simpler cases, the court may require nothing more than a recitation by the Chapter 11 debtor's counsel that each of the sixteen (16) points of § 1129(a) have been met. In other instances, the court will require evidence on each point of § 1129(a) to be established. A creditor who opposes a plan should consult counsel to determine if the plan can be defeated because each point of § 1129(a) has not been met. The primary areas of dispute upon which the courts generally focus are feasibility of a plan and whether the plan has been proposed in good faith.

BAPCPA ADDITIONS TO § 1129

With respect to individual Chapter 11 debtors and small business cases, the BAPCPA has added new provisions to § 1129(a) that must be met in order for a plan to be confirmed. Of particular interest to trade creditors is § 1129(a)(15) which provides that in an individual Chapter 11 case, the value—as of the effective date of the plan—of property to be distributed under the plan to an unsecured claim must equal either the amount of the unsecured claim, or not less than all disposable income to be received during the following five-year period.

Confirmation without Cramdown

If all classes of creditors and interest holders have accepted the plan by the necessary majorities, there is no need to resort to the cramdown process to confirm the plan. Assuming that the court finds that proposed distribution to unsecured creditors will at least equal that which would be made in a Chapter 7 (the liquidation test), the court may confirm the plan as proposed. Only if a class of impaired creditors has rejected the plan is it necessary to refer to the cramdown provisions of the Bankruptcy Code. Note that even a confirmed plan may be subject to postconfirmation modification, however.

Cramdown Process

OVERVIEW

The Bankruptcy Code permits the Bankruptcy Court to confirm a plan with respect to a class or several classes of creditors who reject a plan. Either a class that votes to reject a plan or a class that does not accept by the majority required under 11 USC § 1126 is a rejecting class. *See* the discussion above of the voting process. A class containing a single creditor who fails to vote on the plan is deemed to have rejected the plan since there are no positive acceptances.

Confirmation over a rejecting class's vote is known as cramdown in common parlance. It is a series of three unrelated processes that depend upon the type of class that is involved. The provisions are different for secured creditors, unsecured creditors, and interest holders. The process of forcing rejecting creditors or interest holders to abide by the plan of reorganization is complex and involves many difficult factual and legal issues. The process of cramming down a plan on dissenting creditors or secured creditors is probably threatened more often than it is accomplished. Ideally, of course, the debtor, in proposing a plan, will propose a plan that will be confirmable even if it is not accepted by a majority of the creditors. Cash constraints and the need to write off substantial unsecured debt to make the business viable mean that rarely happens, however. Only rarely is the debtor in a position to propose a full payment plan with an appropriate interest rate that is feasible under market circumstances at the time it is proposed. Anything short of that may require cramdown with all the legal and factual problems that entails. The bottom line is that cramdown is more often threatened than accomplished.

ABSOLUTE PRIORITY RULE

A major creditor protection provision is a codification of the court-developed *absolute priority rule* in 11 USC § 1129(b). In its simplest application it bars confirmation of any plan that preserves the ownership of the equity security holders unless all classes of claims have either voted to accept the plan or will be paid in full. A complete analysis and explanation of the complexities of the absolute priority rule is beyond the scope of this text, but one or two examples should assist you in understanding it. Assume that the debtor is a publicly held corporation operating a chain of retail stores. Aggressive expansion left the debtor with substantial trade debt (all unsecured) and a huge bank debt secured by all of the debtor's real estate, inventory and receivables. There are no assets that are not covered by the bank's lien. The secured debt is undersecured because the value of the collateral is less than the debt. Debtor files for relief and proposes a plan to pay the secured debt in full and trade creditors 15 percent of their claims. Equity holders will retain their stock and make no new capital contributions.

Even though the 15 percent is more than they would receive in liquidation, the trade creditors resoundingly reject the plan, and the creditors' committee files an objection to confirmation. The debtor generally cannot cram down the plan over the rejection of the trade debt because the equity security holders' retention of their stock violates the absolute priority rule.

Assume an individual with a professional practice and substantial personal debt files Chapter 11 and a plan proposing to pay 5 percent of claims to the unsecured creditors and retain the practice. The practice is worth less than the proposed total payment to creditors. The creditors reject the plan. It cannot be confirmed over their rejection because the debtor will retain the business.

While cramdown is usually considered a threat that the debtor makes against creditors, there are situations in which interest holders can cram down a plan against a rejecting class of creditors. Some courts allow what has been called the "new value exception" or the "new value corollary" to the absolute priority rule, under which a plan can be confirmed over the objection of a dissenting class if the owners of the company contribute new value to the reorganization effort. This exception to the absolute priority rule is complicated and has been overly simplified for purposes of this discussion. Indeed, it was hoped that the United States Supreme Court would resolve the issue for once and for all in a case decided in the late 1990s (in which the NACM filed a "friend of the court" brief). Unfortunately, that case raised more questions than it answered and creditors cannot know for certain the extent to which they can rely on the protection set out in the absolute priority rule. If you are faced with a cramdown situation, whether your claim is secured or unsecured, you should consult counsel.

POSTCONFIRMATION PROBLEMS

Plan Modification

Naturally, not all plans work exactly as intended. The Code, therefore, permits the modification of a confirmed plan before it is substantially consummated. Only the proponent of a plan can move for postconfirmation modification. Thus, the creditors, unless they proposed and confirmed the plan, are barred from seeking modifications of the plan. The usual issue is whether the plan has been so substantially consummated that it is not amenable to postconfirmation modification. Generally, if the debtor has transferred all property dealt with under the plan to creditors or other entities and has begun payments to creditors pursuant to the terms of the plan, the plan has been substantially consummated and is not subject to modification. Any default must be dealt with as a breach of contract.

Most often, postconfirmation modifications are minor and will be directed toward correcting technical errors in the plan, such as the omission of a secured creditor or dealing with other details relating to transfer of property. Occasionally, however, the debtor or some other proponent will attempt to redo the plan with major changes in payments to creditors, etc., based on poor postconfirmation operating results. The court will consider this type of major modification if the plan has not been substantially consummated. If the plan modification alters the rights of the creditors under the originally confirmed plan, the modification must generally be submitted to creditors for a vote.

Case Dismissal Postconfirmation

Under very limited circumstances, a court may consider dismissal of a case postconfirmation. Again, assuming that the plan has not been substantially consummated, the court has the option of dismissing a bankruptcy case postconfirmation. The court will rarely consider a motion for dismissal postconfirmation, however, because of the difficulties in unraveling the effects of confirmation.

Postconfirmation Conversion

Under certain limited circumstances, the court will consider postconfirmation conversion of the case to Chapter 7. Generally, conversion will follow on the debtor's failure to effectuate substantial consummation of the confirmed plan or a material default by the debtor with respect to a confirmed plan. Some plans provide for the conversion of the case upon the happening of a specified event. Even in these cases, the conversion will require a motion to the court and notice to creditors.

If the debtor has failed to make payments provided under the confirmed plan, you may also consider suing the debtor under the plan in state court to collect your portion of whatever payments have been missed.

Revocation of Confirmation

The Code specifically provides that the court may, within 180 days of the entry of the order for confirmation, revoke confirmation of the plan if, and only if, the order of confirmation was procured by fraud. 11 USC § 1144. Generally, an adversary complaint to revoke the confirmation order must be filed against the debtor or the proponent of the plan. Note that such a motion must be filed within 180 days after the entry of the order of confirmation.

Enforcing the Plan

While a plan may provide for payments over a period of time, there is some question as to where the suit should be filed to enforce payments. The bankruptcy court may retain jurisdiction after confirmation of the plan to resolve adversary proceedings and claims objections, but generally the bankruptcy court's jurisdiction over the case will terminate once substantial consummation is achieved. Prior to that time, at least theoretically, the bankruptcy court has jurisdiction to entertain a suit against the debtor for any missed payments. There is a split in authority as to whether a creditor may sue for the entire outstanding balance on its claim in the event of default on the plan payments and the plan is silent on acceleration of the plan indebtedness in the event of a default. For example, if the creditor holds a claim of $100,000 and the debtor has agreed to pay 15 percent over three years, the courts are divided on whether the debtor's failure to make the first payment renders the entire $15,000 due under the plan collectible. Some courts have held that only the missed payments can be enforced through legal action. Other courts have found that a default in a single payment renders all payments due under the plan.

The courts are generally in agreement that an action to enforce the plan may be brought in state court. Particularly if substantial consummation has been achieved and the bankruptcy court has terminated its jurisdiction, the state court would be the appropriate forum for collection of the plan payments.

SMALL BUSINESS PROVISIONS OF CHAPTER 11

Statistics have shown that a small business cannot survive a Chapter 11 bankruptcy proceeding unless that small business is able to get in and out of the bankruptcy court within a reasonable period of time.

Definition of Small Business

A "small business debtor" is one engaged in commercial or business activities that has aggregate non-insider, non-affiliate, non-contingent liquidated secured and unsecured debts, as of the date of the commencement of the bankruptcy, of not more than $2 million. Formerly, a "small business debtor" could elect to be treated as a small business or elect to operate as a non-small business Chapter 11. That is no longer an option. A debtor who meets the definition of "small business" must proceed as a "small business". The only exception will be if a creditors' committee is appointed, then the debtor is removed from the definition of "small business."

Duties of a Small Business Debtor

The BAPCPA mandates additional duties for a debtor and a trustee. It remains to be seen whether or not these new duties will result in an orderly use of the Small Business provisions of the legislation or whether the additional duties will, in and of themselves, become a burden that cannot be fulfilled. The additional requirements for a small business debtor are that:

(i)   the most recent balance sheet, statement of operations, cash-flow statement and federal income tax return must be filed with a voluntary Chapter 11 petition. Alternatively, a statement under penalty of perjury must be filed stating that no balance sheet, statement of operations, or cash-flow statement has been prepared and no federal income tax return has been filed;

(ii) the debtor must attend meetings scheduled by the court or the United States Trustee, including the initial debtor interview, the meeting of creditors, and scheduling conferences, unless the court, after notice and hearing, waives this requirement;

(iii) the debtor timely file all schedules and statements of financial affairs, unless the court grants an extension of not more than 30 days, absent extraordinary and compelling circumstances;

(iv) the debtor file all postpetition financial and other reports required by the Bankruptcy Rules or local rules;

(v)   the debtor maintain insurance customary and appropriate to the debtor's industry;

(vi)　the debtor timely file tax returns and other required government filings;

(vii)　the debtor timely pay all taxes except those being appropriately contested; and

(viii)　the debtor allow the United States Trustee, or a designated representative to inspect the debtor's premises, books and records at reasonable times and upon reasonable notice.

The BAPCPA has also instituted supplemental reporting requirements for small business debtors. A small business debtor will now be required to file periodic financial and other reports containing information that includes: (i) the debtor's profitability; (ii) the debtor's projected cash receipts and disbursements over a reasonable period; and (iii) comparisons of actual cash receipts and disbursements with projections in prior reports. The small business debtor must also state in the report whether it is in compliance with all applicable bankruptcy laws and whether it is timely filing tax returns and required government filings. Additionally, the small business debtor must report if it is timely paying taxes and other administrative expenses when due.

If the small business debtor is not timely making required government filings and/or not making tax and other administrative payments when due, the debtor must report what the failures are and how, at what cost, and when the debtor intends to remedy such failures. The effective date of this provision is 60 days after the date of promulgation of the Bankruptcy Rules required under this provision.

Flexible Rules for Disclosure Statement and Plan

The BAPCPA requires that when the bankruptcy court considers a debtor's disclosure statement, it must take into account the complexity of the case, the benefit of additional information to creditors and other parties in interest, and the cost associated with providing any additional information (This also applies in all other Chapter 11s). This section also allows the bankruptcy court to dispense with the requirement of a disclosure statement altogether in cases in which: (i) the debtor is classified as a small business and; (ii) when the debtor's plan itself provides enough adequate information. In a small business case, a court can approve a disclosure statement that has been submitted on standard forms approved by the court or adopted under 28 USC 2075.

Standard Form Disclosure Statement and Plan

It is the intent of the legislation that an official form disclosure statement and plan of reorganization for small business debtors will be created to achieve a practical balance between:

(i)　the reasonable needs of the courts, the United States Trustee, creditors, and other parties in interest for reasonably complete information; and

(ii)　economy and simplicity for debtors.

Small Business Plan Filing and Confirmation Deadlines

The BAPCPA provides that a small business debtor has the exclusive right to file a plan for the first 180 days following the order for relief. This period may be extended after a notice of hearing if: (i) the debtor demonstrates by a preponderance of the evidence that it is more likely than not that the court will confirm a plan within a reasonable period of time; (ii) a new deadline is imposed at the time the extension is granted; and (iii) the order extending the time is signed before expiration of the existing deadline. Alternatively, the 180-day period may be extended if the court so orders "for cause", an easier standard. The amendment further requires that a small business debtor must file a plan and a disclosure statement (if any) within 300 days of the order for relief, subject to extension only if the small business debtor satisfies the tougher requirements contained in (i), (ii) and (iii) above. The passage of these deadlines would result in the debtor's inability to confirm a plan and be grounds for conversion of the case to Chapter 7 or dismissal.

PLAN CONFIRMATION DEADLINE

The court must confirm a plan in a small business case not later than 45 days from the date the plan is filed, provided the plan complies with all applicable provisions of the Bankruptcy Code. This 45-day period may only be extended if: (i) the debtor demonstrates by a preponderance of the evidence that it is more likely than not that the court will confirm a plan within a reasonable period of time; (ii) a new deadline is imposed at the time the extension is granted; and (iii) the order extending the time is signed before the existing deadline expires.

SERIAL "SMALL BUSINESS" FILERS AND THE AUTOMATIC STAY

The BAPCPA has added a new subsection (n) to Bankruptcy Code Section 362 (the automatic stay section) applicable only to small business cases. The amendment provides the automatic stay does not apply in a case in which the debtor: (i) is a debtor in a small business case; (ii) was a debtor in a small business case that was dismissed by an order that became final in the two-year period ending on the commencement of the current bankruptcy case; (iii) was a debtor in a small business case in which a plan was confirmed in the two-year period ending on the commencement date of the current bankruptcy case; or (iv) is an entity that acquired substantially all the assets or business of a small business debtor described in (i) through (iii), above, unless the entity can establish that it acquired substantially all of such assets or such business in good faith.

However, the new subsection (n) does not apply to an involuntary bankruptcy filing where there was no collusion between the debtor and petitioning creditors, or where the debtor can prove: (i) the filing of the petition resulted from circumstances beyond the control of the debtor not foreseeable at the time the case then pending was filed; and (ii) it is more likely than not that the court will confirm a feasible plan, but not a liquidating plan, within a reasonable period of time.

BASICS OF CHAPTER 12

Overview

In the mid-1980s, the farm economy in this country was under a great deal of financial stress. Many farmers and farm lenders were facing bankruptcy or insolvency of one kind or another. Chapter 11 did not work very well to reorganize farmers because of the absolute priority rule (discussed above) and the general complexity of the process. Moreover, the disclosure requirements of Chapter 11 were generally too cumbersome for the individual farmer.

As a result of pressure from various farm groups, Congress adopted Chapter 12 of the Bankruptcy Code in 1986, providing special provisions relating to the reorganization of family farmers. Chapter 12 shares some elements of Chapter 11 and Chapter 13. Although originally intended as a temporary measure for family farmers, the BAPCPA has expanded the provisions of Chapter 12 and is now a permanent part of the Bankruptcy Code.

Eligibility

Eligibility for Chapter 12 has been expanded to include family fisherman in addition to family farmers, yet there are clear distinctions between these two types of Chapter 12 entities.

Definition of Family Farmer and Monetary Requirements. A "family farmer" is defined as an individual or individual and spouse engaged in a farming operation whose aggregate debts do not exceed $3,237,000 and not less than 50 percent of whose aggregate noncontingent, liquidated debts (excluding a debt for the principal residence of such individual or such individual and spouse unless such debt arises out of a farming operation), on the date the case is filed, arise out of a farming operation owned or operated by such individual or such individual and spouse, and such individual or such individual and spouse receive from such farming operation more than 50 percent of such individual's or such individual and spouse's gross income for:

    (i)   the taxable year preceding; or

    (ii) each of the 2d and 3d taxable years preceding; the taxable year in which the case concerning such individual or such individual and spouse was filed; or

  (B) corporation or partnership in which more than 50 percent of the outstanding stock or equity is held by one family, or by one family and the relatives of the members of such family, and such family or such relatives conduct the farming operation, and

    (i)   more than 80 percent of the value of its assets consists of assets related to the farming operation;

    (ii) its aggregate debts do not exceed $3,237,000 and not less than 50 percent of its aggregate noncontingent, liquidated debts (excluding a debt for one dwelling which is owned by such corporation or partnership and which a shareholder or partner maintains as a principal residence, unless such debt arises out of a farming operation), on the date the case is filed, arise out of the farming operation owned or operated by such corporation or such partnership; and

    (iii) if such corporation issues stock, such stock is not publicly traded

These debt limits will be increased periodically based on the Consumer Price Index.

Definition of Farming Operation. The term "farming operation" includes farming, tillage of the soil, dairy farming, ranching, production or raising of crops, poultry, or livestock, and production of poultry or livestock products in an unmanufactured state.

Definition of Family Fisherman and Monetary Limits. "Family fisherman" means –

  (A) an individual or individual and spouse engaged in a commercial fishing operation –

    (i)   whose aggregate debts do not exceed $1,500,000 and not less than 80 percent of whose aggregate noncontingent, liquidated debts (excluding a debt for the principal residence of such individual or such individual and spouse, unless such debt arises out of a commercial fishing operation), on the date the case is filed, arise out of a commercial fishing operation owned or operated by such individual or such individual and spouse; and

    (ii) who receive from such commercial fishing operation more than 50 percent of such individual's or such individual's and spouse's gross income for the taxable year preceding the taxable year in which the case concerning such individual or such individual and spouse was filed.

Similar provisions are included for partnerships and corporations. It is interesting to note that the family fisherman definitions and debt structure are more in line with the original family farmer provisions rather than in conformity with the new modifications to the family farmer definitions and debt structure.

"Commercial fishing operation" means

(A) the catching or harvesting of fish, shrimp, lobsters, urchins, seaweed, shellfish, or other, aquatic species, or products of such species; or

(B) ...aquaculture activities consisting of raising for market any species or product described in subparagraph (A)

"Commercial fishing vessel" means a vessel by a family to carry out a commercial fishing operation

Commencement of the Chapter 12 Case

Chapter 12 is commenced by the filing of a voluntary petition for relief with the bankruptcy court and the payment of the requisite filing fee. An individual, referred to as the standing trustee, is appointed in each Chapter 12 to act as the disbursing agent for payments under the plan. The trustee is paid a fee from the payments to creditors.

The Plan

In order to accelerate the operation of Chapter 12, the Code requires that a Chapter 12 plan be filed no more than 90 days after the filing of the petition for relief. While the court can extend that 90-day deadline, the extension generally occurs only if there is substantial progress toward the formulation of a plan. The extension of the deadline is the exception rather than the rule. Only the debtor may file a plan.

Like a Chapter 11 plan, a Chapter 12 plan must classify creditors and provide for their treatment. Compared to most Chapter 11 plans, Chapter 12 plans are relatively simple and straightforward with a single unsecured class and separate classes for each secured creditor. You should carefully review the classification and treatment of your claim under the plan.

Filing a Proof of Claim

All creditors must file a proof of claim, irrespective of being scheduled by the debtor. The proof of claim must be filed not later than 90 days after the first date for the meeting of creditors as initially set by the court or the office of the United States

Trustee. Other than as contained in the notice of the meeting of creditors, there may be no other notice to creditors warning creditors of the deadline for the filing of proofs of claim.

Trade Creditors' Primary Concerns about Chapter 12 Confirmation

The requirements for confirmation of a Chapter 12 are similar to those in a Chapter 11 proceeding, but with some specific distinctions. Among the requisites for plan confirmation is that the amount to be distributed under the plan on account of each allowed unsecured claim is not less than the amount that would be paid on such claim if the estate were liquidated under Chapter 7. Further, the debtor must show that it will be able to make all payments under the plan and to comply with all other aspects of the plan.

A trade creditor may object to confirmation of a Chapter 12 plan. If a trade creditor or the trustee objects, then the debtor can only confirm a plan if:

(A) the value of the property to be distributed under the plan on account of such objecting creditor is not less than the amount of the claim;

(B) the plan provides that all of the debtor's projected disposable income to be received in a three-year period (or longer period if approved by the court) will be applied to make payments under the plan; or

(C) the value of the property to be distributed under the plan in the three-year period (or longer period if approved by the court) is not less than the debtor's disposable income for that period.

Discharge

A Chapter 12 debtor will be granted a discharge only after all amounts payable under the plan have been made.

The court will not grant a discharge if there is pending any proceeding in which the debtor may be found guilty of specific felonies or liable for specific debts defined in section 522 of the Bankruptcy Code.

BASICS OF CHAPTER 13

Overview

Chapter 13 is denominated "Adjustments of Debts of an Individual with Regular Income" and affords a means of reorganizing the debts of an individual who has regular income from one or more sources, regardless of employment. From a trade creditor's point of view, the likelihood that you will become involved in many Chapter 13s increased when Congress raised the debt limits from $100,000 in unsecured debt and $300,000 in secured debt to an increasing scale of debts, subject to periodic adjustment. Currently, the debt limits are $307,675 for unsecured debts and $922,975 for secured debts. Chapter 13 affords an individual employee, a professional, or a business owner an opportunity to reorganize debts through a plan that classifies and provides for treatment of claims. As in a reorganization case, your primary concern will be monitoring the filing and provisions of the plan for repayment and discharge of the indebtedness.

Eligibility

The Bankruptcy Code places three limitations on eligibility for relief under Chapter 13. First, a debtor must be an *individual*; thus, partnerships, corporations, and other business entities are not eligible for Chapter 13 relief. Second, the individual must have regular income. The income may be derived from such varied sources as wages, the operation of a business, or may come from social security or welfare. Finally, the debtor's indebtedness may not exceed the secured debt and unsecured debt limits as they are periodically adjusted. The first two tests are rarely at issue: (1) whether or not the debtor is an individual, and (2) whether or not the income is sufficiently regular to qualify. If a debt is genuinely contingent or disputed, it is not included in the calculation of the debt total subject to the limit. Debtors, however, often overlook the unsecured portion of a secured claim. For example, if a debtor's homestead has a value of $300,000, but has a $600,000 mortgage against it, there is a $300,000 secured claim and a $300,000 unsecured claim, both held by the mortgagee. Overlooking the unsecured portion of the mortgagee's claim may lead to miscalculating the debt total and may render the debtor ineligible.

Generally, the standing trustee appointed to administer the case will raise the issue of the debt limits or computations.

Summary of a Typical Case

A typical case is commenced by the filing of a Chapter 13 petition with the Bankruptcy Court in the district in which the debtor resides and the payment of the requisite filing fee. The debtor must file a plan for dealing with the debts with the petition. However, if no plan is filed with the petition, the debtor is given 15 days to file a plan. Failure to file a plan by the 15 days deadline will subject the Chapter 13 debtor to a motion to dismiss its petition.

Upon filing, the case is referred to the standing trustee, who is appointed by the United States Trustee to handle Chapter 13s in a particular location. The standing trustee's responsibilities are primarily to collect the money paid in by the debtor and disburse it to creditors in accordance with a confirmed plan. The trustee is paid a percentage, established by the United States Trustee, of the disbursements to creditors. The fee, however, may not exceed five percent of disbursements. A standing trustee should be able to answer questions about the status of the case and provide you with a summary of any payments and other disbursements made by the trustee. The standing trustee presides at the § 341 meeting in Chapter 13 cases and generally makes recommendations to the court concerning confirmation. Rarely will the court confirm a plan if the trustee opposes it.

The standing trustee is also responsible for objecting to claims and other administrative aspects of the case and may, on occasion, bring preference or lien avoidance actions where appropriate.

Filing a Proof of Claim

All creditors must file a proof of claim, irrespective of being scheduled by the debtor. The proof of claim must be filed not later than 90 days after the first date for the meeting of creditors as initially set by the court or the office of the United States Trustee. Other than as contained in the notice of the meeting of creditors, there may be no other notice to creditors warning creditors of the deadline for the filing of proofs of claim.

The Plan

Generally, a plan is filed with the petition for relief under Chapter 13. If the debtor fails to file a plan, the standing trustee will move to dismiss the case.

As in Chapter 11, the plan must classify creditors and provide for their treatment. The rules on classification and treatment of creditors that apply in Chapter 11 also apply in Chapter 13. Although the rules for a Chapter 13 plan have been less complicated than those in Chapter 11, the BAPCPA has put into place specific requirements with respect to the length of payments under a Chapter 13 plan and with respect to an in-depth examination into the Chapter 13 debtor's current monthly income.

A typical Chapter 13 plan will provide for one or two classes of secured creditors, usually the mortgage on the debtor's homestead and the security interest on the debtor's vehicle. Chapter 13 specifically permits the debtor to provide special treatment for certain consumer claims secured by guarantees of relatives. The plan may also provide for a special class of creditors whose continued cooperation is essential to the performance of the Chapter 13 plan.

Since a Chapter 13 plan may provide for the cure of any *monetary* default on a homestead mortgage or other secured debt, Chapter 13 is particularly useful in those states which have creditor-oriented foreclosure systems permitting the creditor to sell the homestead or other property on very short notice. However, any default must be cured within a "reasonable" period of time. Thus, if the debtor is six months delinquent on house payments, the court will generally require that the default be cured within six months to one year. The typical Chapter 13 plan will also provide for payments to the creditor for both the prepetition default and for postpetition payments under the contract. If the creditor has already repossessed the collateral, the bankruptcy court can order the property turned over to the debtor in return for payments under the Chapter 13 plan.

With the new criteria for determining the debtor's disposable income under BAPCPA, it is more likely that unsecured creditors will receive distributions in a Chapter 13 proceeding, especially where the debtor is a business owner.

Chapter 13 sets forth substantial requirements for what must be included in the Chapter 13 plan and additional requirements for those things that may be included in the Chapter 13 plan.

Among other things, the Chapter 13 plan must provide for the submission of all of the debtor's future earnings or future income to the supervision and control of the trustee as is necessary for the execution of the plan. The plan must provide either for full payment to all priority claims or—if less than full payment is proposed—the debtor must contribute all its disposable income for a five-year period in order to make its payments under the plan.

The BAPCPA sets forth criteria based on the current monthly income of the debtor and the debtor's spouse, which combined, the court can determine whether the debtor will be provided with three years to pay its debts or whether the debtor will be permitted five years to pay its debts.

The BAPCPA has imposed special notice provisions that a Chapter 13 trustee must give to any holder of a claim for a domestic support obligation so that full information and protection is provided to that holder of such claim.

A creditor must file a claim in a Chapter 13 case to participate in any distribution under the plan. A debtor will get a windfall if creditors fail to file claims. However, the creditors who do file claims may be paid more of their allowed claim if the debtor is making a fixed monthly payment to the trustee for distribution pro rata among creditors.

Confirmation

The court must hold a confirmation hearing on the plan and any creditor may object to confirmation. The hearing on confirmation may be held not earlier than 20 days and not later than 45 days after the meeting of creditors under section 341(a), unless the court determines that it would be in the best interests of the creditors and the estate to hold such hearing at an earlier date and there is no objection to such earlier date. This is a change made by the BAPCPA.

There are new requirements for confirmation of a plan under the BAPCPA. There are nine requirements for confirmation if no objection to confirmation has been filed. A review by creditor with its counsel should be made of the complete details of these nine requirements when the creditor is faced with a Chapter 13 confirmation hearing. Succinctly stated, the nine requirements are:

1. The plan complies with the Chapter 13 provisions and all other provisions of the Bankruptcy Code
2. Any fee, charge or amount required has been paid
3. The plan has been proposed in good faith and not by any means forbidden by law
4. The value, as of the effective date of the plan, of property to be distributed to each allowed unsecured claim is not less than such claim would receive in a Chapter 7 liquidation
5. With respect to each allowed secured claim, the holder of that secured claim has accepted the plan, retains the lien securing the claim until payment of the debt or discharge, or if the case is dismissed or converted, the secured claim retains the lien. There are additional provisions for secured claims
6. The debtor will be able to make all its plan payments
7. The Chapter 13 petition was filed in good faith
8. All domestic support obligations that arose after the filing of the Chapter 13 petition have been paid
9. All applicable Federal, State and local tax returns have been filed

If an unsecured claimant objects to confirmation, the court may not approve the plan unless:

(A) the value of property to be distributed under the plan is not less than the amount of such claim; or
(B) the plan provides that all of the debtor's projected disposable income to be received during the applicable commitment period of the plan will be applied to make payments to unsecured creditors under the plan.

There are further details to these requirements that should be reviewed by a creditor with its counsel if involved in a Chapter 13 proceeding.

Scope of Discharge

The discharge in Chapter 13, is granted only after the debtor has completed all payments required under the plan. The court may grant a discharge before all plan payments are made only if the failure to complete payments is due to circumstances beyond the control of the debtor and each unsecured claim has received what they would have gotten in a Chapter 7 liquidation, and it is not practicable to modify the Chapter 13 plan.

The BAPCPA has added circumstances under which a discharge shall not be granted. The court shall not granted a discharge if the Chapter 13 debtor has received a discharge:

(1) in a case filed under Chapter 7, 11 or 12 of the Bankruptcy Code during the four-year period preceding the date of the order for relief under this chapter, or

(2) in a case filed under Chapter 13 of the Bankruptcy Code during the two-year period preceding the date of such order.

Further, in order to receive a discharge, the Chapter 13 debtor must complete an instructional course concerning personal financial management (unless the United States Trustee or bankruptcy administrator determines that no such course in their district is adequate).

Finally, the court may not grant a discharge unless notice and a hearing is held if there is reasonable cause to believe that the debtor may be found guilty of certain felonies.

ESTABLISHING A SYSTEMATIC RESPONSE
TO BANKRUPTCY FILINGS

New BAPCPA Notice Provision

The BAPCPA has amended Section 342 of the Bankruptcy Code to expand the notice requirements a debtor has to satisfy in order for the notice to be effective against its creditors. Any notice the debtor is required to provide must contain the name, address and last four digits of the debtor's taxpayer identification number. Any notice that relates to an amendment of the debtor's schedules to add a creditor must contain the debtor's full taxpayer identification number.

Also, where a creditor sends at least two communications to the debtor, containing the debtor's account number and the address at which the creditor wants to receive correspondence from the debtor, within 90 days before the debtor's bankruptcy filing, the debtor is required to send notices containing the debtor's account number to the creditor at the specified address. Any non-complying notice will not be effective until it is brought to the creditor's attention. Where the creditor has established reasonable internal procedures for dealing with bankruptcy notices, the debtor's notice will not be deemed to have been brought to the creditor's attention until receipt by the person in or subdivision designated in the creditor's procedures to receive notice.

A creditor will not be penalized for violating the automatic stay for conduct prior to the creditor's receipt of effective notice of the bankruptcy in accordance with the above-described procedures.

Internal Routing of Bankruptcy Notices

Bankruptcy often involves a number of deadlines for the taking of action or the filing of objections. For example, if a Chapter 11 debtor in possession seeks to sell assets other than in the ordinary course of business, notice must be given to creditors and creditors are given an opportunity to object. If no timely objections are filed, the debtor may go ahead with the sale without further notice.

It is absolutely essential, therefore, that you establish an internal routing system for handling all bankruptcy notices that will get them to the proper decision maker in time to file objections or otherwise respond.

Receipt and Routing of Notices

An internal response system should get the notice from the bankruptcy court matched up with the appropriate file and to the decision maker as soon as possible. Because many of the deadlines are relatively short, you may need to file a change of address form with the bankruptcy court and give notice to the debtor or trustee if notices are being mailed to a lockbox or other office where rerouting may involve unnecessary delay.

Copies should be routed to your sales department with instructions on the effect of the bankruptcy filing on existing credit limits and any need for consultation on postpetition sales. We have seen situations in which the credit department of a particular creditor is opposing the debtor in the bankruptcy court while the sales department, apparently unaware of the bankruptcy filing, is selling goods to the debtor postpetition on credit. Special instructions should, therefore, be prepared on dealing with bankruptcy notices and routing them to all departments that may be affected by the bankruptcy filing.

The credit manager, or other officer that makes decisions on bankruptcy cases, must receive the notice as soon as possible and note deadlines for the meeting of creditors, the meeting of the creditors' committee, filing of a proof of claim, and any objections to sales of assets, use of cash collateral, etc.

A separate system should be established to deal with adversary proceedings, which are lawsuits filed within a bankruptcy case, because the debtor or some other party in the bankruptcy case could sue your company. These will almost always involve reference to counsel. Most adversaries will require the filing of an answer within a specified period of time after service and, therefore, require prompt handling. Since an adversary proceeding may be served by mail or in person, special instructions for routing any legal documents mailed or personally served on the company should be established.

While your particular response to a bankruptcy filing will vary according to the location of the filing, the amount of your claim, and any postpetition relationship with the debtor, you should prepare specific written policies on reviewing existing credit lines, reviewing goods in transit and reviewing any other relationships with the debtor in bankruptcy. In particular, you will need to review what actions you are permitted to take to recover or reclaim goods in transit or recently delivered to the debtor on credit. *See* the discussion of UCC 2-702 and 11 USC § 546 and the rights of reclaiming sellers in Chapter 15.

Education of Sales and Other Contact Personnel

Your bankruptcy system should include a periodic review with the sales and other staff members who have direct contact with a customer of the need to watch for bankruptcy danger signs and what actions to take upon learning of the bankruptcy filing. While you will, of course, develop your own early warning system for anticipating potential bankruptcy problems, your sales and other contact staff people may prove invaluable in avoiding losses. They should, however, be given at least a rudimentary knowledge of the bankruptcy process and, in particular, any limits you will place on postpetition credit sales to the debtor.

Alerting Lockbox Users

If you are using a lockbox system to handle receivables, it may be the only address that the debtor has to mail you notice. Thus, it is imperative for you to establish procedures for the staff that deals with receipts at the lockbox address for handling bankruptcy notices. The staff should contact you *immediately* by phone or fax upon receipt of any bankruptcy notices so that you can take action to protect your position and to be sure you do not run afoul of the automatic stay. If the bankruptcy court has been given the lockbox address as your address, you should immediately file a change of address with the court and with the debtor or trustee so that notices will be routed directly to decision makers.

FILING A PROOF OF CLAIM

Need for Filing

In cases under Chapters 7, 12 and 13, the filing of a proof of claim is required to participate in any distribution of the bankruptcy estate assets to unsecured creditors. A claim is deemed allowed once it is filed unless the trustee, the debtor in possession, or someone else granted standing under the Bankruptcy Code objects to it.

In a Chapter 11 case, a claim is *deemed* to be filed for any claim or interest that the debtor correctly lists in the schedules without indicating that the claim is disputed, contingent or unliquidated. 11 USC § 1111(a). To determine whether it will be necessary to file a proof of claim in a Chapter 11 case, you should carefully review the debtor's listing of your claim in the schedules. If the amount listed is incorrect or the claim is listed as disputed, contingent or unliquidated, you *must* file a proof of claim. If you file a proof of claim in a Chapter 11 case and your claim is scheduled, the filed claim will simply supersede the scheduled claim. Fed. R. Bankr. P. 3003(c)(4). Before filing the proof of claim, you should discuss the case with counsel as filing a claim may subject you to the jurisdiction of the bankruptcy court and waive any right you have to a jury trial on any claim the debtor may make against you.

Section § 506 of the Code determines whether a claim is to be treated as a secured claim, and if so, to what extent. If you have a lien on the debtor's property, you have a secured claim up to the value of your collateral. For example, if you have a claim for $10,000 and the value of the inventory securing the debt is worth $15,000, you have a fully secured claim. If, on the other hand, your claim is for $10,000 and the collateral is worth only $7,500, your secured claim is for $7,500. The remaining $2,500 is an unsecured claim.

Terminology

Technically, any document filed with the bankruptcy court that is intended to set forth your rights to payment of a debt may be considered proof of claim. The document is often referred to as simply a "claim." While some courts have recognized "informal" claims such as letters to the court, you should timely file a proof of claim on the official form to avoid problems.

Deadlines

To be effective, your proof of claim must be *timely* filed with the appropriate bankruptcy court. Federal Rules of Bankruptcy Procedure Rule 3002 establishes the deadlines for the filing of all claims under Chapters 7, 11, 12 and 13. To be considered in a Chapter 7, 11, 12 or 13 case, the proof of claim must be received by the court in which the bankruptcy case is pending on or before the last day for filing claims. Actual receipt is essential; merely mailing it to the court before the date will not suffice. Generally, the original notice of the bankruptcy filing sets out the deadlines for filing a proof of claim. Unless the court establishes other deadlines, the Federal Rules of Bankruptcy Procedure establish the following:

CHAPTER 7

Federal Rules of Bankruptcy Procedures Rule 3002 provides that all claims must be filed within 90 days of the first date set for the § 341 meeting. However, the initial Notice of Commencement, the document that advises you of the filing of the bankruptcy case, will often instruct you *not* to file a proof of claim until the court otherwise advises you. This is because so few Chapter 7 cases result in any distribution to creditors. If the trustee discovers that there are assets available for distribution, you will receive instructions to file a proof of claim along with the deadline for doing so.

CHAPTER 11

Federal Rule of Bankruptcy Procedure Rule 3003(c) grants the Bankruptcy Court the authority to establish a deadline. In some districts, it is customary for the deadline to be established immediately upon the filing of the petition. In other districts, the court will establish and separately notice any deadline. You should review all notices.

CHAPTER 12

As in Chapter 7, Rule 3002(c) provides that all claims must be filed within 90 days of the first date set for the § 341 meeting.

CHAPTER 13

All proofs of claim must be filed within 90 days after the first date set for the § 341 meeting. Again, the deadline is determined by the original date of the § 341 meeting and will not be extended should the § 341 meeting is be rescheduled.

Calculation of Time and Extensions

As stated earlier, the 90 days are calculated from the date the § 341 meeting was initially scheduled and include all calendar days including holidays, Saturdays and Sundays. However, if the 90th day falls on a holiday or weekend day, the next workday is the deadline. For example, the 90th day after the § 341 meeting falls on a Saturday. If the proof of claim form reaches the bankruptcy court by the following Monday, it is timely filed. In a limited number of circumstances in Chapter 11 cases, a late filed claim will be treated as timely if the claim's lateness is due to *excusable neglect*. However, excusable neglect is hard to prove and if you discover you have missed the deadline, consult counsel about whether to file a late claim. The bankruptcy court may extend the deadline for the filing of a proof of claim if a motion requesting the extension is filed *before* the expiration of the original deadline.

Official Proof of Claim Form

Over the last several years the Official Bankruptcy Forms have been under review with an eye toward simplification and clarification. Official Form 10 (Form B10) should be used to file proofs of claim in all cases. Although it is extremely rare for a court to disallow a proof of claim filed on something other than the official form, you should use the latest form included in the proposed Interim Bankruptcy Rules.

GENERAL COMMENT

Not all claims need be on official forms. Virtually any writing, which sets out an enforceable claim against the debtor that is served on the trustee or filed with the court, may be deemed an informal claim. Generally, all it must do is set out that the debtor is somehow indebted to the writer. Filing a letter to the court or trustee may suffice, but there is always some risk that the court will disallow the informal claim. The timely use of Official Form 10 is recommended. Official Form 10 is available at any Bankruptcy Court Clerk's office. Additionally, this form can be found online at www.uscourts.gov/rules/new_and_revised_official_forms.html. If however, you corresponded with the trustee about your claim, but failed to file a formal claim on the official form, consult counsel about the possibility that the correspondence constitutes an informal, but timely claim.

An official claim form may be obtained from the Clerk of the Bankruptcy Court or any office supply company. You may program a computer to prepare the form. Any form used should, however, be identical to the official form. Claims should be prepared in duplicate and signed by an officer or attorney of the company. You should also provide additional copies of the proof of claim to the Clerk's Office with a request that the clerk return at least one filed stamped copy. Be sure to include a self-addressed, stamped envelope. Because of the tremendous caseload in most courts, a proof of claim may be lost or misfiled. Retaining a file stamped copy will eliminate any potential problems if your proof of claim is later missing.

FILLING OUT FORM 10

Identity of the Bankruptcy Court

In the top lefthand corner of the form you will fill in the name of the court in which the case is pending. The form reads, "United States Bankruptcy Court _____ District of _____." The notice will identify the court as the "Northern District of Florida" or the "District of Kansas." Some states are divided into more than one district and the district in which the case is filed should be identified. While some districts are further divided into divisions, it is not necessary to identify the division, however, you should be sure to send the proof of claim to the correct office. Note, in some of the larger cases, the court appoints a claims administrator. In those instances, follow the instructions received as to where to file the claim.

Name of the Debtor

The name of the debtor should be taken from the bankruptcy notice. Usually, this includes the debtor's full name. It is not necessary to include aliases or d/b/a names.

If the court includes a Social Security or tax identification number in the caption, be sure to include it in your proof of claim.

Bankruptcy Case Number

The form also requires you to insert the bankruptcy case number. This number will be set out in the notice you receive. Given the tremendous number of cases filed, it is imperative that you give the correct number. If the case number is not accurately listed, your proof of claim may be filed in the wrong case and never seen again. Both the debtor's name and the case number should be carefully checked and should appear on all correspondence with the court or the trustee.

Creditor Information

The next portion of Official Form 10 requires you to insert your name and address. Where indicated, you will insert the full legal name of the company. Directly below that you will indicate where you want notices to be sent. If you want them sent to you, insert your street address or post office box number. Use the address that will deliver further correspondence to the decision maker most quickly. Never use a lockbox if it is controlled by your bank. You can also designate someone else to receive notices, such as your attorney, in this box, but be sure to include that person's name. In the space provided, insert the telephone number of the person designated to receive notices or responsible for the file.

Immediately below the name and address blocks insert the last four digits of the account number, loan, credit card or other identification number used in connection with the particular debtor. If you have no identifying number for the debtor, insert the word "None."

To the right of the name and address block, you are asked to provide the court with some additional information. The first box asks you if you are aware of anyone else filing a proof of claim relating to your claim. If you check this box, you must provide a copy of the claim or a statement giving the particulars. The second box asks whether you received a notice from the bankruptcy court. If you did not receive notice directly from the court, check the second box. For example, if you file the claim after informally learning of the case from the newspaper, check the second box. You should check the third box if the address you provided to the left is in any way different from the address contained in the notice sent to you from the court. The purpose of the last two boxes is to ensure that you are properly listed on the case mailing matrix so that you receive all subsequent notices.

The final portion of the claim form requesting creditor information asks you to indicate whether this particular claim is an amendment or replacement of a claim you previously filed. For example, if you previously filed a claim listing collateral, and have now recovered and liquidated that collateral, you should check the box stating that this is an amended claim. If you are amending a claim because the amount due has been adjusted, that information should be provided. If, on the other hand, you are filing additional documentation, you should check the "Replaces" box because the proof of claim is replacing the earlier claim. You must provide the date that the previous claim was *filed* with the court. This may require you to obtain a copy of the earlier claim.

Claim Information

- Section 1 of the form asks you to indicate the basis for your claim. There are eight choices: (1) goods sold; (2) services performed; (3) money loaned; (4) personal injury/wrongful death; (5) taxes; (6) retiree benefits as defined in 11 USC § 1114(a); (7) wage, salary, and compensation; or (8) other. Your claim will probably fit within the first three possibilities. If the basis for your claim does not fit within any of the specific boxes, check "Other" and describe the legal basis for your claim against the debtor briefly in the blank provided.
- Section 2 asks you to indicate the date the debt was incurred. This would be the date a promissory note was filed or the date of the last invoice or statement sent to the debtor. Multiple invoices can be totaled and included in a single proof of claim.
- If your claim is based on a court judgment, section 3 asks you to provide the date the judgment was entered.
- In section 4, you must classify your claim. Claims are grouped into three classifications: (1) secured; (2) unsecured priority; and (3) unsecured nonpriority. If you have a security interest in property of the debtor and the value of the collateral securing your loan is greater than the amount of your claim, you have a fully secured claim and may be entitled to include postpetition interest and fees in your claim. If, on the other hand, the value of the collateral securing your claim is worth less than the amount of your claim, your claim will be a secured claim only up to the value of the collateral. The remainder of your claim will be an unsecured, nonpriority claim. For example, if your claim is $10,000, but the collateral is only worth $7,000, you have a secured claim for $7,000 and an unsecured, nonpriority claim for $3,000. In determining the amount of your claim be sure to deduct any precomputed interest.
- The Bankruptcy Code gives certain types of unsecured claims a priority over others. These claims include claims for wages, salary or commissions contributions to employee benefit plans, and taxes. *See* 11 USC § 507. All other types of unsecured claims are nonpriority, unsecured claims. Rarely will a trade claim be entitled to priority.
- Section 5 asks you to set forth the unsecured, secured and priority portions of your claim.
- Section 6 is a statement that all payments on this claim have been credited and deducted for purposes of making a claim
- Section 7 is the Documentation section. It is imperative that you attach copies, not the originals, of all supporting documentation to the proof of claim. These copies must be legible and clear and attached to all copies of the proof of claim filed with the court. Failure to provide legible copies might result in the trustee or the debtor in possession challenging your claim. By providing the necessary documentation, you can save yourself the time and money needed to defend a challenge to your claim.
- Section 8 advises you to enclose a stamped, self-addressed envelope and copy of your claim in order to receive an acknowledgment of the filing of said claim. Some Courts require that you file at least two copies of your proof of claim. To determine the number of copies that must be filed, check the local rules for the district in which the case is pending. When in doubt, send at least three copies: two for the court and one for return for your file.

To protect yourself against the misfiling of the original, provide the court with at least one extra copy of your proof of claim with a self-addressed, stamped envelope and ask the court to return a file stamped copy.

Electronic Filing

You should also check with the court on whether electronic filing of your claim is required.

Certification

At the bottom of the claim, you must sign your name and give your title. You must also date your signature. If for some reason you are signing under a power of attorney, you must attach a copy of that power of attorney.

OBJECTIONS TO PROOFS OF CLAIMS

General Comment

The trustee in bankruptcy in Chapters 7, 11 and 13, and the debtor in possession under Chapter 11 are statutorily responsible for reviewing claims, to determine whether the claims are proper claims against the estate. A properly executed and filed claim is *prima facie* evidence of the validity and amount of the claim. Fed. R. Bankr. P. 3001(f).

Objections range from a simple objection on the grounds that the claim lacks the necessary documentation to a full-blown lawsuit. By far the most common objections are based on a lack of documentation or an assertion that, based on the documentation provided, the debtor is not liable for the claim. These objections are often simply communication problems, and providing the trustee or debtor in possession with the requested documentation will resolve the matter. Failing to attach the required documents to your proof of claim will almost guarantee such an objection.

Another routine objection involves the inclusion of precomputed interest or postpetition interest in a claim. For example, the debtor files bankruptcy on January 1, but the proof of claim indicates that interest is computed through February 1, the date the claim was filed. Postpetition interest is generally not allowed and almost never on unsecured claims. Therefore, if your claim includes interest accrued after the bankruptcy case was filed, an objection will likely be made. Failure to timely file the proof of claim will certainly result in an objection that will be sustained unless your claim is scheduled in the correct amount and not listed as disputed, contingent and unliquidated as in a Chapter 11. Your only recourse is to argue lack of notice of the claims deadline or demonstrate excusable neglect in missing the deadline. While many routine objections are usually easily resolved by providing the debtor in possession with the necessary documentation or agreeing upon the last date through which interest will be computed, there is a cost involved. The trustee will charge the estate for all legal expenses incurred in connection with the claim objection. You ultimately pay for these expenses because they will reduce the amount available for distribution to unsecured creditors. In effect, the trustee or debtor in possession is fighting you with your own money. And of course you might have to incur the expense of retaining counsel.

Procedure

The procedures for objecting to claims and resolving those objections vary from court to court. In some courts, the trustee or debtor in possession will file the claims objection, and the court will send a notice for hearing before the court on a specific date of all objections filed in the case. If you fail to appear or send counsel to the scheduled hearing, the court will sustain the objection and disallow your claim in part or in full. In other courts, the trustee or debtor in possession will file notice of the claim objection and specify a deadline for responding with a request for a hearing. Unless you respond by that date and request a hearing, the court will simply enter an order sustaining the objection and disallowing your claim in full or in part.

On all but the most routine claim objections, you should contact counsel to make sure that your claim is allowed in the proper amount.

DISCHARGE AND DISCHARGEABILITY

Preliminary Comment

A detailed discussion of discharge and dischargeability is beyond the scope of this type of text. You should be aware that the goal of virtually any bankruptcy proceeding is the discharge of some or all of the debtor's debts and obligations. The Bankruptcy Code recognizes that, under certain circumstances, a debtor should be denied a discharge completely in Chapter 7. *See* 11 USC § 727. The bases for denial of discharge generally revolve around fraud, perjury or other misconduct such as concealment of assets or destruction of records in connection with the bankruptcy case itself.

The bases for denial of discharge are generally not major issues in Chapter 11 proceedings. Most major Chapter 11s are filed by corporations, and a corporation does not receive a discharge under Chapter 7. A discharge, however, is granted in Chapter 11, but only to the extent provided in the plan. The fraud that underlies the provisions of 11 USC § 727 would generally bar the confirmation of a plan of reorganization proposed by the debtor itself.

The Code also recognizes that certain types of debts should be excepted from the operation of the discharge. 11 USC § 523. These exceptions to the discharge are primarily policy statements by the Congress that certain types of debt will not be dealt with in bankruptcy. For example, many types of taxes are not discharged in bankruptcy under Chapter 7. Taxes in a Chapter 11 require special treatment under 11 USC § 1129(d). Thus, while taxes may not be dischargeable in a typical Chapter 7, they must be dealt with and generally paid in full in the Chapter 11. Likewise, alimony, child support and maintenance awards by the state courts are generally nondischargeable in bankruptcy, as are debts obtained through fraud or the use of a false financial statement, breaches of fiduciary duty by a fiduciary, certain types of student loans, judgments arising out of accidents where the person at fault was driving while intoxicated and judgments arising out of certain intentional torts and the conversion of collateral. Again, many of these exceptions simply do not arise in Chapter 11 cases. The following discussion will focus primarily on false financial statements and the conversion of collateral.

Before filing a complaint under 11 USC § 727 in any case, you should consider the effect. If the court denies the discharge under that section, no debts are discharged and all creditors are free to pursue their claims against the debtor and the debtor's assets. You may find yourself paying the cost of the legal work without any guarantee that you will either recover on your claim or recover the costs of the 11 USC § 727 complaint. Generally, you will be far better off to pursue a claim that your debt should be excepted from the discharge under 11 USC § 523.

DENIAL OF DISCHARGE UNDER 11 USC § 727

General Background

In order to bar the granting of a discharge in a Chapter 7, a creditor or the trustee must file an adversary complaint alleging one or more of the bases listed in 11 USC § 727. If the court sustains the complaint, the debtor is not discharged even though the trustee may proceed with administration of the estate. In a very general way, the bases listed in 11 USC § 727 involve misconduct or fraud in connection with the bankruptcy case. These bases have relatively little application in Chapter 11 since rather than denying the debtor a general discharge, the court will refuse to confirm a plan.

§ 727 Checklist

CORPORATIONS NOT DISCHARGED

Under 11 USC § 727, the bankruptcy discharge in Chapter 7 is given to individual debtors only. Congress, in enacting 11 USC § 727, concluded that the grant of a discharge to a corporate or limited liability entity was inappropriate. Since the 11 USC § 1141 discharge is applicable to individuals and other entities, § 727 is of relatively little importance. Note, however, that a corporation or limited liability entity can receive a discharge in Chapter 11. The misconduct necessary to deny a discharge would also support the appointment of a trustee.

CONCEALING ASSETS

Pursuant to 11 USC § 727(a)(2), any attempt to transfer or conceal assets prior to the bankruptcy can afford the basis for denial of discharge. The creditor seeking to bar the discharge under this subsection must prove that the debtor intended to defraud creditors or the bankruptcy trustee in making the transfer. This generally involves gratuitous transfers to family members or other insiders on the eve of bankruptcy. The transfer may take the form of an outright gift of property or the creation of a mortgage on property for which the debtor received insufficient consideration.

FAILURE TO KEEP RECORDS

In order to obtain a discharge in bankruptcy, an individual debtor must maintain necessary business records from which the court can determine how the debtor has conducted his or her business. Where the debtor does not maintain appropriate records or destroys the records on the eve of the bankruptcy or after the filing of the bankruptcy, the court may deny the discharge under 11 USC § 727(a)(3).

PERJURY IN CONNECTION WITH THE BANKRUPTCY CASE

The integrity of the bankruptcy system requires that the courts actively discourage perjury, bribery, and failure to obey court orders in connection with the bankruptcy case. An attempt by the debtor to bribe the trustee or other bankruptcy official or outright failure to surrender assets together with perjury in connection with the case may result in the denial of a discharge. *See* 11 USC § 727(a)(4). Perjury and attempted bribery, of course, are also federal criminal offenses. Also keep in mind that the debtor swears to the accuracy of the information contained in the schedules and statement of financial affairs. Failure to be fully candid in supplying information required in these documents may give rise to an action to deny the discharge because, if the debtor acted intentionally, it amounts to a false statement under oath.

FAILURE TO EXPLAIN DISPOSITION OF ASSETS

One of the primary purposes of a bankruptcy proceeding is to ensure equitable distribution of unencumbered assets to unsecured creditors. Initially, the creditor must prove that the debtor had assets prepetition that have not been accounted for. The debtor must then be able to account for those assets that existed prepetition. The debtor must be able to explain what has happened with the assets and their disposition. Under 11 USC § 727(a)(5), the court may deny discharge to a debtor who cannot satisfactorily explain the disposition of assets the creditor has proven were in existence before the bankruptcy was filed.

FAILURE TO OBEY COURT ORDERS TO TESTIFY

Naturally, the bankruptcy court is concerned that its orders be obeyed. Thus, if a debtor refuses to obey a court order or refuses to testify upon being granted immunity against self-incrimination, the court may deny a discharge under 11 USC § 727(a)(6). This generally arises if the debtor refuses to testify concerning transfers of property. Immunity must be obtained from the appropriate federal authorities before the debtor can be found to have refused to testify.

PRIOR BANKRUPTCY PROCEEDINGS

A debtor may only file a Chapter 7 petition and obtain a discharge in bankruptcy at six-year intervals in cases filed prior to the BAPCPA and at eight-year intervals in cases filed under the BAPCPA. A bankruptcy case commenced less than six years pre-BAPCPA and eight years under the BAPCPA after the filing of a petition for relief in bankruptcy is a basis for denying discharge. Generally, of course, the court will dismiss the second Chapter 7 proceeding. The bar, however, does not apply to the filing of Chapter 11, 12 or 13 cases after a discharge in bankruptcy in Chapter 7. Since a Chapter 7 discharge is not available to corporations and limited liability companies, this provision applies only to individuals. Note that the six-year and eight-year period runs from the filing of the first petition in bankruptcy and not from the date the discharge is granted. Generally, in Chapter 7 cases the discharge is granted approximately six months after the petition for relief.

NEW BAPCPA PROVISIONS

A discharge will not be granted if a debtor fails to complete an instructional course concerning personal financial management unless the United States Trustee or bankruptcy administrator determines that no course in their district is adequate.

Further, a discharge will not be granted if, after notice and a hearing, the court determines that there is or may have been a felony as described in section 522(q) committed by the debtor.

WAIVER OF DISCHARGE

An individual debtor may voluntarily waive a discharge if the court approves. *See* 11 USC § 727(a)(10). The waiver is not valid unless it was executed with court approval after the filing of the petition for relief.

REVOCATION OF DISCHARGE

A court has the power to revoke any discharge obtained through the fraud of the debtor if the creditor seeking the revocation did not know of such fraud when the discharge was originally granted. Further, a discharge will be revoked if the debtor knowingly and fraudulently failed to report property that the debtor acquired and which should have become property of the estate. Finally, failure of the debtor to explain satisfactorily a material misstatement in an audit referred to in section 586(f) of title 28, or failure to make all necessary accounts, papers, documents, etc., which are requested in such audit, will result in a revocation of discharge.

These new additions related to financial misstatements were clearly added as a result of various financial and securities frauds that have occurred during the last several years.

DEBTS EXCEPTED FROM DISCHARGE UNDER 11 USC § 523

General Background

Certain debts are excepted from the discharge, but only upon the filing of an adversary proceeding and action by the bankruptcy court. *See generally* 11 USC § 523. A very limited number of debts, including taxes, alimony, child support, and some student loans are automatically excepted from discharge unless the debtor seeks a specific determination of dischargeability. You will, of course, be primarily concerned with those types of debt excepted from discharge upon action by the creditor and the court. As a trade creditor you will be primarily concerned with credit obtained through a false financial statement and conversion of collateral.

§ 523 Checklist

TAXES

Taxes due less than three years before filing of bankruptcy are not discharged in bankruptcy. 11 USC § 523(a)(1). In a Chapter 11 case this often leads to the debtor creating a special class for the payment of tax liabilities that would not otherwise be discharged. Occasionally, the tax authorities have acted promptly and secured a lien on the debtor's property through tax assessments. Taxes subject to liens are treated as secured claims. The treatment of otherwise nondischargeable taxes may be of some importance if you, as a member of a committee, are proposing a plan of reorganization.

CREDIT OBTAINED BY FALSE FINANCIAL STATEMENT OR FRAUD

Since the discharge is intended only for the honest debtor, the Bankruptcy Code specifically excepts an individual debtor from discharge of debts arising from fraud or the use of a false written financial statement. To bring a claim within this section, the creditor must file a timely complaint to determine dischargeability under 11 USC

§ 523(a)(2). This section has two separate parts: one relating to fraud and the other relating to the use of a false written financial statement.

The difficulty facing any creditor seeking to bring a claim within the exception provisions of 11 USC § 523(a)(2) is the need to prove the fraud and the fraudulent intent by a preponderance of the evidence. Often, a financial statement is an exercise in creative writing and contains inflated values. While some courts will deny discharge based on inflated values, many will not. It is more likely that the court will except a claim from discharge if the debtor failed to list material obligations or listed assets that the debtor, in fact, did not own.

UNLISTED CREDITORS

The Bankruptcy Code does not discharge the claim of a creditor who is not given notice of the bankruptcy in time to permit the filing of a proof of claim or to file a proceeding to determine the dischargeability of certain types of debts. Only if the creditor actually had knowledge of the bankruptcy case through other means is the debt discharged. Occasionally, a debtor will fail to list a creditor such as credit card company hoping to retain the credit card. That creditor's claim will not be discharged. Note, however, that in many jurisdictions, the unlisted debt will be discharged if the case is a no asset Chapter 7. These courts reason that the creditor was not denied the opportunity to participate in the distribution of assets because no such distribution was made.

BREACH OF FIDUCIARY DUTY CLAIMS

Certain obligations arising from fraud or defalcation while acting as a fiduciary, embezzlement, or larceny are excepted from discharge. 11 USC § 523(a)(4). Larceny and embezzlement are fairly easily identified. Breach of fiduciary duty is likewise uncommon. However, secured creditors often assume that there is a trust relationship between a debtor and themselves because of the security agreement. Occasionally, this leads to confusion with the creditor claiming that the debtor has sold property out of trust and, therefore, their claim should be excepted from discharge under 11 USC § 523(a)(4). The majority rule is that a secured claim arising from a security agreement does not involve the necessary type of trust to bring the case within the provisions of 11 USC § 523(a)(4).

INTENTIONAL TORTS/CONVERSION OF COLLATERAL

The Bankruptcy Code provides that debts for the willful and malicious injury by the debtor to another entity or property of another entity are not discharged. *See* 11 USC § 523(a)(6).

Unless you are making secured loans to a trade debtor, or you lease property to the debtor, this section will have little impact especially since it is very difficult to win based on a Supreme Court decision requiring proof that the debtor intended the harm that resulted from a willful and malicious act. If the debtor converts property you have leased or in which you have a security interest, you may have a nondischargeable claim. You should consult counsel.

Fines and Penalties/Taxes

Like most taxes, fines and penalties assessed for the benefit of a governmental unit are not discharged in bankruptcy. 11 USC § 523(a)(7). Obviously, this will have little impact in trade debt situations. It may, however, play a role in a Chapter 11 plan where the debtor is seeking to separately classify and treat fines and penalties.

Student Loans

The Bankruptcy Code excepts from discharge student loans owed to nonprofit or governmental lenders unless paying the debt produces an undue hardship on the debtor or the debtor's dependents. 11 USC § 523(a)(8). Obviously, this exception to the discharge will have little effect on the trade creditors.

DUI Liabilities

In an often-amended section to the Bankruptcy Code, debts for personal injury or death arising from the operation of a motor vehicle while the debtor was intoxicated are specifically excepted. 11 USC § 523(a)(9).

Prior Bankruptcy Proceedings

Debts excepted from the discharge in a prior bankruptcy case are not discharged in subsequent bankruptcy. *See* 11 USC § 523(a)(10). This is to prevent a debtor from using serial bankruptcies to escape liability.

FDIC Claims

Certain debts to federally insured institutions are excepted from discharge under 11 USC § 523(a)(11) and (12). These subsections are complex. *Seek counsel.*

Securities Fraud

Enacted in the wake of the corporate scandals that came to light in 2001-02, § 523(a)(19) excepts from discharge certain debts arising from the violation of federal securities laws and those involving fraud, manipulation or other wrongful conduct in securities related transactions.

The BAPCPA modified Section 523(a)(19) to make it retroactively effective as of July 30, 2002, the date of enactment of the Sarbanes-Oxley Act.

COMPLAINTS TO DETERMINE DISCHARGEABILITY/ DENY DISCHARGE/DEADLINES

In order to have a debt excepted from a discharge under 11 USC § 523 or to deny the discharge generally under 11 USC § 727, a creditor, or the trustee, must file a timely complaint under one of those sections. This will generally require the retention of counsel.

Complaints to determine the dischargeability of a particular debt must be filed within 60 days after the first date set for the § 341 meeting of creditors. The relevant dates are listed on the Notice of Commencement, the document you receive that advises you of the bankruptcy filing. Note that a continuance of the actual meeting of creditors does not extend the deadline to file a complaint. However, this deadline applies only to §§ 523(a)(2) (common law fraud and false financial statements), 523(a)(4) (fraud or defalcation while acting in a fiduciary capacity, larceny or embezzlement), 523(a) (6) (willful and malicious injuries to persons or property), and 523(a) (15) (relating to divorce). The remaining sections of § 523 are not subject to the 60-day time limit.

Denial of discharge under § 727 also must be raised within a specific time period, but the period differs for Chapter 7 and Chapter 11. In Chapter 7 cases, the deadline is, as with § 523, 60 days from the first date set for the § 341 meeting of creditors. In Chapter 11, the deadline is the first date set for the hearing on confirmation of the plan.

Any of these deadlines can be extended if you file an appropriate motion with the court. Your motion must be filed before the initial time period expires, however. If not timely, your motion will be denied.

When considering the filing of an 11 USC § 727 complaint, you must consider the impact that denial of discharge will have generally. If you prevail and the court refuses to grant a discharge no claims are discharged and all creditors are free to pursue the debtor as though the bankruptcy had not been filed. While a trustee may continue to administer the estate of the debtor, and any distribution from the estate must be credited against any claim, the general denial of a discharge is of very little benefit to an individual creditor. On the other hand, if you successfully file a complaint to determine dischargeability under 11 USC § 523, your claim alone is excepted from the discharge under that complaint, and you may be the only creditor with a nondischargeable claim. You are, therefore, free to enter judgment against the debtor to pursue future income and assets of the debtor that other creditors will not share in.

PURSUING CLAIMS FOR FALSE FINANCIAL STATEMENTS AND FRAUD

As a trade credit manager you should be familiar with the provisions of 11 USC §§ 523(a)(2)(A) and (a)(2)(B) relating respectively to fraudulent misconduct and the use of false financial statements. These two sections will have their primary impact in Chapter 7 cases involving individual debtors. To begin with, you should note that the Bankruptcy Code places a slightly different emphasis on false financial statements than on general fraudulent misconduct. In a case of a false financial statement the statement must be in writing. All other types of conduct fall into the fraud exception of 11 USC § 523(a)(2)(A).

Fraud Other Than a False Financial Statement

Debts arising from the extension, renewal or refinancing of credit obtained through false pretenses, false representation, or actual fraud are excepted from the discharge under 11 USC § 523(a)(2)(A). To bring your claim within that section you must show that the debtor made a representation he knew at the time was false, that the debtor intended to deceive you, and that you justifiably relied upon the misrepresentation with the resultant loss. Generally, exceptions to discharge of this nature are construed very narrowly against creditors, and you must prove your case by a preponderance of the evidence.

In the course of a busy business world, it is often difficult to determine exactly what occurred in the sale of goods or other extensions of credit. If you routinely ship to an individual or corporation, it will often be particularly difficult to prove fraud or fraudulent misrepresentation. Before pursuing a claim for fraud or false representation, you should very carefully discuss the situation with your attorney.

You should particularly focus on those situations where the debtor has stocked or loaded up on inventory or other goods at your expense on the eve of filing of a bankruptcy petition. Often, a debtor will load up on inventory or other goods prepetition before filing a Chapter 7 case or to insure that debts guaranteed by the debtor's principal are paid in full out of that inventory. This, of course, comes at your expense as a trade creditor. It may be difficult, however, to prove the necessary elements of fraud unless you have a specific misrepresentation of ability to pay. For example, you may have difficulty showing that the debtor specifically misrepresented the intention to pay. This will be particularly true if you have had a course of dealing with the debtor in which you have routinely shipped goods. Your position, of course, is much better if you refuse to ship an unusual order, than rely on the exception to discharge provided by 11 USC § 523(a)(2)(A).

False Financial Statement

Under 11 USC § 523(a)(2)(B), the Bankruptcy Code excepts from discharge claims arising out of the use of a materially false financial statement in writing. The financial statement may relate to the debtor or an insider of the debtor. To bring your claim within the exception of that section you must show that the debt arises from the use of a false financial statement, in writing, which is materially false regarding the debtor's financial condition that the debtor caused to be published with intent to deceive. Any false statements other than in a writing concerning financial condition must be brought within the previous section. Your reliance on the misrepresentation must be reasonable. Again, this section is narrowly construed, and you must prove by a preponderance of the evidence your claim is within the very technical provisions of 11 USC § 523(a)(2)(B) to prevail.

Every case is fact sensitive. Therefore, court decisions in the area are widely divergent. To begin with, a financial statement must be in writing, of course. It does not need to be a formal financial statement, and financial statements submitted to trade reporting agencies, if they contain the necessary falsity, will satisfy the initial requirement. Any financial statement submitted, however, must be substantially inaccurate and must affect your decision-making process in granting credit.

The clearest situation involves the misrepresentation of ownership of assets, or the failure to list substantial noncontingent liabilities. As these omissions often change the net worth of the individual or entity, failure to disclose liabilities or improper listing of assets generally will result in the debt being excepted from discharge if the other elements are met.

The inflation of asset values, unless it can be shown that the debtor deliberately overvalued virtually worthless assets, is a more difficult situation. Generally, the courts will grant great leeway to a debtor in valuing assets for financial statement purposes. Only if the asset value is so clearly overstated that there was no reasonable basis for the debtor's valuation on the financial statement will the courts except the debt from discharge.

The other factor that causes considerable difficulty is the creditor's reliance on the false financial statement. You must show that you relied on the false financial statement and that it influenced your decision to extend credit. Often in the hurly burly of trade, goods are shipped before the financial information can be received. In such situations, the courts routinely hold that the creditor did not rely on the financial statement since it had not been received when the decision to extend credit through the sale of goods was made. Other courts have held that the reliance must be reasonable and that creditors have an obligation to investigate statements in a financial statement. This is more troublesome since, in many cases, you have no way of knowing a debtor's inventory or liabilities. However, if the debtor lists assets, you certainly can require some evidence of ownership.

Conversion of Collateral

Unfortunately, 11 USC § 523(a)(6) has been construed to cover the conversion of collateral in business situations. We say "unfortunately" since the language of the statute does not clearly apply to the sale of collateral in violation of a security agreement. This has led to widely divergent results in the courts. If you are in a situation where you take a security interest in inventory you sell to a particular debtor, and the debtor sells that inventory to third parties without accounting for the proceeds, you may have a claim under 11 USC § 523(a)(6).

The statute requires a showing of conversion of the collateral and a willful conversion of the proceeds. It is often difficult to prove the debtor's intent. Indeed, in most situations, the debtor uses the proceeds from the sale of inventory of goods generally in the operation of the business. Only where the debtor converts the proceeds to personal use, such as the purchase of exempt assets, have the courts generally held that the conversion was willful.

General Comment on Discharge and Dischargeability

Unless an individual debtor is a highly compensated professional, or stands to inherit substantial assets in the future, denying the debtor's discharge or excepting your claim from the operation of the discharge has little value. There is little difference between a claim that is discharged in bankruptcy and one that is uncollectible because of the debtor's lack of funds. You are much better off to control the losses at the point at which the credit is granted rather than seeking to deny a discharge once bankruptcy has been filed.

TRUSTEE'S STRONG ARM AND AVOIDING POWERS

Overview and Historical Background

Bankruptcy evolved from proceedings to gather up a debtor's assets and distribute them among creditors in an equitable fashion. To further the equitable distribution, bankruptcy trustees have historically had the power to recover certain fraudulent transfers, recover preferential payments to creditors, and avoid certain improperly perfected security interests and mortgages. Collectively, these rights or powers are referred to as the trustee's *strong arm* and *avoiding* powers. From your point of view as an unsecured trade creditor, these powers are something of a two-edged sword. If you have recently received a preferential payment, you may find yourself disgorging the payment in return for the dubious right to make a claim against the bankruptcy estate generally. If, however, others have received the preferential payments, you, as an unpaid trade creditor, may find yourself in a position of receiving a dividend where otherwise nothing would have been available. The recovery of preferential and fraudulent transfers is one of the primary reasons for instituting an involuntary bankruptcy against a debtor.

Importance from Unsecured Trade Creditor's Point of View

As a trade credit manager and as a potential member of an unsecured creditors' committee in Chapter 11, your concern about the trustee's powers will relate to the potential for the recovery of assets for a bankruptcy estate. As the trade creditor, you want to make sure that any payments you will receive are not subject to recovery as a preference, fraudulent transfer, or otherwise. As a member of the creditors' committee, on the other hand, you want to make sure that the debtor presses all possible claims for recovery, including preferences or fraudulent transfers that benefit insiders. Thus, while you need not be a lawyer to understand and deal with the trustee's powers, you will have to make business decisions that require some knowledge of the law, and you will have to be able to communicate with your counsel, either in defending actions by the trustee or in prosecuting claims on behalf of the unsecured creditors.

As a trade credit manager in the nonbankruptcy context, you will want to structure your credit terms and payments in such a fashion as to give you the maximum protection against actions for preferences.

Basic Recovery Procedure

ADVERSARY PROCEEDINGS

Whether the action is brought by the trustee in a Chapter 7 or the debtor in possession in a Chapter 11, the procedure for recovering preferential and fraudulent transfers and setting aside improperly perfected security interests requires the filing of an adversary proceeding under Rule 7001 of the Federal Rules of Bankruptcy Procedure. The trustee may bring a single adversary proceeding to recover multiple preferential payments to a single creditor. Alternatively the trustee could object to the creditor's claim.

Under pre-BAPCPA, the adversary proceeding is filed in the bankruptcy court in which the case is pending. The BAPCPA has changed the venue and jurisdiction provisions of the Bankruptcy Code relating to preference litigation. With some limited exceptions, preference actions (or any action by a trustee to recover a money judgment) against a trade creditor of more than $5,000 and less than $10,000 can be commenced only in the district court for the district where that trade creditor is located. A trustee cannot recover an alleged preference (in a non-consumer case), in the aggregate of less than $5,000. Creditors must note, however, that such action may still be commenced and the creditor must affirmatively assert this as a defense to such action.

Occasionally, a debtor in possession will refuse to prosecute a preference or fraudulent transfer action since it involves a major supplier or a relative of an insider. In those cases the court might, upon an appropriate request, authorize the creditors' committee to pursue the action in the name of the debtor for the benefit of the bankruptcy estate. Where the debtor's schedules and statement of affairs suggests that a preference or fraudulent transfer has taken place or that one of the major creditor's security interest is subject to attack under 11 USC § 544, but the debtor in possession either refuses to or shows no sign of prosecuting the action, you should discuss with committee counsel the possibility of pursuing the action with court approval.

Once the adversary proceeding is filed, the trustee or debtor in possession can obtain nationwide service of the summons and complaint pursuant to the Federal Rules of Bankruptcy Procedure. The defendant must then answer in bankruptcy court within the time specified by the bankruptcy court for an answer and, failing an answer, the court will enter a default judgment. Once an answer is filed, the adversary proceeding proceeds as any other lawsuit would through discovery and pretrial preparation. All of the discovery tools, such as depositions, interrogatories, and requests for admission are available in an adversary proceeding.

The United States Supreme Court has ruled that a transferee who has not filed a proof of claim is entitled to a jury trial on the preference or fraudulent transfer action. The bankruptcy court can conduct a jury trial where the parties consent. Absent that consent, any action requiring a jury trial must be transferred to the district court in the district where the bankruptcy case is pending. Generally, the demand for a jury trial is a delaying tactic. The United States District Courts are inundated with criminal work and simply do not have the time to try a fraudulent transfer action in a bankruptcy case. Thus, there may be substantial delay between the filing of the action and its being brought to trial if a jury is demanded. The delays inherent in bringing the case to trial on the jury trial docket may be a major consideration in settlement negotiations.

From a tactical standpoint, there is some risk to demanding a jury trial because juries are generally ill equipped to deal with the complex legal and financial issues involved in a preference or fraudulent transfer action. If no jury trial has been demanded, the adversary proceeding will be tried in the bankruptcy court.

SETTLEMENT CONSIDERATIONS

Settlement should be considered in any preference or strong arm action. As in any litigation, you should always keep your eye on the bottom line: What will the action by the debtor or the committee bring into the bankruptcy estate for distribution to unsecured creditors? Quite often, the payments are relatively small and the cost of complete litigation may outweigh the potential recovery. Unfortunately, in the bigger cases this goal occasionally disappears from sight. Remember, the cost of bringing the action, whether brought by the debtor or the creditors' committee, is paid by the bankruptcy estate. If the plan is a liquidating plan, the cost of pursuing the litigation will be paid out from the pool of money set aside for creditors.

The cost of litigation should also be a consideration on the defense side. If you are defending a preference or other trustee action to recover assets for the estate, unless you have a very clear defense, you should seriously consider settlement. This is particularly true since you may also participate in any distribution of the monies recovered, which will be diminished by litigation costs.

What follows is a discussion of the trustee's strong arm powers, the elements of a preference action and the elements of a fraudulent transfer action with a brief discussion of tactics from the point of view of the unsecured creditors' committee in a Chapter 11 case.

TRUSTEE'S STRONG ARM POWERS

Preliminary Comment

11 USC § 544, the "strong arm clause," empowers a trustee or a debtor in possession to avoid any lien or security interest in personal property or any lien or mortgage on real estate which is not properly perfected as of the date of the filing of the bankruptcy petition. Generally, you must refer to state law to understand the rights given to a trustee or a debtor in possession under 11 USC § 544. For example, most state laws give priority to attaching creditors over improperly perfected security interests and incompletely conveyed real property interests. This type of priority is carried over into the Bankruptcy Code under 11 USC § 544. As under state law, 11 USC § 544 empowers a trustee or a Chapter 11 debtor to avoid any incomplete transfer of real estate or any improperly perfected security interest in personal property. Assume that the debtor has an inventory financing agreement with the First National Bank. The debtor also grants the bank a security interest in equipment, fixtures and accounts receivable. If First National Bank does not properly file its financing statement (UCC-1), the security interest is unperfected and is subject to attack under 11 USC § 544. Similarly, if the debtor grants First National Bank a mortgage on its manufacturing site, but the mortgage incorrectly describes the real estate, even though the mortgage is recorded, the mortgage is subject to attack because of the incorrect legal description.

Section 544 grants to the trustee the rights of three different hypothetical types of creditors or purchasers. First, the trustee or the debtor in possession has the legal standing of a hypothetical judicial lien creditor who extended credit at the time of the filing of the petition, and at the same time obtained a hypothetical judicial lien on all assets of the debtor. This hypothetical judicial lien creditor status permits a trustee to attack any improperly perfected security interest in personal property or real property since, under most state laws on real estate and most versions of the UCC, a judgment lien creditor has priority over an improperly perfected secured creditor. At the same time, the trustee has the rights of any actual creditor with an allowed unsecured claim as of the date of the petition. This permits the trustee to set aside an improper bulk transfer of the debtor's property, located in states with a bulk sale statute, or a fraudulent conveyance under state law, allowing the trustee to take advantage of the longer state law statute of limitations for fraudulent conveyance actions, rather than the shorter period provided in Section 548. Finally, the trustee has the powers of a bona fide purchaser for value of real estate owned by the debtor as of the date of the petition. This allows the trustee to set aside any unrecorded conveyance of real estate and any improperly perfected mortgage. In most states, a judgment lien or a bona fide purchaser for value takes priority over any improperly recorded deed, mortgage, deed of trust or other real estate encumbrance.

Each of these hypothetical situations involves a complex relationship between federal and state law. From the general creditor's point of view, the trustee's avoiding powers under 11 USC § 544 are an important device for recovering assets for the benefit of all creditors. You should have sufficient understanding of the concepts to discuss them with counsel for the creditors' committee in a Chapter 11. Many times, the committee will prosecute actions to set aside certain interests if the debtor fails to do so. The avoidability of security interests is also an important consideration for negotiating a possible plan. An otherwise apparently secured creditor may be persuaded to give up value to unsecured creditors because of a potential challenge to the validity of the security interest.

Again, you must generally refer to applicable state law to determine how these hypothetical standings interrelate in the bankruptcy case. The scope of this work does not contemplate a state-by-state analysis of the trustee's avoidance powers. You should, however, be aware of them, both as a potential defendant if you take a security interest in assets and fail to properly perfect it and, as a member of an unsecured creditors' committee that may pursue avoidable transfers under the strong arm powers.

Hypothetical Judicial Lien Holder

Section 544(a)(1) of the Code grants the trustee the status of a hypothetical judicial lien creditor who extended credit as of the date of the petition and simultaneously obtained a hypothetical judicial lien on the debtor's assets. In some respects the "hypothetical judicial lien holder" is as mythical as the unicorn since it would be virtually impossible to extend credit and at the same time obtain a judicial lien. The legal fiction, however, is necessary to permit the trustee or the debtor in possession to set aside any security interest or mortgage for the benefit of all creditors.

Given the hypothetical status, you must then refer to the applicable state law to determine whether the hypothetical judgment lien creditor has priority over consensual security interests in the debtor's assets. A majority of states give priority to the judicial lien holder over unperfected security interests under the UCC and unrecorded mortgages or other transfers of property.

Even with the hypothetical status granted under the Bankruptcy Code, if a judicial lien holder would not take priority over the mortgagee of real estate or the secured creditor in personal property, 11 USC § 544(a)(1) does not apply. For example, under most versions of the Uniform Commercial Code, although a security interest may be enforced against the debtor even if the creditor fails to properly perfect it by the necessary filing, the unperfected security interest is subordinate to the rights of a judicial lien creditor. *See, e.g.,* UCC § 9-317(a)(2)(A). The judicial lien holder, however, would not be able to set aside a security interest if, on the day before bankruptcy the debtor notifies the unperfected lien holder of the pending bankruptcy and the unperfected secured creditor thereupon files the necessary financing statement. While this may fall within the purview of 11 USC § 547 as a preference (*see below*), the security interest remains perfected and is not subject to avoidance under 11 USC § 544(a)(1).

While we have assumed that generally you will not be making secured advances to a trade customer, you may wish to carefully review your documentation if, on occasion, you do retain a security interest in goods sold on credit to a customer or sell goods on consignment. Finally, in the unlikely event that you take a mortgage on real estate, counsel should review the transaction to ensure not only the proper perfection of the mortgage, but its priority with respect to other potential mortgages on the same property. In sum, you should establish a legal documentation system that will insure the proper creation and perfection of UCC security interests.

From the unsecured trade creditor's point of view, the avoidance provisions of 11 USC § 544(a)(1) are of major importance. They permit the trustee or debtor in possession or the creditors' committee to recover assets from creditors for the benefit of all creditors. If the committee retains counsel, one of the first things that counsel may wish to do is review all loan documentation supporting purportedly secured creditors' positions. If the documentation indicates that the security interests are not properly perfected, the committee at least has a negotiating point with a secured creditor and may be able to avoid the interest of the creditor completely. The bottom line remains that any security interest or lien not properly perfected as of the date of the petition for relief is subject to attack under 11 USC § 544(a)(1).

Unsecured Creditor Status

Pursuant to 11 USC § 544(b), the trustee and the debtor in possession are given the power to avoid any transfer of assets subject to avoidance by an actual creditor with an allowable unsecured claim as of the date of the petition for relief. An actual creditor must exist, however, who could have avoided the transfer. This involves reference to applicable state law to determine the rights of actual creditors with allowed unsecured claims to set aside transfers by the debtor.

State fraudulent transfer law provides a common basis for § 544(b) actions. This is of significant advantage to the bankruptcy estate because the fraudulent transfer law in the Bankruptcy Code affects only those transferred within one year of the filing of the petition and two years after filing under the BAPCPA for bankruptcy cases filed on and after April 20, 2006. State fraudulent transfer law, on the other hand, allows the trustee to avoid transfers made during a longer reach back period.

This provision is also utilized where there has been an improper bulk transfer of the debtor's assets without notice to creditors. This applies only to bulk transfers in states that have a bulk transfer law—Article 6 of the UCC; most states have repealed their bulk transfer statutes. For those states that retain UCC Article 6, notice and other requirements regarding such bulk sales must be satisfied. Otherwise, a creditor that extended credit before the transfer was made and had an outstanding claim at the time of the bankruptcy can unravel the bulk transfer. Because under 11 USC § 544(b) the trustee is given the rights of an actual creditor, the trustee may set aside the bulk transfer. Within the reorganization setting, this avoidance power is of relatively little importance.

Bona Fide Purchaser for Value

Section 544(a)(3) of the Code is an important weapon in the hands of a debtor in possession or creditors' committee. Congress added this provision to the Bankruptcy Code in 1978 to extend the reach of a trustee in setting aside improperly perfected transfers. Under this section, the trustee has the status of a bona fide purchaser for value of any property of the debtor as of the date of the petition.

Under prior case law the trustee's status as a judgment lien creditor might not permit the trustee to set aside unrecorded interests in real estate, depending upon the law in the particular state where the bankruptcy was pending. This caused inconsistent results, depending upon where the case was filed.

In most states the judgment lien holder has priority over any unrecorded deed, mortgage, deed of trust, or other encumbrance or conveyance of the property. However, some states hold that an unrecorded mortgage or deed of trust has priority over a judgment lien holder. The impact of the provision is clearest in the situation where the debtor misdescribes real estate in a conveyance which is actually recorded or where the creditor fails to record an actual conveyance, such as a mortgage or deed. In either case the trustee, as a bona fide purchaser for value, has priority over the interest of the holder of the inaccurate deed or the mortgagee in the unrecorded mortgage.

This section's actual effect in any given case will depend upon the type of the debtor's business. If the debtor's business has little involvement in real estate, 11 USC § 544(a)(3) will be of little importance. If, on the other hand, the debtor's business involves a large number of interests in real estate, the failure to record mortgages, deeds of conveyance, or other transfers of property may substantially increase the value of the bankruptcy estate. For example, in the oil and gas business it is common for a debtor, in drilling wells, to not record assignments of interests in wells until the well has been proven. When the debtor files bankruptcy before recording assignments there may be substantial recovery of assets for the general unsecured creditors.

Legal Audit

No matter what your role in a potential bankruptcy estate, if you are dealing with security interests and mortgages in personal and real property, you will want to be sufficiently familiar with the law governing the creation and perfection of security interests and mortgages to perform a legal audit or review of either your own documentation or documentation of lending creditors in a case.

A legal audit is simply a review of all the documentation to determine whether all security interests were properly perfected and all mortgages were correct and properly recorded, paying special attention to legal descriptions of the covered real estate. If you are extending credit on a secured basis, such as a purchase money security interest, you should be familiar with the UCC provisions governing the steps necessary to create and perfect a purchase money security interest, including the steps necessary to prime any existing security interests. You would be well advised to ask your counsel to periodically review your documentation and procedures to make sure they continue to confirm with the UCC and other statutes.

PREFERENCES

Overview

At common law, nothing barred a merchant from preferring one creditor over another in the payment of debts. Thus, a debtor facing the threat of insolvency would simply pay off relatives and selected creditors, leaving nothing for the bulk of the creditors. Almost from the beginning of the bankruptcy laws in England, a trustee in bankruptcy could recover payments to unsecured creditors deemed preferential. 11 USC § 547 is the bankruptcy provision authorizing the trustee to recover preferential transfers.

From your point of view as an unsecured trade creditor, the preference provisions cut both ways. You may receive preferential treatment and if challenged, you may be required to repay those monies. In other cases, however, others have received preferential treatment and you might want to encourage the trustee to recover those payments from other creditors.

As a member of the creditors' committee, you should be alert to any sign that the debtor made payments to creditors. Since virtually any payment on account of an antecedent debt made within 90 days of the filing of bankruptcy is at least suspect, and further, since the burden of proof is on the recipient to prove the applicability of a preference defense, you should scrutinize all payments very carefully for possible challenge.

Proving a Preference

In order to fall within the definition of a preferential transfer under 11 USC § 547, the trustee or the debtor in possession must prove: (1) that a transfer of the debtor's assets were made to or for the benefit of a creditor; (2) for or on account of an antecedent debt; (3) while the debtor was insolvent; (4) within 90 days of the petition for relief or within one year if the transfer was to an insider; and (5) the effect of which is to give the creditor more than the creditor would otherwise receive in a Chapter 7 liquidation. 11 USC § 547(b). The Bankruptcy Code, for preference purposes, establishes a rebuttable presumption that the debtor is insolvent for the 90 days prior to the filing of a petition for relief. 11 USC § 547(f). The elements are described in more detail below to assist you in assessing the potential for the recovery of a preference and so that you better understand the defenses available.

TRANSFER OF THE DEBTOR'S PROPERTY

"Transfer" is defined broadly in 11 USC § 101(54). The definition covers every mode of disposing of property whether direct or indirect, absolute or conditional, or voluntary or involuntary. Virtually any payment, gift, or other transfer of assets may fall within the provisions, including any voluntary payment by the debtor of an outstanding unsecured bill or the satisfaction of the same debt through the seizure of assets.

Remember, the transfer must be of the debtor's property. Occasionally, there is dispute as to whether the transfer is of the debtor's property. For instance, a payment made by the debtor from the debtor's bank account or a seizure of the debtor's assets are clearly transfers of the debtor's assets. On the other hand, a payment of the debtor's bills by the principal in a partnership or by an affiliate of the corporate debtor is not a transfer of the debtor's assets. If you are dealing with a subsidiary and receive payment directly from the parent corporation, the trustee of the subsidiary will generally not be able to recover that payment from you.

PAYMENT TO OR FOR THE BENEFIT OF A CREDITOR

The transfer must go to the creditor or somehow directly benefit the creditor. Obviously, if the debtor makes payment to the creditor it falls within the scope of 11 USC § 547. Less clear, however, are the situations where the debtor makes payment to an affiliate of the creditor or to a creditor of the creditor. Assume that a creditor owes a bank $15,000 and pledges accounts receivable as security. Debtor owes creditor $15,000. At the direction of the bank, the debtor pays the bank directly as the account receivable is part of its collateral. The transfer to the bank may constitute a transfer for the benefit of the creditor and, therefore, may be a recoverable preference.

In a line of cases prior to 1994, the courts held that payments to a bank might be considered preferential if the bank holds the guarantee of one of the officers or shareholders of the corporate debtor. This was referred to as the *DePrizio Doctrine*. The trustees in these cases were able to recover transfers that occurred up to one year before the bankruptcies were filed because the officers or shareholders were insiders by definition under the Bankruptcy Code. To illustrate, assume the following facts: Shareholder owns 100 percent of the stock of the debtor and has guaranteed the debtor's obligations at the First National Bank. One hundred eighty days before a filing of a petition for relief, the debtor makes a substantial payment on an otherwise unsecured line of credit at the First National Bank. Some cases stood for the proposition that the payment may constitute a preference and that the preference period may be extended because of the relationship between the transferee, the bank, and the shareholder who is an insider with respect to the debtor. In 1994, Congress amended the Bankruptcy Code and it appeared that *DePrizio* had been eliminated. The BAPCPA has reinstated the concept of a *DePrizio* preference. Section 547(i) now states "If the trustee avoids under subsection (b) a transfer made between 90 days and one year before the date of the filing of the petition, by the debtor to an entity that is not an insider for the benefit of a creditor that is an insider, such transfer shall be considered to be avoided under this section only with respect to the creditors that is an insider." This new language seems to imply that a non-insider trade creditor will become involved in a preference litigation because an insider of the debtor benefited from payment by the debtor to the non-insider. However, the language states that the transfer will not be avoided against the non-insider trade creditor. Case law will have to evolve to see how this section will actually impact the non-insider trade creditor.

PAYMENT OF ANTECEDENT DEBT

The third element of a preference action requires that the trustee show that the transfer was made to the creditor for or on account of an antecedent debt. Antecedent debt is not a defined term under the Bankruptcy Code. Generally, an antecedent debt is one that was in existence prior to the alleged preferential payment. For instance, a debtor's payment of trade credit is a payment of antecedent debt. The giving of the collateral for the repayment of a loan, which was initially to be an unsecured loan, constitutes payment on an antecedent debt. Comments in the case law suggest that if a lender makes a loan with the understanding at the outset that it is to be a short, unsecured bridge loan while the debtor obtains other financing, a preference occurs if the bank thereafter demands repayment or the pledge of collateral even if the demand or repayment occurs the same day that the loan was initially made. However, payment prior to delivery of goods (cash in advance/cash before delivery transactions) is not a preference because there is no antecedent debt being paid. A transfer to someone who is not a creditor, as a gift or otherwise, is not a payment on account of antecedent debt. (The latter, of course, would be subject to attack as a fraudulent transfer. *See below.*)

As a potential trade creditor you should be aware of the major exception to the preferential transfer rules which excepts from recovery payments made in the ordinary course of business. These rules have become much more beneficial to trade creditors with the passage of the BAPCPA. *See below.* This exception may provide you with a defense to a preference action if the payment was made in the ordinary course of business even though it was made on account of antecedent debt.

THE DEBTOR MUST BE INSOLVENT

The transfer must be made while the debtor was insolvent. The Bankruptcy Code relies on the balance sheet test of insolvency - the debtor's indebtedness exceeds the fair value of its non-exempt assets. The Code also creates a rebuttable presumption that the debtor is insolvent for the 90 calendar days preceding the filing of the bankruptcy. *See* 11 USC § 547(f). The trustee is likely to rely exclusively on the presumption created by statute to prove the insolvency of the debtor.

The presumption is, however, rebuttable. If you receive a preferential payment, but can show by a balance sheet test that the debtor was solvent when it made the payment, you will defeat the preference action. Generally, however, the presumption is all that is available since the debtor's records are often so incoherent that it is difficult to determine the debtor's financial condition immediately preceding bankruptcy. It is, therefore, very difficult, and frequently very expensive to prove the debtor's solvency at the time of the payment.

90-DAY REACH BACK

The transfer must be effected within 90 days of the bankruptcy filing unless the transfer is to an insider. *See generally* 11 USC § 101(31). If the transferee is an insider, the reach back period is extended to one year, but the presumption of insolvency does not apply unless the transfer took place within 90 days. Therefore, the trustee has the burden of showing the insolvency of the debtor during the time from 90 days to one year prior to the bankruptcy. Note that under the Bankruptcy Code, the reach back period for a preferential transfer was shortened to 90 days from 120 days under the Bankruptcy Act of 1898.

The rules on check clearing have created some interesting case law in the preference area that was settled by the United States Supreme Court. The rule is, if the check clears within 90 days of the filing for relief, a transfer is deemed to have occurred within the 90-day period. For the purposes of § 547(b) and determining when a transfer occurs, the date the check is *honored* is the date the transfer occurs. Thus, if the check is tendered on the 95th day, but does not clear until the 88th day, the payment may be preferential.

Obviously, if you are concerned about preferential payments you may wish to take special steps to expedite payment. Putting the check through normal banking channels for payment may take several days. If you can arrange to do so, you may wish to have the check presented immediately at the drawee bank for payment or have the debtor pay by wire transfer or bank check.

PREFERENTIAL EFFECT

A transfer or payment will not be preferential if it does not result in the creditor transferee getting more than the creditor would have received in a Chapter 7 liquidation. For this reason, payments of proceeds from the liquidation of collateral subject to a properly perfected security interest are generally not preferential since the creditor would receive as much in a Chapter 7 liquidation. If the security interest was improperly perfected, however, such a payment may be a preference.

Since most bankruptcy estates are no asset cases, with no money for distribution to creditors, it would seem logical that almost any payment that meets the other elements also has a preferential effect. The trustee or debtor in possession, however, still has the burden of proving the preferential effect.

In calculating the preferential effect, the potential dividend from the bankruptcy estate as a percentage of claims is compared to a percent of the claim actually received by the transferee. Assume that the sole asset of the bankruptcy estate is a preferential transfer action against the First National Bank. There are no other assets for distribution to unsecured creditors. Thus, the dividend percentage would be zero. Even if the transfer to the bank was only five percent of its unsecured claim, the payment would be a preference since the bank had received more than what would be distributed in a Chapter 7, namely zero.

Defenses and Exceptions to the Preference Rules

OVERVIEW

The Code and the courts have created a number of exceptions to the preference rules, including exceptions for contemporaneous transfers or exchanges; ordinary course of business payments; extensions of enabling loans; subsequent advances of unsecured credit; attachments of floating liens; attachments of certain statutory liens; and small consumer payment preferences. Each of these exceptions creates a potential defense to a preference action that you should bear in mind in reviewing potential preference actions by a debtor in possession, either against you or against other creditors. In particular, as a credit manager for a trade creditor you should pay attention to the contemporaneous exchange the ordinary course of business and subsequent advance of unsecured credit new value defenses discussed below.

CONTEMPORANEOUS EXCHANGE

A transfer to a creditor, which was intended to be contemporaneous with the extension of credit or the delivery of goods by the creditor and was a substantially contemporaneous exchange, is an exception to the preference rule. *See* 11 USC § 547(c)(1). In its simplest form, the contemporaneous exchange exception is illustrated by a COD delivery where the debtor pays for goods delivered COD with a check tendered upon receipt of the goods. Technically, of course, the check is not paid until the check has cleared. While this situation is, in the most technical fashion, a potential preference, the provisions of the Code specifically except it.

Section 547(c)(1) does not require that the exchange be precisely contemporaneous with the creditor's extension of new value. The exchange only has to be substantially contemporaneous, which allows for the possibility of a short variance between payment and the extension of credit.

ORDINARY COURSE OF BUSINESS

The most frequently invoked and litigated preference defense is the ordinary course of business defense under § 547(c)(2) of the Bankruptcy Code. The ordinary course of business defense is intended to protect routine payments of credit transactions from preference exposure in order to encourage creditors to continue doing business with financially distressed debtors. It is also intended to leave normal financial relationships undisturbed since those types of transfers do not detract from the general policy of § 547 to discourage unusual action by either the debtor or its creditors shortly before bankruptcy.

For any bankruptcy case commenced prior to October 17, 2005, the pre-BAPCPA defense requirements remain in place. A creditor defending a preference lawsuit on a pre-October 17, 2005 bankruptcy case still must prove all of the following to take advantage of the ordinary course of business defense: (a) the debt paid by the alleged preference was incurred in the ordinary course of business of the debtor and creditor; (b) the payment or the transfer was made in the ordinary course of business of the debtor and creditor; and (c) the payment or the transfer was made according to ordinary business terms.

The first element of the ordinary course of business defense concerns whether the creation of the debt was within the ordinary course of business of both the debtor and creditor. In a typical extension of trade credit, this would not generally be an issue. Normally you will not sell to anyone who is not in the business of buying your goods or services. Conversely, rarely would someone be purchasing from you who is not in the business of dealing with your particular goods or services.

The second element of the ordinary course of business defense requires proof that the payment was made in the ordinary course of business of the debtor and creditor. The creditor must compare the alleged preference payments to the debtor's payments to the creditor prior to the 90-day preference period. A payment is in the ordinary course of business of the debtor and creditor if is consistent with their payment history; otherwise it is not. Some courts have compared the timing of the preference payments (i.e., the number of days from invoice or due date to date of payment) to the timing of all payments by the debtor to that creditor prior to the preference period. That payment history could be anything from one year prior to the preference period, two years prior to the preference period, or longer. Where the number of days from invoice or due date to the payment date for a particular preference payment falls within the range of the earliest to latest payments characterizing the party's payment history, the payment would be in the ordinary course of business between the debtor and creditor. Other courts have compared the timing of the preference payments to a modified pre-preference period payment history between the parties that excludes payments at the outer points of the range. Other courts have compared the timing of the preference payments to the mean or average time from invoice or due date to payment date during the parties' pre-preference period payment history. Preference payments that significantly deviate from the mean or average historical payment from invoice or due date to payment will not be in the ordinary course of business of the debtor and creditor. The courts also consider, in addition to the timing of the payment, the amount, the form of tender, the circumstances of the transaction and generally the entire course of dealings between the parties.

The simple fact that a payment is late, however, does not necessarily disqualify it from being subject to the ordinary course of business defense. If the practice between the parties has been to accept late payments, many courts have held that the ordinary course of business defense could be satisfied if there is consistency with the parties' prior payment history. However, if there is no evidence that the parties have modified the original terms of payment, the courts will often find the payment is not subject to the ordinary course of business defense. Some courts have gone as far as to hold that a payment by wire transfer or cashier's check is not in the ordinary course of business where the debtor had previously paid in that fashion.

The third element of the ordinary course of business defense requires the creditor to prove that the preference payment is consistent with the payment practices in the applicable industry. That could be the range of payment terms and practices for firms similar to the creditor. This requirement is usually satisfied as long as the payment is not idiosyncratic or unusual when compared to payments to others in the industry.

A review of the case law suggests that the ordinary course of business defense is largely based on the factual dealings between the parties. If there is a lengthy course of business stretching back over a number of years and the particular transfer which is alleged to be preferential is in compliance with those terms, the court is less likely to find it a preference and more likely to find it within the ordinary course of business exception. On the other hand, the less the particular payment looks like the ordinary payment terms developed through practice between the parties, the more likely it is found to be a preference. All of these determinations are, to a certain extent, fact sensitive. Thus, while the parties are permitted to show prior business dealings, the creditor has the burden of showing that the transfer falls within the exception and that the exception applies.

The ordinary course of business defense is more difficult to prove than the other preference defenses. The creditor must produce witnesses and records showing its payment history with the debtor and industry practice. There has been more litigation concerning the ordinary course of business defense than any other preference defense. The courts have reached conflicting decisions that make it difficult to predict how a court will rule in a particular case. That makes litigating this defense very expensive and risky.

Trade creditors must realize that since the statute of limitations to commence a preference case is generally two years, a trade creditor may have to defend against a pre-BAPCPA preference action for longer than two years in the future.

BAPCPA CHANGES TO ORDINARY COURSE OF BUSINESS DEFENSE

For all bankruptcy cases filed on or after October 17, 2005, the ordinary course of business defense has been made more favorable to trade creditors. A trustee may not avoid a transfer to the extent that such transfer was in payment of a debt incurred by the debtor in the ordinary course of business or financial affairs of the debtor and creditor, and was made in the ordinary course of business or financial affairs of the debtor and the creditor or made according to ordinary business terms.

Trade creditors will note that the difference is that under the pre-BAPCPA cases, a trade creditor had to prove ordinary course existed both between the debtor and the creditor (the "subjective" test) as well as throughout the industry (the "objective" test).

Under the BAPCPA changes, the trade creditor can use either the subjective or the objective test.

NEW VALUE DEFENSE

Another frequently asserted preference defense is the new value defense arising under § 547(c)(4) of the Bankruptcy Code. The new value defense reduces preference exposure by the amount of new credit the creditor had extended to or for the debtor's benefit subsequent to the preference. The new value cannot be secured by an otherwise unavoidable security interest and cannot be paid by an otherwise unavoidable transfer to or for the creditor's benefit.

The new value defense, like other preference defenses, is designed to encourage creditors to continue doing business with and extending credit to a company that is in financial distress. The defense protects creditors that replenish the debtor and its bankruptcy estate by extending new credit subsequent to the preference payment. The payment leaves the debtor no worse off because the creditor had subsequently extended new credit that replenished the debtor and its bankruptcy estate.

Section 547(c)(4) does not specify how new value is to be calculated. Most courts permit creditors to offset subsequent new value against the net balance of all prior preferences. This permits preferences to be carried forward until exhausted by subsequent new value and thereby allows the new value to be applied against the immediately preceding preference and all prior preferences. This view allows for a larger deduction for new value. At least one court has limited offsettable new value to any new value granted between each preference received from the debtor. This view divides the preference period into a series of smaller periods in which new value given by the creditor is netted only against the immediately preceding preference. This has the affect of substantially reducing the amount of any new value offset.

There is also a division of authority as to whether the new value defense is available for paid for new value. One view is that in order for the § 547(c)(4) new value defense to apply, the new value must remain unpaid by the debtor. These courts take the view that once the debtor pre-pays the new value, the estate is diminished and the new value defense should not be available to the creditor. An alternate view rejects any requirement that conditions the new value defense on the new value remaining unpaid. These courts rely on § 547(c)(4) which states that the new value cannot be paid by an otherwise unavoidable transfer to or for the creditor's benefit. To the extent the new value is paid by an avoidable transfer (i.e., a preferential transfer not subject to the contemporaneous exchange and/or ordinary course of business defense), it should still count as new value. Again the new value defense would be substantially expanded by the applicability of paid for new value as an additional offset in reduction of the preference claim.

Enabling Loan Defense

When a creditor extends credit that is secured by the asset being sold to the debtor, the security interest is referred to as a purchase money security interest and the credit extended is referred to as an "enabling loan." The security interest may be avoidable as a preference if it was perfected after being granted and perfection occurred within the preference period.

Section 547(c)(3) of the Bankruptcy Code has a 30-day grace period within which a purchase money secured creditor must perfect its security interest in order to avoid the risk avoidance of the security interest as a preference. This larger period of time granted by the BAPCPA is actually longer than the Uniform Commercial Code Article 9 period for perfection.

FRAUDULENT TRANSFERS

Elements

The Bankruptcy Code permits the debtor in possession or the trustee to avoid two different types of fraudulent transfers made within one year prior to the filing of bankruptcy. Under 11 USC § 548(a), transfers of the debtor's property made with the *actual* intent to hinder, delay, or defraud creditors and transfers of property for less than reasonably equivalent value at a time when the debtor was insolvent or inadequately capitalized may be set aside.

To prevail in the first instance, a trustee must show that the debtor transferred property with the actual intent to defraud its creditors. The debtor's intent will generally be inferred from the circumstances surrounding the transfer since the debtor rarely confesses to the necessary intent. Bankruptcy courts consider the following factors: (1) whether the debtor received fair value for the property actually transferred; (2) whether the debtor became insolvent or was insolvent at the time of the transfer; (3) the amount of the property transferred; (4) the length of time that elapsed between the transfer and the filing of the bankruptcy; (5) the remaining assets available to the debtor after making the transfer; (6) the debtor's records of other transactions before filing bankruptcy; and (7) the existence of a relationship between the debtor and the transferee. A court will generally set aside a transfer if it concludes that the debtor had the necessary fraudulent intent unless the debtor clearly received an equivalent value in money or money's worth in return for the transfer of the asset.

As a practical matter, this type of fraudulent transfer action will rarely be brought by a debtor in possession since it would require it to admit fraudulent intent, something that is unlikely to engender a great deal of faith in its ability to carry on in business. If, however, as a member of the creditors' committee, you become aware of facts that suggest that a transfer was made fraudulently, the committee may, with permission from the court, bring the fraudulent transfer action and recover the assets for the estate.

The second type of fraudulent transfer requires no evidence of a fraudulent intent. The debtor in possession may set aside transfers that the Code deems constructively fraudulent where the debtor received less than reasonably equivalent value for the property transferred even if the debtor received legal consideration.

If the court concludes that the debtor received reasonably equivalent value for the transfer, that is the end of the matter. If, however, the debtor received less than reasonably equivalent value, the debtor in possession must additionally show one of the following: (1) that the debtor was insolvent at the time of the transfer or became insolvent as a result of the transfer; (2) that the debtor was in business and an unreasonably small amount of capital remained after the transfer was completed; or (3) that the debtor intended to incur debts beyond the debtor's ability to pay in the future.

The simplest example of a fraudulent transfer of this type is where a debtor transfers an asset to a relative or friend with the understanding that the asset will be retransferred after the bankruptcy case is closed. More complex are the situations where the debtor creates a sham debt and grants a lien on the property to secure the debt.

The BAPCPA modifies Section 548 of the Bankruptcy Code by enabling the trustee to recover avoidable transfers and excessive prepetition compensation, such as bonuses, paid to insiders of a debtor. It effectuates two changes to current law that would make it easier for a trustee to avoid prepetition transfers as fraudulent conveyances. First, it extends Section 548's one-year reach-back period for fraudulent conveyances to two years. This provision takes effect for bankruptcy cases filed on and after April 20, 2006.

It also adds new fraudulent conveyance grounds. A trustee could recover any transfer or avoid any obligation incurred for the benefit of an insider under an employment contract, and not in the ordinary course of business, if the debtor did not receive reasonably equivalent value. There is also a new Section 548(e) that protects against self-settled trusts by allowing a trustee to avoid any transfer of an interest of the debtor in property that was made within 10 years of the date of commencement of the bankruptcy case if the: (i) transfer was made to a self-settled trust or similar device; (ii) transfer was made by the debtor; (iii) debtor was a beneficiary of the trust; and (iv) debtor made the transfer with actual intent to hinder, delay or defraud a present or future creditor. Transfers avoidable by this new subsection include transfers in anticipation of a money judgment, settlement, civil penalty or fine for violation of securities laws and regulations arising out of fraud, deceit, and manipulation in a fiduciary capacity or in connection with the purchase or sale of any regulated security.

Defenses

Under the Bankruptcy Code, a transferee that takes for value and in good faith is entitled to a lien on the property transferred or may retain any interest transferred to the extent that such transferee gave value. 11 USC § 548(c). To fall within this savings provision, the transferee must show that it gave value for the transfer and that the transfer was made in good faith.

Involuntary Bankruptcy

The filing of an involuntary bankruptcy is used by creditors to force recovery of fraudulent and preferential transfers. *See above.* Since the common law does not prevent a debtor from preferring one creditor over others and gives creditors only a limited ability to recover fraudulent transfers, the filing of an involuntary bankruptcy may be the only way of stopping and recovering these types of transfers.

You will want to monitor the debtor. If you become aware of activities that suggest that the debtor is rapidly depleting its assets or if the debtor is preferring creditors through the payment of some unsecured claims over others, including yours, you may wish to consider the filing of an involuntary bankruptcy. As a general rule, if a debtor has 12 or more creditors, you need at least three creditors, with unsecured claims, not contingent as to liability or subject to bona fide dispute, totaling at least $12,300, to be petitioning creditors.

The BAPCPA also modifies Section 303 in connection with the eligibility requirements for a creditor to qualify to join in the filing of an involuntary bankruptcy petition. For cases in which there are more than 12 creditors of the potential debtor, where three or more creditors may file an involuntary petition, each such creditor must hold a claim that is not contingent as to liability and not the subject of a bona fide dispute "as to liability or amount." The petitioning creditors' non-contingent, undisputed claims must total at least $12,300 more than any liens securing such claims. This alters Section 303 by precluding such claims from being subject to bona fide dispute as to liability or amount. This change became effective on April 20, 2005 and applies to all cases commenced before, on or after that date, and therefore, retroactively applied to all involuntary cases pending on April 20, 2005.

The proposed interim bankruptcy rules also include a new form of involuntary bankruptcy petition which can be found at www.uscourts.gov/bkforms/.

You also need to prove that the debtor is generally not paying its undisputed debts as they mature to be successful on an involuntary bankruptcy petition. Remember, however, that if the court fails to order relief, you may be held liable for any loss by or damage to the debtor by the filing of the involuntary bankruptcy petition, including the debtor's professional fees incurred in defending the petition and actual and possibly punitive damages for a bad faith filing.

Tactics

If a customer you suspect is contemplating bankruptcy offers you payment on an unsecured claim, you should generally accept the payment. Although the payment may later be deemed a preference, there is always the possibility that the debtor will not file bankruptcy at all or, if it does file, it will file more than 90 days after the payment is received. In either event, the payment will not be recoverable as a preference. Even if the bankruptcy is filed, the trustee may determine the cost of litigation outweighs any potential recovery or, if the preference action is filed, your payment may fit within one of the statutory exceptions. In other words, the worst that can happen is that you will have to pay the money back. Thus, when offered payment by a debtor in financial difficulties, *accept the payment.*

As a member of the creditors' committee, you will want to carefully review the debtor's security agreements for possible preference and other avoidance actions and scrutinize all transfers made within the year preceding the bankruptcy filing for potential fraudulent transfer actions. Ideally, the debtor in possession will initiate these actions. Realistically, however, the debtor in possession may be unable or unwilling to take action against some of its creditors. If this is the case, the committee may wish to intervene.

Like any lawsuit, it is important to evaluate the case at the outset. Far too often, creditors force the debtor or trustee to litigate actions that have little potential benefit, but involve tremendous expense to the bankruptcy estate. As the debtor's and the committee's legal fees are paid out of the monies available for distribution to the unsecured creditors, pursuit of costly litigation may result in your fighting yourself with your own money. Counsel should be given instructions on time and expense limits in pursuing recovery of transfers.

MASTER CHECKLIST

Caveat

This checklist is primarily aimed at assisting nonlawyers in making an initial evaluation of a bankruptcy case. It is not intended as a substitute for counsel. In many of the cases, the checklist will help you in determining whether you are going to refer the case to counsel or close the case entirely.

Routing System

At the outset it is imperative that you set up an appropriate routing system for *all* bankruptcy notices. You could prescribe the address to which notices are sent by sending at least two letters to the debtor prior to the bankruptcy with the debtor's account number and the creditor's address where notices must be sent. Particularly if your accounts receivable are paid through a lockbox or other direct deposit system, you need to reroute bankruptcy notices *directly* to whoever is responsible for making decisions and taking action in bankruptcy cases. This may involve a change of address with the bankruptcy court at the very beginning of the case to reroute the bankruptcy notices from the lockbox to the responsible party.

Internally, your bankruptcy system should route copies of notices to all individuals who make decisions concerning customers. The sales department, as well as the credit department, may need to know of the bankruptcy filing and should receive copies of any notices. The routing system should establish a single file for all notices. The file should also contain other credit information concerning the debtor and copies of any credit memos or other documentation relating to sales of goods or services to the debtor.

Finally, the file should contain sufficient information for you to determine the amount of your prepetition claim and any postpetition credit extended to a debtor in possession in a Chapter 11. Separate documentation as to postpetition credit is very important, as the postpetition credit will be treated differently from prepetition claims. *See above.*

BANKRUPTCY CHECKLIST

Response to Initial Bankruptcy Notice

1. Stop any collection activity.
2. Review initial bankruptcy notice and determine the size of any claim your company holds against the debtor.
3. If the claim is small and does not justify t.he assistance of counsel in the reorganization process, file a claim and close the file.
4. Gather all documentation relating to the claim for possible transmittal to counsel with instructions for action in the case.
5. Notify the sales department of any restrictions on postpetition credit sales to the debtor in possession.

Reclamation/Goods in Transit/New Administrative Claim

1. Determine whether any goods are in transmit or delivered immediately prior to the petition are subject to reclamation under the Uniform Commercial Code 2-207. *See above.*
2. Stop all goods in transit through notice to the common carrier delivering the goods.
3. Serve a reclamation demand upon the debtor for goods received immediately prior to bankruptcy.
4. Reclamation or stoppage of goods in transit will probably require reference to counsel for further action.
5. There is also the new administrative claim in favor of goods suppliers in the amount of the value of goods received by the debtor within 20 days of bankruptcy (*see* Chapter 15).

Participation in the Chapter 11 Creditors' Committee

If the case is filed under Chapter 11, review the file and the prospects for reorganization to determine whether appointment to the creditors' committee would assist in the reorganization process. If you wish to participate in the reorganization as a member of the creditors' committee, contact the United States Trustee for the district in which the case is pending and volunteer for membership on the committee. You should also fill out and return the solicitation form sent by the United States Trustee to the debtor's larger creditors if your wish to serve on the committee.

Deadline for Filing Claims

Chapter 7

It is not likely that the initial notice of the bankruptcy will indicate a deadline for filing a proof of claim. If the trustee discovers assets available for distribution, you will receive a separate notice advising you that you need to file your proof of claim and the deadline by which you must comply.

NOTE that the filing of a claim submits you to the jurisdiction of the Bankruptcy Court and may constitute the waiver of a right to a jury trial in certain preference and fraudulent transfer actions.

CHAPTER 11

a. Determine the deadline for the filing of claims from the initial notice. If no deadline is established in the initial notice, review the file periodically for deadlines subsequently established by the court.
b. If the court has established a deadline for the filing of claims in the initial notice, review your file and determine whether you intend to file a claim. If so, file the claim within the deadline established.
c. Even if the court does not establish a deadline in the initial notice, you may wish to file a claim immediately.

NOTE that under 11 USC § 1111(b), a claim is deemed filed in Chapter 11 (but not in Chapters 7, 12 or 13) unless the debtor has listed the creditor's claim as disputed, contingent, or unliquidated in the schedules. Since you may not be able to review the court file and determine how you are listed, you may have to file a claim.

NOTE that the filing of a claim submits you to the jurisdiction of the Bankruptcy Court and may constitute the waiver of a right to a jury trial in certain preference and fraudulent transfer actions.

CHAPTER 12

The deadline is 90 days from the date first set for the § 341 meeting. Generally, the notice sent by the Bankruptcy Court will establish the deadline.

NOTE that the filing of a claim submits you to the jurisdiction of the Bankruptcy Court and may constitute the waiver of a right to a jury trial in certain preference and fraudulent transfer actions.

CHAPTER 13

The deadline is 90 days from the date first set for the § 341 meeting. Generally, the notice sent by the bankruptcy court will establish the deadline.

NOTE that the filing of a claim submits you to the jurisdiction of the bankruptcy court and may constitute the waiver of a right to a jury trial in certain preference and fraudulent transfer actions.

Deadlines for Objections to Discharge and Complaints to Determine Dischargeability

Review the initial notice for the deadlines established for any objections to discharge and complaints to determine dischargeability. If the deadlines are established, consult counsel about any complaints to determine dischargeability or objections to discharge well prior to the deadline so counsel can timely file the necessary complaint.

Motions for Trustee or Examiner in Chapter 11

If you intend to participate actively in the case, you may want to review the facts to determine whether the appointment of a trustee or an examiner is warranted. Generally, it will be necessary to consult counsel to file a motion.

Subsequent Notices

Review all other notices received from the court to determine whether action is required.

Notice of Hearing on an Application for Use of Cash Collateral

Generally, the debtor in Chapter 11 will propose to use cash collateral in the continued operation of the business immediately after the filing of the petition. Failure to object to the use of cash collateral may waive the right to object.

Motion for Relief from Stay

Generally, secured creditors will seek relief from the automatic stay to foreclose their security interest in property of the estate shortly after the petition is filed. You may need to consult with counsel to determine how the relief from stay might affect your rights as a secured creditor or consignor in any property of the bankruptcy estate.

Notice of Intended Sale of Estate Assets

If you claim a security interest or other right to property in the possession of the bankruptcy, your rights may be affected and even eliminated through the sale of the property by the debtor. Generally, any sale other than in the ordinary course of business will have to be noticed to all creditors. If you fail to object to the intended sale, you may waive your rights to property in the hands of the estate.

Notice of Hearing on Disclosure Statement

The court will generally require the debtor in Chapter 11 to give notice of the filing of the disclosure statement and plan. You may not actually receive a copy of the disclosure statement and plan at the preliminary stages of the case. Rather, the court will direct that notice be given and, if you want a copy of the disclosure statement and plan, you will have to request them from the debtor.

Once you have received the disclosure statement and plan, you may object to the adequacy of the information furnished, although this will require the assistance of counsel.

Notice of Confirmation Hearing: Chapter 11, 12, or 13

Once a plan has been filed (and a disclosure statement approved in Chapter 11), the court will require the debtor or other proponent of the plan to give notice of the confirmation of the plan. Attached to the notice will be the plan and disclosure statement previously approved by the court. You will also receive a ballot for voting on the plan in Chapter 11. No ballot will be sent in Chapter 12 or 13, as creditors do not vote on plans in those cases.

You should immediately review the notice to establish any deadlines for objections to the plan and the date for the confirmation hearing. You should also review the deadline for the filing of the ballot in connection with the plan in Chapter 11.

You should thereafter review the plan provisions with counsel to determine whether you have any objections to confirmation or, in Chapter 11, how you should vote. Generally, you will want to review the proposed distribution to your claim in making a decision on voting on the plan.

Thereafter, in Chapter 11, you will want to file your ballot in time for the court or proponent to receive it well before the confirmation hearing. You may accept or reject the plan and, if more than one plan is before the creditors, you may accept or reject any of them and indicate a preference for one plan over all others. While the filing of the ballot will not require the assistance of counsel, counsel will be necessary to file objections to confirmation. If you elect to object to confirmation of the proposed plan, consult counsel.

FEE APPLICATIONS

The court must approve all applications for fees and expenses presented by professionals employed by the debtor, the creditors' committee and the trustee, and fee applications from the trustee or examiner, if one is appointed, after notice to creditors. Generally, professionals will be paid on an hourly basis. Hourly rates vary widely from one part of the country to another. As nationwide law firms and accounting firms become more and more common, the bankruptcy courts have become more experienced in awarding fees based on specific criteria set forth by the Office of the United States Trustee. These criteria include the complexity of the case being handled, the experience level of the professional, the uniqueness or routine of a particular matter. A new provision added by the BAPCPA is with respect to a professional person, whether the person is board certified or otherwise has demonstrated skill and experience in the bankruptcy field.

As an unsecured creditor, you will be concerned that the fees not be excessive and that they be reasonably related to the results in the case. You will have an opportunity to object to the award of the fees. The objection will have to be in writing and filed with the bankruptcy court prior to any deadline established in the notice of the fee application. If you are objecting to the hourly rates, the time spent, or the results achieved, you will have to demonstrate that the fee request is unreasonable in light of the size of the case, normal hourly rates in the area where the case is pending, or the results achieved. This may require the employment of an expert witness to testify on any of those issues.

POSTCONFIRMATION MOTIONS

A debtor or other proponent of a plan may propose modifications of the plan up until the time the plan is substantially consummated. Substantial consummation is discussed above and generally involves the transfer of any assets involved in the case and the commencement of payments to creditors pursuant to a confirmed plan. You will be given an opportunity to object to any postconfirmation modification of the plan. Quite often, postconfirmation modifications will be an attempt to delay payments because the operating results have not been as projected.

Refer to Chapter 27 for the following forms:

- Official Form 10 (Form B10)
- Reaffirmation Agreement
- Proof of Claim with Power of Attorney

20 Alternatives to Forcing a Financially Distressed Debtor into Bankruptcy

The story of a debtor's financial struggles is all too common to the credit professional. It begins by the debtor describing that its industry is mired in the trough of a cyclical slowdown, that the slowdown reduced customer demand and created over-capacity in the industry, and more particularly, in the debtor's operations, and that as a result, the debtor experienced operating losses and cash flow difficulties. The debtor then rides this slippery slope of obscurity into an enthusiastic picture of an anticipated turnaround to the profitable days of yesteryear. However, as credit extensions become increasingly rare, and collection actions more familiar, the debtor finally concludes that reorganization is the only avenue to remain in the market-place, but wait, bankruptcy is not the only solution.

Let's face it, bankruptcy does not always work the way that it should. Bankruptcy proceedings are becoming increasingly more expensive and time consuming. As the debtor contemplates its prospects of reorganization through continuing its operations or liquidating its assets, its creditors are often in limbo and holding substantial claims that may never get paid. Still further, a creditor must fret over the concern that payments received pre-petition may be subject to a preference action and returned to the estate for an "equal" distribution.

As cynical as it may sound, bankruptcy effectively distorts state law entitlements, creditors' rights, and penalizes efficient businesses through its preservation of thwarting businesses. Although bankruptcy may have its advantages for the debtor, creditors should encourage a distressed debtor to consider alternatives to formal bankruptcy proceedings such as mediation, arbitration, an out-of-court workout, or an assignment for the benefit of creditors prior to pressuring the debtor into bankruptcy. The use of alternative dispute resolution and non bankruptcy alternatives is becoming increasingly popular as a more expedient and less expensive method to adjusting debts when there is a dispute or an inability to pay. Creditors and debtors alike often overlook these viable alternatives in the heat of collection demands and the debtor's reciprocal delay. However, when properly applied, these alternatives may maximize, or even provide a greater return to creditors by avoiding significant administrative fees and expenses that would otherwise be incurred through a bankruptcy filing. How many times are claims reduced, or not paid at all, while professionals make the big bucks? If it's your debtor in bankruptcy, you probably think this happens all too often.

A bankruptcy filing may be the only viable option as in the case of a large, publicly held corporation or other corporation seeking discharge of its debts, which under the following alternatives, are not possible because state law cannot discharge debts. Nevertheless, there is no harm in inquiring whether any of these alternatives may be a better option, or refraining from a course of conduct that would force the debtor to seek bankruptcy protection.

The intent of this chapter is to inform creditors and debtors of alternatives to bankruptcy proceedings or, in the event that a creditor receives notice that its debtor has elected an alternative to bankruptcy, to inform the creditor of the process in which it is about to embark. In most circumstances, implementation of an alternative is intended to minimize fees and costs associated with the adjustment and the collection of debts. However, in all of these circumstances, the debtor's resources for the payment of its debts are limited and every dollar consumed by professionals to resolve the debt is one less dollar to satisfy creditors' claims. Creditors should keep that simple fact in mind when negotiating with the debtor to resolve its debts with the least amount of litigation as possible.

ALTERNATIVE DISPUTE RESOLUTION

The court system is the traditional method for collecting an outstanding account or resolving other disputes with debtors. However, once a civil action has commenced, lawyers begin to vigorously pursue their client's interest and, of course, usually at the expense of their client. Creditors that have sought to resolve their disputes through commencing litigation are painfully aware that litigation of the dispute takes considerable time and involves escalating costs. The economic consequences of pursuing a debtor are often harsh and resolution of the dispute may be more costly than the value of a judgment itself.

In an effort to minimize the costs of resolving disputes, creditors are frequently turning to Alternative Dispute Resolution ("ADR"). ADR refers to any means of settling disputes outside of the traditional court system. The most common ADR procedures are mediation and arbitration. However, these methods seldom mirror one another in both substance and procedure. In essence, mediation incorporates a flexible structure in which a mediator clarifies the issues between the parties and directs the parties toward settlement. The casual environment of mediation is intended to encourage dialogue between the parties. On the other hand, arbitration is more adversarial and akin to an abbreviated court proceeding or trial. In arbitration, each party presents its side of the story in a courtroom like setting with an arbitrator issuing findings of fact and an award.

Parties can enter into mediation and arbitration voluntarily or through court order once a civil proceeding has commenced. Due to these differences, a creditor should review which method is most beneficial in obtaining a favorable resolution to its claim.

Mediation

Perhaps one of the most beneficial and cost-effective methods of ADR is voluntary mediation. In mediation, the parties to the dispute meet informally with the assistance of a mediator to discuss the dispute and explore the possibility of settlement. In the initial stage of mediation, a mediator will discuss his or her qualifications and knowledge of the dispute, which may be expansive through the submission of mediation briefs, or limited and based on preliminary discussions with the parties. Subsequent to this introduction, a mediator conducts confidential meetings with each party to refine the dispute and assess the risks and strengths of the parties' respective interests. The confidential sessions may continue back and forth culminating into several sessions and, intermittently, may involve meetings between the parties to gauge how far along they have progressed toward settlement. Ultimately, the mediation is intended to assist the parties toward a mutually agreeable settlement of their disputes.The flexibility of mediation permits the parties to enter into mediation proceedings before or after the commencement of litigation. In addition, a majority of jurisdictions have enacted legislation that permits courts to order mediation at the request of the parties, or in some instances, involuntarily. In almost all instances, mediation requires the good faith efforts of all parties to engage in meaningful dialogue with the possibility that settlement will be reached. This is especially so where mediation has been entered into voluntarily prior to the commencement of litigation because there is nothing holding the parties to mediate their dispute.

The selection of a mediator is essential to the success of the mediation. The parties will usually agree to the selection of a mediator that is skilled in the area of law in which the dispute has arisen. At times, selection of a mediator may go through several rounds between the parties. The mediator should not only be a good facilitator with knowledge of particular areas of law, but also have specialized training in the techniques that bring parties to compromise their disputes.

The mediator is a catalyst, and through the use of common mediation techniques, initiates ideas to guide the parties toward settlement. The mediator does not make a decision as to the merits of the parties' respective contentions. Instead, the parties remain in control of their positions and participation in the mediation. The mediator may provide his or her opinion as to the strength of a party's contentions; however, a mediator does not issue formal findings of fact, opinions, or awards. Perhaps the most significant benefit to mediation is that resolution of the dispute is left solely between the parties and they can structure a resolution almost any way that the parties see fit and agree upon.

The casual environment of mediation and confidential communications with the mediator permits the parties to explain their contentions in great detail to the mediator, which will then assist in facilitating dialogue when the parties meet to discuss their dispute. Oftentimes, parties will provide more information between one another, as the mediation environment is not as intimidating as litigation. In addition, since the mediator does not have the authority to make a decision on any matter, the parties are more inclined to share information to bring the dispute to a close. Indeed, the open dialogue is often used by the mediator to point out common ground between the parties and to shrink the differences in opinion that were brought to the mediation table by the parties in the first instance. Further, as the parties remain in control and are not bound to continue mediation, a party may withdraw from mediation at any time without the concern that statements it expressed will be revealed in future proceedings.

The mediator must be a skilled facilitator and interpreter as the mediator will convey positions and proposals to the parties. The mediator uses several techniques to narrow the issues and move the parties toward resolution of their disputes. One technique is to separate the parties from the dispute through actively listening to their contentions while maintaining neutrality. In this respect, the mediator maintains a positive environment through recasting a party's contentions in a way that is non offensive to the other party. Yet another technique involves redirecting the parties to focus on their interests and not their positions. The mediator may provide analogies and metaphors to analyze a dispute and propose solutions that were not previously reviewed because the parties were focused on the dispute instead of their underlying interests. Still another technique is the mediator's focus on proposals in which each party realizes some benefit from settlement. The mediator may use other techniques that are developed entirely through his or her unique experiences in mediating disputes.

Mediation is also a useful tool for parties to assess the likelihood that their case will prevail in litigation. Through the mediator's impartial and confidential position, the mediator is able to assess the strengths and weaknesses of each party's contentions and advise the parties during the mediation process. In some cases, this may reinforce a party's belief that their case is strong, whereas to others, it may serve as a "wake up call" that their case has more holes than "Swiss cheese." However, if a bad case is flushed out, a party holding up settlement may be more willing to resolve the dispute.

Arbitration

To arbitrate or not to arbitrate—that is the question facing many creditors in negotiation of their contracts and commercial disputes. To begin with, arbitration is mostly a creature of contract law and, usually, can only be initiated if the parties agree to it. The decision to arbitrate is dependent on a myriad of factors, including the requirement imposed by contract law, nature of the dispute, or in other cases, by statute. In limited circumstances, arbitration may be compelled after the commencement of litigation by court order or elected by the litigating parties. In any event, arbitration should be considered a valuable method for creditors to resolve their disputes in a cost-effective and expeditious manner.

As briefly discussed above, a decision to arbitrate a dispute is determined at the outset of the parties' relationship and incorporated into an agreement. The arbitration agreement must be in writing and should be signed by the parties. If a decision is made to include an arbitration agreement, then the agreement should state that the arbitration is "binding" on the parties. For example, an arbitration clause may read:

> Any controversy or claim arising out of or relating to this contract, or breach thereof, shall be settled through binding arbitration, in accordance with the rules, then obtaining, of the American Arbitration Association, and judgment on the award rendered may be entered in the highest court of the forum, state, or federal, court having jurisdiction.

It is important to have counsel review the arbitration agreement, as well as other provisions of the contract, to assure that it is in conformity with state law, the Uniform Commercial Code, and any other applicable laws. Furthermore, the agreement should be reviewed in reference to the trade in which it is being applied.

Similar to mediation, the selection of an arbitrator is essential to the success of the arbitration. The arbitrator may be selected in one of many ways. Generally, the contract outlines the selection procedure or references rules that apply. In most cases, arbitrators are selected by the service administrating the arbitration, or the parties may agree to an arbitrator or submit a list of arbitrators to the administrator that will select the arbitrator. In most situations, the arbitration will be conducted with one arbitrator administering the dispute. However, in certain complex cases, a panel of arbitrators may be utilized. As arbitration involves procedures similar to that of court proceedings, the arbitrator should have knowledge of legal procedures and some familiarity with the rules of evidence, though evidentiary rules are loosely applied in arbitration proceedings. Additionally, the arbitrator should have knowledge of particular areas of law and industry practices.

From the commencement of the arbitration, the parties are not bound by the rules of the court. Instead, the parties are bound to the terms of their agreement or the rules adopted by the arbitration administer. For example, arbitrations usually involve limited contact between the parties and the arbitrator prior to the proceeding in which evidence is presented as opposed to court proceedings that may involve numerous hearings on case administration and motions prior to the commencement of trial. Another important aspect of arbitration is its limitation on the right to discovery. Generally, discovery is limited in arbitration unless specifically permitted by the arbitration agreement. Discovery is the method that parties use in litigation to gain information and documents related to the dispute from the opposing party. In contentious matters, discovery can cause significant delay and unreasonably inflate the costs of litigation through numerous disputes and motions. Through arbitration, discovery related matters are minimized or avoided altogether. The abbreviated procedures usually assure that an arbitration proceeding will commence sooner rather than later, and in most events, far in advance of trial if the dispute is litigated. Further, the abbreviated deadlines and speed of the arbitration process usually provide an incentive for the parties to facilitate settlement discussions as the case progresses to the arbitration proceeding.

At the arbitration proceeding, the arbitrator acts in lieu of a judge and presides over evidence introduced by the parties. Unlike court proceedings where judges are bound by rules of procedure and evidence, an arbitrator adheres to relaxed procedures and the rules of evidence are not strictly enforced. For example, evidence relating to "hearsay" is usually admitted, whereas in court proceedings, absent an exception, such evidence would be disregarded. Another example of relaxed evidence standards is the admissibility of "parol evidence" (i.e., evidence outside of a contract used to interpret a contract's provisions). In theory, relaxed evidentiary standards allow the parties to present their cases in a fast and efficient manner.

Once the parties have concluded presentation of their cases, the arbitrator issues the findings of fact and an award. Ordinarily, the parties to the arbitration may not appeal the arbitration's results and the award becomes final. The prevailing party usually registers the arbitration award in the court in which the other party is domiciled or operates its principal place of business. The court gives full force and effect to the arbitrator's findings and award. If execution of the judgment becomes necessary, then the prevailing party may use state law remedies to satisfy its judgment.

In summary, arbitration provides an alternative method to resolve disputes between creditors and debtors. Generally, arbitration is more expeditious and cost effective than traditional court proceedings while maintaining a similar, yet more flexible procedure.

OUT-OF-COURT WORKOUTS

Instead of electing business reorganization under Chapter 11 of the Bankruptcy Code, or an assignment for the benefit of creditors, the debtor and its creditors may elect to "workout" their debts through a contract. An out-of-court workout is usually initiated by the debtor who sends a "confidential communication" requesting that its creditors attend a meeting of creditors to discuss a workout. Should the credit professional be receptive to this request or solicit others to force an involuntary bankruptcy? It all depends on the chances for recovery.

Background

A financially struggling debtor may propose an out of court workout to its creditors to avoid formal relief under the Bankruptcy Code. An out of court workout is a contractual agreement made between the debtor and its creditors to resolve outstanding debt obligations and, at the same time, direct a course toward financial stability. In most instances, a corporation or limited liability company will use an out-of-court workout while other business forms (i.e., proprietorships and partnerships) will seek a discharge of their debts. A credit professional should balance the advantages of a workout agreement against the advantages of reorganization through bankruptcy.

A workout agreement enables a debtor to address its primary concern of burdensome debt without the stigma that a bankruptcy filing may entail. Through a workout, the debtor avoids the public scrutiny of a bankruptcy case, shields its customers from competitors seeking to cash in on the debtor's demise, and manages internal relations with employees in a much less intimidating manner. The positive atmosphere that the workout may accomplish assists all parties in interest by focusing on the issues that led to the debtors' financial difficulties and charting a course to profitability.

More important, a workout is usually expeditious, less expensive, and interferes only minimally with the debtor's operations. Workout agreements are proposed and accepted within a short period of time after the meeting of creditors. In the context of bankruptcy reorganization, a bankruptcy case may take several months, and perhaps years, prior to the acceptance of a plan. Even after a plan is accepted, payment of pre-petition obligations is further delayed through post confirmation litigation of preference actions and other avoidable transactions. The delay of bankruptcy reorganization also has a collateral effect on the expenses to the debtor's estate. In bankruptcy, the debtors are required to pay for the services and costs of professionals through administrative expense claims. As an administrative claim, the professionals are paid prior to the other creditors, which will affect the amount of a distribution. Further, a workout agreement has a minimal affect on the debtors' operations and does not require a court order for use of cash, filing of monthly operating reports, and other operational scrutiny of a court proceeding. Instead, a workout permits the debtor to focus on returning its operations to profitability.

Meeting of Creditors

The first step toward a successful workout will require the debtor to convene a "meeting of creditors." The meeting normally consists of general unsecured creditors only. At the meeting of creditors, the debtor is usually prepared to confidentially discuss the issues that created its financial difficulties, its current revenues and debt structure, prior and future efforts to reorganize its operations, and other information to convince creditors that a workout is the best chance for payment.

Formation of a Creditors' Committee

The formation of a creditors' committee is also of primary importance at the meeting of creditors. The role of a work out creditors' committee is similar to that of a Chapter 11 creditors' committee. Essentially, the creditors' committee serves as the "watchdog" of the debtor's affairs and makes decisions and recommendations to the debtor's creditors. The selection of the committee should closely correspond to the requirement of the Bankruptcy Code since a failed workout or, alternatively, a dissenting creditor group seeking an involuntary bankruptcy petition, may force the debtor into bankruptcy. If the debtor is forced into bankruptcy, then the workout committee may continue its functions and relationship with the debtor as a Chapter 11 creditors' committee. Generally, a creditors' committee should be fairly chosen after notice is given and consist of a fair representation of the creditor body. Similar to the bankruptcy context, the creditors' committee should seek legal counsel and other professionals as soon as practicable. It is imperative in the workout process that the creditors' committee receives competent legal advice since a debtor is subject to less scrutiny than under the administration of a bankruptcy case. Generally, the debtor will compensate the creditors' committee's legal counsel for its costs and services. The individual committee members are also entitled to compensation for expenses.

Workout Agreements and Creditors Subject to the Agreement's Terms and Conditions

There is no strict formula as to the terms and conditions incorporated into an out of court workout agreement. In most circumstances, members of the creditors' committee have experience in negotiating agreements and, with the assistance of professionals, negotiate with the debtor to reach a fair accommodation with creditors. The real benefit of workout agreements is that the agreement is specifically tailored to the needs of the debtor and its creditors and is the sole product of negotiations between the parties.

Generally, there are two types of workout agreements. An "extension agreement" restructures the debtor's obligations for payment in full over a period of time. Alternatively, a "composition" agreement reduces debt obligations and creditors receive only a fraction of their claims. There are also hybrid plans that may pay a fraction of the claim over a period of time or payment may be received in goods or products of the debtor.

A workout agreement is a contract that is only binding on the creditors that accept the agreement. Accordingly, creditors that do not agree with the workout are free to pursue their own agendas. Although unanimity is difficult, if not impossible to reach, the workout agreement should at least seek the approval of one half of the creditors holding claims totaling two thirds in value. Granted the debtor makes adequate disclosures, the terms and conditions of the workout agreement may be incorporated into a plan of reorganization and quickly enforceable if the debtor is forced into bankruptcy. Accordingly, the assistance of professionals is important to assure that the agreement will survive the test of confirmation if recalcitrant creditors force the debtor into an involuntary bankruptcy.

Comparison to the Bankruptcy Code and the Advantages of a Formal Reorganization

Although the informal context of a workout is a valuable method in achieving payment, the more viable alternative may be a formal reorganization. The Bankruptcy Code provides several statutory protections to assist the debtor through its reorganization efforts, which are unavailable through a workout. One of the more useful protections of the Bankruptcy Code is the automatic stay. The automatic stay imposes a freeze on all suits, foreclosures and similar actions against the debtor's assets, which comprise the debtor's bankruptcy "estate." If the debtor is facing a flood of litigation, then the automatic stay creates breathing space for the debtor to focus its attention on the reorganization of its operations. Another operational advantage to reorganization under the Bankruptcy Code is the debtor's ability to reject executory contracts and unexpired leases. Although the newly-enacted Bankruptcy Reform Act has shifted much of the control in assuming or rejecting non-residential real estate from the debtor to the lessor, this is nonetheless an important tool for the debtor if it remains liable for burdensome contracts and unexpired leases, which may be over market or simply no longer a part of its operations or future business plan.

The Bankruptcy Code also offers unique strategies to achieve a successful reorganization that are not always available through a workout. If management concludes that a sale of the debtor's assets is the only way to effectuate reorganization, then the debtor is usually entitled to sell its assets free and clear of liens and encumbrances and, oftentimes, without the consent of secured creditors. This remedy is not available under a workout and may invite protracted litigation by secured parties in an attempt to protect their individual interests. In addition, under certain circumstances, the Bankruptcy Code permits the "cramdown" on dissenting creditors of the provisions of a plan. In the workout setting, creditors may "opt out" of the workout agreement and seek their own recovery. Further, reorganization under the Bankruptcy Code permits recovery of preferential transfers and the avoidance of liens and fraudulent conveyances.

Accordingly, reorganization under Bankruptcy Code provides an even playing field for all creditors to recover their proportionate share of available funds whereas a workout may pay certain creditors ahead of others (i.e., judgment lien creditors).

Conclusion

An out-of-court workout agreement is a valuable method to seek payment from the debtor. The workout may result in a faster plan for payment, reduction in professional fees, and minimal disruption to the debtor's operations. Moreover, it is especially important if creditors do not receive a distribution under a Chapter 11 reorganization since payment may be structured to suit the needs of all parties including the debtor, secured creditors and general unsecured creditors. Furthermore, it is important to underscore the important roles that professionals perform, from the beginning of the workout through the consummation, an agreement that will ultimately assist in a successful workout agreement.

ASSIGNMENTS FOR THE BENEFIT OF CREDITORS

An assignment for the benefit of creditors ("ABC") is an effective, expeditious and cost effective method in liquidating the assets of a distressed debtor without involving the provisions of the Bankruptcy Code. In recent years, the utility of ABCs over a bankruptcy filing has increased, finding particular favor in the technology sector and businesses intending to avoid the stigma of a bankruptcy filing. ABCs also offer the benefit of liquidating assets quickly as the assignee does not need bankruptcy court approval to sell the debtor's assets as would a trustee or debtor in possession.

ABCs are creatures of state law, and as one would anticipate, implementation and the effectiveness of an assignment will vary from state to state. In some states, a contract between the assignee and assignor is all that is required to effectuate an ABC. In other states, the assignee or assignor must register the ABC with a state court of appropriate jurisdiction. However, one nicety remains uniform; by electing an ABC, a debtor avoids the administrative costs and delays that govern bankruptcy proceedings and creditors usually reap the benefit of receiving a greater distribution on their claims.

Assignments for the Benefit of Creditors Are Contractual Transactions

The ABC is a contractual transaction where the debtor, as the assignor, transfers all of its legal and equitable rights in its assets to a third party, as the assignee. The assignee holds that debtor's property in trust and, ultimately, distributes proceeds from the sale of the debtor's assets to creditors in relation to the creditor's priority, which is established by state law.

Assignments for the Benefit of Creditors Minimize Expenses to Provide a Greater Return to Creditors

A main purpose of the ABC is to minimize the administrative expenses associated with bankruptcy proceedings. Although attorneys will likely, and should, become involved in representing parties of interest to the ABC, a debtor would likely incur more significant administrative expenses through bankruptcy proceedings. For example, if the debtor were to file under Chapter 11 of the Bankruptcy Code, then professional fees would be paid directly through the debtor's estate, which become increasingly costly as other professionals are employed and paid through the bankruptcy estate (i.e., a creditors' committee, financial advisors, etc.). In the instance of Chapter 7, a trustee is appointed and paid a fee dependent upon the assets administered through the estate. Bankruptcy also requires, regardless of either Chapter 7 or 11, many procedural filings and appearances that increase costs of administration of the estate including schedules, the statement of financial affairs, and the debtor's examination at the meeting of creditors. As one can see, administrative expenses can add up quickly, even if the bankruptcy case is relatively simple.

On the other hand, administrative expenses associated with ABCs are usually kept to a minimum. The assignee will require a fee, which is paid through the estate's assets and based upon the contractual agreement between the assignor and assignee. The fees may be a retainer with an hourly rate, or contingency rate upon the return of assets to the estate or based on the distribution to creditors, or may be a hybrid or another payment scheme devised under the contract. Professionals assisting the assignee will also likely receive a retainer and any further fees and expenses would be paid through the estate's assets. In this regard, the fees may be similar to that of a Chapter 7 debtor, but the savings will be the "handle," or percentage, that a trustee will receive in administering the assets of the debtor's estate together with the costs of the trustee's counsel and delay of bankruptcy proceedings. Additionally, further savings under an ABC are realized in avoiding the procedural requirements of the Bankruptcy Code.

Duties and Obligations of the Assignee

As discussed above, an ABC is administered by the assignee, which may be an individual or an agent acting on behalf of an entity. In a majority of states, statutes mandate the assignee's duties and obligations, which were previously determined under common law. Additionally, some states have incorporated the common law into its statutory scheme, or have allowed common law and provisions of the Bankruptcy Code to guide courts on the duties and obligations of the assignee.

INVESTIGATING THE TANGIBLE ASSETS OF THE ESTATE

In general, the assignee's foremost duty is its responsibility for investigating, locating and assessing the value of the debtor's assets. The assignee, sometimes with the assistance of the assignor, will then analyze the various options that will maximize the worth of the assets either by sale as a going concern or liquidation.

INVESTIGATING PREFERENCE ACTIONS AND OTHER ACTIONS

The assignee may recover preferential transfers made within a certain number of days preceding the assignment and, likewise, may usually recover payments to insiders made within a longer time period preceding the assignment. In a majority of states, the statutes follow the time periods set under the Bankruptcy Code, which is 90 days and one year (two years under the newly enacted bankruptcy law for fraudulent conveyances in cases commenced one year after the effective date of the new law) preceding the date of the assignment, respectively. In other states, the preference period may be expanded beyond the days set under the Bankruptcy Code (so, creditors "beware"). In addition, a majority of states have adopted the Uniform Fraudulent Transfer Act ("UFTA"), which permits the assignee to "reach back" even further than the assignment statutes and recover for actual and constructive fraudulent conveyances up to four years preceding the assignment.

Unlike the Bankruptcy Code that provides parties in interest (such as creditors) to conduct investigations of the debtor early in the case, most states do not permit the assignee to examine the assignor without first obtaining court order. Accordingly, creditors should monitor the assignment to determine whether the assignee is investigating pre-assignment transfers, especially those to insiders, to assure that the assignment is not simply being used as a ploy to deepen the pockets of insiders outside the scrutiny of bankruptcy proceedings.

In addition to recovery under preference laws and fraudulent conveyance laws, the assignee may be authorized under state statute to perform other duties including, among other things, enjoin an eviction and continue to occupy the debtor's business premises for a period of time after the assignment, prosecute and defend claims as the assignee's successor in interest, set aside unperfected security interests, void attachments and judgment liens, and avoid bulk sales laws (e.g., California). However, as most states have their own statutory scheme, it is important to seek the advice of a professional to determine the powers of the assignee, especially if one of those powers is being asserted adversely against you, the creditor.

INVESTIGATING CREDITORS' CLAIMS, NOTICE OF ASSIGNMENT, AND SETTING A CLAIMS BAR DATE

The assignor provides the assignee with a creditors' listing, contact information and the outstanding balance owed to each creditor. Another one of the assignee's duties is to give notice to creditors of the assignment and an opportunity to file a claim against the assignment estate. Generally, the notice will provide information about the assignee, where to file a claim, and a "bar" date in which claims must be submitted for a creditor to receive a distribution for its claim The notice is similar to the notice that a creditor receives in a bankruptcy proceeding under Chapter 7 of the Bankruptcy Code. However, unlike bankruptcy proceedings in which some flexibility exists for late filed proofs of claims to be considered, ABCs offer less leniency. As a matter of course, a creditor should file a claim with the assignee as soon as practicable and even prior to the notice and bar date if the creditor is aware of the ABC. Moreover, it is always a safe practice to send the claim under registered or certified mail with a return receipt to verify mailing in the event that the claim is inadvertently mishandled. Once the notice and bar date are received, the creditor should verify that its claim purports to the notice and claim requirements. After the bar date passes, the assignee will reconcile the claims and object to those claims deemed improper.

SALE AND DISTRIBUTION OF ASSETS

In most circumstances, the assignee will collect all of the assignor's assets and liquidate the assets either in piecemeal or in bulk, whichever method provides the greatest return to the estate. Although the assignee is not required to comply with the notice and timing requirements of a sale through bankruptcy proceedings, states usually require some reasonable notice to creditors in order to satisfy the assignee's fiduciary duties. In some instances, a buyer may have already been identified, even prior to the entry of the assignment. These "pre packaged" assignments may be beneficial to creditors, as costs associated with the ABC remain very limited; however, a creditor should take great caution that the prepackaged sale is not simply an arrangement with insiders to shave off debt and to continue the business in virtually identical form. In such instances, a liquidation appraisal demonstrating that the prepackaged sale is greater in value than an auction sale should suffice. In all instances, the sale of assets is not free and clear of liens, claims and encumbrances and the purchaser takes possession and title of the assets subject to these interests, which should provide some solace to those creditors holding security interests.

Once the assignee liquidates the assets and has concluded its recovery on other actions, if any, the assignee will prepare to distribute the estate assets pro rata to allowed claims. Generally, it is the assignee's responsibility to distribute the estate's assets. However, in states requiring court supervision, a report is filed with the court and distribution is either ordered or authorized to creditors. The distribution scheme and priority structure follow state law, and unlike the Bankruptcy Code, certain claims, such as tax claims, may not be subordinated and are given a position first in line to other creditors.

Assignments for the Benefit of Creditors and the Involuntary Petition

One of the risks of proceeding with an ABC is that three recalcitrant unsecured creditors of the debtor (or, only one creditor if the debtor has fewer than 12 creditors) may file an involuntary bankruptcy proceeding against the debtor. Bankruptcy courts have been, for the most part, unwilling to unwind the ABC and have dismissed involuntary cases if the assignee can establish that its administration of the estate is competent and the continued administration by the assignee will best serve the interests of the creditors.

RECEIVERSHIP PROCEEDINGS

State or federal court receiverships are a viable non bankruptcy alternative to electing alternative dispute resolution, a workout, or an assignment for the benefit of creditors. Generally, corporations use receiverships because the debtor does not receive a discharge of its debts. Unlike the other alternatives to bankruptcy discussed above, receivership proceedings are rarely voluntary. Receivership proceedings are usually commenced by the filing of an adversary type proceeding and are instituted after the court has made the determination that a receivership is necessary.

Receivership proceedings are not always used to liquidate the assets of insolvent corporations. In some instances, courts may appoint receivers where a corporation is experiencing intra-company disputes between directors, officers, or shareholders. In that respect, receivers act in the capacity of a custodian as opposed to a liquidator. Accordingly, if notified of a receivership proceeding against a debtor, the creditor should carefully review the capacity of the receiver and its duties, which are pre-scribed by court order and state or federal statutes.

Federal Court Receiverships

Pursuant to federal procedural law, the United States District Court may appoint a receiver in the "appropriate circumstance." Generally, federally agencies such as the Internal Revenue Service request the appointment of a receiver. Requests outside of federal agencies are rare. If a party initiates an action to have a receiver appointed, it is necessary for that party to demonstrate an interest in the debtor's property and the court will not appoint a receiver absent some legal justification. In addition, a receiver may be appointed if the debtor's principals have been convicted of criminal activity and the government elects to operate the business to satisfy claims. In federal receiverships, the receiver usually continues the debtor's business operations in order to maximize the recovery for the governmental agency involved. Generally, there are few, if any, creditor interests to protect. Accordingly, federal receiverships deserve less attention from creditors than state court receiverships.

State Court Receiverships

Similar to most other non bankruptcy alternatives state court receiverships are prescribed by statute and vary from state to state. State court receivers are appointed in many situations including to take control of a corporation where disputes exist between directors, officers, or shareholders or, alternatively, in cases where a corporation becomes insolvent and is unable to pay its debts. In these situations, the state court receiver is empowered with the authorities and duties similar to that of an assignee in the assignment for the benefit of creditors. Furthermore, there are many other circumstances in which a state court will appoint a receiver including instances where the corporation is involved in criminal activity. Often times, receivers are attorneys that are selected by the court for their reputation and competence in their respective legal fields.

Although procedures vary from state to state, there are common procedures that apply almost universally. For example, it is common for receivers to post a bond. It is also common for receivers to review the debtor's business operations and hire management and staff to operate the business as an ongoing concern to increase marketability of the business for sale or to preserve the value of its assets in anticipation of liquidation. If a receiver continues to operate the debtor's business, then post receivership debts are often paid in the ordinary course of business. However, unlike administrative claims in a bankruptcy case, there is no guarantee that these claims will be paid or receive priority over pre receivership claims. Accordingly, caution should be taken in transactions made once a debtor goes into receivership.

If a creditor receives notice of a state court receivership proceeding, then it should closely monitor the receivership to determine the requirements for submitting a claim. The court supervises the state court receivership and a court order may set the date in which all claims must be submitted, or alternatively, the claims bar date may be prescribed by statute. If a creditor fails to file a claim with the receiver, then it is precluded from sharing in any distribution through the receivership. Further, if a creditor believes that the state court and receiver are not adequately protecting its interest, the creditor should consult with other creditors to consider the filing of an involuntary bankruptcy case under either Chapter 7 or 11 of the Bankruptcy Code.

In summary, receivership proceedings are the rare exception, rather than the rule. Creditors should monitor state receiverships, and to a lesser extent federal receiverships, to assure that they are not missing the filing date for any proof of claim. Further, if a receivership appears to be infringing on the rights of creditors, then creditors may want to work together to bring an involuntary bankruptcy proceeding, which may protect the interests of creditors through greater supervision of the debtor's business operations.

To find out more or to further answer your questions on alternatives to bankruptcy, contact NACM and its professionals whom will guide you through the process or refer you to other professionals to advise you on the unique circumstances of your situation.

21 Retail Installment Sales Laws

Most states have enacted laws regulating retail installment sales. Retail installment sales are sales of goods or services where the price is payable in periodic installments. Comparable to the retail installment sale is the open-end credit plan. The open-end credit plan allows the buyer to purchase goods or services and have the unpaid balance debited to an account, e.g., credit cards. The balance is then paid off in installments. The application of retail installment sales laws is often limited to certain kinds of goods. In some states they apply to all retail sales payable in installments; in others they apply to only specific types of goods such as automobiles; and in still others they apply only to personal and household goods.

Most commercial credit grantors do not, in their ordinary course of their duties, need to deal with retail installment sales transactions. When such is the case, competent counsel familiar with the unique nature of the transactions must be consulted. The penalties for violation of retail installment sales laws can be very strict and onerous. No short dissertation or chart dealing with retail installments sales laws can be sufficiently complete so as to do away with the necessity for individual competent counsel to provide specialized advice. This chapter is presented for the purpose of an overview only, and should not be relied upon in the absence of individualized legal advice and representation.

A common feature of these laws is a disclosure requirement, by which interest charges must be separately stated. In addition, many statutes specify a particular form of contract, regulate interest rates, and require that sales finance companies be licensed. Civil or criminal penalties may be provided for violations of statutory provisions.

Other state and federal statutes may apply to retail installment sales. A seller is advised to consider the requirements of Article 9 of the Uniform Commercial Code which deals with secured transactions, even though filing may not be required to perfect a security interest. Article 9 underwent a substantial revamping in 2001 and anyone dealing in secured transactions will want to consult with counsel to see whether and how the updates will affect them.

There are a number of other federal statutes that may apply to retail installment sales transactions. Among the better known federal laws are the Truth in Lending Act (TILA), also known as Title I of the Consumer Credit Protection Act (15 USC §§ 1601 et. seq.) and the Equal Credit Opportunity Act (ECOA) (15 USC §§ 1691-1691f). TILA requires that the lender disclose certain terms and costs to the borrower. ECOA prohibits the denial of credit to an individual because of sex, race, national origin, religion or marital status. In addition, the following states have also adopted legislation that prohibits discrimination in granting credit in a similar fashion to the ECOA: Alaska, Arkansas, California, Colorado, Connecticut, Florida, Georgia, Hawaii, Illinois, Indiana, Iowa, Kentucky, Louisiana, Maine, Maryland, Massachusetts, Michigan, Minnesota, Missouri, Montana, Nevada, New

Jersey, New Mexico, New York, North Carolina, North Dakota, Ohio, Oklahoma, Rhode Island, Tennessee, Texas, Utah, Vermont, Virginia, Washington, West Virginia and Wisconsin.

CONTRACT REQUIREMENTS

Most of the state statutes contain specific requirements as to the form and contents of a retail installment sales contract. These include such items as: the contract shall be dated and in writing; the printed portion thereof shall be in at least eight-point type; it shall contain the names of the seller and the buyer, the place of business of the seller, the residence or place of business of the buyer (in some cases, post office addresses), as specified by the buyer; and an adequate description of the goods (including make and model, if any), or services to be rendered. With minor exceptions, the document can contain no blank spaces at the time it is signed by the purchaser. The contract must contain the entire agreement between the parties. The contract must be signed by the buyer and the seller and a copy must be delivered to the buyer at the time of execution or delivery of the goods, or within another specified period of time.

Provisions with respect to price and time payment. Most of the statutes require specifically that the contract set forth the following items:

1. The cash sale price of goods (and/or services)
2. The amount of the buyer's down payment, indicating the amount paid in cash and in goods, and briefly describing the goods traded in
3. The difference between items one and two
4. The amount, if any, included for insurance, specifying the insurance coverage and the cost of each type of coverage
5. The amount, if any, of official fees (filing fees)
6. The principal balance, which is the sum of items three, four and five, above
7. The amount of the credit service charge
8. The time balance, which is the sum of items six and seven, payable by the buyer to the seller, the number of installments required, the amount of each installment expressed in dollars, and the due date or period thereof
9. The time sale price
10. If the installments are not in substantially equal amounts, in some states it is required that the contract contain a statutory statement to this effect in bold type of a stated size

Many of the states require that the contract contain an acknowledgment of receipt of a copy thereof by the buyer, in 10-point bold type or larger. In most cases this is required to appear immediately above the buyer's signature. In Maryland and California, this acknowledgment must be signed specifically by the buyer in addition to his signature at end of contract.

In most of the states, there is also a requirement that a special notice addressed to the buyer be printed in bold type ranging from at least eight to 12 point. The most common form of notice is as follows:

NOTICE TO THE BUYER

1. **Do not sign this agreement before you read it, or if it contains any blank space.**

2. You are entitled to a completely filled-in copy of this agreement.

3. Under the law, you have the right to pay off in advance the full amount due and under certain conditions to obtain a partial refund of the credit service charge.

Some states provide that their disclosure requirements must conform to federal requirements. For example, in Connecticut, disclosure requirements under the state sales act must conform to those requirements in the Truth in Lending Act. *See* Chapter 22.

Contract requirements vary from state to state. The following are offered as examples only. Creditors must be certain to check the applicable law.

Many states permit the buyer in a retail installment sales contract to cancel the contract on written notice mailed to the seller within two or three days after execution of the contract, especially in cases involving house-to-house sales or home improvements.

Many states require periodic statements to be mailed out within a reasonable time at the end of the billing cycle.

In Illinois, a retail installment contract cannot be accelerated unless the buyer has been in default at least 30 days or has abandoned or destroyed the property or the holder believes the buyer is leaving the state. A cosigner, except for a parent or spouse, is liable only if he actually receives the goods sold and the seller must compute the total amount of the finance charges paid by the buyer during the year and furnish such information to the buyer, on request, within 30 days after the end of the year. If a creditor, within 30 days from receipt of a written letter from the debtor concerning an alleged account error sent within 60 days of receipt of the statement containing the alleged error, fails to resolve the allegation, the debtor is excused from paying any service charge on the disputed amount.

In Massachusetts, a statute has been adopted which provides that the default provisions of a retail installment contract are enforceable only to the extent that the default is material and consists of the buyer's failure to make one or more installment payments as required.

Nevada requires that any fee charged to the retail buyer for his cancellation of a retail installment contract within 72 hours after its execution be prohibited unless notice of the fee is clearly set forth in the printed or typed portion of the document.

Delinquency Charges—Attorneys' Fees. Most of the statutes contain provisions authorizing the seller, or holder of the contract, to impose a delinquency charge for late payment of any installment. Generally, the installment must be overdue by at least 10 days, and only one delinquency charge can be made with respect to any one installment. While the charges are based upon the percentage of the installment due, most of the statutes fix a maximum, usually $5. Where the buyer defaults under the contract, and it is necessary to procure the services of an attorney, most of the statutes permit the judgment against the buyer of a reasonable attorney's fee, and costs. In many cases, the statute limits the amount of such fees to approximately 15 percent of the amount then due on the contract. If the terms of the statute are not adhered to, the seller may forfeit the delinquency charge, fees or time price differential.

In New Hampshire, if a contract provides for attorneys' fees to be awarded to the retail seller in any action against the buyer involving a credit transaction, the contract must also provide for reasonable attorneys' fees to be awarded to the buyer in the event the buyer prevails in court. The waiver by a buyer of any such rights is unenforceable and void.

The federal government and a number of states have adopted the Fair Credit Billing Act, discussed in Chapter 22.

LICENSING PROVISIONS

In Alabama, Alaska, Arizona, Connecticut, Delaware, the District of Columbia, Florida, Illinois, Iowa, Kentucky, Louisiana, Maine, Maryland, Massachusetts, Michigan, Minnesota, Mississippi, Missouri, Montana, Nebraska, New Hampshire, New Jersey, New Mexico, New York, North Carolina, Pennsylvania, Rhode Island, South Dakota, Tennessee, Texas, Vermont, West Virginia and Wisconsin, a "sales finance company" (which is defined as a person or firm engaged in the business of purchasing retail installment contracts from one or more retail sellers) is required to be licensed, with an annual license fee frequently required. These statutes also make provision for examination of the books and records of the licensees. Alabama, Florida, Louisiana and Vermont also require annual license fees of retail installment sellers. Under most statutes, banks and other financial institutions are exempted from the licensing provisions.

Most states have separate licensing requirements for sales financing companies purchasing sales contracts from retail sellers of motor vehicles.

The Uniform Consumer Credit Code (UCCC) provides for licensing of certain persons engaged in the business of extending supervised loans. Colorado, Indiana, Iowa, Kansas, Maine, Oklahoma, South Carolina, Utah, Wisconsin and Wyoming have enacted the UCCC. Two states, Idaho and Louisiana have adopted laws that are similar to the UCCC.

INSURANCE PROVISIONS

The statutes of the several states vary as to the contract provisions and requirements or limitations relating to insurance coverage. However, in general, the statutes contain the following requirements:

Contract Provisions. If the cost of insurance is included in the total price, it must be stated as a separate item in the contract together with a description of the coverage. In some states, the contract must indicate whether the insurance is to be procured by the buyer or the seller.

Cost of Insurance. Under most statutes it is provided that the cost of insurance included in the contract cannot exceed the actual cost to the seller, or the usual charges made by the insurance carrier, or charges based upon the carrier's rates filed with the appropriate state agency having jurisdiction.

Copies of Policies. Most statutes provide that within a designated number of days following the making of the contract or delivery of the merchandise, the seller must deliver to the buyer a certificate of insurance, or a copy of the insurance policy, or other statement that will be sufficient to advise the buyer concerning the insurance coverage, and his rights under the policy.

Miscellaneous. Under some statutes it is specifically required that the insurance carrier be licensed to do business in the state, and a number of the statutes provide that the buyer has the right to have the insurance placed with a company of his own choosing, usually subject to the seller's approval. Where the contract is prepaid, or for any other reason there is a refund or rebate in insurance charges, the statutes usually require that they be refunded to the buyer.

PROVISIONS PROHIBITED

The statutes not only make special provisions as to what the contract shall contain, but also specify that which is prohibited. Although the prohibitions vary in the several states, the following are some of the prohibited provisions found:

1. Waiver by the buyer of claims or defenses against the seller of rights under the statute.
2. Acceleration of the maturity of any amount owing under the contract other than for a default on the part of the buyer.
3. Power of attorney to confess judgment or an assignment of wages.
4. Authorization to enter upon the buyer's premises unlawfully and to commit any breach of the peace in repossession of goods.
5. Waiver by the buyer of rights against an assignee of the seller. (However, some of the statutes contain a provision that a notice be sent by the assignee to the buyer informing him of the assignment and notifying him that unless he advises the assignee of any right of action or defense against the seller arising out of the sale, if the buyer does not respond within a limited period of time to this demand, such claims or defenses may not be raised against the assignee.) Many statutes even provide that the assignee of an installment sales contract is not a holder in due course.
6. Power of attorney appointing the seller, or holder of a contract, or other person, as agent of the buyer, in collection of payments under the contract or repossession of the goods.
7. Execution of notes separate from an installment contract which would cut off the buyer's rights or defenses against the seller.

States may prohibit other clauses in a contract. For example, in California, a seller is prohibited from acquiring a lien on goods; in New York, there is a prohibition against liens on goods other than the subject of the sale; in Maryland a seller may not have the buyer open two accounts in order to impose a higher interest rate; in Virginia the maximum late charge is five percent; in Massachusetts a seller cannot permit any buyer to enter into more than one retail installment contract at the same time.

Under some of the statutes the inclusion of such prohibitive provisions is made ineffectual, or void, by the statute. In other cases, penalties may be imposed for failure to comply with the statutory restrictions.

While, as previously noted, some statutes require special contractual provisions and notice with respect to unequal installments, in other states such provisions for irregular or uneven payments or installments, such as "balloon payments" at the maturity date, are prohibited.

Prior to the advent of specific legislation on installment sales, the question was raised as to whether a finance charge that exceeded the legal rate of interest permitted under state statute constituted usury. This question has been litigated over the years in numerous states, and it has invariably been held that the usury statutes are not applicable since the "time price differential" does not constitute interest and the parties could fix, by agreement, such prices as they determined appropriate for a purchase on either a cash or time sale basis. With the advent of legislative controls on installment selling, the states began to impose limits on finance charges. With a few exceptions, all of the state statutes regulating installment selling fix the amounts of the legally permissible "time price differential" or "finance charge."

REFINANCING, EXTENSIONS AND RESCHEDULING

Many of the state statutes contain provisions with respect to refinancing of installment contracts, extension of the period for repayment or rescheduling of installment payments. In some of the states the basic rates set forth in the original contract are applicable to such extension periods. In other cases, the statutes make specific provision for either straight interest charges or combinations of flat charges and specified rates on the extended balances.

Many of the statutes also contain provisions with respect to the inclusion of additional provisions. In New York and some other states, for example, there are provisions for retail installment obligations to cover future purchases of goods or services with or without the use of merchandise certificates.

BUYER'S DEFAULT—REMEDIES OF SELLER

In the event of a default by the buyer in payment of the installments or other breach of the contract, the seller or holder of the contract is afforded certain remedies. In some states these remedies are set forth in the Retail Installment Sales Statute, and in others the statutes relating to conditional sales or secured transactions (under the UCC) will be applicable.

While the statutes vary in the several states, in general the remedies are as follows: (a) sue the buyer for the unpaid installment or balance due under the contract; (b) repossess the goods without process if it can be done peaceably, otherwise repossess by appropriate legal process; (c) sell the goods, after repossession, and hold the buyer for any deficiency in the event that the proceeds of sale are insufficient to cover the costs of repossession, storage, reconditioning, sale, etc.; (d) institute foreclosure, or other special proceeding, as authorized by state statute, in which the rights of the parties will be determined and fixed by court order or decree; (e) after repossession, under some statutes, the seller or the holder of the contract may treat the repossessed property as his own, free of any claim by the buyer, and may dispose of it accordingly.

Under most of the state statutes there are provisions requiring a sale of the goods in cases where the buyer has paid a substantial part of the purchase price (usually more than 50 percent); notice of sale must be given to the buyer, and after all costs and expenses and the balance due on the contract have been paid, any proceeds still remaining from the sale are payable to the buyer.

In most states, the buyer has the right to make good his default by paying past-due installments and reasonable expenses incurred in retaking, storing, etc., although the buyer usually has the right of redemption until the property has been disposed of. Some of the statutes make provision for a notice to be given to the buyer prior to repossession or resale, and in the event that the buyer does not make good his default within a prescribed time limit, his right of redemption will be lost.

Under some statutes the giving of a notice prior to retaking is also a prerequisite to the recovery of the costs of retaking, storing, etc.

While the rights of the seller, or holder of the contract, are generally cumulative where the property is retaken and it is not resold within the time limited by statute, it is usually considered that the seller has elected to accept the goods in full satisfaction of the buyer's obligation, and he is barred from resorting to other remedies.

In many states the assignee of a retail installment sales contract is subject to all claims and defenses that the buyer could have asserted against the original seller.

On March 1, 1985, the Federal Trade Commission's Trade Regulation Rule entitled "The Credit Practices Rule" became effective. This rule specifies remedies that may not be used by lenders and retail installment sellers in consumer credit contracts for use against defaulting buyers. The rule covers contracts offered by finance companies and retail sellers and is designed to protect consumers from unfair or deceptive collection practices by creditors.

The FTC's Credit Practices Rule restricts the use of the following remedies in the consumer credit contracts: confessions of judgment, waivers of exemption, wage assignments, security interests in household goods and certain late charges. The rule further prohibits misrepresentations of cosigner liability and provides that potential cosigners be furnished a "Notice of Cosigner" that explains in general terms their obligations and liabilities.

The rule is applicable industry-wide in all states unless a particular state has requirements that are substantially equivalent to the FTC rule, in which case that state can apply to the FTC for an exemption from the rule.

PENALTIES

Most of the state statutes contain provisions imposing penalties upon the seller or holder of a Retail Installment Contract for failure to comply with statutory requirements. These penalties vary in the several states and range from rendering void any provision contrary to the statute, to the imposition of fines and imprisonment. It is usually provided that the inclusion in the contract of prohibited provisions renders such provision void and unenforceable, but does not otherwise affect the contract.

Where the violations relate to the amount of finance charges and other costs and charges, penalties include the loss of the right to recover such charges, civil action by the buyer to recover overcharges, and prohibitions against enforcement of the contract. In Illinois, a creditor's violations of the state retail installment sales act is an affirmative defense to an action for default on the sales contract.

While the most severe penalties of fines and imprisonment are imposed for violations with respect to licensing provisions, under a number of statutes such penalties are also imposed for willful violations of other provisions. Under the Code, however, no filing is generally required for consumer transactions.

FILING AND RECORDING—GENERAL CONSIDERATIONS

Retail installment sales laws do not provide for the filing or recording of the agreements. However, as previously noted, in those cases where the contract provides for the retention of title or a security interest by the seller there may be compliance with the filing or recording statute, generally the Uniform Commercial Code, in order to afford to the seller, or holder of the contract, protection against the rights of creditors of the buyer or other third parties. In most states, however, no filing is required for purchase money security interests in consumer goods.

The foregoing review of the retail installment sales laws of the various states is not intended to give detailed information for the preparation of agreements or for carrying on installment selling under any specific statute. The statutes are highly technical and it is recommended that competent counsel be consulted in preparing instruments which conform to the various state statutes, as well as to advise on practices and procedures. In some states, operations under the statute are subject to control and regulation by governmental agencies. The state statutes are also subject to periodic revision, and additional states have legislation in this field under consideration.

The following chart illustrates the maximum rates applicable to retail installment sales as well as the scope of coverage of the retail installment sales laws.

RULE OF 78

The Rule of 78 is also known as the "sum of the digits" method. It is an accounting method used to compute prepayment refunds relating to installment credit transactions.

The Rule is applied as follows: The numbers 1 through 12 added together provide the figure 78. This is the denominator. The sum of the months expired at the date of prepayment supplies the numerator. The first month of a 12-month loan is considered as 12 because the outstanding balance is 12 times as large during the first month as it is for the last month. The second month is 11, and so on, to 1. The portion of interest considered earned each month is for the first month, $\frac{12}{78}$; second month, $\frac{11}{78}$; and so on down to the 12th month. The numerator for a 24-month contract is obtained by beginning with 24, instead of 12, as for a 12-month contract, or 36 in the case of a 36-month contract.

Under 15 USC §§ 1690, which was added to the Truth-in-Lending Act as a part of the Housing and Community Development Act of 1992, the use of the Rule of 78s is prohibited in calculating any refund of interest required under TILA if the contract term is greater than 61 months. This provision was effective for transactions consummated after September 30, 1993. Instead the creditor must use a method at last as favorable to the consumer as the actuarial method.

The actuarial method approximates the amount of interest earned on a day-by-day basis.

STATE LAWS CONTROLLING RETAIL INSTALLMENT SALES

Note: State legislatures will, on occasion, modify an area of law without clear delineation as to its content and context. As a result, even the changes which have been enacted prior to placement in the state's Code may be difficult to locate. As a result, the Editors urge all users of the *Manual* to use this publication only as a guide, and consult the latest codified version of the state's law for all recent changes.

State	Coverage	Interest Rate Regulation
Alabama	Statute covers property or services for personal, family, household, or agricultural purpose; bailments or leases with rentals substantially equal to value of property or services and with nominal or no-cost option to become owner; open-end credit plans and credit sales.	Greater of (A) total of (i) $15 per $100 per year to $750, (ii) $10 per $100 per year on over $750 and not over $2,000, and (iii) $8 per $100 per year on over $2,000; or (B) $8 per $100 per year on entire amount financed if originally over $2,000 or 2% above prime rate. Alternative variable rate fixed by statute is also permitted. Open-end credit plan: $1\frac{1}{2}\%$ per month on unpaid balances.
Alaska	Sale (including catalog sale) of goods and services primarily for personal, family, or household use; also includes revolving credit; services for goods and realty.	On retail installment contract $\frac{5}{6}$ of 1% per month on balances not over $1,000, $\frac{2}{3}$ of 1% per month on amounts in excess of $1,000; on retail charge agreements or revolving charge agreements, $1\frac{1}{2}\%$ per month on balances up to $1,000, one-twelfth of the annual rate permitted under the state law.
Arizona	Statute covers tangible chattels, including fixtures and merchandise certificates; services; also includes revolving credit. Separate statute covers motor vehicles not for resale. Vehicle statute does not apply to tractors, buses, trucks, farm machinery or devices on rails.	Maximum rate set by contract applies to retail installment sales, revolving charge agreements, and motor vehicle sales based on a time price differential calculated from date of transaction to date last installment becomes due. Separate rates for motor vehicles.
Arkansas	No statutory enactment.	No statutory enactment.
California	Sale of goods for personal, family, or household use excluding resale; property and services, other than for commercial or business use; also covers revolving credit. Separate statute covers automobiles for personal or family use, required to be registered.	Greater of $\frac{5}{6}$ of 1% per month not over $1,000; $\frac{2}{3}$ of 1% per month over $1,000, or $12; $10 on contract of eight months or less if precomputed. If simple-interest basis, $10 for first $500, $25 if unpaid balance of $500 to $1,000, $50 if over $1,000 up to $2,000, or $75 if over $2,000. For installment accounts, 1.5% on $1,000 or less, 1% on excess.
Colorado	Uniform Consumer Credit Code is in effect.	UCCC finance service charges: Consumer credit sales—Greater of 21% on all unpaid balances or total of 25% of unpaid balance of $630 or less; 20% on amounts over $630 to $2,100, and 15% on amounts over $2,100. Revolving credit: $1\frac{3}{4}\%$ per month on average daily balance.
Connecticut	Consumer goods for personal, family, or household use, motor vehicles, up to $25,000; open end credit plans according to the federal Truth in Lending Act and Regulation Z.	18% per year; special rates for motor vehicles. Revolving credit: $1\frac{1}{4}\%$ per month on average daily balance.

STATE LAWS CONTROLLING RETAIL INSTALLMENT SALES *(Continued)*

State	Coverage	Interest Rate Regulation
Delaware	Retail installment sale of goods for personal, family, or household use, including services or goods for improvement to real property, and services for other than a commercial or business use; also includes revolving credit. Does not apply to goods of which the cash sale price is $75 or less, or where no security interest is retained. Sales of motor vehicles are covered by Motor Vehicle Sales Finance Act.	Rate as specified in contract.
District of Columbia	Statute covers tangible chattels used for personal, family, or household use, merchandise certificates, and revolving credit, not over $25,000. A separate statute covers motor vehicles.	No statute governing retail installment sales except for motor vehicles; revolving credit cannot exceed 2% per month on balance.
Florida	Retail installment sale of goods and services for personal, family, or household use including merchandise certificates excluding resale; also includes revolving credit. Motor vehicles are covered by the Motor Vehicle Sales Finance Act.	12% per $100 per year. Revolving credit: 1.5% per month. Separate rates for motor vehicles. 1.5% on $5,000 maximum for bank loans and credit cards.
Georgia	Retail installment sale of goods and services purchased for personal, family, or household use; also includes revolving credit. Motor vehicles are covered by the Motor Vehicle Sales Finance Act.	13% per year on principal balance. Revolving credit: 1.75% per month on unpaid amounts. Separate rate for motor vehicles.
Hawaii	Sale of personal chattels not for resale including merchandise certificates, emblements, growing crops and fixtures and services for family, household, commercial, or business use on goods or realty; also includes revolving credit.	12% per year for not over 18 months plus; 9% per year for next 12 months plus; 6% per year for next 12 months plus; 3% per year for next six months alternatively 24% per year. Revolving credit: 24% a year. Minimum charge is $10.
Idaho	Idaho Consumer Credit Code is in effect.	ICCC finance service charges: Consumer credit sales—No charge limit. Revolving credit: No charge limit. Charges and fees appear in Uniform Consumer Credit Code.
Illinois	Installment sale of goods for personal, family, or household use and services for use other than in business; exclude services for which charges are subject to state or federal law and professional services unless the subject of a signed retail installment sales contract; also includes revolving credit. Motor vehicles covered by separate statute.	No limit on consumer credit sales or revolving credit. By authorized institutions, certain banks and lenders licensed under state laws, all others maximum rate is 1½%.
Indiana	Indiana Uniform Consumer Credit Code is in effect.	UCCC finance service charges: Consumer credit sales—Greater of 21% on all unpaid balances or total of 36% on all unpaid balances not in excess of $810, 21% on amounts of $810 to $2,700, and 15% on amounts over $2,700. Revolving credit: 1¾% on monthly balance.
Iowa	The State Consumer Credit Code covers goods, services, or interest in land for personal, family, or household use up to $25,000 (no such limit for interest in land sales). Motor vehicles covered by separate statute.	21% per year. Separate rate for motor vehicles. Revolving credit: 1.65% monthly on unpaid balances.

State		
Kansas	Kansas Uniform Consumer Credit Code in effect.	21% on first $1,000, 14.45% on balance over $1,000. Revolving consumer credit sales: 1¾% on first $300, 1½% on $300 to $1,000, 11¼% on excess over $1,000.
Kentucky	Goods and services for personal, family or household use, and revolving credit. Separate statute covers motor vehicles.	No provisions except for motor vehicles.
Louisiana	Goods and services for personal, family, household, or agricultural use; also covers revolving credit. Motor vehicles are covered by Motor Vehicle Sales Finance Act.	On consumer credit sales: greater of (1) 24% per year on balances not over $1,750, 18% on balances over $1,750 but not over $5,000, 12% on balances over $5,000, or (2) 18% per year on amount deferred. Revolving credit: 1½% permitted on average daily balance.
Maine	Maine Consumer Credit Code is in effect. There is a separate Home Repair Financing Act.	Credit sales: 30% per year on unpaid balance of $700 or less, 21% per year on $700 to $2,000, 15% on over $2,000, or 18% per year on total unpaid balance. Revolving credit: charge may not exceed 1½% per month; home repair financing loans—18% on unpaid balance.
Maryland	Installment sales of personal chattels for use or consumption of buyer having a cash price of $25,000 or less. Includes revolving credit.	22% on $1,000 or less; 18% on balance exceeding $1,000. Revolving credit: 1½% a month on outstanding balance not exceeding $700; 1% a month on balance exceeding $700. Separate rates for motor vehicles.
Massachusetts	Retail installment sale of movable goods or services for personal, family, or household use. Agreement must provide finance charge and more than one payment or no finance charge and five or more payments. Exclusion if three or less payments, finance charge under $1, and no security. Includes revolving credit. Separate statute covers motor vehicles.	21% per year. Retail seller on sales agreement may charge a finance charge not in excess of an annual percentage rate of 21% computed from the original amount financed. Applies to new or used motor vehicles.
Michigan	Retail installment sales of chattels for personal, family or household use; includes revolving credit, but not for commercial or business use. Separate statute covers home improvements for sales in excess of $300 and motor vehicle sale.	12% per year on principal balance not in excess of $500; 10% per year on the principal balance in excess of $500. Revolving credit: 1.7% of unpaid balance per month. Separate rates for motor vehicles and home improvement sales.
Minnesota	Open-end credit plan; separate statute covers motor vehicles not for resale only.	On open-end consumer credit sales, a finance charge not to exceed 1½% per month; 1⅓% per month for sellers with gross annual sales over $10 billion. Separate rates for motor vehicles.
Mississippi	Retail installment of tangible property or services other than pursuant to a revolving charge agreement; revolving credit: motor vehicles not for resale.	$2,500 or less—24%, on accounts more than $2,500—21%. None until one month after initial billing statement. 1¾% per month on average daily balance. Separate rates for motor vehicles.
Missouri	Retail installment sales of goods and services. Statute includes revolving credit. Motor vehicles with a maximum cash price of $7,500 or less are covered by the Motor Vehicle Time Sales Act.	15% per year on $750 or less; 12% on $750 to $1,000; 10% on $1,000 to $7,500; by agreement on over $7,500. Charge agreement: 2.218% on unpaid balance per month up to $1,200 and 1.67% for a balance over $1,200.
Montana	Retail installment sale of personal chattels, including motor vehicles and the furnishing of services. Includes revolving credit.	Rate agreed by seller and buyer.

STATE LAWS CONTROLLING RETAIL INSTALLMENT SALES (Continued)

State	Coverage	Interest Rate Regulation
Nebraska	Personal property and services.	18% per year. Revolving charge agreements 1³/₄% on $500 or less and 1¹/₂% on portion over $500.
Nevada	Retail installment sale of goods and services for personal or household use; also covers merchandise certificates and revolving credit, including credit cards.	Any amount agreed upon. Revolving credit: any amount agreed upon.
New Hampshire	Motor vehicles not for resale only with a $7,500 maximum price.	Statutory limitations apply to motor vehicles only. No provision for motor vehicles; any rate agreed upon.
New Jersey	Retail installment sale of goods and services having a cash price of $10,000 or less, other than for a commercial or business use, including motor vehicles; also covers most services to consumers excluding professional services; includes retail charge accounts. Separate statute covers home improvements with minimum cash price of $300.	As agreed by buyer and seller; contract may provide for increase or decrease in rate up to 6% over life of loan, but no more than 3% in any 12-month period. Separate rates for motor vehicles and home improvement sales. Charge account, as agreed to by buyer and seller.
New Mexico	Retail installment use of tangible goods and services other than for a commercial or business use or resale; also covers merchandise certificates and retail charge agreements. Retail installment sales of motor vehicles are covered by separate statute.	No special provision. Interest-usury laws control.
New York	Retail installment sale of goods and services other than for a commercial or business use; also covers revolving credit. Retail installment sales of motor vehicles are covered by separate statute.	Rate agreed to by buyer. Revolving credit: rate agreed to by parties. Separate rates for motor vehicles.
North Carolina	Retail consumers installment sale of movable goods including merchandise certificates, services for personal, family, household, or agricultural purpose, and goods for improvement of real property, in amount less than $25,000. Separate statute covers motor vehicles.	On regular installment sales maximum 24% per year where amount financed is less than $1,500; 22% per year where the amount financed is between $1,500 and $2,000; 20% per year where the amount financed is between $2,000 and $3,000; 18% per year where the amount financed is $3,000 or greater. Motor vehicles have separate rates as do sales secured by interest in real property. Revolving credit charges prescribed by the interest usury statute: 1¹/₂% per month on unpaid balance.
North Dakota	Retail installment sale of personal property, including motor vehicles, for personal, family, or agricultural purposes, up to a value of $25,000 except for purpose of resale.	No provisions. Revolving credit: 1¹/₂% per month on balance.
Ohio	Retail installment sale of personal goods not for resale, motor vehicles, and mobile homes, and revolving credit if the base finance and service charge exceed $15. In Ohio a statute has been enacted to exempt from the retail installment sales law lease-purchase agreements that have an initial term of four months or less and are automatically renewable.	8% per year plus service charge of 50¢ per month for the first $50 unit of the principal balance for each month, and 25¢ per month for each of the next five $50 units. Alternatively, any amount agreed upon not exceeding 25%. Revolving credit, same as retail installment sales but not to exceed 1¹/₂% per month.

State	Coverage	Charges
Oklahoma	Oklahoma Uniform Consumer Credit Code in effect.	UCCC finance-service charges: Consumer credit sales—Greater of 21% on all unpaid balances or total of 30% on unpaid balance of $780 or less, 21% on over $780 and less than $2,600, and 15% on over $2,600. Revolving credit: 1¾% on monthly balance if monthly billing cycles.
Oregon	Retail installment sales of goods and services for personal, family, or household use, including merchandise certificates, and revolving credit. Separate statute covers motor vehicles.	No statutory limitation.
Pennsylvania	Retail installment sale of goods and services bought primarily for personal, family, or household purposes, merchandise certificates, and revolving credit. Motor vehicles, and home improvements costing over $300, are covered by separate statutes.	18% per year, 15% for gasoline credit card issuers. Retail installment account, 1½% per month. Separate statutes for motor vehicles and home improvement rates.
Puerto Rico	Personal property not for resale, exclude intangibles other than merchandise or credit certificates; includes services on goods or realty; motor vehicles; minimum cash price $50.	Rate varies depending on goods sold and type of purchaser, but may not exceed 21% (not for motor vehicles) Revolving Credit: 20.4% or 26% if card issued by financial institution. No limit for new or used motor vehicles, industrial, agricultural and construction machinery and commercial electrical appliances.
Rhode Island	Merchandise and services involving credit. Revolving credit.	18% simple interest per year; rate does not apply if charge of $10 or less is made. Revolving credit: 1½%.
South Carolina	Consumer Protection Code in effect.	Charges and fees appear in the Uniform Consumer Credit Code. 18% per year; revolving credit: 18% per year.
South Dakota	Tangible personal chattels including things that are at time of sale to be affixed to real property. Statute also covers work, labor, and other personal services. Separate statute covers motor vehicles.	Interest rate set by agreement. Revolving charge accounts: as agreed. Delinquency or service charge authorized of greater of $5 or 5 percent of installment which is late for at least 10 days.
Tennessee	Retail installment sales of personalty not for resale and services for goods or realty, excluding commercial and industrial use and motor vehicles. Revolving credit is also covered.	11.75% per year on principal balance of each transaction. Revolving credit: 1.75% per month on balance.
Texas	All tangible personal property and services for personal, family, or household use and not for commercial or business use. Also covers revolving credit and merchandise certificates. Motor vehicles covered by separate statute.	12% per year on principal balance not in excess of $1,800; 10% per year on an amount over $1,800 but not over $3,600; 8% per year on an amount over $3,600. Charge agreement: 1.5% per month on $1,800 or less, 1% on excess. Alternatively, parties may agree to rate not exceeding rate authorized by the interest usury law. Separate rates for motor vehicles.
Utah	Utah Consumer Credit Code in effect.	Consumer credit sales and revolving credit: no charge limit.
Vermont	Sale of tangible goods and services purchased for personal, family, or household use and not for commercial, industrial, or agricultural use; also includes merchandise certificates. Includes revolving credit. Motor vehicles covered by separate statute.	18% per year on amounts of $500 or less; 15% per year on amounts in excess of $500. Revolving credit: rate agreed upon by the parties but not more than 21% per year. Separate rates for motor vehicles.

STATE LAWS CONTROLLING RETAIL INSTALLMENT SALES *(Continued)*

State	Coverage	Interest Rate Regulation
Virginia	Consumer goods. Separate statute covers motor vehicles for buyer use.	As agreed by the parties. Revolving credit: Any amount agreed on, free period 25 days from billing, no charge if bill not mailed within 8 days of the billing date.
Washington	Retail installment sales of goods and services for goods for personal, family, or household use and not for commercial or business use, including merchandise certificates. Includes revolving credit, also lender credit cards.	Higher of 13.75% per year or $10. Revolving credit: 1¹/₂% per month on unpaid balance. Motor vehicles contracts, 12.25%.
West Virginia	Goods, services, or interest in land for personal, family, or household use; value not to exceed $25,000. Includes open-end credit plans and merchandise certificates. Separate statute covers motor vehicles.	18% if $1,500 or less, 12% for excess over $1,500. Alternative rate set by Lending and Credit Rate Board (18% as of June 1, 1990). Revolving credit: 1.5% on first $750, 1% for excess over $750. Separate rates for motor vehicles.
Wisconsin	Goods, services, or an interest in land for personal, family, household, or agricultural purpose; value not to exceed $25,000. Also covers consumer leases and open-end credit plans. Separate statute covers motor vehicles for personal use only.	Limit on the finance charge for consumer credit transactions; revolving credit: 1.5% per month on unpaid balance if billing cycle is monthly.
Wyoming	Wyoming Uniform Consumer Credit Code in effect.	Wyoming UCCC finance-service charges: Consumer credit sales—Greater of 21% on all unpaid balances or total of 36% on unpaid balances of $1,000 or less, 21% on over $1,000; on amounts financed exceeding $25,000 the charge is that specified in the sales agreement. Revolving credit: 1³/₄% on average monthly balance.

22 Consumer Protection Legislation—An Overview

FEDERAL LAW

Federal and state legislation designed to protect the rights of consumers is pervasive and expansive. These statutes stemmed from abuses—both actual and perceived—in creating or enforcing consumer transactions. Consumer transactions are usually defined as those primarily for "personal, family, or household" purposes. Credit grantors must understand that even in the midst of regular commercial transactions with a customer, a consumer transaction may arise which would require the vendor to comply with the provisions of state or federal consumer protection laws. If a business could possibly deal with consumer transactions, understanding consumer protection laws is a necessity.

Both federal and state statutes impose strict limitations with respect to consumer transactions, including limits on the terms of the agreement, the disclosures that must be made in a transaction, the amount of interest or finance charges, the use of credit reports, the reporting of a consumer's credit history, the manner and method of collection activity, and the like. Failure to comply with these laws can lead to penalties under a number of strict liability statutes.

TRUTH IN LENDING ACT

In 1968, Congress enacted the Consumer Credit Protection Act, 15 USC §§ 1601 et seq., which includes the popularly known Truth in Lending Act (TILA). Id. §§ 1601-1615, 1631-1649, 1661-1665b, 1666-1666j, 1667-1667j. The Act is implemented by Regulation Z, 12 CFR § 226.

TILA was a major advance in the law of consumer protection and continues to be amended periodically. The most significant aspect of the Act is the requirement of written disclosure to the borrower of the true cost of credit. The following is a brief summary of the law.

Subchapter I deals with consumer credit costs and disclosure, and concerns "Informed use of credit" and "Terms of personal property leases." With respect to the "Informed use of credit," Congress has declared the following as the purpose of this statute:

The Congress finds that economic stabilization would be enhanced and the competition among the various financial institutions and other firms engaged in the extension of consumer credit would be strengthened by the informed use of credit. The informed use of credit results from an awareness of the cost thereof by consumers. It is the purpose of this subchapter to assure a meaningful disclosure of credit terms so that the consumer will be able to compare more readily the various credit terms available to him and avoid the uninformed use of credit, and to protect the consumer against inaccurate and unfair credit billing and credit card practices.

The Act exempts the following transactions from its scope:

1. Credit transactions involving extensions of credit primarily for business, commercial, or agricultural purposes; or to government or governmental agencies; or instrumentalities; or to organizations, such as cooperatives, partnerships, or trusts
2. Transactions in securities or commodities accounts by a broker-dealer registered with the Securities and Exchange Commission
3. Credit transactions, other than those involving a principal dwelling in which the total amount to be financed exceeds $25,000
4. Transactions under public utility tariffs if it is determined that a state regulatory body regulates the charges for public service
5. Transactions which the Board of Governors of the Federal Reserve Board determines are not necessary to be covered under this subchapter
6. Higher Education loans

The amount of the finance charge in connection with any consumer credit transaction, determined by Section 1605, is to be the sum of all charges, payable directly or indirectly by the borrower or imposed on him by the creditor, including interest charges, service or carrying charges, loan fees, finders' fees, fees for investigation or credit reports, guarantee charges, credit insurance charges, premiums for credit, life, accident or health insurance (unless the issuance of such insurance is not a factor in obtaining the credit, and the borrower is so advised in writing, but nevertheless specifically requests such insurance in writing after disclosure of the cost). Charges or premiums for insurance against loss or damage to property or liability for its use shall be included in the finance charge unless the borrower is advised in writing of the cost of such insurance and the fact that it can be obtained from any person the borrower chooses.

Excluded from the finance charge are the following items, provided a separate disclosure is made: fees prescribed by law that actually are or will be paid to public officials for determining the existence of, or for perfecting or releasing or satisfying any security related to the credit transactions, and premiums for insurance obtained in lieu of perfecting any security interest, provided the cost of such insurance is not in excess of the public official fees stated above, and any tax levied on security instruments if the payment of such taxes is a precondition for recording the instrument securing the evidence of indebtedness.

In connection with real estate loans, the finance charge excludes title examinations and title insurance fees, appraisal and inspection fees, credit reports, notarization fees, escrows for future payment of taxes and insurance and fees for preparation of documents.

Section 1606 of the Act requires that the finance charge for credit sales and loans must be disclosed and expressed as an annual percentage rate, and defines how that rate is computed.

Section 1635 deals with abuses arising from sales on credit for home improvements. It provides that, in the case of any credit transactions in which a security interest is retained or required in any real property the borrower uses as his residence, except for first liens created to finance the acquisition of such property, the borrower shall have the right to rescind the transaction until midnight of the third business day following the consummation of the transaction or the delivery of the making of the disclosures required by the Act, whichever is later. Upon rescission, the borrower is not liable for any finance or any other charge and any security interest becomes void and the creditor is obligated to return the downpayment. Once rescission has been made by the borrower, the creditor has 20 days within which to return any money or property given as earnest money to the borrower. If there is any property in the hands of the borrower, he must offer to return it to the creditor. If the creditor does not take possession of its property within 20 days after the offer to return it has been made, the creditor forfeits its claim to it.

Before any creditor permits a borrower to open an open-end consumer credit plan, he is obligated to advise the borrower of any of the following applicable items:

1. The conditions under which a finance charge may be imposed; the time period, if any, when credit extended may be repaid without incurring a finance charge
2. The method of determining the balance upon which the finance charge is imposed
3. The method of determining the amount of the finance charge
4. Identification of any other charges
5. Whether any security interest is acquired by the creditor

The creditor is also obligated at the end of each billing cycle to submit a statement setting forth, among other information: the outstanding balance at the beginning and end of the period, the credit charges during the period together with a brief identification of the goods or services purchased, the finance charge, and the total amount credited to the account during the period.

In credit sales that are not under an open-end credit plan, the creditor is obligated to disclose:

1. The identity of the creditor
2. The "amount financed," which is to be determined pursuant to 15 USC § 1638(a)(2)(A)(i)(ii) and a written itemization of amount financed if requested by the consumer
3. The "finance charge"
4. The finance charge expressed as an "annual percentage rate" except if amount financed does not exceed $75 and the service charge does not exceed $5 or if amount financed exceeds $75 and finance charge does not exceed $7.50
5. The "total of payments"
6. The number, amount and due dates scheduled to repay the total of payments
7. In a sale of property, the "total sale price"
8. Descriptive explanations of above terms
9. A statement that a security interest has been taken, where appropriate
10. A charge that may be imposed due to a late payment
11. A statement indicating whether the consumer is entitled to a rebate of any finance charge upon prepayment or refinancing
12. A statement referring the consumer to appropriate contract document for information
13. In a residential mortgage transaction, a statement whether the debt is assumable on original terms and conditions
14. In the case of any variable interest rate residential mortgage transaction, a statement that the periodic payments may increase or decrease substantially, and the maximum interest rate and payment for a $10,000 loan originated at a recent interest rate, assuming the maximum periodic increases in rates and payments under the program

If a consumer makes an order or a creditor receives a loan request by mail or telephone without personal solicitation, disclosures must be made no later than the date the first payment is due.

Regulation Z, 12 CFR §§ 226.1-226.33, which implements the provisions of the Truth in Lending Act, provides that a seller that regularly arranges for its customers to obtain outside financing is also required to make TILA disclosures if it is compensated by the bank for its services or participates in the preparation of the contract documents required in procuring a loan. This does not include assisting customers in filling out bank loan applications.

Written acknowledgment by the borrower of receipt of a statement containing the disclosures required to be made under the Act is conclusive proof of compliance as to the assignee of a creditor, without knowledge to the contrary. Therefore, such acknowledgments should be obtained in all transactions covered by the Act.

Common Violations

The following are some of the more commonly encountered violations of Regulation Z and the Truth in Lending Act:

1. The disclosures required by 12 CFR § 226.18 in a closed-end credit transaction are not grouped together, segregated from everything else, or they contain information not directly related to the disclosures required under that section
2. In a closed-end credit transaction there has not been disclosure of the "amount financed," using that term, together with a brief description such as "the amount of credit provided to you or on your behalf"
3. In a closed-end credit transaction the itemization of the amount financed required by 12 CFR § 226.18(c)(1) is not separate from the other required disclosures
4. In a closed-end credit transaction there has not been disclosure of the "finance charge," using that term, together with a brief description such as "the dollar amount the credit will cost you"
5. In a closed-end credit transaction there has not been disclosure of the "annual percentage rate," using that term, together with a brief description such as "the cost of your credit as a yearly rate"
6. In a closed-end credit transaction there has not been disclosure of the payment schedule indicating the number, amounts, and timing of payments scheduled to repay the obligation
7. In a closed-end credit transaction there has not been disclosure of the "total of payments," using that term, and a descriptive explanation such as "the amount you will have paid when you have made all scheduled payments"

Sections 1661 through 1665(b) of the Act establish controls over credit advertising and set forth certain requirements for different types of advertising.

The Act charges various federal agencies with the responsibility of enforcing different parts of the Act, and the Board of Governors of the Federal Reserve System is authorized to prescribe regulations to carry out the purpose of Subchapter I.

Criminal penalties for willful and knowing violation of the Subchapter I are a fine of not more than $5,000 or imprisonment of not more than one year, or both.

A creditor who fails to disclose information properly as required under the Act is liable for an amount equal to any actual damage sustained. Other statutory damages are specified for individual and class actions. In December 2005, the U.S. Supreme

Court upheld earlier case law that limited the amount of statutory penalties that could be assessed by overturning 1995 amendments to § 1640 that may have eliminated some of those limits (*Koons Buick v. Nigh*, 2004 WL 2707418).

Any person engaged in the business of making loans or sales on credit or advertising credit loans is advised to review the specific provisions of the Act to be certain that his practices are in compliance on the effective dates as both the Act and the Regulation Z are amended periodically.

The Act was amended in 1970 to control issuance and misuse of credit cards. Regulation Z, which implements the Truth in Lending Act, has added a provision allowing merchants to give discounts to customers who pay by check or cash rather than by credit card.

Title 18 of the United States Code provides for the control of organized crime in the extension of credit. It is a federal offense to make or finance extortionate extensions of credit or to collect extensions of credit by extortionate means.

Restrictions on Garnishment

Subchapter II of the Act restricts garnishments of wages. 15 USC §§ 1671-1677. Congress found that the unrestricted garnishment of compensation encourages the predatory making of credit and results in the loss of employment by borrowers. The amount of weekly wages subject to garnishment is limited to the lesser of 25 percent of disposable earnings of the debtor or the amount by which the weekly disposable earnings exceed 30 times the federal minimum hourly wage, except that these restrictions do not apply to court orders for support of a person, payments of state or federal taxes or payment pursuant to a Bankruptcy Court order. An employer is also prohibited from discharging any employee because of a garnishment for one indebtedness.

The Act authorizes the Secretary of Labor to enforce this provision and further authorizes him to exempt garnishments in certain states if it is determined that the laws of such states provide restrictions on garnishments substantially similar to those provided for by the Act.

FAIR CREDIT REPORTING ACT AND FACTA

Federal regulators have stated that any use of a consumer credit report without the written consent of the consumer is prohibited unless there exists a legitimate business need for the information. The Federal Trade Commission, in a written opinion letter, dated July 25, 2000, reiterated that all individuals are considered to be "consumers" even when dealing with a sole proprietor, a partner in a partnership, or a guarantor of a business debt. As a result of continued communication to the Federal Trade Commission by various credit organizations, the FTC, on June 22, 2001, issued a revision to its opinion and stated that a permissible business purpose to enable the use of a consumer credit report does exist where the individual in question is or will be personally liable on the debt, such as in the case of an individual proprietor, co-signer, or guarantor.

Subchapter III of the Consumer Credit Protection Act was enacted on October 26, 1970, and became effective on April 25, 1971. It has been amended from time to time. The amendments which have been incorporated into the current statute have come from the Consumer Credit Reporting Reform Act of 1996, the Omnibus Consolidated Appropriations Act for Fiscal Year 1997, Section 311 of the

Intelligence Authorization for Fiscal Year 1998, the Consumer Reporting Employment Clarification Act of 1998 and the Gramm-Leach-Bliley Act. The most recent amendment took place in November 1999. This statute is known as the Fair Credit Reporting Act. 15 USC §§ 1681-1681u. The purpose of the Act is to require that consumer reporting agencies adopt reasonable procedures for meeting the needs of consumer credit, personnel, insurance and other information in an accurate, fair, relevant, confidential, proper and equitable manner. In 2003, Congress passed the Fair and Accurate Credit Transactions Act (HR 2622, known as "FACTA") which implemented numerous changes and additions to FCRA.

The following are three of the most important concepts defined by the Act:

1. A *consumer report* is any written, oral, or other communication of any information by a consumer reporting agency bearing on a consumer's creditworthiness, credit standing, credit capacity, character, general reputation, personal characteristics or mode of living that is used or expected to be used in establishing the consumer's eligibility for (1) credit or insurance primarily for personal, family or household purposes; (2) employment purposes; or (3) other specific purposes authorized by the Act. The term, however, does not include (a) any report containing information solely as to transactions or experience between the consumer and the person making the report, (b) any authorization or approval for a specific extension of credit by the issuer of a credit or debit card, (c) any report made by a person who has been requested by a third party to extend credit to a consumer, provided the third party advised the consumer of the name and address of the person to whom the request is made and such person makes the disclosures to the consumer required by the Act, or (d) any communication to a prospective employer for the purpose of procuring employment whether made directly by the prospective employee or another on his behalf. Credit guides or delinquent creditors' lists, including bad check blacklists, are alphabetical listings rating consumers according to certain criteria, which are assembled into a book and are distributed to credit grantors. Such lists are "consumer reports" according to FTC rulings, and are subject to the Act. No permissible purpose for obtaining the information exists at the time they are distributed to credit grantors since no credit grantor could possibly be considering advancing credit to every consumer listed. Thus, in order to be in compliance with the Fair Credit Reporting Act, these credit guides and bad check blacklists must be coded so that the consumer's identity is not disclosed until decoded. Appropriate identifiers would include Social Security numbers, drivers' licenses and bank account numbers, which a credit grantor could use to decode information concerning specific consumers in whom it was interested.

2. An *investigative consumer report* is a consumer report or portion thereof in which information about a consumer's character, general reputation, personal characteristics or mode of living is obtained through personal interviews with neighbors, friends, or associates of the consumer or with others with whom (s)he is acquainted or who may have knowledge concerning any such items of information. However, this definition does not include specific factual information on a consumer's credit record obtained directly from a creditor of the consumer or from a consumer reporting agency when such information was obtained directly from a creditor of the consumer or from the consumer.

3. A ***consumer reporting agency*** is any entity that, for compensation or on a cooperative nonprofit basis, regularly engages in whole or in part in the practice of assembling or evaluating consumer credit information or other information on consumers for the purpose of furnishing consumer reports to third parties, and which uses any facility of interstate commerce for this purpose.

The Act provides that a consumer reporting agency may furnish a consumer report for the following purposes only:

1. In response to a court order or subpoena in connection with proceedings before a Federal grand jury
2. At the written request of a consumer who is the subject of the report
3. To a person which it has reason to believe intends to use the information on the consumer's behalf in connection with (a) a credit transaction involving the consumer on whom the information is to be furnished and involving the extension of credit to, or review or collection of any account of, the consumer; or (b) for employment purposes; or (c) insurance purposes; or (d) a license granted by a branch of the government; or (e) as a potential investor or servicer, or current insurer, in connection with a valuation of, or an assessment of the credit or prepayment risks associated with, an existing credit obligation; or (f) some other legitimate business purpose
4. In response to a request by a child support enforcement agency (strict guidelines are set forth for this use)
5. In response to a request by an agency administering a State Plan under the Social Security Act for use to set an initial or modified child support award

Once during any 12-month period a consumer reporting agency must, within 15 days of a request, provide a free report to a consumer. The FTC's new regulation provides a centralized source through which consumers can obtain free reports from all reporting agencies with a single request.

One area that will be of concern to the trade credit grantor is the ability—or inability to obtain a consumer report for a legitimate business purpose. The Fair Credit Reporting Act sets forth that the legitimate business need for the information must be in connection with a business transaction that is initiated by the consumer; or to review an account to determine whether the consumer continues to meet the terms of the account.

Although the Federal Trade Commission has now concurred that a permissible business purpose exists in the case of an individual who is or will be liable for the debt, such as a sole proprietor, co-signor or guarantor, the trade credit grantor may still wish to protect itself by obtaining written permission which authorizes the credit grantor to obtain and use a credit report on that sole proprietor, partner or guarantor. Even if the intent is to obtain a business credit report, the credit professional will be wise to obtain this written permission before proceeding.

An investigative consumer report may not be prepared unless it is disclosed in writing to the consumer, within three days after the date on which the report was first requested, that such a report is being prepared, and the consumer is advised that he has a right to certain information. However, such disclosure need not be given to the consumer if the report is to be used for employment purposes for which the consumer has not specifically applied. Any person who prepares an investigative consumer report must upon a written request made by the consumer make a complete and accurate disclosure of the nature and scope of the investigation requested. The disclosure must be made in writing not later than five days after the date of the request from the consumer.

No consumer reporting agency may issue any consumer report containing any of the following items of information which are deemed obsolete:

1. Bankruptcies older than 10 years
2. Suits and judgments older than seven years or until the governing statute of limitation has expired, whichever is the longer period
3. Paid tax liens older than seven years
4. Accounts placed for collection older than seven years
5. Any other adverse information older than seven years (except for records of convictions of crimes)

These prohibitions, however, do not apply to credit or insurance transactions involving more than $150,000 or employment for a salary in excess of $75,000.

Every consumer reporting agency shall, upon the request of and upon the receipt of the proper identification of the consumer, disclose to him:

1. The nature and substance of all information in its files on the consumer
2. The source of the information (except the sources of an investigative consumer report and used solely for that purpose)
3. The recipients of any consumer report which it has furnished for employment purposes within two years, or for any other purpose within one year

The disclosures must be made upon reasonable notice and during normal business hours. They can be made to the consumer in person, by telephone, by electronic means, or by any other reasonable means, including mail. A consumer may be accompanied by one other person of his choice who can furnish reasonable identification.

A consumer reporting agency must make the disclosures required by the Act without charge to the consumer if, within 60 days after receipt by the consumer of notice that his credit rating has been or may be adversely affected, a request for such disclosure is made by the consumer. Otherwise, the consumer reporting agency, after advising the consumer, may impose a charge not to exceed $8.00 on the consumer for making the disclosures of which the consumer shall be advised prior to the furnishing of such information.

If a consumer asks for a credit score, a reporting agency must give the consumer a statement indicating that the information and credit scoring model may be different than the credit score that may be used by the lender, and a notice that gives:

(a) the current credit score of the consumer (or the consumer's most recent credit score that was previously calculated by the reporting agency for a purpose related to the extension of credit);
(b) the range of possible credit scores under the model used;
(c) the key factors (up to a maximum of four) that adversely affected the consumer's credit score in the model used;
(d) the date on which the credit score was created; and
(e) the name of the person that provided the credit score or credit file upon which the credit score was created.

If the consumer requests the credit file and not the credit score, the reporting agency must advise the consumer that (s)he may request and obtain the credit score.

If the completeness or accuracy of any information is disputed by a consumer, the consumer reporting agency must within a reasonable time reinvestigate and record the current status of such information unless it has reasonable grounds to believe that the dispute by the consumer is frivolous or irrelevant. If the agency cannot resolve the dispute by reinvestigation, it must make such an entry in the report. If the information is found to be inaccurate or not capable of being verified, the consumer reporting agency must at the request of the consumer notify the recipient of any report that contained the disputed information received within two years prior thereto for employment purposes, or within six months prior thereto for other purposes.

Whenever any adverse action is taken on the basis of information contained in consumer reports, the user of the consumer report must (a) provide oral, written, or electronic notice of the adverse action to the consumer, (b) advise the consumer orally, in writing, or electronically, of the name and address of the consumer reporting agency making the report and a statement that the consumer reporting agency did not make the decision to take the adverse action and is unable to provide the consumer the specific reasons why the adverse action was taken, and (c) provide oral, written, or electronic notice of the consumer's right to obtain a copy of its report or to dispute the accuracy or completeness of any information in that report.

Adverse action under the Fair Credit Report Act, generally carries the same definition as used in the Equal Credit Opportunity Act and includes a denial or cancellation of, or an increase in any charge for insurance coverage, denial of employment, denial or cancellation of or increase in any charge for a license or benefit, or an action taken or determination that is adverse to the interests of the consumer.

When an adverse action is taken because of information obtained from a person other than a consumer reporting agency, the user of such information must within a reasonable period of time, upon the consumer's written request for the reasons for such adverse action received within 60 days thereafter, disclose the nature of such information. In addition, the user of such information must clearly and accurately disclose to the consumer his right to make such written request at the time such adverse action is communicated to the consumer.

Truncation

On electronically-printed credit card and debit card receipts, FACTA requires truncation of all but the last five digits of any credit or debit card number on any receipt provided to the cardholder at the point of sale. This requirement does not apply to transactions in which the sole means of recording the account number is by handwriting or by an imprint or copy of the card. FACTA also allows consumers to require credit reporting agencies to truncate the first five digits of their Social Security or other identification numbers.

Risk-Based Pricing

FACTA also attempts to deal with "risk-based pricing," which occurs when a person uses a consumer report in connection with an application for—or a grant, extension, or other provision of—credit on material terms that are materially less favorable than the most favorable terms available to a substantial proportion of consumers from or through that person, based in whole or in part on a consumer report.

A consumer must be notified in writing if a creditor uses risk-based pricing. A risk-based pricing notice must:

- Contain a statement informing the consumer that the terms offered are set based on information from a consumer report
- Identify the consumer reporting agency furnishing the report
- Inform the consumer that (s)he can get a copy of a consumer report from that consumer reporting agency for free
- Describe how to get the report
- The notice must be given either at the time of application or at the time that creditor tells the consumer that his/her credit has been approved. The notice can be given orally, in writing, or electronically

Prescreening

FACTA also improves a consumer's right to opt out of prescreening with a requirement to provide the address and toll-free telephone number of the system to use to opt out, which must be presented in a simple and easy to understand form. Furthermore, the opt-out period is extended from two to five years.

Identity Theft

Numerous portions of FACTA deal with the growing problem of identity theft, i.e., fraud committed by the perpetrator using the identifying information of another person. The FCRA provides two different kinds of reports that identity theft victims can file with credit reporting agencies.

The first type of report is a preliminary report that may be filed by a consumer who in good faith suspects that (s)he has been or is about to become a victim of fraud or a related crime, including identity theft. For a period of at least 90 days, unless the consumer requests cancellation of the alert, each credit reporting agency that receives such a report must maintain a fraud alert in the consumer's file and provide that alert with any credit score generated from the consumer's file. An agency that receives the fraud alert must refer information regarding the alert to each of the other credit reporting agencies. It must also notify the victim of the right to obtain a free copy of his or her credit file and it must disclose the file within three business days of any such request. Although this type of report is short-lived, it allows victims to take speedy action to protect themselves.

The second type of report is an extended report that both: (1) alleges that an identity theft has occurred; and (2) includes a copy of an official report filed by the consumer with an appropriate federal, state, or local law enforcement agency. To qualify, the type of official report that must be submitted is one that subjects the person filing it to criminal penalties for the filing of false information.

Upon receipt of the identity theft report, a reporting agency must:

(a) include a fraud alert in victim's file;
(b) provide that alert with any credit score generated from the file for a period of seven years;
(c) exclude the consumer from any prescreening list for a period of five years;
(d) refer the information from the fraud alert to each of the other consumer reporting agencies;

(e) inform the victim of the right to obtain two free copies of the victim's credit file during the first year after the extended alert is placed in the file; and

(f) provide that credit file within three business days of a request.

A victim may request the withdrawal of the report or of some of these protections. Once an extended alert has been initiated, a consumer reporting agency must notify all prospective users of the victim's report that the consumer does not authorize:

(a) establishment of any new credit plan or extension of credit, except under an open-end credit plan;

(b) issuance of any additional cards on a consumer's existing credit account; or

(c) any increase in the credit limit on an existing credit account of the consumer.

If the victim also provides a phone number to be used for identity verification purposes, no credit grantor that uses the consumer's credit report may authorize any new credit plan or extension of credit in the name of the consumer without first either: (1) contacting the consumer at the number that (s)he furnished; or (2) taking reasonable steps to verify the consumer's identity and to confirm that the application for new credit is not a result of identity theft.

FACTA also provides special identity theft protections for military personnel. Under the Act an "active duty military consumer" is a consumer in military service who: (1) is on active duty or is a reservist performing duty under a call or order to active duty; and (2) is assigned to service away from his or her usual duty station.

Upon request, each credit reporting agency must include an active duty alert in the military consumer's file, and it must provide that alert with any credit score generated from the file. Unless the consumer requests earlier removal, an active duty alert must remain in the consumer's file for a minimum of 12 months, and for a period of two years a credit reporting agency must exclude the military consumer from any prescreening list. Active duty alerts must contain warnings of the type used in extended identity theft alerts. If a consumer furnishes a phone number to be used for identity verification, prospective credit grantors may not extend credit unless they first either contact the consumer at that number or take reasonable steps to verify the consumer's identity and confirm that the application for new credit is not the result of identity theft.

"Repollution" of Consumer Reports

FACTA attempts to prevent the "repollution" of reports with blocked information by mandating that a furnisher of information must have in place reasonable procedures to prevent it from refurnishing blocked information resulting from identity theft. If a consumer submits to a furnisher an identity theft report stating that information maintained by the furnisher purportedly relating to the consumer resulted from identity theft, the furnisher may not furnish that information to any reporting agency, unless the furnisher subsequently knows or is informed by the consumer that the information is correct.

Changes of Address

If a card issuer receives notification of an existing customer's change of address and, within 30 days after that notification, receives a request for an additional card or for a replacement card on the same account, the issuer may not issue the additional or replacement card unless it has a good reason to believe that the person requesting the card is the account holder. To determine the identity of the person requesting a new card, the card issuer must:

(a) notify the customer at his/her former address of the request and provide the card holder a means to promptly report any incorrect address changes;
(b) notify the card holder of the request by such other means of communication as has been previously agreed to by the customer and the issuer; or
(c) use another means of assessing the validity of the change of address, in accordance with reasonable policies and procedures established by the card issuer.

FACTA requires that every entity regulated by the Federal Trade Commission, the NCUA, and the federal banking agencies must establish reasonable policies and procedures to identify possible risks to customers and account holders and to the safety and soundness of those institutions and their customers. The Act also requires credit reporting agencies to block (within four business days after receiving notice from the consumer) the reporting of any information in a consumer's file that the consumer identifies as having resulted from alleged identity theft, provided that the consumer's notice includes:

(a) proof of the consumer's identity;
(b) a copy of an identity theft report;
(c) identification of the identity theft-related information; and
(d) a statement that the information does not relate to any transaction by the consumer.

After blocking the information, the reporting agency must promptly notify the furnisher of information identified by the consumer:

(a) that the information may be a result of identity theft;
(b) that an identity theft report has been filed;
(c) that a block has been requested; and
(d) the effective dates of the block.

A reporting agency may refuse to block information or rescind a block if it reasonably determines that:

(a) the information was blocked in error;
(b) a block was requested by the consumer in error;
(c) the information was blocked on the basis of a material misrepresentation of fact by the consumer;
(d) a block was requested on the basis of a material misrepresentation of fact by the consumer; or
(e) the consumer obtained possession of goods, services, or money as a result of the blocked transaction or transactions.

If a credit reporting agency receives a request for a consumer's report containing a different address than the address in its file on the consumer, it must give notice of the discrepancy to the person requesting the report.

Debt Collection and Identity Theft

FACTA also impacts debt collection practices on accounts that allegedly result from identity theft. No person may sell, transfer for consideration, or place for collection a debt that such person has been notified under FACTA Section 605B resulted from identity theft. This restriction necessitates the implementation of new procedures for many sellers and re-sellers of debt.

If a third-party debt collector is notified that information relating to a debt that (s)he is trying to collect may be fraudulent or may be the result of identity theft, the collector must:

(a) notify the creditor that the information may be fraudulent or the result of identity theft; and

(b) upon request of the alleged victim, provide to that person all information to which (s)he would be entitled if (s)he were not a victim of identity theft, but had wished to dispute the debt under provisions of law applicable to that person.

Medical Information

FACTA imposes restrictions on both reporting agencies and users with regard to medical information. Ordinarily, creditors may not use nor obtain medical information to determine consumers' eligibility (or continued eligibility) for credit. Furthermore, consumer reporting agencies may not:

(a) furnish in connection with an insurance transaction a report containing a consumer's medical information without the affirmative consent of the consumer;

(b) furnish for employment purposes a report containing a consumer's medical information unless: (1) the information is relevant to the processing or effectuation of the transaction; and (2) the consumer provides a written consent that clearly and conspicuously states the use of the information;

(c) furnish in connection with a credit transaction a report containing a consumer's medical information unless: (1) the information is relevant to the processing or effectuation of the transaction; and (2) the consumer provides a written consent that clearly and conspicuously states the use of the information;

(d) disclose the name, address, or phone number of a medical information furnisher unless the information either is encoded or is furnished to an insurance company for a business purpose other than property or casualty insurance.

Special Problems for Creditors

FACTA presents some new requirements that will be of particular concern to credit grantors. For example, the sharing of consumer information between affiliated companies is permitted only if the possibility of sharing is clearly and conspicuously disclosed to the consumer and the consumer has the right to opt out.

Any financial institution that: (a) extends credit, (b) regularly and in the ordinary course of business furnishes information to a reporting agency, and (c) furnishes negative information to an agency regarding credit extended to a customer must, within 30 days of sending the information to the reporting agency, give the consumer written notice that it furnished the negative information.

FACTA also requires the FTC, the NCUA, and the federal banking agencies to establish and maintain guidelines for all persons who furnish information to consumer reporting agencies. The guidelines are to address the accuracy and integrity of the information relating to consumers that the furnishers provide to consumer reporting agencies. Those guidelines are to be updated as often as necessary. The agencies are also to prescribe regulations requiring each furnisher to establish reasonable policies and procedures for implementing the guidelines.

In the case of a consumer dispute that results in reinvestigation by a consumer reporting agency, if an item disputed by the consumer is found to be inaccurate or incomplete or cannot be verified after reinvestigation, the furnisher must, before furnishing information on that account to a reporting agency, either modify the information, delete it, or permanently block it, as appropriate, based on the results of the reinvestigation.

Disposal of records is also an issue for creditors. FACTA requires multiple federal agencies to promulgate uniform rules for those creditors seeking to dispose of consumer records.

Liability

The Act imposes civil liability for noncompliance in the amount of any actual damages sustained, of not less than $100 and not more than $1,000 plus punitive damages as the court may allow. In addition, if the consumer has successfully obtained enforcement through a court proceeding, then the court will grant the costs of the action together with reasonable attorneys' fees. The FACTA amendment allows a consumer to sue not later than the earlier of two years from the date (s)he discovers the violation, or five years after the date on which the violation occurs. It also imposes more stringent compliance standards on furnishers of credit information.

Liability is also imposed for negligent failure to comply with the Act. Penalties in the nature of a fine or imprisonment may be imposed on any person who obtained information on a consumer from a consumer reporting agency under false pretenses, or upon any officer or employee of a consumer reporting agency who knowingly and willingly provides information to an unauthorized person.

Under FACTA, the standard of care for a furnisher of information has been toughened. Under the new standard, a person may not furnish any information relating to a consumer to a consumer reporting agency if the person knows or has reasonable cause to believe that the information is inaccurate.

Compliance with the Act is enforced by the Federal Trade Commission and other federal agencies.

FAIR CREDIT BILLING ACT

This Act requires creditors to respond to inquiries by consumers on credit card accounts and other charge accounts in which an allegedly improper or incorrect charge is made on a bill. 15 USC §§ 1666-1666j. Under certain circumstances a card issuer can be subject to many of the claims and defenses that the consumer could assert against the merchant with whom the consumer incurred charges. The Act authorizes creditors to inquire into an applicant's sex, marital status, race, national origin and age, but the applicant is not required to answer these questions. It sets 62 as the age to which the term "elderly" applies and describes the working of a nondiscriminatory credit-scoring system.

CONSUMER LEASING ACT

The Consumer Leasing Act of 1976 added new sections to the Truth in Lending Act, and first became effective March 23, 1977. Id. §§ 1667-1667f. The law:

1. Requires lessors to disclose information affecting the cost of consumer leases defined as leases of personal property, primarily for personal, family, or household use for a term greater than four months where the consumer's total contractual obligation is less than $25,000
2. Sets forth limits of liability of the lessee at the expiration or termination of the lease
3. Seeks to ensure meaningful and accurate disclosure in advertising of leasing terms

CONSUMER PRODUCTS SAFETY ACT

In late 1972 Congress enacted the Consumer Products Safety Act, 15 USC § 2051-2085 which is intended to protect the public against unreasonable risks of injury associated with consumer products, to assist consumers in evaluating the comparative safety of consumer products, to develop uniform safety standards, and to promote research and investigation into product-related deaths, illnesses and injuries.

The Act creates a commission which collects, analyzes and investigates information of injuries associated with consumer products. It may also conduct research studies and investigations and test consumer products. The commission is authorized to make rules with respect to consumer product safety standards and requirements. The Act contains punitive measures for failure to comply with any rules or standards promulgated by the commission and also provides for civil penalties and private enforcement.

EQUAL CREDIT OPPORTUNITY ACT

The Equal Credit Opportunity Act (ECOA), while primarily a consumer law, does impose obligations on business creditors with respect to the extension, modification and termination of credit, as well as notification of credit decisions and record keeping.

Since March 23, 1977, federal law has not only prohibited creditors from discriminating against a person because of sex or marital status, but it has also been unlawful to discriminate because of race, color, religion, national origin, age, welfare assistance or the exercise of debtor's rights assured by the Consumer Credit Protection Act. 15 USC §§ 1601, 1691-1691f. The law, and Regulation B, which implements it (12 CFR §§ 202.1 and 202.17 (2003)) is not limited to consumer transactions but applies to credit extended to any individual, partnership or corporation for any purpose.

It also applies to consumer leases even though the Equal Credit Opportunity Act does not specify that consumer leases are covered by its provisions. If information on a debtor is obtained from a consumer reporting agency, the name and address of such agency must be set forth. The source of such information other than from a consumer reporting agency need not be revealed. When viewed in light of the Consumer

Credit Protection Act, it is clear that the ECOA applies to all transactions covered by Truth in Lending.

As noted below, there are strict requirements for credit grantors with respect to adverse credit decisions. These include the suspension, denial or reduction of credit availability. On March 5, 2003, the Federal Reserve Board of Governors adopted and published its final rule amending Regulation B. Business credit grantors must be aware of the very strict requirements that have been mandated by the ECOA with respect to the establishing of credit, appropriate notifications to customers and retention of records. The mandatory compliance date for amended Regulation B was April 15, 2004.

Under Regulation B, grantors of business credit must notify applicants of a decision on its application for credit within 30 days from receiving a completed application. An application is deemed "completed" when the creditor has received all the information it requires to evaluate an application for credit. At the time of notification to an applicant of an adverse credit decision, the applicant must be provided with a notice of the right to request the reasons for the adverse credit decision. This disclosure must include the name, address and telephone number of the person or office from which the statement of reasons can be obtained. However, business credit grantors are not required to notify an applicant of the reasons for the denial of credit unless the applicant, within 60 days after oral or written notification that adverse action has been taken, requests in writing the reasons for such action. Additionally, the notice must contain certain language, a sample of which is the following:

> The federal Equal Credit Opportunity Act prohibits creditors from discriminating against credit applicants on the basis of race, color, religion, national origin, sex, marital status, age (provided the applicant has the capacity to enter into a binding contract); because all or part of the applicant's income derives from any public assistance program; or because the applicant has in good faith exercised any right under the Consumer Credit Protection Act. The federal agency that administers compliance with this law concerning this creditor is [Different areas of business are regulated by different governmental agencies. Be certain to insert the appropriate agency.]

If a written request for reasons is received, such request must be responded to in writing by a credit grantor within 30 days by advising the inquirer as to the reasons for such denial, which can be expressed in a brief statement such as "insufficient credit references" or "unable to verify credit references." A statement that the adverse action was based on the creditors' internal standards or policies or that the applicant failed to achieve a qualifying score on the creditor's credit scoring system is insufficient.

A written notice of rights of an applicant can be given one of three ways: (1) by providing a written notice of the right to a statement of the specific reasons for credit denial after an adverse decision, (2) by actually providing a written statement of the specific reasons for denial, or (3) giving notice to all business applicants on any document given to the applicant which the applicant can retain.

As stated above, the strict requirements of notification apply to adverse credit decisions. Acceleration of a note that is in default does not constitute an adverse action. Likewise, terminating, or changing credit terms because of a current default is not considered an adverse action.

An oral request for an extension of credit, if made in accordance with the procedures established by the creditor for the type of credit requested, is considered an application.

If an application for business credit is made solely by telephone, then the creditor may provide an oral disclosure of the applicant's right to a written statement of the specific reasons for denial of credit. In such instances, the creditor does not have to recite all of the information normally required with a written notice.

A request for an advance under an existing line of credit is not considered an "application" and therefore does not trigger the notice requirements.

Creditors are prohibited from inquiring about the marital status of a business credit applicant for unsecured credit. Creditors can inquire about the marital status if an applicant resides in a community property state and relies on property located in such a state to repay a debt or applies for secured credit. A creditor can also inquire about ownership rights in, or the name of any co-owner of, property relied upon by a credit applicant to satisfy a debt in the event of default.

For 12 months after the date that a creditor notifies an applicant of action taken on an application or of incompleteness, or of adverse action taken on an existing account, the creditor shall retain in original form or a copy thereof, any application, any information concerning characteristics of the application, any written or recorded information used in evaluating the application, notification of action taken, the statement of specific reasons for adverse action and any written statement submitted by the applicant alleging a violation of the Act or regulation.

For business applicants that had gross revenues in excess of $1 million in its preceding fiscal year, or an extension of trade credit, credit incident to a factoring agreement, or other similar types of business credit, the creditor shall retain records for 60 days. If an applicant requests a written statement of the specific reasons for credit denial, then the creditor must retain the records for not less than 12 months.

FAIR DEBT COLLECTION PRACTICES ACT

The Federal Fair Debt Collection Practices Act, 15 USC §§ 1692-1692o, is commonly known as the FDCPA. Ordinarily, the Act applies only to "consumer" debts, i.e., those incurred primarily for personal, family, or household purposes, even if the debts have been reduced to judgment.

The FDCPA focuses on the collection activities of third-party collectors such as collection agencies and attorneys. Ordinarily, creditors are exempt from the FDCPA if they are collecting their own debts in their own name. However, a creditor will lose this exemption if it uses any name other than its own so as to make it appear that a third party is attempting to collect its debts. Such conduct both violates the Act and renders the creditor liable to the same extent as a third-party debt collector.

Multiple cases have held that a creditor who purchases a debt after it is already in default will be treated as a "debt collector" under the Act and is not entitled to avail itself of the creditor exemption. Therefore, companies that purchase portfolios of bad debts must ensure that their employees comply with the FDCPA.

The Federal Trade Commission has taken the position that the FDCPA may set standards for fair trade practices by creditors. The Commission has stated that under section 5 of the FTC Act it could pursue creditors and collectors of commercial debts for the type conduct that is prohibited by the FDCPA.

In addition to the FDCPA, many state laws restrict the actions of those who collect consumer debts. While there are many variations in the state statutes, both California and Pennsylvania have enacted statutes that apply the bulk of the FDCPA to creditors who are collecting their own debts in their own names. It is therefore clear that a creditor that deals in retail debts would be wise to implement collection procedures that are consistent with the FDCPA. Texas, North Carolina, and Florida have fair debt laws that impose substantial restrictions on creditors.

Common FDCPA Prohibitions

The following is a partial list of the practices prohibited by the FDCPA:

- Misrepresenting the character or amount of a debt
- Threatening to take action prohibited by law
- Threatening to take action that is not intended to be taken
- Using profane, obscene, or abusive language
- Making repeated calls for the purpose of harassment
- Reporting a disputed debt to a credit bureau without disclosing that it is disputed
- Reporting a "stale" debt to a credit bureau
- Suing or threatening to file suit on a time-barred debt (*Kimber v. Federal Financial Corp.*, 668 F. Supp 1480 (M.D. Ala. 1987)
- Continuing to collect without first complying with a verification request.
- Communicating improperly with a third party
- Communicating with a consumer who is known to be represented by an attorney
- Communicating with a consumer at improper hours or at a time or place known to be inconvenient
- Filing suit in an improper venue
- Using any sort of false representations or deceptive means to collect a debt

Businesses that violate the FDCPA can be sued for any actual damages resulting from the violation, together with statutory damages in the amount of $1,000 per suit and the attorneys' fees incurred in prosecuting the suit. The Act also allows for class actions, and in such an action suit the defendant can be held liable for up to $500,000 or one percent of its net worth, whichever is less, plus the named plaintiff's individual claim and the reasonable attorney's fees and costs incurred in pursuing the class action.

PROMISES OF CREDIT REPAIR

The Credit Repair Organizations Act (15 USC § 1679, *et seq.*) imposes a number of severe restrictions upon those who offer to repair or improve a consumer's credit in exchange for valuable consideration. Although creditors are generally exempt from the Act, any business that offers to repair or improve consumers' credit as part of its marketing or collection practices should familiarize itself with CROA. Many states have implemented comparable credit service organization acts that provide similar protections to consumers.

THE FTC HOLDER IN DUE COURSE RULE

16 CFR § 433.2 requires the inclusion of the following disclaimer in certain consumer credit contracts:

<u>NOTICE</u>

ANY HOLDER OF THIS CONSUMER CREDIT CONTRACT IS SUBJECT TO ALL CLAIMS AND DEFENSES WHICH THE DEBTOR COULD ASSERT AGAINST THE SELLER OF GOODS OR SERVICES OBTAINED PURSUANT HERETO OR WITH THE PROCEEDS HEREOF. RECOVERY HEREUNDER BY THE DEBTOR SHALL NOT EXCEED AMOUNTS PAID BY THE DEBTOR HEREUNDER.

A similar disclaimer is required when a seller accepts the proceeds of a purchase money loan in full or partial payment for a sale or lease of goods or services to a consumer. The Rule allows the assertion of defenses to payment and claims for refunds of sums paid against all subsequent holders of a consumer credit contract, even those who have never actually received funds from the debtor. Moreover, the limitation on liability does not limit a creditor's liability on independent state law grounds. Therefore, an assignee of a consumer credit contract can be sued for both its own acts and those of the seller.

Although the Rule is mandated only in consumer transactions, through error or misunderstanding, the disclaimer is sometimes included in commercial agreements. Creditors should be careful to avoid such inadvertent inclusion, as the clause is a contractual provision that, once included, may be asserted by the debtor as in the case of any other part of the contract.

CLAIMS AND DEFENSES ON PURCHASES MADE BY CREDIT CARD

15 USC § 1666i provides a right similar to the Holder in Due Course Rule for claims and defenses arising out of a credit card transaction. A card issued under an open end consumer credit plan is subject to all claims (other than tort claims) and defenses arising out of any transaction in which the credit card is used as an extension of credit if:

(a) the obligor has made a good faith effort to obtain satisfactory resolution of the problem with the merchant honoring the credit card;

(b) the amount of the initial transaction exceeds $50; and

(c) the initial transaction occurred in the same state as the mailing address previously provided by the cardholder or within 100 miles of that address.

The requirements of transaction size and locale do not apply if the merchant honoring the card is the card issuer, a person controlled by the card issuer, a person under direct or indirect common control with the card issuer, a franchised dealer in the card issuer's products or services, or is a person who obtained the order for the transaction through a mail solicitation in which the card issuer participated by soliciting the consumer to use its card in connection with the sale.

The amount of claims or defenses asserted by the consumer may not exceed the amount of credit outstanding with respect to the disputed transaction at the time the consumer first notifies the card issuer or merchant of the claim or defense. The statute sets forth a method of determining the amount of such outstanding credit by applying any payments to all other charges before crediting them against the disputed charge.

FAIR CREDIT AND CHARGE CARD DISCLOSURE ACT

The statute requires credit and charge card issuers to disclose rates and other cost information in a uniform manner.

FEDERAL TRADE COMMISSION'S REGULATION OF CREDIT PRACTICES

The Federal Trade Commission has issued rules regulating credit practices in consumer credit transactions. The rules designate certain practices as unfair credit practices. Such practices include the following:

1. A confession of judgment or warrant of attorney or other waiver of the right to notice and the opportunity to be heard
2. An executory waiver or a limitation of exemption from attachment, execution, or other process, on real or personal property, unless the waiver applies to property subject to a security interest executed in connection with the obligation
3. An assignment of wages or other earnings, unless the assignment is revocable by debtor; the assignment is part of a payroll deduction plan or preauthorized payment plan; or the assignment applies only to wages or other earnings already earned at the time of the assignment
4. A nonpossessory security interest in household goods, other than a purchase money security interest

Deceptive cosigner practices are proscribed. They include misrepresentation by lender or seller of the nature or extent of cosigner liability; and a lender or a retail installment seller obligating a cosigner without the cosigner being informed prior to becoming obligated of the nature of his or her liability. A special notice prescribed by the rules is required to be given to a cosigner to prevent unfair and deceptive cosigner practices.

In connection with collecting a debt arising out of the extension of credit to a consumer, it is an unfair act or practice to collect any delinquency charge on a payment that is otherwise a full payment for the applicable period and is paid on its due date, when the only delinquency is attributable to late fees or delinquency charges assessed on earlier installments.

If there is a state requirement that provides for a level of protection equal to the federal requirement, the state may obtain an exemption from application of these rules to it.

STATE LEGISLATION

The majority of the states, the District of Columbia and Puerto Rico have truth in lending legislation in effect. Their common requirement is that disclosure of the cost of credit be in the form of an annual percentage rate, thus simplifying the task of the consumer when shopping for the best credit purchase.

Most of these states have adopted some version of the disclosure requirements mandated by the federal act, and typically the disclosure requirements are applicable to the types of transactions normally entered into by consumers: sales, loans and revolving credit transactions.

All such states require the creditor to disclose detailed credit information to the debtor, at or before the time when credit is extended. The information required is essentially the same as that in the federal Truth in Lending Act. In some states, creditors need not disclose finance charges on transactions to a certain maximum limit, as in the federal Act. Other states have no such exceptions. (*See below* Summary of State Laws on Truth in Lending.)

Section 111(a) of the federal Truth in Lending Act specifies that it is not intended to preempt state creditor disclosure legislation unless the state provision is inconsistent with federal rules, and then only to the extent of the inconsistency. The Act does not preempt the entire body of state law if an inconsistency arises in one case. The intent of this federal legislation, in fact, is "to encourage as much state legislation in this area as is possible so that the federal law will no longer be necessary." (Senate Committee on Banking and Currency, Report 392, 90th Congress, 1st Session, June 29, 1967, p. 8.)

The annual percentage rate to be disclosed under local law is not a simple interest rate, but, similar to the federal Act, is a complex "finance charge" which includes all costs of credit, including legal interest and other charges incident to the extension of credit.

The Federal Reserve Board of Governors is authorized to exempt any class of credit transactions in any state if it finds that the state requires essentially the same information as the federal Act, and has made adequate provision for enforcement of the state law.

Methods of Determining Annual Percentage Rate

CONSTANT RATIO METHOD

The constant ratio method for determining the annual percentage rate is useful for highly irregular contracts. The constant ratio formula assumes that: (a) all scheduled installments of a credit transaction are equal in amount, payable at equal intervals, and fall on due dates which are the same day of each month or other payment period as that on which the agreement is entered into, and (b) the debtor makes all payments at the times and in the amounts scheduled. The formula is:

$$R = \frac{2PC}{A(N+1)}$$

R equals the percentage rate; P equals the number of payment periods in a year; C equals the finance charge; A equals the principal balance to be paid by the debtor; and N equals the number of installments.

ACTUARIAL METHOD (UNITED STATES RULE)

This is a method for computing the simple annual rate on the declining balance and assumes that a uniform periodic rate is applied to a schedule of installment payments such that the principal is reduced to zero upon completion of the payments. The actuarial rate is the periodic rate multiplied by the number of periods in a year.

Many states that have adopted Retail Installment Sales Acts have a provision in such acts requiring disclosure of the amount of finance charges to a retail buyer on the purchase of consumer goods. However, such statutes do not provide that the disclosure take the form of an annual percentage rate which is required under the federal law or under the state laws set forth in the Summary of State Laws on Truth in Lending. For a more detailed discussion of the disclosure requirements under the Retail Installment Sales Acts *see* Chapter 21.

Those states that require some form of disclosure of finance charges but not an annual percentage rate are Florida, Georgia, Montana, Missouri, Nebraska, Nevada, Ohio, Tennessee and Vermont.

Alaska and New Hampshire have in effect a Retail Installment Sales Act, which allows disclosure either in the form of an annual percentage rate or as a dollar amount. Minnesota and Mississippi have some form of disclosure requirement (although not an annual percentage rate) on sales of vehicles only.

In New York, use of the previous balance method to compute finance charges on retail charge accounts is illegal under the Personal Property Law; sellers are required to use the adjusted balance method.

SUMMARY OF STATE LAWS ON TRUTH IN LENDING

Note: States not listed do not have truth-in-lending provisions. State legislatures will, on occasion, modify an area of law without clear delineation as to its content and context. As a result, even the changes which have been enacted prior to placement in the state's Code may be difficult to locate. As a result, the Editors urge all users of the *Manual* to use this publication only as a guide, and consult the latest codified version of the state's law for all recent changes.

CALIFORNIA

Jurisdiction—Retail Installment Sales Law, Motor Vehicle Sales and Finance Act, Mobile Homes and Manufactured Housing Act. Disclosures made in any retail installment contract, conditional sale contract, or other document may be set forth in terminology required or permitted under Federal Reserve Board Regulation Z. Nothing in the state laws is deemed prohibitive of the disclosure in such contracts or documents of additional information required or permitted under Regulation Z at the time the disclosure is made. Compliance with FRB interpretations of Regulation Z is deemed full compliance with that regulation with respect to the subject matter of the interpretations.

COLORADO

Jurisdiction—UCCC.

Exemptions and Exceptions—Credit to governmental bodies; insurance sales by insurers (except those under UCCC Article 4); regulated public and municipal utilities and common carriers; licensed pawnbrokers; and rates and charges of credit unions under state or federal law.

Transactions Subject to Disclosure Provisions—Sales, loans and revolving credit.

Administration—Assistant attorney general. District attorney with administrator's consent.

Annual Rate Calculation—Actuarial method or other rule prescribed by administrator. Exemptions: charges under $5 for debt under $75; $7.50 for debt over $75 but less than $500; and $15 if amount financed is more than $500.

Civil Penalty—Twice the finance charge, but no less than $100, or more than $1000.

Criminal Penalty—$5,000 maximum fine, one year imprisonment, or both.

Type Size—Clear and conspicuous.

CONNECTICUT

Jurisdiction—Truth in Lending Act. Creditors and lessors are required to comply with the federal Truth in Lending Act and Regulations Z and M by reference.

DELAWARE

Jurisdiction—Retail Installment Sales Act and Motor Vehicle Sales Finance Act. Disclosures made under the federal Truth in Lending Act are compliance with comparable, but literally inconsistent, disclosures under state laws.

DISTRICT OF COLUMBIA

Jurisdiction—Consumer retail credit regulation.

Exemptions and Exceptions—Business credit, credit over $25,000; motor vehicles, 90-day credit if there is no finance charge; prices, tariffs regulated by government.

Transactions Subject to Disclosure Provisions—Sales and revolving credit.

Administration—Officer of Consumer Protection.

Annual Rate Calculation—Actuarial or U.S. Rule. *Exemptions:* Charges under $5 for debt under $75; $7.50 for debt over $75.

Civil Penalty—No provisions.

Criminal Penalty—Loss or suspension of license, $300 maximum fine, or 10 days' imprisonment.

Type Size—Same as federal Truth in Lending Act.

FLORIDA

Jurisdiction—Retail Installment Sales Act. A creditor who discloses all information required by the federal Truth in Lending Act will be deemed in compliance with state contract requirements, except that a separate written itemization of the amount financed must be provided in accordance with state law, and state requirements for revolving accounts.

HAWAII

Jurisdiction—Under the Hawaii Industrial Loan Companies Act, Retail Installment Sales Act, Small Loan Act, and any transaction governed by the federal Truth in Lending Act there is no requirement to have any disclosure when inconsistent with the federal law. The Disclosure of Finance Charges Law does not apply to transactions governed by federal law.

IDAHO

Jurisdiction—Credit Code, effective March 31, 1983. Creditors covered by the federal Truth in Lending Act and the regulations issued pursuant thereto are required to comply with the provisions of the law and regulations administered by the Director of the Department of Finance. Exemptions and advertising standards of the federal Truth in Lending Act and Regulations Z and M apply to creditors in Idaho.

Civil Penalty—Federal civil liability provisions in effect. The liability of a creditor under the federal Truth in Lending Act is in lieu of, not in addition to, liability under the Uniform Commercial Code. No action with respect to the same violation may be maintained under both acts.

Criminal Penalty—$5,000 maximum fine, one year imprisonment, or both.

ILLINOIS

Jurisdiction—Retail Installment Sales Act (RISA), Motor Vehicle Retail Installment Sales Act (MVRISA), Consumer Installment Loan Act (CILA), Revolving Credit Act, Revolving Charge Act, Consumer Finance Act (CFA), Premium Finance Companies Act (PFC), Credit Cards (CC).

Exemptions and Exceptions—*RISA:* Business credit and motor vehicles; retail charge agreements. *MVRISA:* Business credit not including farm or professional. *CILA* and *Revolving Charge Acts* have no exemptions. *Revolving Credit Act:* Accounts without unpaid balances. *CFA:* Business loans by state licensed entities. *PFC:* Financial institutions, insurance companies, consumer finance agencies.

Transactions Subject to Disclosure Provisions—*RISA:* Sales and revolving credit. *MVRISA:* Sales. *CILA:* Loans. *Revolving Credit Act:* Revolving credit (credit card applications). *Revolving Charge Act:* Revolving credit. *CFA* and *PFC:* Loans.

Administration—*RISA:* Commissioner of Bank and Trust Companies. *CILA:* Director of Financial Institutions. *CFA:* Department of Financial Institutions. The other statutes have no provisions.

Annual Rate Calculation—Actuarial or U.S. Rule for RISA, CFA, and MVRISA. Other statutes have no provisions.

Exemptions: *RISA:* Charge under $5 for debt under $75; under $7.50 for debt over $75. *CFA:* Same as RISA.

Civil Penalty—*Revolving Credit Act:* Contract unenforceable. *Revolving Charge Act:* Only balance of cash price is collectible. *CFA:* Balance of cash price minus attorney's fees and only court costs are collectible. *PFC:* Revocation of license. The other statutes have no provisions.

Criminal Penalty—*RISA* and *MVRISA*: $1,000 maximum fine, one year imprisonment, or both. *CFA:* $100 to 1,000 fine; Class A misdemeanor. The other statutes have no provisions.

Type Size—RISA and *MVRISA*: Clear and conspicuous in eight-point type. *CILA:* Clear and conspicuous. *Revolving Charge Act:* Equal prominence. *Revolving Credit Act:* No provision. *CFA* and *MVRISA*: In English. *PFC*: Eight-point type.

INDIANA

*Jurisdiction—*UCCC.

*Exemptions and Exceptions—*Credit to governmental bodies; insurance sales by insurers, except those under UCCC Article 4); regulated public and municipal utilities and common carriers; licensed pawnbrokers.

*Transactions Subject to Disclosure Provisions—*Sales, loans and revolving credit. Sellers, lessors and lendors are required to provide disclosure information pursuant to the federal Consumer Credit Protection Act.

*Administration—*Department of Financial Institutions and Division of Consumer Credit.

*Annual Rate Calculation—*Actuarial method or other prescribed by administrator. *Exemptions:* Charge under $5 for debt under $75; under $7.50 for debt over $75.

*Civil Penalty—*Twice the finance charge; but no less than $100, or more than $1,000.

Criminal Penalty—$5,000 maximum fine, one year imprisonment, or both.

*Type Size—*Clear and conspicuous.

IOWA

*Jurisdiction—*Consumer Credit Code. A creditor must comply with the federal Truth in Lending Act and disclose to the consumer all information required by the Act.

*Exemptions and Exceptions—*Business or governmental credit, insurance sales by insurers, regulated public utilities and common carriers, and nonrealty credit over $35,000.

*Administration—*Attorney General.

*Civil Penalty—*Twice the finance charge, but no less than $100, or more than $1,000.

Criminal Penalty—$5,000 maximum fine, one year imprisonment, or both.

KANSAS

*Jurisdiction—*UCCC and the Insurance Premium Financing Act (IPFCA).

Exemptions and Exceptions—UCCC: Business or governmental credit; nonrealty credit over $25,000, regulated public utilities and common carriers; insurance sales by insurers (except those under UCCC Article 4). *IPFCA:* No provisions.

*Transactions Subject to Disclosure Provisions—*A creditor must comply with the federal Truth in Lending Act and disclose to the consumer all information required by the Act.

Administration—UCCC: Consumer Credit Commissioner and enforcement agencies. *IPFCA:* Commissioner of Insurance.

Annual Rate Calculation—UCCC: A creditor must comply with the federal Truth in Lending Act. *IPFCA:* No provisions.

Civil Penalty—UCCC: Twice the finance charge, but no less than $100, or more than $1,000. $5000 for repeated violations. *IPFCA:* No provision.

Criminal Penalty—UCCC: Class A misdemeanor or federal Truth in Lending penalties. *IPFCA:* No provisions.

Type Size—UCCC: A creditor must comply with the federal Truth in Lending Act. *IPFCA:* Eight-point type.

KENTUCKY

*Jurisdiction—*Credit Disclosure Law, Banking Commission Regulations, Bank Revolving Credit Law, Manufactured

Home Financing Law, and Insurance Premium Finance Companies Regulations.

*Exemptions and Exceptions—*Sales under the Installment Sales Law, motor vehicle sales, pawnbrokers, credit over $25,000 and finance charges. Compliance with federal Truth in Lending Act constitutes compliance with the Kentucky Credit Disclosure Law.

*Transactions Subject to Disclosure Provisions—*Loans and revolving credit sales.

*Administration—*Com. Department of Banking and Securities.

*Annual Rate Calculation—*Constant ratio method.

Civil Penalty—Forfeiture of finance charge.

Criminal Penalty—$500 maximum fine, six months imprisonment, or both.

Type Size—Annual rate must appear at 12-point bold.

MAINE

Jurisdiction—Truth in Lending Law.

Exemptions and Exceptions—Business or commercial credit, agricultural transactions, transactions not secured by realty where amount financed exceeds $25,000, securities or commodities transactions, public utilities, leases of personal property incidental to lease of real property where there is no option to purchase.

Transactions Subject to Disclosure Provisions—Sales, loans, revolving credit.

Administration—Supt. Consumer Credit Protection.

Annual Rate Calculation—Actuarial or U.S. Rule; in unusual circumstances, the constant ratio method. *Exemptions:* Charge under $5 for debt under $75; under $7.50 for debt over $75.

Civil Penalty—Actual damages or twice the finance charge, but no less than $100, or more than $1,000. Leases: 25 percent of total monthly payments.

Criminal Penalty—Organizations may be charged a $5,000 maximum fine, one year imprisonment or both. Natural persons may be charged $1,000, one year imprisonment, or both.

Type Size—Clear and conspicuous.

MARYLAND

Jurisdiction—Interest and usury law, Credit Grantor Revolving Credit and Closed End Credit provisions.

Exemptions and Exceptions—Transactions subject to the Credit Grantor Revolving Credit and Closed End Credit provisions are subject to the disclosures and requirements of that law and the federal Truth in Lending Act.

Transactions Subject to Disclosure Provisions—Loans.

Administration—No provisions.

Annual Rate Calculation—Annual effective rate.

Civil Penalty—No provisions.

Criminal Penalty—$1,000 maximum fine, one year imprisonment, or both.

Type Size—No provisions.

MASSACHUSETTS

Jurisdiction—Truth in Lending Act (TILA), Retail Installment Sales and Service (RISS), Motor Vehicle Retail Installment Sales (MVRIS), Insurance Premium Financing Act (IPFA), and Bank Commission Regulations.

Exemptions and Exceptions—*TILA:* Business or commercial credit, agricultural transactions, transactions not secured by real property, dwellings where amount financed exceeds $25,000, securities or commodities transactions, public utilities, home fuel budget plans. *RISS:* Loans, sales with less than three payments, charge of $1 or less and no collateral. *MVRIS:* No provisions. *IPFA:* Premiums financed at not more than 6 percent per year; life endowment, retirement income insurance.

Transactions Subject to Disclosure Provisions—*TILA:* Sales, loans and revolving credit. *RISS:* Sales and revolving credit. *MVRIS* and *IPFA:* Sales.

Administration—Commissioner of Banks.

Annual Rate Calculation—Actuarial method or U.S. Rule. *Exemption:* Charge under $5 for debt under $75.

Civil Penalty—*TILA:* Actual damages or twice the finance charge, but no less than $100, or more than $1,000. *RISS* and *MVRIS:* Forfeiture of finance charge. *IPFCA:* No provisions.

Criminal Penalty—*TILA:* $5,000 maximum fine, one year imprisonment, or both. *RISS* and *MVRIS:* $500 maximum fine, six months imprisonment, or both. *IPFCA:* No provision.

Type Size—Clear and conspicuous.

MICHIGAN

Jurisdiction—Retail Installment Sales Act, Home Improvement Finance Act, Motor Vehicle Retail Installment Sales Act, Retail Charge Accounts. Michigan creditor compliance with the federal Truth in Lending Act constitutes compliance with the disclosure provision of the listed state acts.

MINNESOTA

Jurisdiction—Regulated Loan Act. Open-end loans made by licensed regulated lenders must comply with the disclosure requirements of the federal Truth in Lending Act and Regulation Z.

NEW JERSEY

Jurisdiction—Designated consumer credit law and retail charge accounts. To the extent that New Jersey laws are inconsistent with disclosure, advertising, terminology, type size, method of computation of finance charges, form, content, or time of delivery provisions and requirements of the federal Truth in Lending Act and Regulation Z, compliance with the federal rules is deemed compliance with the New Jersey laws. Retail charge accounts are subject to the requirements of the federal Truth in Lending Act and Regulation Z applicable to open-end credit.

NEW MEXICO

Jurisdiction—Retail installment sales loans, Motor Vehicle Sales Finance Act (MVSFA), Insurance Premium Finance Act (IPFA) and Interest Usury Act. For retail installment sales loans and MVSFA, compliance with the federal Truth in Lending Act and Regulation Z is deemed compliance with the Retail Installment Sales Law. Premium finance agreements must comply with all applicable federal requirements as to form. Financial disclosure for loans must be made as required by statute.

Exemptions and Exceptions—Business and agricultural credit over $50,000.

Transactions Subject to Disclosure Provisions—Sales, loans and revolving credit.

Administration—Director of financial institutions.

Annual Rate Calculation—No provisions.

Civil Penalty—Forfeiture of all interest charges or other advantages.

Criminal Penalty—No provision.

Type Size—In English.

NEW YORK

Jurisdiction—Retail Installment Sales Act, Motor Vehicle Retail Installment Sales Act, Sales Finance Companies Law, Insurance Premium Financing Law, Small Loan Law, and Penal and Banking Laws. Credit transactions are subject to the federal Truth in Lending Act and the regulations thereunder.

NORTH DAKOTA

Jurisdiction—Retail Installment Sales Act (RISA) and revolving charge accounts.

Exemptions and Exceptions—Sale of personal property for $25,000 or above; property used primarily for business, commercial, or agricultural purposes.

Transactions Subject to Disclosure Provisions—Revolving credit. Sellers may comply with the federal Truth in Lending Act instead of the disclosure provisions of RISA.

Administration—No provisions.

Annual Rate Calculation—Annual simple interest.

Civil Penalty—For revolving charge accounts, forfeiture of finance charge. No provisions for RISA.

Criminal Penalty—Class A misdemeanor for revolving charge accounts. No provision for RISA.

Type Size—No provisions.

OKLAHOMA

Jurisdiction—Uniform Consumer Credit Code, Department of Consumer Affairs and Rules of the Administrator.

Exemptions and Exceptions—Business, commercial, agricultural, or government credit; insurance sales by insurers (except those under UCCC Article 4); licensed pawnbrokers; home fuel budget plans; regulated public utilities; common carriers; and non-realty credit over $45,000.

Transactions Subject to Disclosure Provisions—Sales, loans and revolving credit.

Administration—Administrator of Consumer Credit.

Annual Rate Calculation—Actuarial or U.S. Rule. In certain circumstances, constant ratio method.

Exemptions: Charge under $5 for debt under $75; under $7.50 for debt over $75.

Civil Penalty—Actual damages or twice the finance charge, but no less than $100, or more than $1,000.

Criminal Penalty—$5,000 maximum fine, one year imprisonment, or both.

Type Size—Clear and conspicuous.

OREGON

Jurisdiction—Retail Installment Sales Act (RISA) and Motor Vehicle Retail Installment Sales Act (MVRISA). Any compliance with the disclosure requirements of the federal Truth in Lending Act is deemed compliance with disclosure provisions of the RISA and MVRISA.

Administration—Administrator of Consumer Affairs.

PUERTO RICO

Jurisdiction—Retail installment sales and finance companies.

Exemptions and Exceptions—No provision.

Transactions Subject to Disclosure Provisions—Sales.

Administration—Director of Consumer Service Administration.

Annual Rate Calculation—No provisions.

Civil Penalty—Administrative fine of no less than $100, or more than $1,000.

Criminal Penalty—$1,000 maximum fine, two years imprisonment, or both.

Type Size—10-point type, elite typewritten, or legible handwritten for figures and percentages.

RHODE ISLAND

Jurisdiction—Truth in Lending and Retail Selling Act (TILRSA); general powers and obligations of financial institutions.

Exemptions and Exceptions—*TILRSA:* Oral solicitations on applications through print media distributed in more than one state. *Financial Institutions:* No provisions.

Transactions Subject to Disclosure Provisions—*TILRSA:* Loans and revolving credit. *Financial Institutions:* Sales

Administration—*TILRSA:* No provisions. *Financial Institutions:* Board of Bank Incorporation.

Annual Rate Calculation—*TILRSA:* No provisions. *Financial Institutions:* Annual simple interest.

Civil Penalty—*TILRSA:* $500 to $5,000 per violation. *Financial Institutions:* No provisions.

Criminal Penalty—No provisions.

Type Size—*TILRSA:* Clear and conspicuous. *Financial Institutions:* No provisions.

SOUTH CAROLINA

Jurisdiction—Consumer Protection Code. A creditor must disclose to the consumer all the information required by the federal Truth in Lending Act and otherwise comply with the entire Act.

Administration—Administrator of Consumer Affairs.

Civil Penalty—Twice the finance charge, but no less than $100, or more than $1,000.

Criminal Penalty—$5,000 maximum fine, imprisonment for one year, or both.

Type Size—No provisions.

TENNESSEE

Jurisdiction—Compliance with federal Truth in Lending Act is compliance with state disclosure requirements.

TEXAS

Jurisdiction—Insurance Premium Finance Law, Manufactured Home Credit Transactions Law, and Revolving Loan Accounts Law.

Exemptions and Exceptions—No provisions.

Transactions Subject to Disclosure Provisions—Loans.

Administration—State Board of Insurance.

Annual Rate Calculation—Same as the federal Truth in Lending Act.

Civil Penalty—No provisions.

Criminal Penalty—Class B misdemeanor.

Type Size—10-point type, .075 computer type, elite typewriter or legibly handwritten for figures and percentages.

UTAH

Jurisdiction—UCCC and Department of Financial Institutions.

Exemptions and Exceptions—Business or government credit, sales of insurance by insurers (except under UCCC Article 4), regulated public utilities and common carriers, licensed pawnbrokers, margin accounts, credit for agricultural purposes, transactions in securities.

Transactions Subject to Disclosure Provisions—Sales, loans and revolving credit. The provisions on disclosure of the federal Truth in Lending Act and Regulation Z and M have been adopted by reference.

Administration—Comm. of Financial Institutions.

Annual Rate Calculation—Actuarial or U.S. Rule, under unusual circumstances, the constant ratio method. *Exemptions:* Charge under $5 for debt under $75; under $7.50 for debt over $75.

Civil Penalty—Twice the finance charge, but no less than $100, or more than $1,000. For class actions, there is no minimum charge, with the maximum being the lesser of $500,000 or 1 percent of net worth.

Criminal Penalty—$5,000 maximum fine, one year imprisonment, or both.

Type Size—Clear and conspicuous, 10-point type.

VERMONT

Jurisdiction—Insurance Premium Finance Companies Act.

Exemptions and Exceptions—No provisions.

Transactions Subject to Disclosure Provisions—Loans.

Administration—Commissioner of Banking or Insurance.

Annual Rate Calculation—No provisions.

Civil Penalty—No provisions.

Criminal Penalty—$1,000 maximum fine, 5 years' imprisonment, or both.

Type Size—8-point type.

WASHINGTON

Jurisdiction—Credit Disclosure Act and Consumer Leasing Act.

Exemptions and Exceptions—Home improvement retail sales transactions under FHA. Service contracts are subject to governmental price control and margin accounts. Any lease that complies with the requirements of the federal Consumer Leasing Act shall be deemed in compliance with the requirements of State law.

Transactions Subject to Disclosure Provisions—Sales.

Administration—State Attorney General.

Annual Rate Calculation—Actuarial.

Civil Penalty—Fine up to $1,000 for violation of injunction or order.

Criminal Penalty—$1,000 maximum fine, six months' imprisonment, or both.

Type Size—10-point bold.

WISCONSIN

Jurisdiction—Consumer Act. Creditors are required to comply with disclosure provisions of the federal Truth in Lending Act in addition to those of the Consumer Act.

WYOMING

Jurisdiction—UCCC, Installment Loan Law (ILL).

Exemptions and Exceptions—*UCCC:* Credit to governmental bodies, insurance sales by insurers (except under UCCC Article 4), regulated public utilities and common carriers, licensed pawnbrokers, rates and charges of credit unions under state or federal law, nonrealty credit over $25,000. *ILL:* No provisions.

Transactions Subject to Disclosure Provisions—*UCCC:* Sales, loans, revolving credit. *ILL:* Loans.

Administration—UCCC: State Examiner. *ILL:* No provisions.

Annual Rate Calculation—UCCC: Actuarial or U.S. Rule, under unusual circumstances, the constant ratio method. *Exemptions:* Charge under $5 for debt under $75; under $7.50 for debt over $75. *ILL:* No provisions.

Civil Penalty—UCCC: Twice the finance charge, fine of no less than $100, or more than $1,000. *ILL:* No provisions.

Criminal Penalty—UCCC: $5,000 maximum fine, one year imprisonment, or both. *ILL:* No provision.

Type Size—UCCC: Clear and conspicuous. *ILL:* No provisions.

General Consumer Protection Legislation

In addition to statutes governing disclosures of rates of interest on sales or installment sales, every state in the country has adopted some legislation that can be characterized as "consumer protection." The major types of such legislation are:

Fair Credit Reporting Act—Controls issuance and accuracy of credit reports.

Small Loan Acts—Governs the rates and terms of loans in amounts usually less than $3,000.

Installment, Personal or Consumer Loan Act—Governs the rates and terms of loans for personal or consumer use in amounts usually $5,000 or less.

Revolving Sales Credit Act—Governs the rates and terms of consumer credit sales in which charge accounts are used.

Home Solicitation Act—Governs sales made at home or on the merchant's business premises, usually permitting cancellation of such contract within a short period of time (two-three days).

Home Improvement Loan Act—Governs the terms of contracts for home improvements that are financed, and usually provides for cancellation of such contracts within a short period of time (two-three days).

Unfair Trade or Consumer Protection Act—Comprehensive state legislation that protects the consumer against unfair or deceptive advertising or business practices.

Insurance Premium Financing Act—Governs the rates and terms of financing of insurance premiums.

Unsolicited Merchandise Act—Provides that unsolicited merchandise may be retained by the recipient as a gift.

Consumer Defense—The right of a purchaser to assert against the obligee or his assignee any rights or defenses he might have against the original seller of the goods or services.

Fair Credit Billing Act—Requires a creditor to rectify any error in billing within a specified period of time upon a consumer complaint.

See the below chart for examples of some state consumer protection legislation.

Although not indicated in the chart, many states, such as New York and Delaware, have enacted a "Plain Language" Act in relation to consumer contracts. Such acts require that all language in consumer contracts for less than $50,000 be intelligible and logical as well as easy to understand. Anyone violating these guidelines may be liable for up to three times the amount of actual damages proved plus attorneys' fees. Moreover, a consumer likely to be damaged by a deceptive practice that is governed by this act may be granted an injunction against it under the principles of equity and on terms a court considers reasonable.

Oregon has a statute that abolishes deficiency judgments on consumer goods after repossession if the unpaid balance at the time of default is less than $1,250.

California's Consumer Warranty Act requires manufacturers of consumer goods to maintain sufficient service and repair facilities in the state, and provides remedies for retailers and consumers. California and Illinois require persons conducting or negotiating a retail transaction in a language other than English to provide an unexecuted copy of the agreement to the consumer in that language.

Maryland has a statute that declares the use of a consumer contract that contains a confession of judgment clause that waives the consumer's legal defenses to be an unfair or deceptive trade practice and is subject to certain applicable penalties.

New Hampshire has a Distributorship Disclosure Act that requires those offering distributorships within the state to file certain disclosures to the consumer protection division of the Attorney General's office, and to provide prospective distributors with the same information at least seven days prior to entering into any distributorship agreement. The Act also forbids fraud in advertising or contracting and provides remedies for violations.

Washington has a Financial Institutions Disclosure Act requiring lending institutions with more than $10 million in assets to file information annually with the Secretary of State concerning loans and mortgages rejected and granted. Each financial institution and the Secretary of State are required to make this information available to any interested party. Penalties are provided for failure to file or for furnishing false information.

Iowa's Consumer Rental Purchase Agreement Act provides that a disclosure statement must accompany written agreements with consumers who enter into rental purchase agreements or what would otherwise be deemed a credit sale under its Truth in Lending Act. Lessors who willfully fail to provide disclosure statements are guilty of a misdemeanor.

Florida, Louisiana, Massachusetts, Oklahoma and Virginia have enacted legislation which mandates that before the execution of a contract between a buyer and a credit service organization, the organization must provide the buyer with a statement advising the buyer as to the buyer's right to review any files on the buyer maintained by the consumer reporting agency, the buyer's right to dispute the completeness or accuracy of any item contained in the file, the buyer's right to a description of the services to be performed by the credit service agency, the total cost to the buyer for such services, and the procedures for cancellation of the contract between the buyer and seller of the credit services.

Utah has enacted legislation requiring creditors to provide consumers with written notice within 30 days of a negative credit report before submitting it to a credit reporting agency.

Louisiana provides that a lender may charge a documentation fee as reimbursement for actual costs incurred, not to exceed $5, in connection with consumer loan transactions.

A number of states have regulated the credit service business which involves the performing of services for payment, to obtain credit for a consumer or improve a consumer's credit standing. Such states include Iowa, Michigan, Texas, Virginia and Washington. Hawaii prohibits a person from engaging in the credit repair business.

(Continued on p. 22–34)

STATE CONSUMER PROTECTION LEGISLATION

States	Credit Reporting Act	Small Loan Act	Consumer or Installment Loan Act	Revolving Sales Credit Act*	Home Solicitation Act	Home Improvement Loan Act	Unfair Trade or Consumer Protection Act	Insurance Premium Financing Act*	Unsolicited Merchandise Act	Consumer Defenses against Assignee*	Creditor Billings Error	Credit Services Organizations Act
AL		X	X	X	X	X		X		X		
AK		X	X	X	X		X	X	X	X		
AZ	X	X	X	X	X		X	X	X	X		
AR	X				X		X		X			
CA	X	X		X	X	X	X	X	X	X		
CO**		X	X	X	X		X	X	X	X		
CT	X	X		X	X		X	X	X	X	X	
DE		X	X	X	X		X	X	X	X		
DC		X	X	X	X	X	X	X	X	X		
FL	X	X	X	X	X	X	X	X	X	X		X
GA		X		X	X	X	X	X	X	X		X
HI		X	X	X	X	X	X		X	X		
ID**		X	X	X	X	X	X	X	X	X		
IL***		X	X	X	X	X	X	X	X	X	X	
IN**		X	X	X	X		X	X	X	X		
IA**		X	X	X	X	X	X	X	X	X		
KS	X	X	X	X	X	X	X	X	X	X		
KY	X	X	X	X	X	X	X	X	X	X		
LA	X	X	X	X	X		X	X	X	X		X
ME	X	X	X	X	X		X	X	X	X		
MD	X	X	X	X	X	X	X	X	X	X	X	
MA	X	X		X	X	X	X	X	X	X	X	X

STATE CONSUMER PROTECTION LEGISLATION (Continued)

States	Credit Reporting Act	Small Loan Act	Consumer or Installment Loan Act	Revolving Sales Credit Act*	Home Solicitation Act	Home Improvement Loan Act	Unfair Trade or Consumer Protection Act	Insurance Premium Financing Act*	Unsolicited Merchandise Act	Consumer Defenses against Assignee*	Creditor Billings Error	Credit Services Organizations Act
MI		X	X	X	X	X	X	X	X	X		
MN	X	X	X	X	X		X	X	X	X		
MS		X	X	X	X		X	X	X			
MO		X		X	X		X	X	X	X		
MT	X	X	X	X	X		X	X	X	X		
NE	X	X	X	X	X	X	X		X			
NV		X		X	X	X	X	X	X	X		
NH	X	X	X	X	X	X	X	X	X	X		
NJ		X	X	X	X	X	X	X	X	X	X	
NM	X	X	X	X		X	X	X	X	X		
NY	X	X	X	X	X	X	X	X	X	X	X	
NC		X		X	X	X	X	X	X	X		
ND		X		X	X		X	X		X		
OH		X	X	X	X		X	X		X		
OK**	X	X	X	X	X		X	X	X	X		X
OR		X	X	X	X	X	X	X		X		
PA	X	X	X	X	X	X	X	X	X	X		
RI		X	X	X	X			X	X	X		
SC		X	X	X	X	X	X	X	X			
SD		X	X	X	X		X		X	X		
TN		X	X	X	X	X	X	X	X	X		
TX	X	X	X	X	X	X	X	X	X	X		

State														
UT**	X	X	X	X		X	X	X	X	X	X		X	X
VT	X	X	X	X	X	X	X	X	X	X	X	X	X	X
VA	X	X	X	X	X	X	X	X	X	X	X	X		X
WA	X	X	X	X	X	X	X	X	X	X	X	X		
WV	X	X	X	X	X	X	X	X	X		X		X	
WI	X	X	X	X	X	X	X	X	X	X	X	X	X	
WY**	X	X	X	X	X		X	X	X	X	X	X		

* Many states include revolving credit legislation, insurance premium financing, legislations, home improvement loan legislation and legislation on consumer defense as part of Retail Installment Act or other laws.

** The UCCC has, for the most part, supplanted the Acts listed in the Chart, but the reader is cautioned to check both the UCCC and the statute in question in the specific states. Some of the states adopting the UCCC have not repealed a number of the statutes under consideration, but, rather, have maintained them to be interpreted and applied along with the UCCC.

*** Illinois has enacted the Farm Implement Buyer Protection Act which requires authorized dealers of farm implements to repair or replace non-conforming farm implements (with a reasonable charge for use) or accept the return of the farm implement by the consumer and refund price and sales tax paid for it.

(Continued from p. 22–30)

CAN-SPAM ACT AND DO-NOT-FAX RULE

CAN-SPAM Act

INTRODUCTION

The Controlling the Assault of Non-Solicited Pornography and Marketing Act of 2003, also known as the CAN-SPAM Act (the "Act"), became effective on January 1, 2004. The Act was implemented to restrict the use of commercial electronic mail ("e-mail") through the imposition of specific requirements. More specifically, the Act establishes requirements for those who send commercial e-mail and creates penalties for spammers and companies whose products are advertised in spam in violation of the Act. As a Federal Law, the Act is given preemptive power over state and local laws, with the exception of those laws that prohibit false and deceptive e-mails. The Act gives state attorneys general the power to enforce the civil provisions of the Act and it creates a private right of action for providers of Internet access services.

PURPOSE

The purpose of the Act is to outlaw certain commercial e-mail acts and practices. The Act only applies to messages that fall within the Act's definition of "commercial electronic mail message" and it applies to all commercial e-mail messages, whether or not the e-mail is solicited. The Act defines the term "commercial electronic mail message," as "any electronic mail message, the primary purpose of which is the commercial advertisement or promotion of a commercial product or service." To help determine the "primary purpose" of the e-mail, the Act divides e-mails into four categories based upon their contents as follows:

1. Only commercial content
2. Both commercial content and content that is transactional or relationship in nature
3. Both commercial content and content that is neither commercial nor "transactional or relationship" in nature
4. Only transactional or relationship content

Obviously, if an e-mail message contains only commercial content, the "primary purpose" of the message shall be deemed to be commercial. To determine the "primary purpose" of mixed content e-mails, the FTC has provided additional guidelines. For e-mails containing both commercial and transactional relationship content, they are considered commercial if: (1) a recipient reasonably interpreting the subject line would likely conclude that the message contains commercial content; or (2) the e-mail's transactional relationship content does not appear in whole or substantial part at the beginning of the body of the message. For e-mails that contain both commercial content and content that has neither a commercial nor transactional relationship, the primary purpose will be deemed commercial if a recipient reasonably interpreting the subject line or body of the message would likely conclude the primary purpose is commercial.

The key factors relevant to interpretation of the Act as applied to e-mails that include both commercial content and content that has neither a commercial nor transactional relationship include: the placement of commercial content (whether it is in whole or substantial part in the beginning of the body of the message); the proportion of the message dedicated to commercial content; and how color, graphics, type size, and style are used to highlight commercial content. (Use of the term "substantial" does not refer to volume and there is no minimum number of "transactional or relationship" characters that must appear at the beginning or in the body of the message, but instead the term refers to the nature of the content.) If an e-mail contains only transactional or relationship content, its primary purpose shall be deemed to be "transactional or relationship" and is generally not subject to the Act.

COMPLIANCE

To comply with the Act, commercial e-mail senders must include in the message a "clear and conspicuous" notice that the message is an advertisement or solicitation. The Act defines affirmative consent as an express indication from the recipient of consent to receive commercial messages. Such consent may be obtained via response from an e-mail request by the association for such consent or an indication on a dues statement that the individual expressly consents to receive commercial e-mails from the association. However, if the recipient has given "affirmative consent" prior to the receipt of e-mails from the sender, then the sender does not need to mark the e-mail with clear and conspicuous identification that the message is an advertisement or solicitation. Regardless of consent, all commercial e-mails must include a valid physical mail address of the sender. In addition, there must be a "clear and conspicuous" notice of the recipient's right to opt out of subsequent commercial messages from the same sender. In connection with the Opt-Out requirement, the sender must provide a mechanism through which opt out requests may be made online and opt out preferences must be honored. The Act also prohibits fraudulent or deceptive subject lines, headers, return addresses, etc., and makes it illegal to send e-mails to e-mail addresses that have been "harvested" from websites.

There are some exceptions to the notification rules of the Act. Associations and businesses may contact their past and present customers and members without observing all of the restrictions of the Act if the e-mail fits in the category of "transactional or relationship messages." This narrow definition includes e-mails with the following primary purposes:

1. It facilitates, completes or confirms a commercial transaction that the recipient has previously agreed to enter into with the sender.
2. It provides warranty information, product recall information, or safety and security information with respect to a product or service used or purchased by the recipient.
3. It provides account balance information, or notification concerning a change in the terms or features of, or a change in the standing or status with respect to, an account, account statement, subscription, membership or comparable ongoing commercial relationship involving the ongoing purchase or use by the recipient of products or services offered by the sender.
4. It provides information directly related to an employment relationship or related benefit plan in which the recipient is currently involved, participating, or enrolled.
5. It delivers goods or services, including product updates or upgrades, that the recipient is entitled to receive under the terms of a transaction that the recipi-

ent has previously agreed to enter into with the sender. While transactional or relationship messages are generally exempt from most provisions of the Act, the restrictions on false or misleading header information still applies

ENFORCEMENT

According to the Act, the FTC, which enforces the Act, is restricted to the same jurisdiction and power as it has under the FTC Act. On its face, this provision of the CAN-SPAM Act seems to exclude nonprofit organizations from its scope, as it does under the FTC Act. (The FTC Act states that the FTC does not have jurisdiction over any entity that is not "organized to carry on business for its own profit or that of its members." 15 USC 44.) However, unlike the FTC Act, the CAN-SPAM Act does not affect the ability of other Federal agencies, the States, or providers of Internet access services to bring actions under the Act against any entity within their jurisdiction as authorized. Therefore, nonprofits that are normally outside the FTC's jurisdiction may be subject to an enforcement action for violating the Act. In addition, despite numerous requests, the FTC has declined to implement any interpretation of the law that would specifically exclude nonprofit organizations from the Act.

In contrast with states' laws on e-mail solicitation, which generally do not apply to nonprofit organizations, the Act may affect nonprofits because it affects all organizations that communicate with their members through e-mail. In particular, the Act prohibits organizations, including associations and other nonprofit organizations, from sending commercial e-mails unless: (1) the e-mails include a notice to recipients that they may "opt out" of future e-mails (and there is a mechanism for doing so); or (2) recipients have already given written permission. If a recipient does opt out of a future e-mail, the sender must cease transmissions of e-mail ads to that recipient after 10 business days from the date of receipt of the request. (In the Federal Register, Vol. 70, No. 01, 5/12/05, p. 25442, the FTC proposes shortening the requirement to comply with an opt-out request to three days.)

While the primary regulatory and enforcement body of the Act is the Federal Trade Commission, there are other parties that have the power to enforce the Act. State attorneys general also may bring civil actions and Internet service providers, such as AOL, may bring suit against spammers. However, no one else, including recipients of commercial e-mails, will be able to sue. This significant restriction should help prevent consumer lawsuits, which have been a significant problem for businesses under the federal law prohibiting unsolicited faxes. The penalties for violations of the Act can be severe and there may be fines and criminal penalties for knowing and intentional violations.

AS APPLIED TO NONPROFIT ORGANIZATIONS

While the Act makes no exceptions for nonprofit organizations, the Act should not materially affect associations and other nonprofits because most nonprofit e-mails do not contain commercial material. However, this does not include e-mails that advertise a product or service that would traditionally be considered "unrelated" from a tax standpoint and should be considered a "commercial e-mail" until regulations to the contrary are issued. In addition, there is a slight possibility that a "Do Not E-mail" registry may be established in the future. The registry has been shelved indefinitely because of the possible hazards of the list being obtained by spammers. However, technology may change in the future and it is best to be prepared for any change to the possibility of the registry. And finally, until regulations are issued to the contrary, associations and other nonprofits should assume that "commercial e-mail" includes e-mails, for which the primary purpose is to advertise a product or service that is unrelated to the tax-exempt purpose of the organization.

Alternatively, e-mails that are not primarily advertisements for a product or service and e-mails promoting a product, service, or other offering of the organization that is related to the organization's exempt purpose would not be considered "commercial" if sent from a nonprofit organization. However, pending issuance of regulations, it may be best to assume that third-party companies will need to comply with the Act if they are sending bulk e-mails to an organization's members, supporters, or others promoting a product or service that would be considered "unrelated" to an organization's exempt purposes. If an association or other nonprofit does decide to send bulk e-mails advertising or promoting products or services that are unrelated to the organization's exempt purposes to recipients who have not already given permission, a notice regarding the recipient's ability to opt out of future e-mails and a mechanism for doing so should be included by the sender.

Do-Not-Fax Rule

INTRODUCTION

The Telephone Consumer Protection Act (the "TCPA"), which had existed in relative anonymity since its inception in 1992, first started to gain widespread attention several years ago due to several high profile lawsuits. This shot to the limelight has been the result of lawsuits generated under a previously little used provision of the TCPA, the Do-Not-Fax Rule. Two lawsuits in particular assisted in this rise to fame: the 2002, $650,000 settlement by the Dallas Mavericks NBA basketball team in reaction to a fax class action lawsuit and the 2003 lawsuit by Covington & Burling, a Washington, D.C. law firm, in which the firm claimed to have received over 1,500 fax advertisements from a single entity during one day—and for which the firm secured a $2.2 million court judgment. However, since it has gained notoriety, businesses of all sizes throughout the nation have been sued for TCPA violations. These lawsuits are often referred to as "junk fax" lawsuits. To avoid a "junk fax" lawsuit, one must first understand the basic operation of the TCPA.

PURPOSE AND ENFORCEMENT

The TCPA provision that contains the Do-Not-Fax Rule makes it unlawful for any person to "use a telephone facsimile machine, computer, or other device to send an unsolicited advertisement to a telephone facsimile machine." The TCPA defines an "unsolicited advertisement" broadly as, "any material advertising the commercial availability or quality of any property, goods, or services which is transmitted to any person without that person's prior express invitation or permission." Under the TCPA, if a party can prove that it received an unsolicited fax advertisement, the party may bring an action in state court to enjoin such a violation and/or recover actual damages, or $500 per unsolicited fax (whichever is greater). In addition, the damages may be trebled if the party can also prove that the sender willfully or knowingly violated the TCPA. Parties may state an additional claim for damages if the fax does not clearly contain, either in the margin at the top or bottom of each faxed page or on the first page of the fax, the following information: (1) the date and time of the transmission; (2) the identity of the sender; and (3) and the telephone number of the sending machine or the sender.

JUNK FAX PREVENTION ACT OF 2005

While the only fail-safe mechanism to avoid a lawsuit in the junk fax area is to secure and maintain a written permission on file from any person or entity to which you send a fax advertisement, there is an important provision that may help in avoiding a junk-fax lawsuit. The provision prohibits a fax recipient from filing a suit under the TCPA against a fax sender if an "established business relationship" exists between the sender and the recipient. An "established business relationship" is not well defined by the TCPA, but one would assume the definition includes customers and those who request information from the company, vendors, subcontractors, and similar persons or entities.

The FCC extended the "established business relationship" provision to January 9, 2006 at the request of industries and to give Congress time to draft amendments to the TCPA. These amendments, known as the Junk Fax Prevention Act, were signed into law on July 9, 2005, and provide for a permanent addition of the "established business relationship" exception. However, the Junk Fax Prevention Act also gives the FCC the ability to determine an end date to the "established business relationship" provision if it determines that the provision is being abused. The implementation date for the Junk Fax Prevention Act is to be no later than 270 days after the date of its enactment, which falls on April 5, 2006.

While an extension to the "established business relationship" exception has been granted, it is possible that written consent will become a prerequisite for future fax advertisements. Therefore, organizations may wish to begin the process of securing consent to receive faxes on its order forms, purchase orders, vendor contracts and any other exchange with third parties through which the organization may secure written permission to send future fax advertisements. In fact, even if consent is not required in the future, such consent may support an "established business relationship" defense in the event there is a junk-fax lawsuit against the organization.

In addition to the "established business relationship" exception, the Junk Fax Prevention Act added an Opt-Out notice requirement to the TCPA. Under the Opt-Out notice requirement, a business may only send an unsolicited advertisement if it: (1) is clear and conspicuous and on the first page of the fax; (2) states that the recipient may request that the sender not send any future unsolicited faxes to the sender, and that failure to comply with such a request is unlawful; and (3) provides a domestic contact telephone and fax number to send the request to and a cost-free mechanism to transmit the request at any time and any day of the week. However, a business only has to comply with the Opt-Out request if: (1) the request identifies the telephone number of the fax machine to which the request relates; (2) the request is made to the telephone or fax number of the sender as provided; and (3) the person making the request has not subsequently provided express invitation or permission to send the advertisement. The Junk Fax Prevention Act states that the FCC is to determine the timeframe for when a business must comply with the Opt-Out request and if there is to be a small business exception to the Opt-Out notice requirement.

Finally, the Junk Fax Prevention Act has given the FCC the authority to establish a nonprofit exception to the Do-Not-Fax Rule. Specifically, the Act states that the Commission, "may prescribe, allow professional or trade associations that are tax-exempt nonprofit organizations to send unsolicited advertisements to their members in furtherance of the association's tax-exempt purpose." The FCC will make a determination of whether there shall be an exception based on comments and will give a definitive guideline on April 5, 2006.

The FCC has not yet implemented guidelines on the Junk Fax Prevention Act provisions and has begun to solicit comments. Final guidelines should be ready for the April 5, 2006 implementation date.

Please note that the TCPA does not preempt any state laws governing unsolicited fax advertisements, so it is important to ensure that your company complies with all applicable state or local laws that effect your advertising practices.

Conclusion

Whether the organization is for-profit or nonprofit, there is no surefire way of avoiding potential liabilities when e-mailing or faxing an entity, short of receiving written permission to fax, call, or e-mail beforehand. However, if organizations comply with the guidelines provided, it greatly reduces an opponent's ability to prevail, short of a willful and knowing disregard for the law. Here are a few scenarios that may provide some guidance for avoiding issues.

Commercial E-mail Messages

The simplest scenario that requires the least amount of direction is when e-mails are completely commercial. For example, if an organization sends out e-mails to a list of e-mail addresses that only promotes the services of the organization, they will be viewed as commercial in content and the e-mails must comply with the requirements of the CAN-SPAM Act.

Mixed e-mails are not as straightforward. For example, suppose a credit manager contacts a client about closing an existing account via e-mail at the request of the client, and the e-mail contains some promotional material, such as the services that the credit manager could provide. Assume that the client has not given prior approval to receive commercial e-mails. If the promotional material is at the beginning of the e-mail and is not an insignificant part of the text, it will be considered commercial and will be subject to the restrictions of the Act. In addition, even if the commercial material is not at the beginning or takes up the bulk of the e-mail, it may still be considered commercial if the client believes that the e-mail is commercial after reading the subject line. Therefore, the credit manager must review any e-mails that contain commercial content closely to ensure that it would not be considered primarily of commercial content. Unfortunately, these requirements are very subjective and the FTC has not given a great deal of guidance on determining when an e-mail is commercial or transactional. If there is any doubt on the content of the e-mail, the sender should assume that the e-mail is commercial and comply with the requirements of the Act.

Fax Messages

The restrictions on faxes are much clearer and not as subjective as those provided for e-mails. While the intent of the CAN-SPAM Act is not to prevent commercial e-mails, only restrict how they are presented, the Do-Not-Fax Rule specifically restricts the sending of faxes. Under the Do-Not-Fax Rule, a credit manager would not be allowed to contact a fax recipient unless there was an established business relationship between the parties. For example, a credit manager would not be allowed to fax a potential client with a fax setting out services the credit manager provides unless the client has given prior permission to receive faxes. However, the credit manager would be able to fax an existing client if there is a business relationship. As stated above, the definition of business relationship is ambiguous, but common sense dictates that if the credit manager conservatively does not believe there is a business relationship, then the relationship should not be assumed.

UNIFORM CONSUMER CREDIT CODE

The Uniform Consumer Credit Code (UCCC) is a law similar to the Uniform Commercial Code, which deals with consumer transactions involving small loans, retail installment sales, home solicitation sales and their related activities. The UCCC is a comprehensive consumer protection law prepared by the National Conference of Commissioners on Uniform State Laws. It seeks to codify various state statutes dealing with consumer protection, such as Small Loan Acts, Personal Loan Acts, Installment Loan and Sales Acts, Truth in Lending Acts, Consumer Unfair Trade Practices Acts and Home Solicitation Sales Acts.

The UCCC, to mention a few of its provisions, establishes maximum rates of interest on loans and credit sales, requires disclosure of finance charges and other information and prohibits deceptive advertising and unconscionable contract provisions. Multiple states, including Colorado, Indiana, Iowa, Kansas, Maine, Oklahoma, South Carolina, Utah, Wisconsin and Wyoming have adopted the UCCC in whole or in part. Previously adopted local laws that dealt with consumer protection have been replaced. Idaho, which had adopted the UCCC, has repealed same and replaced it with the Idaho Credit Code, similar to the UCCC. Louisiana has adopted the Louisiana Consumer Credit Law which is similar to the UCCC. In this respect, the situation is comparable to the adoption by a state of the Uniform Commercial Code that similarly necessitated the repeal of a number of statutes encompassed within the scope of the Code.

There is no inherent conflict between the UCCC and the Uniform Commercial Code, and consumer credit transactions may be subject to both statutes. However, in the event of any conflict between the two, the UCCC most often controls.

The UCCC conforms to the requirements of the federal Truth in Lending Act; therefore, any state that adopts it will meet the minimum standards of the federal Act, and be eligible for the exemptions provided by it. The Code applies to consumer credit transactions—including sales, leases and loans—and not to regular business or commercial transactions, and only to individuals and not to business organizations, except for sole proprietors or governmental units. Consumer credit is defined as those transactions not in excess of $25,000 that are for personal, family, household, or agricultural purposes. Colorado, Indiana, Kansas, Maine, Oklahoma and Wyoming exclude agricultural purposes from coverage. Real estate transactions are included irrespective of the $25,000 limit, but only if a rate of interest in excess of 10 percent per year is charged. Idaho, Oklahoma, Colorado and Kansas have alterations in their statutes that include differences regarding interest rates and differ when a mobile home is involved. In addition, the limits of liability differ among several of the states. Consequently, the standard first mortgage is often within the scope of the law, but the second mortgage which is usually at a higher rate of interest and may exceed the monetary limit, may be covered by it.

The following is a brief summary of the Code:

Article 1—General Provisions and Definitions. The statute states that the Code is to be liberally construed and applied to promote its underlying purposes. Simply stated, the purpose of the statute is:

A. To simplify, clarify and modernize the law governing retail installment sales, consumer credit, small loans and usury
B. To provide rate ceilings to assure an adequate supply of credit to consumers
C. To further consumer understanding of the terms of credit transactions and to foster competition among suppliers of consumer credit so that consumers may obtain credit at reasonable cost
D. To protect consumer buyers, lessees and borrowers against unfair practices by some suppliers of consumer credit, having due regard for the interests of legitimate and scrupulous creditors
E. To permit and encourage the development of fair and economically sound consumer credit practices
F. To conform the regulation of consumer credit transactions to the policies of the Federal Truth in Lending Act

In addition, this Article states that a buyer or lessee cannot waive the benefits of the Code.

Article 2—Finance Charges and Related Provisions. This Article applies to consumer credit sales, consumer loans, including loans made by supervised lenders, charges and modifications with respect to consumer credit transactions and other credit transactions. This Article generally provides for maximum charges allowable, including maximum rates of interest on regular consumer credit sales and on consumer sales on revolving charge accounts. All loans may be prepaid without penalty or interest, and in the event of any prepayment, any previously paid finance charge must be rebated.

The maximum rates differ among the states and change from time to time. Therefore, particular state statutes for these maximum interest rates should be checked as the need arises. A seller may also receive a minimum credit service charge of not more than $5 when the amount financed does not exceed $75, or $7.50 when the amount financed exceeds $75. Colorado, Maine and Utah have permitted minimum finance charges which differ from the standard. In addition to the credit service charge, a seller may receive additional charges for official fees and taxes, insurance and charges for other benefits conferred on the buyer if such benefits are of value and if the charges are reasonable to the benefits conferred. This Article also fixes the amount of the maximum delinquency charges on any installments not paid within 10 days after the due date.

For revolving charge accounts, the maximum rate of interest also differs from state to state.

This section also provides that the buyer shall have the right to prepay, without penalty, any amounts due and any unearned credit service charge must be rebated.

Article 3—Regulation of Agreements and Practices deals with disclosure, limitations on agreements and practices, and limitations on consumer's liability with respect to consumer credit transactions and advertising. The disclosure requirements are those of the federal Truth in Lending Law or as established under the Code. The information must be clearly and conspicuously made in writing to the buyer or lessee.

For all consumer credit sales not made pursuant to a revolving charge account, the seller is required to disclose to the buyer certain information, including a description of the goods, cash prices, amount of downpayment, amount financed, amount of the credit service charge, rate of the credit service charge, default charges, number of payments and security interest.

The Code provides for clear and conspicuous disclosure requirements with respect to all loans by which the buyer is to be advised in writing of the annual percentage rate. In addition, the lender is required to so advise the debtor of other information such as net amount to be paid, amount of fees and taxes, description of insurance to be provided, amount of any additional charges, number of payments required, and delinquency charges.

On a revolving loan account, lender must advise buyer of specified information, also to be disclosed on credit card transactions. For revolving charge account sales, the seller is required to provide the buyer with certain information before making a sale, including the conditions under which credit service charge is to be made, method of determining balance upon which service charge will be made, method of determining amount of the service charge and security interest retained. The following information is required to be given to buyer if at the end of any billing cycle there is a balance due: the outstanding balance at the beginning of the billing cycle, price and date of each sale during the cycle, amount credited to the account, amount of credit service charge, balance upon which credit service charge is computed, balance at the end of the billing cycle and date by which payment must be made to avoid additional credit service charges. A lender is prohibited from engaging in false or misleading advertising concerning the terms and conditions of a consumer loan.

The restrictions against balloon payments and the prohibitions of assignment of earnings, and alternatives with respect to attorneys' fees, cited above with respect to consumer sales, also apply to consumer loans.

Specific information is also required to be given to a buyer in the event a loan is refinanced or consolidated. A buyer in a consumer credit sale is given, under the Code, the right to refinance the loan in the event there is any balloon payment required.

The seller or lessor in consumer credit sales or leases, other than those primarily for agricultural purposes, is prohibited from taking a negotiable instrument other than a check, as evidence of an obligation of the buyer or lessee.

The Code provides two alternative sections with respect to the liability of an assignee of a seller to the claims and defenses of the buyer. One alternative proposes that the assignee is subject to all claims and defenses of the buyer, and the other alternative provides that the assignee is not subject to such claims and defenses if he advises the buyer of the assignment, and within three months thereafter is not informed in writing by the buyer of any claim or defense.

A security interest in the property sold is specifically permitted in consumer credit sales, but no assignment of earnings of a buyer or lessee is permitted as security for payment of a debt. Confessions of judgment are also not permitted.

The Code provides alternatives with respect to attorneys' fees. Alternative A prohibits payment of the seller's attorneys' fees by the buyer or lessee. Alternative B provides that the buyer or lessee may pay reasonable attorneys' fees not in excess of 15 percent of the unpaid debt after default.

With respect to home solicitation sales, the buyer is given the right to cancel any home solicitation sale until midnight of the third business day after the day on which he signs the agreement to purchase. Only certain states still provide that the seller must return the downpayment within 10 days except for retention of 5 percent of the cash price. The more common practice is that the seller may not retain any portion of the purchase price.

Article 4—This section regulates sales of insurance on credit.

Article 5—This deals with limitations on creditors' remedies. It limits the rights available to a creditor in the event of a default, and imposes limitations on permissible wage garnishments more severe than those of the federal Truth in Lending Act. Garnishments before judgment are proscribed and an employer cannot discharge an employee because his wages have been subject to one or more garnishments.

In the event a court finds, as a matter of law, any provision in a credit sale, lease or loan unconscionable, the court may refuse to enforce the agreement or the unconscionable provision.

Part 2 of Article 5 provides remedies available to consumers for violations of the Code by creditors, sellers or lenders, including the right to rescind certain transactions, right to demand a refund and penalties for violations of the disclosure provisions of the Code.

Part 3 establishes criminal penalties for violations of the Code.

Article 6 deals with administration of the Code.

Article 7 does not currently exist.

Article 8 generally adopts the Federal Truth in Lending statute.

Certain states which have adopted the UCCC have additional articles as follows:

Article 9 applies to all consumer credit transactions made by creditors that are not supervised financial organizations, that are secured by a first-lien mortgage on real estate.

Article 10 covers credit services organizations.

Article 11 covers rental-purchase practices.

23 Antitrust and Trade Regulation for Credit Groups and Credit Grantors

From railroads to microtechnology, antitrust regulation was created to preserve competition and continues to exist as the guardian of the free enterprise system. Antitrust regulations have been in existence since the late 1800s and the origins of the U.S. Antitrust statutes stem from older English common law. The antitrust lawsuits which tend to make the headlines are those cases involving the giants within industries where the Department of Justice is determined to prevent or curtail monopolization in order to perpetuate healthy competition. Often, it is the political climate of the day which determines whether antitrust actions are hotly pursued by the Department of Justice or whether there is an apparent lack of enforcement of the various statutory requirements.

This chapter cannot cover every aspect of antitrust regulation. It is meant, instead, to provide a compendium of the antitrust statutes with a particular emphasis on how they relate to everyday business credit operations. For too many years, credit professionals believed themselves to be immune from antitrust responsibilities. It was believed to be the sales department that could be culpable for antitrust activity. The courts believed differently. Through the years of case law, the courts have come to hold one doctrine to be true, time and time again. That doctrine is that CREDIT TERMS EQUALS PRICE. Therefore, every credit professional must be knowledgeable as to what constitutes an antitrust violation.

This knowledge must be applied to the everyday business environment. It must always be utilized concerning the exchange of credit information, either with a fellow credit grantor or in conjunction with a trade credit group. An understanding of the existing antitrust laws, their similarities and differences is no longer merely helpful to the credit grantor, it is now imperative.

ANTITRUST STATUTES

Sherman Antitrust Act of 1890

The Sherman Antitrust Act of 1890 (15 USC §§ 1-7) prohibits contracts, combinations in form of trust or otherwise, conspiracies in restraint of trade, in interstate commerce or with foreign nations. Any person (a "person" can be an individual, partnership, corporation, association or other legal entity) who combines, contracts or conspires with another or others to restrain trade or commerce in interstate commerce or with foreign nations, shall be guilty of a felony. A corporation can be penalized for such activity by a fine not exceeding $10,000,000. Any other person convicted of such a felony can be penalized by a fine not exceeding $350,000 or by imprisonment not exceeding three years, or by both punishments.

Likewise, this statute covers any person who contracts, combines or conspires with another or others to monopolize trade or commerce. The crime remains a felony and the parameters of the punishments are the same.

The phrase "Restraint of Trade" often mystifies the credit professional since it seems to encompass many different legal issues. The test of Restraint of Trade is whether the activity which makes up the asserted restraint of trade is "unreasonable." Certain activity is considered to be "per se unreasonable," that is, the mere activity is unreasonable without any query into the surrounding circumstances. Case law has determined that "per se" violations consist of agreements or practices which have no redeeming virtue and have pernicious effects on competition. Of particular concern to credit professionals is the Supreme Court decision in *Catalano, Inc. v. Target Sales, Inc.*, 446 U.S. 643 (1980), which held that agreements between competitors to fix credit terms are *per se* violations of the Sherman Act.

Violations which do not fit the category of "per se unreasonable" must pass a "rule of reason" test. The courts have established that the test to ascertain what is reasonable is "whether restraint imposed is such as merely regulates and perhaps thereby promotes competition or whether it is such as may suppress or even destroy competition."

In understanding Restraint of Trade, it is essential to first understand what is meant by "combination" and/or "conspiracy." In determining when a combination or conspiracy exists, case law has established certain criteria which are essential to determining that a combination and conspiracy exist, they are:

1. All members of combination must know of defendant's purpose to restrain trade
2. At least two members of combination must benefit by restraint of trade and share a common purpose in restraining trade
3. The agreement by two members of combination must actually restrain trade, as opposed to merely facilitating restraint
4. At least two members of combination must intend to restrain trade

These four steps originally identified in 1978 in *Harold Friedman, Inc. v. Kroger Company*, 581 F.2d 1068 seem to make it easy to eliminate circumstances under which an agreement or combination can occur, but that isn't so. Numerous cases have held that an agreement, combination or conspiracy is established where enough evidence is presented to prove that the players had a unity of purpose or common design and understanding or meeting of minds in an unlawful arrangement.

Even if there is not an explicit agreement undertaken, there are three major elements which the courts will look for to determine whether or not there is an unlawful agreement. Those elements may be summarized as: shared knowledge of a proposed plan, a strong motive for concerted action and substantial unanimity of action. Actual agreement is not necessary. In 1939, the United States Supreme Court found that "it was enough that, knowing that concerted action was contemplated and invited, the distributors gave their adherence to the scheme and participated in it." (*Interstate Circuit, et al. v. United States*, 306 U.S. 208, 59 S.Ct. 467. In other cases, the Supreme Court and other courts have held where a "group of competitors enters into series of separate but similar agreements with competitors or others, strong inference arises that such agreements are result of concerted action" (*United States v. Line Material Co.*, 333 U.S. 287, *United States v. United States Gypsum*, 333 U.S. 364 and *United States v. General Electric Co.*, 80 F.Supp. 989).

The description of specific situations described below is not meant to be all-inclusive. Nevertheless, these particular examples will provide the credit professional with a substantial foundation from which to avoid the possibility of falling into an antitrust snare.

EXCHANGE OF PRICING INFORMATION

Criminal proceedings were brought against defendants, leading members of the gypsum board industry, who it was alleged had violated the Sherman Act by engaging in interseller price verification. The defendants interposed a defense under Section 2(b) of the Robinson-Patman Act that such activity was lawful as a good faith effort to verify prices of a competitor before attempting to meet such prices. The court instructions to the jury were that if the exchange of price information had the effect of raising, fixing, maintaining or stabilizing the price of gypsum board, then the parties are presumed, *as a matter of law*, to have intended that result. The Supreme Court rejected the legal presumption approach and held that a defendant's state of mind or intent is an essential element of a criminal antitrust case, which must be established by evidence and inferences drawn therefrom; such criminal intent cannot be based upon a legal presumption of wrongful intent from proof of an effect on prices.

CONSPIRACIES IN RESTRAINT OF TRADE

In another case, a movie exhibitor that controlled first-run movie theaters in six southern cities wrote letters to eight branch managers of major film distributors demanding that they distribute only second-run films to theaters in those cities charging low admission prices or they would lose the exhibitor's first-run business. There was no evidence that the branch managers of the film distributors ever met or conspired together, but in fact all the distributors changed their policies toward second-run movie theaters in accordance with the request. The Supreme Court declared that in order to establish an agreement, the government is compelled to rely on inferences drawn from the course of conduct of the alleged conspirators. The court felt that a mere coincidence could not explain how such a severe departure from standard business practice could be simultaneously undertaken by eight distributors. Noting that each letter from the exhibitor had the names of all eight distributors on its title, that the plan required uniformity of action and that the action of the distributors was unanimous, the court declared that there was a conspiracy and a Sherman Act violation because, knowing that concerted action had been invited, the distributors gave their adherence to and participated in the scheme.

PRICE FIXING

Price fixing is also covered by the Sherman Act. As we already stated, agreements between competitors to fix credit terms are *per se* violations of the Sherman Act. Likewise, an agreement (express or implied) among credit grantors or credit group members to establish or maintain prices constitutes price fixing. The leading case which deals directly with credit granting is the case of *Catalano v. Target Sales* 446 U.S. 643. Beer retailers had been offered varying credit terms ranging from 30 days to 42 days. In 1967, certain wholesalers agreed that they would sell to retailers only on COD terms or with payment in advance. The court opined that the agreement to eliminate credit was no different than a direct agreement to raise prices and is plainly anticompetitive.

An illegal combination to fix prices was found where wholesalers suggested prices and secured compliance in any manner which surpassed a "mere announcement of policy of simple refusal to deal." In at least one particular case, the illegal combination was found to exist where the retailer gave in to "coercion and unwillingly complied with wholesaler's suggested pricing" (*Crown Cent. Petroleum Corp. v. Brice* 427 F.Supp 638).

Fortunately, although a good amount of restraint of trade and price fixing cases are commenced, those cases are not always won. Where certain shippers negotiated more favorable rates than their competitors, unreasonable restraint of trade did not exist. Where a computer manufacturer, franchiser of retail distributors and others were accused of a price-fixing scheme which eliminated mail-order sellers because it offered price discounts on manufacturer's products, evidence that manufacturer's actions were unilateral, manufacturer's competitors were changing their distribution strategies and manufacturer was legitimately concerned about mail-order dealers' effects on local dealers defeated the price-fixing claim.

GROUP BOYCOTTING

Antitrust violations generally exist when firms with sufficient market power boycott suppliers or customers in order to discourage them from doing business with a competitor. Two hallmarks of illegal group boycott are the collective refusal to deal and the resulting denial of access to a competitively useful commodity.

It is quite clear that without the combination/conspiracy among parties, group boycotting cannot exist. Nevertheless the courts have found that even peaceful persuasion of one person to refrain from dealing with another is group boycotting and a violation of the Sherman Act. Some examples of group boycotting include:

1. A refusal to deal with one retailer by manufacturers and distributors at the urging of another retailer
2. Institution and enforced concerted communications to isolate a competitor from contact and communication, not only with manufacturer's distributors but with potential distributors
3. An agreement to refuse to extend credit
4. An agreement to use or join a group service for the purpose of preparing or participating in a "black list"

Clearly, the last two examples cause the most concern among credit professionals. The criteria in a court battle will be whether credit professionals have acted independently or whether creditors belonging to a trade association refused to deal with a mechanical contractor after communicating among themselves and thus violated antitrust laws.

Clayton Act of 1914

The Clayton Act of 1914 (15 USC §§ 12–27, 44 and 29 USC § 52) followed the Sherman Act and was created to "correct" defects in the Sherman Act as well as to supplement the Sherman Act by conferring upon certain administrative agencies the power to stop violations of the law in their incipience and before a threatened conspiracy has ripened into actuality. Congress passed the Clayton Act in order to promote competition through protection of viable, small, locally-owned businesses. One must note that the Clayton Act and the Robinson-Patman Act overlap in that USC § 13 which was originally a section of the Clayton Act was amended by the Robinson-Patman Price Discrimination Act in 1936 and again by the Robinson-Patman Act in 1938. Price discrimination will be discussed under the Robinson-Patman Act, below.

Under the Clayton Act, it is unlawful to enter into (a) leases or sales on condition that lessee or purchaser shall not use or deal in the commodities of a competitor of the lessor or seller, (b) exclusive dealing arrangements, and (c) tying arrangements. In addition, the Clayton Act restricts the acquisition by one corporation of the stock of another where the effect of such acquisition may be substantially to lessen competition, or to tend to create a monopoly. Last, the Clayton act prohibits any person serving as a director or officer in any two corporations under certain conditions where their service would result in an elimination of competition which would violate any of the antitrust laws.

A person injured in his business or property as the result of a violation of the Clayton Act may recover treble damages in a civil action. The Supreme Court interpreted Section 4 of the Clayton Act to allow only those customers who buy directly from proven price fixers to maintain an action for treble damages. The court found that the purpose of the law was better served by holding direct purchasers to be injured to the full extent of the overcharge paid by them, and thus allowing them to recover treble damages, than by attempting to apportion the overcharge among all those that may have indirectly absorbed a part of it.

Violations of the Act may be enjoined either by the government or by private individuals if loss or damage by reason thereof results or is threatened. The Act vests jurisdiction in the Interstate Commerce Commission to enforce its prohibitions in the case of common carriers, the Federal Communications Commission in the case of common carriers engaged in wire or radio communication or radio transmission of energy, the Federal Reserve Board in the case of banks and the Federal Trade Commission in all other cases. Such administrative boards or commissions, upon finding a violation or threatened violation and after hearings on notice to the defendants, may issue an order to cease and desist from the complained act.

Antitrust laws are not applicable to labor organizations or agricultural associations. Nonprofit organizations are exempt from the Act's provisions relating to price discrimination.

Robinson-Patman Act

The Robinson-Patman Act of 1936 was partially an amendment to the Clayton Act. The Robinson-Patman Act makes it unlawful for any person engaged in commerce to "discriminate in price between different purchasers of commodities of like grade and quality... where the effect of such discrimination may be substantially to lessen competition or tend to create a monopoly in any line of commerce, or to injure, destroy, or prevent competition with any person who either grants or knowingly receives the benefit of such discrimination, or with customers of either of them." 15 USC § 13(a). The Robinson-Patman Act is designed to prevent discriminatory practices adversely affecting free competitive enterprise, to preserve competition generally, and to protect small business which is usually unable to buy in quantity against large competitors. It is equally unlawful for any person engaged in commerce "knowingly to induce or receive a discrimination in price which is prohibited by this section." 15 USC § 13(f). The Robinson-Patman Act is designed to afford protection against acts of *individual* competitors.

Case law has clarified this statute so as to make the definition of price discrimination and the kinds of activities which can be included in the term "price discrimination" quite clear. The term "price discrimination" now includes the following types of business practices:

DIFFERENT PRICES CHARGED TO DIFFERENT PURCHASERS

The statute clearly states that a difference in price can only occur when the price difference results from differentials in the "cost of manufacture, sale, or delivery resulting from the differing methods or quantities in which such" goods are sold. Further, price changes are allowable when they result from "changing conditions affecting the market for or the marketability of the goods concerned" (15 USC § 13(a)). It is easy to understand that delivering a full truckload of goods to one customer is less costly than delivering parts of that same truckload to 10 different customers. In that case, the savings can be passed on to the customer who is buying the full truckload (commonly known as a "volume discount").

DIFFERENCES IN TERMS AND CONDITIONS OF SALE

Granting one purchaser free freight while charging freight costs to another purchaser is discriminatory. Charging one price for goods "delivered" to a customer and charging the same price for goods "delivered f.o.b. terminal" has been found to be discriminatory. On the other hand, a promotional two-week discount period for new customers and distributors of its products is not a violation of the Robinson-Patman Act so long as the introductory discount was available to all new customers or customers who secured an additional location and the two-week period involved shows that the discount could not have decreased competition. A price change made in the regular course of business must apply at the same time to all competing purchasers and *customers must be given an equal opportunity* to place orders in advance for future delivery at the old and lower price.

PREFERENTIAL CREDIT TERMS

Requiring one dealer to pay COD while granting another dealer credit terms can support a price discrimination claim. Likewise, granting different credit terms to similar customers can be found to be discriminatory pricing. However, any person is entitled to extend different terms to competing purchasers as long as the credit decision is made in a nondiscriminatory manner so that the same standards of creditworthiness are applied to all customers who compete with each other. For example, history of late payments and financial difficulties are sufficient business justification for denial of credit. In one particular case, a manufacturer abruptly terminated credit and advised its customer that future sales would be on a cash basis. Determining that the customer had prior credit problems with the manufacturer, had little capital and was highly leveraged was good reason for termination of credit. Further, there was no discrimination in the standard of credit applied nor was the customer treated differently than other customers. Other sections of the Robinson-Patman Act provide as follows:

1. It is unlawful to pay, grant, receive or accept a commission, brokerage or other compensation, or an allowance of a discount in lieu thereof, except for services rendered in connection with the sale or purchase of goods, wares or merchandise, either to the other party to such transaction or to an intermediary acting on his behalf

2. It is prohibited to make payments or other transfers of benefit to a customer as compensation for any consideration of services or facilities furnished by or through such customer in connection with the processing, handling, sale or

offering for sale, of any products or commodities manufactured, sold or offered for sale by such person, unless such payment or consideration is available on proportionally equal terms to all competing customers

3. Discrimination in favor of one purchaser as against another of a commodity bought for resale by contracting to furnish or furnishing, any services or facilities not accorded to all purchasers on proportionally equal terms is disallowed

4. It shall be unlawful for any person engaged in commerce, in the course of such commerce, knowingly to induce or receive a discrimination in price which is prohibited by the Act

Nothing in the Robinson-Patman Act denies the right to effect price changes from time to time in response to changing conditions affecting the market for, or the marketability of, the goods concerned, such as actual or imminent deterioration of perishable goods, obsolescence of seasonable goods, distress sales or sales in good faith in discontinuance of business in the goods concerned. Case law has expanded this section to include price differences resulting from technological obsolescence or introduction of new product model.

It is to be noted that to constitute a discrimination in price, within the meaning of the Robinson-Patman Act, there must be actual sales at different prices to at least two different purchasers, and that a prohibited price discrimination must be between purchasers of commodities of *like grade and quality*, and the effect of the discrimination must be to lessen competition or tend to create a monopoly in any line of commerce, or to injure, destroy or prevent competition with any person who either grants or knowingly receives the benefits of such discrimination or with customers of either of them.

The Robinson-Patman Act provides that upon proof that there has been discrimination in price or services or facilities furnished, the burden of proof then shifts to the entity charged with the violation to overcome the initial adversary proof. One of the best-known rebuttals or defenses is to show that the lower price for the furnishing of services or facilities to any purchaser or purchasers was made in good faith to meet an equally low price by a competitor, or to match the services or facilities furnished by a competitor. This is often referred to as the defense of "Good Faith Meeting the Competition." A company will have to be able to demonstrate that, for example, case-by-case discounts were granted in a good-faith effort to meet its competitors' equally low or lower prices.

Often, a supplier is told that a competitor is offering a lower price. The credit professional's dilemma is how to verify that the lower price is indeed being offered. A typical scenario is where a customer implicitly refuses to buy a product unless the manufacturer offers an "X" percent discount. A manufacturer may know that these discounts are available in the marketplace and the customer may repeatedly assure the manufacturer that competitors are offering a similar price. A manufacturer will need to establish that it knew the company and officials with whom it was negotiating and believed them.

While one might think the easiest way in which to confirm that a lower price is being offered by a competitor would be to ask the competitor, that is strictly proscribed. Therefore, sellers who desire to avail themselves of this defense are advised to use all means of verifying or corroborating the alleged lower prices of competitors other than direct contact with competitors. Absolute proof is not necessary. The seller will need to show a good faith effort was made to confirm the offer of a lower price.

The defenses available to a seller charged with violation of Section 2(a) of the Act are based upon the theory that while a seller may not use discrimination in price to grant an unearned competitive advantage as between its customers; nevertheless, if a purchaser, by virtue of the method or quantities in which it buys, creates savings to the seller in the cost of the goods sold, the seller may reflect such savings in the prices which it charges.

A seller has the option either to pass along the cost savings so arising to the purchaser responsible for them, or to sell to all customers at the same price.

It is to be noted, however, that not all differences in a seller's cost of manufacture, sale or delivery in selling goods of like grade and quality to different purchasers may be used to justify a discrimination in price, but cost savings may be reflected in prices *only to the extent that they result from differing methods of delivery or quantities of merchandise being sold*. Thus differences in manufacturing costs resulting from seasonal fluctuations in costs of raw materials, or from varying labor costs, would not in themselves justify the sale of the lower cost goods at a lower price, because such differences in cost do not result from differing methods of delivery or quantities of sale. Nor does the fact that large orders from a single customer may reduce the seller's unit cost of production *of all goods sold* permit a differential in favor of a large purchaser, except to the extent that additional savings may result from such purchaser's method of buying or result in reduced costs of shipment attributable to it alone.

Thus some purchasers order during rush periods and demand immediate delivery while others place their orders well in advance, thereby permitting the manufacturer to produce the goods during off seasons, and resulting cost savings may be treated as resulting from different methods of purchase and may be reflected in the prices charged.

Differences in costs of sale and delivery also result where one customer's order calls for periodic deliveries over a long period of time while another customer places a number of small orders requiring more frequent calls by salesmen. Again, one customer may buy from traveling salesmen, while other customers buy across the counter, and others by mail.

Differences in *cost of production* are infrequent as between separate customers or classes of customers served, because goods and commodities of like grade and quality are usually manufactured to stock and orders are filled from stock. It is, therefore, in the manner of distribution and delivery that cost differences are most likely to arise.

"Quantity or Volume Discounts" is another area that causes concern to the credit professional. The Robinson-Patman Act permits discounts for quantity purchases where they do not tend to stifle competition or create monopoly, or do not discriminate between buyers within the same classification. These "volume discounts" must be available to all customers and should be granted only when the buyer purchases the required amount.

All quantity or volume discounts are closely scrutinized. Much case law exists regarding these discounts.

In one instance price discrimination was not established where a drug manufacturer sold product to warehouse chains under a single-product and global contract. Those prices were lower than the prices offered to its other customers. No predatory intent was found to exist and no competitive injury could be inferred.

In another instance, a manufacturer's use of a trailing credit program resulted in lower prices for some dealers. It was undisputed that the pricing differentials may have been based on the volume of business which is not prohibited under Robinson-Patman.

It is common for sellers to establish price differentials based upon the *distributional function* of the purchasers. Thus, there is usually one price to customers engaged in manufacturing or processing, a different price to wholesalers, another to retailers and another to consumers. These are known as *functional discounts*, which are neither prohibited nor expressly permitted by the statute, and are therefore, subject to the same tests as any other price difference in determining whether they amount to unlawful discrimination. If injury to competition results, the fact that the differential was made in good faith on functional grounds is no defense.

Where a purchaser is engaged in business both as a wholesaler and as a retailer and it receives a wholesale price differential, it obviously has a competitive advantage when selling at retail. Therefore, a supplier selling to this type of customer must keep informed as to the true nature and scope of its customer's business activities, or it may run afoul of the Robinson-Patman Act.

One means of protection in any such case is to bill all goods at the retailer price subject to rebate upon satisfactory proof that the goods were actually resold at wholesale. Functional differentials, if based upon a *bona fide* classification of customers at noncompetitive levels, will not result in unlawful discrimination unless used by recipients of the lower price to create competitive advantage at a lower level of competition, either for themselves or for their customers.

Federal Trade Commission Act of 1914

The Federal Trade Commission Act of 1914 prohibits all "unfair methods of competition in or affecting commerce, and unfair or deceptive acts or practices in or affecting commerce." 15 USC § 45. The Federal Trade Commission Act is the broadest of all antitrust statutes. Its coverage includes acquisitions, mergers, monopolies, unfair trade practices, unfair arrangements between suppliers and dealers, deceptive sales approaches, discrimination in price, services or facilities. Its prohibitions cover false advertising of foods, drugs, devices and cosmetics, and any other practice which is designed to deceive the public. Any practice which violates the Sherman Antitrust Act, Clayton Act or Robinson-Patman Act, or even falls short of an actual violation of those laws but is related to the types of practice which those laws prohibit, may constitute an unfair method of competition under the Federal Trade Commission Act.

With respect to the prohibition of "unfair methods of competition" the Supreme Court has said that these words "are clearly inapplicable to practices never heretofore regarded as opposed to good morals because characterized by deception, bad faith, fraud or oppression, or as against public policy because of their dangerous tendency unduly to hinder competition or create monopoly. The act was certainly not intended to fetter free and fair competition as commonly understood and practiced by honorable opponents in trade."

The Commission is called upon first to determine, as a necessary prerequisite to the issuance of a complaint charging the use of an unfair method of competition, whether there is reason to believe that a given person, partnership, or corporation has been, or is using such unfair method of competition, and, that being determined in the affirmative, the Commission still may not proceed unless it further appears that the proceeding would be in the interest of the public and that such interest is specific and substantial.

The Supreme Court has said:

In a case arising under the Trade Commission Act, the fundamental questions are, whether the methods complained of are 'unfair,' and whether, as in cases under the Sherman Act, they tend to the substantial injury of the public by restricting competition in interstate trade and the 'common liberty' to engage therein. The paramount aim of the Act is the protection of the public from the evils likely to result from the destruction of competition or the restriction of it in a substantial degree, and this presupposes the existence of some substantial competition to be affected, since the public is not concerned in the maintenance of competition which itself is without real substance.

In addition to restraining incipient combinations or conspiracies in restraint of trade, the Commission, under its mandate to prevent unfair and deceptive acts or practices in commerce, has authority to inquire into such matters as false advertising, deceptive brands and similar other matters, and the great majority of the cases coming before the Commission involve practices of this type.

Antitrust Procedure and Penalties Act

The Antitrust Procedure and Penalties Act, codified in 1976, increased penalties for violation of the Sherman Antitrust Act, changed consent decree procedures and revised the provisions for appellate review of antitrust cases.

Since approximately 80 percent of antitrust complaints filed by the United States are settled by consent decree, the Act seeks to reform this procedure. The Act requires that the Justice Department file a "competitive impact statement" concerning the proposed settlement and provide the public with an opportunity to comment on its own. The statute also enables district court judges to determine as a matter of law whether a proposed consent judgment is in the public interest. The Act requires disclosure by the settling defendant of any lobbying with government officials concerning the terms of the consent decree. Previously, judges were required to accept proposed consent decrees.

Neither the judicial determination of public interest nor the statement of competitive impact that the Justice Department must file in consent decrees as required by this statute may be used as evidence against defendants in private antitrust litigation.

The penalties for violation of antitrust laws are severe, including fine, imprisonment and liability for triple damages. The conviction and imprisonment of officers of some of our largest electrical manufacturing companies for violation of the price-fixing provisions of the Sherman Act should serve as a warning to businessmen that these laws are not to be taken lightly.

1976 Antitrust Act

The 1976 Antitrust Act (13 USC §§ 1311–1314) gave the federal government new disclosure powers in antitrust litigation. This statute also permits a state Attorney General to sue for damages on behalf of a particular state's citizens and requires companies of a certain size to file premerger notices.

State Antitrust Statutes

Almost every state has independent laws prohibiting monopolies, contracts, conspiracies and combinations in restraint of trade. Such laws include fair trade or resale price maintenance laws, and prohibitions against price discrimination and sales below cost.

International Antitrust Laws

With international trade an everyday occurrence, it is important to recognize that international transactions are subject to antitrust laws. If a group of U.S. credit grantors exchanges information or there is an industry credit group in the U.S. exchanging information involving foreign trade, the U.S. antitrust laws do apply to the activities of these groups. The federal laws and regulations are not limited to transactions which take place within U.S. borders. When foreign transactions have a substantial and foreseeable effect on U.S. commerce, such transactions are subject to U.S. law, regardless of where they take place.

The Treaty Establishing the European Community contains the "antitrust" law within the European Economic Community. Title VI of that Treaty, "Common rules on competition, taxation and approximation of laws," is comparable to the U.S. statutes. The opening text of Article 81 of that Title states that "all agreements between undertakings, decisions by associations of undertakings and concerted practices which may affect trade between Member States and which have as their object or effect the prevention, restriction or distortion of competition within the common market..." are prohibited.

Particularly prohibited activities are those which:

(1) directly or indirectly fix purchase or selling prices or any other trading conditions;
(2) limit or control production, markets, technical development or investment;
(3) share markets or sources of supply;
(4) apply dissimilar conditions to equivalent transactions with other trading parties, thereby placing them at a competitive disadvantage;
(5) make the conclusion of contracts subject to acceptance by the other parties of supplementary obligations which, by their nature or according to commercial usage, have no connection with the subject of such contracts.

One should note the similarity to the U.S. prohibitions of restraint of trade and the U.S. condemnation of "uniform actions to fix, standardize or otherwise interfere with prices." The object of both U.S. and EEC regulations is free and unrestricted business competition.

It should be further noted, that Title VI Article 82 of the Treaty mirrors U.S. statutes by providing additional prohibitions to those parties of a "dominant position within the common market or in a substantial part of it..." This Article 82 prohibits abuses by *one or more* parties, which consist in:

(1) directly or indirectly imposing unfair purchase or selling prices or other unfair trading conditions;
(2) limiting production, markets or technical development to the prejudice of consumers;
(3) applying dissimilar conditions to equivalent transactions with other trading parties, thereby placing them at a competitive disadvantage;

(4) making the conclusion of contracts subject to acceptance by the other parties of supplementary obligations which, by their nature or according to commercial usage, have no connection with the subject of such contracts.

GOVERNANCE OF ANTITRUST LAWS

It is important for the credit grantor to understand that it is not only the Department of Justice which may pursue antitrust lawsuits. Violations of antitrust statutes may subject the violator to either criminal prosecution, civil prosecution or both. The credit grantor must be warned that certain antitrust violations can result in criminal prosecution against the individual who violates the antitrust laws while the Department of Justice simultaneously pursues the offending company.

The following civil actions can be commenced:

1. Any individual private party claiming injury as a result of antitrust violations can sue for actual damages as well as pecuniary damages (up to triple the amount of actual damages to serve as a punishment to the offender)
2. A class action may be brought by a selected body of injured parties for the same actual damages and pecuniary damages
3. The Attorney General of any state may commence an action for injunctions against further violations and for damages
4. The Antitrust Division of the Department of Justice may bring a civil case to enjoin further violations
5. The Federal Trade Commission can bring a civil case for a violation of certain antitrust statutes

A criminal action under the federal antitrust statutes can only be commenced by the Antitrust Division of the Department of Justice. This action can result in fines against businesses as well as individuals, and jail terms against individuals. Additionally, state attorney generals may bring criminal actions under various state statutes which are similar to the federal antitrust statutes.

Antitrust actions may be brought in the federal court, or sometimes before an administrative law judge. In addition to the Federal Trade Commission, other administrative agencies have specific control over specific industries. The Interstate Commerce Commission is the administrative agency which enforces its prohibitions against common carriers. The Federal Communications Commission is the enforcement agency against common carriers engaged in wire or radio communication or radio transmission of energy. The Federal Reserve Board acts in the case of Banks. The Federal Trade Commission has the ability to hear all other matters.

The International Chamber of Commerce is the counterpart to the United States Chamber of Commerce. The World Trade Organization and the Organization for Economic Cooperation and Development play major roles in providing White Papers and changes in laws in international commerce. The European Commission serves in much the same manner as does the Federal Trade Commission.

Refusal to Deal with Particular Supplier or Customer

The courts have held that a manufacturer has "the right to deal or refuse to deal with a particular distributor as long as it does so unilaterally" (*Terry's Floor Fashions, Inc. v. Burlington Industries, Inc.* 763 F.2d 604). Other cases have found that "a manufacturer generally has the right to independently decide with whom it wants to do business..." (*Pink Supply Corp. v. Hiebert, Inc.* 612 F.Supp. 1334, aff'd (CA8 Minn.) 788 F.2d 1313). Additionally, it is legal to "deal or refuse to deal...as long as it does so independently; unilateral refusal to deal does not constitute illegal contract, combination or conspiracy..." (*Tunis Bros. Co. v. Ford Motor Co.* 763 F.2d 1482). More recently, in 1988, this ability to refuse to deal was upheld. The 5th Circuit Court of Appeals noted that to find an antitrust violation, it would have to be shown that there were joint efforts that resulted in "either directly denying or persuading or coercing suppliers or customers to deny the relationships the competitors needed in the competitive struggle" (*Consolidated Metal Products, Inc. v. American Petroleum Institute* 846 F.2d 284).

EXCHANGE OF CREDIT INFORMATION AND THE ANTITRUST LAWS

It is well established that the extension of credit and terms of sale come within the scope of antitrust laws. In numerous decisions, the courts have recognized the legitimate business interest and need for the exchange of credit information among business people. As early as 1925, the U.S. Supreme Court held:

...The gathering and dissemination of information which will enable sellers to prevent a perpetration of fraud upon them, which information they are free to act upon or not as they choose, cannot be held to be an unlawful restraint upon commerce, even though, in the ordinary course of business, most sellers would act upon the information...We cannot regard the procuring and dissemination of information which tends to prevent the fraudulent securing of deliveries of merchandise... as an unlawful restraint of trade, even though such information be gathered by those who are engaged in the trade or business principally concerned... (*Cement Manufacturers' Protective Association v. United States*, 268 U.S. 588, 603-604 (1925).

More recently, in a 1976 case the U.S. Court of Appeals for the Second Circuit in New York commented on the exchange of credit information by stating the following:

Unlike exchanges regarding prices which usually serve no purpose other than to suppress competition, and hence fall within the ban of the Sherman Act... the dissemination of information concerning the creditworthiness of customers aids sellers in gaining information necessary to protect themselves against fraudulent or insolvent customers... Given the legitimate function of such data, it is not a violation of the Sherman Act to exchange such information, provided that any action taken in reliance upon it is the result of each firm's independent judgment, and not of agreement (*Michelman v. Clark Schwebel Fiberglass Corp.*, 534 F.2d 1036 (1976)).

The objectives and purposes of creditors exchanging credit information and, more importantly, NACM credit groups, are clearly within the scope of this lawful conduct. However, since members of credit groups or creditors who exchange information are generally in competition with one another, the exchange of other information, whether by group meetings or otherwise, appear to provide a ready opportunity for a claim of a violation of the antitrust laws. In a 1982 case, a private plaintiff unsuccessfully argued that attendance at an NACM credit group meeting constituted evidence of a conspiracy to fix prices. It is the responsibility of the creditors exchanging information and sponsoring NACM credit associations to be vigilant and alert to see that no such violations occur. It is further very important that group meetings be held only under the auspices and with the presence of trained NACM personnel and, in many instances, outside counsel to ensure that there is neither the perception nor the reality of a violation of the laws. A case, commenced in 2004 (and still ongoing), alleges that NACM members met at a credit group meeting to discuss with whom credit group members should not do business, thus, alleging a "group boycott" took place. The recently update and revised "Antitrust Guide for NACM Group Members" is available, which clearly outlines what actions need to be taken to protect NACM Group Members and what members may or may not do.

Burden of Defense

For the protection of credit grantors, as well as NACM credit groups, an important factor in an antitrust situation must be understood—the burden and the cost of a defense of any claim. In any antitrust action or investigation, the burden of defending and explaining the activities and/or services of a credit grantor or a credit group will fall upon those being charged with a violation. In any antitrust action brought by the federal government, the government will most likely allege a conspiracy or other illegal action. The evidence or charges presented may impute illegal actions arising from normally and legal proper activities or from legal and proper services used for illegal purposes. The credit grantor or the credit group along with the NACM sponsoring association will then have the responsibility and the burden of explaining those services and activities and defending their legality. The cost of defending an antitrust charge can be substantial and monetary awards can be substantial. Whether such costs or fees can be recovered from any of those involved depends upon the individual circumstances of the case.

Should a credit group be subject to an investigation by the federal trade commission or the antitrust division of the U.S. Department of Justice, or should such entities investigate individual creditors, the investigators will look to those involved to explain the activities and defend their legality.

None of the above is intended to dissuade credit professionals from the legitimate exchange of credit information, either individually or through a credit group. Indeed, since both statute and case law clearly permit such an exchange of information, it should be fully utilized in today's complicated business environment in order to assist the credit grantor in making credit decisions. However, because of the potential danger involved in any such activity, careful attention must be paid to strict compliance with appropriate legal and business standards.

SUMMARY

1. Any agreement, express or implied, among credit grantors or credit group members to establish or maintain prices, payment terms or conditions of sale is an illegal conspiracy in restraint of trade.
2. Any agreement, express or implied, among credit grantors or credit group members to refuse to sell to any person or business is an illegal conspiracy in restraint of trade.

3. Any agreement, express or implied, among credit grantors or credit group members to refuse to extend credit to any person or business is an illegal conspiracy in restraint of trade. Any form of use by credit grantors or credit group members of a group service for illegal purposes, such as treating a delinquent account report as a "black list," may be evidence of an illegal conspiracy in restraint of a trade.

4. *Delinquent Account Reports.* It is lawful to discuss an account which is delinquent or has been delinquent in the past. The safest practice is to:

    a. Limit the information to past and completed transactions
    b. Do not discuss uniform action with any one or several of your competitors
    c. Do not discuss what you will do in the future with respect to prices, payment terms or discounts

5. *Record Keeping.* The maintenance of good records including copies of memoranda and letters as well as records of conversations can be essential in defending an allegation of antitrust violations. The following documentation can be extremely helpful to you:

    a. Suggested price lists to dealers with clear language that the prices are only recommendations
    b. Records of your justification for canceling nonperforming dealers
    c. Credit reports on which you based a decision to restrict a credit line, cancel a credit line or not extend credit
    d. Records to substantiate the manner in which your competitors lower price was brought to your attention which caused you to change your price

24 Escheatment Laws and Unclaimed Property Reporting Requirements

WHAT IS UNCLAIMED PROPERTY?

For most people, the term "unclaimed property" connotes some abandoned piece of property down the street with nothing built on it. The more proper term for the subject of "unclaimed property" should be "unclaimed money," because it generally does not deal at all with real estate. It deals with contract rights, intangible personal property.

The history and background of unclaimed property goes back to the year 1066. That is the foundation of the English common law and the concept of escheat: the crown had the right to reclaim real property when an owner of that property died without heirship or an heir that wasn't capable of taking.

This concept is referred to in the Magna Carta in 1215, and has become statutory law in all 50 states plus the four U.S. legislative jurisdictions of the District of Columbia, Commonwealth of Puerto Rico, Territory of Guam, and the U.S. Virgin Islands.

There are basically 54 different laws. These laws are all at the state level for one simple reason: the framers of the Constitution did not reserve the concept of escheat to the federal government. Under the reservation clause of the U.S. Constitution, all powers not granted to the federal government devolve to the states.

Even though many are called the Uniform Unclaimed Property Act, there is only one thing uniform about them—not any two are the same. If you overlay them, you will find many similarities but no exact duplication. You're dealing with a complex matrix of different provisions.

The formal definition of unclaimed property is "intangible personal property that has gone unclaimed by its rightful owner." A concept that is often misunderstood relates to the activity required by the rightful owner to avoid property being "unclaimed." Activity by a credit manager to attempt to get the rightful owner to act or to maintain accurate records about the account is irrelevant. A credit executive can update the account four times a day. You can write a check for a credit balance. Any internal action that you take on an item does not qualify as contact for the tolling of the periods under the law. Dormancy periods vary from state to state generally from two years to seven years. Consider the bank that posts interest on a savings account every quarter. If you looked at the computer file, it would say "last active June 30, 2005." That's activity generated by the bank, not activity generated by the owner.

So that's one important concept to remember. The activity is owner generated, not something you do.

JURISDICTION ISSUES

In the law of taxation, a fundamental concept is that of "nexus." That basically means that a jurisdiction—a state, a county, a city—has jurisdiction over a business to impose a tax, whether it be property, sales, use, litter, or any of the other hundreds of different taxes.

Nexus means that a business has to have a physical presence in the jurisdiction. It has to have employees and property, as well as, sell product there. There has to be a connection. Nexus is a Latin term meaning "connection."

What if a business is incorporated in Nebraska and does business in Nebraska and Kansas? It has no employees, property or sells product anywhere else. The State of Illinois would not have nexus over that business for imposing a tax.

However, the rules of unclaimed property are very different, because it doesn't deal with a tax. Unclaimed property is not a tax. It is a custodial transfer of money from a private holder to some state government, who then holds it. Once money is transferred to a state, it's claimable by the owner or the heir to the owner forever. There's no cutoff of those rights. If there were, the courts would have held these laws unconstitutional.

Three times since 1965, the U.S. Supreme Court has settled disputes between the states over unclaimed property. In the process, the Court has established certain common law rules that have become precedent in the field of unclaimed property.

The first of these cases, *Texas v. New Jersey*, 379 U.S. 674, 85 S.Ct. 626, 13 L.Ed.2d 596 (1965), addressed escheat of debts owed by Sun Oil Company to its creditors. It addressed what state should receive the abandoned property and established two rules, known simply as the Primary Rule and the Secondary Rule, as follows:

Primary Rule—Escheat to state of creditor's last known address.

Secondary Rule—If no address, escheat to state in which debtor is incorporated.

In the second case, *Pennsylvania v. New York*, 407 U.S. 206, 92 S.Ct. 2075, 32 L.Ed.2d 693 (1972), the Court dealt with money orders for which there was typically no known address. The Court held that the rule established in *Texas v. New Jersey* applied. This distorted the equities laid out in the first decision and Congress shortly thereafter enacted 12 USC 2501-2503 (effective 1974). As a result, abandoned money orders and traveler's checks are specifically subject to federal law for the purpose of allocating escheated funds among the states. If the buyer's address is unknown, the property will escheat to the state where the instrument was sold.

The third Supreme Court case was *Delaware v. New York*, 113 S.Ct. 1550, 123 L.Ed.2d 211 (1993). It dealt with unclaimed securities dividends and interest, where the intermediary securities depository and the securities issuer are in different states. That case held: escheat to the state in which the intermediary, having assumed the position of legal obligor, is incorporated, as argued by Delaware, as opposed to where the intermediary was located, as argued by New York, unless another state can prove that a creditor's last address is in that state.

Escheatable property that is outside the United States generally must go into the company's state of incorporation. However, there are some subtle nuances that should be considered. In order to be escheatable under U.S. law, the credit has to be a U.S. obligation on a U.S. entity's books. For instance, if your company has a subsidiary that is an Argentine entity that has an uncashed check to an employee or to a vendor, that is not reportable because it isn't held by the U.S. entity.

The flip side of the question relates to whether the company would also have to report and remit to the foreign jurisdiction. The only way a U.S. entity would be subject to the reporting to a foreign jurisdiction would be pursuant to a treaty between the U.S. and that foreign government. Currently there are no treaties related to unclaimed property.

CURRENT HOT TOPICS WITH UNCLAIMED PROPERTY

New Technology

There is a big controversy brewing right now over law that Congress enacted in 1974 to deal with money orders. In pertinent part, it applies to "sums payable on money orders, traveler's checks, and similar written instruments deemed abandoned…" The question is whether "other similar written instruments" includes items that did not exist in 1974. Examples are gift certificates, gift cards and stored value cards. These are all going to have unclaimed property implications that probably will require federal intervention to determine to which state the funds should escheat.

Technology is developing at a pace that these statutes never contemplated. The last time the National Conference of Commissioners on Uniform State Laws adopted changes to the Uniform Unclaimed Property Act was in 1995. This amended the act, which had been initially adopted as a uniform act in 1981. This Act is preceded by the 1954 Uniform Disposition of Unclaimed Property Act (1954), which was revised in 1966, and became the Uniform Unclaimed Property Act in 1981.

Sarbanes-Oxley

Because of Sarbanes-Oxley, public companies are in a whole new era. Prior to Sarbanes-Oxley, unclaimed property was below the bottom of the list of priorities at public companies. Now that we have Sarbanes-Oxley, there are a couple of specific sections of the Act that become important in the unclaimed property arena:

Section 302. The certification that the CFO and CEO sign. If the company has not reported or underreported liability for unclaimed property, the certification would be incorrect.

Section 404 reviews. Internal control reviews to ensure the integrity of financial reporting. The company's review of internal controls should include that of unclaimed property.

TYPES OF PROPERTY

For most companies that are not financial institutions, unclaimed property is some kind of check that doesn't get cashed. For example, it could be a payroll check, a vendor check, expense check, a commission check, a rebate check.

What do most companies do with outstanding checks? After six months, they write them off to income. Take a look at commissions, account payable checks, refund checks and credit balances in accounts receivable (under the Fair Credit Reporting Act, a company may be required to refund that credit balance).

If a company is in the rental business or any business where it takes advance money, security deposits become a potential source of unclaimed property.

If a company ever receives unidentified remittances, it could have unclaimed property obligations. If it has a high volume of transactions, it is not unlikely that payments received will not be able to be immediately matched to the correct account. Those responsible for cash management often believe that regardless of who the check is made payable to, it should be cashed and matched up later. This can create a significant number of potential unclaimed property liabilities.

Unfortunately, most states do not have a de minimus rule allowing anything under some threshold to be written off by the company and need not be researched or escheated.

However, a company may nonetheless adopt policies to efficiently and economically deal with the small amount item. Companies have the right to set policy that has economic substance. For example, if the amount is under $25, the item is booked to a special account of items that might need to be escheated. When the items become three years old (or whatever age is mandated by the state in question for the type of property in question), the amount in the account is sent to the state. A rolling three-year period rule keeps it fresh and the company out of trouble.

If indeed someone with a $2.43 check surfaces at some point, they can get their money back from the state if the issuing company has remitted it. Remember, the owner never loses the right when funds are transferred to any one of the states. It's a custodial law. It merely substitutes the state treasurer for the company. What transfers is the right to use the money—from the company to the state.

Property Category/Types

(Source: PEACC.COM—Property Escheatment and Compliance Consulting; 410-552-1340; www.peacc.com.)

MISCELLANEOUS CHECKS AND INTANGIBLE PERSONAL PROPERTY HELD IN THE ORDINARY COURSE OF BUSINESS

Payroll/Wages/Salary
Commissions
Worker's Compensation Benefits
Payments for Goods and/or Services
Customer Overpayments
Unidentified Remittances
Unrefunded Overcharges
Accounts Payable
Credit Balances and Accounts Receivable
Discounts Due
Refunds Due
Unredeemed Gift Certificates
Unclaimed Loan Collateral
Pension and Profit Sharing Plans (IRA, KEOGH)
Dissolutions or Liquidations
Miscellaneous Outstanding Checks
Miscellaneous Intangible Property
Suspense Liabilities

UNCASHED CHECKS

Cashier's Checks
Certified Checks
Registered Checks
Treasurer's Checks
Drafts
Warrants
Traveler's Checks
Bank Money Orders
Personal Money Orders

Foreign Exchange Checks
Expense Checks
Pension Checks
Credit Checks or Memos
Vendor Checks
Checks Written Off to Income
Other Outstanding Official Checks
CD Interest Checks

ACCOUNT BALANCES DUE

Checking Accounts
Savings Accounts
Matured CD or Savings Certificate
Christmas Club Funds
Money on Deposit to Secure Funds
Security Deposits
Unidentified Deposits
Suspense Accounts

SAFE DEPOSIT BOXES AND SAFEKEEPING

Safe Deposit Box Contents
Other Safekeeping Items
Other Tangible Property
Unclaimed Loan Collateral

INSURANCE

Individual Policy Benefits or Claim Payments
Group Policy Benefits or Claim Payments
Proceeds Due Beneficiaries
Proceeds from Matured Policies, Endowments or Annuities
Premium Refunds
Unidentified Remittances
Other Amounts Due Under Policy Terms
Agent Credit Balances

SECURITIES

Dividends
Interest on Registered Bonds
Principal Payments
Equity Payments
Profits
Funds Paid to Purchase Shares
Funds for Stocks and Bonds
Shares of Stock (Returned by Post Office)
Cash for Fractional Shares
Unexchanged Stock of Successor Corporation
Other Certificates of Ownership

Underlying Shares or Other Outstanding Certificates
Funds for Liquidation/Redemption of Unsurrendered Stocks or Bonds
Debentures, Bonds or Coupons
US Government Securities
Mutual Fund Shares
Warrants/Rights
Matured Bond Principal
Dividend Reinvestment Plans
Credit Balances

TRUST, INVESTMENT AND ESCROW ACCOUNTS

Paying Agent Accounts
Undelivered or Uncashed Dividends
Funds Held in a Fiduciary Capacity
Escrow Accounts
Trust Vouchers
Pre-Need Funeral Payments

COURT DEPOSITS/PUBLIC AGENCIES

Escrow Funds
Condemnation Awards
Missing Heirs Funds
Suspense Accounts
Other Court Deposits or w/Public Agencies
Child Support Payments

MINERAL PROCEEDS AND MINERAL INTERESTS

Net Revenue Interest
Royalties
Overriding Royalties
Production Payments
Working/Royalty Interest
Bonuses
Delay Rentals
Shut-In Royalties
Minimum Royalties

UTILITIES

Utility Deposits
Membership Fees
Refunds or Rebates
Unrefunded Overcharges
Capital Credit Distributions

REPORTING TO THE STATES

The laws requiring the report and escheating of funds to the states are not voluntary in nature. The laws create a duty to file a report. They create a duty to perform due diligence. They create a duty to actually send the money to the state. They create, on an inferred basis, a duty to protect the funds and a duty to maintain copies of the report you file.

Unlike tax law, there is no statute of limitations on unclaimed property reporting. If the company doesn't file reports or if the reports aren't complete, the states can go back 50 years if they want to. California, in fact, does go back 50 years.

So one of the primary questions for a company that is addressing compliance for the first time is, how far back in time should the research and reporting go? Some states have what is called a voluntary disclosure program, where a company can contact the state about coming into compliance. What benefits does your state provide for a first-time filer? Some states will say, rather than go back 20 years— the period the state goes back if they sent in an auditor—you only have to go back 10 years.

What to Report

The report is due on the forms or the software prescribed by each state. They're very similar. If a company captures its data, generally the data needed for each occurrence of unclaimed property is the owner's name and address; the kind of property it is (there is a property type code list you can get off the PEAC website); the date it was last active, which on a check, the date is the issue date; the amount of the item due (some ask if any kind of deduction has been made); and a service charge or a fee.

A company can also be penalized for failure to report, or filing a fraudulent report. For example, if a company is a Delaware corporation and the State can prove that it filed a fraudulent report, like a zero, or it owed hundreds of thousands of dollars and only sent in two hundred, the State can charge an additional 75 percent against the liability. That is enormous. There is a 50 percent penalty, 10 percent negligence fee, 5 percent interest, and 75 percent for fraudulent report. Simply put, a Delaware corporation does not want to be in noncompliance.

Electronic reporting is becoming more prevalent, and is sometimes required. For example, if a company has 25 or more owners of unclaimed property, many states require by law that it files electronically because they don't want to reenter all the information and risk chance of incorrect entry.

Due Diligence

Due diligence is a term used in unclaimed property, that requires that if the amount is over a certain amount (usually $50), the company must send one first-class mailing to the last known address, if it has it. Generally the letter should inform the individual that it has an unclaimed check (or an unclaimed credit, or whatever is unclaimed) and that the company is going to be required to send it to its state if the individual does not respond.

Some states, if they find that they become a revolving door and a company "dumps" the property without sending the letters to try to reconcile with the owner, will assess a penalty against that. Virginia and Iowa are noted for doing so.

The best thing to do, is to have an area at the bottom of the letter where the individual can simply sign, date and return the letter. Or, include a postcard in with the notification letter, requesting the owner to sign and send it back. The key element is to not just say, "Dear John Smith, you're a good customer, we haven't heard from you, stop by the store." That's going to go in the trash. Tell the individual that their money will be transferred to the state and they must claim it from the state. If the customer does not take action on that, none will be.

If it comes back "addressee unknown," no forwarding order, addressee deceased, etc., keep it in a file. There's really nothing more that can be done.

Some companies will send a second letter if the amounts involved are particularly high (e.g., over $10,000, $20,000 or $100,000). According to Anthony Andreoli, in a presentation at NACM's 109th Annual Credit Congress, the U.S. Post Office statistics on first-class mailings provide some insight into how you might want to proceed. When a first-class mailing was re-mailed to those returned, 50 percent got through. When it was returned a second time and re-mailed, 20 percent got through.

Duty to Remit

In most states now, when a report is filed, as with a tax return, the money is sent with it. In the old days, a report was sent, a six-month wait followed, then the money was sent. It was an enormous reconciling problem.

There are a few states, including Delaware, for example, that require that an initial report be sent. It then does a publication and funds end up being turned in with the final report. But most states report and remit simultaneously.

Keep Reports Forever

Companies should keep any report filed to any state forever. States can't necessarily be relied on to have accurate records of a company's reporting, particularly from many years ago. Should a company be audited, one of the first things the state auditors will ask for are copies of its old reports. Some states will penalize for not keeping copies of the reports.

Audits by the States

A company should not claim property from a state if it hasn't been filing, it's a big audit target. It needs to make sure its in compliance before commencing the claiming of property.

For a company that have been selected for an audit, either by a state or a contract auditor, it will help if it is well prepared when the auditors come in the door. It should have copies of any prior reports and have its policies and procedures well documented. If the auditor sees that the company has good procedures in place, they literally just walk on and start moving on to another company. There are so many companies that are not in compliance, it is easier to deal with those than a company that has made an effort to comply.

In the absence of records, auditors are permitted to use estimation techniques to determine a holder's liability, and they do. The best form of company defense is its records. When a company has systems conversions like Y2K, has purchased another company and merged all those records into its own, an auditor can now come in and create a statistical sampling based on current data. That can be an enormous liability that's overstated. So a very good job has to be done to show that the company procedures are well written. Not surprisingly, estimation techniques can result in large liability assessments.

There's a difference between a state, joint and contract audit. A company can be selected for any or all of them. One state can select a company for an audit and use an employee of the state to come in and do a review. They can also collaborate with other states.

What's most commonly being used today, especially with the budget crises they are under, is the state will select a company for an audit and they'll assign a contract audit firm.

The contract auditors are reimbursed on a contingency fee basis. They receive anywhere from 12-15 percent of what they find.

Some audit triggers include:

Recent merger/acquisition (M&A) activity. The understanding is, if a company has been acquired by another, they probably haven't been filing reports—the acquiring company just bought the liability in most cases. The states are savvy to that and their contract auditors usually have one person doing nothing but watching activity, so they know that in about two or three years, this will be a good candidate for an audit.

Filing a negative report. If a company files a negative report, or fails to report at all, especially for large corporations, it's going to be on the radar list. If a large transient workforce exists where there is an outstanding payroll—a likelihood that is pretty high—that company will probably be selected for an audit.

Industry type. Car dealerships are now hot on the list as an audit target for many states. Because of gift cards, retail is an industry being looked at, obviously because retailers have been issuing rebates.

UNCLAIMED PROPERTY AUDITS

(Reprinted with permission of PEACC.COM)

Actions a Holder Can Take to Lessen the Chance of an Audit

- Review, research and learn the unclaimed property laws
- Educate all employees responsible for unclaimed property
- Establish and follow written in-house procedures
- Establish and abide to strong internal controls (including for fraud)
- Have internal audit functions in place
- Keep good records that are easily available
- Account for liability
- Conduct research regularly (including voided and outstanding checks)
- Establish communication with property owners
- Research returned mail and correct postal errors
- Make sure all unclaimed property types are being reported
- Perform due diligence (search letter mailings, telephone calls, advertise, etc.)
- Most importantly: file all required unclaimed property reports in a timely manner

Actions Not to Take

- Implement "private escheat" laws
- Deduct unlawful charges from accounts
- Just sitting back and waiting for "them" to come and find you

Some Audit Selection Criteria

- Not filing unclaimed property reports
- Submitting continuously negative reports or even in back-to-back years
- Submitting reports with errors on them
- Lump-sum aggregate totals
- Taking unlawful deductions or service charges
- Poor due diligence efforts or no effort at all
- Reporting property to only one state
- Dollar amounts reported are less than similar types from other company reports
- Not reporting all required property types, or types conducive to industry
- Gaps in reporting history
- Doing business in a state, but not reporting unclaimed property there
- Not filing an unclaimed property report to state of incorporation
- Other state agencies may recommend it
- Company is in the news
- Whistle blower
- Mergers, reorganizations, liquidation, re-incorporations, or acquisitions

How to Prepare for an Audit

- Although it may be hard, prepare a nice, comfortable place for the auditors to use
- Identify and inform key personnel within the organization
- Request records for the years at which the auditors are going to be looking
- Establish an Audit Coordinator to act as contact within the organization
- Coordinate EDP support
- Gather and review all unclaimed property policies and procedures
- Gather and review records
- Notify transfer agents and third-party administrators
- Consult with legal consul
- Take time to prepare before the auditors arrive

CONCLUSION

All companies will have some form of a liability. That's just the nature of the game. There's going to be a check out there that doesn't get cashed. Unclaimed property compliance is mandatory.

UNCLAIMED PROPERTY OFFICES

The following list is the contact information for unclaimed property divisions for the 50 states, District of Columbia, Guam, Puerto Rico and U.S. Virgin Islands. (Provided by National Association of Unclaimed Property Administrators— www.unclaimed.org.)

ALASKA

Department of Revenue
Treasury Division
Unclaimed Property Section
P.O. Box 11040
Juneau, AK 99811-0405
Phone: 907-465-3726
Fax: 907-465-2394

ALABAMA

State Treasury
Unclaimed Property Division
P.O. Box 302520
Montgomery, AL 36130-2520
Phone: 888-844-8400
Fax: 334-242-9620

ARKANSAS

Unclaimed Property Division
Auditor of State
1400 West 3rd Street, Suite 100
Little Rock, AR 72201-1811
Phone: 1-800-252-4648 or 501-682-6000
Fax: 501-682-6005

ARIZONA

Department of Revenue
Unclaimed Property Unit
P.O. Box 29026
Site Code 9026
Phoenix, AZ 85038-9026
Phone: 602-364-0380
Fax: 602-542-2089

CALIFORNIA

State Controller Steve Westly
Division of Collections - Bureau of Unclaimed
Property
3301 C Street, Suite 712
P.O. Box 942850
Sacramento, CA 94250-5873
Phone: 1-800-992-4647 or 916-323-2827
Fax: 916-323-2851

COLORADO

Unclaimed Property Division
1120 Lincoln Street, Suite 1004
Denver, CO 80203
Phone: 303-894-2443
Fax: 303-894-2351

CONNECTICUT

Unclaimed Property Division
Office of State Treasurer
55 Elm Street
Hartford, CT 06106
Phone: 860-702-3050
Fax: 860-702-3044

DISTRICT OF COLUMBIA

Office of Finance & Treasury
Unclaimed Property Unit
1275 K Street, NW - Suite 500B
Washington, DC 20005
Phone: 202-442-8181
Fax: 202-442-8180

DELAWARE

Bureau of Abandoned Property
P.O. Box 8931
Wilmington, DE 19899
Phone: 302-577-8205
Fax: 302-577-8656

FLORIDA

Department of Financial Services
Bureau of Unclaimed Property
P.O. Box 1990
Tallahassee, FL 32302-1990
Phone: 850-410-9253
Fax: 850-410-9728

GEORGIA

Georgia Department of Revenue
Property Tax Division
Unclaimed Property Section
4245 International Parkway, Suite A
Hapeville, GA 30354-3918
Phone: 404-968-0490
Fax: 404-968-0772

GUAM

Treasurer of Guam
P.O. Box 884
Agana, GU 96910
Phone: 671-475-1286

HAWAII

Department of Budget and Finance
Unclaimed Property Program
P.O. Box 150
Honolulu, HI 96810-0150
Phone: 808-586-1589
Fax: 808-586-1644

IOWA

Michael L. Fitzgerald, State Treasurer
The Great Iowa Treasure Hunt
Lucas State Office Building
321 East 12th Street, 1st Floor
Des Moines, IA 50319
Phone: 515-281-5367
Fax: 515-242-6962

IDAHO

Idaho State Tax Commission
Unclaimed Property Section
P.O. BOX 70012
Boise, ID 83707-0112
Phone: 208-334-7623
Fax: 208-364-7392

ILLINOIS

Office of State Treasurer
Unclaimed Property Division
P.O. Box 19495
Springfield, IL 62794-9495
Phone: 217-782-6692
Fax: 217-557-5871

INDIANA

Attorney General's Office
Unclaimed Property Division
402 West Washington, Suite C-531
Indianapolis, IN 46204
Phone: 317-232-6348
Fax: 317-232-7979

KANSAS

Unclaimed Property Division
900 Jackson, Suite 201
Topeka, KS 66612-1235
Phone: 800-432-0386 or 785-296-4165
Fax: 785-296-7950

KENTUCKY

Unclaimed Property Division
Kentucky Department of Treasury
Suite 183, Capitol Annex
Frankfort, KY 40601
Phone: 502-564-4722
Fax: 502-564-4200

LOUISIANA

John Kennedy, State Treasurer
Unclaimed Property Division
P.O. Box 91010
Baton Rouge, LA 70821
Phone: 225-219-9400
Fax: 225-342-0046

MASSACHUSETTS

Abandoned Property Division
1 Ashburton Place, 12th Floor
Boston, MA 02108
Phone: 617-367-0400
Fax: 617-248-3944

MARYLAND

Unclaimed Property Unit
301 W. Preston Street
Baltimore, MD 21201-2385
Phone: 1-800-782-7383 or 410-767-1700
Fax: 410-333-7150

MAINE

State Treasurer's Office
Unclaimed Property Division
39 State House Station
111 Sewall Street, 3rd Floor
Burton M. Cross Building
Augusta, ME 04333-0039
Phone: 207-624-7470
Fax: 207-287-2367

MICHIGAN

Department of Treasury
Unclaimed Property Division
P.O. Box 30756
Lansing, MI 48909
Phone: 517-636-5320
Fax: 517-636-5324

MINNESOTA

Minnesota Department of Commerce
Unclaimed Property Division
85 7th Place East, Suite 600
St. Paul, MN 55101-3165
Phone: 1-800-925-5668 or 651-296-2568
Fax: 651-284-4108

MISSOURI

State Treasurer's Office
Unclaimed Property Section
P.O. Box 1004
Jefferson City, MO 65102
Phone: 573-751-0840
Fax: 573-526-6027

MISSISSIPPI

Treasury Department
Unclaimed Property Division
P.O. Box 138
Jackson, MS 39205-0138
Phone: 601-359-3600
Fax: 601-359-2001

MONTANA

Dept. of Revenue - Unclaimed Property Division
Sam W. Mitchell Bldg.
125 North Roberts, 3rd Floor
P.O. Box 5805
Helena, MT 59604-5805
Phone: 406-444-6900
Fax: 406-444-0722

NORTH CAROLINA

Department of State Treasurer
Unclaimed / Escheats Division
325 North Salisbury Street
Raleigh, NC 27603-1385
Phone: 919-508-1000
Fax: 919-508-5181

NORTH DAKOTA

State Land Department
Unclaimed Property Division
P.O. Box 5523
Bismarck, ND 58506-5523
Phone: 701-328-2800
Fax: 701-328-3650

NEBRASKA

Unclaimed Property Division
P.O. Box 94788
Lincoln, NE 68509
Phone: 402-471-2455
Fax: 402-471-4390

NEW HAMPSHIRE

Treasury Department
Unclaimed Property Division
25 Capitol Street, Room 205
Concord, NH 03301
Phone: 603-271-2649
Fax: 603-271-2730

NEW JERSEY

Department of the Treasury
Unclaimed Property
P.O. Box 214
Trenton, NJ 08695-0214
Phone: 609-292-9200
Fax: 609-984-0593

NEW MEXICO

Taxation & Revenue Department
Unclaimed Property Division
P.O. Box 25123
Santa Fe, NM 87504-5123
Phone: 505-476-1774
Fax: 505-827-1759

NEVADA

Office of the State Treasurer
Unclaimed Property Division
555 East Washington Avenue, Suite 4200
Las Vegas, NV 89101-1070
Phone: 702-486-4140
Fax: 702-486-4177

NEW YORK

State Comptroller
New York State Office of Unclaimed Funds
110 State Street, 8th Floor
Albany, NY 12236
Phone: 518-270-2200
Fax: 518-473-2177

OHIO

Department of Commerce
Division of Unclaimed Funds
77 South High Street, 20th Floor
Columbus, OH 43266-0545
Phone: 614-466-4433
Fax: 614-752-5078

OKLAHOMA

Oklahoma State Treasurer's Office
Unclaimed Property Division
4545 North Lincoln Boulevard, Suite 106
Oklahoma City, OK 73105-3413
Phone: 405-521-4273
Fax: 405-521-2146

OREGON

Department of State Lands - Unclaimed Property
Division
775 Summer Street NE, Suite 100
Salem, OR 97301-1279
Phone: 503-378-3805
Fax: 503-378-4844

PENNSYLVANIA

State Treasurer
Unclaimed Property Bureau
P.O. Box 1837
Harrisburg, PA 17105-1837
Phone: 800-379-3999

PUERTO RICO

Office of the Commissioner of Financial
Institutions
Unclaimed Property Division
P.O. Box 11855
San Juan, PR 00910-3855
Phone: 787-723-3131
Fax: 787-723-4042

RHODE ISLAND
Department of Treasury
Unclaimed Property Division
P.O. Box 1435
Providence, RI 02901-1435
Phone: 401-222-6505
Fax: 401-274-3865

SOUTH CAROLINA
Office of the State Treasurer
Unclaimed Property Division
P.O. Box 11778
Columbia, SC 29211-1778
Phone: 803-737-4771
Fax: 803-734-2668

SOUTH DAKOTA
Office of the State Treasurer
500 East Capitol Ave.
Pierre, SD 57501-5070
Phone: 605-773-3379
Fax: 605-773-3115

TENNESSEE
Treasury Department
Unclaimed Property Division
Andrew Jackson Bldg., 10th Floor
500 Deaderick Street
Nashville, TN 37243-0242
Phone: 615-741-6499
Fax: 615-734-6458

TEXAS
Texas Comptroller of Public Accounts
Unclaimed Property Division
P.O. Box 12019
Austin, TX 78711-2019
Phone: 1-800-321-2274 or 512-936-6246
Fax: 512-936-6224

U.S. VIRGIN ISLANDS
Office of the Lieutenant Governor
Division of Banking
18 Kongens Gade
St. Thomas, VI 00802
Phone: 340-774-7166
Fax: 809-774-9458

UTAH
State Treasurer's Office
Unclaimed Property Division
341 South Main Street, 5th Floor
Salt Lake City, UT 84111
Phone: 801-320-5360 or 888-217-1203
Fax: 801-533-4096

VIRGINIA
Department of Treasury
Unclaimed Property Division
P.O. Box 2478
Richmond, VA 23218-2478
Phone: 800-468-1088 or 804-225-2393
Fax: 804-786-4653

VERMONT
State Treasurer's Office
Unclaimed Property Division
133 State Street
Montpelier, VT 05633-0001
Phone: 802-828-2407
Fax: 802-828-2772

WASHINGTON
Department of Revenue
Unclaimed Property Section
P.O. Box 47489
Olympia, WA 98504-7489
Phone: 800-435-2429 or 360-705-6706
Fax: 360-586-2163

WISCONSIN
State Treasurer's Office
Unclaimed Property Division
P.O. Box 2114
Madison, WI 53701-2114
Phone: 608-267-7977
Fax: 608-261-6799

WEST VIRGINIA
Office of State Treasurer
One Players Club Drive
Charleston, WV 25311
Phone: 800-642-8687
Fax: 304-558-4835

WYOMING
Office of the State Treasurer
Unclaimed Property Division
2515 Warren Avenue, Suite 502
Cheyenne, WY 82002
Phone: 307-777-5590
Fax: 307-777-5430

25 Compliance Issues and Regulations

SARBANES-OXLEY ACT OF 2002

Overview

There is no doubt that the Enron fiasco led to the ultimate passage of the Sarbanes-Oxley Act of 2002. Bala G. Dharan, the J. Howard Creekmore Professor of Accounting at the Jesse H. Jones Graduate School of Management, Rice University, Houston says that "[T]he scandals have become popular 'case studies' for class use in courses such as accounting, auditing, corporate finance, investment banking, business strategy, ethics, and so on." *(ENRON, Corporate Fiascos and Their Implications* by Nancy B. Rapoport and Bala G. Dhaban. Published by Foundation Press, 2004.)

There also is no doubt that since the Enron scandal broke, there is more interest in accounting practices by financial executives and the lay public as well than there ever has been in the past. A recent article from the *Los Angeles Times* is excerpted here just to provide the flavor for what is piquing everyone's interest:

> Michael Eisner and Martha Stewart may have assured that more investors this spring will do something that usually bores them: actually read their companies' proxy statements—and then vote their shares with interest rather than with resignation, or not at all.
>
> The dramatic finish to Walt Disney Co.'s annual shareholder meeting last week, which saw Chief Executive Eisner rebuffed by the holders of 43 percent of the shares voted in his re-election bid as a director, is raising hopes among corporate governance reformers that they're nearing a critical mass of sorts.
>
> The Disney and Stewart cases are energizing those who believe that shareholders, as the suppliers of capital to the capitalist system, must be a louder voice for corporate change on issues including executive compensation, transparent accounting, board independence and basic honesty in business.
>
> Still, the push for greater corporate accountability has been gaining steam for the last two years. The collapse of fraud-ridden Enron Corp. led to the federal Sarbanes-Oxley Act in 2002, which boosted financial disclosure requirements and penalties for executive wrongdoing.
>
> That was followed last year by rule changes at the New York Stock Exchange and the NASDAQ Stock Market requiring that listed companies show that a majority of their directors are independent of management—an attempt to lessen the odds that any CEO could wield imperial power over his board and his company.
>
> For the average investor, all of this ought to raise two main questions: First, can shareholder activism produce meaningful results—in other words, is it worth the effort? And second, is there a danger that activism could get carried away and hamper honest company managers. ["Scandals are Rousing Investors," by Tom Petruno, *Los Angeles Times*, March 8, 2004.]

Definitions Used in the Sarbanes-Oxley Act of 2002

In order to best understand the Sarbanes-Oxley Act, some of the more pertinent definitions are included below:

Audit—An examination of the financial statements of any issuer by an independent public accounting firm in accordance with the rules of the Board or the Commission, for the purpose of expressing an opinion on such statements.

Audit Committee—A committee (or equivalent body) established by and amongst the board of directors of an issuer for the purpose of overseeing the accounting and financial reporting processes of the issuer and audits of the financial statements of the issue; and, if no such committee exists with respect to an issuer, the entire board of directors of the issuer.

Audit Report—A document or other record prepared following an audit performed for purposes of compliance by an issuer with the requirements of the securities law, and in which a public accounting firm either: (1) sets forth the opinion of that firm regarding a financial statement, report, or other documents; or (2) asserts that no such opinion can be expressed.

Board—The Public Company Accounting Oversight Board. This Board will be discussed more fully below.

Commission—The Securities and Exchange Commission.

Issuer—An entity whose securities are registered under section 12 of the Securities Exchange Act of 1934, or that is required to file reports under section 15(d) of the Securities Exchange Act of 1934, or that files or has filed a registration statement that has not yet become effective under the Securities Act of 1933, and that it has not withdrawn. Generally speaking, an "issuer" is a public company.

Non-Audit Services—Any professional services provided to an issuer by a registered public accounting firm, other than those provided to an issuer in connection with an audit or a review of the financial statements of an issuer.

Person Associated with a Public Accounting Firm—Any individual proprietor, partner, shareholder, principal, accountant, or other professional employee of a public accounting firm, or any other independent contractor or entity that, in connection with the preparation or issuance of any audit report: (1) shares in the profits or receives compensation in any other form from that firm; or (2) participates as an agent or otherwise on behalf of such accounting firm in any activity of that firm.

Professional Standards—(1) Accounting principles that are established by the standard setting body described in the Securities Act of 1933, or the Securities Exchange Act of 1934 and relevant to audit reports for particular issuers, or dealt within the quality control system of a particular registered public account firm; and

(2) Auditing standards, standards for attestation engagements, quality control policies and procedures, ethical and competency standards, and independence standards that the Board of Commission determines (a) relate to the preparation or issuance of audit reports for issuers; and (b) are established or adopted by the Board under section 103(a), or are promulgated as rules of the Commission.

Public Accounting Firm—A proprietorship, partnership, incorporated association, corporation, limited liability company, limited liability partnership, or other legal entity that is engaged in the practice of public accounting or preparing or issuing audit reports; and to the extent so designated by the rules of the Board, any associated person of any of these described entities.

Registered Public Accounting Firm—A public accounting firm registered with the Board in accordance with the Sarbanes-Oxley Act.

Security—Same as in section 3(a) of the Securities Exchange Act of 1934.

State—Any State of the United States, the District of Columbia, Puerto Rico, the Virgin Islands, or any other territory or possession of the United States.

Title I: Public Company Accounting Oversight Board

Section 101 provides for the establishment of a Public Company Accounting Oversight Board (the "Board") which is meant to be the watchdog for public companies. The intended result is informative, accurate and independent audit reports.

Section 101(c) details the duties of this Board to include:

1. Register public accounting firms that prepare audit reports for issuers
2. Establish by rule or otherwise auditing, quality control, ethics, independence and other standards relating to the preparation of audit reports for issuers
3. Conduct inspections, investigations and disciplinary proceedings of registered public accounting firms and associated persons where necessary
4. Perform such other duties or functions as appropriate to promote high professional standards among, and improve the quality of audit services offered by registered public accounting firms
5. Enforce compliance with the Sarbanes-Oxley Act

Section 101(e) sets the membership of this Board at five members, only two of whom shall be or shall have been certified public accountants.

Each member of the Board shall serve on a full-time basis and may not, concurrent with service on the Board, be employed by any other person or engage in any other professional or business activity. In addition, no member of the Board may share profits or receive payments from a public account firm (except retirement payments, under strict conditions).

Section 103 directs the Board to establish auditing and related attestation standards, quality control standards, and ethics standards to be used by registered public accounting firms in the preparation and issuance of audit reports. This section holds specific mandates that the auditing standards to be adopted must include requirements for each public accounting firm to:

1. Prepare and maintain all work papers, etc. for not less than seven years
2. Provide a concurring or second partner review of each audit report
3. Describe in each audit report the scope of the auditor's testing of the internal control structure and procedures of the issuer, as required by section 404(b)

This section holds specific mandates that the quality control standards to be adopted must include requirements for each public accounting firm relating to:

1. Monitoring of professional ethics and independence from issues
2. Consultation within such firm on accounting and auditing questions
3. Supervision of audit work
4. Hiring, professional development and advancement of personnel
5. Acceptance and continuation of engagements
6. Internal inspection

Section 104 directs the Board to conduct continuing inspections of registered public accounting firms and associated persons of those firms to insure compliance with the mandates of the Sarbanes-Oxley Act.

Section 105 directs the Board to establish fair procedures for the investigation and disciplining of registered public accounting firms and associated persons of such firms. Included in this section are provisions for sanctions and monetary fines.

Section 106 mandates that any foreign public accounting firm that prepares or furnishes an audit report with respect to any issuer is likewise subject to the provisions of the Sarbanes-Oxley Act. The Board may also determine that a foreign public accounting firm that does not issue audit reports nonetheless plays such a substantial role in the preparation and furnishing of such reports for particular issues, that it is necessary or appropriate that such firm should be treated as a public accounting firm for purposes of registration under, and oversight by, the Board.

Section 107 provides that the Commission shall have oversight of the Board and sets forth the provisions for monitoring, disciplining, sanctioning, etc.

Section 108 provides for the recognition of Accounting Standards. "Generally accepted" accounting principles are those established by a standard setting body (that the Commission determines is capable of improving the accuracy and effectiveness of financial reporting and the protection of investors under the securities laws) and that standard setting body:

1. Is organized as a private entity
2. Has, for administrative and operational purposes, a board of trustees or equivalent body serving in the public interest
3. Is funded as provided in the Sarbanes-Oxley Act
4. Has adopted procedures to ensure prompt consideration of changes to accounting principles necessary to reflect emerging accounting issues and changing business practices
5. Considers, in adopting accounting principles, the need to keep standards current in order to reflect changes in the business environment, the extent to which international convergence on high-quality accounting standards is necessary or appropriate in the public interest and for the protection of investors

Title II: Auditor Independence

Section 201 prohibits any registered public accounting firm (and any person associated with that firm) to provide any non-audit related services, including:

1. Bookkeeping or other services related to the accounting records financial statements of the audit client
2. Financial information systems design and implementation
3. Appraisal or valuation services, fairness opinions, or contribution-in-kind reports
4. Actuarial services
5. Internal audit outsourcing services
6. Management functions or human resources
7. Broker or dealer, investment adviser, or investment banking services
8. Legal services and expert services unrelated to the audit
9. Any other service that the Board determines, by regulation is impermissible

Section 202 requires that all auditing services and non-audit services, other than minor services shall be pre-approved by the audit committee of the issuer.

Section 203 limits the length of time when one auditor may be the lead responsible auditor for a particular issuer. This section provides that "It shall be unlawful for a registered public accounting firm to provide audit services to an issuer if the lead (or coordinating) audit partner (having primary responsibility for the audit), or the audit partner responsible for reviewing the audit, has performed audit services for that issuer in each of the five previous fiscal years of that issuer."

Section 204 requires the registered public accounting firm to timely report to the audit committee of the issuer:

1. All critical accounting policies and practices to be used
2. All alternative treatments of financial information within generally accepted accounting principles that have been discussed with management officials of the issuer, ramifications of the use of such alternative disclosures and treatments, and the treatment preferred by the registered public accounting firm
3. Other material written communications between the registered public accounting firm and the management of the issuer, such as any management letter or schedule of unadjusted differences

Section 206 prohibits any registered public accounting firm from performing any audit service if the CEO, controller, CFO, chief accounting officer, or any equivalent person was employed by that registered independent public accounting firm and participated in any audit capacity during the one-year period prior to the initiation of the audit.

Title III: Corporate Responsibility

The purpose of this Title is to place the onus for proper audit procedures and financial reporting squarely on the shoulders of the principal executive officer or officers and the principal financial officer or officers or other persons performing the duties normally performed by such officers. Each issuer must have an audit committee which shall be directly responsible for the appointment, compensation, and oversight of the work of any registered public accounting firm employed by that issuer for the purpose of preparing or issuing an audit report or related work, and each such registered public accounting firm shall report directly to the audit committee.

Section 301(3) mandates the independence of each member of the audit committee and states: (1) each member of the audit committee of the issuer shall be a member of the board of directors of the issuer, and shall otherwise be independent, and (2) in order to be considered to be independent for purposes of this paragraph, a member of an audit committee of an issuer may not, other than in his or her capacity as a member of the audit committee, the board of directors, or any other board committee (a) accept any consulting, advisory, or other compensatory fee from the issuer; or (b) be an affiliated person of the issuer or any subsidiary thereof.

Section 302 provides, for each company filing periodic reports, the principal executive officer or officers and the principal financial officer or officers, or persons performing similar functions, must certify in each annual or quarterly report that:

1. The signing officer has reviewed the report
2. Based on the officer's knowledge, the report does not contain any untrue statement of a material fact or omit to state a material fact necessary in order to make the statements made, in light of the circumstances under which such statements were made, not misleading
3. Based on such officer's knowledge, the financial statements, and other financial information included in the report, fairly present in all material respects

the financial condition and results of operations of the issuer as of, and for, the periods presented in the report

4. The signing officers: (a) are responsible for establishing and maintaining internal controls; (b) have designed such internal controls to ensure that material information relating to the issuer and its consolidated subsidiaries is made known to such officers by others within those entities, particularly during the period in which the periodic reports are being prepared; (c) have evaluated the effectiveness of the issuer's internal controls as of a date within 90 days prior to the report; and (d) have presented in the report their conclusions about the effectiveness of their internal controls based on their evaluation as of that date

5. The signing officers have disclosed to the issuer's auditors and the audit committee of the board of directors (or persons fulfilling the equivalent function): (a) all significant deficiencies in the design or operation of internal controls which could adversely affect the issuer's ability to record, process, summarize and report financial data and have identified for the issuer's auditors any material weaknesses in internal controls; and (b) any fraud, whether or not material, that involves management or other employees who have a significant role in the issuer's internal controls

6. The signing officers have indicated in the report whether or not there were significant changes in internal controls or in other facts that could significantly affect internal controls subsequent to the date of their evaluation, including any corrective actions with regard to significant deficiencies and material weaknesses

Section 302 is likely the most important section of Sarbanes-Oxley.

Section 303 prohibits any attempt to fraudulently influence, coerce, manipulate, or mislead any independent public or certified accountant engaged in the performance of an audit of the financial statements of that issuer for the purpose of rendering such financial statements materially misleading.

Section 304 provides that if there is material noncompliance of the issuer with any financial reporting requirement that therefore requires the preparation of an accounting restatement, the chief executive officer and chief financial officer shall reimburse the issuer for (1) any bonus or other incentive-based or equity-based compensation received by that person from the issuer during the 12-month period following the first public issuance or filing of the financial document embodying such financial reporting requirement; and (2) any profits realized from the sale of securities of the issuer during that 12-month period.

Title IV: Enhanced Financial Disclosures

Section 401 requires that each financial report that contains financial statements to be prepared in accordance with generally accepted accounting principles and reflect all material correcting adjustments that have been identified by a registered public accounting firm. This title focuses substantially on "off-balance sheet transactions."

Section 401(j) requires disclosure of all material off-balance sheet transactions, arrangements, obligations (including contingent obligations) and other relationships of the issuer with unconsolidated entities or other persons, that may have a material current or future effect on financial conditions, changes in financial conditions, results of operations, liquidity, capital expenditures, capital resources, or significant components of revenues or expenses. The Sarbanes-Oxley Act provided that the Commission would issue final rules that pro forma financial information included in any periodic or other report, or in any public disclosure or press or other release must be presented so that there is no untrue statement of a material fact or omission of a material fact which would make the pro forma financial information misleading, and the pro forma financial information is reconciled with the financial condition and results of operations of the issuer under generally accepted accounting principles.

Effective April 7, 2003, the Commission issued its final rule regarding off-balance sheet transactions which, summary requires:

> As directed by new Section 13(j) of the Securities Exchange Act of 1934, added by Section 401(a) of the Sarbanes-Oxley Act of 2002, we are adopting amendments to our rules to require disclosure of off-balance sheet arrangements. The amendments require a registrant to provide an explanation of its off-balance sheet arrangements in a separately captioned subsection of the "Management's Discussion and Analysis" ("MD&A") section of a registrant's disclosure documents. The amendments also require registrants (other than small business issuers) to provide an overview of certain known contractual obligations in a tabular format.

Section 403 requires the disclosure by every person who is directly or indirectly the beneficial owner of more than 10 percent of any class of any equity security (other than an exempted security) which is registered pursuant to section 12, or who is a director or an officer of the issuer of such security to file registration statements with the Commission.

Section 404 requires each annual report of an issuer to contain an "internal control report", which shall: (1) state the responsibility of management for establishing and maintaining an adequate internal control structure and procedures for financial reporting; and (2) contain an assessment, as of the end of the issuer's fiscal year, of the effectiveness of the internal control structure and procedures of the issuer for financial reporting. Each issuer's auditor shall attest to, and report on, the assessment made by the management of the issuer. An attestation made under this section shall be in accordance with standards for attestation engagements issued or adopted by the Board. An attestation engagement shall not be the subject of a separate engagement.

Title V: Analyst Conflicts of Interest

Section 501 provides for an amendment to the Securities Exchange Act of 1934 to include rules designed to:

1. Foster greater public confidence in securities research, and to protect the objectivity and independence of security analysts
2. Define periods during which brokers or dealers who have participated, or are to participate, in a public offering of securities as underwriters or dealers should not publish or otherwise distribute research reports relating to such securities or to the issuer of such securities
3. Establish structural and institutional safeguards within registered brokers or dealers to assure that securities analysts are separated by appropriate informational partitions with the firm from the review, pressure, or oversight of those

whose involvement in investment banking activities might potentially bias their judgment or supervision

This section further provides for rules requiring each securities analyst to disclose any conflicts of interest that are known or should have been known by the securities analyst at the time of any public appearance or date of distribution of its report. Such conflicts of interest may include:

1. The extent to which the securities analyst has debt or equity investments in the issuer that is the subject of the appearance or research report
2. Whether any compensation has been received by the registered broker or dealer, or any affiliate thereof, including the securities analyst, from the issuer that it's the subject of the appearance or research report
3. Whether an issuer, the securities of which are recommended in the appearance or research report, currently is, or during the one-year period preceding the date of the appearance or date of distribution of the report has been, a client of the registered broker or dealer
4. Whether the securities analyst received compensation with respect to a research report

Title VI: Commission Resources and Authority

Section 601 amends the Securities Exchange Act with respect to authorization of appropriations to enable the Commission to carry out its duties and responsibilities.

Section 602 governs appearance and practice before the Commission.

Section 603 empowers the Federal Court to prohibit persons from participating in an offering of Penny Stock.

Section 604 governs the qualification, suspension or barring of any person to be associated with a broker or dealer.

Title VII: Studies and Reports

Section 701 directs the Comptroller General of the United States to conduct a study to, among other things, identify the factors which have lead to the consolidation of public accounting firms since 1989, the present and future impact of this consolidation on capital formation and securities markets, both domestic and international, and solutions to any problems determined by such consolidation.

Section 702 provides for a study and report regarding credit rating agencies.

Section 703 provides for a study and report on violators and violations among securities professionals who have been found to have aided and abetted a violation of the Federal securities laws, and who have been found to have been primary violators of the Federal securities laws. This study is based upon information from January 1, 1998 to December 2001.

Section 704 directs a review and analysis of all enforcement actions by the Commission involving violations of reporting requirements imposed under the securities laws.

Section 705 directs a study on whether investment banks and financial advisers assisted public companies in manipulating their earnings and obfuscating their true financial condition.

Title VIII: Corporate and Criminal Fraud Accountability

This title governs the criminal penalties for the destruction, alteration, or falsification of records in Federal investigations and bankruptcy.

Section 802 amends title 18 of the United States Code by adding at its end "Whoever knowingly alters, destroys, mutilates, conceals, covers up, falsifies, or makes a false entry in any record, document, or tangible object with the intent to impede, obstruct, or influence the investigation or proper administration of any matter within the jurisdiction of any department or agency of the United States or any case filed under title 11, or in relation to or contemplation of any such matter or case, shall be fined under this title, imprisoned not more than 20 years, or both."

Section 803 provides that debts incurred in violation of securities fraud laws are nondischargeable.

Section 804 sets forth the statute of limitations for securities fraud actions is two years after the discovery of the facts constituting the violation, or five years after such violation.

Section 805 provides for the review and revision of federal sentencing guidelines for obstruction of justice and extensive criminal fraud.

Section 806 is commonly known as the "whistle blower" section. This section protects employees of publicly traded companies who provide evidence of fraud. This section specifically states that no issuer (or any of its officers, employees, contractors, subcontractors, or agents) may discharge, demote, suspend, threaten, harass or in any other manner discriminate against an employee in the terms and conditions of employment because of any lawful act done by the employee:

1. To provide information, cause information to be provided, or otherwise assist in an investigation regarding any conduct which the employee reasonably believes constitutes a violation of…any rule or regulation of the Commission, or any provision of federal law relating to fraud against shareholders, when the information or assistance is provided to or the investigation is conducted by:
   (A) a federal regulatory or law enforcement agency;
   (B) any Member of Congress or any committee of Congress; or
   (C) a person with supervisory authority over the employee (or such other person working for the employer who has the authority to investigate, discover, or terminate misconduct; or
2. To file, cause to be filed, testify, participate in, or otherwise assist in a proceeding filed or about to be filed (with any knowledge of the employer) relating to any alleged violation of…any rule or regulation of the Commission, or any provision of federal law relating to fraud against shareholders

Section 807 provides for the criminal penalties for defrauding shareholders of publicly traded companies.

Title IX: White-Collar Crime Penalty Enhancements

The majority of this title provides amendments to existing statutes and the inclusion of additional statutes relating to penalties for attempts or conspiracy to commit criminal fraud, mail fraud, wire fraud, and violations of the Employee Retirement Income Security Act of 1974. In addition Section 905 amends the sentencing guidelines relating to certain white-collar offenses.

Section 906 is the companion to Title III, Section 302. Section 906 amends title 18 of the United States Code so that there are criminal penalties for failure of corporate officers to certify financial reports. This section (as with Section 302) requires that each periodic report containing financial statements filed by an issuer…shall be accompanied by a written statement by the chief executive officer and chief financial officer (or equivalent thereof) of the issuer that certifies that the periodic report containing the financial statement is fully compliant and that the information contained therein fairly presents, in all material respects, the financial condition and results of operations of the issue. This section further provides criminal penalties for whoever: (1) certifies any statement of this section knowing that the periodic report accompanying the statement does not comport with all the requirements shall be fined not more than $1,000,000 or imprisoned not more than 10 years, or both; or (2) willfully certifies any statement knowing that the periodic report accompanying the statement does not comport with all the requirements set forth in this section shall be fined not more than $5,000,000, or imprisoned not more than 20 years, or both.

Title X: Corporate Tax Returns

This title simply states that "It is the sense of the Senate that the Federal income tax return of a corporation should be signed by the chief executive officer of such corporation.

Title XI: Corporate Fraud Accountability

Section 1102 amends section 1512 of title 18 of the United States Code by adding that whoever corruptly alters, destroys, mutilates, or conceals a record, document, or other object, or attempts to do so, with the intent to impair the object's integrity or availability for use in an official proceeding; or otherwise obstructs, influences, or impedes any official proceeding, or attempts to do so, shall be fined under this title or imprisoned not more than 20 years, or both.

Section 1103 authorizes the Commission to petition a federal district court for a temporary order requiring an issuer to escrow, subject to court supervision, any extraordinary payments into an interest-bearing account for 45 days while an investigation is ongoing. Notice and an opportunity for a hearing will be given to the issuer unless the court determines that such notice and hearing prior to the entry of a temporary order would be impracticable or contrary to the public interest.

Section 1104 issued a request to the United States Sentencing Commission to review the sentencing guidelines for securities and accounting fraud and related offenses and to report to Congress thereon.

Section 1105 authorizes the Commission to prohibit persons from serving as officers or directors of any issuer if the conduct of that person demonstrates unfitness to serve as such officer or director.

Section 1106 increases the criminal penalties under the Securities Exchange Act of 1934.

Section 1107 amends section 1513 of title 18 of the United States Code to provide that whoever knowingly, with the intent to retaliate, takes any action harmful to any person, including interference with the lawful employment or livelihood of any person, for providing to a law enforcement officer any truthful, information relating to the commission or possible commission of any Federal offense, shall be fined under this title or imprisoned not more than 10 years or both.

BUILDING UPON SECTION 404 COMPLIANCE: MOVING BEYOND THE FIRST TWO YEARS[1]

First-year compliance with Sections 302 and 404 of the Sarbanes-Oxley Act of 2002 (SOA) has commanded the attention of CEOs and CFOs (the "certifying officers"). Most U.S. accelerated filers have already completed the "first time through" compliance process and continue the ongoing annual compliance with these SOA sections. Many of these companies are currently focused on second year compliance. As they do so, these companies could face an even more challenging environment in future years for the following reasons:

- Internal control reporting is an open display of management's commitment to quality financial reporting. Investors expect more transparency into the financial reporting process than ever before.
- Many companies have work to do with respect to improving the quality and sustainability of their business and accounting processes and underlying controls. Continued reliance by management on ad hoc, manual processes that foster significant rework will result in increased financial reporting risk during times of change.
- Questions on internal controls from analysts, stockholders and underwriters are fair game. Management can expect to spend more time preparing for these discussions, because representations about internal control will be regarded as much more than implied promises. In effect, they place the company's reputation on the line.
- With the first-year honeymoon over, the jury is out regarding the impact of disclosing material weaknesses in future years. Will an unfavorable auditor opinion have significant negative share price implications given investors' heightened interest in accounting transparency and corporate governance? Will such developments feed class action suits in the event of financial restatements? Only time will tell.
- The call to reduce the cost of compliance is deafening. Developing an efficient compliance process often requires structural improvements in policies, processes, people and systems. For many companies, recognizing the nature of the transition from Year One to an ongoing process in future years is the key to controlling costs. Making this "project to process" transition happen is not possible without some planning and investment.

These emerging dynamics raise many questions about preparing for the future. If the effectiveness of an organization's internal control over financial reporting (ICFR) is questioned, certifying officers should be able to make a convincing case that they did everything they could do to improve or advance the maturity of key business processes, the financial reporting process and the compliance process. Evidence of their personal involvement and commitment to the process will be very important in articulating how they discharged their responsibilities. The suggestions provided here will help make that case.

Most importantly, some companies are making the mistake of delegating responsibility to streamlining the compliance effort to middle management with a mandate to reduce costs. The opportunity is much more than just streamlining the compliance

---

[1] Reprinted, with changes, from *The Bulletin*, Vol. 1, Issue 12, by permission of Protiviti, an internal audit and risk consulting firm. *The Bulletin* is a periodic newsletter from Protiviti focusing on key corporate governance and risk management issues. Copyright 2004 by Protiviti.

effort. The risk is that companies will design an ongoing compliance process around a high-cost internal control structure. That approach will not achieve the results most executives want. The answer is to transition "project to process" with the intent to add value to SOA compliance while improving sustainability.

To begin, a brief review of recent history is appropriate to pick up on some lessons learned.

Lessons Learned from First Adopters

First-year compliance with Section 404 involved a significant amount of work for most companies. Section 404 requires companies and their auditors to evaluate the effectiveness of their ICFR. The first-year costs of Section 404 compliance were significant, ranging from .06 percent of revenues for companies with revenues in excess of $10 billion to 2.65 percent of revenues for companies with revenues of under $100 million. The results indicated that just over 12 percent of first adopters reported material weaknesses, with an impact on shareholder value of generally less than three percent. About 70 percent of the material weaknesses were related to financial accounting issues, such as accounting policies and practices (22 percent), lease accounting (15 percent), tax accounting (9 percent) and revenue recognition (6 percent). Another 14 percent of the issues pertained to personnel matters relating to poor segregation of duties, inadequate staffing, lack of competence in a specific GAAP-reporting area or other related training or supervision problems. The remaining companies disclosing material weaknesses reported issues relating to their IT controls, the control environment or other matters.

According to one study, 9 of 10 CFOs believe the costs of Section 404 compliance exceed the benefits. Many companies reported their personnel were exhausted from the demands of Section 404 compliance. Some of these companies are using the second year of compliance to catch up on systems implementations, merger integration activities and other important things that were deferred to accommodate the allocation of management attention and resources to Section 404 compliance during the first year. Nearly every company has a "spend hangover" from Year One compliance and, as a result, there is a resolve to reduce compliance costs.

Making things up as you go along is rarely a good way to do business. However, that is how many companies were forced to approach their first year of compliance with Section 404. Lack of planning, understaffing and overwork were the result. The Year One compliance activity was largely ad hoc, chaotic and messy—for everyone. Fire drills were the norm. Estimates to complete the work were grossly underestimated throughout the project. Significant systems upgrades and accounting consolidations were often delayed. Resource shortages were acute. Management and auditors were often at odds.

First-year Section 404 compliance was not a model of efficiency. Some first-year adopters simply waited too long to begin. It also took time for the standards-setters to issue guidance to the outside auditors, which meant the process began with many indicating they did not understand exactly what was required. Management had no specific guidance directed to them, leaving them relying on standards written for the auditors and subject to their auditor's interpretation of those standards. Interpretations sometimes differed among and even within the accounting firms, further complicating the environment. Many companies reported significant scope creep as a result. While few disagreed with the overall objectives of SOA, many questioned the cost of complying with Section 404. The debate often heard centers on whether the evaluation process is sufficiently top-down and risk-based and whether the nature, timing and extent of testing ICFR is appropriate.

Year One Lessons Are Just the Beginning

Everyone wants to reduce compliance costs. In addition, everyone wants to discontinue the ad hoc, fire drill mode of Year One, and avoid the hard lessons around Section 404 compliance learned by many companies in their first year. Unfortunately, many of these same lessons will probably be learned again during Year Two. There are several reasons why:

- Most first adopters deferred planning for Year Two compliance until after Year One compliance activities were completed.
- For many first-year adopters, Year One compliance consumed most of the first quarter of Year Two.
- Year One Section 404 compliance was so intensive, responsible personnel insisted on taking a well-deserved break from Section 404 compliance after completing their assignments.
- Assigning Section 404 compliance ownership and budget responsibility has been difficult for some companies.
- Many companies waited for Washington to act following the Securities and Exchange Commission's (SEC) April 2005 roundtable.
- Accounting firms were reluctant to modify their policies and methodologies until the Public Company Accounting Oversight Board (PCAOB) completed and reported on its inspections of the firms' 2004 audits.

As a result, sufficient planning did not happen in advance of Year Two for many accelerated filers. Therefore, Year Two is shaping up to be a year of incremental improvement for many companies as they take a hard look at (1) the number of controls they classified last year as "key controls," (2) their testing scopes and (3) specific testing tools and techniques. This self-examination should increase the efficiency and reduce the cost of testing. However, it will not drive substantive improvements in the financial reporting process and in the underlying control environment. Nor will it drive long-term sustainable changes in the Section 404 compliance process.

This means Year Two could be another year of high costs, strained staffs, excessive emphasis on testing manual controls, and more angst between management and the auditors. And many companies are at risk of vital planning not happening in advance of Year Three, because time is running out. Unless executives start thinking longer term, they and their organizations will repeat, yet again, these expensive lessons.

The difficulty companies are having breaking out of the chains of reaction points out the importance of planning, ideally during the annual budget cycle, so that expectations and appropriate action steps can be built into the business plan. The importance of early planning cannot be overstated, because it is never too early to begin the process.

The points below provide insights as to what companies should be thinking about going forward.

"Tone at the Top" Is Where It All Starts

"Tone at the top" captures the essence of where a commitment to responsible business behavior begins. Through their steady, unrelenting commitment to reliable financial reporting, the certifying officers set the tone that can strengthen or undermine the effectiveness of company accounting policies, disclosure processes and ICFR. More importantly, the tone the certifying officers set helps to influence behavior that may not be subject to even the most elaborate controls and reporting systems.

Reinforce Process Owner Accountability with a Self-Assessment Process

When you want reasonable assurance that something important is happening, do you take someone's word for it that "things are okay" or do you design and implement a management process to make sure it happens? Process owners should be held accountable for the effective functioning of internal controls for which they are responsible. Through an effective self-assessment process, that accountability is reinforced by requiring process owners to respond to specific questions regarding specific controls for which they are responsible, creating a transparent "chain of accountability" for ICFR. The Section 404 compliance process lays the foundation for an effective self-assessment process by providing insights as to the key controls and the owners of those controls.

The Public Company Accounting Oversight Board (PCAOB) has taken the position that company-level controls include "controls to monitor other controls, including…self-assessment programs." Because "process owners" are the men and women closest to the critical control points within the organization, they are best positioned to know what's working and what isn't, when changes are occurring in the process, and what's the impact of systems and other pervasive changes on the controls within the process. Process owners both execute controls and supervise and monitor the owners of controls, and are ultimately responsible for assessing the design and the performance of controls.

What does this mean to certifying officers? If you don't have a self-assessment process, implement one. If you have a self-assessment process already in place, improve it. Make it more robust by linking it to the critical controls identified by the Section 404 compliance process and including it as an integral part of the disclosure process and continuous monitoring required by Section 302 reporting. Look at self-assessment as a management tool that drives the "tone at the top" down to the process owners.

Augment Disclosure Controls with an Effective Change-Recognition Process

Are you confident your disclosure controls won't grow stale over time, i.e., they become so "business as usual" no one is paying attention when something that matters happens? Is there a process for infusing the disclosure controls with new developments and risks on a timely basis? If so, how do you know it is working? These are important questions because SOA Section 302 requires disclosure of changes that materially affect, or are reasonably likely to materially affect, ICFR. The COSO Internal Control–Integrated Framework states that "risk assessment" is a component of ICFR, and provides guidance that an important aspect of assessing risk is identifying and reacting to change. A change-recognition process is not only needed, it is a requirement.

Every company needs a process for identifying environment, operating and other changes that impact the financial statements, other disclosures in public reports and the effectiveness of ICFR. Examples of changes requiring evaluation include mergers and acquisitions, divestitures, new innovative business practices, new systems, changes in personnel (including significant early retirement or personnel reduction programs), significant market declines, and changes in laws and regulations. The disclosure committee, or an equivalent group of executives, should be charged with the responsibility of monitoring change for purposes of identifying material information requiring consideration and possible disclosure.

Certifying officers need a change-recognition process that surfaces new developments and events timely for subsequent follow-up and disclosure. If there is ONE area in the future that is most likely to cause a breakdown in the disclosure process of companies which are strongly committed to reliable financial reporting, it is likely to be that the company did not timely identify the impact of change on the business, the financial statements and the required disclosures.

Implement the Appropriate Organizational Structure to Support Process Owners and Ensure Sustainability of Ongoing Compliance

The importance of (1) a strong tone at the top, (2) process owners who are accountable for the important controls, and (3) an effective change-recognition process have been discussed. While these elements are important, they provide the foundation for something else that is not only as equally important but is also a matter that companies continue to address. Certifying officers should really focus on the matter of organizational structure.

Reflecting on the thousands of hours of effort invested by companies in Year One, and in some cases, the millions spent, going forward it is unrealistic to expect process owners to shoulder the burden of Section 404 compliance by themselves. If there are significant changes, it is inconceivable how they will get the job done without support. It is imperative, therefore, that companies protect their initial year investment by supporting process owners and ensuring ongoing compliance.

The PCAOB requires management to maintain up-to-date compliance documentation to facilitate the attestation process. The good news is that the first-year compliance documentation may be rolled forward if there are no changes in policies, processes, people and systems. That said, who will keep this documentation up-to-date going forward? Who will assess the impact of changes in processes and systems, redesign controls in response to change and update the related controls documentation for changes made? Who will remediate deficiencies when necessary? Do process owners know how to do these things? Who will coach, assist and evaluate them? How will certifying officers know the job gets done? An appropriate organizational structure that facilitates compliance must provide answers to these questions, because process owners are neither auditors nor experts in documentation and remediation.

MANAGE GAPS AND OVERLAPS

An organizational structure that drives effective ICFR is predicated on a sharp delineation of roles and responsibilities. When discussing process owner accountability earlier, it was not pointed out that that the question of "ownership" is often times obscured by the "command and control" structure of most organizations because that structure has always placed strong emphasis on managing silos. For example, the "procure to pay" process is executed by the purchasing, receiving, accounts payable and treasury (cash disbursements) functions. Not only do these functions operate at different levels of the organization, there are critical interfaces or "touch points" among these functions that make the "procure to pay" process work. There must be effective controls over these interfaces, as well as owners of these controls who are accountable for their effective operation.

Certifying officers can benefit from clarifying accountability at all levels and for all key financial reporting processes within the organization. While Section 404 compliance should drive this definition, the ultimate litmus test occurs when management deploys a self-assessment process. To make self-assessment happen, every key control must have a name by it. Gaps (such as when there is no one responsible for executing a control) should be eliminated and overlaps (such as when there are multiple owners of a control) minimized. While easy to say, this kind of clarity is not easy to achieve.

Therefore, many companies face situations in which process ownership must be clarified, particularly at the interface or transition points within processes.

Because Section 404 compliance demands attention to execution, it is important to understand that the process ownership aspects of identifying processes and the controls within processes is a significant change management issue. The mere exercise of assigning responsibility can result in redrawing the scope of control responsibilities that previously existed for specific individuals. Thus, if companies remain in a project mode, it is critical that they consider carefully the transitional organizational structure over the next couple of years to facilitate process owner understanding and acceptance of the scope of their respective responsibilities. Such responsibilities include appropriately testing and self-assessing internal controls to provide assurance that they are operating effectively as designed.

Establish the Appropriate Transitional Organizational Structure

Certifying officers need an organizational structure that facilitates the sustainability of ongoing compliance with SOA Sections 302 and 404. This structure should emphasize the internal audit function, a group of risk control specialists or both. For example, assume an organization contemplates a lot of changes, or the skill sets, capacity and charter of the internal audit function are not conducive to providing the assistance that process owners need with respect to documenting controls, evaluating change, assessing controls design, testing controls operation and remediation. In such instances, certifying officers should consider creating a risk control function or engaging risk control specialists. A risk control group does not execute processes and controls. It may report to and be embedded within the entity's operations. Alternatively, it may be independent of operations, reporting to the chief financial officer, the chief compliance officer or the chief risk officer. In fact, the change management aspects of eliminating gaps and minimizing overlaps suggest a need for risk control specialists to support process owners over a 12- to 24-month period as they assume responsibility for the ongoing operation of specific controls after the first internal control report is filed. Another factor management may choose to consider is the impact on desired objectivity of the internal audit function.

If not much change is contemplated or internal audit has strong requisite process, risk and control skill sets and available capacity, the department may be expanded or redeployed and its charter aligned to provide process owners the assistance they need in lieu of a separate risk control group. If it is desired to deploy risk control specialists, such specialists may be organized as a separate division within the internal audit function, reporting to the chief audit executive, or integrated across the organization. In any event, the internal audit function should align its audit plan with whatever SOA compliance-related monitoring role management has designated for it to fulfill.

Whether embedded or independent, whether reporting to a C-level executive or housed within internal audit, risk control specialists play a vital role. Through their knowledge of risk, SOA requirements and business processes, they ensure consistent compliance enterprisewide and effectively evaluate the risk at critical interface or transition points between business functions. They recommend process innovations on a periodic basis. They facilitate the identification of metrics that will drive operational efficiency and effectiveness. In specialty areas like technology, supply chain, commodity trading and treasury, they have access to organizations with whom they may co-source personnel with expertise that is not deployed daily in most organizations. Most importantly, they give the process owners assistance from someone they respect, which is vital during the early transitional stage as process owners assume new and expanded responsibilities for controls.

In summary, three alternative organizational structures that facilitate ongoing compliance with Sections 404 and 302 have been suggested (*see* illustration on next page):

1. Traditional Internal Audit
2. Independent Risk Control Group
3. Embedded Risk Control Specialists

There are several factors certifying officers should consider as they evaluate the appropriate transitional organizational structure going forward. Following are six:

1. The need to clarify roles and responsibilities of, among others, process owners, operating unit managers and, depending on the selected structure, internal auditors and risk control specialists. As noted earlier, clarity of roles and responsibilities is essential to achieve accountability.
2. As the underlying business processes are simplified, focused and automated, there will be greater emphasis on preventive controls (versus detective controls), systems-based controls (versus manual controls) and continuous process-level monitoring. The state of maturity of the company's processes (meaning the extent to which they are defined and managed) will drive the nature of the skills needed. For example, business processes that rely heavily on automated controls will require less testing. Testing in these environments demands more emphasis on technology-related skills that are not required with respect to processes that rely on manual controls. The more efficient and effective the organization's processes, the more they will depend on preventive and automated controls. Consequently, less testing will be necessary and compliance costs will decline over time.
3. Use of continuous monitoring tools will replace manual testing and reduce substantially the need for periodic auditing. While this exercise reduces the number of hours required to perform manual testing of key controls, the real

(Continued on p. 25–19)

Alternative SOA Compliance Structures

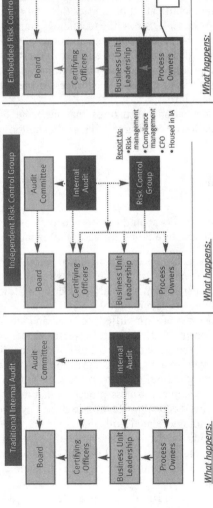

Traditional Internal Audit

Audit Committee • Internal Audit • Board • Certifying Officers • Business Unit Leadership • Process Owners

What happens:
- Internal audit tests
- Internal audit consults on control environment whenever possible

Advantages:
- Internal audit focused on financial reporting controls
- Least amount of internal change from an historical perspective (assuming a competent IA function)

Independent Risk Control Group

Audit Committee • Internal Audit • Risk Control Group • Board • Certifying Officers • Business Unit Leadership • Process Owners

Report to:
- Risk management
- Compliance management
- CFO
- Housed in IA

What happens:
- Risk control group:
  - Coaches process owners
  - Assists with remediation
  - Tests controls
  - May exist with or without an IA function
- IA independently assesses management's compliance process

Advantages:
- Consolidated team of risk specialists promotes consistency of control structure
- Maximize appearance of IA objectivity to increase external auditor reliance

Embedded Risk Control Specialists

Audit Committee • Internal Audit • Business Unit Risk Control Specialists • Board • Certifying Officers • Business Unit Leadership • Process Owners

What happens:
- Risk control specialists:
  - Are embedded within business units
  - Work directly with process owners on control environment
  - Perform testing
- IA independently assesses management's compliance process

Advantages:
- Process owners supported close to the source
- Maximize appearance of IA objectivity

(Continued from p. 25–17)

objective is cost-effective process performance, not cost-effective compliance. The comprehensive coverage of continuous process-level monitoring makes the testing process value-added because it can lead to operational improvements. It enhances the quality of self-assessments because it provides more transparency in the performance of financial reporting processes and controls. This shift from compliance to quality is what the "Project to Process" vision is all about. Evaluators must understand both the financial reporting assertions these tools address as well as how the outputs drive insights for improving operational efficiency and effectiveness.

4. The extent of change expected within the industry should be considered, e.g., regulatory, consolidation and other developments. The more change, the more help process owners will need.

5. A highly competent and objective risk control function (either within internal audit or separate) and a strong internal audit department are management tools recognized by the PCAOB as units whose work the external auditor can rely on to a greater extent than on work performed by others within the company. Going forward, this may be an important factor as companies look for ways to mitigate net audit costs while maintaining audit effectiveness.

6. The choice of using internal audit and risk control specialist(s) to advise and coach process owners and perform testing is based upon:
   - the assigned role and responsibilities of process owners;
   - the capabilities, capacity and cost of deploying process owners; and
   - the capabilities, capacity and cost of deploying internal audit.

If the needs of the organization require expansion of these skill sets, hiring all of the necessary skills may be expensive, particularly in areas of specialized skills such as IT. Therefore, co-sourcing may provide an attractive option to management.

In summary, after the intensity of the first two years of Section 404 compliance winds down, certifying officers face three realities. First, if there is a significant breakdown in ICFR, the company could receive an adverse opinion from the auditor on its internal control. Second, the entity's process owners have a business to run, and due to the day-to-day demands of executing the processes of the business, will be unable to carry the entire compliance load during periods of significant change. Third, there are change management issues that reinforce the need to support process owners, at least on a transitional basis over the next couple of years. Certifying officers need an effective organizational structure that provides them with confidence that what is supposed to be done with respect to ongoing 302 and 404 compliance is in fact being done and reduces the risk of personal exposure going forward.

Think "Project to Process"

"Project to process" is the transition from an ad hoc project, which most first adopters experienced in Year One, to a sustainable, cost-effective and value-added process over time. There are three things companies must do to make the SOA "Project to Process" transition happen:

- *Think longer term.* Companies need to understand the end game and begin the journey to get there. The "end game" consists of three elements: (1) A sustainable internal control structure, (2) clear evidence of value-add and (3) a cost-effective compliance process. Once the end game is understood, senior management must assess the organization's change readiness and begin building expectations and action items into the budget cycle and business plan. As organizations address these three elements of the end game, they will begin taking control of the compliance process and achieve superior results on the cost and value equation.

- *Make the right choice.* It is clear that no one wants to continue the game of reaction played during Year One. Everyone wants to take control of the game. The way most companies take control is through designing an effective process. However, many companies may end up designing their compliance process around the existing internal control structure. This is not the "right choice." The "right choice" is to commit to improving the quality of the internal control structure and design the compliance process around that improved structure. Therefore, companies should make the choices that improve the quality, compress the time and reduce the cost of the financial reporting processes and of the underlying internal controls. These choices reach beyond choosing to design a more repeatable, better defined and effectively managed compliance process. The design decision is obvious; however, if the decision is made around the existing internal control structure, companies are very likely to end up disappointed in the results they achieve.

- *Create value while improving sustainability.* The suggestions in this article provide a roadmap for accomplishing this task. The planning process is the key to making it happen. Management must define and execute the plan to implement near- and longer-term improvements. The action plan should prioritize the improvements and set forth the timeline for implementing them. For strategic longer-term improvements, solutions must be designed according to management's timetable, along with a communications and change management plan. An effective plan supports the alignment of policies, processes, methodologies, tools and technology, together with the resource needs and change management efforts, leading to a sustainable and cost-effective compliance process.

Other Steps Certifying Officers Should Take

Once the appropriate organizational structure to support process owners and ensure ongoing compliance is in place, certifying officers should also do the following:

- *Make sure someone is paying attention to the importance of technology.* In many companies, business processes are very dependent on the technology embedded within them for timely, comprehensive and accurate execution. The processes that initiate, authorize, record, process and report the transactions underlying financial reporting in most, if not all, companies, are accomplished with computers, programs, and other technology-related equipment and software. Many applications and systems also have controls programmed into them, and some of these programmed controls may be critical to the evaluation of ICFR. In addition, technology is also a key enabler for SOA compliance, as there is a wide range of software tools available in the marketplace, either in the form of "point solutions" or "platform solutions." Point solutions are applications designed specifically for SOA compliance. Platform solutions are software infrastructure that is designed for another purpose, such as business process automation, document management, financial management or broader compliance, and is adapted for SOA compliance.

The implication: Technology introduces unique and potentially significant risks affecting security, change management, business continuity and other vital areas. Therefore, certifying officers should ensure the appropriate personnel are considering those risks and the controls that mitigate them. In addition, companies must select the technology solution they need going forward. Depending upon such factors as the organization's size and complexity, the total number and location of individuals involved with the compliance effort, the needs around security and workflow, the existing investments in software (e.g., ERP, content management, process management or compliance software) and other factors, companies will often choose either a "compliance-driven" (short-term) approach or a "value-driven" (long-term) approach to their SOA compliance process.

- *Aggressively dispose of significant deficiencies.* Unfortunately, most material weaknesses do not get reported to management until it is too late to fix them. Simply stated, in many instances management didn't know they even existed. Furthermore, despite the fact that the PCAOB has strived to define the distinction between a significant deficiency and a material weakness, evaluating the severity of deficiencies will require much judgment in practice. As a result, reasonable men and women may differ when applying the Board's rules.

The implication: Someone needs to pay attention when significant control issues arise. Certifying officers shouldn't be surprised by what they don't know. There are four imperatives they should stress:

1. Make sure control deficiencies that could potentially be significant deficiencies or material weaknesses are identified and reported timely. For example, provide process owners and internal audit with a process for escalating potentially significant issues outside the formal reporting process to get them on the table for resolution as soon as practicable, particularly during the quarterly reporting season.

2. Fix control deficiencies that could potentially be significant deficiencies or material weaknesses on a timely basis. If unresolved deficiencies "stack up," there is a risk the external auditor could conclude the deficiencies, in the aggregate, include one or more material weaknesses in ICFR. Recognize that legal counsel may also advise external disclosure of a multitude of unresolved deficiencies to protect management.

3. Evaluate the key business processes not only to assess control design effectiveness but also to assess process maturity as a measure of sustainability. Don't stand pat with your existing processes just because they may be repeatable and may have passed the assessment test in Year One. If processes are heavily dependent on manual and detective controls and on human intervention, your internal control structure may be driving high costs and may not be sustainable during periods of change. Target such processes strategically for improvement and for increased scrutiny by internal audit or risk control specialists.

4. Finally, implement some type of program management around control deficiencies identified by process owner self-assessments, by the Section 404 compliance team, by internal audit and by external audit. This process should report the identified deficiencies by source and track progress from evaluation of the deficiency to completion of remediation or other appropriate disposition.

- *Put in place and support a strong audit committee.* An effectively functioning audit committee provides appropriate oversight with respect to external financial reporting and ICFR. From a Section 404 compliance standpoint, it is important to understand that the external auditor assesses the effectiveness of the committee's oversight role. That assessment is conducted within the broader context of the auditor's evaluation of the company's control environment and entity-level monitoring process. The board retains the overall responsibility to assess the effectiveness of the audit committee.

  The implication: Certifying officers should make sure the audit committee has the resources it needs to play the oversight role it is expected to perform. Management and the audit committee should re-evaluate the committee charter and agenda and the information reported to the committee with the objective of determining that the committee is fully responsive to the expanded requirements set forth by SOA and the applicable exchange listing requirements. A strong audit committee can provide support for diligent certifying officers if unexpected surprises occur.

- *Find the value.* When the final bill is tallied for Section 404 compliance, will the certifying officers ask where the value is? Not only should they ask for value returned just like they do for any other investment or expenditure, they should insist on it.

  The implication: There is a significant opportunity to build-in (versus inspect-in) quality, compress time and reduce costs within the organization's processes while simultaneously reducing its financial reporting risks. With improved financial reporting, companies can also augment the governance process by managing reputation and other business risks to protect and enhance enterprise value. Companies with documented processes can compare and benchmark their processes to improve efficiency, articulate clearer job descriptions, better train their people, design improved metrics, eliminate nonessentials, and simplify, focus and automate manual activities to minimize and eliminate rework.

It Could Be Your Organization

Just as your organization puts its reputation and integrity on the line through its products and services, so it does through its financial reporting. When all is said and done, certifying officers should be in a position to make a convincing case that they have done everything they can to improve or advance the maturity of the financial reporting process and reduce financial reporting risks to an acceptable level. More importantly, they should integrate compliance into existing management processes and plan for a "project to process" shift to add value and increase cost-effectiveness. The steps outlined here are an imperative for certifying officers and are summarized below in "A Call to Act—What Certifying Officers Should Do." By taking these steps, certifying officers demonstrate due care in reinforcing the responsibility and accountability of process owners and in supporting these owners in their respective roles. While companies remediate their control deficiencies with short-term solutions, they are also planning for longer-term improvement in key processes that support financial reporting. Certifying officers should waste no time in giving these and other steps their strongest consideration and in discussing their conclusions with the audit committee and the full board.

Key Questions to Ask

BOARD MEMBERS

- Have you discussed with management their specific plans for complying with SOA Sections 302 and 404 going forward, including how they will reinforce process owner accountability and provide support to the process owners?
- Is the audit committee satisfied that the existing internal control structure is sustainable given management's plans to grow and diversify the business?
- As processes are improved, new systems are implemented and other changes occur in the business, is adequate attention given to the related impact on the internal control structure and the potential disclosure implications?
- What specific steps is management taking to strengthen the tone at the top for reliable financial reporting?

MANAGEMENT

- Have you considered the appropriate structure for ensuring continued compliance with Sections 302 and 404 after Years One and Two of Section 404 compliance?
- Are you satisfied there are no critical gaps and overlaps in the ownership of your financial reporting processes and in the underlying internal controls? How do you know?
- Are you implementing a self-assessment process that engages your process owners and reinforces their accountability for effective internal control over financial reporting?
- Are process owners adequately supported in the fulfillment of their responsibilities on an ongoing basis? How do you know?
- Have you used or are you planning to use the Section 404 documentation to identify opportunities for building in (versus inspecting in) quality, eliminating rework, reducing costs and compressing time, while simultaneously reducing financial reporting risk?
- Does your internal audit function meet the external auditor's tests of competence and objectivity, as specified by PCAOB Auditing Standard No. 2, so that your organization can take advantage of the opportunity to reduce audit costs?

What Will Happen to Costs?

As companies transition from the intense project mode of the first year to an ongoing process in Years Two and Three, they should implement a compliance process that is sustainable, value-added and cost-effective. *See* the chart on the next page for a summary of the cost drivers over the first three years of Section 404 compliance.

(Continued on p. 25–25)

Year 1 Activities

Plan and Organize Project
Manage Project
Document Controls
Evaluate Design Effectiveness
Remediate Design Deficiencies
Test Operating Effectiveness
Remediate Operating Deficiencies

Issue Internal Control Report
Support Attestation Process

Year 2 Activities

Manage Process

Test Operating Effectiveness
Remediate Operating Deficiencies
Design Change-Recognition Process (1)
Evaluate Implications of Change;
  Update Documentation
Design Self-Assessment Process (1)
Execute Self-Assessment Process (1)
Implement Change Management
Improve Efficiency/Effectiveness (2)
Issue Internal Control Report
Support Attestation Process

Year 3 Activities

Manage Process

Test Operating Effectiveness
Remediate Operating Deficiencies
Execute Change-Recognition Process (1)
Evaluate Implications of Change;
  Update Documentation

Execute Self-Assessment Process (1)
Implement Change Management
Improve Efficiency/Effectiveness (2)
Issue Internal Control Report
Support Attestation Process

Notes

(1) A process created, implemented and improved during Years Two and Three.

(2) Improving quality, compressing time and reducing costs while simultaneously reducing risk through simplifying, focusing and automating manual processes and improving the mix of preventive and detective controls can result in improvements in efficiency and effectiveness that will reduce testing scopes over time.

(Continued from p. 25–23)

A Call to Act—What Certifying Officers Should Do

Certifying officers should take the following steps in preparing their organizations for moving beyond the initial year of Section 404 compliance:

- *Pay attention to "tone at the top."* It starts with your personal involvement and commitment. Overtly support a strong control environment through, among other things, the code of conduct, audit committee oversight, an effective process for handling confidential and anonymous complaints, clear policies for assigning authority and responsibility, effective human resource policies and practices, and an organizational structure and management style that is conducive to an open and transparent internal control environment. Speak out about ethics, internal control and personal integrity in company meetings. Let the organization know you won't tolerate ethical violations.
- *Reinforce responsibility and accountability through establishment of a self-assessment process.* If you already have a self-assessment process, make sure it is effective and is linked to specific business processes and critical controls. If you don't have a self-assessment process, conduct one periodically. Provide guidance to your process owners as to what is expected of them in supporting the assessments they submit. Let them know internal audit will periodically review the basis for their assessments. Engage your operating unit managers by making them privy to self-assessment results and request their participation when following-up on matters requiring remediation.
- *Implement a change-recognition process.* When certifying officers have confidence that disclosure controls and internal control over financial reporting are functioning as intended and processes are improved as necessary when changes occur in the business, they will be able to focus on the disclosure implications of change. That is where their focus should be. A formal change-recognition process is needed to identify emerging risks, issues and developments timely for action and disclosure on a quarterly basis.
- *Consider establishing a risk control specialists group to support your process owners with remediation, design changes and documentation updates during times of change and to perform testing of operating effectiveness.* Eliminate gaps and minimize overlaps in process owner accountability for internal control over financial reporting. Decide whether to (1) embed the risk control specialists within operations, or (2) establish an independent risk control function either reporting to a C-suite executive or housed within the internal audit department.
- *Define the ongoing SOA role of the internal audit department.* Focus internal audit's role on evaluating management's assessment process, performing testing in selected areas and reporting results. Define the function's role consistent with its other responsibilities (e.g., to conduct operational and compliance audits in critical risk areas), its capabilities and its available capacity.
- *Formalize a reporting and escalation process that will support management's continuing responsibilities under Section 302 and initiate timely remediation of significant deficiencies.* Management must disclose significant deficiencies and material weaknesses to the audit committee and external auditors on a timely basis. Management must also make sure a process is in place to report and esca-

late significant deficiencies and potentially significant deficiencies to the disclosure committee and to other designated management as soon as practicable.

- *Understand who is taking charge of identifying and controlling the unique technology-related risks.* Don't underestimate the importance of managing IT-related risks. The complexity of technology makes these risks more critical. Confirm that the chief information officer is continuously engaged in the process of evaluating internal control over financial reporting. Also, be sure your software solution for managing compliance satisfies your needs going forward.

- *Insist on getting value for your first-year investment.* Once the first internal control report is filed, ask your people to think "project to process" and mine the value out of the increased transparency into your business processes that the Section 404 compliance documentation provides. If you don't get results, your people aren't looking hard enough.

The above steps lay a strong foundation for ongoing compliance. Because they necessitate advance preparation, some companies must focus on these steps to ensure that appropriate expectations and action items are built into the planning and budgeting process. Effective planning will ensure that the first and second year investments will pay off in the future. (*End of reprint.*)

SAS 70 REPORTS

Service auditor reports are primarily used by service organizations, their clients and the client's auditors. A service organization is an entity (or segment of an entity) that provides services to a user organization (the client) that are part of the user organization's information system and control environment, such as processing transactions or hosting data. The client's auditors can use the Statement on Auditing Standard No. 70 (SAS 70) to gain an understanding of the internal controls in operation at the service organization. Depending on the type of report, the client's auditors may be able to consider the service organization's internal controls in planning and executing Sarbanes-Oxley 404 attestation and financial audit services for that client.

Service organizations are responsible for describing their controls and defining their control objectives. Generally, the control objectives are specific to the service organization and their customers, and a service organization may consult with their service auditor for guidance on the control objectives. However, the American Institute of Certified Public Accountants (AICPA) has released *Service Organizations, Applying SAS No. 70, as Amended* to provide the latest guidance to auditors of companies that use service organizations and service auditors that perform examinations of service organizations. The audit guide can be ordered from the AICPA's website and is listed as publication number 012772SK.

The SAS 70 audit should focus on the control environment surrounding the services an organization provides to its customers. The service auditor's report can also be customized to specifically identify the applicable data centers, operating environments and applications that are covered in the audit. For example, an organization may have many business units, but only one processes transactions or provides data processing services for its customers.

An SAS 70 audit can only performed by an independent certified public accountant (CPA) or firm. CPA firms that perform SAS 70 audits must adhere to AICPA's

Reports on the Processing of Transactions by Service Organizations, which outlines specific guidance related to planning, execution, and supervision of the audit procedures. In addition, they are required to undergo a peer review to ensure that the firm's audits are conducted in accordance with generally accepted auditing standards.

The result of a SAS 70 audit engagement is the issuance of a SAS 70 Report. The SAS 70 Report will then be provided to the service organization for distribution to their respective customers (user organizations), user auditors and other parties. The SAS 70 Report is usually distributed via hardcopy or electronically.

Report Sections

SAS 70 Reports typically include several sections:

1. Independent Service Auditor's Report
2. The Service Organization's Description of Controls
   - Overview
   - Control Environment Elements
   - Description of Computerized Systems
   - Control Objectives, Controls and User Control Considerations for each of the Controls
   - Tests of the Controls and Results of the Tests Performed (For Type II Reports)
3. Other information provided by the Service Organization or Service Auditor

Type I versus Type II

A Type I report is a report on the controls placed in operation as of a specific date. A Type II report is a report on the controls placed in operation and tests of the operating effectiveness of controls during a specified period of time. The period of time for a Type II report is generally six months or one year. Since the Type II report is an extension of the Type I report, if you chose to do a Type I report and opted to switch to Type II, the difference is the application of tests of the operating effectiveness of specific controls

Some clients have opted for a Type I report for the first year and a Type II report in subsequent years. This has the advantage of allowing you to review and improve your controls before undergoing the testing in Type II. (With Sarbanes Oxley 404 time pressures this approach is less of an option.)

SAS 70 Responsibilities

- The service organization is responsible for:
- Description of its own controls
- Features of the control environment that may affect the service provided to user organizations
- Applications and control objectives to be covered by the tests
- Other information it may provide
- The service auditor is responsible for:
- An opinion as to whether the service organization's description of its controls presents fairly those controls that have been placed in operation as of the end of the reporting period

- An opinion as to whether the described controls were suitably designed to achieve the specified control objectives
- Other information that it may provide
- For a Type II Report, the service auditor is responsible for:
- An opinion that the controls that were tested were operating with sufficient effectiveness to provide reasonable, but not absolute, assurance that the control objectives were achieved for the period under review
- Determining which controls are, in his or her judgment, necessary to achieve the control objectives and the nature, timing, and extent of the tests of the selected controls
- A description of the tests of operating effectiveness of controls and the results of those tests

The SAS 70 Audit Process

The general steps within the SAS 70 process follows the traditional audit approach but may differ based on a service organization's current control environment. A typical engagement would include:

1. On-site consultation with service organization management and involved parties to gain an understanding of the service organizations business processes, control environment and control components
2. Provide guidance to management on the adequacy of its control objectives and controls as it relates to its environments and respective industries
3. Perform on-site testing at various points in time to determine the effectiveness of the controls placed in operation and the operating effectiveness of the controls for Type II reports. Testing typically includes inquiry, inspection of documents and records, and observation of activities. The extent of testing will vary depending on the scope of the report (including type and the period covered)
4. Preparation of a draft report to be reviewed by the service organization for accuracy and completeness of the details
5. Delivery of a management letter to management for any control deficiencies uncovered during the course of the review
6. Issuance of the SAS 70 Report in hardcopy and electronic PDF format

Benefits of SAS 70

- Satisfy customer Sarbanes Oxley 404 requirements
- Satisfy customer audit requirements
- Compliance with regulatory requirements
- Satisfy contract requirements
- Documentation and testing of internal control structure
- Streamline business processes and controls

SAS 70 Terminology

User organization: An entity that has engaged a service organization for a service.
User auditor: The auditor who reports on the financial statements of the user organization.
Service organization: An entity that provides services to a user organization.

Service auditor: The auditor who reports on and tests the controls of a service organization.

Service auditor's report: An independent report issued by a service auditor over the internal control structure of a service organization.

26 U.S. District Court System Locator

Set forth in this chapter is a partial listing of the United States District Courts System as authorized by Congress 28 USC §§ 81-131. Court information from the U.S. Federal Court System has been selected to provide the information thought most pertinent to the credit professional.

The first section entitled "Access to the U.S. Courts" provides general information about U.S. Courts and cases available via the Internet, modem and telephone systems. The sources discussed are Public Access to Case Electronic Records (PACER), Case Management/Electronic Case Files (CM/ECF) and Voice Case Information System (VCIS).

The next section provides general information about the U.S. Bankruptcy and District Courts for each state and territory, including court website and e-mail addresses (if available) through which more information may be obtained. The final section provides general and contact information for the U.S. Trustee Regions. This section also provides information about the U.S. Circuit Courts of Appeals.

ACCESS TO THE U.S. COURTS

The Administrative Office of the U.S. Courts maintains the www.uscourts.gov website. This site serves as a clearinghouse for information from and about the Judicial Branch of the U.S. Government. Information on the U.S. Supreme Court, the Courts of Appeal and links to all available online Bankruptcy and District courts can be accessed directly from the home page. To find out more about other services offered outside the scope of this chapter, visit the Directory of Electronic Public Access Services to automated information in the U.S. Federal Courts at http://pacer.psc.uscourts.gov/pubaccess.html.

Public Access to Court Electronic Records (PACER)

PACER allows any user with a personal computer, modem (Internet access isn't required, but as noted below, may be less costly) and a word processor to dial in to a district or bankruptcy court computer and retrieve official electronic case information and court dockets usually in less than a minute. In accordance with Judicial Conference policy, most courts charge a $.60 per minute access fee for dial-up service or $.08 per page for Internet service, not to exceed the fee for 30 pages. District PACER and BANCAP PACER each offer information in a different manner. Some courts have a locally-developed public access systems. These are referred to as NIBS (National Integrated Bulletin Board System) or JAMS (Judicial Automated Management System) courts.

Persons desiring to use PACER service must first register with the PACER Service Center on the Internet at http://pacer.psc.uscourts.gov/register.html or at 1-800-676-6856. The federal courts continue to upgrade equipment and expand data retrieval options and reports. In addition, more jurisdictions will be offering 800 lines in order to eliminate long distance toll charges. Each court controls its own computer system and case information database; therefore, there are some variations among jurisdictions as to the information offered. Direct links to all courts that offer PACER are listed at http://pacer.psc.uscourts.gov/cgi-bin/links.pl. The listing below details whether or not a particular court participates in PACER.

Case Management/Electronic Case Files (CM/ECF)

The federal judiciary's Case Management/Electronic Case Files (CM/ECF) project is designed to replace aging electronic docketing and case management systems in more than 200 bankruptcy, district and appellate courts by 2005. CM/ECF will also provide courts the capability to have case file documents in electronic format, and to accept filings over the Internet if they choose to do so. Many courts have either already instituted mandatory electronic filing and noticing, or are in the process of doing so.

Attorneys practicing in courts offering the electronic filing capability are able to file documents directly with the court over the Internet. The CM/ECF system uses standard computer hardware, an Internet connection and browser, and accepts documents in Portable Document Format (PDF). The system is easy to use—filers prepare a document using conventional word processing software, then convert it to PDF. After logging onto the court's web site with a court-issued password, the filer fills out several screens with information that serves as the basis for the docket entry, attaches the document and submits it to the court. A notice verifying court receipt is generated and sent by e-mail to the filer automatically. Other parties in the case also receive e-mail notification of all action in the case.

There are no electronic filing fees added for filing documents over the Internet using CM/ECF; existing document filing fees do apply. Consistent with Congressional requirements, access to court documents over the Internet will be through the PACER system. The CM/ECF system will provide litigants one free electronic copy of the documents in their cases. **Direct links to all courts that offer CM/ECF are listed at http://pacer.psc.uscourts.gov/cgi-bin/links.pl.** The listing below notes if a particular court does not participate in CM/ECF.

Voice Case Information System (VCIS)

VCIS uses an automated voice response system to provide a limited amount of bankruptcy or appellate case information directly from the court's database in response to telephone inquiries. Access to VCIS is currently offered at no cost. Information for VCIS in each jurisdiction is listed below.

U.S. DISTRICT AND BANKRUPTCY COURTS BY STATE

ALABAMA

Alabama is a member of the 11th Circuit Court and is divided into three judicial districts: Northern, Middle and Southern.

Northern District

The Northern District comprises seven divisions.
(1) Northwestern Division: Colbert, Franklin and Lauderdale counties.
(2) Northeastern Division: Cullman, Jackson, Lawrence, Limestone, Madison and Morgan counties.

(3) Southern Division: Blount, Jefferson and Shelby counties.
(4) Eastern Division: Calhoun, Clay, Cleburne and Talladega counties
(5) Western Division: Bibb, Greene, Pickens, Sumter and Tuscaloosa counties.
(6) Middle Division: Cherokee, De Kalb, Etowah, Marshall and Saint Clair counties.
(7) Jasper Division: Fayette, Lamar, Marion, Walker and Winston counties.

DISTRICT COURT

Court Locations:	Anniston, Birmingham, Decatur, Florence, Gadsden, Huntsville and Tuscaloosa
Contact Information:	U.S. District Court
	Hugo L. Black U.S. Courthouse
	1729 Fifth Avenue, North
	Birmingham, AL 35203
	205-278-1700
	www.alnd.uscourts.gov

BANKRUPTCY COURT

Court Locations:	Anniston, Birmingham, Decatur, Mobile, Montgomery and Tuscaloosa
Contact Information:	U.S. Bankruptcy Court
	Vance Federal Building
	1800 Fifth Avenue, North, Room 120
	Birmingham, AL 35203-2111
	205-714-4000
	www.alnb.uscourts.gov
U.S. Trustee Region:	No U.S. Trustee administration, has Bankruptcy Administrator. *See* trustee listing at end of chapter for contact.
VCIS Phone:	Anniston: 256-240-9191 or 877-466-8879, Birmingham: 205-254-7337 or 877-466-0795, Decautur: 256-351-0539 or 877-466-0796, Tuscaloosa: 205-752-1302 or 877-466-9267

Middle District

The Middle District comprises three divisions.
(1) Northern Division: Autauga, Barbour, Bullock, Butler, Chilton, Coosa, Covington, Crenshaw, Elmore, Lowndes, Montgomery and Pike counties.
(2) Southern Division: Coffee, Dale, Geneva, Henry and Houston counties.
(3) Eastern Division: Chambers, Lee, Macon, Randolph, Russell and Tallapoosa counties.

DISTRICT COURT

Court Locations:	Dothan, Montgomery and Opelika	
Contact Information:	Street Address:	Mailing Address:
	U.S. District Court	U.S. District Court
	One Church Street	P.O. Box 711
	Montgomery, AL 36104	Montgomery, AL 36101-0711
	334-954-3600	
	www.almd.uscourts.gov	

BANKRUPTCY COURT

Court Locations:	Dothan, Montgomery and Opelika	
Contact Information:	Street Address:	Mailing Address:
	U.S. Bankruptcy Court	U.S. Bankruptcy Court
	One Church Street	P.O. Box 1248
	Montgomery, AL 36102-1248	Montgomery, AL 36102
	334-954-3800	
	www.almb.uscourts.gov	
U.S. Trustee Region:	No U.S. Trustee administration, has Bankruptcy Administrator. *See* trustee listing at end of chapter for contact.	
VCIS Phone:	334-954-3868	

Southern District

The Southern District comprises two divisions.

(1) Northern Division: Dallas, Hale, Marengo, Perry and Wilcox counties.

(2) Southern Division: Baldwin, Choctaw, Clarke, Conecuh, Escambia, Mobile, Monroe and Washington counties.

DISTRICT COURT

Court Locations:	Mobile and Selma
Contact Information:	U.S. District Court
	113 St. Joseph Street
	Mobile, AL 36602
	251-690-2371
	www.alsd.uscourts.gov

BANKRUPTCY COURT

Court Locations: Mobile

Contact Information:

Street Address:
U.S. Bankruptcy Court Administrator
Administrator
201 St. Louis Street
Mobile, AL 36602
251-441-5391
www.alsb.uscourts.gov

Mailing Address:
U.S. Bankruptcy Court
Administrator

P.O. Box 3083
Mobile, AL 36652-3083

U.S. Trustee Region: No U.S. Trustee administration, has Bankruptcy Administrator. *See* trustee listing at end of chapter for contact.

VCIS Phone: 251-441-5637 or 251-441-5638

ALASKA

Alaska is a member of the 9th Circuit Court and constitutes one judicial district.

DISTRICT COURT

Court Locations: Anchorage, Fairbanks, Juneau, Ketchikan and Nome

Contact Information:

Street Address:
U.S. District Court
222 West 7th Avenue, Room 229
Anchorage, AK 99513
907-677-6100
866-243-3814 (toll free)
www.akd.uscourts.gov

Mailing Address:
U.S. District Court
222 West 7th Avenue, #4
Anchorage, AK 99513

BANKRUPTCY COURT

Court Locations: Anchorage, Fairbanks, Juneau, Ketchikan and Nome

Contact Information: U.S. Bankruptcy Court
605 West 4th Avenue, Suite 138
Anchorage, AK 99501-2296
970-271-2655 or 800-859-8059 (In Alaska)
www.akb.uscourts.gov

U.S. Trustee Region: 18

VCIS Phone: 907-271-2658 or 888-878-3110

ARIZONA

Arizona is a member of the 9th Circuit Court and constitutes one judicial district.

DISTRICT COURT

Court Locations: Flagstaff, Phoenix, Prescott, Tucson and Yuma

Contact Information: U.S. District Court
                        130 U.S. Courthouse
                        401 West Washington St., SPC 1
                        Phoenix, AZ 85003-2118
                        602-322-7200
                        www.azd.uscourts.gov

BANKRUPTCY COURT
    Court Locations: Phoenix, Tucson and Yuma
    Contact Information: U.S. Bankruptcy Court
                            230 North 1st Avenue, Suite 101
                            P.O. Box 34151
                            Phoenix, AZ 85003
                            602-640-5800
                            www.azb.uscourts.gov
    U.S. Trustee Region: 14
    VCIS Phone: Phoenix: 602-640-5820 or 888-549-5336, Tucson: 520-620-7475 or 888-
                            299-6032, Yuma: 520-783-2474 or 888-298-9465

ARKANSAS

Arkansas is a member of the 8th Circuit Court and is divided into two judicial districts: Eastern and Western.

Eastern District

The Eastern District comprises five divisions.

(1) Eastern Division: Cross, Lee, Monroe, Phillips, Saint Francis and Woodruff counties.

(2) Western Division: Conway, Faulkner, Lonoke, Perry, Pope, Prairie, Pulaski, Saline, Van Buren, White and Yell counties.

(3) Pine Bluff Division: Arkansas, Chicot, Cleveland, Dallas, Desha, Drew, Grant, Jefferson and Lincoln counties.

(4) Northern Division: Cleburne, Fulton, Independence, Izard, Jackson, Sharp and Stone counties.

(5) Jonesboro Division: Clay, Craighead, Crittenden, Greene, Lawrence, Mississippi, Poinsett and Randolph counties.

DISTRICT COURT
    Court Locations: Batesville, Helena, Jonesboro, Little Rock and Pine Bluff
    Contact Information: U.S. District Court
                            600 West Capitol Avenue, Suite 402
                            Little Rock, AR 72201-3325
                            501-604-5351
                            www.are.uscourts.gov

BANKRUPTCY COURT
    Court Locations: Little Rock
    Contact Information: U.S. Bankruptcy Court
                            300 West 2nd Street
                            P.O. Drawer 3777
                            Little Rock, AR 72201
                            501-918-5500
                            vwww.arb.uscourts.gov
    U.S. Trustee Region: 13
    VCIS Phone: 501-918-5555 or 800-891-6741

Western District

The Western District comprises six divisions.

(1) Texarkana Division: Hempstead, Howard, Lafayette, Little River, Miller, Nevada and Sevier counties.

(2) El Dorado Division: Ashley, Bradley, Calhoun, Columbia, Ouachita and Union counties.

(3) Fort Smith Division: Crawford, Franklin, Johnson, Logan, Polk, Scott and Sebastian counties.
(4) Harrison Division: Baxter, Boone, Carroll, Marion, Newton and Searcy counties.
(5) Fayetteville Division: Benton, Madison and Washington counties.
(6) Hot Springs Division: Clark, Garland, Hot Springs, Montgomery and Pike counties.

DISTRICT COURT

Court Locations: El Dorado, Fayetteville, Fort Smith, Harrison, Hot Springs and Texarkana

Contact Information:

Street Address:
1038 U.S. District Court
South 6th Street & Rogers Avenue
Fort Smith, AR 72901
479-783-6833
FSMinfo@arwd.uscourts.gov, CMECFinfo@arwd.uscourts.gov
www.arwd.uscourts.gov

Mailing Address:
U.S. District Court
P.O. Box 1547
Fort Smith, AR 72902

BANKRUPTCY COURT

Court Locations: Fayetteville

Contact Information:

Street Address:
Divisional Office
316 Federal Building
35 East Mountain Street
Fayetteville, AR 72701
479-582-9800
www.arb.uscourts.gov

Mailing Address:
Divisional Office
P.O. Box 3097
Fayetteville, AR 72702

U.S. Trustee Region: 13
VCIS Phone: 501-918-5555 or 800-891-6741

CALIFORNIA

California is a member of the 9th Circuit Court and is divided into four judicial districts: Northern, Eastern, Central and Southern.

Northern District

Alameda, Contra Costa, Del Norte, Humboldt, Lake, Marin, Mendocino, Monterey, Napa, San Benito, Santa Clara, Santa Cruz, San Francisco, San Mateo and Sonoma counties.

DISTRICT COURT

Court Locations: Eureka, Oakland, San Francisco and San Jose
Contact Information: U.S. District Court
450 Golden Gate Avenue, 16th Floor
San Francisco, CA 94102
415-522-2000
www.cand.uscourts.gov

BANKRUPTCY COURT

Court Locations: Oakland, San Francisco, San Jose and Santa Rosa

Contact Information:

Street Address:
U.S. Bankruptcy Court
235 Pine Street, 19th Floor
San Francisco, CA 94104
415-268-2300
www.canb.uscourts.gov

Mailing Address:
U.S. Bankruptcy Court
P.O. Box 7341
San Francisco, CA 94120-7341

U.S. Trustee Region: 17
VCIS Phone: 888-457-0604

Eastern District

Alpine, Amador, Butte, Calaveras, Colusa, El Dorado, Fresno, Glenn, Inyo, Kern, Kings, Lassen, Madera, Mariposa, Merced, Modoc, Mono, Nevada, Placer, Plumas, Sacramento, San Joaquin, Shasta, Sierra, Siskiyou, Solano, Stanislaus, Sutter, Tehama, Trinity, Tulare, Tuolumne, Yolo and Yuba counties.

DISTRICT COURT

Court Locations:	Bakersfield, Fresno, Redding, Sacramento, Tahoe and Yosemite
Contact Information:	U.S. District Court
	501 I Street, Suite 4-401
	Sacramento, CA 95814
	916-930-4000
	www.caed.uscourts.gov

BANKRUPTCY COURT

Court Locations:	Bakersfield, Fresno, Modesto and Sacramento
Contact Information:	U.S. Bankruptcy Court
	501 I Street, Suite 3-200
	Sacramento, CA 95814
	916-930-4400
	www.caeb.uscourts.gov
U.S. Trustee Region:	17
VCIS Phone:	916-498-5583 or 916-498-5584

Central District

The Central District comprises three divisions.
(1) Eastern Division: Riverside and San Bernardino counties.
(2) Southern Division: Orange county.
(3) Western Division: Los Angeles, San Luis Obispo, Santa Barbara and Ventura counties.

DISTRICT COURT

Court Locations:	Los Angeles, Riverside and Santa Ana
Contact Information:	U.S. District Court
	312 North Spring Street
	Los Angeles, CA 90012
	213-894-1565 or 213-894-2215
	www.cacd.uscourts.gov

BANKRUPTCY COURT

Court Locations:	Los Angeles, Riverside, Santa Ana, Santa Barbara and Woodland Hills
Contact Information:	U.S. Bankruptcy Court
	1260 U.S. Courthouse
	255 East Temple Street
	Los Angeles, CA 90012
	213-894-3118
	www.cacb.uscourts.gov
U.S. Trustee Region:	16
VCIS Phone:	213-894-4111
No CM/ECF.	

Southern District

Imperial and San Diego counties.

DISTRICT COURT

Court Locations:	El Centro and San Diego
Contact Information:	U.S. District Court
	880 Front Street, Suite 4290
	San Diego, CA 92101-8900
	619-557-5600
	www.casd.uscourts.gov

BANKRUPTCY COURT

Court Locations: San Diego
Contact Information: U.S. Bankruptcy Court
                    325 West F Street
                    San Diego, CA 92101-6998
                    619-557-5620
                    www.casb.uscourts.gov
U.S. Trustee Region: 15
VCIS Phone: 619-557-6521

COLORADO

Colorado is a member of the 10th Circuit Court and constitutes one judicial district.

DISTRICT COURT

Court Locations: Boulder, Denver, Durango, Grand Junction, Montrose, Pueblo and Sterling
Contact Information: U.S. District Court
                    A-105 U.S. Courthouse
                    901 19th Street
                    Denver, CO 80294-3589
                    303-844-3433
                    www.co.uscourts.gov

BANKRUPTCY COURT

Court Locations: Boulder, Colorado Springs and Denver
Contact Information: U.S. Bankruptcy Court
                    U.S. Custom House
                    721 19th Street
                    Denver, CO 80202-2508
                    303-844-4045
                    www.cob.uscourts.gov
U.S. Trustee Region: 19
VCIS Phone: 303-844-0267

CONNECTICUT

Connecticut is a member of the 2nd Circuit Court and constitutes one judicial district.

DISTRICT COURT

Court Locations: Bridgeport, Hartford, New Haven and Waterbury
Contact Information: U.S. District Court
                    141 Church Street
                    New Haven, CT 06510
                    203-773-2140
                    www.ctd.uscourts.gov

BANKRUPTCY COURT

Court Locations: Bridgeport, Hartford, New Haven and Waterbury
Contact Information: U.S. Bankruptcy Court
                    Federal Building & U.S. Courthouse
                    450 Main Street
                    Hartford, CT 06103
                    860-240-3675
                    www.ctb.uscourts.gov
U.S. Trustee Region: 2
VCIS Phone: 800-800-5113
No CM/ECF.

DELAWARE

Delaware is a member of the 3rd Circuit Court and constitutes one judicial district.

DISTRICT COURT

Court Locations:	Wilmington
Contact Information:	U.S. District Court
	J. Caleb Boggs Federal Building
	844 North King Street
	Lockbox 18
	Wilmington, DE 19801
	302-573-6170
	helpdeskde@debuscourts.gov
	www.ded.uscourts.gov

BANKRUPTCY COURT

Court Locations:	Wilmington
Contact Information:	U.S. Bankruptcy Court
	824 North Market Street, 3rd Floor
	Wilmington, DE 19801
	302-252-2900
	www.deb.uscourts.gov
U.S. Trustee Region:	3
VCIS Phone:	302-252-2560

DISTRICT OF COLUMBIA

The District of Columbia has its own Circuit Court and constitutes one judicial district.

DISTRICT COURT

Court Locations:	Washington
Contact Information:	U.S. District Court
	333 Constitution Avenue, N.W.
	Washington, DC 20001
	202-354-3000
	www.dcd.uscourts.gov

BANKRUPTCY COURT

Court Locations:	Washington
Contact Information:	U.S. Bankruptcy Court
	4400 U.S. Courthouse
	333 Constitution Avenue, N.W.
	Washington, DC 20001
	202-565-2500
	www.dcb.uscourts.gov
U.S. Trustee Region:	4
VCIS Phone:	202-208-1365

FLORIDA

Florida is a member of the 11th Circuit Court and is divided into three judicial districts: Northern, Middle and Southern.

Northern District

Alachua, Bay, Calhoun, Dixie, Escambia, Franklin, Gadsden, Gilchrist, Gulf, Holmes, Jackson, Jefferson, Lafayette, Leon, Levy, Liberty, Madison, Okaloosa, Santa Rosa, Taylor, Wakulla, Walton and Washington counties.

DISTRICT COURT

Court Locations:	Gainesville, Panama City, Pensacola and Tallahassee

Contact Information: U.S. District Court
111 North Adams Street
Tallahassee, FL 32301
850-521-3501-7730
www.flnd.uscourts.gov

BANKRUPTCY COURT

Court Locations: Gainsville, Panama City, Pensacola and Tallahassee
Contact Information: U.S. Bankruptcy Court
110 East Park Avenue, Suite 100
Tallahassee, FL 32301
850-521-5001
www.flnb.uscourts.gov
U.S. Trustee Region: 21
VCIS Phone: Tallahassee: 850-521-5001, Pensacola: 850-435-8477

Middle District

Baker, Bradford, Brevard, Charlotte, Citrus, Clay, Collier, Columbia, De Soto, Duval, Flagler, Glades, Hamilton, Hardee, Hendry, Hernando, Hillsborough, Lake, Lee, Manatee, Marion, Nassau, Orange, Osceola, Pasco, Pinellas, Polk, Putnam, Saint Johns, Sarasota, Seminole, Sumter, Suwannee, Union and Volusia counties.

DISTRICT COURT

Court Locations: Fort Myers, Jacksonville, Ocala, Orlando and Tampa
Contact Information: U.S. District Court
80 North Hughey Avenue
Orlando, FL 32801
407-835-4200
www.flmd.uscourts.gov

BANKRUPTCY COURT

Court Locations: Fort Myers, Jacksonville, Orlando, Tampa and Viera
Contact Information: U.S. Bankruptcy Court
801 North Florida Avenue, Suite 727
Tampa, FL 33602-3899
813-301-5162
www.flmb.uscourts.gov
U.S. Trustee Region: 21
VCIS Phone: 866-879-1286

Southern District

Broward, Dade, Highlands, Indian River, Martin, Monroe, Okeechobee, Palm Beach and Saint Lucie counties.

DISTRICT COURT

Court Locations: Fort Lauderdale, Fort Pierce, Key West, Miami and West Palm Beach
Contact Information: U.S. District Court
301 North Miami Avenue
Miami, FL 33128-7788
305-523-5100
www.flsd.uscourts.gov

BANKRUPTCY COURT

Court Locations: Fort Lauderdale, Miami and West Palm Beach
Contact Information: U.S. Bankruptcy Court
1517 Claude Pepper Federal Building
51 S.W. First Avenue
Miami, FL 33130

305-714-1800
www.flsb.uscourts.gov
U.S. Trustee Region: 21
VCIS Phone: 305-536-5979 or 800-473-0226

GEORGIA

Georgia is a member of the 11th Circuit Court and is divided into three judicial districts: Northern, Middle and Southern.

Northern District

The Northern District comprises four divisions.

(1) Gainesville Division: Banks, Barrow, Dawson, Fannin, Forsyth, Gilmer, Habersham, Hall, Jackson, Lumpkin, Pickens, Rabun, Stephens, Towns, Union and White counties.

(2) Atlanta Division: Cherokee, Clayton, Cobb, De Kalb, Douglas, Fulton, Gwinnett, Henry, Newton and Rockdale counties.

(3) Rome Division: Bartow, Catoosa, Chattooga, Dade, Floyd, Gordon, Murray, Paulding, Polk, Walker and Whitfield counties.

(4) Newnan Division: Carroll, Coweta, Fayette, Haralson, Heard, Meriwether, Pike, Spalding and Troup counties.

DISTRICT COURT

Court Locations: Atlanta, Gainesville, Newnan and Rome
Contact Information: U.S. District Court
2211 U.S. Courthouse
75 Spring Street, S.W.
Atlanta, GA 30303-3361
404-215-1660
www.gand.uscourts.gov

BANKRUPTCY COURT

Court Locations: Atlanta, Gainesville, Newnan and Rome
Contact Information: U.S. Bankruptcy Court
1340 U.S. Courthouse
75 Spring Street, S.W.
Atlanta, GA 30303
404-215-1000
www.ganb.uscourts.gov
U.S. Trustee Region: 21
VCIS Phone: 404-730-2866 or 800-510-8284

Middle District

The Middle District comprises seven divisions.

(1) Athens Division: Clarke, Elbert, Franklin, Greene, Hart, Madison, Morgan, Oconee, Oglethorpe and Walton counties.

(2) Macon Division: Baldwin, Bibb, Bleckley, Butts, Crawford, Hancock, Houston, Jasper, Jones, Lamar, Monroe, Peach, Pulaski, Putnam, Twiggs, Upson, Washington and Wilkinson counties.

(3) Columbus Division: Chattahoochee, Clay, Harris, Marion, Muscogee, Quitman, Randolph, Stewart, Talbot and Taylor.

(4) Americus Division: Ben Hill, Crisp, Dooly, Lee, Macon, Schley, Sumter, Terrell, Webster and Wilcox counties.

(5) Albany Division: Baker, Calhoun, Dougherty, Early, Miller, Mitchell, Turner and Worth counties.

(6) Valdosta Division: Berrien, Clinch, Cook, Echols, Irwin, Lanier, Lowndes and Tift counties.

(7) Thomasville Division: Brooks, Colquitt, Decatur, Grady, Seminole and Thomas counties.

DISTRICT COURT

Court Locations: Albany, Athens, Columbus, Macon, Thomasville and Valdosta

Contact Information: U.S. District Court
                       475 Mulberry Street
                       P.O. Box 128
                       Macon, GA 31202
                       478-752-3497
                       info@gamd.uscourts.gov
                       www.gamd.uscourts.gov

BANKRUPTCY COURT

Court Locations: Albany, Athens, Columbus, Macon, Thomasville and Valdosta
Contact Information: Street Address: Mailing Address:
                       U.S. Bankruptcy Court   U.S. Bankruptcy Court
                       433 Cherry Street   P.O. Box 1957
                       Macon, GA 31202
                       478-752-3506
                       www.gamb.uscourts.gov
U.S. Trustee Region: 21
VCIS Phone: 478-752-8183 or 800-211-3015

Southern District

The Southern District comprises six divisions.

(1) Augusta Division: Burke, Columbia, Glascock, Jefferson, Lincoln, McDuffie, Richmond, Taliaferro, Warren and Wilkes counties.

(2) Dublin Division: Dodge, Johnson, Laurens, Montgomery, Telfair, Treutlen and Wheeler counties.

(3) Savannah Division: Bryan, Chatham, Effingham and Liberty counties.

(4) Waycross Division: Atkinson, Bacon, Brantley, Charlton, Coffee, Pierce and Ware counties.

(5) Brunswick Division: Appling, Camden, Glynn, Jeff Davis, Long, McIntosh and Wayne counties.

(6) Statesboro Division: Bulloch, Candler, Emanual, Evans, Jenkins, Screven, Tattnall and Toombs counties.

DISTRICT COURT

Court Locations: Augusta, Brunswick, Dublin, Savannah, Statesboro and Waycross
Contact Information: U.S. District Court
                       125 Bull Street, Room 304
                       Savannah, GA 31401
                       912-650-4020
                       www.gasd.uscourts.gov

BANKRUPTCY COURT

Court Locations: Augusta, Brunswick, Dublin, Savannah, Statesboro and Waycross
Contact Information: Street Address: Mailing Address:
                       U.S. Bankruptcy Court   U.S. Bankruptcy Court
                       125 Bull Street, Room 213   P.O. Box 8347
                       Savannah, GA 31401   Savannah, GA 31401
                       912-650-4100
                       www.gasb.uscourts.gov
U.S. Trustee Region: 21
VCIS Phone: None

GUAM

Guam is a member of the 9th Circuit Court and constitutes one judicial district.

DISTRICT AND BANKRUPTCY COURTS

Court Locations: Hagatna
Contact Information: U.S. District Court/Bankruptcy Division
                       520 West Soledad Avenue, 4th Floor
                       Hagatna, GU 96910
                       671-473-9100

Charles.White@gud.uscourts.gov
www.gud.uscourts.gov

U.S. Trustee Region:	15
VCIS Phone:	None

HAWAII

Hawaii is a member of the 9th Circuit Court and constitutes one judicial district which includes the Ringman Reef and Baker, Canton, Enderbury, Howland, Jarvis, Johnston, Midway, Palmyra, Sand and Wake Islands.

DISTRICT COURT

Court Locations:	Honolulu
Contact Information:	U.S. District Court
	300 Ala Moana Blvd., Room C338
	Honolulu, HI 96850
	808-541-1300
	www.hid.uscourts.gov

BANKRUPTCY COURT

Court Locations:	Honolulu
Contact Information:	U.S. Bankruptcy Court
	1132 Bishop Street, Suite 250L
	Honolulu, HI 96813
	808-522-8100
	info@hib.uscourts.gov
	www.hib.uscourts.gov
U.S. Trustee Region:	15
VCIS Phone:	808-522-8122

IDAHO

Idaho, exclusive of Yellowstone National Park, is a member of the 9th Circuit Court and constitutes one judicial district comprising four divisions.

(1) Central Division: Clearwater, Idaho, Latah, Lewis and Nez Perce counties.

(2) Eastern Division: Bannock, Bear Lake, Bingham, Bonneville, Butte, Caribou, Cassia, Clark, Custer, Franklin, Fremont, Jefferson, Lemhi, Madison, Minidoka, Oneida, Power and Teton counties.

(3) Northern Division: Benewah, Bonner, Boundary, Kootenai and Shoshone counties.

(4) Southern Division: Ada, Adams, Blaine, Boise, Camas, Canyon, Elmore, Gem, Gooding, Jerome, Lincoln, Owyhee, Payette, Twin Falls, Valley and Washington counties.

DISTRICT COURT

Court Locations:	Boise, Coeur d'Alene, Moscow and Pocatello.
Contact Information:	U.S. District Court
	550 West Fort Street, Room 400
	Boise, ID 83724
	208-334-1361
	www.id.uscourts.gov

BANKRUPTCY COURT

Court Locations:	Boise, Coeur D'Alene, Moscow and Pocatello
Contact Information:	U.S. Bankruptcy Court
	550 West Fort Street, Room 400
	Boise, ID 83724
	208-334-1074
	www.id.uscourts.gov
U.S. Trustee Region:	18
VCIS Phone:	208-334-9386

No PACER, uses RACER.

ILLINOIS

Illinois is a member of the 7th Circuit Court and is divided into three judicial districts: Northern, Central and Southern.

Northern District

The Northern District comprises two divisions.

(1) Eastern Division: Cook, Du Page, Grundy, Kane, Kendall, Lake, La Salle and Will counties.

(2) Western Division: Boone, Carroll, DeKalb, Jo Daviess, Lee, McHenry, Ogle, Stephenson, Whiteside and Winnebago counties.

DISTRICT COURT

Court Locations:	Chicago and Rockford
Contact Information:	U.S. District Court
	219 South Dearborn Street, 20th Floor
	Chicago, IL 60604
	312-435-5670
	www.ilnd.uscourts.gov

BANKRUPTCY COURT

Court Locations:	Chicago and Rockford
Contact Information:	U.S. Bankruptcy Court
	219 South Dearborn Street, Room 710
	Chicago, IL 60604
	312-435-5694
	www.ilnb.uscourts.gov
U.S. Trustee Region:	11
VCIS Phone:	888-232-6814

Central District

Adams, Brown, Bureau, Cass, Champaign, Christian, Coles, De Witt, Douglas, Edgar, Ford, Fulton, Greene, Hancock, Henderson, Henry, Iroquois, Kankakee, Knox, Livingston, Logan, McDonough, McLean, Macoupin, Macon, Marshall, Mason, Menard, Mercer, Montgomery, Morgan, Moultrie, Peoria, Piatt, Pike, Putnam, Rock Island, Sangamon, Schuyler, Scott, Shelby, Stark, Tazewell, Vermilion, Warren and Woodford counties.

DISTRICT COURT

Court Locations:	Peoria, Rock Island, Springfield and Urbana
Contact Information:	U.S. District Court
	151 U.S. Courthouse
	600 East Monroe Street
	Springfield, IL 62701
	217-492-4020
	www.ilcd.uscourts.gov

BANKRUPTCY COURT

Court Locations:	Danville, Peoria and Springfield
Contact Information:	U.S. Bankruptcy Court
	226 U.S. Courthouse
	600 East Monroe Street
	Springfield, IL 62701
	217-492-4551
	www.ilcb.uscourts.gov
U.S. Trustee Region:	10
VCIS Phone:	217-492-4550 or 800-827-9005

Southern District

Alexander, Bond, Calhoun, Clark, Clay, Clinton, Crawford, Cumberland, Edwards, Effingham, Fayette, Franklin, Gallatin, Hamilton, Hardin, Jackson, Jasper, Jefferson, Jersey, Johnson, Lawrence,

Madison, Marion, Massac, Monroe, Perry, Pope, Pulaski, Randolph, Richland, St. Clair, Saline, Union, Wabash, Washington, Wayne, White and Williamson counties.

DISTRICT COURT

Court Locations:	Benton and East St. Louis
Contact Information:	U.S. District Court
	750 Missouri Avenue
	East St. Louis, IL 62201
	618-482-9371
	www.ilsd.uscourts.gov

BANKRUPTCY COURT

Court Locations:	Alton, Benton, East St. Louis and Effingham
Contact Information:	U.S. Bankruptcy Court
	750 Missouri Avenue
	East St. Louis, IL 62201
	618-482-9400
	www.ilsb.uscourts.gov
U.S. Trustee Region:	10
VCIS Phone:	618-482-9365 or 800-726-5622

INDIANA

Indiana is a member of the 7th Circuit Court and is divided into two judicial districts: Northern and Southern.

Northern District

The Northern District comprises three divisions.

(1) Fort Wayne Division: Adams, Allen, Blackford, De Kalb, Grant, Huntington, Jay, Lagrange, Noble, Steuben, Wells and Whitley counties.

(2) South Bend Division: Cass, Elkhart, Fulton, Kosciusko, La Porte, Marshall, Miami, Pulaski, St. Joseph, Starke and Wabash counties.

(3) Hammond Division: Benton, Carroll, Jasper, Lake, Newton, Porter, Tippecanoe, Warren and White counties.

DISTRICT COURT

Court Locations:	Fort Wayne, Hammond, Lafayette and South Bend
Contact Information:	U.S. District Court
	204 South Main Street
	South Bend, IN 46601
	574-246-8000
	www.innd.uscourts.gov

BANKRUPTCY COURT

Court Locations:	Fort Wayne, Hammond, Lafayette and South Bend	
Contact Information:	Street Address:	Mailing Address:
	U.S. Bankruptcy Court	U.S. Bankruptcy Court
	401 South Michigan Street	P.O. Box 7003
	South Bend, IN 46601	South Bend, IN 46634-7003
	574-968-2100	
	http://www.innb.uscourts.govwww.innb.uscourts.gov	
U.S. Trustee Region:	10	
VCIS Phone:	574-968-2275 or 800-755-8393	

Southern District

The Southern District comprises four divisions.

(1) Indianapolis Division: Bartholomew, Boone, Brown, Clinton, Decatur, Delaware, Fayette, Fountain, Franklin, Hamilton, Hancock, Hendricks, Henry, Howard, Johnson, Madison, Marion, Monroe, Montgomery, Morgan, Randolph, Rush, Shelby, Tipton, Union and Wayne counties.

(2) Terre Haute Division: Clay, Greene, Knox, Owen, Parke, Putnam, Sullivan, Vermilion and Vigo counties.

(3) Evansville Division: Davies, Dubois, Gibson, Martin, Perry, Pike, Posey, Spencer, Vanderburgh and Warrick counties.

(4) New Albany Division: Clark, Crawford, Dearborn, Floyd, Harrison, Jackson, Jefferson, Jennings, Lawrence, Ohio, Orange, Ripley, Scott, Switzerland and Washington counties.

DISTRICT COURT

Court Locations:	Evansville, Indianapolis, New Albany and Terre Haute.
Contact Information:	U.S. District Court
	46 East Ohio Street, Room 105
	Indianapolis, IN 46204
	317-229-3700
	www.insd.uscourts.gov

BANKRUPTCY COURT

Court Locations:	Evansville, Indianapolis, New Albany and Terre Haute	
Contact Information:	Street Address:	Mailing Address:
	U.S. Bankruptcy Court	U.S. Bankruptcy Court
	116 U.S. Courthouse	P.O. Box 44978
	46 East Ohio Street	Indianapolis, IN 46244
	Indianapolis, IN 46204	
	317-229-3800	
	www.insb.uscourts.gov	
U.S. Trustee Region:	10	
VCIS Phone:	800-335-8003 or 317-229-3888	

IOWA

Iowa is a member of the 8th Circuit Court and is divided into two judicial districts: Northern and Southern.

Northern District

The Northern District comprises four divisions.

(1) Cedar Rapids Division: Benton, Cedar, Grundy, Hardin, Iowa, Jones, Linn and Tama counties.

(2) Eastern Division: Allamakee, Black Hawk, Bremer, Buchanan, Chickasaw, Clayton, Delaware, Dubuque, Fayette, Floyd, Howard, Jackson, Mitchell and Winneshiek counties.

(3) Western Division: Buena Vista, Cherokee, Clay, Crawford, Dickinson, Ida, Lyon, Monona, O'Brien, Osceola, Plymouth, Sac, Sioux and Woodbury counties.

(4) Central Division: Butler, Calhoun, Carroll, Cerro Gordo, Emmet, Franklin, Hamilton, Hancock, Humboldt, Kossuth, Palo Alto, Pocahontas, Webster, Winnebago, Worth and Wright counties.

DISTRICT COURT

Court Locations:	Cedar Rapids, Fort Dodge and Sioux City	
Contact Information:	Street Address:	Mailing Address:
	U.S. District Court	U.S. District Court
	101 First Street, S.E.	P.O. Box 74710
	Cedar Rapids, IA 52401	Cedar Rapids, IA 52407-4710
	319-286-2300	
	www.iand.uscourts.gov	

BANKRUPTCY COURT

Court Locations:	Cedar Rapids, Dubuque, Fort Dodge, Independence, Mason City and Sioux City	
Contact Information:	Street Address:	Mailing Address:
	U.S. Bankruptcy Court	U.S. Bankruptcy Court
	425 2nd Street, SE	P.O. Box 74890
	Cedar Rapids, IA 52401	Cedar Rapids, IA 52407-4890
	319-286-2200	
	www.ianb.uscourts.gov	

U.S. Trustee Region: 12
VCIS Phone: 319-286-2282 or 800-249-9859

Southern District

The Southern District comprises three divisions.

(1) Davenport Division: Clinton, Des Moines, Henry, Johnson, Lee, Louisa, Muscatine, Scott, Van Buren and Washington counties.

(2) Central Division: Adair, Adams, Appanoose, Boone, Clark, Dallas, Davis, Decatur, Greene, Guthrie, Jasper, Jefferson, Keokuk, Lucas, Madison, Mahaska, Marion, Marshall, Monroe, Polk, Poweshiek, Ringgold, Story, Taylor, Union, Wapelo, Warren and Wayne counties.

(3) Western Division: Audubon, Cass, Fremont, Harrison, Mills, Montgomery, Page, Pottawattamie and Shelby counties.

DISTRICT COURT

Court Locations: Council Bluffs, Davenport and Des Moines
Contact Information: U.S. District Court
U.S. Courthouse
P.O. Box 9344
123 East Walnut Street, Room 300
Des Moines, IA 50306-9344
515-284-6248
www.iasd.uscourts.gov

BANKRUPTCY COURT

Court Locations: Council Bluffs, Davenport and Des Moines
Contact Information:

Street Address:	Mailing Address:
U.S. Bankruptcy Court	U.S. Bankruptcy Court
300 U.S. Courthouse Annex	P.O. Box 9264
110 East Court Avenue	Des Moines, IA 50306-9264
Des Moines, IA 50309	
515-284-6230	

www.iasb.uscourts.gov/courtpages/home/homepage.asp
U.S. Trustee Region: 12
VCIS Phone: 515-323-2962

KANSAS

Kansas is a member of the 10th Circuit Court and constitutes one judicial district.

DISTRICT COURT

Court Locations: Kansas City, Topeka and Wichita
Contact Information: U.S. District Court
259 U.S. Courthouse
500 State Avenue
Kansas City, KS 66101
913-551-6719
www.ksd.uscourts.gov

BANKRUPTCY COURT

Court Locations: Kansas City, Topeka and Wichita
Contact Information: U.S. Bankruptcy Court
167 U.S. Courthouse
401 North Market Street
Wichita, KS 67202
316-269-6486
www.ksb.uscourts.gov
U.S. Trustee Region: 20
VCIS Phone: 800-827-9028

KENTUCKY

Kentucky is a member of the 6th Circuit Court and is divided into two judicial districts: Eastern and Western.

Eastern District

Anderson, Bath, Bell, Boone, Burbon, Boyd, Boyle, Bracken, Breathitt, Campbell, Carroll, Carter, Clark, Clay, Elliott, Estill, Fayette, Fleming, Floyd, Franklin, Gallatin, Garrard, Grant, Greenup, Harlan, Harrison, Henry, Jackson, Jessamine, Johnson, Kenton, Knott, Knox, Laurel, Lawrence, Lee, Leslie, Letcher, Lewis, Lincoln, McCreary, Madison, Magoffin, Martin, Mason, Menifee, Mercer, Montgomery, Morgan, Nicholas, Owen, Owsley, Pendleton, Perry, Pike, Powell, Pulaski, Robertson, Rockcastle, Rowan, Scott, Shelby, Trimble, Wayne, Whitley, Wolfe and Woodford counties.

DISTRICT COURT

Court Locations:	Ashland, Covington, Frankfort, Lexington, London and Pikeville
Contact Information:	Street Address: Mailing Address:

Street Address:
U.S. District Court
101 Barr Street
Lexington, KY 40507
859-233-2503
www.kyed.uscourts.gov

Mailing Address:
U.S. District Court
P.O. Drawer 3074
Lexington, KY 40588-3074

BANKRUPTCY COURT

Court Locations: Ashland, Covington, Frankfort, Lexington, London and Pikeville
Contact Information: Street Address: Mailing Address:
                      U.S. Bankruptcy Court   U.S. Bankruptcy Court
                      100 East Vine Street, Suite 200   P.O. Box 1111
                      Lexington, KY 40507   Lexington, KY 40588-1111
                      859-233-2608
                      www.kyeb.uscourts.gov
U.S. Trustee Region: 8
VCIS Phone: 859-233-2650 or 800-998-2650

Western District

Adair, Allen, Ballard, Barren, Breckenridge, Bullitt, Butler, Caldwell, Calloway, Carlisle, Casey, Christian, Clinton, Crittenden, Cumberland, Daviess, Edmonson, Fulton, Graves, Grayson, Green, Hancock, Hardin, Hart, Henderson, Hickman, Hopkins, Jefferson, Larue, Livingston, Logan, Lyon, McCracken, McLean, Marion, Marshall, Meade, Metcalfe, Monroe, Muhlenberg, Nelson, Ohio, Oldham, Russell, Simpson, Spencer, Taylor, Todd, Trigg, Union, Warren, Washington and Webster counties.

DISTRICT COURT

Court Locations: Bowling Green, Louisville, Owensboro and Paducah
Contact Information: U.S. District Court
                      106 U.S. Courthouse
                      601 West Broadway
                      Louisville, KY 40202
                      502-625-3500
                      www.kywd.uscourts.gov

BANKRUPTCY COURT

Court Locations: Bowling Green, Louisville, Owensboro and Paducah
Contact Information: U.S. Bankruptcy Court
                      601 West Broadway, Suite 450
                      Louisville, KY 40202
                      502-627-5800
                      www.kywb.uscourts.gov
U.S. Trustee Region: 8
VCIS Phone: 502-627-5660 or 800-263-9385

LOUISIANA

Louisiana is a member of the 5th Circuit Court and is divided into three judicial districts: Eastern, Middle and Western.

Eastern District

Assumption, Jefferson, Lafourche, Orleans, Plaquemines, Saint Bernard, Saint Charles, Saint James, Saint John the Baptist, Saint Tammany, Tangipahoa, Terrebonne and Washington parishes.

DISTRICT COURT

Court Locations:	Houma and New Orleans
Contact Information:	U.S. District Court
	500 Poydras Street, Suite C-151
	New Orleans, LA 70130-3313
	504-589-7600
	www.laed.uscourts.gov

BANKRUPTCY COURT

Court Locations:	New Orleans
Contact Information:	U.S. Bankruptcy Court
	500 Poydras Street, Suite B-601
	New Orleans, LA 70130-3386
	504-589-7878
	www.laeb.uscourts.gov
U.S. Trustee Region:	5
VCIS Phone:	504-589-7879

Middle District

Ascension, East Baton Rouge, East Feliciana, Iberville, Livingston, Pointe Coupee, Saint Helena, West Baton Rouge and West Feliciana parishes.

DISTRICT COURT

Court Locations:	Baton Rouge
Contact Information:	U.S. District Court
	777 Florida Street, Suite 139
	Baton Rouge, LA 70801-1712
	225-389-3500
	www.lamd.uscourts.gov

BANKRUPTCY COURT

Court Locations:	Baton Rouge
Contact Information:	U.S. Bankruptcy Court
	707 Florida Street, Room 119
	Baton Rouge, LA 70801
	225-389-0211
	www.lamb.uscourts.gov
U.S. Trustee Region:	5
VCIS Phone:	225-382-2175

Western District

Acadia, Allen, Avoyelles, Beauregard, Bienville, Bossier, Caddo, Calcasieu, Caldwell, Cameron, Catahoula, Claiborne, Concordia, Jefferson Davis, De Soto, East Carroll, Evangeline, Franklin, Grant, Iberia, Jackson, Lafayette, La Salle, Lincoln, Madison, Morehouse, Natchitoches, Ouachita, Rapides, Red River, Richland, Sabine, Saint Landry, Saint Martin, Saint Mary, Tensas, Union, Vermilion, Vernon, Webster, West Carroll and Winn parishes.

DISTRICT COURT

Court Locations:	Alexandria, Lafayette/Opelousas, Lake Charles, Monroe and Shreveport

Contact Information: U.S. District Court
                        300 Fannin Street, Suite 1167
                        Shreveport, LA 71101-3083
                        318-676-4273
                        www.lawd.uscourts.gov

BANKRUPTCY COURT

Court Locations: Alexandria, Opelousas and Shreveport
Contact Information: U.S. Bankruptcy Court
                        300 Fannin Street, Suite 2201
                        Shreveport, LA 71101
                        318-676-4267
                        www.lawb.uscourts.gov
U.S. Trustee Region: 5
VCIS Phone: 318-676-4234 or 800-326-4026

MAINE

Maine is a member of the 1st Circuit Court and constitutes one judicial district.

DISTRICT COURT

Court Locations: Bangor and Portland
Contact Information: U.S. District Court
                        156 Federal Street
                        Portland, ME 04101
                        207-780-3356
                        www.med.uscourts.gov

BANKRUPTCY COURT

Court Locations: Bangor and Portland
Contact Information: U.S. Bankruptcy Court
                        537 Congress Street, 2nd Floor
                        Portland, ME 04101
                        207-780-3482
                        www.meb.uscourts.gov
U.S. Trustee Region: 1
VCIS Phone: 207-780-3755 or 800-650-7253

MARYLAND

Maryland is a member of the 4th Circuit Court and constitutes one judicial district comprising two divisions.

(1) Northern Division: Allegany, Anne Arundel, Baltimore, Caroline, Carroll, Cecil, Dorchester, Frederick, Garrett, Harford, Howard, Kent, Queen Anne's, Somerset, Talbot, Washington, Wicomico and Worcester counties, and the City of Baltimore.

(2) Southern Division: Calvert, Charles, Montgomery, Prince George's and St. Mary's counties.

DISTRICT COURT

Court Locations: Baltimore and Greenbelt
Contact Information: U.S. District Court
                        Garmatz Courthouse
                        101 West Lombard Street
                        Baltimore, MD 21201
                        410-962-2600
                        www.mdd.uscourts.gov

BANKRUPTCY COURT

Court Locations: Baltimore and Greenbelt

Contact Information: U.S. Bankruptcy Court
1 01 W. Lombard St., Suite 8308
Baltimore, MD 21201
410-962-2688
www.mdb.uscourts.gov
U.S. Trustee Region: 4
VCIS Phone: 410-962-0733 or 1-800-829-0145

MASSACHUSETTS

Massachusetts is a member of the 1st Circuit Court and constitutes one judicial district.

DISTRICT COURT

Court Locations: Boston, Springfield and Worcester
Contact Information: U.S. District Court
1 Courthouse Way, Suite 2300
Boston, MA 02210
617-748-9152
www.mad.uscourts.gov

BANKRUPTCY COURT

Court Locations: Boston, Hyannis, Springfield and Worcester
Contact Information: U.S. Bankruptcy Court
1101 O'Neill Federal Building
10 Causeway Street
Boston, MA 02222-1074
617-565-8950
www.mab.uscourts.gov
U.S. Trustee Region: 1
VCIS Phone: 617-565-6025 or 888-201-3572

MICHIGAN

Michigan is a member of the 6th Circuit Court and is divided into two judicial districts: Eastern and Western.

Eastern District

The Eastern District comprises two divisions.

(1) Southern Division: Genesee, Jackson, Lapeer, Lenawee, Livingston, Macomb, Monroe, Oakland, Saint Clair, Sanilac, Shiawassee, Washtenaw and Wayne counties.

(2) Northern Division: Alcona, Alpena, Arenac, Bay, Cheboygan, Clare, Crawford, Gladwin, Gratiot, Huron, Iosco, Isabella, Midland, Montmorency, Ogemaw, Oscoda, Otsego, Presque Isle, Roscommon, Saginaw and Tuscola counties.

DISTRICT COURT

Court Locations: Ann Arbor, Bay City, Detroit, Flint and Port Huron
Contact Information: U.S. District Court
231 West Lafayette Blvd., 5th Floor
Detroit, MI 48226
313-234-5005
www.mied.uscourts.gov

BANKRUPTCY COURT

Court Locations: Bay City, Detroit and Flint
Contact Information: U.S. Bankruptcy Court
211 West Fort Street
Detroit, MI 48226
313-234-0065
www.mieb.uscourts.gov

U.S. Trustee Region: 9
VCIS Phone: 877-422-3066

Western District

The Western District comprises two divisions.

(1) Southern Division: Allegan, Antrim, Barry, Benzie, Berrien, Branch, Calhoun, Cass, Charlevoix, Clinton, Eaton, Emmet, Grand Traverse, Hillsdale, Ingham, Ionia, Kalamazoo, Kalkaska, Kent, Lake, Leelanau, Manistee, Mason, Mecosta, Missaukee, Montcalm, Muskegon, Newaygo, Oceana, Osceola, Ottawa, Saint Joseph, Van Buren and Wexford counties.

(2) Northern Division: Alger, Baraga, Chippewa, Delta, Dickinson, Gogebic, Houghton, Iron, Keweenaw, Luce, Mackinac, Marquette, Menominee, Ontonagon and Schoolcraft counties.

DISTRICT COURT

Court Locations: Grand Rapids, Kalamazoo, Lansing and Marquette
Contact Information: U.S. District Court
                       399 Federal Building
                       110 Michigan Street, NW
                       Grand Rapids, MI 49503
                       616-456-2381
                       info@miwd.uscourts.gov
                       www.miwd.uscourts.gov

BANKRUPTCY COURT

Court Locations: Grand Rapids, Kalamazoo, Lansing, Marquette and Traverse City
Contact Information: Street Address: Mailing Address:
                       299 U.S. Bankruptcy Court   U.S. Bankruptcy Court
                       110 Michigan Street, NW   P.O. Box 3310
                       Grand Rapids, MI 49501   Grand Rapids, MI 49501
                       616-456-2693
                       www.miwb.uscourts.gov
U.S. Trustee Region: 9
VCIS Phone: 616-456-2075

MINNESOTA

Minnesota is a member of the 8th Circuit Court and constitutes one judicial district comprising six divisions.

(1) First Division: Dodge, Fillmore, Houston, Mower, Olmsted, Steele, Wabasha and Winona counties.

(2) Second Division: Blue Earth, Brown, Cottonwood, Faribault, Freeborn, Jackson, Lac qui Parle, Le Sueur, Lincoln, Lyon, Martin, Murray, Nicollet, Nobles, Pipestone, Redwood, Rock, Sibley, Waseca, Watonwan and Yellow Medicine counties.

(3) Third Division: Chisago, Dakota, Goodhue, Ramsey, Rice, Scott and Washington counties.

(4) Fourth Division: Anoka, Carver, Chippewa, Hennepin, Isanti, Kandiyohi, McLeod, Meeker, Renville, Sherburne, Swift and Wright counties.

(5) Fifth Division: Aitkin, Benton, Carlton, Cass, Cook, Crow Wing, Itasca, Kanabec, Koochiching, Lake, Mille Lacs, Morrison, Pine and Saint Louis counties.

(6) Sixth Division: Becker, Beltrami, Big Stone, Clay, Clearwater, Douglas, Grant, Hubbard, Kittson, Lake of the Woods, Mahnomen, Marshall, Norman, Otter Tail, Pennington, Polk, Pope, Red Lake, Roseau, Stearns, Stevens, Todd, Traverse, Wadena and Wilkin counties.

DISTRICT COURT

Court Locations: Duluth, Fergus Falls, Minneapolis and St. Paul
Contact Information: Street Address: Mailing Address:
                       U.S. District Court   U.S. District Court
                       180 East Fifth Street   700 Federal Building
                       St. Paul, MN 55101   316 North Robert Street
                       651-848-1100   St. Paul, MN 55101
                       www.mnd.uscourts.gov

BANKRUPTCY COURT

Court Locations:	Duluth, Fergus Falls, Minneapolis and St. Paul
Contact Information:	U.S. Bankruptcy Court
	300 South 4th Street, Room 301
	Minneapolis, MN 55415
	612-664-5200
	www.mnb.uscourts.gov
U.S. Trustee Region:	12
VCIS Phone:	800-959-9002

MISSISSIPPI

Mississippi is a member of the 5th Circuit Court and is divided into two judicial districts: Northern and Southern.

Northern District

The Northern District comprises four divisions.

(1) Eastern Division: Alcorn, Attala, Chickasaw, Choctaw, Clay, Itawamba, Lee, Lowndes, Monroe, Oktibbeha, Prentiss, Tishomingo and Winston counties.

(2) Western Division: Benton, Calhoun, Grenada, Lafayette, Marshall, Montgomery, Pontotoc, Tippah, Union, Webster and Yalobusha counties.

(3) Delta Division: Bolivar, Coahoma, De Soto, Panola, Quitman, Tallahatchie, Tate and Tunica counties.

(4) Greenville Division: Carroll, Humphreys, Leflore, Sunflower and Washington counties.

DISTRICT COURT

Court Locations:	Aberdeen, Greenville and Oxford
Contact Information:	U.S. District Court
	369 Federal Building
	911 Jackson Avenue
	Oxford, MS 38655
	662-234-1971
	www.msnd.uscourts.gov

BANKRUPTCY COURT

Court Locations:	Aberdeen, Greenville and Oxford
Contact Information:	U.S. Bankruptcy Court
	Thad Cochran U.S. Courthouse
	703 Highway 145 North
	Aberdeen, MS 39730
	662-369-2596
	www.msnb.uscourts.gov
U.S. Trustee Region:	5
VCIS Phone:	662-369-8147 or 800-392-8653

Southern District

The Southern District comprises five divisions.

(1) Jackson Division: Amite, Copiah, Franklin, Hinds, Holmes, Leake, Lincoln, Madison, Pike, Rankin, Scott, Simpson and Smith counties.

(2) Eastern Division: Clarke, Jasper, Kemper, Lauderdale, Neshoba, Newton, Noxubee and Wayne counties.

(3) Western Division: Adams, Claiborne, Issaquena, Jefferson, Sharkey, Warren, Wilkinson and Yazoo counties.

(4) Southern Division: George, Hancock, Harrison, Jackson, Pearl River and Stone counties.

(5) Hattiesburg Division: Covington, Forrest, Greene, Jefferson Davis, Jones, Lamar, Lawrence, Marion, Perry and Walthall counties.

DISTRICT COURT

 Court Locations: Biloxi, Gulfport, Hattiesburg, Jackson, Meridian, Natchez and Vicksburg

 Contact Information: Street Address: Mailing Address:

           U.S. District Court   U.S. District Court

           245 East Capital Street, Suite 316 P.O. Box 23552

           Jackson, MS 39201   Jackson, MS 39225-3552

           601-965-4439

           www.mssd.uscourts.gov

BANKRUPTCY COURT

 Court Locations: Gulfport and Jackson

 Contact Information: U.S. Bankruptcy Court

           100 East Capitol Street

           Jackson, MS 39201

           601-965-5301

           www.mssb.uscourts.gov

 U.S. Trustee Region: 5

 VCIS Phone: Gulfport: 228-563-1822 or 800-293-2723, Jackson: 601-965-6106 or 800-601-8859

MISSOURI

Missouri is a member of the 8th Circuit Court and is divided into two judicial districts: Eastern and Western.

Eastern District

The Eastern District comprises three divisions.

(1) Eastern Division: Crawford, Dent, Franklin, Gasconade, Iron, Jefferson, Lincoln, Maries, Phelps, Saint Charles, Saint Francois, Saint Genevieve, Saint Louis, Warren and Washington counties, and the city of Saint Louis.

(2) Northern Division: Adair, Audrain, Chariton, Clark, Knox, Lewis, Linn, Macon, Marion, Monroe, Montgomery, Pike, Ralls, Randolph, Schuyler, Scotland and Shelby counties.

(3) Southeastern Division: Bollinger, Butler, Cape Girardeau, Carter, Dunklin, Madison, Mississippi, New Madrid, Pemiscot, Perry, Reynolds, Ripley, Scott, Shannon, Stoddard and Wayne counties.

DISTRICT COURT

 Court Locations: Cape Girardeau, Hannibal and St. Louis

 Contact Information: U.S. District Court

           111 South 10th Street, Suite 3.300

           St. Louis, MO 63102

           314-244-7900

           www.moed.uscourts.gov

BANKRUPTCY COURT

 Court Locations: Cape Girardeau, Hannibal and St. Louis

 Contact Information: U.S. Bankruptcy Court

           111 South 10th Street, 4th Floor

           St. Louis, MO 63102

           314-244-4500

           www.moeb.uscourts.gov

 U.S. Trustee Region: 13

 VCIS Phone: 314-244-4999 or 888-223-6431

Western District

The Western District comprises five divisions.

(1) Western Division: Bates, Carroll, Cass, Clay, Henry, Jackson, Johnson, Lafayette, Ray, Saint Clair and Saline counties.

(2) Southwestern Division: Barton, Barry, Jasper, Lawrence, McDonald, Newton, Stone and Vernon counties.

(3) Saint Joseph Division: Andrew, Atchison, Buchanan, Caldwell, Clinton, Daviess, De Kalb, Gentry, Grundy, Harrison, Holt, Livingston, Mercer, Nodaway, Platte, Putnam, Sullivan and Worth counties.

(4) Central Division: Benton, Boone, Callaway, Camden, Cole, Cooper, Hickory, Howard, Miller, Moniteau, Morgan, Osage and Pettis counties.

(5) Southern Division: Cedar, Christian, Dade, Dallas, Douglas, Greene, Howell, Laclede, Oregon, Ozark, Polk, Pulaski, Taney, Texas, Webster and Wright counties.

DISTRICT COURT

Court Locations:	Jefferson City, Joplin, Kansas City, St. Joseph and Springfield
Contact Information:	U.S. District Court
	400 East 9th Street
	Kansas City, MO 64106
	816-512-5000
	www.mow.uscourts.gov

BANKRUPTCY COURT

Court Locations:	Kansas City
Contact Information:	1800 U.S. Bankruptcy Court
	400 East 9th Street
	Kansas City, MO 64106
	816-512-1800
	www.mow.uscourts.gov
U.S. Trustee Region:	13
VCIS Phone:	888-205-2527

MONTANA

Montana, exclusive of Yellowstone National Park, is a member of the 9th Circuit Court and constitutes one judicial district.

DISTRICT COURT

Court Locations:	Billings, Butte, Great Falls, Helena and Missoula
Contact Information:	U.S. District Court
	5405 Federal Building
	316 North 26th Street
	Billings, MT 59101
	406-247-7000
	www.mtd.uscourts.gov

BANKRUPTCY COURT

Court Locations:	Billings, Butte, Great Falls, Kalispell and Missoula
Contact Information:	U.S. Bankruptcy Court
	400 N. Main Street
	Butte, MT 59701
	406-782-3354
	www.mtb.uscourts.gov
U.S. Trustee Region:	18
VCIS Phone:	888-879-0071 or 406-782-1060

NEBRASKA

Nebraska belongs to the 8th Circuit Court and constitutes one judicial district.

DISTRICT COURT

Court Locations:	Lincoln, North Platte and Omaha
Contact Information:	U.S. District Court
	111 South 18th Plaza, Suite 1152
	Omaha, NE 68102

402-661-7350 or 866, 220-4381
www.ned.uscourts.gov

BANKRUPTCY COURT

Court Locations:	Lincoln and Omaha
Contact Information:	U.S. Bankruptcy Court
	111 South 18th Plaza, Suite 1125
	Omaha, NE 68102
	402-661-7444
	www.neb.uscourts.gov
U.S. Trustee Region:	13
VCIS Phone:	402-661-7457 or 800-829-0112

NEVADA

Nevada is a member of the 9th Circuit Court and constitutes one judicial district.

DISTRICT COURT

Court Locations:	Las Vegas and Reno
Contact Information:	U.S. District Court
	333 Las Vegas Blvd., South
	Las Vegas, NV 89101
	702-464-5400
	www.nvd.uscourts.gov

BANKRUPTCY COURT

Court Locations:	Las Vegas and Reno
Contact Information:	U.S. Bankruptcy Court
	300 Las Vegas Blvd., South
	Las Vegas, NV 89101
	702-388-6633
	www.nvb.uscourts.gov
U.S. Trustee Region:	17
VCIS Phone:	702-388-6708, Outside Las Vegas: 800-314-3436

NEW HAMPSHIRE

New Hampshire is a member of the 1st Circuit Court and constitutes one judicial district.

DISTRICT COURT

Court Locations:	Concord
Contact Information:	U.S. District Court
	Warren B. Rudman U.S. Courthouse
	55 Pleasant Street, Room 110
	Concord, NH 03301-3941
	603-225-1423
	www.nhd.uscourts.gov

BANKRUPTCY COURT

Court Locations:	Manchester
Contact Information:	U.S. Bankruptcy Court
	1000 Elm Street, Suite 1001
	Manchester, NH 03101-1708
	603-222-2600
	www.nhb.uscourts.gov
U.S. Trustee Region:	1
VCIS Phone:	603-222-2626 or 800-851-8954

NEW JERSEY

New Jersey is a member of the 3rd Circuit Court and constitutes one judicial district.

DISTRICT COURT

Court Locations: Camden, Newark and Trenton
Contact Information: U.S. District Court
                       50 Walnut Street, Room 4015
                       Newark, NJ 07101
                       973-645-3730
                       www.njd.uscourts.gov

BANKRUPTCY COURT

Court Locations: Camden, Newark and Trenton
Contact Information: Street Address: Mailing Address:
                       U.S. Bankruptcy Court   U.S. Bankruptcy Court
                       MLK, Jr. Federal Building   P.O. Box 1352
                       50 Walnut Street   Newark, NJ 07101-1352
                       Newark, NJ 07102
                       973-645-4764
                       www.njb.uscourts.gov
U.S. Trustee Region: 3
VCIS Phone: 973-645-6044, 973-645-6045 or 877-239-2547

NEW MEXICO

New Mexico is a member of the 10th Circuit Court and constitutes one judicial district.

DISTRICT COURT

Court Locations: Albuquerque, Las Cruces, Roswell and Santa Fe
Contact Information: U.S. District Court
                       333 Lomas Blvd., N.W.
                       Albuquerque, NM 87102
                       505-348-2000
                       www.nmcourt.fed.us

BANKRUPTCY COURT

Court Locations: Albuquerque
Contact Information: Street Address: Mailing Address:
                       U.S. Bankruptcy Court   U.S. Bankruptcy Court
                       500 Gold Avenue, S.W., 10th Floor   P.O. Box 546
                       Albuquerque, NM 87102   Albuquerque, NM 87103-0546
                       505-348-2500 or 866-291-6805
                       www.nmcourt.fed.us
U.S. Trustee Region: 20
VCIS Phone: 505-348-2444 or 888-435-7822
No CM/ECF, uses ACE.

NEW YORK

New York is a member of the 2nd Circuit Court and is divided into four judicial districts: Northern, Southern, Eastern and Western.

Northern District

Albany, Broome, Cayuga, Chenango, Clinton, Columbia, Cortland, Delaware, Essex, Franklin, Fulton, Greene, Hamilton, Herkimer, Jefferson, Lewis, Madison, Montgomery, Oneida, Onondaga, Oswego, Otsego, Rensselaer, Saint Lawrence, Saratoga, Schenectady, Schoharie, Tioga, Tompkins, Ulster, Warren and Washington counties.

DISTRICT COURT

Court Locations:	Albany, Binghamton, Plattsburgh, Syracuse, Utica and Watertown
Contact Information:	U.S. District Court
	445 Broadway, Room 509
	Albany, NY 12207-2924
	518-257-1800
	www.nynd.uscourts.gov

BANKRUPTCY COURT

Court Locations	Albany and Utica
Contact Information:	U.S. Bankruptcy Court
	445 Broadway, Suite 330
	Albany, NY 12207
	518-257-1661
	www.nynb.uscourts.gov
U.S. Trustee Region:	2
VCIS Phone:	800-206-1952

Southern District

Bronx, Dutchess, New York, Orange, Putnam, Rockland, Sullivan and Westchester counties, and concurrently with the Eastern District, the waters within the Eastern District.

DISTRICT COURT

Court Locations:	New York and White Plains
Contact Information:	U.S. District Court
	500 Pearl Street
	New York, NY 10007-1312
	212-805-0136
	www.nysd.uscourts.gov

BANKRUPTCY COURT

Court Locations:	New York, Poughkeepsie and White Plains
Contact Information:	U.S. Bankruptcy Court
	Hamilton Custom House
	One Bowling Green, 6th Floor
	New York, NY 10004-1408
	212-668-2870
	www.nysd.uscourts.gov
U.S. Trustee Region:	2
VCIS Phone:	212-668-2772 or 866-232-1268

Eastern District

Kings, Nassau, Queens, Richmond and Suffolk counties, and concurrently with the Southern District, the waters within the counties of Bronx and New York.

DISTRICT COURT

Court Locations:	Brooklyn and Central Islip
Contact Information:	U.S. District Court
	225 Cadman Plaza East
	Brooklyn, NY 11201
	718-260-2600
	www.nyed.uscourts.gov

BANKRUPTCY COURT

Court Locations:	Brooklyn and Central Islip
Contact Information:	U.S. Bankruptcy Court
	75 Clinton Street
	Brooklyn, NY 11201

718-330-2188
www.nyeb.uscourts.gov
U.S. Trustee Region: 2
VCIS Phone: 718-852-5726, 718-852-5091 or 800-252-2537

Western District

Allegany, Cattaraugus, Chautauqua, Chemung, Erie, Genesee, Livingston, Monroe, Niagara, Ontario, Orleans, Schuyler, Seneca, Steuben, Wayne, Wyoming and Yates counties.

DISTRICT COURT

Court Locations: Batavia, Buffalo, Mayville, Niagara Falls, Olean, Rochester and Watkins
                        Glen
Contact Information: U.S. District Court
                        304 U.S. Courthouse
                        68 Court Street
                        Buffalo, NY 14202
                        716-551-4211
                        www.nywd.uscourts.gov

BANKRUPTCY COURT

Court Locations: Buffalo and Rochester
Contact Information: U.S. Bankruptcy Court
                        300 Pearl Street, Suite 250
                        Buffalo, NY 14202-2501
                        716-551-4130
                        www.nywb.uscourts.gov
U.S. Trustee Region: 2
VCIS Phone: 800-776-9578 or 716-551-5311

NORTH CAROLINA

North Carolina is a member of the 4th Circuit Court and is divided into three judicial districts: Eastern, Middle and Western.

Eastern District

Beaufort, Bertie, Bladen, Brunswick, Camden, Carteret, Chowan, Columbus, Craven, Cumberland, Currituck, Dare, Duplin, Edgecombe, Franklin, Gates, Granville, Greene, Halifax, Harnett, Hertford, Hyde, Johnston, Jones, Lenoir, Martin, Nash, New Hanover, Northampton, Onslow, Pamlico, Pasquotank, Pender, Perquimans, Pitt, Robeson, Sampson, Tyrrell, Vance, Wake, Warren, Washington, Wayne and Wilson counties and that portion of Durham County encompassing the Federal Correctional Institution, Butner, North Carolina.

DISTRICT COURT

Court Locations: Elizabeth City, Fayetteville, Greenville, New Bern, Raleigh and Wilmington
Contact Information: U.S. District Court
                        Terry Sanford Federal Building and Courthouse
                        310 New Bern Avenue
                        Raleigh, NC 27601
                        919-645-1700
                        www.nced.uscourts.gov

BANKRUPTCY COURT

Court Locations: Wilson and Raleigh
Contact Information: U.S. Bankruptcy Court
                        1760-A Parkwood Blvd., West
                        Wilson, NC 27893-3564
                        252-237-0248
                        www.nceb.uscourts.gov

U.S. Trustee Region: No U.S. Trustee administration, has Bankruptcy Administrator. *See* trustee
                        listing at end of chapter for contact.
VCIS Phone: Raleigh: 919-856-4618 or 888-847-9138, Wilson: 252-234-7655 or 888-513-9765
No PACER, using RACER.

Middle District

Alamance, Cabarrus, Caswell, Chatham, Davidson, Davie, Durham (excluding that portion of Durham
County encompassing the Federal Correctional Institution in Butner), Forsythe, Guilford, Hoke, Lee,
Montgomery, Moore, Orange, Person, Randolph, Richmond, Rockingham, Rowan, Scotland, Stanly,
Stokes, Surry and Yadkin counties.

DISTRICT COURT

Court Locations: Durham, Greensboro and Winston-Salem
Contact Information: U.S. District Court
                        324 West Market Street, Suite 401
                        Greensboro, NC 27401
                        336-332-6000
                        www.ncmd.uscourts.gov

BANKRUPTCY COURT

Court Locations: Durham, Greensboro and Winston-Salem
Contact Information: Street Address: Mailing Address:
                        U.S. Bankruptcy Court   U.S. Bankruptcy Court
                        101 South Edgeworth Street   P.O. Box 26100
                        Greensboro, NC 27401   Greensboro, NC 27420-6100
                        336-333-5647
                        www.ncmd.uscourts.gov
U.S. Trustee Region: No U.S. Trustee administration, has Bankruptcy Administrator. *See* trustee
                        listing at end of chapter for contact.
VCIS Phone: 888-319-0455, Greensboro area: 888-333-5532

Western District

Alexander, Alleghany, Anson, Ashe, Avery, Buncombe, Burke, Caldwell, Catawba, Cherokee, Clay,
Cleveland, Gaston, Graham, Haywood, Henderson, Iredell, Jackson, Lincoln, McDowell, Macon,
Madison, Mecklenburg, Mitchell, Polk, Rutherford, Swain, Transylvania, Union, Watauga, Wilkes and
Yancey counties.

DISTRICT COURT

Court Locations: Asheville, Bryson City, Charlotte and Statesville
Contact Information: U.S. District Court
                        309 U.S. Courthouse
                        100 Otis Street
                        Asheville, NC 28801-2611
                        828-771-7200
                        www.ncwd.uscourts.gov

BANKRUPTCY COURT

Court Locations: Asheville, Bryson City, Charlotte, Shelby and Wilkesboro
Contact Information: Street Address: Mailing Address:
                        U.S. Bankruptcy Court   U.S. Bankruptcy Court
                        401 West Trade Street, Room 111   P.O. Box 34189
                        Charlotte, NC 28202   Charlotte, NC 28234-4189
                        704-350-7500
                        www.ncwb.uscourts.gov
U.S. Trustee Region: No U.S. Trustee administration, has Bankruptcy Administrator. *See* trustee
                        listing at end of chapter for contact.
VCIS Phone: 800-884-9868

NORTH DAKOTA

North Dakota is a member of the 8th Circuit Court and constitutes one judicial district comprising four divisions.

(1) Southwestern Division: Adams, Billings, Bowman, Burleigh, Dunn, Emmons, Golden Valley, Grant, Hettinger, Kidder, Logan, McIntosh, McLean, Mercer, Morton, Oliver, Sioux, Slope and Stark counties.

(2) Southeastern Division: Barnes, Cass, Dickey, Eddy, Foster, Griggs, La Moure, Ransom, Richland, Sargent, Steele and Stutsman counties.

(3) Northeastern Division: Benson, Cavalier, Grand Forks, Nelson, Pembina, Ramsey, Rolette, Towner, Traill and Walsh counties.

(4) Northwestern Division: Bottineau, Burke, Divide, McHenry, McKenzie, Mountrail, Pierce, Renville, Sheridan, Ward, Wells and Williams counties.

DISTRICT COURT

Court Locations:	Bismarck, Fargo, Grand Forks and Minot
Contact Information:	U.S. District Court
	220 East Rosser Avenue
	P.O. Box 1193
	Bismarck, ND 58502
	701-530-2300
	www.ndd.uscourts.gov

BANKRUPTCY COURT

Court Locations:	Bismarck and Fargo
Contact Information:	U.S. Bankruptcy Court
	655 First Avenue North, Suite 210
	Fargo, ND 58102-4932
	701-297-7100
	www.ndb.uscourts.gov
U.S. Trustee Region:	12
VCIS Phone:	701-297-7166

NORTHERN MARIANA ISLANDS

Northern Mariana Islands are a member of the 9th Circuit Court and constitute one judicial district.

DISTRICT AND BANKRUPTCY COURTS

Court Locations:	Saipan
Contact Information:x	U.S. District Court
	2nd Floor, Horiguchi Bldg., Garapan
	P.O. Box 500687
	Saipan, MP 96950
	670-236-2902
	www.nmid.uscourts.gov
U.S. Trustee Region:	15
VCIS Phone: None	
No PACER or CM/ECF.	

OHIO

Ohio is a member of the 6th Circuit Court and is divided into two judicial districts: Northern and Southern.

Northern District

The Northern District comprises two divisions.

(1) Eastern Division: Ashland, Ashtabula, Carroll, Columbiana, Crawford, Cuyahoga, Geauga, Holmes, Lake, Lorain, Mahoning, Medina, Portage, Richland, Stark, Summit, Trumbull, Tuscarawas and Wayne counties.

(2) Western Division: Allen, Auglaize, Defiance, Erie, Fulton, Hancock, Hardin, Henry, Huron, Lucas, Marion, Mercer, Ottawa, Paulding, Putnam, Sandusky, Seneca, Van Wert, Williams, Woods and Wyandot counties.

DISTRICT COURT

Court Locations:	Akron, Cleveland, Toledo and Youngstown
Contact Information:	U.S. District Court
	801 West Superior Avenue
	Cleveland, OH 44113-1201
	216-357-7000
	www.ohnd.uscourts.gov

BANKRUPTCY COURT

Court Locations:	Akron, Canton, Cleveland, Toledo and Youngstown
Contact Information:	U.S. Bankruptcy Court
	201 Superior Avenue
	Cleveland, OH 44114
	216-615-4300
	www.ohnb.uscourts.gov
U.S. Trustee Region:	9
VCIS Phone:	800-898-6899

Southern District

The Southern District comprises two divisions.

(1) Western Division: Adams, Brown, Butler, Champaign, Clark, Clermont, Clinton, Darke, Greene, Hamilton, Highland, Lawrence, Miami, Montgomery, Preble, Scioto, Shelby and Warren counties.

(2) Eastern Division: Athens, Belmont, Coshocton, Delaware, Fairfield, Fayette, Franklin, Gallia, Guernsey, Harrison, Hocking, Jackson, Jefferson, Knox, Licking, Logan, Madison, Meigs, Monroe, Morgan, Morrow, Muskingum, Noble, Perry, Pickaway, Pike, Ross, Union, Vinton and Washington counties.

DISTRICT COURT

Court Locations:	Cincinnati, Columbus and Dayton
Contact Information:	U.S. District Court
	260 U.S. Courthouse
	85 Marconi Blvd.
	Columbus, OH 43215
	614-719-3000
	www.ohsd.uscourts.gov

BANKRUPTCY COURT

Court Locations:	Cincinnati, Columbus and Dayton
Contact Information:	U.S. Bankruptcy Court
	124 U.S. Courthouse
	170 North High Street
	Columbus, OH 43215
	614-469-6638
	www.ohsb.uscourts.gov
U.S. Trustee Region:	9
VCIS Phone:	Cincinnati and Dayton: 614-225-2544 or 800-726-1004, Columbus: 800-726-1006

OKLAHOMA

Oklahoma is a member of the 10th Circuit Court and is divided into three judicial districts: Northern, Eastern and Western.

Northern District

Craig, Creek, Delaware, Mayes, Nowata, Osage, Ottawa, Pawnee, Rogers, Tulsa and Washington counties.

DISTRICT COURT

Court Locations: Bartlesville, Miami, Pawhuska, Tulsa and Vinita
Contact Information: U.S. District Court
411 U.S. Courthouse
333 West 4th Street
Tulsa, OK 74103
918-699-4700
www.oknd.uscourts.gov

BANKRUPTCY COURT

Court Locations: Tulsa
Contact Information: U.S. Bankruptcy Court
U.S. Courthouse
224 South Boulder Avenue
Tulsa, OK 74103
918-699-4000
http://www.oknb.uscourts.govwww.oknb.uscourts.gov
U.S. Trustee Region: 20
VCIS Phone: 918-699-4001 or 888-501-6977

Eastern District

Adair, Atoka, Bryan, Carter, Cherokee, Choctaw, Coal, Haskell, Hughes, Johnston, Latimer, Le Flore, Love, McCurtain, McIntosh, Marshall, Murray, Muskogee, Okfuskee, Okmulgee, Pittsburg, Pontotoc, Pushmataha, Seminole, Sequoyah and Wagoner counties.

DISTRICT COURT

Court Locations: Durant, McAlester, Muskogee and Okmulgee
Contact Information: U.S. District Court
101 North 5th Street, Room 208
Muskogee, OK 74401
918-684-7920
www.oked.uscourts.gov

BANKRUPTCY COURT

Court Locations: Okmulgee
Contact Information: U.S. Bankruptcy Court
111 West 4th Street, Room 229
P.O. Box 1347
Okmulgee, OK 74447
918-758-0126
www.okeb.uscourts.gov
U.S. Trustee Region: 20
VCIS Phone: 918-756-8617 or 877-377-1221

Western District

Alfalfa, Beaver, Beckham, Blaine, Caddo, Canadian, Cimarron, Cleveland, Comanche, Cotton, Custer, Dewey, Ellis, Garfield, Garvin, Grady, Grant, Greer, Harmon, Harper, Jackson, Jefferson, Kay, Kingfisher, Kiowa, Lincoln, Logan, Major, McClain, Noble, Oklahoma, Payne, Pottawatomie, Roger Mills, Stephens, Texas, Tillman, Washita, Woods and Woodward counties.

DISTRICT COURT

Court Locations: Chickasha, Enid, Guthrie, Lawton, Mangum, Oklahoma City, Pauls Valley, Ponca City, Shawnee and Woodward
Contact Information: U.S. District Court
1210 U.S. Courthouse
200 N.W. 4th Street
Oklahoma City, OK 73102
405-609-5000
www.okwd.uscourts.gov

BANKRUPTCY COURT

Court Locations:	Oklahoma City
Contact Information:	U.S. Bankruptcy Court
	215 Dean A. McGee Avenue
	Oklahoma City, OK 73102
	405-609-5700
	www.okwb.uscourts.gov
U.S. Trustee Region:	20
VCIS Phone:	405-231-4768 or 800-872-1348

OREGON

Oregon is a member of the 9th Circuit Court and constitutes one judicial district.

DISTRICT COURT

Court Locations:	Eugene, Meford and Portland.
Contact Information:	U.S. District Court
	Hatfield U.S. Courthouse
	1000 S.W. 3rd Avenue
	Portland, OR 97204
	503-326-8008 (Civil Cases)
	503-326-8003 (Criminal Cases)
	www.ord.uscourts.gov

BANKRUPTCY COURT

Court Locations:	Eugene and Portland
Contact Information:	U.S. Bankruptcy Court
	1001 S.W. 5th Avenue, Room 700
	Portland, OR 97204
	503-326-2231
	www.orb.uscourts.gov
U.S. Trustee Region:	18
VCIS Phone:	503-326-2249 or 800-726-2227

PENNSYLVANIA

Pennsylvania is a member of the 3rd Circuit Court and is divided into three judicial districts: Eastern, Middle and Western.

Eastern District

Berks, Bucks, Chester, Delaware, Lancaster, Lehigh, Montgomery, Northampton, Philadelphia and Schuylkill counties.

DISTRICT COURT

Court Locations:	Allentown, Easton, Philadelphia and Reading
Contact Information:	U.S. District Court
	2609 U.S. Courthouse
	601 Market Street
	Philadelphia, PA 19106-1797
	215-597-7704
	www.paed.uscourts.gov

BANKRUPTCY COURT

Court Locations:	Philadelphia and Reading
Contact Information:	U.S. Bankruptcy Court
	400 U.S. Courthouse
	900 Market Street
	Philadelphia, PA 19107

215-408-2800
www.paeb.uscourts.gov

U.S. Trustee Region: 3
VCIS Phone: 215-597-2244 or 888-584-5853

Middle District

Adams, Bradford, Cameron, Carbon, Centre, Clinton, Columbia, Cumberland, Dauphin, Franklin, Fulton, Huntingdon, Juniata, Lackawanna, Lebanon, Luzerne, Lycoming, Mifflin, Monroe, Montour, Northumberland, Perry, Pike, Potter, Schuylkill, Snyder, Sullivan, Susquehanna, Tioga, Union, Wayne, Wyoming and York counties.

DISTRICT COURT

Court Locations: Harrisburg, Scranton, Wilkes-Barre and Williamsport
Contact Information: U.S. District Court
235 North Washington Avenue
P.O. Box 1148
Scranton, PA 18501
570-207-5680
www.pamd.uscourts.gov

BANKRUPTCY COURT

Court Locations: Harrisburg and Wilkes-Barre
Contact Information: U.S. Bankruptcy Court
274 Max Rosenn U.S. Courthouse
197 South Main Street
Wilkes-Barre, PA 18701
570-826-6450
www.pamb.uscourts.gov

U.S. Trustee Region: 3
VCIS Phone: Harrisburg: 888-531-9485, Wilkes Barre: 877-440-2699

Western District

Allegheny, Armstrong, Beaver, Bedford, Blair, Butler, Cambria, Clarion, Clearfield, Crawford, Elk, Erie, Fayette, Forest, Greene, Indiana, Jefferson, Lawrence, McKean, Mercer, Somerset, Venango, Warren, Washington and Westmoreland counties.

DISTRICT COURT

Court Locations: Erie, Johnstown and Pittsburgh
Contact Information:

Street Address: Mailing Address:
U.S. District Court   U.S. District Court
829 U.S. Courthouse   P.O. Box 1805
7th Avenue and Grant Street   Pittsburgh, PA 15230
Pittsburgh, PA 15219
412-208-7500
www.pawd.uscourts.gov

BANKRUPTCY COURT

Court Locations: Erie, Johnstown and Pittsburgh
Contact Information: U.S. Bankruptcy Court
5414 U.S. Steel Tower
600 Grant Street
Pittsburgh, PA 15219
412-644-2700
www.pawb.uscourts.gov

U.S. Trustee Region: 3
VCIS Phone: 412-355-3210

PUERTO RICO

Puerto Rico is a member of the 1st Circuit Court and constitutes one judicial district.

DISTRICT COURT

Court Locations:	Hato Rey and San Juan
Contact Information:	U.S. Courthouse
	150 Carlos Chardon Street
	Hato Rey, PR 00918
	787-772-3000
	www.prd.uscourts.gov

BANKRUPTCY COURT

Court Locations:	San Juan
Contact Information:	U.S. Post Office & Courthouse Building
	300 Recito Sur Street, Suite 109
	San Juan, PR 00901
	787-977-6000
	www.prb.uscourts.gov
U.S. Trustee Region:	21
VCIS Phone:	787-977-6130
No CM/ECF.	

RHODE ISLAND

Rhode Island is a member of the 1st Circuit Court and constitutes one judicial district.

DISTRICT COURT

Court Locations:	Providence
Contact Information:	U.S. District Court
	One Exchange Terrace
	Federal Building & Courthouse
	Providence, RI 02903
	401-752-7200
	www.rid.uscourts.gov

BANKRUPTCY COURT

Court Locations:	Providence
Contact Information:	U.S. Bankruptcy Court
	The Federal Center
	380 Westminster Mall, Suite 615
	Providence, RI 02903
	401-528-4477
	www.rib.uscourts.gov
U.S. Trustee Region:	1
VCIS Phone:	401-528-4476 or 800-843-2841

SOUTH CAROLINA

South Carolina is a member of the 4th Circuit Court and constitutes one judicial district comprising 11 divisions.

(1) Charleston Division: Berkeley, Charleston, Clarendon, Colleton, Dorchester and Georgetown counties.

(2) Columbia Division: Kershaw, Lee, Lexington, Richland and Sumter counties.

(3) Florence Division: Chesterfield, Darlington, Dillon, Florence, Horry, Marion, Marlboro and Williamsburg counties.

(4) Aiken Division: Aiken, Allendale and Barnwell counties.

(5) Orangeburg Division: Bamberg, Calhoun and Orangeburg counties.

(6) Greenville Division: Greenville and Laurens counties.

(7) Rock Hill Division: Chester, Fairfield, Lancaster and York counties.

(8) Greenwood Division: Abbeville, Edgefield, Greenwood, McCormick, Newberry and Saluda counties.

(9) Anderson Division: Anderson, Oconee and Pickens counties.

(10) Spartanburg Division: Cherokee, Spartanburg and Union counties.

(11) Beaufort Division: Beaufort, Hampton and Jasper counties.

DISTRICT COURT

Court Locations:	Aiken, Anderson, Beaufort, Charleston, Columbia, Florence, Greenville and Spartanburg
Contact Information:	U.S. District Court
	901 Richland Street
	Columbia, SC 29201
	803-765-5816
	www.scd.uscourts.gov

BANKRUPTCY COURT

Court Locations:	Charleston, Columbia and Spartanburg
Contact Information:	U.S. Bankruptcy Court
	1100 Laurel Street
	Columbia, SC 29201
	803-765-5436
	www.scb.uscourts.gov
U.S. Trustee Region:	4
VCIS Phone:	803-765-5211 or 800-669-8767

SOUTH DAKOTA

South Dakota is a member of the 8th Circuit Court and constitutes one judicial district comprising four divisions.

(1) Northern Division: Brown, Campbell, Clark, Codington, Corson, Day, Deuel, Edmonds, Grant, Hamlin, McPherson, Marshall, Roberts, Spink and Walworth counties.

(2) Southern Division: Aurora, Beadle, Bon Homme, Brookings, Brule, Charles Mix, Clay, Davison, Douglas, Hanson, Hutchinson, Kingsbury, Lake, Lincoln, McCook, Miner, Minnehaha, Moody, Sanborn, Turner, Union and Yankton counties.

(3) Central Division: Buffalo, Dewey, Faulk, Gregory, Haakon, Hand, Hughes, Hyde, Jackson, Jerauld, Jones, Lyman, Mellette, Potter, Stanley, Sully, Todd, Tripp and Ziebach counties.

(4) Western Division: Bennett, Butte, Custer, Fall River, Harding, Lawrence, Meade, Pennington, Perkins, Shannon, Washabaugh and Washington counties.

DISTRICT COURT

Court Locations:	Aberdeen, Pierre, Rapid City and Sioux Falls
Contact Information:	U.S. District Court
	400 South Phillips Avenue, Room 128
	Sioux Falls, SD 57104
	605-330-4447
	www.sdd.uscourts.gov

BANKRUPTCY COURT

Court Locations:	Aberdeen, Pierre, Rapid City and Sioux Falls
Contact Information:	U.S. Bankruptcy Court
	400 South Phillips Avenue, Room 117
	P.O. Box 5060
	Sioux Falls, SD 57117-5060
	605-330-4544
	www.sdb.uscourts.gov
U.S. Trustee Region:	12
VCIS Phone:	605-330-4559 or 800-768-6218

TENNESSEE

Tennessee is a member of the 6th Circuit Court and is divided into three judicial districts: Eastern, Middle and Western.

Eastern District

The Eastern District comprises four divisions.

(1) Northern Division:Anderson, Blount, Campbell, Claiborne, Grainger, Jefferson, Knox, Loudon, Monroe, Morgan, Roane, Scott, Sevier and Union counties.

(2) Northeastern Division: Carter, Cocke, Greene, Hamblen, Hancock, Hawkins, Johnson, Sullivan, Unicoi and Washington counties.

(3) Southern Division: Bledsoe, Bradley, Hamilton, McMinn, Marion, Meigs, Polk, Rhea and Sequatchie counties.

(4) The Winchester Division: Bedford, Coffee, Franklin, Grundy, Lincoln, Moore, Van Buren and Warren counties.

DISTRICT COURT

Court Locations:	Chattanooga, Greeneville, Knoxville and Winchester
Contact Information:	U.S. District Court
	800 Market Street, Suite 130
	Knoxville, TN 37902
	865-545-4228
	www.tned.uscourts.gov

BANKRUPTCY COURT

Court Locations:	Chattanooga, Greeneville and Knoxville
Contact Information:	U.S. Bankruptcy Court
	31 East 11th Street
	Chattanooga, TN 37402
	423-752-5163
	www.tneb.uscourts.gov
U.S. Trustee Region:	8
VCIS Phone:	423-752-5272 or 800-767-1512

Middle District

The Middle District comprises three divisions.

(1) Nashville Division: Cannon, Cheatham, Davidson, Dickson, Houston, Humphreys, Montgomery, Robertson, Rutherford, Stewart, Sumner, Trousdale, Williamson and Wilson counties.

(2) Northeastern Division: Clay, Cumberland, De Kalb, Fentress, Jackson, Macon, Overton, Pickett, Putnam, Smith and White counties.

(3) Columbia Division: Giles, Hickman, Lawrence, Lewis, Marshall, Maury and Wayne counties.

DISTRICT COURT

Court Locations:	Columbia, Cookeville and Nashville
Contact Information:	U.S. District Court
	800 U.S. Courthouse
	801 Broadway
	Nashville, TN 37203
	615-736-5498
	www.tnmd.uscourts.gov

BANKRUPTCY COURT

Court Locations:	Columbia, Cookeville and Nashville	
Contact Information:	Street Address	Mailing Address
	U.S. Bankruptcy Court	U.S. Bankruptcy Court
	701 Broadway	P.O. Box 24890
	Nashville, TN 37203	Nashville, TN 37202-4890
	615-736-5590	
	www.tnmb.uscourts.gov	

U.S. Trustee Region: 8
VCIS Phone: None

Western District

The Western District comprises two divisions.

(1) Eastern Division: Benton, Carroll, Chester, Crockett, Decatur, Gibson, Hardeman, Hardin, Haywood, Henderson, Henry, Lake, McNairy, Madison, Obion, Perry and Weakley counties. Also includes the waters of Tennessee River to low-water mark on the eastern shore wherever such river forms the boundary between the Western and Middle Districts from the north line of Alabama north to the point in Henry County, Tennessee, where the south boundary of Kentucky strikes the east bank of the river.

(2) Western Division: Dyer, Fayette, Lauderdale, Shelby and Tipton counties.

DISTRICT COURT

Court Locations:	Jackson and Memphis
Contact Information:	U.S. District Court
	242 Federal Building
	167 North Main Street
	Memphis, TN 38103
	901-495-1200
	www.tnwd.uscourts.gov

BANKRUPTCY COURT

Court Locations:	Jackson and Memphis
Contact Information:	U.S. Bankruptcy Court
	200 Jefferson Avenue, Suite 413
	Memphis, TN 38103
	901-328-3500
	www.tnwb.uscourts.gov
U.S. Trustee Region:	8
VCIS Phone:	901-328-3509 or 888-381-4961

TEXAS

Texas is a member of the 5th Circuit Court and is divided into four judicial districts: Northern, Southern, Eastern and Western.

Northern District

The Northern District comprises seven divisions.

(1) Dallas Division: Dallas, Ellis, Hunt, Johnson, Kaufman, Navarro and Rockwall counties.

(2) Fort Worth Division: Comanche, Erath, Hood, Jack, Palo Pinto, Parker, Tarrant and Wise counties.

(3) Abilene Division: Callahan, Eastland, Fisher, Haskell, Howard, Jones, Mitchell, Nolan, Shackleford, Stephens, Stonewall, Taylor and Throckmorton counties.

(4) San Angelo Division: Brown, Coke, Coleman, Concho, Crockett, Glasscock, Irion, Menard, Mills, Reagan, Runnels, Schleicher, Sterling, Sutton and Tom Green counties.

(5) Amarillo Division: Armstrong, Brisco, Carson, Castro, Childress, Collingsworth, Dallam, Deaf Smith, Donley, Gray, Hall, Hansford, Hartley, Hemphill, Hutchinson, Lipscomb, Moore, Ochiltree, Oldham, Parmer, Potter, Randall, Roberts, Sherman, Swisher and Wheeler counties.

(6) Wichita Falls: Archer, Baylor, Clay, Cottle, Foard, Hardeman, King, Knox, Montague, Wichita, Wilbarger and Young counties.

(7) Lubbock Division: Bailey, Borden, Cochran, Crosby, Dawson, Dickens, Floyd, Gaines, Garza, Hale, Hockley, Kent, Lamb, Lubbock, Lynn, Motley, Scurry, Terry and Yoakum counties.

DISTRICT COURT

Court Locations:	Abilene, Amarillo, Dallas, Fort Worth, Lubbock, San Angelo and Wichita Falls
Contact Information:	U.S. District Court
	1100 Commerce Street, 14th Floor
	Dallas, TX 75242

214-753-2200
www.txnd.uscourts.gov

BANKRUPTCY COURT

Court Locations:	Abilene, Amarillo, Dallas, Fort Worth, Lubbock, San Angelo and Wichita Falls
Contact Information:	U.S. Bankruptcy Court
	1100 Commerce Street, Room 1254
	Dallas, TX 75242
	214-753-2000
	www.txnb.uscourts.gov
U.S. Trustee Region:	6
VCIS Phone:	214-753-2128 or 800-886-9008

Southern District

The Southern District comprises seven divisions.

(1) Galveston Division: Brazoria, Chambers, Galveston and Matagorda counties.

(2) Houston Division: Austin, Brazos, Colorado, Fayette, Fort Bend, Grimes, Harris, Madison, Montgomery, San Jacinto, Walker, Waller and Wharton counties.

(3) Laredo Division: Jim Hogg, La Salle, McMullen, Webb and Zapata counties.

(4) Brownsville Division: Cameron and Willacy counties.

(5) Victoria Division: Calhoun, DeWitt, Goliad, Jackson, Lavaca, Refugio and Victoria counties.

(6) Corpus Christi Division: Aransas, Bee, Brooks, Duval, Jim Wells, Kenedy, Kleberg, Live Oak, Nueces and San Patricio counties.

(7) McAllen Division: Hidalgo and Starr counties.

DISTRICT COURT

Court Locations:	Brownsville, Corpus Christi, Galveston, Houston, Laredo, McAllen and Victoria
Contact Information:	5401 U.S. Courthouse
	515 Rusk Avenue
	Houston, TX 77002
	713-250-5500
	www.txs.uscourts.gov

BANKRUPTCY COURT

Court Locations:	Brownsville, Corpus Christi, Galveston, Houston, Laredo, McAllen and Victoria
Contact Information:	U.S. Bankruptcy Court
	5401 U.S. Courthouse
	515 Rusk Avenue
	Houston, TX 77002
	713-250-5500
	www.txs.uscourts.gov
U.S. Trustee Region:	7
VCIS Phone:	713-250-5049 or 800-745-4459

Eastern District

The Eastern District comprises six divisions.

(1) Tyler Division: Anderson, Cherokee, Gregg, Henderson, Panola, Rains, Rusk, Smith, Van Zandt and Wood counties

(2) Beaumont Division: Hardin, Jasper, Jefferson, Liberty, Newton and Orange counties.

(3) Sherman Division: Collin, Cook, Delta, Denton, Fannin, Grayson, Hopkins and Lemar counties.

(4) Marshall Division: Camp, Cass, Harrison, Marion, Morris and Upshur counties.

(5) Texarkana Division: Bowie, Franklin, Red River and Titus counties.

(6) Lufkin Division: Angelina, Houston, Nacogdoches, Polk, Sabine, San Augustine, Shelby, Trinity and Tyler counties.

DISTRICT COURT

Court Locations:	Beaumont, Lufkin, Marshall, Paris, Sherman, Texarkana and Tyler
Contact Information:	U.S. District Court
	211 W. Ferguson Street, Room 106
	Tyler, TX 75702
	903-590-1000
	www.txed.uscourts.gov

BANKRUPTCY COURT

Court Locations:	Beaumont, Plano, Tyler
Contact Information:	U.S. Bankruptcy Court
	110 North College Avenue
	Tyler, TX 75702
	903-590-3200
	www.txeb.uscourts.gov
U.S. Trustee Region:	6
VCIS Phone:	903-590-1217 or 800-466-1694

Western District

The Western District comprises seven divisions.

(1) Austin Division: Bastrop, Blanco, Burleson, Burnet, Caldwell, Gillespie, Hays, Kimble, Lampasas, Lee, Llano, Mason, McCulloch, San Saba, Travis, Washington and Williamson counties.

(2) Waco Division: Bell, Bosque, Coryell, Falls, Freestone, Hamilton, Hill, Leon, Limestone, McLennan, Milam, Robertson and Somervell counties.

(3) El Paso Division: El Paso county.

(4) San Antonio Division: Atascosa, Bandera, Bexar, Comal, Dimmit, Frio, Gonzales, Guadalupe, Karnes, Kendall, Kerr, Medina, Real and Wilson counties.

(5) Del Rio Division: Edwards, Kinney, Maverick, Terrell, Uvalde, Val Verde and Zavalla counties.

(6) Pecos Division: Brewster, Culberson, Jeff Davis, Hudspeth, Loving, Pecos, Presidio, Reeves, Ward and Winkler counties.

(7) Midland-Odessa Division: Andrews, Crane, Ector, Martin, Midland and Upton counties.

DISTRICT COURT

Court Locations:	Austin, Del Rio, El Paso, Midland, Pecos, San Antonio and Waco
Contact Information:	U.S. District Court
	655 East Durango Blvd., Room G65
	San Antonio, TX 78206
	210-472-6550
	www.txwd.uscourts.gov

BANKRUPTCY COURT

Court Locations:	Austin, El Paso, Midland, San Antonio and Waco	
Contact Information:	Street Address:	Mailing Address:
	U.S. Bankruptcy Court	U.S. Bankruptcy Court
	615 East Houston Street, Room 137	P.O. Box 1439
	San Antonio, TX 78205	San Antonio, TX 78295-1439
	210-472-6720	
	www.txwb.uscourts.gov	
U.S. Trustee Region:	7	
VCIS Phone:	210-472-4023 or 888-436-7477	

U.S. VIRGIN ISLANDS

The U.S. Virgin Islands are a member of the 3rd Circuit Court and constitute one judicial district comprising two divisions.

(1) Comprises St. Thomas and St. John.

(2) Comprises St. Croix.

DISTRICT COURT

Court Locations:	St. Croix and St. Thomas
Contact Information:	U.S. District Court
	5500 Veterans Drive, Room 310
	St. Thomas, VI 00802
	340-774-0640
	www.vid.uscourts.gov

BANKRUPTCY COURT

Court Locations:	St. Croix and St. Thomas
Contact Information:	District Court, St. Thomas/St. Croix
	5500 Veterans Drive, Room 310
	St. Thomas, VI 00802
	340-774-8310
	www.vid.uscourts.gov
U.S. Trustee Region:	21

VCIS Phone: None
No CM/ECF.

UTAH

Utah is a member of the 10th Circuit Court and constitutes one judicial district comprising two divisions.

(1) Northern Division: Box Elder, Cache, Davis, Morgan, Rich and Weber counties.

(2) Central Division: Beaver, Carbon, Daggett, Duchesne, Emery, Garfield, Grand, Iron, Juab, Kane, Millard, Piute, Salt Lake, San Juan, Sanpete, Sevier, Summit, Tooele, Uintah, Utah, Wasatch, Washington and Wayne counties.

DISTRICT COURT

Court Locations:	Ogden and Salt Lake City
Contact Information:	U.S. District Court
	150 U.S. Courthouse
	350 South Main Street
	Salt Lake City, UT 84101
	801-524-6100
	www.utd.uscourts.gov

BANKRUPTCY COURT

Court Locations:	Ogden and Salt Lake City
Contact Information:	U.S. Bankruptcy Court
	301 U.S. Courthouse
	350 South Main Street
	Salt Lake City, UT 84101
	801-524-6687
	www.utb.uscourts.gov
U.S. Trustee Region:	19
VCIS Phone:	801-524-3107 or 800-733-6470

VERMONT

Vermont is a member of the 2nd Circuit Court and constitutes one judicial district.

DISTRICT COURT

Court Locations:	Bennington, Brattleboro, Burlington and Rutland	
Contact Information:	Street Address:	Mailing Address:
	U.S. District Court	U.S. District Court
	11 Elmwood Avenue, Room 506	P.O. Box 945
	Burlington, VT 05401	Burlington, VT 05402-0945

802-951-6301
www.vtd.uscourts.gov

BANKRUPTCY COURT

Court Locations:	Burlington and Rutland
Contact Information:	U.S. Bankruptcy Court
	67 Merchants Row
	Post Office Box 6648
	Rutland, VT 05702-6648
	802-776-2000
	www.vtb.uscourts.gov
U.S. Trustee Region:	2
VCIS Phone:	800-260-9956

VIRGINIA

Virginia is a member of the 4th Circuit Court and is divided into two judicial districts: Eastern and Western.

Eastern District

Accomac, Amelia, Arlington, Brunswick, Caroline, Charles City, Chesterfield, Culpeper, Dinwiddie, Elizabeth City, Essex, Fairfax, Fauquier, Gloucester, Goochland, Greensville, Hanover, Henrico, Isle of Wight, James City, King and Queen, King George, King William, Lancaster, Loudoun, Louisa, Lunenburg, Mathews, Mecklenburg, Middlesex, Nansemond, New Kent, Norfolk, Northampton, Northumberland, Nottoway, Orange, Powhatan, Prince Edward, Prince George, Prince William, Princess Anne, Richmond, Southampton, Spotsylvania, Stafford, Surry, Sussex, Warwick, Westmoreland and York counties.

DISTRICT COURT

Court Locations:	Alexandria, Newport News, Norfolk and Richmond
Contact Information:	U.S. District Court
	Albert V. Bryan U.S. Courthouse
	401 Courthouse Square
	Alexandria, VA 22314
	703-299-2100
	www.vaed.uscourts.gov

BANKRUPTCY COURT

Court Locations:	Alexandria, Newport News, Norfolk and Richmond
Contact Information:	U.S. Bankruptcy Court
	1100 East Main Street, Suite 310
	Richmond, VA 23219-3515
	804-916-2400
	www.vaeb.uscourts.gov
U.S. Trustee Region:	4
VCIS Phone:	800-326-5879

Western District

Albermarle, Alleghany, Amherst, Appomattox, Augusta, Bath, Bedford, Bland, Botetourt, Buchanan, Buckingham, Campbell, Carroll, Charlotte, Clarke, Craig, Cumberland, Dickenson, Floyd, Fluvanna, Franklin, Frederick, Giles, Grayson, Greene, Halifax, Henry, Highland, Lee, Madison, Montgomery, Nelson, Page, Patrick, Pittsylvania, Pulaski, Rappahannock, Roanoke, Rockbridge, Rockingham, Russell, Scott, Shenandoah, Smyth, Tazewell, Warren, Washington, Wise and Wythe counties.

DISTRICT COURT

Court Locations:	Abingdon, Big Stone Gap, Charlottesville, Danville, Harrisonburg, Lynchburg and Roanoke	
Contact Information:	Street Address:	Mailing Address:
	U.S. District Court	U.S. District Court
	210 Franklin Road, Room 308	P.O. Box 1234
	Roanoke, VA 24011	Roanoke, VA 24006

540-857-5100
www.vawd.uscourts.gov

BANKRUPTCY COURT

Court Locations:	Abingdon, Big Stone Gap, Charlottesville, Danville, Harrisonburg, Lynchburg, Roanoke and Staunton
Contact Information:	U.S. Bankruptcy Court
	210 Church Avenue, SW - Room 200
	Roanoke, VA 24011
	540-857-2391
	www.vawb.uscourts.gov
U.S. Trustee Region:	4
VCIS Phone:	540-857-2391 ext. 5

WASHINGTON

Washington is a member of the 9th Circuit Court and is divided into two judicial districts: Eastern and Western.

Eastern District

Adams, Asotin, Benton, Chelan, Columbia, Douglas, Ferry, Franklin, Garfield, Grant, Kittitas, Klickitat, Lincoln, Okanogan, Pend Oreille, Spokane, Stevens, Walla Walla, Whitman and Yakima counties.

DISTRICT COURT

Court Locations:	Richland, Spokane, Walla Walla and Yakima	
Contact Information:	Street Address:	Mailing Address:
	U.S. District Court	U.S. District Court
	920 West Riverside, Room 840	P.O. Box 1493
	Spokane, WA 99201	Spokane, WA 99210-1493
	509-353-2150	
	www.waed.uscourts.gov	

BANKRUPTCY COURT

Court Locations:	Spokane and Yakima	
Contact Information:	Street Address:	Mailing Address:
	U.S. Bankruptcy Court	U.S. Bankruptcy Court
	904 West Riverside, Suite 304	P.O. Box 2164
	Spokane, WA 99201	Spokane, WA 99210-2164
	509-353-2404	
	www.waeb.uscourts.gov	
U.S. Trustee Region:	18	
VCIS Phone:	509-353-2404 option 6, or 800-519-2549 option 6	

Western District

Clallam, Clark, Cowlitz, Grays Harbor, Island, Jefferson, King, Kitsap, Lewis, Mason, Pacific, Pierce, San Juan, Skagit, Skamania, Snohomish, Thurston, Wahkiakum and Whatcom counties.

DISTRICT COURT

Court Locations:	Seattle and Tacoma
Contact Information:	U.S. District Court
	700 Stewart Street
	Seattle, WA 98101
	206-370-8400
	www.wawd.uscourts.gov

BANKRUPTCY COURT

Court Locations:	Seattle and Tacoma

Contact Information: U.S. Bankruptcy Court
                      700 Stewart Street, Room 6301
                      1200 Sixth Avenue
                      Seattle, WA 98101-1271
                      206-370-5200
                      www.wawb.uscourts.gov
U.S. Trustee Region: 18
VCIS Phone: 206-370-5285

WEST VIRGINIA

West Virginia is a member of the 4th Circuit Court and is divided into two judicial districts: Northern and Southern.

Northern District

Barbour, Berkeley, Braxton, Brooke, Calhoun, Doddridge, Gilmer, Grant, Hampshire, Hancock, Hardy, Harrison, Jefferson, Lewis, Marion, Marshall, Mineral, Monongalia, Morgan, Ohio, Pendleton, Pleasants, Pocahontas, Preston, Randolph, Ritchie, Taylor, Tucker, Tyler, Upshur, Webster and Wetzel counties.

DISTRICT COURT

Court Locations: Clarksburg, Elkins, Martinsburg and Wheeling
Contact Information: Street Address: Mailing Address:
                      U.S. District Court   U.S. District Court
                      300 Third Street   P.O. Box 1518
                      Elkins, WV 26241   Elkins, WV 26241
                      304-636-1445
                      www.wvnd.uscourts.gov

BANKRUPTCY COURT

Court Locations: Clarksburg, Elking, Martinsburg and Wheeling
Contact Information: Street Address: Mailing Address:
                      U.S. Bankruptcy Court   P.O. Box 70
                      12th and Chapline Streets   Wheeling, WV 26003
                      Wheeling, WV 26003
                      304-233-1655
                      www.wvnb.uscourts.gov
U.S. Trustee Region: 4
VCIS Phone: 800-809-3028

Southern District

The Southern District comprises the counties of Boone, Cabell, Clay, Fayette, Greenbrier, Jackson, Kanawha, Lincoln, Logan, McDowell, Mason, Mercer, Mingo, Monroe, Nicholas, Putnam, Raleigh, Roane, Summers, Wayne, Wirt, Wood and Wyoming counties.

DISTRICT COURT

Court Locations: Beckley, Bluefield, Charleston, Huntington, Lewisburg, and Parkersburg
Contact Information: Street Address: Mailing Address:
                      U.S. District Court   U.S. District Court
                      300 Virginia Street E., Room 2400 P.O. Box 2546
                      Charleston, WV 25301   Charleston, WV 25329
                      304-347-3000
                      www.wvsd.uscourts.gov

BANKRUPTCY COURT

Court Locations: Beckley, Bluefield, Charleston, Huntington and Parkersburg
Contact Information: Street Address: Mailing Address:
                      U.S. Bankruptcy Court   U.S. Bankruptcy Court
                      300 Virginia Street E., Room 2400 P.O. Box 3924
                      Charleston, WV 25301   Charleston, WV 25339

	304-347-3000
	www.wvsb.uscourts.gov
U.S. Trustee Region:	4
VCIS Phone:	304-347-5680

WISCONSIN

Wisconsin is a member of the 7th Circuit Court and is divided into two judicial districts: Eastern and Western.

Eastern District

Brown, Calumet, Dodge, Door, Florence, Fond du Lac, Forest, Green Lake, Kenosha, Kewaunee, Langlade, Manitowoc, Marinette, Marquette, Menominee, Milwaukee, Oconto, Outagamie, Ozaukee, Racine, Shawano, Sheboygan, Walworth, Washington, Waukesha, Waupaca, Waushara and Winnebago counties.

DISTRICT COURT

Court Locations:	Green Bay, Milwaukee and Oshkosh
Contact Information:	U.S. District Court
	362 U.S. Courthouse
	517 East Wisconsin Avenue
	Milwaukee, WI 53202
	414-297-3372
	www.wied.uscourts.gov

BANKRUPTCY COURT

Court Locations:	Milwaukee
Contact Information:	U.S. Bankruptcy Court
	126 U.S. Courthouse
	517 East Wisconsin Avenue
	Milwaukee, WI 53202
	414-297-3291
	www.wieb.uscourts.gov
U.S. Trustee Region:	11
VCIS Phone:	414-297-3582 or 877-781-7277

Western District

Adams, Ashland, Barron, Bayfield, Buffalo, Burnett, Chippewa, Clark, Columbia, Crawford, Dane, Douglas, Dunn, Eau Claire, Grant, Green, Iowa, Iron, Jackson, Jefferson, Juneau, La Crosse, Lafayette, Lincoln, Marathon, Monroe, Oneida, Pepin, Pierce, Polk, Portage, Price, Richland, Rock, Rusk, Saint Croix, Sauk, Sawyer, Taylor, Trempealeau, Vernon, Vilas, Washburn and Wood counties.

DISTRICT COURT

Court Locations:	Eau Claire, La Crosse, Madison, Superior and Wausau
Contact Information:	U.S. District Court
	120 North Henry Street, Room 320
	P.O. Box 432
	Madison, WI 53701-0432
	608-264-5156
	www.wiwd.uscourts.gov

BANKRUPTCY COURT

Court Locations:	Eau Claire and Madison	
Contact Information:	Street Address:	Mailing Address:
	U.S. Bankruptcy Court	P.O. Box 548
	120 North Henry Street, Room 340	Madison, WI 53701-0548
	Madison, WI 53703	
	608-264-5178	
	www.wiwb.uscourts.gov	

U.S. Trustee Region: 11
VCIS Phone: 608-264-5035 or 800-743-8247

WYOMING

Wyoming is a member of the 10th Circuit Court. Wyoming and those portions of Yellowstone National Park situated in Montana and Idaho constitute one judicial district.

DISTRICT COURT

Court Locations: Casper and Cheyenne
Contact Information: U.S. District Court
                        2120 Capitol Avenue, 2nd Floor
                        Cheyenne, WY 82001-3658
                        307-433-2120
                        www.ch10.uscourts.gov/wyoming

BANKRUPTCY COURT

Court Locations: Casper and Cheyenne
Contact Information: U.S. Bankruptcy Court
                        2120 Capitol Avenue, Suite 6004
                        Cheyenne, WY 82001
                        307-433-2200
                        www.wyb.uscourts.gov
U.S. Trustee Region: 19
VCIS Phone: 307-433-2238 or 888-804-5537

U.S. TRUSTEE REGIONAL AND FIELD OFFICES

Region 1—Includes the judicial districts established for the States of Maine, Massachusetts, New Hampshire and Rhode Island.

Regional Office
United States Trustee
10 Causeway Street, Suite 1184
Boston, MA 02222-1043
617-788-0435
www.usdoj.gov/ust/rol/index.htm

Field Offices

Maine
Office of the U.S. Trustee
537 Congress Street, Suite 303
Portland, ME 04100
207-780-3564

Massachusetts
U.S. Trustee, Eastern
10 Causeway Street, Suite 1184
Boston, MA 02222-1043
617-788-0401

U.S. Trustee, Western
446 Main Street, 14th Floor
Worcester, MA 01608
508-793-0555

New Hampshire
U.S. Trustee
66 Hanover Street, Suite 302
Manchester, NH 03101
603-666-7908

Rhode Island
U.S. Trustee
10 Dorrance Street, Suite 910
Providence, RI 02903
401-528-5551

Region 2—Includes the judicial districts established for the States of Connecticut, New York and Vermont.

Regional Office
United States Trustee
33 Whitehall Street, 21st Floor
New York, NY 10004
212-510-0500

Field Offices

Connecticut
Assistant U.S. Trustee
265 Church Street, Suite 1103
New Haven, CT 06510
203-773-2210

New York
Assistant U.S. Trustee
33 Whitehall Street, 21st Floor
New York, NY 10004
212-510-0500

Assistant U.S. Trustee
74 Chapel Street, Suite 200
Albany, NY 12207
518-434-4553

Assistant U.S. Trustee
42 Delaware Avenue, Suite 100
Buffalo, NY 14202
716-551-5541

Assistant U.S. Trustee
560 Federal Plaza
Central Islip, NY 11722
631-715-7800

Assistant U.S. Trustee
100 State Street, Room 609
Rochester, NY 14614
716-263-5812

Assistant U.S. Trustee
10 Broad Street, Room 105
Utica, NY 13501
315-793-8191

Vermont
Assistant U.S. Trustee
74 Chapel Street, Suite 200
Albany, NY 12207
518-434-4553

Region 3—Includes the judicial districts established for the States of Delaware, New Jersey and Pennsylvania.

Regional Office
Acting United States Trustee
833 Chestnut Street, Suite 500
Philadelphia, PA 19107
215-597-4411

Field Offices

Delaware
Assistant U.S. Trustee
844 King Street, Suite 2207
Lockbox 35
Wilmington, DE 19801
302-573-6491

New Jersey
Acting Assistant U.S. Trustee
Assistant U.S. Trustee
One Newark Center, Suite 2100
Newark, NJ 07102
973-645-3014

Pennsylvania
Senior Assistant U.S. Trustee
833 Chestnut Street, Suite 500
Philadelphia, PA 19107
215-597-4411

Assistant U.S. Trustee
228 Walnut Street, Suite 1190
P.O. Box 969
Harrisburg, PA 17101
717-221-4515

Assistant U.S. Trustee
1001 Liberty Avenue, Suite 970
Pittsburgh, PA 15222
412-644-4756

Region 4—Includes the judicial districts established for the States of Maryland, South Carolina, Virginia, West Virginia and for the District of Columbia.

Regional Office
United States Trustee
Regional Assistant U.S. Trustee
1835 Assembly Street, Suite 953
Columbia, SC 29201
803-765-5250

Field Offices

District of Columbia
Assistant U.S. Trustee
115 South Union Street, Room 210
Alexandria, VA 22314
703-557-7176

Maryland
Acting Assistant U.S. Trustee
300 West Pratt Street, Suite 350
Baltimore, MD 21201
410-962-3910

Acting Assistant U.S. Trustee
6305 Ivy Lane, Suite 600
Greenbelt, MD 20770
301-344-6216

South Carolina
Assistant U.S. Trustee
1835 Assembly Street, Suite 953
Columbia, SC 29201
803-765-5250

Virginia
Assistant U.S. Trustee
115 South Union Street, Suite 210
Alexandria, VA 22314
703-557-7176

Assistant U.S. Trustee
200 Granby Street, Room 625
Norfolk, VA 23510
757-441-6012

Acting Assistant U.S. Trustee
600 East Main Street, Suite 301
Richmond, VA 23219
804-771-2310

Assistant U.S. Trustee
210 First Street, S.W., Suite 505
Roanoke, VA 24011
540-857-2806

West Virginia
Assistant U.S. Trustee
300 East Virginia Street, Room 2025
Charleston, WV 25301
304-347-3400

Region 5—Includes the judicial districts established for the States of Louisiana and Mississippi.

Regional Office
United States Trustee
400 Poydras Street, Suite 2110
New Orleans, LA 70130
504-589-4018

Field Offices

Louisiana
Assistant U.S. Trustee
400 Poydras Street, Suite 2110
New Orleans, LA 70130
504-589-4018

Assistant U.S. Trustt
300 Fannin Street, Suite 3196
Shreveport, LA 71101-3079
318-676-3456

Mississippi
Assistant U.S. Trustee
100 West Capitol Street, Suite 706
Jackson, MS 39269
601-965-5241

Region 6—Includes the judicial districts established for the Northern and Eastern Districts of Texas.

Regional Office
United States Trustee
1100 Commerce Street, Room 976
Dallas, TX 75242
214-767-8967

Field Offices

Assistant U.S. Trustee
1100 Commerce Street, Room 976
Dallas, TX 75242
214-767-8967

Assistant U.S. Trustee
110 N. College Avenue, Room 300
Tyler, TX 75702
903-590-1450

Region 7—Includes the judicial districts established for the Southern and Western Districts of Texas.

Regional Office
United States Trustee
515 Rusk Street, Suite 3516
Houston, TX 77002
713-718-4650

Field Offices

Assistant U.S. Trustee
515 Rusk Street, Suite 3516
Houston, TX 77002
713-718-4650

Assistant U.S. Trustee
606 N. Carancahua Street, Suite 1107
Corpus Christi, TX 78476
361-888-3261

Assistant U.S. Trustee
903 San Jacinto, Room 230
Austin, TX 78701
512-916-5328

Assistant U.S. Trustee
615 East Houston Street, Suite 533
San Antonio, TX 78205
210-472-4640

Region 8—Includes the judicial districts established for the States of Kentucky and Tennessee.

Regional Office
United States Trustee
200 Jefferson Avenue, Suite 400
Memphis, TN 38103
901-544-3251

Field Offices

Kentucky
Assistant U.S. Trustee
100 East Vine Street, Suite 803
Lexington, KY 40507
859-233-2822

Assistant U.S. Trustee
601 West Broadway, Suite 512
Louisville, KY 40202
502-582-6000

Tennessee
Assistant U.S. Trustee
200 Jefferson Avenue, Suite 400
Memphis, TN 38103
901-544-3251

Assistant U.S. Trustee
31 East 11th Street, 4th Floor
Chattanooga, TN 37402
423-752-5153

Assistant U.S. Trustee
701 Broadway, Room 318
Nashville, TN 37203
615-736-2254

Region 9—Includes the judicial districts established for the States of Michigan and Ohio.

Regional Office
United States Trustee
200 Public Square, Suite 20-3300
Cleveland, OH 44114
216-522-7800

Field Offices

Michigan
Assistant U.S. Trustee
211 West Fort Street, Suite 700
Detroit, MI 48226
313-226-7999

Assistant U.S. Trustee
330 Ionia Avenue, N.W., Suite 202
Grand Rapids, MI 49503
616-456-2002

Ohio
Assistant U.S. Trustee
201 Superior Avenue East, Suite 441
Cleveland, OH 44114
216-522-7800

Assistant U.S. Trustee
36 East Seventh Street, Suite 2030
Cincinnati, OH 45202
513-684-6988

Assistant U.S. Trustee
170 North High Street, Suite 200
Columbus, OH 43215-2403
614-469-7411

Region 10—Includes the judicial districts established for the Central and Southern District of Illinois and the State of Indiana.

Regional Office
United States Trustee
101 West Ohio Street, Room 1000
Indianapolis, IN 46204
317-226-6101

Field Offices

Illinois
Assistant U.S. Trustee
401 Main Street, Suite 1100
Peoria, IL 61602
309-671-7854

Indiana
Assistant U.S. Trustee
101 West Ohio Street, Room 1000
Indianapolis, IN 46204
317-226-6101

Assistant U.S. Trustee
100 East Wayne Street, Room 555
South Bend, IN 46601
574-236-8105

Region 11—Includes the judicial districts established for the Northern District of Illinois and the State of Wisconsin.

Regional Office
United States Trustee
227 West Monroe Street, Suite 3350
Chicago, IL 60606
312-886-5785

Field Offices

Illinois
Assistant U.S. Trustee
227 West Monroe Street, Suite 3350
Chicago, IL 60606
312-886-5785

Assistant U.S. Trustee
517 East Wisconsin Avenue, Suite 430
Milwaukee, WI 53202
414-297-4499

Wisconsin
Assistant U.S. Trustee
780 Regent Street, Suite 304
Madison, WI 53715
608-264-5522

Region 12—Includes the judicial districts established for the States of Iowa, Minnesota, North Dakota and South Dakota.

Regional Office
United States Trustee
225 Second Street, S.E., Room 400
Cedar Rapids, IA 52401
319-364-2211

Field Offices

Iowa
Assistant U.S. Trustee
225 Second Street, S.E., Room 400
Cedar Rapids, IA 52401
319-364-2211

Assistant U.S. Trustee
210 Walnut Street, Suite 793
Des Moines, IA 50309-2108
515-284-4982

Minnesota
Assistant U.S. Trustee
300 South 4th Street, Suite 1015
Minneapolis, MN 55402
612-644-5500

North Dakota
Assistant U.S. Trustee
230 South Philips Avenue, Room 502
Sioux Falls, SD 57104
605-330-4450

South Dakota
Assistant U.S. Trustee
230 South Philips Avenue, Room 502
Sioux Falls, SD 57104
605-330-4550

Region 13—Includes the judicial districts established for States of Arkansas, Missouri and Nebraska.

Regional Office
United States Trustee
400 East 9th Street, Room 3440
Kansas City, MO 64106
816-512-1940

Field Offices

Arkansas
Assistant U.S. Trustee
200 West Capitol, Suite 1200
Little Rock, AR 72201
501-324-7357

Missouri
Assistant U.S. Trustee
400 East 9th Street, Room 3440
Kansas City, MO 64106
816-512-1940

Assistant U.S. Trustee
111 South 10th Street, Room 6353
St. Louis, MO 63102
314-539-2976

Nebraska
Assistant U.S. Trustee
111 South 18th Plaza, Suite 1148
Omaha, NE 68102
402-221-4300

Region 14—Includes the district of Arizona.

Regional Office
United States Trustee
230 North 1st Avenue, Suite 204
Phoenix, AZ 85003
602-682-2600

Field Offices
Assistant U.S. Trustee
2929 N. Central Avenue, Suite 700
Phoenix, AZ 85012
602-640-2100

Region 15—Includes the judicial districts established for the Southern District of California, the State of Hawaii, and for Guam and the Northern Mariana Islands.

Regional Office
United States Trustee
402 West Broadway, Suite 600
San Diego, CA 92101-8511
619-557-5013

Field Offices

California
Assistant U.S. Trustee
402 W. Broadway, Suite 600
San Diego, CA 92101-8511
619-557-5013

Guam
Assistant U.S. Trustee
108 Hernan Cortez, Suite 131
Sirena Plaza Building
Hagatna, GU 96932
671-472-7336

Hawaii
Assistant U.S. Trustee
1132 Bishop Street, Suite 602
Honolulu, HI 96813-2836
808-522-8150

Northern Mariana Islands
Assistant U.S. Trustee
108 Hernan Cortez, Suite 131
Sirena Plaza Building
Hagatna, GU 96932
671-472-7336

Region 16—Includes the Central District of California.

Regional Office
United States Trustee
725 S. Figueroa Street, Suite 2600
Los Angeles, CA 90017
213-894-6811

Field Offices

Assistant U.S. Trustee
725 S. Figueroa Street, Suite 2600
Los Angeles, CA 90017
213-894-6811

Assistant U.S. Trustee
3685 Main Street, Suite 300
Riverside, CA 92501
951-276-6990

Assistant U.S. Trustee
411 W. Fourth Street, Suite 9041
Santa Ana, CA 92701
714-338-3400

U.S. Trustee
128 East Carrillo Street, Suite 126
Santa Barbara, CA 93101
805-957-4100

Assistant U.S. Trustee
21051 Warner Center Lane
Suite 115
Woodland Hills, CA 91367
818-716-8800

Region 17—Includes the judicial districts established for the Eastern and Northern Districts of California and for the State of Nevada.

Regional Office
United States Trustee
Reg. Asst. U.S. Trustee
235 Pine Street, Suite 700
San Francisco, CA 94104-3401
415-705-3300

Field Offices

California
Assistant U.S. Trustee
235 Pine Street, Suite 700
San Francisco, CA 94104-3401
415-705-3333

Assistant U.S. Trustee
1130 O Street, Suite 1110
Fresno, CA 93721
559-498-7400

Assistant U.S. Trustee
1301 Clay Street, Suite 690N
Oakland, CA 94612-5217
510-637-3200

Assistant U.S. Trustee
501 I Street, Suite 7-500
Sacramento, CA 95814-2322
916-930-2100

Assistant U.S. Trustee
280 South First Street, Room 268
San Jose, CA 95113
408-535-5525

Nevada
Assistant U.S. Trustee
300 Las Vegas Blvd., South
Suite 4300
Las Vegas, NV 89101
702-388-6600

Assistant U.S. Trustee
300 Booth Street, Suite 2129
Reno, NV 89509
775-784-5335

Region 18—Includes the judicial districts established for the States of Alaska, Idaho, Montana, Oregon and Washington.

Regional Office
Acting U.S. Trustee
700 Stewart Street, Suite 5103
Seattle, WA 98101-1271
206-553-2000

Field Offices

Alaska
Assistant U.S. Trustee
605 West Fourth Avenue, Suite 258
Anchorage, AK 99501-2252
907-271-2600

Idaho
Assistant U.S. Trustee
720 Park Blvd., Suite 220
Boise, ID 83712
208-334-1300

Montana
Assistant U.S. Trustee
301 Central Avenue, Suite 204
Great Falls, MT 59401-3113
406-761-8777

Oregon
Assistant U.S. Trustee
211 East 7th Avenue, Suite 285
Eugene, OR 97401-2722
541-465-6330

Assistant U.S. Trustee
620 S.W. Main Street, Suite 213
Portland, OR 97205-3026
503-326-4000

Washington
Assistant U.S. Trustee
920 West Riverside, Room 593
Spokane, WA 99201-1012
509-353-2999

Assistant U.S. Trustee
700 Stewart Street, Suite 5103
Seattle, WA 98101-1271
206-553-2000

Region 19—Includes the judicial districts established for the States of Colorado, Utah and Wyoming.

Regional Office
United States Trustee
999 18th Street, Suite 1551
Denver, CO 80202
303-312-7230

Field Offices

Colorado
Assistant U.S. Trustee
999 18th Street, Suite 1551
Denver, CO 80202
303-312-7230

Utah
Assistant U.S. Trustee
9 Exchange Place, Suite 100
Salt Lake City, UT 84111
801-524-5734

Wyoming
Assistant U.S. Trustee
308 West 21st Street, Suite 203
Cheyenne, WY 82001
307-772-2790

Region 20—Includes the judicial districts established for the States of Kansas, New Mexico and Oklahoma.

Regional Office
United States Trustee
301 North Main Street, Suite 500
Wichita, KS 67202
316-269-6637

Field Offices

Kansas
Assistant U.S. Trustee
301 North Main Street, Suite 500
Wichita, KS 67202
316-269-6637

New Mexico
421 Gold Street, S.W., Suite 112
Albuquerque, NM 87102
505-248-6544

Oklahoma
Assistant U.S. Trustee
215 N.W. Dean A. McGee Avenue,
4th Floor
Oklahoma City, OK 73102
405-231-5950

Assistant U.S. Trustee
224 South Boulder Avenue, Suite 225
Tulsa, OK 74103
918-581-6670

Region 21—Includes the judicial districts established for the States of Florida, Georgia and for the Commonwealth of Puerto Rico and the U.S. Virgin Islands.

Regional Office
United States Trustee
Regional Assistant U.S. Trustee
75 Spring Street, SW, Room 362
Atlanta, GA 30303
404-331-4437

Field Offices

Florida
Assistant U.S. Trustee
51 S.W. First Avenue, Room 1204
Miami, FL 33130
305-536-7285

Assistant U.S. Trustee
135 West Central Blvd., Room 620
Orlando, FL 32801
407-648-6301Assistant U.S. Trustee

110 East Park Avenue, Suite 128
Tallahassee, FL 32301
850-521-5050

Acting Assistant U.S. Trustee
501 East Polk Street, Suite 1200
Tampa, FL 33602
813-228-2000

Georgia
Assistant U.S. Trustee
75 Spring Street, S.W., Room 362
Atlanta, GA 30303
404-331-4437

Assistant U.S. Trustee
433 Cherry Street, Suite 510
Macon, GA 31201-7910
478-752-3544

Assistant U.S. Trustee
222 W. Oglethorpe Avenue, Room 302
Savannah, GA 31401
912-652-4112

Puerto Rico
Assistant U.S. Trustee
Ochoa Building
500 Tanca Street, Suite 301
San Juan, PR 00901-1922
787-729-7444

U.S. Virgin Islands
Assistant U.S. Trustee
75 Spring Street, S.W., Room 362
Atlanta, GA 30303
404-331-4437

The U.S. Trustee Program currently does not administer bankruptcy estates in Alabama and North Carolina. Questions should be addressed to:

Administrative Office of the U.S. Courts
Bankruptcy Judges Division
1 Columbus Circle, N.E. - Suite 4-250
Washington, DC 20544
202-502-1900

U.S. CIRCUIT COURTS

1st Circuit
Maine
Massachusetts
New Hampshire
Puerto Rico
Rhode Island

2nd Circuit
Connecticut
New York
Vermont

3rd Circuit
Delaware
New Jersey
Pennsylvania
U.S. Virgin Islands

4th Circuit
Maryland
North Carolina
South Carolina
Virginia
West Virginia

5th Circuit
Louisiana
Mississippi
Texas

6th Circuit
Kentucky
Michigan
Ohio
Tennessee

7th Circuit
Illinois
Indiana
Wisconsin

8th Circuit
Arkansas
Iowa
Minnesota
Missouri
Nebraska
North Dakota
South Dakota

9th Circuit
Alaska
Arizona
California
Guam
Hawaii
Idaho
Montana
Nevada
No. Mariana Islands
Oregon
Washington

10th Circuit
Colorado
Kansas
New Mexico
Oklahoma
Utah
Wyoming

11th Circuit
Alabama
Florida
Georgia

DC Circuit
District of Columbia

Federal Circuit
U.S. Court of Appeals

27 Forms for Reference and Use

USE OF FORMS

In setting forth specimen forms in this section of the *Manual* our purpose is to familiarize the credit professional with the various types of contracts and instruments that were the subject of discussion in previous chapters of the book. These forms are samples only and should not be used as a substitute for competent professional advice.

In some cases a simple form may satisfy the requirements of the situation in which it is used. In many cases, however, the wrong form, or the failure to properly adapt the form to the needs of the parties, may have disastrous results. Most of the states have statutory forms for specific purposes, or impose requirements about matters which must be set forth in certain types of instruments. In some states, by legislative or judicial decree, a particular form of instrument, such as a judgment note, may be invalid or unenforceable. With competent legal advice, however, an instrument may be drawn that will accomplish the intent of the parties without violating statutory restrictions.

In addition to the forms set forth below, there may have been reproduced throughout the textual material in the various chapters, forms pertinent to the subject matter covered. It is recommended that reference be made to the text material in preceding chapters before using any forms in this chapter.

AFFIDAVIT

STATE OF _____
COUNTY OF _____

(Name of deponent), being duly sworn, deposes and says:

_____
Name

Sworn to before me this _____ day of _____.

_____
Notary Public

AFFIDAVIT OF CAPITAL CONTRIBUTIONS

BEFORE ME, the undersigned authority personally appeared _____ as President of _____, the sole general partner of _____, a limited partnership, who upon being duly sworn, certified as follows:

1. The amount of current and anticipated capital contributions made by the limited partners to the Partnership, in the aggregate, is _____ Dollars ($_____).

2. Except as set forth in paragraph 1, it is not anticipated that additional capital contributions will be made by the limited partners.

By: _____, President

STATE OF _____
COUNTY OF _____

The foregoing instrument was acknowledged before me this _____ day of _____, 20__, by _____, as President of _____, the sole general partner of _____ limited partnership. Said individual is personally known to me; or has produced (type of identification) as identification.

_____
(Signature of Notary Public)

_____
(Print, Type or Stamp Commissioned Name of Notary Public)

Date of Expiration and Number of Commission:_____

AGREEMENT FOR ACCOUNT STATED

(Set forth account as it appears upon the books of the creditor or as agreed upon by the parties.)
An account stated has been given me and I admit that it is true and correct and that I owe to _____the amount stated therein in the sum of _____.
Dated _____, 20__.

(Signature of Debtor)

AGREEMENT OF LIMITED PARTNERSHIP
OF _____ LIMITED PARTNERSHIP
(A _____ LIMITED PARTNERSHIP)

THIS LIMITED PARTNERSHIP AGREEMENT is made and entered into effective the _____ day of _____, 20__, by and among _____ and _____, as General Partners, whose address is _____ and all of the parties listed on Exhibit "A" attached hereto admitted to the Partnership treated hereby as Limited Partners (the "Limited Partners"). All capitalized terms used herein shall have the meaning assigned thereto in Section 1.7 hereof, unless otherwise defined elsewhere herein.

ARTICLE I
GENERAL

1.1. *Formation of Partnership.* The parties hereby form a limited partnership pursuant to the provisions of the Uniform Limited Partnership Act of the State _____ of and in accordance with the further terms and provisions hereof. Each Limited Partner shall immediately execute all such certificates and other documents conforming hereto as necessary for the General Partners to accomplish all filing, recording, publishing, and other acts appropriate to comply with all requirements for the formation and operation of a Limited partnership under the laws of the State of _____and for the formation, qualification, and operation of a limited partnership (or a partnership in which the Limited Partners have limited liability) in all other Jurisdictions where the Partnership shall propose to conduct business.

1.2. *Name.* The name of the Partnership shall be _____ LIMITED PARTNERSHIP.

1.3. *Limited Purpose of the Partnership.* The limited purpose of the Partnership is to acquire, own, hold, manage and maintain the _____ and to hold and manage cash, cash equivalents and readily tradable marketable securities incidental to the ownership and management of the _____s.

1.4. *Authority of the Partnership.* In order to carry out its purpose, the Partnership is empowered to do any and all acts and things necessary, desirable, convenient, incidental, appropriate, proper and advisable for the furtherance and accomplishment of its purpose, and for the protection and benefit of the Partnership.

1.5. *Principal Place of Business.* The location of the principal place of business of the Partnership is _____, _____ or such other place or places as the General Partners determine. The place of residence or principal place of business of each Limited Partner shall be as set forth on Exhibit "A" attached hereto. All such addresses shall be subject to change upon, notice pursuant to Section I hereof.

1.6. *Registered Agent.* The Registered Agent of the Partnership for service is _____. The registered office of the Partnership is _____.

1.7. Term. The Partnership shall be effective from and after the date that first appears on this document. The Partnership shall terminate on the earlier to occur of:

(a) _____, or
(b) such date as is required by Section 9.1 hereof.

1.8. *Definitions.* For the purposes of this Agreement, the following terms shall have the meanings indicated:

"ACT" means the Uniform Limited Partnership Act of the State of _____ as from time to time amended.

"AFFILIATE" with respect to the General Partners, means any person directly or indirectly controlling, controlled by or under common control with the General Partners.

"AGREEMENT" or "PARTNERSHIP AGREEMENT" means this Limited Partnership Agreement between the General Partners and the Limited Partners, together with all amendments hereto.

"CAPITAL ACCOUNTS" of the Partners shall be determined and maintained in accordance with the rules of Treasury Regulation Section 1.704l(b)(2)(iv) and, to the extent consistent therewith, each Partner's Capital Account shall be increased by:

(a) the amount of money contributed by such Partner to the Partnership;

(b) the fair market value of any property contributed by such Partner to the Partnership (net of any liabilities securing such contributed property that the Partnership is considered to assume or take subject to under Code Section 752);

(c) allocations to such Partner of income or gain (including tax exempt income) pursuant to Article VIII but excluding any income or gain described in Treasury Regulation Section 1.704-1 (b)(4)(i);

(d) the amount of Partnership liabilities assumed by such Partner or secured by any Partnership property distributed to such Partner other than the liabilities referred to in paragraph (f) below; and each Partner's Capital Account shall be decreased by:

(e) the amount of any money distributed to such Partner by the Partnership;

(f) the fair market value of any property distributed to such Partner by the Partnership (net of any liabilities securing such distributed property that such Partner is considered to assume or take subject to pursuant to Code Section 752);

(g) the amount of losses, costs and expenses allocated to such Partner under Article VIII:

(h) allocations to such Partner of expenditures of the Partnership described in Code Section 705(a)(2)(B); and

(i) the amount of any liabilities of such Partner assumed by the Partnership or secured by any property such Partner contributes to the Partnership other than the liabilities referred to in paragraph (b) above; subject, however, to such other adjustments as may be required under the Code and Treasury Regulations thereunder, including, but not limited to increases and decreases to reflect a revaluation of the Partnership Property on the Partnership's books in accordance with the rules of Treasury Regulations Section 1.704-1(b)(2)(iv)(f). Generally, a transferee of a Partnership interest shall succeed to the Capital Account relating to the Partnership Interest transferred. The Capital Account is to be determined and maintained at all times in strict accordance with all the provisions of Treasury Regulations Section 1.704-1 (b)(2)(iv). The Capital Account of a Partner may, under certain circumstances, be an amount less than zero.

"CAPITAL TRANSACTIONS" means the sale, exchange or refinancing of all or a portion of the Partnership's Property.

"CAPITAL VALUE" means the fair market value of the Property (net of any liabilities securing such Property that the Partnership is considered to assume or take subject to under Code Section 752) such

Partner is contributing to the Partnership. The Partners agree that the value of the Property contributed to the Partnership by each Partner shall be as set forth on Exhibit "B" attached hereto.

"CERTIFICATE" means the Certificate of Limited Partnership filed with the Secretary of State of the State of _____ as required by the Act and as from time to time amended, or such similar instrument as may be required to be filed by the laws of any other state in which the Partnership intends to conduct business.

"CODE" means the Internal Revenue Code of 1986, as from time to time amended and any federal legislation that may be substituted therefor.

"FEDERAL INCOME TAX ITEMS" means Profits, Losses, Gain From Capital Transactions, and Loss From Capital Transactions.

"GAIN FROM CAPITAL TRANSACTIONS" means income or gain of the Partnership as determined for federal income tax purposes as a result of the sale, exchange, or refinancing of all or a portion of the Partnership's property.

"GENERAL PARTNERS" or General Partner means _____ and _____ and those other persons admitted from time to time as General Partners pursuant hereto or the Act. Whenever the context shall allow, reference to "General Partners" shall be to the General Partner during such times as there shall be a sole General Partner.

"HOLDER OF RECORD" means the person in whose name a Partnership Interest is then registered on the books and records of the Partnership pursuant to Section 2.5 hereof. A Holder of Record does not include any Person who receives the rights to distributions from and allocations of Federal Income Tax Items of the Partnership by levy, foreclosure, charging order, execution or other similar proceeding.

"INCAPACITY" means when (i) an individual is declared or adjudicated as such by a court of competent jurisdiction, (ii) a guardian, conservator, or other personal representative of an individual's person or estate has been appointed by a court of competent jurisdiction, or (iii) an individual is certified as such in writing by at least two licensed physicians.

"LIQUIDATOR" means the Liquidator(s) designated in Section 9.2 hereof to handle the liquidation of the Partnership.

"LIMITED PARTNERS" means those persons herein identified as limited partners herein and listed in Exhibit "A" and those other persons admitted from time to time as limited partners pursuant hereto or the Act.

"LOSSES" means each item of loss, deduction, and credit of the Partnership as determined for federal income tax purposes, but excluding Loss From Capital Transactions.

"LOSS FROM CAPITAL TRANSACTIONS" means any loss of the Partnership as determined for federal income tax purposes as a result of the sale, exchange or refinancing of all or a portion of the Partnership's property.

"NET CASH FLOW" means monies available from the operation of the Partnership for any twelve (12) month period ending December 31st without deduction for depreciation, amortization or any other non-cash expenses, but after deducting monies used to pay or establish a reserve for all other expenses, debt payments, improvements and repairs related to the operation and administration of the Partnership.

"NET PROCEEDS" means the amount realized by the Partnership on the disposition of, or any other capital transaction involving, a Partnership property, less all fees, costs or expenses paid or to be paid with respect thereto and the amount of indebtedness (if any) of the Partnership paid or to be paid from such monies.

"PARTNERS" means the General Partners and all of the Limited Partners of the Partnership. The term "PARTNER" refers to any Limited Partner or to any General Partner of the Partnership, as the context requires.

"PARTNERSHIP" means this partnership formed under the Uniform Limited Partnership Act if the State of _____ in accordance with the terms and provisions of this Agreement and known as Sylvester Group Limited Partnership. "PARTNERSHIP CAPITAL" means the total capital contribution to the Partnership actually made or paid by the General Partners and Limited Partners with respect to the acquisition of a Partnership Interest in the Partnership.

"PARTNERSHIP INTEREST" or "INTEREST" means each Partner's percentage ownership in the Partnership as set forth in Exhibit "A" attached hereto, as adjusted after the Partnership receives the Capital Values of the assets contributed by each Limited Partner to the Partnership.

"PARTY" means a signatory to this Agreement or (during the lifetime of such signatory) a grantor trust created by such signatory.

"PERSON" or "PERSONS" means an individual, corporation, partnership, joint venture, trust or any other entity.

"PROFITS" means each item of income and gain of the Partnership, as determined for federal income tax purposes, but excluding Gain From Capital Transactions.

"PROPERTIES" means the real, personal and intangible assets contributed or to be contributed to the Partnership by the General Partners pursuant to Section 2.4 and by the Limited Partners pursuant to Section 2.3.2, and all other interests, rights and assets of any type owned by the Partnership. The initial Properties shall be as set forth on Exhibit "B" attached hereto. The term "PROPERTY" means a single asset which is included in the Properties.

"SUBSTITUTE LIMITED PARTNER" means any person not previously a Limited Partner who purchases or otherwise acquires from a Limited Partner a Partnership Interest and is admitted to the Partnership as a Substitute Limited Partner in accordance with the terms of this Agreement.

"VOTE" refers to the right of the Partners subject to all limitations set forth below and elsewhere in this Agreement, to decide any matter that may be submitted for decision by the Partners in accordance with the express written terms of this Agreement or under the provisions of the Act. The vote of each General Partner shall constitute one percent (1%) of the total votes cast and the votes of all Limited Partners shall constitute ninety-eight percent (98%) of the total votes cast. Each Limited Partner shall be entitled to cast one vote for every one percent Partnership Interest held of record by him on the date when notice is given of the matter to be voted on or consented to by the Limited Partners. A "Simple Majority Vote" of the Partners means a vote for over fifty percent (50%), a "Required Vote" means a vote of at least sixty-five percent (65%) and a "Unanimous Vote" means a vote of one hundred percent (100%) of the Partners. Except as otherwise expressly provided in this Agreement, a Simple Majority Vote shall be sufficient to pass and approve any matter submitted to a Vote of the Partners. Whenever a Vote of the Partners is required or permitted, a written consent to the action to be taken signed by the Partners holding the required percentage may be used in lieu of holding a formal meeting at which a Vote is taken. The rights of the Limited Partners to require or be permitted to vote on any matter shall be subject to and conditioned on the requirements set forth in Section 4.8 hereof.

ARTICLE II
PARTNERS, CAPITALIZATION AND ASSESSMENTS

2.1 *General Partner's Authority.* Except as otherwise provided in this Agreement, the General Partners of the Partnership shall have the sole, exclusive and absolute right and authority to act for and on behalf of the Partnership and all of the Partners in connection with all aspects of the business of the Partnership.

2.2. *Purchase of Limited Partner's Partnership Interest by General Partners.* The General Partners may purchase a selling. Limited Partner's Partnership Interest pursuant to Article VI hereof. No purchase of any Limited Partnership Interest by the General Partners shall reduce their liability as General Partners of the Partnership.

2.3. *Limited Partner's Partnership Interest.* The Limited Partners in the Partnership shall own ninety-eight percent (98%) of the Partnership Interests.

2.3.1. *Time of Admission.* A person shall be deemed to have been admitted as a Limited Partner:

(a) On the date this Agreement is fully executed by the General Partners and all Limited Partners with respect to all initial Limited Partners and the General Partners execute a certificate of limited partnership which is filed with the Secretary of State of, or

(b) If applicable, with respect to any additional Limited Partners or Substitute Limited Partners on the first day of the calendar month following the month in which such person complies with Article VI hereof.

2.3.2. *Contribution to Capital by Limited Partners.* Each Limited Partner shall contribute those Properties (or portions thereof) set forth opposite each of their respective names on Exhibit "B" attached hereto. Each Limited Partner shall receive such portion of ninety-eight percent (98%) of the Partnership Interests as is equal to the amount that the Capital Value of the portion of the Property contributed by such Limited Partner bears to the sum of the Capital Value of all of the Properties contributed to the Partnership by all Limited Partners. With the prior written consent of the General Partner, a Limited Partner may, if he elects to do so, make additional capital contributions from time to time. No Limited Partner is required to make any additional capital contributions to the Partnership. The Partnership agrees to pay the liabilities of a contributing Partner on all indebtedness secured by liens upon such Properties contributed and agrees to indemnify the contributor with respect thereto. Notwithstanding anything in this Agreement to the contrary, if at any time it is determined by a court of competent jurisdiction that at the time of its contribution to the Partnership the value of a Property did not exceed the total of all indebtedness secured by valid lien(s) upon such Property, then such Property is deemed not to have been contributed to the Partnership and title to said Property shall revert to the Limited Partner who contributed same, effective as of the date of such Property's contribution to the Partnership.

2.3.3. *Execution by Limited Partners.* By executing the Agreement, each Limited Partner subscribes and agrees to contribute to the capital of the Partnership, those amounts of Properties (or portions thereof) as set forth opposite each of their respective names on Exhibit "B" attached hereto.

2.4. *General Partner's Partnership Interest.* Each General Partner in the Partnership shall own one percent (1%) of the Partnership Interests.

2.4.1. *Time of Admission.* A person shall be deemed to have been admitted as a General Partner:

(a) On the date this Agreement is fully executed by the General Partners and all Limited Partners with respect to all initial Limited Partners, and the General Partners execute a certificate of limited partnership which is filed with Secretary of the State of _____, or (b) If applicable, with respect to any new General Partner on the first day of the calendar month following the month in which such person became a General Partner under Article III hereof.

2.4.2. *Contributions to Capital by General Partners; General Partners' Partnership Interest.* Upon the contribution of capital by the Limited Partners, each General Partner shall immediately contribute to the Partnership's capital an amount equal to the lesser of 1.01% of the Limited Partners' capital contribution or an amount that causes the sum of each General Partner's Capital Account balance to equal one percent (1%) of the total positive capital account balances for the Partnership.

2.5. *Registration—Rights of Holders of Record.* Upon the admission of a person as a Limited Partner, such person shall be registered on the records of the Partnership as a Limited Partner and a Holder of Record, together with his address and his amount of Partnership Interest. Upon the assignment of a Limited Partnership Interest pursuant to the terms of Article VI hereof, the assignee of such Partnership Interest shall be registered on the records of the Partnership as a Holder of Record, together with his address and his Partnership Interest.

A Holder of Record shall be entitled to all distributions and all allocations of Net Cash Flow, Net Proceeds, and Federal Income Tax Items with respect to the Partnership Interest registered in his name in the manner specified in Article VIII until his rights in such Partnership Interest have been transferred as permitted by this Agreement and the General Partners have been notified as required herein. The payment to the Holder of Record of any allocation or distribution with respect to such Partnership Interest shall be sufficient to discharge the Partnership's obligation in respect thereto.

2.6. *Continuation of Limited Partner Status.* No event, including but not limited to the admission of a Substitute Limited Partner, the transfer of a Partnership Interest by a Limited Partner, the expulsion of a Limited Partner from the Partnership, the forfeiture of a Partnership Interest, and retirement, death, disability, or bankruptcy of a Limited Partner shall entitle a Limited Partner to withdraw from the Partnership. Once admitted as a Limited Partner, a person shall continue to be a Limited Partner for all purposes of this Agreement and the Act until the General Partner consents in writing to the admission of a Substitute Limited Partner pursuant to Section 6.2 herein.

2.7. *Initial Capitalization.* The Partnership shall have as its initial capitalization an amount equal to the Limited Partners' initial capital contribution plus the General Partners' initial capital contribution. Upon acceptance of Limited Partners, the names, addresses and amount of the capital contributions of each such Limited Partner and the aggregate amount of such initial contributions by the Partners shall be set forth in Exhibits "A" and "B" of this Agreement.

2.8. *Return of Capital.* No Partner has the right to require the return of all or any part of his capital contribution(s) or a distribution of any property from the Partnership prior to its termination and dissolution except as otherwise provided in Section 2.12 herein.

The General Partners shall not be personally liable for the return of the capital contributions of the Partners if and to the extent that any return is required. Any such return shall be made solely from the assets of the Partnership. If any Partner shall receive the return, in whole or in part, of his capital contribution, he shall nevertheless be liable to the Partnership, to the extent provided in the Act, for the sum returned, together with interest thereon, to the extent necessary to discharge the Partnership's liabilities to creditors who extended credit to the Partnership or whose claims against the Partnership arose prior to such return or as otherwise provided under applicable law.

2.9. *Interest on Capital.* No interest shall be payable on any capital contributions made to the Partnership or on any Capital Account.

2.10. *Capital Account.* An individual Capital Account shall be maintained for each of the Partners as provided for in Section 1.7 herein.

2.11. *Liability for Continuing Obligations.* Upon the bankruptcy, insolvency, death, disability, or other change in circumstances of a Partner prior to completion of such Partner's obligations to complete certain payments pursuant to this Section, such Partner's estate, legal representative, or successor shall have the status of the Partner and of such Partner's rights and responsibilities.

2.12. *Status of Partnership Interest.* Except as otherwise provided in this Agreement, the Partnership Interest owned by the Limited Partners shall be fully paid and non-assessable. The Limited Partners shall not have the right to withdraw or reduce their capital contributions to the Partnership except as a result of (i) the dissolution and termination of the Partnership, or (ii) as otherwise provided in this Agreement and in accordance with applicable law.

ARTICLE III
GENERAL PARTNERS

3.1. *Rights and Duties.* At all times during the term of the Partnership, the General Partners shall be the sole managers of the Partnership and shall have the sole, absolute, and exclusive power, authority, and discretion in the conduct of the business and affairs of the Partnership without the concurrence, agreement, or confirmation of any Limited Partner except as expressly provided in Sections 2.3.1(a), 4.6, 9.1(a) and 11.10 of this Agreement. At no time during the term of the Partnership shall any Limited Partner have any authority whatsoever to take any action on behalf of the Partnership or to obligate the Partnership to any third party. Any action by any Limited Partner inconsistent with this Section 3.1 shall subject such Limited Partner to the provisions of Section 5.3 hereof.

3.2. *Reimbursement and Compensation to the General Partners.* The General Partners shall receive as full and complete compensation for their services as general partners the following amounts:

3.2.1. *Management Fees.* The General Partners shall be entitled to receive, in consideration for services to be performed for the Partnership pursuant to the terms and conditions of this Agreement, including without limitation their management of the Partnership and preparation of reports to all Partners, a fair and reasonable management fee, as determined by the General Partners in a manner consistent with their duties to the Partnership, which management fee shall be based upon the General Partners' actual time devoted to the Partnership and administration of the Partnership, the relative financial benefit accruing to the Partnership as the result of the General Partners' management and such other fees as shall be reasonable under all of the facts and circumstances. Such fees shall be paid as, if, and when such funds shall become available to the Partnership.

3.2.2. *Participation in Revenues.* The General Partners will be entitled to receive the allocations and distributions set forth in Article VIII.

3.3. *Interest of the General Partners in Certain Transactions.* The General Partners shall not be deemed to have received commissions, fees or other compensation paid to any firm, proprietorship, partnership or corporation that is an Affiliate, or in which the General Partners, or any partner, officer, director, or employee thereof or any member of any such person's respective immediate family, owns a beneficial interest.

3.4. *Successor General Partner.* In the event of the death or incapacity of both of the General Partners; the removal or withdrawal of both of the General Partners; or the occurrence of any of the events specified in Section 5.5 hereof involving both General Partners, the Limited Partners shall elect by a Simple Majority Vote another successor General Partner. If a new General Partner owns a limited partnership Interest, he shall convert such portion of his limited partnership Interest to a general partnership Interest that equals the amount of the general partnership Interest of the removed, withdrawing General Partner.

3.5. *Voluntary Withdrawal of a General Partner.* A General Partner may voluntarily withdraw from the Partnership upon thirty (30) days written notice to the Partners. Such notice requirement may be shortened or waived by the Partners, in their sole discretion. Upon the withdrawal of a General Partner, the withdrawing General Partner shall not be deemed to be liable with respect to any debts or liabilities that the Partnership incurs subsequent to the date of withdrawal, provided that such withdrawal shall not diminish or in any way affect any debts or liabilities that the Partnership incurred prior to such date.

3.6. *Right of the General Partner Upon Removal or Withdrawal.* If a General Partner is removed in accordance with Section 5.5 hereof, or a General Partner withdraws in accordance with Section 3.5 hereof, or ceases to be a General Partner by operation of law, or otherwise, the Partnership Interest of the removed or withdrawing General Partner shall become a limited partnership Interest and be assigned to the removed or withdrawing General Partner by the Partnership. The removed or withdrawing General Partner holding such limited partnership Interest shall automatically become a Substitute Limited Partner.

ARTICLE IV
MANAGEMENT AND OPERATION

4.1. *General Partners to Manage.* Except as otherwise expressly provided in Sections 2.3.1(a), 4.6, 9.1(a) and 11.11, the General Partners shall make all decisions affecting the business and affairs of the Partnership and use their best efforts to carry out the purposes for which the Partnership was organized. In addition to any other rights and powers which it may possess under applicable law or pursuant to this Agreement, the General Partners shall have all specific rights, powers, and authorities required or appropriate to the management of the Partnership which shall include without limitation the following rights, powers, and authorities to be exercised in such manner, in such form, at such times, and to such extent as the General Partners, in their sole discretion, determine:

(a) to acquire, hold, lease, encumber, pledge, option, sell, exchange, transfer, dispose of or otherwise deal with real or personal property (or rights or interests therein) of any nature whatsoever as may be necessary or advisable for the operation of the Partnership;

(b) to borrow or lend money for Partnership purposes and, if security is required for the borrowing thereof, to execute and deliver all instruments, deeds of trust, mortgages, security agreements, assignments, and other security documents relating to all or a portion of the assets of the Partnership as may be necessary or advisable for the operation of the Partnership. For purposes hereof, the borrowing or lending of money for Partnership purposes shall include: (i) lending money to Partners, Affiliates or other persons or entities, whether related or unrelated, or borrowing from any of the foregoing, upon such terms and conditions as the General Partners shall determine in their sole and absolute discretion; and (ii) the guaranteeing of, or pledging the Partnership Property for any of the foregoing loans, or for loans to or from Partners, to or from Affiliates, or to or from other persons or entities, all as determined in the sole and absolute discretion of the General Partners;

(c) to negotiate and enter into contracts, agreements or arrangements concerning the purposes for which the Partnership is organized and/or concerning assets of the Partnership as may be necessary or advisable for the operation of the Partnership, including, but not limited to purchase, joint venture, development, management and option agreements, deeds, assignments, and leases;

(d) to employ persons, agents, outside consultants and independent contractors as may be necessary or advisable for the operation of the Partnership;

(e) to pay all expenses reasonably incurred in the operation or administration of the Partnership and to establish reserves for liabilities and obligations of the Partnership whether contingent or otherwise, including but not limited to expenses, charges and fees relating to:

(1) the acquisition, preservation, protection or perfection of title to the Partnership's property, including insurance thereon;

(2) the maintenance, operation or management of any Partnership property;

(3) travel expenses, professional fees, attorneys' fees, and court costs;

(4) taxes on real or personal property owned by the Partnership;

(5) interest on any loan to the Partnership;

(6) normal closing costs (in the event of a sale or transfer of all or any part of the Partnership's property);

(7) expenses incurred in connection with the negotiation for, or consummation of financing or renewing, rearranging or refinancing any indebtedness on the Partnership's property; and

(8) the management fees owed to the General Partners pursuant to Section 3.2.1 herein;

(f) to pay on behalf of the Partnership (and be reimbursed for) any and all organizational expenses incurred in the creation of the Partnership including, without limitation, legal and accounting fees;

(g) to take and hold title to property, execute evidences of indebtedness or other obligations or instruments in its name or the name of a nominee all on behalf of the Partnership and with or without disclosing the true owner or party in interest thereto. The Partnership shall be solely entitled to all rights, titles and interests held by a General Partner or nominee on behalf of the Partnership and solely liable for all expenses, costs and other obligations incurred in connection therewith. All such instruments so executed may be transferred into the name of the Partnership by assignment or otherwise or held in the name of a General Partner or nominee as a General Partner determines: provided, always, that the General Partners shall keep as part of the books and records of the Partnership and properly account on its books for each such contract, deed, note or other instrument indicating the nominee parties thereto, date thereof and general description of such document;

(h) to execute and deliver any and all instruments to effectuate the foregoing and to take all such actions as may be necessary or advisable for the operation of the Partnership;

(i) to determine the use of the revenues of the Partnership for Partnership purposes;

(j) to control any matters affecting the rights and obligations of the Partnership, including the employment of attorneys to advise and represent the Partnership, the conduct of any litigation and the settlement thereof, and any other incurring of legal expenses;

(k) to admit one or more additional Limited Partners, at any time or from time to time, without the consent of the Limited Partners, upon such terms and conditions set forth in Article VI hereof and as the General Partners shall deem appropriate in their sole and absolute discretion. Additional Limited Partners shall be entitled to all of the rights and privileges of the original Limited Partners hereunder and shall be subject to all of the obligations and restrictions, and in all other respects their admission shall be subject to all of the terms and provisions of this Agreement;

(l) to act as the "tax matters partners" as described in Code Sections 6221 to 6233. _____ is designated as the tax matters partner (the "Tax Matters Partner"). The Tax Matters Partner is authorized to enter into settlement agreements with the Internal Revenue Service on behalf of all Partners with respect to Partnership Items (as defined in Code Section 6231(a)(3)), and the Limited Partners (except if any Limited Partner has filed a statement described in Code Section 6224(c)(3)(B)) agree to be bound by the terms of any settlement agreement entered into by the Tax Matters Partner on behalf of all Partners. Pursuant to this authorization, the Limited Partners agree to execute such further documents as may be necessary or desirable to cause the settlement agreement to be binding on them and not to exercise any right or undertake any other action which is inconsistent with any settlement agreement entered into by the Tax Matters Partner on their behalf. The Tax Matters Partner shall: (i) keep the Limited Partners reasonably informed as to the status of all administrative and judicial tax proceedings; (ii) file with the Internal Revenue Service a request for administrative adjustment if the Tax Matters Partner deems such to be appropriate; and (iii) file a petition in a court of competent jurisdiction regarding any dispute with respect to Partnership items which the Tax Matters Partner deems appropriate. In the event of the death, incapacity, removal or withdrawal of the Tax Matters Partner (the "Named Tax Matters Partner"), the General Partners shall designate a new Tax Matters Partner; and

(m) to execute powers of attorney, consents, waivers and other documents that may be necessary before any court, administrative board or agency of any governmental authority, affecting the properties owned by the Partnership.

4.2. *Third Parties.* No person dealing with a General Partner shall be required to determine his authority to make any undertaking, or to execute any document or instrument on behalf of the Partnership, nor to determine any fact or circumstance bearing upon the existence of such authority, and any such document, instrument or undertaking shall contain such provisions as a General Partner may deem appropriate or expedient. Any document or instrument, when executed by a General Partner, shall be as to third parties conclusive evidence that the execution of such document or instrument is the act of and binding upon the Partnership. Furthermore, no person dealing with a General Partner shall be required to determine or see to the application or distribution by a General Partner of any sums paid or assets transferred by such person to the Partnership or a General Partner.

4.3. *Obligations of the General Partners as Partnership Manager.* The General Partners shall use their good faith efforts to manage the Partnership affairs in a prudent and businesslike manner, and in accordance with good practices in the industry. The General Partners at all times shall act in the best interests of the Partnership in fulfillment of the purposes herein expressed.

4.4. *Insurance Coverage.* To protect Partnership assets, the General Partners may procure or cause to be procured and maintain or cause to be maintained in force or contract with others to obtain and maintain in force such insurance as in their judgment they deem prudent to serve as protection against liability for loss and damage that may be occasioned by the activities of the Partnership. The cost of obtaining such insurance shall be charged to and borne by the Partnership.

4.5. *Reliance upon Experts.* The General Partners may employ or retain such counsel, accountants, engineers, appraisers or other experts or advisors as they deem appropriate for the purpose of discharging their duties hereunder, and shall be entitled to pay the fees of any such persons from the funds of the Partnership. The General Partners may act and shall be protected in acting in good faith on the opinion or advice of, or information obtained from any such counsel, accountant, engineer, appraiser or other expert or advisor, whether retained or employed by the Partnership, the General Partners, or otherwise, in relation to any matter connected with the administration or operation of the business and affairs of the Partnership.

4.6. *Acts Not Authorized.* The General Partners are expressly not authorized to do any act or enter into any contract or other transaction that would:

(a) Make it impossible to carry on the ordinary business of the Partnership, provided, however, the sale or other disposition of all or any portion of the Partnership Property shall not be deemed to be an act making it impossible for the Partnership to carry on its ordinary business;

(b) Confess a judgment against the Partnership;

(c) Result in a possession of Partnership property or assignment of the Partnership's rights in specific partnership property, other than for a Partnership purpose; or

(d) Admit or substitute a person as a general partner of the Partnership, except with a Simple Majority Vote of the Limited Partners.

4.7. *Other Permissible Activities.* No Partner is prevented hereby from engaging in other activities for profit, whether as an investment, an active business or otherwise. It is expressly understood and agreed that the General Partners shall not be required to devote their entire business time or business resources to the business of the Partnership. The General Partners and their Affiliates have and in the future may engage in other businesses including but not limited to the organization and management of additional partnerships, limited partnerships, or joint ventures for investment in real estate, securities or otherwise, and must necessarily divide their time between the business of the Partnership and their other activities. The General Partners and their Affiliates are hereby authorized, during the life of the Partnership, to acquire real and personal properties and not offer the same to the Partnership.

4.8. *Meetings of Partners.* Except as specifically provided for herein, the General Partners shall not be required to hold meetings of Partners. A quorum for a meeting of Partners shall be (i) all General Partners and (ii) such number of Limited Partners owning no less than sixty-five percent (65%) of the Partnership Interests. Partners may either vote in person at any such meeting or give their proxy to a General Partner which designates the General Partner as their lawful agent to vote on all matters coming before the meeting. Notice of a meeting of Partners shall be given by the General Partners to the Partners at least one (1) day prior to holding the meeting. In lieu of a meeting, the General Partners may obtain a written consent in lieu of a meeting which is executed by Partners owning no less than the required Partnership Interests necessary for a proper Vote.

Notwithstanding the above, the General Partners may, in their sole and absolute discretion, upon one (1) day prior written notice to the Partners, amend the rules and procedures regarding meetings of Partners or written consents of Partners in lieu of meetings Provided, however, the General Partners may not change the specified voting percentage necessary to approve an action.

4.9. *Opinion of Counsel.* Subject to the other provisions of this Agreement, the General Partners may condition the holding of any meeting or the taking of any Vote upon the prior delivery to the Partnership, at the expense of the Partnership, of an opinion of counsel in form and substance satisfactory to the General Partners, to the effect that neither the holding of such meeting nor the Vote of the Partners will:

(a) change the Partnership from a limited partnership to a general partnership or result in the loss of any Limited Partner's limited liability status, or

(b) adversely affect the federal income tax status of the Partnership.

4.10. *Additional Funds.* If the General Partners determine that additional funds are required for the operations of the Partnership, the General Partners shall take the following steps:

4.10.1. *Third-Party Loans.* The General Partners shall attempt to arrange for loan(s) from third-party lenders on the best terms that the General Partners are able to negotiate.

4.10.2. *Notice to Limited Partners.* If the Partnership is not able to obtain loans from third-party lenders, the General Partners shall give notice to the Limited Partners of the amount needed by the Partnership and the purpose for which the Partnership requires such additional funds.

4.10.3. *Loans from Partners.* The General Partners and/or any Limited Partner(s) may loan funds to the Partnership with consent of all Partners at a rate of interest and on such other terms and conditions as may be agreed upon at that time, including with respect to collateral for such loan. As to any funds so loaned, the General Partners or Limited Partner(s) shall be deemed general creditors of the Partnership and shall be entitled to be paid principal and interest thereon without regard to the income or profits of the Partnership.

4.10.4. *Additional Capital Contributions.* If the Partnership is unable to obtain loans from third-party creditors or loans from Partners sufficient to satisfy the Partnerships need for additional funds, the General Partners shall request the Limited Partners to make pro rata additional contributions of cash to the Partnership in the amount necessary to satisfy the Partnership's need for additional funds (the "Funding Shortfall"). All Limited Partners shall have the right (but not tie obligation) to contribute a portion of the Funding Shortfall in the proportion that such Limited Partner's Percentage interest in the Partnership bears to the Percentage Interest of all the Limited Partners (which shall be referred to herein as such Partner's "Proportionate Share"). The Partnership Interest of any Limited Partner failing to contribute his Proportionate Share (a "Non-Contributing Partner") shall be reduced by a percentage (such Partner's "Percentage Reduction") computed by dividing such Partner's Proportionate Share by the sum of all previous contributions (under Sections 2.3 and 2.7 above) to the Partnership plus the amount of the Funding Shortfall actually contributed to the Partnership. A percentage equal to such Non-Contributing Partner's Percentage Reduction shall be added to the Percentage Interest of any Partner(s) contributing the Proportionate Share of such Non-Contributing Partner. If no Partner contributes such Non-Contributing Partner's Proportionate Share, a percentage equal to such Non-Contributing Partner's Percentage Reduction shall be added to the Percentage interest of the Limited Partners who contribute their Proportionate Share. The terms of this provision are solely elective as to the Partners and do not create any rights in any third parties.

4.10.5. *Additional Contribution by General Partners.* Whenever a Limited Partner makes a contribution to the capital of the Partnership, each General Partner shall immediately contribute capital to the Partnership equal to 1.01% of the Limited Partner's capital contribution or a lessor amount (including zero) that causes the General Partner's Capital Account to equal one percent (1%) of the total positive capital account balances for the Partnership. If no Limited Partner Capital Account has a positive balance, then the General Partners need not have a positive Capital Account balance.

ARTICLE V
RIGHTS AND OBLIGATIONS OF LIMITED PARTNERS

5.1. *Limited Liability.* Upon full execution of this Agreement, the General Partners shall file the Certificate and the Limited Partners shall become limited partners within the meaning of the Act.

5.2. *No Management Responsibility.* At no time during the term of the Partnership shall any Limited Partner have any authority or right to take part in the management of the business or transact any business for the Partnership. All management responsibility is vested absolutely and exclusively in the General Partners. Any action by any Limited Partner inconsistent with this Section 5.2 shall subject such acting Limited Partner to the provisions of Section 5.3 hereof.

5.3. *No Authority to Act.* At no time during the term of the Partnership shall a Limited Partner have the power to act on behalf of, sign for, or bind the Partnership. All authority to act on behalf of the Partnership is vested absolutely and exclusively in the General Partners. Any action of a Limited Partner that is inconsistent with the sole, exclusive and absolute right and authority of the General Partners shall:

(a) Constitute a breach of this Agreement on the part of the Limited Partner so acting, and

(b) The General Partners shall provide such Limited Partner with notice (in the manner set forth in Section 11.1) of the breach. Such Limited Partner shall have five (5) days after he receives such notice of the breach to cure the breach (if such breach can be cured). If the breach is not cured within such five (5) day period, such Limited Partner shall be liable for any and all damages that may occur to the Partnership and all of the other Partners, but any such liability shall not extend to any creditor of the Partnership.

5.4. *Rights of Limited Partners.* A Limited Partner shall have the same rights as the General Partners to:

(a) Subject to Section 7.1 hereof, have the Partnership books kept at the principal place of business of the Partnership and at all reasonable times to inspect and copy at his expense any of them either in person or by his authorized representative;

(b) Subject to Section 7.1 hereof, have on demand for a proper purpose, true and full information of all things affecting the Partnership, and a formal accounting of Partnership affairs whenever circumstances render it just and reasonable;

(c) Subject to Section 7.1 hereof, have, on demand for a proper purpose, by mail a copy of the names, addresses and Partnership interests of all Limited Partners; and

(d) Subject to the provisions of Section 4.8 hereof, propose and Vote on certain Partnership matters and amendments to the Agreement as provided herein.

5.5. *Removal of a General Partner.* Limited Partners by obtaining a Simple Majority Vote shall have the right to remove a General Partner in the event that a General Partner:

(a) dies or becomes incapacitated;

(b) makes a general assignment for the benefit of creditors;

(c) files a voluntary bankruptcy petition;

(d) becomes the subject of an order for relief or is declared insolvent in any federal or state bankruptcy or insolvency proceedings;

(e) files a petition or answer seeking for the General Partner a reorganization, arrangement, composition, readjustment, liquidation, dissolution, or similar relief under any law;

(f) files an answer or other pleading admitting or failing to contest the material allegations of a petition filed against it in a proceeding of the type described in paragraphs (a) through (d) above;

(g) seeks, consents to or acquiesces in the appointment of a trustee, receiver or liquidator of all or any substantial part of the General Partner's properties;

(h) commits a crime involving moral turpitude;

(i) is convicted of a felony; or

(j) violates any provision of this Agreement or violates any provision of law applicable to the Partnership and such violation shall not have been cured within ten (10) days after notice of such violation.

ARTICLE VI
TRANSFER AND ASSIGNMENT OF PARTNERSHIP INTERESTS

6.1. *Assignment.* A Partner shall have the right to assign, transfer, encumber or pledge (herein, for purposes of this Article VI, "assign") the whole or any portion of his Partnership Interest by a written assignment, provided that: (i) the terms of such assignment are not in contravention of any of the provisions of this Agreement specifically including, but not limited to, the below provisions of Section 6.1(a)(ii)(A); (ii) such assignment is fully executed by the assignor and assignee; (iii) such assignment is received by the Partnership and recorded on the books thereof; and (iv) the transfer is approved by a Simple Majority Vote of the Partners. In the event of such an assignment, the following rules shall govern:

(a) *Restrictions on Interests During Lifetime.* A Partner shall not during his or her lifetime transfer, encumber of alienate any of his or her Interest in the Partnership except as provided by this Agreement.

(i) Immediate Family. A Partner's Interest in the Partnership may be freely transferred during life or at death to a spouse, children and/or grandchildren of the Partner, or to any trust for the benefit of such persons. In the event of such transfer, the transferee becomes a Partner of the Partnership and shall be bound by this Agreement.

(ii) Sale or Transfer to Persons Other than Immediate Family.

(A) If any Partner should during his or her lifetime desire to transfer, encumber or alienate any of his or her Interest in the Partnership, he or she shall first offer, in writing, to sell all of his or her Interest in the Partnership to the remaining Partners of the Partnership at the price specified in Section 6.1(c). The remaining Partners of the Partnership shall then have thirty (30) days within which to purchase the Interest offered as the total Interest in the Partnership owned by each purchasing Partner of the Partnership on the date of such offer bears to the total Interest in the Partnership owned by all such purchasing Partners of the Partnership. Any Interest in the Partnership not purchased by the remaining Partners of the Partnership by the end of that thirty (30) day period shall be offered at the same price to the Partnership. The Partnership shall then have thirty (30) days within which to purchase such portion of the remaining Interest offered. Any interest in the Partnership not purchased by the remaining Partners of the Partnership, or the Partnership, may then be transferred, encumbered or alienated for a period of thirty (30) days following the expiration of the time hereinabove provided for purchases by the Partnership, but only upon the same terms and conditions as such offer to the remaining Partners of the Partnership, or the Partnership, and only after first securing the written approval of a majority of the remaining Partners of the Partnership, which consent may not be unreasonably withheld; provided, however, that if any Partner has received a bona fide offer for any such Interest, he or she shall not transfer, encumber or alienate any of such Interest except in accordance with the provisions of subparagraph (8) of Section 6.1(a)(ii), below.

(B) If any Partner has received a bona fide offer for all or any part of his or her Interest in the Partnership which the Partner desires to accept, he or she shall first offer in writing to sell all of his or her interest in the Partnership to the remaining Partners of the Partnership at the price specified in such bona fide offer or at the price specified in Section 6.1(c), whichever is the lesser. Attached to such written offer to the remaining Partners of the Partnership shall be a written notice that the Partner has received a bona fide offer for the purchase of all or some part of his or her Interest in the Partnership, stating the name and address of the prospective purchaser, the Interest to be sold, the sales price, and the terms and conditions of such sale. A copy of the written offer to such Partner, if any, shall also be attached to such written offer to the remaining Partners of the Partnership. The remaining Partners of the Partnership, and the Partnership, shall then have the right to purchase all or any part of such Interest in accordance with the procedure set forth in subparagraph (A) of Section 6.1(a)(i), above. Any Interest in the Partnership not purchased by the remaining Partners of the Partnership, the Partnership, may then be transferred, encumbered, or alienated for a period of thirty (30) days following the expiration of the time herein provided for purchases by the Partnership, but only upon the same terms and conditions as such bona fide offer and only after first securing the written approval of a majority of the remaining Partners of the Partnership, which consent may not be unreasonably withheld.

(C) All offers made pursuant to the provisions of Section 6.1(a) shall be irrevocable and shall terminate thirty (30) day period the selling Partner receives another bona fide offer which has a higher purchase price than the previous bona fide offer, then the selling Partner may revoke his prior written offer and substitute the new bona fide offer. A new thirty (30) day period shall start on the date of substitution.

(D) Any Interest in the Partnership which is transferred, encumbered or alienated pursuant to the terms of Section 6.1(a)(ii) shall continue to be subject to all terms and conditions of this Agreement, without regard to whether any such interest was acquired before or after the execution of this Agreement.

(b) *Death.* Upon the death of any Partner, all or any part of the interest in the Partnership owned by the decedent at the time of his or her death may be transferred to a spouse, children, and/or grandchildren of the decedent, or to any trust for the benefit of such persons. In the event of such transfer, the transferee becomes a Partner of the Partnership and shall be bound by this Agreement. If any Interest in the Partnership owned by the decedent at the time of his or her death is not transferred to a spouse, children, and/or grandchildren of the decedent, or to any trust for the benefit of such persons, the remaining Partners of the Partnership, the Partnership, shall have an irrevocable option to purchase any and all of such Interest in accordance with the procedure set forth in Section 6.1(a)(ii) of this Agreement.

(c) *Purchase Price.* The purchase price for each Interest in the Partnership shall be equal to the value of each such Interest, as mutually agreed upon by the remaining Partners of the Partnership, and/or the Partnership, whichever or whoever is purchasing the Interest in the Partnership. If the selling Partner and the remaining Partners of the Partnership, and/or the Partnership, as the case may be, cannot agree on the value of each Interest to be sold, then the fair market value of such interest shall be determined by a qualified appraiser mutually agreeable to the selling Partner, the remaining Partners of the Partnership, and/or the Partnership, whichever or whoever is purchasing such Interest in the Partnership. The appraiser's opinion as to fair market value shall be binding upon all parties. The date of valuation of the fair market value by the appraiser shall be the date the selling Partner offers in writing to sell all or any portion of his or her Interest in the Partnership to the remaining Partners of the Partnership. The appraiser shall render his opinion as to the fair market value of the Interest to be sold within thirty (30) days of being appointed. The determination of the fair market value pursuant to this paragraph shall in every instance be conclusive and binding upon the parties. The cost of the appraiser shall be shared by the selling Partner paying one-half ($\frac{1}{2}$) of such costs and the remaining Partners of the Partnership, the Partnership, paying one-half ($\frac{1}{2}$) of such costs, each to the extent they are purchasing such interest.

(d) *Payment of the Purchase Price.* The purchase price of the Interest in the Partnership shall be payable in full in cash within fifteen (15) days after the expiration of the thirty (30) day period mentioned above for acceptance of an offer to sell by either the remaining Partners of the Partnership, the Partnership, provided, however, in the event of the death of a Partner, the purchase price shall be payable in full in cash within one hundred eighty (180) days after the date of a Partner's death.

(e) *Transfer of Interest.* Upon receipt of the cash by the selling Partner, legal representative of the estate, named legatees or heirs of the deceased Partner, as the case may be, the Partner, or such legal representative, named legatees or heirs of the Partner shall deliver the certificates for the Interest in the Partnership purchased, duly endorsed in blank or with an executed Interest assignment in proper form attached, to the purchasing Partners of the Partnership, the Partnership, as the case may be, together with any and all other documents necessary to carry out the terms of this Agreement. The legal representative of the estate, named legatees or heirs of the deceased Partners shall pay all state and federal taxes imposed upon the transfer of such Interest.

(f) *Legend on Certificate.* Upon the execution of this Agreement, each Certificate for the Partnership held by the Partners and for interests issued by the Partnership in the future shall have placed on it, on the face of the Certificate in bold type, the following legend:

"The Partnership Interest evidenced by this Certificate is subject to the provisions of a Partnership Agreement executed on _____, 20___, by and between the Partners, a copy of which is on file at the principal office of the Partnership."

(g) *Remedies for Enforcement of Agreement.* Each Partner to this Agreement shall have the right to an injunction to prevent any breach of the terms of Section 6.1 and the right to specific performance to enforce compliance with any agreement or covenant contained therein. The prevailing Partner shall be entitled to reimbursement from the nonprevailing party for costs and expenses (including, without implied limitation, reasonable attorneys' fees) incurred in connection with the enforcement of this Section 6.1. Such remedies shall be cumulative and in addition to any rights or remedies which may otherwise be available to any party by law.

(h) *General.* All Interests in the Partnership owned by the Partners, whether acquired before or after the execution of this Agreement, shall be subject to all of the terms and conditions of this Agreement. This Agreement shall inure to the benefit of and be binding upon the Partners, the Partnership, and each of the persons a party to this Agreement, their respective heirs, successors, assigns, and legal representatives.

(i) *Effective Date.* The effective date of an assignment of a Partnership Interest shall be the date set forth on the written date of acceptance.

(j) *Treatment of Assignor.* Notwithstanding anything herein to the contrary, the Partnership and the General Partners shall be entitled to treat the assignor of such interest as the absolute owner thereof in all respects and shall incur no liability for distributions of cash or other property made in good faith to him until such time as the written assignment has been received by and recorded on the books of the Partnership and is otherwise effective in accordance herewith.

(k) *Assignee Distributions.* Except as provided in Section 6.1(i) above, the assignee of a Partnership Interest shall be entitled to receive distributions of cash or other property from the Partnership attributable to the Interest acquired by reason of such assignment from and after the effective date of the assignment of such interest to him.

(l) *Allocation of Profits and Losses.* The division and allocation of Profits and Losses attributable to the Partnership Interest between assignor and assignee during any fiscal year of the Partnership shall be in accordance with the provisions of Section 8.6.6.

6.2. *Substitution.* No assignee of the whole or any portion of a Partnership Interest shall have the right to become a Substituted Limited Partner in place of his assignor unless all of the following conditions are satisfied:

(a) the assignor executes and acknowledges a written instrument of assignment together with such other instruments as the General Partners may deem necessary or desirable to effect the admission of the assignee as a Substituted Limited Partner;

(b) such instrument of assignment has been delivered to, received, and approved in writing by the General Partners; and

(c) the unanimous written consent of all Partners to such substitution has been obtained, the granting or denial of which shall be within the sole and absolute discretion of each Partner and must be given by each Partner free of duress and of each Partner's free will.

6.3. *Amendment of Certificate.* The General Partners shall take such steps as are necessary and/or required by the Act to effect an amendment of the Certificate and Exhibit "A" to this Agreement to reflect the substitution or addition of Limited Partners. For this purpose, the General Partners shall have the authority to sign the amendment of this Agreement and the Certificate as attorney-in-fact for the assigning Limited Partner, the Substitute Limited Partner, and the remaining Limited Partners.

6.4. *Expenses.* The Partnership may charge and receive from the selling Limited Partner an amount not exceeding $3,000.00 to defray its costs and expenses, including attorney's fees, in effecting the transfer and registration on its books of such Interest in the Partnership thus sold.

6.5. *Notice of Assignment.* Notwithstanding anything in the partnership laws of the State of to the contrary, no transfer of any Partnership Interest, although otherwise valid under this Agreement and the Act, shall be recognized by the Partnership until the transferor has given written notice thereof to the General Partners and the transferee has become a Holder of Record.

6.6. *Involuntary Assignment by a General Partner.* Except as provided in Section 9.1(e) hereof, in the event a General Partner's Interest is taken or disturbed by levy, foreclosure, charging order, execution, or other similar proceeding, the Partnership shall not dissolve. The assignee of that General Partner's Interest shall receive only that General Partner's rights to distributions and allocations of Federal Income Tax Items of the Partnership and shall, in no event, have the right to interfere in the management or the administration of the Partnership business or affairs or to act as a General Partner. The assignee shall only have the right to receive distributions and allocations of Federal Income Tax Items attributable to the General Partner's Interest in the Partnership. Any General Partner whose Interest has been taken or disturbed under any circumstances described above shall automatically become a Substitute Limited Partner and the Interest of such General Partner shall become a Limited Partnership Interest.

Any entity to which an Interest under this Agreement is transferred pursuant to the provisions of the Bankruptcy Code, 11 U.S.C. §§ 101 et. seq., shall be deemed without further act to have assumed all of the obligations arising under this Agreement on or after the date of such assignment. Upon demand any such assignees shall execute and deliver to each other party to this Agreement an instrument confirming such assumption. Failure to deliver such instrument shall be deemed a default hereunder by the assignee.

6.7. *Involuntary Assignment by a Limited Partner.* In the event that a Limited Partner's Interest is taken or disturbed by levy, foreclosure, charging order, execution, or other similar proceeding, the Partnership shall not dissolve but the assignee of said Limited Partnership Interest shall be entitled. to no more than to receive distributions and allocations of Federal Income Tax Items attributable to the Limited Partner's Interest in the Partnership, in accordance with the percentages allowed under this Agreement and, in no event, shall said assignee have the right to interfere with the management or administration of the Partnership business or affairs or to become a Substitute Limited Partner except as may otherwise be provided herein.

6.8. *Assignee's Tax Liability.* An assignee of any Partnership Interest, whether of a General Partner or Limited Partner, shall receive the Federal and all relevant state Forms K-1 and report all income and loss on his or her income tax returns each year in accordance with Rev. Rule. 77-137, 1977-1 C.B. 178. A person who becomes an assignee pursuant to Section 6.6 or Section 6.7 will be an assignee and an assignee only for purposes of the other provisions hereof.

6.9. *Death, Incapacity, or Dissolution of a Limited Partner.* Upon the death, adjudication of bankruptcy or Incapacity of a Limited Partner who is an individual, his legally authorized personal representatives shall have all the rights of a Limited Partner for the sole purposes of settling or managing his estate and shall have only such power as the Limited Partner possessed to make an assignment of his Partnership Interest in accordance with the terms hereof and to join with any assignee in making application to substitute such assignee as a Substitute Limited Partner.

Upon the adjudication of bankruptcy, dissolution or other cessation to exist as a legal entity of any Limited Partner which is not an individual, the authorized representative of such entity, possessed of the rights of such Limited Partner for the sole purposes of winding up in an orderly fashion and disposing of the business of such entity, shall have only such power as such entity possessed to make an assignment of its Partnership Interest in accordance with the terms hereof and to join with such assignee in making application to substitute such assignee as a Substitute Limited Partner.

6.10. *Opinion Letter.* In addition to the other requirements of Article VI, notwithstanding anything herein to the contrary, no Limited Partner may sell, transfer, assign, give, bequeath, pledge, encumber, or hypothecate any Partnership Interest without first presenting to the General Partners a written opinion of counsel (in form and substance reasonably acceptable to the General Partners) if requested by the General Partners to the effect that such sale, transfer, assignment, or conveyance:

(a) does not violate any applicable federal or state securities laws, and

(b) will not result in a termination of the Partnership within the meaning of Code Section 708(b).

ARTICLE VII
ACCOUNTING, RECORDS AND REPORTS

7.1. *Books, Records, and Reports.* The General Partners shall maintain at the principal office of the Partnership or at such other place as the General Partners determine:

(a) the books and records of the Partnership, showing all receipts and expenditures, assets and liabilities, profits and losses, and all other records necessary for recording the Partnership's business and affairs including those sufficient to record the allocations and distributions as set forth in Article VIII hereof;

(b) an executed counterpart of this Agreement and all amendments thereto;

(c) a list of the names, residence addresses and Partnership Interests held by each Limited Partner and assignee; and

(d) a copy of the Certificate and all amendments thereto.

Such information shall be open to reasonable inspection and examination by any of the Partners, their agents, accountants, attorneys and other duly authorized representatives during regular business hours upon not less than forty-eight (48) hours prior written request.

7.2. *Accounting Method.* The books and records of the Partnership shall be kept in accordance with the terms of this Agreement and in a manner sufficient to meet the reporting requirements of the Internal Revenue Service. The accounting year of the Partnership shall be the calendar year.

7.3. *Financial Statements and Tax Returns.* At the expense of the Partnership, the General Partners may engage an accountant or other qualified professional to prepare the Partnership's annual income tax return, the return required by Code Section 6050K relating to sales and exchanges of Partnership interests, and such financial statements, if any, as the General Partners in their sole discretion determine appropriate.

The General Partners, in their sole and absolute discretion, may determine the form and amount of detail to be contained in the financial statements and whether or not such financial statements shall be audited or unaudited. Within a reasonable time after the close of each accounting year, the General Partners shall transmit to each person who was a partner (or assignee) during such accounting year, a copy of the Partnership Tax Return (IRS Form 1065) and a report (which may be in the form Schedule K-1 to IRS Form 1065) indicating such persons' respective share of Federal Income Tax Items, tax preference items and investment credits, if any, for such year. Any financial statements which the General Partners cause to be prepared shall be available for inspection at the principal offices of the Partnership.

7.4. *Tax Elections.* In the event of a transfer of all or any part of the Interest of Partner, the Partnership may elect, pursuant to Sections 743 and 754 of the Code, to adjust the basis of the Partnership property if, in the opinion of the General Partners, based upon the advice of the tax counsel for the Partnership, such election would be most advantageous to the Limited Partners. Except insofar as an election pursuant to Section 754 has been made with respect to the Interest of any Partner, the determination of profits, losses, and cash distribution shall be made as provided for in this Agreement. With respect to any Partner whose Interest has been affected by an election pursuant to Section 754, appropriate adjustments may be made with respect to the determination of profits, losses and cash distributions. Each Partner agrees to furnish the Partnership with all information necessary to give effect to such election. Each Partner benefiting from the election will pay or reimburse the Partnership for all additional accounting expenses Occasioned by such election. The Partnership may elect to make any other election permitted under any provision of the Code if in the opinion of the General Partners, based upon the advice of the tax counsel for the Partnership, such election would be advantageous to the Limited Partners as a group or to any Limited Partner without being disadvantageous to any other Limited Partner.

7.5. *Banks.* All funds of the Partnership shall be deposited in a separate bank account or accounts in the name of the Partnership or such other name as may be determined from time to time by the General Partners. Withdrawals from such account or accounts shall be made upon checks or other withdrawal orders executed by a duly authorized representative of the General Partners.

ARTICLE VIII
DISTRIBUTIONS AND ALLOCATIONS TO PARTNERS

8.1. *Distributions of Net Cash Flow and Net Proceeds.* Net Cash Flow and Net Proceeds shall be distributed as follows:

(a) First, the greater of 90% of Net Cash Flow and Net Proceeds, or $250,000 per year to the Partners as a class, in proportion to their Partnership Interest.

(b) The balance shall be distributed at such times and in such amounts as the General Partners, in their sole discretion, shall determine, taking into account the reasonable business needs of the Partnership (including plan for expansion of the Partnership's business).

A General Partner's determination regarding whether or not to make distributions and the amount of distributions to be made shall be final and binding on all Partners. Such distributions shall be made no less than once a year to each Partner in accordance with such Partner's Interest in the Partnership.

8.2. *Distributions in Kind.* Assets of the Partnership may not be distributed in kind.

8.3. *Liquidating Distributions.* Notwithstanding Section 8.2, liquidating distributions may be made and shall be governed by Article IX.

8.4 *Limitations on Cash in Return of Capital.* No Partner shall be entitled to demand and receive property other than cash in return for his capital contribution to the Partnership, and no Partner shall have the right to sue for a partition of Partnership property.

8.5. *No Priority in Distributions Among Limited Partners.* Except as otherwise provide in this Agreement, no limited Partner shall have any priority over any other Limited Partner as to any Partnership distributions or to the return of his contributions to the Partnership capital.

8.6. *Allocation of Federal Income Tax Items.* Except to the extent provided in Subsections 8.6.3 through 8.6.7, the Federal Income Tax Items of the Partnership shall be allocated in the following order and priority:

8.6.1. *Profits and Gain from Capital Transactions:*

(a) First, an amount of Profits and Gain from Capital Transactions equal to the aggregate sum of all the Capital Account balances with a deficit balance shall be allocated among those Partners with a deficit

Capital Account balance, in proportion that each such Partner's deficit Capital Account balance bears to the aggregate sum of all the Capital Account balances with a deficit balance; and

(b) Second, any Profits and Gain from Capital Transactions in excess of the amount allocated in 8.6.1(a) shall be allocated among all Partners in accordance with each Partner's respective percentage Interest in the Partnership.

8.6.2. *Losses and Loss from Capital Transactions:*

(a) First, an amount of Losses and Loss from Capital Transactions equal to the aggregate sum of the Capital Account balances with a positive balance shall be allocated among those Partners with a positive Capital Account balance, in proportion that each such Partner's positive Capital Account balance bears to the aggregate sum of all the Capital Account balances with a positive balance; and

(b) Second, any Losses and Loss from Capital Transactions in excess of the amount allocated in 8.6.2(a) shall be allocated to the General Partners in accordance with each General Partner's respective percentage Interest in the Partnership.

8.6.3. *Qualified Income Offset.* If a Partner unexpectedly receives any adjustments, allocations, or distributions described in Treasury Regulation Section 1.704-1(b)(2)(ii)(d)(4), (5), or (6), which creates a deficit balance in a Partner's Capital Account, such Partner shall be allocated items of Profits and Gains From Capital Transactions of the Partnership in an amount and manner sufficient to eliminate such deficit Capital Account balance as quickly as possible.

8.6.4. *Minimum Gain.* If there is a net decrease in Partnership "minimum gain" during a taxable year of the Partnership, any Partner with a deficit balance in its Capital Account at the end of that year (in excess of its proportionate share of remaining minimum gain at such time) shall be specially allocated, before any other allocation is made under Code Section 704(b), Profits and Gain From Capital Transactions for that taxable year in the amount and proportions necessary to eliminate such deficit as quickly as possible.

8.6.5. *Minimum Allocation to General Partners.* If at any time during the term of the Partnership, the aggregate Federal Income Tax Items allocated to the General Partners do not equal two percent (2%) of the total Federal Income Tax Items allocable to the Partners (other than temporary allocations required under Code Sections 704(b), 704(c), or corresponding Income Tax Regulations), the Partnership shall allocate additional Federal Income Tax Items to the General Partners until such allocation, in the aggregate equals two percent (2%).

8.6.6. *Transfer of Interests.* If a Partnership Interest is transferred during a fiscal year of the Partnership, the Partnership's taxable year shall not close with respect to that Partnership Interest. Instead, all Profits and Losses otherwise attributable to such Partnership Interest for the entire taxable year shall be apportioned between the assigning Partner and his assignee on the basis of the number of days the Partner or his assignee was the Holder of Record during the fiscal year. Gain From Capital Transactions and Loss From Capital Transactions shall be allocated to the Holder of Record on the date of such Capital Transaction.

8.6.7. *Tax Allocation.* In accordance with Code Section 704(c) and the Treasury regulations thereunder, Federal Income Tax Items generated with respect to any property contributed to the capital of the Partnership shall, solely for tax purposes, be allocated among the Partners in a manner so as to take account of any variation between the adjusted basis of such property to the Partnership for federal income tax purposes and its fair market value at the time of contribution. If the Partners' Capital Accounts are adjusted because of any of the events described in Treasury Regulation Section 1.704-1(b)(2)(iv)(f), subsequent allocations of Federal Income Tax Items with respect to the assets giving rise to such adjustment shall take into account any variation between the adjusted basis of such assets and their fair market value at the time of the adjustment in the same manner as under Code Section 704(c) and the regulations thereunder.

8.7. *Compliance with Treasury Regulations.* The foregoing provisions and other provisions of this Agreement relating to the maintenance of Capital Accounts are intended to comply with Treasury Regulations Section 1.704-1(b), and shall be interpreted and applied in a manner consistent with such Regulations. In the event the General Partners determine that it is prudent to modify the manner in which the Capital Accounts, or any debits or credits thereto, are computed in order to comply with such Regulations, the General Partners may make such modifications, provided that it is not likely to have a material effect on the amounts distributable to any Partner pursuant to Article IX hereof upon the dissolution and liquidation of the Partnership. The General Partners shall have the authority in their sole and absolute discretion to make any appropriate modifications if events might otherwise cause this Agreement not to comply with Treasury Regulations Section 1.704-l(b).

ARTICLE IX
TERMINATION AND DISSOLUTION

9.1. *Causes for Termination.* The Partnership shall be dissolved and terminated on the date set forth in Section 1.6 of this Agreement. The Partnership shall be terminated and dissolved prior to such date upon the happening of any of the following events:

(a) a determination by a Simple Majority Vote of the Partners that the Partnership should be dissolved;

(b) the decision of the General Partners to dissolve the Partnership after the disposition and sale of all or substantially all of the assets of the Partnership;

(c) an entry of judicial dissolution under Chapter 9, Section 2 of the Act;

(d) death, insolvency, bankruptcy, removal or withdrawal of all of the General Partners unless within thirty (30) days of such event the Limited Partners elect by a Simple Majority Vote a new general partner to continue the business of the Partnership as set forth in Section 3.4 herein. The new General Partner shall obtain his general partnership Interest in accordance with the terms set forth in Section 3.4 and Section 3.7 herein. Upon the election of a new general partner, the Partnership Interests of the General Partners shall become limited partnership Interests and the General Partners shall automatically become Substitute Limited Partners without any further requirement of any approval of the Limited Partners or of the new general partner as set forth in Section 3.7 herein; or

(e) the involuntary transfer of a general partnership Interest in the Partnership (such as to a trustee in bankruptcy or a purchaser in a creditor's sale) in the event there is only one General Partner of the Partnership, unless within thirty (30) days of such event the Limited Partners elect by a Simple Majority Vote to continue the Partnership.

The Partnership shall not be terminated upon the happening of the insolvency or bankruptcy of the Partnership.

9.2. *Liquidation.* Upon dissolution and termination of the Partnership for any reason, the Partnership shall engage in no further business other than such business as may be necessary to wind up its affairs and to distribute its assets. Such liquidation shall be handled by the General Partners as Liquidator, except that if such dissolution is caused by the bankruptcy, withdrawal or removal of the General Partners as provided in Sections 3.5, 5.5 and 9.1(d) and (e) herein, two Liquidators shall be elected by a Simple Majority Vote of the Limited Partners. Liquidators may be Partners or qualified third parties. No person who is a creditor of the Partnership, a creditor of any Partner or a trustee in a bankruptcy proceeding involving any Partner or the Partnership shall ever serve as a Liquidator.

9.3. *Disposition of Assets.* On the liquidation and dissolution of the Partnership, the Liquidator shall, by the later of the end of the taxable year in which the liquidation occurs or six (6) months after the date of liquidation:

(a) *Determination of Partnership Assets.* Determine the interest of the Partnership in each Partnership property.

(b) *Valuation of Partnership Assets.* Determine the value of the Partnership's properties and adjust the Capital Accounts of the Partners in the manner described in Section 8.2 hereof.

(c) *Final Statement of Account.* As promptly as possible after dissolution, cause a final statement of account to be prepared, which shall show with respect to each Partner the status of such Partner's Capital Account. Such statement of each Partner's Capital Account shall reflect the allocations set forth in Article VIII and the allocation of the gain and losses to the Capital Accounts as provided in subsection (b) above.

(d) *Payment of Third-Party Debts.* Pay all Partnership debts owing to creditors other than Partners, or otherwise make adequate provision therefore.

(e) *Repayment of Loans From Partners.* Obtain repayment of loans, if any, from the Partners to the Partnership, or otherwise make adequate provision therefor.

(f) *Repayment of Capital Accounts.* To the extent of Partnership Property (or cash realized from a sale thereof) available therefor, distribute to each Partner an amount equal to any remaining positive balance of his Capital Account in accordance with Section 8.2(c). If Partnership Property (or cash received from a sale thereof) is insufficient to repay in full the positive Capital Account balances of all Partners, the total amount available for such purpose shall be distributed among the Partners in the proportion that the positive Capital Account balance of each Partner bears to the total positive Capital Account balances of all Partners.

(g) *Indebtedness Owed by Partners.* Notwithstanding the foregoing, if any Partner is indebted to the Partnership, the Liquidator shall, until such debtor Partner has repaid the Partnership, retain such Partner's distributive share of Partnership properties and apply the same to the full discharge and repayment of such indebtedness, and the balance of such distributive share, if any, shall be delivered to such Partner. On dissolution or liquidation of the Partnership, each Partner shall be obligated to restore any negative balance in its Capital Account. No Partner shall be personally liable to return the capital contributions of any other Partner. Capital contributions shall be repaid solely from Partnership assets, if any, that may be available for such purpose pursuant to the terms of this Agreement.

(h) *Compliance Provisions.* The Liquidator shall comply with any requirements of the Act or other applicable law, pertaining to the winding up of a limited partnership, at which time the Partnership shall stand terminated.

9.4. *No Recourse.* On liquidation and dissolution of the Partnership, the Limited Partners shall look solely to the assets of the Partnership for the return of their investment, and if the Partnership assets remaining after payment and discharge of debts and liabilities of the Partnership, including any debts and liabilities owed to any one or more of the Partners, is insufficient to satisfy the rights of the Limited Partners, the Limited Partners shall have no recourse or further right or claim against the Partnership or the General Partners.

9.5. *Reserves.* In winding up the affairs of the Partnership and distributing its assets, the Liquidator shall set up a reserve to meet any contingent or unforeseen liabilities or obligations and deposit funds for such purpose, together with funds held by the Partnership for distribution to Partners which remain unclaimed after a reasonable period of time, with an escrow agent for the purpose of disbursing such reserves and funds. At the expiration of such period the Liquidator deems advisable, the escrow agent shall be authorized and directed to distribute the balance remaining in the manner provided in Section 9.3 above.

9.6. *Statement of Termination.* The Liquidator shall furnish each of the Partners, at the Partnership's expense, with a statement which shall set forth the assets and liabilities of the Partnership as of the date of complete liquidation and distribution as herein provided. Such statement shall also schedule the receipts and disbursements made with respect to the termination hereunder and shall be final and binding upon all persons, except such persons who may file a specific and detailed written protest thereof within ninety (90) days of his receipt of the statement.

9.7. *Deficit Capital Accounts.* Each Partner with a deficit balance in his Capital Account shall have the obligation to restore such deficit balance, or to make any contribution to restore such deficit balance.

ARTICLE X
INDEMNIFICATION

10.1. *Indemnification.* The Partnership shall indemnify any Partner (or employee of a Partner) against reasonable expenses incurred in connection with the defense of any threatened, pending, or completed action, suit, or proceeding, whether civil, criminal, administrative, arbitrative, or investigative, any appeal in such an action, suit, or proceeding, and any inquiry or investigation that could lead to such an action, suit or proceeding, where the Person who was, is, or is threatened to be made a named defendant or respondent in a proceeding was named because the Person is or was a Partner of the Partnership (or employee of the same).

10.2. *Conditions.* The indemnification contained in Section 10.1 is conditioned upon a Simple Majority Vote that such Person:

(a) conducted himself in good faith;

(b) reasonably believed, in the case of conduct in his official capacity as a Partner of the Partnership, that his conduct was in the Partnership's best interest, and in all other cases, that his conduct was at least not opposed to the Partnership's best interest; and

(c) in the case of any criminal proceeding, had no reasonable cause to believe his conduct was unlawful.

10.3. *Successful Defense.* Notwithstanding Section 10.2, the Partnership shall indemnify each Partner (or employee of a Partner) against reasonable expenses incurred in connection with a proceeding in which he is a party because he is or was a Partner (or employee of a Partner) if he has been wholly successful, on the merits or otherwise, in the defense of the proceeding.

10.4. *Exclusions.* A Partner (or employee of Partner) may not be indemnified under this Article X for obligations resulting from a proceeding:

(a) in which the Person is found liable on the basis that personal benefit was improperly received by him, whether or not the benefit resulted from an action taken in the person's official capacity; or

(b) in which the Person is found liable to the Partnership.

10.5. *Expenses.* "Expenses" as used herein means court costs, attorneys' fees, judgments, penalties (including excise and similar taxes), fines, settlements and other reasonable expenditures actually incurred by the Person in connection with the proceeding; provided however, if the proceeding is brought by or in behalf of the Partnership, the indemnification is limited to reasonable expenses actually incurred by the Person in connection with the proceeding of determination of reasonableness of expenses shall be made in the same manner as the determination contained in Section 10.6.

10.6. *Advance Reimbursement.* Reasonable expenses incurred by a Partner who was, is or is threatened to be named a defendant or respondent in a proceeding may be paid or reimbursed by the Partnership in advance of the final disposition of the proceeding after:

(a) the Partnership receives a written affirmation by the Partner of his good faith belief that he has met the standard of conduct necessary for indemnification under this Article X and a written undertaking by or on behalf of the Partner to repay the amount paid or reimbursed if it is ultimately determined that he has not met those requirements, and

(b) a determination is made under Section 10.2 that the facts then known to those making the determination would not preclude indemnification under this Article X.

10.7. *Appearance as Witness or Otherwise.* The Partnership shall pay or reimburse expenses incurred by a Partner (or any employee of a Partner) in connection with his appearance as a witness or other participant in any threatened, pending or completed action, suit or proceeding, whether civil, criminal, administrative, arbitrative, or investigative, any appeal in such action, suit or proceeding, and any inquiry or investigation that could lead to such an action, suit or proceeding, involving or affecting the Partnership at a time when such General Partner is not a named defendant or respondent in the proceeding.

ARTICLE XI
MISCELLANEOUS PROVISIONS

11.1. *Notice.* Any notice, payment, demand or communication required or permitted to be given by any provision of this Agreement shall be in writing and shall be deemed to have been duly given and received for all purposes on the date delivered personally to the party or to an officer of the party to whom the same is directed, or when deposited by registered or certified mail, postage and charges prepaid and addressed as follows:

11.1.1. *Partnership or General Partners.* If to the Partnership or to the General Partners, then to the address of the principal place of business of the Partnership set forth herein or as may be changed from time to time, and

11.1.2. *Limited Partners.* If to a Limited Partner, then to the address of such Limited Partner as set forth on Exhibit "A" attached hereto.

Any party hereto may change his or its address to which notice shall thereafter be given by furnishing written notice to all the Partners and the Partnership in the manner set forth in this Section 11.1.

11.2. *Integration.* This Agreement, constitutes the entire understanding of the parties hereto with respect to the subject matter hereof. No amendment, modification, or alteration of the terms of this Agreement shall be binding unless the same is in writing, dated subsequent to the date hereof and duly adopted by the Partners, as provided herein.

11.3. *Severability.* Each provision of this Agreement is intended to be severable. If any term or provision hereof is illegal or invalid for any reason whatsoever, such illegality or invalidity shall not affect the validity or enforceability of the remainder of this Agreement.

11.4. *Applicable Law.* This Agreement and the application or interpretation hereof shall exclusively be governed by and construed in accordance with the laws of the State of _____.

This Agreement shall be deemed to be performable in and venue shall be mandatory in _____ County, _____.

11.5. *Execution in Counterparts.* This Agreement, the Certificate to be file as provided herein, and any amendment hereto may be executed in any number of counterparts, either by the parties hereto or their duly authorized attorney-in-fact, with the same effect as if all parties had signed the same document. All counterparts shall be construed as and shall constitute one and the same Agreement.

11.6. *Descriptive Heads.* The captions included herein are for administrative convenience only and shall not be considered in interpreting any of the terms or provisions of this Agreement.

11.7. *Gender and Number.* Whenever the context requires, all words used herein in the male, female, or neuter gender shall be deemed to include the male, female, or neuter gender; all singular words shall include the plural, and all plural shall include the singular, as the context may require.

11.8. *Power of Attorney.*

(a) The Limited Partners, by their execution hereof, jointly and severally, hereby make, constitute and appoint the General Partners, as their true and lawful agent and attorney-in-fact, with full power of substitution, in their name, place and stead to make, execute, sign, acknowledge, swear to, record and file, on behalf of them and on behalf of the Partnership;

(i) the Certificate and all amendments thereto required or permitted by law or the provisions of this Agreement; (ii) all certificates or other instruments deemed advisable by the General Partners to permit the Partnership to become or continue as a limited partnership or partnership wherein the Limited Partners have limited liability in the jurisdictions where the Partnership may be conducting its affairs; (iii) all instruments that effect a change or modification of the Partnership in accordance with this Agreement; (iv) any amendment to this Agreement when this Agreement is amended in accordance with the terms hereof or to the extent necessary, in the sole discretion of the General Partners, to comply with Section 704 of the Code; (v) all conveyances and other instruments-deemed advisable by the General Partners to conduct the business of the Partnership (including its liquidation and dissolution); (vi) all fictitious or assumed name certificates required or permitted to be filed on behalf of the Partnership; and (vii) all other documents or instruments which the General Partners deem to be in the best interest of the Partnership and which are not inconsistent with this Agreement.

(b) *The foregoing power of attorney:* (i) is a special power of attorney coupled with an interest and shall be irrevocable and survive the disability, bankruptcy, insanity or incompetency of each Limited Partner; (ii) may be exercised by the General Partners either by signing separately as attorney-in-fact for each Limited Partner or, after listing all of the Limited Partners by a single signature of the General Partners acting as attorney-in-fact for all of them; and (iii) shall survive the delivery of an assignment by a Limited Partner of the whole or any portion of his Partnership Interest, except that where the assignee of the whole of such Partnership interest has been approved by the General Partners for admission to the Partnership as a Substitute Limited Partner, the power of attorney of the assignor shall survive the delivery of such assignment for the sole purpose of enabling the General Partners to execute, acknowledge, and file any instrument necessary to effect such substitutions.

11.9. *Binding Agreement.* Except as otherwise provided herein to the contrary, this Agreement shall be binding upon and inure to the benefit of the parties hereto their personal representatives, successors, assigns, and legal representatives.

11.10 *Amendments to Partnership Agreement.* This Agreement may be amended only by the Simple Majority Vote of the Partners.

11.10.1. *Amendments by General Partners.* Notwithstanding the foregoing, this Agreement may be amended by the General Partners without the approval or Vote of the Limited Partners whenever:

(a) there is a need to provide any provision as may be required by applicable law to be included in this Agreement;

(b) there is a need to correct a false or erroneous statement in this Agreement or to clarify a provision of this Agreement without changing the substance thereof;

(c) it is necessary or appropriate, in the opinion of counsel selected by the General Partners, to satisfy the requirements of the Code, Treasury Regulations thereunder, or administrative guidelines or interpretations relating thereto, to maintain the status of the Partnership, or to comply with the federal tax provisions so as to give effect to any benefits intended thereunder as determined by the General Partners; and

(d) any other term of this Agreement provides for amendments without the approval of the Limited Partners.

11.10.2. *Proposal of Amendments.* Amendments to this Agreement may be proposed by any Partner by submitting a written copy of the proposed amendment to the General Partners, together with a written request that the proposed amendment be submitted to the Partners for a Vote for its adoption.

11.10.3. *Voting on Amendments.* Except as otherwise provided in this Agreement, all proposed amendments shall be submitted to the Partners in the following manner:

(a) Within fifteen (15) days of its proper proposal, notice of the proposed amendment and the text thereof, along with a ballot, shall be sent by the General Partners to each Partner by certified mail, return receipt requested, at the last known address of each Partner; and

(b) The ballot supplied with the notice of the proposed amendment shall state that the written vote of each Partner is due, at the offices of the Partnership, within fifteen (15) days of the date of the notice of proposed amendment (which shall be the date of the postmark of such notice). Ballots not received by said date shall be deemed to have been voted in favor of the proposal.

IN WITNESS WHEREOF, this Agreement has been executed by the General Partners as of the _____ day of _____, 20__, and by each Limited Partner on the date indicated opposite his signature hereto.

GENERAL PARTNERS:

Date:_____　　　_____

　　　　　　　　　　　　　　　　　　_____

Date:_____　　　_____

　　　　　　　　　　　　　　　　　　_____

INITIAL LIMITED PARTNERS:

_____

EXHIBIT "A" TO AGREEMENT OF LIMITED PARTNERSHIP OF
_____, DATED _____, 20__

Name of Limited Partner Partner	Address	Social Security Number	Percent of Limited Partnership Interest
1.			%
2.			%

.... (New Page) ....

EXHIBIT "A" TO AGREEMENT OF LIMITED PARTNERSHIP OF
_____, DATED _____, 20___

Name of Partner	Partnership Interest	Percent of Ownership	Description of Property Contributed	Value of Property Contributed
	General			
	Limited	49.00%		$
	Limited	_____	_____	$

AGREEMENT TO PAY A DEBT CONTRACTED DURING INFANCY

This agreement, made, etc. (parties as in preceding form).

On the _____ day of _____, 20__, the debtor, being then a minor, purchased of the creditor _____ for the sum of _____ dollars, and having now attained his majority and being desirous of ratifying the purchase, to give full effect to this liability for the payment of such debt, proposes to enter into the following agreement: In consideration of the purchase and delivery of _____ to him, and of the agreement on the part of the creditor hereinafter contained, he, the debtor, expressly acknowledges the said debt to be justly due to the said _____ and agrees to pay the same within _____ months from the date hereof, together with interest at the rate of _____ percent per annum.

And the said creditor, in consideration of the promise and agreement hereinbefore contained, hereby agrees that he will not sue for or require payment of the said debt unless and until default shall be made in payment thereof at the time hereinbefore appointed.

In witness, etc.

AGREEMENT TO REVIVE A DEBT
BARRED BY STATUTE OF LIMITATIONS

This agreement, made, etc. (parties as in preceding form).

On the _____ day of _____, 20____, the debtor purchased of the creditor an _____ for the sum of _____ dollars. _____ years have passed and the purchase is unpaid and barred by the statute of limitations. The debtor, desirous to renew the indebtedness to give full effect to his liability for payment of such debt, enters into the following agreement:

In consideration of said purchase and the delivery of said _____ to him and the forbearance of said creditor to sue for said purchase price before recovery was barred by operation of law, the debtor hereby acknowledges the debt to be justly due, and agrees to pay the same within _____ years from the date hereof, together with interest thereon at the rate of _____ percent per annum.

The creditor, in consideration of the agreement hereinbefore contained, hereby agrees not to sue for or require the payment of said debt unless and until default shall be made in the payment at the time herein appointed.

In witness, etc.

APPLICATION FOR EMPLOYER IDENTIFICATION NUMBER

(See next page.)

ARBITRATION CLAUSE FOR DOMESTIC TRADE CONTRACTS

Any controversy or claim arising out of or relating to this contract, or the breach thereof, shall be settled by arbitration, in accordance with the rules, then obtaining, of the American Arbitration Association, and judgment upon the award rendered may be entered in the highest court of the forum, state or federal, having jurisdiction.

ARBITRATION CLAUSE FOR FOREIGN TRADE CONTRACTS

Any controversy or claim arising out of or relating to this contract, or the breach thereof, shall be settled by arbitration, in accordance with the rules, then obtaining, of the American Arbitration Association. This agreement shall be enforceable and judgment upon any reward rendered by all or a majority of the arbitrators may be entered in any court having jurisdiction. The arbitration shall be held in/or where jurisdiction may be obtained over the parties. Three arbitrators shall be selected. Unless the parties have agreed upon qualified persons, one arbitrator shall be appointed by each party and the two so chosen shall designate the third. If either party fails or neglects, within a period of fourteen days after written notice by the other, to select an arbitrator upon its part, or if the two selected by the parties cannot agree upon a third within seven days after they have been chosen, the Arbitration Committee of the American Arbitration Association, upon the request of either party, shall appoint such arbitrator or arbitrators from its National Panel within a period of fourteen days.

(Address inquiries regarding clauses and rules of procedure to the American Arbitration Association, 335 Madison Avenue, Floor 10, New York, NY 10017-4605.)

| Form **SS-4** (Rev. December 2001) Department of the Treasury Internal Revenue Service | **Application for Employer Identification Number** (For use by employers, corporations, partnerships, trusts, estates, churches, government agencies, Indian tribal entities, certain individuals, and others.) ▶ See separate instructions for each line. ▶ Keep a copy for your records. | EIN OMB No. 1545-0003 |

Type or print clearly.

1 Legal name of entity (or individual) for whom the EIN is being requested

2 Trade name of business (if different from name on line 1)

3 Executor, trustee, "care of" name

4a Mailing address (room, apt., suite no. and street, or P.O. box)

5a Street address (if different) (Do not enter a P.O. box.)

4b City, state, and ZIP code

5b City, state, and ZIP code

6 County and state where principal business is located

7a Name of principal officer, general partner, grantor, owner, or trustor

7b SSN, ITIN, or EIN

8a Type of entity (check only one box)
- ☐ Sole proprietor (SSN)
- ☐ Partnership
- ☐ Corporation (enter form number to be filed) ▶
- ☐ Personal service corp.
- ☐ Church or church-controlled organization
- ☐ Other nonprofit organization (specify) ▶
- ☐ Other (specify) ▶
- ☐ Estate (SSN of decedent)
- ☐ Plan administrator (SSN)
- ☐ Trust (SSN of grantor)
- ☐ National Guard ☐ State/local government
- ☐ Farmers' cooperative ☐ Federal government/military
- ☐ REMIC ☐ Indian tribal governments/enterprises
- Group Exemption Number (GEN) ▶

8b If a corporation, name the state or foreign country (if applicable) where incorporated

State

Foreign country

9 Reason for applying (check only one box)
- ☐ Started new business (specify type) ▶
- ☐ Hired employees (Check the box and see line 12.)
- ☐ Compliance with IRS withholding regulations
- ☐ Other (specify) ▶
- ☐ Banking purpose (specify purpose) ▶
- ☐ Changed type of organization (specify new type) ▶
- ☐ Purchased going business
- ☐ Created a trust (specify type) ▶
- ☐ Created a pension plan (specify type) ▶

10 Date business started or acquired (month, day, year)

11 Closing month of accounting year

12 First date wages or annuities were paid or will be paid (month, day, year). Note: If applicant is a withholding agent, enter date income will first be paid to nonresident alien. (month, day, year) . . . . ▶

13 Highest number of employees expected in the next 12 months. Note: If the applicant does not expect to have any employees during the period, enter "-0-." . . . . ▶

| Agricultural | Household | Other |

14 Check **one** box that best describes the principal activity of your business. ☐ Health care & social assistance ☐ Wholesale-agent/broker
- ☐ Construction ☐ Rental & leasing ☐ Transportation & warehousing ☐ Accommodation & food service ☐ Wholesale-other ☐ Retail
- ☐ Real estate ☐ Manufacturing ☐ Finance & insurance ☐ Other (specify)

15 Indicate principal line of merchandise sold; specific construction work done; products produced; or services provided.

16a Has the applicant ever applied for an employer identification number for this or any other business? . . . . ☐ Yes ☐ No
Note: If "Yes," please complete lines 16b and 16c.

16b If you checked "Yes" on line 16a, give applicant's legal name and trade name shown on prior application if different from line 1 or 2 above.
Legal name ▶ Trade name ▶

16c Approximate date when, and city and state where, the application was filed. Enter previous employer identification number if known.

| Approximate date when filed (mo., day, year) | City and state where filed | Previous EIN |

Third Party Designee	Complete this section **only** if you want to authorize the named individual to receive the entity's EIN and answer questions about the completion of this form.
	Designee's name
	Address and ZIP code

Designee's telephone number (include area code) ( )
Designee's fax number (include area code) ( )

Under penalties of perjury, I declare that I have examined this application, and to the best of my knowledge and belief, it is true, correct, and complete.

Applicant's telephone number (include area code) ( )

Name and title (type or print clearly) ▶

Applicant's fax number (include area code) ( )

Signature ▶ Date ▶

For Privacy Act and Paperwork Reduction Act Notice, see separate instructions.   Cat. No. 16055N   Form **SS-4** (Rev. 12-2001)

ARTICLES OF INCORPORATION
OF

_____

ARTICLE I—Name and Address

The name of this corporation is _____. The mailing address of the corporation is: _____. The address of the corporation's principal office is _____.

ARTICLE II—Duration

This corporation shall have perpetual existence.

ARTICLE III—Capital Stock

This corporation is authorized to issue 100,000 shares of common stock, which shall be designated as "Common Shares." The par value of each share of stock shall be One Dollar ($1.00).

ARTICLE IV—Preemptive Rights

Every shareholder, upon an offer for sale for cash of any new stock or authorized but unissued stock of this corporation of the same kind, class or series as that which he already holds, shall have the right to purchase his pro rata share thereof (as nearly as may be done without issuance of fractional shares) at the price at which it is offered to others.

ARTICLE V—Initial Registered Office and Agent

The street address of the initial registered office of this corporation is _____, and the name of the initial registered agent of this corporation at that address is _____.

ARTICLE VI—Incorporator/Incorporators

The name/names and address/addresses of the person/persons signing these Articles is/are:
Name: _____   Address: _____

ARTICLE VII—Indemnification

The corporation shall indemnify any officer or director, or any former officer or director to the full extent permitted by law.

ARTICLE VIII—Amendment

This corporation reserves the right to amend or repeal any provisions contained in these Articles of Incorporation, or any amendment thereto, and any right conferred upon the shareholders is subject to this reservation.

IN WITNESS WHEREOF, the undersigned incorporator/incorporators has/have executed these Articles of Incorporation this _____ day of _____, 20__.

_____

_____

CERTIFICATE DESIGNATING REGISTERED AGENT
AND STREET ADDRESS FOR SERVICE OF PROCESS

Pursuant to Section _____ of the _____, _____ desiring to organize under the laws of the State of _____, _____ hereby designates _____, located at _____, as its registered agent to accept service of process within the State of _____.

ACCEPTANCE OF DESIGNATION

The undersigned hereby accepts the above designation as registered agent to accept service of process for the above-named corporation, at the place designated above, and agrees to comply with the provisions of Section _____ of the _____ relative to maintaining an office for the service of process.

_____

ARTICLES OF ORGANIZATION FOR THE LIMITED LIABILITY COMPANY OF _____

The undersigned, acting as the organizers of a limited liability company to be formed under the _____ Limited Liability Company Act, as amended (the "Act"), hereby form a _____ limited liability company (this "Company") pursuant to the Act and hereby set forth the following Articles of Organization (these "Articles"):

ARTICLE I
Name

The name of this Company shall be: _____.

ARTICLE II
Commencement Date and Duration

This Company shall commence on the date of subscription and acknowledgment in accordance with the provisions of Section _____ of the Act, and shall continue for a period of thirty (30) years from the commencement date, or until dissolved by its members or managers in accordance with Section _____ of the Act or the provisions of these Articles. Subject to the foregoing, this Company shall be dissolved on the happening of any of the following events:

1. Expiration of the term specified above;
2. Withdrawal, retirement, death, resignation, bankruptcy, dissolution or expulsion of any member, unless the business of this Company is continued by the consent of all the remaining members;
3. Unanimous written consent of all of the members; and
4. Unanimous written consent of all of the managers.

ARTICLE III
Purposes

This Company is created and formed for the purpose of engaging in all lawful businesses authorized for a Company pursuant to Section _____ of the Act, including without limitation, the acquisition, disposition, purchase, lease, encumbrance, financing, marketing, promoting, improving, developing, managing, selling, buying, and otherwise dealing with _____ and all such other activities incidental or useful to the foregoing.

ARTICLE IV
Place of Business

The principal place of business of this Company shall be _____, and such other place or places as may be designated by the managers from time to time.

ARTICLE V
Registered Agent and Office

The initial registered agent for this Company shall be _____, and the address of the registered agent for service of process shall be _____.

ARTICLE VI
Capital Contributions

a. *Initial Capital.* The initial capital of this Company shall consist of the sum of cash of _____ Dollars ($_____).

b. *Additional Capital Contributions.* Additional capital contributions, if any, shall be made by the members and at the times as determined by written agreement among the members or in accordance with the Operating Agreement and Regulations adopted and approved by the members, and may be made in cash or in property.

c. *Return of Capital.* The capital contribution of any member may be returned in accordance with the provisions of Section _____ of the Act. A member shall be entitled to a return of his capital contribution by consent of all members.

ARTICLE VII
Admission of Members

The initial members of this Company shall be set forth in the Operating Agreement and Regulations adopted by the members as set forth therein. The admission of additional members shall be accomplished only by the unanimous vote of the members, unless otherwise stated in the Operating Agreement and Regulations.

ARTICLE VIII
Continuation of Business

The members may, by unanimous written consent, continue the business of this Company upon the death, retirement, resignation, expulsion, bankruptcy or dissolution of any member or upon the occurrence of any other event which terminates the continued membership of a member in this Company.

ARTICLE IX
Management of Business

The management of this Company shall be vested entirely in its managers. The name and address of its sole manager who shall serve until the first annual meeting of members or until his successor is duly elected and qualified are as follows:

Name   *Address*

_____   _____

The manager(s) shall be elected by the members of this Company at its annual meeting each year by majority vote relative to their capital interest in this Company as set forth in the Operating Agreement and Regulations.

ARTICLE X
Powers

This Company shall have all of the powers and authorities set forth in Section _____ of the Act.

ARTICLE XI
Property

a. *Ownership.* All property originally paid or brought into, or transferred to, this Company as contributions to capital by the members, or subsequently acquired by purchase or otherwise on account of this Company shall be the property of this Company.

b. *Title.* The title to all property of the Company shall be held in the name of this Company.

c. *Conveyances.* The manager(s) are hereby authorized to convey and obtain title to all real and personal property of whatever nature by the execution on behalf of this Company of any and all agreements, deeds, mortgages, trust agreements, indentures, leases, conveyance documents and all other certificates, instruments and documents as are necessary, reasonable or desirable to obtain title or convey title to any real or personal property whatsoever. Such execution shall be made by a majority of the managers if there is more than one. The signature and execution of such documents shall clearly set forth that the execution is on behalf of this Company and that the manager is signing on its behalf as manager. The following form of signature shall be used for obtaining or conveying title to any real or personal property: _____.

By: _____

_____ as _____

No third party need inquire any further than these Articles of Organization for authorization as to the form of conveyance on documents for title to real or personal property.

ARTICLE XII
Amendments

These Articles of Organization, except with respect to vested rights of the members, may be amended at any time either by (a) vote by a majority in interest of its members, or (b) vote of a majority of its managers; and such amendments shall be filed with the _____ Department of State in accordance with the provision of Section _____ of the Act.

ARTICLE XIII
Regulations

The managers are hereby authorized and directed to prepare and adopt an Operating Agreement and Regulations for the governing of the internal affairs of this Company containing such provisions as they consider necessary, reasonable or desirable, except that no provisions of such Operating Agreement and Regulations may conflict with the provisions of these Articles of Organization, unless otherwise permitted herein. The power to adopt, alter, amend, or repeal the Operating Agreement and Regulations shall be set forth in the Operating Agreement and Regulations, except that the initial form shall be approved by all the members.

ARTICLE XIV
Contracting Debts

No debt shall be contracted nor liability incurred by or on behalf of this Company except by its managers and no member is authorized or empowered to contract debts or incur liabilities on behalf of this Company unless such member is also a manager.

IN WITNESS WHEREOF, the undersigned organizers of _____, L.C. have executed these Articles of Organization this _____ day of _____, 20__.

By: _____

_____

_____

STATE OF _____)

COUNTY OF _____)

Subscribed and sworn to before me on this _____ day of _____, 20__, by _____, who:

[ ] (a) is personally known to me
    OR
[ ] (b) who has produced a _____ (type of identification) as identification.

_____

(Signature of Notary Public)

_____

(Print, Type or Stamp Commissioned Name of Notary Public)

Date of Expiration and Number of Commission:_____

CERTIFICATE OF DESIGNATION AND ACCEPTANCE REGISTERED AGENT

The undersigned, having been named Registered Agent and designated to accept service of process for the above-stated Company, at the place designated herein, hereby agrees to act in this capacity, and further agrees to comply with the provisions of all statutes relative to the proper and complete performance of the duties hereunder.

_____

DATED: _____

ASSIGNMENT OF AN ACCOUNT

I, _____ of _____, in consideration of the sum of _____ dollars paid to me by _____ of _____, the receipt whereof is hereby acknowledged, do hereby sell, assign, and transfer to said _____, all and whatsoever sum or sums of money now due and becoming due to me from _____ of _____; to have and to hold the same to the said _____, with power to collect the same in my name and as my attorney thereunto duly authorized, to his own use.

It is expressly understood, however, that I shall forever be kept and saved harmless by the said _____ from all cost or charge hereafter for and from the expense of the collection of the sum or sums hereby sold and assigned.

In witness, etc.

_____L.S.

ASSIGNMENT BY A CORPORATION

The _____, a corporation organized and existing, under and by virtue of the laws of the state of _____, and having its principal office at _____, in said state, pursuant to a resolution of the board of directors, passed on the _____ day of _____, 20 __, in consideration of _____ dollars, the receipt whereof is hereby acknowledged, does hereby sell, assign, transfer, and set over unto _____ of ._____, all that (here name property assigned) in the hands of (name persons holding the property of company for sale). For a more complete description of the property hereby conveyed reference is made to inventory of said property bearing date of _____ day of _____, 20__, and contained in the inventory book of said company.

Said company has caused this instrument to be signed in its name, by its president, and sealed with its corporate seal, attested by its secretary, this _____ day of _____, 20__.

_____ (Company)

By: _____

President

(Corporate Seal)

Attest: _____

Secretary

(Corporate form of acknowledgment)

ASSIGNMENT OF WAGES DUE AND TO BECOME DUE

I, _____ of _____, in the county of _____, in consideration of _____ dollars to me paid by _____ of _____, the receipt whereof I do hereby acknowledge, do hereby assign and transfer to said _____ all claims and demands which I now have, and all which at any time between the date hereof and the _____ day of _____ I may have against _____ of _____, for all sums of money due, and for all sums of money and demands which, at any time between the date hereof and the said _____ day of _____, may and shall become due to me for services as a _____; to hold the same to the said _____, his executors, administrators, and assigns, forever. And I do hereby constitute and appoint the said _____. to be my attorney irrevocable in the premises, to perform all acts, matters, and things touching the premises in like manner to all intents and purposes as I could if personally present.

In witness, etc.

_____ L.S.

BILL OF SALE

I _____ of _____ in the County of _____ and State of _____ in consideration of the sum of $_____ to me in hand paid by _____ of _____ the receipt of which is hereby acknowledged have granted, bargained, sold, conveyed, transferred and delivered and by this instrument do bargain, sell, grant, convey, transfer and deliver unto the said _____ the following goods and chattels:

TO HAVE AND TO HOLD the same unto the said _____, his executors, administrators and assigns forever;

And I do for myself, my executors, administrators and assigns covenant and agree to and with the said _____ to warrant and defend the said _____ goods and chattels hereby sold to the said _____ his executors, administrators and assigns against all and every person and persons whomsoever.

IN WITNESS WHEREOF, I have hereunto set my hand and seal this _____ day of _____, 20__.

Signed, sealed and delivered in presence of :

_____ L.S.

(Acknowledgment)

STATE OF _____

CITY OF _____

} ss:

COUNTY OF _____

being duly sworn, deposes and says, that _____ resides at _____, in the City of That _____ is the person who executed the within bill of sale.

That _____ is the sole owner of the property described in the bill of sale, and has full right to see and transfer the same.

That the property is free and clear of any liens, mortgages, debts or other encumbrances of whatsoever kind or nature except, _____.

That _____ is not indebted to anyone and has no creditors.

That no judgments exist against _____, in any court, nor are there any replevins, attachments or executions issued against _____ now in force; nor has any petition in bankruptcy been filed by or against

That this affidavit is made to induce _____ to purchase the property described in said bill of sale, knowing that _____ will rely thereon and pay a good and valuable consideration therefor.

Sworn to before me this _____ day of _____ 20__.

(add acknowledgment of subscriber)

BYLAWS
OF

_____

ARTICLE I. Meetings of Shareholders

Section 1. Annual Meeting. The annual meeting of the shareholders of this corporation shall be held at the time and place designated by the Board of Directors of the corporation.

The annual meeting of shareholders for any year shall be held no later than thirteen (13) months after the last preceding annual meeting of shareholders. Business transacted at the annual meeting shall include the election of directors of the corporation.

Section 2. Special Meetings. Special meetings of the shareholders shall be held when directed by the Board of Directors, or when requested in writing by the holders of not less than ten percent (10%) of all the shares entitled to vote at the meeting. A meeting requested by shareholders shall be called for a date not less than ten (10) nor more than sixty (60) days after the request is made, unless the shareholders requesting the meeting designate a later date. The call for the meeting shall be issued by the Secretary, unless the President, Board of Directors, or shareholders requesting the meeting designate another person to do so.

Section 3. Place. Meetings of shareholders may be held within or without the State of
_____.

Section 4. Notice. Written notice stating the place, day and hour of the meeting and, in the case of a special meeting, the purpose or purposes for which the meeting is called, shall be delivered not less than ten (10) nor more than sixty (60) days before the meeting, either personally or by first class mail, by or at the direction of the President, the Secretary, or the officer or persons calling the meeting to each shareholder of record entitled to vote at such meeting. If mailed, such notice shall be deemed to be delivered when deposited in the United States mail addressed to the shareholder at his address as it appears on the stock transfer books of the corporation, with postage thereon prepaid.

Section 5. Notice of Adjourned Meetings. When a meeting is adjourned to another time or place, it shall not be necessary to give any notice of the adjourned meeting if the time and place to which the meeting is adjourned are announced at the meeting at which the adjournment is taken, and at the adjourned meeting any business may be transacted that might have been transacted on the original date of the meeting. If, however, after the adjournment the Board of Directors fixes a new record date for the adjourned meeting, a notice of the adjourned meeting shall be given as provided in this section to each shareholder of record on the new record date entitled to vote at such meeting.

Section 6. Closing of Transfer. Books and Fixing Record Date. For the purpose of determining shareholders entitled to notice of or to vote at any meeting of shareholders or any adjournment thereof, or entitled to receive payment of any dividend, or in order to make a determination of shareholders for any other purpose, the Board of Directors may provide that the stock transfer books shall be closed for a stated period but not to exceed, in any case, sixty (60) days. If the stock transfer books shall be closed for the purpose of determining shareholders entitled to notice of or to vote at a meeting of shareholders, such books shall be closed for at least ten (10) days immediately preceding such meeting.

In lieu of closing the stock transfer books, the Board of Directors may fix in advance a date as the record date for any determination of shareholders, such date in any case to be not more than sixty (60) days and, in case of a meeting of shareholders, not less than ten (10) days prior to the date on which the particular action requiring such determination of shareholders is to be taken.

If the stock transfer books are not closed and no record date is fixed for the determination of shareholders entitled to notice or to vote at a meeting of shareholders, or shareholders entitled to receive payment of a dividend, the date on which notice of the meeting is mailed or the date on which the resolution of the Board of Directors declaring such dividend is adopted, as the case may be, shall be the record date for such determination of shareholders.

When a determination of shareholders entitled to vote at any meeting of shareholders has been made as provided in this section, such determination shall apply to any adjournment thereof, unless the Board of Directors fixes a new record date for the adjourned meeting.

Section 7. Voting Record. The officers or agent having charge of the stock transfer books for shares of the corporation shall make, at least ten (10) days before each meeting of shareholders, a complete list of the shareholders entitled to vote at such meeting or any adjournment thereof, with the address of and the number and class and series, if any, of shares held by each. The list, for a period of ten (10) days prior to such meeting, shall be kept on file at the registered office of the corporation, at the principal place of business of the corporation or at the office of the transfer agent or registrar of the corporation and any shareholder shall be entitled to inspect the list at any time during usual business hours. The list shall also be produced and kept open at the time and place of the meeting and shall be subject to the inspection of any shareholder at any time during the meeting.

If the requirements of this section have not been substantially complied with, the meeting on demand of any shareholder in person or by proxy, shall be adjourned until the requirements are complied with. If no such demand is made, failure to comply with the requirements of this section shall not affect the validity of any action taken at such meeting.

Section 8. Shareholder Quorum and Voting. A majority of the shares entitled to vote, represented in person or by proxy, shall constitute a quorum at a meeting of shareholders. When a specified item of business is required to be voted on by a class or series a majority of the shares of such class or series shall constitute a quorum for the transaction of such item of business by that class or series.

If a quorum is present, the affirmative vote of the majority of the shares represented at the meeting and entitled to vote on the subject matter shall be the act of the shareholders unless otherwise provided by law.

After a quorum has been established at a shareholders' meeting, the subsequent withdrawal of shareholders, so as to reduce the number of shareholders entitled to vote at the meeting below the number required for a quorum, shall not affect the validity of any action taken at the meeting or any adjournment thereof.

Section 9. Voting of Shares. Each outstanding share, regardless of class, shall be entitled to one vote on each matter submitted to a vote at a meeting of shareholders.

Treasury shares, shares of stock of this corporation owned by another corporation the majority of the voting stock of which is owned or controlled by this corporation, and shares of stock of this corporation held by it in a fiduciary capacity shall not be voted, directly or indirectly, at any meeting, and shall not be counted in determining the total number of outstanding shares at any given time.

A shareholder may vote either in person or by proxy executed in writing by the shareholder or his duly authorized attorney-in-fact.

Shares standing in the name of another corporation, domestic or foreign, may be voted by the officer, agent, or proxy designated by the bylaws of the corporate shareholder; or, in the absence of any applicable bylaw, by such person as the Board of Directors of the corporate shareholder may designate. Proof of such designation may be made by presentation of a certified copy of the bylaws or other instrument of the corporate shareholder. In the absence of any such designation, or in case of conflicting designation by the corporate shareholder, the chairman of the board, president, any vice president, secretary and treasurer of the corporate shareholder shall be presumed to possess, in that order, authority to vote such shares.

Shares held by an administrator, executor, guardian or conservator may be voted by him, either in person or by proxy, without a transfer of such shares into his name. Shares standing in the name of a trustee may be voted by him, either in person or by proxy, but no trustee shall be entitled to vote shares held by him without a transfer of such shares into his name.

Shares standing in the name of a receiver may be voted by such receiver, and shares held by or under the control of a receiver may be voted by such receiver without the transfer thereof into his name if authority so to do be contained in an appropriate order of the court by which such receiver was appointed.

A shareholder whose shares are pledged shall be entitled to vote such shares until the shares have been transferred into the name of the pledgee, and thereafter the pledgee or his nominee shall be entitled to vote the shares so transferred.

On and after the date on which written notice of redemption of redeemable shares has been mailed to the holders thereof and a sum sufficient to redeem such shares has been deposited with a bank or trust company with irrevocable instruction and authority to pay the redemption price to the holders thereof upon surrender of certificates therefor, such shares shall not be entitled to vote on any matter and shall not be deemed to be outstanding shares.

Section 10. Proxies. Every shareholder entitled to vote at a meeting of shareholders or to express consent or dissent without a meeting or a shareholder's duly authorized attorney-in-fact may authorize another person or persons to act for him by proxy.

Every proxy must be signed by the shareholder or his attorney-in-fact. No proxy shall be valid after the expiration of eleven (11) months from the date thereof unless otherwise provided in the proxy. Every proxy shall be revocable at the pleasure of the shareholder executing it, except as otherwise provided by law.

The authority of the holder of a proxy to act shall not be revoked by the incompetence or death of the shareholder who executed the proxy unless, before the authority is exercised, written notice of an adjudication of such incompetence or of such death is received by the corporate office responsible for maintaining the list of shareholders.

If a proxy for the same shares confers authority upon two or more persons and does not otherwise provide, a majority of them present at the meeting, or if only one is present then that one, may exercise all the powers conferred by the proxy; but if the proxy holders present at the meeting are equally divided as to the right and manner of voting in any particular case, the voting of such shares shall be prorated.

If a proxy expressly provides, any proxy holder may appoint in writing a substitute to act in his place.

Section 11. Voting Trusts. Any number of shareholders of this corporation may create a voting trust for the purpose of conferring upon a trustee or trustees the right to vote or otherwise represent their shares, as provided by law. Where the counterpart of a voting trust agreement and the copy of the record of the holders of voting trust certificates has been deposited with the corporation as provided by law, such documents shall be subject to the same right of examination by a shareholder of the corporation, in person or by agent or attorney, as are the books and records of the corporation, and such counterpart and such copy of such record shall be subject to examination by any holder of record of voting trust certificates either in person or by agent or attorney, at any reasonable time for any proper purpose.

Section 12. Shareholders' Agreements. Two (2) or more shareholders, of this corporation may enter an agreement providing for the exercise of voting rights in the manner provided in the agreement or relating to any phase of the affairs of the corporation as provided by law. Nothing therein shall impair the right of this corporation to treat the shareholders of record as entitled to vote the shares standing in their names.

Section 13. Action by Shareholders Without a Meeting. Any action required by law, these bylaws, or the articles of incorporation of this corporation to be taken at any annual or special meeting of shareholders of the corporation, or any action which may be taken at any annual or special meeting of such shareholders, may be taken without a meeting, without prior notice and without a vote, if a consent in writing, setting forth the action so taken, shall be signed by the holders of outstanding stock having not less than the minimum number of votes that would be necessary to authorize or take such action at a meeting at which all shares entitled to vote thereon were present and voted. If any class of shares is entitled to vote thereon as a class, such written consent shall be required of the holders of a majority of the shares of each class of shares entitled to vote as a class thereon and of the total shares entitled to vote thereon.

Within ten (10) days after obtaining such authorization by written consent, notice shall be given to those shareholders who have not consented in writing. The notice shall fairly summarize the material features of the authorized action and, if the action be a merger, consolidation or sale or exchange of assets for which dissenters rights are provided under the law, the notice shall contain a clear statement of the right of shareholders dissenting therefrom to be paid the fair value of their shares upon compliance with further provisions of the law regarding the rights of dissenting shareholders.

ARTICLE II. Directors

Section 1. Function. All corporate powers shall be exercised by or under the authority of, and the business and affairs of a corporation shall be managed under the direction of, the Board of Directors.

Section 2. Qualification. Directors need not be residents of this state or shareholders of this corporation.

Section 3. Compensation. The Board of Directors shall have authority to fix the compensation of directors.

Section 4. Duties of Directors. A director shall perform his duties as a director, including his duties as a member of any committee of the board upon which he may serve, in good faith, in a manner he reasonably believes to be in the best interests of the corporation, and with such care as an ordinarily prudent person in a like position would use under similar circumstances.

In performing his duties, a director shall be entitled to rely on information, opinions, reports or statements, including financial statements and other financial data, in each case prepared or presented by:

(a) one or more officers or employees of the corporation whom the director reasonably believes to be reliable and competent in the matters presented,

(b) counsel, public accountants or other persons as to matters which the director reasonably believes to be within such person's professional or expert competence, or

(c) a committee of the board upon which he does not serve, duly designated in accordance with a provision of the articles of incorporation or the bylaws, as to matters within its designated authority, which committee the director reasonably believes to merit confidence.

A director shall not be considered to be acting in good faith if he has knowledge concerning the matter in question that would cause such reliance described above to be unwarranted.

A person who performs his duties in compliance with this section shall have no liability by reason of being or having been a director of the corporation.

Section 5. Presumption of Assent. A director of the corporation who is present at a meeting of its Board of Directors at which action on any corporate matter is taken shall be presumed to have assented to the action taken unless he votes against such action or abstains from voting in respect thereto because of an asserted conflict of interest.

Section 6. Number. This corporation shall have at least one (1) director. The minimum number of directors may be increased or decreased from time to time by amendment to these bylaws, but no decrease shall have the effect of shortening the terms of any incumbent director and no amendment shall decrease the number of directors below one (1), unless the stockholders have voted to operate the corporation.

Section 7. Election and Term. Each person named in the articles of incorporation as a member of the initial Board of Directors shall hold office until the first annual meeting of shareholders, and until his successor shall have been elected and qualified or until his earlier resignation, removal from office, or death.

At the first annual meeting of shareholders and at each annual meeting thereafter the shareholders shall elect directors to hold office until the next succeeding annual meeting. Each director shall hold office for the term for which he is elected and until his successor shall have been elected and qualified or until his earlier resignation, removal from office, or death.

Section 8. Vacancies. Any vacancy occurring in the Board of Directors, including any vacancy created by reason of an increase in the number of directors, may be filled by the affirmative vote of a majority of the remaining directors though less than a quorum of the Board of Directors. A director elected to fill a vacancy shall hold office only until the next election of directors by the shareholders.

Section 9. Removal of Directors. At a meeting of shareholders called expressly for that purpose, any director or the entire Board of Directors may be removed, with or without cause, by a vote of the holders of a majority of the shares then entitled to vote at an election of directors.

Section 10. Quorum and Voting. A majority of the number of directors fixed by these bylaws shall constitute a quorum for the transaction of business. The act of the majority of the directors present at a meeting at which a quorum is present shall be the act of the Board of Directors.

Section 11. Director Conflicts of Interest. No contract or other transaction between this corporation and one (1) or more of its directors or any other corporation, firm, association, or entity in which one or more of the directors are directors or officers or are financially interested, shall be either void or voidable because of such relationship or interest or because such director or directors are present at the meeting of the Board of Directors or a committee thereof which authorizes, approves, or ratifies such contract or transaction or because his or their votes are counted for such purpose, if:

(a) The fact of such relationship or interest is disclosed or known to the Board of Directors or committee which authorizes, approves, or ratifies the contract or transaction by a vote or consent sufficient for the purpose without counting the votes or consents of such interested directors; or

(b) The fact of such relationship or interest is disclosed or known to the shareholders entitled to vote and they authorize, approve, or ratify such contract or transaction by vote or written consent; or

(c) The contract or transaction is fair and reasonable as to the corporation at the time it is authorized by the board, a committee or the shareholders.

Common or interested directors may be counted in determining the presence of a quorum at a meeting of the Board of Directors or a committee thereof which authorizes, approves, or ratifies such contract or transaction.

Section 12. Executive and Other Committees. The Board of Directors, by resolution adopted by a majority of the full Board of Directors, may designate from among its members an executive committee and one or more other committees each of which, to the extent provided in such resolution, shall have and may exercise all the authority of the Board of Directors, except that no committee shall have the authority to:

(a) approve or recommend to shareholders actions or proposals required by law to be approved by shareholders,

(b) designate candidates for the office of director, for purposes of proxy solicitation or otherwise,

(c) fill vacancies on the Board of Directors or any committee thereof,

(d) amend the bylaws,

(e) authorize or approve the reacquisition of shares unless pursuant to a general formula or method specified by the Board of Directors, or

(f) authorize or approve the issuance or sale of, or any contract to issue or sell, shares or designate the terms of a series of a class of shares, except that the Board of Directors, having acted regarding general authorization for the issuance or sale of shares, or any contract therefor, and, in the case of a series, the designation thereof, may, pursuant to a general formula or method specified by the Board of Directors, by resolution or by adoption of a stock option or other plan, authorize a committee to fix the terms of any contract for the sale of the shares and to fix the terms upon which such shares may be issued or sold, including, without limitation, the price, the rate or manner of payment of dividends, provisions for redemption, sinking fund, conversion, voting or preferential rights, and provisions for other features of a class of shares, or a series of a class of shares, with full power in such committee to adopt any final resolution setting forth all the terms thereof and to authorize the statement of the terms of a series for filing with the Department of State.

The Board of Directors, by resolution adopted in accordance with this section, may designate one (1) or more directors as alternate members of any such committee, who may act in the place and stead of any absent member or members at any meeting of such committee.

Section 13. Place of Meetings. Regular and special meetings by the Board of Directors may be held within or without the State of _____.

Section 14. Time, Notice and Call of Meetings. Regular meetings by the Board of Directors shall be held without notice. Written notice of the time and place of special meetings of the Board of Directors shall be given to each director by either personal delivery, telegram or cablegram at least two (2) days before the meeting or by notice mailed to the director at least five (5) days before the meeting.

Notice of a meeting of the Board of Directors need not be given to any director who signs a waiver of notice either before or after the meeting. Attendance of a director at a meeting shall constitute a waiver of notice of such meeting and waiver of any and all objections to the place of the meeting, the time of the meeting, or the manner in which it has been called or convened, except when a director states, at the beginning of the meeting, any objection to the transaction of business because the meeting is not lawfully called or convened.

Neither the business to be transacted at, nor the purpose of, any regular or special meeting of the Board of Directors need be specified in the notice or waiver of notice of such meeting.

A majority of the directors present, whether or not a quorum exists, may adjourn any meeting of the Board of Directors to another time and place. Notice of any such adjourned meeting shall be given to the directors who were not present at the time of the adjournment and, unless the time and place of the adjourned meeting are announced at the time of the adjournment, to the other directors.

Meetings of the Board of Directors may be called by the Chairman of the Board, by the President of the corporation, or by any two (2) directors.

Members of the Board of Directors may participate in a meeting of such board by means of a conference telephone or similar communications equipment by means of which all persons participating in the meeting can hear each other at the same time. Participation by such means shall constitute presence in person at a meeting.

Section 15. Action Without a Meetings. Any action required to be taken at a meeting of the directors of a corporation, or any action which may be taken at a meeting of the directors or a committee thereof, may be taken without a meeting if a consent in writing, setting forth the action so to be taken, signed by all of the directors, or all the members of the committee, as the case may be, is filed in the minutes of the proceedings of the board or of the committee. Such consent shall have the same effect as a unanimous vote.

ARTICLE III. Officers

Section 1. Officers. The officers of this corporation shall consist of a president, a secretary and a treasurer, each of whom shall be elected by the Board of Directors. Such other officers and assistant officers and agents as may be deemed necessary may be elected or appointed by the Board of Directors from time to time. Any two (2) or more offices may be held by the same person. The failure to elect a president, secretary or treasurer shall not affect the existence of this corporation.

Section 2. Duties. The officers of this corporation shall have the following duties:

The President shall be the chief executive officer of the corporation, shall have general and active management of the business and affairs of the corporation subject to the directions of the Board of Directors, and shall preside at all meetings of the stockholders and Board of Directors.

The Secretary shall have custody of, and maintain, all of the corporate records except the financial records; shall record the minutes of all meetings of the stockholders and Board of Directors, send all notice of meetings out, and perform such other duties as may be prescribed by the Board of Directors or the President.

The Treasurer shall have custody of all corporate funds and financial records, shall keep full and accurate accounts of receipts and disbursements and render accounts thereof at the annual meetings of stockholders and whenever else required by the Board of Directors or the President, and shall perform such other duties as may be prescribed by the Board of Directors or the President.

Section 3. Removal of Officers. Any officer or agent elected or appointed by the Board of Directors may be removed by the board whenever in its judgment the best interests of the corporation will be served thereby.

Any officer or agent elected by the shareholders may be removed only by vote of the shareholders, unless the shareholders shall have authorized the directors to remove such officer or agent.

Any vacancy, however occurring, in any office may be filled by the Board of Directors, unless the bylaws shall have expressly reserved such power to the shareholders.

Removal of any officer shall be without prejudice to the contract rights, if any, of the person so removed; however, election or appointment of an officer or agent shall not of itself create contract rights.

ARTICLE IV. Stock Certificates

Section 1. Issuance. Every holder of shares in this corporation shall be entitled to have a certificate, representing all shares to which he is entitled. No certificate shall be issued for any share until such share is fully paid.

Section 2. Form. Certificates representing shares in this corporation shall be signed by the President or Vice President and the Secretary or an Assistant Secretary and may be sealed with the seal of this corporation or a facsimile thereof. The signatures of the President or Vice President and the Secretary or Assistant Secretary may be facsimiled if the certificate is manually signed on behalf of a transfer agent or a registrar, other than the corporation itself or an employee of the corporation. In case any officer who signed or whose facsimile signature has been placed upon such certificate shall have ceased to be such officer before such certificate is issued, it may be issued by the corporation with the same effect as if he were such officer at the date of its issuance.

Every certificate representing shares which are restricted as to the sale, disposition or other transfer of such shares shall state that such shares are restricted as to transfer and shall set forth or fairly summarize upon the certificate, or shall state that the corporation will furnish to any shareholder upon request and without charge a full statement of, such restrictions.

Each certificate representing shares shall state upon the face thereof: the name of the corporation; that the corporation is organized under the laws of this state; the name of the person or persons to whom issued; the number and class of shares, and the designation of the series, if any, which such certificate represents; and the par value of each share represented by such certificate, or a statement that the shares are without par value.

Section 3. Transfer of Stock. The corporation shall register a stock certificate presented to it for transfer if the certificate is properly endorsed by the holder of record or by his duly authorized attorney, and the signature of such person has been guaranteed by a commercial bank or trust company or by a member of the New York or American Stock Exchange.

Section 4. Lost, Stolen, or Destroyed Certificates. The corporation shall issue a new stock certificate in the place of any certificate previously issued if the holder of record of the certificate (a) makes proof in affidavit form that it has been lost, destroyed or wrongfully taken; (b) requests the issue of a new certificate before the corporation has notice that the certificate has been acquired by a purchaser for value in good faith and without notice of any adverse claim; (c) gives bond in such form as the corporation may direct, to indemnify the corporation, the transfer agent, and registrar against any claim that may be made on account of the alleged loss, destruction, or theft of a certificate; and (d) satisfies any other reasonable requirements imposed by the corporation.

ARTICLE V. Books and Records

Section 1. Corporate Records.(a) The corporation shall keep as permanent records minutes of all meetings of its shareholders and Board of Directors, a record of all actions taken by the shareholders or Board of Directors without a meeting, and a record of all actions taken by a committee of the Board of Directors on behalf of the corporation.

(b) The corporation shall maintain accurate accounting records and a record of its shareholders in a form that permits preparation of a list of the names and addresses of all shareholders in alphabetical order by class of shares showing the number and series of shares held by each.

(c) The corporation shall keep a copy of: its articles or restated articles of incorporation and all amendments to them currently in effect; these Bylaws or restated Bylaws and all amendments currently in effect; resolutions adopted by the Board of Directors creating one or more classes or series of shares and fixing their relative rights, preferences, and limitations, if shares issued pursuant to those resolutions are outstanding; the minutes of all shareholders' meetings and records of all actions taken by shareholders without a meeting for the past three years; written communications to all shareholders generally or all shareholders of a class of series within the past three years, including the financial statements furnished for the last three years; a list of names and business street addresses of its current directors and officers; and its most recent annual report delivered to the Department of State.

(d) The corporation shall maintain its records in written form or in another form capable of conversion into written form within a reasonable time.

Section 2. Shareholders' Inspection Rights. A shareholder is entitled to inspect and copy, during regular business hours at the corporation's principal office, any of the corporate records described in Section l(c) of this Article if the shareholder gives the corporation written notice of the demand at least five (5) business days before the date on which he wishes to inspect and copy the records.

A shareholder is entitled to inspect and copy, during regular business hours at a reasonable location specified by the corporation, any of the following records of the corporation if the shareholder gives the corporation written notice of this demand at least five (5) business days before the date on which he wishes to inspect and copy provided (a) the demand is made in good faith and for a proper purpose; (b) the shareholder described with reasonable particularity the purpose and the records he desires to inspects; and (c) the records are directly connected with the purpose: (i) excerpts from minutes of any meeting of the Board of Directors, records of any action of a committee of the Board of Directors while acting in place of the Board on behalf of the corporation; (ii) accounting records; (iii) the record of shareholders; and (iv) any other books and records of the corporation.

This Section 2 does not affect the right of a shareholder to inspect and copy the shareholders' list described in Section 7 of Article 1, if the shareholder is in litigation with the corporation to the same extent as any other litigant or the power of a court to compel the production of corporate records for examination.

The corporation may deny any demand for inspection if the demand was made for an improper purpose, or if the demanding shareholder has within the two (2) years preceding his demand, sold or offered for sale any list of shareholders of the corporation or of any other corporation, has aided or abetted any person in procuring any list of shareholders for that purpose, or has improperly used any information secured through any prior examination of the records of this corporation or any other corporation.

Section 3. Financial Information. Not later than four (4) months after the close of each fiscal year, this corporation shall prepare a balance sheet showing in reasonable detail the financial condition of the corporation as of the close of its fiscal year, and a profit and loss statement showing the results of the operations of the corporation during its fiscal year.

Upon the written request of any shareholder or holder of voting trust certificates for shares of the corporation, the corporation shall mail to such shareholder or holder of voting trust certificates a copy of the most recent such balance sheet and profit and loss statement.

The balance sheets and profit and loss statements shall be filed in the registered office of the corporation in this state, shall be kept for at least five (5) years, and shall be subject to inspection during business hours by any shareholder or holder of voting trust certificates, in person or by agent.

ARTICLE VI. Dividends

The Board of Directors of this corporation may, from time to time, declare, and the corporation may pay dividends on its shares in cash, property or its own shares, except when the corporation is insolvent or when the payment thereof would render the corporation insolvent or when the declaration or payment thereof would be contrary to any restrictions contained in the articles of incorporation, subject to the following provisions:

(a) Dividends in cash or property may be declared and paid, except as otherwise provided in this section, only out of the unreserved and unrestricted earned surplus of the corporation or out of capital surplus, howsoever arising but each dividend paid out of capital surplus, and the amount per share paid from such surplus shall be disclosed to the shareholders receiving the same concurrently with the distribution.

(b) Dividends may be declared and paid in the corporation's own treasury shares.

(c) Dividends may be declared and paid in the corporation's own authorized but unissued shares out of any unreserved and unrestricted surplus of the corporation upon the following conditions:

(1) If a dividend is payable in shares having a par value, such shares shall be issued at not less than the par value thereof and there shall be transferred to stated capital at the time such dividend is paid an amount of surplus equal to the aggregate par value of the shares to be issued as a dividend.

(2) If a dividend is payable in shares without par value, such shares shall be issued at such stated value as shall be fixed by the Board of Directors by resolution adopted at the time such dividend is declared, and there shall be transferred to stated capital at the time such dividend is paid an amount of surplus equal to the aggregate stated value so fixed in respect of such shares; and the amount per share so transferred to stated capital shall be disclosed to the shareholders receiving such dividend concurrently with the payment thereof.

(d) No dividend payable in shares of any class shall be paid to the holders of shares of any other class unless the articles of incorporation so provide or such payment is authorized by the affirmative vote or the written consent of the holders of at least a majority of the outstanding shares of the class in which the payment is to be made.

(e) A split-up or division of the issued shares of any class into a greater number of shares of the same class without increasing the stated capital of the corporation shall not be construed to be a share dividend within the meaning of this section.

ARTICLE VII. Corporate Seal

The Board of Directors shall provide a corporate seal which shall be circular in form and shall have inscribed thereon the name of the corporation as it appears on page 1 of these Bylaws.

ARTICLE VIII. Repayment of Excessive Payments

Any payments made to an employee, officer, director or stockholder of the corporation which shall be disallowed, in whole or in part, as a deductible expense for federal or state income tax purposes, shall be reimbursed by such individual to the corporation to the full extent of such disallowance. If the corporation is not fully reimbursed within a period of thirty (30) days following the final determination of the amount actually disallowed as deduction, the corporation shall have the right to withhold up to fifty percent (50%) of any future compensation or other payments due the individual until the amount owed to the corporation has been paid in full. The corporation shall not be required to defend any proposed disallowance of any payment by the Internal Revenue Service or the Department of Revenue of the State of ____. However, it shall be the duty of the Board of Directors to enforce payment of such amount disallowed.

ARTICLE IX. Amendments

These bylaws may be repealed or amended, and new bylaws may be adopted, by the Board of Directors.

End of Bylaws adopted, by the Board of Directors.

CERTIFICATE OF LIMITED PARTNERSHIP OF
_____ LTD., a limited partnership

The undersigned General Partner, desiring to form a limited partnership pursuant to the laws of the State of _____, hereby states:

1. The name of the Partnership is _____.

2. The mailing address and address of the principal place of business of the Partnership is _____.

3. The name and address of the agent for service of process on the Partnership is:

_____

_____

4. The name and business address of the sole General Partner is:

_____

_____

5. The latest date upon which the Partnership shall dissolve is _____, 20___.

The execution of this Certificate by the undersigned General Partner constitutes an affirmation under the penalties of perjury that the facts stated herein are true.

IN WITNESS WHEREOF, this Certificate of Limited Partnership has been executed by the sole General Partner of _____ this_____ day of _____, 20___.

GENERAL PARTNER:
By: _____
By: _____, President

CERTIFICATE OF SECRETARY

_____ does hereby certify that I am the Secretary of _____ a Corporation, that I am the keeper of the Corporate Records and Seal of said Corporation; that set forth below is a true and correct copy of the resolution adopted at a special meeting of the Board of Directors of said Corporation duly called, convened and held in accordance with its by-laws and the laws of said State at the office of the Corporation at _____ on the _____ day of _____, 20__, as taken and transcribed by me from the minutes of said meeting and compared by me with the original of said minutes recorded in the minute book of said Corporation; that the said resolution was duly adopted at said meeting, and that the same has not been in any way modified, repealed or rescinded, but is in full force and effect; and that all the Directors of the Corporation have duly ratified and affirmed the same in the form aforesaid.

WHEREAS, for and in consideration of the extension of credit by **Creditor**, to _____, the **Debtor** and in order that **Creditor** shall continue to sell and deliver goods and materials to **Debtor**, and for other good and valuable consideration, it is in the best interest of this Corporation to enter into a Cross-Corporate Guarantee Agreement with **Creditor**, and

WHEREAS, the proposed form of the Cross-Corporate Guarantee Agreement has been submitted to this meeting, been duly considered thereat and the execution thereof being deemed to be in the best interest of this Corporation; now, therefore it is

RESOLVED, that any officer of this Corporation be and hereby is authorized and directed on behalf of this Corporation to execute the aforementioned Cross-Corporate Guarantee Agreement, to execute any amendments or supplements to such Cross-Corporate Guarantee Agreement which may be necessary or desirable, and to perform, in such officer's discretion, all other acts which may be necessary or desirable, and convenient or expedient to carry out the provisions, intent and purposes of such Cross-Corporate Guarantee Agreement, and this Corporation and of this Board.

WITNESS my hand and Seal of said Corporation this _____ day of _____, 20__.

By: _____
(Secretary)

COMPROMISE AGREEMENT

AGREEMENT made this _____ day of _____ 20__, between _____ with an address at _____, hereinafter called the Debtor, and _____ with an address at _____, hereinafter called the Creditor, WITNESSETH:

WHEREAS, a dispute has arisen between the Debtor and Creditor with reference to a claim made by the Creditor against the Debtor for _____ in the amount of $_____.

WHEREAS, the parties hereto are desirous of compromising and settling the said dispute,

NOW, THEREFORE, it is agreed that in consideration of the mutual covenants and agreements herein set forth, the Debtor shall pay to the Creditor in full settlement of the claim made against him as hereinbefore stated the sum of $_____.

The Creditor shall accept the said amount of $_____ in full settlement of all claims which he may have against the Debtor and shall upon receiving full payment of such amount execute and deliver to the Debtor a release in due form of law, of all such claims.

IN WITNESS WHEREOF, the parties have signed this document the date first above written.

(Signatures, seals and acknowledgments of parties)

CORPORATE ACKNOWLEDGEMENT

STATE OF _____ }
                          } ss:
COUNTY OF _____ }

On this _____ day of _____, 20__, before me personally came _____ to me personally known, who, being by me duly sworn, did depose and say the (s)he resides at _____, in the State of _____; that (s)he is the _____ of _____ the corporation described in and which executed the foregoing instrument; that (s)he knows the seal of said corporation; that the seal affixed to said instrument is such corporate seal; that it was so affixed by order of the Board of Directors of said corporation; and the (s)he signed his/her name thereto by like order.

_____
NOTARY PUBLIC

CORPORATE GUARANTEE

For and in consideration of the extension of credit by _____ (hereinafter called "Creditor") to _____ a _____ corporation, whose address is _____, (hereinafter called "Debtor") and for other good and valuable consideration, the undersigned, _____, (hereinafter called "**Guarantor**") hereby unconditionally guarantees the payment of all indebtedness, liabilities and obligations of every kind and nature of **Debtor** to **Creditor**, whether existing or to exist in the future, whether absolute or contingent (including liability pursuant to any guarantee or endorsement by **Debtor**) direct or indirect, due or to become due, heretofore or hereafter created, arising or existing, (all hereinafter referred to as the "**Indebtedness**") without limitation as to amount.

The undersigned hereby represents to and covenants and agrees as follows:

1. The within guarantee is a continuing and collateral guarantee, independent of and in addition to any other security, collateral, endorsement or guarantee held by Creditor for the Indebtedness or any part thereof. The undersigned's liability hereunder shall be deemed terminated only upon the actual receipt by **Creditor** of written notice of the revocation of this agreement by the undersigned; provided however that such termination shall be effective only as to any Indebtedness created or arising subsequent to such termination. The payment in full of outstanding Indebtedness at any time shall not discharge or otherwise affect the liability hereunder of the undersigned with respect to indebtedness thereafter created and arising prior to the termination of such liability as herein provided.

2. The liability hereunder of the undersigned shall not be impaired, altered or otherwise affected by the taking of any other or additional security for, or guarantee of the indebtedness or any part thereof, or by any neglect, failure or omission to hold, protect or rely or realize upon any such other or additional security or guarantee, or by any renewal, extension, modification, compounding, compromise or discharge of the indebtedness or any part thereof, whether before or after a termination of the undersigned's liability hereunder as herein provided, or by any other act or thing whatsoever, each and all of which the undersigned hereby consents to without notice to the undersigned. The liability hereunder of the undersigned shall be direct, immediate and absolute and shall not be conditional or contingent upon the pursuit, exercise or prosecution by **Creditor** of any other remedy or remedies whatsoever and **Creditor** shall have and may exercise against the undersigned any and all rights and remedies that it might against a principal **Debtor** upon a past due liquidated obligation.

3. Presentment for payment, demand, protest and notice of protest and nonpayment to the undersigned, to **Debtor** and to all other persons of all bills, notes, checks, drafts, trade acceptances and other orders and promises for the payment of money, notice of the acceptance of this agreement, notice of the extension of credit and making of advances hereunder and notice of default hereunder, are and each and all of them are, hereby waived by the undersigned.

4. If the undersigned is a corporation, partnership or other organization or association, this agreement is made and entered into by it in furtherance of its purposes, the execution of this agreement is not contrary to or a violation of its certificate of incorporation, charter, by-laws or any agreement or indenture to which it or its members are a party or by which it or its property or its members are bound and it and the party executing this agreement on its behalf each represent to **Creditor** that the undersigned is duly authorized to guarantee the indebtedness.

IN WITNESS WHEREOF, the undersigned has caused this agreement to be executed this _____ day of _____, 20__.

_____
{Name of Corporate Guarantor}

By: _____

_____
{Name of Officer signing Guarantee}

_____
{Title}

CORPORATE GUARANTEE OF PAYMENT OF FUTURE DEBTS

The_____ (corporation), organized under the Laws of the State of _____, (address), in consideration of $_____ (or for good and valuable consideration) the receipt of which is hereby acknowledged, does hereby guarantee full payment of any debts that may be incurred by _____ during the period _____, such amounts to be paid in full not later than the _____ day of _____, 20__.

By: _____
(Corporation)

DISPOSITION NOTIFICATION FOR COMMERCIAL TRANSACTION AFTER DEFAULT

[*Name and address of secured party*]

[*Date*]

NOTICE OF OUR PLAN TO SELL PROPERTY

[*Name and address of any obligor who is also a debtor*]

Subject: [*Identification of Transaction*]

We have your [*describe collateral*], because you broke promises in our agreement.

[*For a public disposition:*]

We will sell [*describe collateral*] at public sale. A sale could include a lease or license. The sale will be held as follows:

Date:

Time:

Place:

You may attend the sale and bring bidders if you want.

[*For a private disposition:*]

We will sell [*describe collateral*] at private sale sometime after [*date*]. A sale could include a lease or license.

The money that we get from the sale (after paying our costs) will reduce the amount you owe. If we get less money than you owe, you [*will or* will not, *as applicable*] still owe us the difference. If we get more money than you owe, you will get the extra money, unless we must pay it to someone else.

You can get the property back, at any time before we sell it by paying us the full amount you owe (not just the past due payments), including our expenses. To learn the exact amount you must pay, call us at [*telephone number*].

If you want us to explain to you in writing how we have figured the amount that you owe us, you may call us at [*telephone number*] [or write us at [*secured party's address*]] and request a written explanation.

[We will charge you $_____$ for the explanation if we sent you another written explanation of the amount you owe us within the last six months.]

If you need more information about the sale call us at [*telephone number*] [or write us at [*secured party's address*]].

We are sending this notice to the following other people who have an interest in [describe collateral] or who owe money under your agreement:

[*Names of all other debtors and obligors, if any*]

Includes consumer goods, equipment, farm products and inventory.

Where letter-of-credit rights are "supporting obligations" as defined in § 9-102, perfection as to the related account, chattel paper, document, general intangible, instrument or investment property will perfect as to the letter-of-credit rights.

DISPOSITION NOTIFICATION FOR CONSUMER TRANSACTION AFTER DEFAULT

NOTIFICATION OF DISPOSITION OF COLLATERAL

To: [*Name of debtor, obligor, or other person to which the notification is sent*]

From: [*Name, address, and telephone number of secured party*]

Name of Debtor(s): [*Include only if debtor(s) are not an addressee*]

[*For a public disposition:*]

We will sell [or lease or license, *as applicable*] the [*describe collateral*] to [the highest qualified bidder] in public as follows:

Day and Date:

Time:

Place:

[*For a private disposition:*]

We will sell [or lease or license, *as applicable*] the [*describe collateral*] privately sometime after [*day and date*].

EMPLOYMENT AGREEMENT

THIS AGREEMENT made this _____ day of _____, 20__, by and between _____("Corporation"), a _____ corporation, and _____ ("Employee").

WITNESSETH:

In consideration of the covenants and agreements herein contained and the moneys to be paid hereunder, the Corporation agrees to hire the Employee, and the Employee agrees to work for the Corporation upon the following terms and conditions:

1. *Duties of Employee:* The Employee is employed by the Corporation to render services on behalf of the Corporation as _____.

2. *Devotion of Full-Time to Employment:* The Employee shall not engage in or carry on or be employed by, directly or indirectly, any other business or profession without the consent of the Corporation; provided, however, that nothing herein contained shall prohibit the Employee from investing or trading in stocks, bonds, commodities, or other securities or forms of investments, including real property.

3. *Salary:* The Corporation shall pay to the Employee as compensation for his services a salary of $_____ per year, payable in equal monthly or other convenient installments during the term of this Agreement. Said salary shall be reduced by any payments made to the Employee because of his disability under insurance policies for which the Corporation has paid the premiums. (Any portion of said salary that shall be disallowed in whole or in part as a deductible expense for Federal income tax purposes shall

be reimbursed by the Employee to the Corporation to the full extent of the disallowance.)

The Corporation shall purchase at, its expense, an insurance policy on the life of Employee, payable to the beneficiary or beneficiaries designated in writing by the Employee. Said insurance policy shall be in the face amount of $_____.

The Corporation shall purchase, at its expense, a major medical insurance policy insuring the Employee and his dependents, which policy shall be reasonably acceptable to the parties hereto.

The Corporation shall institute a medical reimbursement plan, mutually acceptable to the parties hereto, providing, among other things, for (1) reimbursement to the Employee of premiums paid by the Employee for a disability insurance policy paying a maximum of $_____ per month after _____ weeks of disability and (2) reimbursement up to the amount of $_____ per year for the medical expenses of the Employee and his dependents not otherwise covered by medical insurance.

ALTERNATE ONE

4. *Term of Agreement:* The effective date of this Agreement shall be _____, and it shall remain effective and continue in force and effect until terminated as hereinafter provided. Notwithstanding the foregoing, the Employee's salary specified above shall be effective only through the end of the Corporation's taxable year, and the same shall be renegotiated in the last month of each taxable year of the Corporation for the following such taxable year until this Agreement is terminated. Said salary shall not be reduced without the written consent of Employee.

ALTERNATE TWO

4. *Term of Agreement:* Subject to the provisions of paragraph _____ hereof regarding termination, the term of this employment shall commence _____, and shall continue thereafter for a period of _____ years until _____. Thereafter, this employment shall be deemed to be renewed automatically, upon the same terms and conditions, for successive periods of one (1) year each until either party, at least thirty (30) days prior to the expiration of the original term or of any extended term, shall give written notice to the other of intention not to renew such employment. Notwithstanding the foregoing, the Employee's salary specified above shall be effective only through the end of the Corporation's taxable year, and the same shall be renegotiated in the last month of each taxable year of the Corporation for the following such taxable year until this Agreement is terminated. Said salary shall not be reduced without the written consent of Employee.

ALTERNATE ONE

5. *Automobile:* The Corporation shall lease or own the automobile used by the Employee in the conduct of the Corporation's business as a condition of his employment, and the Corporation shall pay for all gas, oil, repairs and maintenance, rent (if any), an allowance for depreciation (if any) and insurance in connection therewith.

ALTERNATE TWO

5. *Automobile:* The Employee shall lease or own the automobile used by the Employee in the conduct of the Corporation's business as a condition of his employment, and the Corporation shall pay for all gas, oil, repairs and maintenance, rent (if any), an allowance for depreciation (if any) and insurance in connection therewith.

6. *Reimbursable Expenses:* Except as herein otherwise provided, the Corporation may reimburse the Employee for all pre-approved expenses, or the Employee may be entitled to charge to the Corporation all pre-approved expenses incurred by him, in and about the course of his employment by the Corporation. The Corporation must approve, in advance, all expenses or reimbursements to be paid hereunder. Such expenses shall include but not be limited to:

(a) License fees, membership dues in professional organizations, and subscriptions to professional journals.

(b) The Employee's necessary travel, hotel and entertainment expenses incurred in connection with overnight, out-of-town trips for educational, professional or other related meetings or in connection with other events that contribute to the benefit of the Corporation.

(c) The Employee's necessary travel and entertainment expenses in connection with in-town events for education, professional and other related meetings or in connection with other events that contribute to the benefit of the Corporation.

7. *Vacation:* The Employee shall be entitled to such vacation as is authorized by the Corporation from time to time.

8. *Time Off:* The Employee shall be entitled to such time off as is authorized by the Corporation from time to time.

9. *Termination of Agreement:*

(a) The Corporation may terminate this Agreement at any time if the Employee becomes unfit to properly render services as _____ to the Corporation because of drunkenness, insubordination, gross neglect of his duties, proven dishonesty, or commission of a felony. Such termination shall be effective upon the delivery of written notice thereof to the Employee or at such later time as may be designated in said notice, and the Employee shall vacate the offices of the Corporation on or before such effective date.

(b) The Employee or the Corporation may voluntarily elect to terminate this Agreement, provided that the party electing to terminate must deliver to the other party written notice of such intention to terminate not less than sixty (60) days prior to the date of such termination.

10. *Disability:* If the Employee is unable to fully perform his duties hereunder by reason of illness or incapacity of any kind for a period of more than _____ months, his salary payments may be reduced or terminated by the Corporation in its absolute discretion. The Employee's full salary shall be reinstated upon his return to full time employment and the full discharge of his obligations pursuant to this Agreement.

11. *Bonus:* To provide greater incentive for the Employee by rewarding him with additional compensation, a bonus in the form of cash may be paid to the Employee at any time during the year if he has substantially contributed to the success of the Corporation. Whether or not such bonus shall be paid to the Employee and, if so, the amount thereof, shall be within the sole discretion of the Corporation. In making such determination, the Corporation shall consider the following:

(a) The net profits of the Corporation for such year;
(b) The regular salary of the Employee during such year;
(c) The financial needs of the Employee;
(d) The Employee's knowledge of and skill in performing the tasks assigned to him;
(e) The Employee's overall improvement during such year as an employee of the Corporation;
(f) The Employee's rapport with the customers of the Corporation;
(g) A comparison of the Employee's performance with the performance of other employees of the Corporation based on the foregoing criteria; and
(h) Such other matters as may be considered appropriate by the officers and directors of the Corporation.

12. *Death Benefit:* In the event the Employee should die during the term of this Agreement, the Corporation shall pay, by reason of the death of the Employee and as additional compensation for the services of the Employee to the Corporation hereunder, the sum of $5,000.00 to the beneficiary or beneficiaries designated in writing by the Employee or, in the event of the failure of such designation, to the estate of the Employee. Such death benefit shall be payable on or before the expiration of six (6) months following the death of the Employee. The Employee shall at no time be entitled to receive personally the death benefit provided for hereunder.

13. *Limitations on Authority:* Without the express written consent from the Corporation, the Employee shall have no apparent or implied authority to:

(a) Pledge the credit of the Corporation or any of its other employees.
(b) Bind the Corporation under any contract, agreement, note, mortgage, or otherwise.
(c) Release or discharge any debt due the Corporation unless the Corporation has received the full amount thereof.
(d) Sell, mortgage, transfer, or otherwise dispose of any assets of the Corporation.

14. *Liquidated Damages for Breach:* Notwithstanding anything herein contained to the contrary, if the Employee knowingly breaches this Agreement, and such breach continues unremedied for fifteen (15) days after written notice of such breach has been given to the Employee, the right of such Employee to receive any continued salary payments to which he would otherwise be entitled shall be forfeited as liquidated damages for such breach.

OPTIONAL PARAGRAPH

15. *Disallowance of Expense Deductions.* If any salary or other compensation payments made to the Employee, or, any other payment made to or for the benefit of the Employee is disallowed, in whole or

in part, as a deductible expense by the Internal Revenue Service or the Department of Revenue of the State of _____, such payment shall be reimbursed by the Employee to the Corporation to the full extent of such disallowance. The reimbursement by the Employee shall be made within thirty (30) days after the amount actually disallowed has been finally determined, by agreement or otherwise. If the Corporation is not fully reimbursed within such thirty (30) day period, it shall have the right to withhold all future compensation payments due to the Employee until the amount owed to the Corporation has been paid in full. The Corporation shall not be required to defend any proposed disallowance of any payment by the Internal Revenue Service or by the Department of Revenue of the State of _____.

16. *Covenant Not to Compete:* The Employee agrees that for a period of _____ months following the termination of employment hereunder, whether such termination be with or without cause, and within an area of _____ miles from the corporate limits of _____, the Employee will not enter into the employ of any person, firm or corporation engaged in a similar line of business in competition with the Corporation, nor engage during such period, directly or indirectly, as principal, agent or employee, in any such business in competition with the Corporation. The parties hereto recognize that the services to be performed by the Employee are special and unique, and that by reason of the employment hereunder, the Employee will acquire confidential information as aforesaid. It is agreed that any breach of this agreement by the Employee shall entitle the Corporation, in addition to any other legal remedies available to it, to apply to any court of competent jurisdiction to enjoin any violation of this agreement.

In any action or proceeding relating to or involving enforcement of this covenant, and any counterclaim, crossclaim or other litigation which may be asserted or brought against the Corporation, the Employee hereby expressly waives any and all right to a trial by jury with respect to the action, proceeding or other litigation resulting from or involving the enforcement of the covenant. Further, in any action or proceeding by the Corporation to obtain a temporary restraining order and/or preliminary injunction, the Employee hereby agrees that the Corporation shall not be required to post an injunction bond in excess of the principal sum of Five Thousand Dollars ($5,000.00) in order to obtain the temporary restraining order and/or preliminary injunction. Should the Corporation's action for a temporary restraining order and/or motion for preliminary injunction be granted in whole or in part, and should the Corporation be ultimately unsuccessful in obtaining a permanent injunction to enforce the covenant, the Employee hereby waives any and all rights the Employee may have against the Corporation for any injuries or damages, including consequential damages, sustained by the Employee and arising directly or indirectly from the issuance of the temporary restraining order and/or preliminary injunction.

The Employee acknowledges that when this Agreement is concluded, the Employee will be able to earn a living without violating the restrictions contained in this Paragraph and that the Employee's recognition and representation of this fact is a material condition to the execution of this Agreement and to the Employee's continued employment with the Corporation.

17. *Invalid Provision:* The validity or unenforceability of a particular provision of this Agreement shall not affect the other provisions hereof, and the Agreement shall be construed in all respects as if such invalid or unenforceable provisions were omitted.

18. *Modification:* No change or modification of this Agreement shall be valid unless the same be in writing and signed by the parties hereto.

19. *Applicable Law and Binding Effect:* This Agreement shall be construed and regulated under and by the laws of the State of _____, and shall inure to the benefit of and be binding upon the parties hereto and their heirs, personal representatives, successors and assigns.

20. *Costs and Attorneys' Fees.* If the obligations of the parties expressed herein are the subject of litigation, the prevailing party shall be entitled to recover from the other party all reasonable costs and expenses of such litigation, including reasonable attorneys' fees and costs of appeal.

IN WITNESS WHEREOF, the undersigned have hereunto caused this Agreement to be executed the day and year first above written.

CORPORATION:

By:_____
     President

Attest:_____
          Secretary

WITNESSES:

EMPLOYEE:

_____

_____

_____

As to Employee

You are entitled to an accounting of the unpaid indebtedness secured by the property that we intend to sell [or lease or license, *as applicable*] [for a charge of $]. You may request an accounting by calling us at [*telephone number*].

ENDORSEMENT ON CHECK CONSTITUTING ACCORD AND SATISFACTION

This check is in full payment and settlement of the following items: (Insert items); Endorsement will constitute acceptance in full settlement of (all) (the following) claims against the undersigned.

INSTALLMENT NOTE

$_____.   _____, 20__.
_____ after date I _____ promise to pay to the order of _____, _____ dollars with interest at the rate of _____ percent, per annum, in _____ equal installments as follows:

      On _____, 20__, _____ Dollars
      On _____, 20__, _____ Dollars
      On _____, 20__, _____ Dollars

It is hereby expressly agreed that upon default in payment of any one of said installments, which default shall extend over a period of more than _____(___) days, then all subsequent installments on this note, with interest, shall at once become due and payable at the option of the legal holder thereof without demand or notice, demand and notice being hereby expressly waived. The makers, endorsers and all guarantors of this note severally waive demand, protest and presentation for payment and notice of nonpayment and protest, and also waive any and all defenses on the ground of any extensions or partial payment which may be granted or accepted by the holder before or after the maturity of this note or any part thereof.

We also agree that if proceedings are commenced to collect this note by process of law ___ percent shall be allowed and included in the judgment thereon as attorney's fees. Value received

_____
(Signature)

Signed, sealed, and delivered in the presence of

_____

JUDGMENT NOTE

$_____   _____, 20__
_____ after date for value received I _____ promise to pay to the order of _____,
_____dollars, at _____ with interest at _____ percent, per annum, from and after date, until paid. And to further secure the payment of said sum, _____ authorize, irrevocably, any attorney of any court of record to appear for _____ in said court, and confess judgment without process in favor of the holder of this note for such amount as may appear to be unpaid thereon, hereby expressly waiving all benefit under the exemption laws of _____ with costs and ___ percent, attorneys' fees, and to waive all errors in any such proceedings, and to consent to immediate execution upon such judgment, hereby ratifying and confirming all that _____ said attorney may do by virtue hereof.

Signed _____

(NOTE: Check local law to determine if permissible. *See* **table in Appendix B. Some states do not permit recovery of attorneys' fees in a fixed percentage of the debt, but will only allow reasonable attorneys' fees.)**

LEASE OF PERSONAL PROPERTY

Agreement of Lease dated _____, 20__, between _____ CORPORATION, having its principal place of business at No. _____ Street, _____, herein called "Lessor," and _____ residing at No. _____ Street, _____, herein called "Lessee."

Lessor hereby leases to Lessee the following personal property which property together with all replacement parts, additions, repairs and accessories heretofore or hereafter incorporated therein or affixed thereto are herein called "equipment";

Make _____ Model _____ Serial No. (Set forth in complete detail)

1. *Term*. The term of this lease commences upon _____.

2. *Rent*. As rent for said equipment, Lessee shall pay Lessor, at the address above, the sum of _____ Dollars ($_____) which Lessee hereby promises to pay to Lessor in _____ installments commencing on_____, 20__, as follows:

$_____ on the _____ day of _____, 20__, (In same manner set forth other amounts and dates)

3. *Location*. The equipment shall be located at _____ and shall not be removed therefrom without Lessor's prior written consent.

4. *Use*. Lessor shall comply with all laws relating to the use, operation or maintenance of the equipment. If Lessor supplies Lessee with labels stating that the equipment is owned by Lessor, Lessee shall affix and keep the same upon a prominent place on the equipment.

5. *Acceptance*. Lessee acknowledges that he has fully inspected and accepted said equipment in good condition and repair.

6. *Inspection*. At all times during business hours, Lessor shall have the right to inspect the equipment or observe its use.

7. *Alterations*. Without the prior written consent of Lessor, Lessee shall not make any alterations, additions, or improvements to the equipment. All additions and improvements of whatsoever kind or nature made to the equipment shall belong to and become the property of Lessor upon the expiration, or earlier termination of this lease.

8. *Repairs*. Lessee, at its own cost and expense, shall keep the equipment in good repair, condition and working order and shall furnish any and all parts, mechanisms, and devices required to keep the equipment in good mechanical and working order.

9. *Loss and Damage*. Lessee hereby assumes and shall bear the entire risk of loss and damage to the equipment from any and every cause whatsoever. No loss or damage to the equipment or any part thereof shall impair any obligation of Lessee under this lease which shall continue in full force and effect. In the event of loss or damage of any kind whatever to any item of equipment, Lessee at the option of Lessor shall: (a) place the same in good repair, condition, and working order; or (b) replace the same with like equipment in good repair, condition and working order.

10. *Insurance*. Lessee agrees to take out insurance against risks of fire, malicious mischief and theft in the equipment which names the Lessor as an insured, and to send copies of such policy or certificates thereof to Lessor.

11. *Surrender*. Upon the expiration or earlier termination of this lease, Lessee shall return the equipment to Lessor in good repair, condition and working order, ordinary wear and tear resulting from proper use thereof alone excepted.

12. *Taxes*. Lessee shall keep the equipment free and clear of all levies, liens, and encumbrances and shall pay all license fees, assessments, charges and taxes (municipal, state and federal) which may now or hereafter be imposed upon the ownership, leasing, renting, sale, possession or use of the equipment. If Lessee fails to pay any said fees, assessments, charges, or taxes, Lessor shall have the right, but shall not be obligated, to pay the same. In such event, the cost thereof shall be repayable to Lessor with the next installment of rent, and failure to repay the same shall carry with it the same consequence, including interest at ____ percent (__%) per annum, as failure to pay any installment of rent.

13. *Indemnity*. Lessee shall indemnify Lessor against, and hold Lessor harmless from, any and all claims, actions, suits, proceedings, costs, expenses, damages and liabilities, including attorney's fees, arising out of, connected with, or resulting from the equipment, including without limitation the manufacture, selection, delivery, possession, use, operation or return of the equipment.

14. *Default*. If Lessee with regard to any item or items of equipment fails to pay any rent or other amount herein provided within ten (10) days after the same is due and payable, or if Lessee with regard to any item or items of equipment fails to observe, keep, or perform any other provision of this lease required to be observed, kept or performed by Lessee, Lessor shall have the right to exercise any one or more of the following remedies:

(a) To declare the entire amount of rent hereunder immediately due and payable as to any or all items of equipment, without notice or demand to Lessee.

(b)To sue for and recover all rents, and other payments, then accrued or thereafter accruing, with respect to any or all items of equipment.

(c)To take possession of any or all items of equipment without demand or notice, wherever same may be located, without any court order or other process of law. Lessee hereby waives any and all damages occasioned by such taking of possession. Any said taking of possession shall not constitute a termination of this lease as to any or all items of equipment unless Lessor expressly so notifies Lessee in writing.

(d)To terminate this lease as to any or all items of equipment.

(e)To pursue any other remedy at law or in equity. Notwithstanding any said repossession, or any other action which Lessor may take, Lessee shall be and remain liable for the full performance of all obligations on the part of Lessee to be performed under this lease.

All such remedies are cumulative, and may be exercised concurrently or separately.

15. *Bankruptcy.* Neither this lease nor any interest therein is assignable or transferable by operation of law. If any proceeding under the Bankruptcy Code, as amended, is commenced by or against the Lessee, or if the Lessee is adjudged insolvent, or if the Lessee makes any assignment for the benefit of his creditors, or if a writ of attachment or execution is levied on any item or items of the equipment and is not released or satisfied within ten (10) days thereafter, or if a receiver is appointed in any proceeding or action to which the Lessee is a party with authority to take possession or control of any item or items of the equipment, Lessor shall have and may exercise any one or more of the remedies set forth in paragraph 14 hereof; and this lease shall, at the option of lessor, without notice, immediately terminate and shall not be treated as an asset of Lessee after the exercise of said option.

16. *Lessor's Expenses.* Lessee shall pay Lessor all costs and expenses, including attorney's fees, incurred by Lessor in exercising any of its rights or remedies hereunder or enforcing any of the terms, conditions, or provisions hereof.

17. *Assignment.* Without the prior written consent of Lessor, Lessee shall not (a) assign, transfer, pledge, or hypothecate this lease, the equipment or any part thereof, or any interest therein or (b) sublet or lend the equipment or any part thereof, or permit the equipment or any part thereof to be used by anyone other than Lessee or Lessee's employees. Consent to any of the foregoing prohibited acts applies only in the given instance; and is not a consent to any subsequent like act by Lessee or any other person. Subject always to the foregoing, this lease inures to the benefit of, and is binding upon, the heirs, legatees, personal representatives, successors, and assigns of the parties hereto.

18. *Lessor's Assignment.* It is understood that Lessor contemplates assigning this lease and/or mortgaging the equipment, and that said assignee may assign the same. All rights of Lessor in the equipment and hereunder may be assigned, pledged, mortgaged, transferred, or otherwise disposed of, either in whole or in part, without notice to Lessee. The assignee's rights shall be free from all defenses, setoffs or counterclaims which Lessee may be entitled to assert against Lessor. No such assignee shall be obligated to perform any duty, covenant or condition required to be performed by Lessor under the terms of this lease.

19. *Ownership.* The equipment is, and shall at all times be and remain, the sole and exclusive personal property of Lessor; and the Lessee shall have no right, title or interest therein or thereto except as expressly set forth in this lease.

20. *Interest.* Should Lessee fail to pay any part of the rent herein reserved or any other sum required by Lessee to be paid to Lessor, within ten (10) days after the due date thereof, Lessee shall pay unto the Lessor interest on such delinquent payment from the expiration of said ten (10) days until paid at the rate of _____ percent (___ %) per annum.

21. *Notices.* Service of all notices under this agreement shall be sufficient if given personally or mailed to the party involved at its respective address hereinafter set forth, or at such address as such party may provide in writing from time to time. Any such notice mailed to such address shall be effective when deposited in the United States mail, duly addressed and with postage prepaid.

22. *Gender; Number.* Whenever the context of this lease requires, the masculine gender includes the feminine or neuter, and the singular number includes the plural; and whenever the word "lessor" is used herein shall include all assignees of lessor. If there is more than one lessee named in this lease, the liability of each shall be joint and several.

IN WITNESS WHEREOF the parties hereto have executed these presents this _____ of _____, 20__.

(Signatures, seals and acknowledgments of parties)

LETTER OF CREDIT

Sir:

We hereby agree to accept and pay at maturity any draft or drafts on us at _____ days sight, issued by _____ located at _____ to the extent of $_____ and negotiated through your bank.

Any draft drawn under this letter must state that it is drawn under Letter of Credit issued by _____ No._____ Date _____

This Letter of Credit shall be valid to and until the day of _____, 20___

Very truly yours,

_____

(NOTE: Banks usually insist on the use of their own Letter of Credit form and the creditor will have little ability to change the form.)

NEGOTIABLE PROMISSORY NOTE

City, State, _____, 20__

Sixty days after date, (or, on the _____ day of _____, 20__ or, on demand), I promise (or, we promise, or, we jointly and severally promise) to pay to A. B., or order (or, to A. B. or bearer), one thousand dollars (with interest), for value received.

_____
(Signature)

Signed, sealed and delivered in the presence of

_____

NOTICE BY ASSIGNEE TO DEBTOR OF ASSIGNMENT OF A DEBT

To: _____

I hereby give you notice that by an agreement in writing, dated the _____ day of _____, 20__, and made between _____ of _____, of the one part, and myself of the other part, the debt of _____ dollars owing by you to the said _____ has been absolutely assigned to me, my executors, administrators, and assigns; and further take notice that you are hereby required to pay to me, or such person as I may appoint, the said debt of _____ dollars on or before the _____ day of _____ next, and in default thereof I shall pursue such remedies as are allowed by law for recovery of the said debt.

Dated this _____ day of _____, 20__.

_____ L.S.

NOTICE TO DEBTOR BY HIS OR HER CREDITOR OF THE ASSIGNMENT OF A DEBT

Sir: I have this day assigned the debt of _____ dollars now due from you to me to _____ of _____ and I hereby request you to pay the said sum to him forthwith, and I declare that his receipt for the same shall be a sufficient discharge to you from said debt.

Yours, etc.

_____ L.S.

OPERATING AGREEMENT AND REGULATIONS
OF

_____

This OPERATING AGREEMENT AND REGULATIONS, effective as of _____, 20__, is made by and among those persons listed on Schedule "A" attached hereto (hereinafter collectively referred to as the "Members") to govern the operation and management of a _____limited liability company known as _____. ("_____").

WITNESSETH:

WHEREAS, Articles of Organization were filed on _____ with the office of the Secretary of State of the State of _____ in order to form _____ as a _____ limited liability company pursuant to the provisions of Chapter _____, _____ Statutes;

WHEREAS, pursuant to such Articles of Organization, the business and management of _____ is to be conducted in accordance with such Articles of Organization and in accordance with the provisions of this Operating Agreement and Regulations; and

WHEREAS, the Members desire to enter into this Operating Agreement and Regulations in order to codify the terms and conditions that will regulate and govern the operation and management of _____ and regulate and govern the respective rights and obligations of the Members with respect to _____.

NOW, THEREFORE, in consideration of the foregoing and the mutual covenants contained hereinbelow, and other good and valuable consideration, the receipt and sufficiency of which hereby is acknowledged by each Member to each other Member, the Members (for themselves and their respective successors and assigns), hereby agree as follows:

ARTICLE I
Certain Defined Terms

As used herein, the following terms shall have the following meanings:

1.1. **"Act"** shall mean the _____ Limited Liability Company Act enacted under Chapter _____, _____ Statutes, as amended from time to time.

1.2. **"Agreement"** shall mean this Operating Agreement and Regulations, as amended from time to time, as the context requires. Words such as "herein," "hereinafter," "hereof," "hereto," "hereby" and "hereunder," when used with reference to this Agreement, refer to this Agreement as a whole, unless the context otherwise requires.

1.3. **"Business"** shall mean the business of _____ authorized in Section 2.2 of this Agreement.

1.4. **"Capital Account"** shall mean the Capital Account that shall be established, maintained and adjusted for each Member in accordance with the rules of Section 1.704-l(b)(2)(iv) of the Treasury Regulations. To that end, each Member's Capital Account shall be credited with: (a) the amount of cash contributed to _____ by the Member; (b) additional money contributed to _____ by the Member; (c) the distributive share of _____ Taxable Profits allocated to the Member pursuant to Article VI; (d) the distributive share of _____'s Gross Income allocated to him pursuant to Article IV; and (e) the basis adjustment under Section 48(q)(2) of the Code allocated to him pursuant to Article VI hereof. Each Capital Account shall be debited by: (i) Distributions made to the Member pursuant to Article VI; (ii) the distributive share of _____'s Tax Loss allocated to the Member pursuant to Article VI; (iii) the distributive share of _____'s Non-recourse Deductions allocated to the Member pursuant to Article VI; (iv) the distributive share of any expenditures described in Section 705(a)(2)(B) of the Code or treated as Section 705(a)(2)(B) expenses pursuant to Section 1. 704-1 (b)(2)(iv)(i) of the Treasury Regulations and not otherwise taken into account in computing the Taxable Profit and Tax Loss, allocated to the Member pursuant to Article VI; and (v) the basis adjustment under Section 48(q)(1) and (3) of the Code allocated to the Member pursuant to Article VI hereof. Increases or decreases in the Capital Accounts of the Members to reflect a revaluation of _____ assets shall be made at the sole and absolute discretion of the Managers and in accordance with Section 1.704-1(b)(2)(iv)(f) of the Treasury Regulations. To the extent that any provision of this Agreement is inconsistent with such Regulations, the Treasury Regulations (as the same may be amended or revised hereafter) shall control. Any references in this Agreement to the Capital Account of a Member shall be deemed to refer to such Capital Account as the same may be credited or debited from time to time in the manner set forth above.

1.5. **"Cash Flow"** shall mean in any fiscal year the net income in such period from operations of _____ determined in accordance with Federal income tax principles consistently applied (not including Sale Proceeds Refinancing Proceeds) plus:

(a) depreciation;
(b) amortization of capitalized costs;
(c) other non-cash charges deducted in determining such net income, and;
(d) the net reduction in the amount of any reserves or escrows described in "(f)" below, if distributable;
(e) principal payments on all secured and unsecured borrowings of _____ and any other indebtedness of the _____ including that to the Managers;   (f) the amount reasonably

determined by the Managers to be necessary to fund the opening and start-up expenditures of the second Business after distribution of Cash Flow to Members in an amount necessary to fund the tax liability on Taxable Profits of Members for the prior year, assuming Members pay tax at the maximum federal income tax rate then in effect; and (g)
any other cash expenditures or escrows (except Distributions or payments to Members) which have not been deducted in determining the net income of the _____ which were not funded by borrowings.

1.6. **"Code"** shall mean the United States Internal Revenue Code of 1986, as amended from time to time (or any corresponding provisions of succeeding law).

1.7. **"Distribution"** shall mean any funds distributed to the Members pursuant to this Agreement.

1.8. **"Interests"** shall mean the percentage interest in _____ in the amount specified on Schedule "A", as amended from time to time.

1.9. **"Managers"** shall mean collectively any Person or Persons who or which, at the time of reference thereto, have been admitted as a successor to the Interest of the Managers set forth in Article IV hereof or as an additional Managers.

1.10. **"Member"** shall mean the Managers and Members owning Interests in _____.

1.11. **"Treasury Regulations"** means the Income Tax Regulations promulgated under the Code (as amended from time to time including corresponding provisions of succeeding regulations).

ARTICLE II
CONTINUATION, PURPOSES, AND TERM

2.1. *Name and Principal Place of Business.* _____ shall conduct its business and promote its purpose under the firm name and style "_____," or such other name or names as the Managers or Members may select from time to time. _____'s principal office for the transaction of business shall be maintained at _____.

2.2. *Purposes.* The purposes of _____ shall be limited to _____ and other activities involving real estate and to conduct such other business activities and operations as are consistent with and reasonably related to the foregoing purpose.

2.3. *Term.* The term of _____ shall commence as of _____, the date the Articles of Organization filed with the Secretary of State of _____ were subscribed and acknowledged, and shall continue and extend to and including a period of thirty (30) years thereafter, or until such earlier date as _____ is dissolved and terminated pursuant to the laws of the State of _____, the Articles of Organization, or Article IX hereof.

ARTICLE III
MEMBERS AND CAPITAL

3.1. *Members' Initial Capital Contribution.* The capital of _____ shall consist initially of the initial Capital Contributions of the Members, whose names are set forth on Schedule "A" attached hereto.

3.2. *No Withdrawal from Capital Accounts.* No Member shall have the right, at any time during the term hereof to withdraw or borrow against any part of its Capital Account without the unanimous vote of the Members. If such consent is granted, then each other Member shall have the right to withdraw the same percentage of his Capital Account as all other Members.

3.3. *Interest and Right to Property for Capital.* A Member shall not demand or receive any interest or draw with respect to any Capital Contribution or Capital Account. A Member shall not take and receive (or attempt to take or receive) any property other than cash in return for his or its Capital Contribution or Capital Account. Except as provided in Article IV, no Member shall be entitled to salary for services rendered to or for _____.

3.4. *Additional Capital Contributions.* If _____ needs sums in excess of the initial Capital Contributions, the Members shall make additional Capital Contributions or loans to _____ in such amounts and at such times as all of the Members, collectively, determine by a vote of Members owning 75% of the Interests. If any Member does not make the additional Capital Contribution or loan as determined by the vote of the Members, _____ and the other Members may repurchase all of the Interest held by such Member on the terms and conditions of Section 5.9, as if such Member had died or dissolved.

ARTICLE IV
MANAGEMENT, RIGHTS OF MEMBERS,
FEES AND EXPENSES

4.1. *Interest of Members.* The Members shall be entitled to the Interest set forth on Schedule "A" attached hereto.

4.2. *Management.* (a) The day-to-day business of _____ shall be managed by a management committee which shall consist of two (2) members (collectively the "Managers"). The Managers shall be appointed annually by the unanimous vote of all of the Members. In the event that any Manager ceases to serve, a successor Manager shall be appointed by the unanimous vote of all the Members. At the time of appointment of Managers, the members shall designate one of the serving Managers as President of _____.

(b) The Managers shall be fully accountable to the Members for the operation of the business.

(c) The Managers shall keep the Members fully and regularly advised of all matters affecting or involving _____ shall provide to all Members free and unfettered access to all books and records of _____.

(d) The Members may direct the Managers to take such actions with respect to the operation of the business as the Members shall see fit.

(e) Except for the actions as set forth below for which unanimous consent is required, any other action for which a vote other than a majority vote is specified elsewhere in this Agreement, and all other actions which require the vote of Members owning 75% of the Interests, decisions shall be made by unanimous vote of the Managers. The following actions shall require the unanimous vote of all the Members:

(i) Selling more interests in _____.
(ii) Borrowing to make distributions to any Member or pay any compensation to any Member.
(iii) Borrowing from_____ by any Member.
(iv) Increasing the number of Managers to more than two Managers.
(v) Selling all or substantially all of the assets of _____.
(vi) Doing or taking any action which would make it impossible to carry on the business of _____ in the ordinary course.
(vii) Hiring any professional or non-professional employee.
(viii) Adopting any retirement or other employee benefit plan.
(ix) Entering into any covenants for the provision of medical services.

4.3. *Expulsion of a Member.* A Member may be expelled from , with or without cause, upon the vote of all of the other Members.

4.4. *Removal of Manager.* (a) A Manager may be removed by unanimous vote of all the other Members.

(b) If a Manager is removed from _____ pursuant to paragraph (a) of this Section 4.4, he shall retain his or its percentage Interest as a Member in _____ Taxable Profits and Losses, Cash Flow, Sale Proceeds, Refinancing Proceeds, and any other allocations, payments or distributions hereunder to which he was entitled as a Manager through date of removal. For all purposes of this Agreement, a Manager so removed shall be deemed to have involuntarily withdrawn from _____ as a Manager effective, as of the date of such removal, but shall remain a Member of _____ and such withdrawal as a Manager shall not be deemed to have constituted a violation of this Agreement.

4.5. *Limited Liability.* Performance of one or more of the acts described in this Article IV or contemplated to be performed by the Managers or by the Members shall not impose any personal liability on any Member. No Member shall be liable for any debts or obligations of _____ in excess of his respective Capital Contribution, including any portion of such capital plus interest or any other amount which has been returned to him and with respect to which, by the terms of the Limited Liability Company Act, he shall remain liable. The Capital Contributions of the Members shall be available for the debts, liabilities or other obligations of _____. All undistributed Cash Flow or Sale Proceeds or Refinancing Proceeds which would typically or generally be distributed to the Members shall not be available to creditors to satisfy the debts and obligations of _____ until the time of actual distribution.

4.6. *Meetings of, or Actions by, the Members.* (a) Meetings of the Members to vote upon any matters as to which the Members are authorized to take action under this Agreement may be called at any time by the Managers or by one or more Members holding ten percent (10%) or more of the outstanding interests at a reasonably convenient time and place, by delivering written notice (either in person or by certified mail, return receipt requested) to the Members entitled to vote at such meeting to the effect that a meeting will be held at a designated time and place. Upon receipt of a written request by a proper number of Members, or, by the determination of the Members to hold a meeting, the Managers shall provide to all Members, within 10 days after receipt of said request, written notice (either in person or by certified mail, return receipt requested) of a meeting and the purpose of such meeting to be held on a date not less than 15 days nor more than 60 days after receipt of said request. All expenses of the meeting and notification shall be borne by _____.

(b) Members shall be entitled to one (1) vote for each one percent (1%) Interest in _____ as set forth on Schedule "A." There are no fractional votes. As used herein, the term "Majority Vote" shall mean more than fifty percent (50%) of the votes actually cast for a particular matter. As used herein, the terms "unanimous vote" and "unanimous vote of all the Members" shall mean 100% of the votes entitled to be cast for a particular matter. As used herein, the term "super majority vote" shall mean the vote of at least 75% of the votes entitled to be cast for a particular matter. Members present in person or by proxy, holding in excess of fifty percent (50%) of the voting rights, shall constitute a quorum at any meeting. Attendance by a Member at any meeting and his voting in person shall revoke any written proxy submitted with respect to any action proposed to be taken at such meeting. Any matters as to which the Members are authorized to take action under this Agreement or under the law may be acted upon by the Members without a meeting. Any such action shall be valid and effective as action taken by the Members at a meeting assembled, provided that written consents to such action by the Members are signed by Members who hold the number of voting rights required to authorize such action and such written consents are delivered to the Managers before any such action is taken or becomes binding. In the event that there shall be no Managers, the Members may take action without a meeting by the unanimous written consent of all the Members entitled to vote. All Members shall be bound by actions taken in accordance with the provisions of this Agreement.

4.7. *No Third Party Rights.* The right of _____ to require any additional contributions or loans under the terms of this Agreement shall not be construed as conferring any rights or benefits to or upon any party not a party to this Agreement, including, but not limited to, the holder of any obligations secured by a mortgage, deed of trust, security interest or other lien or encumbrance upon or affecting or any Interest of a Member therein or the Business or improvements on the Business, or any part therefor or interest therein. Such provisions may be amended at any time and from time to time without the approval or consent of such other person.

4.8. *Salary for Managers.* The Managers shall initially not receive any salary or additional compensation except as they may otherwise be entitled to as Members. However, the Managers shall be entitled to reimbursed for expenses they incur in connection with filling their management duties to _____. After the first six (6) months of operations, the Members shall decide upon an appropriate amount of compensation, if any, for the Managers.

ARTICLE V
TRANSFER OF MEMBERSHIP INTERESTS

5.1. *Withdrawal of Members.* A Member may resign, withdraw or retire voluntarily from _____ in accordance with and pursuant to the laws of the State of _____ and subject to the Non-Competition covenant in Section 5.9 and such other reasonable limitations that may be imposed by a vote of the Members.

5.2. *Additional Members.* _____ shall not (and shall hereby be divested of all right to) sell or issue additional Interests or admit additional Members to _____ without the unanimous vote of all the Members. Any new Interests sold will be at such price and on such terms, and shall receive such allocations and Distributions as a unanimous vote of the Members shall determine.

5.3. *Transfers by Members.* A Member shall not sell, transfer, collaterally assign, pledge, hypothecate, grant a security interest in, encumber or in any other manner dispose of all or any part of his or its Interest in and to _____ its capital, profits and losses, without the vote of all of the Members. In the event that any Member at any time attempts to make a sale, assignment, transfer, pledge, hypothecation, mortgage, encumbrance or other disposition of his interest in and to _____'s capital, profits and losses, or any part thereof, in violation of the provisions of this Agreement, the other Members or any one of them, shall in addition to all other rights and remedies which they may have in law, in equity or under the provisions of this Agreement, be entitled to a decree or order restraining and enjoining such attempted sale, assignment, transfer, pledge, hypothecation, mortgage, encumbrance or other disposition. The offending Member shall not plead in defense thereto that there would be an adequate remedy at law, it being recognized and agreed that the injury and damage resulting from such a breach would be impossible to measure monetarily. Any transfer made in violation of the provisions of this Agreement shall be void ab initio.

5.4. *Withdrawal, Dissolution or Bankruptcy of a Member.* The withdrawal, expulsion, dissolution or bankruptcy of a Member shall not cause a dissolution or termination of _____ and _____ shall continue to exist as a separate and distinct entity regardless of the particular composition of the Members and regardless of their particular status. A change in the Members or the Managers shall not cause a discontinuation or interruption of _____'s existence and shall not affect title to or ownership of property held in the name of _____. The legal representatives or successors-in-interest, as the case may be, of the former Member shall be admitted to as a Substituted Member upon compliance with Section 5.5 hereof, provided, however, that in the event of the bankruptcy of a Member, if such representative or successor-in-interest shall not comply with Section 5.5 hereof, then the Interest of the bankrupt Member shall be dealt with in accordance with applicable law at the earliest practicable time. Anything herein contained to the contrary notwithstanding, such reconstituted Interest shall not affect the rights of the Members with respect to distributions or return of their Capital Contributions or otherwise.

5.5. *Substituted Members.* Anything herein contained to the contrary notwithstanding:

(a) No successor-in-interest of a Member and no assignee or transferee of all or any part of a Member's Interest in and to _____, its capital, profits and losses, shall be admitted to the _____ as a Member except upon:

(i) submitting to the Managers a duly executed and acknowledged counterpart of the instrument or instruments making such transfer, together with such other instrument or (including a counterpart of this Agreement as it then may have been amended) signifying such transferee's agreement to be bound by all of the provisions of this Agreement (including the restrictions upon transfers of Interests herein and thereto), all of the foregoing in such form and substance as shall be reasonably satisfactory to the Managers;

(ii) obtaining the unanimous vote of all the Members thereto; and

(iii) bearing all reasonable costs and expenses, incurred by _____ in effecting such substitution.

Upon the transferee's compliance with the foregoing provisions, each of the Members shall take all actions reasonably required to effectuate the recognition of the effectiveness of such transfer and the admission of such transferee to _____ as a Substituted Member including, but not limited to, transferring such Interest in and to _____, its capital, profits and losses upon the books thereof and executing, acknowledging and causing to be filed any necessary or desirable amendment to this Agreement.

(b) The Members shall not consent to the admission of any such assignee as a substituted Member if, in the reasonable opinion of the Members, such admission:

(i) would jeopardize the status of _____ as a partnership for Federal income tax purposes;

(ii) would cause a termination of _____ within the meaning of Section 708(b) of the code; or

(iii) would violate, or cause _____ to violate, any applicable law or governmental rule or regulation.

(c) An assignment or attempted assignment of an Interest to a non-resident alien, minor or incompetent shall be ineffective and void ab initio in all respects.

5.6. *Non-Complying Assignments.* Any assignment, sale, exchange or other transfer in contravention of any of the provisions of this Article V shall be ineffective and void ab initio. An unauthorized assignment shall not bind or be recognized by _____.

5.7. *Obligations of Successor.* Any person who acquires an Interest in _____ by assignment or is admitted to as a Substituted Member shall be subject to and bound by all the provisions of this Agreement as if originally a party to this Agreement. All Substituted Members shall and hereby do waive all objections to this Agreement and the enforceability hereof.

5.8. *Certain Purchases.* (a) Total Purchase Price. For each Interest in _____, the purchase price for such Interest in the event of the death, disability or involuntary termination of employment, if applicable, of a Member shall be the Fair Market Value of such interest in _____ as of the day of the month immediately preceding the month in which the event causing the sale occurs. Such Fair Market Value shall be determined by _____'s certified public accountant. In computing such Fair Market Value, the accountant shall consider among other factors the following:

(i) the Fair Market Value of all assets rather than their respective depreciated values as shown on the books and records of _____.

(ii) all taxes and assessments, including federal and state income taxes, shall be considered liabilities; and

(iii) all actual or contingent liabilities.

(b) Death or Dissolution.

(i) Upon the death of a Member, or, the appointment of a receiver for a Member, first _____ and then the surviving Members shall have the option to purchase and, upon the exercise of the option, the estate of the deceased or the receiver for the Member shall be required to sell, all and not less than all of the Interest in _____ owned by such Member. The surviving Members shall have the right to purchase any such Interest which _____ elects not to purchase. The purchase price for such deceased or dissolved Member's Interest shall be as specified in paragraph 5.8(a) above.

(ii) and the Members shall exercise their respective options to purchase by sending written notice to that effect within ninety (90) days after the qualification of the personal representative of the estate of the deceased Member, or, the appointment of a receiver, or, if no personal representative or receiver has been appointed within one hundred twenty (120) days after the death of the Member or the appointment of the receiver of the Member. If _____ does not exercise its right of purchase within sixty (60) days of the start of such option period, the Members shall then have the balance of such option period to exercise their purchase rights.

(iii) Within thirty (30) days of the expiration of the option periods as specified in paragraph 5.8(b)(ii) above, the closing related to the purchase of such Member's Interest shall occur. At the time of the closing, _____ or the remaining Members shall purchase such Member's Interest by delivering twenty percent (20%) of the purchase price for said Interest in cash or check to the estate or receiver of the Member, and the balance shall be evidenced by the promissory note of the respective purchaser or purchasers. Such promissory note shall provide for four (4) equal annual installments of principal, plus accrued simple interest on the outstanding principal balance at the annual rate of ten percent (10%), and all installments of principal plus accrued interest shall be paid on the fifth. anniversary date of the initial down payment to such Member. Each promissory note may be prepaid in whole or in part without premium or penalty. At the time of the closing, the personal representative of the deceased Member or receiver of the Member shall execute and deliver to the purchaser all such instruments as shall be necessary to transfer title to the interest in _____.

ARTICLE VI
ALLOCATION OF INCOME, LOSS AND DISTRIBUTIONS

6.1. *General Apportionment Provisions.* (a) In the case of a proper transfer of an Interest validly consummated in accordance with this Agreement:

(i) a Substituted Member will be recognized as owning transfer interests; and
(ii) an Assignee will be recognized as being entitled to receive Distributions and allocations of Taxable Profits, Tax Loss, and other tax items attributable to the assigned Interest in the same manner as a substitute Member would be so entitled with respect to transferred Interest, at the time determined in accordance with the following:

> Taxable Profits or Tax Losses from current operations for any year will be allocated between a transferor and a transferee based upon the number of days during the calendar year that each was recognized as the holder of the Interest, without regard to whether the operation of _____ during particular periods of such year produced a profit or loss. Cash distribution of Net Proceeds of Sale or Refinancing, if any, arising from the sale or refinancing of a Property will be distributed, and all related Taxable Profits or Tax Losses will be allocated to the person recognized as holder of the Interest on the date on which the sale or refinancing occurred. For this purpose, transfers will be recognized as of the date specified by the transferor and the transferee in the instrument of assignment or, if no date is specified, the date of the last acknowledgment of such instrument.

> Neither _____ nor any Manager shall incur any liability for making allocation and distribution in accordance with the provisions of this Article VI, notwithstanding that any Manager has knowledge of any transfer of ownership of any Interest.

(b) Notwithstanding anything to the contrary herein, the Managers, after sixty (60) days prior written notice to the Members (sent by certified mail, return receipt requested), but without the vote or consent of any of the Members, may:

(i) adopt a convention other than a "record date" convention for determining the recognition of the Members entitled to Distributions;
(ii) allocate Taxable Profits, Tax Loss, and other _____ tax items among the Members during the fiscal year of _____ in a manner other than that set forth in this Section 6.1 that the Managers, in their sole discretion, determine satisfies the requirements of Section 706 of the Code and any Treasury Regulations promulgated thereunder.

6.2. *Distributions.* (a) All Distributions are subject to the payment of the operating expenses of _____ (including salaries and other compensation for Managers, Physician Members, and others) and to the maintenance of the reserves in amounts determined appropriate by the Managers. Such determinations shall be binding upon _____ and upon the Members. No Distributions may be made without the approval of the Managers. Any Cash Flow from Operations, Sale Proceeds, and Refinancing Proceedings not distributed shall be accounted for in a separate account on books and records. Any positive balance in such accounts may be distributed to the Members in accordance with their Interest as set forth on Schedule "A" upon a unanimous of all the Members or as may be approved by the Managers. Notwithstanding the foregoing, if funds are available for Distribution, Distributions shall be made at such times as required for the payment of personal income taxes in an amount equal to the estimated federal and state tax liability owed as a result of the activities of the business of _____ assuming a maximum marginal tax bracket of each Member.

(b) Distributions from Operations, Sales Proceeds and Refinancing Proceeds. Distributions of Cash Flow from Operations or from other sources, and Distributions of Sales or Refinancing Proceeds, will be made to the Members in accordance with their respective percentage Interests set forth on Schedule "A" attached hereto.

(c) *Zeroing Out the Capital Accounts.* Notwithstanding the preceding provisions of this Section 6.2, when _____ is wound up and dissolved pursuant to Article IX and all of its remaining assets are to be distributed, all items of income, gain, loss and deduction shall first be allocated to the Members' Capital Accounts under Sections 6.3 and 6.4, and other credits and deductions to the Members' Capital Accounts shall be taken before the final Distribution is made. The final Distribution, when made, shall be made to the Members in accordance with and in an amount equal to their positive Capital Account balances pursuant to Sections 9.3 and 9.9, thereby adjusting each Member's Capital Account to zero.

(d) *Compensation Not to be Deemed Distributions.* Any compensation paid to the Managers shall not be deemed to be Distributions for purposes of Article VI of this Agreement, regardless of how such Distributions are characterized for federal income tax purposes. As used in this subsection, the term "Compensation" shall mean any monies paid to the Members for their medical services (whether as salary or as bonus).

6.3. Allocation of Partnership Tax Items. (a) Taxable Profits, Tax Loss, and other tax items shall be determined as of the end of each taxable year of _____ and allocated as set forth in this Section 6.3.

(b) Taxable Profits of _____ not arising from a sale or refinancing of property shall be allocated to the Members in proportion to the Distributions of Cash Flow with respect to which such Taxable Profits relate.

(c) (i) Taxable Profits arising from a sale or refinancing of _____ property which does not result in a "liquidation" within the meaning of Treasury Regulation Section 1.704-1(b)(2)(ii)(g) shall be allocated to the Members in proportion to the distributions of Sales Proceeds and Refinancing Proceeds to which such Taxable Profits relate.

(ii) Taxable Profits arising from a sale or refinancing of property which results in a liquidation as set forth in Section 6.3(d)(i) above shall be allocated as follows:

a. First, to those Members who have negative Capital Accounts pro rata to the extent of such Members' negative Capital Accounts; and

b. Then, to the Members in amounts such that the positive balance of each Member's Capital Account is equal to the amount of the Distributions of Sales Proceeds and Refinancing Proceeds to be made to such Member resulting from the transaction to which the allocation of such Taxable Profits relate.

c. Then to the Members in accordance with their percentage Interest.

If the total gain to be allocated under this Section 6.3(c) includes any item of ordinary income arising under Code Sections 1245 or 1250, as amended, or any similar recapture provision, such items shall be allocated among the Members in the same amount (or ratable proportion thereof, if less) as the tax benefit which created such recapture. If such total gain includes interest income on any deferred sales proceeds, such interest income shall be allocated among the Members in the same proportion as the total gain is allocated under this Section 6.3(c).

For purposes of determining Capital Account balances, all Distributions previously made, as well as all other adjustments to Capital Account balances pursuant to the definition thereof in Article Ill and the other provisions of this Section 6.3 shall be taken into account "other than an adjustment for the allocation of Taxable Profits under this Section 6.3(c)."

If, prior to the allocation in Section 6.3(c)(ii)(b) above, a Member has a positive Capital Account balance ("Excess Capital Account Balance") greater than the amount of Sales Proceeds or Refinancing Proceeds to be distributed to such Member resulting from the transaction to which the allocation of such Taxable Profits relates, then there shall be no additional allocation of Taxable Profits to such Member and the remaining Taxable Profits shall be allocated to the other Members such that their positive Capital Account balances equals as closely as possible the amount of Sales Proceeds or Refinancing Proceeds which would have been distributed to such Members if there were no Excess Capital Account Balance.

(d) (i) Tax Loss from a transaction not constituting a dissolution of as defined in Article 6.3(d)(i) shall be allocated to the Members in accordance, with their percentage Interest.

(ii) After giving effect to the allocations set forth in Section 6.3(f) hereof, Tax Loss from the sale or other disposition of all or substantially all of the Business which results in a liquidation of _____ (as such term is defined in SS6.3(d)(i)) shall be allocated:

a. first, among those Members having positive Capital Accounts, so as to bring, as nearly as possible, their Capital Accounts into, and maintain their Capital Accounts in, the same ratios as the Distribution that they would receive if an amount equal to the aggregate amount of their Capital Accounts (but not below zero) by such loss, were distributed among them in the manner and order of priority prescribed for a distribution of Sale Proceeds or Refinancing Proceeds under Section 9.2(c) hereof until no Member has a positive Capital Account; and

b. then, to the Members in accordance with their percentage Interest.

(e) If the taxing authorities ignore the characterization of the amounts paid to Members as compensation and refuse to treat such payments either as guaranteed payments with the meaning of Section 707(c) of the Code, or payments made to the Members other than in its capacity as a Member within the meaning of Section 707(a) of the Code, and, as a result, such payments are charged to its Capital Account, then the Members shall be allocated the first available Taxable Profits of in an amount equal to the amount so charged, and the Member's Capital Account shall be adjusted to reflect the payment of such amount.

6.4. *Miscellaneous Allocation Matters.* It is intended that the allocation rules set forth in Section 6.3, together with Article II hereof, shall result in the Capital Accounts of the Members equalizing zero following the complete winding up of _____ and the distributions provided for in Section 6.2. The allocation provisions of this Agreement in Section 6.3 shall be construed in such a way by the Managers in order to validate the Distributions provided for in Section 6.2.

6.5. *Members' Consent to Distributions and Allocation Methods.* The methods hereinabove set forth in this Article VI by which Distributions and allocations of income, gain, loss, deductions, tax credits and other tax items are made and apportioned are hereby expressly consented to by each Member as an express condition to becoming a Member.

6.6. *Liquidation Distribution.* In the event that _____ is terminated, Distributions shall be applied in the manner set forth in Article IX hereof.

6.7. *Members' Opinion Final.* A unanimous of all the Members shall be final and conclusive with respect to all disputes as to computation and determinations required to be made under this Article and Articles VII and IX.

ARTICLE VII
AMOUNTS WITHHELD

All amounts which _____ is required by law to withhold pursuant to the Code or any provision of any state or tax law with respect to any payment or distribution to _____ or to the Members shall be treated as amounts distributed to the Members pursuant to Article VI for all purposes under this Agreement. The Managers may allocate any such amounts among the Members in any equitable manner that complies with the letter and spirit of applicable law.

ARTICLE VIII
RECORDS AND BOOKS OF ACCOUNT;
FISCAL YEAR, BANKING, REPORTS TO MEMBERS

8.1. *Records and Books of Account.* The Managers shall maintain or cause to be maintained at _____'s principal office or at such other place or places as the Managers from time to time may determine, full and accurate records and books of account of _____ business. Such records and books of account shall be maintained on the method of accounting determined by the Managers to be most advantageous to _____. Each Member shall be afforded full and complete access to all such records and books of account during reasonable business hours and, at such hours, shall have the right of inspection and the right to copy such records and books of account, at his or its expense.

8.2. *Fiscal Year.* The fiscal year of _____ shall be the calendar year.

8.3. *Banking.* An account or accounts in the name of _____ shall be maintained at such financial institution as the Managers may select. All uninvested funds of _____ shall be deposited in an account of _____. All funds so credited to _____ in any such account shall be subject to withdrawal by checks made in the name of _____ and signed by one of the Managers of such person or persons as the Managers may from time to time designate.

8.4. *Reports to Members.* (a) As soon and as often as reasonably practical, but in no event later than forty-five (45) days after the end of each fiscal quarter of the Managers shall cause to be prepared and furnished to each Member:

(i) The information necessary for the preparation by such Member of his or its Federal, state and other income tax returns;

(ii) The amount in the Capital Account of such Member as of the last day of such fiscal year;

(iii) An income statement and balance sheet of _____ as of the last day of such fiscal year, which shall be prepared by a certified public accountant if timely and requested in writing by any Member; and

(iv) Such other reports as the Managers deem reasonably necessary for the Members to be advised of the current status of _____ and its business.

ARTICLE IX
DISSOLUTION, LIQUIDATION, AND TERMINATION

9.1. *Dissolution.* Subject to the provisions of the Act, _____ shall be dissolved upon the first to occur of any of the following events:

(a) The expiration of the term provided for in Section 2.3 of Article II hereof,

(b) The sale of all or substantially an of its assets, including, but not limited to, the Business, and the collection and distributions the proceeds thereof;

(c) The unanimous consent of all the Members; or

(d) When required by a court of competent jurisdiction.

9.2. *Liquidation.* (a) Upon dissolution of the _____ the Managers shall take or cause to be taken a full account of _____ assets and liabilities as of the date of such dissolution and shall proceed with reasonable promptness to liquidate _____ assets and to terminate its business. The cash proceeds from the liquidation, as and when available hereof, shall be applied and distributed in the following order:

(i) to the payment of all taxes, debts and other obligations and liabilities of _____, including the necessary expenses of liquidation, but excluding therefrom secured creditors whose obligations continue in existence after the liquidation of _____ assets; provided, however, that all debts and other obligations and liabilities of _____ as to which personal liability exists with respect to any Member or Manager shall be satisfied or a reserve established therefor, prior to the satisfaction of any debt or other obligation or liability of as to which no such personal liability exists for either _____ or any Member; provided, however, that where a contingent debt, obligation or liability exists, a reserve, in such amount as the Managers deem reasonable, shall be established to meet such contingent debt, obligation or liability, which reserve shall be distributed as provided in this paragraph (a) only upon the termination of such contingency; and

(ii) all remaining proceeds in liquidation of shall be distributable pursuant to the provisions of Article VI and Section 9.9 hereof.

(b) The Managers shall administer the liquidation of _____ and the termination of its business. The Managers shall be allowed a reasonable time for the orderly liquidation of assets and the discharge of liabilities to creditors, so as to minimize losses resulting from the liquidation of _____ assets.

(c) Anything herein contained to the contrary notwithstanding, the Managers shall not be personally liable for the return of the Members' Capital Contributions, or any part thereof. Any such return shall be made solely from _____'s assets. (d) Except as otherwise provided herein, no dissolution or termination of _____ shall relieve, release, or discharge any Member, or any of his or its successors, assigns, heirs or legal representatives, from any previous breach or default any obligation theretofore incurred or accrued under any provision of this Agreement, and any and all such liabilities, claims, demands or causes of action arising from any such breaches or defaults shall survive such dissolution and termination.

(e) Each Member shall look solely to the assets of _____ for the return of his Capital Account. If _____'s property remaining after the payment or discharge of the debts and liabilities of _____ is insufficient to return the Capital Account of each Member, such Member shall have no recourse against the Managers or any other Member. The winding up of the affairs of _____ and the distribution of its funds shall be conducted exclusively by the Managers, except as provided herein.

9.3. *Members' Rights.* If necessary, a special liquidator may be appointed by a unanimous vote or consent of all the Members. In connection with any such winding up and liquidation, an independent certified public accountant retained by _____ shall, if requested by Members owning more than fifty percent (50%) of the Interests of _____, prepare financial statements regarding such termination for all Members.

9.4. *Gains or Losses in Process of Liquidation.* Any gains or losses on disposition of the Business in the process of liquidation shall be credited or charged to the Members in the manner specified in Article VII. No property shall be distributed in kind.

9.5. *Instruments of Termination.* Upon the termination of _____, the Managers (or special liquidator, as the case may be) shall make such filings and do such other acts as shall be required by _____ or federal law, and the Members shall execute and deliver to the Managers (or special liquidator, as the case may be) such certificates or documents as may be so required.

9.6. *Time of Liquidation.* A reasonable time shall be allowed for the orderly liquidation of the assets of _____ and the discharge of liabilities to creditors so as to enable the Managers to minimize the losses attendant upon a liquidation.

9.7. *No Right of Partition.* The Members and Assignees and their estates or representative upon death or the receiver upon bankruptcy or dissolution shall have no rights to receive _____'s property in kind, nor shall such Members or Assignees have the right to partition or sale of _____'s property, whether or not upon dissolution and termination of _____, notwithstanding any provision of law to the contrary. Each of the Members, as a condition of Membership, waives any and all rights that he or it has or may have to require a partition with respect to any property of _____.

Notwithstanding the foregoing, if any Member shall be indebted to _____, then until payment of such amount by him, the liquidator shall retain such Member's distributive share of property or assets and apply the income therefrom to the liquidation of such indebtedness and the cost of operation of such property or assets during the period of such liquidation; provided, however, if at the expiration of six (6) months after the statement for which provision is made herein has been given to such Member, such amount has not been paid or otherwise liquidated, the liquidator may sell the Interest of such Member at public or private sale at the best price immediately obtainable which shall be determined in the sole judgment of the liquidator. The proceeds of such sale shall be applied to the liquidation of the amount then due under this Article and the balance of such proceeds, if any, shall be delivered to such Member.

9.8. *Termination.* Upon compliance with the foregoing plan of liquidation and distribution, the Managers shall file or cause to be filed any and all documents required to effectuate the dissolution and termination of _____ thereupon shall be terminated.

ARTICLE X
PARTNERSHIP STATUS

Anything in this Agreement to the contrary notwithstanding, it is expressly intended that the entity formed hereby be a partnership for tax purposes as determined by the applicable provisions of the Code, the rules and regulations promulgated thereunder, and other laws pertaining thereto, and that in every respect all of the terms and provisions hereof shall at all times be so construed and interpreted as to give effect to this intent; provided, however, that for purposes of requiring or mandating additional capital contributions, the unanimous vote or unanimous written consent of all the Members shall be required. In the event that the Internal Revenue Service or any other governmental authority having jurisdiction shall in any way or at any time determine that any provision or provisions of this Agreement affects the status of this entity, the Managers shall amend or modify the terms and provisions of this Agreement to the extent necessary to comply with the rules, regulations, and requirements of the Internal Revenue Service or any other government authority having jurisdiction, in order that the entity formed hereby be treated as a partnership, be taxable as such, and the Members hereof taxable as Members of a partnership.

ARTICLE XI
GENERAL PROVISIONS

11.1. *Notices.* Except as otherwise provided herein, any notice, payment, distribution or other communication which shall be required to be given to any Member in connection with the business of _____ shall be duly given in writing sent by certified United States mail, return receipt requested, to the last address furnished by such Member. Written notice to the Managers or _____ shall be given when actually received at the principal office of _____.

11.2. *Survival of Rights.* This Agreement shall be binding upon and inure to the benefit of the Members and their respective heirs, legatees, legal representatives, successors, and rights.

11.3. *Headings.* The headings of the Articles and subparagraphs of this Agreement are for convenience only and shall not be deemed part of the text of this Agreement.

11.4. *Agreement in Counterparts.* This Agreement, or any amendment hereto, may be executed in multiple counterparts, each of which shall be deemed an original agreement, and all of which shall constitute one agreement, by each of the parties hereto on the dates respectively indicated in the acknowledgments of said parties, notwithstanding that all of the parties are not signatories to the original or the same counterpart, to be effective as of the day and year first above written.

11.5. *Governing Law.* This Agreement is enforceable in accordance with its terms and shall be governed, construed and enforced according to the laws of the State of _____.

11.6. *Validity.* Should any portion of this Agreement be declared invalid and unenforceable, then such portion shall be deemed several from this Agreement and shall not affect the remainder hereof.

11.7. *Amendment.* Except as otherwise provided in this Agreement, this Agreement may be amended by a super majority vote of the Members at a meeting called pursuant to this Agreement.

11.8. *Pronouns.* All pronouns and any variations thereof shall be deemed to refer to the masculine, feminine, or neuter, singular or plural, as the identity of the person or persons may require.

11.9. *Loan Restrictions.* A creditor who makes a non-recourse loan to _____ must not have, or acquire, at any time as a result of making the loan, any direct or indirect Interest greater than 20% in the profits, capital, or property of _____ other than as a secured creditor.

11.10. *Merger.* This Agreement contains the entire understanding among the parties and supersedes any prior understanding and agreements between them respecting the matters described herein. This Agreement cannot and shall not be amended, modified, or altered except in writing signed by all of the Members.

11.11. *Arbitration.* Any controversy or claim arising out of or relating to this Agreement or any _____, _____, in a manner agreed upon by the Managers and all the Members directly affected, or if not otherwise agreed upon, then in accordance with the rules of the American Arbitration Association in effect at that time. Judgment upon the award so rendered may be entered in any court having competent jurisdiction therefor. The costs of the arbitration shall be borne equally by the parties, provided that the prevailing parties shall recover attorneys' fees, court costs, and expert compensation.

11.12. *Tax Matters Partner.* (a) _____ is hereby designated as the Tax Matters Partner of _____ as provided in regulations pursuant to Section 6231 of the Code (the "Tax Matters Partner."). Each Member, by the execution of this Agreement, consents to such designation of the Tax Matters Partner and agrees to execute, certify, acknowledge, deliver, swear to, file and record at the appropriate public offices such documents as may be necessary or appropriate to evidence such consent.

(b) The duties of the Tax Matters Partner may include the following:

(1) To the extent and in the manner provided by applicable law and regulations, the Tax Matters Partner shall furnish the name, address, profits, interest, and taxpayer identification number of each Member to the Secretary of the Treasury or his delegate (the "Secretary").

(2) To the extent and in the manner provided by applicable law and regulations, the Tax Matters Partner shall keep each Member informed of the administrative and judicial proceedings for the adjustment at the _____ level of any item required to be taken into account by a Member for income tax purposes (such administrative proceeding being referred to hereinafter as a "Tax Audit" and such judicial proceeding being referred to hereinafter as "Judicial Review").

(3) If the Tax Matters Partner, on behalf of receives a notice with respect to 's tax audit from the Secretary, the Tax Matters Partner shall, within thirty (30) days of receiving such notice, forward a copy of such notice to the Members who hold or held an Interest (through their Interests) in the profits or losses of for the taxable year to which the notice relates.

(c) The Tax Matters Partner is hereby authorized, but not required:

(1) To enter into any settlement agreement with the Internal Revenue Service or the Secretary of Treasury ("Secretary") with respect to any Tax Audit or Judicial Review, in which agreement the Tax Matters Partner may expressly state that such agreement shall bind the other Members, except that such agreement shall not bind any Member who (within the time prescribed pursuant to the Code and Treasury Regulations thereunder) files a statement with the Internal Revenue Service providing that the Tax Matters Partner shall not have the authority to enter into a settlement agreement on behalf of such Member;

(2) In the event that a notice of a final administrative adjustment at the _____ level of any item required to be taken into account by a Member for tax purposes (a "Final Adjustment") is mailed to the Tax Matters Partner, to seek Judicial Review of such Final Adjustment, including the filing of a petition for readjustment with the Tax Court, the District Court of the Interested States for the district in which _____'s principal place of business is located, or the Court of Claims;

(3) To intervene in any action brought by any other Member for Judicial Review of a Final Adjustment;

(4) To file a request for an administrative adjustment with the Secretary at any time and, if any part of such request is not allowed by the Secretary, to file a petition for Judicial Review with respect to such request;

(5) To enter into an agreement with the Service to extend the period for assessing any tax which is attributable to any item required to be taken into account by a Member for tax purposes, or an item affected by such item; and

(6) To take any other action on behalf of the Members or in connection with any administrative or judicial tax proceeding to the extent permitted by applicable laws or regulations.

(d) _____ shall indemnify and reimburse the Tax Matters Partner for all expenses, including legal and accounting fees, claims, liabilities, losses, and damages incurred in connection with any Tax Audit or Judicial Review with respect to the tax liabilities of the Members. The payment of all such expenses shall be made before any distributions are made of Cash Flow any discretionary reserves are set aside by the Managers. Neither the Managers nor any other person or entity shall have any obligation to provide funds for such purpose. The taking of any action and the incurring of any expense by the Tax Matters Partner in connection with any such proceeding, except to the extent required by law, is a matter in the sole discretion of the Tax Matters Partner, and the provisions on limitations of liability of the Managers and indemnification set forth in this Agreement shall be fully applicable to the Tax Matters Partner in its capacity as such.

11.13. *Binding Effect.* Except as otherwise provided in this Agreement, every covenant, term, and provision of this Agreement shall be binding upon and inure to the benefit of the Members and their respective partners, heirs, legatees, legal representatives, agents, successors, and assigns.

11.14. *Construction.* Every covenant, term, and provision of this Agreement shall be construed simply according to its fair meaning and not strictly for or against any Member. In the event of any conflict of the terms of this Agreement with any other oral or written agreement or document of any kind, this Agreement shall control.

11.15. *Severability.* Every provision of this Agreement is intended to be severable. If any term or provision hereof is illegal or invalid for any reason whatsoever, such illegality or invalidity shall not affect the validity or legality of the remainder of this Agreement.

11.16. *Incorporation by Reference.* Every exhibit, schedule, and other appendix attached to this Agreement and referred to herein is hereby incorporated into this Agreement by reference.

11.17. *Additional Documents.* Each Member, upon the request of any Manager, shall agree to perform all further acts and execute, acknowledge, and deliver any documents that may be reasonably necessary, appropriate, or desirable to carry out the provisions of this Agreement.

IN WITNESS WHEREOF, the Members have hereunto set their hands and seals the day and year first above written.

WITNESSES:

_____   _____

_____   _____

_____

_____

Schedule "A"

Name   *Percentage of Interest*

_____   _____%

_____   _____%

PARTNERSHIP AGREEMENT

THIS AGREEMENT made this _____ day of 20__, by and between _____ and _____ (the "Partners").

WITNESSETH:

WHEREAS, the Partners have formed a partnership for the purpose of owning one or more parcels of real estate and the improvements thereon and certain items of tangible personal property ("Property"); and

WHEREAS, the Partners each have a _____ percent (___%) interest in the Partnership and desire to set forth their respective rights, obligations and interests in respect to the Partnership and Property;

NOW, THEREFORE, in consideration of the mutual covenants herein contained, it is agreed as follows:

1. *Recitations.* The above recitations are true and correct.

2. *Formation, Name, Purposes, and Term.* The Partners hereby form and establish a partnership (the "Partnership") to be conducted under the name and style of "_____" or such other name as the Partners may from time to time determine, such Partnership to be under the terms and provisions set forth in this Agreement. The principal office and place of business of the Partnership shall be located at such place in _____ County, _____, as the Partners may from time to time determine.

The purposes of the Partnership are:

a. To purchase or receive as a contribution the Property described on Exhibit "A" and such other properties as the Partners deem desirable;

b. To own, maintain, renovate, lease, sell, manage, develop, and operate the Property and the improvements presently; and

c. To engage in such other business or activities or do such other things as the Partners may unanimously hereinafter decide.

The term of this Partnership shall be from the date hereof to _____, unless sooner terminated, as hereinafter provided.

3. *Percentage of Ownership in the Partnership.* The Partners own the following percentage of interest in and to the Partnership and its property and assets:

4. *Capital and Loans to the Partnership.* The Partners shall each make initial capital contributions of _____ to the Partnership on or before _____. In the event the Partnership shall need sums in excess of the initial capital contributions, the Partners hereby agree to make additional capital contributions and/or loans to the Partnership in such amounts and at such times as a majority in interest of the Partners shall agree.

Loans to the Partnership by the Partners shall be repaid in full before any payments pursuant to paragraph 6 hereof may be made. Additional capital contributions and/or loans to the Partnership shall be made in good faith and shall only be required in order to carry out the business of the Partnership. In the event a call for a capital contribution or a call for a loan is made, each Partner shall have thirty (30) days from the date of receipt of such written notice to pay his percentage (as determined by his percentage of Partnership interest) share of such amount requested. In the event that any Partner does not advance his share of the capital contribution and/or loan within the time provided, the other Partner shall have the right to advance such funds not advanced by the defaulting Partner in the proportion of their Partnership interests, or such other proportions as they may agree among themselves.

The refusal or failure of any Partner to advance the capital contribution and/or loan within the time required hereunder shall cause the Partnership interest of such defaulting Partner to be adjusted downward to the percentage that is equivalent to the following fraction:

The numerator shall be the sum of such Partner's capital contributions to the Partnership and his loans advanced to date to the Partnership, and the denominator shall be the sum of the capital contributions and the loans of the Partnership of all the Partners to date.

—For example, assume Mr. X, a twenty (20%) percent Partner who has paid in his share ($1,800.00) of the Partner's total contributions to capital ($9,000.00) would be required to contribute twenty (20%) percent of a capital contributions called for by the Partners. If there was a call for a capital contribution of $9,000.00, and all Partners except Mr. X advanced his respective share, Mr. X's interest in the Partnership would equal the following percentage:

$1,800.00　(Mr. X's capital contribution)
$9,000.00　(Total initial capital contribution)
　　　　　plus $7,200.00
　　　　　(contributions by non-defaulting Partners)

　　　　　　　　　　　　　　$ 1,800.00
　　　　　　　　　　　　　　$16,200.00

The Partnership interest of the non-defaulting Partners shall be increased by the percentage decrease in the defaulting Partner's interest, such interest to be allocated among them in proportion to their respective interest in the Partnership prior to such default; provided, however, that if a non-defaulting Partner advances part or all of the called for capital contribution and/or loan not advanced by the defaulting Partner hereunder, and if such advances are not made in proportion to their respective Partnership interests, any increases in the Partnership interest of the non-defaulting Partners shall be first allocated among them in proportion to the fraction of the amount of the capital contribution and/ or loan not made by the defaulting Partner that each non-defaulting Partner actually paid.

5. *Capital Account.* A capital account shall be established for each Partner on the books of the Partnership, and there shall be credited to each Partner's capital account, any additional capital contributions and his share of undistributed profits of the Partnership. There shall be charged against each Partner's capital account the amount of all distributions made by the Partnership to each Partner and his share of any losses of the Partnership. No Partner shall have the right to withdraw any capital which he has paid to the Partnership, except in accordance with the provisions of this Agreement. No additional capital contributions shall be made or shall be required to be made to the Partnership, except as expressly set forth in this Agreement.

Upon a distribution of property to a Partner other than in liquidation of such Partner's interest in the Partnership, the Partnership, for capital account purposes, will be deemed to have disposed of the property for its fair market value in a taxable transaction. The gain or loss from the deemed sale shall be allocated among the capital accounts of all Partners in such a manner as gain or loss would be allocated among the Partners had there been an actual taxable disposition of such property.

In the event of a property distribution to a Partner in liquidation of such Partner's interest in the Partnership, the gain or loss from the deemed sale shall be first allocated to the liquidating Partner to the extent needed to cause such Partner's capital account to equal the fair market value of the property distributed. The remaining gain or loss from the deemed sale shall be allocated to the remaining Partners in accordance with a partner's capital account.

For example, assume partnership X has three partners, A, B and C who each have a $100.00 capital account. Further, assume X owns the following assets:

	Book Value	FMV	Gain on Deemed Sale
Property (1)	$100	$200	$100
Property (2)	50	200	150
Property (3)	150	200	50

If X distributes property (2) to A in liquidation of his interest in the Partnership, $100.00 of the gain on the deemed sale would be allocated to A so as to cause A's capital account to equal the fair market value of the distributed property. The remaining $50.00 of gain would be allocated equally to B and C. The sum of B and C's capital accounts would then equal $250.00 which would balance with X's book value of its remaining assets.

In the event the allocation of such gain is not sufficient to cause the capital account of the liquidating Partner to equal the fair market value of the distributed property (for example, if X distributed property (3) to A), the Partnership, if permitted by Treas. Reg. 1____704-1(b)(2)(iv)(f), shall cause a "gross up" of the book value of the remaining Partnership assets to their respective fair market values with a corresponding adjustment to the capital accounts of the remaining Partners.

6. *Allocation of Profits and Losses, Cash Flow and Distribution Thereof.* All profits, losses and cash flow (as hereinafter defined) of the Partnership shall be allocated and distributed annually on a pro rata basis in accordance with the percentages of interest of each Partner in the Partnership.

Cash Flow shall be defined for the purposes of this Agreement as the taxable income for federal income tax purposes as shown on the books of the Partnership increased by:

　　a. the amount of depreciation deductions taken in computing such taxable income; and

　　b. non-taxable income or receipts of the Partnership (excluding capital contributions), and reduced by:

　　(1) payments upon the principal of any mortgages upon Partnership Property or of any other Partnership obligations or loans which are not otherwise tax deductible; and

(2) expenditures for the acquisition of replacements or capital improvements (except to the extent already deducted in arriving at taxable income referred to above).

7. *Powers.* The Partnership shall have authority and power to:

a. acquire real or personal property or any interest therein;

b. lease all or any part of its property for terms which may extend beyond the duration of the Partnership;

c. borrow money and, as security therefor, mortgage all or any part of its property, obtain any replacement of any such mortgage, prepay in whole or in part, refinance, recast, increase or modify any mortgages or security affecting its property, all for terms which may extend beyond the duration of the Partnership;

d. sell, assign or convey all or any part of its property;

e. lend its funds or make guarantees of obligations of others upon such terms as the Partners shall determine;

f. employ such persons, firms, or companies as the Partners shall determine for the operation and management of the Partnership's Property and business on such terms and for such compensation as the Partners shall determine;

g. retain counsel, accountants, financial advisors, and other professional personnel; and

h. engage in such other activities and incur such other expenses as may be necessary or appropriate for the furtherance of the Partnership's purposes, and execute, acknowledge and deliver any and all instruments necessary to the foregoing.

All real and personal property owned by the Partnership shall be kept in such names as the Partners may determine from time to time.

8. *Decisions.* All decisions, approvals, consents, or authorizations of the Partnership shall require and be made by the concurrence or approval by _____ percent (____%) in interest of the Partners, except as otherwise specifically provided in this Agreement.

9. *Management.* A Managing Partner will be selected by a majority in interest of the Partners, and he shall receive no compensation from the Partnership for services rendered to the Partnership, but shall be entitled to reimbursement for expenses reasonably incurred or monies expended on behalf of the Partnership. A management company may be employed to operate the Partnership Property, and the cost thereof shall be considered an expense of the Partnership and not as compensation or payment of services to any Partner. The Managing Partner shall have the full authority and responsibility for the day-to-day operation of Partnership. The Managing Partner shall serve until removed by a majority in interest of the Partners or until he resigns.

10. *Accounting.* The books and records of the Partnership shall be maintained in accordance with proper accounting principles. The fiscal year of the Partnership shall be the calendar year. Periodically, as determined by the Partners and their accountants, there shall be prepared and delivered to each partner a statement showing the results of operations during such determined period. The Partnership may employ as its accountants a firm of certified public accountants satisfactory to the Partners. Each Partner shall be furnished with copies of all statements prepared by the accountants for the Partnership and shall have access to all of the Partnership books and records. The Partnership shall furnish to each Partner such reports on the Partnership's operation and condition as may be reasonably requested by any Partner.

All receipts, funds and income of the Partnership shall be deposited in such banks as are mutually determined by the Partners. Single withdrawals in excess of $1,000.00 (of multiple withdrawals in excess of $1,000.00 within a three (3) day period) from said banks shall be made only with the consent of all the Partners, and there shall be no commingling of the monies and funds of the Partnership with monies and funds of any other entity, and said monies and funds shall be maintained in separate and distinct accounts of the Partnership.

11. *Restriction of Transfer or Pledge of Interests in the Partnership.* Except as expressly provided herein, no Partner shall sell, transfer, assign, syndicate, pledge or otherwise dispose of or encumber any interest in the Partnership, its property or assets without prior written consent of all the Partners.

a. In the event a Partner desires to make a gift of part or all of his Partnership interest to his wife and/or his children and/or an entity in which his wife and/or children have a beneficial or equitable interest of at least _____ percent (%) of such entity, the transferring Partner shall secure the written approval of the other Partners before effectuating such transfer. In the event one or more of the other Partners do not agree to such transfer, the transferring Partner shall be prohibited from making such transfer, but shall have the right to again propose a transfer identical to, or substantially similar to, the prohibited transfer after six (6) months have expired from the date that such proposed transfer was not approved.

b. In the event a Partner desires to transfer a part or all of his Partnership interest to a party who is not presently a Partner (except for a transfer under Subparagraph 11(a) hereof), the transfer shall be subject to the following terms and conditions:

(1) If the proposed transfer occurs within two (2) years from the date of this Agreement, the Partnership shall have the right to purchase the Partnership interest being offered for sale at a purchase price equal to the total amount of capital contributions to the Partnership by the selling Partner. The purchase price shall be paid by the Partnership paying twenty-five (25%) percent of the purchase price at Closing, and the remainder shall be paid in three (3) equal annual installments commencing one (1) year after the date of Closing with subsequent payments on each anniversary date thereafter until fully paid. The interest rate for such preferred payments shall be at the rate of nine (9%) percent per annum and shall be paid with each principal installment. If the Partnership desires to purchase the interest of the selling Partner, it must do so within thirty (30) days of the date that the selling Partner gives written notice of his desire to transfer his interest to the non-Partner.

(2) If the proposed transfer occurs subsequent to the two (2) year period from the date of this Agreement, the Partnership shall have the right to purchase the interest of the selling Partner in the same manner as provided in subparagraph (i) of this Paragraph (b) of this Article 11, except that the purchase price shall be equal to the greater of the capital contributions to the Partnership of the selling Partner or the fair market value of the Partner's Partnership Interest as determined herein by the accountant of the Partnership, and such determination shall be binding upon all Partners. _____ fair market value of such Partnership Interest, as determined by the certified public accountant regularly utilized by the Partnership, and such determination shall be binding upon all parties.

c. Upon the death of a Partner, the Partnership shall purchase the interest of such deceased Partner for a purchase price which is equal to the greater of the amount of such deceased Partner's capital contributions to the Partnership or the fair market of the Partner's Partnership Interest as determined herein by the accountant of the Partnership, and such determination shall be binding upon all parties. The purchase price shall be paid to the estate of such deceased Partner by the Partnership paying twenty-five (25%) percent of such purchase price at the Closing of such transaction, which shall be within sixty (60) days after the death of the deceased Partner, and the remainder shall be paid by the Partnership making three (3) annual installment payments commencing on the first anniversary of the Closing and each subsequent anniversary date thereafter until the purchase price is fully paid. Such installment payments shall bear interest at the rate of nine (9%) percent per annum, and such accrued interest payments shall accompany each installment payment.

d. In the event the relationship between one Partner and another Partner is such that they can no longer work together as Partners in order to operate the Partnership, each such dissenting Partner shall deliver to the certified public accountant employed by the Partnership a seated bid setting forth the price at which he is willing to purchase the Partnership interest of the other dissenting Partner. The bids shall be submitted by each Partner within thirty (30) days after the date that such dissenting Partners determine that they can no longer work together, provided, however, that each such Partner shall give notice to the other dissenting Partner that he has submitted his respective bid. The certified public accountant shall open the bids on such thirtieth (30th) day, and the Partner submitting the higher sealed bid shall have the right to purchase the Partnership interest of the other dissenting Partner by a full cash payment within sixty (60) days after the bids are unsealed, subject to a thirty (30) day option of the non-dissenting Partners to purchase their respective pro rata share of the Partnership interest being sold. If a non-dissenting Partner does not properly exercise his option by giving written notice to the selling Partner, the Partner who is required to purchase the interest of the selling Partner shall purchase such unexercised share. If either Partner fails to submit a bid on or before the date scheduled for opening the bids, the Partner submitting a bid shall be deemed to be the higher bidder. If neither Partner submits a bid, the Partnership shall continue in full force and effect as if such disagreement had never occurred.

The provisions of this paragraph notwithstanding, any assignee who shall have acquired an interest in the Partnership in accordance with the provisions of this agreement shall be bound by and shall hold his interest subject to all of the provisions of this Agreement, and no conveyance or assignment to such assignee shall be valid unless concurrently therewith the assignee shall deliver to the other Partners an agreement assuming and agreeing to be bound by all of the provisions of this Agreement with respect to the interest acquired.

The computation of the fair market value of a Partner's Partnership Interest shall be made in accordance with generally accepted accounting principles consistently applied giving due regard to prior accounting methods of the Partnership, and the following shall be observed:

a. No allowance of any kind shall be made for good will or any similar asset of the Partnership.

b. All accounts payable shall be taken at face amount, less discounts deductible therefrom and all accounts receivable shall be taken at the fair amount thereof, unless in the opinion of the accountant a reserve is necessary.

c. All furniture and fixtures and equipment are to be computed at the depreciated value appearing on the books of the Partnership.

d. Inventory of supplies shall be computed at cost or market, whichever is lower.

e. All unpaid and accrued federal, state, city, and municipal taxes shall be deducted as liabilities.

f. Death proceeds of Partnership-owner insurance insuring the life of a deceased Partner whose Partnership Interest is being valued for purchase under this Agreement shall not be included in "book value" to the extent such proceeds exceed the prepaid premiums and cash value on the policy or policies of the insured Partner.

g. Real estate and securities of the Partnership shall be valued at fair market value, and the accountant of the Partnership may select qualified appraisers to assist him in determining the fair market value of such items.

h. In the event of any pending or known claims for liability which are not fully insured, the accountant, if the same is in keeping with good business practices, may establish such reserves as he deems necessary as a liability of a Partnership.

Except as proved herein, the date of determination of "fair market value" and the adjustments proved hereunder shall be the last day of the calendar month immediately preceding the notice of the Partner's desire to gift or transfer his Partnership Interest or the death of a Partner, whichever shall apply.

12. *Termination.*

a. This Partnership shall terminate upon the first to occur of the following events:

(1) upon the sale of all or substantially all of the Partnership Property and assets;
(2) by mutual agreement of the Partners; and
(3) upon the expiration of the term of the Partnership.

b. *Distributions on Termination.* Upon termination of the Partnership, a final audit shall be made by the Partnership's accountants, and all of the property and assets of the Partnership shall be distributed as follows:

(1) All of the property and assets, if any, other than cash, shall be sold and collected to the extent feasible, and turned into cash within a period of one (1) year from the date of such termination. Any Partner shall have the right to bid on and purchase any of the property and assets being sold, provided any accepted bid of a Partner shall be payable in cash and may not be paid by a debit against the Partner's capital account.

(2) All of the Partnership's debts, liabilities and obligations, including any loans or advances from any Partner, shall be paid in full or reserves therefor shall be set aside.

(3) The balance of the assets, if any shall be distributed in the percentages of ownership in the Partnership. A reasonable time shall be allowed for the orderly liquidation and discharge of the liabilities of the Partnership. Each Partner shall be furnished with a statement, prepared by the Partnership's accountants, setting forth the total amount of the assets available for distribution after satisfaction of all liabilities. In the event that the liabilities of the Partnership shall exceed the assets available for distribution, the Partners shall assume and pay the excess in the percentages of ownership in the Partnership, and in the event that any Partner does not so pay his full pro rata share of such excess and the other Partners are required to do so, then the other Partners shall be entitled to contribution from the defaulting Partner. If the assets of the Partnership are not sold in liquidation, they shall be distributed in kind to the Partners in proportion to their percentages of ownership in the Partnership, subject to all then existing encumbrances thereon.

13. *Disputes.* Where specified in this Agreement, certain controversies or disputes shall be settled by arbitration if a majority in interest of the Partners agree in writing to submit such controversy or dispute to arbitration. Such arbitration shall be effected by arbitration in , in accordance with the rules existing at such time of the American Arbitration Association. Judgment may be entered on any award rendered by the arbitrators in any federal or state court having jurisdiction over the site of the property. The fees and expenses of arbitration shall be borne by the Partner demanding arbitration.

14. *Liabilities and Indemnification.*

a. *Liability.* It is specifically understood and agreed between the Partners that this Partnership extends only to and is limited to the rights and obligations under this Agreement, and nothing herein shall be construed to constitute any Partner the agent or general partner of any other Partner, nor in any manner to limit the Partners in the carrying on of their respective businesses or activities, other than the activities included within the scope of the Partnership. Nothing herein shall deprive or otherwise affect the right of any Partner to own, invest in, manage, or operate property or to transact business activities which are not competitive with the business of the Partnership.

b. *Indemnification.* Each Partner shall be indemnified by each other Partner and held harmless against and from all claims, demands, actions, and rights of action which shall or may arise by virtue of anything done or omitted to be done by each other Partner (directly or through or by agents, employees or other representatives) outside the scope of, or in breach of the terms of this agreement, provided that each other Partner shall be promptly notified of the existence of the claim, demand, action, or right of action, and shall be given reasonable opportunity to participate in the defense thereof, and further provided that failure to give such notice shall not affect each other Partner's obligations hereunder, except to the extent of any actual prejudice to them resulting therefrom. In the event of joint and several liability by reason of notes or mortgages executed on behalf of the Partnership by the individual Partners, each Partner agrees to hold the other harmless to the extent of any claims, demands, actions, and rights of action or judgments obtained in excess of the percentage interest of each such Partner in this Partnership.

15. *Inspection.* Each Partner or his authorized representative may examine any of the books and records of the Partnership at any time without notice.

16. *Integration.* This Agreement is the entire agreement between the parties with respect to the subject matter hereof and cancels all prior agreements with respect to the subject matter hereof, and no alteration, modification, or interpretation hereof shall be binding unless in writing and signed by each party.

17. *Remedies.* Subject to the provisions of this Agreement requiring arbitration, each Partner acknowledges and agrees that the remedy at law for any breach of any terms of this Agreement would be inadequate, and agrees and consents that temporary and permanent injunctive and other equitable relief may be granted in any proceeding which may be brought to enforce any provision hereof, including within such other equitable relief, specific performance, without the necessity of proof of actual damage or inadequacy of any legal remedy.

18. *Notices.* All notices or demands required or permitted by this Agreement shall be in writing and shall be sent by registered mail addressed to the addresses on file with the Managing Partner, or to such other address as shall from time to time be supplied in writing by any party to the other.

19. *Benefits and Obligations.* The covenants and agreements herein contained shall inure to the benefit of, and be binding upon, the parties hereto and their respective successors and assigns. Any person succeeding to the interest of a Partner shall succeed to all of such Partner's rights, interests and obligations hereunder, subject to and with the benefit of all terms and conditions of this Agreement, except as hereinabove set forth, including the restrictive conditions contained herein.

20. *Severability.* If any provision of this Agreement or application to any party or circumstances shall be determined by any court of competent jurisdiction to be invalid and unenforceable to any extent, the remainder of this Agreement or the application of such provision to such person or circumstance other than those as to which it is so determined invalid or unenforceable, shall not be affected thereby, and each provision hereof shall be valid and shall be enforced to the fullest extent permitted by law.

21. *Applicable Law.* This Agreement shall be construed and enforced in accordance with the laws of the State of _____.

IN WITNESS WHEREOF, the parties hereto have hereunto set their hands and seals the day and year first above written.

_____

_____   _____

POWER OF ATTORNEY

(Short Form)

I, _____, of the town of _____ in the county of _____ and state of _____, do hereby make, constitute and appoint _____, of the town of _____, in the county of _____, and state of _____, my true, sufficient and lawful attorney, for me and in my name to (here state subject matter of power); and to do and perform all necessary acts in the execution and prosecution of the aforesaid business in as full and ample a manner as I might do if I were personally present.

In Witness Whereof, I have hereunto set my hand and seal the _____ day of _____, in the year two thousand _____.

Signed, sealed and delivered in presence of

_____L.S.

_____

PROOF OF CLAIM

(See next page for form.)

PROOF OF CLAIM WITH POWER OF ATTORNEY

(Not to be used in bankruptcy cases.)

County of _____

} ss:

State of _____

    On this _____ day of _____, 20__, personally appeared _____ the subscriber, and made oath that the account hereto annexed is just and proper and that he has not directly or indirectly, to his knowledge, received any part of the money charged as due by such account, nor any security or satisfaction for the same, nor any promissory note or other negotiable instrument for the said debt, other than that which is annexed hereto. The subscriber hereby appoints _____ or his representatives, and each of them, attorneys in fact authorizing them and each of them to receive and collect the aforesaid debt, or any payments of dividends thereon, with power to compromise, settle or adjust the claim upon such terms as the attorney may deem best, as fully as the subscriber could do if personally present.

    Subscribed and sworn to before me this _____ day of _____, 20__.

_____

    Notary Public

REAFFIRMATION AGREEMENT

Note: This revised Form B 240 can be used when a bankruptcy debtor has agreed to reaffirm a debt to a creditor under Sec. 524(c) of the Bankruptcy Code, 11 USC 524(c). This form was developed by the Advisory Committee on Bankruptcy Rules and is issued as a service to the Court and the parties in bankruptcy proceedings under Rule 9009 of the Federal Rules of Bankruptcy Procedure. This is a procedural form, rather than an official bankruptcy form; therefore, use of this form is not mandatory but is strongly recommended.

UNITED STATES BANKRUPTCY COURT
DISTRICT OF _____

Debtor's Name	Bankruptcy Case No.
	Chapter
Creditor's Name and Address	

<u>Instructions:</u> (1) Attach a copy of all court judgments, security agreements, and evidence of their perfection. (2) File all the documents by mailing them or delivering them to the Clerk of the Bankruptcy Court.

(Continued on p. 27-69)

FORM B10 (Official Form 10) (10/05)

UNITED STATES BANKRUPTCY COURT _____ DISTRICT OF _____	PROOF OF CLAIM

Name of Debtor	Case Number

NOTE: This form should not be used to make a claim for an administrative expense arising after the commencement of the case. A "request" for payment of an administrative expense may be filed pursuant to 11 U.S.C. § 503.

Name of Creditor (The person or other entity to whom the debtor owes money or property): Name and address where notices should be sent: Telephone number:	☐ Check box if you are aware that anyone else has filed a proof of claim relating to your claim. Attach copy of statement giving particulars. ☐ Check box if you have never received any notices from the bankruptcy court in this case. ☐ Check box if the address differs from the address on the envelope sent to you by the court.	THIS SPACE IS FOR COURT USE ONLY

Last four digits of account or other number by which creditor identifies debtor:	Check here ☐ replaces if this claim ☐ amends a previously filed claim, dated:_____	

1. Basis for Claim
- ☐ Goods sold
- ☐ Services performed
- ☐ Money loaned
- ☐ Personal injury/wrongful death
- ☐ Taxes
- ☐ Other ————————————

- ☐ Retiree benefits as defined in 11 U.S.C. § 1114(a)
- ☐ Wages, salaries, and compensation (fill out below)
  - Last four digits of your SS #: _____
  - Unpaid compensation for services performed
  - from _____ to _____
  -      (date)   (date)

2. Date debt was incurred:	**3. If court judgment, date obtained:**

4. Classification of Claim. Check the appropriate box or boxes that best describe your claim and state the amount of the claim at the time case filed. See reverse side for important explanations.

Unsecured Nonpriority Claim $_____
- ☐ Check this box if: a) there is no collateral or lien securing your claim, or b) your claim exceeds the value of the property securing it, or if c) none or only part of your claim is entitled to priority.

Unsecured Priority Claim
- ☐ Check this box if you have an unsecured claim, all or part of which is entitled to priority.

Amount entitled to priority $_____

Specify the priority of the claim:
- ☐ Domestic support obligations under 11 U.S.C. § 507(a)(1)(A) or (a)(1)(B)
- ☐ Wages, salaries, or commissions (up to $10,000),* earned within 180 days before filing of the bankruptcy petition or cessation of the debtor's business, whichever is earlier - 11 U.S.C. § 507(a)(4).
- ☐ Contributions to an employee benefit plan - 11 U.S.C. § 507(a)(5).

Secured Claim
- ☐ Check this box if your claim is secured by collateral (including a right of setoff).

Brief Description of Collateral:
- ☐ Real Estate   ☐ Motor Vehicle   ☐ Other _____

Value of Collateral: $_____

Amount of arrearage and other charges at time case filed included in secured claim, if any: $_____

- ☐ Up to $2,225* of deposits toward purchase, lease, or rental of property or services for personal, family, or household use - 11 U.S.C. § 507(a)(7).
- ☐ Taxes or penalties owed to governmental units - 11 U.S.C. § 507(a)(8).
- ☐ Other - Specify applicable paragraph of 11 U.S.C. § 507(a)(___).

*Amounts are subject to adjustment on 4/1/07 and every 3 years thereafter with respect to cases commenced on or after the date of adjustment.

5. Total Amount of Claim at Time Case Filed: $ _____ _____ _____ _____
      (unsecured)   (secured)   (priority)   (Total)
- ☐ Check this box if claim includes interest or other charges in addition to the principal amount of the claim. Attach itemized statement of all interest or additional charges.

6. Credits: The amount of all payments on this claim has been credited and deducted for the purpose of making this proof of claim. **7. Supporting Documents:** Attach copies of supporting documents, such as promissory notes, purchase orders, invoices, itemized statements of running accounts, contracts, court judgments, mortgages, security agreements, and evidence of perfection of lien. DO NOT SEND ORIGINAL DOCUMENTS. If the documents are not available, explain. If the documents are voluminous, attach a summary. **8. Date-Stamped Copy:** To receive an acknowledgment of the filing of your claim, enclose a stamped, self-addressed envelope and copy of this proof of claim.	THIS SPACE IS FOR COURT USE ONLY

Date	Sign and print the name and title, if any, of the creditor or other person authorized to file this claim (attach copy of power of attorney, if any):

Penalty for presenting fraudulent claim: Fine of up to $500,000 or imprisonment for up to 5 years, or both. 18 U.S.C. §§ 152 and 3571.

(Continued from p. 27-67)

NOTICE TO DEBTOR:

This agreement <u>gives up the protection of your bankruptcy discharge</u> for this debt.

<u>As a result of this agreement, the creditor may be able to take your property or wages</u> if you do not pay the agreed amounts. The creditor may also act to collect the debt in other ways.

<u>You may rescind (cancel) this agreement at any time before the bankruptcy court enters a discharge order or within 60 days after this agreement is filed with the court, whichever is later,</u> by notifying the creditor that the agreement is canceled.

<u>You are not required to enter into this agreement by any law.</u> It is not required by the Bankruptcy Code, by any other law, or by any contract (except another reaffirmation agreement made in accordance with Bankruptcy Code § 524(c)).

<u>You are allowed to pay this debt without signing this agreement.</u> However, if you do not sign this agreement and are later unwilling or unable to pay the full amount, the creditor will not be able to collect it from you. The creditor also will not be allowed to take your property to pay the debt unless the creditor has a lien on that property.

If the creditor has a lien on your personal property, you may have a right to <u>redeem</u> the property and eliminate the lien by making a single payment to the creditor equal to the current value of the property, as agreed by the parties or determined by the court.

This agreement is not valid or binding unless it is filed with clerk of the bankruptcy court. If you were not represented by an attorney during the negotiation of this reaffirmation agreement, the agreement cannot be enforced by the creditor unless (1) you have attended a reaffirmation hearing in the bankruptcy court, and (2) the agreement has been approved by the bankruptcy court. (Court approval is not required if this is a consumer debt secured by a mortgage or other lien on your real estate.)

REAFFIRMATION AGREEMENT

The debtor and creditor named above agree to reaffirm the debt described in this agreement as follows.

THE DEBT

Total Amount of Debt When Case Was Filed $_____

Total Amount of Debt Reaffirmed $_____

Above Total Includes the Following:

    Interest Accrued to Date of Agreement $_____

    Attorney Fees $_____

    Late Fees $_____

    Other Expenses or Costs Relating to the

    Collection of This Debt (Describe) $_____

Annual Percentage Rate (APR) _____ %

Amount of Monthly Payment $_____

Date Payments Start _____

Total Number of Payments to Be Made _____

Total of Payments If Paid According to Schedule _____

Date Any Lien Is to Be Released If Paid According to Schedule _____

The debtor agrees that any and all remedies available to the creditor under the security agreement remain available.

All additional terms agreed to by the parties (if any): _____

Payments on this debt [were][were not] in default on the date on which this bankruptcy case was filed.

This agreement differs from the original agreement with the creditor as follows:

CREDITOR'S STATEMENT CONCERNING AGREEMENT AND
SECURITY/COLLATERAL (IF ANY)

Description of Collateral. If applicable, list manufacturer, year and model.

Value $_____

Basis or Source for Valuation _____

Current Location and Use of Collateral _____

Expected Future Use of Collateral _____

Check Applicable Boxes: _____

Any lien described herein is valid and perfected.

This agreement is part of a settlement of a dispute regarding the dischargeability of this debt under section 523 of the Bankruptcy Code (11 USC § 523) or any other dispute. The nature of dispute is

_____

DEBTOR'S STATEMENT OF
EFFECT OF AGREEMENT ON DEBTOR'S FINANCES

My Monthly Income (take home pay plus any other income received) is $_____.

My current monthly expenses total $_____, not including any payment due under this agreement or any debt to be discharged in this bankruptcy case.

I believe this agreement [will][will not] impose an undue hardship on me or my dependents.

DEBTOR'S STATEMENT CONCERNING DECISION TO REAFFIRM

I agreed to reaffirm this debt because _____

_____

I believe this agreement is in my best interest because _____

_____

I [considered][did not consider] redeeming the collateral under section 722 of the Bankruptcy Code (11 USC § 722). I chose not to redeem because ____

I [was][was not] represented by an attorney during negotiations on this agreement.

CERTIFICATION OF ATTACHMENTS

Any documents which created and perfected the security interest or lien [are][are not] attached. [*If documents are not attached:* The documents which created and perfected the security interest or lien are not attached because _____

_____]

SIGNATURES

_____   _____
(Signature of Debtor)   (Name of Creditor)

Date _____

                                _____
                                (Signature of Creditor Representative)

                                Date _____

_____
(Signature of Joint Debtor)

Date _____

CERTIFICATION BY DEBTOR'S ATTORNEY (IF ANY)

I hereby certify that (1) this agreement represents a fully informed and voluntary agreement by the debtor(s); (2) this agreement does not impose a hardship on the debtor or any dependent of the debtor; and (3) I have fully advised the debtor of the legal effect and consequences of this agreement and any default under this agreement.

_____   _____
(Signature of Debtor's Attorney, if any)   Date

RECLAMATION DEMAND

[LETTERHEAD]

_____, 20__

Re: Reclamation Demand by _____

Gentlemen:

Demand is hereby made upon you pursuant to § 2-702 of the Uniform Commercial Code and § 546(c) of the United States Bankruptcy Code for the return of all goods consisting of received during the applicable periods referred to in the above-cited sections and specifically including but not limited to goods described in the Schedule enclosed herewith.

Please contact the undersigned for instructions in connection with the return of the goods.

In light of your recent bankruptcy filing, you are further notified that all goods subject to _____'s right of reclamation should be protected and segregated by you and are not to be used for any purpose whatsoever except those specifically authorized following notice and a hearing by the Bankruptcy Court.

Very truly yours,

By: _____

SCHEDULE

Vendor	Invoice No.	Invoice Date	Amount

RELEASE (GENERAL)

I, _____ for and in consideration of the sum of $_____ in hand paid by _____ have remised, released, and forever discharged and by these presents for _____ heirs, executors, and administrators remise, release, and forever discharge the said _____ heirs, executors and administrators of and from any and all manner of action and actions, cause and causes of action, suits, debts, dues, sums of money, accounts, reckonings, bonds, bills, specialties, covenants, contracts, controversies, agreements, premises, variances, trespasses, damages, judgments, extents, executions, claims, and demands whatsoever, in law or in equity which against _____ ever had, now have, or which _____ heirs, executors, or administrators hereafter can, shall or may have, for, upon or by reason of any matter, cause or thing whatsoever, from the beginning of the world to the day of the date of these Presents.

In Witness Whereof, _____ have hereunto set hand and seal the _____ day of _____ 20__.

Sealed and delivered in the presence of

_____

_____

(Acknowledgment)

RELEASE OF LEASE OF PERSONAL PROPERTY

I, _____, of _____, do hereby certify that a certain lease of personal property dated _____ day of _____, 20__, and filed in the Office of the County Clerk of _____ county _____, the _____. day of _____, 20__, No. _____, for the lease of property therein described by the undersigned, as lessor, to _____ as lessee, to secure the payment of $_____, has been satisfied, paid and discharged in full, and the County Clerk of said county is hereby authorized to satisfy and cancel the same of record. Dated: _____, 20__.

Witnesses:

_____

(Signature of Lessor)

(If the person executing this release does not personally appear before the clerk, the release must be acknowledged.)

SATISFACTION OF MECHANICS' LIEN

I, _____, do hereby certify that a certain mechanics' lien, filed in the office of the clerk of the county of _____, the _____ day of _____, 20__, at _____ o'clock in the _____ noon, in favor of _____ claimant, against the building and lot situated on the _____ street, in _____between _____ and _____ streets, and known as No. _____ in said street, _____ owner and contractor, is discharged.

SECURITY AGREEMENT FOR ACCOUNTS RECEIVABLE

AGREEMENT made this _____ day of _____, 20__, by and between _____, a corporation duly organized to do business in the State of _____ with its principal place of business at _____ hereinafter called the "Secured Party," and _____ with its principal place of business at _____ hereinafter called the "Debtor."

I. *Creation of Security Interest*

Debtor hereby grants a personal security interest in and assigns to the Secured Party the collateral described in paragraph II below to secure payment and performance of all debts, liabilities and obligations of Debtor of any kind whenever and however incurred to Secured Party.

II. *Collateral*

The collateral of this security agreement is all of the accounts receivable presently existing and hereafter arising of the Debtor, and all personal property in which the Debtor has an interest now or hereafter in the control or possession of the Secured Party and the proceeds of the above described collateral.

III. *Obligations of Debtor*

A. Debtor shall pay to, turn over to and deposit with the Secured Party all proceeds in the form of cash and negotiable instruments for the payment of money received by Debtor from an Account Debtor in payment of or on Account and the Secured Party shall have the exclusive right in accordance with this Security Agreement to the proceeds paid, turned over or deposited by Debtor.

B. Debtor shall pay immediately without notice and irrespective of any credit term in any instrument or writing evidencing indebtedness, if Secured Party so elects, any or all indebtedness, of Debtor to Secured Party upon Debtor's default under this Security Agreement or if Secured Party deems itself insecure.

C. Debtor shall pay on demand all expenses and expenditures of Secured Party, including reasonable attorneys' fees and legal expenses incurred or paid by Secured Party in protecting, enforcing or exercising its interests, rights or remedies created by, connected with or provided in this Security Agreement or performance pursuant to this Security Agreement.

D. Debtor shall pay to Secured Party upon demand, any balance due to Secured Party in the event that the account debtors fail to pay on the due date, the respective accounts in satisfaction of Debtor's obligation to the Secured Party.

E. Debtor shall not voluntarily or involuntarily subject the collateral or its proceeds or allow the collateral or its proceeds to be subjected to any interest of any transferee, buyer, secured party, encumbrancer, or other third person, shall not modify the contracts with the Account Debtors or diminish any security for any Account, and shall not bring suit to enforce payment of an Account without giving Secured Party notice in advance in writing and without first receiving written consent from Secured Party.

F. Debtor shall, at its expense, do, make, procure, execute and deliver all acts, things, writings and assurances as Secured Party may at any time require to protect, assure or enforce its interests, rights and remedies created by, provided in or emanating from this Security Agreement.

G. Until deposit in accordance with this Security Agreement, Debtor shall hold all proceeds received in payment of or on an Account, and shall hold all other collateral of this Security Agreement for or on behalf of Secured Party separate and apart from and shall not commingle the proceeds or collateral with any of Debtor's funds or property.

IV. *Debtor represents and warrants that:* (A) its principal place of business is in the _____. (B) the accounts that form the basis of this Security Agreement represent goods sold or services performed as follows: _____ and (C) the account is not subject to any prior or subsequent assignment, claim, lien or security interest other than that of the Secured Party, nor is the claim subject to setoff or counterclaim, defense, allowance or judgment.

V. *Default.* Debtor shall be in default under this Security Agreement if any one of the following occurs:

A. When there is misstatement or false statement in connection with, noncompliance with, or non-performance of any of the Debtor's obligations, agreements or affirmations under or emanating from this Security Agreement.

B. Upon death, dissolution, termination of existence, insolvency, business failure, appointment of a receiver of the Debtor or any surety of Debtor, making of an assignment for the benefit of creditors by Debtor, the calling of a meeting of creditors of, or the commencement of any proceeding under any bankruptcy or insolvency laws by or against Debtor or any surety for Debtor, or the termination by a surety for Debtor's obligations of its contract of suretyship.

VI. *Secured Party's Rights and Remedies*

A. Rights and Remedies Exclusive of Default. Secured Party or its nominee or agent may (1) upon written notice to Debtor notify or require Debtor to notify Account Debtors obligated on any or all of Debtor's Accounts to make payment directly to Secured Party, and may take possession of all proceeds of any Accounts in Debtor's possession; (2) take any steps which Secured Party deems necessary or advisable to collect discharge or extend the whole or any part of the Accounts or other collateral or proceeds, and to apply the proceeds to Debtor's indebtedness to Secured Party in accordance with the provisions of this Security Agreement; (3) call at Debtor's place or places of business at intervals to be determined by Secured Party and, without hindrance or delay, inspect, audit, check and make extracts from the books, records, journals, orders, receipts, correspondence and other data relating to the collateral or to any transaction between Debtor and Secured Party; (4) subrogate to all of Debtor's interests, rights and remedies in respect to any Account, including the right to stop delivery and upon notice from Debtor that the Account Debtor has returned, rejected, revoked acceptance of or failed to return the goods or that the goods have been re-consigned or diverted, the right to take possession of and to sell or dispose of the goods, unless Secured Party fails to advise Debtor of its intended exercise of such rights within five business days after receipt of notice.

B. Upon Debtor's Default, Secured Party shall have all of the rights and remedies provided in this Security Agreement and in the Uniform Commercial Code in force in _____ at the date of this Security Agreement.

VII. *Debtor's Rights and Remedies.*

Debtor shall have the right to collect and enforce at its own expense as agent for Secured Party all Accounts until Debtor is in default hereunder or until Secured Party notifies Debtor that it will collect any or all Accounts pursuant to this Security Agreement.

VIII. *Additional Agreements and Affirmations.*

Debtor's Agreements and Affirmations. Debtor agrees and affirms: (1) that its only places of business are those appearing beneath his signature below and that he will promptly notify Secured Party of any change of location of any place of business or of the addition of any new place of business; and (2) that at the time Secured Party's security interest attaches to any of the collateral or its proceeds, Debtor is the lawful owner with the right to transfer any interest therein, that the collateral and its proceeds are not and will not be the subject of any financing statement on file or subject to the interest of any person except under this Security Agreement and that Debtor will defend the collateral and its proceeds against the lawful claims and demands of all persons.

IX. *Mutual Agreements.*

A. "Secured Party" and "Debtor" as used in this Security Agreement shall include the heirs, executors, administrators, successors, representatives, receivers, trustees, and assigns of those parties.

B. The laws of _____ shall govern the construction of and the rights and duties of the parties to this Security Agreement.

C. This Security Agreement includes all amendments and supplements thereto, and all assignments, instruments, documents, Accounts and other writings submitted by Debtor to Secured Party pursuant to this Security Agreement, but neither Debtor nor Secured Party shall be bound by an undertaking not expressed in writing.

D. If any of the provisions of this Security Agreement shall contravene or be held invalid under the laws of any jurisdiction, the Security Agreement shall be construed as if not containing such provisions and the rights and obligations of the parties shall be construed and enforced accordingly. This Agreement is executed this _____ day of _____, 20__.

By _____   By _____

           Secured Party   Debtor

_____   _____

SECURITY AGREEMENT FOR EQUIPMENT

This agreement made this _____ day of _____, by and between _____ with an address a _____ hereinafter called the "Secured Party" and _____ with an address at _____ hereinafter called the "Debtor."

I. *Creation of Security Interest.*

Debtor hereby grants a personal security interest in and assigns to the Secured Party the Collateral described in paragraph II below to secure payment and performance of all debts, liabilities and obligations of Debtor of any kind whenever and however incurred to Secured Party.

II. *Collateral.*

III. *Debtor's Obligations.*

A. Debtor shall pay to Secured Party the sum or sums evidenced by the promissory note or notes executed pursuant to this security agreement in accord with the terms of such note or notes.

B. The Collateral will not be misused or abused, wasted or allowed to deteriorate, except for the ordinary wear and tear of its intended primary use.

C. The Collateral will be insured until this security agreement is terminated against all expected risks to which it is exposed and those which Secured Party may designate, with policies acceptable to Secured Party and payable to both Secured Party and Debtor as their interests appear, and with duplicate policies deposited with the Secured Party.

D. The Collateral will be kept at the Debtor's place of business, aforementioned, where Secured Party may inspect it at any time.

E. The Collateral will not be sold, transferred or disposed, or subject to any paid charge, including taxes of any subsequent interest of a third party created or suffered by Debtor, voluntary or involuntary, unless Secured Party consents in writing to such charge, transfer or disposition.

F. Debtor will sign and execute any financing statement or other document or procure any document and pay all connected costs necessary to protect the security agreement against the rights of interests of a third person.

G. Debtor will reimburse Secured Party for any action to remedy a default under this agreement.

IV. *Secured Party's Obligations.*

Secured Party hereby sells the Collateral and shall transfer possession thereof to Debtor on _____, 20__.

V. *Default.*

Misrepresentation or misstatement in connection with, noncompliance with or nonperformance of any of Debtor's obligations or agreements under paragraphs III and VIII shall constitute default under this Security Agreement. In addition, Debtor shall be in default if bankruptcy or insolvency proceedings are instituted by or against the Debtor or if Debtor makes any assignment for the benefit of creditors.

VI. *Secured Party's Rights and Remedies.*

A. Secured Party may assign this security agreement, and _____.

(1) If Secured Party does assign this security agreement, the assignee shall be entitled, upon notifying the Debtor, to performance of all of Debtor's obligations and agreements under paragraphs III and VIII, and assignee shall be entitled to all of the rights and remedies of Secured Party under this paragraph VI, and

(2) Debtor will assert no claims or defenses he may have against Secured Party or against its assignee except those granted in this security agreement, and _____. Upon Debtor's default, Secured Party may exercise his rights of enforcement under the Uniform Commercial Code in force in the State of _____ at the date of this security agreement and, in conjunction with, addition to or substitution for those rights, at Secured Party's discretion, may

(1) Enter upon Debtor's premises to take possession of, assemble and collect the Collateral or to render it unusable, and

(2) Require Debtor to assemble the Collateral and make it available at a place Secured Party designates which is mutually convenient, to allow Secured Party to take possessions or dispose of the Collateral, and

(3) Waive any default or remedy any default in any reasonable manner without any or all Accounts or other collateral or proceeds, or to sell, transfer, compromise, waiving the default remedied and without waiving any other prior or subsequent default.

VII. *Rights and Remedies of Debtor.*

Debtor shall have all of the rights and remedies before or after default provided in Article 9 of the Uniform Commercial Code in force in the State of _____ at the date of this security agreement.

VIII. *Additional Agreements and Affirmations.*

A. Debtor Agrees and Affirms: (1) that information supplied and statements made by him in any financial or credit statement or application for credit prior to this security agreement are true and correct, (2) that no financing statement covering the Collateral or its proceeds is on file in any public office and that, except for the security interest granted in this security agreement, there is no adverse lien, security interest or encumbrance in or on the Collateral, (3) that the addresses of Debtor's residence and place or places of business, if any, are those appearing below his signature, and (4) that if Debtor is also buyer of the Collateral, there are no express warranties unless they appear in writing signed by the seller and there are no implied warranties of merchant ability or fitness for a particular purpose in connection with the sale of the Collateral.

B. Mutual Agreements. (1) "Debtor" and "Secured Party" as used in this security agreement include the heirs, executors or administrators, successors or assigns of those parties. (2) The law governing this secured transaction shall be that of the State of _____ in force at the date of this security agreement. (3) If more than one Debtor executes the security agreement; their obligations hereunder shall be joint and several.

Executed in triplicate this _____ day of _____, 20__.

By_____   By_____
        Secured Party   Debtor

_____   _____
                                          Debtor's Residence

_____   _____
        Address   Address of Chief Place of Business

                                   _____
                                   Addresses of other places of business

SECURITY AGREEMENT UNDER ARTICLE 9 OF THE UNIFORM COMMERCIAL CODE

LENDER hereby agrees to lend to BORROWER such amounts as may from time to time be agreed upon. To secure its obligation to repay such indebtedness in accordance with the schedule hereinafter set forth, BORROWER hereby creates in favor of LENDER a security interest in all of BORROWER'S present and future accounts, chattel paper, contract rights, documents of title, equipment inventory and general intangibles. BORROWER shall be free to process, use and sell or otherwise dispose of any of the collateral hereunder but the security interest hereby created shall continue in the proceeds and products of any such collateral and in any other personal property hereafter acquired whether as replacements or substitutes for such collateral or otherwise.

Signature and address of Borrower

_____

_____

Date:_____, 20__

Accepted:

Signature and address of Lender

_____

_____

SERIES OF NOTES WITH DEFAULT CLAUSES

$_____.   _____, 20___.

_____ after date I _____ promise to pay to the order of _____ Dollars, payable at _____.
Value received.

    This note is No. _____ of a series of _____ notes for _____ each due as follows: _____. It is hereby specifically agreed that in case of the nonpayment at maturity of this note or any of the notes of this series, then all of the said notes shall immediately become due and payable at the option of the legal holder thereof.

_____
(Signature)

No.: _____ Date: _____

Signed, sealed and delivered in the presence of

_____

    (Note: A series of notes which do not contain a default clause are separate instruments and non-payment of one such note gives the holder of the others no right of action prior to maturity thereof.)

SIMPLE LOAN AGREEMENT (WITH PROMISSORY NOTE)

    Agreement made this _____ day of _____, 20__ by and between _____ residing at _____ Street, City of _____, State of_____, (hereinafter referred to as the "Debtor") and _____ whose office and principal place of business is located at _____ Street, City of _____, State of _____, (hereinafter referred to as the "Creditor").

    WHEREAS, the Debtor is desirous of borrowing money from the Creditor; and

    WHEREAS, the Creditor desires to lend such funds to the Debtor on the terms and conditions herein set forth.

    IN CONSIDERATION OF THE MUTUAL PROMISES HEREIN CONTAINED, IT IS HEREBY AGREED AS FOLLOWS:

    (1) The Creditor does hereby agree to loan to the Debtor the sum of _____ ($_____) Dollars, on or before _____.

    (2) The Debtor agrees, upon receipt of the sum of _____ ($_____) Dollars, to deliver to the Creditor a promissory note. Said promissory note shall provide for the repayment of the sum of _____ ($_____) Dollars to the Creditor within _____ days from the date of this agreement and shall bear interest at the rate of _____ (_____%) per centum per annum. Payment of principal and interest shall be payable at the office of the Creditor at the address hereinabove set forth.

    The provisions of this agreement shall be obligatory and binding upon and shall serve to the use or benefit of the Parties hereto, their heirs, executors, administrators, successors and assigns.

    IN WITNESS WHEREOF, the Parties have hereunto set their hands and seals. In the Presence of:

_____   _____
                                  _____
_____   _____
                                  _____

SIMPLE SECURITY AGREEMENT

DEBTOR(S)_____   CREDITOR_____

_____   _____

_____   _____

_____   _____

SECURITY AGREEMENT

    WHEREAS the above listed DEBTOR(S) are indebted to the above identified CREDITOR as evidenced by one or more promissory notes or other debt instruments dated _____ and

    WHEREAS the DEBTOR(S) may incur further indebtedness to the CREDITOR in the future.

NOW, THEREFORE in consideration of the existing and any future indebtedness to the CREDITOR, to secure the payment of all existing or future debts, advances and liabilities of the DEBTOR(S) to the CREDITOR, the DEBTOR(S) hereby GRANT to the CREDITOR a security interest in the collateral of the type or kind described below, together with any products, proceeds, accessions and replacements, now owned or hereafter acquired.

DESCRIPTION OF THE COLLATERAL

[ ] Second sheet attached with continuation of description of collateral.

DEBTOR(S) WARRANT, COVENANT AND AGREE THAT:

1. The DEBTOR(S) are the absolute and sole owners of the collateral described herein and that the collateral is free from all liens, encumbrances, security interests except those described in the written financial statements submitted to the CREDITOR.

2. The DEBTOR(S) shall remain in possession of the collateral until a default occurs and shall care for, maintain, and insure the collateral. DEBTOR(S) shall further permit the CREDITOR to inspect the collateral at any time during normal business hours. That except for collateral classified as inventory, the DEBTOR(S) shall not sell, dispose of or encumber or permit to become encumbered any of the collateral without the express written consent of the creditor.

3. The DEBTOR(S) shall be in default hereunder if the DEBTOR(S) fail to perform or discharge any obligation or pay any debts secured hereby or fail to perform any covenant or agreement herein or in any other agreement between the DEBTOR(S) and the CREDITOR. Upon default CREDITOR MAY, WITH OR WITHOUT NOTICE, ACCELERATE THE ENTIRE INDEBTEDNESS SECURED HEREBY. No waiver by the CREDITOR of any default shall be effective unless in writing nor shall such waiver operate as a waiver of any other default or of the same default on a future occasion. DEBTOR(S) agree to assemble the collateral and make it available to the CREDITOR at such time and place as designated by the CREDITOR in the event of default and further waive notice of default.

4. This security agreement and the debt instrument secured hereby shall constitute the entire agreement between the DEBTOR(S) and the CREDITOR, unless modified in writing and signed by the party against whom the modification is to be enforced. The agreement between the DEBTOR(S) and the CREDITOR shall be construed under the law of the state of _____ as of the date hereof. Failure of the CREDITOR to exercise any right under this security agreement and the debt instrument shall not be construed as a waiver of any condition or covenant herein.

5. DEBTOR(S) have been advised and understand that DISPOSAL OF THE COLLATERAL COVERED BY THIS SECURITY AGREEMENT MAY CONSTITUTE A VIOLATION OF STATE AND/ OR FEDERAL CRIMINAL LAW. DEBTOR(S) FURTHER ACKNOWLEDGE THAT THEY HAVE READ THIS SECURITY AGREEMENT BEFORE SIGNING IT AND RECEIVED A COPY THEREOF.

DEBTOR(S) _____   DEBTOR(S) _____

DEBTOR(S) _____

DATE _____

(The above described collateral is subject to the security agreement dated _____, 20__ between _____ as debtor and _____ as creditor and all the terms and conditions thereof. _____ debtors' initials

SPECIMEN FORMS OF ACKNOWLEDGMENT AS PRESCRIBED BY THE UNIFORM ACKNOWLEDGMENT ACT

(1) For an individual acting in his own right:

> State of _____
> County of _____
>   The foregoing instrument was acknowledged before me this (date) by (name of person acknowledged).
>   (Signature of person taking acknowledgment)
>   (Title or rank)
>   (Serial number, if any)

(2) For a corporation:

> State of _____
> County of _____
>   The foregoing instrument was acknowledged before me this (date) by (name of officer or agent, title of officer or agent) of (name of corporation acknowledging) a (state or place of incorporation) corporation, on behalf of the corporation.
>   (Signature of person taking acknowledgment)
>   (Title or rank)
>   (Serial number, if any)

(3) For a partnership:

> State of _____
> County of _____
>   The foregoing instrument was acknowledged before me this (date) by (name of acknowledging partner or agent), partner (or agent) on behalf of (name of partnership), a partnership.
>   (Signature of person taking acknowledgment)
>   (Title or rank)
>   (Serial number, if any)

(4) For an individual acting as principal by an attorney in fact:

> State of _____
> County of _____
>   The foregoing instrument was acknowledged before me this (date) by (name of attorney in fact) as attorney in fact on behalf of (name of principal).
>   (Signature of person taking acknowledgment)
>   (Title or rank)
>   (Serial number, if any)

(5) By any public officer, trustee, or personal representative:

> State of _____
> County of _____
>   The foregoing instrument was acknowledged before me this (date) by (name and title of position).
>   (Signature of person taking acknowledgment)
>   (Title or rank)
>   (Serial number, if any)

SUBORDINATION AGREEMENT

In order to induce (name of bank or other lender), hereinafter referred to as "Bank," to make and renew loans and extend credit to (name of borrower) _____ hereinafter called "Borrower," in such manner and amounts and upon such terms and conditions as the Borrower may from time to time request or agree to, and in consideration of any such loan, renewal or extension of credit which the Bank may make, (name of creditor or creditors) _____ hereinafter called "Creditor," hereby agrees, forthwith upon the making of any such loan, renewal or extension of credit, to subordinate and does hereby wholly subordinate, as herein provided, any and all claims which the Creditor may now or hereafter have against the Borrower to any and all claims which the Bank may now or hereafter have against the Borrower.

Until payment in full with interest of all of said claims of the Bank, the Creditor agrees not to accept any payment or satisfaction of any kind of, or any security for, and not to surrender or release, any of said claims hereby subordinated. If the Creditor should so receive any such payment, satisfaction or security, the Creditor agrees forthwith to deliver the same to the Bank in the form received, endorsed or assigned as may be appropriate, for application on account of, or as security for, said claims of the Bank and until so delivered agrees to hold the same in trust for the Bank. At any time and insofar as any of said claims hereby subordinated may be evidenced by any instrument in writing the Creditor agrees to affix to every such instrument, in form and manner satisfactory to the Bank, a statement to the effect that the same is subject to this agreement and, upon request, agrees to assign or endorse and deliver any such instrument to the Bank.

The Creditor hereby assigns, transfers and sets over to the Bank all of said claims hereby subordinated, effective at the option of the Bank in event of default by the Creditor or the Borrower with respect to any obligation to or agreement with the Bank or in event of the commencement of any liquidation, bankruptcy, insolvency, reorganization, or dissolution proceedings by or against the Creditor or the Borrower or of the death of either thereof or of any partner of either thereof. In any such event all of said claims of the Bank and all of said claims hereby subordinated shall, at the option of the Bank, forthwith become due and payable, without demand or notice, and the Bank may, in its absolute discretion, in its own name or the name of the Creditor or otherwise, take any action for the collection of said claims hereby subordinated by process of law, by proof of debt in any proceedings or otherwise, may receive the proceeds thereof and give acquittance therefor and, after deducting the costs and expenses of any action taken, including reasonable counsel fees, may apply the proceeds on account of said claims of the Bank and shall account to the Creditor for any balance remaining.

The Bank shall not be under any duty to take any action in connection with any of said instruments delivered or claims assigned to it and shall not be responsible in any respect in connection therewith, whether for action it may take or refrain from taking or otherwise, except for willful malfeasance.

The Creditor agrees from time to time, upon request, to make, execute and deliver any endorsements, assignments, proofs of claim, affidavits, consents, agreements or other instruments which the Bank may, in its absolute discretion, deem necessary or desirable in order to effectuate the purposes of this agreement in accordance with its true intent and meaning and the Creditor hereby irrevocably constitutes and appoints the Bank and any of its present or future officers severally attorneys in fact for and on behalf of the Creditor, with full power of substitution and revocation, in its own name or in the name of the Creditor or otherwise, so to do, in the exercise of which discretion and power the decision of the Bank or the decision of any of its said officers shall be conclusive as to all persons and for all purposes.

Without notice of the Creditor and without in any way impairing or affecting this agreement, the Bank may from time to time, in its absolute discretion, for value or without value, renew or extend the time of payment of any said claims of the Bank, modify in any manner or release in whole or in part any security therefor or the obligations of any endorsers, sureties or guarantors thereof or release from the terms of this or of any other subordination agreement any claims subordinated. The Borrower, for the consideration hereinabove stated, authorizes and approves any act or thing which may be done in accordance herewith and agrees not to make any payment of or on account of, give any security for, or accept any surrender or release in whole or in part, of any of said claims hereby subordinated.

The Creditor and the Borrower agree to make and maintain in their books of account notations satisfactory to the Bank of the rights and priorities of the Bank hereunder and from time to time on request, to furnish the Bank with sworn financial statements. The Bank may inspect the books of account and any records of the Creditor or the Borrower at any time during business hours. The Creditor and the Borrower waive notice of acceptance hereof and all other notice or demand whatever. No waiver by the Bank of any right hereunder shall be valid unless in writing and no waiver of any right shall be deemed a waiver of any other right. Nothing herein shall limit or affect in any manner any right the Bank may have by virtue of any other instrument or agreement. The words "Creditor" and "Borrower" as herein used shall include the plural as well as the singular and if "Creditor" or "Borrower" includes two or more they shall be jointly and severally bound hereby. The word "claims" as herein used shall mean all liabilities without limitation, whether due or not due, direct or contingent, determined or undetermined in amount, however acquired, evidenced or arising and any part thereof.

This agreement shall inure to the benefit of the Bank, its successors and assigns, and shall be binding upon the Creditor and the Borrower and their respective legal representatives, successors and assigns. It shall be a continuing agreement and shall be irrevocable and shall remain in full force and effect until all of said claims of the Bank shall have been paid in full and until the Bank shall have received notice in writing of election to terminate it as to future loans or extensions of credit but, notwithstanding such notice or any other notice or the death or incompetency of any party hereto, this agreement shall continue to remain in full force and effect as to all said claims of the Bank then outstanding and any renewals or extensions thereof theretofore or thereafter made.

In witness whereof, this agreement has been duly executed this _____ day of _____, 20__.

Creditor: _____

Borrower: _____

(Acknowledgments)

TRUST FUND JOINT CHECK AGREEMENT

In consideration of the sum of one dollar cash in hand paid and the supply of labor and/or materials by Seller on the Project, the receipt and sufficiency of which is hereby acknowledged _____ owner or general contractor ("Owner/G.C."), _____ (Seller) and _____ contractor or Seller's customer ("Contractor") and _____ ("Seller"), agree as follows:

1. All checks issued by Owner/G.C. to Contractor for (all labor or materials supplied) or (only for the Seller's sales price of material supplied by Seller) on the _____ construction project ("Project") shall be made jointly payable to Contractor and Seller and shall be promptly delivered to Seller. Owner/G.C. may rely on any written notice provided by Seller, stating the total current indebtedness of Contractor to Seller and limiting any obligation under this Agreement for any current requisition. Contractor appoints Seller its attorney in fact to sign or endorse on behalf of Contractor all checks received from Owner/G.C.

2. Contractor agrees that all funds owed to Contractor from anyone or received by Contractor to the extent those funds result from the labor or materials supplied by Seller shall be held in trust for the benefit of Seller ("Trust Funds"). **Contractor agrees it has no interest in Trust Funds held by anyone and to promptly account for and pay to Seller all such Trust Funds. Customer irrevocably assigns to Seller any interest it may have in its Trust Fund account receivable.**

3. Seller agrees to supply labor and/or materials to the Project in accordance with Seller's contract.

4. This Agreement is not in payment of obligations of Contractor to Seller and will not affect Seller's rights to withdraw or refuse further credit, or Seller's rights to any payment bond, mechanics' lien, trust fund or other legal rights.

UCC FINANCING STATEMENT

UCC FINANCING STATEMENT

FOLLOW INSTRUCTIONS (front and back) CAREFULLY

A. NAME & PHONE OF CONTACT AT FILER [optional]

B. SEND ACKNOWLEDGMENT TO: (Name and Address)

THE ABOVE SPACE IS FOR FILING OFFICE USE ONLY

1. DEBTOR'S EXACT FULL LEGAL NAME - insert only one debtor name (1a or 1b) - do not abbreviate or combine names

1a. ORGANIZATION'S NAME

OR 1b. INDIVIDUAL'S LAST NAME | FIRST NAME | MIDDLE NAME | SUFFIX

1c. MAILING ADDRESS | CITY | STATE | POSTAL CODE | COUNTRY

| 1d. TAX ID #:   SSN OR EIN | ADD'L INFO RE ORGANIZATION DEBTOR | 1e. TYPE OF ORGANIZATION | 1f. JURISDICTION OF ORGANIZATION | 1g. ORGANIZATIONAL ID #, if any ☐ NONE |

2. ADDITIONAL DEBTOR'S EXACT FULL LEGAL NAME - insert only one debtor name (2a or 2b) - do not abbreviate or combine names

2a. ORGANIZATION'S NAME

OR 2b. INDIVIDUAL'S LAST NAME | FIRST NAME | MIDDLE NAME | SUFFIX

2c. MAILING ADDRESS | CITY | STATE | POSTAL CODE | COUNTRY

| 2d. TAX ID #:   SSN OR EIN | ADD'L INFO RE ORGANIZATION DEBTOR | 2e. TYPE OF ORGANIZATION | 2f. JURISDICTION OF ORGANIZATION | 2g. ORGANIZATIONAL ID #, if any ☐ NONE |

3. SECURED PARTY'S NAME (or NAME of TOTAL ASSIGNEE of ASSIGNOR S/P) - insert only one secured party name (3a or 3b)

3a. ORGANIZATION'S NAME

OR 3b. INDIVIDUAL'S LAST NAME | FIRST NAME | MIDDLE NAME | SUFFIX

3c. MAILING ADDRESS | CITY | STATE | POSTAL CODE | COUNTRY

4. This FINANCING STATEMENT covers the following collateral:

5. ALTERNATIVE DESIGNATION [if applicable]: ☐ LESSEE/LESSOR ☐ CONSIGNEE/CONSIGNOR ☐ BAILEE/BAILOR ☐ SELLER/BUYER ☐ AG. LIEN ☐ NON-UCC FILING

6. ☐ This FINANCING STATEMENT is to be filed [for record] (or recorded) in the REAL ESTATE RECORDS.   Attach Addendum [if applicable] | 7. Check to REQUEST SEARCH REPORT(S) on Debtor(s) [ADDITIONAL FEE]   [optional] ☐ All Debtors ☐ Debtor 1 ☐ Debtor 2

8. OPTIONAL FILER REFERENCE DATA

FILING OFFICE COPY — NATIONAL UCC FINANCING STATEMENT (FORM UCC1) (REV. 07/29/98)

UCC FINANCING STATEMENT ADDENDUM

UCC FINANCING STATEMENT ADDENDUM
FOLLOW INSTRUCTIONS (front and back) CAREFULLY
9. NAME OF FIRST DEBTOR (1a or 1b) ON RELATED FINANCING STATEMENT

	9a. ORGANIZATION'S NAME		
OR	9b. INDIVIDUAL'S LAST NAME	FIRST NAME	MIDDLE NAME,SUFFIX

10. MISCELLANEOUS:

THE ABOVE SPACE IS FOR FILING OFFICE USE ONLY

11. ADDITIONAL DEBTOR'S EXACT FULL LEGAL NAME - insert only one name (11a or 11b) - do not abbreviate or combine names

	11a. ORGANIZATION'S NAME			
OR	11b. INDIVIDUAL'S LAST NAME	FIRST NAME	MIDDLE NAME	SUFFIX
	11c. MAILING ADDRESS	CITY	STATE POSTAL CODE	COUNTRY

11d. TAX ID #: SSN OR EIN	ADD'L INFO RE ORGANIZATION DEBTOR	11e. TYPE OF ORGANIZATION	11f. JURISDICTION OF ORGANIZATION	11g. ORGANIZATIONAL ID #, if any	
					☐ NONE

12. ☐ ADDITIONAL SECURED PARTY'S or ☐ ASSIGNOR S/P'S NAME - insert only one name (12a or 12b)

	12a. ORGANIZATION'S NAME			
OR	12b. INDIVIDUAL'S LAST NAME	FIRST NAME	MIDDLE NAME	SUFFIX
	12c. MAILING ADDRESS	CITY	STATE POSTAL CODE	COUNTRY

13. This FINANCING STATEMENT covers ☐ timber to be cut or ☐ as-extracted collateral, or is filed as a ☐ fixture filing.
14. Description of real estate:

16. Additional collateral description:

15. Name and address of a RECORD OWNER of above-described real estate (if Debtor does not have a record interest):

17. Check only if applicable and check only one box.
Debtor is a ☐ Trust or ☐ Trustee acting with respect to property held in trust or ☐ Decedent's Estate
18. Check only if applicable and check only one box.
☐ Debtor is a TRANSMITTING UTILITY
☐ Filed in connection with a Manufactured-Home Transaction — effective 30 years
☐ Filed in connection with a Public-Finance Transaction — effective 30 years

FILING OFFICE COPY — NATIONAL UCC FINANCING STATEMENT ADDENDUM (FORM UCC1Ad) (REV. 07/29/98)

UCC FINANCING STATEMENT AMENDMENT

UCC FINANCING STATEMENT AMENDMENT
FOLLOW INSTRUCTIONS (front and back) CAREFULLY

A. NAME & PHONE OF CONTACT AT FILER [optional]

B. SEND ACKNOWLEDGMENT TO: (Name and Address)

THE ABOVE SPACE IS FOR FILING OFFICE USE ONLY

1a. INITIAL FINANCING STATEMENT FILE #

1b. This FINANCING STATEMENT AMENDMENT is to be filed [for record] (or recorded) in the REAL ESTATE RECORDS.

2. ☐ TERMINATION: Effectiveness of the Financing Statement identified above is terminated with respect to security interest(s) of the Secured Party authorizing this Termination Statement.

3. ☐ CONTINUATION: Effectiveness of the Financing Statement identified above with respect to security interest(s) of the Secured Party authorizing this Continuation Statement is continued for the additional period provided by applicable law.

4. ☐ ASSIGNMENT (full or partial): Give name of assignee in item 7a or 7b and address of assignee in item 7c; and also give name of assignor in item 9.

5. AMENDMENT (PARTY INFORMATION): This Amendment affects ☐ Debtor or ☐ Secured Party of record. Check only one of these two boxes.
Also check one of the following three boxes and provide appropriate information in items 6 and/or 7.

☐ CHANGE name and/or address: Give current record name in item 6a or 6b; also give new name (if name change) in item 7a or 7b and/or new address (if address change) in item 7c. ☐ DELETE name: Give record name to be deleted in item 6a or 6b. ☐ ADD name: Complete item 7a or 7b, and also item 7c; also complete items 7d-7g (if applicable).

6. CURRENT RECORD INFORMATION:

6a. ORGANIZATION'S NAME

OR 6b. INDIVIDUAL'S LAST NAME | FIRST NAME | MIDDLE NAME | SUFFIX

7. CHANGED (NEW) OR ADDED INFORMATION:

7a. ORGANIZATION'S NAME

OR 7b. INDIVIDUAL'S LAST NAME | FIRST NAME | MIDDLE NAME | SUFFIX

7c. MAILING ADDRESS | CITY | STATE | POSTAL CODE | COUNTRY

7d. TAX ID #: SSN OR EIN | ADD'L INFO RE ORGANIZATION DEBTOR | 7e. TYPE OF ORGANIZATION | 7f. JURISDICTION OF ORGANIZATION | 7g. ORGANIZATIONAL ID #, if any ☐ NONE

8. AMENDMENT (COLLATERAL CHANGE): check only one box.
Describe collateral ☐ deleted or ☐ added, or give entire ☐ restated collateral description, or describe collateral ☐ assigned.

9. NAME OF SECURED PARTY OF RECORD AUTHORIZING THIS AMENDMENT (name of assignor, if this is an Assignment). If this is an Amendment authorized by a Debtor which adds collateral or adds the authorizing Debtor, or if this is a Termination authorized by a Debtor, check here ☐ and enter name of DEBTOR authorizing this Amendment.

9a. ORGANIZATION'S NAME

OR 9b. INDIVIDUAL'S LAST NAME | FIRST NAME | MIDDLE NAME | SUFFIX

10. OPTIONAL FILER REFERENCE DATA

FILING OFFICE COPY — NATIONAL UCC FINANCING STATEMENT AMENDMENT (FORM UCC3) (REV. 07/29/98)

UCC FINANCING STATEMENT AMENDMENT ADDENDUM

UCC FINANCING STATEMENT AMENDMENT ADDENDUM
FOLLOW INSTRUCTIONS (front and back) CAREFULLY

11. INITIAL FINANCING STATEMENT FILE # (same as item 1a on Amendment form)

12. NAME OF PARTY AUTHORIZING THIS AMENDMENT (same as item 9 on Amendment form)

12a. ORGANIZATION'S NAME

OR
12b. INDIVIDUAL'S LAST NAME   FIRST NAME   MIDDLE NAME,SUFFIX

13. Use this space for additional information

THE ABOVE SPACE IS FOR FILING OFFICE USE ONLY

FILING OFFICE COPY — NATIONAL UCC FINANCING STATEMENT AMENDMENT ADDENDUM (FORM UCC3Ad) (REV. 07/29/98)

UCC "IN LIEU" FINANCING STATEMENT

(This attachment is to be filed with the UCC Financing Statement.)

ATTACHMENT

NAME OF FIRST DEBTOR (1a or 1b) ON RELATED FINANCING STATEMENT

ORGANIZATION'S NAME

INDIVIDUAL'S LAST NAME	FIRST NAME	MIDDLE NAME, SUFFIX

This FINANCING STATEMENT is filed in lieu of continuation for the following previously filed financing statement(s), each of which remains effective:

ORIGINAL FINANCING STATEMENT			MOST RECENT CONTINUATION STATEMENT	
FILING OFFICE	ORIGINAL DATE	ORIGINAL NUMBER	CONTINUATION DATE	CONTINUATION NUMBER

UNCONDITIONAL PERSONAL GUARANTEE

FOR VALUE RECEIVED from {Creditor}, and to induce {Creditor} to sell goods on credit to {company} (hereinafter referred to as the "Customer"), the **Guarantor** acknowledges that this Guarantee is a Guarantee of Payment, and the **Guarantor's** obligations under this Guarantee are and shall at all times continue to be absolute and unconditional in all respects, and shall at all times be valid and enforceable irrespective of any other agreements or circumstances of any nature whatsoever which might otherwise constitute a defense to this Guarantee and the obligations of the Guarantor under this Guarantee or the obligations of any other person or party (including, without limitation, the **Customer**) relating to this Guarantee or the obligations of the **Guarantor** hereunder.

This Guarantee sets forth the entire understanding of **Creditor** and **Guarantor**, and **Guarantor** absolutely, unconditionally and irrevocably waives any and all right to assert any defense, set-off, counterclaim or cross-claim of any nature whatsoever with respect to this Guarantee or the obligations of the **Guarantor** under this Guarantee or the obligations of any other person or party (including, without limitation, **Customer**) relating to this **Guarantee** or the obligations of the **Guarantor** under the Guarantee or otherwise with respect to the indebtedness due to **Creditor** ("Debt") in any action or proceeding brought by the holder hereof to collect the Debt or any portion thereof, or to enforce, the obligations of the **Guarantor** under this Guarantee. The **Guarantor** acknowledges that no oral or other agreements, understandings, representations or warranties exist with respect to this Guarantee or with respect to the obligations of the **Guarantor** under this Guarantee, except as specifically set forth in this Guarantee.

Creditor shall have the right to extend the time of payment, modify terms, and grant indulgences with respect to the indebtedness due or to become due from **Customer**, all without releasing me from the provisions of this Guarantee. **Guarantor** authorizes **Creditor** to obtain a credit report on **Guarantor** personally and utilize that credit report in determining the creditworthiness of **Guarantor**.

This personal Guarantee may only be revoked on (ten) days' notice to **Creditor** or by registered mail, at the above address, and said revocation shall become effective (ten) days after the receipt of said notice and shall not discharge any liabilities arising prior to the effective date of the revocation.

The **Guarantor** agrees that whenever an attorney is used to obtain payment under or otherwise to enforce, declare or adjudicate any rights or obligations under this Guarantee, said personal **Guarantor** shall pay said attorney reasonable attorney fees in the sum of (25%) and agrees to reimburse said attorney out of pocket costs and expenses.

In witness of the above understanding, I have hereunto set by hand this _____ day of _____, 20__ .

      (Individually)

Home Address:
Home Telephone Number:
Social Security Number:
STATE OF _____
COUNTY OF _____

On this _____ day of _____, 20__ before me personally appeared _____ residing at _____, to me known and known by me to be the individual(s) described in and who executed the foregoing personal guarantee and (he/she) duly acknowledged to me that (he/she) executed same.

      (Notary Public)

WAIVER OF RIGHT TO FILE MECHANICS' LIEN

Whereas the undersigned _____, residing (or, _____ with principal place of business) at _____ Street, _____, is about to furnish certain materials and to perform certain labor (or, _____ is furnishing materials and performing labor; or, _____ has furnished certain materials and performed certain labor) in the matter of improvement of certain real property owned by _____ of _____ Street, _____, _____, which real property is designated and known as (give brief description of realty).

Now, therefore, in consideration of the sum of One (1.00) Dollar and other valuable considerations received by the undersigned, he hereby covenants and agrees that he shall not in any manner claim or file a mechanics' or other lien against the aforesaid premises or any part thereof of any of the materials hereto-fore or hereafter furnished by him or for any work or labor heretofore or hereafter performed or furnished by him in connection with the improvement of said premises aforesaid by the erection thereon of a two-story dwelling house and garage and the undersigned hereby formally and irrevocably releases and waives in writing any and every lien, charge or claim of any nature whatsoever that he has or may at any time be entitled to have against said premises in connection with the said improvement: (excepting and reserving, however, to the undersigned all right that he has to receive and enforce payment of said account by _____).

In witness whereof, this instrument has been executed and delivered the _____ day of _____, 20__.

_____

_____
(Acknowledgment)

(Some states, such as New York, do not permit a waiver of a mechanics' lien.)

WRITTEN ACTION OF SUBSCRIBER, FIRST BOARD OF DIRECTORS AND STOCKHOLDERS _____

The undersigned, being all of the members of the first Board of Directors of _____, a _____ cor-poration, as well as the subscribers to shares to be issued by the corporation and the persons first acquir-ing said shares, hereby take the following written actions in lieu of holding a meeting regarding same, all pursuant to the terms of § _____ and § _____.0704, inclusive, of the _____ Statutes:

1. *Certificate of Incorporation:* It is noted that the corporation's Certificate of Incorporation, previously subscribed to by _____, was duly filed in the office of the Secretary of State of the state of _____ on _____, 20__, and a certified copy thereof, together with a letter from the Secretary of State acknowledging receipt and filing of such certificate and full payment of all charter fees and all money due the State of _____ incident to the corporation in the amount of $_____, were returned to the offices of _____, at _____.

2. *Date of Activation:* It is noted that pursuant to the corporation's Articles of Incorporation, the cor-poration was activated as of _____.

3. *Subscriptions and Issuance of Shares:* _____ and _____ have each subscribed to purchase _____ (_____)shares of the corporation's capital stock. It is acknowledged by the undersigned direc-tors that each such offer has been accepted by the corporation; that the consideration offered by each sub-scriber has been received in full and has been determined by the Board of Directors as having the value subscribed to it by such subscriber; that an appropriate share certificate shall be issued in favor of each subscriber as soon as possible to reflect ownership of the shares so purchased; and that each subscriber constitutes a shareholder of the corporation that is entitled to take part in the written action hereinafter set forth.

4. *Bylaws:* A draft of a code of Bylaws, in the form set forth in the Minute Book, has been duly reviewed in its entirety by the undersigned directors and stockholders, and they, by proper action, hereby adopt such draft as the official bylaws of the corporation.

5. *Directors:* The following individuals shall be and they are hereby elected as Directors until their successors are duly elected, qualified, and seated:
Name

_____

6. *Officers:* The following individuals shall be and they are hereby elected to the offices set forth oppo-site their names, to serve until their successors are duly elected, qualified and seated:
Name   Office

_____   _____

7. *Registered Office and Registered Agent:* The registered office and registered agent of the corporation, initially fixed by the terms of Article VI of the corporation's Articles of Incorporation, shall be retained pending further action of this Board of Directors.

8. *Financial Records:* Since _____ is a closely held corporation, and all shareholders will be fully aware of its financial condition at all times, balance sheets and profit and loss statements need not be pre-pared for the benefit of the shareholders, and therefore the shareholders hereby waive the requirements of § _____, _____ Statutes.

ALTERNATE PARAGRAPH

9. *S Election:* The proper officers of the corporation are hereby authorized to take any and all action necessary to comply with the requirements of the Internal Revenue Service for making an election pursuant to Subchapter S of the Internal Revenue Code §1362, and the signing of this document by the directors and shareholders shall full ratification thereof.

10. *Seal:* The seal, an impression of which is made in the margin adjacent to this paragraph, is hereby adopted as the seal of this corporation.

11. *Stock Certificate:* The specimen certificate for shares of _____, which is attached to this document, is the form to be used by the corporation in issuing shares of the capital stock of the corporation.

12. *Disallowance of Expense Deductions:* Any salary payments or other payments made to an employee, director or stockholder of the corporation that shall be disallowed in whole or in part as a deductible expense for federal or state income tax purposes shall be reimbursed by such individual to the corporation. The corporation shall not be required to defend legally any proposed disallowance by the Internal Revenue Service or the Department of Revenue of the State of _____, and the amount required to be reimbursed by the individual shall be the amount, as finally determined by agreement or otherwise, actually disallowed as a deduction. It shall be the duty of the Board of Directors to enforce payment of each such amount disallowed.

Dated this _____ day of _____, 20__.

_____

(Signatures of Board of Directors)

Appendix A
Secretaries of State

HEADQUARTERS

National Association of Secretaries of State (NASS)

Leslie Reynolds
Executive Director
reynolds@sso.org

Kay Albowicz
Communications/Marketing Director
kay@sso.org

Hall of States
Suite 401
444 N. Capitol Street, N.W.
Washington, DC 20001
202-624-3525
202-624-3527 Fax
www.nass.org

ALABAMA
Secretary of State
State House
600 Dexter Avenue
Montgomery, AL 36104
334-242-7205
334-242-4993 Fax
www.sos.state.al.us

ALASKA
Lieutenant Governor
P.O. Box 110015
Juneau, AK 99811-0015
907-465-3520
907-465-5400 Fax
www.gov.state.ak.us/ltgov

AMERICAN SAMOA
Lieutenant Governor
Office of the Governor
Pago Pago, AS 96799
684-633-4116
684-633-2269 Fax

ARIZONA
Secretary of State
7th Floor, State Capitol
1700 W. Washington
Phoenix, AZ 85007-2808
602-542-3012
602-542-1575 Fax
www.azsos.gov

ARKANSAS
Secretary of State
256 State Capitol Building
Little Rock, AR 72201
501-682-1010
501-682-3510 Fax
www.sosweb.state.ar.us

CALIFORNIA
Secretary of State
1500 11th Street
Sacramento, CA 95814
916-653-7244
916-653-4620 Fax
www.ss.ca.gov

COLORADO
Secretary of State
Suite 200, 1700 Broadway
Denver, CO 80290
303-894-2200
303-869-4860 Fax
www.sos.state.co.us

CONNECTICUT
Secretary of State
State Capitol, Room 104
Hartford, CT 06106
860-509-6200
860-509-6209 Fax
www.sots.state.ct.us

DELAWARE
Secretary of State
Townsend Building
P.O. Box 898
Dover, DE 19903
302-739-4111
302-739-3811 Fax
www.state.de.us/sos

DISTRICT OF COLUMBIA
Secretary of the District
1350 Pennsylvania Ave., N.W.
Room 419
Washington, DC 20004
202-727-6306
202-727-3582 Fax
http://os.dc.gov/os/site/default.asp

FLORIDA
Secretary of State
R.A. Gray Building
500 South Bronough
Tallahassee, FL 32399-0250
850-245-6500
850-414-5526 Fax
www.dos.state.fl.us

GEORGIA
Secretary of State
State Capitol, Room 214
Atlanta, GA 30334
404-656-2881
404-656-0513 Fax
www.sos.state.ga.us/default800.asp

GUAM
Lieutenant Governor
Executive Chambers
P.O. Box 2950
Agana, GU 96910
671-474-8931
671-477-4826 Fax
http://ns.gov.gu

HAWAII
Lieutenant Governor
State Capitol, Fifth Floor
Honolulu, HI 96813
808-586-0255
808-586-0231 Fax
www.hawaii.gov/ltgov

IDAHO
Secretary of State
State Capitol, Room 203
Boise, ID 83720
208-334-2300
208-334-2282 Fax
www.idsos.state.id.us

ILLINOIS
Secretary of State
213 State Capitol
Springfield, IL 62706
217-782-2201 or 800-252-8980
217-785-0358 Fax
www.sos.state.il.us

INDIANA
Secretary of State
201 State House
Indianapolis, IN 46204
317-232-6531
317-233-3283 Fax
www.in.gov/sos

IOWA
Secretary of State
State House
Des Moines, IA 50319
515-281-5204
515-242-5952/5953 Fax
www.sos.state.ia.us

KANSAS

Secretary of State
120 S.W. 10th Ave.
Memorial Hall
Topeka, KS 66612-1594
785-296-4575
785-368-8033 Fax
www.kssos.org/main.html

KENTUCKY

Secretary of State
State Capitol, Room 150
Frankfort, KY 40601-3493
502-564-3490
502-564-5687 Fax
www.sos.state.ky.us

LOUISIANA

Secretary of State
P.O. Box 94125
Baton Rouge, LA 70804
225-342-4479
225-342-5577 Fax
http://sec.state.la.us

MAINE

Secretary of State
148 State House Station
Augusta, ME 04333-0148
207-626-8400
207-287-8598 Fax
www.state.me.us/sos

MARYLAND

Secretary of State
State House
Annapolis, MD 21401
410-974-5521 or 888-874-0013
410-974-5190 Fax
www.sos.state.md.us

MASSACHUSETTS

Sec. of the Commonwealth
One Ashburton Place, Room 1611
Boston, MA 02108-1512
617-727-7030 or 800-392-6090
617-742-4528 Fax
www.sec.state.ma.us

MICHIGAN

Secretary of State
Treasury Building, 1st Floor
430 W. Allegan Street
Lansing, MI 48918
517-322-1460
517-373-0727 Fax
www.michigan.gov/sos

MINNESOTA

Secretary of State
180 State Office Building
Rev. Dr. Martin Luther King Jr. Blvd.
St. Paul, MN 55155-1299
651-296-2083 or 877-551-6767
651-297-7067 Fax
www.sos.state.mn.us

MISSISSIPPI

Secretary of State
P.O. Box 136
Jackson, MS 39205-0136
601-359-1350
601-359-1499 Fax
www.sos.state.ms.us

MISSOURI

Secretary of State
208 State Capitol
P.O. Box 778
Jefferson City, MO 65102-0778
573-751-4153 or 866-223-6535
573-751-5841 Fax
www.sos.mo.gov

MONTANA

Secretary of State
P.O. Box 202801
Helena, MT 59620
406-444-2034
406-444-3976 Fax
www.sos.state.mt.us

NEBRASKA

Secretary of State
State Capitol, Room 1301
P.O. Box 94608
Lincoln, NE 68509-4608
402-471-4079
402-471-3666 Fax
www.sos.state.ne.us

NEVADA
Secretary of State
101 N. Carson St., Suite 3
Carson City, NV 89701
775-684-5708
775-684-5725 Fax
www.sos.state.nv.us

NEW HAMPSHIRE
Secretary of State
State House, Rm. 204
Concord, NH 03301
603-271-3242
603-271-6316 Fax
www.sos.nh.gov

NEW JERSEY
Secretary of State
P.O. Box 300
Trenton, NJ 08625-0300
609-984-1900
609-292-7665 Fax
www.state.nj.us/state

NEW MEXICO
Secretary of State
State Capitol North Annex, Suite 300
Santa Fe, NM 87503
505-827-3600
505-827-3634 Fax
www.sos.state.nm.us

NEW YORK
Secretary of State
41 State Street
Albany, NY 12231-0001
518-474-0050
518-474-4765 Fax
www.dos.state.ny.us

NORTH CAROLINA
Secretary of State
P.O. Box 29622
Raleigh, NC 27626-0622
919-807-2000
919-807-2010 Fax
www.secstate.state.nc.us

NORTH DAKOTA
Secretary of State
600 East Boulevard, Dept. 108
Bismarck, ND 58505-0500
701-328-2900 or 800-352-0867
701-328-2992 Fax
www.nd.gov/sos

OHIO
Secretary of State
180 E. Broad Street
Columbus, OH 43215
614-466-2655
614-644-0649 Fax
www.sos.state.oh.us/sos

OKLAHOMA
Secretary of State
220 Will Rogers Building
2401 North Lincoln Blvd.
Oklahoma City, OK 73105
405-521-3912
405-521-3771 Fax
www.sos.state.ok.us

OREGON
Secretary of State
136 State Capitol
Salem, OR 97310
503-986-1523
503-986-1616 Fax
www.sos.state.or.us

PENNSYLVANIA
Secretary of Commonwealth
302 North Office Building
Harrisburg, PA 17120
717-787-6458
717-787-1734 Fax
www.dos.state.pa.us

PUERTO RICO
Secretary of State
Department of State
P.O. Box 9023271
San Juan, PR 00902-3271
787-722-2121
787-725-7303 Fax
www.estado.gobierno.pr

RHODE ISLAND
Secretary of State
217 State House
Providence, RI 02903
401-222-2357
401-222-1356 Fax
www.state.ri.us

SOUTH CAROLINA
Secretary of State
Edgar Brown Bldg., 5th Floor
P.O. Box 11350
Columbia, SC 29211
803-734-2170
803-734-1661 Fax
www.scsos.com

SOUTH DAKOTA
Secretary of State
500 E. Capitol Building
Suite 204
Pierre, SD 57501-5070
605-773-3537
605-773-6580 Fax
www.sdsos.gov

TENNESSEE
Secretary of State
312 8th Avenue North
Nashville, TN 37243
615-741-2819
615-741-5962 Fax
www.state.tn.us/sos

TEXAS
P.O. Box 12887
Austin, TX 78711
512-463-5770
512-475-2761 Fax
www.sos.state.tx.us

U.S. VIRGIN ISLANDS
Lieutenant Governor
18 Kongens Gade
St. Thomas, VI 00802
340-774-2991
340-774-6953 Fax
www.ltg.gov.vi

UTAH
Lieutenant Governor
E220 State Capitol Complex
P.O. Box 142220
Salt Lake City, UT 84114
801-538-1000
801-538-1557 Fax
www.utah.gov/governor/

VERMONT
Secretary of State
26 Terrace St., Drawer 09
Montpelier, VT 05609-1101
802-828-2363
802-828-2496 Fax
www.sec.state.vt.us

VIRGINIA
Secretary of Commonwealth
Executive Office Building, 4th Floor
1111 East Broad Street
Richmond, VA 23219
804-786-2441
804-371-0017 Fax
www.soc.state.va.us

WASHINGTON
Secretary of State
Legislative Building
P.O. Box 40220
Olympia, WA 98504-0220
360-902-4151
360-586-5629 Fax
www.secstate.wa.gov

WEST VIRGINIA
Secretary of State
Building 1, Suite-157K
1900 Kanawha Blvd., E.
Charleston, WV 25305-0770
304-558-6000
304-558-0900 Fax
www.wvsos.com

WISCONSIN
Secretary of State
30 W. Mifflin Street
10th Floor
Madison, WI 53702
608-266-8888
608-266-3159 Fax
www.sos.state.wi.us/

WYOMING
Secretary of State
State Capitol Building
Cheyenne, WY 82002
307-777-7378
307-777-6217 Fax
http://soswy.state.wy.us

Appendix B
More Statutory Summaries

INTEREST TABLE

Note: State legislatures will, on occasion, modify an area of law without clear delineation as to its content and context. As a result, even the changes which have been enacted prior to placement in a state's Code may be difficult to locate. As a result, the Editors urge all users of the *Manual* to use this publication only as a guide, and to consult the latest codified version of the state's law for all recent changes.

The following table sets forth the legal rate of interest and the rate which may be charged by special agreement. Usually such agreements must be in writing. Many of the statutes contain special provisions with reference to call loans and in favor of banks, trust companies, pawnbrokers, etc., and with respect to interest on small loans, usually of $5,000 or less, installment loans, student loans, or credit card loans. These provisions are generally not summarized. *See* footnote references (a) through (v) at end of chart. Many states have special legislation limiting the maximum interest rate which can be charged on consumer transactions.

Interest rates fluctuate so it is advisable to verify, during the course of the year, the maximum rate in effect in any state.

Attention is also called to the federal law, outlined above, which preempts state usury laws with regard to certain transactions and lenders.

Besides listing the specific state limitations, the Editors have included the section numbers for the appropriate statutory materials. Because this area of the law changes quite frequently, the Editors suggest that the reader check the appropriate statutory section to ensure that recent changes have not been made.

State	Legal Rate (a)	Contract Rate (b)	Contract Rate (c)	Judgment Rate	Civil Penalty (d)	State Citation
AL (u)	6%	8% or any rate contracted for, so long as the original principal balance is in excess of $2,000	any rate if over $2,000	12% (f)	forfeit all interest, payments applied on principal (i)	legal rate – § 8-8-1; contract rate – §§ 8-8-1 and 8-8-5; corporate rate – § 8-8-5; judgment rate – § 8-8-10; civil penalty – § 8-8-12
AK	10.5%	cannot be more than 5% plus the annual rate charged member banks for advances by the 12th Federal Reserve District; any rate if over $25,000	no special rate	3% above the 12th Federal Reserve District discount rate	forfeit all interest	legal rate – § 45.45.010; contract rate – § 45.45.010; corporate rate – none; judgment rate – 9.30.070; civil penalty – § 45.45.040
AZ	10%	rate agreed to in writing	no special rate	10% or as set forth in instrument	forfeit all interest; interest paid may be applied to principal, or recovered	legal rate – § 44-1201(A); contract rate – § 44-1201(A); corporate rate – none; judgment rate – §§ 44-1201(B) and (C); civil penalty – §§ 44-1202 and 44-1203

AR	6%	The maximum rate on any contract shall not exceed 5% per annum above the Federal Reserve discount rate at the time of the contract; where no rate of interest is agreed upon the maximum shall be 6%. For consumer loans, the maximum shall be 17%	no special rate	10% (r) or as provided in contract up to contract rate, whichever is greater	contract is void for unpaid interest; may recover twice interest paid	legal rate, contract rate, corporate rate and civil penalty – Arkansas Constitution, Article 19 Section 13; contract rate – 4-57-104 judicial rate – Section 16-65-114
CA	7%	loans for personal, family or household uses (real property excluded), 10%; for other uses it cannot exceed the greater of 10% or 5% plus the rate by the Federal Reserve Bank of San Francisco for member banks on the 25th day of the month preceding the earlier of the date of execution of the contract for the loan or the date of the making of the loan	no special rate	7%	forfeit all interest; recover three times amount within one year of payment	legal rate, contract rate and judicial rate – Constitution Article 15 Section 1, Civil Code Section 1916-1; corporate rate – none; judgment rate – Constitution Article 15 Section 1; civil penalty – Civil Code Sections 1916-2 and 1916-3
CO	8% compounded annually	as set out in instrument, except as limited by UCCC, which may be up to 45%	no special rate	8% or higher if specified in contract or note	no statutory provision except with reference to UCCC transactions	legal rate – § 5-12-101; contract rate – § 5-12-103; corporate rate – none; judgment rate – § 5-12-101; civil penalty – none
CT	8%	12% (h)	any rate if over $10,000 or revolving charge agreement with debt over $10,000	10%	forfeit all principal and interest; no recovery of interest paid (i)	legal rate – § 37-1; contract rate – § 37-4; corporate rate – § 37-9; judgment rate – § 37-3a; civil penalty – §§ 37-2 and 37-7

INTEREST TABLE (Continued)

State	Legal Rate (a)	Contract Rate (b)	Contract Rate (c)	Judgment Rate	Civil Penalty (d)	State Citation
DE	5% over the federal discount rate plus applicable surcharge	5% over the federal discount rate plus applicable surcharge, if any; any rate if over $100,000 and not secured by a principal residence mortgage	no special rate	5% over the federal discount rate unless otherwise specified in the contract sued upon	all excess forfeited or applied to principal; recover greater of treble excess interest paid or $500, if action is brought within one year after payment	legal rate, contract rate and judgment rate – Title 6 § 2301; corporate rate – Title 6 § 2306; civil penalty – Title 6 § 2304
DC	6%	24% on secured transactions, but there is no limit on loans in excess of $1,000 which are secured and the borrower is a not for profit corporation, the loan is made for business purposes or conducting an investment activity	no special rate	6% for loans, forbearance of money, or things in the absence of expressed contract; 4% for judgments against DC, its officers and employees; 70% if not against DC, its offices or employees; for underpayments of tax to the IRS, rounded to the nearest full %	forfeit all interest, recover unlawful interest within one year of payment	legal rate – § 28-3302; contract rate – § 28-3301; corporate rate – § 28-3301; judgment rate – § 28-3302; civil penalty – § 28-3303/4/5
FL	7%	18% on loans under $500,000 and a maximum 25% on loans over $500,000	no special rate	6%; average of the federal reserve discount of the Bank of NY for the previous year plus 500 basis points calculated January 1 of every year, or the contracted, if less	forfeit all interest; double recovery of interest actually collected or penalty	legal rate – §§ 687.01 and 55.03; contract rate – § 687.02; judgment rate – § 55-03; corporate rate – none; civil penalty – § 687.0

State	Legal rate		Usury limit	Penalty	Statutory citations
GA	7%	any rate if over $3,000; where $3,000 or less, any rate not in excess of 16%	no special rate	3% over prime rate as published by the Federal Reserve System on the day judgment is entered	forfeit all interest; interest paid can be recovered or pleaded within one year	legal rate and contract rate – § 7-4-2; corporate rate – none; judgment rate – § 7-4-12; civil penalty – § 7-4-10
HI	10%	with respect to consumer loans 12%, 24% if made by a bank. With respect to credit card transactions, 18%	no special rate	10%	all interest forfeited; interest paid applied to reduce principal; borrower recovers costs (i)	legal rate – § 478-2; contract rate – § 478-4; corporate rate – § 478-4; judgment rate – § 478-3; civil penalty – §§ 478-5 and 478-6
ID	12%	no limit	no special rate	5% plus the average weekly yield on U.S. Treasury securities averaged to constant maturity of one year and rounded up to the nearest .13%, deter-mined July 1 of every year	none	legal rate, judgment rate and contract rate – § 28-22-104; corporate rate – none; judgment rate – § 28-22-104; civil penalty – none
IL	5%	9%; any rate on residential mortgage loans, state bank loans and business loans	no special rate	Weekly average of 1-year constant maturity Treasury yield as published by the FRS	forfeit all interest; recover twice total interest on contract or payment, whichever is greater, within two years of last payment plus attorneys fees and court costs	legal rate – 815 ILCS 205/1; contract rate and corporate rate – 815 ILCS 205/4; judgment rate – 735 ILCS 5/2-1303; civil penalty – 205/5 and 205/6

INTEREST TABLE (Continued)

State	Legal Rate (a)	Contract Rate (b)	Contract Rate (c)	Judgment Rate	Civil Penalty (d)	State Citation
IN	8%	for consumer loans, the maximum amount is 21% as promulgated by the UCCC	no special rate	judgment rate can be the amount of the contract so long as that amount does not exceed 8%	up to three times the amount of the total finance charge. For credit card transactions, special rules apply	legal rate – § 24-4.6-1-102; contract rate – § 24-4.5-3-201; corporate rate – none; judgment rate – § 24-4.6-1-101; civil penalty – § 24-4.5-5-202
IA	5%	2% above the monthly average 10-year constant maturity interest rate of U.S. government notes and bonds as published by the federal reserve for the second month preceding the month during which maximum rates will be effective, rounded to the nearest 1/4% per year; any rate for amounts greater than $25,000	no special rate	weekly average of 1-year Constant Maturity Treasury Yield plus 2%	all interest and 8% of all unpaid principal forfeited to the state for the general fund of the state	legal rate, contract rate and corporate rate – § 535.2; judgment rate – §§ 535.3 and 668.13; civil penalty – § 535.5
KS	10%	15% unless UCCC provides otherwise; when residential mortgage loans, 1.5% plus 30 year fixed rate mortgage for federal home loan mortgage for the preceding month	no special rate	4% above federal discount rate	forfeit all interest in excess of maximum equivalent amount deductible from principal and lawful interest	legal rate – § 16-201; contract rate – § 16-207; corporate rate – none; judgment rate – § 16-204; civil penalty – § 16-205

KY	8%	either 19% or 4% plus the federal discount rate on 90-day commercial paper whichever is less on loans of $15,000 or less; others, any rate	no special rate	12%	forfeit all interest; recover twice interest paid within two years of transaction (i)	legal rate and contract rate – § 360.010; corporate rate – § 360.025; judgment rate – § 360.040; civil penalty – § 360.020
LA	12%	12%; 12% if secured by immovable property; any rate for business or commercial purpose loans except for adjustable rate loans (t) there are numerous inconsistencies in various parts of the code and many discrepancies result	no special rate	3¼% above the federal discount rate	forfeit all interest; recover interest within two years of payment	legal rate – R.S. 9:3503; contract rate – R.S. 9:3503 and 9:3504; corporate rate – R.S. 9:3509; judgment rate – R.S. 13.4202; civil penalty – R.S. 9:3501 and C.C. Art. 2924
ME	6%	noncommercial or consumer loans (excluding financial institutions loans secured by a first mortgage on real estate) subject to limitation of Maine UCCC	no special rate	contract or note rate or the 1-year U.S. Treasury bill rate plus 6%, whichever is greater	no provisions	legal rate – 9B § 432; contract rate – 9A §§ 2-601 and 2-401; corporate rate – none; judgment rate – 14 § 1602-C; civil penalty – none
MD	6%	8%; unlimited for business loans over $15,000 if not secured by residential real property or $75,000 if secured by residential real property. Any rate for residential mortgages	no special rate	contract rate or 10%	forfeit three times excess collected, or $500, whichever is greater	legal rate – CL § 12-102; contract rate – CL § 12-103; corporate rate – CL § 12-103; judgment rate – CJ §§ 11-106 and 11-107; civil penalty – CL § 12-114
MA	6%	any rate	no special rate, but any amount greater than 20% per annum constitutes criminal usury	12% on contractual obligations	court may void a criminally usurious loan contract	legal rate – Chap 140 § 1; civil penalty – Chap 271 § 49; contract and legal rate – Chap 231 §6C; judgment rate – Chap 107 § 3

INTEREST TABLE *(Continued)*

State	Legal Rate (a)	Contract Rate (b)	Contract Rate (c)	Judgment Rate	Civil Penalty (d)	State Citation
MI	5%	rate agreed to in writing not exceeding 7%; any rate on business loans by state or national banks, insurance carrier or finance subsidiary of manufacturing corp. not exceeding 25%; business loans by other entities 15%; any rate on realty-secured loans, federal or state regulated loans, land leases with tenant-owned improvements, loans or land contracts of $100,000 or over and secured by non-single-family residence realty	no special rate	12% or contract rate from date of complaint to date of judgment; 13% after judgment date	forfeit interest, pay court fees, costs, attorney's fees	legal rate – § 438.31; contract rate – § 438.5; corporate rate – § 438.61; judgment rate – § 438.7; civil penalty – § 438.32
MN	6%	8%; any rate agreed to in writing on loans or forbearances of $100,000 or more; loan for forbearance of $100,000 or less for business or agricultural purpose, and loan by bank or savings bank not more than 4.5% plus the discount rate on 90 day commercial paper in effect at the Federal Reserve Bank for Minnesota	no special rate	the secondary market yield of U.S. Treasury bills calculated on a bank discount basis on or before the 20th day of December of each year	contract void except as to bona fide purchaser; may recover twice the amount of interest within two years	legal rate and contract rate – §§ 334.01 and 334.011; corporate rate – § 302A.501; judgment rate – § 549.09(c); civil penalty – §§ 334.02, 334.03 and 334.011

State	Legal rate	Maximum contract rate	Corporate rate	Judgment rate	Penalty	Statutory references
MS	8%	not to exceed the greater of 10% or 5% plus the discount rate for the federal reserve in the district where the lender is located; cannot be exceeding greater of 10% or 5% plus the index of market yields of monthly 20 year constant maturity index of long-term U.S. government bond yields using the actuarial method for mortgage for residential land; if the principal balance exceeds $2,000, any rate agreed to		contract rate, or rate set in judgment	forfeit all interest for evasion of 6% interest paid law; interest paid may be recovered; forfeit all interest, principal and finance charges if the finance charge received exceeds the maximum amount authorized by law by more than 100%	legal rate, contract rate and corporate rate – § 75-17-1; judgment rate – § 75-17-7; civil penalty – § 75-17-3
MO	9%	a rate not to exceed the greater of 10%, or 3% plus the monthly index of long-term U.S. government bond yields for the second month preceding the month prior to the beginning of the calendar quarter; any rate for securities pledged as collateral, business loans of $5,000 or more, and loans of $5,000 or more secured by negotiable instruments	no special rate	9% (f)	all moneys paid in excess of the principal and legal rate of any loan plus court costs and attorney fees	legal rate – § 408.020; contract rate – §§ 408.030 and 408.35; corporate rate – § 408.035; judgment rate – § 408.040; civil penalty – § 408.050
MT	10%	the greater of 15% or 6 points over the prime rate of the major banks as published in *The Wall Street Journal* three days prior to the agreement	no special rate	10% or the amount specified in the contract	forfeit double interest charged, recoverable within two years after payment	legal rate – § 31-1-106; contract rate – § 31-1-107; corporate rate – none; judgment rate – § 25-9-205; civil penalty – § 31-1-108

INTEREST TABLE (Continued)

State	Legal Rate (a)	Contract Rate (b)	Contract Rate (c)	Judgment Rate	Civil Penalty (d)	State Citation
NE	6%	16% per annum; maximum does not apply to loans made to any corporation, partnership or trust, guarantor or surety of corporate loans, loans of $25,000 or more, federal insured loans, loans repayable on demand made solely with securities as collateral, with loan used only for the purchase of securities and certain agricultural loans the maximum rates do not apply to business or agricultural loans or loans secured by real estate when made by a federally or state chartered bank or savings and loan association. Consumer interest rates cannot exceed 1⅓% per month	no special rate	2% plus bond investment yield of average accepted auction price for first auction of each annual quarter of 26-week U.S. Treasury bills in effect on the day of the judgment	forfeit all interest and costs	legal rate – § 45-102; contract rate and corporate rate – §§ 45-101.03 and 45-101.04; judgment rate – § 45-103; civil penalty – § 45-105
NV	2% above the current prime rate of the largest bank of NV	any rate agreed on in writing	no special rate	2% above the current prime rate of the largest bank of NV, or contract rate	the Nevada Supreme Court has stated that Nevada has no statute regarding usurious interest rates (812 P.2d 1274)	legal rate – § 99.040; contract rate – § 99.050; corporate rate – none; judgment rate – § 17.130; civil penalty – none

	Legal rate	Contract rate	Judgment rate	Penalty for usury	Citations
NH	10%	any rate agreed on in writing	determined by the State Treasurer as the prevailing discount rate of interest on 26-week UST-bills at the last auction preceding the last day of September in each year, plus 2% rounded to the nearest 10th of a percentage point, effective from January 1 of the following year through December 31 in each year	no special rate	no statutory provision	legal rate, contract rate and judgment rate – § 336.1; corporate rate – none; civil penalty – none
NJ	6%	where there is a written contract, the maximum rate is 16%. Separate regulations apply to certain types of multiple dwelling units on real estate. For loans of $50,000 or more may be at any rate. For consumer loans under $50,000, whatever rate agreed upon	no statutory provision	no special rate	forfeit all interest and costs, but corporations, limited liability companies, and limited liability partnerships may not assert the defense of usury	legal rate, contract rate, corporate rate and judgment rate – §§ 31:1-1 and 17:11C-32; civil penalty – § 31:1-3
NM	15%	as agreed by parties in writing	8.75% (f) the court has the discretion to raise the rate of interest on judgments to 10% under certain circumstances, and up to 15% if bad faith is involved	no special rate	forfeit all interest; recover double interest within two years of time of transaction (i)	legal rate and contract rate – § 56-8-3; corporate rate – § 56-8-9; judgment rate – § 56-8-4; civil penalty – § 56-8-13

INTEREST TABLE *(Continued)*

State	Legal Rate (a)	Contract Rate (b)	Contract Rate (c)	Judgment Rate	Civil Penalty (d)	State Citation
NY	16%	16% (generally same as legal rate); no limit on loans over $2.5 million	no special rate	9% or the contract rate specified until the judgment is paid	contract void and unenforceable, recover excess over lawful rate	legal rate, contract rate and corporate rate – § 5-501; judgment rate – CPLR § 5004; civil penalty – § 5-511
NC	8%	greater of 16% or noncompetitive rate for U.S. treasury bills with a six month maturity plus 6% rounded off by .5% as of the 15th day of each month for contracts less than $25,000; any rate agreed by parties where greater than $25,000; no limit on first mortgage	any rate agreed to	8% or the contract rate	forfeit all interest; recover double interest paid	legal rate – § 24-1; contract rate – § 24-1.1; corporate rate – § 24-9; judgment rate – § 24-5; civil penalty – § 24-2
ND	6%	where the parties agree in writing, interest may be charged at a rate up to 5½% higher than the then current six-month Treasury bills in effect for the six months prior to the transaction. The limitation cannot fall below 7%. Does not apply to loans in excess of $35,000	no special rate	based upon the rates stated in the instrument on which the action is based, but not over the maximum contract rate. If there is no agreement, the judgment rate is 12%, which may not be compounded	forfeit all interest and 25% of principal or double interest paid applied on principal; recover double plus 25% of principal within four years or offset against any indebtedness (i)	legal rate – § 47-14-05; contract rate and corporate rate – § 47-14-09; judgment rate – § 28-20-34; civil penalty – § 47-14-10 consumer loans – § 13-03.1-15

	Legal rate	Rate description		Penalty rate	Usury penalty	Citations
OH	10%	8%; any rate on loans over $100,000; any rate for business loans or for demand notes secured by stocks or bonds if made by registered securities dealer, or secured by certain real estate	no special rate	10% or the contract rate	excess applied to principal	legal rate – § 1343.03; contract rate – § 1343.01; corporate rate – § 1343.01; judgment rate – §§ 1343.02 and 1343.03; civil penalty – § 1343.04 small loans – §§ 1321.13 and 1321.13.1
OK	6%	any rate agreed to; special rates as determined by UCCC; generally no limit on nonconsumer or consumer related loans (e.g... loans in excess of $25,000 are nonconsumer loans)	no special rate	4% over the Treasury bill rate for the prior calendar year, unless the contact specifies a rate of interest in which case the contract will apply	greater of excess interest charged or 10 times excess of refund refused within reasonable time after demand Uniform Consumer Credit Code applies	legal rate – Title 15 §§ 265 and 266; contract rate – Title 15 § 266; corporate rate – Title 15 § 266; judgment rate – Title 12 § 727; civil penalty – Constitution Article 14 § 3
OR	9%	for loans of $50,000 or less, 12% or 5% above the discount rate on 90-day commercial paper rates of the Federal Reserve bank	no special rate	9% (f)	forfeit all interest	legal rate, contract rate, judgment rate and civil penalty – §§ 82.010 and 82.025; corporate rate – none
PA	6% to $50,000	2.5% plus the monthly index of long-term U.S. government bond yields for the second month preceding the calendar month rounded to the nearest ¼% for residential loans; no rate for loans over $50,000, secured principal amount of $50,000 or less secured by realty other than residential, corporate loans over $35,000 and business loans over $10,000	no special rate	6%	forfeit excess over lawful rate; recover three times excess of lawful rate in action brought within four years; excess applied to principal	legal rate – Title 41 § 202; contract rate and corporate rate – Title 41 § 301; judgment rate – Title 42 § 8101; civil penalty – Title 41 §§ 501 and 502

INTEREST TABLE (Continued)

State	Legal Rate (a)	Contract Rate (b)	Contract Rate (c)	Judgment Rate	Civil Penalty (d)	State Citation
PR	6%	9% up to $3,000; over $3,000, 8%. Special rates for mortgages connected to the FHLMC	no special rate	17% over average New York prime rate; special rates for government offices	forfeits all interest; 25% of principal to Commonwealth; recover excess after one year of payment	all – Title 10 § 998
RI	12%	21% or alternate rate of 9% above index on Treasury bills of less than one-year maturity whichever is greater; any rate for loans greater than $1,000,000	no special rate	12%	recover payments; contract void (i)	legal rate and judgment rate – § 6-26-1; contract rate and corporate rate – § 6-26-2; civil penalty – § 6-26-4
SC	6% or 8¾% when term "legal rate" or "lawful rate" used in contract	6% or any rate agreed to in writing	no special rate	12% (f)	forfeit all interest plus costs; recover double interest paid	legal rate – §§ 34-31-20 and 37-10-106; contract rate – §§ 34-29-140 and 37-10-106; corporate rate – none; judgment rate – § 34-31-20; civil penalty – § 37-10-105
SD	12%	any rate unless specifically limited by Code	no special rate	10%	no statutory provision	legal rate – §§ 54-3-4 and 54-3-16(A); contract rate and corporate rate – § 54-3-1.1; judgment rate – §§ 54-3-5.1 and 54-3-16; civil penalty – formerly § 54-3-12 (repealed)
TN	10%	on loans in excess of $100 the maximum rate is 24%. A separate rate applies to home loans. Agreements for variable rates of interest are permitted	no special rate	10% or the rate listed in the contract as long as it is not above the legal contract rate	recover excess over lawful rate within three years (i)	legal rate – §§ 47-14-102 and 47-14-103; contract rate – §§ 47-14-106 and 47-14-103; corporate rate – none; judgment rate – § 47-14-121; civil penalty – §§ 47-14-110, 47-14-111 and 47-14-118

State					
TX	6%	for commercial transactions, up to 1½% per month on obligations with the original principal of $5,000 or more. Additionally, a corporation may agree to pay any rate of interest that does not exceed the 26-week Treasury bill rate. The maximum rate for loans in excess of $250,000 is 28%	18% if loan is greater than $5,000	18% or rate specified in contract, whichever is less; if no contract then rate is based on discount rate for 52-week Treasury bills but not less than 10% nor more than 20%	forfeit triple amount of interest charges plus attorney's fees; amount forfeited may not be less than $2,000 or 20% of the principal, whichever is less; forfeit principal and interest if the interest is double the lawful rate; recoverable within four years of payment	legal rate – §§ 5069-1.02 and 5069-1.08; contract rate – § 5069-1.04; corporate rate – § 1302-209; judgment rate – § 5069-1.05; civil penalty – § 5069-1.06 **Texas law is extremely confusing and somewhat inconsistent. Careful attention must be paid to every provision of the Texas law dealing with interest rates**
UT	10%	agreed rate	no special rate	rate listed in the contract, or if not, rate is agreed upon, the federal post judgment interest rate (28 U.S.C. § 1961) plus 2%	no statutory provision	legal rate and contract rate – § 15-1-1; corporate rate – none; judgment rate – § 15-1-4; civil penalty – none
VT	12%	12% except as provided by law; certain types of loans may not exceed 18%	no special rate	12%	for contracts, forfeit all interest and 50% of principal; recover excess paid with interest from date of payment plus costs and fees (i)	legal rate and contract rate – Title 9 § 41(a); corporate rate – Title 9 § 46; judgment rate – none; civil penalty – Title 9 § 50
VA	6%	12%	no special rate	6% or the legal rate in the contract, whichever is higher	forfeit all interest; recover two times total interest paid within two years of transaction	legal rate – § 6.1-330.53; contract rate – § 6.1-330.55; corporate rate – § 6.1-330.76; judgment rate – § 6.1-330.54; civil penalty – § 6.1-330.57

INTEREST TABLE (Continued)

State	Legal Rate (a)	Contract Rate (b)	Contract Rate (c)	Judgment Rate	Civil Penalty (d)	State Citation
WA	12%	12% or 4% above the yield for 26 week treasury bills, whichever is higher. Treasury bills are measured at the first bill auction during the calendar month preceding the later of the establishment of a rate by written agreement of the parties or any adjustment in the rate	no special rate	12%; legal or contract rate, whichever is higher	forfeit all interest; deduct from principal twice interest where paid plus all accrued and unpaid interest, costs, attorney's fees, and amount by which contract exceeds adjusted liability	legal rate – § 19.52.010; contract rate – § 19.52.020; corporate rate – § 19.52.030; judgment rate – § 4.56.110; civil penalty – § 19.52.030
WV	6%	8%	no special rate	10%	all interest void; recover four times all interest agreed to be paid, minimum $100; recover payment over unlawful rate	legal rate and contract rate – § 47-6-5 (non pre-computed loans – § 47-6-5b); corporate rate – none; judgment rate – § 56-6-31; civil penalty – § 47-6-6
WI	5%	12% except in specifically delineated circumstances. See statute	no special rate	12%	forfeit all interest and principal up to $2000	legal rate – § 138.04; contract rate and corporate rate – § 138.05; judgment rate – §§ 138.03 and 806.38; civil penalty – § 138.06
WY	7%	10% except in specifically designated circumstances and exceptions	no special rate	10% or agreed legal contract rate	greater of excess interest charged or 10 times excess of refund refused within reasonable time after demand Uniform Consumer Credit Code applies	legal rate – § 40-14-106; contract rate – §§ 40-14-304 and 40-14-310; corporate rate – none; judgment rate – §§ 1.16-102 and 40-14-106; civil penalty – § 40-14-52(l)

(a) Maximum rate permitted by state law absent any agreement to the contrary.

(b) Maximum rate that can be charged individuals by agreement.

(c) Rate which may be charged to corporations is controlled by contract rate. "No special rate" means that corporation is controlled by contract rate. "No limit" means that corporations can be charged any rate of interest.

(d) Excludes criminal penalties and multiple damages.

(e) Special statute controls consumer transactions.

(f) Unless otherwise provided, up to maximum contract rate permitted by law and provided for in contract.

(g) Special statutory provisions concerning maximum interest on loans by personal property brokers and industrial lenders, and premiums for mortgage loans.

(h) Maximum rate does not apply to loans by Conn. banks, trust companies, or private bankers, or to any real estate mortgage loan in excess of $5,000 or to any loan carrying an interest rate of not more than 18% made to any corp. engaged primarily in commercial, manufacturing, or industrial pursuits provided original indebtedness is in excess of $10,000, or to any one advance of less than $10,000 made pursuant to revolving loan agreement, provided all loans to borrower are in excess of $10,000.

(i) Violator deemed guilty of misdemeanor.

(j) Florida's contract and corporate rates do not apply to loans or other advances of credit insured by FHA, guaranteed by VA, or made by a financial institution at the time of originating loan to FNMA, GNMA, or FHLMC or its successor, pursuant to act of Congress or federal regulation.

(k) Does not include loans by state and national banks, or such chartered savings and loans, credit unions, pawnbrokers, and interest charges by reg. brk.-dlrs. and lenders approved by the NHA. Loans sec. by a first lien on real property, or insured by FHA, VA, or Farmers Home Administration are also not subject to these rates.

(l) Vermont statute provides that lender shall make no charges to the borrower for the use or forbearance of money other than reasonable cost of credit investigation and appraisal fees, cost of title evidence, cost of protection against insurable hazards, cost of creditor life or disability insurance, filing fees, reasonable value of services rendered in connection with loans of $2,000 or less subject to limitations as determined by the Commissioner of Banking, reasonable cost of private mortgage guarantee insurance subject to limitations of the Commissioner of Banking.

(m) Judgment bears interest at contract rate not in excess of 12%; if not founded on contract then interest is 10%.

(n) All interest void; in addition, from original lender or creditor, amount equal to four times all interest or minimum of $100.

(o) Wisconsin law requires certain contract provisions and disclosure relating to use of interest adjustment clauses and variable rate contracts in connection with certain first lien residential mortgage loans. Penalty for intentional violation is liability to borrower for all excess interest collected, plus interest thereon at 5%. Borrower may also recover damages.

(p) Defense of usury not available for loans of $5,000 and more for business purposes secured by second mortgages.

(q) New York permits a variable interest rate not in excess of the maximum rate permitted at the time the loan of forebearance is made on demand loans which have an initial principal of more than $5,000 and which the borrower has the right to repay at any time without penalty.

(r) A judgment on a contract for the loan of money shall earn the contract rate of interest upon the unpaid principal until maturity.

(s) A financial institution may, on a loan secured by a savings or time account, charge interest 2% above the interest payable on the account.

(t) No limit on mortgages on immovable property which are guaranteed by the VA or insured by the FHA. It is sufficient if the mortgage was eligible to be so guaranteed or insured but the application was denied for reasons other than the rate of interest.

(u) Alternative rate on loans, lease or sales—2% above prime rate.

(v) If a judgment in a civil case is appealed by judgment debtor and judgment affirmed, rate of interest is 2% above discount rate. As of 1/1/83, rate is 11%.

VALIDITY OF JUDGMENT NOTES AND STIPULATION
FOR ATTORNEY'S FEE

	VALIDITY OF JUDGMENT NOTES	PROVISION FOR ATTORNEY'S FEE
ALABAMA	Judgment notes are void. Foreign judgment notes if they are valid in that state will be enforced.	Enforceable.
ALASKA	Judgment notes not authorized by statute.	No statutory provisions.
ARIZONA	No provision.	Enforceable.
ARKANSAS	Judgment notes are not permitted. Will give full faith and credit to foreign note executed in a state where such notes are valid.	Enforceable.
CALIFORNIA	No provision. Foreign judgment on a judgment note made in California but payable in the foreign jurisdiction where such notes are valid is enforceable.	Enforceable.
COLORADO	Judgment notes are recognized but strictly construed against parties in whose favor they are made. Foreign judgment note enforceable if recognized in that state.	Enforceable; provision in consumer credit sales (including instalment sale of a motor vehicle) consumer leases and consumer loans valid up to 15% of amount due.
CONNECTICUT	Judgment notes are authorized.	Enforceable to the extent of reasonable compensation determined by court; instalment contract provision valid up to 15% of amount due.
DELAWARE	Judgment notes are authorized.	No statutory provisions.
DISTRICT OF COLUMBIA	Judgment notes not recognized.	Enforceable for reasonable amount.
FLORIDA	Judgment notes not recognized. Foreign notes are enforceable if they are recognized in that state.	Enforceable where note is turned over to attorney for collection after maturity. Reasonableness of amount within discretion of court.
GEORGIA	No provision.	Void and unenforceable unless defendant is given written notice of intention to bring suit 10 days prior thereto and defendant fails to pay obligation on or before return day of the court in which the suit is filed.

VALIDITY OF JUDGMENT NOTES AND STIPULATION
FOR ATTORNEY'S FEE *(Continued)*

	VALIDITY OF JUDGMENT NOTES	PROVISION FOR ATTORNEY'S FEE
HAWAII	Judgment notes are not recognized.	In district or circuit court, where 25% fee or more is specified, 25% fee is enforceable; less than 25%, then specified fee is allowable; however, fee is not to exceed $250 in district court nor what is deemed reasonable by court.
IDAHO	No provision.	No provision.
ILLINOIS	Judgment notes are recognized by statute.	Enforceable.
INDIANA	Void.	If payment is contingent upon condition set forth in a note the provision is void; otherwise enforceable.
IOWA	No provision. Foreign judgment on a judgment note, executed and made payable in the foreign jurisdiction, is enforceable.	Enforceable but limited to 10% on first $200; 5% on $200 to $500; 3% on $500 to $1,000; 1% on excess.
KANSAS	No statutory provisions. Foreign judgment on a judgment note, executed and made payable in the foreign jurisdiction, is enforceable.	Enforceable in notes, drafts, bonds, or mortgages. Unenforceable in consumer credit transactions.
KENTUCKY	Judgment notes are void. Foreign judgment on a judgment note, executed and made payable in the foreign jurisdiction, is enforceable.	Invalid and unenforceable except in a motor vehicle retail installment contract where an attorney's fee of 15% of amount due is valid.
LOUISIANA	Judgment notes are not recognized.	Enforceable.
MAINE	No statutory provisions.	Valid.
MARYLAND	Judgment notes are recognized.	Enforceable.
MASSACHUSETTS	Judgment notes are void.	Enforceable.
MICHIGAN	Judgment notes are not recognized.	Enforceable.
MINNESOTA	Judgment notes are not recognized. Foreign judgment on a judgment note, executed and made payable in the foreign jurisdiction, is enforceable.	Enforceable. A motor vehicle retail installment contract may provide for payment of attorneys' fees not to exceed 15%.

VALIDITY OF JUDGMENT NOTES AND STIPULATION
FOR ATTORNEY'S FEE *(Continued)*

	VALIDITY OF JUDGMENT NOTES	PROVISION FOR ATTORNEY'S FEE
MISSISSIPPI	Judgment notes are prohibited.	Enforceable. A motor vehicle retail installment contract may provide for payment of attorneys' fees not to exceed 15%.
MISSOURI	Judgment notes are against public policy, but not invalid.	Enforceable.
MONTANA	Judgment notes are not recognized by statute. Mont. Code Ann. § 28-2-709.	Enforceable.
NEBRASKA	No provision. Foreign judgment on a judgment note, executed and made payable in the foreign jurisdiction, is enforceable.	Void.
NEVADA	No statutory provisions.	Enforceable only in retail installment sales contract and only for reasonable costs in the event of delinquency.
NEW HAMPSHIRE	Judgment notes are recognized by implication. N.H. Rev. Stat. Ann. 382A:3-104(a)(3).	Valid in motor vehicle time sales contract only if provision is for a reasonable fee.
NEW JERSEY	Judgment notes are not recognized unless in a separate instrument. Foreign judgment on a judgment note, executed and made payable in the foreign jurisdiction, is enforceable. N.J. Rev. Stat. § 2A: 16-9; N.J. Court Rules 4:45-2	Valid. Also, the Retail Instalment Statute permits a retail installment contract, or a retail charge account to provide for attorney's fee not to exceed 20% of the first $500 and 10% on any excess. *See Alcoa Edgewater No. 1 Federal Credit Union v. Carroll,* 210 A.2d 68 (1965).
NEW MEXICO	Judgment notes are prohibited by statute. It is a misdemeanor to procure another to make, indorse, or assign a cognovit note or to accept such note. Foreign: unenforceable.	Enforceable. *See Edwards v. Mesch,* 763 P.2d 1169 (1988).
NEW YORK	No statutory provisions. Judgment notes may be recognized under case law.	Enforceable. N.Y. UCC 3-106. (Old Code; NY has not adopted Revised Art. 3.) On retail installment contract on a motor vehicle may provide up to a 15% attorney's fee on the amount due; for other goods, up to 20%. On commercial contracts, up to 25% has been allowed.

VALIDITY OF JUDGMENT NOTES AND STIPULATION
FOR ATTORNEY'S FEE *(Continued)*

	VALIDITY OF JUDGMENT NOTES	PROVISION FOR ATTORNEY'S FEE
NORTH CAROLINA	Judgment notes are not recognized.	Enforceable by statute up to 15% of outstanding balance.
NORTH DAKOTA	Judgment notes are not recognized.	Void.
OHIO	Judgment notes are recognized. On a consumer transaction or loan, judgment notes are not enforceable. On all other instruments, judgment notes are enforceable only if they provide notice of loss of rights by a conspicuous warning on the document. *See Vannoy v. Capital Lincoln-Mercury Sales Inc.,* 623 N.E. 2d 177 (1993).	Void.
OKLAHOMA	Judgment notes recognized.	Enforceable.
OREGON	Judgment notes are not recognized.	Enforceable by either party to contract. *See Taylor v. McCollom,* 958 P.2d 207 (1998).
PENNSYLVANIA	No statutory provision	Enforceable. *See Wrenfield Homeowners Assn., Inc. v. DeYoung,* 600 A.2d 960 (1991).
PUERTO RICO	Judgment notes are of doubtful validity.	Enforceable.
RHODE ISLAND	No statutory provision for judgment notes.	Enforceable. *See Stewart v. Industrial Nat'l Bank of Rhode Island,* 458 A.2d 675 (1983).
SOUTH CAROLINA	Judgment notes are not recognized.	Reasonable fees enforceable. *See The South Carolina National Bank v. S&L Investment Partnership,* 419 S.E. 2D 243 (1992).
SOUTH DAKOTA	Judgment notes are not recognized.	Void. Not generally enforceable, except in mortgage foreclosure actions. S.D. Code §§ 21-48-15, 21-49-23.
TENNESSEE	Judgment notes are forbidden.	Enforceable. *See Young v. Jones,* 255 S.W. 2d 703 (1952).
TEXAS	Judgment notes are forbidden.	Enforceable. *See F.R. Hernandez Constr. & Supply Co., Inc. v. National Bank of Commerce of Brownsville,* 578 S.W. 2d 675 (1975).

VALIDITY OF JUDGMENT NOTES AND STIPULATION
FOR ATTORNEY'S FEE *(Continued)*

	VALIDITY OF JUDGMENT NOTES	PROVISION FOR ATTORNEY'S FEE
UTAH	Judgment notes are recognized.	Enforceable.
VERMONT	Judgment notes are not recognized.	Enforceable; however, enforcement has been refused by Vermont Supreme Court in a case involving a note with a 10% attorney's fee provision. The court concluded that "something must more be shown than the mere agreement."
VIRGINIA	Judgment notes are recognized if the warrant to confess judgment in the note names the attorney who will confess judgment in the court in which it will be made and debtor is notified of the confession of judgment against him; may be set aside within 21 days after notice of entry on any valid defense to an action on the note. Va. Code Ann. § 8.01-432.	Enforceable. *See Schwab v. Norris,* 231 S.E. 2d 222 (1977).
WASHINGTON	Judgment notes are recognized.	Enforceable. Wash. Rev. Code Ann. § 4.84.330.
WEST VIRGINIA	Judgment notes are not recognized. Foreign judgment on a judgment note, executed and made payable in the foreign jurisdiction, is enforceable.	Unenforceable.
WISCONSIN	Judgment notes are void and unenforceable. Foreign judgment on a judgment note, executed and made payable in the foreign jurisdiction, is enforceable.	Enforceable, other than transactions under the Wisconsin Consumer Act. Wis. Stat. Ann. § 422.411.
WYOMING	Judgment notes are recognized by implication.	In foreclosure or public advertisement sale cannot add a fee provided in a mortgage or note securing it unless it appears in affidavit of attorney representing mortgagee.

Sales Tax Institute:
Sales and Use Tax Rates
As of 10/31/2005

The following chart lists the standard state level sales and use tax rates. Many states allow non-standard rates on many items including meals, lodging, telecommunications and specific items and services. These rates are not represented in this chart. The range of local taxes is also included as a quick reference. This can be used to determine the combined state and local tax rate maximums and minimums. However, for accurate tax calculation, the specific jurisdiction tax rate should be used. The information concerning local use tax rates can be used to determine whether the use tax also applies to local taxes. If this column contains a "YES," then local taxes apply to both intra-state and inter-state transactions. If this column contains a "NO", then local taxes only apply to intra-state transactions. Please refer to the footnotes, as they are an integral part of this chart. Sales and use tax rates change on a monthly basis, for an updated chart, please visit our webpage at http://www.salestax nstitute.com/sales_tax_rates.jsp. This chart is for informational purposes only. Specific questions should be addressed to your tax advisor. Rate information is gathered from various State Department of Revenue materials and Vertex, Inc.

State	State Rate	Range of Local Rates	Local Rates Apply To Use Tax
Alabama	4.000%	0%–8% (7)	Yes/No (1)
Alaska	0.000%	0%–7% (4), (7)	Yes/No (1)
Arizona	5.600%	0%–4.50% (4), (7)	Yes/No (2)
Arkansas	6.000%	0%–5.50% (4), (7)	Yes
California	6.250%	1.00%–2.5%	Yes
Colorado	2.900%	0%–7% (7)	Yes/No (1)
Connecticut	6.000% (10)	0%	N/A
Delaware	0.000% (3)	0%	N/A
District of Columbia	5.750%	0%	N/A
Florida	6.000% (10)	0%–1.50% (4), (7)	Yes
Georgia	4.000% (10)	1%–3%	Yes
Hawaii	4.000% (5), (10)	0%	N/A
Idaho	6.000%	0%–3% (7)	No
Illinois	6.250% (10)	0%–3.00% (7)	No
Indiana	6.000%	0%	N/A
Iowa	5.000%	0%–2% (7)	No
Kansas	5.300% (10)	0%–3% (7)	Yes
Kentucky	6.000%	0%	N/A
Louisiana	4.000% (10)	0%–6.75% (6) (7)	Yes
Maine	5.000% (10)	0%	N/A
Maryland	5.000%	0%	N/A
Massachusetts	5.000%	0%	N/A
Michigan	6.000% (10)	0%	N/A
Minnesota	6.500% (10)	0%–1% (7)	Yes

(continued)

State	State Rate	Range of Local Rates	Local Rates Apply To Use Tax
Mississippi	7.000% (10)	0%–.25% (7)	No
Missouri	4.225%	.5%–4.375%	Yes/No (1)
Montana	0.000%	0%	N/A
Nebraska	5.50%	0%–1.5% (7)	Yes
Nevada	6.500%	0%–1%	Yes
New Hampshire	0.000%	0%	N/A
New Jersey	6.000% (8)	0%	N/A
New Mexico	5.000% (9)	.125%–2.813%	No
New York	4.00%	0%–4.625%	Yes
North Carolina	4.500% (10)	2%–3%	Yes
North Dakota	5.000% (10)	0%–2.50% (4), (7)	Yes
Ohio	5.500%	.25%–2%	Yes
Oklahoma	4.500%	0%–6% (7)	Yes/No (1)
Oregon	0.000%	0%	N/A
Pennsylvania	6.000%	0%–1% (7)	No
Rhode Island	7.000%	0%	N/A
South Carolina	5.000% (10)	0%–2% (7)	Yes
South Dakota	4.000% (10), (11)	0%–2% (7)	Yes
Tennessee	7.000% (10)	1.5%–2.75% (4)	Yes
Texas	6.250%	0%–2% (7)	Yes
Utah	4.750% (10)	1%–3.25%	Yes
Vermont	6.000% (10)	0%–1% (7)	No
Virginia	4.000% (10)	1%	Yes
Washington	6.500%	.5%–2.40%	Yes
West Virginia	6.000%	0%	N/A
Wisconsin	5.000%	0%–1% (7)	Yes/No (1)
Wyoming	4.000% (10)	0%–2% (7)	Yes

1. Some of the cities and counties do apply use tax.

2. Some of the cities do apply use tax. The counties do not apply a use tax.

3. Delaware does not have a sales tax. They do have a rental tax of 1.92%.

4. A cap on the local sales/use tax applies on sales of any item of tangible personal property.

5. There is a .500% use tax on merchandise imported into the state for resale purposes. Imports for consumption are taxed at the same rate as the sales tax.

6. The combined local rates for a particular city range from 1.8% to 6.75%.

7. Some local jurisdictions do not impose a sales tax.

8. Effective 7/1/94, sales occurring in Salem County will be taxed at the reduced state sales tax rate of 3%.

9. The basic state gross receipts tax rate is 5%. The law provides for an automatic credit of up to .5% for municipally imposed gross receipts taxes. The credit is incorporated in the combined tax rate.

10. The state has reduced rates for sales of certain types of items.

11. Sales and deliveries to certain Indian reservations are subject to the Tribal sales, use and excise taxes in lieu of the state sales, use and excise tax. City sales tax may still apply.

12. The Nevada Minimum Statewide Tax rate of 6.5% consists of several taxes combined: Two state taxes apply — 2.00% Sales Tax and the 2.25% Local School Support Tax which equal the state rate of 4.25%. Two county taxes also apply — 0.50% Basic City-County Relief Tax and 1.75% Supplemental City-County Relief Tax equals an additional city/county rate of 2.25% for a total of 6.5%. Previously, the matrix displayed only these rates state level taxes. However, since the two county taxes apply to every county in the state, Nevada's minimum statewide tax rate is considered to be 6.5%.

Appendix C

Selected Text of the Uniform Commercial Code

The text in this appendix has been reproduced from various states' officially adopted versions of the UCC laws and may differ slightly from section numbers referred to in the rest of this manual. The reader should consult their own state's adopted versions for specific questions about their state's law. The official UCC text can be obtained from the NCCUSL (www.nccusl.org).

UNIFORM COMMERCIAL CODE

The Uniform Commercial Code plays such an important role in the everyday transactions handled by the credit executive that the actual text of many portions of the UCC are included in this book. It is imperative that the credit executive realize each state has the ability to add provisions to the UCC or adopt, delete and revise sections of the UCC as a particular state may find the need to do so exists. Except for Article 6, the statute covering Bulk Transfers, no references to specific state variances to the uniform statute will be included within this chapter. Further, the text included herein is not the entire Uniform Commercial Code. The complete text of the Uniform Commercial Code is available in print form and online. Most importantly, the complete local statute for any particular jurisdiction should be consulted by a credit executive to determine the local variations of moderate or substantive importance.

ARTICLE 1: GENERAL PROVISIONS

Part 1: Short Title, Construction, Application, and Subject Matter of the Act

Section 1-101. *Short Title*—This Act shall be known and may be cited as Uniform Commercial Code.

Section 1-102. *Purposes; Rules of Construction; Variation by Agreement*—(1) This Act shall be liberally construed and applied to promote its underlying purposes and policies.
(2) Underlying purposes and policies of this Act are
(a) to simplify, clarify and modernize the law governing commercial transactions;
(b) to permit the continued expansion of commercial practices through custom, usage and agreement of the parties; and
(c) to make uniform the law among the various jurisdictions.
(3) The effect of provisions of this Act may be varied by agreement, except as otherwise provided in this Act and except that the obligations of good faith, diligence, reasonableness and care prescribed by this Act may not be disclaimed by agreement but the parties may by agreement determine the standards by which the performance of such obligations is to be measured if such standards are not manifestly unreasonable.
(4) The presence in certain provisions of this Act of the words "unless otherwise agreed" or words of similar import does not imply that the effect of other provisions may not be varied by agreement under subsection (3).
(5) In this Act, unless the context otherwise requires
(a) words in the singular number include the plural, and in the plural include the singular;

(b) words of the masculine gender include the feminine and the neuter, and when the sense so indicates words of the neuter gender may refer to any gender.

Section 1-103. *Supplementary General Principles of Law Applicable*—Unless displaced by the particular provisions of this Act, the principles of law and equity, including the law merchant and the law relative to capacity to contract, principal and agent, estoppel fraud, misrepresentation, duress, coercion, mistake, bankruptcy, or other validating or invalidating cause shall supplement its provisions.

Section 1-104. *Construction against Implicit Repeal*—This Act being a general act intended as a unified coverage of its subject matter, no part of it shall be deemed to be impliedly repealed by subsequent legislation if such construction can reasonably be avoided.

Section 1-105. *Territorial Application of the Act; Parties' Power to Choose Applicable Law*—(1) Except as provided hereafter in this section, when a transaction bears a reasonable relation to this state and also to another state or nation the parties may agree that the law either of this state or of such other state or nation shall govern their rights and duties. Failing such agreement this Act applies to transactions bearing an appropriate relation to this state.

(2) Where one of the following provisions of this Act specifies the applicable law, that provision governs and a contrary agreement is effective only to the extent permitted by the law (including the conflict of law rules) so specified:

Rights of creditors against sold goods. Section 2-402.

Applicability of the Article on Leases. Sections 2A-105 and 2A-106.

Applicability of the Article on Bank Deposits and Collections. Section 4-102.

Governing law in the Article on Funds Transfers. Section 4A-507.

Bulk transfers subject to the Article on Bulk Transfers. Section 6-103.

[**Note:** *If a state adopts the repealer of Article 6 Bulk Transfers (Alternative A), there should not be any item relating to bulk transfers. If, however, a state adopts Revised Article 6-Bulk Sales (Alternative B), then this line relating to bulk sales should be included.*]

Applicability of the Article on Investment Securities. Section 8-106.

Perfection provisions of the Article on Secured Transactions. Sections 9-103.

Section 1-106. *Remedies to Be Liberally Administered*—(1) The remedies provided by this Act shall be liberally administered to the end that the aggrieved party may be put in as good a position as if the other party had fully performed but neither consequential or special nor penal damages may be had except as specifically provided in this Act or by other rule of law.

(2) Any right or obligation declared by this Act is enforceable by action unless the provision declaring it specifies a different and limited effect.

Section 1-107. *Waiver or Renunciation of Claim or Right after Breach*—Any claim or right arising out of an alleged breach can be discharged in whole or in part without consideration by a written waiver or renunciation signed and delivered by the aggrieved party.

Section 1-108. *Severability*—If any provision or clause of this Act or application thereof to any person or circumstances is held invalid, such invalidity shall not affect other provisions or applications of the Act which can be given effect without the invalid provision or application, and to this end the provisions of this Act are declared to be severable.

Section 1-109. *Section Captions*—Section captions are parts of this Act.

Part 2: General Definitions and Principles of Interpretation

Section 1-201. *General Definitions*—Subject to additional definitions contained in the subsequent Articles of this Act which are applicable to specific Articles or Parts thereof, and unless the context otherwise requires, in this Act

(1)   "Action" in the sense of a judicial proceeding includes recoupment, counterclaim, setoff, suit in equity and any other proceedings in which rights are determined.

(2)   "Aggrieved party" means a party entitled to resort to a remedy.

(3)   "Agreement" means the bargain of the parties in fact as found in their language or by implication from other circumstances including course of dealing or usage of trade or course of performance as provided in this Act (§§ 1-205 and 2-206). Whether an agreement has legal consequences is determined by the provisions of this Act, if applicable; otherwise by the law of contracts (§ 1-103). (Compare "Contract.")

(4)   "Bank" means any person engaged in the business of banking.

(5)   "Bearer" means the person in possession of an instrument, document of title, or certificated security payable to bearer or endorsed in blank.

(6)   "Bill of lading" means a document evidencing the receipt of goods for shipment issued by a person engaged in the business of transporting or forwarding goods, and includes an airbill. "Airbill" means a document serving for air transportation as a bill of lading does for marine or rail transportation, and includes an air consignment note or air waybill.

(7)   "Branch" includes a separately incorporated foreign branch of a bank.

(8)   "Burden of establishing" a fact means the burden of persuading the triers of fact that the existence of the fact is more probable than its nonexistence.

(9)   "Buyer in ordinary course of business" means a person who in good faith and without knowledge that the sale to him is in violation of the ownership rights or security interest of a third party in the goods buys in ordinary course from a person in the business of selling goods of that kind but does not include a pawnbroker. All persons who sell minerals or the like (including oil and gas) at wellhead or minehead shall be deemed to be persons in the business of selling goods of that kind. "Buying" may be for cash or by exchange of other property or on secured or unsecured credit and includes receiving goods or documents of title under a pre-existing contract for sale but does not include a transfer in bulk or as security for or in total or partial satisfaction of a money debt.

(10)   "Conspicuous": A term or clause is conspicuous when it is so written that a reasonable person against whom it is to operate ought to have noticed it. A printed heading in capitals (as: Nonnegotiable Bill of Lading) is conspicuous. Language in the body of a form is "conspicuous" if it is in larger or other contrasting type or color. But in a telegram any stated term is "conspicuous." Whether a term or clause is "conspicuous" or not is for decision by the court.

(11)   "Contract" means the total obligation in law which results from the parties' agreement as affected by this Act and any other applicable rules of law. (Compare "Agreement.")

(12)   "Creditor" includes a general creditor, a secured creditor, a lien creditor and any representative of creditors, including an assignee for the benefit of creditors, a trustee in bankruptcy, a receiver in equity and an executor or administrator of an insolvent debtor's or assignor's estate.

(13)   "Defendant" includes a person in the position of defendant in a cross-action or counterclaim.

(14)   "Delivery" with respect to instruments, documents of title, chattel paper or certificated securities means voluntary transfer of possession.

(15)   "Document of the title" includes bill of lading, dock warrant, dock receipt, warehouse receipt or order for the delivery of goods, and also any other document which in the regular course of business or financing is treated as adequately evidencing that the person in possession of it is entitled to receive, hold and dispose of the document and the goods it covers. To be a document of title a document must purport to be issued by or addressed to a bailee and purport to cover goods in the bailee's possession which are either identified or are fungible portions of an identified mass.

(16)   "Fault" means wrongful act, omission or breach.

(17)   "Fungible" with respect to goods or securities means goods or securities of which any unit is, by nature or usage of trade, the equivalent of any other like unit. Goods which are not fungible shall be deemed fungible for the purposes of this Act to the extent that under a particular agreement or document unlike units are treated as equivalents.

(18)   "Genuine" means free of forgery or counterfeiting.

(19) "Good faith" means honesty in fact in the conduct or transaction concerned.

(20) "Holder" with respect to a negotiable instrument, means the person in possession if the instrument is payable to bearer or, in the case of an instrument payable to an identified person, if the identified person is in possession. "Holder" with respect to a document of title means the person in possession if the goods are deliverable to bearer or to the order of the person in possession.

(21) To "honor" is to pay or to accept and pay, or where a credit so engages to purchase or discount a draft complying with the terms of the credit.

(22) "Insolvency proceedings" includes any assignment for the benefit of creditors or other proceedings intended to liquidate or rehabilitate the estate of the person involved.

(23) A person is "insolvent" who either has ceased to pay his debts in the ordinary course of business or cannot pay his debts as they become due or is insolvent within the meaning of the federal bankruptcy law.

(24) "Money" means a medium of exchange authorized or adopted by a domestic or foreign government and includes a monetary unit of account established by an intergovernmental organization or by agreement between two or more nations.

(25) A person has "notice" of a fact when

(a) he has actual knowledge of it; or

(b) he has received a notice or notification of it; or

(c) from all the facts and circumstances known to him at the time in question he has reason to know that it exists.

A person "knows" or has "knowledge" of a fact when he has actual knowledge of it. "Discover" or "learn" or a word or phrase of similar import refers to knowledge rather than to reason to know. The time and circumstances under which a notice or notification may cease to be effective are not determined by this Act.

(26) A person "notifies" or "gives" a notice or notification to another by taking such steps as may be reasonably required to inform the other in ordinary course whether or not such other actually comes to know of it. A person "receives" a notice or notification when

(a) it comes to his attention; or

(b) it is duly delivered at the place of business through which the contract was made or at any other place held out by him as the place for receipt of such communications.

(27) Notice, knowledge or a notice or notification received by an organization is effective for a particular transaction from the time when it is brought to the attention of the individual conducting that transaction, and in any event from the time when it would have been brought to his attention if the organization had exercised due diligence. An organization exercises due diligence if it maintains reasonable routines for communicating significant information to the person conducting the transaction and there is reasonable compliance with the routines. Due diligence does not require an individual acting for the organization to communicate information unless such communication is part of his regular duties or unless he has reason to know of the transaction and that the transaction would be materially affected by the information.

(28) "Organization" includes a corporation, government or governmental subdivision or agency, business trust, estate, trust, partnership or association, two or more persons having a joint or common interest, or any other legal or commercial entity.

(29) "Party," as distinct from "third party," means a person who has engaged in a transaction or made an agreement within this Act.

(30) "Person" includes an individual or an organization (*see* § 1-102).

(31) "Presumption" or "presumed" means that the trier of fact must find the existence of the fact presumed unless and until evidence is introduced which would support a finding of its nonexistence.

(32) "Purchase" includes taking by sale, discount, negotiation, mortgage, pledge, lien, issue or reissue, gift or any other voluntary transaction creating an interest in property.

(33) "Purchaser" means a person who takes by purchase.

(34) "Remedy" means any remedial right to which an aggrieved party is entitled with or without resort to a tribunal.

(35) "Representative" includes an agent, an officer of a corporation or association, and a trustee, executor or administrator of an estate, or any other person empowered to act for another.

(36) "Rights" includes remedies.

(37) "Security interest" means an interest in personal property or fixtures which secures payment or performance of an obligation. The retention or reservation of title by a seller of goods notwithstanding shipment or delivery to the buyer (§ 2401) is limited in effect to a reservation of a "security interest." The term also includes any interest of a buyer of accounts or chattel paper which is subject to Article 9. The special property interest of a buyer of goods on identification of those goods to a contract for sale under Section 2-401 is not a "security interest," but a buyer may also acquire a "security interest" by complying with Article 9. Unless a consignment is intended as security, reservation of title thereunder is not a "security interest" but a consignment is in any event subject to the provisions on consignment sales (§ 2-326).

Whether a transaction creates a lease or security interest is determined by the facts of each case; however, a transaction creates a security interest if the consideration the lessee is to pay the lessor for the right to possession and use of the goods is an obligation for the term of the lease not subject to termination by the lessee, and

(a) the original term of the lease is equal to or greater than the remaining economic life of the goods;

(b) the lessee is bound to renew the lease for the remaining economic life of the goods or is bound to become the owner of the goods;

(c) the lessee has an option to renew the lease for the remaining economic life of the goods for no additional consideration or nominal additional consideration upon compliance with the lease agreement; or

(d) the lessee has an option to become the owner of the goods for no additional consideration or nominal additional consideration upon compliance with the lease agreement.

A transaction does not create a security interest merely because it provides that

(a) the present value of the consideration the lessee is obligated to pay the lessor for the right to possession and use of the goods is substantially equal to or is greater than the fair market value of the goods at the time the lease is entered into;

(b) the lessee assumes risk of loss of the goods, or agrees to pay taxes, insurance, filing, recording, or registration fees, or service or maintenance costs with respect to the goods;

(c) the lessee has an option to renew the lease or to become the owner of the goods;

(d) the lessee has an option to renew the lease for a fixed rent that is equal to or greater than the reasonably predictable fair market rent for the use of the goods for the term of the renewal at the time the option is to be performed; or

(e) the lessee has an option to become the owner of the goods for a fixed price that is equal to or greater than the reasonably predictable fair market value of the goods at the time the option is to be performed.

For purposes of this subsection (37):

(x) Additional consideration is not nominal if (i) when the option to renew the lease is granted to the lessee the rent is stated to be the fair market rent for the use of the goods for the term of the renewal determined at the time the option is to be performed, or (ii) when the option to become the owner of the goods is granted to the lessee the price is stated to be the fair market value of the goods determined at the time the option is to be performed. Additional consideration is nominal if it is less than the lessee's reasonably predictable cost of performing under the lease agreement if the option is not exercised;

(y) "Reasonably predictable" and "remaining economic life of the goods" are to be determined with reference to the facts and circumstances at the time the transaction is entered into; and

(z) "Present Value" means the amount as of a date certain of one or more sums payable in the future, discounted to the date certain. The discount is determined by the interest rate specified by the parties if the rate is not manifestly unreasonable at the time the transaction is entered into; otherwise, the discount is determined by a commercially reasonable rate that takes into account the facts and circumstances of each case at the time the transaction was entered into.

(38) "Send" in connection with any writing or notice means to deposit in the mail or deliver for transmission by any other usual means of communication with postage or cost of transmission provided for and properly addressed and in the case of an instrument to an address specified thereon or otherwise agreed, or if there be none to any address reasonable under the circumstances. The receipt of any writing or notice within the time at which it would have arrived if properly sent has the effect of a proper sending.

(39) "Signed" includes any symbol executed or adopted by a party with present intention to authenticate a writing.

(40) "Surety" includes guarantor.

(41) "Telegram" includes a message transmitted by radio, teletype, cable, any mechanical method of transmission, or the like.

(42) "Term" means that portion of an agreement which relates to a particular matter.

(43) "Unauthorized" signature means one made without actual, implied or apparent authority and includes a forgery.

(44) "Value." Except as otherwise provided with respect to negotiable instruments and bank collections (§§ 3-303, 4-208 and 4-209), a person gives "value" for rights if he acquires them.

(a) in return for a binding commitment to extend credit or for the extension of immediately available credit whether or not drawn upon and whether or not a charge back is provided for in the event of difficulties in collection; or

(b) as security for or in total or partial satisfaction of a preexisting claim; or

(c) by accepting delivery pursuant to a preexisting contract for purchase; or

(d) generally, in return for any consideration sufficient to support a simple contract.

(45) "Warehouse receipt" means a receipt issued by a person engaged in the business of storing goods for hire.

(46) "Written" or "writing" includes printing, typewriting or any other intentional reduction to tangible form.

Section 1-202. *Prima Facie Evidence by Third Party Documents*—A document in due form purporting to be a bill of lading, policy or certificate of insurance, official weigher's or inspector's certificate, consular invoice, or any other document authorized or required by the contract to be issued by a third party shall be prima facie evidence of its own authenticity and genuineness and of the fact stated in the document by the third party.

Section 1-203. *Obligation of Good Faith*—Every contract or duty within this Act imposes an obligation of good faith in its performance or enforcement.

Section 1-204. *Time; Reasonable Time; "Seasonably"*—(1) Whenever this Act requires any action to be taken within a reasonable time, any time which is not manifestly unreasonable may be fixed by agreement.

(2) What is a reasonable time for taking any action depends on the nature, purpose and circumstances of such action.

(3) An action is taken "seasonably" when it is taken at or within the time agreed or if no time is agreed at or within a reasonable time.

Section 1-205. *Course of Dealing and Usage of Trade*—(1) A course of dealing is a sequence of previous conduct between the parties to a particular transaction which is fairly to be regarded as establishing a common basis of understanding for interpreting their expressions and other conduct.

(2) A usage of trade is any practice or method of dealing having such regularity of observance in a place, vocation or trade as to justify an expectation that it will be observed with

respect to the transaction in question. The existence and scope of such a usage are to be proved as facts. If it is established that such a usage is embodied in a written trade code or similar writing the interpretation of the writing is for the court.

(3)   A course of dealing between parties and any usage of trade in the vocation or trade in which they are engaged or of which they are or should be aware give particular meaning to and supplement or qualify terms of an agreement.

(4)   The express terms of an agreement and an applicable course of dealing or usage of trade shall be construed wherever reasonable as consistent with each other; but when such construction is unreasonable express terms control both course of dealing and usage of trade and course of dealing controls usage of trade.

(5)   An applicable usage of trade in the place where any part of performance is to occur shall be used in interpreting the agreement as to that part of the performance.

(6)   Evidence of a relevant usage of trade offered by one party is not admissible unless and until he has given the other party such notice as the court finds sufficient to prevent unfair surprise to the latter.

Section 1-206. *Statute of Frauds for Kinds of Personal Property Not Otherwise Covered*—(1) Except in the cases described in subsection (2) of this section a contract for the sale of personal property is not enforceable by way of action or defense beyond five thousand dollars in amount or value of remedy unless there is some writing which indicates that a contract for sale has been made between the parties at a defined or stated price, reasonably identifies the subject matter, and is signed by the party against whom enforcement is sought or by his authorized agent.

(2)   Subsection (1) of this section does not apply to contracts for the sale of goods (§ 2-201) nor of securities (§ 8-319) nor to security agreements (§ 9-203).

Section 1-207. *Performance or Acceptance under Reservation of Rights*—(1) A party who with explicit reservation of rights performs or promises performance or assents to performance in a manner demanded or offered by the other party does not thereby prejudice the rights reserved. Such words as "without prejudice," "under protest" or the like are sufficient.

(2)   Subsection (1) does not apply to an accord and satisfaction.

Section 1-208. *Option to Accelerate at Will*—A term providing that one party or his successor in interest may accelerate payment or performance or require collateral or additional collateral "at will" or "when he deems himself insecure" or in words of similar import shall be construed to mean that he shall have power to do so only if he in good faith believes that the prospect of payment or performance is impaired. The burden of establishing lack of good faith is on the party against whom the power has been exercised.

Section 1-209. *Subordinated Obligations*—An obligation may be issued as subordinated to payment of another obligation of the person obligated, or a creditor may subordinate his right to payment of an obligation by agreement with either the person obligated or another creditor of the person obligated. Such a subordination does not create a security interest as against either the common debtor or a subordinated creditor. This section shall be construed as declaring the law as it existed prior to the enactment of this section and not as modifying it.

ARTICLE 2: SALES

Part 1: General Provisions

Part 1 consists of definitions of terms used in Article 2 and an index to terms defined in other sections of the Code. The text of four of the more significant sections of Part 1 is reprinted here.

Section 2-104. *Definitions: "Merchant"; "Between Merchants"; "Financing Agency"*—(1) "Merchant" means a person who deals in goods of the kind or otherwise by his occupation holds himself out as having knowledge or skill peculiar to the practices or goods involved in the transaction or to whom such knowledge or skill may be attributed by his employment of an agent or broker or other intermediary who by his occupation holds himself out as having such knowledge or skill.

(2)   "Financing agency" means a bank, finance company or other person who in the ordinary course of business makes advances against goods or documents of title or who by arrangement with either the seller or the buyer intervenes in ordinary course to make or collect payment due or claimed under the contract for sale, as by purchasing or paying the seller's draft or making advances against it or by merely taking it for collection whether or not documents of title accompany the draft. "Financing agency" includes also a bank or other person who similarly intervenes between persons who are in the position of seller and buyer in respect to the goods (§ 2-707).

(3)   "Between merchants" means in any transaction with respect to which both parties are chargeable with the knowledge or skill of merchants.

Section 2-105. *Definitions: Transferability; "Goods"; "Future" Goods; "Lot"; "Commercial Unit"*—(1) "Goods" means all things (including specially manufactured goods) which are movable at the time of identification to the contract for sale other than the money in which the price is to be paid, investment securities (Article 8) and things in action. "Goods" also includes the unborn young of animals and growing crops and other identified things attached to realty as described in the section on goods to be severed from realty (§ 2-107).

(2)   Goods must be both existing and identified before any interest in them can pass. Goods which are not both existing and identified are "future" goods. A purported present sale of future goods or of any interest therein operates as a contract to sell.

(3)   There may be a sale of a part interest in existing identified goods.

(4)   An undivided share in an identified bulk of fungible goods is sufficiently identified to be sold although the quantity of the bulk is not determined. Any agreed proportion of such a bulk or any quantity thereof agreed upon by number, weight or other measure may to the extent of the seller's interest in the bulk be sold to the buyer who then becomes an owner in common.

(5)   "Lot" means a parcel or a single article which is the subject matter of a separate sale or delivery, whether or not it is sufficient to perform the contract.

(6)   "Commercial unit" means such a unit of goods as by commercial usage is a single whole for purposes of sale and division of which materially impairs its character or value on the market or in use. A commercial unit may be a single article (as a machine) or a set of articles (as a suite of furniture or an assortment of sizes) or a quantity (as a bale, gross, or carload) or any other unit treated in use or in the relevant market as a single whole.

Section 2-106. *Definitions: "Contract"; "Agreement"; "Contract for Sale"; "Sale"; "Present Sale"; "Conforming" to Contract; "Termination"; "Cancellation"*—(1) In this Article unless the context otherwise requires "contract" and "agreement" are limited to those relating to the present or future sale of goods. "Contract for sale" includes both a present sale of goods and a contract to sell goods at a future time. A "sale" consists in the passing of title from the seller to the buyer for a price (§ 2-401). A "present sale" means a sale which is accomplished by the making of the contract.

(2)   Goods or conduct including any part of a performance are "conforming" or conform to the contract when they are in accordance with the obligations under the contract.

(3)   "Termination" occurs when either party pursuant to a power created by agreement or law puts an end to the contract otherwise than for its breach. On "termination" all obligations which are still executory on both sides are discharged but any right based on prior breach or performance survives.

(4)   "Cancellation" occurs when either party puts an end to the contract for breach by the other and its effect is the same as that of "termination" except that the canceling party also retains any remedy for breach of the whole contract or any unperformed balance.

Section 2-107. *Goods to Be Severed from Realty: Recording*—(1) A contract for the sale of minerals or the like (including oil and gas) or a structure or its materials to be removed from realty is a contract for the sale of goods within this Article if they are to be severed by the seller but until severance a purported present sale thereof which is not effective as a transfer of an interest in land is effective only as a contract to sell.

(2)   A contract for the sale apart from the land of growing crops or other things attached to realty and capable of severance without material harm thereto but not described in subsection (1) or of timber to be cut is a contract for the sale of goods within this Article whether the subject matter is to be severed by the buyer or by the seller even though it forms part of the realty at the time of contracting, and the parties can by identification effect a present sale before severance.

(3)   The provisions of this section are subject to any third party rights provided by the law relating to reality records, and the contract for sale may be executed and recorded as a document transferring an interest in land and shall then constitute notice to third parties of the buyer's rights under the contract for sale.

Part 2: Form, Formation, and Readjustment of Contract

Section 2-201. *Formal Requirements; Statute of Frauds*—(1) Except as otherwise provided in this section a contract for the sale of goods for the price of $500 or more is not enforceable by way of action or defense unless there is some writing sufficient to indicate that a contract for sale has been made between the parties and signed by the party against whom enforcement is sought or by his authorized agent or broker. A writing is not insufficient because it omits or incorrectly states a term agreed upon but the contract is not enforceable under this paragraph beyond the quantity of goods shown in such writing.

(2)   Between merchants if within a reasonable time a writing in confirmation of the contract and sufficient against the sender is received, and the party receiving it has reason to know its contents, it satisfies the requirements of subsection (1) against such party unless written notice of objection to its contents is given within 10 days after it is received.

(3)   A contract which does not satisfy the requirements of subsection (1) but which is valid in other respects is enforceable

(a)   if the goods are to be specially manufactured for the buyer and are not suitable for sale to others in the ordinary course of the seller's business and the seller, before notice of repudiation is received and under circumstances which reasonably indicate that the goods are for the buyer, has made either a substantial beginning of their manufacture or commitments for their procurement; or

(b)   if the party against whom enforcement is sought admits in his pleading, testimony or otherwise in court that a contract for sale was made, but the contract is not enforceable under this provision beyond the quantity of goods admitted; or

(c)   with respect to goods for which payment has been made and accepted or which have been received and accepted (§ 2-606).

Section 2-202. *Final Written Expression: Parol or Extrinsic Evidence*—Terms with respect to which the confirmatory memoranda of the parties agree or which are otherwise set forth in a writing intended by the parties as a final expression of their agreement with respect to such terms as are included therein may not be contradicted by evidence of any prior agreement or of a contemporaneous oral agreement but may be explained or supplemented

(a)   by course of dealing or usage of trade (§ 1-205) or by course of performance (§ 2-208); and

(b)   by evidence of consistent additional terms unless the court finds the writing to have been intended also as a complete and exclusive statement of the terms of the agreement.

Section 2-203. *Seals Inoperative*—The affixing of a seal to a writing evidencing a contract for sale or an offer to buy or sell goods does not constitute the writing a sealed instrument and the law with respect to sealed instruments does not apply to such a contract or offer.

Section 2-204. *Formation in General*—(1) A contract for sale of goods may be made in any manner sufficient to show agreement, including conduct by both parties which recognizes the existence of such a contract.

(2)　An agreement sufficient to constitute a contract for sale may be found even though the moment of its making is undetermined.

(3)　Even though one or more terms are left open, a contract for sale does not fail for indefiniteness if the parties have intended to make a contract and there is a reasonably certain basis for giving an appropriate remedy.

Section 2-205. *Firm Offers*—An offer by a merchant to buy or sell goods in a signed writing which by its terms gives assurance that it will be held open is not revocable, for lack of consideration, during the time stated or if no time is stated for a reasonable time, but in no event may such period of irrevocability exceed three months; but any such term of assurance on a form supplied by the offeree must be separately signed by the offeror.

Section 2-206. *Offer and Acceptance in Formation of Contract*—(1) Unless otherwise unambiguously indicated by the language or circumstances

(a)　an offer to make a contract shall be construed as inviting acceptance in any manner and by any medium reasonable in the circumstances;

(b)　an order or other offer to buy goods for prompt or current shipment shall be construed as inviting acceptance either by a prompt promise to ship or by the prompt or current shipment of conforming or non-conforming goods, but such a shipment of nonconforming goods does not constitute an acceptance if the seller seasonably notifies the buyer that the shipment is offered only as an accommodation to the buyer.

(2)　Where the beginning of a requested performance is a reasonable mode of acceptance, an offeror who is not notified of acceptance within a reasonable time may treat the offer as having lapsed before acceptance.

Section 2-207. *Additional Terms in Acceptance or Confirmation*—(1) A definite and seasonable expression of acceptance or a written confirmation which is sent within a reasonable time operates as an acceptance even though it states terms additional to or different from those offered or agreed upon, unless acceptance is expressly made conditional on assent to the additional or different terms.

(2)　The additional terms are to be construed as proposals for addition to the contract. Between merchants such terms become part of the contract unless

(a)　the offer expressly limits acceptance to the terms of the offer;

(b)　they materially alter it; or

(c)　notification of objection to them has already been given or is given within a reasonable time after notice of them is received.

(3)　Conduct by both parties which recognizes the existence of a contract is sufficient to establish a contract for sale although the writings of the parties do not otherwise establish a contract. In such case the terms of the particular contract consist of those terms on which the writings of the parties agree, together with any supplementary terms incorporated under any other provisions of this Act.

Section 2-208. *Course of Performance or Practical Construction*—(1) Where the contract for sale involves repeated occasions for performance by either party with knowledge of the nature of the performance and opportunity for objection to it by the other, any course of performance accepted or acquiesced in without objection shall be relevant to determine the meaning of the agreement.

(2) The express terms of the agreement and any such course of performance, as well as any course of dealing and usage of trade, shall be construed whenever reasonable as consistent with each other; but when such construction is unreasonable, express terms shall control course of performance and course of performance shall control both course of dealing and usage of trade (§ 1-205).

(3) Subject to the provisions of the next section on modification and waiver, such course of performance shall be relevant to show a waiver or modification of any term inconsistent with such course of performance.

Section 2-209. *Modification, Rescission, and Waiver*—(1) An agreement modifying a contract within this Article needs no consideration to be binding.

(2) A signed agreement which excludes modification or rescission except by a signed writing cannot be otherwise modified or rescinded, but except as between merchants such a requirement on a form supplied by the merchant must be separately signed by the other party.

(3) The requirements of the statute of frauds section of this Article (§ 2-201) must be satisfied if the contract as modified is within its provisions.

(4) Although an attempt at modification or rescission does not satisfy the requirements of subsection (2) or (3) it can operate as a waiver.

(5) A party who has made a waiver affecting an executory portion of the contract may retract the waiver by reasonable notification received by the other party that strict performance will be required of any term waived, unless the retraction would be unjust in view of a material change of position in reliance on the waiver.

Section 2-210. *Delegation of Performance; Assignment of Rights*—(1) A party may perform his duty through a delegate unless otherwise agreed or unless the other party has a substantial interest in having his original promisor perform or control the acts required by the contract. No delegation of performance relieves the party delegating of any duty to perform or any liability for breach.

(2) Unless otherwise agreed all rights of either seller or buyer can be assigned except where the assignment would materially change the duty of the other party, or increase materially the burden or risk imposed on him by his contract, or impair materially his chance of obtaining return performance. A right to damages for breach of the whole contract or a right arising out of the assignor's due performance of his entire obligation can be assigned despite agreement otherwise.

(3) Unless the circumstances indicate the contrary a prohibition of assignment of "the contract" is to be construed as barring only the delegation to the assignee of the assignor's performance.

(4) An assignment of "the contract" or of "all my rights under the contract" or an assignment in similar general terms is an assignment of rights and unless the language or the circumstances (as in an assignment for security) indicate the contrary, it is a delegation of performance of the duties of the assignor and its acceptance by the assignee constitutes a promise by him to perform those duties. This promise is enforceable by either the assignor or the other party to the original contract.

(5) The other party may treat any assignment which delegates performance as creating reasonable grounds for insecurity and may without prejudice to his rights against the assignor demand assurances from the assignee (Section 2-609).

Part 3: General Obligation and Construction of Contract

Section 2-301. *General Obligations of Parties*—The obligation of the seller is to transfer and deliver and that of the buyer is to accept and pay in accordance with the contract.

Section 2-302. *Unconscionable Contract or Clause*—(1) If the court as a matter of law finds the contract or any clause of the contract to have been unconscionable at the time it was made the court may refuse to enforce the contract, or it may enforce the remainder of the contract without the unconscionable clause, or it may so limit the application of any unconscionable clause as to avoid any unconscionable result.

(2) When it is claimed or appears to the court that the contract or any clause thereof may be unconscionable the parties shall be afforded a reasonable opportunity to present evidence as to its commercial setting, purpose and effect to aid the court in making the determination.

Section 2-303. *Allocation or Division of Risks*—Where this Article allocates a risk or a burden as between the parties "unless otherwise agreed", the agreement may not only shift the allocation but may also divide the risk or burden.

Section 2-304. *Price Payable in Money, Goods, Realty, or Otherwise*—(1) The price can be made payable in money or otherwise. If it is payable in whole or in part in goods each party is a seller of the goods which he is to transfer.

(2) Even though all or part of the price is payable in an interest in realty the transfer of the goods and the seller's obligations with reference to them are subject to this Article, but not the transfer of the interest in realty or the transferor's obligations in connection therewith.

Section 2-305. *Open Price Term*—(1) The parties if they so intend can conclude a contract for sale even though the price is not settled. In such a case the price is a reasonable price at the time for delivery if

(a)   nothing is said as to price; or

(b)   the price is left to be agreed by the parties and they fail to agree; or

(c)   the price is to be fixed in terms of some agreed market or other standard as set or recorded by a third person or agency and it is not so set or recorded.

(2)   A price to be fixed by the seller or by the buyer means a price for him to fix in good faith.

(3)   When a price left to be fixed otherwise than by agreement of the parties fails to be fixed through fault of one party the other may at his option treat the contract as canceled or himself fix a reasonable price.

(4)   Where, however, the parties intend not to be bound unless the price be fixed or agreed and it is not fixed or agreed there is no contract. In such a case the buyer must return any goods already received or if unable so to do must pay their reasonable value at the time of delivery and the seller must return any portion of the price paid on account.

Section 2-306. *Output, Requirements, and Exclusive Dealings*—(1) A term which measures the quantity by the output of the seller or the requirements of the buyer means such actual output or requirements as may occur in good faith, except that no quantity unreasonably disproportionate to any stated estimate or in the absence of a stated estimate to any normal or otherwise comparable prior output or requirements may be tendered or demanded.

(2)   A lawful agreement by either the seller or the buyer for exclusive dealing in the kind of goods concerned imposes unless otherwise agreed an obligation by the seller to use best efforts to supply the goods and by the buyer to use best efforts to promote their sale.

Section 2-307. *Delivery in Single Lot or Several Lots*—Unless otherwise agreed, all goods called for by a contract for sale must be tendered in a single delivery and payment is due only on such tender but where the circumstances give either party the right to make or demand delivery in lots the price if it can be apportioned may be demanded for each lot.

Section 2-308. *Absence of Specified Place for Delivery*—Unless otherwise agreed

(a)   the place for delivery of goods is the seller's place of business or if he has none his residence; but

(b)   in a contract for sale of identified goods which to the knowledge of the parties at the time of contracting are in some other place, that place is the place for their delivery; and

(c)   documents of title may be delivered through customary banking channels.

Section 2-309. *Absence of Specific Time Provisions; Notice of Termination*—(1) The time for shipment or delivery or any other action under a contract if not provided in this Article or agreed upon shall be a reasonable time.

(2)   Where the contract provides for successive performances but is indefinite in duration it is valid for a reasonable time but unless otherwise agreed may be terminated at any time by either party.

(3)   Termination of a contract by one party except on the happening of an agreed event requires that reasonable notification be received by the other party and an agreement dispensing with notification is invalid if its operation would be unconscionable.

Section 2-310. *Open Time for Payment or Running of Credit; Authority to Ship Under Reservation*—Unless otherwise agreed
- (a)   payment is due at the time and place at which the buyer is to receive the goods even though the place of shipment is the place of delivery; and
- (b)   if the seller is authorized to send the goods he may ship them under reservation, and may tender the documents of title, but the buyer may inspect the goods after their arrival before payment is due unless such inspection is inconsistent with the terms of the contract (§ 2-513); and
- (c)   if delivery is authorized and made by way of documents of title otherwise than by subsection (b) then payment is due at the time and place at which the buyer is to receive the documents regardless of where the goods are to be received; and
- (d)   where the seller is required or authorized to ship the goods on credit the credit period runs from the time of shipment but postdating the invoice or delaying its dispatch will correspondingly delay the starting of the credit period.

Section 2-311. *Options and Cooperation Respecting Performance*—(1) An agreement for sale which is otherwise sufficiently definite (subsection (3) of § 2204) to be a contract is not made invalid by the fact that the agreement leaves particulars of performance to be specified by one of the parties. Any such specification must be made in good faith and within limits set by commercial reasonableness.

(2)   Unless otherwise agreed, specifications relating to assortment of the goods are at the buyer's option and except as otherwise provided in subsections (1)(c) and (3) of Section 2-319, specifications or arrangements relating to shipment are at the seller's option.

(3)   Where such specification would materially affect the other party's performance but is not seasonably made or where one party's cooperation is necessary to the agreed performance of the other but is not seasonably forthcoming, the other party in addition to all other remedies
- (a)   is excused for any resulting delay in his own performance; and
- (b)   may also either proceed to perform in any reasonable manner or after the time for a material part of his own performance treat the failure to specify or to cooperate as a breach by failure to deliver or accept the goods.

Section 2-312. *Warranty of Title and Against Infringement; Buyer's Obligation Against Infringement*—(1) Subject to subsection (2) there is in a contract for sale a warranty by the seller that
- (a)   the title conveyed shall be good, and its transfer rightful; and
- (b)   the goods shall be delivered free from any security interest or other lien or encumbrance of which the buyer at the time of contracting has no knowledge.

(2)   A warranty under subsection (1) will be excluded or modified only by specific language or by circumstances which give the buyer reason to know that the person selling does not claim title in himself or that he is purporting to sell only such right or title as he or a third person may have.

(3)   Unless otherwise agreed a seller who is a merchant regularly dealing in goods of the kind warrants that the goods shall be delivered free of the rightful claim of any third person by way of infringement or the like but a buyer who furnishes specifications to the seller must hold the seller harmless against any such claim which arises out of compliance with the specifications.

Section 2-313. *Express Warranties by Affirmation, Promise, Description, Sample*—(1) Express warranties by the seller are created as follows:
- (a)   Any affirmation of fact or promise made by the seller to the buyer which relates to the goods and becomes part of the basis of the bargain creates an express warranty that the goods shall conform to the affirmation or promise.

(b)   Any description of the goods which is made part of the basis of the bargain creates an express warranty that the goods shall conform to the description.

(c)   Any sample or model which is made part of the basis of the bargain creates an express warranty that the whole of the goods shall conform to the sample or model.

(2) It is not necessary to the creation of an express warranty that the seller use formal words such as "warrant" or "guarantee" or that he have a specific intention to make a warranty, but an affirmation merely of the value of the goods or a statement purporting to be merely the seller's opinion or commendation of the goods does not create a warranty.

Section 2-314. *Implied Warranty: Merchantability; Usage of Trade*—(1) Unless excluded or modified (§ 2-316), a warranty that the goods shall be merchantable is implied in a contract for their sale if the seller is a merchant with respect to goods of that kind. Under this section the serving for value of food or drink to be consumed either on the premises or elsewhere is a sale.

(2)   Goods to be merchantable must at least be such as

(a)   pass without objection in the trade under the contract description; and

(b)   in the case of fungible goods, are of fair average quality within the description; and

(c)   are fit for the ordinary purposes for which such goods are used; and

(d)   run, within the variations permitted by the agreement, of even kind, quality and quantity within each unit and among all units involved; and

(e)   are adequately contained, packaged, and labeled as the agreement may require; and

(f)   conform to the promises or affirmations of fact made on the container or label if any.

(3)   Unless excluded or modified (§ 2-316) other implied warranties may arise from course of dealing or usage of trade.

Section 2-315. *Implied Warranty: Fitness for Particular Purpose*—Where the seller at the time of contracting has reason to know any particular purpose for which the goods are required and that the buyer is relying on the seller's skill or judgment to select or furnish suitable goods, there is unless excluded or modified under the next section an implied warranty that the goods shall be fit for such purpose.

Section 2-316. *Exclusion or Modification of Warranties*—(1) Words or conduct relevant to the creation of an express warranty and words or conduct tending to negate or limit warranty shall be construed wherever reasonable as consistent with each other; but subject to the provisions of this Article on parol or extrinsic evidence (§ 2-202) negation or limitation is inoperative to the extent that such construction is unreasonable.

(2)   Subject to subsection (3), to exclude or modify the implied warranty of merchantability or any part of it the language must mention merchantability and in case of a writing must be conspicuous, and to exclude or modify any implied warranty of fitness the exclusion must be by a writing and conspicuous. Language to exclude all implied warranties of fitness is sufficient if it states, for example, that "There are no warranties which extend beyond the description on the face hereof."

(3)   Notwithstanding subsection (2)

(a)   unless the circumstances indicate otherwise, all implied warranties are excluded by expressions like "as is," "with all faults" or other language which is common understanding calls the buyer's attention to the exclusion of warranties and makes plain that there is no implied warranty; and

(b)   when the buyer before entering into the contract has examined the goods or the sample or model as fully as he desired or has refused to examine the goods there is no implied warranty with regard to defects which an examination ought in the circumstances to have revealed to him; and

(c)   an implied warranty can also be excluded or modified by course of dealing or course of performance or usage of trade.

(4)   Remedies for breach of warranty can be limited in accordance with the provisions of this Article on liquidation or limitation of damages and on contractual modifications of remedy (§§ 2-718 and 2-719).

Section 2-317. *Cumulation and Conflict of Warranties Express or Implied*—Warranties whether express or implied shall be construed as consistent with each other and as cumulative, but if such construction is unreasonable the intention of the parties shall determine which warranty is dominant. In ascertaining that intention the following rules apply:

(a)   Exact or technical specifications displace an inconsistent sample or model or general language of description.

(b)   A sample from an existing bulk displaces inconsistent general language of description.

(c)   Express warranties displace inconsistent implied warranties other than an implied warranty of fitness for a particular purpose.

Section 2-318. *Third-Party Beneficiaries of Warranties Express or Implied*—
NOTE: Each state determines which alternative to adopt.

Alternative A

A seller's warranty whether express or implied extends to any natural person who is in the family or household of his buyer or who is a guest in his home if it is reasonable to expect that such person may use, consume or be affected by the goods and who is injured in person by breach of the warranty. A seller may not exclude or limit the operation of this section.

Alternative B

A seller's warranty whether express or implied extends to any natural person who may reasonably be expected to use, consume or be affected by the goods and who is injured in person by breach of the warranty. A seller may not exclude or limit the operation of this section.

Alternative C

A seller's warranty whether express or implied extends to any person who may reasonably be expected to use, consume or be affected by the goods and who is injured by breach of the warranty. A seller may not exclude or limit the operation of this section with respect to injury to the person of an individual to whom the warranty extends.

Section 2-319. *F.O.B. and F.A.S. Terms*—(1) Unless otherwise agreed the term F.O.B. (which means "free on board") at a named place, even though used only in connection with the stated price, is a delivery term under which

(a)   when the term is F.O.B. the place of shipment, the seller must at that place ship the goods in the manner provided in this Article (§ 2-504) and bear the expense and risk of putting them into the possession of the carrier; or

(b)   when the term is F.O.B. the place of destination, the seller must at his own expense and risk transport the goods to that place and there tender delivery of them in the manner provided in this Article (§ 2-503);

(c)   when under either (a) or (b) the term is also F.O.B. vessel, car or other vehicle, the seller must in addition at his own expense and risk load the goods on board. If the term is F.O.B. vessel the buyer must name the vessel and in an appropriate case the seller must comply with the provisions of this Article on the form of bill of lading (§ 2-323).

(2)   Unless otherwise agreed, the term F.A.S. vessel (which means "free alongside") at a named port, even though used only in connection with the stated price, is a delivery term under which the seller must

(a)   at his own expense and risk deliver the goods alongside the vessel in the manner usual in that port or on a dock designated and provided by the buyer; and

(b)   obtain and tender a receipt for the goods in exchange for which the carrier is under a duty to issue a bill of lading.

(3) Unless otherwise agreed in any case falling within subsection (1)(a) or (c) or subsection (2), the buyer must seasonably give any needed instructions for making delivery, including when the term is F.A.S. or F.O.B. the loading berth of the vessel and in an appropriate case its name and sailing date. The seller may treat the failure of needed instructions as a failure of cooperation under this Article (§ 2-311). He may also at his option move the goods in any reasonable manner preparatory to delivery or shipment.

(4) Under the term F.O.B. vessel or F.A.S. unless otherwise agreed the buyer must make payment against tender of the required documents and the seller may not tender nor the buyer demand delivery of the goods in substitution for the documents.

Section 2-320. *C.I.F. and C. & F. Terms*—(1) The term C.I.F. means that the price includes in a lump sum the cost of the goods and the insurance and freight to the named destination. The term C. & F. or C.F. means that the price so includes cost and freight to the named destination.

(2) Unless otherwise agreed and even though used only in connection with the stated price and destination, the term C.I.F. destination or its equivalent requires the seller at his own expense and risk to

(a) put the goods into the possession of a carrier at the port for shipment and obtain a negotiable bill or bills of lading covering the entire transportation to the named destination; and

(b) load the goods and obtain a receipt from the carrier (which may be contained in the bill of lading) showing that the freight has been paid or provided for; and

(c) obtain a policy or certificate of insurance, including any war risk insurance, of a kind and on terms then current at the port of shipment in the usual amount, in the currency of the contract, shown to cover the same goods covered by the bill of lading and providing for payment of loss to the order of the buyer or for the account of whom it may concern; but the seller may add to the price the amount of the premium for any such war risk insurance; and

(d) prepare an invoice of the goods and procure any other documents required to effect shipment or to comply with the contract; and

(e) forward and tender with commercial promptness all the documents in due form and with any endorsement necessary to perfect the buyer's rights.

(3) Unless otherwise agreed the term C. & F. or its equivalent has the same effect and imposes upon the seller the same obligations and risks as a C.I.F. term except the obligation as to insurance.

(4) Under the term C.I.F. or C. & F. unless otherwise agreed the buyer must make payment against tender of the required documents and the seller may not tender nor the buyer demand delivery of the goods in substitution for the documents.

Section 2-321. *C.I.F. or C. & F.: "Net Landed Weights"; "Payment on Arrival"; Warranty of Condition on Arrival*—Under a contract containing a term C.I.F., or C. & F.:

(1) Where the price is based on or is to be adjusted according to "net landed weights," "delivered weights," "out turn" quantity or quality or the like, unless otherwise agreed the seller must reasonably estimate the price. The payment due on tender of the documents called for by the contract is the amount so estimated, but after final adjustment of the price a settlement must be made with commercial promptness.

(2) An agreement described in subsection (1) or any warranty of quality or condition of the goods on arrival places upon the seller the risk of ordinary deterioration, shrinkage and the like in transportation but has no effect on the place or time of identification to the contract for sale or delivery or on the passing of the risk of loss.

(3) Unless otherwise agreed where the contract provides for payment on or after arrival of the goods the seller must before payment allow such preliminary inspection as is feasible; but if the goods are lost delivery of the documents and payment are due when the goods should have arrived.

Section 2-322. *Delivery "Ex-Ship"*—(1) Unless otherwise agreed a term for delivery of goods "ex-ship" (which means from the carrying vessel) or in equivalent language is not restricted to a particular ship and requires delivery from a ship which has reached a place at the named port of destination where goods of the kind are usually discharged.

(2) Under such a term, unless otherwise agreed

(a) the seller must discharge all liens arising out of the carriage and furnish the buyer with a direction which puts the carrier under a duty to deliver the goods; and

(b)   the risk of loss does not pass to the buyer until the goods leave the ship's tackle or are otherwise properly unloaded.

Section 2-323. *Form of Bill of Lading Required in Overseas Shipment; "Overseas"*—(1) Where the contract contemplates overseas shipment and contains a term C.I.F. or C. & F. or F.O.B. vessel, the seller unless otherwise agreed must obtain a negotiable bill of lading stating that the goods have been loaded on board or, in the case of a term C.I.F. or C. & F., received for shipment.

(2)   Where in a case within subsection (1) a bill of lading has been issued in a set of parts, unless otherwise agreed if the documents are not to be sent from abroad the buyer may demand tender of the full set; otherwise only one part of the bill of lading need be tendered. Even if the agreement expressly requires a full set

(a)   due tender of a single part is acceptable within the provisions of this Article on cure of improper delivery (subsection (1) of § 2-508); and

(b)   even though the full set is demanded, if the documents are sent from abroad the person tendering an incomplete set may nevertheless require payment upon furnishing and indemnity which the buyer in good faith deems adequate.

(3)   A shipment by water or by air or a contract contemplating such shipment is "overseas" insofar as by usage of trade or agreement it is subject to the commercial, financing or shipping practices characteristic of international deep water commerce.

Section 2-324. *"No Arrival, No Sale" Term*—Under a term "no sale no arrival" or terms of like meaning, unless otherwise agreed

(a)   the seller must properly ship conforming goods and if they arrive by any means he must tender them on arrival but he assumes no obligation that the goods will arrive unless he has caused the nonarrival; and

(b)   where without fault of the seller the goods are in part lost or have so deteriorated as no longer to conform to the contract or arrive after the contract time, the buyer may proceed as if there had been casualty to identified goods (§ 2-613).

Section 2-325. *"Letter of Credit" Term; "Confirmed Credit"*—(1) Failure of the buyer seasonably to furnish an agreed letter of credit is a breach of the contract for sale.

(2)   The delivery to seller of a proper letter of credit suspends the buyer's obligation to pay. If the letter of credit is dishonored, the seller may on seasonable notification to the buyer require payment directly from him.

(3)   Unless otherwise agreed the term "letter of credit" or "banker's credit" in a contract for sale means an irrevocable credit issued by a financing agency of good repute and, where the shipment is overseas, of good international repute. The term "confirmed credit" means that the credit must also carry the direct obligation of such an agency which does business in the seller's financial market.

Section 2-326. *Sale on Approval and Sale or Return; Consignment Sales and Rights of Creditors*—(1) Unless otherwise agreed, if delivered goods may be returned by the buyer even though they conform to the contract, the transaction is

(a)   a "sale on approval" if the goods are delivered primarily for use, and

(b)   a "sale or return" if the goods are delivered primarily for resale.

(2)   Except as provided in subsection (3), goods held on approval are not subject to the claims of the buyer's creditors until acceptance; goods held on sale or return are subject to such claims while in the buyer's possession.

(3)   Where goods are delivered to a person for sale and such person maintains a place of business at which he deals in goods of the kind involved, under a name other than the name of the person making delivery, then with respect to claims of creditors of the person conducting the business the goods are deemed to be on sale or return. The provisions of this subsection are applicable even though an agreement purports to reserve title to the person making delivery until payment or resale or uses such words as "on consignment" or "on memorandum." However, this subsection is not applicable if the person making delivery

(a) complies with an applicable law providing for a consignor's interest or the like to be evidenced by a sign, or

(b) establishes that the person conducting the business is generally known by his creditors to be substantially engaged in selling the goods of others, or

(c) complies with the filing provisions of the Article on Secured Transactions (Article 9).

(4) Any "or return" term of a contract for sale is to be treated as a separate contract for sale within the statute of frauds section of this Article (§ 2-201) and as contradicting the sale aspect of the contract within the provisions of this Article on parol or extrinsic evidence (§ 2-202).

Section 2-327. *Special Incidents of Sale on Approval and Sale or Return*—(1) Under a sale on approval unless otherwise agreed

(a) although the goods are identified to the contract the risk of loss and the title do not pass to the buyer until acceptance; and

(b) use of the goods consistent with the purpose of trial is not acceptance but failure seasonably to notify the seller of election to return the goods is acceptance, and if the goods conform to the contract acceptance of any part is acceptance of the whole; and

(c) after due notification of election to return, the return is at the seller's risk and expense but a merchant buyer must follow any reasonable instructions.

(2) Under a sale or return unless otherwise agreed

(a) the option to return extends to the whole or any commercial unit of the goods while in substantially their original condition, but must be exercised seasonably; and

(b) the return is at the buyer's risk and expense.

Section 2-328. *Sale by Auction*—(1) In a sale by auction if goods are put up in lots each lot is the subject of a separate sale.

(2) A sale by auction is complete when the auctioneer so announces by the fall of the hammer or in other customary manner. Where a bid is made while the hammer is falling in acceptance of a prior bid the auctioneer may in his discretion reopen the bidding or declare the goods sold under the bid on which the hammer was falling.

(3) Such a sale is with reserve unless the goods are in explicit terms put up without reserve. In an auction with reserve the auctioneer may withdraw the goods at any time until he announces completion of the sale. In an auction without reserve, after the auctioneer calls for bids on an article or lot, that article or lot cannot be withdrawn unless no bid is made within a reasonable time. In either case a bidder may retract his bid until the auctioneer's announcement of completion of the sale, but a bidder's retraction does not revive any previous bid.

(4) If the auctioneer knowingly receives a bid on the seller's behalf or the seller makes or procures such a bid, and notice has not been given that liberty for such bidding is reserved, the buyer may at his option avoid the sale or take the goods at the price of the last good faith bid prior to the completion of the sale. This subsection shall not apply to any bid at a forced sale.

Part 4: Title, Creditors, and Good Faith Purchasers

Section 2-401. *Passing of Title; Reservation for Security; Limited Application of This Section*—Each provision of this Article with regard to the rights, obligations and remedies of the seller, the buyer, purchasers or other third parties applies irrespective of title to the goods except where the provision refers to such title. Insofar as situations are not covered by the other provisions of this Article and matters concerning title become material the following rules apply:

(1) Title to goods cannot pass under a contract for sale prior to their identification to the contract (§ 2-501), and unless otherwise explicitly agreed the buyer acquires by their identification a special property as limited by this Act. Any retention or reservation by the seller of the title (property) in goods shipped or delivered to the buyer is limited in effect to a reserva-

tion of a security interest. Subject to these provisions and to the provisions of the Article on Secured Transactions (Article 9), title to goods passes from the seller to the buyer in any manner and on any conditions explicitly agreed on by the parties.

(2) Unless otherwise explicitly agreed, title passes to the buyer at the time and place at which the seller completes his performance with reference to the physical delivery of the goods, despite any reservation of a security interest and even though a document of title is to be delivered at a different time or place; and in particular and despite any reservation of a security interest by the bill of lading

   (a) if the contract requires or authorizes the seller to send the goods to the buyer but does not require him to deliver them at destination, title passes to the buyer at the time and place of shipment; but

   (b) if the contract requires delivery at destination, title passes on tender there.

(3) Unless otherwise explicitly agreed where delivery is to be made without moving the goods

   (a) if the seller is to deliver a document of title, title passes at the time when and the place where he delivers such documents; or

   (b) if the goods are at the time of contracting already identified and no documents are to be delivered, title passes at the time and place of contracting.

(4) A rejection or other refusal by the buyer to receive or retain the goods, whether or not justified, or a justified revocation of acceptance revests title to the goods in the seller. Such revesting occurs by operation of law and is not a "sale."

Section 2-402. *Rights of Seller's Creditors Against Sold Goods*—(1) Except as provided in subsections (2) and (3), rights of unsecured creditors of the seller with respect to goods which have been identified to a contract for sale are subject to the buyer's rights to recover the goods under this Article (§§ 2-502 and 2-716).

(2) A creditor of the seller may treat a sale or an identification of goods to a contract for sale as void if as against him a retention of possession by the seller is fraudulent under any rule of law of the state where the goods are situated, except that retention of possession in good faith and current course of trade by a merchant-seller for a commercially reasonable time after a sale or identification is not fraudulent.

(3) Nothing in this Article shall be deemed to impair the rights of creditors of the seller.

   (a) under the provisions of the Article on Secured Transactions (Article 9); or

   (b) where identification to the contract or delivery is made not in current course of trade but in satisfaction of or as security for a preexisting claim for money, security or the like and is made under circumstances which under any rule of law of the state where the goods are situated would apart from this Article constitute the transaction a fraudulent transfer or voidable preference.

Section 2-403. *Power to Transfer; Good Faith Purchase of Goods; "Entrusting"*—(1) A purchaser of goods acquires all title which his transferor had or had power to transfer except that a purchaser of a limited interest acquires rights only to the extent of the interest purchased. A person with voidable title has power to transfer a good title to a good faith purchaser for value. When goods have been delivered under a transaction of purchase the purchaser has such power even though

   (a) the transferor was deceived as to the identity of the purchaser, or

   (b) the delivery was in exchange for a check which is later dishonored, or

   (c) it was agreed that the transaction was to be a "cash sale," or

   (d) the delivery was procured through fraud punishable as larcenous under the criminal law.

(2) Any entrusting of possession of goods to a merchant who deals in goods of that kind gives him power to transfer all rights of the entruster to a buyer in ordinary course of business.

(3) "Entrusting" includes any delivery and any acquiescence in retention of possession regardless of any condition expressed between the parties to the delivery or acquiescence and

regardless of whether the procurement of the entrusting or the possessor's disposition of the goods has been such as to be larcenous under the criminal law.

[Note: If a state adopts the repealer of Article 6-Bulk Transfers (Alternative A), subsec. (4) should read as follows:]

(4) The rights of other purchasers of goods and of lien creditors are governed by the Articles on Secured Transactions (Article 9) and Documents of Title (Article 7).

[Note: If a state adopts Revised Article 6-Bulk Sales (Alternative B), subsec. (4) should read as follows:]

(4) The rights of other purchasers of goods and of lien creditors are governed by the Articles on Secured Transactions (Article 9), Bulk Sales (Article 6) and Documents of Title (Article 7).

Part 5: Performance

Section 2-501. *Insurable Interest in Goods; Manner of Identification of Goods*—(1) The buyer obtains a special property and an insurable interest in goods by identification of existing goods as goods to which the contract refers even though the goods so identified are nonconforming and he has an option to return or reject them. Such identification can be made at any time and in any manner explicitly agreed to by the parties. In the absence of explicit agreement identification occurs

    (a)   when the contract is made if it is for the sale of goods already existing and identified

    (b)   if the contract is for the sale of future goods other than those described in paragraph (c), when goods are shipped, marked or otherwise designated by the seller as goods to which the contract refers;

    (c)   when the crops are planted or otherwise become growing crops or the young are conceived if the contract is for the sale of unborn young to be born within 12 months after contracting or for the sale of crops to be harvested within 12 months or the next normal harvest season after contracting whichever is longer.

(2) The seller retains an insurable interest in goods so long as title to or any security interest in the goods remains in him and where the identification is by the seller alone he may until default or insolvency or notification to the buyer that the identification is final substitute other goods for those identified.

(3) Nothing in this section impairs any insurable interest recognized under any other statute or rule of law.

Section 2-502. *Buyer's Rights to Goods on Seller's Insolvency*—(1) Subject to subsection (2) and even though the goods have not been shipped a buyer who has paid a part or all of the price of goods in which he has a special property under the provisions of the immediately preceding section may on making and keeping good a tender of any unpaid portion of their price recover them from the seller if the seller becomes insolvent within 10 days after receipt of the first installment on their price.

(2) If the identification creating his special property has been made by the buyer he acquires the right to recover the goods only if they conform to the contract for sale.

Section 2-503. *Manner of Seller's Tender of Delivery*—(1) Tender of delivery requires that the seller put and hold conforming goods at the buyer's disposition and give the buyer any notification reasonably necessary to enable him to take delivery. The manner, time and place for tender are determined by the agreement and this Article, and in particular

    (a)   tender must be at a reasonable hour, and if it is of goods they must be kept available for the period reasonably necessary to enable the buyer to take possession; but

    (b)   unless otherwise agreed the buyer must furnish facilities reasonably suited to the receipt of the goods.

(2) Where the case is within the next section respecting shipment tender requires that the seller comply with its provisions.

(3)   Where the seller is required to deliver at a particular destination tender requires that he comply with subsection (1) and also in any appropriate case tender documents as described in subsections (4) and (5) of this section.

(4)   Where goods are in the possession of a bailee and are to be delivered without being moved

(a)   tender requires that the seller either tender a negotiable document of title covering such goods or procure acknowledgment by the bailee of the buyer's right to possession of the goods; but

(b)   tender to the buyer of a nonnegotiable document of title or of a written direction to the bailee to deliver is sufficient tender unless the buyer seasonably objects, and receipt by the bailee of notification of the buyer's rights fixes those rights as against the bailee and all third persons; but risk of loss of the goods and of any failure by the bailee to honor the nonnegotiable document of title or to obey the direction remains on the seller until the buyer has had a reasonable time to present the document or direction, and a refusal by the bailee to honor the document or to obey the direction defeats the tender.

(5)   Where the contract requires the seller to deliver documents

(a)   he must tender all such documents in correct form, except as provided in this Article with respect to bills of lading in a set (subsection (2) of § 2-323); and

(b)   tender through customary banking channels is sufficient and dishonor of a draft accompanying the documents constitutes nonacceptance or rejection.

Section 2-504. *Shipment by Seller*—Where the seller is required or authorized to send the goods to the buyer and the contract does not require him to deliver them at a particular destination, then unless otherwise agreed he must

(a)   put the goods in the possession of such a carrier and make such a contract for their transportation as may be reasonable having regard to the nature of the goods and other circumstances of the case; and

(b)   obtain and promptly deliver or tender in due form any document necessary to enable the buyer to obtain possession of the goods or otherwise required by the agreement or by usage of trade; and

(c)   promptly notify the buyer of the shipment.

Failure to notify the buyer under paragraph (c) or to make a proper contract under paragraph (a) is a ground for rejection only if material delay or loss ensues.

Section 2-505. *Seller's Shipment under Reservation*—(1) Where the seller has identified goods to the contract by or before shipment:

(a)   His procurement of a negotiable bill of lading to his own order or otherwise reserves in him a security interest in the goods. His procurement of the bill to the order of a financing agency or of the buyer indicates in addition only the seller's expectation of transferring that interest to the person named.

(b)   A nonnegotiable bill of lading to himself or his nominee reserves possession of the goods as security but except in a case of conditional delivery (subsection (2) of § 2-507) a nonnegotiable bill of lading naming the buyer as consignee reserves no security interest even though the seller retains possession of the bill of lading.

(2)   When shipment by the seller with reservation of a security interest is in violation of the contract for sale it constitutes an improper contract for transportation within the preceding section but impairs neither the rights given to the buyer by shipment and identification of the goods to the contract nor the seller's powers as a holder of a negotiable document.

Section 2-506. *Rights of Financing Agency*—(1) A financing agency by paying or purchasing for value a draft which relates to a shipment of goods acquires to the extent of the payment or purchase and in addition to its own rights under the draft and any document of title securing it any rights of the shipper in the goods including the right to stop delivery and the shipper's right to have the draft honored by the buyer.

(2)   The right to reimbursement of a financing agency which has in good faith honored or purchased the draft under commitment to or authority from the buyer is not impaired by subsequent discovery of defects with reference to any relevant document which was apparently regular on its face.

Section 2-507. *Effect of Seller's Tender; Delivery on Condition*—(1) Tender of delivery is a condition to the buyer's duty to accept the goods and, unless otherwise agreed, to his duty to pay for them. Tender entitles the seller to acceptance of the goods and to payment according to the contract.

(2)   Where payment is due and demanded on the delivery to the buyer of goods or documents of title, his right as against the seller to retain or dispose of them is conditional upon his making the payment due.

Section 2-508. *Cure by Seller of Improper Tender or Delivery; Replacement*—(1) Where any tender or delivery by the seller is rejected because nonconforming and the time for performance has not yet expired, the seller may seasonably notify the buyer of his intention to cure and may then within the contract time make a conforming delivery.

(2)   Where the buyer rejects a nonconforming tender which the seller had reasonable grounds to believe would be acceptable with or without money allowance the seller may if he reasonably notifies the buyer have a further reasonable time to substitute a conforming tender.

Section 2-509. *Risk of Loss in the Absence of Breach*—(1) Where the contract requires or authorizes the seller to ship the goods by carrier
(a)   if it does not require him to deliver them at a particular destination, the risk of loss passes to the buyer when the goods are duly delivered to the carrier even though the shipment is under reservation (§ 2-205); but
(b)   if it does require him to deliver them at a particular destination and the goods are there duly tendered while in the possession of the carrier, the risk of loss passes to the buyer when the goods are there duly so tendered as to enable the buyer to take delivery.
(2)   Where the goods are held by a bailee to be delivered without being moved, the risk of loss passes to the buyer
(a)   on his receipt of a negotiable document of title covering the goods; or
(b)   on acknowledgment by the bailee of the buyer's right to possession of the goods; or
(c)   after his receipt of a nonnegotiable document of title or other written direction to deliver, as provided in subsection (4)(b) of Section 2-503.
(3)   In any case not within subsection (1) or (2), the risk of loss passes to the buyer on his receipt of the goods if the seller is a merchant; otherwise the risk passes to the buyer on tender of delivery.
(4)   The provisions of this section are subject to contrary agreement of the parties and to the provisions of this Article on sale on approval (§ 2-327) and on effect of breach on risk of loss (§ 2-510).

Section 2-510. *Effect of Breach on Risk of Loss*—(1) Where a tender or delivery of goods so fails to conform to the contract as to give a right of rejection the risk of their loss remains on the seller until cure or acceptance.

(2)   Where the buyer rightfully revokes acceptance he may to the extent of any deficiency in his effective insurance coverage treat the risk of loss as having rested on the seller from the beginning.

(3)   Where the buyer as to conforming goods already identified to the contract for sale repudiates or is otherwise in breach before risk of their loss has passed to him, the seller may to the extent of any deficiency in his effective insurance coverage treat the risk of loss as resting on the buyer for a commercially reasonable time.

Section 2-511. *Tender of Payment by Buyer; Payment by Check*—(1) Unless otherwise agreed tender of payment is a condition to the seller's duty to tender and complete any delivery.

(2)   Tender of payment is sufficient when made by any means or in any manner current in the ordinary course of business unless the seller demands payment in legal tender and gives any extension of time reasonably necessary to procure it.

(3)   Subject to the provisions of this Act on the effect of an instrument on an obligation (§ 3-802), payment by check is conditional and is defeated as between the parties by dishonor of the check on due presentment.

Section 2-512. *Payment by Buyer before Inspection*—(1) Where the contract requires payment before inspection nonconformity of the goods does not excuse the buyer from so making payment unless
(a)   the nonconformity appears without inspection; or
(b)   despite tender of the required documents the circumstances would justify injunction against honor under the provisions of this Act (§ 5-114).
(2)   Payment pursuant to subsection (1) does not constitute an acceptance of the goods or impair the buyer's right to inspect or any of his remedies.

Section 2-513. *Buyer's Right to Inspection of Goods*—(1) Unless otherwise agreed and subject to subsection (3), where goods are tendered or delivered or identified to the contract for sale, the buyer has a right before payment or acceptance to inspect them at any reasonable place and time and in any reasonable manner. When the seller is required or authorized to send the goods to the buyer, the inspection may be after their arrival.
(2)   Expenses of inspection must be borne by the buyer but may be recovered from the seller if the goods do not conform and are rejected.
(3)   Unless otherwise agreed and subject to the provisions of this Article on C.I.F. contracts (subsection (3) of § 2-321), the buyer is not entitled to inspect the goods before payment of the price when the contract provides
(a)   for delivery "C.O.D." or on like terms; or
(b)   for payment against documents of title, except where such payment is due only after the goods are to become available for inspection.
(4)   A place or method of inspection fixed by the parties is presumed to be exclusive, but unless otherwise expressly agreed it does not postpone identification or shift the place for delivery or for passing the risk of loss. If compliance becomes impossible, inspection shall be as provided in this section unless the place or method fixed was clearly intended as an indispensable condition failure of which avoids the contract.

Section 2-514. *When Documents Deliverable on Acceptance; When on Payment*—Unless otherwise agreed documents against which a draft is drawn are to be delivered to the drawee on acceptance of the draft if it is payable more than three days after presentment; otherwise, only on payment.

Section 2-515. *Preserving Evidence of Goods in Dispute*—In furtherance of the adjustment of any claim or dispute
(a)   either party on reasonable notification to the other and for the purpose of ascertaining the facts and preserving evidence has the right to inspect, test and sample the goods including such of them as may be in the possession or control of the other; and
(b)   the parties may agree to a third-party inspection or survey to determine the conformity or condition of the goods and may agree that the findings shall be binding upon them in any subsequent litigation or adjustment.

Part 6: Breach, Repudiation, and Excuse

Section 2-601. *Buyer's Rights on Improper Delivery*—Subject to the provisions of this Article on breach in installment contracts (§ 2-612) and unless otherwise agreed under the sections on contractual limitation of remedy (§§ 2-718 and 2-719), if the goods or the tender of delivery fail in any respect to conform to the contract, the buyer may
(a)   reject the whole; or

(b)   accept the whole; or

(c)   accept any commercial unit or units and reject the rest.

Section 2-602. *Manner and Effect of Rightful Rejection*—(1) Rejection of goods must be within a reasonable time after their delivery or tender. It is ineffective unless the buyer seasonably notifies the seller. This is particularly important for sellers and credit grantors who long after the sale is made when they are experiencing collection problems first have an attempted rejection by the buyer of nonconforming goods. The UCC requires any rejection for nonconforming goods to be within a reasonable time, and there must be a reasonable notification to the seller. Absent this, the seller may appropriately object to the claimed rejection of the goods.

(2)   Subject to the provisions of the two following sections on rejected goods (§§ 2-603 and 2-604),

(a)   after rejection any exercise of ownership by the buyer with respect to any commercial unit is wrongful as against the seller; and

(b)   if the buyer has before rejection taken physical possession of goods in which he does not have a security interest under the provisions of this Article (subsection (3) of § 2-711), he is under a duty after rejection to hold them with reasonable care at the seller's disposition for a time sufficient to permit the seller to remove them; but

(c)   the buyer has no further obligations with regard to goods rightfully rejected.

(3)   The seller's rights with respect to goods wrongfully rejected are governed by the provisions of this Article on seller's remedies in general (§ 2-703).

Section 2-603. *Merchant Buyer's Duties as to Rightfully Rejected Goods*—(1) Subject to any security interest in the buyer (subsection (3) of § 2-711), when the seller has no agent or place of business at the market of rejection a merchant buyer is under a duty after rejection of goods in his possession or control to follow any reasonable instructions received from the seller with respect to the goods and in the absence of such instructions to make reasonable efforts to sell them for the seller's account if they are perishable or threaten to decline in value speedily. Instructions are not reasonable if on demand indemnity for expenses is not forthcoming.

(2)   When the buyer sells goods under subsection (1), he is entitled to reimbursement from the seller or out of the proceeds for reasonable expenses of caring for and selling them, and if the expenses include no selling commission then to such commission as is usual in the trade or if there is none to a reasonable sum not exceeding 10 percent on the gross proceeds.

(3)   In complying with this section the buyer is held only to good faith and good faith conduct hereunder is neither acceptance nor conversion nor the basis of an action for damages.

Section 2-604. *Buyer's Options As to Salvage of Rightfully Rejected Goods*—Subject to the provisions of the immediately preceding section on perishables if the seller gives no instructions within a reasonable time after notification of rejection the buyer may store the rejected goods for the seller's account or reship them to him or resell them for the seller's account with reimbursement as provided in the preceding section. Such action is not acceptance or conversion.

Section 2-605. *Waiver of Buyer's Objections by Failure to Particularize*—(1) The buyer's failure to state in connection with rejection a particular defect which is ascertainable by reasonable inspection precludes him from relying on the unstated defect to justify rejection or to establish breach

(a)   where the seller could have cured it if stated seasonably; or

(b)   between merchants when the seller has after rejection made a request in writing for a full and final written statement of all defects on which the buyer proposes to rely.

(2)   Payment against documents made without reservation of rights precludes recovery of the payment for defects apparent on the face of the documents.

Section 2-606. *What Constitutes Acceptance of Goods*—(1) Acceptance of goods occurs when the buyer

(a)   after a reasonable opportunity to inspect the goods signifies to the seller that the goods are conforming or that he will take or retain them in spite of their nonconformity; or

(b)   fails to make an effective rejection (subsection (1) of § 2-602), but such acceptance does not occur until the buyer has had a reasonable opportunity to inspect them; or

(c)   does any act inconsistent with the seller's ownership; but if such act is wrongful as against the seller it is an acceptance only if ratified by him.

(2)   Acceptance of a part of any commercial unit is acceptance of that entire unit.

Section 2-607. *Effect of Acceptance; Notice of Breach; Burden of Establishing Breach after Acceptance; Notice of Claim or Litigation to Person Answerable Over*—(1) The buyer must pay at the contract rate for any goods accepted.

(2)   Acceptance of goods by the buyer precludes rejection of the goods accepted and if made with knowledge of a nonconformity cannot be revoked because of it unless the acceptance was on the reasonable assumption that the nonconformity would be seasonably cured but acceptance does not of itself impair any other remedy provided by this Article for nonconformity.

(3)   Where a tender has been accepted

(a)   the buyer must within a reasonable time after he discovers or should have discovered any breach notify the seller of breach or be barred from any remedy; and

(b)   if the claim is one for infringement or the like (subsection (3) of § 2-312) and the buyer is sued as a result of such breach he must so notify the seller within a reasonable time after he receives notice of the litigation or be barred from any remedy over for liability established by the litigation.

(4)   The burden is on the buyer to establish any breach with respect to the goods accepted.

(5)   Where the buyer is sued for breach of a warranty or other obligation for which his seller is answerable over:

(a)   He may give his seller written notice of the litigation. If the notice states that the seller may come in and defend and that if the seller does not do so he will be bound in any action against him by his buyer by any determination of fact common to the two litigations, then unless the seller after seasonable receipt of the notice does come in and defend he is so bound.

(b)   If the claim is one for infringement or the like (subsection (3) of § 2-312) the original seller may demand in writing that his buyer turn over to him control of the litigation including settlement or else be barred from any remedy over and if he also agrees to bear all expense and to satisfy any adverse judgment, then unless the buyer after seasonable receipt of the demand does turn over control the buyer is so barred.

(6)   The provisions of subsections (3), (4) and (5) apply to any obligation of a buyer to hold a seller harmless against infringement or the like (subsection (3) of § 2-312).

Section 2-608. *Revocation of Acceptance in Whole or in Part*—(1) The buyer may revoke his acceptance of a lot or commercial unit whose nonconformity substantially impairs its value to him if he has accepted it

(a)   on the reasonable assumption that its nonconformity would be cured and it has not been seasonably cured; or

(b)   without discovery of such nonconformity if his acceptance was reasonably induced either by the difficulty of discovery before acceptance or by the seller's assurances.

(2)   Revocation of acceptance must occur within a reasonable time after the buyer discovers or should have discovered the ground for it and before any substantial change in condition of the goods which is not caused by their own defects. It is not effective until the buyer notifies the seller of it.

(3)   A buyer who so revokes has the same rights and duties with regard to the goods involved as if he had rejected them.

Section 2-609. *Right to Adequate Assurance of Performance*—(1) A contract for sale imposes an obligation on each party that the other's expectation of receiving due performance will not be impaired. When reasonable grounds for insecurity arise with respect to the performance of either party the other may in writing demand adequate assurance of due perform-ance and until he receives such assurance may if commercially reasonable suspend any per-formance for which he has not already received the agreed return.

(2) Between merchants the reasonableness of grounds for insecurity and the adequacy of any assurance offered shall be determined according to commercial standards.

(3) Acceptance of any improper delivery or payment does not prejudice the aggrieved party's right to demand adequate assurance of future performance.

(4) After receipt of a justified demand failure to provide within a reasonable time not exceeding 30 days such assurance of due performance as is adequate under the circumstances of the particular case is a repudiation of the contract.

Section 2-610. *Anticipatory Repudiation*—When either party repudiates the contract with respect to a performance not yet due the loss of which will substantially impair the value of the contract to the other, the aggrieved party may

(a) for a commercially reasonable time await performance by the repudiating party; or

(b) resort to any remedy for breach (§ 2-703 or § 2-711), even though he has notified the repudiating party that he would await the latter's performance, and has urged retrac-tion; and

(c) in either case suspend his own performance or proceed in accordance with the provi-sions of this Article on the seller's right to identify goods to the contract notwithstand-ing breach or to salvage unfinished goods (§ 2-704).

Section 2-611. *Retraction of Anticipatory Repudiation*—(1) Until the repudiating party's next performance is due he can retract his repudiation unless the aggrieved party has since the repudiation canceled or materially changed his position or otherwise indicated that he consid-ers the repudiation final.

(2) Retraction may be by any method which clearly indicates to the aggrieved party that the repudiating party intends to perform, but must include any assurance justifiably demanded under the provisions of this Article (§ 2-609).

(3) Retraction reinstates the repudiating party's rights under the contract with due excuse and allowance to the aggrieved party for any delay occasioned by the repudiation.

Section 2-612. *"Installment Contract"; Breach*—(1) An "installment contract" is one which requires or authorizes the delivery of goods in separate lots to be separately accepted, even though the contract contains a clause "each delivery is a separate contract" or its equivalent.

(2) The buyer may reject any installment which is nonconforming if the nonconformity substantially impairs the value of that installment and cannot be cured or if the nonconformity is a defect in the required documents; but if the nonconformity does not fall within subsection (3) and the seller gives adequate assurance of its cure the buyer must accept that installment.

(3) Whenever nonconformity or default with respect to one or more installments substan-tially impairs the value of the whole contract there is a breach of the whole. But the aggrieved party reinstates the contract if he accepts a nonconforming installment without seasonably notifying of cancellation or if he brings an action with respect only to past installments or demands performance as to future installments.

Section 2-613. *Casualty to Identified Goods*—Where the contract requires for its perform-ance goods identified when the contract is made, and the goods suffer casualty without fault of either party before the risk of loss passes to the buyer, or in a proper case under a "no arrival, no sale" term (§ 2-324) then

(a) if the loss is total the contract is avoided; and

(b) if the loss is partial or the goods have so deteriorated as no longer to conform to the contract the buyer may nevertheless demand inspection and at his option either treat the contract as avoided or accept the goods with due allowance from the contract price for the deterioration or the deficiency in quantity but without further right against the seller.

Section 2-614. *Substituted Performance*—(1) Where without fault of either party the agreed berthing, loading, or unloading facilities fail or an agreed type of carrier becomes unavailable or the agreed manner of delivery otherwise becomes commercially impracticable but a commercially reasonable substitute is available, such substitute performance must be tendered and accepted.

(2) If the agreed means or manner of payment fails because of domestic or foreign governmental regulation, the seller may withhold or stop delivery unless the buyer provides a means or manner of payment which is commercially a substantial equivalent. If delivery has already been taken, payment by the means in the manner provided by the regulation discharges the buyer's obligation unless the regulation is discriminatory, oppressive or predatory.

Section 2-615. *Excuse by Failure of Presupposed Conditions*—Except so far as a seller may have assumed a greater obligation and subject to the preceding section on substituted performance:

(a) Delay in delivery or nondelivery in whole or in part by a seller who complies with paragraphs (b) and (c) is not a breach of his duty under a contract for sale if performance as agreed has been made impracticable by the occurrence of a contingency the nonoccurrence of which was a basic assumption on which the contract was made or by compliance in good faith with any applicable foreign or domestic governmental regulation or order whether or not it later proves to be invalid.

(b) Where the causes mentioned in paragraph (a) affect only a part of the seller's capacity to perform, he must allocate production and deliveries among his customers but may at his option include regular customers not then under contract as well as his own requirements for further manufacture. He may so allocate in any manner which is fair and reasonable.

(c) The seller must notify the buyer seasonably that there will be delay or nondelivery and, when allocation is required under paragraph (b), of the estimated quota thus made available for the buyer.

Section 2-616. *Procedure on Notice Claiming Excuse*—(1) Where the buyer receives notification of a material or indefinite delay or an allocation justified under the preceding section he may by written notification to the seller as to any delivery concerned, and where the prospective deficiency substantially impairs the value of the whole contract under the provisions of this Article relating to breach of installment contracts (§ 2-612), then also as to the whole,

(a) terminate and thereby discharge any unexecuted portion of the contract; or

(b) modify the contract by agreeing to take his available quota in substitution.

(2) If after receipt of such notification from the seller the buyer fails so to modify the contract within a reasonable time not exceeding 30 days the contract lapses with respect to any deliveries affected.

(3) The provisions of this section may not be negated by agreement except insofar as seller has assumed greater obligation under preceding section.

Part 7: Remedies

Section 2-701. *Remedies for Breach of Collateral Contracts Not Impaired*—Remedies for breach of any obligation or promise collateral or ancillary to a contract for sale are not impaired by the provisions of this Article.

Section 2-702. *Seller's Remedies on Discovery of Buyer's Insolvency*—(1) Where the seller discovers the buyer to be insolvent he may refuse delivery except for cash including payment for all goods theretofore delivered under the contract, and stop delivery under this Article (§ 2-705).

(2) Where the seller discovers that the buyer has received goods on credit while insolvent he may reclaim the goods upon demand made within 10 days after the receipt, but if misrepresentation of solvency has been made to the particular seller in writing within three months

before delivery, the 10-day limitation does not apply. Except as provided in this subsection the seller may not base a right to reclaim goods on the buyer's fraudulent or innocent misrepresentation of solvency or of intent to pay.

(3) The seller's right to reclaim under subsection (2) is subject to the rights of a buyer in ordinary course or other good faith purchase or lien creditor under this Article (§ 2-403). Successful reclamation of goods excludes all other remedies with respect to them.

Section 2-703. *Seller's Remedies in General*—Where the buyer wrongfully rejects or revokes acceptance of goods or fails to make a payment due on or before delivery or repudiates with respect to a part or the whole, then with respect to any goods directly affected and, if the breach is of the whole contract (§ 2-612), then also with respect to the whole undelivered balance, the aggrieved seller may

(a) withhold delivery of such goods;
(b) stop delivery by any bailee as hereafter provided (§ 2-705);
(c) proceed under the next section respecting goods still unidentified to the contract;
(d) resell and recover damages as hereafter provided (§ 2-706);
(e) recover damages for nonacceptance (§ 2-708) or in a proper case the price (§ 2-709);
(f) cancel.

Section 2-704. *Seller's Right to Identify Goods to the Contract Notwithstanding Breach or to Salvage Unfinished Goods*—(1) An aggrieved seller under the preceding section may

(a) identify to the contract conforming goods not already identified if at the time he learned of the breach they are in his possession or control;
(b) treat as the subject of resale goods which have demonstrably been intended for the particular contract even though those goods are unfinished.

(2) Where the goods are unfinished an aggrieved seller may in the exercise of reasonable commercial judgment for the purposes of avoiding loss and of effective realization either complete the manufacture and wholly identify the goods to the contract or cease manufacture and resell for scrap or salvage value or proceed in any other reasonable manner.

Section 2-705. *Seller's Stoppage of Delivery in Transit or Otherwise*—(1) The seller may stop delivery of goods in the possession of a carrier or other bailee when he discovers the buyer to be insolvent (§ 2-702) and may stop delivery of carload, truckload, planeload or larger shipments of express or freight when the buyer repudiates or fails to make a payment due before delivery or if for any other reason the seller has a right to withhold or reclaim the goods.

(2) As against such buyer the seller may stop delivery until
(a) receipt of the goods by the buyer; or
(b) acknowledgment to the buyer by any bailee of the goods except a carrier that the bailee holds the goods for the buyer; or
(c) such acknowledgment to the buyer by a carrier by reshipment or as warehouseman; or
(d) negotiation to the buyer of any negotiable document of title covering the goods.

(3)(a) To stop delivery the seller must so notify as to enable the bailee by reasonable diligence to prevent delivery of the goods.
(b) After such notification the bailee must hold and deliver the goods according to the directions of the seller but the seller is liable to the bailee for any ensuing charges or damages.
(c) If a negotiable document of title has been issued for goods the bailee is not obliged to obey a notification to stop until surrender of the document.
(d) A carrier who has issued a nonnegotiable bill of lading is not obliged to obey a notification to stop received from a person other than the consigner.

Section 2-706. *Seller's Resale Including Contract for Resale*—(1) Under the conditions stated in Section 2-703 on seller's remedies, the seller may resell the goods concerned or the undelivered balance thereof. Where the resale is made in good faith and in a commercially reasonable manner the seller may recover the difference between the resale price and the contract price together with any incidental damages allowed under the provisions of this Article (Section 2-710), but less expenses saved in consequence of the buyer's breach.

(2)   Except as otherwise provided in subsection (3) or unless otherwise agreed resale may be at public or private sale including sale by way of one or more contracts to sell or of identification to an existing contract of the seller. Sale may be as a unit or in parcels and at any time and place and on any terms but every aspect of the sale including the method, manner, time, place and terms must be commercially reasonable. The resale must be reasonably identified as referring to the broken contract, but it is not necessary that the goods be in existence or that any or all of them have been identified to the contract before the breach.

(3)   Where the resale is at private sale the seller must give the buyer reasonable notification of his intention to resell.

(4)   Where the resale is at public sale

(a)   only identified goods can be sold except where there is a recognized market for a public sale of futures in goods of the kind; and

(b)   it must be made at a usual place or market for public sale if one is reasonably available and except in the case of goods which are perishable or threaten to decline in value speedily the seller must give the buyer reasonable notice of the time and place of the resale; and

(c)   if the goods are not to be within the view of those attending the sale the notification of sale must state the place where the goods are located and provide for their reasonable inspection by prospective bidders; and

(d)   the seller may buy.

(5)   A purchaser who buys in good faith at a resale takes the goods free of any rights of the original buyer even though the seller fails to comply with one or more of the requirements of this section.

(6)   The seller is not accountable to the buyer for any profit made on any resale. A person in the position of a seller (Section 2-707) or a buyer who has rightfully rejected or justifiably revoked acceptance must account for any excess over the amount of his security interest, as hereinafter defined (subsection (3) of Section 2-711).

Section 2-707. *Person in the Position of a Seller*—(1) A "person in the position of a seller" includes as against a principal an agent who has paid or become responsible for the price of goods on behalf of his principal or anyone who otherwise holds a security interest or other right in goods similar to that of a seller.

(2)   A person in the position of a seller may as provided in this Article withhold or stop delivery (Section 2-705) and resell (Section 2-706) and recover incidental damages (Section 2-710).

Section 2-708. *Seller's Damages for Nonacceptance or Repudiation*—(1) Subject to subsection (2) and to the provisions of this Article with respect to proof of market price (§ 2-723), the measure of damages for nonacceptance or repudiation by the buyer is the difference between the market price at the time and place for tender and the unpaid contract price together with any incidental damages provided in this Article (§ 2-710), but less expenses saved in consequence of the buyer's breach.

(2)   If the measure of damages provided in subsection (1) is inadequate to put the seller in as good a position as performance would have done then the measure of damages is the profit (including reasonable overhead) which the seller would have made from full performance by the buyer, together with any incidental damages provided in this Article (§ 2-710), due allowance for costs reasonably incurred and due credit for payments or proceeds of resale.

Section 2-709. *Action for the Price*—(1) When the buyer fails to pay the price as it becomes due the seller may recover, together with any incidental damages under the next section, the price

(a)   of goods accepted or of conforming goods lost or damaged within a commercially reasonable time after risk of their loss has passed to the buyer; and

(b)   of goods identified to the contract if the seller is unable after reasonable effort to resell them at a reasonable price or the circumstances reasonably indicate that such effort will be unavailing.

(2)   Where the seller sues for the price he must hold for the buyer any goods which have been identified to the contract and are still in his control except that if resale becomes possible he may resell them at any time prior to the collection of the judgment. The net proceeds of any such resale must be credited to the buyer and payment of the judgment entitles him to any goods not resold.

(3)   After the buyer has wrongfully rejected or revoked acceptance of the goods or has failed to make a payment due or has repudiated (§ 2-610), a seller who is held not entitled to the price under this section shall nevertheless be awarded damages for nonacceptance under the preceding section.

Section 2-710. *Seller's Incidental Damages*—Incidental damages to an aggrieved seller include any commercially reasonable charges, expenses or commissions incurred in stopping delivery, in the transportation, care and custody of goods after the buyer's breach, in connection with return or resale of the goods or otherwise resulting from the breach.

Section 2-711. *Buyer's Remedies in General; Buyer's Security Interest in Rejected Goods*—(1) Where the seller fails to make delivery or repudiates or the buyer rightfully rejects or justifiably revokes acceptance then with respect to any goods involved, and with respect to the whole if the breach goes to the whole contract (§ 2-612), the buyer may cancel and whether or not he has done so may in addition to recovering so much of the price as has been paid
   (a)   "cover" and have damages under the next section as to all the goods affected whether or not they have been identified to the contract; or
   (b)   recover damages for nondelivery as provided in this Article (§ 2-713).
   (2) Where the seller fails to deliver or repudiates the buyer may also
   (a)   if the goods have been identified recover them as provided in this Article (§ 2-502); or
   (b)   in a proper case obtain specific performance or replevy the goods as provided in this Article (§ 2-716).
   (3)   On rightful rejection or justifiable revocation of acceptance a buyer has a security interest in goods in his possession or control for any payments made on their price and any expenses reasonably incurred in their inspection, receipt, transportation, care and custody and may hold such goods and resell them in like manner as an aggrieved seller (§ 2-706).

Section 2-712. *"Cover"; Buyer's Procurement of Substitute Goods*—(1) After a breach within the preceding section the buyer may "cover" by making in good faith and without unreasonable delay any reasonable purchase of or contract to purchase goods in substitution for those due from seller.

(2)   The buyer may recover from the seller as damages the difference between the cost of cover and the contract price together with any incidental or consequential damages as hereinafter defined (§ 2-715), but less expenses saved in consequence of the seller's breach.

(3)   Failure of the buyer to effect cover within this section does not bar him from any other remedy.

Section 2-713. *Buyer's Damages for Nondelivery or Repudiation*—(1) Subject to the provisions of this Article with respect to proof of market price (§ 2-723), the measure of damages for nondelivery or repudiation by the seller is the difference between the market price at the time the buyer learned of the breach and the contract price together with any incidental and consequential damages as provided in this Article (§ 2-715), but less expenses saved in consequence of the seller's breach.

(2)   Market price is to be determined as of the place for tender or, in cases of rejection after arrival or revocation of acceptance, as of the place of arrival.

Section 2-714. *Buyer's Damages for Breach in Regard to Accepted Goods*—(1) Where the buyer has accepted goods and given notification (subsection (3) of § 2-607) he may recover as damages for any nonconformity of tender the loss resulting in the ordinary course of events from the seller's breach as determined in any manner which is reasonable.

(2) The measure of damages for breach of warranty is the difference at the time and place of acceptance between the value of the goods accepted and the value they would have had if they had been as warranted, unless special circumstances show proximate damages of a different amount.

(3) In a proper case any incidental and consequential damages under the next section may also be recovered.

Section 2-715. *Buyer's Incidental and Consequential Damages*—(1) Incidental damages resulting from the seller's breach include expenses reasonably incurred in inspection, receipt, transportation and care and custody of goods rightfully rejected, any commercially reasonable charges, expenses or commissions in connection with effecting cover and any other reasonable expense incident to the delay or other breach.

(2) Consequential damages resulting from the seller's breach include

(a) any loss resulting from general or particular requirements and needs of which the seller at the time of contracting had reason to know and which could not reasonably be prevented by cover or otherwise; and

(b) injury to person or property proximately resulting from any breach of warranty.

Section 2-716. *Buyer's Right to Specific Performance or Replevin*—(1) Specific performance may be decreed where the goods are unique or in other proper circumstances.

(2) The decree for specific performance may include such terms and conditions as to payment of the price, damages, or other relief as the court may deem just.

(3) The buyer has a right of replevin for goods identified to the contract if after reasonable effort he is unable to effect cover for such goods or the circumstances reasonably indicate that such effort will be unavailing or if the goods have been shipped under reservation and satisfaction of the security interest in them has been made or tendered.

Section 2-717. *Deduction of Damages from Price*—The buyer on notifying the seller of his intention to do so may deduct all or any part of the damages resulting from any breach of the contract from any part of the price still due under the same contract.

Section 2-718. *Liquidation or Limitation of Damages; Deposits*—(1) Damages for breach by either party may be liquidated in the agreement but only at an amount which is reasonable in the light of the anticipated or actual harm caused by the breach, the difficulties of proof of loss, and the inconvenience or nonfeasibility of otherwise obtaining an adequate remedy. A term fixing unreasonably large liquidated damages is void as a penalty.

(2) Where the seller justifiably withholds delivery of goods because of the buyer's breach, the buyer is entitled to restitution of any amount by which the sum of his payments exceeds

(a) the amount to which the seller is entitled by virtue of terms liquidating the seller's damages in accordance with subsection (1); or

(b) in the absence of such terms, 20 percent of the value of the total performance for which the buyer is obligated under the contract or $500, whichever is smaller.

(3) The buyer's right to restitution under subsection (2) is subject to offset to the extent that the seller establishes

(a) a right to recover damages under the provisions of this Article other than subsection (1); and

(b) the amount or value of any benefits received by the buyer directly or indirectly by reason of the contract.

(4) Where a seller has received payment in goods their reasonable value or the proceeds of their resale shall be treated as payments for the purposes of subsection (2); but if the seller has notice of the buyer's breach before reselling goods received in part performance, his

resale is subject to the conditions laid down in this Article on resale by an aggrieved seller (§ 2-706).

Section 2-719. *Contractual Modification or Limitation of Remedy*—(1) Subject to the provisions of subsections (2) and (3) of this section and of the preceding section on liquidation and limitation of damages,

(a) the agreement may provide for remedies in addition to or in substitution for those provided in this Article and may limit or alter the measure of damages recoverable under this Article, as by limiting the buyer's remedies to return of the goods and repayment of the price or to repair and replacement of nonconforming goods or parts; and

(b) resort to a remedy as provided is optional unless the remedy is expressly agreed to be exclusive, in which case it is the sole remedy.

(2) Where circumstances cause an exclusive or limited remedy to fail of its essential purpose remedy may be had as provided in this Act.

(3) Consequential damages may be limited or excluded unless the limitation or exclusion is unconscionable. Limitation of consequential damages for injury to the person in the case of consumer goods is prima facie unconscionable but limitation of damages where the loss is commercial is not.

Section 2-720. *Effect of "Cancellation" or "Rescission" on Claims for Antecedent Breach*—Unless the contrary intention clearly appears, expressions of "cancellation" or "rescission" of the contract or the like shall not be construed as a renunciation or discharge of any claim in damages for an antecedent breach.

Section 2-721. *Remedies for Fraud*—Remedies for material misrepresentation or fraud include all remedies available under this Article for nonfraudulent breach. Neither rescission nor a claim for rescission of the contract for sale nor rejection or return of the goods shall bar or be deemed inconsistent with a claim for damages or other remedy.

Section 2-722. *Who Can Sue Third Parties for Injury to Goods*—Where a third party so deals with goods which have been identified to a contract for sale as to cause actionable injury to a party to that contract

(1) a right of action against the third party is in either party to the contract for sale who has title to or a security interest or a special property or an insurable interest in the goods; and if the goods have been destroyed or converted a right of action is also in the party who either bore the risk of loss under the contract for sale or has since the injury assumed that risk as against the other;

(2) if at the time of the injury the party plaintiff did not bear the risk of loss as against the other party to the contract for sale and there is no arrangement between them for disposition of the recovery, his suit or settlement is, subject to his own interest, as a fiduciary for the other party to the contract;

(3) either party may with the consent of the other sue for the benefit of whom it may concern.

Section 2-723. *Proof of Market Price: Time and Place*—(1) If an action based on anticipatory repudiation comes to trial before the time for performance with respect to some or all of the goods, any damages based on market price (Section 2-708 or Section 2-713) shall be determined according to the price of such goods prevailing at the time when the aggrieved party learned of the repudiation.

(2) If evidence of a price prevailing at the times or places described in this Article is not readily available the price prevailing within any reasonable time before or after the time described or at any other place which in commercial judgment or under usage of trade would serve as a reasonable substitute for the one described may be used, making any proper allowance for the cost of transporting the goods to or from such other place.

(3) Evidence of a relevant price prevailing at a time or place other than the one described in this Article offered by one party is not admissible unless and until he has given the other party such notice as the court finds sufficient to prevent unfair surprise.

Section 2-724. *Admissibility of Market Quotations*—Whenever the prevailing price or value of any goods regularly bought and sold in any established commodity market is in issue, reports in official publications or trade journals or in newspapers or periodicals of general circulation published as the reports of such market shall be admissible in evidence. The circumstances of the preparation of such a report may be shown to affect its weight but not its admissibility.

Section 2-725. *Statute of Limitations in Contracts for Sale*—(1) This is the statute of limitations section for all of Article 2 dealing with sales. This four-year statute of limitations is that which is applicable for any contract involving the sale of goods. A state's statute of limitation which is general in nature and different does not apply with respect to an agreement for the sale of goods. An action for breach of any contract for sale must be commenced within four years after the cause of action has accrued. By the original agreement the parties may reduce the period of limitation to not less than one year but may not extend it.

(2) A cause of action accrues when the breach occurs, regardless of the aggrieved party's lack of knowledge of the breach. A breach of warranty occurs when tender of delivery is made, except that where a warranty explicitly extends to future performance of the goods and discovery of the breach must await the time of such performance the cause of action accrues when the breach is or should have been discovered.

(3) Where an action commenced within the time limited by subsection (1) is so terminated as to leave available a remedy by another action for the same breach such other action may be commenced after the expiration of the time limited and within six months after the termination of the first action unless the termination resulted from voluntary discontinuance or from dismissal for failure or neglect to prosecute.

(4) This section does not alter the law on tolling of the statute of limitations nor does it apply to causes of action which have accrued before this Act becomes effective.

ARTICLE 2A: LEASES

Part 1: General Provisions

Section 2A-101. *Short Title*—This Article shall be known and may be cited as the Uniform Commercial Code—Leases.

Section 2A-102. *Scope*—This Article applies to any transaction, regardless of form, that creates a lease.

Section 2A-103. *Definitions and Index of Definitions*—(1) In this Article unless the context otherwise requires:

(a) "Buyer in ordinary course of business" means a person who in good faith and without knowledge that the sale to him [or her] is in violation of the ownership rights or security interest or leasehold interest of a third party in the goods, buys in ordinary course from a person in the business of selling goods of that kind but does not include a pawnbroker. "Buying" may be for cash or by exchange of other property or on secured or unsecured credit and includes receiving goods or documents of title under a preexisting contract for sale but does not include a transfer in bulk or as security for or in total or partial satisfaction of a money debt.

(b) "Cancellation" occurs when either party puts an end to the lease contract for default by the other party.

(c) "Commercial unit" means such a unit of goods as by commercial usage is a single whole for purposes of lease and division of which materially impairs its character or value on the market or in use. A commercial unit may be a single article, as a machine, or a set of articles, as a suite of furniture or a line of machinery, or a quantity, as a gross or carload, or any other unit treated in use or in the relevant market as a single whole.

(d) "Conforming" goods or performance under a lease contract means goods or performance that are in accordance with the obligations under the lease contract.

(e) "Consumer lease" means a lease that a lessor regularly engaged in the business of leasing or selling makes to a lessee, except an organization, who takes under the lease primarily for a personal, family, or household purpose, if the total payments to be made under the lease contract, excluding payments for options to renew or buy, do not exceed $25,000.

(f) "Fault" means wrongful act, omission, breach, or default.

(g) "Finance lease" means a lease in which (i) the lessor does not select, manufacture or supply the goods, (ii) the lessor acquires the goods or the right to possession and use of the goods in connection with the lease, and (iii) either the lessee receives a copy of the contract evidencing the lessor's purchase of the goods on or before signing the lease contract, or the lessee's approval of the contract evidencing the lessor's purchase of the goods is a condition to effectiveness of the lease contract.

(h) "Goods" means all things that are movable at the time of identification to the lease contract, or are fixtures (§ 2A-309), but the term does not include money, documents, instruments, accounts, chattel paper, general intangibles, or minerals or the like, including oil and gas, before extraction. The term also includes the unborn young of animals.

(i) "Installment lease contract" means a lease contract that authorizes or requires the delivery of goods in separate lots to be separately accepted, even though the lease contract contains a clause "each delivery is a separate lease" or its equivalent.

(j) "Lease" means a transfer of the right to possession and use of goods for a term in return for consideration, but a sale, including a sale on approval or a sale or return, or retention or creation of a security interest is not a lease. Unless the context clearly indicates otherwise, the term includes a sublease.

(k) "Lease agreement" means the bargain, with respect to the lease, of the lessor and the lessee in fact as found in their language or by implication from other circumstances including course of dealing or usage of trade or course of performance as provided in this Article. Unless the context clearly indicates otherwise, the term includes a sublease agreement.

(l) "Lease contract" means the total legal obligation that results from the lease agreement as affected by this Article and any other applicable rules of law. Unless the context clearly indicates otherwise, the term includes a sublease contract.

(m) "Leasehold interest" means the interest of the lessor or the lessee under a lease contract.

(n) "Lessee" means a person who acquires the right to possession and use of goods under a lease. Unless the context clearly indicates otherwise, the term includes a sublessee.

(o) "Lessee in ordinary course of business" means a person who in good faith and without knowledge that the lease to him [or her] is in violation of the ownership rights or security interest or leasehold interest of a third party in the goods, leases in ordinary course from a person in the business of selling or leasing goods of that kind but does not include a pawnbroker. "Leasing" may be for cash or by exchange of other property or on secured or unsecured credit and includes receiving goods or documents of title under a preexisting lease contract but does not include a transfer in bulk or as security for or in total or partial satisfaction of a money debt.

(p) "Lessor" means a person who transfers the right to possession and use of goods under a lease. Unless the context clearly indicates otherwise, the term includes a sublessor.

(q) "Lessor's residual interest" means the lessor's interest in the goods after expiration, termination, or cancellation of the lease contract.

(r) "Lien" means a charge against or interest in goods to secure payment of a debt or performance of an obligation, but the term does not include a security interest.

(s) "Lot" means a parcel or a single article that is the subject matter of a separate lease or delivery, whether or not it is sufficient to perform the lease contract.

(t) "Merchant lessee" means a lessee that is a merchant with respect to goods of the kind subject to the lease.

(u) "Present value" means the amount as of a date certain of one or more sums payable in the future, discounted to the date certain. The discount is determined by the interest rate specified by the parties if the rate was not manifestly unreasonable at the time the transaction was entered into; otherwise, the discount is determined by a commercially reasonable rate that takes into account the facts and circumstances of each case at the time the transaction was entered into.

(v) "Purchase" includes taking by sale, lease, mortgage, security interest, pledge, gift, or any other voluntary transaction creating an interest in goods.

(w) "Sublease" means a lease of goods the right to possession and use of which was acquired by the lessor as a lessee under an existing lease.

(x) "Supplier" means a person from whom a lessor buys or leases goods to be leased under a finance lease.

(y) "Supply contract" means a contract under which a lessor buys or leases goods to be leased.

(z) "Termination" occurs when either party pursuant to a power created by agreement or law puts an end to the lease contract otherwise than for default.

(2) Other definitions applying to this Article and the sections in which they appear are:
"Accessions." Section 2A-310(1)
"Construction mortgage." Section 2A-309(1)(d)
"Encumbrance." Section 2A-309(1)(e)
"Fixtures." Section 2A-309(1)(a)
"Fixture filing." Section 2A-309(1)(b)
"Purchase money lease." Section 2A-309(1)(c).

(3) The following definitions in other Articles apply to this Article:
"Accounts." Section 9-106
"Between merchants." Section 2-104(3)
"Buyer." Section 2-103(1)(a)   "Chattel paper." Section 9-105(1)(b)
"Consumer goods." Section 9-109(1)
"Documents." Section 9-105(1)(f)
"Entrusting." Section 2-403(3)
"General intangibles." Section 9-106
"Good faith." Section 2-103(1)(b)
"Instruments." Section 9-105(1)(i)
"Merchant." Section 2-104(1)
"Mortgage." Section 9-105(1)(j)
"Pursuant to commitment." Section 9-105(1)(k)
"Receipt." Section 2-103(1)(c)
"Sale." Section 2-106(1)
"Sale on approval." Section 2-326
"Sale or return." Section 2-326
"Seller." Section 2-103(1)(d).

(4) In addition Article 1 contains general definitions and principles of construction and interpretation applicable throughout this Article.

Section 2A-104. *Leases Subject to Other Statutes*—(1) A lease, although subject to this Article, is also subject to any applicable:

(a) statute of the United States;

(b) certificate of title statute of this State: (list any certificate of title statutes covering automobiles, trailers, mobile homes, boats, farm tractors, and the like);

(c) certificate of title statute of another jurisdiction (§ 2A-105); or

(d) consumer protection statute of this State.

(2) In case of conflict between the provisions of this Article, other than Sections 2A-105, 2A-304(3) and 2A-305(3), and any statute referred to in subsection (1), the provisions of that statute control.

(3) Failure to comply with any applicable statute has only the effect specified therein.

Section 2A-105. *Territorial Application of Article to Goods Covered by Certificate of Title*—Subject to the provisions of Sections 2A-304(3) and 2A-305(3), with respect to goods covered by a certificate of title issued under a statute of this State or of another jurisdiction, compliance and the effect of compliance or noncompliance with a certificate of title statute are governed by the law (including the conflict of laws rules) of the jurisdiction issuing the certificate until the earlier of (a) surrender of the certificate, or (b) four months after the goods are removed from that jurisdiction and thereafter until a new certificate of title is issued by another jurisdiction.

Section 2A-106. *Limitation on Power of Parties to Consumer Lease to Choose Applicable Law and Judicial Forum*—(1) If the law chosen by the parties to a consumer lease is that of a jurisdiction other than a jurisdiction in which the lessee resides at the time the lease agreement becomes enforceable or within 30 days thereafter or in which the goods are to be used, the choice is not enforceable.

(2)   If the judicial forum chosen by the parties to a consumer lease is a forum that would not otherwise have jurisdiction over the lessee, the choice is not enforceable.

Section 2A-107. *Waiver or Renunciation of Claim or Right After Default*—Any claim or right arising out of an alleged default or breach of warranty may be discharged in whole or in part without consideration by a written waiver or renunciation signed and delivered by the aggrieved party.

Section 2A-108. *Unconscionability*—(1) If the court as a matter of law finds a lease contract or any clause of a lease contract to have been unconscionable at the time it was made, the court may refuse to enforce the lease contract, or it may enforce the remainder of the lease contract without the unconscionable clause, or it may so limit the application of any unconscionable clause as to avoid any unconscionable result.

(2)   With respect to a consumer lease, if the court as a matter of law finds that a lease contract or any clause of a lease contract has been induced by unconscionable conduct or that unconscionable conduct has occurred in the collection of a claim arising from a lease contract, the court may grant appropriate relief.

(3)   Before making a finding of unconscionability under subsection (1) or (2), the court, on its own motion or that of a party, shall afford the parties a reasonable opportunity to present evidence as to the setting, purpose, and effect of the lease contract or clause thereof, or of the conduct.

(4)   In an action in which the lessee claims unconscionability with respect to a consumer lease:

(a)   If the court finds unconscionability under subsection (1) or (2), the court shall award reasonable attorney's fees to the lessee.

(b)   If the court does not find unconscionability and the lessee claiming unconscionability has brought or maintained an action he [or she] knew to be groundless, the court shall award reasonable attorney's fees to the party against whom the claim is made.

(c)   In determining attorney's fees, the amount of the recovery on behalf of the claimant under subsections (1) and (2) is not controlling.

Section 2A-109. *Option to Accelerate at Will*—(1) A term providing that one party or his [or her] successor in interest may accelerate payment or performance or require collateral or additional collateral "at will" or "when he [or she] deems himself [or herself] insecure" or in words of similar import must be construed to mean that he [or she] has power to do so only if he [or she] in good faith believes that the prospect of payment or performance is impaired.

(2)   With respect to a consumer lease, the burden of establishing good faith under subsection (1) is on the party who exercised the power; otherwise the burden of establishing lack of good faith is on the party against whom the power has been exercised.

Part 2: Formation and Construction of Lease Contract

Section 2A-201. *Statute of Frauds*—(1) A lease contract is not enforceable by way of action or defense unless:

    (a)   the total payments to be made under the lease contract, excluding payments for options to renew or buy, are less than $1,000; or

    (b)   there is a writing, signed by the party against whom enforcement is sought or by that party's authorized agent, sufficient to indicate that a lease contract has been made between the parties and to describe the goods leased and the lease term.

(2)   Any description of leased goods or of the lease term is sufficient and satisfies subsection (1)(b), whether or not it is specific, if it reasonably identifies what is described.

(3)   A writing is not insufficient because it omits or incorrectly states a term agreed upon, but the lease contract is not enforceable under subsection (1)(b) beyond the lease term and the quantity of goods shown in the writing.

(4)   A lease contract that does not satisfy the requirements of subsection (1), but which is valid in other respects, is enforceable:

    (a)   if the goods are to be specially manufactured or obtained for the lessee and are not suitable for lease or sale to others in the ordinary course of the lessor's business, and the lessor, before notice of repudiation is received and under circumstances that reasonably indicate that the goods are for the lessee, has made either a substantial beginning of their manufacture or commitments for their procurement;

    (b)   if the party against whom enforcement is sought admits in that party's pleading, testimony or otherwise in court that a lease contract was made, but the lease contract is not enforceable under this provision beyond the quantity of goods admitted; or

    (c)   with respect to goods that have been received and accepted by the lessee.

(5)   The lease term under a lease contract referred to in subsection (4) is:

    (a)   if there is a writing signed by the party against whom enforcement is sought or by that party's authorized agent specifying the lease term, the term so specified;

    (b)   if the party against whom enforcement is sought admits in that party's pleading, testimony, or otherwise in court a lease term, the term so admitted; or

    (c)   a reasonable lease term.

Section 2A-202. *Final Written Expression: Parol or Extrinsic Evidence*—Terms with respect to which the confirmatory memoranda of the parties agree or which are otherwise set forth in a writing intended by the parties as a final expression of their agreement with respect to such terms as are included therein may not be contradicted by evidence of any prior agreement or of a contemporaneous oral agreement but may be explained or supplemented:

    (a)   by course of dealing or usage of trade or by course of performance; and

    (b)   by evidence of consistent additional terms unless the court finds the writing to have been intended also as a complete and exclusive statement of the terms of the agreement.

Section 2A-203. *Seals Inoperative*—The affixing of a seal to a writing evidencing a lease contract or an offer to enter into a lease contract does not render the writing a sealed instrument and the law with respect to sealed instruments does not apply to the lease contract or offer.

Section 2A-204. *Formation in General*—(1) A lease contract may be made in any manner sufficient to show agreement, including conduct by both parties which recognizes the existence of a lease contract.

(2)   An agreement sufficient to constitute a lease contract may be found although the moment of its making is undetermined.

(3)   Although one or more terms are left open, a lease contract does not fail for indefiniteness if the parties have intended to make a lease contract and there is a reasonably certain basis for giving an appropriate remedy.

Section 2A-205. *Firm Offers*—An offer by a merchant to lease goods to or from another person in a signed writing that by its terms gives assurance it will be held open is not revocable, for lack of consideration, during the time stated or, if no time is stated, for a reasonable time, but in no event may the period of irrevocability exceed 3 months. Any such term of assurance on a form supplied by the offeree must be separately signed by the offeror.

Section 2A-206. *Offer and Acceptance in Formation of Lease Contract*—(1) Unless otherwise unambiguously indicated by the language or circumstances, an offer to make a lease contract must be construed as inviting acceptance in any manner and by any medium reasonable in the circumstances.

(2) If the beginning of a requested performance is a reasonable mode of acceptance, an offeror who is not notified of acceptance within a reasonable time may treat the offer as having lapsed before acceptance.

Section 2A-207. *Course of Performance or Practical Construction*—(1) If a lease contract involves repeated occasions for performance by either party with knowledge of the nature of the performance and opportunity for objection to it by the other, any course of performance accepted or acquiesced in without objection is relevant to determine the meaning of the lease agreement.

(2) The express terms of a lease agreement and any course of performance, as well as any course of dealing and usage of trade, must be construed whenever reasonable as consistent with each other; but if that construction is unreasonable, express terms control course of performance, course of performance controls both course of dealing and usage of trade, and course of dealing controls usage of trade.

(3) Subject to the provisions of Section 2A-208 on modification and waiver, course of performance is relevant to show a waiver or modification of any term inconsistent with the course of performance.

Section 2A-208. *Modification, Rescission and Waiver*—(1) An agreement modifying a lease contract needs no consideration to be binding.

(2) A signed lease agreement that excludes modification or rescission except by a signed writing may not be otherwise modified or rescinded, but, except as between merchants, such a requirement on a form supplied by a merchant must be separately signed by the other party.

(3) Although an attempt at modification or rescission does not satisfy the requirements of subsection (2), it may operate as a waiver.

(4) A party who has made a waiver affecting an executory portion of a lease contract may retract the waiver by reasonable notification received by the other party that strict performance will be required of any term waived, unless the retraction would be unjust in view of a material change of position in reliance on the waiver.

Section 2A-209. *Lessee under Finance Lease as Beneficiary of Supply Contract*—(1) The benefit of the supplier's promises to the lessor under the supply contract and of all warranties, whether express or implied, under the supply contract, extends to the lessee to the extent of the lessee's leasehold interest under a finance lease related to the supply contract, but subject to the terms of the supply contract and all of the supplier's defenses or claims arising therefrom.

(2) The extension of the benefit of the supplier's promises to the lessee does not: (a) modify the rights and obligations of the parties to the supply contract, whether arising therefrom or otherwise, or (b) impose any duty or liability under the supply contract on the lessee.

(3) Any modification or rescission of the supply contract by the supplier and the lessor is effective against the lessee unless, prior to the modification or rescission, the supplier has received notice that the lessee has entered into a finance lease related to the supply contract. If the supply contract is modified or rescinded after the lessee enters the finance lease, the lessee has a cause of action against the lessor, and against the supplier if the supplier has notice of the lessee's entering the finance lease when the supply contract is modified or rescinded. The resulting judgment shall put the lessee in as good a position as if the modification or rescission had not occurred.

Section 2A-210. *Express Warranties*—(1) Express warranties by the lessor are created as follows:

(a) Any affirmation of fact or promise made by the lessor to the lessee which relates to the goods and becomes part of the basis of the bargain creates an express warranty that the goods will conform to the affirmation or promise.

(b) Any description of the goods which is made part of the basis of the bargain creates an express warranty that the goods will conform to the description.

(c) Any sample or model that is made part of the basis of the bargain creates an express warranty that the whole of the goods will conform to the sample or model.

(2) It is not necessary to the creation of an express warranty that the lessor use formal words, such as "warrant" or "guarantee," or that the lessor have a specific intention to make a warranty, but an affirmation merely of the value of the goods or a statement purporting to be merely the lessor's opinion or commendation of the goods does not create a warranty.

Section 2A-211. *Warranties against Interference and against Infringement; Lessee's Obligation against Infringement*—(1) There is in a lease contract a warranty that for the lease term no person holds a claim to or interest in the goods that arose from an act or omission of the lessor, other than a claim by way of infringement or the like, which will interfere with the lessee's enjoyment of its leasehold interest.

(2) Except in a finance lease there is in a lease contract by a lessor who is a merchant regularly dealing in goods of the kind, a warranty that the goods are delivered free of the rightful claim of any person by way of infringement or the like.

(3) A lessee who furnishes specifications to a lessor or a supplier shall hold the lessor and the supplier harmless against any claim by way of infringement or the like that arises out of compliance with the specifications.

Section 2A-212. *Implied Warranty of Merchantability*—(1) Except in a finance lease, a warranty that the goods will be merchantable is implied in a lease contract if the lessor is a merchant with respect to goods of that kind.

(2) Goods to be merchantable must be at least such as

(a) pass without objection in the trade under the description in the lease agreement;

(b) in the case of fungible goods, are of fair average quality within the description;

(c) are fit for the ordinary purposes for which goods of that type are used;

(d) run, within the variation permitted by the lease agreement, of even kind, quality, and quantity within each unit and among all units involved;

(e) are adequately contained, packaged, and labeled as the lease agreement may require; and

(f) conform to any promises or affirmations of fact made on the container or label.

(3) Other implied warranties may arise from course of dealing or usage of trade.

Section 2A-213. *Implied Warranty of Fitness for Particular Purpose*—Except in a finance lease, if the lessor at the time the lease contract is made has reason to know of any particular purpose for which the goods are required and that the lessee is relying on the lessor's skill or judgment to select or furnish suitable goods, there is in the lease contract an implied warranty that the goods will be fit for that purpose.

Section 2A-214. *Exclusion or Modification of Warranties*—(1) Words or conduct relevant to the creation of an express warranty and words or conduct tending to negate or limit a warranty must be construed wherever reasonable as consistent with each other; but, subject to the provisions of Section 2A-202 on parol or extrinsic evidence, negation or limitation is inoperative to the extent that the construction is unreasonable.

(2) Subject to subsection (3), to exclude or modify the implied warranty of merchantability or any part of it the language must mention "merchantability," be by a writing, and be conspicuous. Subject to subsection (3), to exclude or modify any implied warranty of fitness the exclusion must be by a writing and be conspicuous. Language to exclude all implied warranties of fitness is sufficient if it is conspicuous and states, for example, "There is no warranty that the goods will be fit for a particular purpose."

(3) Notwithstanding subsection (2), but subject to subsection (4),

(a) unless the circumstances indicate otherwise, all implied warranties are excluded by expressions like "as is" or "with all faults" or by other language that in common understanding calls the lessee's attention to the exclusion of warranties, makes plain that there is no implied warranty, and is conspicuous;

(b) if the lessee before entering into the lease contract has examined the goods or the sample or model as fully as desired or has refused to examine the goods, there is no implied warranty with regard to defects that an examination ought in the circumstances to have revealed; and

(c) an implied warranty may also be excluded or modified by course of dealing, course of performance, or usage of trade.

(4) To exclude or modify a warranty against interference or against infringement (§ 2A-211) or any part of it, the language must be specific, be by a writing, and be conspicuous, unless the circumstances, including course of performance, course of dealing, or usage of trade, give the lessee reason to know that the goods are being leased subject to a claim or interest of any person.

Section 2A-215. *Cumulation and Conflict of Warranties Express or Implied*—Warranties, whether express or implied, must be construed as consistent with each other and as cumulative, but if that construction is unreasonable, the intention of the parties determines which warranty is dominant. In ascertaining that intention the following rules apply:

(a) Exact or technical specifications displace an inconsistent sample or model or general language of description.

(b) A sample from an existing bulk displaces inconsistent general language of description.

(c) Express warranties displace inconsistent implied warranties other than an implied warranty of fitness for a particular purpose.

Section 2A-216. *Third-Party Beneficiaries of Express and Implied Warranties.*

Alternative A

A warranty to or for the benefit of a lessee under this Article, whether express or implied, extends to any natural person who is in the family or household of the lessee or who is a guest in the lessee's home if it is reasonable to expect that such person may use, consume, or be affected by the goods and who is injured in person by breach of the warranty. This section does not displace principles of law and equity that extend a warranty to or for the benefit of a lessee to other persons. The operation of this section may not be excluded, modified, or limited, but an exclusion, modification, or limitation of the warranty, including any with respect to rights and remedies, effective against the lessee is also effective against any beneficiary designated under this section.

Alternative B

A warranty to or for the benefit of a lessee under this Article, whether express or implied, extends to any natural person who may reasonably be expected to use, consume, or be affected by the goods and who is injured in person by breach of the warranty. This section does not displace principles of law and equity that extend a warranty to or for the benefit of a lessee to other persons. The operation of this section may not be excluded, modified, or limited, but an exclusion, modification, or limitation of the warranty, including any with respect to rights and remedies, effective against the lessee is also effective against the beneficiary designated under this section.

Alternative C

A warranty to or for the benefit of a lessee under this Article, whether express or implied, extends to any person who may reasonably be expected to use, consume, or be affected by the goods and who is injured by breach of the warranty. The operation of this section may not be excluded, modified, or limited with respect to injury to the person of an individual to whom the warranty extends, but an exclusion, modification, or limitation of the warranty, including any with respect to rights and remedies, effective against the lessee is also effective against the beneficiary designated under this section.

Section 2A-217. *Identification*—Identification of goods as goods to which a lease contract refers may be made at any time and in any manner explicitly agreed to by the parties. In the absence of explicit agreement, identification occurs:

(a) when the lease contract is made if the lease contract is for a lease of goods that are existing and identified;

(b) when the goods are shipped, marked, or otherwise designated by the lessor as goods to which the lease contract refers, if the lease contract is for a lease of goods that are not existing and identified; or

(c) when the young are conceived, if the lease contract is for a lease of unborn young of animals.

Section 2A-218. *Insurance and Proceeds*—(1) A lessee obtains an insurable interest when existing goods are identified to the lease contract even though the goods identified are non-conforming and the lessee has an option to reject them.

(2) If a lessee has an insurable interest only by reason of the lessor's identification of the goods, the lessor, until default or insolvency or notification to the lessee that identification is final, may substitute other goods for those identified.

(3) Notwithstanding a lessee's insurable interest under subsections (1) and (2), the lessor retains an insurable interest until an option to buy has been exercised by the lessee and risk of loss has passed to the lessee.

(4) Nothing in this section impairs any insurable interest recognized under any other statute or rule of law.

(5) The parties by agreement may determine that one or more parties have an obligation to obtain and pay for insurance covering the goods and by agreement may determine the beneficiary of the proceeds of the insurance.

Section 2A-219. *Risk of Loss*—(1) Except in the case of a finance lease, risk of loss is retained by the lessor and does not pass to the lessee. In the case of a finance lease, risk of loss passes to the lessee.

(2) Subject to the provisions of this Article on the effect of default on risk of loss (§ 2A-220), if risk of loss is to pass to the lessee and the time of passage is not stated, the following rules apply:

(a) If the lease contract requires or authorizes the goods to be shipped by carrier

    (i) and it does not require delivery at a particular destination, the risk of loss passes to the lessee when the goods are duly delivered to the carrier; but

    (ii) if it does require delivery at a particular destination and the goods are there duly tendered while in the possession of the carrier, the risk of loss passes to the lessee when the goods are there duly so tendered as to enable the lessee to take delivery.

(b) If the goods are held by a bailee to be delivered without being moved, the risk of loss passes to the lessee on acknowledgment by the bailee of the lessee's right to possession of the goods.

(c) In any case not within subsection (a) or (b), the risk of loss passes to the lessee on the lessee's receipt of the goods if the lessor, or, in the case of a finance lease, the supplier, is a merchant; otherwise the risk passes to the lessee on tender of delivery.

Section 2A-220. *Effect of Default on Risk of Loss*—(1) Where risk of loss is to pass to the lessee and the time of passage is not stated:

(a) If a tender or delivery of goods so fails to conform to the lease contract as to give a right of rejection, the risk of their loss remains with the lessor, or, in the case of a finance lease, the supplier, until cure or acceptance.

(b) If the lessee rightfully revokes acceptance, he [or she], to the extent of any deficiency in his [or her] effective insurance coverage, may treat the risk of loss as having remained with the lessor from the beginning.

(2) Whether or not risk of loss is to pass to the lessee, if the lessee as to conforming goods already identified to a lease contract repudiates or is otherwise in default under the lease contract, the lessor, or, in the case of a finance lease, the supplier, to the extent of any deficiency in his [or her] effective insurance coverage may treat the risk of loss as resting on the lessee for a commercially reasonable time.

Section 2A-221. *Casualty to Identified Goods*—If a lease contract requires goods identified when the lease contract is made, and the goods suffer casualty without fault of the lessee, the lessor or the supplier before delivery, or the goods suffer casualty before risk of loss passes to the lessee pursuant to the lease agreement or Section 2A-219, then:

(a) if the loss is total, the lease contract is avoided; and

(b) if the loss is partial or the goods have so deteriorated as to no longer conform to the lease contract, the lessee may nevertheless demand inspection and at his [or her] option either treat the lease contract as avoided or, except in a finance lease that is not a consumer lease, accept the goods with due allowance from the rent payable for the balance of the lease term for the deterioration or the deficiency in quantity but without further right against the lessor.

Part 3: Effect of Lease Contract

Section 2A-301. *Enforceability of Lease Contract*—Except as otherwise provided in this Article, a lease contract is effective and enforceable according to its terms between the parties, against purchasers of the goods and against creditors of the parties.

Section 2A-302. *Title to and Possession of Goods*—Except as otherwise provided in this Article, each provision of this Article applies whether the lessor or a third party has title to the goods, and whether the lessor, the lessee, or a third party has possession of the goods, notwithstanding any statute or rule of law that possession or the absence of possession is fraudulent.

Section 2A-303. *Alienability of Party's Interest Under Lease Contract or of Lessor's Residual Interest in Goods; Delegation of Performance; Assignment of Rights*—(1) Any interest of a party under a lease contract and the lessor's residual interest in the goods may be transferred unless:

(a) the transfer is voluntary and the lease contract prohibits the transfer; or

(b) the transfer materially changes the duty of or materially increases the burden or risk imposed on the other party to the lease contract, and within a reasonable time after notice of the transfer the other party demands that the transferee comply with subsection (2) and the transferee fails to comply.

(2) Within a reasonable time after demand pursuant to subsection (1)(b), the transferee shall:

(a) cure or provide adequate assurance that he [or she] will promptly cure any default other than one arising from the transfer;

(b) compensate or provide adequate assurance that he [or she] will promptly compensate the other party to the lease contract and any other person holding an interest in the lease contract, except the party whose interest is being transferred, for any loss to that party resulting from the transfer;

(c) provide adequate assurance of future due performance under the lease contract; and

(d) assume the lease contract.

(3) Demand pursuant to subsection (1)(b) is without prejudice to the other party's rights against the transferee and the party whose interest is transferred.

(4) An assignment of "the lease" or of "all my rights under the lease" or an assignment in similar general terms is a transfer of rights, and unless the language or the circumstances, as in an assignment for security, indicate the contrary, the assignment is a delegation of duties

by the assignor to the assignee and acceptance by the assignee constitutes a promise by him [or her] to perform those duties. This promise is enforceable by either the assignor or the other party to the lease contract.

(5) Unless otherwise agreed by the lessor and the lessee, no delegation of performance relieves the assignor as against the other party of any duty to perform or any liability for default.

(6) A right to damages for default with respect to the whole lease contract or a right arising out of the assignor's due performance of his [or her] entire obligation can be assigned despite agreement otherwise.

Section 2A-304. *Subsequent Lease of Goods by Lessor*—(1) Subject to the provisions of Section 2A-303, a subsequent lessee from a lessor of goods under an existing lease contract obtains, to the extent of the leasehold interest transferred, the leasehold interest in the goods that the lessor had or had power to transfer, and except as provided in subsection (2) and Section 2A-527(4), takes subject to the existing lease contract. A lessor with voidable title has power to transfer a good leasehold interest to a good faith subsequent lessee for value, but only to the extent set forth in the preceding sentence. When goods have been delivered under a transaction of purchase the lessor has that power even though:

(a) the lessor's transferor was deceived as to the identity of the lessor;
(b) the delivery was in exchange for a check which is later dishonored;
(c) it was agreed that the transaction was to be a "cash sale"; or
(d) the delivery was procured through fraud punishable as larcenous under the criminal law.

(2) A subsequent lessee in the ordinary course of business from a lessor who is a merchant dealing in goods of that kind to whom the goods were entrusted by the existing lessee before the interest of the subsequent lessee became enforceable against the lessor obtains, to the extent of the leasehold interest transferred, all of the lessor's and the existing lessee's rights to the goods, and takes free of the existing lease contract.

(3) A subsequent lessee from the lessor of goods that are subject to an existing lease contract and are covered by a certificate of title issued under a statute of this State or of another jurisdiction takes no greater rights than those provided both by this section and by the certificate of title statute.

Section 2A-305. *Sale or Sublease of Goods by Lessee*—(1) Subject to the provisions of Section 2A-303, a buyer or sublessee from the lessee of goods under an existing lease contract obtains, to the extent of the interest transferred, the leasehold interest in the goods that the lessee had or had power to transfer, and except as provided in subsection (2) and Section 2A-511(4), takes subject to the existing lease contract. A lessee with a voidable leasehold interest has power to transfer a good leasehold interest to a good faith buyer for value or a good faith sublessee for value, but only to the extent set forth in the preceding sentence. When goods have been delivered under a transaction of lease the lessee has that power even though:

(a) the lessor was deceived as to the identity of the lessee;
(b) the delivery was in exchange for a check which is later dishonored; or
(c) the delivery was procured through fraud punishable as larcenous under the criminal law.

(2) A buyer in the ordinary course of business or a sublessee in the ordinary course of business from a lessee who is a merchant dealing in goods of that kind to whom the goods were entrusted by the lessor obtains, to the extent of the interest transferred, all of the lessor's and lessee's rights to the goods, and takes free of the existing lease contract.

(3) A buyer or sublessee from the lessee of goods that are subject to an existing lease contract and are covered by a certificate of title issued under a statute of this State or of another jurisdiction takes no greater rights than those provided both by this section and by the certificate of title statute.

Section 2A-306. *Priority of Certain Liens Arising by Operation of Law*—If a person in the ordinary course of his [or her] business furnishes services or materials with respect to goods subject to a lease contract, a lien upon those goods in the possession of that person given by statute or rule of law for those materials or services is enforceable and takes priority over any interest of the lessor or lessee under the lease contract or this Article unless the lien is created by statute and the statute provides otherwise or unless the lien is created by rule of law and the rule of law provides otherwise.

Section 2A-307. *Priority of Liens Arising by Attachment or Levy on, Security Interests in, and Other Claims to Goods*—(1) Except as otherwise provided in Section 2A-306, a creditor of a lessee takes subject to the lease contract.

(2)   Except as otherwise provided in subsections (3) and (4) of this section and in Sections 2A-306 and 2A-308, a creditor of a lessor takes subject to the lease contract:

(a)   unless the creditor holds a lien that attached to the goods before the lease contract became enforceable, or

(b)   unless the creditor holds a security interest in the goods that under the Article on Secured Transactions (Article 9) would have priority over any other security interest in the goods perfected by a filing covering the goods and made at the time the lease contract became enforceable, whether or not any other security interest existed.

(3)   A lessee in the ordinary course of business takes the leasehold interest free of a security interest in the goods created by the lessor even though the security interest is perfected and the lessee knows of its existence.

(4)   A lessee other than a lessee in the ordinary course of business takes the leasehold interest free of a security interest to the extent that it secures future advances made after the secured party acquires knowledge of the lease or more than 45 days after the lease contract becomes enforceable, whichever first occurs, unless the future advances are made pursuant to a commitment entered into without knowledge of the lease and before the expiration of the 45-day period.

Section 2A-308. *Special Rights of Creditors*—(1) A creditor of a lessor in possession of goods subject to a lease contract may treat the lease contract as void if as against the creditor retention of possession by the lessor is fraudulent under any statute or rule of law, but retention of possession in good faith and current course of trade by the lessor for a commercially reasonable time after the lease contract becomes enforceable is not fraudulent.

(2)   Nothing in this Article impairs the rights of creditors of a lessor if the lease contract (a) becomes enforceable, not in current course of trade but in satisfaction of or as security for a pre-existing claim for money, security, or the like, and (b) is made under circumstances which under any statute or rule of law apart from this Article would constitute the transaction a fraudulent transfer or voidable preference.

(3)   creditor of a seller may treat a sale or an identification of goods to a contract for sale as void if as against the creditor retention of possession by the seller is fraudulent under any statute or rule of law, but retention of possession of the goods pursuant to a lease contract entered into by the seller as lessee and the buyer as lessor in connection with the sale or identification of the goods is not fraudulent if the buyer bought for value and in good faith.

Section 2A-309. *Lessor's and Lessee's Rights When Goods Become Fixtures*—(1) In this section:

(a)   goods are "fixtures" when they become so related to particular real estate that an interest in them arises under real estate law;

(b)   a "fixture filing" is the filing, in the office where a mortgage on the real estate would be recorded or registered, of a financing statement concerning goods that are or are to become fixtures and conforming to the requirements of subsection (5) of Section 9-402;

(c)   a lease is a "purchase money lease" unless the lessee has possession or use of the goods or the right to possession or use of the goods before the lease agreement is enforceable;

(d)　a mortgage is a "construction mortgage" to the extent it secures an obligation incurred for the construction of an improvement on land including the acquisition cost of the land, if the recorded writing so indicates; and

(e)　"encumbrance" includes real estate mortgages and other liens on real estate and all other rights in real estate that are not ownership interests.

(2)　Under this Article a lease may be of goods that are fixtures or may continue in goods that become fixtures, but no lease exists under this Article of ordinary building materials incorporated into an improvement on land.

(3)　This Article does not prevent creation of a lease of fixtures pursuant to real estate law.

(4)　The perfected interest of a lessor of fixtures has priority over a conflicting interest of an encumbrancer or owner of the real estate if:

(a)　the lease is a purchase money lease, the conflicting interest of the encumbrancer or owner arises before the goods become fixtures, the interest of the lessor is perfected by a fixture filing before the goods become fixtures or within 10 days thereafter, and the lessee has an interest of record in the real estate or is in possession of the real estate; or

(b)　the interest of the lessor is perfected by a fixture filing before the interest of the encumbrancer or owner is of record, the lessor's interest has priority over any conflicting interest of a predecessor in title of the encumbrancer or owner, and the lessee has an interest of record in the real estate or is in possession of the real estate.

(5)　The interest of a lessor of fixtures, whether or not perfected, has priority over the conflicting interest of an encumbrancer or owner of the real estate if:

(a)　the fixtures are readily removable factory or office machines, readily removable equipment that is not primarily used or leased for use in the operation of the real estate, or readily removable replacements of domestic appliances that are goods subject to a consumer lease, and before the goods become fixtures the lease contract is enforceable; or

(b)　the conflicting interest is a lien on the real estate obtained by legal or equitable proceedings after the lease contract is enforceable; or

(c)　the encumbrancer or owner has consented in writing to the lease or has disclaimed an interest in the goods as fixtures; or

(d)　the lessee has a right to remove the goods as against the encumbrancer or owner. If the lessee's right to remove terminates, the priority of the interest of the lessor continues for a reasonable time.

(6)　Notwithstanding paragraph (a) of subsection (4) but otherwise subject to subsections (4) and (5), the interest of a lessor of fixtures is subordinate to the conflicting interest of an encumbrancer of the real estate under a construction mortgage recorded before the goods become fixtures if the goods become fixtures before the completion of the construction. To the extent given to refinance a construction mortgage, the conflicting interest of an encumbrancer of the real estate under a mortgage has this priority to the same extent as the encumbrancer of the real estate under the construction mortgage.

(7)　In cases not within the preceding subsections, priority between the interest of a lessor of fixtures and the conflicting interest of an encumbrancer or owner of the real estate who is not the lessee is determined by the priority rules governing conflicting interests in real estate.

(8)　If the interest of a lessor has priority over all conflicting interests of all owners and encumbrancers of the real estate, the lessor or the lessee may (a) on default, expiration, termination, or cancellation of the lease agreement by the other party but subject to the provisions of the lease agreement and this Article, or (b) if necessary to enforce his [or her] other rights and remedies under this Article, remove the goods from the real estate, free and clear of all conflicting interests of all owners and encumbrancers of the real estate, but he [or she] must reimburse any encumbrancer or owner of the real estate who is not the lessee and who has not otherwise agreed for the cost of repair of any physical injury, but not for any diminution in value of the real estate caused by the absence of the goods removed or by any necessity of replacing them. A person entitled to reimbursement may refuse permission to remove until the party seeking removal gives adequate security for the performance of this obligation.

(9)   Even though the lease agreement does not create a security interest, the interest of a lessor of fixtures is perfected by filing a financing statement as a fixture filing for leased goods that are or are to become fixtures in accordance with the relevant provisions of the Article on Secured Transactions (Article 9).

Section 2A-310. *Lessor's and Lessee's Rights When Goods Become Accessions*—(1) Goods are "accessions" when they are installed in or affixed to other goods.

(2)   The interest of a lessor or a lessee under a lease contract entered into before the goods became accessions is superior to all interests in the whole except as stated in subsection (4).

(3)   The interest of a lessor or a lessee under a lease contract entered into at the time or after the goods became accessions is superior to all subsequently acquired interests in the whole except as stated in subsection (4) but is subordinate to interests in the whole existing at the time the lease contract was made unless the holders of such interests in the whole have in writing consented to the lease or disclaimed an interest in the goods as part of the whole.

(4)   The interest of a lessor or a lessee under a lease contract described in subsection (2) or (3) is subordinate to the interest of:

(a)   a buyer in the ordinary course of business or a lessee in the ordinary course of business of any interest in the whole acquired after the goods became accessions; or

(b)   a creditor with a security interest in the whole perfected before the lease contract was made to the extent that the creditor makes subsequent advances without knowledge of the lease contract.

(5)   Then under subsections (2) or (3) and (4) a lessor or a lessee of accessions holds an interest that is superior to all interests in the whole, the lessor or the lessee may (a) on default, expiration, termination, or cancellation of the lease contract by the other party but subject to the provisions of the lease contract and this Article, or (b) if necessary to enforce his [or her] other rights and remedies under this Article, remove the goods from the whole, free and clear of all interests in the whole, but he [or she] must reimburse any holder of an interest in the whole who is not the lessee and who has not otherwise agreed for the cost of repair of any physical injury but not for any diminution in value of the whole caused by the absence of the goods removed or by any necessity for replacing them. A person entitled to reimbursement may refuse permission to remove until the party seeking removal gives adequate security for the performance of this obligation.

Part 4: Performance of Lease Contract: Repudiated, Substituted, and Excused

Section 2A-401. *Insecurity: Adequate Assurance of Performance*—(1) A lease contract imposes an obligation on each party that the other's expectation of receiving due performance will not be impaired.

(2)   If reasonable grounds for insecurity arise with respect to the performance of either party, the insecure party may demand in writing adequate assurance of due performance. Until the insecure party receives that assurance, if commercially reasonable the insecure party may suspend any performance for which he [or she] has not already received the agreed return.

(3)   A repudiation of the lease contract occurs if assurance of due performance adequate under the circumstances of the particular case is not provided to the insecure party within a reasonable time, not to exceed 30 days after receipt of a demand by the other party.

(4)   Between merchants, the reasonableness of grounds for insecurity and the adequacy of any assurance offered must be determined according to commercial standards.

(5)   Acceptance of any nonconforming delivery or payment does not prejudice the aggrieved party's right to demand adequate assurance of future performance.

Section 2A-402. *Anticipatory Repudiation*—If either party repudiates a lease contract with respect to a performance not yet due under the lease contract, the loss of which performance will substantially impair the value of the lease contract to the other, the aggrieved party may:

(a)   for a commercially reasonable time, await retraction of repudiation and performance by the repudiating party;

(b)   make demand pursuant to Section 2A-401 and await assurance of future performance adequate under the circumstances of the particular case; or

(c)   resort to any right or remedy upon default under the lease contract or this Article, even though the aggrieved party has notified the repudiating party that the aggrieved party would await the repudiating party's performance and assurance and has urged retraction. In addition, whether or not the aggrieved party is pursuing one of the foregoing remedies, the aggrieved party may suspend performance or, if the aggrieved party is the lessor, proceed in accordance with the provisions of this Article on the lessor's right to identify goods to the lease contract notwithstanding default or to salvage unfinished goods (§ 2A-524).

Section 2A-403. *Retraction of Anticipatory Repudiation*—(1) Until the repudiating party's next performance is due, the repudiating party can retract the repudiation unless, since the repudiation, the aggrieved party has canceled the lease contract or materially changed the aggrieved party's position or otherwise indicated that the aggrieved party considers the repudiation final.

(2)   Retraction may be by any method that clearly indicates to the aggrieved party that the repudiating party intends to perform under the lease contract and includes any assurance demanded under Section 2A-401.

Section 2A-404. *Substituted Performance*—(1) If without fault of the lessee, the lessor and the supplier, the agreed berthing, loading, or unloading facilities fail or the agreed type of carrier becomes unavailable or the agreed manner of delivery otherwise becomes commercially impracticable, but a commercially reasonable substitute is available, the substitute performance must be tendered and accepted.

(2)   If the agreed means or manner of payment fails because of domestic or foreign governmental regulation:

(a)   the lessor may withhold or stop delivery or cause the supplier to withhold or stop delivery unless the lessee provides a means or manner of payment that is commercially a substantial equivalent; and

(b)   if delivery has already been taken, payment by the means or in the manner provided by the regulation discharges the lessee's obligation unless the regulation is discriminatory, oppressive, or predatory.

Section 2A-405. *Excused Performance*—Subject to Section 2A-404 on substituted performance, the following rules apply:

(a)   Delay in delivery or nondelivery in whole or in part by a lessor or a supplier who complies with paragraphs (b) and (c) is not a default under the lease contract if performance as agreed has been made impracticable by the occurrence of a contingency the nonoccurrence of which was a basic assumption on which the lease contract was made or by compliance in good faith with any applicable foreign or domestic governmental regulation or order, whether or not the regulation or order later proves to be invalid.

(b)   If the causes mentioned in paragraph (a) affect only part of the lessor's or the supplier's capacity to perform, he [or she] shall allocate production and deliveries among his [or her] customers but at his [or her] option may include regular customers not then under contract for sale or lease as well as his [or her] own requirements for further manufacture. He [or she] may so allocate in any manner that is fair and reasonable.

(c)   The lessor seasonably shall notify the lessee and in the case of a finance lease the supplier seasonably shall notify the lessor and the lessee, if known, that there will be delay or nondelivery and, if allocation is required under paragraph (b), of the estimated quota thus made available for the lessee.

Section 2A-406. *Procedure on Excused Performance*—(1) If the lessee receives notification of a material or indefinite delay or an allocation justified under Section 2A-405, the lessee may by written notification to the lessor as to any goods involved, and with respect to all of the goods if under an installment lease contract the value of the whole lease contract is substantially impaired (§ 2A-510):

   (a)   terminate the lease contract (§ 2A-505(2)); or

   (b)   except in a finance lease that is not a consumer lease, modify the lease contract by accepting the available quota in substitution, with due allowance from the rent payable for the balance of the lease term for the deficiency but without further right against the lessor.

(2)   If, after receipt of a notification from the lessor under Section 2A-405, the lessee fails so to modify the lease agreement within a reasonable time not exceeding 30 days, the lease contract lapses with respect to any deliveries affected.

Section 2A-407. *Irrevocable Promises: Finance Leases*—(1) In the case of a finance lease that is not a consumer lease the lessee's promises under the lease contract become irrevocable and independent upon the lessee's acceptance of the goods.

(2)   A promise that has become irrevocable and independent under subsection (1):

   (a)   is effective and enforceable between the parties by or against third parties including assignees of the parties, and

   (b)   is not subject to cancellation, termination, modification, repudiation, excuse, or substitution without the consent of the party to whom the promise runs.

Part 5: Default

A. In General

Section 2A-501. *Default: Procedure*—(1) Whether the lessor or the lessee is in default under a lease contract is determined by the lease agreement and this Article.

(2)   If the lessor or the lessee is in default under the lease contract, the party seeking enforcement has rights and remedies as provided in this Article and, except as limited by this Article, as provided in the lease agreement.

(3)   If the lessor or the lessee is in default under the lease contract, the party seeking enforcement may reduce the party's claim to judgment, or otherwise enforce the lease contract by self-help or any available judicial procedure or nonjudicial procedure, including administrative proceeding, arbitration, or the like, in accordance with this Article.

(4)   Except as otherwise provided in this Article or the lease agreement, the rights and remedies referred to in subsections (2) and (3) are cumulative.

(5)   If the lease agreement covers both real property and goods, the party seeking enforcement may proceed under this Part as to the goods, or under other applicable law as to both the real property and the goods in accordance with his [or her] rights and remedies in respect of the real property, in which case this Part does not apply.

Section 2A-502. *Notice after Default*—Except as otherwise provided in this Article or the lease agreement, the lessor or lessee in default under the lease contract is not entitled to notice of default or notice of enforcement from the other party to the lease agreement.

Section 2A-503. *Modification or Impairment of Rights and Remedies*—(1) Except as otherwise provided in this Article, the lease agreement may include rights and remedies for default in addition to or in substitution for those provided in this Article and may limit or alter the measure of damages recoverable under this Article.

(2)   Resort to a remedy provided under this Article or in the lease agreement is optional unless the remedy is expressly agreed to be exclusive. If circumstances cause an exclusive or limited remedy to fail of its essential purpose, or provision for an exclusive remedy is unconscionable, remedy may be had as provided in this Article.

(3)   Consequential damages may be liquidated under Section 2A-504, or may otherwise be limited, altered, or excluded unless the limitation, alteration, or exclusion is unconscionable. Limitation of consequential damages for injury to the person in the case of con-

sumer goods is prima facie unconscionable but limitation of damages where the loss is commercial is not.

(4) Rights and remedies on default by the lessor or the lessee with respect to any obligation or promise collateral or ancillary to the lease contract are not impaired by this Article.

Section 2A-504. *Liquidation of Damages*—(1) Damages payable by either party for default, or any other act or omission, including indemnity for loss or diminution of anticipated tax benefits or loss or damage to lessor's residual interest, may be liquidated in the lease agreement but only at an amount or by a formula that is reasonable in light of the then anticipated harm caused by the default or other act or omission.

(2) If the lease agreement provides for liquidation of damages, and such provision does not comply with subsection (1), or such provision is an exclusive or limited remedy that circumstances cause to fail of its essential purpose, remedy may be had as provided in this Article.

(3) If the lessor justifiably withholds or stops delivery of goods because of the lessee's default or insolvency (§ 2A-525 or 2A-526), the lessee is entitled to restitution of any amount by which the sum of his [or her] payments exceeds:

(a) the amount to which the lessor is entitled by virtue of terms liquidating the lessor's damages in accordance with subsection (1); or

(b) in the absence of those terms, 20 percent of the then present value of the total rent the lessee was obligated to pay for the balance of the lease term, or, in the case of a consumer lease, the lesser of such amount or $500.

(4) A lessee's right to restitution under subsection (3) is subject to offset to the extent the lessor establishes:

(a) a right to recover damages under the provisions of this Article other than subsection (1); and

(b) the amount or value of any benefits received by the lessee directly or indirectly by reason of the lease contract.

Section 2A-505. *Cancellation and Termination and Effect of Cancellation, Termination, Rescission, or Fraud on Rights and Remedies*—(1) On cancellation of the lease contract, all obligations that are still executory on both sides are discharged, but any right based on prior default or performance survives, and the canceling party also retains any remedy for default of the whole lease contract or any unperformed balance.

(2) On termination of the lease contract, all obligations that are still executory on both sides are discharged but any right based on prior default or performance survives.

(3) Unless the contrary intention clearly appears, expressions of "cancellation," "rescission," or the like of the lease contract may not be construed as a renunciation or discharge of any claim in damages for an antecedent default.

(4) Rights and remedies for material misrepresentation or fraud include all rights and remedies available under this Article for default.

(5) Neither rescission nor a claim for rescission of the lease contract nor rejection or return of the goods may bar or be deemed inconsistent with a claim for damages or other right or remedy.

Section 2A-506. *Statute of Limitations*—(1) An action for default under a lease contract, including breach of warranty or indemnity, must be commenced within four years after the cause of action accrued. By the original lease contract the parties may reduce the period of limitation to not less than one year.

(2) A cause of action for default accrues when the act or omission on which the default or breach of warranty is based is or should have been discovered by the aggrieved party, or when the default occurs, whichever is later. A cause of action for indemnity accrues when the act or omission on which the claim for indemnity is based is or should have been discovered by the indemnified party, whichever is later.

(3) If an action commenced within the time limited by subsection (1) is so terminated as to leave available a remedy by another action for the same default or breach of warranty or

indemnity, the other action may be commenced after the expiration of the time limited and within six months after the termination of the first action unless the termination resulted from voluntary discontinuance or from dismissal for failure or neglect to prosecute.

(4)   This section does not alter the law on tolling of the statute of limitations nor does it apply to causes of action that have accrued before this Article becomes effective.

Section 2A-507. *Proof of Market Rent: Time and Place*—(1) Damages based on market rent (§ 2A-519 or 2A-528) are determined according to the rent for the use of the goods concerned for a lease term identical to the remaining lease term of the original lease agreement and prevailing at the time of the default.

(2)   If evidence of rent for the use of the goods concerned for a lease term identical to the remaining lease term of the original lease agreement and prevailing at the times or places described in this Article is not readily available, the rent prevailing within any reasonable time before or after the time described or at any other place or for a different lease term which in commercial judgment or under usage of trade would serve as a reasonable substitute for the one described may be used, making any proper allowance for the difference, including the cost of transporting the goods to or from the other place.

(3) Evidence of a relevant rent prevailing at a time or place or for a lease term other than the one described in this Article offered by one party is not admissible unless and until he [or she] has given the other party notice the court finds sufficient to prevent unfair surprise.

(4)   If the prevailing rent or value of any goods regularly leased in any established market is in issue, reports in official publications or trade journals or in newspapers or periodicals of general circulation published as the reports of that market are admissible in evidence. The circumstances of the preparation of the report may be shown to affect its weight but not its admissibility.

B. Default by Lessor

Section 2A-508. *Lessee's Remedies*—(1) If a lessor fails to deliver the goods in conformity to the lease contract (§ 2A-509) or repudiates the lease contract (§ 2A-502), or a lessee rightfully rejects the goods (§ 2A-509) or justifiably revokes acceptance of the goods (§ 2A-517), then with respect to any goods involved, and with respect to all of the goods if under an installment lease contract the value of the whole lease contract is substantially impaired (§ 2A-510), the lessor is in default under the lease contract and the lessee may:

(a)   cancel the lease contract (§ 2A-505(1));

(b)   recover so much of the rent and security as has been paid, but in the case of an installment lease contract the recovery is that which is just under the circumstances;

(c)   cover and recover damages as to all goods affected whether or not they have been identified to the lease contract (§§ 2A-518 and 2A-520), or recover damages for nondelivery (§§ 2A-519 and 2A-520).

(2)   If a lessor fails to deliver the goods in conformity to the lease contract or repudiates the lease contract, the lessee may also:

(a)   if the goods have been identified, recover them (§ 2A-522); or

(b)   in a proper case, obtain specific performance or replevy the goods (§ 2A-521).

(3)   If a lessor is otherwise in default under a lease contract, the lessee may exercise the rights and remedies provided in the lease contract and this Article.

(4)   If a lessor has breached a warranty, whether express or implied, the lessee may recover damages (§ 2A-519(4)).

(5)   On rightful rejection or justifiable revocation of acceptance, a lessee has a security interest in goods in the lessee's possession or control for any rent and security that has been paid and any expenses reasonably incurred in their inspection, receipt, transportation, and care and custody and may hold those goods and dispose of them in good faith and in a commercially reasonable manner, subject to the provisions of Section 2A-527(5).

(6)   Subject to the provisions of Section 2A-407, a lessee, on notifying the lessor of the lessee's intention to do so, may deduct all or any part of the damages resulting from any default under the lease contract from any part of the rent still due under the same lease contract.

Section 2A-509. *Lessee's Rights on Improper Delivery; Rightful Rejection*—(1) Subject to the provisions of Section 2A-510 on default in installment lease contracts, if the goods or the tender or delivery fail in any respect to conform to the lease contract, the lessee may reject or accept the goods or accept any commercial unit or units and reject the rest of the goods.

(2) Rejection of goods is ineffective unless it is within a reasonable time after tender or delivery of the goods and the lessee seasonably notifies the lessor.

Section 2A-510. *Installment Lease Contracts: Rejection and Default*—(1) Under an installment lease contract a lessee may reject any delivery that is nonconforming if the nonconformity substantially impairs the value of that delivery and cannot be cured or the nonconformity is a defect in the required documents; but if the nonconformity does not fall within subsection (2) and the lessor or the supplier gives adequate assurance of its cure, the lessee must accept that delivery.

(2) Whenever nonconformity or default with respect to one or more deliveries substantially impairs the value of the installment lease contract as a whole there is a default with respect to the whole. But, the aggrieved party reinstates the installment lease contract as a whole if the aggrieved party accepts a nonconforming delivery without seasonably notifying of cancellation or brings an action with respect only to past deliveries or demands performance as to future deliveries.

Section 2A-511. *Merchant Lessee's Duties as to Rightfully Rejected Goods*—(1) Subject to any security interest of a lessee (§ 2A-508(5)), if a lessor or a supplier has no agent or place of business at the market of rejection, a merchant lessee, after rejection of goods in his [or her] possession or control, shall follow any reasonable instructions received from the lessor or the supplier with respect to the goods. In the absence of those instructions, a merchant lessee shall make reasonable efforts to sell, lease, or otherwise dispose of the goods for the lessor's account if they threaten to decline in value speedily. Instructions are not reasonable if on demand indemnity for expenses is not forthcoming.

(2) If a merchant lessee (subsection (1)) or any other lessee (§ 2A-512) disposes of goods, he [or she] is entitled to reimbursement either from the lessor or the supplier or out of the proceeds for reasonable expenses of caring for and disposing of the goods and, if the expenses include no disposition commission, to such commission as is usual in the trade, or if there is none, to a reasonable sum not exceeding 10 percent of the gross proceeds.

(3) In complying with this section or Section 2A-512, the lessee is held only to good faith. Good faith conduct hereunder is neither acceptance or conversion nor the basis of an action for damages.

(4) A purchaser who purchases in good faith from a lessee pursuant to this section or Section 2A-512 takes the goods free of any rights of the lessor and the supplier even though the lessee fails to comply with one or more of the requirements of this Article.

Section 2A-512. *Lessee's Duties as to Rightfully Rejected Goods*—(1) Except as otherwise provided with respect to goods that threaten to decline in value speedily (§ 2A-511) and subject to any security interest of a lessee (§ 2A-508(5)):

(a) the lessee, after rejection of goods in the lessee's possession, shall hold them with reasonable care at the lessor's or the supplier's disposition for a reasonable time after the lessee's seasonable notification of rejection;

(b) if the lessor or the supplier gives no instructions within a reasonable time after notification of rejection, the lessee may store the rejected goods for the lessor's or the supplier's account or ship them to the lessor or the supplier or dispose of them for the lessor's or the supplier's account with reimbursement in the manner provided in Section 2A-511; but

(c) the lessee has no further obligations with regard to goods rightfully rejected.

(2) Action by the lessee pursuant to subsection (1) is not acceptance or conversion.

Section 2A-513. *Cure by Lessor of Improper Tender or Delivery; Replacement*—(1) If any tender or delivery by the lessor or the supplier is rejected because nonconforming and the time for performance has not yet expired, the lessor or the supplier may seasonably notify the lessee of the lessor's or the supplier's intention to cure and may then make a conforming delivery within the time provided in the lease contract.

(2) If the lessee rejects a nonconforming tender that the lessor or the supplier had reasonable grounds to believe would be acceptable with or without money allowance, the lessor or the supplier may have a further reasonable time to substitute a conforming tender if he [or she] seasonably notifies the lessee.

Section 2A-514. *Waiver of Lessee's Objections*—(1) In rejecting goods, a lessee's failure to state a particular defect that is ascertainable by reasonable inspection precludes the lessee from relying on the defect to justify rejection or to establish default:

(a) if, stated seasonably, the lessor or the supplier could have cured it (§ 2A513); or

(b) between merchants if the lessor or the supplier after rejection has made a request in writing for a full and final written statement of all defects on which the lessee proposes to rely.

(2) A lessee's failure to reserve rights when paying rent or other consideration against documents precludes recovery of the payment for defects apparent on the face of the documents.

Section 2A-515. *Acceptance of Goods*—(1) Acceptance of goods occurs after the lessee has had a reasonable opportunity to inspect the goods and:

(a) the lessee signifies or acts with respect to the goods in a manner that signifies to the lessor or the supplier that the goods are conforming or that the lessee will take or retain them in spite of their nonconformity; or

(b) the lessee fails to make an effective rejection of the goods (§ 2A-509(2)).

(2) Acceptance of a part of any commercial unit is acceptance of that entire unit.

Section 2A-516. *Effect of Acceptance of Goods; Notice of Default; Burden of Establishing Default after Acceptance; Notice of Claim or Litigation to Person Answerable Over*—(1) A lessee must pay rent for any goods accepted in accordance with the lease contract, with due allowance for goods rightfully rejected or not delivered.

(2) A lessee's acceptance of goods precludes rejection of the goods accepted. In the case of a finance lease, if made with knowledge of a nonconformity, acceptance cannot be revoked because of it. In any other case, if made with knowledge of a nonconformity, acceptance cannot be revoked because of it unless the acceptance was on the reasonable assumption that the nonconformity would be seasonably cured. Acceptance does not of itself impair any other remedy provided by this Article or the lease agreement for nonconformity.

(3) If a tender has been accepted:

(a) within a reasonable time after the lessee discovers or should have discovered any default, the lessee shall notify the lessor or the supplier, or be barred from any remedy;

(b) except in the case of a consumer lease, within a reasonable time after the lessee receives notice of litigation for infringement or the like (§ 2A-211) the lessee shall notify the lessor or be barred from any remedy over for liability established by the litigation; and

(c) the burden is on the lessee to establish any default.

(4) If a lessee is sued for breach of a warranty or other obligation for which a lessor or a supplier is answerable over:

(a) The lessee may give the lessor or the supplier written notice of the litigation. If the notice states that the lessor or the supplier may come in and defend and that if the lessor or the supplier does not do so he [or she] will be bound in any action against him [or her] by the lessee by any determination of fact common to the two litigations, then unless the lessor or the supplier after seasonable receipt of the notice does come in and defend he [or she] is so bound.

(b) The lessor or the supplier may demand in writing that the lessee turn over control of the litigation including settlement if the claim is one for infringement or the like (§ 2A-211) or else be barred from any remedy over. If the demand states that the lessor or the supplier agrees to bear all expense and to satisfy any adverse judgment, then unless the lessee after seasonable receipt of the demand does turn over control the lessee is so barred.

(5)   The provisions of subsections (3) and (4) apply to any obligation of a lessee to hold the lessor or the supplier harmless against infringement or the like (§ 2A-211).

Section 2A-517. *Revocation of Acceptance of Goods*—(1) A lessee may revoke acceptance of a lot or commercial unit whose nonconformity substantially impairs its value to the lessee if he [or she] has accepted it:

(a)   except in the case of a finance lease, on the reasonable assumption that its nonconformity would be cured and it has not been seasonably cured; or

(b)   without discovery of the nonconformity if the lessee's acceptance was reasonably induced either by the lessor's assurances or, except in the case of a finance lease, by the difficulty of discovery before acceptance.

(2)   Revocation of acceptance must occur within a reasonable time after the lessee discovers or should have discovered the ground for it and before any substantial change in condition of the goods which is not caused by the nonconformity. Revocation is not effective until the lessee notifies the lessor.

(3)   A lessee who so revokes has the same rights and duties with regard to the goods involved as if the lessee had rejected them.

Section 2A-518. *Cover; Substitute Goods*—(1) After default by a lessor under the lease contract (§ 2A-508(1)), the lessee may cover by making in good faith and without unreasonable delay any purchase or lease of or contract to purchase or lease goods in substitution for those due from the lessor.

(2)   Except as otherwise provided with respect to damages liquidated in the lease agreement (§ 2A-504) or determined by agreement of the parties (§ 1-102(3)), if a lessee's cover is by lease agreement substantially similar to the original lease agreement and the lease agreement is made in good faith and in a commercially reasonable manner, the lessee may recover from the lessor as damages (a) the present value, as of the date of default, of the difference between the total rent for the lease term of the new lease agreement and the total rent for the remaining lease term of the original lease agreement and (b) any incidental or consequential damages less expenses saved in consequence of the lessor's default.

(3)   If a lessee's cover does not qualify for treatment under subsection (2), the lessee may recover from the lessor as if the lessee had elected not to cover and Section 2A-519 governs.

Section 2A-519. *Lessee's Damages for Non-Delivery, Repudiation, Default and Breach of Warranty in Regard to Accepted Goods*—(1) If a lessee elects not to cover or a lessee elects to cover and the cover does not qualify for treatment under Section 2A-518(2), the measure of damages for non-delivery or repudiation by the lessor or for rejection or revocation of acceptance by the lessee is the present value as of the date of the default of the difference between the then market rent and the original rent, computed for the remaining lease term of the original lease agreement together with incidental and consequential damages, less expenses saved in consequence of the lessor's default.

(2)   Market rent is to be determined as of the place for tender or, in cases of rejection after arrival or revocation of acceptance, as of the place of arrival.

(3)   If the lessee has accepted goods and given notification (§ 2A-516(3)), the measure of damages for nonconforming tender or delivery by a lessor is the loss resulting in the ordinary course of events from the lessor's default as determined in any manner that is reasonable together with incidental and consequential damages, less expenses saved in consequence of the lessor's default.

(4)   The measure of damages for breach of warranty is the present value at the time and place of acceptance of the difference between the value of the use of the goods accepted and the value if they had been as warranted for the lease term, unless special circumstances show proximate damages of a different amount, together with incidental and consequential damages, less expenses saved in consequence of the lessor's default or breach of warranty.

Section 2A-520. *Lessee's Incidental and Consequential Damages*—(1) Incidental damages resulting from a lessor's default include expenses reasonably incurred in inspection, receipt, transportation, and care and custody of goods rightfully rejected or goods the acceptance of which is justifiably revoked, any commercially reasonable charges, expenses or commissions in connection with effecting cover, and any other reasonable expense incident to the default.

(2) Consequential damages resulting from a lessor's default include:

(a) any loss resulting from general or particular requirements and needs of which the lessor at the time of contracting had reason to know and which could not reasonably be prevented by cover or otherwise; and

(b) injury to person or property proximately resulting from any breach of warranty.

Section 2A-521. *Lessee's Right to Specific Performance or Replevin*—(1) Specific performance may be decreed if the goods are unique or in other proper circumstances.

(2) A decree for specific performance may include any terms and conditions as to payment of the rent, damages, or other relief that the court deems just.

(3) A lessee has a right of replevin, detinue, sequestration, claim and delivery, or the like for goods identified to the lease contract if after reasonable effort the lessee is unable to effect cover for those goods or the circumstances reasonably indicate that the effort will be unavailing.

Section 2A-522. *Lessee's Right to Goods on Lessor's Insolvency*—(1) Subject to subsection (2) and even though the goods have not been shipped, a lessee who has paid a part or all of the rent and security for goods identified to a lease contract (§ 2A-217) on making and keeping good a tender of any unpaid portion of the rent and security due under the lease contract may recover the goods identified from the lessor if the lessor becomes insolvent within 10 days after receipt of the first installment of rent and security.

(2) A lessee acquires the right to recover goods identified to a lease contract only if they conform to the lease contract.

C. Default by Lessee

Section 2A-523. *Lessor's Remedies*—(1) If a lessee wrongfully rejects or revokes acceptance of goods or fails to make a payment when due or repudiates with respect to a part or the whole, then, with respect to any goods involved, and with respect to all of the goods if under an installment lease contract the value of the whole lease contract is substantially impaired (§ 2A-510), the lessee is in default under the lease contract and the lessor may:

(a) cancel the lease contract (§ 2A-505(1));

(b) proceed respecting goods not identified to the lease contract (§ 2A-524);

(c) withhold delivery of the goods and take possession of goods previously delivered (§ 2A-525);

(d) stop delivery of the goods by any bailee (§ 2A-526);

(e) dispose of the goods and recover damages (§ 2A-527), or retain the goods and recover damages (§ 2A-528), or in a proper case recover rent (§ 2A-529).

(2) If a lessee is otherwise in default under a lease contract, the lessor may exercise the rights and remedies provided in the lease contract and this Article.

Section 2A-524. *Lessor's Right to Identify Goods to Lease Contract*—(1) A lessor aggrieved under Section 2A-523(1) may:

(a) identify to the lease contract conforming goods not already identified if at the time the lessor learned of the default they were in the lessor's or the supplier's possession or control; and

(b) dispose of goods (§ 2A-527(1)) that demonstrably have been intended for the particular lease contract even though those goods are unfinished.

(2) If the goods are unfinished, in the exercise of reasonable commercial judgment for the purposes of avoiding loss and of effective realization, an aggrieved lessor or the supplier may either complete manufacture and wholly identify the goods to the lease contract or cease man-

ufacture and lease, sell, or otherwise dispose of the goods for scrap or salvage value or proceed in any other reasonable manner.

Section 2A-525. *Lessor's Right to Possession of Goods*—(1) If a lessor discovers the lessee to be insolvent, the lessor may refuse to deliver the goods.

(2) The lessor has on default by the lessee under the lease contract the right to take possession of the goods. If the lease contract so provides, the lessor may require the lessee to assemble the goods and make them available to the lessor at a place to be designated by the lessor which is reasonably convenient to both parties. Without removal, the lessor may render unusable any goods employed in trade or business, and may dispose of goods on the lessee's premises (§ 2A-527).

(3) The lessor may proceed under subsection (2) without judicial process if that can be done without breach of the peace or the lessor may proceed by action.

Section 2A-526. *Lessor's Stoppage of Delivery in Transit or Otherwise*—(1) A lessor may stop delivery of goods in the possession of a carrier or other bailee if the lessor discovers the lessee to be insolvent and may stop delivery of carload, truckload, planeload, or larger shipments of express or freight if the lessee repudiates or fails to make a payment due before delivery, whether for rent, security or otherwise under the lease contract, or for any other reason the lessor has a right to withhold or take possession of the goods.

(2) In pursuing its remedies under subsection (1), the lessor may stop delivery until:

(a) receipt of the goods by the lessee;

(b) acknowledgment to the lessee by any bailee of the goods, except a carrier, that the bailee holds the goods for the lessee; or

(c) such an acknowledgment to the lessee by a carrier via reshipment or as warehouseman.

(3)(a) To stop delivery, a lessor shall so notify as to enable the bailee by reasonable diligence to prevent delivery of the goods.

(b) After notification, the bailee shall hold and deliver the goods according to the directions of the lessor, but the lessor is liable to the bailee for any ensuing charges or damages.

(c) A carrier who has issued a nonnegotiable bill of lading is not obliged to obey a notification to stop received from a person other than the consignor.

Section 2A-527. *Lessor's Rights to Dispose of Goods*—(1) After a default by a lessee under the lease contract (§ 2A-523(1)) or after the lessor refuses to deliver or takes possession of goods (§ 2A-525 or 2A-526), the lessor may dispose of the goods concerned or the undelivered balance thereof in good faith and without unreasonable delay by lease, sale or otherwise.

(2) If the disposition is by lease contract substantially similar to the original lease contract and the lease contract is made in good faith and in a commercially reasonable manner, the lessor may recover from the lessee as damages (a) accrued and unpaid rent as of the date of default, (b) the present value as of the date of default of the difference between the total rent for the remaining lease term of the original lease contract and the total rent for the lease term of the new lease contract, and (c) any incidental damages allowed under Section 2A-530, less expenses saved in consequence of the lessee's default.

(3) If the lessor's disposition is by lease contract that for any reason does not qualify for treatment under subsection (2), or is by sale or otherwise, the lessor may recover from the lessee as if the lessor had elected not to dispose of the goods and Section 2A-528 governs.

(4) A subsequent buyer or lessee who buys or leases from the lessor in good faith for value as a result of a disposition under this section takes the goods free of the original lease contract and any rights of the original lessee even though the lessor fails to comply with one or more of the requirements of this Article.

(5) The lessor is not accountable to the lessee for any profit made on any disposition. A lessee who has rightfully rejected or justifiably revoked acceptance shall account to the lessor for any excess over the amount of the lessee's security interest (§ 2A-508(5)).

Section 2A-528. *Lessor's Damages for Non-Acceptance or Repudiation*—(1) Except as otherwise provided with respect to damages liquidated in the lease agreement (§ 2A-504) or determined by agreement of the parties (§ 1-102(3)), if a lessor elects to retain the goods or a lessor elects to dispose of the goods and disposition is by lease agreement that for any reason does not qualify for treatment under Section 2A-527(2), or is by sale or otherwise, the lessor may recover from the lessee as damages for non-acceptance or repudiation by the lessee (a) accrued and unpaid rent as of the date of default, (b) the present value as of the date of default of the difference between the total rent for the remaining lease term of the original lease agreement and the market rent at the time and place for tender computed for the same lease term, and (c) any incidental damages allowed under Section 2A-530, less expenses saved in consequence of the lessee's default.

(2) If the measure of damages provided in subsection (1) is inadequate to put a lessor in as good a position as performance would have, the measure of damages is the profit, including reasonable overhead, the lessor would have made from full performance by the lessee, together with any incidental damages allowed under Section 2A-530, due allowance for costs reasonably incurred and due credit for payments or proceeds of disposition.

Section 2A-529. *Lessor's Action for the Rent*—(1) After default by the lessee under the lease contract (§ 2A-523(1)), if the lessor complies with subsection (2), the lessor may recover from the lessee as damages:

(a)   for goods accepted by the lessee and for conforming goods lost or damaged within a commercially reasonable time after risk of loss passes to the lessee (§ 2A-219), (i) accrued and unpaid rent as of the date of default, (ii) the present value as of the date of default of the rent for the remaining lease term of the lease agreement, and (iii) any incidental damages allowed under Section 2A-530, less expenses saved in consequence of the lessee's default; and

(b)   for goods identified to the lease contract if the lessor is unable after reasonable effort to dispose of them at a reasonable price or the circumstances reasonably indicate that effort will be unavailing, (i) accrued and unpaid rent as of the date of default, (ii) the present value as of the date of default of the rent for the remaining lease term of the lease agreement, and (iii) any incidental damages allowed under Section 2A-530, less expenses saved in consequence of the lessee's default.

(2) Except as provided in subsection (3), the lessor shall hold for the lessee for the remaining lease term of the lease agreement any goods that have been identified to the lease contract and are in the lessor's control.

(3) The lessor may dispose of the goods at any time before collection of the judgment for damages obtained pursuant to subsection (1), and the lessor may proceed against the lessee for damages pursuant to Sections 2A-527 and 2A-528.

(4) Payment of the judgment for damages obtained pursuant to subsection (1) entitles the lessee to use and possession of the goods not then disposed of for the remaining lease term of the lease agreement.

(5) After a lessee has wrongfully rejected or revoked acceptance of goods, has failed to pay rent then due, or has repudiated (§ 2A-402), a lessor who is held not entitled to rent under this section must nevertheless be awarded damages for non-acceptance under Sections 2A-527 and 2A-528.

ARTICLE 3: COMMERCIAL PAPER

Article 3 of the Uniform Commercial Code was thoroughly recently revised. These 1990 revisions were adopted by all states except Massachusetts, New York, Rhode Island, South Carolina, and Utah. Much of what is contained in Article 3 is superseded by federal statute. Nevertheless, understanding the numerous definitions which are provided within Article 3 will prove useful to the credit executive. Other pertinent provisions are cited as well.

Section 3-103. *Definitions*—(a) In this Article:

(1)   "Acceptor" means a drawee who has accepted a draft.

(2)   "Drawee" means a person ordered in a draft to make payment.

(3)   "Drawer" means a person who signs or is identified in a draft as a person ordering payment.

(4)   "Good faith" means honesty in fact and the observance of reasonable commercial standards of fair dealing.

(5)   "Maker" means a person who signs or is identified in a note as a person undertaking to pay.

(6)   "Order" means a written instruction to pay money signed by the person giving the instruction. The instruction may be addressed to any person, including the person giving the instruction, or to one or more persons jointly or in the alternative but not in succession. An authorization to pay is not an order unless the person authorized to pay is also instructed to pay.

(7)   "Ordinary care" in the case of a person engaged in business means observance of reasonable commercial standards, prevailing in the area in which the person is located, with respect to the business in which the person is engaged. In the case of a bank that takes an instrument for processing for collection or payment by automated means, reasonable commercial standards do not require the bank to examine the instrument if the failure to examine does not violate the bank's prescribed procedures and the bank's procedures do not vary unreasonably from general banking usage not disapproved by this Article or Article 4.

(8)   "Party" means a party to an instrument.

(9)   "Promise" means a written undertaking to pay money signed by the person undertaking to pay. An acknowledgment of an obligation by the obligor is not a promise unless the obligor also undertakes to pay the obligation.

(10)   "Prove" with respect to a fact means to meet the burden of establishing the fact (Section 1-201(8)).

(11)   "Remitter" means a person who purchases an instrument from its issuer if the instrument is payable to an identified person other than the purchaser.

(b)   Other definitions applying to this Article and the sections in which they appear are:

"Acceptance"–Section 3-409

"Accommodated party"–Section 3-419

"Accommodation party"–Section 3-419

"Alteration"–Section 3-407

"Anomalous indorsement"–Section 3-205

"Blank indorsement"–Section 3-205

"Cashier's check"–Section 3-104

"Certificate of deposit"–Section 3-104

"Certified check"–Section 3-409

"Check"–Section 3-104

"Consideration"–Section 3-303

"Draft"–Section 3-104

"Holder in due course"–Section 3-302

"Incomplete instrument"–Section 3-115

"Indorsement"–Section 3-204

"Indorser"–Section 3-204

"Instrument"–Section 3-104

"Issue"–Section 3-105

"Issuer"–Section 3-105

"Negotiable instrument"–Section 3-104

"Negotiation"–Section 3-201

"Note"–Section 3-104

"Payable at a definite time"–Section 3-108

"Payable on demand"–Section 3-108

"Payable to bearer"–Section 3-109

"Payable to order"–Section 3-109
"Payment"–Section 3-602
"Person entitled to enforce"–Section 3-301
"Presentment"–Section 3-501
"Reacquisition"–Section 3-207
"Special indorsement"–Section 3-205
"Teller's check"–Section 3-104
"Transfer of instrument"–Section 3-203
"Traveler's check"–Section 3-104
"Value"–Section 3-303

(c)   The following definitions in other Articles apply to this Article:
"Bank"–Section 4-105
"Banking day"–Section 4-104
"Clearing house"–Section 4-104
"Collecting bank"–Section 4-105
"Depositary bank"–Section 4-105
"Documentary draft"–Section 4-104
"Intermediary bank"–Section 4-105
"Item"–Section 4-104
"Payor bank"–Section 4-105
"Suspends payments"–Section 4-104

(d)   In addition, Article 1 contains general definitions and principles of construction and interpretation applicable throughout this Article.

Section 3-104. *Negotiable Instrument*—(a) Except as provided in subsections (c) and (d), "negotiable instrument" means an unconditional promise or order to pay a fixed amount of money, with or without interest or other charges described in the promise or order, if it:

(1)   is payable to bearer or to order at the time it is issued or first comes into possession of a holder;

(2)   is payable on demand or at a definite time; and

(3)   does not state any other undertaking or instruction by the person promising or ordering payment to do any act in addition to the payment of money, but the promise or order may contain (i) an undertaking or power to give, maintain, or protect collateral to secure payment, (ii) an authorization or power to the holder to confess judgment or realize on or dispose of collateral, or (iii) a waiver of the benefit of any law intended for the advantage or protection of an obligor.

(b)   "Instrument" means a negotiable instrument.

(c)   An order that meets all of the requirements of subsection (a), except paragraph (1), and otherwise falls within the definition of "check" in subsection (f) is a negotiable instrument and a check.

(d)   A promise or order other than a check is not an instrument if, at the time it is issued or first comes into possession of a holder, it contains a conspicuous statement, however expressed, to the effect that the promise or order is not negotiable or is not an instrument governed by this Article.

(e)   An instrument is a "note" if it is a promise and is a "draft" if it is an order. If an instrument falls within the definition of both "note" and "draft," a person entitled to enforce the instrument may treat it as either.

(f)   "Check" means (i) a draft, other than a documentary draft, payable on demand and drawn on a bank or (ii) a cashier's check or teller's check. An instrument may be a check even though it is described on its face by another term, such as "money order."

(g)   "Cashier's check" means a draft with respect to which the drawer and drawee are the same bank or branches of the same bank.

(h)   "Teller's check" means a draft drawn by a bank (i) on another bank, or (ii) payable at or through a bank.

(i)   "Traveler's check" means an instrument that (i) is payable on demand, (ii) is drawn on or payable at or through a bank, (iii) is designated by the term "traveler's check" or by a substantially similar term, and (iv) requires, as a condition to payment, a countersignature by a person whose specimen signature appears on the instrument.

(j)   "Certificate of deposit" means an instrument containing an acknowledgment by a bank that a sum of money has been received by the bank and a promise by the bank to repay the sum of money. A certificate of deposit is a note of the bank.

Section 3-114. *Contradictory Terms of Instrument*—If an instrument contains contradictory terms, typewritten terms prevail over printed terms, handwritten terms prevail over both, and words prevail over numbers.

Section 3-118. *Statute of Limitations*—(a) Except as provided in subsection (e), an action to enforce the obligation of a party to pay a note payable at a definite time must be commenced within six years after the due date or dates stated in the note or, if a due date is accelerated, within six years after the accelerated due date.

(b)   Except as provided in subsection (d) or (e), if demand for payment is made to the maker of a note payable on demand, an action to enforce the obligation of a party to pay the note must be commenced within six years after the demand. If no demand for payment is made to the maker, an action to enforce the note is barred if neither principal nor interest on the note has been paid for a continuous period of 10 years.

(c)   Except as provided in subsection (d), an action to enforce the obligation of a party to an unaccepted draft to pay the draft must be commenced within three years after dishonor of the draft or 10 years after the date of the draft, whichever period expires first.

(d)   An action to enforce the obligation of the acceptor of a certified check or the issuer of a teller's check, cashier's check, or traveler's check must be commenced within three years after demand for payment is made to the acceptor or issuer, as the case may be.

(e)   An action to enforce the obligation of a party to a certificate of deposit to pay the instrument must be commenced within six years after demand for payment is made to the maker, but if the instrument states a due date and the maker is not required to pay before that date, the six-year period begins when a demand for payment is in effect and the due date has passed.

(f)   An action to enforce the obligation of a party to pay an accepted draft, other than a certified check, must be commenced (i) within six years after the due date or dates stated in the draft or acceptance if the obligation of the acceptor is payable at a definite time, or (ii) within six years after the date of the acceptance if the obligation of the acceptor is payable on demand.

(g)   Unless governed by other law regarding claims for indemnity or contribution, an action (i) for conversion of an instrument, for money had and received, or like action based on conversion, (ii) for breach of warranty, or (iii) to enforce an obligation, duty, or right arising under this Article and not governed by this section must be commenced within three years after the [cause of action] accrues.

Section 3-311. *Accord and Satisfaction by Use of Instrument*—(a) If a person against whom a claim is asserted proves that (i) that person in good faith tendered an instrument to the claimant as full satisfaction of the claim, (ii) the amount of the claim was unliquidated or subject to a bona fide dispute, and (iii) the claimant obtained payment of the instrument, the following subsections apply.

(b)   Unless subsection (c) applies, the claim is discharged if the person against whom the claim is asserted proves that the instrument or an accompanying written communication contained a conspicuous statement to the effect that the instrument was tendered as full satisfaction of the claim.

(c)   Subject to subsection (d), a claim is not discharged under subsection (b) if either of the following applies: (1) The claimant, if an organization, proves that (i) within a reasonable time before the tender, the claimant sent a conspicuous statement to the person against whom the claim is asserted that communications concerning disputed debts, including an instrument tendered as full satisfaction of a debt, are to be sent to a designated person, office, or place, and (ii) the instrument or accompanying communication was not received by that designated person, office, or place. (2) The claimant, whether or not an organization, proves that within 90 days after payment of the instrument, the claimant tendered repayment of the amount of the instrument to the person against whom the claim is asserted. This paragraph does not apply if the claimant is an organization that sent a statement complying with paragraph (1)(i).

(d)　A claim is discharged if the person against whom the claim is asserted proves that within a reasonable time before collection of the instrument was initiated, the claimant, or an agent of the claimant having direct responsibility with respect to the disputed obligation, knew that the instrument was tendered in full satisfaction of the claim.

ARTICLE 4: BANK DEPOSITS AND COLLECTIONS

This Article deals with matters relating to dealings between banks and their customers, other banks and third parties. It covers such matters as deposits and collection of negotiable instruments, the relationship between a bank and its customers, and the dealings between banks. As a result of federal statutes, as well as Regulations CC and J of the Code of Federal Regulations, many provisions contained within Article 4 of the UCC have been superseded. Therefore, the text of this Article is not reproduced in this volume.

Chapter 9 "Negotiable Instruments: Notes, Checks, Drafts—How They Work—And Interest Rates" contains substantive discussion of Article 4 of the UCC in conjunction with Regulations CC and J of the Code of Federal Regulations and the Expedited Funds Availability Act (EFAA).

As a result of the adoption of the Expedited Funds Availability Act (EFAA), parts of Article 4 of the UCC have been superseded. Since there is no readily available text which sets forth where and how these superseded changes are effected, the following is a list of federal changes created by the EFAA which supersede any provisions of the UCC to the contrary.

Some of the pertinent provisions are set forth.

4-104(a)(c) Regulation CC (as promulgated by the EFAA) defines "banking day" as "business day."

4-202(b) Regulation CC may affect time limits required by this section of the UCC because of the additional requirement to make an expeditious return of dishonored checks. A paying bank is still subject to the midnight deadline rule under this section of the UCC.

4-204(b)(1) Under Regulation CC, a presenting bank may not send a check for same-day settlement directly to a paying bank if the paying bank designates a different location in accordance with the provisions of the EFAA.

Section 4-213. *Medium and Time of Settlement by Bank*—(a) With respect to settlement by a bank, the medium and time of settlement may be prescribed by Federal Reserve regulations or circulars, clearing-house rules, and the like, or agreement. In the absence of such prescription:

(1)　the medium of settlement is cash or credit to an account in a Federal Reserve bank of or specified by the person to receive settlement; and

(2)　the time of settlement, is: (i) with respect to tender of settlement by cash, a cashier's check, or teller's check, when the cash or check is sent or delivered; (ii) with respect to tender of settlement by credit in an account in a Federal Reserve Bank, when the credit is made; (iii) with respect to tender of settlement by a credit or debit to an account in a bank, when the credit or debit is made or, in the case of tender of settlement by authority to charge an account, when the authority is sent or delivered; or (iv) with respect to tender of settlement by a funds transfer, when payment is made pursuant to Section 4A-406(a) to the person receiving settlement.

(b)　If the tender of settlement is not by a medium authorized by subsection (a) or the time of settlement is not fixed by subsection (a), no settlement occurs until the tender of settlement is accepted by the person receiving settlement.

(c)　If settlement for an item is made by cashier's check or teller's check and the person receiving settlement, before its midnight deadline:

(1)   presents or forwards the check for collection, settlement is final when the check is finally paid; or

(2)   fails to present or forward the check for collection, settlement is final at the midnight deadline of the person receiving settlement.

(d)   If settlement for an item is made by giving authority to charge the account of the bank giving settlement in the bank receiving settlement, settlement is final when the charge is made by the bank receiving settlement if there are funds available in the account for the amount of the item.

4-213(a) Regulation CC limits the medium of settlement for checks to credit to an account at a federal reserve bank, and provides that for checks presented after the deadline for same-day settlement and before the paying bank's cut-off hour, the presenting bank may receive settlement on the next business day of presentment by cash.

4-214(a) Regulation CC may affect time limits required by this section because of the additional requirement to make an expeditious return and settlement for return checks made under the EFAA may not be charged back the provisional credit. Therefore, recovery can be had from any prior bank.

4-215 Regulation CC eliminates the concept of provisional credit as it relates to the payment of interest by depository banks.

4-301(a) Regulation CC may affect the time limits in this section because of the additional requirement to make an expeditious return. As to the form and information required by this section for a notice of dishonor or nonpayment, Regulation CC supersedes the UCC in that it allows notice in lieu of returning a check by sending a legible copy of both sides of the check or a written notice of nonpayment containing the information specified in the EFAA. Additionally, this section of the UCC is superseded in that in order to preserve the ability to exercise deferred posting, the time limit specified for settlement or return by a paying bank on the banking day a check is received is superseded by Regulation CC's requirement to settle for checks by the close of the "Fedwire." This change also affects UCC Section 4-302(a).

4-301(d) Regulation CC allows a paying bank to return a check directly to the depository bank or a returning bank, unlike the UCC which has checks returning through a clearing house or to the presenting bank.

4-302(a) *See* the section relating to 4-301(a) above.

In addition to the above changes of the UCC by the EFAA, 12 CFR 210, Regulation J, affects the UCC in how checks are handled by the federal reserve banks. Regulation J preempts the UCC in such ways as requiring the federal reserve bank to be paid by other banks by the end of the banking day rather than by midnight. In addition, Regulation J allows the federal reserve bank to charge overdraft fees on intraday overdrafts. Finally, relating to intraday posting, Regulation J mandates that a paying bank must settle by the next clock hour that is at least one hour after the paying bank receives the check.

ARTICLE 4A: FUNDS TRANSFERS

Part 1: Subject Matter and Definitions

Section 4A-101. *Short Title*—This Article may be cited as Uniform Commercial Code—Funds Transfers.

Section 4A-102. *Subject Matter*—Except as otherwise provided in Section 4A-108, this Article applies to funds transfers defined in Section 4A-104.

Section 4A-103. *Payment Order*—Definitions—(a) In this Article:

(1)   "Payment order" means an instruction of a sender to a receiving bank, transmitted orally, electronically, or in writing, to pay, or to cause another bank to pay, a fixed or determinable amount of money to a beneficiary if:

(i)   the instruction does not state a condition to payment to the beneficiary other than time of payment;

(ii) the receiving bank is to be reimbursed by debiting an account of, or otherwise receiving payment from, the sender; and

(iii) the instruction is transmitted by the sender directly to the receiving bank or to an agent, funds-transfer system, or communication system for transmittal to the receiving bank.

(2) "Beneficiary" means the person to be paid by the beneficiary's bank.

(3) "Beneficiary's bank" means the bank identified in a payment order in which an account of the beneficiary is to be credited pursuant to the order or which otherwise is to make payment to the beneficiary if the order does not provide for payment to an account.

(4) "Receiving bank" means the bank to which the sender's instruction is addressed.

(5) "Sender" means the person giving the instruction to the receiving bank.

(b) If an instruction complying with subsection (a)(1) is to make more than one payment to a beneficiary, the instruction is a separate payment order with respect to each payment.

(c) A payment order is issued when it is sent to the receiving bank.

Section 4A-104. *Funds Transfer*—Definitions—In this Article: (a) "Funds transfer" means the series of transactions, beginning with the originator's payment order, made for the purpose of making payment to the beneficiary of the order. The term includes any payment order issued by the originator's bank or an intermediary bank intended to carry out the originator's payment order. A funds transfer is completed by acceptance by the beneficiary's bank of a payment order for the benefit of the beneficiary of the originator's payment order.

(b) "Intermediary bank" means a receiving bank other than the originator's bank or the beneficiary's bank.

(c) "Originator" means the sender of the first payment order in a funds transfer.

(d) "Originator's bank" means (i) the receiving bank to which the payment order of the originator is issued if the originator is not a bank, or (ii) the originator if the originator is a bank.

Section 4A-105. *Other Definitions*—(a) In this Article:

(1) "Authorized account" means a deposit account of a customer in a bank designated by the customer as a source of payment of payment orders issued by the customer to the bank. If a customer does not so designate an account, any account of the customer is an authorized account if payment of a payment order from that account is not inconsistent with a restriction on the use of that account.

(2) "Bank" means a person engaged in the business of banking and includes a savings bank, savings and loan association, credit union, and trust company. A branch or separate office of a bank is a separate bank for purposes of this Article.

(3) "Customer" means a person, including a bank, having an account with a bank or from whom a bank has agreed to receive payment orders.

(4) "Funds-transfer business day" of a receiving bank means the part of a day during which the receiving bank is open for the receipt, processing, and transmittal of payment orders and cancellations and amendments of payment orders.

(5) "Funds-transfer system" means a wire transfer network, automated clearing house, or other communication system of a clearing house or other association of banks through which a payment order by a bank may be transmitted to the bank to which the order is addressed.

(6) "Good faith" means honesty in fact and the observance of reasonable commercial standards of fair dealing.

(7) "Prove" with respect to a fact means to meet the burden of establishing the fact (§ 1-201(8)).

(b) Other definitions applying to this Article and the sections in which they appear are:

"Acceptance"–Section 4A-209
"Beneficiary"–Section 4A-103
"Beneficiary's bank"–Section 4A-103
"Executed"–Section 4A-301

"Execution date"–Section 4A-301
"Funds transfer"–Section 4A-104
"Funds-transfer system rule"–Section 4A-501
"Intermediary bank"–Section 4A-104
"Originator"–Section 4A-104
"Originator's bank"–Section 4A-104
"Payment by beneficiary's bank to beneficiary"–Section 4A-405
"Payment by originator to beneficiary"–Section 4A-406
"Payment by sender to receiving bank"–Section 4A-403
"Payment date"–Section 4A-401
"Payment order"–Section 4A-103
"Receiving bank"–Section 4A-103
"Security procedure"–Section 4A-201
"Sender"–Section 4A-103

(c)   The following definitions in Article 4 apply to this Article:
"Clearinghouse"–Section 4-104
"Item"–Section 4-104
"Suspends payments"–Section 4-104

(d)   In addition Article 1 contains general definitions and principles of construction and interpretation applicable throughout this Article.

Section 4A-106. *Time Payment Order Is Received*—(a) The time of receipt of a payment order or communication canceling or amending a payment order is determined by the rules applicable to receipt of a notice stated in Section 1-201(27). A receiving bank may fix a cut-off time or times on a funds-transfer business day for the receipt and processing of payment orders and communications canceling or amending payment orders. Different cut-off times may apply to payment orders, cancellations, or amendments, or to difference categories of payment orders, cancellations, or amendments. A cut-off time may apply to senders generally or different cut-off times may apply to different senders or categories of payment orders. If a payment order or communication canceling or amending a payment order is received after the close of a funds-transfer business day or after the appropriate cut-off time on a funds-transfer business day, the receiving bank may treat the payment order or communication as received at the opening of the next funds-transfer business day.

(b) If this Article refers to an execution date or payment date or states a day on which a receiving bank is required to take action, and the date or day does not fall on a funds-transfer business day, the next day that is a funds-transfer business day is treated as the date or day stated, unless the contrary is stated in this Article.

Section 4A-107. *Federal Reserve Regulations and Operating Circulars*—Regulations of the Board of Governors of the Federal Reserve System and operating circulars of the Federal Reserve Banks supersede any inconsistent provision of this Article to the extent of the inconsistency.

Section 4A-108. *Exclusion of Consumer Transactions Governed by Federal Law*—This Article does not apply to a funds transfer any part of which is governed by the Electronic Funds Transfer Act of 1978 (Title XX, Public Law 95-630, 92 Stat, 3728, 15 USC § 1693 et seq.) as amended from time to time.

Part 2: Issue and Acceptance of Payment Order

Section 4A-201. *Security Procedure*—"Security procedure" means a procedure established by agreement of a customer and a receiving bank of the purpose of (i) verifying that a payment order or communication amending or canceling a payment order is that of the customer, or (ii) detecting error in the transmission or the content of the payment order or communication. A security procedure may require the use of algorithms or other codes, identifying words or numbers, encryption, callback procedures, or similar security devices. Comparison of a signature on a payment order or communication with an authorized specimen signature of the customer is not by itself a security procedure.

Section 4A-202. *Authorized and Verified Payment Orders*—(a) A payment order received by the receiving bank is the authorized order of the person identified as sender if that person authorized the order is otherwise bound by it under the law of agency.

(b) If a bank and its customer have agreed that the authenticity of payment orders issued to the bank in the name of the customer as sender will be verified pursuant to a security procedure, a payment order received by the receiving bank is effective as the order of the customer, whether or not authorized, if (i) the security procedure is a commercially reasonable method of providing security against unauthorized payment orders, and (ii) the bank proves that it accepted the payment order in good faith and in compliance with the security procedure and any written agreement or instruction of the customer restricting acceptance of payment orders issued in the name of the customer. The bank is not required to follow an instruction that violates a written agreement with the customer or notice of which is not received at a time and in a manner affording the bank a reasonable opportunity to act on it before the payment order is accepted.

(c) Commercial reasonableness of a security procedure is a question of law to be determined by considering the wishes of the customer expressed to the bank, the circumstances of the customer known to the bank, including the size, type, and frequency of payment orders, normally issued by the customer to the bank, alternative security procedures offered to the customer, and security procedures in general use by customers and receiving banks similarly situated. A security procedure is deemed to be commercially reasonable if (i) the security procedure was chosen by the customer after the bank offered, and the customer refused, a security procedure that was commercially reasonable for that customer, and (ii) the customer expressly agreed in writing to be bound by any payment order, whether or not authorized, issued in its name and accepted by the bank in compliance with the security procedure chosen by the customer.

(d) The term "sender" in this Article includes the customer in whose name a payment order is issued if the order is the authorized order of the customer under subsection (a), or it is effective as the order of the customer under subsection (b).

(e) This section applies to amendments and cancellations of payment orders to the same extent it applies to payment orders.

(f) Except as provided in this section and in Section 4A-203(a)(1), rights and obligations arising under this section or Section 4A-203 may not be varied by agreement.

Section 4A-203. *Unenforceability of Certain Verified Payment Orders*—(a) If an accepted payment order is not, under Section 4A-202(a), an authorized order of a customer identified as sender, but is effective as an order of the customer pursuant to Section 4A-202(b), the following rules apply:

(1) By express written agreement, the receiving bank may limit the extent to which it is entitled to enforce or retain payment of the payment order.

(2) The receiving bank is not entitled to enforce or retain payment of the payment order if the customer proves that the order was not caused, directly or indirectly, by a person (i) entrusted at any time with duties to act for the customer with respect to payment orders or the security procedure, or (ii) who obtained access to transmitting facilities of the customer or who obtained, from a source controlled by the customer and without authority of the receiving bank, information facilitating breach of the security procedure, regardless of how the information was obtained or whether the customer was at fault. Information includes any access device, computer software, or the like.

(b) The section applies to amendments of payment orders to the same extent it applies to payment orders.

Section 4A-204. *Refund of Payment and Duty of Customer to Report with Respect to Unauthorized Payment Order*—(a) If a receiving bank accepts a payment order issued in the name of its customer as sender which is (i) not authorized and not effective as the order of the customer under Section 4A-202, or (ii) not enforceable, in whole or in part, against the customer under Section 4A-203, the bank shall refund any payment of the payment order received from the customer to the extent the bank is not entitled to enforce payment and shall pay interest on the refundable amount calculated from the date the bank received payment to the date of the refund. However, the customer is not entitled to interest from the bank on the amount to be refunded if the customer fails to exercise ordinary care to determine that the order was not authorized by the customer and to notify the bank of the relevant facts within a reasonable time not exceeding 90 days after the date the customer received notification from the bank that the order was accepted or that the customer's account was debited with respect to the order. The bank is not entitled to any recovery from the customer on account of a failure by the customer to give notification as stated in this section.

(b) Reasonable time under subsection (a) may be fixed by agreement as stated in Section 1-204(1), but the obligation of a receiving bank to refund payment as stated in subsection (a) may not otherwise be varied by agreement.

Section 4A-205. *Erroneous Payment Orders*—(a) If an accepted payment order was transmitted pursuant to a security procedure for the detection of error and the payment order (i) erroneously instructed payment to a beneficiary not intended by the sender, (ii) erroneously instructed payment in an amount greater than the amount intended by the sender, or (iii) was an erroneously transmitted duplicate of a payment order previously sent by the sender, the following rules apply:

(1) If the sender proves that the sender or a person acting on behalf of the sender pursuant to Section 4A-206 complied with the security procedure and that the error would have been detected if the receiving bank had also complied, the sender is not obliged to pay the order to the extent stated in paragraph (2) and (3).

(2) If the funds transfer is completed on the basis of an erroneous payment order described in clause (i) or (iii) of subsection (a), the sender is not obliged to pay the order and the receiving bank is entitled to recover from the beneficiary any amount paid to the beneficiary to the extent allowed by the law governing mistake and restitution.

(3) If the funds transfer is completed on the basis of a payment order described in clause (ii) of subsection (a), the sender is not obliged to pay the order to the extent the amount received by the beneficiary is greater than the amount intended by the sender. In that case, the receiving bank is entitled to recover from the beneficiary the excess amount received to the extent allowed by the law governing mistake and restitution.

(b) If (i) the sender of an erroneous payment order described in subsection (a) is not obliged to pay all or part of the order and (ii) the sender receives notification from the receiving bank that the order was accepted by the bank or that the sender's account was debited with respect to the order, the sender has a duty to exercise ordinary care, on the basis of information available to the sender, to discover the error with respect to the order and to advise the bank of the relevant facts within a reasonable time, not exceeding 90 days, after the bank's notification was received by the sender. If the bank proves that the sender failed to perform that duty, the sender is liable to the bank for the loss the bank proves it incurred as a result of the failure, but the liability of the sender may not exceed the amount of the sender's order.

(c) This section applies to amendments to payment orders to the same extent it applies to payment orders.

Section 4A-206. *Transmission of Payment Order through Funds-Transfer or Other Communication System*—(a) If a payment order addressed to a receiving bank is transmitted to a funds-transfer system or other third-party communication system for transmittal to the bank, the system is deemed to be an agent of the sender for the purpose of transmitting the payment order to the bank. If there is a discrepancy between the terms of the payment order transmitted to the systems and the terms of the payment order transmitted by the system to the bank, the terms of the payment order of the sender are those transmitted by the system. This section does not apply to a funds-transfer system of the Federal Reserve Banks.

(b) This section applies to cancellations and amendments of payment orders to the same extent it applies to payment orders.

Section 4A-207. *Misdescription of Beneficiary*—(a) Subject to subsection (b), if, in a payment order received by the beneficiary's bank, the name, bank account number, other identification of the beneficiary refers to a nonexistent or unidentifiable person or account, no person has rights as a beneficiary of the order and acceptance of the order cannot occur.

(b) If a payment order received by the beneficiary's bank identifies the beneficiary both by name and by an identifying or bank account number and the name and number identify different persons, the following rules apply:

(1) Except as otherwise provided in subsection (c), if the beneficiary's bank does not know that the name and number refer to different persons, it may rely on the number as the proper identification of the beneficiary of the order. The beneficiary's bank need not determine whether the name and number refer to the same person.

(2) If the beneficiary's bank pays the person identified by name or knows that the name and number identify different persons, no person has rights as beneficiary except the person paid by the beneficiary's bank if that person was entitled to receive payment from the originator of the funds transfer. If no person has rights as beneficiary, acceptance of the order cannot occur.

(c) If (i) a payment order described in subsection (b) is accepted, (ii) the originator's payment order described the beneficiary inconsistently by name and number, and (iii) the beneficiary's bank pays the person identified by number as permitted by subsection (b)(1), the following rules apply:

(1) If the originator is a bank, the originator is obliged to pay its order.

(2) If the originator is not a bank and proves that the person identified by number was not entitled to receive payment from the originator, the originator is not obliged to pay its order unless the originator's bank proves that the originator, before acceptance of the originator's order, had notice that payment of a payment order issued by the originator might be made by the beneficiary's bank on the basis of an identifying or bank account number even if it identifies a person different from the named beneficiary. Proof of notice may be made by any admissible evidence. The originator's bank satisfies the burden of proof if it proves that the originator, before the payment order was accepted, signed a writing stating the information to which the notice relates.

(d) In a case governed by subsection (b)(1), if the beneficiary's bank rightfully pays the person identified by number and that person was not entitled to receive payment from the originator, the amount paid may be recovered from that person to the extent allowed by the law governing mistake and restitution as follows:

(1) If the originator is obliged to pay its payment order as stated in subsection (c), the originator has the right to recover.

(2) If the originator is not a bank and is not obliged to pay its payment order, the originator's bank has the right to recover.

Section 4A-208. *Misdescription of Intermediary Bank or Beneficiary's Bank*—(a) This subsection applies to a payment order identifying an intermediary bank or the beneficiary's bank only by an identifying number.

(1) The receiving bank may rely on the number as the proper identification of the intermediary or beneficiary's bank and need not determine whether the number identifies a bank.

(2) The sender is obliged to compensate the receiving bank for any loss and expenses incurred by the receiving bank as a result of its reliance on the number in executing or attempting to execute the order.

(b) This subsection applies to a payment order identifying an intermediary bank or the beneficiary's bank both by name and an identifying number if the name and number identify different persons.

(1) If the sender is a bank, the receiving bank may rely on the number as the proper identification of the intermediary or beneficiary's bank if the receiving bank, when it executes the sender's order, does not know that the name and number identify different persons. The receiving bank need not determine whether the name and number refer to the same person or whether the number refers to a bank. The sender is obliged to compensate the receiving bank for any loss and expenses incurred by the receiving bank as a result of its reliance on the number in executing or attempting to execute the order.

(2) If the sender is not a bank and the receiving bank proves that the sender, before the payment order was accepted, had notice that the receiving bank might rely on the number as the proper identification of the intermediary or beneficiary's bank even if it identifies a person different from the bank identified by name, the rights and obligations of the sender and the receiving bank are governed by subsection (b)(1), as though the sender were a bank. Proof of notice may be made by any admissible evidence. The receiving bank satisfies the burden or proof if it proves that the sender, before the payment order was accepted, signed a writing stating the information to which the notice relates.

(3) Regardless of whether the sender is a bank, the receiving bank may rely on the name as the proper identification of the intermediary or beneficiary's bank if the receiving bank, at the time it executes the sender's order, does not know that the name and number identify different persons. The receiving bank need not determine whether the name and number refer to the same person.

(4) If the receiving bank knows that the name and number identify different persons, reliance on either the name or the number in executing the sender's payment order is a breach of the obligation stated in Section 4A-302(a)(1).

Section 4A-209. *Acceptance of Payment Order*—(a) Subject to subsection (d), a receiving bank other than the beneficiary's bank accepts a payment order when it executes the order.

(b) Subject to subsections (c) and (d), a beneficiary's bank accepts a payment order at the earliest of the following times:

(1) when the bank (i) pays the beneficiary as stated in Section 4A-405(a) or 4A-405(b), or (ii) notifies the beneficiary of receipt of the order or that the account of the beneficiary has been credited with respect to the order unless the notice indicates that the bank is rejecting the order or that funds with respect to the order may not be withdrawn or used until receipt of payment from the sender of the order;

(2) when the bank receives payment of the entire amount of the sender's order pursuant to Section 4A-403(a)(1) or 4A-403(a)(2); or

(3) the opening of the next funds-transfer business day of the bank following the payment date of the order if, at that time, the amount of the sender's order is fully covered by a withdrawable credit balance in an authorized account of the sender or the bank has otherwise received full payment from the sender, unless the order was rejected before that time or is rejected within (i) one hour after that time, or (ii) one hour after the opening of the next business day of the sender following the payment date if that time is later. If notice of rejection is received by the sender after the payment date and the authorized account of the sender does not bear interest, the bank is obliged to pay interest to the sender on the amount of the order for the number of days elapsing after the payment date to the day the sender receives notice or learns that the order was not accepted, counting that day as an elapsed day. If the withdrawable credit balance during that period falls below the amount of the order, the amount of interest payable is reduced accordingly.

(c) Acceptance of a payment order cannot occur before the order is received by the receiving bank. Acceptance does not occur under subsection (b)(2) or (b)(3) if the beneficiary of the payment order does not have an account with the receiving bank, the account has been closed, or the receiving bank is not permitted by law to receive credits for the beneficiary's account.

(d)　A payment order issued to the originator's bank cannot be accepted until the payment date if the bank is the beneficiary's bank, or the execution date if the bank is not the beneficiary's bank. If the originator's bank executes the originator's payment order before the execution date or pays the beneficiary of the originator's payment order before the payment date and the payment order is subsequently canceled pursuant to Section 4A-211(b), the bank may recover from the beneficiary any payment received to the extent allowed by the law governing mistake and restitution.

Section 4A-210. *Rejection of Payment Order*—(a) A payment order is rejected by the receiving bank by a notice of rejection transmitted to the sender orally, electronically, or in writing. A notice of rejection need not use any particular words and is sufficient if it indicates that the receiving bank is rejecting the order or will not execute or pay the order. Rejection is effective when the notice is given if transmission is by a means that is reasonable in the circumstances. If notice of rejection is given by a means that is not reasonable, rejection is effective when the notice is received. If an agreement of the sender and receiving bank establishes the means to be used to reject a payment order, (i) any means complying with the agreement is reasonable and (ii) any means not complying is not reasonable unless no significant delay in receipt of the notice resulted from the use of the noncomplying means.

(b)　This subsection applies if a receiving bank other than the beneficiary's bank fails to execute a payment order despite the existence on the execution date of a withdrawable credit balance in an authorized account of the sender sufficient to cover the order. If the sender does not receive notice of rejection of the order on the execution date and the authorized account of the sender does not bear interest, the bank is obliged to pay interest to the sender on the amount of the order for the number of days elapsing after the execution date to the earlier of the day the order is canceled pursuant to Section 4A-211(d) or the day the sender receives notice or learns that the order was not executed, counting the final day of the period as an elapsed day. If the withdrawable credit balance during that period falls below the amount of the order, the amount of interest is reduced accordingly.

(c)　If a receiving bank suspends payment, all unaccepted payment orders issued to it are deemed rejected at the time the bank suspends payments.

(d)　Acceptance of a payment order precludes a later rejection of the order. Rejection of a payment order precludes a later acceptance of the order.

Section 4A-211. *Cancellation and Amendment of Payment Order*—(a) A communication of the sender of a payment order canceling or amending the order may be transmitted to the receiving bank orally, electronically, or in writing. If a security procedure is in effect between the sender and the receiving bank, the communication is not effective to cancel or amend the order unless the communication is verified pursuant to the security procedure or the bank agrees to the cancellation or amendment.

(b)　Subject to subsection (a), a communication by the sender canceling or amending a payment order is effective to cancel or amend the order if notice of the communication is received at a time and in a manner affording the receiving bank a reasonable opportunity to act on the communication before the bank accepts the payment order.

(c)　After a payment order has been accepted, cancellation or amendment of the order is not effective unless the receiving bank agrees or a funds-transfer system rule allows cancellation or amendment without agreement of the bank.

(1)　With respect to a payment order accepted by a receiving bank other than the beneficiary's bank, cancellation or amendment is not effective unless a conforming cancellation or amendment of the payment order issued by the receiving bank is also made.

(2)　With respect to a payment order accepted by the beneficiary's bank, cancellation or amendment is not effective unless the order was issued in execution of an unauthorized payment order, or because of a mistake by a sender in the funds transfer which resulted in the issuance of a payment order (i) that is a duplicate of a payment order previously issued by the sender, (ii) that orders payment to a beneficiary not entitled to receive payment from the originator, or (iii) that orders payment in an amount greater than the amount the beneficiary was entitled to receive from the originator. If the payment order is canceled or amended, the beneficiary's bank is entitled to recover from the beneficiary any amount paid to the beneficiary to the extent allowed by the law governing mistake and restitution.

(d)   An unaccepted payment order is canceled by operation of law at the close of the fifth funds-transfer business day of the receiving bank after the execution date or payment date of the order.

(e)   A canceled payment order cannot be accepted. If an accepted payment order is canceled, the acceptance is nullified and no person has any right or obligation based on the acceptance. Amendment of a payment order is deemed to be cancellation of the original order at the time of amendment and issue of a new payment order in the amended form at the same time.

(f)   Unless otherwise provided in an agreement of the parties or in a funds-transfer system rule, if the receiving bank, after accepting a payment order, agrees to cancellation or amendment of the order by the sender or is bound by a funds-transfer system rule allowing cancellation or amendment without the bank's agreement, the sender, whether or not cancellation or amendment is effective, is liable to the bank for any loss and expenses, including reasonable attorney's fees, incurred by the bank as a result of the cancellation or amendment or attempted cancellation or amendment.

(g)   A payment order is not revoked by the death or legal incapacity of the sender unless the receiving bank knows of the death or of an adjudication of incapacity by a court of competent jurisdiction and has reasonable opportunity to act before acceptance of the order.

(h)   A funds-transfer system rule is not effective to the extent it conflicts with subsection (c)(2).

Section 4A-212. *Liability and Duty of Receiving Bank Regarding Unaccepted Payment Order*—If a receiving bank fails to accept a payment order that it is obliged by express agreement to accept, the bank is liable for breach of the agreement to the extent provided in the agreement or in this Article, but does not otherwise have any duty to accept a payment order, or before acceptance, to take any action, or refrain from taking action, with respect to the order except as provided in this Article or by express agreement. Liability based on acceptance arises only when acceptance occurs as stated in Section 4A-209, and liability is limited to that provided in this Article. A receiving bank is not the agent of the sender or beneficiary of the payment order it accepts, or of any other party to the funds transfer, and the bank owes no duty to any party to the funds transfer except as provided in this Article or by express agreement.

Part 3: Execution of Sender's Payment Order by Receiving Bank

Section 4A-301. *Execution and Execution Date*—(a) A payment order is "executed" by the receiving bank when it issues a payment order intended to carry out the payment order received by the bank. A payment order received by the beneficiary's bank can be accepted but cannot be executed.

(b)   "Execution date" of a payment order means the day on which the receiving bank may properly issue a payment order in execution of the sender's order. The execution date may be determined by instruction of the sender but cannot be earlier than the day the order is received and, unless otherwise determined, is the day the order is received. If the sender's instruction states a payment date, the execution date is the payment date or an earlier date on which execution is reasonably necessary to allow payment to the beneficiary on the payment date.

Section 4A-302. *Obligations of Receiving Bank in Execution of Payment Order*—(a) Except as provided in subsections (b) through (d), if the receiving bank accepts a payment order pursuant to Section 4A-209(a), the bank has the following obligations in executing the order:

(1)   The receiving bank is obliged to issue, on the execution date, a payment order complying with the sender's order and to follow the sender's instructions concerning (i) any

intermediary bank or funds-transfer system to be used in carrying out the funds transfer, or (ii) the means by which payment orders are to be transmitted in the funds transfer. If the originator's bank issues a payment order to an intermediary bank according to the instruction of the originator. A intermediary bank in the funds transfer is similarly bound by an instruction given to it by the sender of the payment order it accepts.

(2)   If the sender's instruction states that the funds transfer is to be carried out telephonically or by wire transfer or otherwise indicates that the funds transfer is to be carried out by the most expeditious means, the receiving bank is obliged to transmit its payment by the most expeditious available means, and to instruct any intermediary bank accordingly. If a sender's instruction states a payment date, the receiving bank is obliged to transmit its payment order at a time and by means reasonably necessary to allow payment to the beneficiary on the payment date or as soon thereafter as is feasible.

(b)   Unless otherwise instructed, a receiving bank executing a payment order may (i) use any funds-transfer system if use of that system is reasonable in the circumstances, and (ii) issue a payment order to the beneficiary's bank or to an intermediary bank through which a payment order conforming to the sender's order can expeditiously be issued to the beneficiary's bank if the receiving bank. A receiving bank is not required to follow an instruction of the sender designating a funds-transfer system to be used in carrying out the funds transfer if the receiving bank, in good faith, determines that it is not feasible to follow the instruction or that following the instruction would unduly delay completion of the funds transfer.

(c)   Unless subsection (a)(2) applies or the receiving bank is otherwise instructed, the bank may execute a payment order by transmitting its payment order by first class mail or by any means reasonable in the circumstances. If the receiving bank is instructed to execute the sender's order by transmitting its payment order by a particular means, the receiving bank may issue its payment order by the means stated or by any means as expeditious as the means stated.

(d)   Unless instructed by the sender, (i) the receiving bank may not obtain payment of its charges for services and expenses in connection with the execution of the sender's order by issuing a payment order in an amount equal to the amount of the sender's order less the amount of the charges, and (ii) may not instruct a subsequent receiving bank to obtain payment of its charges in the same manner.

Section 4A-303. *Erroneous Execution of Payment Order*—(a) A receiving bank that (i) executes the payment order of the sender by issuing a payment order in an amount greater than the amount of the sender's order, or (ii) issues a payment order in execution of the sender's order and then issues a duplicate order, is entitled to payment of the amount of the sender's order under Section 4A-402(c) if that subsection is otherwise satisfied. The bank is entitled to recover from the beneficiary of the erroneous order the excess payment received to the extent allowed by the law governing mistake and restitution.

(b)   A receiving bank that executes the payment order of the sender by issuing a payment order in an amount less than the amount of the sender's order is entitled to payment of the amount of the sender's order under Section 4A-402(c) is (i) that subsection is otherwise satisfied and (ii) the bank corrects its mistake by issuing an additional payment order for the benefit of the beneficiary of the sender's order. If the error is not corrected, the issuer of the erroneous order is entitled to receive or retain payment from the sender of the order it accepted only to the extent of the amount of the erroneous order. This subsection does not apply if the receiving bank executes the sender's payment order by issuing a payment order in an amount less than the amount of the sender's order for the purpose of obtaining payment of its charges for services and expenses pursuant to instruction of the sender.

(c)   If a receiving bank executes the payment order of the sender by issuing a payment order to a beneficiary different from the beneficiary of the sender's order and the funds transfer is completed on the basis of that error, the sender of the payment order that was erroneously executed and all previous senders in the funds transfer are not obliged to pay the payment orders they issued. The issuer of the erroneous order is entitled to recover from the beneficiary of the order the payment received to the extent allowed by the law governing mistake and restitution.

Section 4A-304. *Duty of Sender to Report Erroneously Executed Payment Order*—If the sender of a payment order that is erroneously executed as stated in Section 4A-303 receives notification from the receiving bank that the order was executed or that the sender's account was debited with respect to the order, the sender has a duty to exercise ordinary care to determine, on the basis of information available to the sender, that the order was erroneously executed and to notify the bank of the relevant facts within a reasonable time not exceeding 90 days after the notification from the bank was received by the sender. If the sender fails to perform that duty, the bank is not obliged to pay interest on any amount refundable to the sender under Section 4A-402(d) for the period before the bank learns of the execution error. The bank is not entitled to any recovery from the sender on account of a failure by the sender to perform the duty stated in this section.

Section 4A-305. *Liability for Late or Improper Execution or Failure to Execute Payment Order*—(a) If a funds transfer is completed but execution of a payment order by the receiving bank in breach of Section 4A-302 results in delay in payment to the beneficiary, the bank is obliged to pay interest to either the originator or the beneficiary of the funds transfer for the period of delay caused by the improper execution. Except as provided in subsection (c), additional damages are not recoverable.

(b) If execution of a payment order by a receiving bank in breach of Section 4A-302 results in (i) noncompletion of the funds transfer, (ii) failure to use an intermediary bank designated by the originator, or (iii) issuance of a payment order that does not comply with the terms of the payment order of the originator, the bank is liable to the originator for its expenses in the funds transfer and for incidental expenses and interest losses, to the extent not covered by subsection (a), resulting from the improper execution. Except as provided in subsection (c), additional damages are not recoverable.

(c) In addition to the amounts payable under subsections (a) and (b), damages, including consequential damages, are recoverable to the extent provided in an express written agreement of the receiving bank.

(d) If a receiving bank fails to execute a payment order it was obliged by express agreement to execute, the receiving bank is liable to the sender for its expenses in the transaction and for incidental expenses and interest losses resulting from the failure to execute. Additional damages, including consequential damages, are recoverable to the extent provided in an express written agreement of the receiving bank, but are not otherwise recoverable.

(e) Reasonable attorney's fees are recoverable if demand for compensation under subsection (a) or (b) is made and requested before an action is brought on the claim. If a claim is made for breach of an agreement under subsection (d) and the agreement does not provide for damages, reasonable attorney's fees are recoverable if demand for compensation under subsection (d) is made and refused before an action is brought on the claim.

(f) Except as stated in this section, the liability of a receiving bank under subsections (a) and (b) may not be varied by agreement.

Part 4: Payment

Section 4A-401. *Payment Date*—"Payment date" of a payment order means the day on which the amount of the order is payable to the beneficiary by the beneficiary's bank. The payment date may be determined by instruction of the sender but cannot be earlier than the day the order is received by the beneficiary's bank and, unless otherwise determined, is the day the order is received by the beneficiary's bank.

Section 4A-402. *Obligation of Sender to Pay Receiving Bank*—(a) This section is subject to Sections 4A-205 and 4A-207.

(b) With respect to a payment order issued to the beneficiary's bank, acceptance of the order by the bank obliges the sender to pay the amount of the order, but payment is not due until the payment date of the order.

(c) This subsection is subject to subsection (e) and to Section 4A-303. With respect to a payment order issued to a receiving bank other than the beneficiary's bank, acceptance of the order by the receiving bank obliges the sender to pay the bank the amount of the sender's order. Payment by the sender is not due until the execution date of the sender's order. The obligation of that sender to pay its payment order is excused if the funds transfer is not completed by acceptance by the beneficiary's bank of a payment order instructing payment to the beneficiary of that sender's payment order.

(d) If the sender of a payment order pays the order and was not obliged to pay all or part of the amount paid, the bank receiving payment is obliged to refund payment to the extent the sender was not obliged to pay. Except as provided in Sections 4A-204 and 4A-304, interest is payable on the refundable amount from the date of payment.

(e) If a funds transfer is not completed as stated in subsection (c) and an intermediary bank is obliged to refund payment as stated in subsection (d) but is unable to do so because not permitted by applicable law or because the bank suspends payments, a sender in the funds transfer that executed a payment order in compliance with an instruction, as stated in Section 4A-302(a)(1), to route the funds transfer through that intermediary bank is entitled to receive or retain payment from the sender of the payment order that it accepted. The first sender in the funds transfer that issued an instruction requiring routing through that intermediary bank is subrogated to the right of the bank that paid the intermediary bank to refund as stated in subsection (d).

(f) The right of the sender of a payment order to be excused from the obligation to pay the order as stated in subsection (c) or to receive refund under subsection (d) may not be varied by agreement.

Section 4A-403. *Payment by Sender to Receiving Bank*—(a) Payment of the sender's obligation under Section 4A-402 to pay the receiving bank occurs as follows:

(1) If the sender is a bank, payment occurs when the receiving bank receives final settlement of the obligation through a Federal Reserve Bank or through a funds-transfer system.

(2) If the sender is a bank and the sender (i) credited an account of the receiving bank with the sender, or (ii) caused an account of the receiving bank in another bank to be credited, payment occurs when the credit is withdrawn or, if not withdrawn, at midnight of the day on which the credit is withdrawable and the receiving bank learns of that fact.

(3) If the receiving bank debits an account of the sender with the receiving bank, payment occurs when the debit is made to the extent the debit is covered by a withdrawable credit balance in the account.

(b) If the sender and receiving bank are members of a funds-transfer system that nets obligations multilaterally among participants, the receiving bank receives final settlement when settlement is complete in accordance with the rules of the system. The obligation of the sender to pay the amount of a payment order transmitted through the funds-transfer system may be satisfied, to the extent permitted by the rules of the system, by setting off and applying against the sender's obligation the right of the sender to receive payment from the receiving bank of the amount of any other payment order transmitted to the sender by the receiving bank through the funds-transfer system. The aggregate balance of obligations owed by each sender to each receiving bank in the funds-transfer system may be satisfied, to the extent permitted by the rules of the system, by setting off and applying against that balance the aggregate balance of obligations owed to the sender by other members of the system. The aggregate balance is determined after the right of setoff stated in the second sentence of this subsection has been exercised.

(c) If two banks transmit payment orders to each other under an agreement that settlement of the obligations of each bank to the other under Section 4A-402 will be made at the end of the day or other period, the total amount owed with respect to all orders transmitted by one bank shall be set off against the total amount owed with respect to all orders transmitted by the other bank. To the extent of the setoff, each bank has made payment to the other.

(d)   In a case not covered by subsection (a), the time when payment of the sender's obligation under Section 4A-402(b) or 4A-402(c) occurs is governed by applicable principles of law that determine when an obligation is satisfied.

Section 4A-404. *Obligation of Beneficiary's Bank to Pay and Give Notice to Beneficiary*— (a) Subject to Sections 4A-211(e), 4A-405(d), and 4A-405(e), if a beneficiary's bank accepts a payment order, the bank is obliged to pay the amount of the order to the beneficiary of the order. Payment is due on the payment date of the order, but if acceptance occurs on the payment date after the close of the funds-transfer business day of the bank, payment is due on the next funds-transfer business day. If the bank refuses to pay after demand by the beneficiary and receipt of notice of particular circumstances that will give rise to consequential damages as a result of nonpayment, the beneficiary may recover damages resulting from the refusal to pay to the extent the bank had notice of the damages, unless the bank proves that it did not pay because of a reasonable doubt concerning the right of the beneficiary to payment.

(b)   If a payment order accepted by the beneficiary's bank instructs payment to an account of the beneficiary, the bank is obliged to notify the beneficiary of receipt of the order before midnight of the next funds-transfer business day following the payment date. If the payment order does not instruct payment to an account of the beneficiary, the bank is required to notify the beneficiary only if notice is required by the order. Notice may be given by first class mail or any other means reasonable in the circumstances. If the bank fails to give the required notice, the bank is obliged to pay interest to the beneficiary on the amount of the payment order from the day notice should have been given until the day the beneficiary learned of receipt of the payment order by the bank. No other damages are recoverable. Reasonable attorney's fees are also recoverable if demand for interest is made and refused before an action is brought on the claim.

(c)   The right of a beneficiary to receive payment and damages as stated in subsection (a) may not be varied, by agreement or a funds-transfer system rule. The right of a beneficiary to be notified as stated in subsection (b) may be varied by agreement of the beneficiary or by a funds-transfer system rule if the beneficiary is notified of the rule before initiation of the funds transfer.

Section 4A-405. *Payment by Beneficiary's Bank to Beneficiary*—(a) If the beneficiary's bank credits an account of the beneficiary of a payment order, payment of the bank's obligation under Section 4A-404(a) occurs when and to the extent (i) the beneficiary is notified of the right to withdraw the credit, (ii) the bank lawfully applies the credit to a debt of the beneficiary, or (iii) funds with respect to the order are otherwise made available to the beneficiary by the bank.

(b)   If the beneficiary's bank does not credit an account of the beneficiary of a payment order, the time when payment of the bank's obligation under Section 4A-404(a) occurs is governed by principles of law that determine when an obligation is satisfied.

(c)   Except as stated in subsections (d) and (e), if the beneficiary's bank pays the beneficiary of a payment order under a condition to payment or agreement of the beneficiary giving the bank the right to recover payment from the beneficiary if the bank does not receive payment of the order, the condition to payment or agreement is not enforceable.

(d)   A funds-transfer system rule may provide that payments made to beneficiaries of funds transfers made through the system are provisional until receipt of payment by the beneficiary's bank of the payment order is accepted. A beneficiary's bank that makes a payment that is provisional under the rule is entitled to refund from the beneficiary if (i) the rule requires that both the beneficiary and the originator be given notice of the provisional nature of the payment before the funds transfer is initiated, (ii) the beneficiary, the beneficiary's bank and the originator's bank agreed to be bound by the rule, and (iii) the beneficiary's bank did not receive payment of the payment order that it accepted. If the beneficiary is obliged to refund payment to the beneficiary's bank, acceptance of the payment order by the beneficiary's bank is nullified and no payment by the originator of the funds transfer to the beneficiary occurs under Section 4A-406.

(e) This subsection applies to a funds transfer that includes a payment order transmitted over a funds-transfer system that (i) nets obligations multilaterally among participants, and (ii) has in effect a loss-sharing agreement among participants for the purpose of providing funds necessary to complete settlement of the obligations of one or more participants that do not meet their settlement obligations. If the beneficiary's bank in the funds transfer accepts a payment order and the system fails to complete settlement pursuant to its rules with respect to any payment order in the funds transfer, (i) the acceptance by the beneficiary's bank is nullified and no person has any right or obligation based on the acceptance, (ii) the beneficiary's bank is entitled to recover payment from the beneficiary, (iii) no payment by the originator to the beneficiary occurs under Section 4A-406, and (iv) subject to Section 4A-402(e), each sender in the funds transfer is excused from its obligation to pay its payment order under Section 4A-402(c) because the funds transfer has not been completed.

Section 4A-406. *Payment by Originator to Beneficiary; Discharge of Underlying Obligation*—(a) Subject to Sections 4A-211(e), 4A-504(d), and 4A-405(e), the originator of a funds transfer pays the beneficiary of the originator's payment order (i) at the time a payment order for the benefit of the beneficiary is accepted by the beneficiary's bank in the funds transfer and (ii) in an amount equal to the amount of the order accepted by the beneficiary's bank, but not more than the amount of the originator's order.

(b) If payment under subsection (a) is made to satisfy an obligation, the obligation is discharged to the same extent discharge would result from payment to the beneficiary of the same amount in money, unless (i) the payment under subsection (a) was made by a means prohibited by the contract of the beneficiary with respect to the obligation, (ii) the beneficiary, within a reasonable time after receiving notice of receipt of the order by the beneficiary's bank, notified the originator of the beneficiary's refusal of the payment, (iii) funds with respect to the order were not withdrawn by the beneficiary or applied to a debt of the beneficiary, and (iv) the beneficiary would suffer a loss that could reasonably have been avoided if payment had been made by a means complying with the contract. If payment by the originator does not result in discharge under this section, the originator is subrogated to the rights of the beneficiary to receive payment from the beneficiary's bank under Section 4A-404(a).

(c) For the purpose of determining whether discharge of an obligation occurs under subsection (b), if the beneficiary's bank accepts a payment order in an amount equal to the amount of the originator's payment order less charges of one or more receiving banks in the funds transfer, payment to the beneficiary is deemed to be in the amount of the originator's order unless upon demand by the beneficiary the originator does not pay the beneficiary the amount of the deducted charges.

(d) Rights of the originator or of the beneficiary of a funds transfer under this section may be varied only by agreement of the originator and the beneficiary.

Part 5: Miscellaneous Provisions

Section 4A-501. *Variation by Agreement and Effect of Funds-Transfer System Rule*—(a) Except as otherwise provided in this Article, the rights and obligations of a party to a funds transfer may be varied by agreement of the affected party.

(b) "Funds-transfer system rule" means a rule of an association of banks (i) governing transmission of payment orders by means of a funds-transfer system of the association or rights and obligations with respect to those orders, or (ii) to the extent the rule governs rights and obligations between banks that are parties to a funds transfer in which a Federal Reserve Bank, acting as an intermediary bank, sends a payment order to the beneficiary's bank. Except as otherwise provided in this Article, a funds-transfer system rule governing rights and obligations between participating banks using the system may be effective even if the rule conflicts with this Article and indirectly affects even if the rule conflicts with this Article and indirectly affects another party to the funds transfer who does not consent to the rule. A funds-transfer system rule may also govern rights and obligations of parties other than participating banks using the system to the extent stated in Sections 4A-404(c), 4A-405(d), and 4A-507(c).

Section 4A-502. *Creditor Process Served on Receiving Bank; Setoff by Beneficiary's Bank*—(a) As used in this section, "creditor process" means levy, attachment, garnishment, notice of lien, sequestration, or similar process issued by or on behalf of a creditor or other claimant with respect to an account.

(b) This subsection applies to creditor process with respect to an authorized account of the sender of a payment order if the creditor process is served on the receiving bank. For the purpose of determining rights with respect to the creditor process, if the receiving bank accepts the payment order the balance in the authorized account is deemed to be reduced by the amount of the payment order to the extent the bank did not otherwise receive payment of the order, unless the creditor process is served at a time and in a manner affording the bank a reasonable opportunity to act on it before the bank accepts the payment order.

(c) If a beneficiary's bank has received a payment order for payment to the beneficiary's account in the bank, the following rules apply:

(1) The bank may credit the beneficiary's account. The amount credited may be set off against an obligation owed by the beneficiary to the bank or may be applied to satisfy creditor process served on the bank with respect to the account.

(2) The bank may credit the beneficiary's account and allow withdrawal of the amount credited unless creditor process with respect to the account is served at a time and in a manner affording the bank a reasonable opportunity to act to prevent withdrawal.

(3) If creditor process with respect to the beneficiary's account has been served and the bank has had a reasonable opportunity to act on it, the bank may not reject the payment order except for a reason unrelated to the service of process.

(d) Creditor process with respect to a payment by the originator to the beneficiary pursuant to a funds transfer may be served only on the beneficiary's bank with respect to the debt owed by that bank to the beneficiary. Any other bank served with the creditor process is not obliged to act with respect to the process.

Section 4A-503. *Injunction or Restraining Order with Respect to Funds Transfer*—For proper cause and in compliance with applicable law, a court may restrain (i) a person from issuing a payment order to initiate a funds transfer, (ii) an originator's bank from executing the payment order of the originator, or (iii) the beneficiary's bank from releasing funds to the beneficiary or the beneficiary from withdrawing the funds. A court may not otherwise restrain a person from issuing a payment order, paying or receiving payment of a payment order, or otherwise acting with respect to a funds transfer.

Section 4A-504. *Order in Which Items and Payment Orders May Be Charged to Account; Order of Withdrawals from Account*—(a) If a receiving bank has received more than one payment order of the sender or one or more payment orders and other items that are payable from the sender's account, the bank may charge the sender's account with respect to the various orders and items in any sequence.

(b) In determining whether a credit to an account has been withdrawn by the holder of the account or applied to a debt of the holder of the account, credits first made to the account are first withdrawn or applied.

Section 4A-505. *Preclusion of Objection to Debit of Customer's Account*—If a receiving bank has received payment from its customer with respect to a payment order issued in the name of the customer as sender and accepted by the bank, and the customer received notification reasonably identifying the order, the customer is precluded from asserting that the bank is not entitled to retain the payment unless the customer notifies the bank of the customer's objection to the payment within one year after the notification was received by the customer.

Section 4A-506. *Rate of Interest*—(a) If, under this Article, a receiving bank is obliged to pay interest with respect to a payment order issued to the bank, the amount payable may be determined (i) by agreement of the sender and receiving bank, or (ii) by a funds-transfer system rule if the payment order is transmitted through a funds-transfer system.

(b)   If the amount of interest is not determined by an agreement or rule as stated in subsection (a), the amount is calculated by multiplying the applicable Federal Funds rate by the amount on which interest is payable, and then multiplying the product by the number of days for which interest is payable. The applicable Federal Funds rate is the average of the Federal Funds rates published by the Federal Reserve Bank of New York for each of the days for which interest is payable divided by 360. The Federal Funds rate for any date on which a published rate is not available is the same as the published rate for the next preceding day for which there is a published rate. If a receiving bank that accepted a payment order is required to refund payment to the sender of the order because the funds transfer was not completed, but the failure to complete was not due to any fault by the bank, the interest payable is reduced by a percentage equal to the reserve requirement on deposits of the receiving bank.

Section 4A-507. *Choice of Law*—(a) The following rules apply unless the affected parties otherwise agree or subsection (c) applies:
(1)   The rights and obligations between the sender of a payment order and the receiving bank are governed by the law of the jurisdiction in which the receiving bank is located.
(2)   The rights and obligations between the beneficiary's bank and the beneficiary are governed by the law of the jurisdiction in which the beneficiary's bank is located.
(3)   The issue of when payment is made pursuant to a funds transfer by the originator to the beneficiary is governed by the law of the jurisdiction in which the beneficiary's bank is located.
(b)   If the parties described in each paragraph of subsection (a) have made an agreement selecting the law of a particular jurisdiction to govern rights and obligations between each other, the law of that jurisdiction governs those rights and obligations, whether or not the payment order or the funds transfer bears a reasonable relation to that jurisdiction.
(c)   A funds-transfer system rule may select the law of a particular jurisdiction to govern (i) rights and obligations between participating banks with respect to payment orders transmitted or processed through the system, or (ii) the rights and obligations of some or all parties to a funds transfer any part of which is carried out by means of the system. A choice of law made pursuant to clause (i) is binding on participating banks. A choice of law made pursuant to clause (ii) is binding on the originator, other sender, or a receiving bank having notice that the funds-transfer system might be used in the funds transfer and of the choice of law by the system when the originator, other sender, or receiving bank issued or accepted a payment order. The beneficiary of a funds transfer is bound by the choice of law if, when the funds transfer is initiated, the beneficiary has notice that the funds-transfer system might be used in the funds transfer and of the choice of law by the system. The law of a jurisdiction selected pursuant to this subsection may govern, whether or not that law bears a reasonable relation to the matter in issue.
(d)   In the event of inconsistency between an agreement under subsection (b) and a choice-of-law rule under subsection (c), the agreement under subsection (b) prevails.
(e)   If a funds transfer is made by use of more than one funds-transfer system and there is inconsistency between choice-of-law rules of the systems, the matter in issue is governed by the law of the selected jurisdiction that has the most significant relationship to the matter in issue.

ARTICLE 5: LETTERS OF CREDIT

Section 5-101. *Short Title*—This article may be cited as Uniform Commercial Code—Letters of Credit.

Section 5-102. *Definitions*—(a) In this article:
(1)   "Adviser" means a person who, at the request of the issuer, a confirmer, or another adviser, notifies or requests another adviser to notify the beneficiary that a letter of credit has been issued, confirmed, or amended.

(2) "Applicant" means a person at whose request or for whose account a letter of credit is issued. The term includes a person who requests an issuer to issue a letter of credit on behalf of another if the person making the request undertakes an obligation to reimburse the issuer.

(3) "Beneficiary" means a person who under the terms of a letter of credit is entitled to have its complying presentation honored. The term includes a person to whom drawing rights have been transferred under a transferable letter of credit.

(4) "Confirmer" means a nominated person who undertakes, at the request or with the consent of the issuer, to honor a presentation under a letter of credit issued by another.

(5) "Dishonor" of a letter of credit means failure to timely honor or to take an interim action, such as acceptance of a draft, that may be required by the letter of credit.

(6) "Document" means a draft or other demand, document of title, investment security, certificate, invoice, or other record, statement, or representation of fact, law, right, or opinion (i) which is presented in a written or other medium permitted by the letter of credit or, unless prohibited by the letter of credit, by the standard practice referred to in Section 5-108(e) and (ii) which is capable of being examined for compliance with the terms and conditions of the letter of credit. A document may not be oral.

(7) "Good faith" means honesty in fact in the conduct or transaction concerned.

(8) "Honor" of a letter of credit means performance of the issuer's undertaking in the letter of credit to pay or deliver an item of value. Unless the letter of credit otherwise provides, "honor" occurs
(i) upon payment,
(ii) if the letter of credit provides for acceptance, upon acceptance of a draft and, at maturity, its payment, or
(iii) if the letter of credit provides for incurring a deferred obligation, upon incurring the obligation and, at maturity, its performance.

(9) "Issuer" means a bank or other person that issues a letter of credit, but does not include an individual who makes an engagement for personal, family, or household purposes.

(10) "Letter of credit" means a definite undertaking that satisfies the requirements of Section 5-104 by an issuer to a beneficiary at the request or for the account of an applicant or, in the case of a financial institution, to itself or for its own account, to honor a documentary presentation by payment or delivery of an item of value.

(11) "Nominated person" means a person whom the issuer (i) designates or authorizes to pay, accept, negotiate, or otherwise give value under a letter of credit and (ii) undertakes by agreement or custom and practice to reimburse.

(12) "Presentation" means delivery of a document to an issuer or nominated person for honor or giving of value under a letter of credit.

(13) "Presenter" means a person making a presentation as or on behalf of a beneficiary or nominated person.

(14) "Record" means information that is inscribed on a tangible medium, or that is stored in an electronic or other medium, and is retrievable in perceivable form.

(15) "Successor of a beneficiary" means a person who succeeds to substantially all of the rights of a beneficiary by operation of law, including a corporation with or into which the beneficiary has been merged or consolidated, an administrator, executor, personal representative, trustee in bankruptcy, debtor in possession, liquidator, or receiver.

(b) Definitions in other Articles applying to this article and the sections in which they appear are:

"Accept" or "Acceptance"–Section 3-409

"Value"–Sections 3-303, 4-211

(c) Article 1 contains certain additional general definitions and principles of construction and interpretation applicable throughout this article.

Section 5-103. *Scope*—(a) This article applies to letters of credit and to certain rights and obligations arising out of transactions involving letters of credit.

(b)   The statement of a rule in this article does not by itself require, imply, or negate application of the same or a different rule to a situation not provided for, or to a person not specified, in this article.

(c)   With the exception of this subsection, subsections (a) and (d), Sections 5-102(a)(9) and (10), 5-106(d), and 5-114(d), and except to the extent prohibited in Sections 1-102(3) and 5-117(d), the effect of this article may be varied by agreement or by a provision stated or incorporated by reference in an undertaking. A term in an agreement or undertaking generally excusing liability or generally limiting remedies for failure to perform obligations is not sufficient to vary obligations prescribed by this article.

(d)   Rights and obligations of an issuer to a beneficiary or a nominated person under a letter of credit are independent of the existence, performance, or nonperformance of a contract or arrangement out of which the letter of credit arises or which underlies it, including contracts or arrangements between the issuer and the applicant and between the applicant and the beneficiary.

Section 5-104. *Formal Requirements*—A letter of credit, confirmation, advice, transfer, amendment, or cancellation may be issued in any form that is a record and is authenticated (i) by a signature or (ii) in accordance with the agreement of the parties or the standard practice referred to in Section 5-108(e).

Section 5-105. *Consideration*—Consideration is not required to issue, amend, transfer, or cancel a letter of credit, advice, or confirmation.

Section 5-106. *Issuance, Amendment, Cancellation, and Duration*—(a) A letter of credit is issued and becomes enforceable according to its terms against the issuer when the issuer sends or otherwise transmits it to the person requested to advise or to the beneficiary. A letter of credit is revocable only if it so provides.

(b)   After a letter of credit is issued, rights and obligations of a beneficiary, applicant, confirmer, and issuer are not affected by an amendment or cancellation to which that person has not consented except to the extent the letter of credit provides that it is revocable or that the issuer may amend or cancel the letter of credit without that consent.

(c)   If there is no stated expiration date or other provision that determines its duration, a letter of credit expires one year after its stated date of issuance or, if none is stated, after the date on which it is issued.

(d)   A letter of credit that states that it is perpetual expires five years after its stated date of issuance, or if none is stated, after the date on which it is issued.

Section 5-107. *Confirmer, Nominated Person, and Adviser*—(a) A confirmer is directly obligated on a letter of credit and has the rights and obligations of an issuer to the extent of its confirmation. The confirmer also has rights against and obligations to the issuer as if the issuer were an applicant and the confirmer had issued the letter of credit at the request and for the account of the issuer.

(b)   A nominated person who is not a confirmer is not obligated to honor or otherwise give value for a presentation.

(c)   A person requested to advise may decline to act as an adviser. An adviser that is not a confirmer is not obligated to honor or give value for a presentation. An adviser undertakes to the issuer and to the beneficiary accurately to advise the terms of the letter of credit, confirmation, amendment, or advice received by that person and undertakes to the beneficiary to check the apparent authenticity of the request to advise. Even if the advice is inaccurate, the letter of credit, confirmation, or amendment is enforceable as issued.

(d)   A person who notifies a transferee beneficiary of the terms of a letter of credit, confirmation, amendment, or advice has the rights and obligations of an adviser under subsection (c). The terms in the notice to the transferee beneficiary may differ from the terms in any notice to the transferor beneficiary to the extent permitted by the letter of credit, confirmation, amendment, or advice received by the person who so notifies.

Section 5-108. *Issuer's Rights and Obligations*—(a) Except as otherwise provided in Section 5-109, an issuer shall honor a presentation that, as determined by the standard practice referred to in subsection (e), appears on its face strictly to comply with the terms and conditions of the letter of credit. Except as otherwise provided in Section 5-113 and unless otherwise agreed with the applicant, an issuer shall dishonor a presentation that does not appear so to comply.

(b) An issuer has a reasonable time after presentation, but not beyond the end of the seventh business day of the issuer after the day of its receipt of documents:

(1)   to honor,

(2)   if the letter of credit provides for honor to be completed more than seven business days after presentation, to accept a draft or incur a deferred obligation, or

(3)   to give notice to the presenter of discrepancies in the presentation.

(c)   Except as otherwise provided in subsection (d), an issuer is precluded from asserting as a basis for dishonor any discrepancy if timely notice is not given, or any discrepancy not stated in the notice if timely notice is given.

(d)   Failure to give the notice specified in subsection (b) or to mention fraud, forgery, or expiration in the notice does not preclude the issuer from asserting as a basis for dishonor fraud or forgery as described in Section 5-109(a) or expiration of the letter of credit before presentation.

(e)   An issuer shall observe standard practice of financial institutions that regularly issue letters of credit. Determination of the issuer's observance of the standard practice is a matter of interpretation for the court. The court shall offer the parties a reasonable opportunity to present evidence of the standard practice.

(f)   An issuer is not responsible for:

(1)   the performance or nonperformance of the underlying contract, arrangement, or transaction,

(2)   an act or omission of others, or

(3)   observance or knowledge of the usage of a particular trade other than the standard practice referred to in subsection (e).

(g)   If an undertaking constituting a letter of credit under Section 5-102(a)(10) contains nondocumentary conditions, an issuer shall disregard the nondocumentary conditions and treat them as if they were not stated.

(h)   An issuer that has dishonored a presentation shall return the documents or hold them at the disposal of, and send advice to that effect to, the presenter.

(i)   An issuer that has honored a presentation as permitted or required by this article:

(1)   is entitled to be reimbursed by the applicant in immediately available funds not later than the date of its payment of funds;

(2)   takes the documents free of claims of the beneficiary or presenter;

(3)   is precluded from asserting a right of recourse on a draft under Sections 3-414 and 3-415;

(4)   except as otherwise provided in Sections 5-110 and 5-117, is precluded from restitution of money paid or other value given by mistake to the extent the mistake concerns discrepancies in the documents or tender which are apparent on the face of the presentation; and

(5)   is discharged to the extent of its performance under the letter of credit unless the issuer honored a presentation in which a required signature of a beneficiary was forged.

Section 5-109. *Fraud and Forgery*—(a) If a presentation is made that appears on its face strictly to comply with the terms and conditions of the letter of credit, but a required document is forged or materially fraudulent, or honor of the presentation would facilitate a material fraud by the beneficiary on the issuer or applicant:

(1)   the issuer shall honor the presentation, if honor is demanded by (i) a nominated person who has given value in good faith and without notice of forgery or material fraud, (ii) a confirmer who has honored its confirmation in good faith, (iii) a holder in due course of a draft drawn under the letter of credit which was taken after acceptance by

the issuer or nominated person, or (iv) an assignee of the issuer's or nominated person's deferred obligation that was taken for value and without notice of forgery or material fraud after the obligation was incurred by the issuer or nominated person; and

(2) the issuer, acting in good faith, may honor or dishonor the presentation in any other case.

(b) If an applicant claims that a required document is forged or materially fraudulent or that honor of the presentation would facilitate a material fraud by the beneficiary on the issuer or applicant, a court of competent jurisdiction may temporarily or permanently enjoin the issuer from honoring a presentation or grant similar relief against the issuer or other persons only if the court finds that:

(1) the relief is not prohibited under the law applicable to an accepted draft or deferred obligation incurred by the issuer;

(2) a beneficiary, issuer, or nominated person who may be adversely affected is adequately protected against loss that it may suffer because the relief is granted;

(3) all of the conditions to entitle a person to the relief under the law of this State have been met; and

(4) on the basis of the information submitted to the court, the applicant is more likely than not to succeed under its claim of forgery or material fraud and the person demanding honor does not qualify for protection under subsection (a)(1).

Section 5-110. *Warranties*—(a) If its presentation is honored, the beneficiary warrants:

(1) to the issuer, any other person to whom presentation is made, and the applicant that there is no fraud or forgery of the kind described in Section 5-109(a); and

(2) to the applicant that the drawing does not violate any agreement between the applicant and beneficiary or any other agreement intended by them to be augmented by the letter of credit.

(b) The warranties in subsection (a) are in addition to warranties arising under Article 3, 4, 7, and 8 because of the presentation or transfer of documents covered by any of those articles.

Section 5-111. *Remedies*—(a) If an issuer wrongfully dishonors or repudiates its obligation to pay money under a letter of credit before presentation, the beneficiary, successor, or nominated person presenting on its own behalf may recover from the issuer the amount that is the subject of the dishonor or repudiation. If the issuer's obligation under the letter of credit is not for the payment of money, the claimant may obtain specific performance or, at the claimant's election, recover an amount equal to the value of performance from the issuer. In either case, the claimant may also recover incidental but not consequential damages. The claimant is not obligated to take action to avoid damages that might be due from the issuer under this subsection. If, although not obligated to do so, the claimant avoids damages, the claimant's recovery from the issuer must be reduced by the amount of damages avoided. The issuer has the burden of proving the amount of damages avoided. In the case of repudiation the claimant need not present any document.

(b) If an issuer wrongfully dishonors a draft or demand presented under a letter of credit or honors a draft or demand in breach of its obligation to the applicant, the applicant may recover damages resulting from the breach, including incidental but not consequential damages, less any amount saved as a result of the breach.

(c) If an adviser or nominated person other than a confirmer breaches an obligation under this article or an issuer breaches an obligation not covered in subsection (a) or (b), a person to whom the obligation is owed may recover damages resulting from the breach, including incidental but not consequential damages, less any amount saved as a result of the breach. To the extent of the confirmation, a confirmer has the liability of an issuer specified in this subsection and subsections (a) and (b).

(d) An issuer, nominated person, or adviser who is found liable under subsection (a), (b), or (c) shall pay interest on the amount owed thereunder from the date of wrongful dishonor or other appropriate date.

(e) Reasonable attorney's fees and other expenses of litigation must be awarded to the prevailing party in an action in which a remedy is sought under this article.

(f) Damages that would otherwise be payable by a party for breach of an obligation under this article may be liquidated by agreement or undertaking, but only in an amount or by a formula that is reasonable in light of the harm anticipated.

Section 5-112. Transfer of Letter of Credit—(a) Except as otherwise provided in Section 5-113, unless a letter of credit provides that it is transferable, the right of a beneficiary to draw or otherwise demand performance under a letter of credit may not be transferred.

(b) Even if a letter of credit provides that it is transferable, the issuer may refuse to recognize or carry out a transfer if:

(1) the transfer would violate applicable law; or

(2) the transferor or transferee has failed to comply with any requirement stated in the letter of credit or any other requirement relating to transfer imposed by the issuer which is within the standard practice referred to in Section 5-108(e) or is otherwise reasonable under the circumstances.

Section 5-113. *Transfer by Operation of Law*—(a) A successor of a beneficiary may consent to amendments, sign and present documents, and receive payment or other items of value in the name of the beneficiary without disclosing its status as a successor.

(b) A successor of a beneficiary may consent to amendments, sign and present documents, and receive payment or other items of value in its own name as the disclosed successor of the beneficiary. Except as otherwise provided in subsection (e), an issuer shall recognize a disclosed successor of a beneficiary as beneficiary in full substitution for its predecessor upon compliance with the requirements for recognition by the issuer of a transfer of drawing rights by operation of law under the standard practice referred to in Section 5-108(e) or, in the absence of such a practice, compliance with other reasonable procedures sufficient to protect the issuer.

(c) An issuer is not obliged to determine whether a purported successor is a successor of a beneficiary or whether the signature of a purported successor is genuine or authorized.

(d) Honor of a purported successor's apparently complying presentation under subsection (a) or (b) has the consequences specified in Section 5-108(i) even if the purported successor is not the successor of a beneficiary. Documents signed in the name of the beneficiary or of a disclosed successor by a person who is neither the beneficiary nor the successor of the beneficiary are forged documents for the purposes of Section 5-109.

(e) An issuer whose rights of reimbursement are not covered by subsection (d) or substantially similar law and any confirmer or nominated person may decline to recognize a presentation under subsection (b).

(f) A beneficiary whose name is changed after the issuance of a letter of credit has the same rights and obligations as a successor of a beneficiary under this section.

Section 5-114. *Assignment of Proceeds*—(a) In this section, "proceeds of a letter of credit" means the cash, check, accepted draft, or other item of value paid or delivered upon honor or giving of value by the issuer or any nominated person under the letter of credit. The term does not include a beneficiary's drawing rights or documents presented by the beneficiary.

(b) A beneficiary may assign its right to part or all of the proceeds of a letter of credit. The beneficiary may do so before presentation as a present assignment of its right to receive proceeds contingent upon its compliance with the terms and conditions of the letter of credit.

(c) An issuer or nominated person need not recognize an assignment of proceeds of a letter of credit until it consents to the assignment.

(d) An issuer or nominated person has no obligation to give or withhold its consent to an assignment of proceeds of a letter of credit, but consent may not be unreasonably withheld if the assignee possesses and exhibits the letter of credit and presentation of the letter of credit is a condition to honor.

(e) Rights of a transferee beneficiary or nominated person are independent of the beneficiary's assignment of the proceeds of a letter of credit and are superior to the assignee's right to the proceeds.

(f) Neither the rights recognized by this section between an assignee and an issuer, transferee beneficiary, or nominated person nor the issuer's or nominated person's payment of proceeds to an assignee or a third person affect the rights between the assignee and any person other than the issuer, transferee beneficiary, or nominated person. The mode of creating and perfecting a security interest in or granting an assignment of a beneficiary's rights to proceeds is governed by Article 9 or other law. Against persons other than the issuer, transferee beneficiary, or nominated person, the rights and obligations arising upon the creation of a security interest or other assignment of a beneficiary's right to proceeds and its perfection are governed by Article 9 or other law.

Section 5-115. *Statute of Limitations*—An action to enforce a right or obligation arising under this article must be commenced within one year after the expiration date of the relevant letter of credit or one year after the [claim for relief] [cause of action] accrues, whichever occurs later. A [claim for relief] [cause of action] accrues when the breach occurs, regardless of the aggrieved party's lack of knowledge of the breach.

Section 5-116. *Choice of Law and Forum*—(a) The liability of an issuer, nominated person, or adviser for action or omission is governed by the law of the jurisdiction chosen by an agreement in the form of a record signed or otherwise authenticated by the affected parties in the manner provided in Section 5-104 or by a provision in the person's letter of credit, confirmation, or other undertaking. The jurisdiction whose law is chosen need not bear any relation to the transaction.

(b) Unless subsection (a) applies, the liability of an issuer, nominated person, or adviser for action or omission is governed by the law of the jurisdiction in which the person is located. The person is considered to be located at the address indicated in the person's undertaking. If more than one address is indicated, the person is considered to be located at the address from which the person's undertaking was issued. For the purpose of jurisdiction, choice of law, and recognition of interbranch letters of credit, but not enforcement of a judgment, all branches of a bank are considered separate juridical entities and a bank is considered to be located at the place where its relevant branch is considered to be located under this subsection.

(c) Except as otherwise provided in this subsection, the liability of an issuer, nominated person, or adviser is governed by any rules of custom or practice, such as the Uniform Customs and Practice for Documentary Credits, to which the letter of credit, confirmation, or other undertaking is expressly made subject. If (i) this article would govern the liability of an issuer, nominated person, or adviser under subsection (a) or (b), (ii) the relevant undertaking incorporates rules of custom or practice, and (iii) there is conflict between this article and those rules as applied to that undertaking, those rules govern except to the extent of any conflict with the nonvariable provisions specified in Section 5-103(c).

(d) If there is conflict between this article and Article 3, 4, 4A, or 9, this article governs.

(e) The forum for settling disputes arising out of an undertaking within this article may be chosen in the manner and with the binding effect that governing law may be chosen in accordance with subsection (a).

Section 5-117. *Subrogation of Issuer, Applicant, and Nominated Person*—(a) An issuer that honors a beneficiary's presentation is subrogated to the rights of the beneficiary to the same extent as if the issuer were a secondary obligor of the underlying obligation owed to the beneficiary and of the applicant to the same extent as if the issuer were the secondary obligor of the underlying obligation owed to the applicant.

(b)   An applicant that reimburses an issuer is subrogated to the rights of the issuer against any beneficiary, presenter, or nominated person to the same extent as if the applicant were the secondary obligor of the obligations owed to the issuer and has the rights of subrogation of the issuer to the rights of the beneficiary stated in subsection (a).

(c)   A nominated person who pays or gives value against a draft or demand presented under a letter of credit is subrogated to the rights of:

  (1)   the issuer against the applicant to the same extent as if the nominated person were a secondary obligor of the obligation owed to the issuer by the applicant;

  (2)   the beneficiary to the same extent as if the nominated person were a secondary obligor of the underlying obligation owed to the beneficiary; and

  (3)   the applicant to same extent as if the nominated person were a secondary obligor of the underlying obligation owed to the applicant.

(d)   Notwithstanding any agreement or term to the contrary, the rights of subrogation stated in subsections (a) and (b) do not arise until the issuer honors the letter of credit or otherwise pays and the rights in subsection (c) do not arise until the nominated person pays or otherwise gives value. Until then, the issuer, nominated person, and the applicant do not derive under this section present or prospective rights forming the basis of a claim, defense, or excuse.

ARTICLE 6: BULK TRANSFERS

Repealer of Article 6—Bulk Transfers and [Revised] Article 6—Bulk Sales (States to Select One Alternative)

ALTERNATIVE A

Section
1.   Repeal.
2.   Amendment.
3.   Amendment.
4.   Savings Clause.

Section 1. *Repeal*. Article 6 and Section 9-111 of the Uniform Commercial Code are hereby repealed, effective .

Section 2. *Amendment*. Section 1-105(2) of the Uniform Commercial Code is hereby amended to read as follows:

(2)   Where one of the following provisions of this Act specifies the applicable law, that provision governs and a contrary agreement is effective only to the extent permitted by the law (including the conflict of laws rules) so specified:

Rights of creditors against sold goods. Section 2-402.

Applicability of the Article on Leases. Sections 2A-105 and 2A-106.

Applicability of the Article on Bank Deposits and Collections. Section 4-102.

Applicability of the Article on Investment Securities. Section 8-106.

Perfection provisions of the Article on Secured Transactions. Section 9-103.

Section 3. *Amendment*. Section 2-403(4) of the Uniform Commercial Code is hereby amended to read as follows:

(4)   The rights of other purchasers of goods and of lien creditors are governed by the Articles on Secured Transactions (Article 9) and Documents of Title (Article 7).

Section 4. *Savings Clause*. Rights and obligations that arose under Article 6 and Section 9-111 of the Uniform Commercial Code before their repeal remain valid and may be enforced as though those statutes had not been repealed.

[End of Alternative A]

ALTERNATIVE B

Section

Section 6-101. *Short Title.* This Article shall be known and may be cited as Uniform Commercial Code—Bulk Sales.

Section 6-102. *Definitions and Index of Definitions.* (1) In this Article, unless the context otherwise requires:

(a) "Assets" means the inventory that is the subject of a bulk sale and any tangible and intangible personal property used or held for use primarily in, or arising from, the seller's business and sold in connection with that inventory, but the term does not include:

    (i) fixtures (§ 9-313(1)(a)) other than readily removable factory and office machines;

    (ii) the lessee's interest in a lease of real property; or

    (iii) property to the extent it is generally exempt from creditor process under nonbankruptcy law.

(b) "Auctioneer" means a person whom the seller engages to direct, conduct, control, or be responsible for a sale by auction.

(c) "Bulk sale" means:

    (i) in the case of a sale by auction or a sale or series of sales conducted by a liquidator on the seller's behalf, a sale or series of sales not in the ordinary course of the seller's business of more than half of the seller's inventory, as measured by value on the date of the bulk-sale agreement, if on that date the auctioneer or liquidator has notice, or after reasonable inquiry would have had notice, that the seller will not continue to operate the same or a similar kind of business after the sale or series of sales; and

    (ii) in all other cases, a sale not in the ordinary course of the seller's business of more than half the seller's inventory, as measured by value on the date of the bulk-sale agreement, if on that date the buyer has notice, or after reasonable inquiry would have had notice, that the seller will not continue to operate the same or a similar kind of business after the sale.

(d) "Claim" means a right to payment from the seller, whether or not the right is reduced to judgment, liquidated, fixed, matured, disputed, secured, legal, or equitable. The term includes costs of collection and attorney's fees only to the extent that the laws of this state permit the holder of the claim to recover them in an action against the obligor.

(e) "Claimant" means a person holding a claim incurred in the seller's business other than:

    (i) an unsecured and unmatured claim for employment compensation and benefits, including commissions and vacation, severance, and sick leave pay;

    (ii) a claim for injury to an individual or to property, or for breach of warranty, unless:

        (A) a right of action for the claim has accrued;

        (B) the claim has been asserted against the seller; and

(C) the seller knows the identity of the person asserting the claim and the basis upon which the person has asserted it; and

(States to Select One Alternative)

ALTERNATIVE A

[(iii) a claim for taxes owing to a governmental unit.]

ALTERNATIVE B

[(iii) a claim for taxes owing to a governmental unit, if:

    (A) a statute governing the enforcement of the claim permits or requires notice of the bulk sale to be given to the governmental unit in a manner other than by compliance with the requirements of this Article; and

    (B) notice is given in accordance with the statute.]

(f) "Creditor" means a claimant or other person holding a claim.

(g) (i)   "Date of the bulk sale" means:

    (A) if the sale is by auction or is conducted by a liquidator on the seller's behalf, the date on which more than 10 percent of the net proceeds is paid to or for the benefit of the seller; and

    (B) in all other cases, the later of the date on which: (I) more than 10 percent of the net contract price is paid to or for the benefit of the seller; or (II) more than 10 percent of the assets, as measured by value, are transferred to the buyer.

(ii) For purposes of this subsection:

    (A) Delivery of a negotiable instrument (§ 3-104(1)) to or for the benefit of the seller in exchange for assets constitutes payment of the contract price pro tanto;

    (B) To the extent that the contract price is deposited in an escrow, the contract price is paid to or for the benefit of the seller when the seller acquires the unconditional right to receive the deposit or when the deposit is delivered to the seller or for the benefit of the seller, whichever is earlier; and

    (C) An asset is transferred when a person holding an unsecured claim can no longer obtain through judicial proceedings rights to the asset that are superior to those of the buyer arising as a result of the bulk sale. A person holding an unsecured claim can obtain those superior rights to a tangible asset at least until the buyer has an unconditional right, under the bulk-sale agreement, to possess the asset, and a person holding an unsecured claim can obtain those superior rights to an intangible asset at least until the buyer has an unconditional right, under the bulk-sale agreement, to use the asset.

(h) "Date of the bulk-sale agreement" means:

(i) in the case of a sale by auction or conducted by a liquidator (subsection (c)(i)), the date on which the seller engages the auctioneer or liquidator; and

(ii) in all other cases, the date on which a bulk-sale agreement becomes enforceable between the buyer and the seller.

(i) "Debt" means liability on a claim.

(j) "Liquidator" means a person who is regularly engaged in the business of disposing of assets for businesses contemplating liquidation or dissolution.

(k) "Net contract price" means the new consideration the buyer is obligated to pay for the assets less:

(i) the amount of any proceeds of the sale of an asset, to the extent the proceeds are applied in partial or total satisfaction of a debt secured by the asset; and

(ii) the amount of any debt to the extent it is secured by a security interest or lien that is enforceable against the asset before and after it has been sold to a buyer. If a debt is secured by an asset and other property of the seller, the amount of the debt secured by a security interest or lien that is enforceable against the asset is determined by multiplying the debt by a fraction, the numerator of which is the value of the new consideration for the asset on the date of the bulk sale and the denominator of which is the value of all property securing the debt on the date of the bulk sale.

(l) "Net proceeds" means the new consideration received for assets sold at a sale by auction or a sale conducted by a liquidator on the seller's behalf less:

    (i) commissions and reasonable expenses of the sale;

    (ii) the amount of any proceeds of the sale of an asset, to the extent the proceeds are applied in partial or total satisfaction of a debt secured by the asset; and

    (iii) the amount of any debt to the extent it is secured by a security interest or lien that is enforceable against the asset before and after it has been sold to a buyer. If a debt is secured by an asset and other property of the seller, the amount of the debt secured by a security interest or lien that is enforceable against the asset is determined by multiplying the debt by a fraction, the numerator of which is the value of the new consideration for the asset on the date of the bulk sale and the denominator of which is the value of all property securing the debt on the date of the bulk sale.

(m) A sale is "in the ordinary course of the seller's business" if the sale comports with usual or customary practices in the kind of business in which the seller is engaged or with the seller's own usual or customary practices.

(n) "United States" includes its territories and possessions and the Commonwealth of Puerto Rico.

(o) "Value" means fair market value.

(p) "Verified" means signed and sworn to or affirmed.

(2) The following definitions in other Articles apply to this article.

(a) "Buyer." Section 2-103(1)(a).

(b) "Equipment." Section 9-109(2).

(c) "Inventory." Section 9-109(4).

(d) "Sale." Section 2-106(1).

(e) "Seller." Section 2-103(1)(d).

(3) In addition, Article 1 contains general definitions and principles of construction and interpretation applicable throughout this Article.

Section 6-103. *Applicability of Article.* (1) Except as otherwise provided in subsection (3), this Article applies to a bulk sale if:

(a) the seller's principal business is the sale of inventory from stock; and

(b) on the date of the bulk-sale agreement the seller is located in this state or, if the seller is located in a jurisdiction that is not a part of the United States, the seller's major executive office in the United States is in this state.

(2) A seller is deemed to be located at his [or her] place of business. If a seller has more than one place of business, the seller is deemed located at his [or her] chief executive office.

(3) This Article does not apply to:

(a) a transfer made to secure payment or performance of an obligation;

(b) a transfer of collateral to a secured party pursuant to Section 9-503;

(c) a sale of collateral pursuant to Section 9-504;

(d) retention of collateral pursuant to Section 9-505;

(e) a sale of an asset encumbered by a security interest or lien if (i) all the proceeds of the sale are applied in partial or total satisfaction of the debt secured by the security interest or lien or (ii) the security interest or lien is enforceable against the asset after it has been sold to the buyer and the net contract price is zero;

(f) a general assignment for the benefit of creditors or to a subsequent transfer by the assignee;

(g) a sale by an executor, administrator, receiver, trustee in bankruptcy, or any public officer under judicial process;

(h) a sale made in the course of judicial or administrative proceedings for the dissolution or reorganization of an organization;

(i)   a sale to a buyer whose principal place of business is in the United States and who

    (i)   not earlier than 21 days before the date of the bulk sale, (A) obtains from the seller a verified and dated list of claimants of whom the seller has notice three days before the seller sends or delivers the list to the buyer or (B) conducts a reasonable inquiry to discover the claimants;

    (ii)   assumes in full the debts owed to claimants of whom the buyer has knowledge on the date the buyer receives the list of claimants from the seller or on the date the buyer completes the reasonable inquiry, as the case may be;

    (iii)   is not insolvent after the assumption; and

    (iv)   gives written notice of the assumption not later than 30 days after the date of the bulk sale by sending or delivering a notice to the claimants identified in subparagraph (ii) or by filing a notice in the office of the [Secretary of State];

(j)   a sale to a buyer whose principal place of business is in the United States and who:

    (i)   assumes in full the debts that were incurred in the seller's business before the date of the bulk sale;

    (ii)   is not insolvent after the assumption; and

    (iii)   gives written notice of the assumption not later than 30 days after the date of the bulk sale by sending or delivering a notice to each creditor whose debt is assumed or by filing a notice in the office of the [Secretary of State];

(k)   a sale to a new organization that is organized to take over and continue the business of the seller and that has its principal place of business in the United States if:

    (i)   the buyer assumes in full the debts that were incurred in the seller's business before the date of the bulk sale;

    (ii)   the seller receives nothing from the sale except an interest in the new organization that is subordinate to the claims against the organization arising from the assumption; and

    (iii)   the buyer gives written notice of the assumption not later than 30 days after the date of the bulk sale by sending or delivering a notice to each creditor whose debt is assumed or by filing a notice in the office of the [Secretary of State];

(l)   a sale of assets having:

    (i)   a value, net of liens and security interests, of less than $10,000. If a debt is secured by assets and other property of the seller, the net value of the assets is determined by subtracting from their value an amount equal to the product of the debt multiplied by a fraction, the numerator of which is the value of the assets on the date of the bulk sale and the denominator of which is the value of all property securing the debt on the date of the bulk sale; or

    (ii)   a value of more than $25,000,000 on the date of the bulk-sale agreement; or

(m) a sale required by, and made pursuant to, statute.

(4)   The notice under subsection (3)(i)(iv) must state: (i) that a sale that may constitute a bulk sale has been or will be made; (ii) the date or prospective date of the bulk sale; (iii) the individual, partnership, or corporate names and the addresses of the seller and buyer; (iv) the address to which inquiries about the sale may be made, if different from the seller's address; and (v) that the buyer has assumed or will assume in full the debts owed to claimants of whom the buyer has knowledge on the date the buyer receives the list of claimants from the seller or completes a reasonable inquiry to discover the claimants.

(5)   The notice under subsections (3)(j)(iii) and (3)(k)(iii) must state: (i) that a sale that may constitute a bulk sale has been or will be made; (ii) the date or prospective date of the bulk sale; (iii) the individual, partnership, or corporate names and the addresses of the seller and buyer; (iv) the address to which inquiries about the sale may be made, if different from the seller's address; and (v) that the buyer has assumed or will assume the debts that were incurred in the seller's business before the date of the bulk sale.

(6)   For purposes of subsection (3)(l), the value of assets is presumed to be equal to the price the buyer agrees to pay for the assets. However, in a sale by auction or a sale conducted by a liquidator on the seller's behalf, the value of assets is presumed to be the amount the auctioneer or liquidator reasonably estimates the assets will bring at auction or upon liquidation.

Section 6-104. *Obligations of Buyer.* (1) In a bulk sale as defined in Section 6-102(1)(c)(ii) the buyer shall:

(a) obtain from the seller a list of all business names and addresses used by the seller within three years before the date the list is sent or delivered to the buyer;

(b) unless excused under subsection (2), obtain from the seller a verified and dated list of claimants of whom the seller has notice three days before the seller sends or delivers the list to the buyer and including, to the extent known by the seller, the address of and the amount claimed by each claimant;

(c) obtain from the seller or prepare a schedule of distribution (§ 6-106(1));

(d) give notice of the bulk sale in accordance with Section 6-105;

(e) unless excused under Section 6-106(4), distribute the net contract price in accordance with the undertakings of the buyer in the schedule of distribution; and

(f) unless excused under subsection (2), make available the list of claimants (subsection (1)(b)) by:

    (i) promptly sending or delivering a copy of the list without charge to any claimant whose written request is received by the buyer no later than six months after the date of the bulk sale;

    (ii) permitting any claimant to inspect and copy the list at any reasonable hour upon request received by the buyer no later than six months after the date of the bulk sale; or

    (iii) filing a copy of the list in the office of the [Secretary of State] no later than the time for giving a notice of the bulk sale (§ 6-105(5)). A list filed in accordance with this subparagraph must state the individual, partnership, or corporate name and a mailing address of the seller.

(2) A buyer who gives notice in accordance with Section 6-105(2) is excused from complying with the requirements of subsections (1)(b) and (1)(f).

Section 6-105. *Notice to Claimants.* (1) Except as otherwise provided in subsection (2), to comply with Section 6-104(1)(d) the buyer shall send or deliver a written notice of the bulk sale to each claimant on the list of claimants (§ 6-104(1)(b)) and to any other claimant of whom the buyer has knowledge at the time the notice of the bulk sale is sent or delivered.

(2) A buyer may comply with Section 6-104(1)(d) by filing a written notice of the bulk sale in the office of the [Secretary of State] if:

(a) on the date of the bulk-sale agreement the seller has 200 or more claimants, exclusive of claimants holding secured or matured claims for employment compensation and benefits, including commissions and vacation, severance, and sick-leave pay; or

(b) the buyer has received a verified statement from the seller stating that, as of the date of the bulk-sale agreement, the number of claimants, exclusive of claimants holding secured or matured claims for employment compensation and benefits, including commissions and vacation, severance, and sick-leave pay, is 200 or more.

(3) The written notice of the bulk sale must be accompanied by a copy of the schedule of distribution (§ 6-106(1)) and state at least:

(a) that the seller and buyer have entered into an agreement for a sale that may constitute a bulk sale under the laws of the State of ;

(b) the date of the agreement;

(c) the date on or after which more than 10 percent of the assets were or will be transferred;

(d) the date on or after which more than 10 percent of the net contract price was or will be paid, if the date is not stated in the schedule of distribution;

(e) the name and a mailing address of the seller;

(f) any other business name and address listed by the seller pursuant to Section 6-104(1)(a);

(g) the name of the buyer and an address of the buyer from which information concerning the sale can be obtained;

(h) a statement indicating the type of assets or describing the assets item by item;

SELECTED TEXT OF THE UNIFORM COMMERCIAL CODE Appendix C–89

(i) the manner in which the buyer will make available the list of claimants (§ 6-104(1)(f)), if applicable; and

(j) if the sale is in total or partial satisfaction of an antecedent debt owed by the seller, the amount of the debt to be satisfied and the name of the person to whom it is owed.

(4) For purposes of subsections (3)(e) and (3)(g), the name of a person is the person's individual, partnership, or corporate name.

(5) The buyer shall give notice of the bulk sale not less than 45 days before the date of the bulk sale and, if the buyer gives notice in accordance with subsection (1), not more than 30 days after obtaining the list of claimants.

(6) A written notice substantially complying with the requirements of subsection (3) is effective even though it contains minor errors that are not seriously misleading.

(7) A form substantially as follows is sufficient to comply with subsection (3):

Notice of Sale

(1) _____, whose address is _____, is described in this notice as the "seller."

(2) _____, whose address is _____, is described in this notice as the "buyer."

(3) The seller has disclosed to the buyer that within the past three years the seller has used other business names, operated at other addresses, or both, as follows:

(4) The seller and the buyer have entered into an agreement dated _____, for a sale that may constitute a bulk sale under the laws of the state of _____.

(5) The date on or after which more than 10 percent of the assets that are the subject of the sale were or will be transferred is _____ and [if not stated in the schedule of distribution] the date on or after which more than 10 percent of the net contract price was or will be paid is _____.

(6) The following assets are the subject of the sale: _____.

(7) [If applicable] The buyer will make available to claimants of the seller a list of the seller's claimants in the following manner: _____.

(8) [If applicable] The sale is to satisfy $_____ of an antecedent debt owed by the seller to _____.

(9) A copy of the schedule of distribution of the net contract price accompanies this notice.

Section 6-106. *Schedule of Distribution.* (1) The seller and buyer shall agree on how the net contract price is to be distributed and set forth their agreement in a written schedule of distribution.

(2) The schedule of distribution may provide for distribution to any person at any time, including distribution of the entire net contract price to the seller.

(3) The buyer's undertakings in the schedule of distribution run only to the seller. However, a buyer who fails to distribute the net contract price in accordance with the buyer's undertakings in the schedule of distribution is liable to a creditor only as provided in Section 6-107(1).

(4) If the buyer undertakes in the schedule of distribution to distribute any part of the net contract price to a person other than the seller, and, after the buyer has given notice in accordance with Section 6-105, some or all of the anticipated net contract price is or becomes unavailable for distribution as a consequence of the buyer's or seller's having complied with an order of court, legal process, statute, or rule of law, the buyer is excused from any obligation arising under this Article or under any contract with the seller to distribute the net contract price in accordance with the buyer's undertakings in the schedule if the buyer:

(a) distributes the net contract price remaining available in accordance with any priorities for payment stated in the schedule of distribution and, to the extent that the price is insufficient to pay all the debts having a given priority, distributes the price pro rata among those debts shown in the schedule as having the same priority;

(b) distributes the net contract price remaining available in accordance with an order of court;

   (c)   commences a proceeding for interpleader in a court of competent jurisdiction and is discharged from the proceeding; or

   (d)   reaches a new agreement with the seller for the distribution of the net contract price remaining available, sets forth the new agreement in an amended schedule of distribution, gives notice of the amended schedule, and distributes the net contract price remaining available in accordance with the buyer's undertakings in the amended schedule.

   (5) The notice under subsection (4)(d) must identify the buyer and the seller, state the filing number, if any, of the original notice, set forth the amended schedule, and be given in accordance with subsection (1) or (2) of Section 6-105, whichever is applicable, at least 14 days before the buyer distributes any part of the net contract price remaining available.

   (6) If the seller undertakes in the schedule of distribution to distribute any part of the net contract price, and, after the buyer has given notice in accordance with Section 6-105, some or all of the anticipated net contract price is or becomes unavailable for distribution as a consequence of the buyer's or seller's having complied with an order of court, legal process, statute, or rule of law, the seller and any person in control of the seller are excused from any obligation arising under this Article or under any agreement with the buyer to distribute the net contract price in accordance with the seller's undertakings in the schedule if the seller:

   (a)   distributes the net contract price remaining available in accordance with any priorities for payment stated in the schedule of distribution and, to the extent that the price is insufficient to pay all the debts having a given priority, distributes the price pro rata among those debts shown in the schedule as having the same priority;

   (b)   distributes the net contract price remaining available in accordance with an order of court;

   (c)   commences a proceeding for interpleader in a court of competent jurisdiction and is discharged from the proceeding; or

   (d)   prepares a written amended schedule of distribution of the net contract price remaining available for distribution, gives notice of the amended schedule, and distributes the net contract price remaining available in accordance with the amended schedule.

   (7) The notice under subsection (6)(d) must identify the buyer and the seller, state the filing number, if any, of the original notice, set forth the amended schedule, and be given in accordance with subsection (1) or (2) of Section 6-105, whichever is applicable, at least 14 days before the seller distributes any part of the net contract price remaining available.

   Section 6-107. *Liability for Noncompliance.* (1) Except as provided in subsection (3), and subject to the limitation in subsection (4):

   (a)   a buyer who fails to comply with the requirements of Section 6-104(1)(e) with respect to a creditor is liable to the creditor for damages in the amount of the claim, reduced by any amount that the creditor would not have realized if the buyer had complied; and

   (b)   a buyer who fails to comply with the requirements of any other subsection of Section 6-104 with respect to a claimant is liable to the claimant for damages in the amount of the claim, reduced by any amount that the claimant would not have realized if the buyer had complied.

   (2) In an action under subsection (1), the creditor has the burden of establishing the validity and amount of the claim, and the buyer has the burden of establishing the amount that the creditor would not have realized if the buyer had complied.

   (3) A buyer who:

   (a)   made a good faith and commercially reasonable effort to comply with the requirements of Section 6-104(1) or to exclude the sale from the application of this Article under Section 6-103(3); or

   (b)   on or after the date of the bulk-sale agreement, but before the date of the bulk sale, held a good faith and commercially reasonable belief that this Article does not apply to the particular sale is not liable to creditors for failure to comply with the requirements of Section 6-104. The buyer has the burden of establishing the good faith and commercial reasonableness of the effort or belief.

(4) In a single bulk sale the cumulative liability of the buyer for failure to comply with the requirements of Section 6-104(1) may not exceed an amount equal to:

(a) if the assets consist only of inventory and equipment, twice the net contract price, less the amount of any part of the net contract price paid to or applied for the benefit of the seller or a creditor; or

(b) if the assets include property other than inventory and equipment, twice the net value of the inventory and equipment less the amount of the portion of any part of the net contract price paid to or applied for the benefit of the seller or a creditor which is allocable to the inventory and equipment.

(5) For the purposes of subsection (4)(b), the "net value" of an asset is the value of the asset less (i) the amount of any proceeds of the sale of an asset, to the extent the proceeds are applied in partial or total satisfaction of a debt secured by the asset and (ii) the amount of any debt to the extent it is secured by a security interest or lien that is enforceable against the asset before and after it has been sold to a buyer. If a debt is secured by an asset and other property of the seller, the amount of the debt secured by a security interest or lien that is enforceable against the asset is determined by multiplying the debt by a fraction, the numerator of which is the value of the asset on the date of the bulk sale and the denominator of which is the value of all property securing the debt on the date of the bulk sale. The portion of a part of the net contract price paid to or applied for the benefit of the seller or a creditor that is "allocable to the inventory and equipment" is the portion that bears the same ratio to that part of the net contract price as the net value of the inventory and equipment bears to the net value of all of the assets.

(6) A payment made by the buyer to a person to whom the buyer is, or believes he [or she] is, liable under subsection (1) reduces pro tanto the buyer's cumulative liability under subsection (4).

(7) No action may be brought under subsection (1)(b) by or on behalf of a claimant whose claim is unliquidated or contingent.

(8) A buyer's failure to comply with the requirements of Section 6-104(1) does not (i) impair the buyer's rights in or title to the assets, (ii) render the sale ineffective, void, or voidable, (iii) entitle a creditor to more than a single satisfaction of his [or her] claim, or (iv) create liability other than as provided in this Article.

(9) Payment of the buyer's liability under subsection (1) discharges pro tanto the seller's debt to the creditor.

(10) Unless otherwise agreed, a buyer has an immediate right of reimbursement from the seller for any amount paid to a creditor in partial or total satisfaction of the buyer's liability under subsection (1).

(11) If the seller is an organization, a person who is in direct or indirect control of the seller, and who knowingly, intentionally, and without legal justification fails, or causes the seller to fail, to distribute the net contract price in accordance with the schedule of distribution is liable to any creditor to whom the seller undertook to make payment under the schedule for damages caused by the failure.

Official Comment

Prior Uniform Statutory Provision: None.

Purposes: 1. This section sets forth the consequences of noncompliance with the requirements of Section 6-104. Although other legal consequences may result from a bulk sale, for example, the buyer may be liable to the seller under Article 2 or to the seller's creditors under the Uniform Fraudulent Transfer Act—no other consequences may be imposed by reason of the buyer's failure to comply with the requirements of this Article.

The two subsections of Section 6-107(1) reflect the duties set forth in Section 6-104. The duties generally run only to claimants, but the duty to distribute the net contract price in accordance with the schedule of distribution (§ 6104(1)(e)) may run also to certain creditors.

2.   Article 6 (1987 Official Text), like many of its nonuniform predecessors makes a non-complying transfer ineffective against aggrieved creditors. In contrast, noncompliance with this Article neither renders the sale ineffective nor otherwise affects the buyer's rights in or title to the assets.

Liability under this Article is for breach of a statutory duty. The buyer's only liability is personal (*in personam*) liability. Aggrieved creditors may only recover money damages. *In rem* remedies, which are available upon noncompliance with Article 6 (1987 Official Text), are not available under this Article. Thus, aggrieved creditors no longer may treat the sale as if it had not occurred and use the judicial process to apply assets purchased by the buyer toward the satisfaction of their claims against the seller.

The change in the theory of liability and in the available remedy should be of particular significance if the seller enters bankruptcy after the sale is consummated. When an aggrieved creditor of the transferor has a nonbankruptcy right to avoid a transfer in whole or in part, as may be the case under Article 6 (1987 Official Text), the transferor's bankruptcy trustee may avoid the entire transfer. *See* Bankruptcy Code 544(b), 11 U.S.C. 544(b). Under this Article, a person who is aggrieved by the buyer's noncompliance may not avoid the sale. Rather the person is entitled only to recover damages as provided in this section. Because no creditor has the right to avoid the transaction or to assert a remedy that is the functional equivalent of avoidance, the seller's bankruptcy trustee likewise should be unable to do so.

3.   This Article makes explicit what is implicit in Article 6 (1987 Official Text): only those persons as to whom there has been noncompliance are entitled to a remedy. For example, if notices are sent to each claimant other than claimant A, claimant B cannot recover. Similarly, a creditor who acquires a claim after notice is given has no remedy unless the buyer undertakes in the schedule of distribution to pay that creditor and the buyer fails to meet the obligation.

4.   Unlike Article 6 (1987 Official Text), which imposes strict liability upon a noncomplying transferee, this Article imposes liability for noncompliance only when the failure to comply actually has injured a creditor and only to the extent of the injury. Each creditor's damages are measured by the injury that the particular creditor sustained as a consequence of the buyer's failure to comply. This measure is stated as the amount of the debt reduced by any amount that the person would not have realized if the buyer had complied. Compare Section 6-103(5).

5.   A buyer is liable only for the buyer's own noncompliance with the requirements of Section 6-104. Under that section, the only step the buyer must take to discover the identity of the seller's claimants is to obtain a list of claimants from the seller. If the seller's list is incomplete and the buyer lacks knowledge of claimant C, then claimant C has no remedy under subsection (1)(b) of this section.

6.   The creditor has the burden of establishing the validity and amount of the debt owed by the seller as well as the fact of the buyer's noncompliance. In contesting the allegation of noncompliance, the buyer may introduce evidence tending to show either that the sale was not a bulk sale or that the sale was a bulk sale to which this Article does not apply. In contesting the validity and amount of the debt, the buyer may introduce evidence tending to show that the seller had a defense to the debt. The buyer has the burden of establishing the amount that the creditor would not have realized even if the buyer had complied. Implicit in subsection (2) is that certain failures to comply with the requirements of this Article will cause no injury and thus result in no liability.

The following examples illustrate the operation of subsection (2):

Example 1: The buyer fails to give notice of the bulk sale. Claimant D, who appears on seller's list of claimants, admits to having had actual knowledge of the impending sale two months before it occurred. The buyer is likely to be able to meet the burden of establishing that even had the buyer given notice of the sale, claimant D would not have recovered any more than the claimant actually recovered.

Example 2: The buyer failed to obtain a list of seller's business names (§ 6-104(1)(a)) or to make available the list of claimants (§ 6-104(1)(f)). In many cases, the buyer may be able to meet the burden of establishing that compliance with those subsections would not have enabled claimants to recover any more than they actually recovered.

7.   Subsection (3) may afford a complete defense to a noncomplying buyer. This defense is available to buyers who establish that they made a good faith effort to comply with the requirements of this Article or made a good faith effort to exclude the sale from the application of this Article (e.g., by assuming debts and attempting to comply with the notice requirements of § 6-103(3)(i), (j), or (k)). When a buyer makes a good faith effort to comply with this Article or to exclude the transaction from its coverage, the injury caused by noncompliance is likely to be de minimis. In any event, the primary responsibility for satisfying claims rests with the creditors, and this Article imposes no greater duty upon buyers who attempt to comply with this Article or to exclude a sale from its application than to make a good faith effort to do so.

The defense of subsection (3) also is available to buyers who act on the good faith belief that this Article does not apply to the sale (e.g., because the sale is not a bulk sale or is excluded under § 6-103). The good-faith-belief defense is an acknowledgment that reasonable people may disagree over whether a given transaction is or is not a bulk sale and over whether Section 6-103 excludes a particular transaction. A buyer acting in good faith should be protected from the liability that this Article otherwise would impose on buyers who may be completely innocent of wrongdoing. A buyer who is unaware of the requirements of this Article holds no belief concerning the applicability of the Article and so may not use the defense.

8.   Even a buyer who completely fails to comply with this Article may not be liable in an amount equal to sum of the seller's debts. Subsection (4) limits the aggregate recovery for "any one bulk sale," which term includes a series of sales by a liquidator. The maximum cumulative liability for noncompliance with this Article parallels the maximum recovery generally available to creditors under the 1987 Official Text of Article 6. Under that Article, the noncomplying transferee may have to "pay twice" for the goods. First, the transferee may pay the purchase price to the transferor; then, the transferee may lose the goods to aggrieved creditors.

Under this Article, the maximum cumulative liability is an amount equal to twice the net contract price of the inventory and equipment (i.e., twice the amount that would be available to unsecured creditors from the inventory and equipment), less the amount of any portion of that net contract price paid to or applied for the benefit of the seller or a creditor of the seller. Unless the buyer receives credit for amounts paid to the seller (which amounts the creditors have a right to apply to payment of their claims), the buyer might wind up paying an amount equal to the net contract price three times (once to the seller and twice to aggrieved creditors). The grant of credit for amounts paid to the seller's creditors recognizes that ordinarily the seller has no obligation to pay creditors pro rata.

When the assets sold consist of only inventory and equipment, calculation of the maximum cumulative liability is relatively simple. But when the assets sold include property in addition to inventory and equipment, the calculation becomes more difficult. When inventory or equipment secures a debt that also is secured by other collateral and the aggregate value of the collateral exceeds the secured debt, a determination of the amount in clause (ii) of subsection (5) may require an allocation of the collateral to the debt in accordance with the statutory formula. In addition, one may need to determine which portion of payments of the net contract price is allocable to inventory and equipment. Subsection (5) directs that this allocation be made by multiplying the part of the net contract price paid to or applied for the benefit of the seller or a creditor by a fraction whose nominator is the net value of the inventory and equipment and whose denominator is the net value of all the assets.

Sometimes the seller may receive the net contract price and pay some or all of it to one or more creditors. In determining whether a payment to a creditor was made from the net contract price or from another source, courts are free to employ tracing rules. Amounts paid to secured parties usually are taken into account in determining the net contract price; if so, the buyer should not receive credit for them.

9.   The buyer need not wait for judgment to be entered before paying a person believed to be a creditor of the seller. Indeed, the buyer is entitled to credit for amounts paid to persons who in fact may not be creditors of the seller, as long as the buyer acts with the belief that the

seller is so indebted. As is the case with respect to all obligations under the Code, the buyer's belief must be held in good faith.

10. Any amounts paid by the buyer in satisfaction of the liability created by Section 6-107(1) reduce the seller's liability to the recipient pro tanto. Consequently, the buyer is entitled to immediate reimbursement of those amounts from the seller. The right of reimbursement is available only for amounts paid to actual creditors. Amounts paid to those whom the buyer incorrectly believes to be creditors ordinarily are not recoverable from the seller, although the buyer is entitled to credit for those amounts against the aggregate liability in subsection (4). Of course, the buyer and seller may vary the seller's reimbursement obligation by agreement.

11. Because of the difficulty in valuing claims that are unliquidated or contingent, persons holding claims of that kind may not bring an action under subsection (1)(b). If the claim remains unliquidated or contingent throughout the limitation period in Section 6-110, then these creditors have no remedy for noncompliance under that subsection. They may, however, be entitled to a remedy under subsection (1)(a) or (11) for failure to distribute the net contract price in accordance with the schedule of distribution.

12. In certain circumstances, subsection (11) imposes liability on a person in direct or indirect control of a seller that is an organization. Excuse under Section 6-106(6) is a "legal justification" that prevents liability from attaching under subsection (11). No special provision applies to the seller who fails to comply with the schedule. The seller already owes the debt to the creditor, and other law governs the consequences of a debtor who fails to pay a debt when promised.

Cross References:

Point 1:   Section 6-104.
Point 4:   Section 4-103.
Point 5:   Sections 6-104 and 6-105.
Point 6:   Sections 1-201, 6-102, 6-103, and 6-104.
Point 7:   Sections 1-102, 1-201, 6-102 and 6-103.
Point 8:   Section 6-102.
Point 9:   Section 1-203.
Point 10: Section 1-102.
Point 11: Sections 6-102 and 6-110.
Point 12: Section 6-106.

Definitional Cross-References:

"Assets." Section 6-102.

Section 6-108. *Bulk Sales by Auction; Bulk Sales Conducted by Liquidator.* (1) Sections 6-104, 6-105, 6-106, and 6-107 apply to a bulk sale by auction and a bulk sale conducted by a liquidator on the seller's behalf with the following modifications:
  (a) "buyer" refers to auctioneer or liquidator, as the case may be;
  (b) "net contract price" refers to net proceeds of the auction or net proceeds of the sale, as the case may be;
  (c) the written notice required under Section 6-105(3) must be accompanied by a copy of the schedule of distribution (§ 6-106(1)) and state at least:
      (i)   that the seller and the auctioneer or liquidator have entered into an agreement for auction or liquidation services that may constitute an agreement to make a bulk sale under the laws of the State of ;
      (ii) the date of the agreement;
      (iii) the date on or after which the auction began or will begin or the date on or after which the liquidator began or will begin to sell assets on the seller's behalf;

    (iv) the date on or after which more than 10 percent of the net proceeds of the sale were or will be paid, if the date is not stated in the schedule of distribution;

    (v) the name and a mailing address of the seller;

    (vi) any other business name and address listed by the seller pursuant to Section 6-104(1)(a);

    (vii) the name of the auctioneer or liquidator and an address of the auctioneer or liquidator from which information concerning the sale can be obtained;

    (viii)a statement indicating the type of assets or describing the assets item by item;

    (ix) the manner in which the auctioneer or liquidator will make available the list of claimants (§ 6-104(1)(f)), if applicable; and

    (x) if the sale is in total or partial satisfaction of an antecedent debt owed by the seller, the amount of the debt to be satisfied and the name of the person to whom it is owed; and

  (d) in a single bulk sale the cumulative liability of the auctioneer or liquidator for failure to comply with the requirements of this section may not exceed the amount of the net proceeds of the sale allocable to inventory and equipment sold less the amount of the portion of any part of the net proceeds paid to or applied for the benefit of a creditor which is allocable to the inventory and equipment.

  (2) A payment made by the auctioneer or liquidator to a person to whom the auctioneer or liquidator is, or believes he [or she] is, liable under this section reduces pro tanto the auctioneer's or liquidator's cumulative liability under subsection (1)(d).

  (3) A form substantially as follows is sufficient to comply with subsection (1)(c):

Notice of Sale

  (1) _____, whose address is _____, is described in this notice as the "seller."

  (2) _____, whose address is _____, is described in this notice as the "auctioneer" or "liquidator"

  (3) The seller has disclosed to the auctioneer or liquidator that within the past three years the seller has used other business names, operated at other addresses, or both, as follows:

  (4) The seller and the auctioneer or liquidator have entered into an agreement dated _____ for auction or liquidation services that may constitute an agreement to make a bulk sale under the laws of the State of _____.

  (5) The date on or after which the auction began or will begin or the date on or after which the liquidator began or will begin to sell assets on the seller's behalf is and [if not stated in the schedule of distribution] the date on or after which more than 10 percent of the net proceeds of the sale were or will be paid is

  (6) The following assets are the subject of the sale:

  (7) [If applicable] The auctioneer or liquidator will make available to claimants of the seller a list of the seller's claimants in the following manner: _____.

  (8) [If applicable] The sale is to satisfy $_____ of an antecedent debt owed by the seller to _____.

  (9) A copy of the schedule of distribution of the net proceeds accompanies this notice.

[End of Notice]

  (4) A person who buys at a bulk sale by auction or conducted by a liquidator need not comply with the requirements of Section 6-104(1) and is not liable for the failure of an auctioneer or liquidator to comply with the requirements of this section.

Official Comment

Prior Uniform Statutory Provision: Section 6-108.

Changes: Revised, expanded to include sales conducted by a liquidator on the seller's behalf, and form of notice added.

Purposes of Changes and New Matter:

1.   This section applies only to bulk sales by auction or conducted by a liquidator on the seller's behalf, as defined in Section 6-102(1)(c). Bulk sales conducted by an auctioneer or liquidation its own behalf are treated as ordinary bulk sales and are not subject to this section.

2.   Regardless of whether the assets are sold directly from the seller to the buyer, are sold to a variety of buyers at auction, or are sold on the seller's behalf by a liquidator to one or more buyers, a going-out-of-business sale of inventory presents similar risks to claimants. Auctioneers and liquidators are likely to be in a better position to ascertain whether the sale they are conducting is, or is part of, a bulk sale than are their customers. Accordingly, buyers at auctions and from liquidators selling assets of others need not be concerned with complying with this Article. Instead, this Section imposes upon auctioneers and liquidators duties and liabilities that are similar, but not always identical, to those of a buyer under Sections 6-104(1) and 6-107. Except to the extent that this section treats bulk sales by auctioneers and liquidators differently from those conducted by the seller on its own behalf, the Official Comments to Sections 6-105(1) and 6-107, as well as the Comments to Sections 6-105 and 6-106, which those sections incorporate by reference, are applicable to sales to which this section applies.

3.   Subsection (1)(d) sets forth the maximum cumulative liability for auctioneers and liquidators "in any one bulk sale," which term includes a series of sales by a liquidator. This liability is to be calculated in a manner similar to that set forth in Sections 6-107(4) and 6107(5). The term "net proceeds of the auction or sale allocable to inventory and equipment" is analogous to the term "net value of the inventory and equipment"; however, the former takes into account the reasonable expenses of the auction or sale whereas the latter does not. Also, the latter is doubled whereas the former is not. The "amount of the portion of any part of the net proceeds paid to or applied for the benefit of a creditor which is allocable to inventory and equipment" is determined by multiplying the part of the net proceeds paid to or applied for the benefit of a creditor by a fraction whose numerator is the net proceeds of the sale allocable to inventory and equipment and whose denominator is the total net proceeds of the auction or sale. Because the amount of the net proceeds allocable to inventory and equipment is not doubled, the auctioneer or liquidator is not entitled to credit for payments made to the seller.

4.   Section 6-107(3) applies to all bulk sales. Accordingly, an auctioneer or liquidator who makes a good faith effort to comply with the requirements of this Article or to exclude the sale from this Article or who acts under a good faith belief that this Article does not apply to the sale faces no liability whatsoever.

Cross-References:

Point 1: Section 6-102.
Point 2: Sections 6-102, 6-104, 6-105, 6-106, and 6-107.
Point 3: Sections 6-102 and 6-107.
Point 4: Section 6-107.

Definitional Cross-References:

"Assets." Section 6-102.
"Auctioneer." Section 6-102.
"Bulk sale." Section 6-102.
"Claimants." Section 6-102.
"Creditor." Section 6-102.
"Debt." Section 6-102.
"Equipment." Section 9-109.
"Inventory." Section 9-109.
"Liquidator." Section 6-102.
"Net proceeds." Section 6-102.
"Person." Section 1-201.
"Seller." Section 2-103.
"Written." Section 1-201.

Section 6-109. *What Constitutes Filing; Duties of Filing Officer; Information from Filing Officer.* (1) Presentation of a notice or list of claimants for filing and tender of the filing fee or acceptance of the notice or list by the filing officer constitutes filing under this Article.

(2)   The filing officer shall:
  (a)   mark each notice or list with a file number and with the date and hour of filing;
  (b)   hold the notice or list or a copy for public inspection;
  (c)   index the notice or list according to each name given for the seller and for the buyer; and
  (d)   note in the index the file number and the addresses of the seller and buyer given in the notice of list.

(3)   If the person filing a notice or list furnished the filing officer with a copy, the filing officer upon request shall note upon the copy the file number and date and hour of the filing of the original and send or deliver the copy to the person.

(4)   The fee for filing and indexing and for stamping a copy furnished by the person filing to show the date and place of filing is $ for the first page and $ for each additional page. The fee for indexing each name more that two is $.

(5)   Upon request of any person, the filing officer shall issue a certificate showing whether any notice of list with respect to a particular seller or buyer is on file on the date and hour stated in the certificate. If a notice or list is on file on the date and hour stated in the certificate. If a notice or list is on file, the certificate must give the date and hour of filing of each notice or list and the name and address of each seller, buyer, auctioneer, or liquidator. The fee for the certificate is $ if the request for the certificate is in the standard form prescribed by the [Secretary of State] and otherwise is $. Upon request of any person, the filing officer shall furnish a copy of any filed notice of list for a fee of $.

(6)   The filing officer shall keep each notice or list for two years after it is filed.

Section 6-110. *Limitation of Actions.* (1) Except as provided in subsection (2), and action under this Article against a buyer, auctioneer, or liquidator must be commenced within one year after the date of the bulk sale.

(2)   If the buyer, auctioneer, or liquidator conceals the fact that the sale has occurred, the limitation is tolled and an action under this Article may be commenced within the earlier of (i) one year after the person bringing the action discovers that the sale has occurred or (ii) one year after the person bringing the action should have discovered that the sale has occurred, but no later than two years after the date of the bulk sale. Complete noncompliance with requirements of this Article doe not of itself constitute concealment.

(3)   An action under Section 6-107(11) must be commenced within one year after the alleged violation occurs.

Additional Sections Included in Article 6 of the Codes of Certain Jurisdictions Which Are Not Contained in the Official Text

California. Adds sections as follows:

Section 6106.2. *Payment of Consideration to Satisfy Claims of Seller's Creditors; Disputed Claims; Attachment; Interpleader; Notice; Security Interest.* (a) This section applies only to a bulk sale where the consideration is two million dollars ($2,000,000) or less and is substantially all cash or an obligation of the buyer to pay cash in the future to the seller or a combination thereof.

(b)   Upon every bulk sale subject to this section except one made by sale at auction or a sale or series of sales conducted by a liquidator on the seller's behalf, it is the duty of the buyer or, if the transaction is handled through an escrow, the escrow agent to apply the cash consideration in accordance with this section so far as necessary to pay those debts of the seller for which claims are due and payable on or before the date of the bulk sale and are received in writing on or prior to the date specified as the last date to file claims with the person designated in the notice to receive claims. This duty of the buyer or escrow agent runs to each claimant timely filing the claim.

(c) If the seller disputes whether a claim is due and payable on the date of the bulk sale or the amount of any claim, the buyer or escrow agent shall withhold from distribution an amount equal to (1) 125 percent of the first seven thousand five hundred dollars ($7,500) of the claim, and (2) an amount equal to that portion of the claim in excess of the first seven thousand five hundred dollars (57,500), or the pro rata amount under subdivision (b) of Section 6106.4 if applicable, and shall send a written notice to the claimant filing the claim on or before two business days after the distribution that the amount will be paid to the seller, or to the other claimants in accordance with subdivision (b) of Section 6106.4, as the case may be, unless attached within 25 days from the mailing of the notice. Any portion of the amount withheld which is not attached by the claimant within that time shall be paid by the buyer or escrow agent to the seller, or to the other claimants in accordance with subdivision (b) of Section 6106.4 if they have not been paid in full. An attachment of any amount so withheld shall be limited in its effect to the amount withheld for the attaching claimant and shall give the attaching claimant no greater priority or rights with respect to its claim than the claimant would have had if the claim had not been disputed. For purposes of this subdivision, a claimant may obtain the issuance of an attachment for a claim which is less than five hundred dollars ($500) and which otherwise meets the requirements of Section 483.010 of the Code of Civil Procedure or which is a secured claim or lien of the type described in Section 483.010 of the Code of Civil Procedure. The remedy in this subdivision shall be in addition to any other remedies the claimant may have, including any right to attach the property intended to be transferred or any other property.

(d) If the cash consideration payable is not sufficient to pay all of the claims received in full, where no escrow has been established pursuant to Section 6106.4, the buyer shall follow the procedures specified in subdivisions (a) to (c), inclusive, of Section 6106.4, and the immunity established by paragraph (3) of subdivision (a) of that section shall apply to the buyer.

(e) The buyer or escrow agent shall, within 45 days after the buyer takes legal title to any of the goods, either pay to the extent of the cash consideration the claims filed and not disputed, or the applicable portion thereof to the extent of the cash consideration under subdivision (b) of Section 6106.4, or institute an action in interpleader pursuant to subdivision (b) of Section 386 of the Code of Civil Procedure and deposit the consideration with the clerk of the court pursuant to subdivision (c) of that section. The action shall be brought in the appropriate court in the county where the seller had its principal place of business in this state. Sections 386.1 and 386.6 of the Code of Civil Procedure shall apply in the action.

(f) The notice shall state, in addition to the matters required by Section 6105, the name and address of the person with whom claims may be filed and the last date for filing claims, which shall be the business day before the date stated in the notice pursuant to paragraph (4) of subdivision (a) of Section 6105. Claims shall be deemed timely filed only if actually received by the person designated in the notice to receive claims before the close of business on the day specified in the notice as the last date for filing claims.

(g) This section shall not be construed to release any security interest or other lien on the property which is the subject of the bulk sale except upon a voluntary release by the secured party or lienholder.

Section 6106.4. *Escrow; Filing Claims; Distribution; Notice.* In any case where the notice of a bulk sale subject to Section 6106.2 states that claims may be filed with an escrow agent, the intended buyer shall deposit with the escrow agent the full amount of the purchase price or consideration. If, at the time the bulk sale is otherwise ready to be consummated, the amount of cash deposited or agreed to be deposited at or prior to consummation in the escrow is insufficient to pay in full all of the claims filed with the escrow agent, the escrow agent shall do each of the following:

(a)(1) Delay the distribution of the consideration and the passing of legal title for a period of not less than 25 days nor more than 30 days from the date the notice required in paragraph (2) is mailed.

(2) Within five business days after the time the bulk sale would otherwise have been consummated, send a written notice to each claimant who has filed a claim stating the total consideration deposited or agreed to be deposited in the escrow, the name of each

claimant who filed a claim against the escrow and the amount of each claim, the amount proposed to be paid to each claimant, the new date scheduled for the passing of legal title pursuant to paragraph (1) and the date on or before which distribution will be made to claimants which shall not be more than five days after the new date specified for the passing of legal title.

(3) If no written objection to the distribution described in the notice required by paragraph (2) is received by the escrow agent prior to the new date specified in the notice for the passing of legal title, the escrow agent shall not be liable to any person to whom the notice required by paragraph (2) was sent for any good faith error which may have been committed in allocating and distributing the consideration as stated in the notice.

(b) Distribute the consideration in the following order of priorities:

(1) All obligations owing to the United States, to the extent given priority by federal

(2) Secured claims, including statutory and judicial liens, to the extent of the consideration fairly attributable to the value of the properties securing the claims and in accordance with the priorities provided by law. A secured creditor shall participate in the distribution pursuant to this subdivision only if a release of lien is deposited by the secured creditor conditioned only upon receiving an amount equal to the distribution.

(3) Escrow and professional charges and brokers' fees attributable directly to the sale.

(4) Wage claims given priority by Section 1205 of the Code of Civil Procedure.

Amendments to other Articles of Uniform Commercial Code Conforming to Revised Article 6 [Alternative B]

CONFORMING AMENDMENT TO SECTION 1-105

States adopting Alternative B should amend Section 1-105(2) of the Uniform Commercial Code to read as follows:

(2) Where one of the following provisions of this Act specifies the applicable law, that provision governs and a contrary agreement is effective only to the extent permitted by the law (including the conflict of laws rules) so specified:

Rights of creditors against sold goods. Section 2-402.

Applicability of the Article on Leases. Sections 2A-105 and 2A-106.

Applicability of the Article on Bank Deposits and Collections. Section 4-102.

Bulk Transfers Sales subject to the Article on Bulk Transfers Sales. Section 6-103.

Applicability of the Article on Investment Securities. Section 8-106.

Perfection provisions of the Article on Secured Transactions. Section 9-103.

CONFORMING AMENDMENT TO SECTION 2-403

States adopting Alternative B should amend Section 2-403(4) of the Uniform Commercial Code to read as follows:

(4) The rights of other purchasers of goods and of lien creditors are governed by the Articles on Secured Transactions (Article 9), Bulk Transfers Sales (Article 6) and Documents of Title (Article 7).

ARTICLE 7: WAREHOUSE RECEIPTS, BILLS OF LADING, AND OTHER DOCUMENTS OF TITLE

(This Article is a consolidation and revision of the Uniform Warehouse Receipts Act and the Uniform Bill of Ladings Act and contains some provisions of the Uniform Sales Act relating to negotiation of documents of title. A portion of this Article, but not the complete text, is set forth below.)

Part 1: General

Section 7-102. *Definitions and Index of Definitions*—(1) In this Article, unless the context otherwise requires:

(a) "Bailee" means the person who by a warehouse receipt, bill of lading or other document of title acknowledges possession of goods and contracts to deliver them.

(b) "Consignee" means the person named in a bill to whom or to whose order the bill promises delivery.

(c) "Consignor" means the person named in a bill as the person from whom the goods have been received for shipment.

(d) "Delivery order" means a written order to deliver goods directed to a warehouseman, carrier or other person who in the ordinary course of business issues warehouse receipts or bills of lading.

(e) "Document" means document of title as defined in the general definitions in Article 1 (§1-201).

(f) "Goods" means all things which are treated as movable for the purposes of a contract of storage or transportation.

(g) "Issuer" means a bailee who issues a document except that in relation to an unaccepted delivery order it means the person who orders the possessor of goods to deliver. Issuer includes any person for whom an agent or employee purports to act in issuing a document if the agent or employee has real or apparent authority to issue documents, notwithstanding that the issuer received no goods or that the goods were misdescribed or that in any other respect the agent or employee violated his instructions.

(h) "Warehouseman" is a person engaged in the business of storing goods for hire.

(2) Other definitions applying to this Article or to specified Parts thereof, and the sections in which they appear are:

"Duly negotiate." Section 7-501.

"Person entitled under the document." Section 7-403(4).

(3) Definitions in other Articles applying to this Article and the sections in which they appear are:

"Contract for sale." Section 2-106.

"Overseas." Section 2-323.

"Receipt" of goods. Section 2-103.

(4) In addition Article 1 contains general definitions and principles of construction and interpretation applicable throughout this Article.

Section 7-104. *Negotiable and Nonnegotiable Warehouse Receipt, Bill of Lading, or Other Document of Title*—(1) A warehouse receipt, bill of lading, or other document of title is negotiable

(a) if by its terms the goods are to be delivered to bearer or to the order of a named person; or

(b) where recognized in overseas trade, if it runs to a named person or assigns.

(2) Any other document is nonnegotiable. A bill of lading in which it is stated that the goods are consigned to a named person is not made negotiable by a provision that the goods are to be delivered only against a written order signed by the same or another named person.

Part 2: Warehouse Receipts: Special Provisions

Section 7-201. *Who May Issue a Warehouse Receipt; Storage under Government Bond*—(1) A warehouse receipt may be issued by any warehouseman.

(2) Where goods including distilled spirits and agricultural commodities are stored under a statute requiring a bond against withdrawal or a license for the issuance of receipts in the nature of warehouse receipts, a receipt issued for the goods has like effect as a warehouse receipt even though issued by a person who is the owner of the goods and is not a warehouseman.

Section 7-202. *Form of Warehouse Receipt; Essential Terms; Optional Terms*—(1) A warehouse receipt need not be in any particular form.

(2)   Unless a warehouse receipt embodies within its written or printed terms each of the following, the warehouseman is liable for damages caused by the omission to a person injured thereby:

(a)   the location of the warehouse where the goods are stored;

(b)   the date of issue of the receipt;

(c)   the consecutive number of the receipt;

(d)   a statement whether the goods received will be delivered to the bearer, to a specified person, or to a specified person or his order;

(e)   the rate of storage and handling charges, except that where goods are stored under a field warehousing arrangement a statement of that fact is sufficient on a nonnegotiable receipt;

(f)   a description of the goods or of the packages containing them;

(g)   the signature of the warehouseman, which may be made by his authorized agent;

(h)   if the receipt is issued for goods of which the warehouseman is owner, either solely or jointly or in common with others, the fact of such ownership; and

(i)   a statement of the amount of advances made and of liabilities incurred for which the warehouseman claims a lien or security interest (§ 7-209). If the precise amount of such advances made or of such liabilities incurred is, at the time of the issue of the receipt, unknown to the warehouseman or to his agent who issues it, a statement of the fact that advances have been made or liabilities incurred and the purpose thereof is sufficient.

(3)   A warehouseman may insert in his receipt any other terms which are not contrary to the provisions of this Act and do not impair his obligation of delivery (§ 7-403) or his duty of care (§ 7-204). Any contrary provisions shall be ineffective.

Section 7-203. *Liability for Non-Receipt or Misdescription*—A party to or purchaser for value in good faith of a document of title other than a bill of lading relying in either case upon the description therein of the goods may recover from the issuer damages caused by the non-receipt or misdescription of the goods, except to the extent that the document conspicuously indicates that the issuer does not know whether any part or all of the goods in fact were received or conform to the description, as where the description is in terms of marks or labels or kind, quantity or condition, or the receipt or description is qualified by "contents, condition and quality unknown," "said to contain" or the like, if such indication be true, or the party or purchaser otherwise has notice.

Section 7-204. *Duty of Care; Contractual Limitation of Warehouseman's Liability*—(This section sets forth the liability for loss or injury to property which is in the possession of a warehouseman. There are many variations on this section so the state code should be checked.)

Section 7-205. *Title under Warehouse Receipt Defeated in Certain Cases*—A buyer in the ordinary course of business of fungible goods sold and delivered by a warehouseman who is also in the business of buying and selling such goods takes free of any claim under a warehouse receipt even though it has been duly negotiated.

Section 7-209. *Lien of Warehouseman*—(1) A warehouseman has a lien against the bailor on the goods covered by a warehouse receipt or on the proceeds thereof in his possession for charges for storage or transportation (including demurrage and terminal charges), insurance, labor, or charges present or future in relation to the goods, and for expenses necessary for preservation of the goods or reasonably incurred in their sale pursuant to law. If the person on whose account the goods are held is liable for like charges or expenses in relation to other goods whenever deposited and it is stated in the receipt that a lien is claimed for charges and expenses in relation to other goods, the warehouseman also has a lien against him for such charges and expenses whether or not the other goods have been delivered by the warehouseman. But against a person to whom a negotiable warehouse receipt is duly negotiated a warehouseman's lien is limited to charges in an amount or at a rate specified on the receipt or if no charges are so specified then to a reasonable charge for storage of the goods covered by the receipt subsequent to the date of the receipt.

(2) The warehouseman may also reserve a security interest against the bailor for a maximum amount specified on the receipt for charges other than those specified in subsection (1), such as for money advanced and interest. Such a security interest is governed by the Article on Secured Transactions (Article 9).

(3)(a) A warehouseman's lien for charges and expenses under subsection (1) or a security interest under subsection (2) is also effective against any person who so entrusted the bailor with possession of the goods that a pledge of them by him to a good faith purchaser for value would have been valid but is not effective against a person as to whom the document confers no right in the goods covered by it under Section 7-503.

    (b) A warehouseman's lien on household goods for charges and expenses in relation to the goods under subsection (1) is also effective against all persons if the depositor was the legal possessor of the goods at the time of deposit. "Household goods" means furniture, furnishings and personal effects used by the depositor in a dwelling.

(4) A warehouseman loses his lien on any goods which he voluntarily delivers or which he unjustifiably refuses to deliver.

Part 3: Bills of Lading: Special Provisions

(The sections of this part of Article 7, with the exception of § 7-307, are not reproduced.)

Section 7-307. *Lien of Carrier*—(1) A carrier has a lien on the goods covered by a bill of lading for charges subsequent to the date of its receipt of the goods for storage or transportation (including demurrage and terminal charges) and for expenses necessary for preservation of the goods incident to their transportation or reasonably incurred in their sale pursuant to law. But against a purchaser for value of a negotiable bill of lading a carrier's lien is limited to charges stated in the bill or the applicable tariffs, or if no charges are stated then to reasonable charge.

(2) A lien for charges and expenses under subsection (1) on goods which the carrier was required by law to receive for transportation is effective against the consignor or any person entitled to the goods unless the carrier had notice that the consignor lacked authority to subject the goods to such charges and expenses. Any other lien under subsection (1) is effective against the consignor, and any person who permitted the bailor to have control or possession of the goods unless the carrier had notice that the bailor lacked such authority.

(3) A carrier loses his lien on any goods which he voluntarily delivers or which he unjustifiably refuses to deliver.

Part 4: Warehouse Receipts and Bills of Lading: General Obligations

(Sections 7-401 through 7-404, which are not reproduced, cover irregularities in issue of documents of title, obligations of warehouseman or carrier to deliver, and nonliability for good faith delivery pursuant to document of title.)

Part 5: Warehouse Receipts and Bills of Lading: Negotiation and Transfer

(Sections 7-501 and 7-502, which are not reproduced, cover form of negotiation of documents of title and the requirements of and rights acquired by "due negotiation." It accords to the payee who meets the necessary requirements, the rights of a holder in due course of a negotiable instrument.)

Section 7-503. *Document of Title to Goods Defeated in Certain Cases*—(1) A document of title confers no right in goods against a person who before issuance of the document had a legal interest or a perfected security interest in them and who neither

  (a) delivered nor entrusted them or any document of title covering them to the bailor or his nominee with actual or apparent authority to ship, store or sell or with power to obtain delivery under this Article (§ 7-403) or with power of disposition under this Act (§§ 2-403 and 9-307) or other statute or rule of law; nor

  (b) acquiesced in the procurement by the bailor or his nominee of any document of title.

(2) Title to goods based upon an unaccepted delivery order is subject to the rights of anyone to whom a negotiable warehouse receipt or bill of lading covering the goods has been duly negotiated. Such a title may be defeated under the next section to the same extent as the rights of the issuer or a transferee from the issuer.

(3) Title to goods based upon a bill of lading issued to a freight forwarder is subject to the rights of anyone to whom a bill issued by the freight forwarder is duly negotiated; but delivery by the carrier in accordance with Part 4 of this Article pursuant to its own bill of lading discharges the carrier's obligation to deliver.

Section 7-504. *Rights Acquired in the Absence of Due Negotiation; Effect of Diversion; Seller's Stoppage of Delivery*—(1) A transferee of a document, whether negotiable or non-negotiable, to whom the document has been delivered but not duly negotiated, acquires the title and rights which his transferor had or had actual authority to convey.

(2) In the case of a nonnegotiable document, until, but not after, the bailee receives notification of the transfer, the rights of the transferee may be defeated

  (a) by those creditors of the transferor who could treat the sale as void under Section 2-402; or

  (b) by a buyer from the transferor in ordinary course of business if the bailee has delivered the goods to the buyer or received notification of his rights; or

  (c) as against the bailee by good faith dealings of the bailee with the transferor.

(3) A diversion or other change of shipping instructions by the consignor in a nonnegotiable bill of lading which causes the bailee not to deliver to the consignee defeats the consignee's title to the goods if they have been delivered to a buyer in ordinary course of business and in any event defeats the consignee's rights against the bailee.

(4) Delivery pursuant to a nonnegotiable document may be stopped by a seller under Section 2-705, and subject to the requirement of due notification there provided. A bailee honoring the seller's instructions is entitled to be indemnified by the seller against any resulting loss or expense.

Section 7-505. *Endorser Not a Guarantor for Other Parties*—The endorsement of a document of title issued by a bailee does not make the endorser liable for any default by the bailee or by previous endorsers.

Section 7-506. *Delivery without Endorsement: Right to Compel Endorsement*—The transferee of a negotiable document of title has a specifically enforceable right to have his transferor supply any necessary endorsement but the transfer becomes a negotiation only as of the time the endorsement is supplied.

Section 7-507. *Warranties on Negotiation or Transfer of Receipt or Bill*—Where a person negotiates or transfers a document of title for value otherwise than as a mere intermediary under the next following section, then unless otherwise agreed he warrants to his immediate purchaser only in addition to any warranty made in selling the goods

  (a) that the document is genuine; and

  (b) that he has no knowledge of any fact which would impair its validity or worth; and

  (c) that this negotiation or transfer is rightful and fully effective with respect to the title to the document and the goods it represents.

Part 6: Warehouse Receipts and Bills of Lading: Miscellaneous Provisions

(Sections 7-601 through 7-603, which are not reproduced, cover lost and missing documents, attachment of goods, and conflicting claims to goods.)

ARTICLE 8: INVESTMENT SECURITIES

(This Article, which is not reproduced, deals with bearer bonds, registered bonds, and certificates of stock. Portions of this Article were formerly covered by provisions of the Uniform Negotiable Instruments Law and Uniform Stock Transfer Act.)

ARTICLE 9: SECURED TRANSACTIONS

The statute excerpts of the Revised Article 9 of the Uniform Commercial Code include the full text of:

UCC 9-101 through 9-110: Title, Definitions, General Concepts, Scope and Applicability of Article

UCC 9-201 through 9-206: Effectiveness and Attachment

UCC 9-207 through 9-210: Rights and Duties

UCC 9-301 through 9-339: Perfection and Priority

UCC 9-501 through 9-518: Filing

Note, this text has been taken from the New York State Consolidated Laws and is virtually identical to the original revised statute as recommended by the Commission on Uniform Laws. Each state may modify, delete from or add to these sections. Credit executives should consult the specific Revised Article 9 within the pertinent state to determine any differences from the revised statute.

Part 1: General Provisions

SUBPART 1: SHORT TITLE, DEFINITIONS, AND GENERAL CONCEPTS

Section 9-101. *Short Title.* This article may be cited as Uniform Commercial Code—Secured Transactions.

Section 9-102. *Definitions and Index of Definitions.* (a) Article 9 definitions. In this article:

(1) "Accession" means goods that are physically united with other goods in such a manner that the identity of the original goods is not lost.

(2) "Account", except as used in "account for", means a right to payment of a monetary obligation, whether or not earned by performance, (i) for property that has been or is to be sold, leased, licensed, assigned, or otherwise disposed of, (ii) for services rendered or to be rendered, (iii) for a policy of insurance issued or to be issued, (iv) for a secondary obligation incurred or to be incurred, (v) for energy provided or to be provided, (vi) for the use or hire of a vessel under a charter or other contract, (vii) arising out of the use of a credit or charge card or information contained on or for use with the card, or (viii) as winnings in a lottery or other game of chance operated or sponsored by a state, governmental unit of a State, or person licensed or authorized to operate the game by a State or governmental unit of a State. The term includes health-care-insurance receivables. The term does not include (i) rights to payment evidenced by chattel paper or an instrument, (ii) commercial tort claims, (iii) deposit accounts, (iv) investment property, (v) letter-of-credit rights or letters of credit, or (vi) rights to payment for money or funds advanced or sold, other than rights arising out of the use of a credit or charge card or information contained on or for use with the card.

(3) "Account debtor" means a person obligated on an account, chattel paper, or general intangible. The term does not include persons obligated to pay a negotiable instrument, even if the instrument constitutes part of chattel paper.

(4) "Accounting", except as used in "accounting for", means a record:
   (A) authenticated by a secured party;
   (B) indicating the aggregate unpaid secured obligations as of a date not more than 35 days earlier or 35 days later than the date of the record; and
   (C) identifying the components of the obligations in reasonable detail.

(5) "Agricultural lien" means an interest, other than a security interest, in farm products:
   (A) which secures payment or performance of an obligation for:
      (i) goods or services furnished in connection with a debtor's farming operation; or
      (ii) rent on real property leased by a debtor in connection with its farming operation; and
   (B) which is created by statute in favor of a person that:
      (i) in the ordinary course of its business furnished goods or services to a debtor in connection with a debtor's farming operation; or
      (ii) leased real property to a debtor in connection with the debtor's farming operation; and
   (C) whose effectiveness does not depend on the person's possession of the personal property.

(6) "As-extracted collateral" means:
   (A) oil, gas, or other minerals that are subject to a security interest that:
      (i) is created by a debtor having an interest in the minerals before extraction; and
      (ii) attaches to the minerals as extracted; or
   (B) accounts arising out of the sale at the wellhead or minehead of oil, gas, or other minerals in which the debtor had an interest before extraction.

(7) "Authenticate" means:
   (A) to sign; or
   (B) to execute or otherwise adopt a symbol, or encrypt or similarly process a record in whole or in part, with the present intent of the authenticating person to identify the person and adopt or accept a record.

(8) "Bank" means an organization that is engaged in the business of banking. The term includes savings banks, savings and loan associations, credit unions, and trust companies.

(9) "Cash proceeds" means proceeds that are money, checks, deposit accounts, or the like.

(10) "Certificate of title" means a certificate of title with respect to which a statute provides for the security interest in question to be indicated on the certificate as a condition or result of the security interest's obtaining priority over the rights of a lien creditor with respect to the collateral.

(11) "Chattel paper" means a record or records that evidence both a monetary obligation and a security interest in specific goods, a security interest in specific goods and software used in the goods, a security interest in specific goods and license of software used in the goods, a lease of specific goods, or a lease of specific goods and license of software used in the goods. In this paragraph, "monetary obligation" means a monetary obligation secured by the goods or owed under a lease of the goods and includes a monetary obligation with respect to software used in the goods. The term does not include (i) charters or other contracts involving the use or hire of a vessel or (ii) records that evidence a right to payment arising out of the use of a credit or charge card or information contained on or for use with the card. If a transaction is evidenced by records that include an instrument or series of instruments, the group of records taken together constitutes chattel paper.

(11-a) "Check" means (i) a draft, other than a documentary draft, payable on demand and drawn on a bank or (ii) a cashier's check or a teller's check. An instrument may be a check even though it is described on its face by another term, such as "money order". An instrument that (i) meets all of the requirements stated in Article 3 of this chapter to be a negotiable instrument other than stating that it is payable to order or bearer and (ii) otherwise qualifies as a check is a negotiable instrument and a check.

(12) "Collateral" means the property subject to a security interest or agricultural lien. The term includes:

    (A) proceeds to which a security interest attaches;

    (B) accounts, chattel paper, payment intangibles, and promissory notes that have been sold; and

    (C) goods that are the subject of a consignment.

(13) "Commercial tort claim" means a claim arising in tort with respect to which:

    (A) the claimant is an organization; or

    (B) the claimant is an individual and the claim:

        (i) arose in the course of the claimant's business or profession; and

        (ii) does not include damages arising out of personal injury to or the death of an individual.

(14) "Commodity account" means an account maintained by a commodity intermediary in which a commodity contract is carried for a commodity customer.

(15) "Commodity contract" means a commodity futures contract, an option on a commodity futures contract, a commodity option, or another contract if the contract or option is:

    (A) traded on or subject to the rules of a board of trade that has been designated as a contract market for such a contract pursuant to federal commodities laws; or

    (B) traded on a foreign commodity board of trade, exchange, or market, and is carried on the books of a commodity intermediary for a commodity customer.

(16) "Commodity customer" means a person for which a commodity intermediary carries a commodity contract on its books.

(17) "Commodity intermediary" means a person that:

    (A) is registered as a futures commission merchant under federal commodities law; or

    (B) in the ordinary course of its business provides clearance or settlement services for a board of trade that has been designated as a contract market pursuant to federal commodities law.

(18) "Communicate" means:

    (A) to send a written or other tangible record;

    (B) to transmit a record by any means agreed upon by the persons sending and receiving the record; or

    (C) in the case of transmission of a record to or by a filing office, to transmit a record by any means prescribed by filing-office rule.

(19) "Consignee" means a merchant to which goods are delivered in a consignment.

(20) "Consignment" means a transaction, regardless of its form, in which a person delivers goods to a merchant for the purpose of sale and:

    (A) the merchant:

        (i) ideals in goods of that kind under a name other than the name of the person making delivery;

        (ii) is not an auctioneer; and

        (iii) is not generally known by its creditors to be substantially engaged in selling the goods of others;

    (B) with respect to each delivery, the aggregate value of the goods is $1,000 or more at the time of delivery;

    (C) the goods are not consumer goods immediately before delivery; and

    (D) the transaction does not create a security interest that secures an obligation.

(21) "Consignor" means a person that delivers goods to a consignee in a consignment.

(22) "Consumer debtor" means a debtor in a consumer transaction.

(23) "Consumer goods" means goods that are used or bought for use primarily for personal, family, or household purposes.

(24) "Consumer-goods transaction" means a consumer transaction in which:
  (A) an individual incurs an obligation primarily for personal, family, or household purposes; and
  (B) a security interest in consumer goods secures the obligation.

(25) "Consumer obligor" means an obligor who is an individual and who incurred the obligation as part of a transaction entered into primarily for personal, family, or household purposes.

(26) "Consumer transaction" means a transaction in which (i) an individual incurs an obligation primarily for personal, family, or household purposes, (ii) a security interest secures the obligation, and (iii) the collateral is held or acquired primarily for personal, family, or household purposes. The term includes consumer-goods transactions.

(27) "Continuation statement" means an amendment of a financing statement which:
  (A) identifies, by its file number, the initial financing statement to which it relates; and
  (B) indicates that it is a continuation statement for, or that it is filed to continue the effectiveness of, the identified financing statement.

(27-a) "Cooperative addendum" means a record that satisfies Section 9—502(e).

(27-b) "Cooperative interest" means an ownership interest in a cooperative organization, which interest, when created, is coupled with possessory rights of a proprietary nature in identified physical space belonging to the cooperative organization. A subsequent termination of the possessory rights shall not cause an ownership interest to cease being a cooperative interest.

(27-c) "Cooperative organization" means an organization which has as its principal asset an interest in real property in this state and in which organization all ownership interests are cooperative interests.

(27-d) "Cooperative organization security interest" means a security interest which is in a cooperative interest, is in favor of the cooperative organization, is created by the cooperative record, and secures only obligations incident to ownership of that cooperative interest.

(27-e) "Cooperative record" means those records which, as a whole, evidence cooperative interests and define the mutual rights and obligations of the owners of the cooperative interests and the cooperative organization.

(27-f) "Cooperative unit" means the physical space associated with a cooperative interest.

(28) "Debtor" means:
  (A) a person having an interest, other than a security interest or other lien, in the collateral, whether or not the person is an obligor;
  (B) a seller of accounts, chattel paper, payment intangibles, or promissory notes; or
  (C) a consignee.

(29) "Deposit account" means a demand, time, savings, passbook, or similar account maintained with a bank. The term does not include investment property or accounts evidenced by an instrument.

(30) "Document" means a document of title or a receipt of the type described in Section 7-201(2).

(31) "Electronic chattel paper" means chattel paper evidenced by a record or records consisting of information stored in an electronic medium.

(32) "Encumbrance" means a right, other than an ownership interest, in real property. The term includes mortgages and other liens on real property.

(33) "Equipment" means goods other than inventory, farm products, or consumer goods.

(34) "Farm products" means goods, other than standing timber, with respect to which the debtor is engaged in a farming operation and which are:
  (A) crops grown, growing, or to be grown, including:
    (i) crops produced on trees, vines, and bushes; and

(ii) aquatic goods produced in aquacultural operations;

(B) livestock, born or unborn, including aquatic goods produced in aquacultural operations;

(C) supplies used or produced in a farming operation; or

(D) products of crops or livestock in their unmanufactured states.

(35) "Farming operation" means raising, cultivating, propagating, fattening, grazing, or any other farming, livestock, or aquacultural operation.

(36) "File number" means the number assigned to an initial financing statement pursuant to Section 9—519(a).

(37) "Filing office" means an office designated in Section 9—501 as the place to file a financing statement.

(38) "Filing-office rule" means a rule adopted pursuant to Section 9-526.

(39) "Financing statement" means a record or records composed of an initial financing statement and any filed record relating to the initial financing statement.

(40) "Fixture filing" means the filing of a financing statement covering goods that are or are to become fixtures and satisfying Section 9-502(a) and (b). The term includes the filing of a financing statement covering goods of a transmitting utility which are or are to become fixtures.

(41) "Fixtures" means goods that have become so related to particular real property that an interest in them arises under real property law.

(42) "General intangible" means any personal property, including things in action, other than accounts, chattel paper, commercial tort claims, deposit accounts, documents, goods, instruments, investment property, letter-of-credit rights, letters of credit, money, and oil, gas, or other minerals before extraction. The term includes payment intangibles and software.

(43) "Good faith" means honesty in fact and the observance of reasonable commercial standards of fair dealing.

(44) "Goods" means all things that are movable when a security interest attaches. The term includes (i) fixtures, (ii) standing timber that is to be cut and removed under a conveyance or contract for sale, (iii) the unborn young of animals, (iv) crops grown, growing, or to be grown, even if the crops are produced on trees, vines, or bushes, and (v) manufactured homes. The term also includes a computer program embedded in goods and any supporting information provided in connection with a transaction relating to the program if (i) the program is associated with the goods in such a manner that it customarily is considered part of the goods, or (ii) by becoming the owner of the goods, a person acquires a right to use the program in connection with the goods. The term does not include a computer program embedded in goods that consists solely of the medium in which the program is embedded. The term also does not include accounts, chattel paper, commercial tort claims, deposit accounts, documents, general intangibles, instruments, investment property, letter-of-credit rights, letters of credit, money, or oil, gas, or other minerals before extraction.

(45) "Governmental unit" means a subdivision, agency, department, county, parish, municipality, or other unit of the government of the United States, a state, or a foreign country. The term includes an organization having a separate corporate existence if the organization is eligible to issue debt on which interest is exempt from income taxation under the laws of the United States.

(46) "Healthcare-insurance receivable" means an interest in or claim under a policy of insurance which is a right to payment of a monetary obligation for healthcare goods or services provided.

(47) "Instrument" means a negotiable instrument or any other writing that evidences a right to the payment of a monetary obligation, is not itself a security agreement or lease, and is of a type that in ordinary course of business is transferred by delivery with any necessary indorsement or assignment. The term does not include (i) investment property, (ii) letters of credit, or (iii) writings that evidence a right to payment

arising out of the use of a credit or charge card or information contained on or for use with the card.

(48) "Inventory" means goods, other than farm products, which:

(A) are leased by a person as lessor;

(B) are held by a person for sale or lease or to be furnished under a contract of service;

(C) are furnished by a person under a contract of service; or

(D) consist of raw materials, work in process, or materials used or consumed in a business.

(49) "Investment property" means a security, whether certificated or uncertificated, security entitlement, securities account, commodity contract, or commodity account.

(50) "Jurisdiction of organization", with respect to a registered organization, means the jurisdiction under whose law the organization is organized.

(51) "Letter-of-credit right" means a right to payment or performance under a letter of credit, whether or not the beneficiary has demanded or is at the time entitled to demand payment or performance. The term does not include the right of a beneficiary to demand payment or performance under a letter of credit.

(52) "Lien creditor" means:

(A) a creditor that has acquired a lien on the property involved by attachment, levy, or the like;

(B) an assignee for benefit of creditors from the time of assignment;

(C) a trustee in bankruptcy from the date of the filing of the petition; or

(D) a receiver in equity from the time of appointment.

(53) "Manufactured home" means a structure, transportable in one or more sections, which, in the traveling mode, is eight body feet or more in width or 40 body feet or more in length, or, when erected on site, is 320 or more square feet, and which is built on a permanent chassis and designed to be used as a dwelling with or without a permanent foundation when connected to the required utilities, and includes the plumbing, heating, air-conditioning, and electrical systems contained therein. The term includes any structure that meets all of the requirements of this paragraph except the size requirements and with respect to which the manufacturer voluntarily files a certification required by the United States Secretary of Housing and Urban Development and complies with the standards established under Title 42 of the United States Code.

(54) "Manufactured-home transaction" means a secured transaction:

(A) that creates a purchase-money security interest in a manufactured home, other than a manufactured home held as inventory; or

(B) in which a manufactured home, other than a manufactured home held as inventory, is the primary collateral.

(55) "Mortgage" means a consensual interest in real property, including fixtures, which secures payment or performance of an obligation.

(56) "New debtor" means a person that becomes bound as debtor under Section 9-203(d) by a security agreement previously entered into by another person.

(57) "New value" means (i) money, (ii) money's worth in property, services, or new credit, or (iii) release by a transferee of an interest in property previously transferred to the transferee. The term does not include an obligation substituted for another obligation.

(58) "Noncash proceeds" means proceeds other than cash proceeds.

(59) "Obligor" means a person that, with respect to an obligation secured by a security interest in or an agricultural lien on the collateral, (i) owes payment or other performance of the obligation, (ii) has provided property other than the collateral to secure payment or other performance of the obligation, or (iii) is otherwise accountable in whole or in part for payment or other performance of the obligation. The term does not include issuers or nominated persons under a letter of credit.

(60) "Original debtor", except as used in Section 9-310(c), means a person that, as debtor, entered into a security agreement to which a new debtor has become bound under Section 9-203(d).

(61) "Payment intangible" means a general intangible under which the account debtor's principal obligation is a monetary obligation.

(62) "Person related to", with respect to an individual, means:
- (A) the spouse of the individual;
- (B) a brother, brother-in-law, sister, or sister-in-law of the individual;
- (C) an ancestor or lineal descendant of the individual or the individual's spouse; or
- (D) any other relative, by blood or marriage, of the individual or the individual's spouse who shares the same home with the individual.

(63) "Person related to", with respect to an organization, means:
- (A) a person directly or indirectly controlling, controlled by, or under common control with the organization;
- (B) an officer or director of, or a person performing similar functions with respect to, the organization;
- (C) an officer or director of, or a person performing similar functions with respect to, a person described in subparagraph (A);
- (D) the spouse of an individual described in subparagraph (A), (B), or (C); or
- (E) an individual who is related by blood or marriage to an individual described in subparagraph (A), (B), (C), or (D) and shares the same home with the individual.

(64) "Proceeds", except as used in Section 9-609(b), means the following property:
- (A) whatever is acquired upon the sale, lease, license, exchange, or other disposition of collateral;
- (B) whatever is collected on, or distributed on account of, collateral;
- (C) rights arising out of collateral;
- (D) to the extent of the value of collateral, claims arising out of the loss, nonconformity, or interference with the use of, defects or infringement of rights in, or damage to, the collateral; or
- (E) to the extent of the value of collateral and to the extent payable to the debtor or the secured party, insurance payable by reason of the loss or nonconformity of, defects or infringement of rights in, or damage to, the collateral.

(65) "Promissory note" means an instrument that evidences a promise to pay a monetary obligation, does not evidence an order to pay, and does not contain an acknowledgment by a bank that the bank has received for deposit a sum of money or funds.

(66) "Proposal" means a record authenticated by a secured party which includes the terms on which the secured party is willing to accept collateral in full or partial satisfaction of the obligation it secures pursuant to Sections 9-620, 9-621, and 9-622.

(66-a) "Prove" with respect to a fact means to meet the burden of establishing the fact (Section 1-201(8)).

(67) "Public-finance transaction" means a secured transaction in connection with which:
- (A) debt securities are issued;
- (B) all or a portion of the securities issued have an initial stated maturity of at least 20 years; and
- (C) the debtor, obligor, secured party, account debtor or other person obligated on collateral, assignor or assignee of a secured obligation, or assignor or assignee of a security interest is a state or a governmental unit of a state.

(68) "Pursuant to commitment", with respect to an advance made or other value given by a secured party, means pursuant to the secured party's obligation, whether or not a subsequent event of default or other event not within the secured party's control has relieved or may relieve the secured party from its obligation.

(69) "Record", except as used in "for record", "of record", "record or legal title", and "record owner", means information that is inscribed on a tangible medium or which is stored in an electronic or other medium and is retrievable in perceivable form.

(70) "Registered organization" means an organization organized solely under the law of a single state or the United States and as to which the state or the United States must maintain a public record showing the organization to have been organized.

(71) "Secondary obligor" means an obligor to the extent that:

    (A) the obligor's obligation is secondary; or

    (B) the obligor has a right of recourse with respect to an obligation secured by collateral against the debtor, another obligor, or property of either.

(72) "Secured party" means:

    (A) a person in whose favor a security interest is created or provided for under a security agreement, whether or not any obligation to be secured is outstanding;

    (B) a person that holds an agricultural lien;

    (C) a consignor;

    (D) a person to which accounts, chattel paper, payment intangibles, or promissory notes have been sold;

    (E) a trustee, indenture trustee, agent, collateral agent, or other representative in whose favor a security interest or agricultural lien is created or provided for; or

    (F) a person that holds a security interest arising under Section 2-401, 2-505, 2-711(3), 2-A-508(5), 4-210, or 5-118.

(73) "Security agreement" means an agreement that creates or provides for a security interest. A cooperative record that provides that the owner of a cooperative interest has an obligation to pay amounts to the cooperative organization incident to ownership of that cooperative interest and which states that the cooperative organization has a direct remedy against that cooperative interest if such amounts are not paid is a security agreement creating a cooperative organization security interest.

(74) "Send", in connection with a record or notification, means:

    (A) to deposit in the mail, deliver for transmission, or transmit by any other usual means of communication, with postage or cost of transmission provided for, addressed to any address reasonable under the circumstances; or

    (B) to cause the record or notification to be received within the time that it would have been received if properly sent under subparagraph (A).

(75) "Software" means a computer program and any supporting information provided in connection with a transaction relating to the program. The term does not include a computer program that is included in the definition of goods.

(76) "State" means a state of the United States, the District of Columbia, Puerto Rico, the United States Virgin Islands, or any territory or insular possession subject to the jurisdiction of the United States.

(77) "Supporting obligation" means a letter-of-credit right or secondary obligation that supports the payment or performance of an account, chattel paper, a document, a general intangible, an instrument, or investment property.

(78) "Tangible chattel paper" means chattel paper evidenced by a record or records consisting of information that is inscribed on a tangible medium.

(79) "Termination statement" means an amendment of a financing statement which:

    (A) identifies, by its file number, the initial financing statement to which it relates; and

    (B) indicates either that it is a termination statement or that the identified financing statement is no longer effective.

(80) "Transmitting utility" means a person primarily engaged in the business of:

    (A) operating a railroad, subway, street railway, or trolley bus;

    (B) transmitting communications electrically, electromagnetically, or by light;

    (C) transmitting goods by pipeline or sewer; or

    (D) transmitting or producing and transmitting electricity, steam, gas, or water.

(b) Definitions in other articles. The following definitions in other articles apply to this article:

"Applicant." Section 5-102.

"Beneficiary." Section 5-102.

"Broker." Section 8-102.

"Certificated security." Section 8-102.

"Clearing corporation." Section 8-102.

"Contract for sale." Section 2-106.

"Customer." Section 4-104.
"Entitlement holder." Section 8-102.
"Financial asset." Section 8-102.
"Holder in due course." Section 3-302.
"Issuer" (with respect to a letter of credit or letter-of-credit right). Section 5-102.
"Issuer" (with respect to a security). Section 8-201.
"Lease." Section 2-A-103.
"Lease agreement." Section 2-A-103.
"Lease contract." Section 2-A-103.
"Leasehold interest." Section 2-A-103.
"Lessee." Section 2-A-103.
"Lessee in ordinary course of business." Section 2-A-103.
"Lessor." Section 2-A-103.
"Lessor's residual interest." Section 2-A-103.
"Letter of credit." Section 5-102.
"Merchant." Section 2-104.
"Negotiable instrument." Section 3-104.
"Nominated person." Section 5-102.
"Note." Section 3-104.
"Proceeds of a letter of credit." Section 5-114.
"Sale." Section 2-106.
"Securities account." Section 8-501.
"Securities intermediary." Section 8-102.
"Security." Section 8-102.
"Security certificate." Section 8-102.
"Security entitlement." Section 8-102.
"Uncertificated security." Section 8-102.

(c)   Article 1 definitions and principles. Article 1 contains general definitions and principles of construction and interpretation applicable throughout this article.

Section 9-103. *Purchase-money Security Interest; Application of Payments; Burden of Establishing.* (a) Definitions. In this section:

(1)   "purchase-money collateral" means goods or software that secures a purchase-money obligation incurred with respect to that collateral; and

(2)   "purchase-money obligation" means an obligation of an obligor incurred as all or part of the price of the collateral or for value given to enable the debtor to acquire rights in or the use of the collateral if the value is in fact so used.

(b)   Purchase-money security interest in goods. A security interest in goods is a purchase-money security interest:

(1)   to the extent that the goods are purchase-money collateral with respect to that security interest;

(2)   if the security interest is in inventory that is or was purchase-money collateral, also to the extent that the security interest secures a purchase-money obligation incurred with respect to other inventory in which the secured party holds or held a purchase-money security interest; and

(3)   also to the extent that the security interest secures a purchase-money obligation incurred with respect to software in which the secured party holds or held a purchase-money security interest.

(c)   Purchase-money security interest in software. A security interest in software is a purchase-money security interest to the extent that the security interest also secures a purchase-money obligation incurred with respect to goods in which the secured party holds or held a purchase-money security interest if:

(1)   the debtor acquired its interest in the software in an integrated transaction in which it acquired an interest in the goods; and

(2) the debtor acquired its interest in the software for the principal purpose of using the software in the goods.

(d) Consignor's inventory purchase-money security interest. The security interest of a consignor in goods that are the subject of a consignment is a purchase-money security interest in inventory.

(e) Application of payment in non-consumer-goods transaction. In a transaction other than a consumer-goods transaction, if the extent to which a security interest is a purchase-money security interest depends on the application of a payment to a particular obligation, the payment must be applied:
(1) in accordance with any reasonable method of application to which the parties agree;
(2) in the absence of the parties' agreement to a reasonable method, in accordance with any intention of the obligor manifested at or before the time of payment; or
(3) in the absence of an agreement to a reasonable method and a timely manifestation of the obligor's intention, in the following order:
(A) to obligations that are not secured; and
(B) if more than one obligation is secured, to obligations secured by purchase-money security interests in the order in which those obligations were incurred.

(f) No loss of status of purchase-money security interest in non-consumer-goods transaction. In a transaction other than a consumer-goods transaction, a purchase-money security interest does not lose its status as such, even if:
(1) the purchase-money collateral also secures an obligation that is not a purchase-money obligation;
(2) collateral that is not purchase-money collateral also secures the purchase-money obligation; or
(3) the purchase-money obligation has been renewed, refinanced, consolidated, or restructured.

(g) Burden of proof in non-consumer-goods transaction. In a transaction other than a consumer-goods transaction, a secured party claiming a purchase-money security interest has the burden of establishing the extent to which the security interest is a purchase-money security interest.

(h) Non-consumer-goods transactions; no inference. The limitation of the rules in subsections (e), (f), and (g) to transactions other than consumer-goods transactions is intended to leave to the court the determination of the proper rules in consumer-goods transactions. The court may not infer from that limitation the nature of the proper rule in consumer-goods transactions and may continue to apply established approaches.

Section 9-104. *Control of Deposit Account.* (a) Requirements for control. A secured party has control of a deposit account if:
(1) the secured party is the bank with which the deposit account is maintained;
(2) the debtor, secured party, and bank have agreed in an authenticated record that the bank will comply with instructions originated by the secured party directing disposition of the funds in the deposit account without further consent by the debtor; or
(3) the secured party becomes the bank's customer with respect to the deposit account.

(b) Debtor's right to direct disposition. A secured party that has satisfied subsection (a) has control, even if the debtor retains the right to direct the disposition of funds from the deposit account.

Section 9-105. *Control of Electronic Chattel Paper.* A secured party has control of electronic chattel paper if the record or records comprising the chattel paper are created, stored, and assigned in such a manner that:
(1) a single authoritative copy of the record or records exists which is unique, identifiable and, except as otherwise provided in paragraphs (4), (5), and (6), unalterable;
(2) the authoritative copy identifies the secured party as the assignee of the record or records;

(3) the authoritative copy is communicated to and maintained by the secured party or its designated custodian;

(4) copies or revisions that add or change an identified assignee of the authoritative copy can be made only with the participation of the secured party;

(5) each copy of the authoritative copy and any copy of a copy is readily identifiable as a copy that is not the authoritative copy; and

(6) any revision of the authoritative copy is readily identifiable as an authorized or unauthorized revision.

Section 9-106. *Control of Investment Property.* (a) Control under Section 8-106. A person has control of a certificated security, uncertificated security, or security entitlement as provided in Section 8-106.

(b) Control of commodity contract. A secured party has control of a commodity contract if:

(1) the secured party is the commodity intermediary with which the commodity contract is carried; or

(2) the commodity customer, secured party, and commodity intermediary have agreed that the commodity intermediary will apply any value distributed on account of the commodity contract as directed by the secured party without further consent by the commodity customer.

(c) Effect of control of securities account or commodity account. A secured party having control of all security entitlements or commodity contracts carried in a securities account or commodity account has control over the securities account or commodity account.

Section 9-107. *Control of Letter-of-Credit Right.* A secured party has control of a letter-of-credit right to the extent of any right to payment or performance by the issuer or any nominated person if the issuer or nominated person has consented to an assignment of proceeds of the letter of credit under Section 5-114(c) or otherwise applicable law or practice.

Section 9-108. *Sufficiency of Description.* (a) Sufficiency of description. Except as otherwise provided in subsections (c), (d), and (e), a description of personal or real property is sufficient, whether or not it is specific, if it reasonably identifies what is described.

(b) Examples of reasonable identification. Except as otherwise provided in Section 9-502 and subsection (d), a description of collateral reasonably identifies the collateral if it identifies the collateral by:

(1) specific listing;

(2) category;

(3) except as otherwise provided in subsection (e), a type of collateral defined in this chapter;

(4) quantity;

(5) computational or allocational formula or procedure; or

(6) except as otherwise provided in subsection (c), any other method, if the identity of the collateral is objectively determinable.

(c) Supergeneric description not sufficient. A description of collateral as "all the debtor's assets" or "all the debtor's personal property" or using words of similar import does not reasonably identify the collateral.

(d) Investment property. Except as otherwise provided in subsection (e), a description of a security entitlement, securities account, or commodity account is sufficient if it describes:

(1) the collateral by those terms or as investment property; or

(2) the underlying financial asset or commodity contract.

(e) When description by type insufficient. A description only by type of collateral defined in this chapter is an insufficient description of:

(1) a commercial tort claim;

(2) in a consumer transaction, consumer goods, a security entitlement, a securities account, or a commodity account; or

(3) a cooperative interest.

SUBPART 2: APPLICABILITY OF ARTICLE

Section 9-109. *Scope.* (a) General scope of article. Except as otherwise provided in subsections (c) and (d), this article applies to:

(1) a transaction, regardless of its form, that creates a security interest in personal property or fixtures by contract;

(2) an agricultural lien;

(3) a sale of accounts, chattel paper, payment intangibles, or promissory notes;

(4) a consignment;

(5) a security interest arising under Section 2-401, 2-505, 2-711(3), or 2-A-508(5), as provided in Section 9-110;

(6) a security interest arising under Section 4-210 or 5-118; and

(7) a security interest in a cooperative interest.

(b) Security interest in secured obligation. The application of this article to a security interest in a secured obligation is not affected by the fact that the obligation is itself secured by a transaction or interest to which this article does not apply.

(c) Extent to which article does not apply. This article does not apply to the extent that:

(1) a statute, regulation, or treaty of the United States preempts this article;

(2) another statute of this State expressly governs the creation, perfection, priority, or enforcement of a security interest created by this state or a governmental unit of this state;

(3) a statute of another state, a foreign country, or a govern mental unit of another state or a foreign country, other than a statute generally applicable to security interests, expressly governs creation, perfection, priority, or enforcement of a security interest created by the state, country, or governmental unit; or

(4) the rights of a transferee beneficiary or nominated person under a letter of credit are independent and superior under Section 5-114.

(d) Inapplicability of article. This article does not apply to:

(1) a landlord's lien, other than an agricultural lien, or a security interest in a cooperative interest;

(2) a lien, other than an agricultural lien, given by statute or other rule of law for services or materials, but Section 9-333 applies with respect to priority of the lien;

(3) an assignment of a claim for wages, salary, or other compensation of an employee;

(4) a sale of accounts, chattel paper, payment intangibles, or promissory notes as part of a sale of the business out of which they arose;

(5) an assignment of accounts, chattel paper, payment intangibles, or promissory notes which is for the purpose of collection only;

(6) an assignment of a right to payment under a contract to an assignee that is also obligated to perform under the contract;

(7) an assignment of a single account, payment intangible, or promissory note to an assignee in full or partial satisfaction of a preexisting indebtedness;

(8) a transfer of an interest in or an assignment of a claim under a policy of insurance or contract for an annuity including a variable annuity other than an assignment by or to a healthcare provider of a healthcare-insurance receivable and any subsequent assignment of the right to payment, but Sections 9-315 and 9-322 apply with respect to proceeds and priorities in proceeds;

(9) an assignment of a right represented by a judgment, other than a judgment taken on a right to payment that was collateral;

(10) a right of recoupment or set-off, but:

(A) Section 9-340 applies with respect to the effectiveness of rights of recoupment or set-off against deposit accounts; and

(B) Section 9-404 applies with respect to defenses or claims of an account debtor;

(11) the creation or transfer of an interest in or lien on real property, including a lease or rents thereunder, except to the extent that provision is made for:

(A) liens on real property in Section 9-203 and 9-308;

    (B) fixtures in Section 9-334;

    (C) fixture filings in Sections 9-501, 9-502, 9-512, 9-516, and 9-519;

    (D) security agreements covering personal and real property in Section 9-604; and

    (E) security interests in cooperative interests;

(12) an assignment of a claim arising in tort, other than a commercial tort claim, but Sections 9-315 and 9-322 apply with respect to proceeds and priorities in proceeds; or

(13) an assignment of a deposit account in a consumer trans action, but Sections 9-315 and 9-322 apply with respect to proceeds and priorities in proceeds.

Section 9-110. *Security Interests Arising Under Article 2 or 2-A.* A security interest arising under Section 2-401, 2-505, 2-711(3),or 2-A-508(5) is subject to this article. However, until the debtor obtains possession of the goods:

(1) the security interest is enforceable, even if Section 9-203(b)(3) has not been satisfied;

(2) filing is not required to perfect the security interest;

(3) the rights of the secured party after default by the debtor are governed by Article 2 or 2-A; and

(4) the security interest has priority over a conflicting security interest created by the debtor.

Part 2: Effectiveness of Security Agreement; Attachment of Security Interest; Rights of Parties to Security Agreement

SUBPART 1: EFFECTIVENESS AND ATTACHMENT

Section 9-201. *General Effectiveness of Security Agreement.* (a) General effectiveness. Except as otherwise provided in this chapter, a security agreement is effective according to its terms between the parties, against purchasers of the collateral, and against creditors.

(b) Applicable consumer laws and other law. A transaction subject to this article is subject to:

(1) any applicable rule of law which establishes a different rule for consumers;

(2) any other statute or regulation of this state which regulates the rates, charges, agreements and practices for loans, credit sales or other extensions of credit;

(3) any consumer protection statute or regulation of this state.

(c) Other applicable law controls. In case of conflict between this article and a rule of law, statute, or regulation described in subsection (b), the rule of law, statute, or regulation controls. Failure to comply with a statute or regulation described in subsection (b) has only the effect the statute or regulation specifies.

(d) Further deference to other applicable law. This article does not:

(1) validate any rate, charge, agreement, or practice that violates a rule of law, statute, or regulation described in subsection (b); or

(2) extend the application of the rule of law, statute, or regulation to a transaction not otherwise subject to it.

Section 9-202. *Title to Collateral Immaterial.* Except as otherwise provided with respect to consignments or sales of accounts, chattel paper, payment intangibles, or promissory notes, the provisions of this article with regard to rights and obligations apply whether title to collateral is in the secured party or the debtor.

Section 9-203. *Attachment and Enforceability of Security Interest; Proceeds; Supporting Obligations; Formal Requisites.* (a) Attachment. A security interest attaches to collateral when it becomes enforceable against the debtor with respect to the collateral, unless an agreement expressly postpones the time of attachment.

(b) Enforceability. Except as otherwise provided in subsections (c) through (i), a security interest is enforceable against the debtor and third parties with respect to the collateral only if:

(1) value has been given;

(2) the debtor has rights in the collateral or the power to transfer rights in the collateral to a secured party; and

(3) one of the following conditions is met:

    (A) the debtor has authenticated a security agreement that provides a description of the collateral and, if the security interest covers timber to be cut, a description of the land concerned;

    (B) the collateral is not a certificated security and is in the possession of the secured party under Section 9-313 pursuant to the debtor's security agreement;

    (C) the collateral is a certificated security in registered form and the security certificate has been delivered to the secured party under Section 8-301 pursuant to the debtor's security agreement; or

    (D) the collateral is deposit accounts, electronic chattel paper, investment property, or letter-of-credit rights, and the secured party has control under Section 9-104, 9-105, 9-106, or 9-107 pursuant to the debtor's security agreement.

(c) Other UCC provisions. Subsection (b) is subject to Section 4-210 on the security interest of a collecting bank, Section 5-118 on the security interest of a letter-of-credit issuer or nominated person, Section 9-110 on a security interest arising under Article 2 or 2-A, and Section 9-206 on security interests in investment property.

(d) When a person becomes bound by another person's security agreement. A person becomes bound as debtor by a security agreement entered into by another person if, by operation of law other than this article or by contract:

(1) the security agreement becomes effective to create a security interest in the person's property; or

(2) the person becomes generally obligated for the obligations of the other person, including the obligation secured under the security agreement, and acquires or succeeds to all or substantially all of the assets of the other person.

(e) Effect of new debtor becoming bound. If a new debtor becomes bound as debtor by a security agreement entered into by another person:

(1) the agreement satisfies subsection (b)(3) with respect to existing or after-acquired property of the new debtor to the extent the property is described in the agreement; and

(2) another agreement is not necessary to make a security interest in the property enforceable.

(f) Proceeds and supporting obligations. The attachment of a security interest in collateral gives the secured party the rights to proceeds provided by Section 9-315 and is also attachment of a security interest in a supporting obligation for the collateral.

(g) Lien securing right to payment. The attachment of a security interest in a right to payment or performance secured by a security interest or other lien on personal or real property is also attachment of a security interest in the security interest, mortgage, or other lien.

(h) Security entitlement carried in securities account. The attachment of a security interest in a securities account is also attachment of a security interest in the security entitlements carried in the securities account.

(i) Commodity contracts carried in commodity account. The attachment of a security interest in a commodity account is also attachment of a security interest in the commodity contracts carried in the commodity account.

Section 9-204. *After-acquired Property; Future Advances.* (a) After-acquired collateral. Except as otherwise provided in subsection (b), a security agreement may create or provide for a security interest in after-acquired collateral.

(b) When after-acquired property clause not effective. A security interest does not attach under a term constituting an after-acquired property clause to:

(1) consumer goods, other than an accession when given as additional security, unless the debtor acquires rights in them within 10 days after the secured party gives value; or

(2) a commercial tort claim.

(c) Future advances and other value. A security agreement may provide that collateral secures, or that accounts, chattel paper, payment intangibles, or promissory notes are sold in connection with, future advances or other value, whether or not the advances or value are given pursuant to commitment.

Section 9-205. *Use or Disposition of Collateral Permissible.* (a) When security interest not invalid or fraudulent. A security interest is not invalid or fraudulent against creditors solely because:
(1) the debtor has the right or ability to:
    (A) use, commingle, or dispose of all or part of the collateral, including returned or repossessed goods;
    (B) collect, compromise, enforce, or otherwise deal with collateral;
    (C) accept the return of collateral or make repossessions; or
    (D) use, commingle, or dispose of proceeds; or
(2) the secured party fails to require the debtor to account for proceeds or replace collateral.
(b) Requirements of possession not relaxed. This section does not relax the requirements of possession if attachment, perfection, or enforcement of a security interest depends upon possession of the collateral by the secured party.

Section 9-206. *Security Interest Arising in Purchase or Delivery of Financial Asset.* (a) Security interest when person buys through securities intermediary. A security interest in favor of a securities intermediary attaches to a person's security entitlement if:
(1) the person buys a financial asset through the securities intermediary in a transaction in which the person is obligated to pay the purchase price to the securities intermediary at the time of the purchase; and
(2) the securities intermediary credits the financial asset to the buyer's securities account before the buyer pays the securities intermediary.
(b) Security interest secures obligation to pay for financial asset. The security interest described in subsection (a) secures the person's obligation to pay for the financial asset.
(c) Security interest in payment against delivery transaction. A security interest in favor of a person that delivers a certificated security or other financial asset represented by a writing attaches to the security or other financial asset if:
(1) the security or other financial asset:
    (A) in the ordinary course of business is transferred by delivery with any necessary indorsement or assignment; and
    (B) is delivered under an agreement between persons in the business of dealing with such securities or financial assets; and
(2) the agreement calls for delivery against payment.
(d) Security interest secures obligation to pay for delivery. The security interest described in subsection (c) secures the obligation to make payment for the delivery.

SUBPART 2: RIGHTS AND DUTIES

Section 9-207. *Rights and Duties of Secured Party Having Possession or Control of Collateral.* (a) Duty of care when secured party in possession. Except as otherwise provided in subsection (d), a secured party shall use reasonable care in the custody and preservation of collateral in the secured party's possession. In the case of chattel paper or an instrument, reasonable care includes taking necessary steps to preserve rights against prior parties unless otherwise agreed.
(b) Expenses, risks, duties, and rights when secured party in possession. Except as otherwise provided in subsection (d), if a secured party has possession of collateral:
(1) reasonable expenses, including the cost of insurance and payment of taxes or other charges, incurred in the custody, preservation, use, or operation of the collateral are charge able to the debtor and are secured by the collateral;

(2) the risk of accidental loss or damage is on the debtor to the extent of a deficiency in any effective insurance coverage;

(3) the secured party shall keep the collateral identifiable, but fungible collateral may be commingled; and

(4) the secured party may use or operate the collateral:

(A) for the purpose of preserving the collateral or its value;

(B) as permitted by an order of a court having competent jurisdiction; or

(C) except in the case of consumer goods, in the manner and to the extent agreed by the debtor.

(c) Duties and rights when secured party in possession or control. Except as otherwise provided in subsection (d), a secured party having possession of collateral or control of collateral under Section 9-104, 9-105, 9-106, or 9-107:

(1) may hold as additional security any proceeds, except money or funds, received from the collateral;

(2) shall apply money or funds received from the collateral to reduce the secured obligation, unless remitted to the debtor; and

(3) may create a security interest in the collateral.

(d) Buyer of certain rights to payment. If the secured party is a buyer of accounts, chattel paper, payment intangibles, or promissory notes or a consignor:

(1) subsection (a) does not apply unless the secured party is entitled under an agreement:

(A) to charge back uncollected collateral; or

(B) otherwise to full or limited recourse against the debtor or a secondary obligor based on the nonpayment or other default of an account debtor or other obligor on the collateral; and

(2) subsections (b) and (c) do not apply.

Section 9-208. *Additional Duties of Secured Party Having Control of Collateral.* (a) Applicability of section. This section applies to cases in which there is no outstanding secured obligation and the secured party is not committed to make advances, incur obligations, or otherwise give value.

(b) Duties of secured party after receiving demand from debtor. Within 10 days after receiving an authenticated demand by the debtor:

(1) a secured party having control of a deposit account under Section 9-104(a)(2) shall send to the bank with which the deposit account is maintained an authenticated statement that releases the bank from any further obligation to comply with instructions originated by the secured party;

(2) a secured party having control of a deposit account under Section 9-104(a)(3) shall:

(A) pay the debtor the balance on deposit in the deposit account; or

(B) transfer the balance on deposit into a deposit account in the debtor's name;

(3) a secured party, other than a buyer, having control of electronic chattel paper under Section 9-105 shall:

(A) communicate the authoritative copy of the electronic chattel paper to the debtor or its designated custodian;

(B) if the debtor designates a custodian that is the designated custodian with which the authoritative copy of the electronic chattel paper is maintained for the secured party, communicate to the custodian an authenticated record releasing the designated custodial from any further obligation to comply with instructions originated by the secured party and instructing the custodian to comply with instructions originated by the debtor; and

(C) take appropriate action to enable the debtor or its designated custodian to make copies of or revisions to the authoritative copy which add or change an identified assignee of the authoritative copy without the consent of the secured party;

(4) a secured party having control of investment property under Section 8-106(d)(2) or 9-106(b) shall send to the securities intermediary or commodity intermediary with which the security entitlement or commodity contract is maintained an authenticated

record that releases the securities intermediary or commodity intermediary from any further obligation to comply with entitlement orders or directions originated by the secured party; and

(5) a secured party having control of a letter-of-credit right under Section 9-107 shall send to each person having an unfulfilled obligation to pay or deliver proceeds of the letter-of-credit to the secured party an authenticated release from any further obligation to pay or deliver proceeds of the letter-of-credit to the secured party.

Section 9-209. *Duties of Secured Party If Account Debtor Has Been Notified of Assignment.* (a) Applicability of section. Except as otherwise provided in subsection (c), this section applies if:

(1) there is no outstanding secured obligation; and

(2) the secured party is not committed to make advances, incur obligations, or otherwise give value.

(b) Duties of secured party after receiving demand from debtor. Within 10 days after receiving an authenticated demand by the debtor, a secured party shall send to an account debtor that has received notification of an assignment to the secured party as assignee under Section 9-406(a) an authenticated record that releases the account debtor from any further obligation to the secured party.

(c) Inapplicability to sales. This section does not apply to an assignment constituting the sale of an account, chattel paper, or payment intangible.

Section 9-210. *Request for Accounting; Request Regarding List of Collateral or Statement of Account.* (a) Definitions in this section:

(1) "Request" means a record of a type described in paragraph (2), (3), or (4).

(2) "Request for an accounting" means a record authenticated by a debtor requesting that the recipient provide an accounting of the unpaid obligations secured by collateral and reasonably identifying the transaction or relationship that is the subject of the request.

(3) "Request regarding a list of collateral" means a record authenticated by a debtor requesting that the recipient approve or correct a list of what the debtor believes to be the collateral securing an obligation and reasonably identifying the transaction or relationship that is the subject of the request.

(4) "Request regarding a statement of account" means a record authenticated by a debtor requesting that the recipient approve or correct a statement indicating what the debtor believes to be the aggregate amount of unpaid obligations secured by collateral as of a specified date and reasonably identifying the transaction or relationship that is the subject of the request.

(b) Duty to respond to requests. Subject to subsections (c), (d), (e), and (f), a secured party, other than a buyer of accounts, chattel paper, payment intangibles, or promissory notes or a consignor, shall comply with a request within 14 days after receipt:

(1) in the case of a request for an accounting, by authenticating and sending to the debtor an accounting; and (2) in the case of a request regarding a list of collateral or a request regarding a statement of account, by authenticating and sending to the debtor an approval or correction.

(c) Request regarding list of collateral; statement concerning type of collateral. A secured party that claims a security interest in all of a particular type of collateral owned by the debtor may comply with a request regarding a list of collateral by sending to the debtor an authenticated record including a statement to that effect within 14 days after receipt.

(d) Request regarding list of collateral; no interest claimed. A person that receives a request regarding a list of collateral, claims no interest in the collateral when it receives the request, and claimed an interest in the collateral at an earlier time shall comply with the request within 14 days after receipt by sending to the debtor an authenticated record:

(1) disclaiming any interest in the collateral; and

(2) if known to the recipient, providing the name and mailing address of any assignee of or successor to the recipient's interest in the collateral.

(e)   Request for accounting or regarding statement of account; no interest in obligation claimed. A person that receives a request for an accounting or a request regarding a statement of account, claims no interest in the obligations when it receives the request, and claimed an interest in the obligations at an earlier time shall comply with the request within 14 days after receipt by sending to the debtor an authenticated record:

(1)   disclaiming any interest in the obligations; and

(2)   if known to the recipient, providing the name and mailing address of any assignee of or successor to the recipient's interest in the obligations.

(f)   Charges for responses. A debtor is entitled without charge to one response to a request under this section during any six-month period. The secured party may require payment of a charge not exceeding $25 for each additional response.

Part 3: Perfection and Priority

SUBPART 1: LAW GOVERNING PERFECTION AND PRIORITY

Section 9-301. *Law Governing Perfection and Priority of Security Interests.* Except as otherwise provided in Sections 9-303 through 9-306, the following rules determine the law governing perfection, the effect of perfection or nonperfection, and the priority of a security interest in collateral:

(a)   Except as otherwise provided in this section, while a debtor is located in a jurisdiction, the local law of that jurisdiction governs perfection, the effect of perfection or nonperfection, and the priority of a security interest in collateral.

(b)   While collateral is located in a jurisdiction, the local law of that jurisdiction governs perfection, the effect of perfection or nonperfection, and the priority of a possessory security interest in that collateral.

(c)   Except as otherwise provided in paragraph (d), while negotiable documents, goods, instruments, money, or tangible chattel paper is located in a jurisdiction, the local law of that jurisdiction governs:

(1)   perfection of a security interest in the goods by filing a fixture filing;

(2)   perfection of a security interest in timber to be cut; and

(3)   the effect of perfection or nonperfection and the priority of a nonpossessory security interest in the collateral.

(d)   The local law of the jurisdiction in which the wellhead or minehead is located governs perfection, the effect of perfection or nonperfection, and the priority of a security interest in as-extracted collateral.

(e)   When collateral is a cooperative interest, the law of this state governs perfection, the effect of perfection or nonperfection, and the priority of the security interest in such collateral.

Section 9-302. *Law Governing Perfection and Priority of Agricultural Liens.* While farm products are located in a jurisdiction, the local law of that jurisdiction governs perfection, the effect of perfection or nonperfection, and the priority of an agricultural lien on the farm products.

Section 9-303. *Law Governing Perfection and Priority of Security Interests in Goods Covered by a Certificate of Title.* (a) Applicability of section. This section applies to goods covered by a certificate of title, even if there is no other relationship between the jurisdiction under whose certificate of title the goods are covered and the goods or the debtor.

(b)   When goods covered by certificate of title. Goods become covered by a certificate of title when a valid application for the certificate of title and the applicable fee are delivered to the appropriate authority. Goods cease to be covered by a certificate of title at the earlier of the time the certificate of title ceases to be effective under the law of the issuing jurisdiction or the time the goods become covered subsequently by a certificate of title issued by another jurisdiction.

(c)   Applicable law. The local law of the jurisdiction under whose certificate of title the goods are covered governs perfection, the effect of perfection or nonperfection, and the priority of a security interest in goods covered by a certificate of title from the time the goods become covered by the certificate of title until the goods cease to be covered by the certificate of title.

Section 9-304. *Law Governing Perfection and Priority of Security Interests in Deposit Accounts.* (a) Law of bank's jurisdiction governs. The local law of a bank's jurisdiction governs perfection, the effect of perfection or nonperfection, and the priority of a security interest in a deposit account maintained with that bank.

(b)   Bank's jurisdiction. The following rules determine a bank's jurisdiction for purposes of this part:

(1)   If an agreement between the bank and the debtor governing the deposit account expressly provides that a particular jurisdiction is the bank's jurisdiction for purposes of this part, this article, or this chapter, that jurisdiction is the bank's jurisdiction.

(2)   If paragraph (1) does not apply and an agreement between the bank and its customer governing the deposit account expressly provides that the agreement is governed by the law of a particular jurisdiction, that jurisdiction is the bank's jurisdiction.

(3)   If neither paragraph (1) nor paragraph (2) applies and an agreement between the bank and its customer governing the deposit account expressly provides that the deposit account is maintained at an office in a particular jurisdiction, that jurisdiction is the bank's jurisdiction.

(4)   If none of the preceding paragraphs apply, the bank's jurisdiction is the jurisdiction in which the office identified in an account statement as the office serving the customer's account is located.

(5)   If none of the preceding paragraphs apply, the bank's jurisdiction is the jurisdiction in which the chief executive office of the bank is located.

Section 9-305. *Law Governing Perfection and Priority of Security Interests in Investment Property.* (a) Governing law: general rules. Except as otherwise provided in subsections (c) and (d), the following rules apply:

(1)   While a security certificate is located in a jurisdiction, the local law of that jurisdiction governs perfection, the effect of perfection or nonperfection, and the priority of a security interest in the certificated security represented thereby.

(2)   The local law of the issuer's jurisdiction as specified in Section 8-110(d) governs perfection, the effect of perfection or nonperfection, and the priority of a security interest in an uncertificated security.

(3)   The local law of the securities intermediary's jurisdiction as specified in Section 8-110(e) governs perfection, the effect of perfection or nonperfection, and the priority of a security interest in a security entitlement or securities account.

(4)   The local law of the commodity intermediary's jurisdiction governs perfection, the effect of perfection or nonperfection, and the priority of a security interest in a commodity contract or commodity account.

(b)   Commodity intermediary's jurisdiction. The following rules determine a commodity intermediary's jurisdiction for purposes of this part:

(1)   If an agreement between the commodity intermediary and commodity customer governing the commodity account expressly provides that a particular jurisdiction is the commodity intermediary's jurisdiction for purposes of this part, this article, or this chapter, that jurisdiction is the commodity intermediary's jurisdiction.

(2)   If paragraph (1) does not apply and an agreement between the commodity intermediary and commodity customer governing the commodity account expressly provides that the agreement is governed by the law of a particular jurisdiction, that jurisdiction is the commodity intermediary's jurisdiction.

(3)   If neither paragraph (1) nor paragraph (2) applies and an agreement between the commodity intermediary and commodity customer governing the commodity account

expressly provides that the commodity account is maintained at an office in a particular jurisdiction, that jurisdiction is the commodity intermediary's jurisdiction.

(4) If none of the preceding paragraphs apply, the commodity intermediary's jurisdiction is the jurisdiction in which the office identified in an account statement as the office serving the commodity customer's account is located.

(5) If none of the preceding paragraphs apply, the commodity intermediary's jurisdiction is the jurisdiction in which the chief executive office of the commodity intermediary is located.

(c) When perfection governed by law of jurisdiction where debtor located. The local law of the jurisdiction in which the debtor is located governs:

(1) perfection of a security interest in investment property by filing;

(2) automatic perfection of a security interest in investment property created by a broker or securities intermediary; and

(3) automatic perfection of a security interest in a commodity contract or commodity account created by a commodity intermediary.

(d) Cooperative interests. Subsections (a) through (c) do not apply to cooperative interests.

Section 9-306. *Law Governing Perfection and Priority of Security Interests in Letter-of-Credit Rights.* (a) Governing law: issuer's or nominated person's jurisdiction. Subject to subsection (c), the local law of the issuer's jurisdiction or a nominated person's jurisdiction governs perfection, the effect of perfection or nonperfection, and the priority of a security interest in a letter-of-credit right if the issuer's jurisdiction or nominated person's jurisdiction is a state.

(b) Issuer's or nominated person's jurisdiction. For purposes of this part, an issuer's jurisdiction or nominated person's jurisdiction is the jurisdiction whose law governs the liability of the issuer or nominated person with respect to the letter-of-credit right as provided in Section 5-116.

(c) When section not applicable. This section does not apply to a security interest that is perfected only under Section 9-308(d).

Section 9-307. *Location of Debtor.* (a) "Place of business." In this section, "place of business" means a place where a debtor conducts its affairs.

(b) Debtor's location: general rules. Except as otherwise provided in this section, the following rules determine a debtor's location:

(1) A debtor who is an individual is located at the individual's principal residence.

(2) A debtor that is an organization and has only one place of business is located at its place of business.

(3) A debtor that is an organization and has more than one place of business is located at its chief executive office.

(c) Limitation of applicability of subsection (b). Subsection (b) applies only if a debtor's residence, place of business, or chief executive office, as applicable, is located in a jurisdiction whose law generally requires information concerning the existence of a nonpossessory security interest to be made generally available in a filing, recording, or registration system as a condition or result of the security interest's obtaining priority over the rights of a lien creditor with respect to the collateral. If subsection (b) does not apply, the debtor is located in the District of Columbia.

(d) Continuation of location: cessation of existence, etc. A person that ceases to exist, have a residence, or have a place of business continues to be located in the jurisdiction specified by subsections (b) and (c).

(e) Location of registered organization organized under state law. A registered organization that is organized under the law of a state is located in that state.

(f) Location of registered organization organized under federal law; bank branches and agencies. Except as otherwise provided in subsection (i), a registered organization that is organized under the law of the United States and a branch or agency of a bank that is not organized under the law of the United States or a state are located:

    (1) in the state that the law of the United States designates, if the law designates a state of location;

    (2) in the state that the registered organization, branch, or agency designates, if the law of the United States authorizes the registered organization, branch, or agency to designate its state of location; or

    (3) in the District of Columbia, if neither paragraph (1) nor paragraph (2) applies.

    (g) Continuation of location: change in status of registered organization. A registered organization continues to be located in the jurisdiction specified by subsection (e) or (f) notwithstanding:

    (1) the suspension, revocation, forfeiture, or lapse of the registered organization's status as such in its jurisdiction of organization; or

    (2) the dissolution, winding up, or cancellation of the existence of the registered organization.

    (h) Location of United States. The United States is located in the District of Columbia.

    (i) Location of foreign bank branch or agency if licensed in only one state. A branch or agency of a bank that is not organized under the law of the United States or a state is located in the state in which the branch or agency is licensed, if all branches and agencies of the bank are licensed in only one state.

    (j) Location of foreign air carrier. A foreign air carrier under the Federal Aviation Act of 1958, as amended, is located at the designated office of the agent upon which service of process may be made on behalf of the carrier.

    (k) Section applies only to this part. This section applies only for purposes of this part.

SUBPART 2: PERFECTION

Section 9-308. *When Security Interest or Agricultural Lien Is Perfected; Continuity of Perfection.* (a) Perfection of security interest. Except as otherwise provided in this section and Section 9-309, a security interest is perfected if it has attached and all of the applicable requirements for perfection in Sections 9-310 through 9-316 have been satisfied. A security interest is perfected when it attaches if the applicable requirements are satisfied before the security interest attaches.

    (b) Perfection of agricultural lien. An agricultural lien is perfected if it has become effective and all of the applicable requirements for perfection in Section 9-310 have been satisfied. An agricultural lien is perfected when it becomes effective if the applicable requirements are satisfied before the agricultural lien becomes effective.

    (c) Continuous perfection; perfection by different methods. A security interest or agricultural lien is perfected continuously if it is originally perfected by one method under this article and is later perfected by another method under this article, without an intermediate period when it was unperfected.

    (d) Supporting obligation. Perfection of a security interest in collateral also perfects a security interest in a supporting obligation for the collateral.

    (e) Lien securing right to payment. Perfection of a security interest in a right to payment or performance also perfects a security interest in a security interest, mortgage, or other lien on personal or real property securing the right.

    (f) Security entitlement carried in securities account. Perfection of a security interest in a securities account also perfects a security interest in the security entitlements carried in the securities account.

    (g) Commodity contract carried in commodity account. Perfection of a security interest in a commodity account also perfects a security interest in the commodity contracts carried in the commodity account.

    (h) Cooperative organization security interest. A cooperative organization security interest becomes perfected when the cooperative interest first comes into existence and remains perfected so long as the cooperative interest exists.

Section 9-309. *Security Interest Perfected upon Attachment.* The following security interests are perfected when they attach:

(1) a purchase-money security interest in consumer goods, except as otherwise provided in Section 9-311(b) with respect to consumer goods that are subject to a statute or treaty described in Section 9-311(a);

(2) an assignment of accounts or payment intangibles which does not by itself or in conjunction with other assignments to the same assignee transfer a significant part of the assignor's outstanding accounts or payment intangibles;

(3) a sale of a payment intangible;

(4) a sale of a promissory note;

(5) a security interest created by the assignment of a healthcare-insurance receivable to the provider of the healthcare goods or services;

(6) a security interest arising under Section 2-401, 2-505, 2-711(3), or 2-A-508(5), until the debtor obtains possession of the collateral;

(7) a security interest of a collecting bank arising under Section 4-210;

(8) a security interest of an issuer or nominated person arising under Section 5-118;

(9) a security interest arising in the delivery of a financial asset under Section 9-206(c);

(10) a security interest in investment property created by a broker or securities intermediary;

(11) a security interest in a commodity contract or a commodity account created by a commodity intermediary;

(12) an assignment for the benefit of all creditors of the transferor and subsequent transfers by the assignee thereunder; and

(13) a security interest created by an assignment of a beneficial interest in a decedent's estate.

Section 9-310. *When Filing Required to Perfect Security Interest or Agricultural Lien; Security Interests and Agricultural Liens to Which Filing Provisions Do Not Apply.* (a) General rule: perfection by filing. Except as otherwise provided in subsection (b) and Section 9-312(b), a financing statement must be filed to perfect all security interests and agricultural liens.

(b) Exceptions: filing not necessary. Except as provided in subsection (d), the filing of a financing statement is not necessary to perfect a security interest:

(1) that is perfected under Section 9-308(d), (e), (f), or (g);

(2) that is perfected under Section 9-309 when it attaches;

(3) in property subject to a statute, regulation, or treaty described in Section 9-311(a);

(4) in goods in possession of a bailee which is perfected under Section 9-312(d)(1) or (2);

(5) in certificated securities, documents, goods, or instruments which is perfected without filing or possession under Section 9-312(e), (f), or (g);

(6) in collateral in the secured party's possession under Section 9-313;

(7) in a certificated security which is perfected by delivery of the security certificate to the secured party under Section 9-313;

(8) in deposit accounts, electronic chattel paper, investment property, or letter-of-credit rights which is perfected by control under Section 9-314;

(9) in proceeds which is perfected under Section 9-315;

(10) that is perfected under Section 9-316; or

(11) that is a cooperative organization security interest.

(c) Assignment of perfected security interest. If a secured party assigns a perfected security interest or agricultural lien, a filing under this article is not required to continue the perfected status of the security interest against creditors of and transferees from the original debtor.

(d) Special rule for cooperative interests. Except for a cooperative organization security interest, a security interest in a cooperative interest may be perfected only by filing a financing statement.

Section 9-311. *Perfection of Security Interests in Property Subject to Certain Statutes, Regulations, and Treaties.* (a) Security interest subject to other law. Except as otherwise provided in subsection (d), the filing of a financing statement is not necessary or effective to perfect a security interest in property subject to:

(1) a statute, regulation, or treaty of the United States whose requirements for a security interest's obtaining priority over the rights of a lien creditor with respect to the property preempt Section 9-310(a);

(2) a certificate-of-title statute of this state or regulations promulgated thereunder, to the extent such statute or regulations provide for a security interest to be indicated on the certificate as a condition or result of perfection; or

(3) a certificate-of-title statute of another jurisdiction which provides for a security interest to be indicated on the certificate as a condition or result of the security interest's obtaining priority over the rights of a lien creditor with respect to the property.

(b) Compliance with other law. Compliance with the requirements of a statute, regulation, or treaty described in subsection (a) for obtaining priority over the rights of a lien creditor is equivalent to the filing of a financing statement under this article. Except as otherwise provided in subsection (d) and Sections 9-313 and 9-316(d) and (e) for goods covered by a certificate of title, a security interest in property subject to a statute, regulation, or treaty described in subsection (a) may be perfected only by compliance with those requirements, and a security interest so perfected remains perfected notwithstanding a change in the use or transfer of possession of the collateral.

(c) Duration and renewal of perfection. Except as otherwise provided in subsection (d) and Section 9-316(d) and (e), duration and renewal of perfection of a security interest perfected by compliance with the requirements prescribed by a statute, regulation, or treaty described in subsection (a) are governed by the statute, regulation, or treaty. In other respects, the security interest is subject to this article.

(d) Inapplicability to certain inventory. During any period in which collateral subject to a statute specified in subsection (a)(2) is inventory held for sale or lease by a person or leased by that person as lessor and that person is in the business of selling goods of that kind, this section does not apply to a security interest in that collateral created by that person.

Section 9-312. *Perfection of Security Interests in Chattel Paper, Deposit Accounts, Documents, Goods Covered by Documents, Instruments, Investment Property, Letter-of-credit Rights, and Money; Perfection by Permissive Filing; Temporary Perfection Without Filing or Transfer of Possession.* (a) Perfection by filing permitted. A security interest in chattel paper, negotiable documents, instruments, or investment property may be perfected by filing.

(b) Control or possession of certain collateral. Except as otherwise provided in Section 9-315(c) and (d) for proceeds:

(1) a security interest in a deposit account may be perfected only by control under Section 9-314;

(2) and except as otherwise provided in Section 9-308(d), a security interest in a letter-of-credit right may be perfected only by control under Section 9-314; and

(3) a security interest in money may be perfected only by the secured party's taking possession under Section 9-313.

(c) Goods covered by negotiable document. While goods are in the possession of a bailee that has issued a negotiable document covering the goods:

(1) a security interest in the goods may be perfected by perfecting a security interest in the document; and

(2) a security interest perfected in the document has priority over any security interest that becomes perfected in the goods by another method during that time.

(d) Goods covered by nonnegotiable document. While goods are in the possession of a bailee that has issued a non-negotiable document covering the goods, a security interest in the goods may be perfected by:

(1) issuance of a document in the name of the secured party;

(2) the bailee's receipt of notification of the secured party's interest; or

(3)   filing as to the goods.

(e)   Temporary perfection: new value. A security interest in certificated securities, negotiable documents, or instruments is perfected without filing or the taking of possession for a period of 20 days from the time it attaches to the extent that it arises for new value given under an authenticated security agreement.

(f)   Temporary perfection: goods or documents made available to debtor. A perfected security interest in a negotiable document or goods in possession of a bailee, other than one that has issued a negotiable document for the goods, remains perfected for 20 days without filing if the secured party makes available to the debtor the goods or documents representing the goods for the purpose of:

(1)   ultimate sale or exchange; or

(2)   loading, unloading, storing, shipping, transshipping, manufacturing, processing, or otherwise dealing with them in a manner preliminary to their sale or exchange.

(g)   Temporary perfection: delivery of security certificate or instrument to debtor. A perfected security interest in a certificated security or instrument remains perfected for 20 days without filing if the secured party delivers the security certificate or instrument to the debtor for the purpose of:

(1)   ultimate sale or exchange; or

(2)   presentation, collection, enforcement, renewal, or registration of transfer.

(h)   Expiration of temporary perfection. After the 20-day period specified in subsection (e), (f), or (g) expires, perfection depends upon compliance with this article.

(i)   Cooperative interests. Subsections (a) through (h) do not apply to cooperative interests.

Section 9-313. When Possession by or Delivery to Secured Party Perfects Security Interest Without Filing. (a) Perfection by possession or delivery. Except as otherwise provided in subsection (b), a secured party may perfect a security interest in negotiable documents, goods, instruments, money, or tangible chattel paper by taking possession of the collateral. A secured party may perfect a security interest in certificated securities by taking delivery of the certificated securities under Section 8-301.

(b)   Goods covered by certificate of title. With respect to goods covered by a certificate of title issued by this state, a secured party may perfect a security interest in the goods by taking possession of the goods only in the circumstances described in Section 9-316(d).

(c)   Collateral in possession of person other than debtor. With respect to collateral other than certificated securities and goods covered by a document, a secured party takes possession of collateral in the possession of a person other than the debtor, the secured party, or a lessee of the collateral from the debtor in the ordinary course of the debtor's business, when:

(1)   the person in possession authenticates a record acknowledging that it holds possession of the collateral for the secured party's benefit; or

(2)   the person takes possession of the collateral after having authenticated a record acknowledging that it will hold possession of collateral for the secured party's benefit.

(d)   Time of perfection by possession; continuation of perfection. If perfection of a security interest depends upon possession of the collateral by a secured party, perfection occurs no earlier than the time the secured party takes possession and continues only while the secured party retains possession.

(e)   Time of perfection by delivery; continuation of perfection. A security interest in a certificated security in registered form is perfected by delivery when delivery of the certificated security occurs under Section 8-301 and remains perfected by delivery until the debtor obtains possession of the security certificate.

(f)   Acknowledgment not required. A person in possession of collateral is not required to acknowledge that it holds possession for a secured party's benefit.

(g)   Effectiveness of acknowledgment; no duties or confirmation. If a person acknowledges that it holds possession for the secured party's benefit:

(1)   the acknowledgment is effective under subsection (c) or Section 8-301(a), even if the acknowledgment violates the rights of a debtor; and

(2) unless the person otherwise agrees or law other than this article otherwise provides, the person does not owe any duty to the secured party and is not required to confirm the acknowledgment to another person.

(h) Secured party's delivery to person other than debtor. A secured party having possession of collateral does not relinquish possession by delivering the collateral to a person other than the debtor or a lessee of the collateral from the debtor in the ordinary course of the debtor's business if the person was instructed before the delivery or is instructed contemporaneously with the delivery:

(1) to hold possession of the collateral for the secured party's benefit; or

(2) to redeliver the collateral to the secured party.

(i) Effect of delivery under subsection (h); no duties or confirmation. A secured party does not relinquish possession, even if a delivery under subsection (h) violates the rights of a debtor. A person to which collateral is delivered under subsection (h) does not owe any duty to the secured party and is not required to confirm the delivery to another person unless the person otherwise agrees or law other than this article otherwise provides.

(j) Cooperative interests. Subsections (a) through (i) do not apply to cooperative interests.

Section 9-314. *Perfection by Control.* (a) Perfection by control. A security interest in investment property, deposit accounts, letter-of-credit rights, or electronic chattel paper may be perfected by control of the collateral under Section 9-104, 9-105, 9-106, or 9-107.

(b) Specified collateral: time of perfection by control; continuation of perfection. A security interest in deposit accounts, electronic chattel paper, or letter-of-credit rights is perfected by control under Section 9-104, 9-105, or 9-107 when the secured party obtains control and remains perfected by control only while the secured party retains control.

(c) Investment property: time of perfection by control; continuation of perfection. A security interest in investment property is perfected by control under Section 9-106 from the time the secured party obtains control and remains perfected by control until:

(1) the secured party does not have control; and

(2) one of the following occurs:

(A) if the collateral is a certificated security, the debtor has or acquires possession of the security certificate;

(B) if the collateral is an uncertificated security, the issuer has registered or registers the debtor as the registered owner; or

(C) if the collateral is a security entitlement, the debtor is or becomes the entitlement holder.

(d) Cooperative interests. Subsections (a) through (c) do not apply to cooperative interests.

Section 9-315. *Secured Party's Rights on Disposition of Collateral and in Proceeds.* (a) Disposition of collateral: continuation of security interest or agricultural lien; proceeds. Except as otherwise provided in this article and in Section 2-403(2):

(1) a security interest or agricultural lien continues in collateral notwithstanding sale, lease, license, exchange, or other disposition thereof unless the secured party authorized the disposition free of the security interest or agricultural lien; and

(2) a security interest attaches to any identifiable proceeds of collateral.

(b) When commingled proceeds identifiable. Proceeds that are commingled with other property are identifiable proceeds:

(1) if the proceeds are goods, to the extent provided by Section 9-336; and

(2) if the proceeds are not goods, to the extent that the secured party identifies the proceeds by a method of tracing, including application of equitable principles, that is permitted under law other than this article with respect to commingled property of the type involved.

(c)   Perfection of security interest in proceeds. A security interest in proceeds is a perfected security interest if the security interest in the original collateral was perfected.

(d)   Continuation of perfection. A perfected security interest in proceeds becomes unperfected on the 21st day after the security interest attaches to the proceeds unless:
(1)   the following conditions are satisfied:
    (A)   a filed financing statement covers the original collateral;
    (B)   the proceeds are collateral in which a security interest may be perfected by filing in the office in which the financing statement has been filed; and
    (C)   the proceeds are not acquired with cash proceeds;
(2)   the proceeds are identifiable cash proceeds; or
(3)   the security interest in the proceeds is perfected other than under subsection (c) when the security interest attaches to the proceeds or within 20 days thereafter.

(e)   When perfected security interest in proceeds becomes unperfected. If a filed financing statement covers the original collateral, a security interest in proceeds which remains perfected under subsection (d)(1) becomes unperfected at the later of:
(1)   when the effectiveness of the filed financing statement lapses under Section 9-515 or is terminated under Section 9-513; or
(2)   the 21st day after the security interest attaches to the proceeds.

Section 9-316. *Continued Perfection of Security Interest Following Change in Governing Law.* (a) General rule: effect on perfection of change in governing law. A security interest perfected pursuant to the law of the jurisdiction designated in Section 9-301(a) or 9-305(c) remains perfected until the earliest of:
(1)   the time perfection would have ceased under the law of that jurisdiction;
(2)   the expiration of four months after a change of the debtor's location to another jurisdiction; or
(3)   the expiration of one year after a transfer of collateral to a person that thereby becomes a debtor and is located in another jurisdiction.

(b)   Security interest perfected or unperfected under law of new jurisdiction. If a security interest described in subsection (a) becomes perfected under the law of the other jurisdiction before the earliest time or event described in that subsection, it remains perfected thereafter. If the security interest does not become perfected under the law of the other jurisdiction before the earliest time or event, it becomes unperfected and is deemed never to have been perfected as against a purchaser of the collateral for value.

(c)   Possessory security interest in collateral moved to new jurisdiction. A possessory security interest in collateral, other than goods covered by a certificate of title and as-extracted collateral consisting of goods, remains continuously perfected if:
(1)   the collateral is located in one jurisdiction and subject to a security interest perfected under the law of that jurisdiction;
(2)   thereafter the collateral is brought into another jurisdiction; and
(3)   upon entry into the other jurisdiction, the security interest is perfected under the law of the other jurisdiction.

(d)   Goods covered by certificate of title from this state. Except as otherwise provided in subsection (e), a security interest in goods covered by a certificate of title which is perfected by any method under the law of another jurisdiction when the goods become covered by a certificate of title from this state remains perfected until the security interest would have become unperfected under the law of the other jurisdiction had the goods not become so covered.

(e)   When subsection (d) security interest becomes unperfected against purchasers. A security interest described in subsection (d) becomes unperfected as against a purchaser of the goods for value and is deemed never to have been perfected as against a purchaser of the goods for value if the applicable requirements for perfection under Section 9-311(b) or 9-313 are not satisfied before the earlier of:
(1)   the time the security interest would have become unperfected under the law of the other jurisdiction had the goods not become covered by a certificate of title from this state; or

(2) the expiration of four months after the goods had become so covered.

(f) Change in jurisdiction of bank, issuer, nominated person, securities intermediary, or commodity intermediary. A security interest in deposit accounts, letter-of-credit rights, or investment property which is perfected under the law of the bank's jurisdiction, the issuer's jurisdiction, a nominated person's jurisdiction, the securities intermediary's jurisdiction, or the commodity intermediary's jurisdiction, as applicable, remains perfected until the earlier of:

(1) the time the security interest would have become unperfected under the law of that jurisdiction; or

(2) the expiration of four months after a change of the applicable jurisdiction to another jurisdiction.

(g) Subsection (f) security interest perfected or unperfected under law of new jurisdiction. If a security interest described in subsection (f) becomes perfected under the law of the other jurisdiction before the earlier of the time or the end of the period described in that subsection, it remains perfected thereafter. If the security interest does not become perfected under the law of the other jurisdiction before the earlier of that time or the end of that period, it becomes unperfected and is deemed never to have been perfected as against a purchaser of the collateral for value.

SUBPART 3: PRIORITY

Section 9-317. *Interests That Take Priority over or Take Free of Security Interest or Agricultural Lien.* (a) Conflicting security interests and rights of lien creditors. A security interest or agricultural lien is subordinate to the rights of:

(1) a person entitled to priority under Section 9-322; and

(2) except as otherwise provided in subsection (e), a person that becomes a lien creditor before the earlier of the time:

(A) the security interest or agricultural lien is perfected; or

(B) one of the conditions specified in Section 9-203(b)(3) is met and a financing statement covering the collateral is filed.

(b) Buyers that receive delivery. Except as otherwise provided in subsection (e), a buyer, other than a secured party, of tangible chattel paper, documents, goods, instruments, or a security certificate takes free of a security interest or agricultural lien if the buyer gives value and receives delivery of the collateral without knowledge of the security interest or agricultural lien and before it is perfected.

(c) Lessees that receive delivery. Except as otherwise provided in subsection (e), a lessee of goods takes free of a security interest or agricultural lien if the lessee gives value and receives delivery of the collateral without knowledge of the security interest or agricultural lien and before it is perfected.

(d) Licensees and buyers of certain collateral. A licensee of a general intangible or a buyer, other than a secured party, of accounts, electronic chattel paper, general intangibles, or investment property other than a certificated security takes free of a security interest if the licensee or buyer gives value without knowledge of the security interest and before it is perfected.

(e) Purchase-money security interest. Except as otherwise provided in Sections 9-320 and 9-321, if a person files a financing statement with respect to a purchase-money security interest before or within 20 days after the debtor receives delivery of the collateral, the security interest takes priority over the rights of a buyer, lessee, or lien creditor which arise between the time the security interest attaches and the time of filing. The preceding sentence does not apply to cooperative interests.

Section 9-318. *No Interest Retained in Right to Payment That Is Sold; Rights and Title of Seller of Account or Chattel Paper with Respect to Creditors and Purchasers.* (a) Seller retains no interest. A debtor that has sold an account, chattel paper, payment intangible, or promissory note does not retain a legal or equitable interest in the collateral sold.

(b) Deemed rights of debtor if buyer's security interest unperfected. For purposes of determining the rights of creditors of, and purchasers for value of an account or chattel paper from, a debtor that has sold an account or chattel paper, while the buyer's security interest is unperfected, the debtor is deemed to have rights and title to the account or chattel paper identical to those the debtor sold.

Section 9-319. *Rights and Title of Consignee with Respect to Creditors and Purchasers.* (a) Consignee has consignor's rights. Except as otherwise provided in subsection (b), for purposes of determining the rights of creditors of, and purchasers for value of goods from, a consignee, while the goods are in the possession of the consignee, the consignee is deemed to have rights and title to the goods identical to those the consignor had or had power to transfer.

(b) Applicability of other law. For purposes of determining the rights of a creditor of a consignee, law other than this article determines the rights and title of a consignee while goods are in the consignee's possession if, under this part, a perfected security interest held by the consignor would have priority over the rights of the creditor.

Section 9-320. *Buyer of Goods.* (a) Buyer in ordinary course of business. Except as otherwise provided in subsection (e), a buyer in ordinary course of business, other than a person buying farm products from a person engaged in farming operations, takes free of a security interest created by the buyer's seller, even if the security interest is perfected and the buyer knows of its existence.

(b) Buyer of consumer goods. Except as otherwise provided in subsection (e), a buyer of goods from a person who used or bought the goods for use primarily for personal, family, or household purposes takes free of a security interest, even if perfected, if the buyer buys:

(1) without knowledge of the security interest;

(2) for value;

(3) primarily for the buyer's personal, family, or household purposes; and

(4) before the filing of a financing statement covering the goods.

(c) Effectiveness of filing for subsection (b). To the extent that it affects the priority of a security interest over a buyer of goods under subsection (b), the period of effectiveness of a filing made in the jurisdiction in which the seller is located is governed by Section 9-316(a) and (b).

(d) Buyer in ordinary course of business at wellhead or minehead. A buyer in ordinary course of business buying oil, gas, or other minerals at the wellhead or minehead or after extraction takes free of an interest arising out of an encumbrance.

(e) Possessory security interest not affected. Subsections (a) and (b) do not affect a security interest in goods in the possession of the secured party under Section 9-313.

Section 9-321. *Licensee of General Intangible and Lessee of Goods in Ordinary Course of Business.* (a) "Licensee in ordinary course of business." In this section, "licensee in ordinary course of business" means a person that becomes a licensee of a general intangible in good faith, without knowledge that the license violates the rights of another person in the general intangible, and in the ordinary course from a person in the business of licensing general intangibles of that kind. A person becomes a licensee in the ordinary course if the license to the person comports with the usual or customary practices in the kind of business in which the licensor is engaged or with the licensor's own usual or customary practices.

(b) Rights of licensee in ordinary course of business. A licensee in ordinary course of business takes its rights under a nonexclusive license free of a security interest in the general intangible created by the licensor, even if the security interest is perfected and the licensee knows of its existence.

(c) Rights of lessee in ordinary course of business. A lessee in ordinary course of business takes its leasehold interest free of a security interest in the goods created by the lessor, even if the security interest is perfected and the lessee knows of its existence.

Section 9-322. *Priorities among Conflicting Security Interests in and Agricultural Liens on Same Collateral.* (a) General priority rules. Except as otherwise provided in this section, priority among conflicting security interests and agricultural liens in the same collateral is determined according to the following rules:

(1) Conflicting perfected security interests and agricultural liens rank according to priority in time of filing or perfection. Priority dates from the earlier of the time a filing covering the collateral is first made or the security interest or agricultural lien is first perfected, if there is no period thereafter when there is neither filing nor perfection.

(2) A perfected security interest or agricultural lien has priority over a conflicting unperfected security interest or agricultural lien.

(3) The first security interest or agricultural lien to attach or become effective has priority if conflicting security interests and agricultural liens are unperfected.

(b) Time of perfection: proceeds and supporting obligations. For the purposes of subsection (a)(1):

(1) the time of filing or perfection as to a security interest in collateral is also the time of filing or perfection as to a security interest in proceeds; and

(2) the time of filing or perfection as to a security interest in collateral supported by a supporting obligation is also the time of filing or perfection as to a security interest in the supporting obligation.

(c) Special priority rules: proceeds and supporting obligations. Except as otherwise provided in subsection (f), a security interest in collateral which qualifies for priority over a conflicting security interest under Section 9-327, 9-328, 9-329, 9-330, or 9-331 also has priority over a conflicting security interest in:

(1) any supporting obligation for the collateral; and

(2) proceeds of the collateral if:

(A) the security interest in proceeds is perfected;

(B) the proceeds are cash proceeds or of the same type as the collateral; and

(C) in the case of proceeds that are proceeds of proceeds, all intervening proceeds are cash proceeds, proceeds of the same type as the collateral, or an account relating to the collateral.

(d) First-to-file priority rule for certain collateral. Subject to subsection (e) and except as otherwise provided in subsection (f), if a security interest in chattel paper, deposit accounts, negotiable documents, instruments, investment property, or letter-of-credit rights is perfected by a method other than filing, conflicting perfected security interests in proceeds of the collateral rank according to priority in time of filing.

(e) Applicability of subsection (d). Subsection (d) applies only if the proceeds of the collateral are not cash proceeds, chattel paper, negotiable documents, instruments, investment property, or letter-of-credit rights.

(f) Limitations on subsections (a) through (e). Subsections (a) through (e) are subject to:

(1) subsection (g) and the other provisions of this part;

(2) Section 4-210 with respect to a security interest of a collecting bank;

(3) Section 5-118 with respect to a security interest of an issuer or nominated person; and

(4) Section 9-110 with respect to a security interest arising under Article 2 or 2-A.

(g) Priority under agricultural lien statute. A perfected agricultural lien on collateral has priority over a conflicting security interest in or agricultural lien on the same collateral if the statute creating the agricultural lien so provides.

(h) Special priority rules: cooperative interests.

(1) With respect to all amounts secured, a cooperative organization security interest has priority over all other security interests in a cooperative interest.

(2) As to security interests in cooperative interests other than cooperative organization security interests, Section 9-323(h) provides special rules for future advances.

Section 9-323. *Future Advances.* (a) When priority based on time of advance. Except as otherwise provided in subsection (c), for purposes of determining the priority of a perfected security interest under Section 9-322(a)(1), perfection of the security interest dates from the time an advance is made to the extent that the security interest secures an advance that:

   (1) is made while the security interest is perfected only:

      (A) under Section 9-309 when it attaches; or

      (B) temporarily under Section 9-312(e), (f), or (g); and

   (2) is not made pursuant to a commitment entered into before or while the security interest is perfected by a method other than under Section 9-309 or 9-312(e), (f), or (g).

   (b) Lien creditor. Except as otherwise provided in subsections (c) and (h), a security interest is subordinate to the rights of a person that becomes a lien creditor to the extent that the security interest secures an advance made more than 45 days after the person becomes a lien creditor unless the advance is made:

   (1) without knowledge of the lien; or

   (2) pursuant to a commitment entered into without knowledge of the lien.

   (c) Buyer of receivables. Subsections (a) and (b) do not apply to a security interest held by a secured party that is a buyer of accounts, chattel paper, payment intangibles, or promissory notes or a consignor.

   (d) Buyer of goods. Except as otherwise provided in subsection (e), a buyer of goods other than a buyer in ordinary course of business takes free of a security interest to the extent that it secures advances made after the earlier of:

   (1) the time the secured party acquires knowledge of the buyer's purchase; or

   (2) 45 days after the purchase.

   (e) Advances made pursuant to commitment: priority of buyer of goods. Subsection (d) does not apply if the advance is made pursuant to a commitment entered into without knowledge of the buyer's purchase and before the expiration of the 45 day period.

   (f) Lessee of goods. Except as otherwise provided in subsection (g), a lessee of goods, other than a lessee in ordinary course of business, takes the leasehold interest free of a security interest to the extent that it secures advances made after the earlier of:

   (1) the time the secured party acquires knowledge of the lease; or

   (2) 45 days after the lease contract becomes enforceable.

   (g) Advances made pursuant to commitment: priority of lessee of goods. Subsection (f) does not apply if the advance is made pursuant to a commitment entered into without knowledge of the lease and before the expiration of the 45 day period.

   (h) Priority with respect to cooperative interests. The following rules apply for purposes of determining under Section 9-322(a)(1) the priority of a perfected security interest in a cooperative interest:

   (1) Perfection of the security interest with respect to a future advance dates from the time of the filing under Section 9-310(d) if all of the following are true:

      (A) The security agreement states the maximum amount to be advanced pursuant to commitment;

      (B) The future advance is made pursuant to that commitment;

      (C) The future advance plus the outstanding sum of any prior advances is not more than the stated maximum amount; and

      (D) The filed financing statement includes a cooperative addendum disclosing that the security agreement contains a commitment to make future advances.

   (2) Except as provided in paragraph (1), perfection of the security interest with respect to a future advance dates from the time the advance is made.

   (3) For purposes of paragraph (1), no amendment of a security agreement shall adversely affect the priority of any other security interest in the same cooperative interest that was perfected prior to the amendment.

   (4) This subsection applies only to advances made subsequent to an initial advance.

   Section 9-324. *Priority of Purchase-money Security Interests.* (a) General rule: purchase-money priority. Except as otherwise provided in subsection (g), a perfected purchase-money security interest in goods other than inventory or livestock has priority over a conflicting security interest in the same goods, and, except as otherwise provided in Section 9-327, a perfected security interest in its identifiable proceeds also has priority, if the purchase-money security interest is perfected when the debtor receives possession of the collateral or within 20 days thereafter.

(b) Inventory purchase-money priority. Subject to subsection (c) and except as otherwise provided in subsection (g), a perfected purchase-money security interest in inventory has priority over a conflicting security interest in the same inventory, has priority over a conflicting security interest in chattel paper or an instrument constituting proceeds of the inventory and in proceeds of the chattel paper, if so provided in Section 9-330, and, except as otherwise provided in Section 9-327, also has priority in identifiable cash proceeds of the inventory to the extent the identifiable cash proceeds are received on or before the delivery of the inventory to a buyer, if:

(1) the purchase-money security interest is perfected when the debtor receives possession of the inventory;

(2) the purchase-money secured party sends an authenticated notification to the holder of the conflicting security interest;

(3) the holder of the conflicting security interest receives the notification within five years before the debtor receives possession of the inventory; and

(4) the notification states that the person sending the notification has or expects to acquire a purchase-money security interest in inventory of the debtor and describes the inventory.

(c) Holders of conflicting inventory security interests to be notified. Subsections (b)(2) through (4) apply only if the holder of the conflicting security interest had filed a financing statement covering the same types of inventory:

(1) if the purchase-money security interest is perfected by filing, before the date of the filing; or

(2) if the purchase-money security interest is temporarily perfected without filing or possession under Section 9-312(f), before the beginning of the 20-day period there under.

(d) Livestock purchase-money priority. Subject to subsection (e) and except as otherwise provided in subsection (g), a perfected purchase-money security interest in livestock that are farm products has priority over a conflicting security interest in the same livestock, and, except as otherwise provided in Section 9-327, a perfected security interest in their identifiable proceeds and identifiable products in their unmanufactured states also has priority, if:

(1) the purchase-money security interest is perfected when the debtor receives possession of the livestock;

(2) the purchase-money secured party sends an authenticated notification to the holder of the conflicting security inter est;

(3) the holder of the conflicting security interest receives the notification within six months before the debtor receives possession of the livestock; and

(4) the notification states that the person sending the notification has or expects to acquire a purchase-money security interest in livestock of the debtor and describes the live stock.

(e) Holders of conflicting livestock security interests to be notified. Subsections (d)(2) through (4) apply only if the holder of the conflicting security interest had filed a financing statement covering the same types of livestock:

(1) if the purchase-money security interest is perfected by filing, before the date of the filing; or

(2) if the purchase-money security interest is temporarily perfected without filing or possession under Section 9-312(f), before the beginning of the 20-day period there under.

(f) Software purchase-money priority. Except as otherwise provided in subsection (g), a perfected purchase-money security interest in software has priority over a conflicting security interest in the same collateral, and, except as otherwise provided in Section 9-327, a perfected security interest in its identifiable proceeds also has priority, to the extent that the purchase-money security interest in the goods in which the software was acquired for use has priority in the goods and proceeds of the goods under this section.

(g) Conflicting purchase-money security interests. If more than one security interest qualifies for priority in the same collateral under subsection (a), (b), (d), or (f):

(1) a security interest securing an obligation incurred as all or part of the price of the collateral has priority over a security interest securing an obligation incurred for value given to enable the debtor to acquire rights in or the use of collateral; and

(2) in all other cases, Section 9-322(a) applies to the qualifying security interests.

Section 9-325. *Priority of Security Interests in Transferred Collateral.* (a) Subordination of security interest in transferred collateral. Except as otherwise provided in subsection (b), a security interest created by a debtor is subordinate to a security interest in the same collateral created by another person if:

(1) the debtor acquired the collateral subject to the security interest created by the other person;

(2) the security interest created by the other person was perfected when the debtor acquired the collateral; and

(3) there is no period thereafter when the security interest is unperfected.

(b) Limitation of subsection (a) subordination. Subsection (a) subordinates a security interest only if the security interest:

(1) otherwise would have priority solely under Section 9-322(a) or 9-324; or

(2) arose solely under Section 2-711(3) or 2-A-508(5).

Section 9-326. *Priority of Security Interests Created by New Debtor.* (a) Subordination of security interest created by new debtor. Subject to subsection (b), a security interest created by a new debtor which is perfected by a filed financing statement that is effective solely under Section 9-508 in collateral in which a new debtor has or acquires rights is subordinate to a security interest in the same collateral which is perfected other than by a filed financing statement that is effective solely under Section 9-508.

(b) Priority under other provisions; multiple original debtors. The other provisions of this part determine the priority among conflicting security interests in the same collateral perfected by filed financing statements that are effective solely under Section 9-508. However, if the security agreements to which a new debtor became bound as debtor were not entered into by the same original debtor, the conflicting security interests rank according to priority in time of the new debtor's having become bound.

Section 9-327. *Priority of Security Interests in Deposit Account.* The following rules govern priority among conflicting security interests in the same deposit account:

(a) A security interest held by a secured party having control of the deposit account under Section 9-104 has priority over a conflicting security interest held by a secured party that does not have control.

(b) Except as otherwise provided in subsections (c) and (d), security interests perfected by control under Section 9-314 rank according to priority in time of obtaining control.

(c) Except as otherwise provided in subsection (d), a security interest held by the bank with which the deposit account is maintained has priority over a conflicting security interest held by another secured party.

(d) A security interest perfected by control under Section 9-104(a)(3) has priority over a security interest held by the bank with which the deposit account is maintained.

Section 9-328. *Priority of Security Interests in Investment Property.* The following rules govern priority among conflicting security interests in the same investment property:

(a) A security interest held by a secured party having control of investment property under Section 9-106 has priority over a security interest held by a secured party that does not have control of the investment property.

(b) Except as otherwise provided in paragraphs (c) and (d), conflicting security interests held by secured parties each of which has control under Section 9-106 rank according to priority in time of:

(1) if the collateral is a security, obtaining control;

(2)   if the collateral is a security entitlement carried in a securities account and:

    (A)   if the secured party obtained control under Section 8-106(d)(1), the secured party's becoming the person for which the securities account is maintained;

    (B)   if the secured party obtained control under Section 8-106(d)(2), the securities intermediary's agreement to comply with the secured party's entitlement orders with respect to security entitlements carried or to be carried in the securities account; or

    (C)   if the secured party obtained control through another person under Section 8-106(d)(3), the time on which priority would be based under this paragraph if the other person were the secured party; or

(3)   if the collateral is a commodity contract carried with a commodity intermediary, the satisfaction of the requirement for control specified in Section 9-106(b)(2) with respect to commodity contracts carried or to be carried with the commodity intermediary.

(c)   A security interest held by a securities intermediary in a security entitlement or a securities account maintained with the securities intermediary has priority over a conflicting security interest held by another secured party.

(d)   A security interest held by a commodity intermediary in a commodity contract or a commodity account maintained with the commodity intermediary has priority over a conflicting security interest held by another secured party.

(e)   A security interest in a certificated security in registered form which is perfected by taking delivery under Section 9-313(a) and not by control under Section 9-314 has priority over a conflicting security interest perfected by a method other than control.

(f)   Conflicting security interests created by a broker, securities intermediary, or commodity intermediary which are perfected without control under Section 9-106 rank equally.

(g)   In all other cases, priority among conflicting security interests in investment property is governed by Sections 9-322 and 9-323.

(h)   Subsections (a) through (g) do not apply to cooperative interests.

Section 9-329. *Priority of Security Interests in Letter-of-Credit Right.* The following rules govern priority among conflicting security interests in the same letter-of-credit right:

(a)   A security interest held by a secured party having control of the letter-of-credit right under Section 9-107 has priority to the extent of its control over a conflicting security interest held by a secured party that does not have control.

(b)   Security interests perfected by control under Section 9-314 rank according to priority in time of obtaining control.

Section 9-330. *Priority of Purchaser of Chattel Paper or Instrument.* (a) Purchaser's priority: security interest claimed merely as proceeds. A purchaser of chattel paper has priority over a security interest in the chattel paper which is claimed merely as proceeds of inventory subject to a security interest if:

(1)   in good faith and in the ordinary course of the purchaser's business, the purchaser gives new value and takes possession of the chattel paper or obtains control of the chattel paper under Section 9-105; and

(2)   the chattel paper does not indicate that it has been assigned to an identified assignee other than the purchaser.

(b)   Purchaser's priority: other security interests. A purchaser of chattel paper has priority over a security interest in the chattel paper which is claimed other than merely as proceeds of inventory subject to a security interest if the purchaser gives new value and takes possession of the chattel paper or obtains control of the chattel paper under Section 9-105 in good faith, in the ordinary course of the purchaser's business, and without knowledge that the purchase violates the rights of the secured party.

(c)   Chattel paper purchaser's priority in proceeds. Except as otherwise provided in Section 9-327, a purchaser having priority in chattel paper under subsection (a) or (b) also has priority in proceeds of the chattel paper to the extent that:

(1)   Section 9-322 provides for priority in the proceeds; or

(2)   the proceeds consist of the specific goods covered by the chattel paper or cash proceeds of the specific goods, even if the purchaser's security interest in the proceeds is unperfected.

(d)   Instrument purchaser's priority. Except as otherwise provided in Section 9-331(a), a purchaser of an instrument has priority over a security interest in the instrument perfected by a method other than possession if the purchaser gives value and takes possession of the instrument in good faith and without knowledge that the purchase violates the rights of the secured party.

(e)   Holder of purchase-money security interest gives new value. For purposes of subsections (a) and (b), the holder of a purchase-money security interest in inventory gives new value for chattel paper constituting proceeds of the inventory.

(f)   Indication of assignment gives knowledge. For purposes of subsections (b) and (d), if chattel paper or an instrument indicates that it has been assigned to an identified secured party other than the purchaser, a purchaser of the chattel paper or instrument has knowledge that the purchase violates the rights of the secured party.

Section 9-331. *Priority of Rights of Purchasers of Instruments, Documents, and Securities under Other Articles; Priority of Interests in Financial Assets and Security Entitlements under Article 8.* (a) Rights under Articles 3, 7, and 8 not limited. This article does not limit the rights of a holder in due course of a negotiable instrument, a holder to which a negotiable document of title has been duly negotiated, or a protected purchaser of a security. These holders or purchasers take priority over an earlier security interest, even if perfected, to the extent provided in Articles 3, 7, and 8.

(b)   Protection under Article 8. This article does not limit the rights of or impose liability on a person to the extent that the person is protected against the assertion of a claim under Article 8.

(c)   Filing not notice. Filing under this article does not constitute notice of a claim or defense to the holders, or purchasers, or persons described in subsections (a) and (b).

(d)   Section not applicable to cooperative interests. Subsections (a), (b), and (c) do not apply to cooperative interests.

Section 9-332. *Transfer of Money; Transfer of Funds from Deposit Account.* (a) Transferee of money. A transferee of money takes the money free of a security interest unless the transferee acts in collusion with the debtor in violating the rights of the secured party.

(b)   Transferee of funds from deposit account. A transferee of funds from a deposit account takes the funds free of a security interest in the deposit account unless the transferee acts in collusion with the debtor in violating the rights of the secured party.

Section 9-333. *Priority of Certain Liens Arising by Operation of Law.* (a) "Possessory lien." In this section, "possessory lien" means an interest, other than a security interest or an agricultural lien:

(1)   which secures payment or performance of an obligation for services or materials furnished with respect to goods by a person in the ordinary course of the person's business;

(2)   which is created by statute or rule of law in favor of the person; and

(3)   whose effectiveness depends on the person's possession of the goods.

(b)   Priority of possessory lien. A possessory lien on goods has priority over a security interest in the goods unless the lien is created by a statute that expressly provides otherwise.

Section 9-334. *Priority of Security Interests in Fixtures and Crops.* (a) Security interest in fixtures under this article. A security interest under this article may be created in goods that are fixtures or may continue in goods that become fixtures. A security interest does not exist under this article in ordinary building materials incorporated into an improvement on land.

(b)   Security interest in fixtures under real property law. This article does not prevent creation of an encumbrance upon fixtures under real property law.

(c) General rule: subordination of security interest in fixtures. In cases not governed by subsections (d) through (h), a security interest in fixtures is subordinate to a conflicting interest of an encumbrancer or owner of the related real property other than the debtor.

(d) Fixtures purchase-money priority. Except as otherwise provided in subsection (h), a perfected security interest in fixtures has priority over a conflicting interest of an encumbrancer or owner of the real property if the debtor has an interest of record in or is in possession of the real property and:

(1) the security interest is a purchase-money security interest;

(2) the interest of the encumbrancer or owner arises before the goods become fixtures; and

(3) the security interest is perfected by a fixture filing before the goods become fixtures or within 20 days thereafter.

(e) Priority of security interest in fixtures over interests in real property. A perfected security interest in fixtures has priority over a conflicting interest of an encumbrancer or owner of the real property if:

(1) the debtor has an interest of record in the real property or is in possession of the real property and the security interest:

(A) is perfected by a fixture filing before the interest of the encumbrancer or owner is of record; and

(B) has priority over any conflicting interest of a predecessor in title of the encumbrancer or owner;

(2) before the goods become fixtures, the security interest is perfected by any method permitted by this article and the fixtures are readily removable:

(A) factory or office machines;

(B) equipment that is not primarily used or leased for use in the operation of the real property; or

(C) replacements of domestic appliances that are consumer goods;

(3) the conflicting interest is a lien on the real property obtained by legal or equitable proceedings after the security interest was perfected by any method permitted by this article; or

(4) the security interest is:

(A) created in a manufactured home in a manufactured-home transaction; and

(B) perfected pursuant to a statute described in Section 9-311(a)(2).

(f) Priority based on consent, disclaimer, or right to remove. A security interest in fixtures, whether or not perfected, has priority over a conflicting interest of an encumbrancer or owner of the real property if:

(1) the encumbrancer or owner has, in an authenticated record, consented to the security interest or disclaimed an interest in the goods as fixtures; or

(2) the debtor has a right to remove the goods as against the encumbrancer or owner.

(g) Continuation of paragraph (f)(2) priority. The priority of the security interest under paragraph (f)(2) continues for a reasonable time if the debtor's right to remove the goods as against the encumbrancer or owner terminates.

(h) Priority of construction mortgage. A mortgage is a construction mortgage to the extent that it secures an obligation incurred for the construction of an improvement on land, including the acquisition cost of the land, if a recorded record of the mortgage so indicates. Except as otherwise provided in subsections (e) and (f), a security interest in fixtures is subordinate to a construction mortgage if a record of the mortgage is recorded before the goods become fixtures and the goods become fixtures before the completion of the construction. A mortgage has this priority to the same extent as a construction mortgage to the extent that it is given to refinance a construction mortgage.

(i) Priority of security interest in crops. A perfected security interest in crops growing on real property has priority over a conflicting interest of an encumbrancer or owner of the real property if the debtor has an interest of record in or is in possession of the real property.

(j) Subsection (i) prevails. Subsection (i) prevails over any inconsistent provisions with this article or any other chapter of law.

Section 9-335. *Accessions.* (a) Creation of security interest in accession. A security interest may be created in an accession and continues in collateral that becomes an accession.

(b) Perfection of security interest. If a security interest is perfected when the collateral becomes an accession, the security interest remains perfected in the collateral.

(c) Priority of security interest. Except as otherwise provided in subsection (d), the other provisions of this part determine the priority of a security interest in an accession.

(d) Compliance with certificate-of-title statute. A security interest in an accession is subordinate to a security interest in the whole which is perfected by compliance with the requirements of a certificate-of-title statute under Section 9-311 (b).

(e) Removal of accession after default. After default, subject to Part 6, a secured party may remove an accession from other goods if the security interest in the accession has priority over the claims of every person having an interest in the whole.

(f) Reimbursement following removal. A secured party that removes an accession from other goods under subsection (e) shall promptly reimburse any holder of a security interest or other lien on, or owner of, the whole or of the other goods, other than the debtor, for the cost of repair of any physical injury to the whole or the other goods. The secured party need not reimburse the holder or owner for any diminution in value of the whole or the other goods caused by the absence of the accession removed or by any necessity for replacing it. A person entitled to reimbursement may refuse permission to remove until the secured party gives adequate assurance for the performance of the obligation to reimburse.

Section 9-336. *Commingled Goods.* (a) "Commingled goods." In this section, "commingled goods" means goods that are physically united with other goods in such a manner that their identity is lost in a product or mass.

(b) No security interest in commingled goods as such. A security interest does not exist in commingled goods as such. However, a security interest may attach to a product or mass that results when goods become commingled goods.

(c) Attachment of security interest to product or mass. If collateral becomes commingled goods, a security interest attaches to the product or mass.

(d) Perfection of security interest. If a security interest in collateral is perfected before the collateral becomes commingled goods, the security interest that attaches to the product or mass under subsection (c) is perfected.

(e) Priority of security interest. Except as otherwise provided in subsection (f), the other provisions of this part determine the priority of a security interest that attaches to the product or mass under subsection (c).

(f) Conflicting security interests in product or mass. If more than one security interest attaches to the product or mass under subsection (c), the following rules determine priority:

(1) A security interest that is perfected under subsection (d) has priority over a security interest that is unperfected at the time the collateral becomes commingled goods.

(2) If more than one security interest is perfected under subsection (d), the security interests rank equally in proportion to the value of the collateral at the time it became commingled goods.

Section 9-337. *Priority of Security Interests in Goods Covered by Certificate of Title.* If, while a security interest in goods is perfected by any method under the law of another jurisdiction, this state issues a certificate of title that does not show that the goods are subject to the security interest or contain a statement that they may be subject to security interests not shown on the certificate:

(a) a buyer of the goods, other than a person in the business of selling goods of that kind, takes free of the security interest if the buyer gives value and receives delivery of the goods after issuance of the certificate and without knowledge of the security interest; and

(b) the security interest is subordinate to a conflicting security interest in the goods that attaches, and is perfected under Section 9-311(b), after issuance of the certificate and without the conflicting secured party's knowledge of the security interest.

Section 9-338. *Priority of Security Interest or Agricultural Lien Perfected by Filed Financing Statement Providing Certain Incorrect Information.* If a security interest or agricultural lien is perfected by a filed financing statement providing information described in Section 9-516(b)(5) which is incorrect at the time the financing statement is filed:

(a) the security interest or agricultural lien is subordinate to a conflicting perfected security interest in the collateral to the extent that the holder of the conflicting security interest gives value in reasonable reliance upon the incorrect information; and

(b) a purchaser, other than a secured party, of the collateral takes free of the security interest or agricultural lien to the extent that, in reasonable reliance upon the incorrect information, the purchaser gives value and, in the case of chattel paper, documents, goods, instruments, or a security certificate, receives delivery of the collateral.

Section 9-339. *Priority Subject to Subordination.* This article does not preclude subordination by agreement by a person entitled to priority.

Part 5: Filing

SUBPART 1. FILING OFFICE; CONTENTS AND EFFECTIVENESS OF FINANCING STATEMENT

Section 9-501. *Filing Office.* (a) Filing offices. Except as otherwise provided in subsection (b), if the law of this state governs perfection of a security interest or agricultural lien, the office in which to file a financing statement to perfect the security interest or agricultural lien is:

(1) the office designated for the filing or recording of a record of a mortgage on the related real property, if:

(A) the collateral is as-extracted collateral or timber to be cut; or

(B) the financing statement is filed as a fixture filing and the collateral is goods that are or are to become fixtures; or

(C) the collateral is a cooperative interest; or

(2) the office of the secretary of state, in all other cases, including a case in which the collateral is goods that are or are to become fixtures and the financing statement is not filed as a fixture filing.

(b) Filing office for transmitting utilities. The office in which to file a financing statement to perfect a security interest in collateral, including fixtures, of a transmitting utility is the office of the secretary of state. The financing statement also constitutes a fixture filing as to the collateral indicated in the financing statement which is or is to become fixtures.

(c) The term "filing officer" or "recording officer" means the county clerk of the county, except in the counties of Bronx, Kings, New York, and Queens where it means the city register in the county; and the term "filing officer" includes the secretary of state where a filing is made in the department of state.

Section 9-502. *Contents of Financing Statement; Record of Mortgage as Financing Statement; Time of Filing Financing Statement; Contents of Cooperative Addendum.* (a) Sufficiency of financing statement. Subject to subsection (b), a financing statement is sufficient only if it:

(1) provides the name of the debtor;

(2) provides the name of the secured party or a representative of the secured party;

(3) indicates the collateral covered by the financing statement; and

(4) in the case of a cooperative interest, indicates the number or other designation and the street address of the cooperative unit.

(b) Real-property-related financing statements. Except as otherwise provided in Section 9-501(b), to be sufficient, a financing statement that covers as-extracted collateral or timber to be cut, or which is filed as a fixture filing and covers goods that are or are to become fixtures, or, unless a cooperative addendum is filed, which covers a cooperative interest, must satisfy subsection (a) and also:

(1) indicate that it covers this type of collateral;

(2)   indicate that it is to be filed in the real property records;

(3)   provide a description of the real property to which the collateral is related, including the location of the real estate by reference to a book and page number in a deed or mortgage index maintained in the county clerk's office in the county where the property is situate or by street and number and town or city, or, if the real estate is in the city of New York, by county, except that if the real estate is in the city of New York or counties of Nassau or Onondaga, where the block system of recording or registering and indexing conveyances is in use, the statement must also specify the block and lot number in which the real estate is situated; and

(4)   if the debtor does not have an interest of record in the real property, provide the name of a record owner.

(c)   Record of mortgage as financing statement. A record of a mortgage is effective, from the date of recording, as a financing statement filed as a fixture filing or as a financing statement covering as-extracted collateral or timber to be cut only if:

(1)   the record indicates the goods or accounts that it covers;

(2)   the goods are or are to become fixtures related to the real property described in the record or the collateral is related to the real property described in the record and is as-extracted collateral or timber to be cut;

(3)   the record satisfies the requirements for a financing statement in this section other than an indication that it is to be filed in the real property records; and

(4)   the record is duly recorded.

(d)   Filing before security agreement or attachment. A financing statement may be filed before a security agreement is made or a security interest otherwise attaches.

(e)   Contents of cooperative addendum. A cooperative addendum is sufficient only if it satisfies subsection (a) and also:

(1)   if not filed simultaneously with the initial financing statement, identifies, by its file number, the initial financing statement to which the addendum relates;

(2)   indicates the street address of the cooperative unit;

(3)   indicates the county in which the cooperative unit is located;

(4)   indicates the city, town, or village in which the cooperative unit is located;

(5)   indicates the real property tax designation associated with the real property in which the cooperative unit is located as assigned by the local real property tax assessing authority; and

(6)   indicates the name of the cooperative organization.

Section 9-503. *Name of Debtor and Secured Party.* (a) Sufficiency of debtor's name. A financing statement sufficiently provides the name of the debtor:

(1)   if the debtor is a registered organization, only if the financing statement provides the name of the debtor indicated on the public record of the debtor's jurisdiction of organization which shows the debtor to have been organized;

(2)   if the debtor is a decedent's estate, only if the financing statement provides the name of the decedent and indicates that the debtor is an estate;

(3)   if the debtor is a trust or a trustee acting with respect to property held in trust, only if the financing statement:

(A)   provides the name specified for the trust in its organic documents or, if no name is specified, provides the name of the settlor and additional information sufficient to distinguish the debtor from other trusts having one or more of the same settlors; and

(B)   indicates, in the debtor's name or otherwise, that the debtor is a trust or is a trustee acting with respect to property held in trust; and

(4)   in other cases:

(A)   if the debtor has a name, only if it provides the individual or organizational name of the debtor; and

(B)   if the debtor does not have a name, only if it provides the names of the partners, members, associates, or other persons comprising the debtor.

(b) Additional debtor-related information. A financing statement that provides the name of the debtor in accordance with subsection (a) is not rendered ineffective by the absence of:

(1) a trade name or other name of the debtor; or

(2) unless required under subsection (a)(4)(B), names of partners, members, associates, or other persons comprising the debtor.

(c) Debtor's trade name insufficient. A financing statement that provides only the debtor's trade name does not sufficiently provide the name of the debtor.

(d) Representative capacity. Failure to indicate the representative capacity of a secured party or representative of a secured party does not affect the sufficiency of a financing statement.

(e) Multiple debtors and secured parties. A financing statement may provide the name of more than one debtor and the name of more than one secured party.

Section 9-504. *Indication of Collateral.* A financing statement sufficiently indicates the collateral that it covers if the financing statement provides:

(1) a description of the collateral pursuant to Section 9-108; or

(2) an indication that the financing statement covers all assets or all personal property.

Section 9-505. *Filing and Compliance with Other Statutes and Treaties for Consignments, Leases, Other Bailments, and Other Transactions.* (a) Use of terms other than "debtor" and "secured party." A consignor, lessor, or other bailor of goods, a licensor, or a buyer of a payment intangible or promissory note may file a financing statement, or may comply with a statute or treaty described in Section 9-311(a), using the terms "consignor", "consignee", "lessor", "lessee", "bailor", "bailee", "licensor", "licensee", "owner", "registered owner", "buyer", "seller", or words of similar import, instead of the terms "secured party" and "debtor".

(b) Effect of financing statement under subsection (a). This part applies to the filing of a financing statement under subsection (a) and, as appropriate, to compliance that is equivalent to filing a financing statement under Section 9-311(b), but the filing or compliance is not of itself a factor in determining whether the collateral secures an obligation. If it is determined for another reason that the collateral secures an obligation, a security interest held by the consignor, lessor, bailor, licensor, owner, or buyer which attaches to the collateral is perfected by the filing or compliance.

Section 9-506. *Effect of Errors or Omissions.* (a) Minor errors and omissions. A financing statement substantially satisfying the requirements of this part is effective, even if it has minor errors or omissions, unless the errors or omissions make the financing statement seriously misleading.

(b) Financing statement seriously misleading. Except as otherwise provided in subsection (c), a financing statement that fails sufficiently to provide the name of the debtor in accordance with Section 9-503(a) is seriously misleading.

(c) Financing statement not seriously misleading. If a search of the records of the filing office under the debtor's correct name, using the filing office's standard search logic, if any, would disclose a financing statement that fails sufficiently to provide the name of the debtor in accordance with Section 9-503(a), the name provided does not make the financing statement seriously misleading.

(d) "Debtor's correct name." For purposes of Section 9-508(b), the "debtor's correct name" in subsection (c) means the correct name of the new debtor.

Section 9-507. *Effect of Certain Events on Effectiveness of Financing Statement.* (a) Disposition. A filed financing statement remains effective with respect to collateral that is sold, exchanged, leased, licensed, or otherwise disposed of and in which a security interest or agricultural lien continues, even if the secured party knows of or consents to the disposition.

(b) Information becoming seriously misleading. Except as otherwise provided in subsection (c) and Section 9-508, a financing statement is not rendered ineffective if, after the financing statement is filed, the information provided in the financing statement becomes seriously misleading under Section 9-506.

(c) Change in debtor's name. If a debtor so changes its name that a filed financing statement becomes seriously misleading under Section 9-506:

(1) the financing statement is effective to perfect a security interest in collateral acquired by the debtor before, or within four months after, the change; and

(2) the financing statement is not effective to perfect a security interest in collateral acquired by the debtor more than four months after the change, unless an amendment to the financing statement which renders the financing statement not seriously misleading is filed within four months after the change.

Section 9-508. *Effectiveness of Financing Statement If New Debtor Becomes Bound by Security Agreement.* (a) Financing statement naming original debtor. Except as otherwise provided in this section, a filed financing statement naming an original debtor is effective to perfect a security interest in collateral in which a new debtor has or acquires rights to the extent that the financing statement would have been effective had the original debtor acquired rights in the collateral.

(b) Financing statement becoming seriously misleading. If the difference between the name of the original debtor and that of the new debtor causes a filed financing statement that is effective under subsection (a) to be seriously misleading under Section 9-506:

(1) the financing statement is effective to perfect a security interest in collateral acquired by the new debtor before, and within four months after, the new debtor becomes bound under Section 9-203(d); and

(2) the financing statement is not effective to perfect a security interest in collateral acquired by the new debtor more than four months after the new debtor becomes bound under Section 9-203(d) unless an initial financing statement providing the name of the new debtor is filed before the expiration of that time.

(c) When section not applicable. This section does not apply to collateral as to which a filed financing statement remains effective against the new debtor under Section 9-507(a).

Section 9-509. *Persons Entitled to File a Record.* (a) Person entitled to file record. A person may file an initial financing statement, amendment that adds collateral covered by a financing statement, or amendment that adds a debtor to a financing statement only if:

(1) the debtor authorizes the filing in an authenticated record or pursuant to subsection (b) or (c); or

(2) the person holds an agricultural lien that has become effective at the time of filing and the financing statement covers only collateral in which the person holds an agricultural lien.

(b) Security agreement as authorization. By authenticating or becoming bound as debtor by a security agreement, a debtor or new debtor authorizes the filing of an initial financing statement, and an amendment, covering:

(1) the collateral described in the security agreement; and

(2) property that becomes collateral under Section 9-315(a)(2), whether or not the security agreement expressly covers proceeds.

(c) Acquisition of collateral as authorization. By acquiring collateral in which a security interest or agricultural lien continues under Section 9-315(a)(1), a debtor authorizes the filing of an initial financing statement, and an amendment, covering the collateral and property that becomes collateral under Section 9-315(a)(2).

(d) Person entitled to file certain amendments. A person may file an amendment other than an amendment that adds collateral covered by a financing statement or an amendment that adds a debtor to a financing statement only if:

(1) the secured party of record authorizes the filing; or

(2) the amendment is a termination statement for a financing statement as to which the secured party of record has failed to file or send a termination statement as required

by Section 9-513(a) or (c), the debtor authorizes the filing, and the termination statement indicates that the debtor authorized it to be filed.

(e)   Multiple secured parties of record. If there is more than one secured party of record for a financing statement, each secured party of record may authorize the filing of an amendment under subsection (d).

Section 9-510. *Effectiveness of Filed Record.* (a) Filed record effective if authorized. A filed record is effective only to the extent that it was filed by a person that may file it under Section 9-509.

(b)   Authorization by one secured party of record. A record authorized by one secured party of record does not affect the financing statement with respect to another secured party of record.

(c)   Continuation statement not timely filed. A continuation statement that is not filed within the six-month period prescribed by Section 9-515(d) is ineffective.

Section 9-511. *Secured Party of Record.* (a) Secured party of record. A secured party of record with respect to a financing statement is a person whose name is provided as the name of the secured party or a representative of the secured party in an initial financing statement that has been filed. If an initial financing statement is filed under Section 9-514(a), the assignee named in the initial financing statement is the secured party of record with respect to the financing statement.

(b)   Amendment naming secured party of record. If an amendment of a financing statement which provides the name of a person as a secured party or a representative of a secured party is filed, the person named in the amendment is a secured party of record. If an amendment is filed under Section 9-514(b), the assignee named in the amendment is a secured party of record.

(c)   Amendment deleting secured party of record. A person remains a secured party of record until the filing of an amendment of the financing statement which deletes the person.

Section 9-512. *Amendment of Financing Statement.* (a) Amendment of information in financing statement. Subject to Section 9-509, a person may add or delete collateral covered by, continue or terminate the effectiveness of, or, subject to subsection (e), otherwise amend the information provided in, a financing statement by filing an amendment that:

(1)   identifies, by its file number, the initial financing statement to which the amendment relates; and

(2)   if the amendment relates to an initial financing statement filed in a filing office described in Section 9-501(a)(1), provides the date and time that the initial financing statement was filed and the information specified in Section 9-502(b).

(b)   Period of effectiveness not affected. Except as otherwise provided in Section 9-515, the filing of an amendment does not extend the period of effectiveness of the financing statement.

(c)   Effectiveness of amendment adding collateral. A financing statement that is amended by an amendment that adds collateral is effective as to the added collateral only from the date of the filing of the amendment.

(d)   Effectiveness of amendment adding debtor. A financing statement that is amended by an amendment that adds a debtor is effective as to the added debtor only from the date of the filing of the amendment.

(e)   Certain amendments ineffective. An amendment is ineffective to the extent it:

(1)   purports to delete all debtors and fails to provide the name of a debtor to be covered by the financing statement; or

(2)   purports to delete all secured parties of record and fails to provide the name of a new secured party of record.

Section 9-513. *Termination Statement.* (a) Consumer goods. A secured party shall cause the secured party of record for a financing statement to file a termination statement for the financing statement if the financing statement covers consumer goods and:

(1)　there is no obligation secured by the collateral covered by the financing statement and no commitment to make an advance, incur an obligation, or otherwise give value; or

(2)　the debtor did not authorize the filing of the initial financing statement.

(b)　Time for compliance with subsection (a). To comply with subsection (a), a secured party shall cause the secured party of record to file the termination statement:

(1)　within one month after there is no obligation secured by the collateral covered by the financing statement and no commitment to make an advance, incur an obligation, or otherwise give value; or

(2)　if earlier, within 20 days after the secured party receives an authenticated demand from a debtor.

(c)　Other collateral. In cases not governed by subsection (a), within 20 days after a secured party receives an authenticated demand from a debtor, the secured party shall cause the secured party of record for a financing statement to send to the debtor a termination statement for the financing statement or file the termination statement in the filing office if:

(1)　except in the case of a financing statement covering accounts or chattel paper that has been sold or goods that are the subject of a consignment, there is no obligation secured by the collateral covered by the financing statement and no commitment to make an advance, incur an obligation, or other wise give value;

(2)　the financing statement covers accounts or chattel paper that has been sold but as to which the account debtor or other person obligated has discharged its obligation;

(3)　the financing statement covers goods that were the subject of a consignment to the debtor but are not in the debtor's possession; or

(4)　the debtor did not authorize the filing of the initial financing statement.

(d)　Effect of filing termination statement. Except as otherwise provided in Section 9-510, upon the filing of a termination statement with the filing office, the financing statement to which the termination statement relates ceases to be effective. Except as otherwise provided in Section 9-510, for purposes of Section 9-519(g), 9-522(a), and 9-523(c), the filing with the filing office of a termination statement relating to a financing statement that indicates that the debtor is a transmitting utility also causes the effectiveness of the financing statement to lapse.

(e)　Cooperative Interests.

(1)　"Cooperative Interest Settlement" means the time and place at which an owner of a cooperative interest transfers the cooperative interest, or refinances or pays off the debt secured by the cooperative interest.

(2)　Upon an authenticated demand with sufficient notice by a debtor, the secured party shall deliver to a cooperative interest settlement a termination statement or partial release and any component of the cooperative record of which it took possession, which shall be released to the debtor upon payment of the debt secured by the cooperative interest and the discharge of any obligation of the secured party to make further advances. Unless the secured party has agreed otherwise or the cooperative interest settlement takes place at the offices of the secured party, the secured party or its agent shall be entitled to a reasonable fee for attendance at the cooperative interest settlement.

(3)　Upon payment of the debt secured by a cooperative interest other than at a cooperative interest settlement and the discharge of any obligation of the secured party to make further advances, the secured party shall arrange for a termination statement or partial release to be filed within one month of receipt of the payment or discharge of the obligation to make further advances, whichever is later, and shall send to the debtor any component of the cooperative record of which it took possession.

Section 9-514. *Assignment of Powers of Secured Party of Record.* (a) Assignment reflected on initial financing statement. Except as otherwise provided in subsection (c), an initial financing statement may reflect an assignment of all of the secured party's power to authorize an amendment to the financing statement by providing the name and mailing address of the assignee as the name and address of the secured party.

(b) Assignment of filed financing statement. Except as otherwise provided in subsection (c), a secured party of record may assign of record all or part of its power to authorize an amendment to a financing statement by filing in the filing office an amendment of the financing statement which:

(1) identifies, by its file number, the initial financing statement to which it relates;

(2) provides the name of the assignor; and

(3) provides the name and mailing address of the assignee.

(c) Assignment of record of mortgage. An assignment of record of a security interest in a fixture covered by a record of a mortgage which is effective as a financing statement filed as a fixture filing under Section 9-502(c) may be made only by an assignment of record of the mortgage in the manner provided by law of this state other than this chapter.

Section 9-515. *Duration and Effectiveness of Financing Statement; Effect of Lapsed Financing Statement.* (a) Five-year effectiveness. Except as otherwise provided in subsections (b), (e), (f), (g), and (h), a filed financing statement is effective for a period of five years after the date of filing.

(b) Public-financed or manufactured-home transaction. Except as otherwise provided in subsections (e), (f), (g), and (h), an initial financing statement filed in connection with a public-financed transaction or manufactured-home transaction is effective for a period of 30 years after the date of filing if it indicates that it is filed in connection with a public-financed transaction or manufactured-home transaction.

(c) Lapse and continuation of financing statement. The effectiveness of a filed financing statement lapses on the expiration of the period of its effectiveness unless before the lapse a continuation statement is filed pursuant to subsection(d). Upon lapse, a financing statement ceases to be effective and any security interest or agricultural lien that was perfected by the financing statement becomes unperfected, unless the security interest is perfected otherwise. If the security interest or agricultural lien becomes unperfected upon lapse, it is deemed never to have been perfected as against a purchaser of the collateral for value.

(d) When continuation statement may be filed. A continuation statement may be filed only within six months before the expiration of the five-year period specified in subsection (a) or the thirty-year period specified in subsection (b) or the 50-year period specified in subsection (h), whichever is applicable.

(e) Effect of filing continuation statement. Except as otherwise provided in Section 9-510, upon timely filing of a continuation statement, the effectiveness of the initial financing statement continues for a period of five years commencing on the day on which the financing statement would have become ineffective in the absence of the filing. Upon the expiration of the five-year period, the financing statement lapses in the same manner as provided in subsection (c), unless, before the lapse, another continuation statement is filed pursuant to subsection (d). Succeeding continuation statements may be filed in the same manner to continue the effectiveness of the initial financing statement.

(f) Transmitting utility financing statement. If a debtor is a transmitting utility and a filed financing statement so indicates, the financing statement is effective until a termination statement is filed.

(g) Record of mortgage as financing statement. A record of a mortgage that is effective as a financing statement filed as a fixture filing under Section 9-502(c) remains effective as a financing statement filed as a fixture filing until the mortgage is released or satisfied of record or its effectiveness otherwise terminates as to the real property.

(h) Cooperative interest transaction. An initial financing statement covering a cooperative interest is effective for a period of 50 years after the date of the filing of the initial financing statement if a cooperative addendum is filed simultaneously with the initial financing statement or is filed before the financing statement lapses.

Section 9-516. *What Constitutes Filing; Effectiveness of Filing.* (a) What constitutes filing. Except as otherwise provided in subsection (b), communication of a record to a filing office and tender of the filing fee or acceptance of the record by the filing office constitutes filing.

(b) Refusal to accept record; filing does not occur. Filing does not occur with respect to a record that a filing office refuses to accept because:

(1) the record is not communicated by a method or medium of communication authorized by the filing office;

(2) an amount equal to or greater than the applicable filing fee is not tendered;

(3) the filing office is unable to index the record because:

(A) in the case of an initial financing statement, the record does not provide a name for the debtor;

(B) in the case of an amendment or correction statement, the record:

(i) does not identify the initial financing statement as required by Section 9-512 or 9-518, as applicable; or

(ii) identifies an initial financing statement whose effectiveness has lapsed under Section 9-515;

(C) in the case of an initial financing statement that provides the name of a debtor identified as an individual or an amendment that provides a name of a debtor identified as an individual which was not previously provided in the financing statement to which the record relates, the record does not identify the debtor's last name; or

(D) in the case of a record filed in the filing office described in Section 9-501(a)(1), the record does not provide a sufficient description of the real property to which it relates;

(4) in the case of an initial financing statement or an amendment that adds a secured party of record, the record does not provide a name and mailing address for the secured party of record;

(5) in the case of an initial financing statement or an amendment that provides a name of a debtor which was not previously provided in the financing statement to which the amendment relates, the record does not:

(A) provide a mailing address for the debtor; or

(B) indicate whether the debtor is an individual or an organization;

(C) if the financing statement indicates that the debtor is an organization, provide:

(i) a type of organization for the debtor, or

(ii) a jurisdiction of organization for the debtor; or

(6) in the case of an assignment reflected in an initial financing statement under Section 9-514(a) or an amendment filed under Section 9-514(b), the record does not provide a name and mailing address for the assignee; or

(7) in the case of a continuation statement, the record is not filed within the six-month period prescribed by Section 9-515(d).

(c) Rules applicable to subsection (b). For purposes of subsection (b):

(1) a record does not provide information if the filing office is unable to read or decipher the information; and

(2) a record that does not indicate that it is an amendment or identify an initial financing statement to which it relates, as required by Section 9-512, 9-514, or 9-518, is an initial financing statement.

(d) Refusal to accept record; record effective as filed record. A record that is communicated to the filing office with tender of the filing fee, but which the filing office refuses to accept for a reason other than one set forth in subsection (b), is effective as a filed record except as against a purchaser of the collateral which gives value in reasonable reliance upon the absence of the record from the files.

(e) Special rule for cooperative interests; record effective as notice. A filing that includes a cooperative addendum covering a cooperative interest constitutes notice of the existence of the security interest in the cooperative interest as of the date of the filing of the cooperative addendum, except as against a purchaser of the collateral which gives value in reasonable reliance upon the absence of the record from the files.

Section 9-517. *Effect of Indexing Errors.* The failure of the filing office to index a record correctly does not affect the effectiveness of the filed record.

Section 9-518. *Claim Concerning Inaccurate or Wrongfully Filed Record.* (a) Correction statement. A person may file in the filing office a correction statement with respect to a record indexed there under the person's name if the person believes that the record is inaccurate or was wrongfully filed.

(b)   Sufficiency of correction statement. A correction statement must:

(1)   identify the record to which it relates by:

    (A)   the file number assigned to the initial financing statement to which the record relates; and

    (B)   if the correction statement relates to a record filed in a filing office described in Section 9-501(a)(1), the date and time that the initial financing statement was filed and the information specified in Section 9-502(b);

(2)   indicate that it is a correction statement; and

(3)   provide the basis for the person's belief that the record is inaccurate and indicate the manner in which the person believes the record should be amended to cure any inaccuracy or provide the basis for the person's belief that the record was wrongfully filed.

(c)   Record not affected by correction statement. The filing of a correction statement does not affect the effectiveness of an initial financing statement or other filed record.

ARTICLE 10: EFFECTIVE DATE AND REPEALER

(This Article, which of necessity varies in the several states which have enacted the Code, provides the date as of which it became effective and the repeal of various Uniform Laws and other statutes which it supersedes.)

ARTICLE 11: EFFECTIVE DATE AND TRANSITION PROVISIONS

(This Article includes provisions which cover the transition from the original version of the Code and the subsequent changes which have been made.)

Index

References are to chapter and page numbers (e.g., 5-42 refers to page 42 in Chapter 5).
References starting with a letter (A, B, or C) indicate the appendices.